INSTRUCTOR'S SOLUTIONS MANUAL

DAVID C. LAY
University of Maryland – College Park

THOMAS POLASKI
Winthrop University

LINEAR ALGEBRA AND ITS APPLICATIONS

THIRD EDITION UPDATE

David C. Lay
University of Maryland – College Park

PEARSON

Addison
Wesley

Boston San Francisco New York
London Toronto Sydney Tokyo Singapore Madrid
Mexico City Munich Paris Cape Town Hong Kong Montreal

Reproduced by Pearson Addison-Wesley from electronic files supplied by the author.

Copyright © 2006 Pearson Education, Inc.
Publishing as Pearson Addison-Wesley, 75 Arlington Street, Boston, MA 02116.

ISBN   0-321-28065-2

1 2 3 4 5 6 BB 08 07 06 05

PEARSON
Addison
Wesley

CONTENTS

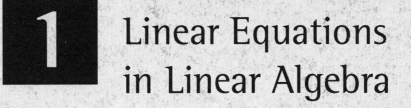

1 Linear Equations in Linear Algebra

1.1 SOLUTIONS

Notes: The key exercises are 7 (or 11 or 12), 19–22, and 25. For brevity, the symbols R1, R2,…, stand for row 1 (or equation 1), row 2 (or equation 2), and so on. Additional notes are at the end of the section.

1.
$$\begin{aligned} x_1 + 5x_2 &= 7 \\ -2x_1 - 7x_2 &= -5 \end{aligned} \qquad \begin{bmatrix} 1 & 5 & 7 \\ -2 & -7 & -5 \end{bmatrix}$$

Replace R2 by R2 + (2)R1 and obtain:
$$\begin{aligned} x_1 + 5x_2 &= 7 \\ 3x_2 &= 9 \end{aligned} \qquad \begin{bmatrix} 1 & 5 & 7 \\ 0 & 3 & 9 \end{bmatrix}$$

Scale R2 by 1/3:
$$\begin{aligned} x_1 + 5x_2 &= 7 \\ x_2 &= 3 \end{aligned} \qquad \begin{bmatrix} 1 & 5 & 7 \\ 0 & 1 & 3 \end{bmatrix}$$

Replace R1 by R1 + (–5)R2:
$$\begin{aligned} x_1 &= -8 \\ x_2 &= 3 \end{aligned} \qquad \begin{bmatrix} 1 & 0 & -8 \\ 0 & 1 & 3 \end{bmatrix}$$

The solution is $(x_1, x_2) = (-8, 3)$, or simply $(-8, 3)$.

2.
$$\begin{aligned} 2x_1 + 4x_2 &= -4 \\ 5x_1 + 7x_2 &= 11 \end{aligned} \qquad \begin{bmatrix} 2 & 4 & -4 \\ 5 & 7 & 11 \end{bmatrix}$$

Scale R1 by 1/2 and obtain:
$$\begin{aligned} x_1 + 2x_2 &= -2 \\ 5x_1 + 7x_2 &= 11 \end{aligned} \qquad \begin{bmatrix} 1 & 2 & -2 \\ 5 & 7 & 11 \end{bmatrix}$$

Replace R2 by R2 + (–5)R1:
$$\begin{aligned} x_1 + 2x_2 &= -2 \\ -3x_2 &= 21 \end{aligned} \qquad \begin{bmatrix} 1 & 2 & -2 \\ 0 & -3 & 21 \end{bmatrix}$$

Scale R2 by –1/3:
$$\begin{aligned} x_1 + 2x_2 &= -2 \\ x_2 &= -7 \end{aligned} \qquad \begin{bmatrix} 1 & 2 & -2 \\ 0 & 1 & -7 \end{bmatrix}$$

Replace R1 by R1 + (–2)R2:
$$\begin{aligned} x_1 &= 12 \\ x_2 &= -7 \end{aligned} \qquad \begin{bmatrix} 1 & 0 & 12 \\ 0 & 1 & -7 \end{bmatrix}$$

The solution is $(x_1, x_2) = (12, -7)$, or simply $(12, -7)$.

3. The point of intersection satisfies the system of two linear equations:

$$\begin{aligned} x_1 + 5x_2 &= 7 \\ x_1 - 2x_2 &= -2 \end{aligned} \qquad \begin{bmatrix} 1 & 5 & 7 \\ 1 & -2 & -2 \end{bmatrix}$$

Replace R2 by R2 + (–1)R1 and obtain:

$$\begin{aligned} x_1 + 5x_2 &= 7 \\ -7x_2 &= -9 \end{aligned} \qquad \begin{bmatrix} 1 & 5 & 7 \\ 0 & -7 & -9 \end{bmatrix}$$

Scale R2 by –1/7:

$$\begin{aligned} x_1 + 5x_2 &= 7 \\ x_2 &= 9/7 \end{aligned} \qquad \begin{bmatrix} 1 & 5 & 7 \\ 0 & 1 & 9/7 \end{bmatrix}$$

Replace R1 by R1 + (–5)R2:

$$\begin{aligned} x_1 &= 4/7 \\ x_2 &= 9/7 \end{aligned} \qquad \begin{bmatrix} 1 & 0 & 4/7 \\ 0 & 1 & 9/7 \end{bmatrix}$$

The point of intersection is $(x_1, x_2) = (4/7, 9/7)$.

4. The point of intersection satisfies the system of two linear equations:

$$\begin{aligned} x_1 - 5x_2 &= 1 \\ 3x_1 - 7x_2 &= 5 \end{aligned} \qquad \begin{bmatrix} 1 & -5 & 1 \\ 3 & -7 & 5 \end{bmatrix}$$

Replace R2 by R2 + (–3)R1 and obtain:

$$\begin{aligned} x_1 - 5x_2 &= 1 \\ 8x_2 &= 2 \end{aligned} \qquad \begin{bmatrix} 1 & -5 & 1 \\ 0 & 8 & 2 \end{bmatrix}$$

Scale R2 by 1/8:

$$\begin{aligned} x_1 - 5x_2 &= 1 \\ x_2 &= 1/4 \end{aligned} \qquad \begin{bmatrix} 1 & -5 & 1 \\ 0 & 1 & 1/4 \end{bmatrix}$$

Replace R1 by R1 + (5)R2:

$$\begin{aligned} x_1 &= 9/4 \\ x_2 &= 1/4 \end{aligned} \qquad \begin{bmatrix} 1 & 0 & 9/4 \\ 0 & 1 & 1/4 \end{bmatrix}$$

The point of intersection is $(x_1, x_2) = (9/4, 1/4)$.

5. The system is already in "triangular" form. The fourth equation is $x_4 = -5$, and the other equations do not contain the variable x_4. The next two steps should be to use the variable x_3 in the third equation to eliminate that variable from the first two equations. In matrix notation, that means to replace R2 by its sum with 3 times R3, and then replace R1 by its sum with –5 times R3.

6. One more step will put the system in triangular form. Replace R4 by its sum with –3 times R3, which

produces $\begin{bmatrix} 1 & -6 & 4 & 0 & -1 \\ 0 & 2 & -7 & 0 & 4 \\ 0 & 0 & 1 & 2 & -3 \\ 0 & 0 & 0 & -5 & 15 \end{bmatrix}$. After that, the next step is to scale the fourth row by –1/5.

7. Ordinarily, the next step would be to interchange R3 and R4, to put a 1 in the third row and third column. But in this case, the third row of the augmented matrix corresponds to the equation $0\,x_1 + 0\,x_2 + 0\,x_3 = 1$, or simply, $0 = 1$. A system containing this condition has no solution. Further row operations are unnecessary once an equation such as $0 = 1$ is evident.
The solution set is empty.

8. The standard row operations are:

$$\begin{bmatrix} 1 & -4 & 9 & 0 \\ 0 & 1 & 7 & 0 \\ 0 & 0 & 2 & 0 \end{bmatrix} \sim \begin{bmatrix} 1 & -4 & 9 & 0 \\ 0 & 1 & 7 & 0 \\ 0 & 0 & 1 & 0 \end{bmatrix} \sim \begin{bmatrix} 1 & -4 & 0 & 0 \\ 0 & 1 & 0 & 0 \\ 0 & 0 & 1 & 0 \end{bmatrix} \sim \begin{bmatrix} 1 & 0 & 0 & 0 \\ 0 & 1 & 0 & 0 \\ 0 & 0 & 1 & 0 \end{bmatrix}$$

The solution set contains one solution: (0, 0, 0).

9. The system has already been reduced to triangular form. Begin by scaling the fourth row by 1/2 and then replacing R3 by R3 + (3)R4:

$$\begin{bmatrix} 1 & -1 & 0 & 0 & -4 \\ 0 & 1 & -3 & 0 & -7 \\ 0 & 0 & 1 & -3 & -1 \\ 0 & 0 & 0 & 2 & 4 \end{bmatrix} \sim \begin{bmatrix} 1 & -1 & 0 & 0 & -4 \\ 0 & 1 & -3 & 0 & 7 \\ 0 & 0 & 1 & -3 & -1 \\ 0 & 0 & 0 & 1 & 2 \end{bmatrix} \sim \begin{bmatrix} 1 & -1 & 0 & 0 & -4 \\ 0 & 1 & -3 & 0 & -7 \\ 0 & 0 & 1 & 0 & 5 \\ 0 & 0 & 0 & 1 & 2 \end{bmatrix}$$

Next, replace R2 by R2 + (3)R3. Finally, replace R1 by R1 + R2:

$$\sim \begin{bmatrix} 1 & -1 & 0 & 0 & -4 \\ 0 & 1 & 0 & 0 & 8 \\ 0 & 0 & 1 & 0 & 5 \\ 0 & 0 & 0 & 1 & 2 \end{bmatrix} \sim \begin{bmatrix} 1 & 0 & 0 & 0 & 4 \\ 0 & 1 & 0 & 0 & 8 \\ 0 & 0 & 1 & 0 & 5 \\ 0 & 0 & 0 & 1 & 2 \end{bmatrix}$$

The solution set contains one solution: (4, 8, 5, 2).

10. The system has already been reduced to triangular form. Use the 1 in the fourth row to change the –4 and 3 above it to zeros. That is, replace R2 by R2 + (4)R4 and replace R1 by R1 + (–3)R4. For the final step, replace R1 by R1 + (2)R2.

$$\begin{bmatrix} 1 & -2 & 0 & 3 & -2 \\ 0 & 1 & 0 & -4 & 7 \\ 0 & 0 & 1 & 0 & 6 \\ 0 & 0 & 0 & 1 & -3 \end{bmatrix} \sim \begin{bmatrix} 1 & -2 & 0 & 0 & 7 \\ 0 & 1 & 0 & 0 & -5 \\ 0 & 0 & 1 & 0 & 6 \\ 0 & 0 & 0 & 1 & -3 \end{bmatrix} \sim \begin{bmatrix} 1 & 0 & 0 & 0 & -3 \\ 0 & 1 & 0 & 0 & -5 \\ 0 & 0 & 1 & 0 & 6 \\ 0 & 0 & 0 & 1 & -3 \end{bmatrix}$$

The solution set contains one solution: (–3, –5, 6, –3).

11. First, swap R1 and R2. Then replace R3 by R3 + (–3)R1. Finally, replace R3 by R3 + (2)R2.

$$\begin{bmatrix} 0 & 1 & 4 & -5 \\ 1 & 3 & 5 & -2 \\ 3 & 7 & 7 & 6 \end{bmatrix} \sim \begin{bmatrix} 1 & 3 & 5 & -2 \\ 0 & 1 & 4 & -5 \\ 3 & 7 & 7 & 6 \end{bmatrix} \sim \begin{bmatrix} 1 & 3 & 5 & -2 \\ 0 & 1 & 4 & -5 \\ 0 & -2 & -8 & 12 \end{bmatrix} \sim \begin{bmatrix} 1 & 3 & 5 & -2 \\ 0 & 1 & 4 & -5 \\ 0 & 0 & 0 & 2 \end{bmatrix}$$

The system is inconsistent, because the last row would require that 0 = 2 if there were a solution. The solution set is empty.

12. Replace R2 by R2 + (–3)R1 and replace R3 by R3 + (4)R1. Finally, replace R3 by R3 + (3)R2.

$$\begin{bmatrix} 1 & -3 & 4 & -4 \\ 3 & -7 & 7 & -8 \\ -4 & 6 & -1 & 7 \end{bmatrix} \sim \begin{bmatrix} 1 & -3 & 4 & -4 \\ 0 & 2 & -5 & 4 \\ 0 & -6 & 15 & -9 \end{bmatrix} \sim \begin{bmatrix} 1 & -3 & 4 & -4 \\ 0 & 2 & -5 & 4 \\ 0 & 0 & 0 & 3 \end{bmatrix}$$

The system is inconsistent, because the last row would require that 0 = 3 if there were a solution. The solution set is empty.

13. $\begin{bmatrix} 1 & 0 & -3 & 8 \\ 2 & 2 & 9 & 7 \\ 0 & 1 & 5 & -2 \end{bmatrix} \sim \begin{bmatrix} 1 & 0 & -3 & 8 \\ 0 & 2 & 15 & -9 \\ 0 & 1 & 5 & -2 \end{bmatrix} \sim \begin{bmatrix} 1 & 0 & -3 & 8 \\ 0 & 1 & 5 & -2 \\ 0 & 2 & 15 & -9 \end{bmatrix} \sim \begin{bmatrix} 1 & 0 & -3 & 8 \\ 0 & 1 & 5 & -2 \\ 0 & 0 & 5 & -5 \end{bmatrix}$

$\sim \begin{bmatrix} 1 & 0 & -3 & 8 \\ 0 & 1 & 5 & -2 \\ 0 & 0 & 1 & -1 \end{bmatrix} \sim \begin{bmatrix} 1 & 0 & 0 & 5 \\ 0 & 1 & 0 & 3 \\ 0 & 0 & 1 & -1 \end{bmatrix}$. The solution is $(5, 3, -1)$.

14. $\begin{bmatrix} 1 & -3 & 0 & 5 \\ -1 & 1 & 5 & 2 \\ 0 & 1 & 1 & 0 \end{bmatrix} \sim \begin{bmatrix} 1 & -3 & 0 & 5 \\ 0 & -2 & 5 & 7 \\ 0 & 1 & 1 & 0 \end{bmatrix} \sim \begin{bmatrix} 1 & -3 & 0 & 5 \\ 0 & 1 & 1 & 0 \\ 0 & -2 & 5 & 7 \end{bmatrix} \sim \begin{bmatrix} 1 & -3 & 0 & 5 \\ 0 & 1 & 1 & 0 \\ 0 & 0 & 7 & 7 \end{bmatrix}$

$\sim \begin{bmatrix} 1 & -3 & 0 & 5 \\ 0 & 1 & 1 & 0 \\ 0 & 0 & 1 & 1 \end{bmatrix} \sim \begin{bmatrix} 1 & -3 & 0 & 5 \\ 0 & 1 & 0 & -1 \\ 0 & 0 & 1 & 1 \end{bmatrix} \sim \begin{bmatrix} 1 & 0 & 0 & 2 \\ 0 & 1 & 0 & -1 \\ 0 & 0 & 1 & 1 \end{bmatrix}$. The solution is $(2, -1, 1)$.

15. First, replace R4 by R4 + (–3)R1, then replace R3 by R3 + (2)R2, and finally replace R4 by R4 + (3)R3.

$\begin{bmatrix} 1 & 0 & 3 & 0 & 2 \\ 0 & 1 & 0 & -3 & 3 \\ 0 & -2 & 3 & 2 & 1 \\ 3 & 0 & 0 & 7 & -5 \end{bmatrix} \sim \begin{bmatrix} 1 & 0 & 3 & 0 & 2 \\ 0 & 1 & 0 & -3 & 3 \\ 0 & -2 & 3 & 2 & 1 \\ 0 & 0 & -9 & 7 & -11 \end{bmatrix}$

$\sim \begin{bmatrix} 1 & 0 & 3 & 0 & 2 \\ 0 & 1 & 0 & -3 & 3 \\ 0 & 0 & 3 & -4 & 7 \\ 0 & 0 & -9 & 7 & -11 \end{bmatrix} \sim \begin{bmatrix} 1 & 0 & 3 & 0 & 2 \\ 0 & 1 & 0 & -3 & 3 \\ 0 & 0 & 3 & -4 & 7 \\ 0 & 0 & 0 & -5 & 10 \end{bmatrix}$

The resulting triangular system indicates that a solution exists. In fact, using the argument from Example 2, one can see that the solution is unique.

16. First replace R4 by R4 + (2)R1 and replace R4 by R4 + (–3/2)R2. (One could also scale R2 before adding to R4, but the arithmetic is rather easy keeping R2 unchanged.) Finally, replace R4 by R4 + R3.

$\begin{bmatrix} 1 & 0 & 0 & -2 & -3 \\ 0 & 2 & 2 & 0 & 0 \\ 0 & 0 & 1 & 3 & 1 \\ -2 & 3 & 2 & 1 & 5 \end{bmatrix} \sim \begin{bmatrix} 1 & 0 & 0 & -2 & -3 \\ 0 & 2 & 2 & 0 & 0 \\ 0 & 0 & 1 & 3 & 1 \\ 0 & 3 & 2 & -3 & -1 \end{bmatrix}$

$\sim \begin{bmatrix} 1 & 0 & 0 & -2 & -3 \\ 0 & 2 & 2 & 0 & 0 \\ 0 & 0 & 1 & 3 & 1 \\ 0 & 0 & -1 & -3 & -1 \end{bmatrix} \sim \begin{bmatrix} 1 & 0 & 0 & -2 & -3 \\ 0 & 2 & 2 & 0 & 0 \\ 0 & 0 & 1 & 3 & 1 \\ 0 & 0 & 0 & 0 & 0 \end{bmatrix}$

The system is now in triangular form and has a solution. The next section discusses how to continue with this type of system.

17. Row reduce the augmented matrix corresponding to the given system of three equations:

$$\begin{bmatrix} 1 & -4 & 1 \\ 2 & -1 & -3 \\ -1 & -3 & 4 \end{bmatrix} \sim \begin{bmatrix} 1 & -4 & 1 \\ 0 & 7 & -5 \\ 0 & -7 & 5 \end{bmatrix} \sim \begin{bmatrix} 1 & -4 & 1 \\ 0 & 7 & -5 \\ 0 & 0 & 0 \end{bmatrix}$$

The system is consistent, and using the argument from Example 2, there is only one solution. So the three lines have only one point in common.

18. Row reduce the augmented matrix corresponding to the given system of three equations:

$$\begin{bmatrix} 1 & 2 & 1 & 4 \\ 0 & 1 & -1 & 1 \\ 1 & 3 & 0 & 0 \end{bmatrix} \sim \begin{bmatrix} 1 & 2 & 1 & 4 \\ 0 & 1 & -1 & 1 \\ 0 & 1 & -1 & -4 \end{bmatrix} \sim \begin{bmatrix} 1 & 2 & 1 & 4 \\ 0 & 1 & -1 & 1 \\ 0 & 0 & 0 & -5 \end{bmatrix}$$

The third equation, $0 = -5$, shows that the system is inconsistent, so the three planes have no point in common.

19. $\begin{bmatrix} 1 & h & 4 \\ 3 & 6 & 8 \end{bmatrix} \sim \begin{bmatrix} 1 & h & 4 \\ 0 & 6-3h & -4 \end{bmatrix}$ Write c for $6 - 3h$. If $c = 0$, that is, if $h = 2$, then the system has no solution, because 0 cannot equal -4. Otherwise, when $h \neq 2$, the system has a solution.

20. $\begin{bmatrix} 1 & h & -3 \\ -2 & 4 & 6 \end{bmatrix} \sim \begin{bmatrix} 1 & h & -3 \\ 0 & 4+2h & 0 \end{bmatrix}$. Write c for $4 + 2h$. Then the second equation $cx_2 = 0$ has a solution for every value of c. So the system is consistent for all h.

21. $\begin{bmatrix} 1 & 3 & -2 \\ -4 & h & 8 \end{bmatrix} \sim \begin{bmatrix} 1 & 3 & -2 \\ 0 & h+12 & 0 \end{bmatrix}$. Write c for $h + 12$. Then the second equation $cx_2 = 0$ has a solution for every value of c. So the system is consistent for all h.

22. $\begin{bmatrix} 2 & -3 & h \\ -6 & 9 & 5 \end{bmatrix} \sim \begin{bmatrix} 2 & -3 & h \\ 0 & 0 & 5+3h \end{bmatrix}$. The system is consistent if and only if $5 + 3h = 0$, that is, if and only if $h = -5/3$.

23. **a**. True. See the remarks following the box titled *Elementary Row Operations*.

   b. False. A 5×6 matrix has five rows.

   c. False. The description given applied to a single solution. The solution *set* consists of all possible solutions. Only in special cases does the solution set consist of exactly one solution. Mark a statement True only if the statement is *always* true.

   d. True. See the box before Example 2.

24. **a**. True. See the box preceding the subsection titled *Existence and Uniqueness Questions*.

   b. False. The definition of *row equivalent* requires that there exist a sequence of row operations that transforms one matrix into the other.

   c. False. By definition, an inconsistent system has *no* solution.

   d. True. This definition of *equivalent systems* is in the second paragraph after equation (2).

25.
$$\begin{bmatrix} 1 & -4 & 7 & g \\ 0 & 3 & -5 & h \\ -2 & 5 & -9 & k \end{bmatrix} \sim \begin{bmatrix} 1 & -4 & 7 & g \\ 0 & 3 & -5 & h \\ 0 & -3 & 5 & k+2g \end{bmatrix} \sim \begin{bmatrix} 1 & -4 & 7 & g \\ 0 & 3 & -5 & h \\ 0 & 0 & 0 & k+2g+h \end{bmatrix}$$

Let b denote the number $k + 2g + h$. Then the third equation represented by the augmented matrix above is $0 = b$. This equation is possible if and only if b is zero. So the original system has a solution if and only if $k + 2g + h = 0$.

26. A basic principle of this section is that row operations do not affect the solution set of a linear system. Begin with a simple augmented matrix for which the solution is obviously $(-2, 1, 0)$, and then perform any elementary row operations to produce other augmented matrices. Here are three examples. The fact that they are all row equivalent proves that they all have the solution set $(-2, 1, 0)$.

$$\begin{bmatrix} 1 & 0 & 0 & -2 \\ 0 & 1 & 0 & 1 \\ 0 & 0 & 1 & 0 \end{bmatrix} \sim \begin{bmatrix} 1 & 0 & 0 & -2 \\ 2 & 1 & 0 & -3 \\ 0 & 0 & 1 & 0 \end{bmatrix} \sim \begin{bmatrix} 1 & 0 & 0 & -2 \\ 2 & 1 & 0 & -3 \\ 2 & 0 & 1 & -4 \end{bmatrix}$$

27. Study the augmented matrix for the given system, replacing R2 by R2 + (−c)R1:

$$\begin{bmatrix} 1 & 3 & f \\ c & d & g \end{bmatrix} \sim \begin{bmatrix} 1 & 3 & f \\ 0 & d-3c & g-cf \end{bmatrix}$$

This shows that shows $d - 3c$ must be nonzero, since f and g are arbitrary. Otherwise, for some choices of f and g the second row would correspond to an equation of the form $0 = b$, where b is nonzero. Thus $d \neq 3c$.

28. Row reduce the augmented matrix for the given system. Scale the first row by $1/a$, which is possible since a is nonzero. Then replace R2 by R2 + (−c)R1.

$$\begin{bmatrix} a & b & f \\ c & d & g \end{bmatrix} \sim \begin{bmatrix} 1 & b/a & f/a \\ c & d & g \end{bmatrix} \sim \begin{bmatrix} 1 & b/a & f/a \\ 0 & d-c(b/a) & g-c(f/a) \end{bmatrix}$$

The quantity $d - c(b/a)$ must be nonzero, in order for the system to be consistent when the quantity $g - c(f/a)$ is nonzero (which can certainly happen). The condition that $d - c(b/a) \neq 0$ can also be written as $ad - bc \neq 0$, or $ad \neq bc$.

29. Swap R1 and R2; swap R1 and R2.

30. Multiply R2 by −1/2; multiply R2 by −2.

31. Replace R3 by R3 + (−4)R1; replace R3 by R3 + (4)R1.

32. Replace R3 by R3 + (3)R2; replace R3 by R3 + (−3)R2.

33. The first equation was given. The others are:

$$T_2 = (T_1 + 20 + 40 + T_3)/4, \quad \text{or} \quad 4T_2 - T_1 - T_3 = 60$$

$$T_3 = (T_4 + T_2 + 40 + 30)/4, \quad \text{or} \quad 4T_3 - T_4 - T_2 = 70$$

$$T_4 = (10 + T_1 + T_3 + 30)/4, \quad \text{or} \quad 4T_4 - T_1 - T_3 = 40$$

Rearranging,

$$
\begin{array}{rcrcrcrcl}
4T_1 & - & T_2 & & & - & T_4 & = & 30 \\
-T_1 & + & 4T_2 & - & T_3 & & & = & 60 \\
& & -T_2 & + & 4T_3 & - & T_4 & = & 70 \\
-T_1 & & & - & T_3 & + & 4T_4 & = & 40
\end{array}
$$

34. Begin by interchanging R1 and R4, then create zeros in the first column:

$$
\begin{bmatrix}
4 & -1 & 0 & -1 & 30 \\
-1 & 4 & -1 & 0 & 60 \\
0 & -1 & 4 & -1 & 70 \\
-1 & 0 & -1 & 4 & 40
\end{bmatrix}
\sim
\begin{bmatrix}
-1 & 0 & -1 & 4 & 40 \\
-1 & 4 & -1 & 0 & 60 \\
0 & -1 & 4 & -1 & 70 \\
4 & -1 & 0 & -1 & 30
\end{bmatrix}
\sim
\begin{bmatrix}
-1 & 0 & -1 & 4 & 40 \\
0 & 4 & 0 & -4 & 20 \\
0 & -1 & 4 & -1 & 70 \\
0 & -1 & -4 & 15 & 190
\end{bmatrix}
$$

Scale R1 by −1 and R2 by 1/4, create zeros in the second column, and replace R4 by R4 + R3:

$$
\sim
\begin{bmatrix}
1 & 0 & 1 & -4 & -40 \\
0 & 1 & 0 & -1 & 5 \\
0 & -1 & 4 & -1 & 70 \\
0 & -1 & -4 & 15 & 190
\end{bmatrix}
\sim
\begin{bmatrix}
1 & 0 & 1 & -4 & -40 \\
0 & 1 & 0 & -1 & 5 \\
0 & 0 & 4 & -2 & 75 \\
0 & 0 & -4 & 14 & 195
\end{bmatrix}
\sim
\begin{bmatrix}
1 & 0 & 1 & -4 & -40 \\
0 & 1 & 0 & -1 & 5 \\
0 & 0 & 4 & -2 & 75 \\
0 & 0 & 0 & 12 & 270
\end{bmatrix}
$$

Scale R4 by 1/12, use R4 to create zeros in column 4, and then scale R3 by 1/4:

$$
\sim
\begin{bmatrix}
1 & 0 & 1 & -4 & -40 \\
0 & 1 & 0 & -1 & 5 \\
0 & 0 & 4 & -2 & 75 \\
0 & 0 & 0 & 1 & 22.5
\end{bmatrix}
\sim
\begin{bmatrix}
1 & 0 & 1 & 0 & 50 \\
0 & 1 & 0 & 0 & 27.5 \\
0 & 0 & 4 & 0 & 120 \\
0 & 0 & 0 & 1 & 22.5
\end{bmatrix}
\sim
\begin{bmatrix}
1 & 0 & 1 & 0 & 50 \\
0 & 1 & 0 & 0 & 27.5 \\
0 & 0 & 1 & 0 & 30 \\
0 & 0 & 0 & 1 & 22.5
\end{bmatrix}
$$

The last step is to replace R1 by R1 + (−1)R3:

$$
\sim
\begin{bmatrix}
1 & 0 & 0 & 0 & 20.0 \\
0 & 1 & 0 & 0 & 27.5 \\
0 & 0 & 1 & 0 & 30.0 \\
0 & 0 & 0 & 1 & 22.5
\end{bmatrix}
$$

. The solution is (20, 27.5, 30, 22.5).

Notes: The *Study Guide* includes a "Mathematical Note" about statements, "If … , then … ."

This early in the course, students typically use single row operations to reduce a matrix. As a result, even the small grid for Exercise 34 leads to about 25 multiplications or additions (not counting operations with zero). This exercise should give students an appreciation for matrix programs such as MATLAB. Exercise 14 in Section 1.10 returns to this problem and states the solution in case students have not already solved the system of equations. Exercise 31 in Section 2.5 uses this same type of problem in connection with an LU factorization.

For instructors who wish to use technology in the course, the *Study Guide* provides boxed MATLAB notes at the ends of many sections. Parallel notes for Maple, Mathematica, and the TI-83+/86/89 and HP-48G calculators appear in separate appendices at the end of the *Study Guide*. The MATLAB box for Section 1.1 describes how to access the data that is available for all numerical exercises in the text. This feature has the ability to save students time if they regularly have their matrix program at hand when studying linear algebra. The MATLAB box also explains the basic commands **replace**, **swap**, and **scale**. These commands are included in the text data sets, available from the text web site, www.laylinalgebra.com.

1.2 SOLUTIONS

Notes: The key exercises are 1–20 and 23–28. (Students should work at least four or five from Exercises 7–14, in preparation for Section 1.5.)

1. Reduced echelon form: a and b. Echelon form: d. Not echelon: c.

2. Reduced echelon form: a. Echelon form: b and d. Not echelon: c.

3. $\begin{bmatrix} 1 & 2 & 3 & 4 \\ 4 & 5 & 6 & 7 \\ 6 & 7 & 8 & 9 \end{bmatrix} \sim \begin{bmatrix} 1 & 2 & 3 & 4 \\ 0 & -3 & -6 & -9 \\ 0 & -5 & -10 & -15 \end{bmatrix} \sim \begin{bmatrix} 1 & 2 & 3 & 4 \\ 0 & 1 & 2 & 3 \\ 0 & -5 & -10 & -15 \end{bmatrix}$

$\sim \begin{bmatrix} 1 & 2 & 3 & 4 \\ 0 & 1 & 2 & 3 \\ 0 & 0 & 0 & 0 \end{bmatrix} \sim \begin{bmatrix} ① & 0 & -1 & -2 \\ 0 & ① & 2 & 3 \\ 0 & 0 & 0 & 0 \end{bmatrix}$. Pivot cols 1 and 2. $\begin{bmatrix} ① & 2 & 3 & 4 \\ 4 & ⑤ & 6 & 7 \\ 6 & 7 & 8 & 9 \end{bmatrix}$

4. $\begin{bmatrix} 1 & 3 & 5 & 7 \\ 3 & 5 & 7 & 9 \\ 5 & 7 & 9 & 1 \end{bmatrix} \sim \begin{bmatrix} 1 & 3 & 5 & 7 \\ 0 & -4 & -8 & -12 \\ 0 & -8 & -16 & -34 \end{bmatrix} \sim \begin{bmatrix} 1 & 3 & 5 & 7 \\ 0 & 1 & 2 & 3 \\ 0 & -8 & -16 & -34 \end{bmatrix} \sim \begin{bmatrix} 1 & 3 & 5 & 7 \\ 0 & 1 & 2 & 3 \\ 0 & 0 & 0 & -10 \end{bmatrix}$

$\sim \begin{bmatrix} 1 & 3 & 5 & 7 \\ 0 & 1 & 2 & 3 \\ 0 & 0 & 0 & 1 \end{bmatrix} \sim \begin{bmatrix} 1 & 3 & 5 & 0 \\ 0 & 1 & 2 & 0 \\ 0 & 0 & 0 & 1 \end{bmatrix} \sim \begin{bmatrix} ① & 0 & -1 & 0 \\ 0 & ① & 2 & 0 \\ 0 & 0 & 0 & ① \end{bmatrix}$. Pivot cols 1, 2, and 4 $\begin{bmatrix} ① & 3 & 5 & 7 \\ 3 & ⑤ & 7 & 9 \\ 5 & 7 & 9 & ① \end{bmatrix}$

5. $\begin{bmatrix} ■ & * \\ 0 & ■ \end{bmatrix}, \begin{bmatrix} ■ & * \\ 0 & 0 \end{bmatrix}, \begin{bmatrix} 0 & ■ \\ 0 & 0 \end{bmatrix}$

6. $\begin{bmatrix} ■ & * \\ 0 & ■ \\ 0 & 0 \end{bmatrix}, \begin{bmatrix} ■ & * \\ 0 & 0 \\ 0 & 0 \end{bmatrix}, \begin{bmatrix} 0 & ■ \\ 0 & 0 \\ 0 & 0 \end{bmatrix}$

7. $\begin{bmatrix} 1 & 3 & 4 & 7 \\ 3 & 9 & 7 & 6 \end{bmatrix} \sim \begin{bmatrix} 1 & 3 & 4 & 7 \\ 0 & 0 & -5 & -15 \end{bmatrix} \sim \begin{bmatrix} 1 & 3 & 4 & 7 \\ 0 & 0 & 1 & 3 \end{bmatrix} \sim \begin{bmatrix} ① & 3 & 0 & -5 \\ 0 & 0 & ① & 3 \end{bmatrix}$

Corresponding system of equations: $\begin{array}{rcr} ⓧ_1 + 3x_2 & = & -5 \\ ⓧ_3 & = & 3 \end{array}$

The basic variables (corresponding to the pivot positions) are x_1 and x_3. The remaining variable x_2 is free. Solve for the basic variables in terms of the free variable. The general solution is

$$\begin{cases} x_1 = -5 - 3x_2 \\ x_2 \text{ is free} \\ x_3 = 3 \end{cases}$$

Note: Exercise 7 is paired with Exercise 10.

8. $\begin{bmatrix} 1 & 4 & 0 & 7 \\ 2 & 7 & 0 & 10 \end{bmatrix} \sim \begin{bmatrix} 1 & 4 & 0 & 7 \\ 0 & -1 & 0 & -4 \end{bmatrix} \sim \begin{bmatrix} 1 & 4 & 0 & 7 \\ 0 & 1 & 0 & 4 \end{bmatrix} \sim \begin{bmatrix} ① & 0 & 0 & -9 \\ 0 & ① & 0 & 4 \end{bmatrix}$

Corresponding system of equations:
$$\begin{aligned} x_1 \qquad &= -9 \\ x_2 \quad &= 4 \end{aligned}$$

The basic variables (corresponding to the pivot positions) are x_1 and x_2. The remaining variable x_3 is free. Solve for the basic variables in terms of the free variable. In this particular problem, the basic variables do not depend on the value of the free variable.

General solution: $\begin{cases} x_1 = -9 \\ x_2 = 4 \\ x_3 \text{ is free} \end{cases}$

Note: A common error in Exercise 8 is to assume that x_3 is zero. To avoid this, identify the basic variables first. Any remaining variables are *free*. (This type of computation will arise in Chapter 5.)

9. $\begin{bmatrix} 0 & 1 & -6 & 5 \\ 1 & -2 & 7 & -6 \end{bmatrix} \sim \begin{bmatrix} 1 & -2 & 7 & -6 \\ 0 & 1 & -6 & 5 \end{bmatrix} \sim \begin{bmatrix} ① & 0 & -5 & 4 \\ 0 & ① & -6 & 5 \end{bmatrix}$

Corresponding system:
$$\begin{aligned} x_1 \qquad - 5x_3 &= 4 \\ x_2 - 6x_3 &= 5 \end{aligned}$$

Basic variables: x_1, x_2; free variable: x_3. General solution: $\begin{cases} x_1 = 4 + 5x_3 \\ x_2 = 5 + 6x_3 \\ x_3 \text{ is free} \end{cases}$

10. $\begin{bmatrix} 1 & -2 & -1 & 3 \\ 3 & -6 & -2 & 2 \end{bmatrix} \sim \begin{bmatrix} 1 & -2 & -1 & 3 \\ 0 & 0 & 1 & -7 \end{bmatrix} \sim \begin{bmatrix} ① & -2 & 0 & -4 \\ 0 & 0 & ① & -7 \end{bmatrix}$

Corresponding system:
$$\begin{aligned} x_1 - 2x_2 \qquad &= -4 \\ x_3 &= -7 \end{aligned}$$

Basic variables: x_1, x_3; free variable: x_2. General solution: $\begin{cases} x_1 = -4 + 2x_2 \\ x_2 \text{ is free} \\ x_3 = -7 \end{cases}$

11. $\begin{bmatrix} 3 & -4 & 2 & 0 \\ -9 & 12 & -6 & 0 \\ -6 & 8 & -4 & 0 \end{bmatrix} \sim \begin{bmatrix} 3 & -4 & 2 & 0 \\ 0 & 0 & 0 & 0 \\ 0 & 0 & 0 & 0 \end{bmatrix} \sim \begin{bmatrix} ① & -4/3 & 2/3 & 0 \\ 0 & 0 & 0 & 0 \\ 0 & 0 & 0 & 0 \end{bmatrix}$

Corresponding system:
$$\begin{aligned} x_1 - \frac{4}{3}x_2 + \frac{2}{3}x_3 &= 0 \\ 0 &= 0 \\ 0 &= 0 \end{aligned}$$

Basic variable: x_1; free variables x_2, x_3. General solution: $\begin{cases} x_1 = \dfrac{4}{3}x_2 - \dfrac{2}{3}x_3 \\ x_2 \text{ is free} \\ x_3 \text{ is free} \end{cases}$

12. $\begin{bmatrix} 1 & -7 & 0 & 6 & 5 \\ 0 & 0 & 1 & -2 & -3 \\ -1 & 7 & -4 & 2 & 7 \end{bmatrix} \sim \begin{bmatrix} 1 & -7 & 0 & 6 & 5 \\ 0 & 0 & 1 & -2 & -3 \\ 0 & 0 & -4 & 8 & 12 \end{bmatrix} \sim \begin{bmatrix} ① & -7 & 0 & 6 & 5 \\ 0 & 0 & ① & -2 & -3 \\ 0 & 0 & 0 & 0 & 0 \end{bmatrix}$

Corresponding system: $\begin{aligned} Ⓧₗ \ - \ 7x_2 \quad\quad\ + \ 6x_4 &= \ 5 \\ Ⓧ_3 \ - \ 2x_4 &= \ -3 \\ 0 &= \ 0 \end{aligned}$

Basic variables: x_1 and x_3; free variables: x_2, x_4. General solution: $\begin{cases} x_1 = 5 + 7x_2 - 6x_4 \\ x_2 \text{ is free} \\ x_3 = -3 + 2x_4 \\ x_4 \text{ is free} \end{cases}$

13. $\begin{bmatrix} 1 & -3 & 0 & -1 & 0 & -2 \\ 0 & 1 & 0 & 0 & -4 & 1 \\ 0 & 0 & 0 & 1 & 9 & 4 \\ 0 & 0 & 0 & 0 & 0 & 0 \end{bmatrix} \sim \begin{bmatrix} 1 & -3 & 0 & 0 & 9 & 2 \\ 0 & 1 & 0 & 0 & -4 & 1 \\ 0 & 0 & 0 & 1 & 9 & 4 \\ 0 & 0 & 0 & 0 & 0 & 0 \end{bmatrix} \sim \begin{bmatrix} ① & 0 & 0 & 0 & -3 & 5 \\ 0 & ① & 0 & 0 & -4 & 1 \\ 0 & 0 & 0 & ① & 9 & 4 \\ 0 & 0 & 0 & 0 & 0 & 0 \end{bmatrix}$

Corresponding system: $\begin{aligned} Ⓧₗ \quad\quad\quad - \ 3x_5 &= \ 5 \\ Ⓧ_2 \quad\quad - \ 4x_5 &= \ 1 \\ Ⓧ_4 \ + \ 9x_5 &= \ 4 \\ 0 &= \ 0 \end{aligned}$

Basic variables: x_1, x_2, x_4; free variables: x_3, x_5. General solution: $\begin{cases} x_1 = 5 + 3x_5 \\ x_2 = 1 + 4x_5 \\ x_3 \text{ is free} \\ x_4 = 4 - 9x_5 \\ x_5 \text{ is free} \end{cases}$

Note: The *Study Guide* discusses the common mistake $x_3 = 0$.

14. $\begin{bmatrix} 1 & 2 & -5 & -6 & 0 & -5 \\ 0 & 1 & -6 & -3 & 0 & 2 \\ 0 & 0 & 0 & 0 & 1 & 0 \\ 0 & 0 & 0 & 0 & 0 & 0 \end{bmatrix} \sim \begin{bmatrix} ① & 0 & 7 & 0 & 0 & -9 \\ 0 & ① & -6 & -3 & 0 & 2 \\ 0 & 0 & 0 & 0 & ① & 0 \\ 0 & 0 & 0 & 0 & 0 & 0 \end{bmatrix}$

Corresponding system:

$$\begin{aligned}
\boxed{x_1} \quad + \quad 7x_3 \qquad\qquad &= \;-9 \\
\boxed{x_2} \;-\; 6x_3 \;-\; 3x_4 \quad &= \;\;\;2 \\
\boxed{x_5} &= \;\;\;0 \\
0 &= \;\;\;0
\end{aligned}$$

Basic variables: x_1, x_2, x_5; free variables: x_3, x_4. General solution:
$$\begin{cases}
x_1 = -9 - 7x_3 \\
x_2 = 2 + 6x_3 + 3x_4 \\
x_3 \text{ is free} \\
x_4 \text{ is free} \\
x_5 = 0
\end{cases}$$

15. **a.** The system is consistent, with a unique solution.

    b. The system is inconsistent. (The rightmost column of the augmented matrix is a pivot column).

16. **a.** The system is consistent, with a unique solution.

    b. The system is consistent. There are many solutions because x_2 is a free variable.

17. $\begin{bmatrix} 2 & 3 & h \\ 4 & 6 & 7 \end{bmatrix} \sim \begin{bmatrix} \boxed{2} & 3 & h \\ 0 & 0 & 7-2h \end{bmatrix}$ The system has a solution only if $7 - 2h = 0$, that is, if $h = 7/2$.

18. $\begin{bmatrix} 1 & -3 & -2 \\ 5 & h & -7 \end{bmatrix} \sim \begin{bmatrix} \boxed{1} & -3 & -2 \\ 0 & h+15 & 3 \end{bmatrix}$ If $h + 15$ is zero, that is, if $h = -15$, then the system has no solution, because 0 cannot equal 3. Otherwise, when $h \neq -15$, the system has a solution.

19. $\begin{bmatrix} 1 & h & 2 \\ 4 & 8 & k \end{bmatrix} \sim \begin{bmatrix} \boxed{1} & h & 2 \\ 0 & 8-4h & k-8 \end{bmatrix}$

    a. When $h = 2$ and $k \neq 8$, the augmented column is a pivot column, and the system is inconsistent.

    b. When $h \neq 2$, the system is consistent and has a unique solution. There are no free variables.

    c. When $h = 2$ and $k = 8$, the system is consistent and has many solutions.

20. $\begin{bmatrix} 1 & 3 & 2 \\ 3 & h & k \end{bmatrix} \sim \begin{bmatrix} \boxed{1} & 3 & 2 \\ 0 & h-9 & k-6 \end{bmatrix}$

    a. When $h = 9$ and $k \neq 6$, the system is inconsistent, because the augmented column is a pivot column.

    b. When $h \neq 9$, the system is consistent and has a unique solution. There are no free variables.

    c. When $h = 9$ and $k = 6$, the system is consistent and has many solutions.

21. **a.** False. See Theorem 1.

    b. False. See the second paragraph of the section.

    c. True. Basic variables are defined after equation (4).

    d. True. This statement is at the beginning of *Parametric Descriptions of Solution Sets*.

    e. False. The row shown corresponds to the equation $5x_4 = 0$, which does not by itself lead to a contradiction. So the system might be consistent or it might be inconsistent.

22. a. False. See the statement preceding Theorem 1. Only the *reduced* echelon form is unique.

   b. False. See the beginning of the subsection *Pivot Positions*. The pivot positions in a matrix are determined completely by the positions of the leading entries in the nonzero rows of any echelon form obtained from the matrix.

   c. True. See the paragraph after Example 3.

   d. False. The existence of at least one solution is not related to the presence or absence of free variables. If the system is inconsistent, the solution set is empty. See the solution of Practice Problem 2.

   e. True. See the paragraph just before Example 4.

23. Yes. The system is consistent because with three pivots, there must be a pivot in the third (bottom) row of the coefficient matrix. The reduced echelon form cannot contain a row of the form $[0 \ 0 \ 0 \ 0 \ 0 \ 1]$.

24. The system is inconsistent because the pivot in column 5 means that there is a row of the form $[0 \ 0 \ 0 \ 0 \ 1]$. Since the matrix is the *augmented* matrix for a system, Theorem 2 shows that the system has no solution.

25. If the coefficient matrix has a pivot position in every row, then there is a pivot position in the bottom row, and there is no room for a pivot in the augmented column. So, the system is consistent, by Theorem 2.

26. Since there are three pivots (one in each row), the augmented matrix must reduce to the form

$$\begin{bmatrix} ① & 0 & 0 & a \\ 0 & ① & 0 & b \\ 0 & 0 & ① & c \end{bmatrix} \text{ and so } \begin{array}{ccc} ⓧ_1 & = & a \\ ⓧ_2 & = & b \\ ⓧ_3 & = & c \end{array}$$

No matter what the values of a, b, and c, the solution exists and is unique.

27. *"If a linear system is consistent, then the solution is unique if and only if every column in the coefficient matrix is a pivot column; otherwise there are infinitely many solutions."*

This statement is true because the free variables correspond to *nonpivot* columns of the coefficient matrix. The columns are all pivot columns if and only if there are no free variables. And there are no free variables if and only if the solution is unique, by Theorem 2.

28. Every column in the augmented matrix *except the rightmost column* is a pivot column, and the rightmost column is *not* a pivot column.

29. An underdetermined system always has more variables than equations. There cannot be more basic variables than there are equations, so there must be at least one free variable. Such a variable may be assigned infinitely many different values. If the system is consistent, each different value of a free variable will produce a different solution.

30. Example:
$$\begin{array}{ccccccc} x_1 & + & x_2 & + & x_3 & = & 4 \\ 2x_1 & + & 2x_2 & + & 2x_3 & = & 5 \end{array}$$

31. Yes, a system of linear equations with more equations than unknowns can be consistent.

Example (in which $x_1 = x_2 = 1$):
$$\begin{array}{ccccc} x_1 & + & x_2 & = & 2 \\ x_1 & - & x_2 & = & 0 \\ 3x_1 & + & 2x_2 & = & 5 \end{array}$$

32. According to the numerical note in Section 1.2, when $n = 30$ the reduction to echelon form takes about $2(30)^3/3 = 18{,}000$ flops, while further reduction to reduced echelon form needs at most $(30)^2 = 900$ flops. Of the total flops, the "backward phase" is about $900/18900 = .048$ or about 5%.

When $n = 300$, the estimates are $2(300)^3/3 = 18{,}000{,}000$ phase for the reduction to echelon form and $(300)^2 = 90{,}000$ flops for the backward phase. The fraction associated with the backward phase is about $(9 \times 10^4)/(18 \times 10^6) = .005$, or about .5%.

33. For a quadratic polynomial $p(t) = a_0 + a_1 t + a_2 t^2$ to exactly fit the data $(1, 12)$, $(2, 15)$, and $(3, 16)$, the coefficients a_0, a_1, a_2 must satisfy the systems of equations given in the text. Row reduce the augmented matrix:

$$\begin{bmatrix} 1 & 1 & 1 & 12 \\ 1 & 2 & 4 & 15 \\ 1 & 3 & 9 & 16 \end{bmatrix} \sim \begin{bmatrix} 1 & 1 & 1 & 12 \\ 0 & 1 & 3 & 3 \\ 0 & 2 & 8 & 4 \end{bmatrix} \sim \begin{bmatrix} 1 & 1 & 1 & 12 \\ 0 & 1 & 3 & 3 \\ 0 & 0 & 2 & -2 \end{bmatrix} \sim \begin{bmatrix} 1 & 1 & 1 & 12 \\ 0 & 1 & 3 & 3 \\ 0 & 0 & 1 & -1 \end{bmatrix}$$

$$\sim \begin{bmatrix} 1 & 1 & 0 & 13 \\ 0 & 1 & 0 & 6 \\ 0 & 0 & 1 & -1 \end{bmatrix} \sim \begin{bmatrix} ① & 0 & 0 & 7 \\ 0 & ① & 0 & 6 \\ 0 & 0 & ① & -1 \end{bmatrix}$$

The polynomial is $p(t) = 7 + 6t - t^2$.

34. **[M]** The system of equations to be solved is:

$$a_0 + a_1 \cdot 0 + a_2 \cdot 0^2 + a_3 \cdot 0^3 + a_4 \cdot 0^4 + a_5 \cdot 0^5 = 0$$
$$a_0 + a_1 \cdot 2 + a_2 \cdot 2^2 + a_3 \cdot 2^3 + a_4 \cdot 2^4 + a_5 \cdot 2^5 = 2.90$$
$$a_0 + a_1 \cdot 4 + a_2 \cdot 4^2 + a_3 \cdot 4^3 + a_4 \cdot 4^4 + a_5 \cdot 4^5 = 14.8$$
$$a_0 + a_1 \cdot 6 + a_2 \cdot 6^2 + a_3 \cdot 6^3 + a_4 \cdot 6^4 + a_5 \cdot 6^5 = 39.6$$
$$a_0 + a_1 \cdot 8 + a_2 \cdot 8^2 + a_3 \cdot 8^3 + a_4 \cdot 8^4 + a_5 \cdot 8^5 = 74.3$$
$$a_0 + a_1 \cdot 10 + a_2 \cdot 10^2 + a_3 \cdot 10^3 + a_4 \cdot 10^4 + a_5 \cdot 10^5 = 119$$

The unknowns are $a_0, a_1, \ldots, a_5$. Use technology to compute the reduced echelon of the augmented matrix:

$$\begin{bmatrix} 1 & 0 & 0 & 0 & 0 & 0 & 0 \\ 1 & 2 & 4 & 8 & 16 & 32 & 2.9 \\ 1 & 4 & 16 & 64 & 256 & 1024 & 14.8 \\ 1 & 6 & 36 & 216 & 1296 & 7776 & 39.6 \\ 1 & 8 & 64 & 512 & 4096 & 32768 & 74.3 \\ 1 & 10 & 10^2 & 10^3 & 10^4 & 10^5 & 119 \end{bmatrix} \sim \begin{bmatrix} 1 & 0 & 0 & 0 & 0 & 0 & 0 \\ 0 & 2 & 4 & 8 & 16 & 32 & 2.9 \\ 0 & 0 & 8 & 48 & 224 & 960 & 9 \\ 0 & 0 & 24 & 192 & 1248 & 7680 & 30.9 \\ 0 & 0 & 48 & 480 & 4032 & 32640 & 62.7 \\ 0 & 0 & 80 & 960 & 9920 & 99840 & 104.5 \end{bmatrix}$$

$$\sim \begin{bmatrix} 1 & 0 & 0 & 0 & 0 & 0 & 0 \\ 0 & 2 & 4 & 8 & 16 & 32 & 2.9 \\ 0 & 0 & 8 & 48 & 224 & 960 & 9 \\ 0 & 0 & 0 & 48 & 576 & 4800 & 3.9 \\ 0 & 0 & 0 & 192 & 2688 & 26880 & 8.7 \\ 0 & 0 & 0 & 480 & 7680 & 90240 & 14.5 \end{bmatrix} \sim \begin{bmatrix} 1 & 0 & 0 & 0 & 0 & 0 & 0 \\ 0 & 2 & 4 & 8 & 16 & 32 & 2.9 \\ 0 & 0 & 8 & 48 & 224 & 960 & 9 \\ 0 & 0 & 0 & 48 & 576 & 4800 & 3.9 \\ 0 & 0 & 0 & 0 & 384 & 7680 & -6.9 \\ 0 & 0 & 0 & 0 & 1920 & 42240 & -24.5 \end{bmatrix}$$

$$\sim \begin{bmatrix} 1 & 0 & 0 & 0 & 0 & 0 & 0 \\ 0 & 2 & 4 & 8 & 16 & 32 & 2.9 \\ 0 & 0 & 8 & 48 & 224 & 960 & 9 \\ 0 & 0 & 0 & 48 & 576 & 4800 & 3.9 \\ 0 & 0 & 0 & 0 & 384 & 7680 & -6.9 \\ 0 & 0 & 0 & 0 & 0 & 3840 & 10 \end{bmatrix} \sim \begin{bmatrix} 1 & 0 & 0 & 0 & 0 & 0 & 0 \\ 0 & 2 & 4 & 8 & 16 & 32 & 2.9 \\ 0 & 0 & 8 & 48 & 224 & 960 & 9 \\ 0 & 0 & 0 & 48 & 576 & 4800 & 3.9 \\ 0 & 0 & 0 & 0 & 384 & 7680 & -6.9 \\ 0 & 0 & 0 & 0 & 0 & 1 & .0026 \end{bmatrix}$$

$$\sim \begin{bmatrix} 1 & 0 & 0 & 0 & 0 & 0 & 0 \\ 0 & 2 & 4 & 8 & 16 & 0 & 2.8167 \\ 0 & 0 & 8 & 48 & 224 & 0 & 6.5000 \\ 0 & 0 & 0 & 48 & 576 & 0 & -8.6000 \\ 0 & 0 & 0 & 0 & 384 & 0 & -26.900 \\ 0 & 0 & 0 & 0 & 0 & 1 & .002604 \end{bmatrix} \sim \cdots \sim \begin{bmatrix} 1 & 0 & 0 & 0 & 0 & 0 & 0 \\ 0 & 1 & 0 & 0 & 0 & 0 & 1.7125 \\ 0 & 0 & 1 & 0 & 0 & 0 & -1.1948 \\ 0 & 0 & 0 & 1 & 0 & 0 & .6615 \\ 0 & 0 & 0 & 0 & 1 & 0 & -.0701 \\ 0 & 0 & 0 & 0 & 0 & 1 & .0026 \end{bmatrix}$$

Thus $p(t) = 1.7125t - 1.1948t^2 + .6615t^3 - .0701t^4 + .0026t^5$, and $p(7.5) = 64.6$ hundred lb.

Notes: In Exercise 34, if the coefficients are retained to higher accuracy than shown here, then $p(7.5) = 64.8$. If a polynomial of lower degree is used, the resulting system of equations is overdetermined. The augmented matrix for such a system is the same as the one used to find p, except that at least column 6 is missing. When the augmented matrix is row reduced, the sixth row of the augmented matrix will be entirely zero except for a nonzero entry in the augmented column, indicating that no solution exists.

Exercise 34 requires 25 row operations. It should give students an appreciation for higher-level commands such as **gauss** and **bgauss**, discussed in Section 1.4 of the *Study Guide*. The command **ref** (reduced echelon form) is available, but I recommend postponing that command until Chapter 2.

The *Study Guide* includes a "Mathematical Note" about the phrase, "If and only if," used in Theorem 2.

1.3   SOLUTIONS

Notes: The key exercises are 11–14, 17–22, 25, and 26. A discussion of Exercise 25 will help students understand the notation $[\mathbf{a}_1 \ \ \mathbf{a}_2 \ \ \mathbf{a}_3]$, $\{\mathbf{a}_1, \mathbf{a}_2, \mathbf{a}_3\}$, and Span$\{\mathbf{a}_1, \mathbf{a}_2, \mathbf{a}_3\}$.

1. $\mathbf{u} + \mathbf{v} = \begin{bmatrix} -1 \\ 2 \end{bmatrix} + \begin{bmatrix} -3 \\ -1 \end{bmatrix} = \begin{bmatrix} -1 + (-3) \\ 2 + (-1) \end{bmatrix} = \begin{bmatrix} -4 \\ 1 \end{bmatrix}$.

Using the definitions carefully,

$\mathbf{u} - 2\mathbf{v} = \begin{bmatrix} -1 \\ 2 \end{bmatrix} + (-2)\begin{bmatrix} -3 \\ -1 \end{bmatrix} = \begin{bmatrix} -1 \\ 2 \end{bmatrix} + \begin{bmatrix} (-2)(-3) \\ (-2)(-1) \end{bmatrix} = \begin{bmatrix} -1+6 \\ 2+2 \end{bmatrix} = \begin{bmatrix} 5 \\ 4 \end{bmatrix}$, or, more quickly,

$\mathbf{u} - 2\mathbf{v} = \begin{bmatrix} -1 \\ 2 \end{bmatrix} - 2\begin{bmatrix} -3 \\ -1 \end{bmatrix} = \begin{bmatrix} -1+6 \\ 2+2 \end{bmatrix} = \begin{bmatrix} 5 \\ 4 \end{bmatrix}$. The intermediate step is often not written.

2. $\mathbf{u} + \mathbf{v} = \begin{bmatrix} 3 \\ 2 \end{bmatrix} + \begin{bmatrix} 2 \\ -1 \end{bmatrix} = \begin{bmatrix} 3+2 \\ 2+(-1) \end{bmatrix} = \begin{bmatrix} 5 \\ 1 \end{bmatrix}$.

Using the definitions carefully,

$$\mathbf{u} - 2\mathbf{v} = \begin{bmatrix} 3 \\ 2 \end{bmatrix} + (-2)\begin{bmatrix} 2 \\ -1 \end{bmatrix} = \begin{bmatrix} 3 \\ 2 \end{bmatrix} + \begin{bmatrix} (-2)(2) \\ (-2)(-1) \end{bmatrix} = \begin{bmatrix} 3 + (-4) \\ 2 + 2 \end{bmatrix} = \begin{bmatrix} -1 \\ 4 \end{bmatrix}, \text{ or, more quickly,}$$

$$\mathbf{u} - 2\mathbf{v} = \begin{bmatrix} 3 \\ 2 \end{bmatrix} - 2\begin{bmatrix} 2 \\ -1 \end{bmatrix} = \begin{bmatrix} 3 - 4 \\ 2 + 2 \end{bmatrix} = \begin{bmatrix} -1 \\ 4 \end{bmatrix}. \text{ The intermediate step is often not written.}$$

3.

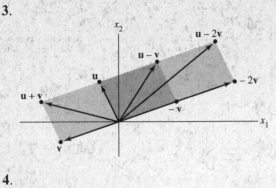

4.

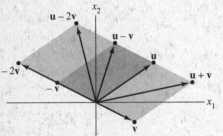

5. $x_1 \begin{bmatrix} 6 \\ -1 \\ 5 \end{bmatrix} + x_2 \begin{bmatrix} -3 \\ 4 \\ 0 \end{bmatrix} = \begin{bmatrix} 1 \\ -7 \\ -5 \end{bmatrix}$, $\begin{bmatrix} 6x_1 \\ -x_1 \\ 5x_1 \end{bmatrix} + \begin{bmatrix} -3x_2 \\ 4x_2 \\ 0 \end{bmatrix} = \begin{bmatrix} 1 \\ -7 \\ -5 \end{bmatrix}$, $\begin{bmatrix} 6x_1 - 3x_2 \\ -x_1 + 4x_2 \\ 5x_1 \end{bmatrix} = \begin{bmatrix} 1 \\ -7 \\ -5 \end{bmatrix}$

$$\begin{array}{rcrcr} 6x_1 & - & 3x_2 & = & 1 \\ -x_1 & + & 4x_2 & = & -7 \\ 5x_1 & & & = & -5 \end{array}$$

Usually the intermediate steps are not displayed.

6. $x_1 \begin{bmatrix} -2 \\ 3 \end{bmatrix} + x_2 \begin{bmatrix} 8 \\ 5 \end{bmatrix} + x_3 \begin{bmatrix} 1 \\ -6 \end{bmatrix} = \begin{bmatrix} 0 \\ 0 \end{bmatrix}$, $\begin{bmatrix} -2x_1 \\ 3x_1 \end{bmatrix} + \begin{bmatrix} 8x_2 \\ 5x_2 \end{bmatrix} + \begin{bmatrix} x_3 \\ -6x_3 \end{bmatrix} = \begin{bmatrix} 0 \\ 0 \end{bmatrix}$, $\begin{bmatrix} -2x_1 + 8x_2 + x_3 \\ 3x_1 + 5x_2 - 6x_3 \end{bmatrix} = \begin{bmatrix} 0 \\ 0 \end{bmatrix}$

$$\begin{array}{rcrcrcr} -2x_2 & + & 8x_2 & + & x_3 & = & 0 \\ 3x_1 & + & 5x_2 & - & 6x_3 & = & 0 \end{array}$$

Usually the intermediate steps are not displayed.

7. See the figure below. Since the grid can be extended in every direction, the figure suggests that every vector in $\mathbf{R}^2$ can be written as a linear combination of $\mathbf{u}$ and $\mathbf{v}$.

To write a vector $\mathbf{a}$ as a linear combination of $\mathbf{u}$ and $\mathbf{v}$, imagine walking from the origin to $\mathbf{a}$ along the grid "streets" and keep track of how many "blocks" you travel in the $\mathbf{u}$-direction and how many in the $\mathbf{v}$-direction.

a. To reach $\mathbf{a}$ from the origin, you might travel 1 unit in the $\mathbf{u}$-direction and -2 units in the $\mathbf{v}$-direction (that is, 2 units in the negative $\mathbf{v}$-direction). Hence $\mathbf{a} = \mathbf{u} - 2\mathbf{v}$.

b. To reach **b** from the origin, travel 2 units in the **u**-direction and –2 units in the **v**-direction. So **b** = 2**u** – 2**v**. Or, use the fact that **b** is 1 unit in the **u**-direction from **a**, so that

$$\mathbf{b} = \mathbf{a} + \mathbf{u} = (\mathbf{u} - 2\mathbf{v}) + \mathbf{u} = 2\mathbf{u} - 2\mathbf{v}$$

c. The vector **c** is –1.5 units from **b** in the **v**-direction, so

$$\mathbf{c} = \mathbf{b} - 1.5\mathbf{v} = (2\mathbf{u} - 2\mathbf{v}) - 1.5\mathbf{v} = 2\mathbf{u} - 3.5\mathbf{v}$$

d. The "map" suggests that you can reach **d** if you travel 3 units in the **u**-direction and –4 units in the **v**-direction. If you prefer to stay on the paths displayed on the map, you might travel from the origin to –3**v**, then move 3 units in the **u**-direction, and finally move –1 unit in the **v**-direction. So

$$\mathbf{d} = -3\mathbf{v} + 3\mathbf{u} - \mathbf{v} = 3\mathbf{u} - 4\mathbf{v}$$

Another solution is

$$\mathbf{d} = \mathbf{b} - 2\mathbf{v} + \mathbf{u} = (2\mathbf{u} - 2\mathbf{v}) - 2\mathbf{v} + \mathbf{u} = 3\mathbf{u} - 4\mathbf{v}$$

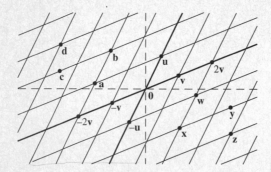

Figure for Exercises 7 and 8

8. See the figure above. Since the grid can be extended in every direction, the figure suggests that every vector in $\mathbf{R}^2$ can be written as a linear combination of **u** and **v**.

w. To reach **w** from the origin, travel –1 units in the **u**-direction (that is, 1 unit in the negative **u**-direction) and travel 2 units in the **v**-direction. Thus, **w** = (–1)**u** + 2**v**, or **w** = 2**v** – **u**.

x. To reach **x** from the origin, travel 2 units in the **v**-direction and –2 units in the **u**-direction. Thus, **x** = –2**u** + 2**v**. Or, use the fact that **x** is –1 units in the **u**-direction from **w**, so that

$$\mathbf{x} = \mathbf{w} - \mathbf{u} = (-\mathbf{u} + 2\mathbf{v}) - \mathbf{u} = -2\mathbf{u} + 2\mathbf{v}$$

y. The vector **y** is 1.5 units from **x** in the **v**-direction, so

$$\mathbf{y} = \mathbf{x} + 1.5\mathbf{v} = (-2\mathbf{u} + 2\mathbf{v}) + 1.5\mathbf{v} = -2\mathbf{u} + 3.5\mathbf{v}$$

z. The map suggests that you can reach **z** if you travel 4 units in the **v**-direction and –3 units in the **u**-direction. So **z** = 4**v** – 3**u** = –3**u** + 4**v**. If you prefer to stay on the paths displayed on the "map," you might travel from the origin to –2**u**, then 4 units in the **v**-direction, and finally move –1 unit in the **u**-direction. So

$$\mathbf{z} = -2\mathbf{u} + 4\mathbf{v} - \mathbf{u} = -3\mathbf{u} + 4\mathbf{v}$$

9.
$$\begin{array}{rcrcrcl} & & x_2 & + & 5x_3 & = & 0 \\ 4x_1 & + & 6x_2 & - & x_3 & = & 0, \\ -x_1 & + & 3x_2 & - & 8x_3 & = & 0 \end{array} \qquad \begin{bmatrix} x_2 + 5x_3 \\ 4x_1 + 6x_2 - x_3 \\ -x_1 + 3x_2 - 8x_3 \end{bmatrix} = \begin{bmatrix} 0 \\ 0 \\ 0 \end{bmatrix}$$

$$\begin{bmatrix} 0 \\ 4x_1 \\ -x_1 \end{bmatrix} + \begin{bmatrix} x_2 \\ 6x_2 \\ 3x_2 \end{bmatrix} + \begin{bmatrix} 5x_3 \\ -x_3 \\ -8x_3 \end{bmatrix} = \begin{bmatrix} 0 \\ 0 \\ 0 \end{bmatrix}, \qquad x_1 \begin{bmatrix} 0 \\ 4 \\ -1 \end{bmatrix} + x_2 \begin{bmatrix} 1 \\ 6 \\ 3 \end{bmatrix} + x_3 \begin{bmatrix} 5 \\ -1 \\ -8 \end{bmatrix} = \begin{bmatrix} 0 \\ 0 \\ 0 \end{bmatrix}$$

Usually, the intermediate calculations are not displayed.

Note: The *Study Guide* says, "Check with your instructor whether you need to "show work" on a problem such as Exercise 9."

$$
\begin{aligned}
4x_1 &+ x_2 + 3x_3 = 9 \\
10. \quad x_1 &- 7x_2 - 2x_3 = 2, \\
8x_1 &+ 6x_2 - 5x_3 = 15
\end{aligned}
\qquad
\begin{bmatrix} 4x_1 + x_2 + 3x_3 \\ x_1 - 7x_2 - 2x_3 \\ 8x_1 + 6x_2 - 5x_3 \end{bmatrix} = \begin{bmatrix} 9 \\ 2 \\ 15 \end{bmatrix}
$$

$$
\begin{bmatrix} 4x_1 \\ x_1 \\ 8x_1 \end{bmatrix} + \begin{bmatrix} x_2 \\ -7x_2 \\ 6x_2 \end{bmatrix} + \begin{bmatrix} 3x_3 \\ -2x_3 \\ -5x_3 \end{bmatrix} = \begin{bmatrix} 9 \\ 2 \\ 15 \end{bmatrix},
\qquad
x_1 \begin{bmatrix} 4 \\ 1 \\ 8 \end{bmatrix} + x_2 \begin{bmatrix} 1 \\ -7 \\ 6 \end{bmatrix} + x_3 \begin{bmatrix} 3 \\ -2 \\ -5 \end{bmatrix} = \begin{bmatrix} 9 \\ 2 \\ 15 \end{bmatrix}
$$

Usually, the intermediate calculations are not displayed.

11. The question

> Is $\mathbf{b}$ a linear combination of $\mathbf{a}_1$, $\mathbf{a}_2$, and $\mathbf{a}_3$?

is equivalent to the question

> Does the vector equation $x_1\mathbf{a}_1 + x_2\mathbf{a}_2 + x_3\mathbf{a}_3 = \mathbf{b}$ have a solution?

The equation

$$
x_1 \begin{bmatrix} 1 \\ -2 \\ 0 \end{bmatrix} + x_2 \begin{bmatrix} 0 \\ 1 \\ 2 \end{bmatrix} + x_3 \begin{bmatrix} 5 \\ -6 \\ 8 \end{bmatrix} = \begin{bmatrix} 2 \\ -1 \\ 6 \end{bmatrix} \qquad (*)
$$
$$
\quad\;\uparrow \qquad\quad \uparrow \qquad\quad \uparrow \qquad\; \uparrow
$$
$$
\quad\;\mathbf{a}_1 \qquad\; \mathbf{a}_2 \qquad\; \mathbf{a}_3 \qquad \mathbf{b}
$$

has the same solution set as the linear system whose augmented matrix is

$$
M = \begin{bmatrix} 1 & 0 & 5 & 2 \\ -2 & 1 & -6 & -1 \\ 0 & 2 & 8 & 6 \end{bmatrix}
$$

Row reduce M until the pivot positions are visible:

$$
M \sim \begin{bmatrix} 1 & 0 & 5 & 2 \\ 0 & 1 & 4 & 3 \\ 0 & 2 & 8 & 6 \end{bmatrix} \sim \begin{bmatrix} ① & 0 & 5 & 2 \\ 0 & ① & 4 & 3 \\ 0 & 0 & 0 & 0 \end{bmatrix}
$$

The linear system corresponding to M *has* a solution, so the vector equation (*) has a solution, and therefore $\mathbf{b}$ *is* a linear combination of $\mathbf{a}_1$, $\mathbf{a}_2$, and $\mathbf{a}_3$.

12. The equation

$$
x_1 \begin{bmatrix} 1 \\ -2 \\ 2 \end{bmatrix} + x_2 \begin{bmatrix} 0 \\ 5 \\ 5 \end{bmatrix} + x_3 \begin{bmatrix} 2 \\ 0 \\ 8 \end{bmatrix} = \begin{bmatrix} -5 \\ 11 \\ -7 \end{bmatrix} \qquad (*)
$$
$$
\quad\;\uparrow \qquad\quad \uparrow \qquad\quad \uparrow \qquad\; \uparrow
$$
$$
\quad\;\mathbf{a}_1 \qquad\; \mathbf{a}_2 \qquad\; \mathbf{a}_3 \qquad \mathbf{b}
$$

has the same solution set as the linear system whose augmented matrix is

$$M = \begin{bmatrix} 1 & 0 & 2 & -5 \\ -2 & 5 & 0 & 11 \\ 2 & 5 & 8 & -7 \end{bmatrix}$$

Row reduce M until the pivot positions are visible:

$$M \sim \begin{bmatrix} 1 & 0 & 2 & -5 \\ 0 & 5 & 4 & 1 \\ 0 & 5 & 4 & 3 \end{bmatrix} \sim \begin{bmatrix} ① & 0 & 2 & -5 \\ 0 & ⑤ & 4 & 1 \\ 0 & 0 & 0 & ② \end{bmatrix}$$

The linear system corresponding to M has *no* solution, so the vector equation (*) has no solution, and therefore **b** is *not* a linear combination of $\mathbf{a}_1$, $\mathbf{a}_2$, and $\mathbf{a}_3$.

13. Denote the columns of A by $\mathbf{a}_1$, $\mathbf{a}_2$, $\mathbf{a}_3$. To determine if **b** is a linear combination of these columns, use the boxed fact on page 34. Row reduced the augmented matrix until you reach echelon form:

$$\begin{bmatrix} 1 & -4 & 2 & 3 \\ 0 & 3 & 5 & -7 \\ -2 & 8 & -4 & -3 \end{bmatrix} \sim \begin{bmatrix} ① & -4 & 2 & 3 \\ 0 & ③ & 5 & -7 \\ 0 & 0 & 0 & ③ \end{bmatrix}$$

The system for this augmented matrix is inconsistent, so **b** is *not* a linear combination of the columns of A.

14. $[\mathbf{a}_1 \quad \mathbf{a}_2 \quad \mathbf{a}_3 \quad \mathbf{b}] = \begin{bmatrix} 1 & -2 & -6 & 11 \\ 0 & 3 & 7 & -5 \\ 1 & -2 & 5 & 9 \end{bmatrix} \sim \begin{bmatrix} ① & -2 & -6 & 11 \\ 0 & ③ & 7 & -5 \\ 0 & 0 & ⑪ & -2 \end{bmatrix}$. The linear system corresponding to this

matrix *has* a solution, so **b** is a linear combination of the columns of A.

15. Noninteger weights are acceptable, of course, but some simple choices are $0 \cdot \mathbf{v}_1 + 0 \cdot \mathbf{v}_2 = \mathbf{0}$, and

$$1 \cdot \mathbf{v}_1 + 0 \cdot \mathbf{v}_2 = \begin{bmatrix} 7 \\ 1 \\ -6 \end{bmatrix}, \quad 0 \cdot \mathbf{v}_1 + 1 \cdot \mathbf{v}_2 = \begin{bmatrix} -5 \\ 3 \\ 0 \end{bmatrix}$$

$$1 \cdot \mathbf{v}_1 + 1 \cdot \mathbf{v}_2 = \begin{bmatrix} 2 \\ 4 \\ -6 \end{bmatrix}, \quad 1 \cdot \mathbf{v}_1 - 1 \cdot \mathbf{v}_2 = \begin{bmatrix} 12 \\ -2 \\ -6 \end{bmatrix}$$

16. Some likely choices are $0 \cdot \mathbf{v}_1 + 0 \cdot \mathbf{v}_2 = \mathbf{0}$, and

$$1 \cdot \mathbf{v}_1 + 0 \cdot \mathbf{v}_2 = \begin{bmatrix} 3 \\ 0 \\ 2 \end{bmatrix}, \quad 0 \cdot \mathbf{v}_1 + 1 \cdot \mathbf{v}_2 = \begin{bmatrix} -2 \\ 0 \\ 3 \end{bmatrix}$$

$$1 \cdot \mathbf{v}_1 + 1 \cdot \mathbf{v}_2 = \begin{bmatrix} 1 \\ 0 \\ 5 \end{bmatrix}, \quad 1 \cdot \mathbf{v}_1 - 1 \cdot \mathbf{v}_2 = \begin{bmatrix} 5 \\ 0 \\ -1 \end{bmatrix}$$

17. $[\mathbf{a}_1 \quad \mathbf{a}_2 \quad \mathbf{b}] = \begin{bmatrix} 1 & -2 & 4 \\ 4 & -3 & 1 \\ -2 & 7 & h \end{bmatrix} \sim \begin{bmatrix} 1 & -2 & 4 \\ 0 & 5 & -15 \\ 0 & 3 & h+8 \end{bmatrix} \sim \begin{bmatrix} 1 & -2 & 4 \\ 0 & 1 & -3 \\ 0 & 3 & h+8 \end{bmatrix} \sim \begin{bmatrix} ① & -2 & 4 \\ 0 & ① & -3 \\ 0 & 0 & h+17 \end{bmatrix}$. The vector **b** is

in Span$\{\mathbf{a}_1, \mathbf{a}_2\}$ when $h + 17$ is zero, that is, when $h = -17$.

18. $[\mathbf{v}_1 \quad \mathbf{v}_2 \quad \mathbf{y}] = \begin{bmatrix} 1 & -3 & h \\ 0 & 1 & -5 \\ -2 & 8 & -3 \end{bmatrix} \sim \begin{bmatrix} 1 & -3 & h \\ 0 & 1 & -5 \\ 0 & 2 & -3+2h \end{bmatrix} \sim \begin{bmatrix} ① & -3 & h \\ 0 & ① & -5 \\ 0 & 0 & 7+2h \end{bmatrix}$. The vector **y** is in

Span$\{\mathbf{v}_1, \mathbf{v}_2\}$ when $7 + 2h$ is zero, that is, when $h = -7/2$.

19. By inspection, $\mathbf{v}_2 = (3/2)\mathbf{v}_1$. Any linear combination of $\mathbf{v}_1$ and $\mathbf{v}_2$ is actually just a multiple of $\mathbf{v}_1$. For instance,

$$a\mathbf{v}_1 + b\mathbf{v}_2 = a\mathbf{v}_1 + b(3/2)\mathbf{v}_2 = (a + 3b/2)\mathbf{v}_1$$

So Span$\{\mathbf{v}_1, \mathbf{v}_2\}$ is the set of points on the line through $\mathbf{v}_1$ and **0**.

Note: Exercises 19 and 20 prepare the way for ideas in Sections 1.4 and 1.7.

20. Span$\{\mathbf{v}_1, \mathbf{v}_2\}$ is a plane in $\mathbf{R}^3$ through the origin, because the neither vector in this problem is a multiple of the other. Every vector in the set has 0 as its second entry and so lies in the *xz*-plane in ordinary 3-space. So Span$\{\mathbf{v}_1, \mathbf{v}_2\}$ *is* the *xz*-plane.

21. Let $\mathbf{y} = \begin{bmatrix} h \\ k \end{bmatrix}$. Then $[\mathbf{u} \quad \mathbf{v} \quad \mathbf{y}] = \begin{bmatrix} 2 & 2 & h \\ -1 & 1 & k \end{bmatrix} \sim \begin{bmatrix} ② & 2 & h \\ 0 & ② & k+h/2 \end{bmatrix}$. This augmented matrix corresponds to

a consistent system for all h and k. So **y** is in Span$\{\mathbf{u}, \mathbf{v}\}$ for all h and k.

22. Construct any 3×4 matrix in echelon form that corresponds to an inconsistent system. Perform sufficient row operations on the matrix to eliminate all zero entries in the first three columns.

23. a. False. The alternative notation for a (column) vector is (–4, 3), using parentheses and commas.

b. False. Plot the points to verify this. Or, see the statement preceding Example 3. If $\begin{bmatrix} -5 \\ 2 \end{bmatrix}$ were on

the line through $\begin{bmatrix} -2 \\ 5 \end{bmatrix}$ and the origin, then $\begin{bmatrix} -5 \\ 2 \end{bmatrix}$ would have to be a multiple of $\begin{bmatrix} -2 \\ 5 \end{bmatrix}$, which is not

the case.

c. True. See the line displayed just before Example 4.

d. True. See the box that discusses the matrix in (5).

e. False. The statement is often true, but Span$\{\mathbf{u}, \mathbf{v}\}$ is not a plane when **v** is a multiple of **u**, or when **u** is the zero vector.

24. a. True. See the beginning of the subsection *Vectors in* $\mathbf{R}^n$.

b. True. Use Fig. 7 to draw the parallelogram determined by $\mathbf{u} - \mathbf{v}$ and **v**.

c. False. See the first paragraph of the subsection *Linear Combinations*.

d. True. See the statement that refers to Fig. 11.

e. True. See the paragraph following the definition of Span$\{\mathbf{v}_1, \dots, \mathbf{v}_p\}$.

25. a. There are only three vectors in the set $\{a_1, a_2, a_3\}$, and b is not one of them.

b. There are infinitely many vectors in $W = \text{Span}\{a_1, a_2, a_3\}$. To determine if b is in W, use the method of Exercise 13.

$$\begin{bmatrix} 1 & 0 & -4 & 4 \\ 0 & 3 & -2 & 1 \\ -2 & 6 & 3 & -4 \end{bmatrix} \sim \begin{bmatrix} 1 & 0 & -4 & 4 \\ 0 & 3 & -2 & 1 \\ 0 & 6 & -5 & 4 \end{bmatrix} \sim \begin{bmatrix} ① & 0 & -4 & 4 \\ 0 & ③ & -2 & 1 \\ 0 & 0 & ㊀① & 2 \end{bmatrix}$$

$$\uparrow \quad \uparrow \quad \uparrow \quad \uparrow$$

$$a_1 \quad a_2 \quad a_3 \quad b$$

The system for this augmented matrix is consistent, so b is in W.

c. $a_1 = 1a_1 + 0a_2 + 0a_3$. See the discussion in the text following the definition of $\text{Span}\{v_1, \ldots, v_p\}$.

26. a. $[a_1 \ a_2 \ a_3 \ b] = \begin{bmatrix} 2 & 0 & 6 & 10 \\ -1 & 8 & 5 & 3 \\ 1 & -2 & 1 & 3 \end{bmatrix} \sim \begin{bmatrix} 1 & 0 & 3 & 5 \\ -1 & 8 & 5 & 3 \\ 1 & -2 & 1 & 3 \end{bmatrix} \sim \begin{bmatrix} 1 & 0 & 3 & 5 \\ 0 & 8 & 8 & 8 \\ 0 & -2 & -2 & -2 \end{bmatrix} \sim \begin{bmatrix} 1 & 0 & 3 & 5 \\ 0 & 8 & 8 & 8 \\ 0 & 0 & 0 & 0 \end{bmatrix}$

Yes, b is a linear combination of the columns of A, that is, b is in W.

b. The third column of A is in W because $a_3 = 0 \cdot a_1 + 0 \cdot a_2 + 1 \cdot a_3$.

27. a. $5v_1$ is the output of 5 days' operation of mine #1.

b. The total output is $x_1 v_1 + x_2 v_2$, so x_1 and x_2 should satisfy $x_1 v_1 + x_2 v_2 = \begin{bmatrix} 150 \\ 2825 \end{bmatrix}$.

c. [M] Reduce the augmented matrix $\begin{bmatrix} 20 & 30 & 150 \\ 550 & 500 & 2825 \end{bmatrix} \sim \begin{bmatrix} 1 & 0 & 1.5 \\ 0 & 1 & 4.0 \end{bmatrix}$.

Operate mine #1 for 1.5 days and mine #2 for 4 days. (This is the exact solution.)

28. a. The amount of heat produced when the steam plant burns x_1 tons of anthracite and x_2 tons of bituminous coal is $27.6x_1 + 30.2x_2$ million Btu.

b. The total output produced by x_1 tons of anthracite and x_2 tons of bituminous coal is given by the vector $x_1 \begin{bmatrix} 27.6 \\ 3100 \\ 250 \end{bmatrix} + x_2 \begin{bmatrix} 30.2 \\ 6400 \\ 360 \end{bmatrix}$.

c. [M] The appropriate values for x_1 and x_2 satisfy $x_1 \begin{bmatrix} 27.6 \\ 3100 \\ 250 \end{bmatrix} + x_2 \begin{bmatrix} 30.2 \\ 6400 \\ 360 \end{bmatrix} = \begin{bmatrix} 162 \\ 23,610 \\ 1,623 \end{bmatrix}$.

To solve, row reduce the augmented matrix:

$$\begin{bmatrix} 27.6 & 30.2 & 162 \\ 3100 & 6400 & 23610 \\ 250 & 360 & 1623 \end{bmatrix} \sim \begin{bmatrix} 1.000 & 0 & 3.900 \\ 0 & 1.000 & 1.800 \\ 0 & 0 & 0 \end{bmatrix}$$

The steam plant burned 3.9 tons of anthracite coal and 1.8 tons of bituminous coal.

29. The total mass is $2 + 5 + 2 + 1 = 10$. So $\mathbf{v} = (2\mathbf{v}_1 + 5\mathbf{v}_2 + 2\mathbf{v}_3 + \mathbf{v}_4)/10$. That is,

$$\mathbf{v} = \frac{1}{10}\left(2\begin{bmatrix}5\\-4\\3\end{bmatrix} + 5\begin{bmatrix}4\\3\\-2\end{bmatrix} + 2\begin{bmatrix}-4\\-3\\-1\end{bmatrix} + \begin{bmatrix}-9\\8\\6\end{bmatrix}\right) = \frac{1}{10}\begin{bmatrix}10+20-8-9\\-8+15-6+8\\6-10-2+6\end{bmatrix} = \begin{bmatrix}1.3\\.9\\0\end{bmatrix}$$

30. Let m be the total mass of the system. By definition,

$$\mathbf{v} = \frac{1}{m}(m_1\mathbf{v}_1 + \cdots + m_k\mathbf{v}_k) = \frac{m_1}{m}\mathbf{v}_1 + \cdots + \frac{m_k}{m}\mathbf{v}_k$$

The second expression displays $\mathbf{v}$ as a linear combination of $\mathbf{v}_1, \ldots, \mathbf{v}_k$, which shows that $\mathbf{v}$ is in $\text{Span}\{\mathbf{v}_1, \ldots, \mathbf{v}_k\}$.

31. a. The center of mass is $\dfrac{1}{3}\left(1\cdot\begin{bmatrix}0\\1\end{bmatrix} + 1\cdot\begin{bmatrix}8\\1\end{bmatrix} + 1\cdot\begin{bmatrix}2\\4\end{bmatrix}\right) = \begin{bmatrix}10/3\\2\end{bmatrix}$.

b. The total mass of the new system is 9 grams. The three masses added, w_1, w_2, and w_3, satisfy the equation

$$\frac{1}{9}\left((w_1 + 1)\cdot\begin{bmatrix}0\\1\end{bmatrix} + (w_2 + 1)\cdot\begin{bmatrix}8\\1\end{bmatrix} + (w_3 + 1)\cdot\begin{bmatrix}2\\4\end{bmatrix}\right) = \begin{bmatrix}2\\2\end{bmatrix}$$

which can be rearranged to

$$(w_1 + 1)\cdot\begin{bmatrix}0\\1\end{bmatrix} + (w_2 + 1)\cdot\begin{bmatrix}8\\1\end{bmatrix} + (w_3 + 1)\cdot\begin{bmatrix}2\\4\end{bmatrix} = \begin{bmatrix}18\\18\end{bmatrix}$$

and

$$w_1\cdot\begin{bmatrix}0\\1\end{bmatrix} + w_2\cdot\begin{bmatrix}8\\1\end{bmatrix} + w_3\cdot\begin{bmatrix}2\\4\end{bmatrix} = \begin{bmatrix}8\\12\end{bmatrix}$$

The condition $w_1 + w_2 + w_3 = 6$ and the vector equation above combine to produce a system of three equations whose augmented matrix is shown below, along with a sequence of row operations:

$$\begin{bmatrix}1&1&1&6\\0&8&2&8\\1&1&4&12\end{bmatrix} \sim \begin{bmatrix}1&1&1&6\\0&8&2&8\\0&0&3&6\end{bmatrix} \sim \begin{bmatrix}1&1&1&6\\0&8&2&8\\0&0&1&2\end{bmatrix}$$

$$\sim \begin{bmatrix}1&1&0&4\\0&8&0&4\\0&0&1&2\end{bmatrix} \sim \begin{bmatrix}1&0&0&3.5\\0&8&0&4\\0&0&1&2\end{bmatrix} \sim \begin{bmatrix}1&0&0&3.5\\0&1&0&.5\\0&0&1&2\end{bmatrix}$$

Answer: Add 3.5 g at (0, 1), add .5 g at (8, 1), and add 2 g at (2, 4).

Extra problem: Ignore the mass of the plate, and distribute 6 gm at the three vertices to make the center of mass at (2, 2). Answer: Place 3 g at (0, 1), 1 g at (8, 1), and 2 g at (2, 4).

32. See the parallelograms drawn on Fig. 15 from the text. Here c_1, c_2, c_3, and c_4 are suitable scalars. The darker parallelogram shows that $\mathbf{b}$ is a linear combination of $\mathbf{v}_1$ and $\mathbf{v}_2$, that is

$$c_1\mathbf{v}_1 + c_2\mathbf{v}_2 + 0\cdot\mathbf{v}_3 = \mathbf{b}$$

The larger parallelogram shows that **b** is a linear combination of $\mathbf{v}_1$ and $\mathbf{v}_3$, that is,

$$c_4\mathbf{v}_1 + 0\cdot\mathbf{v}_2 + c_3\mathbf{v}_3 = \mathbf{b}$$

So the equation $x_1\mathbf{v}_1 + x_2\mathbf{v}_2 + x_3\mathbf{v}_3 = \mathbf{b}$ has at least two solutions, not just one solution. (In fact, the equation has infinitely many solutions.)

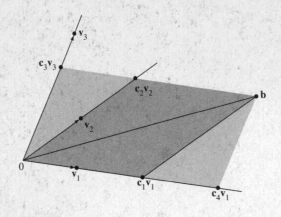

33. **a.** For $j = 1,\ldots, n$, the jth entry of $(\mathbf{u} + \mathbf{v}) + \mathbf{w}$ is $(u_j + v_j) + w_j$. By associativity of addition in **R**, this entry equals $u_j + (v_j + w_j)$, which is the jth entry of $\mathbf{u} + (\mathbf{v} + \mathbf{w})$. By definition of equality of vectors, $(\mathbf{u} + \mathbf{v}) + \mathbf{w} = \mathbf{u} + (\mathbf{v} + \mathbf{w})$.

   b. For any scalar c, the jth entry of $c(\mathbf{u} + \mathbf{v})$ is $c(u_j + v_j)$, and the jth entry of $c\mathbf{u} + c\mathbf{v}$ is $cu_j + cv_j$ (by definition of scalar multiplication and vector addition). These entries are equal, by a distributive law in **R**. So $c(\mathbf{u} + \mathbf{v}) = c\mathbf{u} + c\mathbf{v}$.

34. **a.** For $j = 1,\ldots, n$, $u_j + (-1)u_j = (-1)u_j + u_j = 0$, by properties of **R**. By vector equality,

   $$\mathbf{u} + (-1)\mathbf{u} = (-1)\mathbf{u} + \mathbf{u} = \mathbf{0}.$$

   b. For scalars c and d, the jth entries of $c(d\mathbf{u})$ and $(cd)\mathbf{u}$ are $c(du_j)$ and $(cd)u_j$, respectively. These entries in **R** are equal, so the vectors $c(d\mathbf{u})$ and $(cd)\mathbf{u}$ are equal.

Note: When an exercise in this section involves a vector equation, the corresponding technology data (in the data files on the web) is usually presented as a set of (column) vectors. To use MATLAB or other technology, a student must first construct an augmented matrix from these vectors. The MATLAB note in the *Study Guide* describes how to do this. The appendices in the *Study Guide* give corresponding information about Maple, Mathematica, and the TI and HP calculators.

1.4   SOLUTIONS

Notes: Key exercises are 1–20, 27, 28, 31 and 32. Exercises 29, 30, 33, and 34 are harder. Exercise 34 anticipates the Invertible Matrix Theorem but is not used in the proof of that theorem.

1. The matrix-vector product $A\mathbf{x}$ product is not defined because the number of columns (2) in the 3×2

   matrix $\begin{bmatrix} -4 & 2 \\ 1 & 6 \\ 0 & 1 \end{bmatrix}$ does not match the number of entries (3) in the vector $\begin{bmatrix} 3 \\ -2 \\ 7 \end{bmatrix}$.

2. The matrix-vector product $A\mathbf{x}$ product is not defined because the number of columns (1) in the 3×1 matrix $\begin{bmatrix} 2 \\ 6 \\ -1 \end{bmatrix}$ does not match the number of entries (2) in the vector $\begin{bmatrix} 5 \\ -1 \end{bmatrix}$.

3. $A\mathbf{x} = \begin{bmatrix} 6 & 5 \\ -4 & -3 \\ 7 & 6 \end{bmatrix} \begin{bmatrix} 2 \\ -3 \end{bmatrix} = 2\begin{bmatrix} 6 \\ -4 \\ 7 \end{bmatrix} - 3\begin{bmatrix} 5 \\ -3 \\ 6 \end{bmatrix} = \begin{bmatrix} 12 \\ -8 \\ 14 \end{bmatrix} + \begin{bmatrix} -15 \\ 9 \\ -18 \end{bmatrix} = \begin{bmatrix} -3 \\ 1 \\ -4 \end{bmatrix}$, and

$$A\mathbf{x} = \begin{bmatrix} 6 & 5 \\ -4 & -3 \\ 7 & 6 \end{bmatrix} \begin{bmatrix} 2 \\ -3 \end{bmatrix} = \begin{bmatrix} 6\cdot 2 + 5\cdot(-3) \\ (-4)\cdot 2 + (-3)\cdot(-3) \\ 7\cdot 2 + 6\cdot(-3) \end{bmatrix} = \begin{bmatrix} -3 \\ 1 \\ -4 \end{bmatrix}$$

4. $A\mathbf{x} = \begin{bmatrix} 8 & 3 & -4 \\ 5 & 1 & 2 \end{bmatrix} \begin{bmatrix} 1 \\ 1 \\ 1 \end{bmatrix} = 1\cdot\begin{bmatrix} 8 \\ 5 \end{bmatrix} + 1\cdot\begin{bmatrix} 3 \\ 1 \end{bmatrix} + 1\cdot\begin{bmatrix} -4 \\ 2 \end{bmatrix} = \begin{bmatrix} 8+3-4 \\ 5+1+2 \end{bmatrix} = \begin{bmatrix} 7 \\ 8 \end{bmatrix}$, and

$$A\mathbf{x} = \begin{bmatrix} 8 & 3 & -4 \\ 5 & 1 & 2 \end{bmatrix} \begin{bmatrix} 1 \\ 1 \\ 1 \end{bmatrix} = \begin{bmatrix} 8\cdot 1 + 3\cdot 1 + (-4)\cdot 1 \\ 5\cdot 1 + 1\cdot 1 + 2\cdot 1 \end{bmatrix} = \begin{bmatrix} 7 \\ 8 \end{bmatrix}$$

5. On the left side of the matrix equation, use the entries in the vector $\mathbf{x}$ as the weights in a linear combination of the columns of the matrix A:

$$5\cdot\begin{bmatrix} 5 \\ -2 \end{bmatrix} - 1\cdot\begin{bmatrix} 1 \\ -7 \end{bmatrix} + 3\cdot\begin{bmatrix} -8 \\ 3 \end{bmatrix} - 2\cdot\begin{bmatrix} 4 \\ -5 \end{bmatrix} = \begin{bmatrix} -8 \\ 16 \end{bmatrix}$$

6. On the left side of the matrix equation, use the entries in the vector $\mathbf{x}$ as the weights in a linear combination of the columns of the matrix A:

$$-2\cdot\begin{bmatrix} 7 \\ 2 \\ 9 \\ -3 \end{bmatrix} - 5\cdot\begin{bmatrix} -3 \\ 1 \\ -6 \\ 2 \end{bmatrix} = \begin{bmatrix} 1 \\ -9 \\ 12 \\ -4 \end{bmatrix}$$

7. The left side of the equation is a linear combination of three vectors. Write the matrix A whose columns are those three vectors, and create a variable vector $\mathbf{x}$ with three entries:

$$A = \begin{bmatrix} \begin{bmatrix} 4 \\ -1 \\ 7 \\ -4 \end{bmatrix} & \begin{bmatrix} -5 \\ 3 \\ -5 \\ 1 \end{bmatrix} & \begin{bmatrix} 7 \\ -8 \\ 0 \\ 2 \end{bmatrix} \end{bmatrix} = \begin{bmatrix} 4 & -5 & 7 \\ -1 & 3 & -8 \\ 7 & -5 & 0 \\ -4 & 1 & 2 \end{bmatrix} \text{ and } \mathbf{x} = \begin{bmatrix} x_1 \\ x_2 \\ x_3 \end{bmatrix}.$$ Thus the equation $A\mathbf{x} = \mathbf{b}$ is

$$\begin{bmatrix} 4 & -5 & 7 \\ -1 & 3 & -8 \\ 7 & -5 & 0 \\ -4 & 1 & 2 \end{bmatrix} \begin{bmatrix} x_1 \\ x_2 \\ x_3 \end{bmatrix} = \begin{bmatrix} 6 \\ -8 \\ 0 \\ -7 \end{bmatrix}$$

For your information: The unique solution of this equation is (5, 7, 3). Finding the solution by hand would be time-consuming.

Note: The skill of writing a vector equation as a matrix equation will be important for both theory and application throughout the text. See also Exercises 27 and 28.

8. The left side of the equation is a linear combination of four vectors. Write the matrix A whose columns are those four vectors, and create a variable vector with four entries:

$$A = \begin{bmatrix} \begin{bmatrix} 4 \\ -2 \end{bmatrix} & \begin{bmatrix} -4 \\ 5 \end{bmatrix} & \begin{bmatrix} -5 \\ 4 \end{bmatrix} & \begin{bmatrix} 3 \\ 0 \end{bmatrix} \end{bmatrix} = \begin{bmatrix} 4 & -4 & -5 & 3 \\ -2 & 5 & 4 & 0 \end{bmatrix}, \text{ and } \mathbf{z} = \begin{bmatrix} z_1 \\ z_2 \\ z_3 \\ z_4 \end{bmatrix}. \text{ Then the equation } A\mathbf{z} = \mathbf{b}$$

is $\begin{bmatrix} 4 & -4 & -5 & 3 \\ -2 & 5 & 4 & 0 \end{bmatrix} \begin{bmatrix} z_1 \\ z_2 \\ z_3 \\ z_4 \end{bmatrix} = \begin{bmatrix} 4 \\ 13 \end{bmatrix}.$

For your information: One solution is (7, 3, 3, 1). The general solution is $z_1 = 6 + .75z_3 - 1.25z_4$, $z_2 = 5 - .5z_3 - .5z_4$, with z_3 and z_4 free.

9. The system has the same solution set as the vector equation

$$x_1 \begin{bmatrix} 3 \\ 0 \end{bmatrix} + x_2 \begin{bmatrix} 1 \\ 1 \end{bmatrix} + x_3 \begin{bmatrix} -5 \\ 4 \end{bmatrix} = \begin{bmatrix} 9 \\ 0 \end{bmatrix}$$

and this equation has the same solution set as the matrix equation

$$\begin{bmatrix} 3 & 1 & -5 \\ 0 & 1 & 4 \end{bmatrix} \begin{bmatrix} x_1 \\ x_2 \\ x_3 \end{bmatrix} = \begin{bmatrix} 9 \\ 0 \end{bmatrix}$$

10. The system has the same solution set as the vector equation

$$x_1 \begin{bmatrix} 8 \\ 5 \\ 1 \end{bmatrix} + x_2 \begin{bmatrix} -1 \\ 4 \\ -3 \end{bmatrix} = \begin{bmatrix} 4 \\ 1 \\ 2 \end{bmatrix}$$

and this equation has the same solution set as the matrix equation

$$\begin{bmatrix} 8 & -1 \\ 5 & 4 \\ 1 & -3 \end{bmatrix} \begin{bmatrix} x_1 \\ x_2 \end{bmatrix} = \begin{bmatrix} 4 \\ 1 \\ 2 \end{bmatrix}$$

11. To solve $A\mathbf{x} = \mathbf{b}$, row reduce the augmented matrix $[\mathbf{a}_1 \ \mathbf{a}_2 \ \mathbf{a}_3 \ \mathbf{b}]$ for the corresponding linear system:

$$\begin{bmatrix} 1 & 2 & 4 & -2 \\ 0 & 1 & 5 & 2 \\ -2 & -4 & -3 & 9 \end{bmatrix} \sim \begin{bmatrix} 1 & 2 & 4 & -2 \\ 0 & 1 & 5 & 2 \\ 0 & 0 & 5 & 5 \end{bmatrix} \sim \begin{bmatrix} 1 & 2 & 4 & -2 \\ 0 & 1 & 5 & 2 \\ 0 & 0 & 1 & 1 \end{bmatrix} \sim \begin{bmatrix} 1 & 2 & 0 & -6 \\ 0 & 1 & 0 & -3 \\ 0 & 0 & 1 & 1 \end{bmatrix} \sim \begin{bmatrix} ① & 0 & 0 & 0 \\ 0 & ① & 0 & -3 \\ 0 & 0 & ① & 1 \end{bmatrix}$$

The solution is $\begin{cases} x_1 &=& 0 \\ x_2 &=& -3 \\ x_3 &=& 1 \end{cases}$. As a vector, the solution is $\mathbf{x} = \begin{bmatrix} x_1 \\ x_2 \\ x_3 \end{bmatrix} = \begin{bmatrix} 0 \\ -3 \\ 1 \end{bmatrix}$.

12. To solve $A\mathbf{x} = \mathbf{b}$, row reduce the augmented matrix $[\mathbf{a}_1 \ \ \mathbf{a}_2 \ \ \mathbf{a}_3 \ \ \mathbf{b}]$ for the corresponding linear system:

$$\begin{bmatrix} 1 & 2 & 1 & 0 \\ -3 & -1 & 2 & 1 \\ 0 & 5 & 3 & -1 \end{bmatrix} \sim \begin{bmatrix} 1 & 2 & 1 & 0 \\ 0 & 5 & 5 & 1 \\ 0 & 5 & 3 & -1 \end{bmatrix} \sim \begin{bmatrix} 1 & 2 & 1 & 0 \\ 0 & 5 & 5 & 1 \\ 0 & 0 & -2 & -2 \end{bmatrix} \sim \begin{bmatrix} 1 & 2 & 1 & 0 \\ 0 & 5 & 5 & 1 \\ 0 & 0 & 1 & 1 \end{bmatrix}$$

$$\sim \begin{bmatrix} 1 & 2 & 0 & -1 \\ 0 & 5 & 0 & -4 \\ 0 & 0 & 1 & 1 \end{bmatrix} \sim \begin{bmatrix} 1 & 2 & 0 & -1 \\ 0 & 1 & 0 & -4/5 \\ 0 & 0 & 1 & 1 \end{bmatrix} \sim \begin{bmatrix} ① & 0 & 0 & 3/5 \\ 0 & ① & 0 & -4/5 \\ 0 & 0 & ① & 1 \end{bmatrix}$$

The solution is $\begin{cases} x_1 &=& 3/5 \\ x_2 &=& -4/5 \\ x_3 &=& 1 \end{cases}$. As a vector, the solution is $\mathbf{x} = \begin{bmatrix} x_1 \\ x_2 \\ x_3 \end{bmatrix} = \begin{bmatrix} 3/5 \\ -4/5 \\ 1 \end{bmatrix}$.

13. The vector $\mathbf{u}$ is in the plane spanned by the columns of A if and only if $\mathbf{u}$ is a linear combination of the columns of A. This happens if and only if the equation $A\mathbf{x} = \mathbf{u}$ has a solution. (See the box preceding Example 3 in Section 1.4.) To study this equation, reduce the augmented matrix $[A \ \ \mathbf{u}]$

$$\begin{bmatrix} 3 & -5 & 0 \\ -2 & 6 & 4 \\ 1 & 1 & 4 \end{bmatrix} \sim \begin{bmatrix} 1 & 1 & 4 \\ -2 & 6 & 4 \\ 3 & -5 & 0 \end{bmatrix} \sim \begin{bmatrix} 1 & 1 & 4 \\ 0 & 8 & 12 \\ 0 & -8 & -12 \end{bmatrix} \sim \begin{bmatrix} ① & 1 & 4 \\ 0 & ⑧ & 12 \\ 0 & 0 & 0 \end{bmatrix}$$

The equation $A\mathbf{x} = \mathbf{u}$ has a solution, so $\mathbf{u}$ is in the plane spanned by the columns of A.

For your information: The unique solution of $A\mathbf{x} = \mathbf{u}$ is $(5/2, 3/2)$.

14. Reduce the augmented matrix $[A \ \ \mathbf{u}]$ to echelon form:

$$\begin{bmatrix} 5 & 8 & 7 & 2 \\ 0 & 1 & -1 & -3 \\ 1 & 3 & 0 & 2 \end{bmatrix} \sim \begin{bmatrix} 1 & 3 & 0 & 2 \\ 0 & 1 & -1 & -3 \\ 5 & 8 & 7 & 2 \end{bmatrix} \sim \begin{bmatrix} 1 & 3 & 0 & 2 \\ 0 & 1 & -1 & -3 \\ 0 & -7 & 7 & -8 \end{bmatrix} \sim \begin{bmatrix} ① & 3 & 0 & 2 \\ 0 & ① & -1 & -3 \\ 0 & 0 & 0 & ㊋-29 \end{bmatrix}$$

The equation $A\mathbf{x} = \mathbf{u}$ has no solution, so $\mathbf{u}$ is not in the subset spanned by the columns of A.

15. The augmented matrix for $A\mathbf{x} = \mathbf{b}$ is $\begin{bmatrix} 2 & -1 & b_1 \\ -6 & 3 & b_2 \end{bmatrix}$, which is row equivalent to $\begin{bmatrix} ② & -1 & b_1 \\ 0 & 0 & b_2 + 3b_1 \end{bmatrix}$.

This shows that the equation $A\mathbf{x} = \mathbf{b}$ is not consistent when $3b_1 + b_2$ is nonzero. The set of $\mathbf{b}$ for which the equation *is* consistent is a line through the origin–the set of all points (b_1, b_2) satisfying $b_2 = -3b_1$.

16. Row reduce the augmented matrix $[A \ \ \mathbf{b}]$: $A = \begin{bmatrix} 1 & -3 & -4 \\ -3 & 2 & 6 \\ 5 & -1 & -8 \end{bmatrix}, \mathbf{b} = \begin{bmatrix} b_1 \\ b_2 \\ b_3 \end{bmatrix}$.

$$\begin{bmatrix} 1 & -3 & -4 & b_1 \\ -3 & 2 & 6 & b_2 \\ 5 & -1 & -8 & b_3 \end{bmatrix} \sim \begin{bmatrix} 1 & -3 & -4 & b_1 \\ 0 & -7 & -6 & b_2 + 3b_1 \\ 0 & 14 & 12 & b_3 - 5b_1 \end{bmatrix}$$

$$\sim \begin{bmatrix} 1 & -3 & -4 & b_1 \\ 0 & -7 & -6 & b_2 + 3b_1 \\ 0 & 0 & 0 & b_3 - 5b_1 + 2(b_2 + 3b_1) \end{bmatrix} = \begin{bmatrix} ① & -3 & -4 & b_1 \\ 0 & ⑦ & -6 & b_2 + 3b_1 \\ 0 & 0 & 0 & b_1 + 2b_2 + b_3 \end{bmatrix}$$

The equation $A\mathbf{x} = \mathbf{b}$ is consistent if and only if $b_1 + 2b_2 + b_3 = 0$. The set of such $\mathbf{b}$ is a plane through the origin in $\mathbf{R}^3$.

17. Row reduction shows that only three rows of A contain a pivot position:

$$A = \begin{bmatrix} 1 & 3 & 0 & 3 \\ -1 & -1 & -1 & 1 \\ 0 & -4 & 2 & -8 \\ 2 & 0 & 3 & -1 \end{bmatrix} \sim \begin{bmatrix} 1 & 3 & 0 & 3 \\ 0 & 2 & -1 & 4 \\ 0 & -4 & 2 & -8 \\ 0 & -6 & 3 & -7 \end{bmatrix} \sim \begin{bmatrix} 1 & 3 & 0 & 3 \\ 0 & 2 & -1 & 4 \\ 0 & 0 & 0 & 0 \\ 0 & 0 & 0 & 5 \end{bmatrix} \sim \begin{bmatrix} ① & 3 & 0 & 3 \\ 0 & ② & -1 & 4 \\ 0 & 0 & 0 & ⑤ \\ 0 & 0 & 0 & 0 \end{bmatrix}$$

Because not every row of A contains a pivot position, Theorem 4 in Section 1.4 shows that the equation $A\mathbf{x} = \mathbf{b}$ does *not* have a solution for each $\mathbf{b}$ in $\mathbf{R}^4$.

18. Row reduction shows that only three rows of B contain a pivot position:

$$B = \begin{bmatrix} 1 & 3 & -2 & 2 \\ 0 & 1 & 1 & -5 \\ 1 & 2 & -3 & 7 \\ -2 & -8 & 2 & -1 \end{bmatrix} \sim \begin{bmatrix} 1 & 3 & -2 & 2 \\ 0 & 1 & 1 & -5 \\ 0 & -1 & -1 & 5 \\ 0 & -2 & -2 & 3 \end{bmatrix} \sim \begin{bmatrix} 1 & 3 & -2 & 2 \\ 0 & 1 & 1 & -5 \\ 0 & 0 & 0 & 0 \\ 0 & 0 & 0 & -7 \end{bmatrix} \sim \begin{bmatrix} ① & 3 & -2 & 2 \\ 0 & ① & 1 & -5 \\ 0 & 0 & 0 & ⑦ \\ 0 & 0 & 0 & 0 \end{bmatrix}$$

Because not every row of B contains a pivot position, Theorem 4 in Section 1.4 shows that the equation $B\mathbf{x} = \mathbf{y}$ does *not* have a solution for each $\mathbf{y}$ in $\mathbf{R}^4$.

19. The work in Exercise 17 shows that statement (d) in Theorem 4 is false. So all four statements in Theorem 4 are false. Thus, not all vectors in $\mathbf{R}^4$ can be written as a linear combination of the columns of A. Also, the columns of A do *not* span $\mathbf{R}^4$.

20. The work in Exercise 18 shows that statement (d) in Theorem 4 is false. So all four statements in Theorem 4 are false. Thus, not all vectors in $\mathbf{R}^4$ can be written as a linear combination of the columns of B. The columns of B certainly do *not* span $\mathbf{R}^3$, because each column of B is in $\mathbf{R}^4$, not $\mathbf{R}^3$. (This question was asked to alert students to a fairly common misconception among students who are just learning about spanning.)

21. Row reduce the matrix $[\mathbf{v}_1 \ \mathbf{v}_2 \ \mathbf{v}_3]$ to determine whether it has a pivot in each row.

$$\begin{bmatrix} 1 & 0 & 1 \\ 0 & -1 & 0 \\ -1 & 0 & 0 \\ 0 & 1 & -1 \end{bmatrix} \sim \begin{bmatrix} 1 & 0 & 1 \\ 0 & -1 & 0 \\ 0 & 0 & 1 \\ 0 & 1 & -1 \end{bmatrix} \sim \begin{bmatrix} 1 & 0 & 1 \\ 0 & -1 & 0 \\ 0 & 0 & 1 \\ 0 & 0 & -1 \end{bmatrix} \sim \begin{bmatrix} ① & 0 & 1 \\ 0 & ① & 0 \\ 0 & 0 & ① \\ 0 & 0 & 0 \end{bmatrix}.$$

The matrix $[\mathbf{v}_1 \ \mathbf{v}_2 \ \mathbf{v}_3]$ does not have a pivot in each row, so the columns of the matrix do not span $\mathbf{R}^4$, by Theorem 4. That is, $\{\mathbf{v}_1, \mathbf{v}_2, \mathbf{v}_3\}$ does not span $\mathbf{R}^4$.

Note: Some students may realize that row operations are not needed, and thereby discover the principle covered in Exercises 31 and 32.

22. Row reduce the matrix $[\mathbf{v}_1 \ \mathbf{v}_2 \ \mathbf{v}_3]$ to determine whether it has a pivot in each row.

$$\begin{bmatrix} 0 & 0 & 4 \\ 0 & -3 & -1 \\ -2 & 8 & -5 \end{bmatrix} \sim \begin{bmatrix} \boxed{-2} & 8 & -5 \\ 0 & \boxed{-3} & -1 \\ 0 & 0 & \boxed{4} \end{bmatrix}$$

The matrix $[\mathbf{v}_1 \ \mathbf{v}_2 \ \mathbf{v}_3]$ has a pivot in each row, so the columns of the matrix span $\mathbf{R}^4$, by Theorem 4. That is, $\{\mathbf{v}_1, \mathbf{v}_2, \mathbf{v}_3\}$ spans $\mathbf{R}^4$.

23. a. False. See the paragraph following equation (3). The text calls $A\mathbf{x} = \mathbf{b}$ a *matrix equation*.

    b. True. See the box before Example 3.

    c. False. See the warning following Theorem 4.

    d. True. See Example 4.

    e. True. See parts (c) and (a) in Theorem 4.

    f. True. In Theorem 4, statement (a) is false if and only if statement (d) is also false.

24. a. True. This statement is in Theorem 3. However, the statement is true without any "proof" because, by definition, $A\mathbf{x}$ is simply a notation for $x_1\mathbf{a}_1 + \cdots + x_n\mathbf{a}_n$, where $\mathbf{a}_1, \ldots, \mathbf{a}_n$ are the columns of A.

    b. True. See Example 2.

    c. True, by Theorem 3.

    d. True. See the box before Example 2. Saying that $\mathbf{b}$ is not in the set spanned by the columns of A is the same a saying that $\mathbf{b}$ is not a linear combination of the columns of A.

    e. False. See the warning that follows Theorem 4.

    f. True. In Theorem 4, statement (c) is false if and only if statement (a) is also false.

25. By definition, the matrix-vector product on the left is a linear combination of the columns of the matrix, in this case using weights –3, –1, and 2. So $c_1 = -3$, $c_2 = -1$, and $c_3 = 2$.

26. The equation in x_1 and x_2 involves the vectors $\mathbf{u}$, $\mathbf{v}$, and $\mathbf{w}$, and it may be viewed as

$$\begin{bmatrix} \mathbf{u} & \mathbf{v} \end{bmatrix} \begin{bmatrix} x_1 \\ x_2 \end{bmatrix} = \mathbf{w}.$$ By definition of a matrix-vector product, $x_1\mathbf{u} + x_2\mathbf{v} = \mathbf{w}$. The stated fact that

$3\mathbf{u} - 5\mathbf{v} - \mathbf{w} = \mathbf{0}$ can be rewritten as $3\mathbf{u} - 5\mathbf{v} = \mathbf{w}$. So, a solution is $x_1 = 3$, $x_2 = -5$.

27. Place the vectors $\mathbf{q}_1$, $\mathbf{q}_2$, and $\mathbf{q}_3$ into the columns of a matrix, say, Q and place the weights x_1, x_2, and x_3 into a vector, say, $\mathbf{x}$. Then the vector equation becomes

$$Q\mathbf{x} = \mathbf{v}, \text{ where } Q = \begin{bmatrix} \mathbf{q}_1 & \mathbf{q}_2 & \mathbf{q}_3 \end{bmatrix} \text{ and } \mathbf{x} = \begin{bmatrix} x_1 \\ x_2 \\ x_3 \end{bmatrix}$$

Note: If your answer is the equation $A\mathbf{x} = \mathbf{b}$, you need to specify what A and $\mathbf{b}$ are.

28. The matrix equation can be written as $c_1\mathbf{v}_1 + c_2\mathbf{v}_2 + c_3\mathbf{v}_3 + c_4\mathbf{v}_4 + c_5\mathbf{v}_5 = \mathbf{v}_6$, where

$c_1 = -3$, $c_2 = 2$, $c_3 = 4$, $c_4 = -1$, $c_5 = 2$, and

$$\mathbf{v}_1 = \begin{bmatrix} -3 \\ 5 \end{bmatrix}, \mathbf{v}_2 = \begin{bmatrix} 5 \\ 8 \end{bmatrix}, \mathbf{v}_3 = \begin{bmatrix} -4 \\ 1 \end{bmatrix}, \mathbf{v}_4 = \begin{bmatrix} 9 \\ -2 \end{bmatrix}, \mathbf{v}_5 = \begin{bmatrix} 7 \\ -4 \end{bmatrix}, \mathbf{v}_6 = \begin{bmatrix} 8 \\ -1 \end{bmatrix}$$

29. Start with any 3×3 matrix B in echelon form that has three pivot positions. Perform a row operation (a row interchange or a row replacement) that creates a matrix A that is *not* in echelon form. Then A has the desired property. The justification is given by row reducing A to B, in order to display the pivot positions. Since A has a pivot position in every row, the columns of A span $\mathbf{R}^3$, by Theorem 4.

30. Start with any nonzero 3×3 matrix B in echelon form that has fewer than three pivot positions. Perform a row operation that creates a matrix A that is *not* in echelon form. Then A has the desired property. Since A does not have a pivot position in every row, the columns of A do not span $\mathbf{R}^3$, by Theorem 4.

31. A 3×2 matrix has three rows and two columns. With only two columns, A can have at most two pivot columns, and so A has at most two pivot positions, which is not enough to fill all three rows. By Theorem 4, the equation $A\mathbf{x} = \mathbf{b}$ cannot be consistent for all $\mathbf{b}$ in $\mathbf{R}^3$. Generally, if A is an $m{\times}n$ matrix with $m > n$, then A can have at most n pivot positions, which is not enough to fill all m rows. Thus, the equation $A\mathbf{x} = \mathbf{b}$ cannot be consistent for all $\mathbf{b}$ in $\mathbf{R}^3$.

32. A set of three vectors in cannot span $\mathbf{R}^4$. Reason: the matrix A whose columns are these three vectors has four rows. To have a pivot in each row, A would have to have at least four columns (one for each pivot), which is not the case. Since A does not have a pivot in every row, its columns do not span $\mathbf{R}^4$, by Theorem 4. In general, a set of n vectors in $\mathbf{R}^m$ cannot span $\mathbf{R}^m$ when n is less than m.

33. If the equation $A\mathbf{x} = \mathbf{b}$ has a unique solution, then the associated system of equations does not have any free variables. If every variable is a basic variable, then each column of A is a pivot column. So the reduced echelon form of A must be $\begin{bmatrix} ① & 0 & 0 \\ 0 & ① & 0 \\ 0 & 0 & ① \\ 0 & 0 & 0 \end{bmatrix}$.

Note: Exercises 33 and 34 are difficult in the context of this section because the focus in Section 1.4 is on existence of solutions, not uniqueness. However, these exercises serve to review ideas from Section 1.2, and they anticipate ideas that will come later.

34. If the equation $A\mathbf{x} = \mathbf{b}$ has a unique solution, then the associated system of equations does not have any free variables. If every variable is a basic variable, then each column of A is a pivot column. So the reduced echelon form of A must be $\begin{bmatrix} ① & 0 & 0 \\ 0 & ① & 0 \\ 0 & 0 & ① \end{bmatrix}$. Now it is clear that A has a pivot position in each *row*. By Theorem 4, the columns of A span $\mathbf{R}^3$.

35. Given $A\mathbf{x}_1 = \mathbf{y}_1$ and $A\mathbf{x}_2 = \mathbf{y}_2$, you are asked to show that the equation $A\mathbf{x} = \mathbf{w}$ has a solution, where $\mathbf{w} = \mathbf{y}_1 + \mathbf{y}_2$. Observe that $\mathbf{w} = A\mathbf{x}_1 + A\mathbf{x}_2$ and use Theorem 5(a) with $\mathbf{x}_1$ and $\mathbf{x}_2$ in place of $\mathbf{u}$ and $\mathbf{v}$, respectively. That is, $\mathbf{w} = A\mathbf{x}_1 + A\mathbf{x}_2 = A(\mathbf{x}_1 + \mathbf{x}_2)$. So the vector $\mathbf{x} = \mathbf{x}_1 + \mathbf{x}_2$ is a solution of $\mathbf{w} = A\mathbf{x}$.

36. Suppose that y and z satisfy $A\mathbf{y} = \mathbf{z}$. Then $4\mathbf{z} = 4A\mathbf{y}$. By Theorem 5(b), $4A\mathbf{y} = A(4\mathbf{y})$. So $4\mathbf{z} = A(4\mathbf{y})$, which shows that $4\mathbf{y}$ is a solution of $A\mathbf{x} = 4\mathbf{z}$. Thus, the equation $A\mathbf{x} = 4\mathbf{z}$ is consistent.

37. [M] $\begin{bmatrix} 7 & 2 & -5 & 8 \\ -5 & -3 & 4 & -9 \\ 6 & 10 & -2 & 7 \\ -7 & 9 & 2 & 15 \end{bmatrix} \sim \begin{bmatrix} 7 & 2 & -5 & 8 \\ 0 & -11/7 & 3/7 & -23/7 \\ 0 & 58/7 & 16/7 & 1/7 \\ 0 & 11 & -3 & 23 \end{bmatrix} \sim \begin{bmatrix} ⑦ & 2 & -5 & 8 \\ 0 & \boxed{-11/7} & 3/7 & -23/7 \\ 0 & 0 & \boxed{50/11} & -189/11 \\ 0 & 0 & 0 & 0 \end{bmatrix}$

or, approximately $\begin{bmatrix} ⑦ & 2 & -5 & 8 \\ 0 & \boxed{-1.57} & .429 & -3.29 \\ 0 & 0 & \boxed{4.55} & -17.2 \\ 0 & 0 & 0 & 0 \end{bmatrix}$, to three significant figures. The original matrix does not

have a pivot in every row, so its columns do not span $\mathbf{R}^4$, by Theorem 4.

38. [M]
$$\begin{bmatrix} 5 & -7 & -4 & 9 \\ 6 & -8 & -7 & 5 \\ 4 & -4 & -9 & -9 \\ -9 & 11 & 16 & 7 \end{bmatrix} \sim \begin{bmatrix} 5 & -7 & -4 & 9 \\ 0 & 2/5 & -11/5 & -29/5 \\ 0 & 8/5 & -29/5 & -81/5 \\ 0 & -8/5 & 44/5 & 116/5 \end{bmatrix} \sim \begin{bmatrix} ⑤ & -7 & -4 & 9 \\ 0 & ②/⑤ & -11/5 & -29/5 \\ 0 & 0 & ③ & 7 \\ 0 & 0 & * & * \end{bmatrix}$$

MATLAB shows starred entries for numbers that are essentially zero (to many decimal places). So, with pivots only in the first three rows, the original matrix has columns that do not span $\mathbf{R}^4$, by Theorem 4.

39. [M]
$$\begin{bmatrix} 12 & -7 & 11 & -9 & 5 \\ -9 & 4 & -8 & 7 & -3 \\ -6 & 11 & -7 & 3 & -9 \\ 4 & -6 & 10 & -5 & 12 \end{bmatrix} \sim \begin{bmatrix} 12 & -7 & 11 & -9 & 5 \\ 0 & -5/4 & 1/4 & 1/4 & 3/4 \\ 0 & 15/2 & -3/2 & -3/2 & -13/2 \\ 0 & -11/3 & 19/3 & -2 & 31/3 \end{bmatrix}$$

$$\sim \begin{bmatrix} 12 & -7 & 11 & -9 & 5 \\ 0 & -5/4 & 1/4 & 1/4 & 3/4 \\ 0 & 0 & 0 & 0 & -2 \\ 0 & 0 & 28/5 & -41/15 & 122/15 \end{bmatrix} \sim \begin{bmatrix} ⑫ & -7 & 11 & -9 & 5 \\ 0 & \boxed{-5/4} & 1/4 & 1/4 & 3/4 \\ 0 & 0 & \boxed{28/5} & -41/15 & 122/15 \\ 0 & 0 & 0 & 0 & \boxed{-2} \end{bmatrix}$$

The original matrix has a pivot in every row, so its columns span $\mathbf{R}^4$, by Theorem 4.

40. [M]
$$\begin{bmatrix} 8 & 11 & -6 & -7 & 13 \\ -7 & -8 & 5 & 6 & -9 \\ 11 & 7 & -7 & -9 & -6 \\ -3 & 4 & 1 & 8 & 7 \end{bmatrix} \sim \begin{bmatrix} 8 & 11 & -6 & -7 & 13 \\ 0 & 13/8 & -1/4 & -1/8 & 19/8 \\ 0 & -65/8 & 5/4 & 5/8 & -191/8 \\ 0 & 65/8 & -5/4 & 43/8 & 95/8 \end{bmatrix}$$

$$\sim \begin{bmatrix} 8 & 11 & -6 & -7 & 13 \\ 0 & 13/8 & -1/4 & -1/8 & 19/8 \\ 0 & 0 & 0 & 0 & -12 \\ 0 & 0 & 0 & 6 & 0 \end{bmatrix} \sim \begin{bmatrix} ⑧ & 11 & -6 & -7 & 13 \\ 0 & \boxed{13/8} & -1/4 & -1/8 & 19/8 \\ 0 & 0 & 0 & ⑥ & 0 \\ 0 & 0 & 0 & 0 & \boxed{-12} \end{bmatrix}$$

The original matrix has a pivot in every row, so its columns span $\mathbf{R}^4$, by Theorem 4.

41. [M] Examine the calculations in Exercise 39. Notice that the fourth column of the original matrix, say A, is not a pivot column. Let A° be the matrix formed by deleting column 4 of A, let B be the echelon form obtained from A, and let B° be the matrix obtained by deleting column 4 of B. The sequence of row operations that reduces A to B also reduces A° to B°. Since B° is in echelon form, it shows that A° has a pivot position in each row. Therefore, the columns of A° span $\mathbf{R}^4$.

It is possible to delete column 3 of A instead of column 4. In this case, the fourth column of A becomes a pivot column of A°, as you can see by looking at what happens when column 3 of B is deleted. For later work, it is desirable to delete a nonpivot column.

Note: Exercises 41 and 42 help to prepare for later work on the column space of a matrix. (See Section 2.9 or 4.6.) The *Study Guide* points out that these exercises depend on the following idea, not explicitly mentioned in the text: when a row operation is performed on a matrix A, the calculations for each new entry depend only on the other entries in the *same column*. If a column of A is removed, forming a new matrix, the absence of this column has no affect on any row-operation calculations for entries in the other columns of A. (The absence of a column might affect the particular *choice* of row operations performed for some purpose, but that is not being considered here.)

42. **[M]** Examine the calculations in Exercise 40. The third column of the original matrix, say A, is not a pivot column. Let A° be the matrix formed by deleting column 3 of A, let B be the echelon form obtained from A, and let B° be the matrix obtained by deleting column 3 of B. The sequence of row operations that reduces A to B also reduces A° to B°. Since B° is in echelon form, it shows that A° has a pivot position in each row. Therefore, the columns of A° span $\mathbf{R}^4$.

It is possible to delete column 2 of A instead of column 3. (See the remark for Exercise 41.) However, only *one* column can be deleted. If two or more columns were deleted from A, the resulting matrix would have fewer than four columns, so it would have fewer than four pivot positions. In such a case, not every row could contain a pivot position, and the columns of the matrix would not span $\mathbf{R}^4$, by Theorem 4.

Notes: At the end of Section 1.4, the *Study Guide* gives students a method for learning and mastering linear algebra concepts. Specific directions are given for constructing a review sheet that connects the basic definition of "span" with related ideas: equivalent descriptions, theorems, geometric interpretations, special cases, algorithms, and typical computations. I require my students to prepare such a sheet that reflects their choices of material connected with "span", and I make comments on their sheets to help them refine their review. Later, the students use these sheets when studying for exams.

The MATLAB box for Section 1.4 introduces two useful commands `gauss` and `bgauss` that allow a student to speed up row reduction while still visualizing all the steps involved. The command `B = gauss(A,1)` causes MATLAB to find the left-most nonzero entry in row 1 of matrix A, and use that entry as a pivot to create zeros in the entries below, using row replacement operations. The result is a matrix that a student might write next to A as the first stage of row reduction, since there is no need to write a new matrix after each separate row replacement. I use the `gauss` command frequently in lectures to obtain an echelon form that provides data for solving various problems. For instance, if a matrix has 5 rows, and if row swaps are not needed, the following commands produce an echelon form of A:

$$B = \texttt{gauss(A,1)}, \quad B = \texttt{gauss(B,2)}, \quad B = \texttt{gauss(B,3)}, \quad B = \texttt{gauss(B,4)}$$

If an interchange is required, I can insert a command such as `B = swap(B,2,5)`. The command `bgauss` uses the left-most nonzero entry in a row to produce zeros *above* that entry. This command, together with `scale`, can change an echelon form into reduced echelon form.

The use of `gauss` and `bgauss` creates an environment in which students use their computer program the same way they work a problem by hand on an exam. Unless you are able to conduct your exams in a computer laboratory, it may be unwise to give students too early the power to obtain reduced echelon forms with one command—they may have difficulty performing row reduction by hand during an exam. Instructors whose students use a graphic calculator in class each day do not face this problem. In such a case, you may wish to introduce `rref` earlier in the course than Chapter 4 (or Section 2.8), which is where I finally allow students to use that command.

1.5   SOLUTIONS

Notes: The geometry helps students understand Span$\{\mathbf{u}, \mathbf{v}\}$, in preparation for later discussions of subspaces. The parametric vector form of a solution set will be used throughout the text. Figure 6 will appear again in Sections 2.9 and 4.8.

For solving homogeneous systems, the text recommends working with the augmented matrix, although no calculations take place in the augmented column. See the *Study Guide* comments on Exercise 7 that illustrate two common student errors.

All students need the practice of Exercises 1–14. (Assign all odd, all even, or a mixture. If you do not assign Exercise 7, be sure to assign both 8 and 10.) Otherwise, a few students may be unable later to find a basis for a null space or an eigenspace. Exercises 29–34 are important. Exercises 33 and 34 help students later understand how solutions of $A\mathbf{x} = \mathbf{0}$ encode linear dependence relations among the columns of A. Exercises 35–38 are more challenging. Exercise 37 will help students avoid the standard mistake of forgetting that Theorem 6 applies only to a *consistent* equation $A\mathbf{x} = \mathbf{b}$.

1. Reduce the augmented matrix to echelon form and circle the pivot positions. If a column of the *coefficient* matrix is not a pivot column, the corresponding variable is free and the system of equations has a nontrivial solution. Otherwise, the system has *only* the trivial solution.

$$\begin{bmatrix} 2 & -5 & 8 & 0 \\ -2 & -7 & 1 & 0 \\ 4 & 2 & 7 & 0 \end{bmatrix} \sim \begin{bmatrix} 2 & -5 & 8 & 0 \\ 0 & -12 & 9 & 0 \\ 0 & 12 & -9 & 0 \end{bmatrix} \sim \begin{bmatrix} ② & -5 & 8 & 0 \\ 0 & ⑫ & 9 & 0 \\ 0 & 0 & 0 & 0 \end{bmatrix}$$

The variable x_3 is free, so the system has a nontrivial solution.

2. $\begin{bmatrix} 1 & -3 & 7 & 0 \\ -2 & 1 & -4 & 0 \\ 1 & 2 & 9 & 0 \end{bmatrix} \sim \begin{bmatrix} 1 & -3 & 7 & 0 \\ 0 & -5 & 10 & 0 \\ 0 & 5 & 2 & 0 \end{bmatrix} \sim \begin{bmatrix} ① & -3 & 7 & 0 \\ 0 & ⑤ & 10 & 0 \\ 0 & 0 & ⑫ & 0 \end{bmatrix}$

There is no free variable; the system has only the trivial solution.

3. $\begin{bmatrix} -3 & 5 & -7 & 0 \\ -6 & 7 & 1 & 0 \end{bmatrix} \sim \begin{bmatrix} ③ & 5 & -7 & 0 \\ 0 & ③ & 15 & 0 \end{bmatrix}$. The variable x_3 is free; the system has nontrivial solutions.

An alert student will realize that row operations are unnecessary. With only two equations, there can be at most two basic variables. One variable *must* be free. Refer to Exercise 31 in Section 1.2.

4. $\begin{bmatrix} -5 & 7 & 9 & 0 \\ 1 & -2 & 6 & 0 \end{bmatrix} \sim \begin{bmatrix} 1 & -2 & 6 & 0 \\ -5 & 7 & 9 & 0 \end{bmatrix} \sim \begin{bmatrix} ① & -2 & 6 & 0 \\ 0 & ③ & 39 & 0 \end{bmatrix}$. x_3 is a free variable; the system has nontrivial solutions. As in Exercise 3, row operations are unnecessary.

5. $\begin{bmatrix} 1 & 3 & 1 & 0 \\ -4 & -9 & 2 & 0 \\ 0 & -3 & -6 & 0 \end{bmatrix} \sim \begin{bmatrix} 1 & 3 & 1 & 0 \\ 0 & 3 & 6 & 0 \\ 0 & -3 & -6 & 0 \end{bmatrix} \sim \begin{bmatrix} 1 & 0 & -5 & 0 \\ 0 & 3 & 6 & 0 \\ 0 & 0 & 0 & 0 \end{bmatrix} \sim \begin{bmatrix} ① & 0 & -5 & 0 \\ 0 & ① & 2 & 0 \\ 0 & 0 & 0 & 0 \end{bmatrix}$

$\;\;①\;\;\;- 5x_3 = 0$

$\;\;\;\;②\;+ 2x_3 = 0$. The variable x_3 is free, $x_1 = 5x_3$, and $x_2 = -2x_3$.

$\;\;\;\;\;\;\;\;0 = 0$

In parametric vector form, the general solution is $\mathbf{x} = \begin{bmatrix} x_1 \\ x_2 \\ x_3 \end{bmatrix} = \begin{bmatrix} 5x_3 \\ -2x_3 \\ x_3 \end{bmatrix} = x_3 \begin{bmatrix} 5 \\ -2 \\ 1 \end{bmatrix}$.

6. $\begin{bmatrix} 1 & 3 & -5 & 0 \\ 1 & 4 & -8 & 0 \\ -3 & -7 & 9 & 0 \end{bmatrix} \sim \begin{bmatrix} 1 & 3 & -5 & 0 \\ 0 & 1 & -3 & 0 \\ 0 & 2 & -6 & 0 \end{bmatrix} \sim \begin{bmatrix} 1 & 3 & -5 & 0 \\ 0 & 1 & -3 & 0 \\ 0 & 0 & 0 & 0 \end{bmatrix} \sim \begin{bmatrix} ① & 0 & 4 & 0 \\ 0 & ① & -3 & 0 \\ 0 & 0 & 0 & 0 \end{bmatrix}$

$$\boxed{x_1} + 4x_3 = 0$$
$$\boxed{x_2} - 3x_3 = 0 . \text{ The variable } x_3 \text{ is free, } x_1 = -4x_3, \text{ and } x_2 = 3x_3.$$
$$0 = 0$$

In parametric vector form, the general solution is $\mathbf{x} = \begin{bmatrix} x_1 \\ x_2 \\ x_3 \end{bmatrix} = \begin{bmatrix} -4x_3 \\ 3x_3 \\ x_3 \end{bmatrix} = x_3 \begin{bmatrix} -4 \\ 3 \\ 1 \end{bmatrix}.$

7. $\begin{bmatrix} 1 & 3 & -3 & 7 & 0 \\ 0 & 1 & -4 & 5 & 0 \end{bmatrix} \sim \begin{bmatrix} ① & 0 & 9 & -8 & 0 \\ 0 & ① & -4 & 5 & 0 \end{bmatrix}.$ $\quad \boxed{x_1} + 9x_3 - 8x_4 = 0$
$$\boxed{x_2} - 4x_3 + 5x_4 = 0$$

The basic variables are x_1 and x_2, with x_3 and x_4 free. Next, $x_1 = -9x_3 + 8x_4$, and $x_2 = 4x_3 - 5x_4$. The general solution is

$$\mathbf{x} = \begin{bmatrix} x_1 \\ x_2 \\ x_3 \\ x_4 \end{bmatrix} = \begin{bmatrix} -9x_3 + 8x_4 \\ 4x_3 - 5x_4 \\ x_3 \\ x_4 \end{bmatrix} = \begin{bmatrix} -9x_3 \\ 4x_3 \\ x_3 \\ 0 \end{bmatrix} + \begin{bmatrix} 8x_4 \\ -5x_4 \\ 0 \\ x_4 \end{bmatrix} = x_3 \begin{bmatrix} -9 \\ 4 \\ 1 \\ 0 \end{bmatrix} + x_4 \begin{bmatrix} 8 \\ -5 \\ 0 \\ 1 \end{bmatrix}$$

8. $\begin{bmatrix} 1 & -2 & -9 & 5 & 0 \\ 0 & 1 & 2 & -6 & 0 \end{bmatrix} \sim \begin{bmatrix} ① & 0 & -5 & -7 & 0 \\ 0 & ① & 2 & -6 & 0 \end{bmatrix}.$ $\quad \boxed{x_1} - 5x_3 - 7x_4 = 0$
$$\boxed{x_2} + 2x_3 - 6x_4 = 0$$

The basic variables are x_1 and x_2, with x_3 and x_4 free. Next, $x_1 = 5x_3 + 7x_4$ and $x_2 = -2x_3 + 6x_4$. The general solution in parametric vector form is

$$\mathbf{x} = \begin{bmatrix} x_1 \\ x_2 \\ x_3 \\ x_4 \end{bmatrix} = \begin{bmatrix} 5x_3 + 7x_4 \\ -2x_3 + 6x_4 \\ x_3 \\ x_4 \end{bmatrix} = \begin{bmatrix} 5x_3 \\ -2x_3 \\ x_3 \\ 0 \end{bmatrix} + \begin{bmatrix} 7x_4 \\ 6x_4 \\ 0 \\ x_4 \end{bmatrix} = x_3 \begin{bmatrix} 5 \\ -2 \\ 1 \\ 0 \end{bmatrix} + x_4 \begin{bmatrix} 7 \\ 6 \\ 0 \\ 1 \end{bmatrix}$$

9. $\begin{bmatrix} 3 & -9 & 6 & 0 \\ -1 & 3 & -2 & 0 \end{bmatrix} \sim \begin{bmatrix} 1 & -3 & 2 & 0 \\ 3 & -9 & 6 & 0 \end{bmatrix} \sim \begin{bmatrix} ① & -3 & 2 & 0 \\ 0 & 0 & 0 & 0 \end{bmatrix}$ $\quad \boxed{x_1} - 3x_2 + 2x_3 = 0$
$$0 = 0 .$$

The solution is $x_1 = 3x_2 - 2x_3$, with x_2 and x_3 free. In parametric vector form,

$$\mathbf{x} = \begin{bmatrix} 3x_2 - 2x_3 \\ x_2 \\ x_3 \end{bmatrix} = \begin{bmatrix} 3x_2 \\ x_2 \\ 0 \end{bmatrix} + \begin{bmatrix} -2x_3 \\ 0 \\ x_3 \end{bmatrix} = x_2 \begin{bmatrix} 3 \\ 1 \\ 0 \end{bmatrix} + x_3 \begin{bmatrix} -2 \\ 0 \\ 1 \end{bmatrix}.$$

10. $\begin{bmatrix} 1 & 3 & 0 & -4 & 0 \\ 2 & 6 & 0 & -8 & 0 \end{bmatrix} \sim \begin{bmatrix} ① & 3 & 0 & -4 & 0 \\ 0 & 0 & 0 & 0 & 0 \end{bmatrix}$ $\quad \boxed{x_1} - 3x_2 - 4x_4 = 0$
$$0 = 0 .$$

The only basic variable is x_1, so $x_2, x_3,$ and x_4 are free. (Note that x_3 is not zero.) Also, $x_1 = 3x_2 + 4x_4$. The general solution is

$$
\mathbf{x} = \begin{bmatrix} x_1 \\ x_2 \\ x_3 \\ x_4 \end{bmatrix} = \begin{bmatrix} 3x_2 + 4x_4 \\ x_2 \\ x_3 \\ x_4 \end{bmatrix} = \begin{bmatrix} 3x_2 \\ x_2 \\ 0 \\ 0 \end{bmatrix} + \begin{bmatrix} 0 \\ 0 \\ x_3 \\ 0 \end{bmatrix} + \begin{bmatrix} 4x_4 \\ 0 \\ 0 \\ x_4 \end{bmatrix} = x_2 \begin{bmatrix} 3 \\ 1 \\ 0 \\ 0 \end{bmatrix} + x_3 \begin{bmatrix} 0 \\ 0 \\ 1 \\ 0 \end{bmatrix} + x_4 \begin{bmatrix} 4 \\ 0 \\ 0 \\ 1 \end{bmatrix}
$$

11. $\begin{bmatrix} 1 & -4 & -2 & 0 & 3 & -5 & 0 \\ 0 & 0 & 1 & 0 & 0 & -1 & 0 \\ 0 & 0 & 0 & 0 & 1 & -4 & 0 \\ 0 & 0 & 0 & 0 & 0 & 0 & 0 \end{bmatrix} \sim \begin{bmatrix} 1 & -4 & -2 & 0 & 0 & 7 & 0 \\ 0 & 0 & 1 & 0 & 0 & -1 & 0 \\ 0 & 0 & 0 & 0 & 1 & -4 & 0 \\ 0 & 0 & 0 & 0 & 0 & 0 & 0 \end{bmatrix} \sim \begin{bmatrix} ① & -4 & 0 & 0 & 0 & 5 & 0 \\ 0 & 0 & ① & 0 & 0 & -1 & 0 \\ 0 & 0 & 0 & 0 & ① & -4 & 0 \\ 0 & 0 & 0 & 0 & 0 & 0 & 0 \end{bmatrix}$

$$
\begin{array}{ll}
①x_1 - 4x_2 \qquad\qquad\quad + 5x_6 = 0 & \\
\qquad\quad ③x_3 \qquad\quad - x_6 = 0 & \\
\qquad\qquad\quad ⑤x_5 - 4x_6 = 0 & \\
\qquad\qquad\qquad\qquad 0 = 0 &
\end{array}
$$. The basic variables are x_1, x_3, and x_5. The remaining variables are free.

In particular, x_4 is free (and not zero as some may assume). The solution is $x_1 = 4x_2 - 5x_6$, $x_3 = x_6$, $x_5 = 4x_6$, with x_2, x_4, and x_6 free. In parametric vector form,

$$
\mathbf{x} = \begin{bmatrix} x_1 \\ x_2 \\ x_3 \\ x_4 \\ x_5 \\ x_6 \end{bmatrix} = \begin{bmatrix} 4x_2 - 5x_6 \\ x_2 \\ x_6 \\ x_4 \\ 4x_6 \\ x_6 \end{bmatrix} = \begin{bmatrix} 4x_2 \\ x_2 \\ 0 \\ 0 \\ 0 \\ 0 \end{bmatrix} + \begin{bmatrix} 0 \\ 0 \\ 0 \\ x_4 \\ 0 \\ 0 \end{bmatrix} + \begin{bmatrix} -5x_6 \\ 0 \\ x_6 \\ 0 \\ 4x_6 \\ x_6 \end{bmatrix} = x_2 \begin{bmatrix} 4 \\ 1 \\ 0 \\ 0 \\ 0 \\ 0 \end{bmatrix} + x_4 \begin{bmatrix} 0 \\ 0 \\ 0 \\ 1 \\ 0 \\ 0 \end{bmatrix} + x_6 \begin{bmatrix} -5 \\ 0 \\ 1 \\ 0 \\ 4 \\ 1 \end{bmatrix}
$$
$$
\qquad\qquad\qquad\qquad\qquad\qquad\qquad\qquad\qquad\qquad\qquad\qquad\qquad\qquad\quad \uparrow \qquad\quad \uparrow \qquad\quad \uparrow
$$
$$
\qquad\qquad\qquad\qquad\qquad\qquad\qquad\qquad\qquad\qquad\qquad\qquad\qquad\qquad\quad \mathbf{u} \qquad\quad \mathbf{v} \qquad\quad \mathbf{w}
$$

Note: The *Study Guide* discusses two mistakes that students often make on this type of problem.

12. $\begin{bmatrix} 1 & 5 & 2 & -6 & 9 & 0 & 0 \\ 0 & 0 & 1 & -7 & 4 & -8 & 0 \\ 0 & 0 & 0 & 0 & 0 & 1 & 0 \\ 0 & 0 & 0 & 0 & 0 & 0 & 0 \end{bmatrix} \sim \begin{bmatrix} 1 & 5 & 2 & -6 & 9 & 0 & 0 \\ 0 & 0 & 1 & -7 & 4 & 0 & 0 \\ 0 & 0 & 0 & 0 & 0 & 1 & 0 \\ 0 & 0 & 0 & 0 & 0 & 0 & 0 \end{bmatrix} \sim \begin{bmatrix} ① & 5 & 0 & 8 & 1 & 0 & 0 \\ 0 & 0 & ① & -7 & 4 & 0 & 0 \\ 0 & 0 & 0 & 0 & 0 & ① & 0 \\ 0 & 0 & 0 & 0 & 0 & 0 & 0 \end{bmatrix}$

$$
\begin{array}{l}
①x_1 + 5x_2 \qquad + 8x_4 + x_5 \qquad = 0 \\
\qquad\quad ③x_3 - 7x_4 + 4x_5 \qquad = 0 \\
\qquad\qquad\qquad\qquad\qquad ⑥x_6 = 0 \\
\qquad\qquad\qquad\qquad\qquad 0 = 0
\end{array}
$$.

The basic variables are x_1, x_3, and x_6; the free variables are x_2, x_4, and x_5. The general solution is $x_1 = -5x_2 - 8x_4 - x_5$, $x_3 = 7x_4 - 4x_5$, and $x_6 = 0$. In parametric vector form, the solution is

$$\mathbf{x} = \begin{bmatrix} x_1 \\ x_2 \\ x_3 \\ x_4 \\ x_5 \\ x_6 \end{bmatrix} = \begin{bmatrix} -5x_2 - 8x_4 - x_5 \\ x_2 \\ 7x_4 - 4x_5 \\ x_4 \\ x_5 \\ 0 \end{bmatrix} = \begin{bmatrix} -5x_2 \\ x_2 \\ 0 \\ 0 \\ 0 \\ 0 \end{bmatrix} + \begin{bmatrix} -8x_4 \\ 0 \\ 7x_4 \\ x_4 \\ 0 \\ 0 \end{bmatrix} + \begin{bmatrix} -x_5 \\ 0 \\ -4x_5 \\ 0 \\ x_5 \\ 0 \end{bmatrix} = x_2 \begin{bmatrix} -5 \\ 1 \\ 0 \\ 0 \\ 0 \\ 0 \end{bmatrix} + x_4 \begin{bmatrix} -8 \\ 0 \\ 7 \\ 1 \\ 0 \\ 0 \end{bmatrix} + x_5 \begin{bmatrix} -1 \\ 0 \\ -4 \\ 0 \\ 1 \\ 0 \end{bmatrix}$$

13. To write the general solution in parametric vector form, pull out the constant terms that do not involve the free variable:

$$\mathbf{x} = \begin{bmatrix} x_1 \\ x_2 \\ x_3 \end{bmatrix} = \begin{bmatrix} 5 + 4x_3 \\ -2 - 7x_3 \\ x_3 \end{bmatrix} = \begin{bmatrix} 5 \\ -2 \\ 0 \end{bmatrix} + \begin{bmatrix} 4x_3 \\ -7x_3 \\ x_3 \end{bmatrix} = \begin{bmatrix} 5 \\ -2 \\ 0 \end{bmatrix} + x_3 \begin{bmatrix} 4 \\ -7 \\ 1 \end{bmatrix} = \mathbf{p} + x_3\mathbf{q}.$$
$$\qquad\qquad\qquad\qquad\qquad\qquad\qquad\qquad\qquad\qquad\uparrow\qquad\quad\;\uparrow$$
$$\qquad\qquad\qquad\qquad\qquad\qquad\qquad\qquad\qquad\qquad\mathbf{p}\qquad\;\;\mathbf{q}$$

Geometrically, the solution set is the line through $\begin{bmatrix} 5 \\ -2 \\ 0 \end{bmatrix}$ in the direction of $\begin{bmatrix} 4 \\ -7 \\ 1 \end{bmatrix}$.

14. To write the general solution in parametric vector form, pull out the constant terms that do not involve the free variable:

$$\mathbf{x} = \begin{bmatrix} x_1 \\ x_2 \\ x_3 \\ x_4 \end{bmatrix} = \begin{bmatrix} 3x_4 \\ 8 + x_4 \\ 2 - 5x_4 \\ x_4 \end{bmatrix} = \begin{bmatrix} 0 \\ 8 \\ 2 \\ 0 \end{bmatrix} + \begin{bmatrix} 3x_4 \\ x_4 \\ -5x_4 \\ x_4 \end{bmatrix} = \begin{bmatrix} 0 \\ 8 \\ 2 \\ 0 \end{bmatrix} + x_4 \begin{bmatrix} 3 \\ 1 \\ -5 \\ 1 \end{bmatrix} = \mathbf{p} + x_4\mathbf{q}$$
$$\qquad\qquad\qquad\qquad\qquad\qquad\qquad\qquad\qquad\qquad\uparrow\qquad\quad\;\uparrow$$
$$\qquad\qquad\qquad\qquad\qquad\qquad\qquad\qquad\qquad\qquad\mathbf{p}\qquad\;\;\mathbf{q}$$

The solution set is the line through $\mathbf{p}$ in the direction of $\mathbf{q}$.

15. Row reduce the augmented matrix for the system:

$$\begin{bmatrix} 1 & 3 & 1 & 1 \\ -4 & -9 & 2 & -1 \\ 0 & -3 & -6 & -3 \end{bmatrix} \sim \begin{bmatrix} 1 & 3 & 1 & 1 \\ 0 & 3 & 6 & 3 \\ 0 & -3 & -6 & -3 \end{bmatrix} \sim \begin{bmatrix} 1 & 3 & 1 & 1 \\ 0 & 3 & 6 & 3 \\ 0 & 0 & 0 & 0 \end{bmatrix}$$

$$\sim \begin{bmatrix} 1 & 3 & 1 & 1 \\ 0 & 1 & 2 & 1 \\ 0 & 0 & 0 & 0 \end{bmatrix} \sim \begin{bmatrix} ① & 0 & -5 & -2 \\ 0 & ① & 2 & 1 \\ 0 & 0 & 0 & 0 \end{bmatrix}. \qquad \begin{matrix} ⓧ_1 \quad\;\; - 5x_3 = -2 \\ \quad ⓧ_2 + 2x_3 = \;\; 1 \\ 0 = \;\; 0 \end{matrix}$$

Thus $x_1 = -2 + 5x_3$, $x_2 = 1 - 2x_3$, and x_3 is free. In parametric vector form,

$$\mathbf{x} = \begin{bmatrix} x_1 \\ x_2 \\ x_3 \end{bmatrix} = \begin{bmatrix} -2 + 5x_3 \\ 1 - 2x_3 \\ x_3 \end{bmatrix} = \begin{bmatrix} -2 \\ 1 \\ 0 \end{bmatrix} + \begin{bmatrix} 5x_3 \\ -2x_3 \\ x_3 \end{bmatrix} = \begin{bmatrix} -2 \\ 1 \\ 0 \end{bmatrix} + x_3 \begin{bmatrix} 5 \\ -2 \\ 1 \end{bmatrix}$$

The solution set is the line through $\begin{bmatrix} -2 \\ 1 \\ 0 \end{bmatrix}$, parallel to the line that is the solution set of the homogeneous

system in Exercise 5.

16. Row reduce the augmented matrix for the system:

$$\begin{bmatrix} 1 & 3 & -5 & 4 \\ 1 & 4 & -8 & 7 \\ -3 & -7 & 9 & -6 \end{bmatrix} \sim \begin{bmatrix} 1 & 3 & -5 & 4 \\ 0 & 1 & -3 & 3 \\ 0 & 2 & -6 & 6 \end{bmatrix} \sim \begin{bmatrix} 1 & 3 & -5 & 4 \\ 0 & 1 & -3 & 3 \\ 0 & 0 & 0 & 0 \end{bmatrix} \sim \begin{bmatrix} ① & 0 & 4 & -5 \\ 0 & ① & -3 & 3 \\ 0 & 0 & 0 & 0 \end{bmatrix}$$

$\begin{aligned} Ⓧ_1 \quad + 4x_3 &= -5 \\ Ⓧ_2 - 3x_3 &= 3 \\ 0 &= 0 \end{aligned}$. Thus $x_1 = -5 - 4x_3$, $x_2 = 3 + 3x_3$, and x_3 is free. In parametric vector form,

$$\mathbf{x} = \begin{bmatrix} x_1 \\ x_2 \\ x_3 \end{bmatrix} = \begin{bmatrix} -5 - 4x_3 \\ 3 + 3x_3 \\ x_3 \end{bmatrix} = \begin{bmatrix} -5 \\ 3 \\ 0 \end{bmatrix} + \begin{bmatrix} -4x_3 \\ 3x_3 \\ x_3 \end{bmatrix} = \begin{bmatrix} -5 \\ 3 \\ 0 \end{bmatrix} + x_3 \begin{bmatrix} -4 \\ 3 \\ 1 \end{bmatrix}$$

The solution set is the line through $\begin{bmatrix} -5 \\ 3 \\ 0 \end{bmatrix}$, parallel to the line that is the solution set of the homogeneous

system in Exercise 6.

17. Solve $x_1 + 9x_2 - 4x_3 = -2$ for the basic variable: $x_1 = -2 - 9x_2 + 4x_3$, with x_2 and x_3 free. In vector form, the solution is

$$\mathbf{x} = \begin{bmatrix} x_1 \\ x_2 \\ x_3 \end{bmatrix} = \begin{bmatrix} -2 - 9x_2 + 4x_3 \\ x_2 \\ x_3 \end{bmatrix} = \begin{bmatrix} -2 \\ 0 \\ 0 \end{bmatrix} + \begin{bmatrix} -9x_2 \\ x_2 \\ 0 \end{bmatrix} + \begin{bmatrix} 4x_3 \\ 0 \\ x_3 \end{bmatrix} = \begin{bmatrix} -2 \\ 0 \\ 0 \end{bmatrix} + x_2 \begin{bmatrix} -9 \\ 1 \\ 0 \end{bmatrix} + x_3 \begin{bmatrix} 4 \\ 0 \\ 1 \end{bmatrix}$$

The solution of $x_1 + 9x_2 - 4x_3 = 0$ is $x_1 = -9x_2 + 4x_3$, with x_2 and x_3 free. In vector form,

$$\mathbf{x} = \begin{bmatrix} x_1 \\ x_2 \\ x_3 \end{bmatrix} = \begin{bmatrix} -9x_2 + 4x_3 \\ x_2 \\ x_3 \end{bmatrix} = \begin{bmatrix} -9x_2 \\ x_2 \\ 0 \end{bmatrix} + \begin{bmatrix} 4x_3 \\ 0 \\ x_3 \end{bmatrix} = x_2 \begin{bmatrix} -9 \\ 1 \\ 0 \end{bmatrix} + x_3 \begin{bmatrix} 4 \\ 0 \\ 1 \end{bmatrix} = x_2 \mathbf{u} + x_3 \mathbf{v}$$

The solution set of the homogeneous equation is the plane through the origin in $\mathbf{R}^3$ spanned by $\mathbf{u}$ and $\mathbf{v}$. The solution set of the nonhomogeneous equation is parallel to this plane and passes through the point $\mathbf{p} = \begin{bmatrix} -2 \\ 0 \\ 0 \end{bmatrix}$.

18. Solve $x_1 - 3x_2 + 5x_3 = 4$ for the basic variable: $x_1 = 4 + 3x_2 - 5x_3$, with x_2 and x_3 free. In vector form, the solution is

$$\mathbf{x} = \begin{bmatrix} x_1 \\ x_2 \\ x_3 \end{bmatrix} = \begin{bmatrix} 4 + 3x_2 - 5x_3 \\ x_2 \\ x_3 \end{bmatrix} = \begin{bmatrix} 4 \\ 0 \\ 0 \end{bmatrix} + \begin{bmatrix} 3x_2 \\ x_2 \\ 0 \end{bmatrix} + \begin{bmatrix} -5x_3 \\ 0 \\ x_3 \end{bmatrix} = \begin{bmatrix} 4 \\ 0 \\ 0 \end{bmatrix} + x_2 \begin{bmatrix} 3 \\ 1 \\ 0 \end{bmatrix} + x_3 \begin{bmatrix} -5 \\ 0 \\ 1 \end{bmatrix}$$

The solution of $x_1 - 3x_2 + 5x_3 = 0$ is $x_1 = 3x_2 - 5x_3$, with x_2 and x_3 free. In vector form,

$$\mathbf{x} = \begin{bmatrix} x_1 \\ x_2 \\ x_3 \end{bmatrix} = \begin{bmatrix} 3x_2 - 5x_3 \\ x_2 \\ x_3 \end{bmatrix} = \begin{bmatrix} 3x_2 \\ x_2 \\ 0 \end{bmatrix} + \begin{bmatrix} -5x_3 \\ 0 \\ x_3 \end{bmatrix} = x_2 \begin{bmatrix} 3 \\ 1 \\ 0 \end{bmatrix} + x_3 \begin{bmatrix} -5 \\ 0 \\ 1 \end{bmatrix} = x_2 \mathbf{u} + x_3 \mathbf{v}$$

The solution set of the homogeneous equation is the plane through the origin in $\mathbf{R}^3$ spanned by $\mathbf{u}$ and $\mathbf{v}$. The solution set of the nonhomogeneous equation is parallel to this plane and passes through the

point $\mathbf{p} = \begin{bmatrix} 4 \\ 0 \\ 0 \end{bmatrix}$.

19. The line through $\mathbf{a}$ parallel to $\mathbf{b}$ can be written as $\mathbf{x} = \mathbf{a} + t\,\mathbf{b}$, where t represents a parameter:

$$\mathbf{x} = \begin{bmatrix} x_1 \\ x_2 \end{bmatrix} = \begin{bmatrix} -2 \\ 0 \end{bmatrix} + t \begin{bmatrix} -5 \\ 3 \end{bmatrix}, \text{ or } \begin{cases} x_1 = -2 - 5t \\ x_2 = 3t \end{cases}$$

20. The line through $\mathbf{a}$ parallel to $\mathbf{b}$ can be written as $\mathbf{x} = \mathbf{a} + t\mathbf{b}$, where t represents a parameter:

$$\mathbf{x} = \begin{bmatrix} x_1 \\ x_2 \end{bmatrix} = \begin{bmatrix} 3 \\ -4 \end{bmatrix} + t \begin{bmatrix} -7 \\ 8 \end{bmatrix}, \text{ or } \begin{cases} x_1 = 3 - 7t \\ x_2 = -4 + 8t \end{cases}$$

21. The line through $\mathbf{p}$ and $\mathbf{q}$ is parallel to $\mathbf{q} - \mathbf{p}$. So, given $\mathbf{p} = \begin{bmatrix} 2 \\ -5 \end{bmatrix}$ and $\mathbf{q} = \begin{bmatrix} -3 \\ 1 \end{bmatrix}$, form

$$\mathbf{q} - \mathbf{p} = \begin{bmatrix} -3 - 2 \\ 1 - (-5) \end{bmatrix} = \begin{bmatrix} -5 \\ 6 \end{bmatrix}, \text{ and write the line as } \mathbf{x} = \mathbf{p} + t(\mathbf{q} - \mathbf{p}) = \begin{bmatrix} 2 \\ -5 \end{bmatrix} + t \begin{bmatrix} -5 \\ 6 \end{bmatrix}.$$

22. The line through $\mathbf{p}$ and $\mathbf{q}$ is parallel to $\mathbf{q} - \mathbf{p}$. So, given $\mathbf{p} = \begin{bmatrix} -6 \\ 3 \end{bmatrix}$ and $\mathbf{q} = \begin{bmatrix} 0 \\ -4 \end{bmatrix}$, form

$$\mathbf{q} - \mathbf{p} = \begin{bmatrix} 0 - (-6) \\ -4 - 3 \end{bmatrix} = \begin{bmatrix} 6 \\ -7 \end{bmatrix}, \text{ and write the line as } \mathbf{x} = \mathbf{p} + t(\mathbf{q} - \mathbf{p}) = \begin{bmatrix} -6 \\ 3 \end{bmatrix} + t \begin{bmatrix} 6 \\ -7 \end{bmatrix}$$

Note: Exercises 21 and 22 prepare for Exercise 27 in Section 1.8.

23. **a.** True. See the first paragraph of the subsection titled *Homogeneous Linear Systems*.

 b. False. The equation $A\mathbf{x} = \mathbf{0}$ gives an *implicit* description of its solution set. See the subsection entitled *Parametric Vector Form*.

 c. False. The equation $A\mathbf{x} = \mathbf{0}$ *always* has the trivial solution. The box before Example 1 uses the word *nontrivial* instead of *trivial*.

 d. False. The line goes through $\mathbf{p}$ parallel to $\mathbf{v}$. See the paragraph that precedes Fig. 5.

 e. False. The solution set could be *empty*! The statement (from Theorem 6) is true only when there exists a vector $\mathbf{p}$ such that $A\mathbf{p} = \mathbf{b}$.

24. **a.** False. A nontrivial solution of $A\mathbf{x} = \mathbf{0}$ is any nonzero $\mathbf{x}$ that satisfies the equation. See the sentence before Example 2.

 b. True. See Example 2 and the paragraph following it.

c. True. If the zero vector is a solution, then $\mathbf{b} = A\mathbf{x} = A\mathbf{0} = \mathbf{0}$.

d. True. See the paragraph following Example 3.

e. False. The statement is true only when the solution set of $A\mathbf{x} = \mathbf{0}$ is nonempty. Theorem 6 applies only to a consistent system.

25. Suppose $\mathbf{p}$ satisfies $A\mathbf{x} = \mathbf{b}$. Then $A\mathbf{p} = \mathbf{b}$. Theorem 6 says that the solution set of $A\mathbf{x} = \mathbf{b}$ equals the set $S = \{\mathbf{w} : \mathbf{w} = \mathbf{p} + \mathbf{v}_h$ for some $\mathbf{v}_h$ such that $A\mathbf{v}_h = \mathbf{0}\}$. There are two things to prove: (a) every vector in S satisfies $A\mathbf{x} = \mathbf{b}$, (b) every vector that satisfies $A\mathbf{x} = \mathbf{b}$ is in S.

  a. Let $\mathbf{w}$ have the form $\mathbf{w} = \mathbf{p} + \mathbf{v}_h$, where $A\mathbf{v}_h = \mathbf{0}$. Then

  $A\mathbf{w} = A(\mathbf{p} + \mathbf{v}_h) = A\mathbf{p} + A\mathbf{v}_h$. By Theorem 5(a) in section 1.4

  $\quad = \mathbf{b} + \mathbf{0} = \mathbf{b}$

  So every vector of the form $\mathbf{p} + \mathbf{v}_h$ satisfies $A\mathbf{x} = \mathbf{b}$.

  b. Now let $\mathbf{w}$ be any solution of $A\mathbf{x} = \mathbf{b}$, and set $\mathbf{v}_h = \mathbf{w} - \mathbf{p}$. Then

  $A\mathbf{v}_h = A(\mathbf{w} - \mathbf{p}) = A\mathbf{w} - A\mathbf{p} = \mathbf{b} - \mathbf{b} = \mathbf{0}$

  So $\mathbf{v}_h$ satisfies $A\mathbf{x} = \mathbf{0}$. Thus every solution of $A\mathbf{x} = \mathbf{b}$ has the form $\mathbf{w} = \mathbf{p} + \mathbf{v}_h$.

26. (*Geometric argument using Theorem* 6.) Since $A\mathbf{x} = \mathbf{b}$ is consistent, its solution set is obtained by translating the solution set of $A\mathbf{x} = \mathbf{0}$, by Theorem 6. So the solution set of $A\mathbf{x} = \mathbf{b}$ is a single vector if and only if the solution set of $A\mathbf{x} = \mathbf{0}$ is a single vector, and that happens if and only if $A\mathbf{x} = \mathbf{0}$ has only the trivial solution.

  (*Proof using free variables.*) If $A\mathbf{x} = \mathbf{b}$ has a solution, then the solution is unique if and only if there are no free variables in the corresponding system of equations, that is, if and only if every column of A is a pivot column. This happens if and only if the equation $A\mathbf{x} = \mathbf{0}$ has only the trivial solution.

27. When A is the 3×3 zero matrix, *every* $\mathbf{x}$ in $\mathbf{R}^3$ satisfies $A\mathbf{x} = \mathbf{0}$. So the solution set is all vectors in $\mathbf{R}^3$.

28. No. If the solution set of $A\mathbf{x} = \mathbf{b}$ contained the origin, then $\mathbf{0}$ would satisfy $A\mathbf{0} = \mathbf{b}$, which is not true since $\mathbf{b}$ is not the zero vector.

29. **a.** When A is a 3×3 matrix with three pivot positions, the equation $A\mathbf{x} = \mathbf{0}$ has no free variables and hence has no nontrivial solution.

  b. With three pivot positions, A has a pivot position in each of its three rows. By Theorem 4 in Section 1.4, the equation $A\mathbf{x} = \mathbf{b}$ has a solution for every possible $\mathbf{b}$. The term "possible" in the exercise means that the only vectors considered in this case are those in $\mathbf{R}^3$, because A has three rows.

30. **a.** When A is a 3×3 matrix with two pivot positions, the equation $A\mathbf{x} = \mathbf{0}$ has two basic variables and one free variable. So $A\mathbf{x} = \mathbf{0}$ has a nontrivial solution.

  b. With only two pivot positions, A cannot have a pivot in every row, so by Theorem 4 in Section 1.4, the equation $A\mathbf{x} = \mathbf{b}$ cannot have a solution for every possible $\mathbf{b}$ (in $\mathbf{R}^3$).

31. **a.** When A is a 3×2 matrix with two pivot positions, each column is a pivot column. So the equation $A\mathbf{x} = \mathbf{0}$ has no free variables and hence no nontrivial solution.

  b. With two pivot positions and three rows, A cannot have a pivot in every row. So the equation $A\mathbf{x} = \mathbf{b}$ cannot have a solution for every possible $\mathbf{b}$ (in $\mathbf{R}^3$), by Theorem 4 in Section 1.4.

32. **a.** When A is a 2×4 matrix with two pivot positions, the equation $A\mathbf{x} = \mathbf{0}$ has two basic variables and two free variables. So $A\mathbf{x} = \mathbf{0}$ has a nontrivial solution.

  b. With two pivot positions and only two rows, A has a pivot position in every row. By Theorem 4 in Section 1.4, the equation $A\mathbf{x} = \mathbf{b}$ has a solution for every possible $\mathbf{b}$ (in $\mathbf{R}^2$).

33. Look at $x_1 \begin{bmatrix} -2 \\ 7 \\ -3 \end{bmatrix} + x_2 \begin{bmatrix} -6 \\ 21 \\ -9 \end{bmatrix}$ and notice that the second column is 3 times the first. So suitable values for

x_1 and x_2 would be 3 and –1 respectively. (Another pair would be 6 and –2, etc.) Thus $\mathbf{x} = \begin{bmatrix} 3 \\ -1 \end{bmatrix}$

satisfies $A\mathbf{x} = \mathbf{0}$.

34. Inspect how the columns $\mathbf{a}_1$ and $\mathbf{a}_2$ of A are related. The second column is –3/2 times the first. Put

another way, $3\mathbf{a}_1 + 2\mathbf{a}_2 = \mathbf{0}$. Thus $\begin{bmatrix} 3 \\ 2 \end{bmatrix}$ satisfies $A\mathbf{x} = \mathbf{0}$.

Note: Exercises 33 and 34 set the stage for the concept of linear dependence.

35. Look for $A = [\mathbf{a}_1 \quad \mathbf{a}_2 \quad \mathbf{a}_3]$ such that $1 \cdot \mathbf{a}_1 + 1 \cdot \mathbf{a}_2 + 1 \cdot \mathbf{a}_3 = \mathbf{0}$. That is, construct A so that each row sum (the sum of the entries in a row) is zero.

36. Look for $A = [\mathbf{a}_1 \quad \mathbf{a}_2 \quad \mathbf{a}_3]$ such that $1 \cdot \mathbf{a}_1 - 2 \cdot \mathbf{a}_2 + 1 \cdot \mathbf{a}_3 = \mathbf{0}$. That is, construct A so that the sum of the first and third columns is twice the second column.

37. Since the solution set of $A\mathbf{x} = \mathbf{0}$ contains the point (4,1), the vector $\mathbf{x} = (4,1)$ satisfies $A\mathbf{x} = \mathbf{0}$. Write this equation as a vector equation, using $\mathbf{a}_1$ and $\mathbf{a}_2$ for the columns of A:

$$4 \cdot \mathbf{a}_1 + 1 \cdot \mathbf{a}_2 = \mathbf{0}$$

Then $\mathbf{a}_2 = -4\mathbf{a}_1$. So choose any nonzero vector for the first column of A and multiply that column by -4

to get the second column of A. For example, set $A = \begin{bmatrix} 1 & -4 \\ 1 & -4 \end{bmatrix}$.

Finally, the only way the solution set of $A\mathbf{x} = \mathbf{b}$ could *not* be parallel to the line through (1,4) and the origin is for the solution set of $A\mathbf{x} = \mathbf{b}$ to be *empty*. This does not contradict Theorem 6, because that theorem applies only to the case when the equation $A\mathbf{x} = \mathbf{b}$ has a nonempty solution set. For $\mathbf{b}$, take any vector that is *not* a multiple of the columns of A.

Note: In the *Study Guide*, a "Checkpoint" for Section 1.5 will help students with Exercise 37.

38. No. If $A\mathbf{x} = \mathbf{y}$ has no solution, then A cannot have a pivot in each row. Since A is 3×3, it has at most two pivot positions. So the equation $A\mathbf{x} = \mathbf{z}$ for any $\mathbf{z}$ has at most two basic variables and at least one free variable. Thus, the solution set for $A\mathbf{x} = \mathbf{z}$ is either empty or has infinitely many elements.

39. If $\mathbf{u}$ satisfies $A\mathbf{x} = \mathbf{0}$, then $A\mathbf{u} = \mathbf{0}$. For any scalar c, Theorem 5(b) in Section 1.4 shows that $A(c\mathbf{u}) = cA\mathbf{u} = c \cdot \mathbf{0} = \mathbf{0}$.

40. Suppose $A\mathbf{u} = \mathbf{0}$ and $A\mathbf{v} = \mathbf{0}$. Then, since $A(\mathbf{u} + \mathbf{v}) = A\mathbf{u} + A\mathbf{v}$ by Theorem 5(a) in Section 1.4,

$$A(\mathbf{u} + \mathbf{v}) = A\mathbf{u} + A\mathbf{v} = \mathbf{0} + \mathbf{0} = \mathbf{0}.$$

Now, let c and d be scalars. Using both parts of Theorem 5,

$$A(c\mathbf{u} + d\mathbf{v}) = A(c\mathbf{u}) + A(d\mathbf{v}) = cA\mathbf{u} + dA\mathbf{v} = c\mathbf{0} + d\mathbf{0} = \mathbf{0}.$$

Note: The MATLAB box in the *Study Guide* introduces the `zeros` command, in order to augment a matrix with a column of zeros.

1.6   SOLUTIONS _____

1. Fill in the exchange table one column at a time. The entries in a column describe where a sector's output goes. The decimal fractions in each column sum to 1.

Distribution of

Output From:

	Goods	Services		Purchased by:
output	↓	↓	input	
	.2	.7	→	Goods
	.8	.3	→	Services

Denote the total annual output (in dollars) of the sectors by p_G and p_S. From the first row, the total input to the Goods sector is $.2\,p_G + .7\,p_S$. The Goods sector must pay for that. So the equilibrium prices must satisfy

income   expenses

$$p_G \quad = \quad .2p_G + .7p_S$$

From the second row, the input (that is, the expense) of the Services sector is $.8\,p_G + .3\,p_S$. The equilibrium equation for the Services sector is

income   expenses

$$p_S \quad = \quad .8p_G + .3p_S$$

Move all variables to the left side and combine like terms:

$$.8p_G \quad - \quad .7p_S \quad = \quad 0$$
$$-.8p_G \quad + \quad .7p_S \quad = \quad 0$$

Row reduce the augmented matrix:

$$\begin{bmatrix} .8 & -.7 & 0 \\ -.8 & .7 & 0 \end{bmatrix} \sim \begin{bmatrix} .8 & -.7 & 0 \\ 0 & 0 & 0 \end{bmatrix} \sim \begin{bmatrix} ① & -.875 & 0 \\ 0 & 0 & 0 \end{bmatrix}$$

The general solution is $p_G = .875\,p_S$, with p_S free. One equilibrium solution is $p_S = 1000$ and $p_G = 875$. If one uses fractions instead of decimals in the calculations, the general solution would be written $p_G = (7/8)\,p_S$, and a natural choice of prices might be $p_S = 80$ and $p_G = 70$. Only the *ratio* of the prices is important: $p_G = .875\,p_S$. The economic equilibrium is unaffected by a proportional change in prices.

2. Take some other value for p_S, say 200 million dollars. The other equilibrium prices are then $p_C = 188$ million, $p_E = 170$ million. Any constant nonnegative multiple of these prices is a set of equilibrium prices, because the solution set of the system of equations consists of all multiples of one vector. Changing the unit of measurement to, say, European euros has the same effect as multiplying all equilibrium prices by a constant. The *ratios* of the prices remain the same, no matter what currency is used.

3. **a**. Fill in the exchange table one column at a time. The entries in a column describe where a sector's output goes. The decimal fractions in each column sum to 1.

Distribution of Output From:				Purchased
Chemicals	Fuels	Machinery		by:
output ↓	↓	↓	input	
.2	.8	.4	⟶	Chemicals
.3	.1	.4	⟶	Fuels
.5	.1	.2	⟶	Machinery

b. Denote the total annual output (in dollars) of the sectors by p_C, p_F, and p_M. From the first row of the table, the total input to the Chemical & Metals sector is $.2\,p_C + .8\,p_F + .4\,p_M$. So the equillibrium prices must satisfy

$$\underset{\text{income}}{p_C} \;=\; \underset{\text{expenses}}{.2p_C + .8p_F + .4p_M}$$

From the second and third rows of the table, the income/expense requirements for the Fuels & Power sector and the Machinery sector are, respectively,

$$p_F = .3p_C + .1p_F + .4p_M$$
$$p_M = .5p_C + .1p_F + .2p_M$$

Move all variables to the left side and combine like terms:

$$.8p_C - .8p_F - .4p_M = 0$$
$$-.3p_C + .9p_F - .4p_M = 0$$
$$-.5p_C - .1p_F + .8p_M = 0$$

c. **[M]** You can obtain the reduced echelon form with a matrix program. Actually, hand calculations are not too messy. To simplify the calculations, first scale each row of the augmented matrix by 10, then continue as usual.

$$\begin{bmatrix} 8 & -8 & -4 & 0 \\ -3 & 9 & -4 & 0 \\ -5 & -1 & 8 & 0 \end{bmatrix} \sim \begin{bmatrix} 1 & -1 & -.5 & 0 \\ -3 & 9 & -4 & 0 \\ -5 & -1 & 8 & 0 \end{bmatrix} \sim \begin{bmatrix} 1 & -1 & -.5 & 0 \\ 0 & 6 & -5.5 & 0 \\ 0 & -6 & 5.5 & 0 \end{bmatrix}$$

$$\sim \begin{bmatrix} 1 & -1 & -.5 & 0 \\ 0 & 1 & -.917 & 0 \\ 0 & 0 & 0 & 0 \end{bmatrix} \sim \begin{bmatrix} ① & 0 & -1.417 & 0 \\ 0 & ① & -.917 & 0 \\ 0 & 0 & 0 & 0 \end{bmatrix}$$
The number of decimal places displayed is somewhat arbitrary.

The general solution is $p_C = 1.417\,p_M$, $p_F = .917\,p_M$, with p_M free. If p_M is assigned the value 100, then $p_C = 141.7$ and $p_F = 91.7$. Note that only the *ratios* of the prices are determined. This makes sense, for if the were converted from, say, dollars to yen or Euros, the inputs and outputs of each sector would still balance. The economic equilibrium is not affected by a proportional change in prices.

4. a. Fill in the exchange table one column at a time. The entries in each column must sum to 1.

Distribution of Output From:

output	Agric. ↓	Energy ↓	Manuf. ↓	Transp. ↓	input	Purchased by:
	.65	.30	.30	.20	→	Agric.
	.10	.10	.15	.10	→	Energy
	.25	.35	.15	.30	→	Manuf.
	0	.25	.40	.40	→	Transp.

b. Denote the total annual output of the sectors by p_A, p_E, p_M, and p_T, respectively. From the first row of the table, the total input to Agriculture is $.65p_A + .30p_E + .30p_M + .20\, p_T$. So the equilibrium prices must satisfy

income   expenses

$$p_A \;=\; .65\,p_A + .30\,p_E + .30\,p_M + .20\,p_T$$

From the second, third, and fourth rows of the table, the equilibrium equations are

$$
\begin{aligned}
p_E &= \;\;.10\,p_A + .10\,p_E + .15\,p_M + .10\,p_T\\
p_M &= \;\;.25\,p_A + .35\,p_E + .15\,p_M + .30\,p_T\\
p_T &= \;\;\qquad\;\; .25\,p_E + .40\,p_M + .40\,p_T
\end{aligned}
$$

Move all variables to the left side and combine like terms:

$$
\begin{aligned}
.35\,p_A - .30\,p_E - .30\,p_M - .20\,p_T &= 0\\
-.10\,p_A + .90\,p_E - .15\,p_M - .10\,p_T &= 0\\
-.25\,p_A - .35\,p_E + .85\,p_M - .30\,p_T &= 0\\
-.25\,p_E - .40\,p_M + .60\,p_T &= 0
\end{aligned}
$$

Use gauss, bgauss, and scale operations to reduce the augmented matrix to reduced echelon form

$$
\begin{bmatrix}
.35 & -.3 & -.3 & -.2 & 0\\
0 & .81 & -.24 & -.16 & 0\\
0 & 0 & 1.0 & -1.17 & 0\\
0 & 0 & 0 & 0 & 0
\end{bmatrix}
\sim
\begin{bmatrix}
.35 & -.3 & 0 & -.55 & 0\\
0 & .81 & 0 & -.43 & 0\\
0 & 0 & 1 & -1.17 & 0\\
0 & 0 & 0 & 0 & 0
\end{bmatrix}
\sim
\begin{bmatrix}
\boxed{35} & 0 & 0 & -.71 & 0\\
0 & \textcircled{1} & 0 & -.53 & 0\\
0 & 0 & \textcircled{1} & -1.17 & 0\\
0 & 0 & 0 & 0 & 0
\end{bmatrix}
$$

Scale the first row and solve for the basic variables in terms of the free variable p_T, and obtain $p_A = 2.03p_T$, $p_E = .53p_T$, and $p_M = 1.17p_T$. The data probably justifies at most two significant figures, so take $p_T = 100$ and round off the other prices to $p_A = 200$, $p_E = 53$, and $p_M = 120$.

5. The following vectors list the numbers of atoms of boron (B), sulfur (S), hydrogen (H), and oxygen (O):

$$
B_2S_3:\begin{bmatrix}2\\3\\0\\0\end{bmatrix},\quad
H_2O:\begin{bmatrix}0\\0\\2\\1\end{bmatrix},\quad
H_3BO_3:\begin{bmatrix}1\\0\\3\\3\end{bmatrix},\quad
H_2S:\begin{bmatrix}0\\1\\2\\0\end{bmatrix}
\begin{array}{l}\text{boron}\\\text{sulfur}\\\text{hydrogen}\\\text{oxygen}\end{array}
$$

The coefficients in the equation $x_1{\cdot}B_2S_3 + x_2{\cdot}H_2O \;\rightarrow\; x_3{\cdot}H_3BO_3 + x_4{\cdot}H_2S$ satisfy

$$x_1 \begin{bmatrix} 2 \\ 3 \\ 0 \\ 0 \end{bmatrix} + x_2 \begin{bmatrix} 0 \\ 0 \\ 2 \\ 1 \end{bmatrix} = x_3 \begin{bmatrix} 1 \\ 0 \\ 3 \\ 3 \end{bmatrix} + x_4 \begin{bmatrix} 0 \\ 1 \\ 2 \\ 0 \end{bmatrix}$$

Move the right terms to the left side (changing the sign of each entry in the third and fourth vectors) and row reduce the augmented matrix of the homogeneous system:

$$\begin{bmatrix} 2 & 0 & -1 & 0 & 0 \\ 3 & 0 & 0 & -1 & 0 \\ 0 & 2 & -3 & -2 & 0 \\ 0 & 1 & -3 & 0 & 0 \end{bmatrix} \sim \begin{bmatrix} 2 & 0 & -1 & 0 & 0 \\ 0 & 0 & 3/2 & -1 & 0 \\ 0 & 2 & -3 & -2 & 0 \\ 0 & 1 & -3 & 0 & 0 \end{bmatrix} \sim \begin{bmatrix} 2 & 0 & -1 & 0 & 0 \\ 0 & 1 & -3 & 0 & 0 \\ 0 & 0 & 3/2 & -1 & 0 \\ 0 & 2 & -3 & -2 & 0 \end{bmatrix} \sim \begin{bmatrix} 2 & 0 & -1 & 0 & 0 \\ 0 & 1 & -3 & 0 & 0 \\ 0 & 0 & 3/2 & -1 & 0 \\ 0 & 0 & 3 & -2 & 0 \end{bmatrix}$$

$$\sim \begin{bmatrix} 2 & 0 & -1 & 0 & 0 \\ 0 & 1 & -3 & 0 & 0 \\ 0 & 0 & 1 & -2/3 & 0 \\ 0 & 0 & 3 & -2 & 0 \end{bmatrix} \sim \begin{bmatrix} 2 & 0 & 0 & -2/3 & 0 \\ 0 & 1 & 0 & -2 & 0 \\ 0 & 0 & 1 & -2/3 & 0 \\ 0 & 0 & 0 & 0 & 0 \end{bmatrix} \sim \begin{bmatrix} 1 & 0 & 0 & -1/3 & 0 \\ 0 & 1 & 0 & -2 & 0 \\ 0 & 0 & 1 & -2/3 & 0 \\ 0 & 0 & 0 & 0 & 0 \end{bmatrix}$$

The general solution is $x_1 = (1/3) x_4$, $x_2 = 2x_4$, $x_3 = (2/3) x_4$, with x_4 free. Take $x_4 = 3$. Then $x_1 = 1$, $x_2 = 6$, and $x_3 = 2$. The balanced equation is

$$B_2S_3 + 6H_2O \;\rightarrow\; 2H_3BO_3 + 3H_2S$$

6. The following vectors list the numbers of atoms of sodium (Na), phosphorus (P), oxygen (O), barium (Ba), and nitrogen(N):

$$Na_3PO_4: \begin{bmatrix} 3 \\ 1 \\ 4 \\ 0 \\ 0 \end{bmatrix}, \quad Ba(NO_3)_2: \begin{bmatrix} 0 \\ 0 \\ 6 \\ 1 \\ 2 \end{bmatrix}, \quad Ba_3(PO_4)_2: \begin{bmatrix} 0 \\ 2 \\ 8 \\ 3 \\ 0 \end{bmatrix}, \quad NaNO_3: \begin{bmatrix} 1 \\ 0 \\ 3 \\ 0 \\ 1 \end{bmatrix} \quad \begin{matrix} \text{sodium} \\ \text{phosphorus} \\ \text{oxygen} \\ \text{barium} \\ \text{nitrogen} \end{matrix}$$

The coefficients in the equation $x_1 \cdot Na_3PO_4 + x_2 \cdot Ba(NO_3)_2 \;\rightarrow\; x_3 \cdot Ba_3(PO_4)_2 + x_4 \cdot NaNO_3$ satisfy

$$x_1 \begin{bmatrix} 3 \\ 1 \\ 4 \\ 0 \\ 0 \end{bmatrix} + x_2 \begin{bmatrix} 0 \\ 0 \\ 6 \\ 1 \\ 2 \end{bmatrix} = x_3 \begin{bmatrix} 0 \\ 2 \\ 8 \\ 3 \\ 0 \end{bmatrix} + x_4 \begin{bmatrix} 1 \\ 0 \\ 3 \\ 0 \\ 1 \end{bmatrix}$$

Move the right terms to the left side (changing the sign of each entry in the third and fourth vectors) and row reduce the augmented matrix of the homogeneous system:

$$\begin{bmatrix} 3 & 0 & 0 & -1 & 0 \\ 1 & 0 & -2 & 0 & 0 \\ 4 & 6 & -8 & -3 & 0 \\ 0 & 1 & -3 & 0 & 0 \\ 0 & 2 & 0 & -1 & 0 \end{bmatrix} \sim \begin{bmatrix} 1 & 0 & -2 & 0 & 0 \\ 3 & 0 & 0 & -1 & 0 \\ 4 & 6 & -8 & -3 & 0 \\ 0 & 1 & -3 & 0 & 0 \\ 0 & 2 & 0 & -1 & 0 \end{bmatrix} \sim \begin{bmatrix} 1 & 0 & -2 & 0 & 0 \\ 0 & 0 & 6 & -1 & 0 \\ 0 & 6 & 0 & -3 & 0 \\ 0 & 1 & -3 & 0 & 0 \\ 0 & 2 & 0 & -1 & 0 \end{bmatrix} \sim \begin{bmatrix} 1 & 0 & -2 & 0 & 0 \\ 0 & 1 & -3 & 0 & 0 \\ 0 & 6 & 0 & -3 & 0 \\ 0 & 0 & 6 & -1 & 0 \\ 0 & 2 & 0 & -1 & 0 \end{bmatrix}$$

$$\sim \begin{bmatrix} 1 & 0 & -2 & 0 & 0 \\ 0 & 1 & -3 & 0 & 0 \\ 0 & 0 & 18 & -3 & 0 \\ 0 & 0 & 6 & -1 & 0 \\ 0 & 0 & 6 & -1 & 0 \end{bmatrix} \sim \begin{bmatrix} 1 & 0 & -2 & 0 & 0 \\ 0 & 1 & -3 & 0 & 0 \\ 0 & 0 & 1 & -1/6 & 0 \\ 0 & 0 & 0 & 0 & 0 \\ 0 & 0 & 0 & 0 & 0 \end{bmatrix} \sim \begin{bmatrix} 1 & 0 & 0 & -1/3 & 0 \\ 0 & 1 & 0 & -1/2 & 0 \\ 0 & 0 & 1 & -1/6 & 0 \\ 0 & 0 & 0 & 0 & 0 \\ 0 & 0 & 0 & 0 & 0 \end{bmatrix}$$

The general solution is $x_1 = (1/3)x_4$, $x_2 = (1/2)x_4$, $x_3 = (1/6)x_4$, with x_4 free. Take $x_4 = 6$. Then $x_1 = 2$, $x_2 = 3$, and $x_3 = 1$. The balanced equation is

$$2Na_3PO_4 + 3Ba(NO_3)_2 \rightarrow Ba_3(PO_4)_2 + 6NaNO_3$$

7. The following vectors list the numbers of atoms of sodium (Na), hydrogen (H), carbon (C), and oxygen (O):

$$NaHCO_3: \begin{bmatrix} 1 \\ 1 \\ 1 \\ 3 \end{bmatrix}, \ H_3C_6H_5O_7: \begin{bmatrix} 0 \\ 8 \\ 6 \\ 7 \end{bmatrix}, \ Na_3C_6H_5O_7: \begin{bmatrix} 3 \\ 5 \\ 6 \\ 7 \end{bmatrix}, \ H_2O: \begin{bmatrix} 0 \\ 2 \\ 0 \\ 1 \end{bmatrix}, \ CO_2: \begin{bmatrix} 0 \\ 0 \\ 1 \\ 2 \end{bmatrix} \begin{matrix} \text{sodium} \\ \text{hydrogen} \\ \text{carbon} \\ \text{oxygen} \end{matrix}$$

The order of the various atoms is not important. The list here was selected by writing the elements in the order in which they first appear in the chemical equation, reading left to right:

$$x_1 \cdot NaHCO_3 + x_2 \cdot H_3C_6H_5O_7 \rightarrow x_3 \cdot Na_3C_6H_5O_7 + x_4 \cdot H_2O + x_5 \cdot CO_2.$$

The coefficients $x_1, \ldots, x_5$ satisfy the vector equation

$$x_1 \begin{bmatrix} 1 \\ 1 \\ 1 \\ 3 \end{bmatrix} + x_2 \begin{bmatrix} 0 \\ 8 \\ 6 \\ 7 \end{bmatrix} = x_3 \begin{bmatrix} 3 \\ 5 \\ 6 \\ 7 \end{bmatrix} + x_4 \begin{bmatrix} 0 \\ 2 \\ 0 \\ 1 \end{bmatrix} + x_5 \begin{bmatrix} 0 \\ 0 \\ 1 \\ 2 \end{bmatrix}$$

Move all the terms to the left side (changing the sign of each entry in the third, fourth, and fifth vectors) and reduce the augmented matrix:

$$\begin{bmatrix} 1 & 0 & -3 & 0 & 0 & 0 \\ 1 & 8 & -5 & -2 & 0 & 0 \\ 1 & 6 & -6 & 0 & -1 & 0 \\ 3 & 7 & -7 & -1 & -2 & 0 \end{bmatrix} \sim \cdots \sim \begin{bmatrix} 1 & 0 & 0 & 0 & -1 & 0 \\ 0 & 1 & 0 & 0 & -1/3 & 0 \\ 0 & 0 & 1 & 0 & -1/3 & 0 \\ 0 & 0 & 0 & 1 & -1 & 0 \end{bmatrix}$$

The general solution is $x_1 = x_5$, $x_2 = (1/3)x_5$, $x_3 = (1/3)x_5$, $x_4 = x_5$, and x_5 is free. Take $x_5 = 3$. Then $x_1 = x_4 = 3$, and $x_2 = x_3 = 1$. The balanced equation is

$$3NaHCO_3 + H_3C_6H_5O_7 \rightarrow Na_3C_6H_5O_7 + 3H_2O + 3CO_2$$

8. The following vectors list the numbers of atoms of potassium (K), manganese (Mn), oxygen (O), sulfur (S), and hydrogen (H):

$$KMnO_4: \begin{bmatrix} 1 \\ 1 \\ 4 \\ 0 \\ 0 \end{bmatrix}, \ MnSO_4: \begin{bmatrix} 0 \\ 1 \\ 4 \\ 1 \\ 0 \end{bmatrix}, \ H_2O: \begin{bmatrix} 0 \\ 0 \\ 1 \\ 0 \\ 2 \end{bmatrix}, \ MnO_2: \begin{bmatrix} 0 \\ 1 \\ 2 \\ 0 \\ 0 \end{bmatrix}, \ K_2SO_4: \begin{bmatrix} 2 \\ 0 \\ 4 \\ 1 \\ 0 \end{bmatrix}, \ H_2SO_4: \begin{bmatrix} 0 \\ 0 \\ 4 \\ 1 \\ 2 \end{bmatrix} \begin{matrix} \text{potassium} \\ \text{manganese} \\ \text{oxygen} \\ \text{sulfur} \\ \text{hydrogen} \end{matrix}$$

The coefficients in the chemical equation

$$x_1 \cdot KMnO_4 + x_2 \cdot MnSO_4 + x_3 \cdot H_2O \rightarrow x_4 \cdot MnO_2 + x_5 \cdot K_2SO_4 + x_6 \cdot H_2SO_4$$

satisfy the vector equation

$$x_1 \begin{bmatrix} 1 \\ 1 \\ 4 \\ 0 \\ 0 \end{bmatrix} + x_2 \begin{bmatrix} 0 \\ 1 \\ 4 \\ 1 \\ 0 \end{bmatrix} + x_3 \begin{bmatrix} 0 \\ 0 \\ 1 \\ 0 \\ 2 \end{bmatrix} = x_4 \begin{bmatrix} 0 \\ 1 \\ 2 \\ 0 \\ 0 \end{bmatrix} + x_5 \begin{bmatrix} 2 \\ 0 \\ 4 \\ 1 \\ 0 \end{bmatrix} + x_6 \begin{bmatrix} 0 \\ 0 \\ 4 \\ 1 \\ 2 \end{bmatrix}$$

Move the terms to the left side (changing the sign of each entry in the last three vectors) and reduce the augmented matrix:

$$\begin{bmatrix} 1 & 0 & 0 & 0 & -2 & 0 & 0 \\ 1 & 1 & 0 & -1 & 0 & 0 & 0 \\ 4 & 4 & 1 & -2 & -4 & -4 & 0 \\ 0 & 1 & 0 & 0 & -1 & -1 & 0 \\ 0 & 0 & 2 & 0 & 0 & -2 & 0 \end{bmatrix} \sim \begin{bmatrix} \textcircled{1} & 0 & 0 & 0 & 0 & -1.0 & 0 \\ 0 & \textcircled{1} & 0 & 0 & 0 & -1.5 & 0 \\ 0 & 0 & \textcircled{1} & 0 & 0 & -1.0 & 0 \\ 0 & 0 & 0 & \textcircled{1} & 0 & -2.5 & 0 \\ 0 & 0 & 0 & 0 & \textcircled{1} & -.5 & 0 \end{bmatrix}$$

The general solution is $x_1 = x_6$, $x_2 = (1.5)x_6$, $x_3 = x_6$, $x_4 = (2.5)x_6$, $x_5 = .5x_6$, and x_6 is free. Take $x_6 = 2$. Then $x_1 = x_3 = 2$, and $x_2 = 3$, $x_4 = 5$, and $x_5 = 1$. The balanced equation is

$$2KMnO_4 + 3MnSO_4 + 2H_2O \rightarrow 5MnO_2 + K_2SO_4 + 2H_2SO_4$$

9. **[M]** Set up vectors that list the atoms per molecule. Using the order lead (Pb), nitrogen (N), chromium (Cr), manganese (Mn), and oxygen (O), the vector equation to be solved is

$$x_1 \begin{bmatrix} 1 \\ 6 \\ 0 \\ 0 \\ 0 \end{bmatrix} + x_2 \begin{bmatrix} 0 \\ 0 \\ 1 \\ 2 \\ 8 \end{bmatrix} = x_3 \begin{bmatrix} 3 \\ 0 \\ 0 \\ 0 \\ 4 \end{bmatrix} + x_4 \begin{bmatrix} 0 \\ 0 \\ 2 \\ 0 \\ 3 \end{bmatrix} + x_5 \begin{bmatrix} 0 \\ 0 \\ 0 \\ 1 \\ 2 \end{bmatrix} + x_6 \begin{bmatrix} 0 \\ 1 \\ 0 \\ 0 \\ 1 \end{bmatrix} \quad \begin{matrix} \text{lead} \\ \text{nitrogen} \\ \text{chromium} \\ \text{manganese} \\ \text{oxygen} \end{matrix}$$

The general solution is $x_1 = (1/6)x_6$, $x_2 = (22/45)x_6$, $x_3 = (1/18)x_6$, $x_4 = (11/45)x_6$, $x_5 = (44/45)x_6$, and x_6 is free. Take $x_6 = 90$. Then $x_1 = 15$, $x_2 = 44$, $x_3 = 5$, $x_4 = 22$, and $x_5 = 88$. The balanced equation is

$$15PbN_6 + 44CrMn_2O_8 \rightarrow 5Pb_3O_4 + 22Cr_2O_3 + 88MnO_2 + 90NO$$

10. **[M]** Set up vectors that list the atoms per molecule. Using the order manganese (Mn), sulfur (S), arsenic (As), chromium (Cr), oxygen (O), and hydrogen (H), the vector equation to be solved is

$$x_1 \begin{bmatrix} 1 \\ 1 \\ 0 \\ 0 \\ 0 \\ 0 \end{bmatrix} + x_2 \begin{bmatrix} 0 \\ 0 \\ 2 \\ 10 \\ 35 \\ 0 \end{bmatrix} + x_3 \begin{bmatrix} 0 \\ 1 \\ 0 \\ 0 \\ 4 \\ 2 \end{bmatrix} = x_4 \begin{bmatrix} 1 \\ 0 \\ 0 \\ 0 \\ 4 \\ 1 \end{bmatrix} + x_5 \begin{bmatrix} 0 \\ 0 \\ 1 \\ 0 \\ 0 \\ 3 \end{bmatrix} + x_6 \begin{bmatrix} 0 \\ 3 \\ 0 \\ 1 \\ 12 \\ 0 \end{bmatrix} + x_7 \begin{bmatrix} 0 \\ 0 \\ 0 \\ 0 \\ 1 \\ 2 \end{bmatrix} \quad \begin{matrix} \text{manganese} \\ \text{sulfur} \\ \text{arsenic} \\ \text{chromium} \\ \text{oxygen} \\ \text{hydrogen} \end{matrix}$$

In rational format, the general solution is $x_1 = (16/327)x_7$, $x_2 = (13/327)x_7$, $x_3 = (374/327)x_7$, $x_4 = (16/327)x_7$, $x_5 = (26/327)x_7$, $x_6 = (130/327)x_7$, and x_7 is free. Take $x_7 = 327$ to make the other variables whole numbers. The balanced equation is

$$16MnS + 13As_2Cr_{10}O_{35} + 374H_2SO_4 \rightarrow 16HMnO_4 + 26AsH_3 + 130CrS_3O_{12} + 327H_2O$$

Note that some students may use decimal calculation and simply "round off" the fractions that relate x_1, ..., x_6 to x_7. The equations they construct may balance most of the elements but miss an atom or two. Here is a solution submitted by two of my students:

$$5MnS + 4As_2Cr_{10}O_{35} + 115H_2SO_4 \rightarrow 5HMnO_4 + 8AsH_3 + 40CrS_3O_{12} + 100H_2O$$

Everything balances except the hydrogen. The right side is short 8 hydrogen atoms. Perhaps the students thought that the $4H_2$ (hydrogen gas) escaped!

11. Write the equations for each node:

Node	Flow in		Flow out
A	$x_1 + x_3$	$=$	20
B	x_2	$=$	$x_3 + x_4$
C	80	$=$	$x_1 + x_2$
Total flow:	80	$=$	$x_4 + 20$

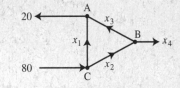

Rearrange the equations:

$$
\begin{array}{rcl}
x_1 \qquad\quad + \quad x_3 \qquad\qquad &=& 20 \\
x_2 \; - \; x_3 \; - \; x_4 &=& 0 \\
x_1 \; + \; x_2 \qquad\qquad\qquad &=& 80 \\
x_4 &=& 60
\end{array}
$$

Reduce the augmented matrix:

$$
\begin{bmatrix}
1 & 0 & 1 & 0 & 20 \\
0 & 1 & -1 & -1 & 0 \\
1 & 1 & 0 & 0 & 80 \\
0 & 0 & 0 & 1 & 60
\end{bmatrix}
\sim \cdots \sim
\begin{bmatrix}
① & 0 & 1 & 0 & 20 \\
0 & ① & -1 & 0 & 60 \\
0 & 0 & 0 & ① & 60 \\
0 & 0 & 0 & 0 & 0
\end{bmatrix}
$$

For this type of problem, the best description of the general solution uses the style of Section 1.2 rather than parametric vector form:

$$
\begin{cases}
x_1 = 20 - x_3 \\
x_2 = 60 + x_3 \\
x_3 \text{ is free} \\
x_4 = 60
\end{cases}
$$
. Since x_1 cannot be negative, the largest value of x_3 is 20.

12. Write the equations for each intersection:

Intersection	Flow in		Flow out
A	x_1	$=$	$x_3 + x_4 + 40$
B	200	$=$	$x_1 + x_2$
C	$x_2 + x_3$	$=$	$x_5 + 100$
D	$x_4 + x_5$	$=$	60
Total flow:	200	$=$	200

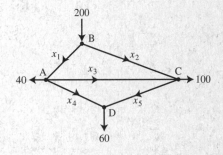

Rearrange the equations:

$$
\begin{array}{rcr}
x_1 \qquad - x_3 - x_4 \qquad\qquad &=& 40 \\
x_1 + x_2 \qquad\qquad\qquad &=& 200 \\
x_2 + x_3 \qquad - x_5 &=& 100 \\
x_4 + x_5 &=& 60
\end{array}
$$

Reduce the augmented matrix:

$$
\begin{bmatrix}
1 & 0 & -1 & -1 & 0 & 40 \\
1 & 1 & 0 & 0 & 0 & 200 \\
0 & 1 & 1 & 0 & -1 & 100 \\
0 & 0 & 0 & 1 & 1 & 60
\end{bmatrix}
\sim
\begin{bmatrix}
① & 0 & -1 & 0 & 1 & 100 \\
0 & ① & 1 & 0 & -1 & 100 \\
0 & 0 & 0 & ① & 1 & 60 \\
0 & 0 & 0 & 0 & 0 & 0
\end{bmatrix}
$$

The general solution (written in the style of Section 1.2) is

$$
\begin{cases}
x_1 = 100 + x_3 - x_5 \\
x_2 = 100 - x_3 + x_5 \\
x_3 \text{ is free} \\
x_4 = 60 - x_5 \\
x_5 \text{ is free}
\end{cases}
$$

b. When $x_4 = 0$, x_5 must be 60, and
$$
\begin{cases}
x_1 = 40 + x_3 \\
x_2 = 160 - x_3 \\
x_3 \text{ is free} \\
x_4 = 0 \\
x_5 = 60
\end{cases}
$$

c. The minimum value of x_1 is 40 cars/minute, because x_3 cannot be negative.

13. Write the equations for each intersection:

Intersection	Flow in		Flow out
A	$x_2 + 30$	$=$	$x_1 + 80$
B	$x_3 + x_5$	$=$	$x_2 + x_4$
C	$x_6 + 100$	$=$	$x_5 + 40$
D	$x_4 + 40$	$=$	$x_6 + 90$
E	$x_1 + 60$	$=$	$x_3 + 20$
Total flow:	230	$=$	230

Rearrange the equations:

$$
\begin{array}{rcr}
x_1 - x_2 \qquad\qquad\qquad\qquad\quad &=& -50 \\
x_2 - x_3 + x_4 - x_5 \qquad &=& 0 \\
x_5 - x_6 &=& 60 \\
x_4 \qquad - x_6 &=& 50 \\
x_1 \qquad - x_3 \qquad\qquad\qquad &=& -40
\end{array}
$$

Reduce the augmented matrix:

$$
\begin{bmatrix}
1 & -1 & 0 & 0 & 0 & 0 & -50 \\
0 & 1 & -1 & 1 & -1 & 0 & 0 \\
0 & 0 & 0 & 0 & 1 & -1 & 60 \\
0 & 0 & 0 & 1 & 0 & -1 & 50 \\
1 & 0 & -1 & 0 & 0 & 0 & -40
\end{bmatrix}
\sim \cdots \sim
\begin{bmatrix}
1 & -1 & 0 & 0 & 0 & 0 & -50 \\
0 & 1 & -1 & 1 & -1 & 0 & 0 \\
0 & 0 & 0 & 1 & 0 & -1 & 50 \\
0 & 0 & 0 & 0 & 1 & -1 & 60 \\
0 & 0 & 0 & 0 & 0 & 0 & 0
\end{bmatrix}
$$

$$\sim\cdots\sim\begin{bmatrix} ① & 0 & -1 & 0 & 0 & 0 & -40 \\ 0 & ① & -1 & 0 & 0 & 0 & 10 \\ 0 & 0 & 0 & ① & 0 & -1 & 50 \\ 0 & 0 & 0 & 0 & ① & -1 & 60 \\ 0 & 0 & 0 & 0 & 0 & 0 & 0 \end{bmatrix}$$

a. The general solution is $\begin{cases} x_1 = x_3 - 40 \\ x_2 = x_3 + 10 \\ x_3 \text{ is free} \\ x_4 = x_6 + 50 \\ x_5 = x_6 + 60 \\ x_6 \text{ is free} \end{cases}$

b. To find minimum flows, note that since x_1 cannot be negative, $x_3 \geq 40$. This implies that $x_2 \geq 50$. Also, since x_6 cannot be negative, $x_4 \geq 50$ and $x_5 \geq 60$. The minimum flows are $x_2 = 50$, $x_3 = 40$, $x_4 = 50$, $x_5 = 60$ (when $x_1 = 0$ and $x_6 = 0$).

14. Write the equations for each intersection.

Intersection	Flow in		Flow out
A	x_1	=	$x_2 + 100$
B	$x_2 + 50$	=	x_3
C	x_3	=	$x_4 + 120$
D	$x_4 + 150$	=	x_5
E	x_5	=	$x_6 + 80$
F	$x_6 + 100$	=	x_1

Rearrange the equations:

$$\begin{array}{rcr} x_1 - x_2 & = & 100 \\ x_2 - x_3 & = & -50 \\ x_3 - x_4 & = & 120 \\ x_4 - x_5 & = & -150 \\ x_5 - x_6 & = & 80 \\ -x_1 + x_6 & = & -100 \end{array}$$

Reduce the augmented matrix:

$$\begin{bmatrix} 1 & -1 & 0 & 0 & 0 & 0 & 100 \\ 0 & 1 & -1 & 0 & 0 & 0 & -50 \\ 0 & 0 & 1 & -1 & 0 & 0 & 120 \\ 0 & 0 & 0 & 1 & -1 & 0 & -150 \\ 0 & 0 & 0 & 0 & 1 & -1 & 80 \\ -1 & 0 & 0 & 0 & 0 & 1 & -100 \end{bmatrix} \sim\cdots\sim \begin{bmatrix} 1 & -1 & 0 & 0 & 0 & 0 & 100 \\ 0 & 1 & -1 & 0 & 0 & 0 & -50 \\ 0 & 0 & 1 & -1 & 0 & 0 & 120 \\ 0 & 0 & 0 & 1 & -1 & 0 & -150 \\ 0 & 0 & 0 & 0 & 1 & -1 & 80 \\ 0 & 0 & 0 & 0 & 0 & 0 & 0 \end{bmatrix}$$

$$\sim \cdots \sim \begin{bmatrix} 1 & 0 & 0 & 0 & 0 & -1 & 100 \\ 0 & 1 & 0 & 0 & 0 & -1 & 0 \\ 0 & 0 & 1 & 0 & 0 & -1 & 50 \\ 0 & 0 & 0 & 1 & 0 & -1 & -70 \\ 0 & 0 & 0 & 0 & 1 & -1 & 80 \\ 0 & 0 & 0 & 0 & 0 & 0 & 0 \end{bmatrix}. \text{ The general solution is } \begin{cases} x_1 = 100 + x_6 \\ x_2 = x_6 \\ x_3 = 50 + x_6 \\ x_4 = -70 + x_6 \\ x_5 = 80 + x_6 \\ x_6 \text{ is free} \end{cases}.$$

Since x_4 cannot be negative, the minimum value of x_6 is 70.

Note: The MATLAB box in the *Study Guide* discusses rational calculations, needed for balancing the chemical equations in Exercises 9 and 10. As usual, the appendices cover this material for Maple, Mathematica, and the TI and HP graphic calculators.

1.7   SOLUTIONS

Note: Key exercises are 9–20 and 23–30. Exercise 30 states a result that could be a theorem in the text. There is a danger, however, that students will memorize the result without understanding the proof, and then later mix up the words row and column. Exercises 37 and 38 anticipate the discussion in Section 1.9 of one-to-one transformations. Exercise 44 is fairly difficult for my students.

1. Use an augmented matrix to study the solution set of $x_1\mathbf{u} + x_2\mathbf{v} + x_3\mathbf{w} = \mathbf{0}$ (*), where $\mathbf{u}$, $\mathbf{v}$, and $\mathbf{w}$ are the

    three given vectors. Since $\begin{bmatrix} 5 & 7 & 9 & 0 \\ 0 & 2 & 4 & 0 \\ 0 & -6 & -8 & 0 \end{bmatrix} \sim \begin{bmatrix} ⑤ & 7 & 9 & 0 \\ 0 & ② & 4 & 0 \\ 0 & 0 & ④ & 0 \end{bmatrix}$, there are no free variables. So the

    homogeneous equation (*) has only the trivial solution. The vectors are linearly independent.

2. Use an augmented matrix to study the solution set of $x_1\mathbf{u} + x_2\mathbf{v} + x_3\mathbf{w} = \mathbf{0}$ (*), where $\mathbf{u}$, $\mathbf{v}$, and $\mathbf{w}$ are the

    three given vectors. Since $\begin{bmatrix} 0 & 0 & -3 & 0 \\ 0 & 5 & 4 & 0 \\ 2 & -8 & 1 & 0 \end{bmatrix} \sim \begin{bmatrix} ② & -8 & 1 & 0 \\ 0 & ⑤ & 4 & 0 \\ 0 & 0 & ㉛ & 0 \end{bmatrix}$, there are no free variables. So the

    homogeneous equation (*) has only the trivial solution. The vectors are linearly independent.

3. Use the method of Example 3 (or the box following the example). By comparing entries of the vectors, one sees that the second vector is −3 times the first vector. Thus, the two vectors are linearly dependent.

4. From the first entries in the vectors, it seems that the second vector of the pair $\begin{bmatrix} -1 \\ 4 \end{bmatrix}, \begin{bmatrix} -2 \\ -8 \end{bmatrix}$ may be 2

    times the first vector. But there is a sign problem with the second entries. So neither of the vectors is a multiple of the other. The vectors are linearly independent.

5. Use the method of Example 2. Row reduce the augmented matrix for $A\mathbf{x} = \mathbf{0}$:

    $$\begin{bmatrix} 0 & -8 & 5 & 0 \\ 3 & -7 & 4 & 0 \\ -1 & 5 & -4 & 0 \\ 1 & -3 & 2 & 0 \end{bmatrix} \sim \begin{bmatrix} 1 & -3 & 2 & 0 \\ 3 & -7 & 4 & 0 \\ -1 & 5 & -4 & 0 \\ 0 & -8 & 5 & 0 \end{bmatrix} \sim \begin{bmatrix} 1 & -3 & 2 & 0 \\ 0 & 2 & -2 & 0 \\ 0 & 2 & -2 & 0 \\ 0 & -8 & 5 & 0 \end{bmatrix} \sim \begin{bmatrix} 1 & -3 & 2 & 0 \\ 0 & 2 & -2 & 0 \\ 0 & 0 & 0 & 0 \\ 0 & 0 & -3 & 0 \end{bmatrix} \sim \begin{bmatrix} ① & -3 & 2 & 0 \\ 0 & ② & -2 & 0 \\ 0 & 0 & ㉛ & 0 \\ 0 & 0 & 0 & 0 \end{bmatrix}$$

There are no free variables. The equation $A\mathbf{x} = \mathbf{0}$ has only the trivial solution and so the columns of A are linearly independent.

6. Use the method of Example 2. Row reduce the augmented matrix for $A\mathbf{x} = \mathbf{0}$:

$$\begin{bmatrix} -4 & -3 & 0 & 0 \\ 0 & -1 & 4 & 0 \\ 1 & 0 & 3 & 0 \\ 5 & 4 & 6 & 0 \end{bmatrix} \sim \begin{bmatrix} 1 & 0 & 3 & 0 \\ 0 & -1 & 4 & 0 \\ -4 & -3 & 0 & 0 \\ 5 & 4 & 6 & 0 \end{bmatrix} \sim \begin{bmatrix} 1 & 0 & 3 & 0 \\ 0 & -1 & 4 & 0 \\ 0 & -3 & 12 & 0 \\ 0 & 4 & -9 & 0 \end{bmatrix} \sim \begin{bmatrix} 1 & 0 & 3 & 0 \\ 0 & -1 & 4 & 0 \\ 0 & 0 & 0 & 0 \\ 0 & 0 & 7 & 0 \end{bmatrix} \sim \begin{bmatrix} ① & 0 & 3 & 0 \\ 0 & ⊖1 & 4 & 0 \\ 0 & 0 & ⑦ & 0 \\ 0 & 0 & 0 & 0 \end{bmatrix}$$

There are no free variables. The equation $A\mathbf{x} = \mathbf{0}$ has only the trivial solution and so the columns of A are linearly independent.

7. Study the equation $A\mathbf{x} = \mathbf{0}$. Some people may start with the method of Example 2:

$$\begin{bmatrix} 1 & 4 & -3 & 0 & 0 \\ -2 & -7 & 5 & 1 & 0 \\ -4 & -5 & 7 & 5 & 0 \end{bmatrix} \sim \begin{bmatrix} 1 & 4 & -3 & 0 & 0 \\ 0 & 1 & -1 & 1 & 0 \\ 0 & 11 & -5 & 5 & 0 \end{bmatrix} \sim \begin{bmatrix} ① & 4 & -3 & 0 & 0 \\ 0 & ① & -1 & 1 & 0 \\ 0 & 0 & ⑥ & -6 & 0 \end{bmatrix}$$

But this is a waste of time. There are only 3 rows, so there are at most three pivot positions. Hence, at least one of the four variables must be free. So the equation $A\mathbf{x} = \mathbf{0}$ has a nontrivial solution and the columns of A are linearly dependent.

8. Same situation as with Exercise 7. The (unnecessary) row operations are

$$\begin{bmatrix} 1 & -3 & 3 & -2 & 0 \\ -3 & 7 & -1 & 2 & 0 \\ 0 & 1 & -4 & 3 & 0 \end{bmatrix} \sim \begin{bmatrix} 1 & -3 & 3 & -2 & 0 \\ 0 & -2 & 8 & -4 & 0 \\ 0 & 1 & -4 & 3 & 0 \end{bmatrix} \sim \begin{bmatrix} ① & -3 & 3 & -2 & 0 \\ 0 & ⊖2 & 8 & -4 & 0 \\ 0 & 0 & 0 & ① & 0 \end{bmatrix}$$

Again, because there are at most three pivot positions yet there are four variables, the equation $A\mathbf{x} = \mathbf{0}$ has a nontrivial solution and the columns of A are linearly dependent.

9. a. The vector $\mathbf{v}_3$ is in Span$\{\mathbf{v}_1, \mathbf{v}_2\}$ if and only if the equation $x_1\mathbf{v}_1 + x_2\mathbf{v}_2 = \mathbf{v}_3$ has a solution. To find out, row reduce $[\mathbf{v}_1 \ \ \mathbf{v}_2 \ \ \mathbf{v}_3]$, considered as an augmented matrix:

$$\begin{bmatrix} 1 & -3 & 5 \\ -3 & 9 & -7 \\ 2 & -6 & h \end{bmatrix} \sim \begin{bmatrix} ① & -3 & 5 \\ 0 & 0 & ⑧ \\ 0 & 0 & h-10 \end{bmatrix}$$

At this point, the equation $0 = 8$ shows that the original vector equation has no solution. So $\mathbf{v}_3$ is in Span$\{\mathbf{v}_1, \mathbf{v}_2\}$ for *no* value of h.

b. For $\{\mathbf{v}_1, \mathbf{v}_2, \mathbf{v}_3\}$ to be linearly independent, the equation $x_1\mathbf{v}_1 + x_2\mathbf{v}_2 + x_3\mathbf{v}_3 = \mathbf{0}$ must have only the trivial solution. Row reduce the augmented matrix $[\mathbf{v}_1 \ \ \mathbf{v}_2 \ \ \mathbf{v}_3 \ \ \mathbf{0}]$

$$\begin{bmatrix} 1 & -3 & 5 & 0 \\ -3 & 9 & -7 & 0 \\ 2 & -6 & h & 0 \end{bmatrix} \sim \begin{bmatrix} 1 & -3 & 5 & 0 \\ 0 & 0 & 8 & 0 \\ 0 & 0 & h-10 & 0 \end{bmatrix} \sim \begin{bmatrix} ① & -3 & 5 & 0 \\ 0 & 0 & ⑧ & 0 \\ 0 & 0 & 0 & 0 \end{bmatrix}$$

For every value of h, x_2 is a free variable, and so the homogeneous equation has a nontrivial solution. Thus $\{\mathbf{v}_1, \mathbf{v}_2, \mathbf{v}_3\}$ is a linearly dependent set for all h.

10. a. The vector $\mathbf{v}_3$ is in Span$\{\mathbf{v}_1, \mathbf{v}_2\}$ if and only if the equation $x_1\mathbf{v}_1 + x_2\mathbf{v}_2 = \mathbf{v}_3$ has a solution. To find out, row reduce $[\mathbf{v}_1\ \ \mathbf{v}_2\ \ \mathbf{v}_3]$, considered as an augmented matrix:

$$\begin{bmatrix} 1 & -2 & 2 \\ -5 & 10 & -9 \\ -3 & 6 & h \end{bmatrix} \sim \begin{bmatrix} \textcircled{1} & -2 & 2 \\ 0 & 0 & \textcircled{1} \\ 0 & 0 & h+6 \end{bmatrix}$$

At this point, the equation $0 = 1$ shows that the original vector equation has no solution. So $\mathbf{v}_3$ is in Span$\{\mathbf{v}_1, \mathbf{v}_2\}$ for *no* value of h.

b. For $\{\mathbf{v}_1, \mathbf{v}_2, \mathbf{v}_3\}$ to be linearly independent, the equation $x_1\mathbf{v}_1 + x_2\mathbf{v}_2 + x_3\mathbf{v}_3 = \mathbf{0}$ must have only the trivial solution. Row reduce the augmented matrix $[\mathbf{v}_1\ \ \mathbf{v}_2\ \ \mathbf{v}_3\ \ \mathbf{0}]$

$$\begin{bmatrix} 1 & -2 & 2 & 0 \\ -5 & 10 & -9 & 0 \\ -3 & 6 & h & 0 \end{bmatrix} \sim \begin{bmatrix} 1 & -2 & 2 & 0 \\ 0 & 0 & 1 & 0 \\ 0 & 0 & h+6 & 0 \end{bmatrix} \sim \begin{bmatrix} \textcircled{1} & -2 & 2 & 0 \\ 0 & 0 & \textcircled{1} & 0 \\ 0 & 0 & 0 & 0 \end{bmatrix}$$

For every value of h, x_2 is a free variable, and so the homogeneous equation has a nontrivial solution. Thus $\{\mathbf{v}_1, \mathbf{v}_2, \mathbf{v}_3\}$ is a linearly dependent set for all h.

11. To study the linear dependence of three vectors, say $\mathbf{v}_1, \mathbf{v}_2, \mathbf{v}_3$, row reduce the augmented matrix $[\mathbf{v}_1\ \ \mathbf{v}_2\ \ \mathbf{v}_3\ \ \mathbf{0}]$:

$$\begin{bmatrix} 1 & 3 & -1 & 0 \\ -1 & -5 & 5 & 0 \\ 4 & 7 & h & 0 \end{bmatrix} \sim \begin{bmatrix} 1 & 3 & -1 & 0 \\ 0 & -2 & 4 & 0 \\ 0 & -5 & h+4 & 0 \end{bmatrix} \sim \begin{bmatrix} \textcircled{1} & 3 & -1 & 0 \\ 0 & \textcircled{-2} & 4 & 0 \\ 0 & 0 & h-6 & 0 \end{bmatrix}$$

The equation $x_1\mathbf{v}_1 + x_2\mathbf{v}_2 + x_3\mathbf{v}_3 = \mathbf{0}$ has a nontrivial solution if and only if $h - 6 = 0$ (which corresponds to x_3 being a free variable). Thus, the vectors are linearly dependent if and only if $h = 6$.

12. To study the linear dependence of three vectors, say $\mathbf{v}_1, \mathbf{v}_2, \mathbf{v}_3$, row reduce the augmented matrix $[\mathbf{v}_1\ \ \mathbf{v}_2\ \ \mathbf{v}_3\ \ \mathbf{0}]$:

$$\begin{bmatrix} 2 & -6 & 8 & 0 \\ -4 & 7 & h & 0 \\ 1 & -3 & 4 & 0 \end{bmatrix} \sim \begin{bmatrix} \textcircled{2} & -6 & 8 & 0 \\ 0 & \textcircled{-5} & h+16 & 0 \\ 0 & 0 & 0 & 0 \end{bmatrix}$$

The equation $x_1\mathbf{v}_1 + x_2\mathbf{v}_2 + x_3\mathbf{v}_3 = \mathbf{0}$ has a free variable and hence a nontrivial solution no matter what the value of h. So the vectors are linearly dependent for all values of h.

13. To study the linear dependence of three vectors, say $\mathbf{v}_1, \mathbf{v}_2, \mathbf{v}_3$, row reduce the augmented matrix $[\mathbf{v}_1\ \ \mathbf{v}_2\ \ \mathbf{v}_3\ \ \mathbf{0}]$:

$$\begin{bmatrix} 1 & -2 & 3 & 0 \\ 5 & -9 & h & 0 \\ -3 & 6 & -9 & 0 \end{bmatrix} \sim \begin{bmatrix} \textcircled{1} & -2 & 3 & 0 \\ 0 & \textcircled{1} & h-15 & 0 \\ 0 & 0 & 0 & 0 \end{bmatrix}$$

The equation $x_1\mathbf{v}_1 + x_2\mathbf{v}_2 + x_3\mathbf{v}_3 = \mathbf{0}$ has a free variable and hence a nontrivial solution no matter what the value of h. So the vectors are linearly dependent for all values of h.

14. To study the linear dependence of three vectors, say $\mathbf{v}_1$, $\mathbf{v}_2$, $\mathbf{v}_3$, row reduce the augmented matrix
$[\mathbf{v}_1 \quad \mathbf{v}_2 \quad \mathbf{v}_3 \quad \mathbf{0}]$:

$$\begin{bmatrix} 1 & -5 & 1 & 0 \\ -1 & 7 & 1 & 0 \\ -3 & 8 & h & 0 \end{bmatrix} \sim \begin{bmatrix} 1 & -5 & 1 & 0 \\ 0 & 2 & 2 & 0 \\ 0 & -7 & h+3 & 0 \end{bmatrix} \sim \begin{bmatrix} ① & -5 & 1 & 0 \\ 0 & ② & 2 & 0 \\ 0 & 0 & h+10 & 0 \end{bmatrix}$$

The equation $x_1\mathbf{v}_1 + x_2\mathbf{v}_2 + x_3\mathbf{v}_3 = \mathbf{0}$ has a nontrivial solution if and only if $h + 10 = 0$ (which corresponds to x_3 being a free variable). Thus, the vectors are linearly dependent if and only if $h = -10$.

15. The set is linearly dependent, by Theorem 8, because there are four vectors in the set but only two entries in each vector.

16. The set is linearly dependent because the second vector is 3/2 times the first vector.

17. The set is linearly dependent, by Theorem 9, because the list of vectors contains a zero vector.

18. The set is linearly dependent, by Theorem 8, because there are four vectors in the set but only two entries in each vector.

19. The set is linearly independent because neither vector is a multiple of the other vector. [Two of the entries in the first vector are -4 times the corresponding entry in the second vector. But this multiple does not work for the third entries.]

20. The set is linearly dependent, by Theorem 9, because the list of vectors contains a zero vector.

21. a. False. A homogeneous system *always* has the trivial solution. See the box before Example 2.

    b. False. See the warning after Theorem 7.

    c. True. See Fig. 3, after Theorem 8.

    d. True. See the remark following Example 4.

22. a. True. See Fig. 1.

    b. False. For instance, the set consisting of $\begin{bmatrix} 1 \\ -2 \\ 3 \end{bmatrix}$ and $\begin{bmatrix} 2 \\ -4 \\ 6 \end{bmatrix}$ is linearly dependent. See the warning after Theorem 8.

    c. True. See the remark following Example 4.

    d. False. See Example 3(a).

23. $\begin{bmatrix} ■ & * & * \\ 0 & ■ & * \\ 0 & 0 & ■ \end{bmatrix}$
    24. $\begin{bmatrix} ■ & * \\ 0 & 0 \end{bmatrix}, \begin{bmatrix} 0 & ■ \\ 0 & 0 \end{bmatrix}, \begin{bmatrix} 0 & 0 \\ 0 & 0 \end{bmatrix}$
    25. $\begin{bmatrix} ■ & * \\ 0 & ■ \\ 0 & 0 \\ 0 & 0 \end{bmatrix}$ and $\begin{bmatrix} 0 & ■ \\ 0 & 0 \\ 0 & 0 \\ 0 & 0 \end{bmatrix}$

26. $\begin{bmatrix} \blacksquare & * & * \\ 0 & \blacksquare & * \\ 0 & 0 & \blacksquare \\ 0 & 0 & 0 \end{bmatrix}$. The columns must linearly independent, by Theorem 7, because the first column is not

zero, the second column is not a multiple of the first, and the third column is not a linear combination of the preceding two columns (because $\mathbf{a}_3$ is not in Span$\{\mathbf{a}_1, \mathbf{a}_2\}$).

27. All five columns of the 7×5 matrix A must be pivot columns. Otherwise, the equation $A\mathbf{x} = \mathbf{0}$ would have a free variable, in which case the columns of A would be linearly dependent.

28. If the columns of a 5×7 matrix A span $\mathbf{R}^5$, then A has a pivot in each row, by Theorem 4. Since each pivot position is in a different column, A has five pivot columns.

29. A: any 3×2 matrix with two nonzero columns such that neither column is a multiple of the other. In this case the columns are linearly independent and so the equation $A\mathbf{x} = \mathbf{0}$ has only the trivial solution. B: any 3×2 matrix with one column a multiple of the other.

30. **a.** n

 b. The columns of A are linearly independent if and only if the equation $A\mathbf{x} = \mathbf{0}$ has only the trivial solution. This happens if and only if $A\mathbf{x} = \mathbf{0}$ has no free variables, which in turn happens if and only if every variable is a basic variable, that is, if and only if every column of A is a pivot column.

31. Think of $A = [\mathbf{a}_1 \quad \mathbf{a}_2 \quad \mathbf{a}_3]$. The text points out that $\mathbf{a}_3 = \mathbf{a}_1 + \mathbf{a}_2$. Rewrite this as $\mathbf{a}_1 + \mathbf{a}_2 - \mathbf{a}_3 = \mathbf{0}$. As a matrix equation, $A\mathbf{x} = \mathbf{0}$ for $\mathbf{x} = (1, 1, -1)$.

32. Think of $A = [\mathbf{a}_1 \quad \mathbf{a}_2 \quad \mathbf{a}_3]$. The text points out that $\mathbf{a}_1 + 2\mathbf{a}_2 = \mathbf{a}_3$. Rewrite this as $\mathbf{a}_1 + 2\mathbf{a}_2 - \mathbf{a}_3 = \mathbf{0}$. As a matrix equation, $A\mathbf{x} = \mathbf{0}$ for $\mathbf{x} = (1, 2, -1)$.

33. True, by Theorem 7. (The *Study Guide* adds another justification.)

34. True, by Theorem 9.

35. False. The vector $\mathbf{v}_1$ could be the zero vector.

36. False. Counterexample: Take $\mathbf{v}_1$, $\mathbf{v}_2$, and $\mathbf{v}_4$ all to be multiples of one vector. Take $\mathbf{v}_3$ to be *not* a multiple of that vector. For example,

$$\mathbf{v}_1 = \begin{bmatrix} 1 \\ 1 \\ 1 \\ 1 \end{bmatrix}, \mathbf{v}_2 = \begin{bmatrix} 2 \\ 2 \\ 2 \\ 2 \end{bmatrix}, \mathbf{v}_3 = \begin{bmatrix} 1 \\ 0 \\ 0 \\ 0 \end{bmatrix}, \mathbf{v}_4 = \begin{bmatrix} 4 \\ 4 \\ 4 \\ 4 \end{bmatrix}$$

37. True. A linear dependence relation among $\mathbf{v}_1$, $\mathbf{v}_2$, $\mathbf{v}_3$ may be extended to a linear dependence relation among $\mathbf{v}_1$, $\mathbf{v}_2$, $\mathbf{v}_3$, $\mathbf{v}_4$ by placing a zero weight on $\mathbf{v}_4$.

38. True. If the equation $x_1\mathbf{v}_1 + x_2\mathbf{v}_2 + x_3\mathbf{v}_3 = \mathbf{0}$ had a nontrivial solution (with at least one of x_1, x_2, x_3 nonzero), then so would the equation $x_1\mathbf{v}_1 + x_2\mathbf{v}_2 + x_3\mathbf{v}_3 + 0 \cdot \mathbf{v}_4 = \mathbf{0}$. But that cannot happen because $\{\mathbf{v}_1, \mathbf{v}_2, \mathbf{v}_3, \mathbf{v}_4\}$ is linearly independent. So $\{\mathbf{v}_1, \mathbf{v}_2, \mathbf{v}_3\}$ must be linearly independent. This problem can also be solved using Exercise 37, if you know that the statement there is true.

39. If for all **b** the equation $A\mathbf{x} = \mathbf{b}$ has at most one solution, then take $\mathbf{b} = \mathbf{0}$, and conclude that the equation $A\mathbf{x} = \mathbf{0}$ has at most one solution. Then the trivial solution is the only solution, and so the columns of A are linearly independent.

40. An $m \times n$ matrix with n pivot columns has a pivot in each column. So the equation $A\mathbf{x} = \mathbf{b}$ has no free variables. If there is a solution, it must be unique.

41. [M] $A = \begin{bmatrix} 8 & -3 & 0 & -7 & 2 \\ -9 & 4 & 5 & 11 & -7 \\ 6 & -2 & 2 & -4 & 4 \\ 5 & -1 & 7 & 0 & 10 \end{bmatrix} \sim \begin{bmatrix} 8 & -3 & 0 & -7 & 2 \\ 0 & 5/8 & 5 & 25/8 & -19/4 \\ 0 & 1/4 & 2 & 5/4 & 5/2 \\ 0 & 7/8 & 7 & 35/8 & 35/4 \end{bmatrix}$

$\sim \begin{bmatrix} 8 & -3 & 0 & -7 & 2 \\ 0 & 5/8 & 5 & 25/8 & -19/4 \\ 0 & 0 & 0 & 0 & 22/5 \\ 0 & 0 & 0 & 0 & 77/5 \end{bmatrix} \sim \begin{bmatrix} ⑧ & -3 & 0 & -7 & 2 \\ 0 & ⑤/⑧ & 5 & 25/8 & -19/4 \\ 0 & 0 & 0 & 0 & ㉒/⑤ \\ 0 & 0 & 0 & 0 & 0 \end{bmatrix}$

The pivot columns of A are 1, 2, and 5. Use them to form $B = \begin{bmatrix} 8 & -3 & 2 \\ -9 & 4 & -7 \\ 6 & -2 & 4 \\ 5 & -1 & 10 \end{bmatrix}$.

Other likely choices use columns 3 or 4 of A instead of 2: $\begin{bmatrix} 8 & 0 & 2 \\ -9 & 5 & -7 \\ 6 & 2 & 4 \\ 5 & 7 & 10 \end{bmatrix}, \begin{bmatrix} 8 & -7 & 2 \\ -9 & 11 & -7 \\ 6 & -4 & 4 \\ 5 & 0 & 10 \end{bmatrix}$.

Actually, any set of three columns of A that includes column 5 will work for B, but the concepts needed to prove that are not available now. (Column 5 is not in the two-dimensional subspace spanned by the first four columns.)

42. [M]

$\begin{bmatrix} 12 & 10 & -6 & -3 & 7 & 10 \\ -7 & -6 & 4 & 7 & -9 & 5 \\ 9 & 9 & -9 & -5 & 5 & -1 \\ -4 & -3 & 1 & 6 & -8 & 9 \\ 8 & 7 & -5 & -9 & 11 & -8 \end{bmatrix} \sim \cdots \sim \begin{bmatrix} ⑫ & 10 & -6 & -3 & 7 & 10 \\ 0 & ㊀⅙ & 1/2 & 21/4 & -59/12 & 65/6 \\ 0 & 0 & 0 & ㊙/② & -89/2 & 89 \\ 0 & 0 & 0 & 0 & 0 & ③ \\ 0 & 0 & 0 & 0 & 0 & 0 \end{bmatrix}$

The pivot columns of A are 1, 2, 4, and 6. Use them to form $B = \begin{bmatrix} 12 & 10 & -3 & 10 \\ -7 & -6 & 7 & 5 \\ 9 & 9 & -5 & -1 \\ -4 & -3 & 6 & 9 \\ 8 & 7 & -9 & -8 \end{bmatrix}$.

Other likely choices might use column 3 of A instead of 2, and/or use column 5 instead of 4.

43. **[M]** Make **v** any one of the columns of A that is not in B and row reduce the augmented matrix $[B \quad \mathbf{v}]$. The calculations will show that the equation $B\mathbf{x} = \mathbf{v}$ is consistent, which means that **v** is a linear combination of the columns of B. Thus, each column of A that is not a column of B is in the set spanned by the columns of B.

44. **[M]** Calculations made as for Exercise 43 will show that each column of A that is not a column of B is in the set spanned by the columns of B. *Reason*: The original matrix A has only four pivot columns. If one or more columns of A are removed, the resulting matrix will have at most four pivot columns. (Use exactly the same row operations on the new matrix that were used to reduce A to echelon form.) If **v** is a column of A that is not in B, then row reduction of the augmented matrix $[B \quad \mathbf{v}]$ will display at most four pivot columns. Since B itself was constructed to have four pivot columns, adjoining **v** cannot produce a fifth pivot column. Thus the first four columns of $[B \quad \mathbf{v}]$ are the pivot columns. This implies that the equation $B\mathbf{x} = \mathbf{v}$ has a solution.

Note: At the end of Section 1.7, the *Study Guide* has another note to students about "Mastering Linear Algebra Concepts." The note describes how to organize a review sheet that will help students form a mental image of linear independence. The note also lists typical misuses of terminology, in which an adjective is applied to an inappropriate noun. (This is a major problem for my students.) I require my students to prepare a review sheet as described in the *Study Guide*, and I try to make helpful comments on their sheets. I am convinced, through personal observation and student surveys, that the students who prepare many of these review sheets consistently perform better than other students. Hopefully, these students will remember important concepts for some time beyond the final exam.

1.8   SOLUTIONS

Notes: The key exercises are 17–20, 25 and 31. Exercise 20 is worth assigning even if you normally assign only odd exercises. Exercise 25 (and 27) can be used to make a few comments about computer graphics, even if you do not plan to cover Section 2.6. For Exercise 31, the *Study Guide* encourages students *not* to look at the proof before trying hard to construct it. Then the *Guide* explains how to create the proof.

Exercises 19 and 20 provide a natural segue into Section 1.9. I arrange to discuss the homework on these exercises when I am ready to begin Section 1.9. The definition of the standard matrix in Section 1.9 follows naturally from the homework, and so I've covered the first page of Section 1.9 before students realize we are working on new material.

The text does not provide much practice determining whether a transformation is linear, because the time needed to develop this skill would have to be taken away from some other topic. If you want your students to be able to do this, you may need to supplement Exercises 29, 30, 32 and 33.

If you skip the concepts of one-to-one and "onto" in Section 1.9, you can use the result of Exercise 31 to show that the coordinate mapping from a vector space onto $\mathbf{R}^n$ (in Section 4.4) preserves linear independence and dependence of sets of vectors. (See Example 6 in Section 4.4.)

1. $T(\mathbf{u}) = A\mathbf{u} = \begin{bmatrix} 2 & 0 \\ 0 & 2 \end{bmatrix} \begin{bmatrix} 1 \\ -3 \end{bmatrix} = \begin{bmatrix} 2 \\ -6 \end{bmatrix}$, $T(\mathbf{v}) = \begin{bmatrix} 2 & 0 \\ 0 & 2 \end{bmatrix} \begin{bmatrix} a \\ b \end{bmatrix} = \begin{bmatrix} 2a \\ 2b \end{bmatrix}$

2. $T(\mathbf{u}) = A\mathbf{u} = \begin{bmatrix} .5 & 0 & 0 \\ 0 & .5 & 0 \\ 0 & 0 & .5 \end{bmatrix} \begin{bmatrix} 1 \\ 0 \\ -4 \end{bmatrix} = \begin{bmatrix} .5 \\ 0 \\ -2 \end{bmatrix}$, $T(\mathbf{v}) = \begin{bmatrix} .5 & 0 & 0 \\ 0 & .5 & 0 \\ 0 & 0 & .5 \end{bmatrix} \begin{bmatrix} a \\ b \\ c \end{bmatrix} = \begin{bmatrix} .5a \\ .5b \\ .5c \end{bmatrix}$

3. $[A \quad \mathbf{b}] = \begin{bmatrix} 1 & 0 & -2 & -1 \\ -2 & 1 & 6 & 7 \\ 3 & -2 & -5 & -3 \end{bmatrix} \sim \begin{bmatrix} 1 & 0 & -2 & -1 \\ 0 & 1 & 2 & 5 \\ 0 & -2 & 1 & 0 \end{bmatrix} \sim \begin{bmatrix} 1 & 0 & -2 & -1 \\ 0 & 1 & 2 & 5 \\ 0 & 0 & 5 & 10 \end{bmatrix}$

$\sim \begin{bmatrix} 1 & 0 & -2 & -1 \\ 0 & 1 & 2 & 5 \\ 0 & 0 & 1 & 2 \end{bmatrix} \sim \begin{bmatrix} 1 & 0 & 0 & 3 \\ 0 & 1 & 0 & 1 \\ 0 & 0 & 1 & 2 \end{bmatrix} \quad \mathbf{x} = \begin{bmatrix} 3 \\ 1 \\ 2 \end{bmatrix}$, unique solution

4. $[A \quad \mathbf{b}] = \begin{bmatrix} 1 & -3 & 2 & 6 \\ 0 & 1 & -4 & -7 \\ 3 & -5 & -9 & -9 \end{bmatrix} \sim \begin{bmatrix} 1 & -3 & 2 & 6 \\ 0 & 1 & -4 & -7 \\ 0 & 4 & -15 & -27 \end{bmatrix} \sim \begin{bmatrix} 1 & -3 & 2 & 6 \\ 0 & 1 & -4 & -7 \\ 0 & 0 & 1 & 1 \end{bmatrix}$

$\sim \begin{bmatrix} 1 & -3 & 0 & 4 \\ 0 & 1 & 0 & -3 \\ 0 & 0 & 1 & 1 \end{bmatrix} \sim \begin{bmatrix} 1 & 0 & 0 & -5 \\ 0 & 1 & 0 & -3 \\ 0 & 0 & 1 & 1 \end{bmatrix} \quad \mathbf{x} = \begin{bmatrix} -5 \\ -3 \\ 1 \end{bmatrix}$, unique solution

5. $[A \quad \mathbf{b}] = \begin{bmatrix} 1 & -5 & -7 & -2 \\ -3 & 7 & 5 & -2 \end{bmatrix} \sim \begin{bmatrix} 1 & -5 & -7 & -2 \\ 0 & 1 & 2 & 1 \end{bmatrix} \sim \begin{bmatrix} ① & 0 & 3 & 3 \\ 0 & ① & 2 & 1 \end{bmatrix}$

Note that a solution is *not* $\begin{bmatrix} 3 \\ 1 \end{bmatrix}$. To avoid this common error, write the equations:

$\begin{array}{rrcl} ⓧ_1 & + \ 3x_3 & = & 3 \\ & ⓧ_2 + \ 2x_3 & = & 1 \end{array}$ and solve for the basic variables: $\begin{cases} x_1 = 3 - 3x_3 \\ x_2 = 1 - 2x_3 \\ x_3 \text{ is free} \end{cases}$

General solution $\mathbf{x} = \begin{bmatrix} x_1 \\ x_2 \\ x_3 \end{bmatrix} = \begin{bmatrix} 3 - 3x_3 \\ 1 - 2x_3 \\ x_3 \end{bmatrix} = \begin{bmatrix} 3 \\ 1 \\ 0 \end{bmatrix} + x_3 \begin{bmatrix} -3 \\ -2 \\ 1 \end{bmatrix}$. For a particular solution, one might choose

$x_3 = 0$ and $\mathbf{x} = \begin{bmatrix} 3 \\ 1 \\ 0 \end{bmatrix}$.

6. $[A \quad \mathbf{b}] = \begin{bmatrix} 1 & -2 & 1 & 1 \\ 3 & -4 & 5 & 9 \\ 0 & 1 & 1 & 3 \\ -3 & 5 & -4 & -6 \end{bmatrix} \sim \begin{bmatrix} 1 & -2 & 1 & 1 \\ 0 & 2 & 2 & 6 \\ 0 & 1 & 1 & 3 \\ 0 & -1 & -1 & -3 \end{bmatrix} \sim \begin{bmatrix} 1 & -2 & 1 & 1 \\ 0 & 1 & 1 & 3 \\ 0 & 0 & 0 & 0 \\ 0 & 0 & 0 & 0 \end{bmatrix} \sim \begin{bmatrix} ① & 0 & 3 & 7 \\ 0 & ① & 1 & 3 \\ 0 & 0 & 0 & 0 \\ 0 & 0 & 0 & 0 \end{bmatrix}$

$\begin{array}{rrcl} ⓧ_1 & + \ 3x_3 & = & 7 \\ & ⓧ_2 + \ x_3 & = & 3 \end{array}$. $\begin{cases} x_1 = 7 - 3x_3 \\ x_2 = 3 - x_3 \\ x_3 \text{ is free} \end{cases}$

General solution: $\mathbf{x} = \begin{bmatrix} x_1 \\ x_2 \\ x_3 \end{bmatrix} = \begin{bmatrix} 7 - 3x_3 \\ 3 - x_3 \\ x_3 \end{bmatrix} = \begin{bmatrix} 7 \\ 3 \\ 0 \end{bmatrix} + x_3 \begin{bmatrix} -3 \\ -1 \\ 1 \end{bmatrix}$, one choice: $\begin{bmatrix} 7 \\ 3 \\ 0 \end{bmatrix}$.

7. $a = 5$; the domain of T is $\mathbf{R}^5$, because a 6×5 matrix has 5 columns and for $A\mathbf{x}$ to be defined, $\mathbf{x}$ must be in $\mathbf{R}^5$. $b = 6$; the codomain of T is $\mathbf{R}^6$, because $A\mathbf{x}$ is a linear combination of the columns of A, and each column of A is in $\mathbf{R}^6$.

8. A must have 5 rows and 4 columns. For the domain of T to be $\mathbf{R}^4$, A must have four columns so that $A\mathbf{x}$ is defined for $\mathbf{x}$ in $\mathbf{R}^4$. For the codomain of T to be $\mathbf{R}^5$, the columns of A must have five entries (in which case A must have five rows), because $A\mathbf{x}$ is a linear combination of the columns of A.

9. Solve $A\mathbf{x} = \mathbf{0}$.
$$\begin{bmatrix} 1 & -4 & 7 & -5 & 0 \\ 0 & 1 & -4 & 3 & 0 \\ 2 & -6 & 6 & -4 & 0 \end{bmatrix} \sim \begin{bmatrix} 1 & -4 & 7 & -5 & 0 \\ 0 & 1 & -4 & 3 & 0 \\ 0 & 2 & -8 & 6 & 0 \end{bmatrix} \sim \begin{bmatrix} 1 & -4 & 7 & -5 & 0 \\ 0 & 1 & -4 & 3 & 0 \\ 0 & 0 & 0 & 0 & 0 \end{bmatrix}$$

$$\sim \begin{bmatrix} \textcircled{1} & 0 & -9 & 7 & 0 \\ 0 & \textcircled{1} & -4 & 3 & 0 \\ 0 & 0 & 0 & 0 & 0 \end{bmatrix} \quad \begin{array}{rcl} \textcircled{x_1} & - 9x_3 + 7x_4 &= 0 \\ \textcircled{x_2} & - 4x_3 + 3x_4 &= 0, \\ & 0 &= 0 \end{array} \quad \begin{cases} x_1 = 9x_3 - 7x_4 \\ x_2 = 4x_3 - 3x_4 \\ x_3 \text{ is free} \\ x_4 \text{ is free} \end{cases}$$

$$\mathbf{x} = \begin{bmatrix} x_1 \\ x_2 \\ x_3 \\ x_4 \end{bmatrix} = \begin{bmatrix} 9x_3 - 7x_4 \\ 4x_3 - 3x_4 \\ x_3 \\ x_4 \end{bmatrix} = x_3 \begin{bmatrix} 9 \\ 4 \\ 1 \\ 0 \end{bmatrix} + x_4 \begin{bmatrix} -7 \\ -3 \\ 0 \\ 1 \end{bmatrix}$$

10. Solve $A\mathbf{x} = \mathbf{0}$.
$$\begin{bmatrix} 1 & 3 & 9 & 2 & 0 \\ 1 & 0 & 3 & -4 & 0 \\ 0 & 1 & 2 & 3 & 0 \\ -2 & 3 & 0 & 5 & 0 \end{bmatrix} \sim \begin{bmatrix} 1 & 3 & 9 & 2 & 0 \\ 0 & -3 & -6 & -6 & 0 \\ 0 & 1 & 2 & 3 & 0 \\ 0 & 9 & 18 & 9 & 0 \end{bmatrix} \sim \begin{bmatrix} 1 & 3 & 9 & 2 & 0 \\ 0 & 1 & 2 & 3 & 0 \\ 0 & -3 & -6 & -6 & 0 \\ 0 & 9 & 18 & 9 & 0 \end{bmatrix}$$

$$\sim \begin{bmatrix} 1 & 3 & 9 & 2 & 0 \\ 0 & 1 & 2 & 3 & 0 \\ 0 & 0 & 0 & 3 & 0 \\ 0 & 0 & 0 & -18 & 0 \end{bmatrix} \sim \begin{bmatrix} 1 & 3 & 9 & 0 & 0 \\ 0 & 1 & 2 & 0 & 0 \\ 0 & 0 & 0 & 1 & 0 \\ 0 & 0 & 0 & 0 & 0 \end{bmatrix} \sim \begin{bmatrix} \textcircled{1} & 0 & 3 & 0 & 0 \\ 0 & \textcircled{1} & 2 & 0 & 0 \\ 0 & 0 & 0 & \textcircled{1} & 0 \\ 0 & 0 & 0 & 0 & 0 \end{bmatrix}$$

$$\begin{array}{rcl} \textcircled{x_1} + 3x_3 &= 0 \\ \textcircled{x_2} + 2x_3 &= 0 \\ \textcircled{x_4} &= 0 \end{array} \quad \begin{cases} x_1 = -3x_3 \\ x_2 = -2x_3 \\ x_3 \text{ is free} \\ x_4 = 0 \end{cases} \quad \mathbf{x} = \begin{bmatrix} -3x_3 \\ -2x_3 \\ x_3 \\ 0 \end{bmatrix} = x_3 \begin{bmatrix} -3 \\ -2 \\ 1 \\ 0 \end{bmatrix}$$

11. Is the system represented by $[A \quad \mathbf{b}]$ consistent? Yes, as the following calculation shows.
$$\begin{bmatrix} 1 & -4 & 7 & -5 & -1 \\ 0 & 1 & -4 & 3 & 1 \\ 2 & -6 & 6 & -4 & 0 \end{bmatrix} \sim \begin{bmatrix} 1 & -4 & 7 & -5 & -1 \\ 0 & 1 & -4 & 3 & 1 \\ 0 & 2 & -8 & 6 & 2 \end{bmatrix} \sim \begin{bmatrix} \textcircled{1} & -4 & 7 & -5 & -1 \\ 0 & \textcircled{1} & -4 & 3 & 1 \\ 0 & 0 & 0 & 0 & 0 \end{bmatrix}$$

The system is consistent, so $\mathbf{b}$ is in the range of the transformation $\mathbf{x} \mapsto A\mathbf{x}$.

12. Is the system represented by $[A \quad \mathbf{b}]$ consistent?

$$\begin{bmatrix} 1 & 3 & 9 & 2 & -1 \\ 1 & 0 & 3 & -4 & 3 \\ 0 & 1 & 2 & 3 & -1 \\ -2 & 3 & 0 & 5 & 4 \end{bmatrix} \sim \begin{bmatrix} 1 & 3 & 9 & 2 & -1 \\ 0 & -3 & -6 & -6 & 4 \\ 0 & 1 & 2 & 3 & -1 \\ 0 & 9 & 18 & 9 & 2 \end{bmatrix} \sim \begin{bmatrix} 1 & 3 & 9 & 2 & -1 \\ 0 & 1 & 2 & 3 & -1 \\ 0 & -3 & -6 & -6 & 4 \\ 0 & 9 & 18 & 9 & 2 \end{bmatrix}$$

$$\sim \begin{bmatrix} 1 & 3 & 9 & 2 & -1 \\ 0 & 1 & 2 & 3 & -1 \\ 0 & 0 & 0 & 3 & 1 \\ 0 & 0 & 0 & -18 & 11 \end{bmatrix} \sim \begin{bmatrix} 1 & 3 & 9 & 2 & -1 \\ 0 & 1 & 2 & 3 & -1 \\ 0 & 0 & 0 & 3 & 1 \\ 0 & 0 & 0 & 0 & 17 \end{bmatrix}$$

The system is inconsistent, so $\mathbf{b}$ is not in the range of the transformation $\mathbf{x} \mapsto A\mathbf{x}$.

13.

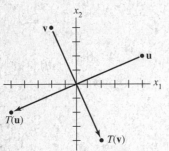

A reflection through the origin.

14.

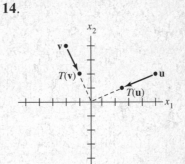

A contraction by the factor .5.

The transformation in Exercise 13 may also be described as a rotation of π radians about the origin or a rotation of $-\pi$ radians about the origin.

15.

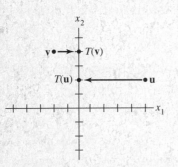

A projection onto the x_2-axis

16.

A reflection through the line $x_2 = x_1$.

17. $T(3\mathbf{u}) = 3T(\mathbf{u}) = 3\begin{bmatrix} 2 \\ 1 \end{bmatrix} = \begin{bmatrix} 6 \\ 3 \end{bmatrix}$, $T(2\mathbf{v}) = 2T(\mathbf{v}) = 2\begin{bmatrix} -1 \\ 3 \end{bmatrix} = \begin{bmatrix} -2 \\ 6 \end{bmatrix}$, and

$$T(3\mathbf{u} + 2\mathbf{v}) = 3T(\mathbf{u}) = 2T(\mathbf{v}) = \begin{bmatrix} 6 \\ 3 \end{bmatrix} + \begin{bmatrix} -2 \\ 6 \end{bmatrix} = \begin{bmatrix} 4 \\ 9 \end{bmatrix}.$$

18. Draw a line through **w** parallel to **v**, and draw a line through **w** parallel to **u**. See the left part of the figure below. From this, estimate that $\mathbf{w} = \mathbf{u} + 2\mathbf{v}$. Since T is linear, $T(\mathbf{w}) = T(\mathbf{u}) + 2T(\mathbf{v})$. Locate $T(\mathbf{u})$ and $2T(\mathbf{v})$ as in the right part of the figure and form the associated parallelogram to locate $T(\mathbf{w})$.

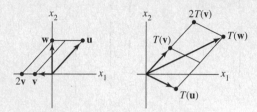

19. All we know are the images of $\mathbf{e}_1$ and $\mathbf{e}_2$ and the fact that T is linear. The key idea is to write

$$\mathbf{x} = \begin{bmatrix} 5 \\ -3 \end{bmatrix} = 5\begin{bmatrix} 1 \\ 0 \end{bmatrix} - 3\begin{bmatrix} 0 \\ 1 \end{bmatrix} = 5\mathbf{e}_1 - 3\mathbf{e}_2.$$ Then, from the linearity of T, write

$$T(\mathbf{x}) = T(5\mathbf{e}_1 - 3\mathbf{e}_2) = 5T(\mathbf{e}_1) - 3T(\mathbf{e}_2) = 5\mathbf{y}_1 - 3\mathbf{y}_2 = 5\begin{bmatrix} 2 \\ 5 \end{bmatrix} - 3\begin{bmatrix} -1 \\ 6 \end{bmatrix} = \begin{bmatrix} 13 \\ 7 \end{bmatrix}.$$

To find the image of $\begin{bmatrix} x_1 \\ x_2 \end{bmatrix}$, observe that $\mathbf{x} = \begin{bmatrix} x_1 \\ x_2 \end{bmatrix} = x_1\begin{bmatrix} 1 \\ 0 \end{bmatrix} + x_2\begin{bmatrix} 0 \\ 1 \end{bmatrix} = x_1\mathbf{e}_1 + x_2\mathbf{e}_2$. Then

$$T(\mathbf{x}) = T(x_1\mathbf{e}_1 + x_2\mathbf{e}_2) = x_1T(\mathbf{e}_1) + x_2T(\mathbf{e}_2) = x_1\begin{bmatrix} 2 \\ 5 \end{bmatrix} + x_2\begin{bmatrix} -1 \\ 6 \end{bmatrix} = \begin{bmatrix} 2x_1 - x_2 \\ 5x_1 + 6x_2 \end{bmatrix}$$

20. Use the basic definition of $A\mathbf{x}$ to construct A. Write

$$T(\mathbf{x}) = x_1\mathbf{v}_1 + x_2\mathbf{v}_2 = \begin{bmatrix} \mathbf{v}_1 & \mathbf{v}_2 \end{bmatrix}\begin{bmatrix} x_1 \\ x_2 \end{bmatrix} = \begin{bmatrix} -2 & 7 \\ 5 & -3 \end{bmatrix}\mathbf{x}, \quad A = \begin{bmatrix} -2 & 7 \\ 5 & -3 \end{bmatrix}$$

21. a. True. Functions from $\mathbf{R}^n$ to $\mathbf{R}^m$ are defined before Fig. 2. A linear transformation is a function with certain properties.

   b. False. The domain is $\mathbf{R}^5$. See the paragraph before Example 1.

   c. False. The range is the set of all linear combinations of the columns of A. See the paragraph before Example 1.

   d. False. See the paragraph after the definition of a linear transformation.

   e. True. See the paragraph following the box that contains equation (4).

22. a. True. See the paragraph following the definition of a linear transformation.

   b. False. If A is an $m \times n$ matrix, the codomain is $\mathbf{R}^m$. See the paragraph before Example 1.

   c. False. The question is an existence question. See the remark about Example 1(d), following the solution of Example 1.

   d. True. See the discussion following the definition of a linear transformation.

   e. True. See the paragraph following equation (5).

23.

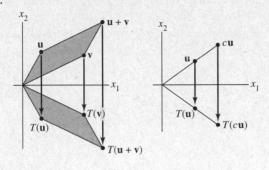

24. Given any $\mathbf{x}$ in $\mathbf{R}^n$, there are constants $c_1, \ldots, c_p$ such that $\mathbf{x} = c_1\mathbf{v}_1 + \cdots c_p\mathbf{v}_p$, because $\mathbf{v}_1, \ldots, \mathbf{v}_p$ span $\mathbf{R}^n$. Then, from property (5) of a linear transformation,

$$T(\mathbf{x}) = c_1 T(\mathbf{v}_1) + \cdots + c_p T(\mathbf{v}_p) = c_1\mathbf{0} + \cdots + c_p\mathbf{0} = \mathbf{0}$$

25. Any point $\mathbf{x}$ on the line through $\mathbf{p}$ in the direction of $\mathbf{v}$ satisfies the parametric equation $\mathbf{x} = \mathbf{p} + t\mathbf{v}$ for some value of t. By linearity, the image $T(\mathbf{x})$ satisfies the parametric equation

$$T(\mathbf{x}) = T(\mathbf{p} + t\mathbf{v}) = T(\mathbf{p}) + tT(\mathbf{v}) \tag{*}$$

If $T(\mathbf{v}) = \mathbf{0}$, then $T(\mathbf{x}) = T(\mathbf{p})$ for all values of t, and the image of the original line is just a single point. Otherwise, (*) is the parametric equation of a line through $T(\mathbf{p})$ in the direction of $T(\mathbf{v})$.

26. Any point $\mathbf{x}$ on the plane P satisfies the parametric equation $\mathbf{x} = s\mathbf{u} + t\mathbf{v}$ for some values of s and t. By linearity, the image $T(\mathbf{x})$ satisfies the parametric equation

$$T(\mathbf{x}) = sT(\mathbf{u}) + tT(\mathbf{v}) \qquad (s, t \text{ in } \mathbf{R}) \tag{*}$$

The set of images is just Span$\{T(\mathbf{u}), T(\mathbf{v})\}$. If $T(\mathbf{u})$ and $T(\mathbf{v})$ are linearly independent, Span$\{T(\mathbf{u}), T(\mathbf{v})\}$ is a plane through $T(\mathbf{u})$, $T(\mathbf{v})$, and $\mathbf{0}$. If $T(\mathbf{u})$ and $T(\mathbf{v})$ are linearly dependent and not both zero, then Span$\{T(\mathbf{u}), T(\mathbf{v})\}$ is a line through $\mathbf{0}$. If $T(\mathbf{u}) = T(\mathbf{v}) = \mathbf{0}$, then Span$\{T(\mathbf{u}), T(\mathbf{v})\}$ is $\{\mathbf{0}\}$.

27. a. From Fig. 7 in the exercises for Section 1.5, the line through $T(\mathbf{p})$ and $T(\mathbf{q})$ is in the direction of $\mathbf{q} - \mathbf{p}$, and so the equation of the line is $\mathbf{x} = \mathbf{p} + t(\mathbf{q} - \mathbf{p}) = \mathbf{p} + t\mathbf{q} - t\mathbf{p} = (1 - t)\mathbf{p} + t\mathbf{q}$.

b. Consider $\mathbf{x} = (1 - t)\mathbf{p} + t\mathbf{q}$ for t such that $0 \le t \le 1$. Then, by linearity of T,

$$T(\mathbf{x}) = T((1 - t)\mathbf{p} + t\mathbf{q}) = (1 - t)T(\mathbf{p}) + tT(\mathbf{q}) \qquad 0 \le t \le 1 \tag{*}$$

If $T(\mathbf{p})$ and $T(\mathbf{q})$ are distinct, then (*) is the equation for the line segment between $T(\mathbf{p})$ and $T(\mathbf{q})$, as shown in part (a) Otherwise, the set of images is just the single point $T(\mathbf{p})$, because

$$(1 - t)T(\mathbf{p}) + tT(\mathbf{q}) = (1 - t)T(\mathbf{p}) + tT(\mathbf{p}) = T(\mathbf{p})$$

28. Consider a point $\mathbf{x}$ in the parallelogram determined by $\mathbf{u}$ and $\mathbf{v}$, say $\mathbf{x} = a\mathbf{u} + b\mathbf{v}$ for $0 \le a \le 1, 0 \le b \le 1$. By linearity of T, the image of $\mathbf{x}$ is

$$T(\mathbf{x}) = T(a\mathbf{u} + b\mathbf{v}) = aT(\mathbf{u}) + bT(\mathbf{v}), \text{ for } 0 \le a \le 1, 0 \le b \le 1 \tag{*}$$

This image point lies in the parallelogram determined by $T(\mathbf{u})$ and $T(\mathbf{v})$.

Special "degenerate" cases arise when $T(\mathbf{u})$ and $T(\mathbf{v})$ are linearly dependent. If one of the images is not zero, then the "parallelogram" is actually the line segment from $\mathbf{0}$ to $T(\mathbf{u}) + T(\mathbf{v})$. If both $T(\mathbf{u})$ and $T(\mathbf{v})$ are zero, then the parallelogram is just $\{\mathbf{0}\}$. Another possibility is that even $\mathbf{u}$ and $\mathbf{v}$ are linearly dependent, in which case the original parallelogram is degenerate (either a line segment or the zero vector). In this case, the set of images must be degenerate, too.

29. a. When $b = 0$, $f(x) = mx$. In this case, for all x, y in $\mathbf{R}$ and all scalars c and d,

$$f(cx + dy) = m(cx + dy) = mcx + mdy = c(mx) + d(my) = c \cdot f(x) + d \cdot f(y)$$

This shows that f is linear.

    b. When $f(x) = mx + b$, with b nonzero, $f(0) = m(0) = b = b \neq 0$. This shows that f is not linear, because every linear transformation maps the zero vector in its domain into the zero vector in the codomain. (In this case, both zero vectors are just the number 0.) Another argument, for instance, would be to calculate $f(2x) = m(2x) + b$ and $2f(x) = 2mx + 2b$. If b is nonzero, then $f(2x)$ is not equal to $2f(x)$ and so f is not a linear transformation.

    c. In calculus, f is called a "linear function" because the graph of f is a line.

30. Let $T(\mathbf{x}) = A\mathbf{x} + \mathbf{b}$ for $\mathbf{x}$ in $\mathbf{R}^n$. If $\mathbf{b}$ is not zero, $T(\mathbf{0}) = A\mathbf{0} + \mathbf{b} = \mathbf{b} \neq \mathbf{0}$. Actually, T fails both properties of a linear transformation. For instance, $T(2\mathbf{x}) = A(2\mathbf{x}) + \mathbf{b} = 2A\mathbf{x} + \mathbf{b}$, which is not the same as $2T(\mathbf{x}) = 2(A\mathbf{x} + \mathbf{b}) = 2A\mathbf{x} + 2\mathbf{b}$. Also,

$$T(\mathbf{x} + \mathbf{y}) = A(\mathbf{x} + \mathbf{y}) + \mathbf{b} = A\mathbf{x} + A\mathbf{y} + \mathbf{b}$$

which is not the same as

$$T(\mathbf{x}) + T(\mathbf{y}) = A\mathbf{x} + \mathbf{b} + A\mathbf{y} + \mathbf{b}$$

31. (The *Study Guide* has a more detailed discussion of the proof.) Suppose that $\{\mathbf{v}_1, \mathbf{v}_2, \mathbf{v}_3\}$ is linearly dependent. Then there exist scalars c_1, c_2, c_3, not all zero, such that

$$c_1\mathbf{v}_1 + c_2\mathbf{v}_2 + c_3\mathbf{v}_3 = \mathbf{0}$$

Then $T(c_1\mathbf{v}_1 + c_2\mathbf{v}_2 + c_3\mathbf{v}_3) = T(\mathbf{0}) = \mathbf{0}$. Since T is linear,

$$c_1 T(\mathbf{v}_1) + c_2 T(\mathbf{v}_2) + c_3 T(\mathbf{v}_3) = \mathbf{0}$$

Since not all the weights are zero, $\{T(\mathbf{v}_1), T(\mathbf{v}_2), T(\mathbf{v}_3)\}$ is a linearly dependent set.

32. Take any vector (x_1, x_2) with $x_2 \neq 0$, and use a negative scalar. For instance, $T(0, 1) = (-2, 3)$, but $T(-1 \cdot (0, 1)) = T(0, -1) = (2, 3) \neq (-1) \cdot T(0, 1)$.

33. One possibility is to show that T does not map the zero vector into the zero vector, something that every linear transformation *does* do. $T(0, 0) = (0, 4, 0)$.

34. Suppose that $\{\mathbf{u}, \mathbf{v}\}$ is a linearly independent set in $\mathbf{R}^n$ and yet $T(\mathbf{u})$ and $T(\mathbf{v})$ are linearly dependent. Then there exist weights c_1, c_2, not both zero, such that

$$c_1 T(\mathbf{u}) + c_2 T(\mathbf{v}) = \mathbf{0}$$

Because T is linear, $T(c_1\mathbf{u} + c_2\mathbf{v}) = \mathbf{0}$. That is, the vector $\mathbf{x} = c_1\mathbf{u} + c_2\mathbf{v}$ satisfies $T(\mathbf{x}) = \mathbf{0}$. Furthermore, $\mathbf{x}$ cannot be the zero vector, since that would mean that a nontrivial linear combination of $\mathbf{u}$ and $\mathbf{v}$ is zero, which is impossible because $\mathbf{u}$ and $\mathbf{v}$ are linearly independent. Thus, the equation $T(\mathbf{x}) = \mathbf{0}$ has a nontrivial solution.

35. Take $\mathbf{u}$ and $\mathbf{v}$ in $\mathbf{R}^3$ and let c and d be scalars. Then

$c\mathbf{u} + d\mathbf{v} = (cu_1 + dv_1, cu_2 + dv_2, cu_3 + dv_3)$. The transformation T is linear because

$$
\begin{aligned}
T(c\mathbf{u} + d\mathbf{v}) &= (cu_1 + dv_1, cu_2 + dv_2, -(cu_3 + dv_3)) = (cu_1 + dv_1, cu_2 + dv_2, \ cu_3 \ dv_3) \\
&= (cu_1, cu_2, \ cu_3) + (dv_1, dv_2, \ dv_3) = c(u_1, u_2, \ u_3) + d(v_1, v_2, \ v_3) \\
&= cT(\mathbf{u}) + dT(\mathbf{v})
\end{aligned}
$$

36. Take $\mathbf{u}$ and $\mathbf{v}$ in $\mathbf{R}^3$ and let c and d be scalars. Then

$c\mathbf{u} + d\mathbf{v} = (cu_1 + dv_1, cu_2 + dv_2, cu_3 + dv_3)$. The transformation T is linear because

$$
\begin{aligned}
T(c\mathbf{u} + d\mathbf{v}) &= (cu_1 + dv_1, 0, cu_3 + dv_3) = (cu_1, 0, cu_3) + (dv_1, 0, dv_3) \\
&= c(u_1, 0, u_3) + d(v_1, 0, v_3) \\
&= cT(\mathbf{u}) + dT(\mathbf{v})
\end{aligned}
$$

37. [M]
$$\begin{bmatrix} 4 & -2 & 5 & -5 & 0 \\ -9 & 7 & -8 & 0 & 0 \\ -6 & 4 & 5 & 3 & 0 \\ 5 & -3 & 8 & -4 & 0 \end{bmatrix} \sim \begin{bmatrix} ① & 0 & 0 & -7/2 & 0 \\ 0 & ① & 0 & -9/2 & 0 \\ 0 & 0 & ① & 0 & 0 \\ 0 & 0 & 0 & 0 & 0 \end{bmatrix}, \quad \begin{cases} x_1 = (7/2)x_4 \\ x_2 = (9/2)x_4 \\ x_3 = 0 \\ x_4 \text{ is free} \end{cases} \quad \mathbf{x} = x_4 \begin{bmatrix} 7/2 \\ 9/2 \\ 0 \\ 1 \end{bmatrix}$$

38. [M]
$$\begin{bmatrix} -9 & -4 & -9 & 4 & 0 \\ 5 & -8 & -7 & 6 & 0 \\ 7 & 11 & 16 & -9 & 0 \\ 9 & -7 & -4 & 5 & 0 \end{bmatrix} \sim \begin{bmatrix} ① & 0 & 0 & 3/4 & 0 \\ 0 & ① & 0 & 5/4 & 0 \\ 0 & 0 & ① & -7/4 & 0 \\ 0 & 0 & 0 & 0 & 0 \end{bmatrix}, \quad \begin{cases} x_1 = -(3/4)x_4 \\ x_2 = -(5/4)x_4 \\ x_3 = (7/4)x_4 \\ x_4 \text{ is free} \end{cases} \quad \mathbf{x} = x_4 \begin{bmatrix} -3/4 \\ -5/4 \\ 7/4 \\ 1 \end{bmatrix}$$

39. [M]
$$\begin{bmatrix} 4 & -2 & 5 & -5 & 7 \\ -9 & 7 & -8 & 0 & 5 \\ -6 & 4 & 5 & 3 & 9 \\ 5 & -3 & 8 & -4 & 7 \end{bmatrix} \sim \begin{bmatrix} ① & 0 & 0 & -7/2 & 4 \\ 0 & ① & 0 & -9/2 & 7 \\ 0 & 0 & ① & 0 & 1 \\ 0 & 0 & 0 & 0 & 0 \end{bmatrix}$$, yes, **b** is in the range of the transformation,

because the augmented matrix shows a consistent system. In fact,

the general solution is $\begin{cases} x_1 = 4 + (7/2)x_4 \\ x_2 = 7 + (9/2)x_4 \\ x_3 = 1 \\ x_4 \text{ is free} \end{cases}$; when $x_4 = 0$ a solution is $\mathbf{x} = \begin{bmatrix} 4 \\ 7 \\ 1 \\ 0 \end{bmatrix}$.

40. [M]
$$\begin{bmatrix} -9 & -4 & -9 & 4 & -7 \\ 5 & -8 & -7 & 6 & -7 \\ 7 & 11 & 16 & -9 & 13 \\ 9 & -7 & -4 & 5 & -5 \end{bmatrix} \sim \begin{bmatrix} ① & 0 & 0 & 3/4 & -5/4 \\ 0 & ① & 0 & 5/4 & -11/4 \\ 0 & 0 & ① & -7/4 & 13/4 \\ 0 & 0 & 0 & 0 & 0 \end{bmatrix}$$, yes, **b** is in the range of the

transformation, because the augmented matrix shows a consistent system. In fact,

the general solution is $\begin{cases} x_1 = -5/4 - (3/4)x_4 \\ x_2 = -11/4 - (5/4)x_4 \\ x_3 = 13/4 + (7/4)x_4 \\ x_4 \text{ is free} \end{cases}$; when $x_4 = 1$ a solution is $\mathbf{x} = \begin{bmatrix} -2 \\ -4 \\ 5 \\ 1 \end{bmatrix}$.

Notes: At the end of Section 1.8, the *Study Guide* provides a list of equations, figures, examples, and connections with concepts that will strengthen a student's understanding of linear transformations. I encourage my students to continue the construction of review sheets similar to those for "span" and "linear independence," but I refrain from collecting these sheets. At some point the students have to assume the responsibility for mastering this material.

If your students are using MATLAB or another matrix program, you might insert the definition of matrix multiplication after this section, and then assign a project that uses random matrices to explore properties of matrix multiplication. See Exercises 34–36 in Section 2.1. Meanwhile, in class you can continue with your plans for finishing Chapter 1. When you get to Section 2.1, you won't have much to do. The *Study Guide*'s MATLAB note for Section 2.1 contains the matrix notation students will need for a project on matrix multiplication. The appendices in the *Study Guide* have the corresponding material for Mathematica, Maple, and the T-83+/86/89 and HP-48G graphic calculators.

1.9   SOLUTIONS

Notes: This section is optional if you plan to treat linear transformations only lightly, but many instructors will want to cover at least Theorem 10 and a few geometric examples. Exercises 15 and 16 illustrate a fast way to solve Exercises 17–22 without explicitly computing the images of the standard basis.

The purpose of introducing *one-to-one* and *onto* is to prepare for the term *isomorphism* (in Section 4.4) and to acquaint math majors with these terms. Mastery of these concepts would require a substantial digression, and some instructors prefer to omit these topics (and Exercises 25–40). In this case, you can use the result of Exercise 31 in Section 1.8 to show that the coordinate mapping from a vector space onto $\mathbf{R}^n$ (in Section 4.4) preserves linear independence and dependence of sets of vectors. (See Example 6 in Section 4.4.) The notions of one-to-one and onto appear in the Invertible Matrix Theorem (Section 2.3), but can be omitted there if desired

Exercises 25–28 and 31–36 offer fairly easy writing practice. Exercises 31, 32, and 35 provide important links to earlier material.

1. $A = [T(\mathbf{e}_1) \quad T(\mathbf{e}_2)] = \begin{bmatrix} 3 & -5 \\ 1 & 2 \\ 3 & 0 \\ 1 & 0 \end{bmatrix}$

2. $A = [T(\mathbf{e}_1) \quad T(\mathbf{e}_2) \quad T(\mathbf{e}_3)] = \begin{bmatrix} 1 & 4 & -5 \\ 3 & -7 & 4 \end{bmatrix}$

3. $T(\mathbf{e}_1) = -\mathbf{e}_2, \ T(\mathbf{e}_2) = \mathbf{e}_1. \ A = [-\mathbf{e}_2 \quad \mathbf{e}_1] = \begin{bmatrix} 0 & 1 \\ -1 & 0 \end{bmatrix}$

4. $T(\mathbf{e}_1) = \begin{bmatrix} 1/\sqrt{2} \\ -1/\sqrt{2} \end{bmatrix}, \ T(\mathbf{e}_2) = \begin{bmatrix} 1/\sqrt{2} \\ 1/\sqrt{2} \end{bmatrix}, \ A = \begin{bmatrix} 1/\sqrt{2} & 1/\sqrt{2} \\ -1/\sqrt{2} & 1/\sqrt{2} \end{bmatrix}$

5. $T(\mathbf{e}_1) = \mathbf{e}_1 - 2\mathbf{e}_2 = \begin{bmatrix} 1 \\ -2 \end{bmatrix}, \ T(\mathbf{e}_2) = \mathbf{e}_2, \ A = \begin{bmatrix} 1 & 0 \\ -2 & 1 \end{bmatrix}$

6. $T(\mathbf{e}_1) = \mathbf{e}_1, \ T(\mathbf{e}_2) = \mathbf{e}_2 + 3\mathbf{e}_1 = \begin{bmatrix} 3 \\ 1 \end{bmatrix}, \ A = \begin{bmatrix} 1 & 3 \\ 0 & 1 \end{bmatrix}$

7. Follow what happens to $\mathbf{e}_1$ and $\mathbf{e}_2$. Since $\mathbf{e}_1$ is on the unit circle in the plane, it rotates through $-3\pi/4$ radians into a point on the unit circle that lies in the third quadrant and on the line $x_2 = x_1$ (that is, $y = x$ in more familiar notation). The point $(-1,-1)$ is on the ine $x_2 = x_1$, but its distance from the origin is $\sqrt{2}$. So the rotational image of $\mathbf{e}_1$ is $(-1/\sqrt{2}, -1/\sqrt{2})$. Then this image reflects in the horizontal axis to $(-1/\sqrt{2}, 1/\sqrt{2})$.

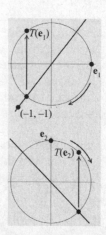

Similarly, $\mathbf{e}_2$ rotates into a point on the unit circle that lies in the second quadrant and on the line $x_2 = x_1$, namely,

$(-1/\sqrt{2}, -1/\sqrt{2})$. Then this image reflects in the horizontal axis to $(-1/\sqrt{2}, 1/\sqrt{2})$.

When the two calculations described above are written in vertical vector notation, the transformation's standard matrix $[T(\mathbf{e}_1)\ \ T(\mathbf{e}_2)]$ is easily seen:

$$\mathbf{e}_1 \rightarrow \begin{bmatrix} -1/\sqrt{2} \\ -1/\sqrt{2} \end{bmatrix} \rightarrow \begin{bmatrix} -1/\sqrt{2} \\ 1/\sqrt{2} \end{bmatrix},\ \mathbf{e}_2 \rightarrow \begin{bmatrix} 1/\sqrt{2} \\ -1/\sqrt{2} \end{bmatrix} \rightarrow \begin{bmatrix} 1/\sqrt{2} \\ 1/\sqrt{2} \end{bmatrix},\ A = \begin{bmatrix} -1/\sqrt{2} & 1/\sqrt{2} \\ 1/\sqrt{2} & 1/\sqrt{2} \end{bmatrix}$$

8. $\mathbf{e}_1 \rightarrow \mathbf{e}_1 \rightarrow \mathbf{e}_2$ and $\mathbf{e}_2 \rightarrow -\mathbf{e}_2 \rightarrow -\mathbf{e}_1$, so $A = [\mathbf{e}_2 \ \ -\mathbf{e}_1] = \begin{bmatrix} 0 & -1 \\ 1 & 0 \end{bmatrix}$

9. The horizontal shear maps $\mathbf{e}_1$ into $\mathbf{e}_1$, and then the reflection in the line $x_2 = -x_1$ maps $\mathbf{e}_1$ into $-\mathbf{e}_2$. (See Table 1.) The horizontal shear maps $\mathbf{e}_2$ into $\mathbf{e}_2$ into $\mathbf{e}_2 - 2\mathbf{e}_1$. To find the image of $\mathbf{e}_2 - 2\mathbf{e}_1$ when it is reflected in the line $x_2 = -x_1$, use the fact that such a reflection is a linear transformation. So, the image of $\mathbf{e}_2 - 2\mathbf{e}_1$ is the same linear combination of the images of $\mathbf{e}_2$ and $\mathbf{e}_1$, namely, $-\mathbf{e}_1 - 2(-\mathbf{e}_2) = -\mathbf{e}_1 + 2\mathbf{e}_2$. To summarize,

$$\mathbf{e}_1 \rightarrow \mathbf{e}_1 \rightarrow -\mathbf{e}_2 \text{ and } \mathbf{e}_2 \rightarrow \mathbf{e}_2 - 2\mathbf{e}_1 \rightarrow -\mathbf{e}_1 + 2\mathbf{e}_2, \text{ so } A = \begin{bmatrix} 0 & -1 \\ -1 & 2 \end{bmatrix}$$

To find the image of $\mathbf{e}_2 - 2\mathbf{e}_1$ when it is reflected through the vertical axis use the fact that such a reflection is a linear transformation. So, the image of $\mathbf{e}_2 - 2\mathbf{e}_1$ is the same linear combination of the images of $\mathbf{e}_2$ and $\mathbf{e}_1$, namely, $\mathbf{e}_2 + 2\mathbf{e}_1$.

10. $\mathbf{e}_1 \rightarrow -\mathbf{e}_1 \rightarrow -\mathbf{e}_2$ and $\mathbf{e}_2 \rightarrow \mathbf{e}_2 \rightarrow -\mathbf{e}_1$, so $A = \begin{bmatrix} 0 & -1 \\ -1 & 0 \end{bmatrix}$

11. The transformation T described maps $\mathbf{e}_1 \rightarrow \mathbf{e}_1 \rightarrow -\mathbf{e}_1$ and maps $\mathbf{e}_2 \rightarrow -\mathbf{e}_2 \rightarrow -\mathbf{e}_2$. A rotation through π radians also maps $\mathbf{e}_1$ into $-\mathbf{e}_1$ and maps $\mathbf{e}_2$ into $-\mathbf{e}_2$. Since a linear transformation is completely determined by what it does to the columns of the identity matrix, the rotation transformation has the same effect as T on every vector in $\mathbb{R}^2$.

12. The transformation T in Exercise 8 maps $\mathbf{e}_1 \rightarrow \mathbf{e}_1 \rightarrow \mathbf{e}_2$ and maps $\mathbf{e}_2 \rightarrow -\mathbf{e}_2 \rightarrow -\mathbf{e}_1$. A rotation about the origin through $\pi/2$ radians also maps $\mathbf{e}_1$ into $\mathbf{e}_2$ and maps $\mathbf{e}_2$ into $-\mathbf{e}_1$. Since a linear transformation is completely determined by what it does to the columns of the identity matrix, the rotation transformation has the same effect as T on every vector in $\mathbb{R}^2$.

13. Since $(2, 1) = 2\mathbf{e}_1 + \mathbf{e}_2$, the image of $(2, 1)$ under T is $2T(\mathbf{e}_1) + T(\mathbf{e}_2)$, by linearity of T. On the figure in the exercise, locate $2T(\mathbf{e}_1)$ and use it with $T(\mathbf{e}_2)$ to form the parallelogram shown below.

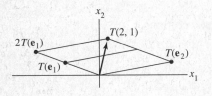

14. Since $T(\mathbf{x}) = A\mathbf{x} = [\mathbf{a}_1 \quad \mathbf{a}_2]\mathbf{x} = x_1\mathbf{a}_1 + x_2\mathbf{a}_2 = -\mathbf{a}_1 + 3\mathbf{a}_2$, when $\mathbf{x} = (-1, 3)$, the image of $\mathbf{x}$ is located by forming the parallelogram shown below.

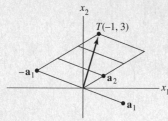

15. By inspection, $\begin{bmatrix} 3 & 0 & -2 \\ 4 & 0 & 0 \\ 1 & -1 & 1 \end{bmatrix} \begin{bmatrix} x_1 \\ x_2 \\ x_3 \end{bmatrix} = \begin{bmatrix} 3x_1 - 2x_3 \\ 4x_1 \\ x_1 - x_2 + x_3 \end{bmatrix}$

16. By inspection, $\begin{bmatrix} 1 & -1 \\ -2 & 1 \\ 1 & 0 \end{bmatrix} \begin{bmatrix} x_1 \\ x_2 \end{bmatrix} = \begin{bmatrix} x_1 - x_2 \\ -2x_1 + x_2 \\ x_1 \end{bmatrix}$

17. To express $T(\mathbf{x})$ as $A\mathbf{x}$, write $T(\mathbf{x})$ and $\mathbf{x}$ as column vectors, and then fill in the entries in A by inspection, as done in Exercises 15 and 16. Note that since $T(\mathbf{x})$ and $\mathbf{x}$ have four entries, A must be a 4×4 matrix.

$$T(\mathbf{x}) = \begin{bmatrix} 0 \\ x_1 + x_2 \\ x_2 + x_3 \\ x_3 + x_4 \end{bmatrix} = \begin{bmatrix} & & A & \end{bmatrix} \begin{bmatrix} x_1 \\ x_2 \\ x_3 \\ x_4 \end{bmatrix} = \begin{bmatrix} 0 & 0 & 0 & 0 \\ 1 & 1 & 0 & 0 \\ 0 & 1 & 1 & 0 \\ 0 & 0 & 1 & 1 \end{bmatrix} \begin{bmatrix} x_1 \\ x_2 \\ x_3 \\ x_4 \end{bmatrix}$$

18. As in Exercise 17, write $T(\mathbf{x})$ and $\mathbf{x}$ as column vectors. Since $\mathbf{x}$ has 2 entries, A has 2 columns. Since $T(\mathbf{x})$ has 4 entries, A has 4 rows.

$$\begin{bmatrix} 2x_2 - 3x_1 \\ x_1 - 4x_2 \\ 0 \\ x_2 \end{bmatrix} = \begin{bmatrix} & A & \end{bmatrix} \begin{bmatrix} x_1 \\ x_2 \end{bmatrix} = \begin{bmatrix} -3 & 2 \\ 1 & -4 \\ 0 & 0 \\ 0 & 1 \end{bmatrix} \begin{bmatrix} x_1 \\ x_2 \end{bmatrix}$$

19. Since $T(\mathbf{x})$ has 2 entries, A has 2 rows. Since $\mathbf{x}$ has 3 entries, A has 3 columns.

$$\begin{bmatrix} x_1 - 5x_2 + 4x_3 \\ x_2 - 6x_3 \end{bmatrix} = \begin{bmatrix} & A & \end{bmatrix} \begin{bmatrix} x_1 \\ x_2 \\ x_3 \end{bmatrix} = \begin{bmatrix} 1 & -5 & 4 \\ 0 & 1 & -6 \end{bmatrix} \begin{bmatrix} x_1 \\ x_2 \\ x_3 \end{bmatrix}$$

20. Since $T(\mathbf{x})$ has 1 entry, A has 1 row. Since $\mathbf{x}$ has 4 entries, A has 4 columns.

$$[2x_1 + 3x_3 - 4x_4] = [\quad A \quad] \begin{bmatrix} x_1 \\ x_2 \\ x_3 \\ x_4 \end{bmatrix} = [2 \quad 0 \quad 3 \quad -4] \begin{bmatrix} x_1 \\ x_2 \\ x_3 \\ x_4 \end{bmatrix}$$

21. $T(\mathbf{x}) = \begin{bmatrix} x_1 + x_2 \\ 4x_1 + 5x_2 \end{bmatrix} = \begin{bmatrix} & A & \\ & & \end{bmatrix}\begin{bmatrix} x_1 \\ x_2 \end{bmatrix} = \begin{bmatrix} 1 & 1 \\ 4 & 5 \end{bmatrix}\begin{bmatrix} x_1 \\ x_2 \end{bmatrix}$. To solve $T(\mathbf{x}) = \begin{bmatrix} 3 \\ 8 \end{bmatrix}$, row reduce the augmented matrix:

$$\begin{bmatrix} 1 & 1 & 3 \\ 4 & 5 & 8 \end{bmatrix} \sim \begin{bmatrix} 1 & 1 & 3 \\ 0 & 1 & -4 \end{bmatrix} \sim \begin{bmatrix} ① & 0 & 7 \\ 0 & ① & -4 \end{bmatrix}, \quad \mathbf{x} = \begin{bmatrix} 7 \\ -4 \end{bmatrix}.$$

22. $T(\mathbf{x}) = \begin{bmatrix} x_1 - 2x_2 \\ -x_1 + 3x_2 \\ 3x_1 - 2x_2 \end{bmatrix} = \begin{bmatrix} & A & \\ & & \\ & & \end{bmatrix}\begin{bmatrix} x_1 \\ x_2 \end{bmatrix} = \begin{bmatrix} 1 & -2 \\ -1 & 3 \\ 3 & -2 \end{bmatrix}\begin{bmatrix} x_1 \\ x_2 \end{bmatrix}$. To solve $T(\mathbf{x}) = \begin{bmatrix} -1 \\ 4 \\ 9 \end{bmatrix}$, row reduce the augmented

matrix:

$$\begin{bmatrix} 1 & -2 & -1 \\ -1 & 3 & 4 \\ 3 & -2 & 9 \end{bmatrix} \sim \begin{bmatrix} 1 & -2 & -1 \\ 0 & 1 & 3 \\ 0 & 4 & 12 \end{bmatrix} \sim \begin{bmatrix} 1 & -2 & -1 \\ 0 & 1 & 3 \\ 0 & 0 & 0 \end{bmatrix} \sim \begin{bmatrix} ① & 0 & 5 \\ 0 & ① & 3 \\ 0 & 0 & 0 \end{bmatrix}, \quad \mathbf{x} = \begin{bmatrix} 5 \\ 3 \end{bmatrix}.$$

23. **a.** True. See Theorem 10.

b. True. See Example 3.

c. False. See the paragraph before Table 1.

d. False. See the definition of *onto*. *Any* function from $\mathbf{R}^n$ to $\mathbf{R}^m$ maps each vector onto another vector.

e. False. See Example 5.

24. **a.** False. See the paragraph preceding Example 2.

b. True. See Theorem 10.

c. True. See Table 1.

d. False. See the definition of one-to-one. Any *function* from $\mathbf{R}^n$ to $\mathbf{R}^m$ maps a vector onto a single (unique) vector.

e. True. See the solution of Example 5.

25. Three row interchanges on the standard matrix A of the transformation T in Exercise 17 produce

$\begin{bmatrix} ① & 1 & 0 & 0 \\ 0 & ① & 1 & 0 \\ 0 & 0 & ① & 1 \\ 0 & 0 & 0 & 0 \end{bmatrix}$. This matrix shows that A has only three pivot positions, so the equation $A\mathbf{x} = \mathbf{0}$ has a

nontrivial solution. By Theorem 11, the transformation T is *not* one-to-one. Also, since A does not have a pivot in each row, the columns of A do not span $\mathbf{R}^4$. By Theorem 12, T does *not* map $\mathbf{R}^4$ onto $\mathbf{R}^4$.

26. The standard matrix A of the transformation T in Exercise 2 is 2×3. Its columns are linearly dependent because A has more columns than rows. So T is *not* one-to-one, by Theorem 12. Also, A is row

equivalent to $\begin{bmatrix} ① & 4 & -5 \\ 0 & -19 & 19 \end{bmatrix}$, which shows that the rows of A span $\mathbf{R}^2$. By Theorem 12, T maps $\mathbf{R}^3$

onto $\mathbf{R}^2$.

27. The standard matrix A of the transformation T in Exercise 19 is $\begin{bmatrix} ① & -5 & 4 \\ 0 & ① & -6 \end{bmatrix}$. The columns of A are

linearly dependent because A has more columns than rows. So T is *not* one-to-one, by Theorem 12. Also, A has a pivot in each row, so the rows of A span $\mathbf{R}^2$. By Theorem 12, T maps $\mathbf{R}^3$ onto $\mathbf{R}^2$.

28. The standard matrix A of the transformation T in Exercise 14 has linearly independent columns, because the figure in that exercise shows that $\mathbf{a}_1$ and $\mathbf{a}_2$ are not multiples. So T is one-to-one, by Theorem 12. Also, A must have a pivot in each column because the equation $A\mathbf{x} = \mathbf{0}$ has no free variables. Thus, the echelon form of A is $\begin{bmatrix} \blacksquare & * \\ 0 & \blacksquare \end{bmatrix}$. Since A has a pivot in each row, the columns of A span $\mathbf{R}^2$. So T maps $\mathbf{R}^2$ onto $\mathbf{R}^2$. An alternate argument for the second part is to observe directly from the figure in Exercise 14 that $\mathbf{a}_1$ and $\mathbf{a}_2$ span $\mathbf{R}^2$. This is more or less evident, based on experience with grids such as those in Figure 8 and Exercise 7 of Section 1.3.

29. By Theorem 12, the columns of the standard matrix A must be linearly independent and hence the equation $A\mathbf{x} = \mathbf{0}$ has no free variables. So each column of A must be a pivot column: $A \sim \begin{bmatrix} \blacksquare & * & * \\ 0 & \blacksquare & * \\ 0 & 0 & \blacksquare \\ 0 & 0 & 0 \end{bmatrix}$.

Note that T cannot be onto because of the shape of A.

30. By Theorem 12, the columns of the standard matrix A must span $\mathbb{R}^3$. By Theorem 4, the matrix must have a pivot in each row. There are four possibilities for the echelon form:

$$\begin{bmatrix} \blacksquare & * & * & * \\ 0 & \blacksquare & * & * \\ 0 & 0 & \blacksquare & * \end{bmatrix}, \begin{bmatrix} \blacksquare & * & * & * \\ 0 & \blacksquare & * & * \\ 0 & 0 & 0 & \blacksquare \end{bmatrix}, \begin{bmatrix} \blacksquare & * & * & * \\ 0 & 0 & \blacksquare & * \\ 0 & 0 & 0 & \blacksquare \end{bmatrix}, \begin{bmatrix} 0 & \blacksquare & * & * \\ 0 & 0 & \blacksquare & * \\ 0 & 0 & 0 & \blacksquare \end{bmatrix}$$

Note that T cannot be one-to-one because of the shape of A.

31. "T is one-to-one if and only if A has n pivot columns." By Theorem 12(b), T is one-to-one if and only if the columns of A are linearly independent. And from the statement in Exercise 30 in Section 1.7, the columns of A are linearly independent if and only if A has n pivot columns.

32. The transformation T maps $\mathbf{R}^n$ onto $\mathbf{R}^m$ if and only if the columns of A span $\mathbf{R}^m$, by Theorem 12. This happens if and only if A has a pivot position in each row, by Theorem 4 in Section 1.4. Since A has m rows, this happens if and only if A has m pivot columns. Thus, "T maps $\mathbf{R}^n$ onto $\mathbf{R}^m$ if and only A has m pivot columns."

33. Define $T : \mathbb{R}^n \to \mathbb{R}^m$ by $T(\mathbf{x}) = B\mathbf{x}$ for some $m \times n$ matrix B, and let A be the standard matrix for T. By definition, $A = [T(\mathbf{e}_1) \ \cdots \ T(\mathbf{e}_n)]$, where $\mathbf{e}_j$ is the jth column of I_n. However, by matrix-vector multiplication, $T(\mathbf{e}_j) = B\mathbf{e}_j = \mathbf{b}_j$, the jth column of B. So $A = [\mathbf{b}_1 \ \cdots \ \mathbf{b}_n] = B$.

34. The transformation T maps $\mathbf{R}^n$ *onto* $\mathbf{R}^m$ if and only if for each $\mathbf{y}$ in $\mathbf{R}^m$ *there exists* an $\mathbf{x}$ in $\mathbf{R}^n$ such that $\mathbf{y} = T(\mathbf{x})$.

35. If $T : \mathbb{R}^n \to \mathbb{R}^m$ maps $\mathbb{R}^n$ onto $\mathbb{R}^m$, then its standard matrix A has a pivot in each row, by Theorem 12 and by Theorem 4 in Section 1.4. So A must have at least as many columns as rows. That is, $m \le n$. When T is one-to-one, A must have a pivot in each column, by Theorem 12, so $m \ge n$.

36. Take $\mathbf{u}$ and $\mathbf{v}$ in $\mathbf{R}^p$ and let c and d be scalars. Then

$$T(S(c\mathbf{u} + d\mathbf{v})) = T(c \cdot S(\mathbf{u}) + d \cdot S(\mathbf{v})) \qquad \text{because } S \text{ is linear}$$
$$= c \cdot T(S(\mathbf{u})) + d \cdot T(S(\mathbf{v})) \qquad \text{because } T \text{ is linear}$$

This calculation shows that the mapping $\mathbf{x} \to T(S(\mathbf{x}))$ is linear. See equation (4) in Section 1.8.

37. [M]
$$\begin{bmatrix} -5 & 10 & -5 & 4 \\ 8 & 3 & -4 & 7 \\ 4 & -9 & 5 & -3 \\ -3 & -2 & 5 & 4 \end{bmatrix} \sim \cdots \sim \begin{bmatrix} 1 & 0 & 0 & 44/35 \\ 0 & 1 & 0 & 79/35 \\ 0 & 0 & 1 & 86/35 \\ 0 & 0 & 0 & 0 \end{bmatrix} \sim \begin{bmatrix} ① & 0 & 0 & 1.2571 \\ 0 & ① & 0 & 2.2571 \\ 0 & 0 & ① & 2.4571 \\ 0 & 0 & 0 & 0 \end{bmatrix}$$. There is no pivot in the

fourth column of the standard matrix A, so the equation $A\mathbf{x} = \mathbf{0}$ has a nontrivial solution. By Theorem 11, the transformation T is *not* one-to-one. (For a shorter argument, use the result of Exercise 31.)

38. [M]
$$\begin{bmatrix} 7 & 5 & 4 & -9 \\ 10 & 6 & 16 & -4 \\ 12 & 8 & 12 & 7 \\ -8 & -6 & -2 & 5 \end{bmatrix} \sim \cdots \sim \begin{bmatrix} ① & 0 & 7 & 0 \\ 0 & ① & -9 & 0 \\ 0 & 0 & 0 & ① \\ 0 & 0 & 0 & 0 \end{bmatrix}$$. No. There is no pivot in the third column of the

standard matrix A, so the equation $A\mathbf{x} = \mathbf{0}$ has a nontrivial solution. By Theorem 11, the transformation T is *not* one-to-one. (For a shorter argument, use the result of Exercise 31.)

39. [M]
$$\begin{bmatrix} 4 & -7 & 3 & 7 & 5 \\ 6 & -8 & 5 & 12 & -8 \\ -7 & 10 & -8 & -9 & 14 \\ 3 & -5 & 4 & 2 & -6 \\ -5 & 6 & -6 & -7 & 3 \end{bmatrix} \sim \cdots \sim \begin{bmatrix} ① & 0 & 0 & 5 & 0 \\ 0 & ① & 0 & 1 & 0 \\ 0 & 0 & ① & -2 & 0 \\ 0 & 0 & 0 & 0 & ① \\ 0 & 0 & 0 & 0 & 0 \end{bmatrix}$$. There is not a pivot in every row, so

the columns of the standard matrix do not span $\mathbf{R}^5$. By Theorem 12, the transformation T does *not* map $\mathbf{R}^5$ onto $\mathbf{R}^5$.

40. [M]
$$\begin{bmatrix} 9 & 13 & 5 & 6 & -1 \\ 14 & 15 & -7 & -6 & 4 \\ -8 & -9 & 12 & -5 & -9 \\ -5 & -6 & -8 & 9 & 8 \\ 13 & 14 & 15 & 2 & 11 \end{bmatrix} \sim \cdots \sim \begin{bmatrix} ① & 0 & 0 & 0 & 5 \\ 0 & ① & 0 & 0 & -4 \\ 0 & 0 & ① & 0 & 0 \\ 0 & 0 & 0 & ① & 1 \\ 0 & 0 & 0 & 0 & 0 \end{bmatrix}$$. There is not a pivot in every row, so

the columns of the standard matrix do not span $\mathbf{R}^5$. By Theorem 12, the transformation T does *not* map $\mathbf{R}^5$ onto $\mathbf{R}^5$.

1.10 SOLUTIONS

1. a. If x_1 is the number of servings of Cheerios and x_2 is the number of servings of 100% Natural Cereal, then x_1 and x_2 should satisfy

$$x_1 \begin{bmatrix} \text{nutrients} \\ \text{per serving} \\ \text{of Cheerios} \end{bmatrix} + x_2 \begin{bmatrix} \text{nutrients} \\ \text{per serving of} \\ \text{100\% Natural} \end{bmatrix} = \begin{bmatrix} \text{quantities} \\ \text{of nutrients} \\ \text{required} \end{bmatrix}$$

That is,

$$x_1 \begin{bmatrix} 110 \\ 4 \\ 20 \\ 2 \end{bmatrix} + x_2 \begin{bmatrix} 130 \\ 3 \\ 18 \\ 5 \end{bmatrix} = \begin{bmatrix} 295 \\ 9 \\ 48 \\ 8 \end{bmatrix}$$

b. The equivalent matrix equation is $\begin{bmatrix} 110 & 130 \\ 4 & 3 \\ 20 & 18 \\ 2 & 5 \end{bmatrix} \begin{bmatrix} x_1 \\ x_2 \end{bmatrix} = \begin{bmatrix} 295 \\ 9 \\ 48 \\ 8 \end{bmatrix}$. To solve this, row reduce the augmented

matrix for this equation.

$$\begin{bmatrix} 110 & 130 & 295 \\ 4 & 3 & 9 \\ 20 & 18 & 48 \\ 2 & 5 & 8 \end{bmatrix} \sim \begin{bmatrix} 2 & 5 & 8 \\ 4 & 3 & 9 \\ 20 & 18 & 48 \\ 110 & 130 & 295 \end{bmatrix} \sim \begin{bmatrix} 1 & 2.5 & 4 \\ 4 & 3 & 9 \\ 10 & 9 & 24 \\ 110 & 130 & 295 \end{bmatrix}$$

$$\sim \begin{bmatrix} 1 & 2.5 & 4 \\ 0 & -7 & -7 \\ 0 & -16 & -16 \\ 0 & -145 & -145 \end{bmatrix} \sim \begin{bmatrix} 1 & 2.5 & 4 \\ 0 & 1 & 1 \\ 0 & 0 & 0 \\ 0 & 0 & 0 \end{bmatrix} \sim \begin{bmatrix} 1 & 0 & 1.5 \\ 0 & 1 & 1 \\ 0 & 0 & 0 \\ 0 & 0 & 0 \end{bmatrix}$$

The desired nutrients are provided by 1.5 servings of Cheerios together with 1 serving of 100% Natural Cereal.

2. Set up nutrient vectors for one serving of Kellogg's Cracklin' Oat Bran (COB) and Kellogg's Crispix (Crp):

Nutrients: COB   Crp

calories $\begin{bmatrix} 110 \\ 3 \\ 21 \\ 3 \end{bmatrix}$ $\begin{bmatrix} 110 \\ 2 \\ 25 \\ .4 \end{bmatrix}$.

protein

carbohydrate

fat

a. Let $B = \begin{bmatrix} COB & Crp \end{bmatrix} = \begin{bmatrix} 110 & 110 \\ 3 & 2 \\ 21 & 25 \\ 3 & .4 \end{bmatrix}$, $\mathbf{u} = \begin{bmatrix} 3 \\ 2 \end{bmatrix}$.

Then $B\mathbf{u}$ lists the amounts of calories, protein, carbohydrate, and fat in a mixture of three servings of Cracklin' Oat Bran and two servings of Crispix.

b. Let u_1 and u_2 be the number of servings of Cracklin' Oat Bran and Crispix, respectively. Can these

numbers satisfy the equation $B \begin{bmatrix} u_1 \\ u_2 \end{bmatrix} = \begin{bmatrix} 110 \\ 2.25 \\ 24 \\ 1 \end{bmatrix}$? To find out, row reduce the augmented matrix

$$\begin{bmatrix} 110 & 110 & 110 \\ 3 & 2 & 2.25 \\ 21 & 25 & 24 \\ 3 & .4 & 1 \end{bmatrix} \sim \begin{bmatrix} 1 & 1 & 1 \\ 3 & 2 & 2.25 \\ 21 & 25 & 24 \\ 3 & .4 & 1 \end{bmatrix} \sim \begin{bmatrix} 1 & 1 & 1 \\ 0 & -1 & -.75 \\ 0 & 4 & 3 \\ 0 & -2.6 & -2 \end{bmatrix} \sim \begin{bmatrix} 1 & 1 & 1 \\ 0 & -1 & -.75 \\ 0 & 0 & 0 \\ 0 & 0 & -.05 \end{bmatrix}$$

The last row identifies an inconsistent system, because $0 = -.05$ is impossible. So, technically, there is no mixture of the two cereals that will supply *exactly* the desired list of nutrients. However, one could tentatively ignore the final equation and see what the other equations prescribe. They reduce to $u_1 = .25$ and $u_2 = .75$. What does the corresponding mixture provide?

$$.25 \cdot \text{COB} + .75 \cdot \text{Crp} = .25 \begin{bmatrix} 110 \\ 3 \\ 21 \\ 3 \end{bmatrix} + .75 \begin{bmatrix} 110 \\ 2 \\ 25 \\ .4 \end{bmatrix} = \begin{bmatrix} 110 \\ 2.25 \\ 24 \\ 1.05 \end{bmatrix}$$

The error of 5% for fat might be acceptable for practical purposes. Actually, the data in COB and Crp are certainly not precise and may have some errors even greater than 5%.

3. Here are the data, assembled from Table 1 and Exercise 3:

Nutrient	Mg of Nutrients/Unit				Nutrients Required (milligrams)
	milk	soy flour	whey	soy prot.	
protein	36	51	13	80	33
carboh.	52	34	74	0	45
fat	0	7	1.1	3.4	3
calcium	1.26	.19	.8	.18	.8

a. Let x_1, x_2, x_3, x_4 represent the number of units of nonfat milk, soy flour, whey, and isolated soy protein, respectively. These amounts must satisfy the following matrix equation

$$\begin{bmatrix} 36 & 51 & 13 & 80 \\ 52 & 34 & 74 & 0 \\ 0 & 7 & 1.1 & 3.4 \\ 1.26 & .19 & .8 & .18 \end{bmatrix} \begin{bmatrix} x_1 \\ x_2 \\ x_3 \\ x_4 \end{bmatrix} = \begin{bmatrix} 33 \\ 45 \\ 3 \\ .8 \end{bmatrix}$$

b. [M]
$$\begin{bmatrix} 36 & 51 & 13 & 80 & 33 \\ 52 & 34 & 74 & 0 & 45 \\ 0 & 7 & 1.1 & 3.4 & 3 \\ 1.26 & .19 & .8 & .18 & .8 \end{bmatrix} \sim \cdots \sim \begin{bmatrix} 1 & 0 & 0 & 0 & .64 \\ 0 & 1 & 0 & 0 & .54 \\ 0 & 0 & 1 & 0 & -.09 \\ 0 & 0 & 0 & 1 & -.21 \end{bmatrix}$$

The "solution" is $x_1 = .64$, $x_2 = .54$, $x_3 = -.09$, $x_4 = -.21$. This solution is not feasible, because the mixture cannot include negative amounts of whey and isolated soy protein. Although the coefficients of these two ingredients are fairly small, they cannot be ignored. The mixture of .64 units of nonfat milk and .54 units of soy flour provide 50.6 g of protein, 51.6 g of carbohydrate, 3.8 g of fat, and .9 g of calcium. Some of these nutrients are nowhere close to the desired amounts.

4. Let x_1, x_2, and x_3 be the number of units of foods 1, 2, and 3, respectively, needed for a meal. The values of x_1, x_2, and x_3 should satisfy

$$x_1 \begin{bmatrix} \text{nutrients} \\ \text{(in mg)} \\ \text{per unit} \\ \text{of Food 1} \end{bmatrix} + x_2 \begin{bmatrix} \text{nutrients} \\ \text{(in mg)} \\ \text{per unit} \\ \text{of Food 2} \end{bmatrix} + x_3 \begin{bmatrix} \text{nutrients} \\ \text{(in mg)} \\ \text{per unit} \\ \text{of Food 3} \end{bmatrix} = \begin{bmatrix} \text{milligrams} \\ \text{of nutrients} \\ \text{required} \end{bmatrix}$$

From the given data,

$$x_1 \begin{bmatrix} 10 \\ 50 \\ 30 \end{bmatrix} + x_2 \begin{bmatrix} 20 \\ 40 \\ 10 \end{bmatrix} + x_3 \begin{bmatrix} 20 \\ 10 \\ 40 \end{bmatrix} = \begin{bmatrix} 100 \\ 300 \\ 200 \end{bmatrix}$$

To solve, row reduce the corresponding augmented matrix:

$$\begin{bmatrix} 10 & 20 & 20 & 100 \\ 50 & 40 & 10 & 300 \\ 30 & 10 & 40 & 200 \end{bmatrix} \sim \begin{bmatrix} 10 & 20 & 20 & 100 \\ 0 & -60 & -90 & -200 \\ 0 & -50 & -20 & -100 \end{bmatrix} \sim \begin{bmatrix} 1 & 2 & 2 & 10 \\ 0 & 1 & 3/2 & 10/3 \\ 0 & 5 & 2 & 10 \end{bmatrix}$$

$$\sim \begin{bmatrix} 1 & 2 & 2 & 10 \\ 0 & 1 & 3/2 & 10/3 \\ 0 & 0 & 1 & 40/33 \end{bmatrix} \sim \begin{bmatrix} 1 & 2 & 0 & 250/33 \\ 0 & 1 & 0 & 50/33 \\ 0 & 0 & 1 & 40/33 \end{bmatrix} \sim \begin{bmatrix} 1 & 0 & 0 & 50/11 \\ 0 & 1 & 0 & 50/33 \\ 0 & 0 & 1 & 40/33 \end{bmatrix}$$

$$\mathbf{x} = \begin{bmatrix} 50/11 \\ 50/33 \\ 40/33 \end{bmatrix} \doteq \begin{bmatrix} 4.55 \\ 1.52 \\ 1.21 \end{bmatrix} = \begin{bmatrix} \text{units of Food 1} \\ \text{units of Food 2} \\ \text{units of Food 3} \end{bmatrix}$$

5. Loop 1: The resistance vector is

$$\mathbf{r}_1 = \begin{bmatrix} 5 \\ -2 \\ 0 \\ 0 \end{bmatrix} \quad \begin{array}{l} \text{Total of four } RI \text{ voltage drops for current } I_1 \\ \text{Voltage drop for } I_2 \text{ is negative; } I_2 \text{ flows in opposite direction} \\ \text{Current } I_3 \text{ does not flow in loop 1} \\ \text{Current } I_4 \text{ does not flow in loop 1} \end{array}$$

Loop 2: The resistance vector is

$$\mathbf{r}_2 = \begin{bmatrix} -2 \\ 11 \\ -3 \\ 0 \end{bmatrix} \quad \begin{array}{l} \text{Voltage drop for } I_1 \text{ is negative; } I_1 \text{ flows in opposite direction} \\ \text{Total of four } RI \text{ voltage drops for current } I_2 \\ \text{Voltage drop for } I_3 \text{ is negative; } I_3 \text{ flows in opposite direction} \\ \text{Current } I_4 \text{ does not flow in loop 2} \end{array}$$

Also, $\mathbf{r}_3 = \begin{bmatrix} 0 \\ -3 \\ 17 \\ -4 \end{bmatrix}$, $\mathbf{r}_4 = \begin{bmatrix} 0 \\ 0 \\ -4 \\ 25 \end{bmatrix}$, and $R = [\mathbf{r}_1 \quad \mathbf{r}_2 \quad \mathbf{r}_3 \quad \mathbf{r}_4] = \begin{bmatrix} 5 & -2 & 0 & 0 \\ -2 & 11 & -3 & 0 \\ 0 & -3 & 17 & -4 \\ 0 & 0 & -4 & 25 \end{bmatrix}$.

Notice that each off-diagonal entry of R is negative (or zero). This happens because the loop current directions are all chosen in the same direction on the figure. (For each loop j, this choice forces the currents in other loops adjacent to loop j to flow in the direction opposite to current I_j.)

Next, set $\mathbf{v} = \begin{bmatrix} 40 \\ -30 \\ 20 \\ -10 \end{bmatrix}$. The voltages in loops 2 and 4 are negative because the battery orientation in each

loop is opposite to the direction chosen for positive current flow. Thus, the equation $R\mathbf{i} = \mathbf{v}$ becomes

$$\begin{bmatrix} 5 & -2 & 0 & 0 \\ -2 & 11 & -3 & 0 \\ 0 & -3 & 17 & -4 \\ 0 & 0 & -4 & 25 \end{bmatrix} \begin{bmatrix} I_1 \\ I_2 \\ I_3 \\ I_4 \end{bmatrix} = \begin{bmatrix} 40 \\ -30 \\ 20 \\ -10 \end{bmatrix} .$$
[M]: The solution is $\mathbf{i} = \begin{bmatrix} I_1 \\ I_2 \\ I_3 \\ I_4 \end{bmatrix} = \begin{bmatrix} 7.56 \\ -1.10 \\ .93 \\ -.25 \end{bmatrix} .$

6. Loop 1: The resistance vector is

$$\mathbf{r}_1 = \begin{bmatrix} 4 \\ -1 \\ 0 \\ 0 \end{bmatrix}$$
  Total of four RI voltage drops for current I_1
  Voltage drop for I_2 is negative; I_2 flows in opposite direction
  Current I_3 does not flow in loop 1
  Current I_4 does not flow in loop 1

Loop 2: The resistance vector is

$$\mathbf{r}_2 = \begin{bmatrix} -1 \\ 6 \\ -2 \\ 0 \end{bmatrix}$$
  Voltage drop for I_1 is negative; I_1 flows in opposite direction
  Total of four RI voltage drops for current I_2
  Voltage drop for I_3 is negative; I_3 flows in opposite direction
  Current I_4 does not flow in loop 2

Also, $\mathbf{r}_3 = \begin{bmatrix} 0 \\ -2 \\ 10 \\ -3 \end{bmatrix}$, $\mathbf{r}_4 = \begin{bmatrix} 0 \\ 0 \\ -3 \\ 12 \end{bmatrix}$, and $R = [\mathbf{r}_1 \ \mathbf{r}_2 \ \mathbf{r}_3 \ \mathbf{r}_4]$. Set $\mathbf{v} = \begin{bmatrix} 40 \\ 30 \\ 20 \\ 10 \end{bmatrix}$. Then $R\mathbf{i} = \mathbf{v}$ becomes

$$\begin{bmatrix} 4 & -1 & 0 & 0 \\ -1 & 6 & -2 & 0 \\ 0 & -2 & 10 & -3 \\ 0 & 0 & -3 & 12 \end{bmatrix} \begin{bmatrix} I_1 \\ I_2 \\ I_3 \\ I_4 \end{bmatrix} = \begin{bmatrix} 40 \\ 30 \\ 20 \\ 10 \end{bmatrix} .$$
[M]: The solution is $\mathbf{i} = \begin{bmatrix} I_1 \\ I_2 \\ I_3 \\ I_4 \end{bmatrix} = \begin{bmatrix} 12.11 \\ 8.44 \\ 4.26 \\ 1.90 \end{bmatrix} .$

7. Loop 1: The resistance vector is

$$\mathbf{r}_1 = \begin{bmatrix} 12 \\ -7 \\ 0 \\ -4 \end{bmatrix}$$
  Total of three RI voltage drops for current I_1
  Voltage drop for I_2 is negative; I_2 flows in opposite direction
  Current I_3 does not flow in loop 1
  Voltage drop for I_4 is negative; I_4 flows in opposite direction

Loop 2: The resistance vector is

$$\mathbf{r}_2 = \begin{bmatrix} -7 \\ 15 \\ -6 \\ 0 \end{bmatrix}$$
  Voltage drop for I_1 is negative; I_1 flows in opposite direction
  Total of three RI voltage drops for current I_2
  Voltage drop for I_3 is negative; I_3 flows in opposite direction
  Current I_4 does not flow in loop 2

Also, $\mathbf{r}_3 = \begin{bmatrix} 0 \\ -6 \\ 14 \\ -5 \end{bmatrix}$, $\mathbf{r}_4 = \begin{bmatrix} -4 \\ 0 \\ -5 \\ 13 \end{bmatrix}$, and $R = [\mathbf{r}_1 \ \ \mathbf{r}_2 \ \ \mathbf{r}_3 \ \ \mathbf{r}_4] = \begin{bmatrix} 12 & -7 & 0 & -4 \\ -7 & 15 & -6 & 0 \\ 0 & -6 & 14 & -5 \\ -4 & 0 & -5 & 13 \end{bmatrix}$.

Notice that each off-diagonal entry of R is negative (or zero). This happens because the loop current directions are all chosen in the same direction on the figure. (For each loop j, this choice forces the currents in other loops adjacent to loop j to flow in the direction opposite to current I_j.)

Next, set $\mathbf{v} = \begin{bmatrix} 40 \\ 30 \\ 20 \\ -10 \end{bmatrix}$. Note the negative voltage in loop 4. The current direction chosen in loop 4 is

opposed by the orientation of the voltage source in that loop. Thus $R\mathbf{i} = \mathbf{v}$ becomes

$$\begin{bmatrix} 12 & -7 & 0 & -4 \\ -7 & 15 & -6 & 0 \\ 0 & -6 & 14 & -5 \\ -4 & 0 & -5 & 13 \end{bmatrix} \begin{bmatrix} I_1 \\ I_2 \\ I_3 \\ I_4 \end{bmatrix} = \begin{bmatrix} 40 \\ 30 \\ 20 \\ -10 \end{bmatrix}. \quad [\mathbf{M}]\text{: The solution is } \mathbf{i} = \begin{bmatrix} I_1 \\ I_2 \\ I_3 \\ I_4 \end{bmatrix} = \begin{bmatrix} 11.43 \\ 10.55 \\ 8.04 \\ 5.84 \end{bmatrix}.$$

8. Loop 1: The resistance vector is

$\mathbf{r}_1 = \begin{bmatrix} 15 \\ -5 \\ 0 \\ -5 \\ -1 \end{bmatrix}$
  Total of four RI voltage drops for current I_1
  Voltage drop for I_2 is negative; I_2 flows in opposite direction
  Current I_3 does not flow in loop 1
  Voltage drop for I_4 is negative; I_4 flows in opposite direction
  Voltage drop for I_5 is negative; I_5 flows in opposite direction

Loop 2: The resistance vector is

$\mathbf{r}_2 = \begin{bmatrix} -5 \\ 15 \\ -5 \\ 0 \\ -2 \end{bmatrix}$
  Voltage drop for I_1 is negative; I_1 flows in opposite direction
  Total of four RI voltage drops for current I_2
  Voltage drop for I_3 is negative; I_3 flows in opposite direction
  Current I_4 does not flow in loop 2
  Voltage drop for I_5 is negative; I_5 flows in opposite direction

Also, $\mathbf{r}_3 = \begin{bmatrix} 0 \\ -5 \\ 15 \\ -5 \\ -3 \end{bmatrix}$, $\mathbf{r}_4 = \begin{bmatrix} -5 \\ 0 \\ -5 \\ 15 \\ -4 \end{bmatrix}$, $\mathbf{r}_5 = \begin{bmatrix} -1 \\ -2 \\ -3 \\ -4 \\ 10 \end{bmatrix}$, and $R = \begin{bmatrix} 15 & -5 & 0 & -5 & -1 \\ -5 & 15 & -5 & 0 & -2 \\ 0 & -5 & 15 & -5 & -3 \\ -5 & 0 & -5 & 15 & -4 \\ -1 & -2 & -3 & -4 & 10 \end{bmatrix}$. Set $\mathbf{v} = \begin{bmatrix} 40 \\ -30 \\ 20 \\ -10 \\ 0 \end{bmatrix}$. Note the

negative voltages for loops where the chosen current direction is opposed by the orientation of the voltage source in that loop. Thus $R\mathbf{i} = \mathbf{v}$ becomes:

$$\begin{bmatrix} 15 & -5 & 0 & -5 & -1 \\ -5 & 15 & -5 & 0 & -2 \\ 0 & -5 & 15 & -5 & -3 \\ -5 & 0 & -5 & 15 & -4 \\ -1 & -2 & -3 & -4 & 10 \end{bmatrix} \begin{bmatrix} I_1 \\ I_2 \\ I_3 \\ I_4 \\ I_5 \end{bmatrix} = \begin{bmatrix} 40 \\ -30 \\ 20 \\ -10 \\ 0 \end{bmatrix}. \quad \textbf{[M]} \text{ The solution is } \begin{bmatrix} I_1 \\ I_2 \\ I_3 \\ I_4 \\ I_5 \end{bmatrix} = \begin{bmatrix} 3.37 \\ .11 \\ 2.27 \\ 1.67 \\ 1.70 \end{bmatrix}.$$

9. The population movement problems in this section assume that the total population is constant, with no migration or immigration. The statement that "about 5% of the city's population moves to the suburbs" means also that the rest of the city's population (95%) remain in the city. This determines the entries in the first column of the migration matrix (which concerns movement *from* the city).

From:

City   Suburbs   To:

$$\begin{bmatrix} .95 & \\ .05 & \end{bmatrix} \quad \begin{matrix} \text{City} \\ \text{Suburbs} \end{matrix}$$

Likewise, if 4% of the suburban population moves to the city, then the other 96% remain in the suburbs. This determines the second column of the migration matrix:, $M = \begin{bmatrix} .95 & .04 \\ .05 & .96 \end{bmatrix}$. The difference equation is

$$\mathbf{x}_{k+1} = M\mathbf{x}_k \text{ for } k = 0, 1, 2, \ldots. \text{ Also, } \mathbf{x}_0 = \begin{bmatrix} 600,000 \\ 400,000 \end{bmatrix}$$

The population in 2001 (when $k = 1$) is $\mathbf{x}_1 = M\mathbf{x}_0 = \begin{bmatrix} .95 & .04 \\ .05 & .96 \end{bmatrix} \begin{bmatrix} 600,000 \\ 400,000 \end{bmatrix} = \begin{bmatrix} 586,000 \\ 414,000 \end{bmatrix}$

The population in 2002 (when $k = 2$) is $\mathbf{x}_2 = M\mathbf{x}_1 = \begin{bmatrix} .95 & .04 \\ .05 & .96 \end{bmatrix} \begin{bmatrix} 586,000 \\ 414,000 \end{bmatrix} = \begin{bmatrix} 573,260 \\ 426,740 \end{bmatrix}$

10. The data in the first sentence implies that the migration matrix has the form:

From:

City   Suburbs   To:

$$\begin{bmatrix} & .03 \\ .07 & \end{bmatrix} \quad \begin{matrix} \text{City} \\ \text{Suburbs} \end{matrix}$$

The remaining entries are determined by the fact that the numbers in each column must sum to 1. (For instance, if 7% of the city people move to the suburbs, then the rest, or 93%, remain in the city.) So the migration matrix is $M = \begin{bmatrix} .93 & .03 \\ .07 & .97 \end{bmatrix}$. The initial population is $\mathbf{x}_0 = \begin{bmatrix} 800,000 \\ 500,000 \end{bmatrix}$.

The population in 2001 (when $k = 1$) is $\mathbf{x}_1 = M\mathbf{x}_0 = \begin{bmatrix} .93 & .03 \\ .07 & .97 \end{bmatrix} \begin{bmatrix} 800,000 \\ 500,000 \end{bmatrix} = \begin{bmatrix} 759,000 \\ 541,000 \end{bmatrix}$

The population in 2002 (when $k = 2$) is $\mathbf{x}_2 = M\mathbf{x}_1 = \begin{bmatrix} .93 & .03 \\ .07 & .97 \end{bmatrix} \begin{bmatrix} 759,000 \\ 541,000 \end{bmatrix} = \begin{bmatrix} 722,100 \\ 577,900 \end{bmatrix}$

11. The problem concerns two groups of people–those living in California and those living outside California (and in the United States). It is reasonable, but not essential, to consider the people living inside

California first. That is, the first entry in a column or row of a vector will concern the people living in California. With this choice, the migration matrix has the form:

From:

Calif.   Outside   To:

$$\begin{bmatrix} & \\ & \end{bmatrix} \begin{matrix} \text{Calif.} \\ \text{Outside} \end{matrix}$$

a. For the first column of the migration matrix M, compute

$$\frac{\left\{\begin{matrix}\text{Calif. persons} \\ \text{who moved}\end{matrix}\right\}}{\{\text{Total Calif. pop.}\}} = \frac{509,500}{29,726,000} = .017146$$

The other entry in the first column is $1 - .017146 = .982854$. The exercise requests that 5 decimal places be used. So this number should be rounded to .98285. Whatever number of decimal places is used, it is important that the two entries sum to 1. So, for the first fraction, use .01715.

For the second column of M, compute $\dfrac{\left\{\begin{matrix}\text{outside persons} \\ \text{who moved}\end{matrix}\right\}}{\{\text{Total outside pop.}\}} = \dfrac{564,100}{218,994,000} = .00258$. The other entry

is $1 - .00258 = .99742$. Thus, the migration matrix is

From:

Calif.   Outside   To:

$$\begin{bmatrix} .98285 & .00258 \\ .01715 & .99742 \end{bmatrix} \begin{matrix} \text{Calif.} \\ \text{Outside} \end{matrix}$$

b. **[M]** The initial vector is $\mathbf{x}_0 = (29.716, 218.994)$, with data in millions of persons. Since $\mathbf{x}_0$ describes the population in 1990, and $\mathbf{x}_1$ describes the population in 1991, the vector $\mathbf{x}_{10}$ describes the projected population for the year 2000, assuming that the migration rates remain constant and there are no deaths, births, or migration. Here are some of the vectors in the calculation, with only the first 4 or 5 figures displayed. Numbers are in millions of persons:

$$\begin{bmatrix} 29.7 \\ 219.0 \end{bmatrix}, \begin{bmatrix} 29.8 \\ 218.9 \end{bmatrix}, \begin{bmatrix} 29.8 \\ 218.9 \end{bmatrix}, \dots, \begin{bmatrix} 30.1 \\ 218.6 \end{bmatrix}, \begin{bmatrix} 30.18 \\ 218.53 \end{bmatrix}, \begin{bmatrix} 30.223 \\ 218.487 \end{bmatrix} = \mathbf{x}_{10}.$$

12. Set $M = \begin{bmatrix} .97 & .05 & .10 \\ .00 & .90 & .05 \\ .03 & .05 & .85 \end{bmatrix}$ and $\mathbf{x}_0 = \begin{bmatrix} 305 \\ 48 \\ 98 \end{bmatrix}$. Then $\mathbf{x}_1 = \begin{bmatrix} .97 & .05 & .10 \\ .00 & .90 & .05 \\ .03 & .05 & .85 \end{bmatrix}\begin{bmatrix} 305 \\ 48 \\ 98 \end{bmatrix} \approx \begin{bmatrix} 308 \\ 48 \\ 95 \end{bmatrix}$, and

$\mathbf{x}_2 = \begin{bmatrix} .97 & .05 & .10 \\ .00 & .90 & .05 \\ .03 & .05 & .85 \end{bmatrix}\begin{bmatrix} 308 \\ 48 \\ 95 \end{bmatrix} \approx \begin{bmatrix} 311 \\ 48 \\ 92 \end{bmatrix}$. The entries in $\mathbf{x}_2$ give the approximate distribution of cars on

Wednesday, two days after Monday.

13. **[M]** The order of entries in a column of a migration matrix must match the order of the columns. For instance, if the first column concerns the population in the city, then the first entry in *each* column must be the fraction of the population that moves to (or remains in) the city. In this case, the data in the

exercise leads to $M = \begin{bmatrix} .95 & .03 \\ .05 & .97 \end{bmatrix}$ and $\mathbf{x}_0 = \begin{bmatrix} 600,000 \\ 400,000 \end{bmatrix}$

a. Some of the population vectors are

$$\mathbf{x}_5 = \begin{bmatrix} 523{,}293 \\ 476{,}707 \end{bmatrix}, \ \mathbf{x}_{10} = \begin{bmatrix} 472{,}737 \\ 527{,}263 \end{bmatrix}, \ \mathbf{x}_{15} = \begin{bmatrix} 439{,}417 \\ 560{,}583 \end{bmatrix}, \ \mathbf{x}_{20} = \begin{bmatrix} 417{,}456 \\ 582{,}544 \end{bmatrix}$$

The data here shows that the city population is declining and the suburban population is increasing, but the changes in population each year seem to grow smaller.

b. When $\mathbf{x}_0 = \begin{bmatrix} 350{,}000 \\ 650{,}000 \end{bmatrix}$, the situation is different. Now

$$\mathbf{x}_5 = \begin{bmatrix} 358{,}523 \\ 641{,}477 \end{bmatrix}, \ \mathbf{x}_{10} = \begin{bmatrix} 364{,}140 \\ 635{,}860 \end{bmatrix}, \ \mathbf{x}_{15} = \begin{bmatrix} 367{,}843 \\ 632{,}157 \end{bmatrix}, \ \mathbf{x}_{20} = \begin{bmatrix} 370{,}283 \\ 629{,}717 \end{bmatrix}$$

The city population is increasing slowly and the suburban population is decreasing. No other conclusions are expected. (This example will be analyzed in greater detail later in the text.)

14. Here are Figs. (a) and (b) for Exercise 13, followed by the figure for Exercise 34 in Section 1.1:

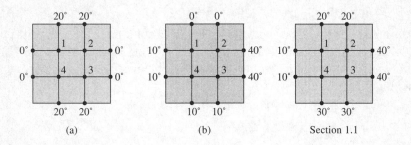

(a)   (b)   Section 1.1

For Fig. (a), the equations are:

$$4T_1 = 0 + 20 + T_2 + T_4$$
$$4T_2 = T_1 + 20 + 0 + T_3$$
$$4T_3 = T_4 + T_2 + 0 + 20$$
$$4T_4 = 0 + T_1 + T_3 + 20$$

To solve the system, rearrange the equations and row reduce the augmented matrix. Interchanging rows 1 and 4 speeds up the calculations. The first five steps are shown in detail.

$$\begin{bmatrix} 4 & -1 & 0 & -1 & 20 \\ -1 & 4 & -1 & 0 & 20 \\ 0 & -1 & 4 & -1 & 20 \\ -1 & 0 & -1 & 4 & 20 \end{bmatrix} \sim \begin{bmatrix} 1 & 0 & 1 & -4 & -20 \\ -1 & 4 & -1 & 0 & 20 \\ 0 & -1 & 4 & -1 & 20 \\ 4 & -1 & 0 & -1 & 20 \end{bmatrix} \sim \begin{bmatrix} 1 & 0 & 1 & -4 & -20 \\ 0 & 4 & 0 & -4 & 0 \\ 0 & -1 & 4 & -1 & 20 \\ 0 & -1 & -4 & 15 & 100 \end{bmatrix} \sim \begin{bmatrix} 1 & 0 & 1 & -4 & -20 \\ 0 & 1 & 0 & -1 & 0 \\ 0 & -1 & 4 & -1 & 20 \\ 0 & -1 & -4 & 15 & 100 \end{bmatrix}$$

$$\sim \begin{bmatrix} 1 & 0 & 1 & -4 & -20 \\ 0 & 1 & 0 & -1 & 0 \\ 0 & 0 & 4 & -2 & 20 \\ 0 & 0 & -4 & 14 & 100 \end{bmatrix} \sim \begin{bmatrix} 1 & 0 & 1 & -4 & -20 \\ 0 & 1 & 0 & -1 & 0 \\ 0 & 0 & 4 & -2 & 20 \\ 0 & 0 & 0 & 12 & 120 \end{bmatrix} \sim \cdots \sim \begin{bmatrix} 1 & 0 & 0 & 0 & 10 \\ 0 & 1 & 0 & 0 & 10 \\ 0 & 0 & 1 & 0 & 10 \\ 0 & 0 & 0 & 1 & 10 \end{bmatrix}$$

For Fig (b), the equations are

$$4T_1 = 10 + 0 + T_2 + T_4$$
$$4T_2 = T_1 + 0 + 40 + T_3$$
$$4T_3 = T_4 + T_2 + 40 + 10$$
$$4T_4 = 10 + T_1 + T_3 + 10$$

Rearrange the equations and row reduce the augmented matrix:

$$\begin{bmatrix} 4 & -1 & 0 & -1 & 10 \\ -1 & 4 & -1 & 0 & 40 \\ 0 & -1 & 4 & -1 & 50 \\ -1 & 0 & -1 & 4 & 20 \end{bmatrix} \sim \cdots \sim \begin{bmatrix} 1 & 0 & 0 & 0 & 10 \\ 0 & 1 & 0 & 0 & 17.5 \\ 0 & 0 & 1 & 0 & 20 \\ 0 & 0 & 0 & 1 & 12.5 \end{bmatrix}$$

a. Here are the solution temperatures for the three problems studied:

Fig. (a) in Exercise 14 of Section 1.10: $(10,\ 10,\ 10,\ 10)$

Fig. (b) in Exercise 14 of Section 1.10: $(10, 17.5, 20, 12.5)$

Figure for Exercises 34 in Section 1.1 $(20, 27.5, 30, 22.5)$

When the solutions are arranged this way, it is evident that the third solution is the sum of the first two solutions. What might not be so evident is that list of boundary temperatures of the third problem is the sum of the lists of boundary temperatures of the first two problems. (The temperatures are listed clockwise, starting at the left of T_1.)

Fig. (a): $(\ 0, 20, 20,\ 0,\ 0, 20, 20,\ 0)$

Fig. (b): $(10,\ 0,\ 0, 40, 40, 10, 10, 10)$

Fig. from Section 1.1: $(10, 20, 20, 40, 40, 30, 30, 10)$

b. When the boundary temperatures in Fig. (a) are multiplied by 3, the new interior temperatures are also multiplied by 3.

c. The correspondence from the list of eight boundary temperatures to the list of four interior temperatures is a linear transformation. A verification of this statement is not expected. However, it can be shown that the solutions of the steady-state temperature problem here satisfy a superposition principle. The system of equations that approximate the interior temperatures can be written in the form $A\mathbf{x} = \mathbf{b}$, where A is determined by the arrangement of the four interior points on the plate and $\mathbf{b}$ is a vector in $\mathbf{R}^4$ determined by the boundary temperatures.

Note: The MATLAB box in the *Study Guide* for Section 1.10 discusses scientific notation and shows how to generate a matrix whose columns list the vectors $\mathbf{x}_0$, $\mathbf{x}_1$, $\mathbf{x}_2$, ..., determined by an equation $\mathbf{x}_{k+1} = M\mathbf{x}_k$ for $k = 0, 1, \ldots$.

Chapter 1   SUPPLEMENTARY EXERCISES _____

1. a. False. (The word "reduced" is missing.) Counterexample:

$$A = \begin{bmatrix} 1 & 2 \\ 3 & 4 \end{bmatrix},\ B = \begin{bmatrix} 1 & 2 \\ 0 & -2 \end{bmatrix},\ C = \begin{bmatrix} 1 & 2 \\ 0 & 1 \end{bmatrix}$$

The matrix A is row equivalent to matrices B and C, both in echelon form.

b. False. Counterexample: Let A be any $n \times n$ matrix with fewer than n pivot columns. Then the equation $A\mathbf{x} = \mathbf{0}$ has infinitely many solutions. (Theorem 2 in Section 1.2 says that a system has either zero, one, or infinitely many solutions, but it does not say that a system with infinitely many solutions exists. Some counterexample is needed.)

c. True. If a linear system has more than one solution, it is a consistent system and has a free variable. By the Existence and Uniqueness Theorem in Section 1.2, the system has infinitely many solutions.

d. False. Counterexample: The following system has no free variables and no solution:

$$
\begin{array}{rcrcl}
x_1 & + & x_2 & = & 1 \\
  &   & x_2 & = & 5 \\
x_1 & + & x_2 & = & 2
\end{array}
$$

e. True. See the box after the definition of elementary row operations, in Section 1.1. If $[A \quad \mathbf{b}]$ is transformed into $[C \quad \mathbf{d}]$ by elementary row operations, then the two augmented matrices are row equivalent.

f. True. Theorem 6 in Section 1.5 essentially says that when $A\mathbf{x} = \mathbf{b}$ is consistent, the solution sets of the nonhomogeneous equation and the homogeneous equation are translates of each other. In this case, the two equations have the same number of solutions.

g. False. For the columns of A to span $\mathbf{R}^m$, the equation $A\mathbf{x} = \mathbf{b}$ must be consistent for *all* $\mathbf{b}$ in $\mathbf{R}^m$, not for just one vector $\mathbf{b}$ in $\mathbf{R}^m$.

h. False. *Any* matrix can be transformed by elementary row operations into reduced echelon form, but not every matrix equation $A\mathbf{x} = \mathbf{b}$ is consistent.

i. True. If A is row equivalent to B, then A can be transformed by elementary row operations first into B and then further transformed into the reduced echelon form U of B. Since the reduced echelon form of A is unique, it must be U.

j. False. Every equation $A\mathbf{x} = \mathbf{0}$ has the trivial solution whether or not some variables are free.

k. True, by Theorem 4 in Section 1.4. If the equation $A\mathbf{x} = \mathbf{b}$ is consistent for every $\mathbf{b}$ in $\mathbf{R}^m$, then A must have a position in every one of its m rows. If A has m pivot positions, then A has m pivot columns, each containing one pivot position.

l. False. The word "unique" should be deleted. Let A be any matrix with m pivot columns but more than m columns altogether. Then the equation $A\mathbf{x} = \mathbf{b}$ is consistent and has m basic variables and at least one free variable. Thus the equation does not does not have a unique solution.

m. True. If A has n pivot positions, it has a pivot in each of its n columns and in each of its n rows. The reduced echelon form has a 1 in each pivot position, so the reduced echelon form is the $n \times n$ identity matrix.

n. True. Both matrices A and B can be row reduced to the 3×3 identity matrix, as discussed in the previous question. Since the row operations that transform B into I_3 are reversible, A can be transformed first into I_3 and then into B.

o. True. The reason is essentially the same as that given for question f.

p. True. If the columns of A span $\mathbf{R}^m$, then the reduced echelon form of A is a matrix U with a pivot in each row, by Theorem 4 in Section 1.4. Since B is row equivalent to A, B can be transformed by row operations first into A and then further transformed into U. Since U has a pivot in each row, so does B. By Theorem 4, the columns of B span $\mathbf{R}^m$.

q. False. See Example 5 in Section 1.6.

r. True. Any set of three vectors in $\mathbf{R}^2$ would have to be linearly dependent, by Theorem 8 in Section 1.6.

s. False. If a set $\{\mathbf{v}_1, \mathbf{v}_2, \mathbf{v}_3, \mathbf{v}_4\}$ were to span $\mathbf{R}^5$, then the matrix $A = [\mathbf{v}_1 \;\; \mathbf{v}_2 \;\; \mathbf{v}_3 \;\; \mathbf{v}_4]$ would have a pivot position in each of its five rows, which is impossible since A has only four columns.

t. True. The vector $-\mathbf{u}$ is a linear combination of $\mathbf{u}$ and $\mathbf{v}$, namely, $-\mathbf{u} = (-1)\mathbf{u} + 0\mathbf{v}$.

u. False. If $\mathbf{u}$ and $\mathbf{v}$ are multiples, then Span$\{\mathbf{u}, \mathbf{v}\}$ is a line, and $\mathbf{w}$ need not be on that line.

v. False. Let $\mathbf{u}$ and $\mathbf{v}$ be any linearly independent pair of vectors and let $\mathbf{w} = 2\mathbf{v}$. Then $\mathbf{w} = 0\mathbf{u} + 2\mathbf{v}$, so $\mathbf{w}$ is a linear combination of $\mathbf{u}$ and $\mathbf{v}$. However, $\mathbf{u}$ cannot be a linear combination of $\mathbf{v}$ and $\mathbf{w}$ because if it were, $\mathbf{u}$ would be a multiple of $\mathbf{v}$. That is not possible since $\{\mathbf{u}, \mathbf{v}\}$ is linearly independent.

w. False. The statement would be true if the condition $\mathbf{v}_1$ is not zero were present. See Theorem 7 in Section 1.7. However, if $\mathbf{v}_1 = \mathbf{0}$, then $\{\mathbf{v}_1, \mathbf{v}_2, \mathbf{v}_3\}$ is linearly dependent, no matter what else might be true about $\mathbf{v}_2$ and $\mathbf{v}_3$.

x. True. "Function" is another word used for "transformation" (as mentioned in the definition of "transformation" in Section 1.8), and a linear transformation is a special type of transformation.

y. True. For the transformation $\mathbf{x} \mapsto A\mathbf{x}$ to map $\mathbf{R}^5$ onto $\mathbf{R}^6$, the matrix A would have to have a pivot in every row and hence have six pivot columns. This is impossible because A has only five columns.

z. False. For the transformation $\mathbf{x} \mapsto A\mathbf{x}$ to be one-to-one, A must have a pivot in each column. Since A has n columns and m pivots, m might be less than n.

2. If $a \neq 0$, then $x = b/a$; the solution is unique. If $a = 0$, and $b \neq 0$, the solution set is empty, because $0x = 0 \neq b$. If $a = 0$ and $b = 0$, the equation $0x = 0$ has infinitely many solutions.

3. **a.** Any consistent linear system whose echelon form is

$$\begin{bmatrix} \blacksquare & * & * & * \\ 0 & \blacksquare & * & * \\ 0 & 0 & 0 & 0 \end{bmatrix} \text{ or } \begin{bmatrix} \blacksquare & * & * & * \\ 0 & 0 & \blacksquare & * \\ 0 & 0 & 0 & 0 \end{bmatrix} \text{ or } \begin{bmatrix} 0 & \blacksquare & * & * \\ 0 & 0 & \blacksquare & * \\ 0 & 0 & 0 & 0 \end{bmatrix}$$

   b. Any consistent linear system whose coefficient matrix has reduced echelon form I_3.

   c. Any inconsistent linear system of three equations in three variables.

4. Since there are three pivots (one in each row), the augmented matrix must reduce to the form

$$\begin{bmatrix} \blacksquare & * & * & * \\ 0 & \blacksquare & * & * \\ 0 & 0 & \blacksquare & * \end{bmatrix}$$. A solution of $A\mathbf{x} = \mathbf{b}$ exists for all $\mathbf{b}$ because there is a pivot in each row of A. Each

solution is unique because there are no free variables.

5. **a.** $\begin{bmatrix} 1 & 3 & k \\ 4 & h & 8 \end{bmatrix} \sim \begin{bmatrix} ① & 3 & k \\ 0 & h-12 & 8-4k \end{bmatrix}$. If $h = 12$ and $k \neq 2$, the second row of the augmented matrix

indicates an inconsistent system of the form $0x_2 = b$, with b nonzero. If $h = 12$, and $k = 2$, there is only one nonzero equation, and the system has infinitely many solutions. Finally, if $h \neq 12$, the coefficient matrix has two pivots and the system has a unique solution.

   b. $\begin{bmatrix} -2 & h & 1 \\ 6 & k & -2 \end{bmatrix} \sim \begin{bmatrix} ⓐ & h & 1 \\ 0 & k+3h & 1 \end{bmatrix}$. If $k + 3h = 0$, the system is inconsistent. Otherwise, the

coefficient matrix has two pivots and the system has a unique solution.

6. a. Set $\mathbf{v}_1 = \begin{bmatrix} 4 \\ 8 \end{bmatrix}$, $\mathbf{v}_2 = \begin{bmatrix} -2 \\ -3 \end{bmatrix}$, $\mathbf{v}_3 = \begin{bmatrix} 7 \\ 10 \end{bmatrix}$, and $\mathbf{b} = \begin{bmatrix} -5 \\ -3 \end{bmatrix}$. "Determine if $\mathbf{b}$ is a linear combination of $\mathbf{v}_1$, $\mathbf{v}_2$, $\mathbf{v}_3$." Or, "Determine if $\mathbf{b}$ is in Span$\{\mathbf{v}_1, \mathbf{v}_2, \mathbf{v}_3\}$." To do this, compute

$$\begin{bmatrix} 4 & -2 & 7 & -5 \\ 8 & -3 & 10 & -3 \end{bmatrix} \sim \begin{bmatrix} ④ & -2 & 7 & -5 \\ 0 & ① & -4 & 7 \end{bmatrix}.$$ The system is consistent, so $\mathbf{b}$ *is* in Span$\{\mathbf{v}_1, \mathbf{v}_2, \mathbf{v}_3\}$.

b. Set $A = \begin{bmatrix} 4 & -2 & 7 \\ 8 & -3 & 10 \end{bmatrix}$, $\mathbf{b} = \begin{bmatrix} -5 \\ -3 \end{bmatrix}$. "Determine if $\mathbf{b}$ is a linear combination of the columns of A."

c. Define $T(\mathbf{x}) = A\mathbf{x}$. "Determine if $\mathbf{b}$ is in the range of T."

7. a. Set $\mathbf{v}_1 = \begin{bmatrix} 2 \\ -5 \\ 7 \end{bmatrix}$, $\mathbf{v}_2 = \begin{bmatrix} -4 \\ 1 \\ -5 \end{bmatrix}$, $\mathbf{v}_3 = \begin{bmatrix} -2 \\ 1 \\ -3 \end{bmatrix}$ and $\mathbf{b} = \begin{bmatrix} b_1 \\ b_2 \\ b_3 \end{bmatrix}$. "Determine if $\mathbf{v}_1$, $\mathbf{v}_2$, $\mathbf{v}_3$ span $\mathbf{R}^3$." To do this, row

reduce $[\mathbf{v}_1 \ \mathbf{v}_2 \ \mathbf{v}_3]$:

$$\begin{bmatrix} 2 & -4 & -2 \\ -5 & 1 & 1 \\ 7 & -5 & -3 \end{bmatrix} \sim \begin{bmatrix} 2 & -4 & -2 \\ 0 & -9 & -4 \\ 0 & 9 & 4 \end{bmatrix} \sim \begin{bmatrix} ② & -4 & -2 \\ 0 & ⑨ & -4 \\ 0 & 0 & 0 \end{bmatrix}.$$ The matrix does not have a pivot in each row, so

its columns do not span $\mathbf{R}^3$, by Theorem 4 in Section 1.4.

b. Set $A = \begin{bmatrix} 2 & -4 & -2 \\ -5 & 1 & 1 \\ 7 & -5 & -3 \end{bmatrix}$. "Determine if the columns of A span $\mathbf{R}^3$."

c. Define $T(\mathbf{x}) = A\mathbf{x}$. "Determine if T maps $\mathbf{R}^3$ onto $\mathbf{R}^3$."

8. a. $\begin{bmatrix} ■ & * & * \\ 0 & ■ & * \end{bmatrix}, \begin{bmatrix} ■ & * & * \\ 0 & 0 & ■ \end{bmatrix}, \begin{bmatrix} 0 & ■ & * \\ 0 & 0 & ■ \end{bmatrix}$ **b.** $\begin{bmatrix} ■ & * & * \\ 0 & ■ & * \\ 0 & 0 & ■ \end{bmatrix}$

9. The first line is the line spanned by $\begin{bmatrix} 1 \\ 2 \end{bmatrix}$. The second line is spanned by $\begin{bmatrix} 2 \\ 1 \end{bmatrix}$. So the problem is to write

$\begin{bmatrix} 5 \\ 6 \end{bmatrix}$ as the sum of a multiple of $\begin{bmatrix} 1 \\ 2 \end{bmatrix}$ and a multiple of $\begin{bmatrix} 2 \\ 1 \end{bmatrix}$. That is, find x_1 and x_2 such that

$x_1 \begin{bmatrix} 2 \\ 1 \end{bmatrix} + x_2 \begin{bmatrix} 1 \\ 2 \end{bmatrix} = \begin{bmatrix} 5 \\ 6 \end{bmatrix}$. Reduce the augmented matrix for this equation:

$$\begin{bmatrix} 2 & 1 & 5 \\ 1 & 2 & 6 \end{bmatrix} \sim \begin{bmatrix} 1 & 2 & 6 \\ 2 & 1 & 5 \end{bmatrix} \sim \begin{bmatrix} 1 & 2 & 6 \\ 0 & -3 & -7 \end{bmatrix} \sim \begin{bmatrix} 1 & 2 & 6 \\ 0 & 1 & 7/3 \end{bmatrix} \sim \begin{bmatrix} 1 & 0 & 4/3 \\ 0 & 1 & 7/3 \end{bmatrix}$$

Thus, $\begin{bmatrix} 5 \\ 6 \end{bmatrix} = \frac{4}{3} \begin{bmatrix} 2 \\ 1 \end{bmatrix} + \frac{7}{3} \begin{bmatrix} 1 \\ 2 \end{bmatrix}$ or $\begin{bmatrix} 5 \\ 6 \end{bmatrix} = \begin{bmatrix} 8/3 \\ 4/3 \end{bmatrix} + \begin{bmatrix} 7/3 \\ 14/3 \end{bmatrix}$.

10. The line through $\mathbf{a}_1$ and the origin and the line through $\mathbf{a}_2$ and the origin determine a "grid" on the $x_1 x_2$-plane as shown below. Every point in $\mathbf{R}^2$ can be described uniquely in terms of this grid. Thus, $\mathbf{b}$ can be reached from the origin by traveling a certain number of units in the $\mathbf{a}_1$-direction and a certain number of units in the $\mathbf{a}_2$-direction.

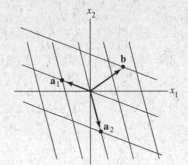

11. A solution set is a line when the system has one free variable. If the coefficient matrix is 2×3, then two of the columns should be pivot columns. For instance, take $\begin{bmatrix} 1 & 2 & * \\ 0 & 3 & * \end{bmatrix}$. Put anything in column 3. The resulting matrix will be in echelon form. Make one row replacement operation on the second row to create a matrix *not* in echelon form, such as $\begin{bmatrix} 1 & 2 & 1 \\ 0 & 3 & 1 \end{bmatrix} \sim \begin{bmatrix} 1 & 2 & 1 \\ 1 & 5 & 2 \end{bmatrix}$

12. A solution set is a plane where there are two free variables. If the coefficient matrix is 2×3, then only one column can be a pivot column. The echelon form will have all zeros in the second row. Use a row replacement to create a matrix not in echelon form. For instance, let $A = \begin{bmatrix} 1 & 2 & 3 \\ 1 & 2 & 3 \end{bmatrix}$.

13. The reduced echelon form of A looks like $E = \begin{bmatrix} 1 & 0 & * \\ 0 & 1 & * \\ 0 & 0 & 0 \end{bmatrix}$. Since E is row equivalent to A, the equation $E\mathbf{x} = \mathbf{0}$ has the same solutions as $A\mathbf{x} = \mathbf{0}$. Thus $\begin{bmatrix} 1 & 0 & * \\ 0 & 1 & * \\ 0 & 0 & 0 \end{bmatrix} \begin{bmatrix} 3 \\ -2 \\ 1 \end{bmatrix} = \begin{bmatrix} 0 \\ 0 \\ 0 \end{bmatrix}$.

By inspection, $E = \begin{bmatrix} 1 & 0 & -3 \\ 0 & 1 & 2 \\ 0 & 0 & 0 \end{bmatrix}$.

14. Row reduce the augmented matrix for $x_1 \begin{bmatrix} 1 \\ a \end{bmatrix} + x_2 \begin{bmatrix} a \\ a+2 \end{bmatrix} = \begin{bmatrix} 0 \\ 0 \end{bmatrix}$ (*).

$$\begin{bmatrix} 1 & a & 0 \\ a & a+2 & 0 \end{bmatrix} \sim \begin{bmatrix} 1 & a & 0 \\ 0 & a+2-a^2 & 0 \end{bmatrix} = \begin{bmatrix} 1 & a & 0 \\ 0 & (2-a)(1+a) & 0 \end{bmatrix}$$

The equation (*) has a nontrivial solution only when $(2 - a)(1 + a) = 0$. So the vectors are linearly independent for all a except $a = 2$ and $a = -1$.

15. **a.** If the three vectors are linearly independent, then a, c, and f must all be nonzero. (The converse is true, too.) Let A be the matrix whose columns are the three linearly independent vectors. Then

A must have three pivot columns. (See Exercise 30 in Section 1.7, or realize that the equation $A\mathbf{x} = \mathbf{0}$ has only the trivial solution and so there can be no free variables in the system of equations.) Since A is 3×3, the pivot positions are exactly where a, c, and f are located.

b. The numbers $a, \ldots, f$ can have any values. Here's why. Denote the columns by $\mathbf{v}_1$, $\mathbf{v}_2$, and $\mathbf{v}_3$. Observe that $\mathbf{v}_1$ is not the zero vector. Next, $\mathbf{v}_2$ is not a multiple of $\mathbf{v}_1$ because the third entry of $\mathbf{v}_2$ is nonzero. Finally, $\mathbf{v}_3$ is not a linear combination of $\mathbf{v}_1$ and $\mathbf{v}_2$ because the fourth entry of $\mathbf{v}_3$ is nonzero. By Theorem 7 in Section 1.7, $\{\mathbf{v}_1, \mathbf{v}_2, \mathbf{v}_3\}$ is linearly independent.

16. Denote the columns from right to left by $\mathbf{v}_1, \ldots, \mathbf{v}_4$. The "first" vector $\mathbf{v}_1$ is nonzero, $\mathbf{v}_2$ is not a multiple of $\mathbf{v}_1$ (because the third entry of $\mathbf{v}_2$ is nonzero), and $\mathbf{v}_3$ is not a linear combination of $\mathbf{v}_1$ and $\mathbf{v}_2$ (because the second entry of $\mathbf{v}_3$ is nonzero). Finally, by looking at first entries in the vectors, $\mathbf{v}_4$ cannot be a linear combination of $\mathbf{v}_1$, $\mathbf{v}_2$, and $\mathbf{v}_3$. By Theorem 7 in Section 1.7, the columns are linearly independent.

17. Here are two arguments. The first is a "direct" proof. The second is called a "proof by contradiction."

    i. Since $\{\mathbf{v}_1, \mathbf{v}_2, \mathbf{v}_3\}$ is a linearly independent set, $\mathbf{v}_1 \neq \mathbf{0}$. Also, Theorem 7 shows that $\mathbf{v}_2$ cannot be a multiple of $\mathbf{v}_1$, and $\mathbf{v}_3$ cannot be a linear combination of $\mathbf{v}_1$ and $\mathbf{v}_2$. By hypothesis, $\mathbf{v}_4$ is not a linear combination of $\mathbf{v}_1$, $\mathbf{v}_2$, and $\mathbf{v}_3$. Thus, by Theorem 7, $\{\mathbf{v}_1, \mathbf{v}_2, \mathbf{v}_3, \mathbf{v}_4\}$ cannot be a linearly dependent set and so must be linearly independent.

    ii. Suppose that $\{\mathbf{v}_1, \mathbf{v}_2, \mathbf{v}_3, \mathbf{v}_4\}$ is linearly dependent. Then by Theorem 7, one of the vectors in the set is a linear combination of the preceding vectors. This vector cannot be $\mathbf{v}_4$ because $\mathbf{v}_4$ is *not* in Span$\{\mathbf{v}_1, \mathbf{v}_2, \mathbf{v}_3\}$. Also, none of the vectors in $\{\mathbf{v}_1, \mathbf{v}_2, \mathbf{v}_3\}$ is a linear combinations of the preceding vectors, by Theorem 7. So the linear dependence of $\{\mathbf{v}_1, \mathbf{v}_2, \mathbf{v}_3, \mathbf{v}_4\}$ is impossible. Thus $\{\mathbf{v}_1, \mathbf{v}_2, \mathbf{v}_3, \mathbf{v}_4\}$ is linearly independent.

18. Suppose that c_1 and c_2 are constants such that

    $$c_1 \mathbf{v}_1 + c_2(\mathbf{v}_1 + \mathbf{v}_2) = \mathbf{0} \quad (*)$$

    Then $(c_1 + c_2)\mathbf{v}_1 + c_2 \mathbf{v}_2 = \mathbf{0}$. Since $\mathbf{v}_1$ and $\mathbf{v}_2$ are linearly independent, both $c_1 + c_2 = 0$ and $c_2 = 0$. It follows that both c_1 and c_2 in $(*)$ must be zero, which shows that $\{\mathbf{v}_1, \mathbf{v}_1 + \mathbf{v}_2\}$ is linearly independent.

19. Let M be the line through the origin that is parallel to the line through $\mathbf{v}_1$, $\mathbf{v}_2$, and $\mathbf{v}_3$. Then $\mathbf{v}_2 - \mathbf{v}_1$ and $\mathbf{v}_3 - \mathbf{v}_1$ are both on M. So one of these two vectors is a multiple of the other, say $\mathbf{v}_2 - \mathbf{v}_1 = k(\mathbf{v}_3 - \mathbf{v}_1)$. This equation produces a linear dependence relation $(k - 1)\mathbf{v}_1 + \mathbf{v}_2 - k\mathbf{v}_3 = \mathbf{0}$.

    A second solution: A parametric equation of the line is $\mathbf{x} = \mathbf{v}_1 + t(\mathbf{v}_2 - \mathbf{v}_1)$. Since $\mathbf{v}_3$ is on the line, there is some t_0 such that $\mathbf{v}_3 = \mathbf{v}_1 + t_0(\mathbf{v}_2 - \mathbf{v}_1) = (1 - t_0)\mathbf{v}_1 + t_0\mathbf{v}_2$. So $\mathbf{v}_3$ is a linear combination of $\mathbf{v}_1$ and $\mathbf{v}_2$, and $\{\mathbf{v}_1, \mathbf{v}_2, \mathbf{v}_3\}$ is linearly dependent.

20. If $T(\mathbf{u}) = \mathbf{v}$, then since T is linear,

    $$T(-\mathbf{u}) = T((-1)\mathbf{u}) = (-1)T(\mathbf{u}) = -\mathbf{v}.$$

21. Either compute $T(\mathbf{e}_1)$, $T(\mathbf{e}_2)$, and $T(\mathbf{e}_3)$ to make the columns of A, or write the vectors vertically in the definition of T and fill in the entries of A by inspection:

    $$A\mathbf{x} = \begin{bmatrix} ? & ? & ? \\ ? & A & ? \\ ? & ? & ? \end{bmatrix} \begin{bmatrix} x_1 \\ x_2 \\ x_3 \end{bmatrix} = \begin{bmatrix} x_1 \\ -x_2 \\ x_3 \end{bmatrix}, \quad A = \begin{bmatrix} 1 & 0 & 0 \\ 0 & -1 & 0 \\ 0 & 0 & 1 \end{bmatrix}$$

22. By Theorem 12 in Section 1.9, the columns of A span $\mathbf{R}^3$. By Theorem 4 in Section 1.4, A has a pivot in each of its three rows. Since A has three columns, each column must be a pivot column. So the equation

$A\mathbf{x} = \mathbf{0}$ has no free variables, and the columns of A are linearly independent. By Theorem 12 in Section 1.9, the transformation $\mathbf{x} \mapsto A\mathbf{x}$ is one-to-one.

23. $\begin{bmatrix} a & -b \\ b & a \end{bmatrix}\begin{bmatrix} 4 \\ 3 \end{bmatrix} = \begin{bmatrix} 5 \\ 0 \end{bmatrix}$ implies that $\begin{array}{rcrcl} 4a & - & 3b & = & 5 \\ 3a & + & 4b & = & 0 \end{array}$. Solve:

$$\begin{bmatrix} 4 & -3 & 5 \\ 3 & 4 & 0 \end{bmatrix} \sim \begin{bmatrix} 4 & -3 & 5 \\ 0 & 25/4 & -15/4 \end{bmatrix} \sim \begin{bmatrix} 4 & -3 & 5 \\ 0 & 1 & -3/5 \end{bmatrix} \sim \begin{bmatrix} 4 & 0 & 16/5 \\ 0 & 1 & -3/5 \end{bmatrix} \sim \begin{bmatrix} 1 & 0 & 4/5 \\ 0 & 1 & -3/5 \end{bmatrix}$$

Thus $a = 4/5$ and $b = -3/5$.

24. The matrix equation displayed gives the information $2a - 4b = 2\sqrt{5}$ and $4a + 2b = 0$. Solve for a and b:

$$\begin{bmatrix} 2 & -4 & 2\sqrt{5} \\ 4 & 2 & 0 \end{bmatrix} \sim \begin{bmatrix} 2 & -4 & 2\sqrt{5} \\ 0 & 10 & -4\sqrt{5} \end{bmatrix} \sim \begin{bmatrix} 1 & -2 & \sqrt{5} \\ 0 & 1 & -2/\sqrt{5} \end{bmatrix} \sim \begin{bmatrix} 1 & 0 & 1/\sqrt{5} \\ 0 & 1 & -2/\sqrt{5} \end{bmatrix}$$

So $a = 1/\sqrt{5}$, $b = -2/\sqrt{5}$.

25. a. The vector lists the number of three-, two-, and one-bedroom apartments provided when x_1 floors of plan A are constructed.

b. $x_1 \begin{bmatrix} 3 \\ 7 \\ 8 \end{bmatrix} + x_2 \begin{bmatrix} 4 \\ 4 \\ 8 \end{bmatrix} + x_3 \begin{bmatrix} 5 \\ 3 \\ 9 \end{bmatrix}$

c. [M] Solve $x_1 \begin{bmatrix} 3 \\ 7 \\ 8 \end{bmatrix} + x_2 \begin{bmatrix} 4 \\ 4 \\ 8 \end{bmatrix} + x_3 \begin{bmatrix} 5 \\ 3 \\ 9 \end{bmatrix} = \begin{bmatrix} 66 \\ 74 \\ 136 \end{bmatrix}$

$$\begin{bmatrix} 3 & 4 & 5 & 66 \\ 7 & 4 & 3 & 74 \\ 8 & 8 & 9 & 136 \end{bmatrix} \sim \cdots \begin{bmatrix} 1 & 0 & -1/2 & 2 \\ 0 & 1 & 13/8 & 15 \\ 0 & 0 & 0 & 0 \end{bmatrix} \qquad \begin{array}{rcrcl} x_1 & - & (1/2)x_3 & = & 2 \\ x_2 & + & (13/8)x_3 & = & 15 \\ & & 0 & = & 0 \end{array}$$

The general solution is

$$\mathbf{x} = \begin{bmatrix} x_1 \\ x_2 \\ x_3 \end{bmatrix} = \begin{bmatrix} 2 + (1/2)x_3 \\ 15 - (13/8)x_3 \\ x_3 \end{bmatrix} = \begin{bmatrix} 2 \\ 15 \\ 0 \end{bmatrix} + x_3 \begin{bmatrix} 1/2 \\ -13/8 \\ 1 \end{bmatrix}$$

However, the only feasible solutions must have whole numbers of floors for each plan. Thus, x_3 must be a multiple of 8, to avoid fractions. One solution, for $x_3 = 0$, is to use 2 floors of plan A and 15 floors of plan B. Another solution, for $x_3 = 8$, is to use 6 floors of plan A , 2 floors of plan B, and 8 floors of plan C. These are the only feasible solutions. A larger positive multiple of 8 for x_3 makes x_2 negative. A negative value for x_3, of course, is not feasible either.

2 Matrix Algebra

2.1 SOLUTIONS

Notes: The definition here of a matrix product AB gives the proper view of AB for nearly all matrix calculations. (The dual fact about the rows of A and the rows of AB is seldom needed, mainly because vectors here are usually written as columns.) I assign Exercise 13 and most of Exercises 17–22 to reinforce the definition of AB.

Exercises 23 and 24 are used in the proof of the Invertible Matrix Theorem, in Section 2.3. Exercises 23–25 are mentioned in a footnote in Section 2.2. A class discussion of the solutions of Exercises 23–25 can provide a transition to Section 2.2. Or, these exercises could be assigned after starting Section 2.2.

Exercises 27 and 28 are optional, but they are mentioned in Example 4 of Section 2.4. Outer products also appear in Exercises 31–34 of Section 4.6 and in the spectral decomposition of a symmetric matrix, in Section 7.1. Exercises 29–33 provide good training for mathematics majors.

1. $-2A = (-2)\begin{bmatrix} 2 & 0 & -1 \\ 4 & -5 & 2 \end{bmatrix} = \begin{bmatrix} -4 & 0 & 2 \\ -8 & 10 & -4 \end{bmatrix}$. Next, use $B - 2A = B + (-2A)$:

$$B - 2A = \begin{bmatrix} 7 & -5 & 1 \\ 1 & -4 & -3 \end{bmatrix} + \begin{bmatrix} -4 & 0 & 2 \\ -8 & 10 & -4 \end{bmatrix} = \begin{bmatrix} 3 & -5 & 3 \\ -7 & 6 & -7 \end{bmatrix}$$

The product AC is not defined because the number of columns of A does not match the number of rows of C. $CD = \begin{bmatrix} 1 & 2 \\ -2 & 1 \end{bmatrix}\begin{bmatrix} 3 & 5 \\ -1 & 4 \end{bmatrix} = \begin{bmatrix} 1 \cdot 3 + 2(-1) & 1 \cdot 5 + 2 \cdot 4 \\ -2 \cdot 3 + 1(-1) & -2 \cdot 5 + 1 \cdot 4 \end{bmatrix} = \begin{bmatrix} 1 & 13 \\ -7 & -6 \end{bmatrix}$. For mental computation, the row-column rule is probably easier to use than the definition.

2. $A + 2B = \begin{bmatrix} 2 & 0 & -1 \\ 4 & -5 & 2 \end{bmatrix} + 2\begin{bmatrix} 7 & -5 & 1 \\ 1 & -4 & -3 \end{bmatrix} = \begin{bmatrix} 2+14 & 0-10 & -1+2 \\ 4+2 & -5-8 & 2-6 \end{bmatrix} = \begin{bmatrix} 16 & -10 & 1 \\ 6 & -13 & -4 \end{bmatrix}$

The expression $3C - E$ is not defined because $3C$ has 2 columns and $-E$ has only 1 column.

$$CB = \begin{bmatrix} 1 & 2 \\ -2 & 1 \end{bmatrix}\begin{bmatrix} 7 & -5 & 1 \\ 1 & -4 & -3 \end{bmatrix} = \begin{bmatrix} 1 \cdot 7 + 2 \cdot 1 & 1(-5) + 2(-4) & 1 \cdot 1 + 2(-3) \\ -2 \cdot 7 + 1 \cdot 1 & -2(-5) + 1(-4) & -2 \cdot 1 + 1(-3) \end{bmatrix} = \begin{bmatrix} 9 & -13 & -5 \\ -13 & 6 & -5 \end{bmatrix}$$

The product EB is not defined because the number of columns of E does not match the number of rows of R.

3. $3I_2 - A = \begin{bmatrix} 3 & 0 \\ 0 & 3 \end{bmatrix} - \begin{bmatrix} 4 & -1 \\ 5 & -2 \end{bmatrix} = \begin{bmatrix} 3-4 & 0-(-1) \\ 0-5 & 3-(-2) \end{bmatrix} = \begin{bmatrix} -1 & 1 \\ -5 & 5 \end{bmatrix}$

$(3I_2)A = 3(I_2 A) = 3\begin{bmatrix} 4 & -1 \\ 5 & -2 \end{bmatrix} = \begin{bmatrix} 12 & -3 \\ 15 & -6 \end{bmatrix}$, or

$(3I_2)A = \begin{bmatrix} 3 & 0 \\ 0 & 3 \end{bmatrix}\begin{bmatrix} 4 & -1 \\ 5 & -2 \end{bmatrix} = \begin{bmatrix} 3\cdot4+0 & 3(-1)+0 \\ 0+3\cdot5 & 0+3(-2) \end{bmatrix} = \begin{bmatrix} 12 & -3 \\ 15 & -6 \end{bmatrix}$

4. $A - 5I_3 = \begin{bmatrix} 9 & -1 & 3 \\ -8 & 7 & -6 \\ -4 & 1 & 8 \end{bmatrix} - \begin{bmatrix} 5 & 0 & 0 \\ 0 & 5 & 0 \\ 0 & 0 & 5 \end{bmatrix} = \begin{bmatrix} 4 & -1 & 3 \\ -8 & 2 & -6 \\ -4 & 1 & 3 \end{bmatrix}$

$(5I_3)A = 5(I_3 A) = 5A = 5\begin{bmatrix} 9 & -1 & 3 \\ -8 & 7 & -6 \\ -4 & 1 & 8 \end{bmatrix} = \begin{bmatrix} 45 & -5 & 15 \\ -40 & 35 & -30 \\ -20 & 5 & 40 \end{bmatrix}$, or

$(5I_3)A = \begin{bmatrix} 5 & 0 & 0 \\ 0 & 5 & 0 \\ 0 & 0 & 5 \end{bmatrix}\begin{bmatrix} 9 & -1 & 3 \\ -8 & 7 & -6 \\ -4 & 1 & 8 \end{bmatrix}$

$= \begin{bmatrix} 5\cdot9+0+0 & 5(-1)+0+0 & 5\cdot3+0+0 \\ 0+5(-8)+0 & 0+5\cdot7+0 & 0+5(-6)+0 \\ 0+0+5(-4) & 0+0+5\cdot1 & 0+0+5\cdot8 \end{bmatrix} = \begin{bmatrix} 45 & -5 & 15 \\ -45 & 35 & -30 \\ -20 & 5 & 40 \end{bmatrix}$

5. a. $A\mathbf{b}_1 = \begin{bmatrix} -1 & 2 \\ 5 & 4 \\ 2 & -3 \end{bmatrix}\begin{bmatrix} 3 \\ -2 \end{bmatrix} = \begin{bmatrix} -7 \\ 7 \\ 12 \end{bmatrix}$, $A\mathbf{b}_2 = \begin{bmatrix} -1 & 2 \\ 5 & 4 \\ 2 & -3 \end{bmatrix}\begin{bmatrix} -2 \\ 1 \end{bmatrix} = \begin{bmatrix} 4 \\ -6 \\ -7 \end{bmatrix}$

$AB = \begin{bmatrix} A\mathbf{b}_1 & A\mathbf{b}_2 \end{bmatrix} = \begin{bmatrix} -7 & 4 \\ 7 & -6 \\ 12 & -7 \end{bmatrix}$

b. $\begin{bmatrix} -1 & 2 \\ 5 & 4 \\ 2 & -3 \end{bmatrix}\begin{bmatrix} 3 & -2 \\ -2 & 1 \end{bmatrix} = \begin{bmatrix} -1\cdot3+2(-2) & -1(-2)+2\cdot1 \\ 5\cdot3+4(-2) & 5(-2)+4\cdot1 \\ 2\cdot3-3(-2) & 2(-2)-3\cdot1 \end{bmatrix} = \begin{bmatrix} -7 & 4 \\ 7 & -6 \\ 12 & -7 \end{bmatrix}$

6. a. $A\mathbf{b}_1 = \begin{bmatrix} 4 & -2 \\ -3 & 0 \\ 3 & 5 \end{bmatrix}\begin{bmatrix} 1 \\ 2 \end{bmatrix} = \begin{bmatrix} 0 \\ -3 \\ 13 \end{bmatrix}$, $A\mathbf{b}_2 = \begin{bmatrix} 4 & -2 \\ -3 & 0 \\ 3 & 5 \end{bmatrix}\begin{bmatrix} 3 \\ -1 \end{bmatrix} = \begin{bmatrix} 14 \\ -9 \\ 4 \end{bmatrix}$

$AB = \begin{bmatrix} A\mathbf{b}_1 & A\mathbf{b}_2 \end{bmatrix} = \begin{bmatrix} 0 & 14 \\ -3 & -9 \\ 13 & 4 \end{bmatrix}$

b. $\begin{bmatrix} 4 & -2 \\ -3 & 0 \\ 3 & 5 \end{bmatrix}\begin{bmatrix} 1 & 3 \\ 2 & -1 \end{bmatrix} = \begin{bmatrix} 4\cdot1-2\cdot2 & 4\cdot3-2(-1) \\ -3\cdot1+0\cdot2 & -3\cdot3+0(-1) \\ 3\cdot1+5\cdot2 & 3\cdot3+5(-1) \end{bmatrix} = \begin{bmatrix} 0 & 14 \\ -3 & -9 \\ 13 & 4 \end{bmatrix}$

7. Since A has 3 columns, B must match with 3 rows. Otherwise, AB is undefined. Since AB has 7 columns, so does B. Thus, B is 3×7.

8. The number of rows of B matches the number of rows of BC, so B has 3 rows.

9. $AB = \begin{bmatrix} 2 & 5 \\ -3 & 1 \end{bmatrix} \begin{bmatrix} 4 & -5 \\ 3 & k \end{bmatrix} = \begin{bmatrix} 23 & -10+5k \\ -9 & 15+k \end{bmatrix}$, while $BA = \begin{bmatrix} 4 & -5 \\ 3 & k \end{bmatrix} \begin{bmatrix} 2 & 5 \\ -3 & 1 \end{bmatrix} = \begin{bmatrix} 23 & 15 \\ 6-3k & 15+k \end{bmatrix}$.

Then $AB = BA$ if and only if $-10 + 5k = 15$ and $-9 = 6 - 3k$, which happens if and only if $k = 5$.

10. $AB = \begin{bmatrix} 2 & -3 \\ -4 & 6 \end{bmatrix} \begin{bmatrix} 8 & 4 \\ 5 & 5 \end{bmatrix} = \begin{bmatrix} 1 & -7 \\ -2 & 14 \end{bmatrix}$, $AC = \begin{bmatrix} 2 & -3 \\ -4 & 6 \end{bmatrix} \begin{bmatrix} 5 & -2 \\ 3 & 1 \end{bmatrix} = \begin{bmatrix} 1 & -7 \\ -2 & 14 \end{bmatrix}$

11. $AD = \begin{bmatrix} 1 & 1 & 1 \\ 1 & 2 & 3 \\ 1 & 4 & 5 \end{bmatrix} \begin{bmatrix} 2 & 0 & 0 \\ 0 & 3 & 0 \\ 0 & 0 & 5 \end{bmatrix} = \begin{bmatrix} 2 & 3 & 5 \\ 2 & 6 & 15 \\ 2 & 12 & 25 \end{bmatrix}$

$DA = \begin{bmatrix} 2 & 0 & 0 \\ 0 & 3 & 0 \\ 0 & 0 & 5 \end{bmatrix} \begin{bmatrix} 1 & 1 & 1 \\ 1 & 2 & 3 \\ 1 & 4 & 5 \end{bmatrix} = \begin{bmatrix} 2 & 2 & 2 \\ 3 & 6 & 9 \\ 5 & 20 & 25 \end{bmatrix}$

Right-multiplication (that is, multiplication on the right) by the diagonal matrix D multiplies each *column* of A by the corresponding diagonal entry of D. Left-multiplication by D multiplies each *row* of A by the corresponding diagonal entry of D. To make $AB = BA$, one can take B to be a multiple of I_3. For instance, if $B = 4I_3$, then AB and BA are both the same as $4A$.

12. Consider $B = [\mathbf{b}_1 \ \mathbf{b}_2]$. To make $AB = 0$, one needs $A\mathbf{b}_1 = \mathbf{0}$ and $A\mathbf{b}_2 = \mathbf{0}$. By inspection of A, a suitable $\mathbf{b}_1$ is $\begin{bmatrix} 2 \\ 1 \end{bmatrix}$, or any multiple of $\begin{bmatrix} 2 \\ 1 \end{bmatrix}$. Example: $B = \begin{bmatrix} 2 & 6 \\ 1 & 3 \end{bmatrix}$.

13. Use the definition of AB written in reverse order: $[A\mathbf{b}_1 \ \cdots \ A\mathbf{b}_p] = A[\mathbf{b}_1 \ \cdots \ \mathbf{b}_p]$. Thus
$[Q\mathbf{r}_1 \ \cdots \ Q\mathbf{r}_p] = QR$, when $R = [\mathbf{r}_1 \ \cdots \ \mathbf{r}_p]$.

14. By definition, $UQ = U[\mathbf{q}_1 \ \cdots \ \mathbf{q}_4] = [U\mathbf{q}_1 \ \cdots \ U\mathbf{q}_4]$. From Example 6 of Section 1.8, the vector $U\mathbf{q}_1$ lists the total costs (material, labor, and overhead) corresponding to the amounts of products B and C specified in the vector $\mathbf{q}_1$. That is, the first column of UQ lists the total costs for materials, labor, and overhead used to manufacture products B and C during the first quarter of the year. Columns 2, 3, and 4 of UQ list the total amounts spent to manufacture B and C during the 2nd, 3rd, and 4th quarters, respectively.

15. a. False. See the definition of AB.

   b. False. The roles of A and B should be reversed in the second half of the statement. See the box after Example 3.

   c. True. See Theorem 2(b), read right to left.

   d. True. See Theorem 3(b), read right to left.

   e. False. The phrase "in the same order" should be "in the reverse order." See the box after Theorem 3.

16. a. False. AB must be a 3×3 matrix, but the formula for AB implies that it is 3×1. The plus signs should be just spaces (between columns). This is a common mistake.

   b. True. See the box after Example 6.

   c. False. The left-to-right order of B and C cannot be changed, in general.

d. False. See Theorem 3(d).

e. True. This general statement follows from Theorem 3(b).

17. Since $\begin{bmatrix} -1 & 2 & -1 \\ 6 & -9 & 3 \end{bmatrix} = AB = \begin{bmatrix} A\mathbf{b}_1 & A\mathbf{b}_2 & A\mathbf{b}_3 \end{bmatrix}$, the first column of B satisfies the equation

$A\mathbf{x} = \begin{bmatrix} -1 \\ 6 \end{bmatrix}$. Row reduction: $\begin{bmatrix} A & A\mathbf{b}_1 \end{bmatrix} \sim \begin{bmatrix} 1 & -2 & -1 \\ -2 & 5 & 6 \end{bmatrix} \sim \begin{bmatrix} 1 & 0 & 7 \\ 0 & 1 & 4 \end{bmatrix}$. So $\mathbf{b}_1 = \begin{bmatrix} 7 \\ 4 \end{bmatrix}$. Similarly,

$\begin{bmatrix} A & A\mathbf{b}_2 \end{bmatrix} \sim \begin{bmatrix} 1 & -2 & 2 \\ -2 & 5 & -9 \end{bmatrix} \sim \begin{bmatrix} 1 & 0 & -8 \\ 0 & 1 & -5 \end{bmatrix}$ and $\mathbf{b}_2 = \begin{bmatrix} -8 \\ -5 \end{bmatrix}$.

Note: An alternative solution of Exercise 17 is to row reduce $\begin{bmatrix} A & A\mathbf{b}_1 & A\mathbf{b}_2 \end{bmatrix}$ with one sequence of row operations. This observation can prepare the way for the inversion algorithm in Section 2.2.

18. The first two columns of AB are $A\mathbf{b}_1$ and $A\mathbf{b}_2$. They are equal since $\mathbf{b}_1$ and $\mathbf{b}_2$ are equal.

19. (A solution is in the text). Write $B = [\mathbf{b}_1 \ \mathbf{b}_2 \ \mathbf{b}_3]$. By definition, the third column of AB is $A\mathbf{b}_3$. By hypothesis, $\mathbf{b}_3 = \mathbf{b}_1 + \mathbf{b}_2$. So $A\mathbf{b}_3 = A(\mathbf{b}_1 + \mathbf{b}_2) = A\mathbf{b}_1 + A\mathbf{b}_2$, by a property of matrix-vector multiplication. Thus, the third column of AB is the sum of the first two columns of AB.

20. The second column of AB is also all zeros because $A\mathbf{b}_2 = A\mathbf{0} = \mathbf{0}$.

21. Let $\mathbf{b}_p$ be the last column of B. By hypothesis, the last column of AB is zero. Thus, $A\mathbf{b}_p = \mathbf{0}$. However, $\mathbf{b}_p$ is not the zero vector, because B has no column of zeros. Thus, the equation $A\mathbf{b}_p = \mathbf{0}$ is a linear dependence relation among the columns of A, and so the columns of A are linearly dependent.

Note: The text answer for Exercise 21 is, "The columns of A are linearly dependent. Why?" The *Study Guide* supplies the argument above, in case a student needs help.

22. If the columns of B are linearly dependent, then there exists a nonzero vector $\mathbf{x}$ such that $B\mathbf{x} = \mathbf{0}$. From this, $A(B\mathbf{x}) = A\mathbf{0}$ and $(AB)\mathbf{x} = \mathbf{0}$ (by associativity). Since $\mathbf{x}$ is nonzero, the columns of AB must be linearly dependent.

23. If $\mathbf{x}$ satisfies $A\mathbf{x} = \mathbf{0}$, then $CA\mathbf{x} = C\mathbf{0} = \mathbf{0}$ and so $I_n\mathbf{x} = \mathbf{0}$ and $\mathbf{x} = \mathbf{0}$. This shows that the equation $A\mathbf{x} = \mathbf{0}$ has no free variables. So every variable is a basic variable and every column of A is a pivot column. (A variation of this argument could be made using linear independence and Exercise 30 in Section 1.7.) Since each pivot is in a different row, A must have at least as many rows as columns.

24. Take any $\mathbf{b}$ in $\mathbf{R}^m$. By hypothesis, $AD\mathbf{b} = I_m\mathbf{b} = \mathbf{b}$. Rewrite this equation as $A(D\mathbf{b}) = \mathbf{b}$. Thus, the vector $\mathbf{x} = D\mathbf{b}$ satisfies $A\mathbf{x} = \mathbf{b}$. This proves that the equation $A\mathbf{x} = \mathbf{b}$ has a solution for each $\mathbf{b}$ in $\mathbf{R}^m$. By Theorem 4 in Section 1.4, A has a pivot position in each row. Since each pivot is in a different column, A must have at least as many columns as rows.

25. By Exercise 23, the equation $CA = I_n$ implies that (number of rows in A) $\geq$ (number of columns), that is, $m \geq n$. By Exercise 24, the equation $AD = I_m$ implies that (number of rows in A) $\leq$ (number of columns), that is, $m \leq n$. Thus $m = n$. To prove the second statement, observe that $DAC = (DA)C = I_nC = C$, and also $DAC = D(AC) = DI_m = D$. Thus $C = D$. A shorter calculation is

$$C = I_nC = (DA)C = D(AC) = DI_n = D$$

26. Write $I_3 = [\mathbf{e}_1 \ \mathbf{e}_2 \ \mathbf{e}_3]$ and $D = [\mathbf{d}_1 \ \mathbf{d}_2 \ \mathbf{d}_3]$. By definition of AD, the equation $AD = I_3$ is equivalent to the three equations $A\mathbf{d}_1 = \mathbf{e}_1$, $A\mathbf{d}_2 = \mathbf{e}_2$, and $A\mathbf{d}_3 = \mathbf{e}_3$. Each of these equations has at least one solution because the columns of A span $\mathbf{R}^3$. (See Theorem 4 in Section 1.4.) Select one solution of each equation and use them for the columns of D. Then $AD = I_3$.

27. The product $\mathbf{u}^T\mathbf{v}$ is a 1×1 matrix, which usually is identified with a real number and is written without the matrix brackets.

$$\mathbf{u}^T\mathbf{v} = \begin{bmatrix} -2 & 3 & -4 \end{bmatrix} \begin{bmatrix} a \\ b \\ c \end{bmatrix} = -2a + 3b - 4c, \quad \mathbf{v}^T\mathbf{u} = \begin{bmatrix} a & b & c \end{bmatrix} \begin{bmatrix} -2 \\ 3 \\ -4 \end{bmatrix} = -2a + 3b - 4c$$

$$\mathbf{u}\mathbf{v}^T = \begin{bmatrix} -2 \\ 3 \\ -4 \end{bmatrix} \begin{bmatrix} a & b & c \end{bmatrix} = \begin{bmatrix} -2a & -2b & -2c \\ 3a & 3b & 3c \\ -4a & -4b & -4c \end{bmatrix}$$

$$\mathbf{v}\mathbf{u}^T = \begin{bmatrix} a \\ b \\ c \end{bmatrix} \begin{bmatrix} -2 & 3 & -4 \end{bmatrix} = \begin{bmatrix} -2a & 3a & -4a \\ -2b & 3b & -4b \\ -2c & 3c & -4c \end{bmatrix}$$

28. Since the inner product $\mathbf{u}^T\mathbf{v}$ is a real number, it equals its transpose. That is,
$\mathbf{u}^T\mathbf{v} = (\mathbf{u}^T\mathbf{v})^T = \mathbf{v}^T(\mathbf{u}^T)^T = \mathbf{v}^T\mathbf{u}$, by Theorem 3(d) regarding the transpose of a product of matrices and by Theorem 3(a). The outer product $\mathbf{u}\mathbf{v}^T$ is an $n\times n$ matrix. By Theorem 3, $(\mathbf{u}\mathbf{v}^T)^T = (\mathbf{v}^T)^T\mathbf{u}^T = \mathbf{v}\mathbf{u}^T$.

29. The (i, j)-entry of $A(B + C)$ equals the (i, j)-entry of $AB + AC$, because

$$\sum_{k=1}^{n} a_{ik}(b_{kj} + c_{kj}) = \sum_{k=1}^{n} a_{ik}b_{kj} + \sum_{k=1}^{n} a_{ik}c_{kj}$$

The (i, j)-entry of $(B + C)A$ equals the (i, j)-entry of $BA + CA$, because

$$\sum_{k=1}^{n} (b_{ik} + c_{ik})a_{kj} = \sum_{k=1}^{n} b_{ik}a_{kj} + \sum_{k=1}^{n} c_{ik}a_{kj}$$

30. The (i, j)-entries of $r(AB)$, $(rA)B$, and $A(rB)$ are all equal, because

$$r\sum_{k=1}^{n} a_{ik}b_{kj} = \sum_{k=1}^{n} (ra_{ik})b_{kj} = \sum_{k=1}^{n} a_{ik}(rb_{kj})$$

31. Use the definition of the product I_mA and the fact that $I_m\mathbf{x} = \mathbf{x}$ for $\mathbf{x}$ in $\mathbf{R}^m$.
$$I_mA = I_m[\mathbf{a}_1 \ \cdots \ \mathbf{a}_n] = [I_m\mathbf{a}_1 \ \cdots \ I_m\mathbf{a}_n] = [\mathbf{a}_1 \ \cdots \ \mathbf{a}_n] = A$$

32. Let $\mathbf{e}_j$ and $\mathbf{a}_j$ denote the jth columns of I_n and A, respectively. By definition, the jth column of AI_n is $A\mathbf{e}_j$, which is simply $\mathbf{a}_j$ because $\mathbf{e}_j$ has 1 in the jth position and zeros elsewhere. Thus corresponding columns of AI_n and A are equal. Hence $AI_n = A$.

33. The (i, j)-entry of $(AB)^T$ is the (j, i)-entry of AB, which is
$$a_{j1}b_{1i} + \cdots + a_{jn}b_{ni}$$

The entries in row i of B^T are $b_{1i}, \ldots, b_{ni}$, because they come from column i of B. Likewise, the entries in column j of A^T are $a_{j1}, \ldots, a_{jn}$, because they come from row j of A. Thus the (i, j)-entry in B^TA^T is $a_{j1}b_{1i} + \cdots + a_{jn}b_{ni}$, as above.

34. Use Theorem 3(d), treating $\mathbf{x}$ as an $n\times1$ matrix: $(AB\mathbf{x})^T = \mathbf{x}^T(AB)^T = \mathbf{x}^TB^TA^T$.

35. **[M]** The answer here depends on the choice of matrix program. For MATLAB, use the **help** command to read about **zeros**, **ones**, **eye**, and **diag**. For other programs see the appendices in the *Study Guide*. (The TI calculators have fewer single commands that produce special matrices.)

36. [M] The answer depends on the choice of matrix program. In MATLAB, the command `rand(6,4)` creates a 6×4 matrix with random entries uniformly distributed between 0 and 1. The command

   `round(19*(rand(6,4)-.5))`

creates a random 6×4 matrix with integer entries between –9 and 9. The same result is produced by the command `randomint` in the Laydata Toolbox on text website. For other matrix programs see the appendices in the *Study Guide*.

37. [M] $(A + I)(A - I) - (A^2 - I) = 0$ for all 4×4 matrices. However, $(A + B)(A - B) - A^2 - B^2$ is the zero matrix only in the special cases when $AB = BA$. In general,

$$(A + B)(A - B) = A(A - B) + B(A - B) = AA - AB + BA - BB.$$

38. [M] The equality $(AB)^T = A^T B^T$ is very likely to be false for 4×4 matrices selected at random.

39. [M] The matrix S "shifts" the entries in a vector (a, b, c, d, e) to yield $(b, c, d, e, 0)$. The entries in S^2 result from applying S to the columns of S, and similarly for S^3, and so on. This explains the patterns of entries in the powers of S:

$$S^2 = \begin{bmatrix} 0 & 0 & 1 & 0 & 0 \\ 0 & 0 & 0 & 1 & 0 \\ 0 & 0 & 0 & 0 & 1 \\ 0 & 0 & 0 & 0 & 0 \\ 0 & 0 & 0 & 0 & 0 \end{bmatrix}, S^3 = \begin{bmatrix} 0 & 0 & 0 & 1 & 0 \\ 0 & 0 & 0 & 0 & 1 \\ 0 & 0 & 0 & 0 & 0 \\ 0 & 0 & 0 & 0 & 0 \\ 0 & 0 & 0 & 0 & 0 \end{bmatrix}, S^4 = \begin{bmatrix} 0 & 0 & 0 & 0 & 1 \\ 0 & 0 & 0 & 0 & 0 \\ 0 & 0 & 0 & 0 & 0 \\ 0 & 0 & 0 & 0 & 0 \\ 0 & 0 & 0 & 0 & 0 \end{bmatrix}$$

S^5 is the 5×5 zero matrix. S^6 is also the 5×5 zero matrix.

40. [M] $A^5 = \begin{bmatrix} .3318 & .3346 & .3336 \\ .3346 & .3323 & .3331 \\ .3336 & .3331 & .3333 \end{bmatrix}, A^{10} = \begin{bmatrix} .333337 & .333330 & .333333 \\ .333330 & .333336 & .333334 \\ .333333 & .333334 & .333333 \end{bmatrix}$

The entries in A^{20} all agree with .3333333333 to 9 or 10 decimal places. The entries in A^{30} all agree with .33333333333333 to at least 14 decimal places. The matrices appear to approach the matrix $\begin{bmatrix} 1/3 & 1/3 & 1/3 \\ 1/3 & 1/3 & 1/3 \\ 1/3 & 1/3 & 1/3 \end{bmatrix}$. Further exploration of this behavior appears in Sections 4.9 and 5.2.

Note: The MATLAB box in the *Study Guide* introduces basic matrix notation and operations, including the commands that create special matrices needed in Exercises 35, 36 and elsewhere. The *Study Guide* appendices treat the corresponding information for the other matrix programs.

2.2   SOLUTIONS

Notes: The text includes the matrix inversion algorithm at the end of the section because this topic is popular. Students like it because it is a simple mechanical procedure. However, I no longer cover it in my classes because technology is readily available to invert a matrix whenever needed, and class time is better spent on more useful topics such as partitioned matrices. The final subsection is independent of the inversion algorithm and is needed for Exercises 35 and 36.

Key Exercises: 8, 11–24, 35. (Actually, Exercise 8 is only helpful for some exercises in this section. Section 2.3 has a stronger result.) Exercises 23 and 24 are used in the proof of the Invertible Matrix Theorem (IMT) in Section 2.3, along with Exercises 23 and 24 in Section 2.1. I recommend letting students work on two or more of these four exercises before proceeding to Section 2.3. In this way students *participate* in the proof of the IMT rather than simply watch an instructor carry out the proof. Also, this activity will help students understand *why* the theorem is true.

1. $\begin{bmatrix} 8 & 6 \\ 5 & 4 \end{bmatrix}^{-1} = \dfrac{1}{32-30}\begin{bmatrix} 4 & -6 \\ -5 & 8 \end{bmatrix} = \begin{bmatrix} 2 & -3 \\ -5/2 & 4 \end{bmatrix}$

2. $\begin{bmatrix} 3 & 2 \\ 7 & 4 \end{bmatrix}^{-1} = \dfrac{1}{12-14}\begin{bmatrix} 4 & -2 \\ -7 & 3 \end{bmatrix} = \begin{bmatrix} -2 & 1 \\ 7/2 & -3/2 \end{bmatrix}$

3. $\begin{bmatrix} 8 & 5 \\ -7 & -5 \end{bmatrix}^{-1} = \dfrac{1}{-40-(-35)}\begin{bmatrix} -5 & -5 \\ 7 & 8 \end{bmatrix} = -\dfrac{1}{5}\begin{bmatrix} -5 & -5 \\ 7 & 8 \end{bmatrix}$ or $\begin{bmatrix} 1 & 1 \\ -1.4 & -1.6 \end{bmatrix}$

4. $\begin{bmatrix} 3 & -4 \\ 7 & -8 \end{bmatrix}^{-1} = \dfrac{1}{-24-(-28)}\begin{bmatrix} -8 & 4 \\ -7 & 3 \end{bmatrix} = \dfrac{1}{4}\begin{bmatrix} -8 & 4 \\ -7 & 3 \end{bmatrix}$ or $\begin{bmatrix} -2 & 1 \\ -7/4 & 3/4 \end{bmatrix}$

5. The system is equivalent to $A\mathbf{x} = \mathbf{b}$, where $A = \begin{bmatrix} 8 & 6 \\ 5 & 4 \end{bmatrix}$ and $\mathbf{b} = \begin{bmatrix} 2 \\ -1 \end{bmatrix}$, and the solution is

$\mathbf{x} = A^{-1}\mathbf{b} = \begin{bmatrix} 2 & -3 \\ -5/2 & 4 \end{bmatrix}\begin{bmatrix} 2 \\ -1 \end{bmatrix} = \begin{bmatrix} 7 \\ -9 \end{bmatrix}$. Thus $x_1 = 7$ and $x_2 = -9$.

6. The system is equivalent to $A\mathbf{x} = \mathbf{b}$, where $A = \begin{bmatrix} 8 & 5 \\ -7 & -5 \end{bmatrix}$ and $\mathbf{b} = \begin{bmatrix} 9 \\ 11 \end{bmatrix}$, and the solution is $\mathbf{x} = A^{-1}\mathbf{b}$. To

compute this by hand, the arithmetic is simplified by keeping the fraction $1/\det(A)$ in front of the matrix for A^{-1}. (The *Study Guide* comments on this in its discussion of Exercise 7.) From Exercise 3,

$\mathbf{x} = A^{-1}\mathbf{b} = -\dfrac{1}{5}\begin{bmatrix} -5 & -5 \\ 7 & 8 \end{bmatrix}\begin{bmatrix} -9 \\ 11 \end{bmatrix} = -\dfrac{1}{5}\begin{bmatrix} -10 \\ 25 \end{bmatrix} = \begin{bmatrix} 2 \\ -5 \end{bmatrix}$. Thus $x_1 = 2$ and $x_2 = -5$.

7. **a.** $\begin{bmatrix} 1 & 2 \\ 5 & 12 \end{bmatrix}^{-1} = \dfrac{1}{1\cdot 12 - 2\cdot 5}\begin{bmatrix} 12 & -2 \\ -5 & 1 \end{bmatrix} = \dfrac{1}{2}\begin{bmatrix} 12 & -2 \\ -5 & 1 \end{bmatrix}$ or $\begin{bmatrix} 6 & -1 \\ -2.5 & .5 \end{bmatrix}$

$\mathbf{x} = A^{-1}\mathbf{b}_1 = \dfrac{1}{2}\begin{bmatrix} 12 & -2 \\ -5 & 1 \end{bmatrix}\begin{bmatrix} -1 \\ 3 \end{bmatrix} = \dfrac{1}{2}\begin{bmatrix} -18 \\ 8 \end{bmatrix} = \begin{bmatrix} -9 \\ 4 \end{bmatrix}$. Similar calculations give

$A^{-1}\mathbf{b}_2 = \begin{bmatrix} 11 \\ -5 \end{bmatrix}, A^{-1}\mathbf{b}_3 = \begin{bmatrix} 6 \\ -2 \end{bmatrix}, A^{-1}\mathbf{b}_4 = \begin{bmatrix} 13 \\ -5 \end{bmatrix}$.

b. $[A \ \mathbf{b}_1 \ \mathbf{b}_2 \ \mathbf{b}_3 \ \mathbf{b}_4] = \begin{bmatrix} 1 & 2 & -1 & 1 & 2 & 3 \\ 5 & 12 & 3 & -5 & 6 & 5 \end{bmatrix}$

$\sim \begin{bmatrix} 1 & 2 & -1 & 1 & 2 & 3 \\ 0 & 2 & 8 & -10 & -4 & -10 \end{bmatrix} \sim \begin{bmatrix} 1 & 2 & -1 & 1 & 2 & 3 \\ 0 & 1 & 4 & -5 & -2 & -5 \end{bmatrix}$

$\sim \begin{bmatrix} 1 & 0 & -9 & 11 & 6 & 13 \\ 0 & 1 & 4 & -5 & -2 & -5 \end{bmatrix}$

The solutions are $\begin{bmatrix} -9 \\ 4 \end{bmatrix}, \begin{bmatrix} 11 \\ -5 \end{bmatrix}, \begin{bmatrix} 6 \\ -2 \end{bmatrix}$, and $\begin{bmatrix} 13 \\ -5 \end{bmatrix}$, the same as in part (a).

Note: The *Study Guide* also discusses the number of arithmetic calculations for this Exercise 7, stating that when A is large, the method used in (b) is much faster than using A^{-1}.

8. Left-multiply each side of the equation $AD = I$ by A^{-1} to obtain
$$A^{-1}AD = A^{-1}I, \; ID = A^{-1}, \text{ and } D = A^{-1}.$$
Parentheses are routinely suppressed because of the associative property of matrix multiplication.

9. **a**. True, by definition of *invertible*.   **b**. False. See Theorem 6(b).

   c. False. If $A = \begin{bmatrix} 1 & 1 \\ 0 & 0 \end{bmatrix}$, then $ab - cd = 1 - 0 \neq 0$, but Theorem 4 shows that this matrix is not invertible, because $ad - bc = 0$.

   d. True. This follows from Theorem 5, which also says that the solution of $A\mathbf{x} = \mathbf{b}$ is unique, for each $\mathbf{b}$.

   e. True, by the box just before Example 6.

10. **a**. False. The product matrix is invertible, but the product of inverses should be in the *reverse* order. See Theorem 6(b).

   b. True, by Theorem 6(a).   **c**. True, by Theorem 4.

   d. True, by Theorem 7.   **e**. False. The last part of Theorem 7 is misstated here.

11. (The proof can be modeled after the proof of Theorem 5.) The $n \times p$ matrix B is given (but is arbitrary). Since A is invertible, the matrix $A^{-1}B$ satisfies $AX = B$, because $A(A^{-1}B) = A\, A^{-1}B = IB = B$. To show this solution is unique, let X be any solution of $AX = B$. Then, left-multiplication of each side by A^{-1} shows that X must be $A^{-1}B$:
$$A^{-1}(AX) = A^{-1}B, \quad IX = A^{-1}B, \quad \text{and} \quad X = A^{-1}B.$$

12. If you assign this exercise, consider giving the following *Hint*: Use elementary matrices and imitate the proof of Theorem 7. The solution in the Instructor's Edition follows this hint. Here is another solution, based on the idea at the end of Section 2.2.

   Write $B = [\mathbf{b}_1 \; \cdots \; \mathbf{b}_p]$ and $X = [\mathbf{u}_1 \; \cdots \; \mathbf{u}_p]$. By definition of matrix multiplication, $AX = [A\mathbf{u}_1 \; \cdots \; A\mathbf{u}_p]$. Thus, the equation $AX = B$ is equivalent to the p systems:
$$A\mathbf{u}_1 = \mathbf{b}_1, \quad \ldots \quad A\mathbf{u}_p = \mathbf{b}_p$$
Since A is the coefficient matrix in each system, these systems may be solved simultaneously, placing the augmented columns of these systems next to A to form $[A \; \mathbf{b}_1 \; \cdots \; \mathbf{b}_p] = [A \; B]$. Since A is invertible, the solutions $\mathbf{u}_1, \ldots, \mathbf{u}_p$ are uniquely determined, and $[A \; \mathbf{b}_1 \; \cdots \; \mathbf{b}_p]$ must row reduce to $[I \; \mathbf{u}_1 \; \cdots \; \mathbf{u}_p] = [I \; X]$. By Exercise 11, X is the unique solution $A^{-1}B$ of $AX = B$.

13. Left-multiply each side of the equation $AB = AC$ by A^{-1} to obtain
$$A^{-1}AB = A^{-1}AC, \quad IB = IC, \quad \text{and} \quad B = C.$$
This conclusion does not always follow when A is singular. Exercise 10 of Section 2.1 provides a counterexample.

14. Right-multiply each side of the equation $(B - C)D = 0$ by D^{-1} to obtain
$$(B - C)DD^{-1} = 0D^{-1}, \quad (B - C)I = 0, \quad B - C = 0, \quad \text{and} \quad B = C.$$

15. The box following Theorem 6 suggests what the inverse of ABC should be, namely, $C^{-1}B^{-1}A^{-1}$. To verify that this is correct, compute:
$$(ABC)\, C^{-1}B^{-1}A^{-1} = ABCC^{-1}B^{-1}A^{-1} = ABIB^{-1}A^{-1} = ABB^{-1}A^{-1} = AIA^{-1} = AA^{-1} = I$$
and
$$C^{-1}B^{-1}A^{-1}(ABC) = C^{-1}B^{-1}A^{-1}ABC = C^{-1}B^{-1}IBC = C^{-1}B^{-1}BC = C^{-1}IC = C^{-1}C = I$$

16. Let $C = AB$. Then $CB^{-1} = ABB^{-1}$, so $CB^{-1} = AI = A$. This shows that A is the product of invertible matrices and hence is invertible, by Theorem 6.

Note: The *Study Guide* warns against using the formula $(AB)^{-1} = B^{-1}A^{-1}$ here, because this formula can be used only when both A and B are already known to be invertible.

17. Right-multiply each side of $AB = BC$ by B^{-1}:

$$ABB^{-1} = BCB^{-1}, \quad AI = BCB^{-1}, \quad A = BCB^{-1}.$$

18. Left-multiply each side of $A = PBP^{-1}$ by P^{-1}:

$$P^{-1}A = P^{-1}PBP^{-1}, \quad P^{-1}A = IBP^{-1}, \quad P^{-1}A = BP^{-1}$$

Then right-multiply each side of the result by P:

$$P^{-1}AP = BP^{-1}P, \quad P^{-1}AP = BI, \quad P^{-1}AP = B$$

19. Unlike Exercise 17, this exercise asks two things, "Does a solution exist and what is it?" First, find what the solution must be, if it exists. That is, suppose X satisfies the equation $C^{-1}(A + X)B^{-1} = I$. Left-multiply each side by C, and then right-multiply each side by B:

$$CC^{-1}(A + X)B^{-1} = CI, \quad I(A + X)B^{-1} = C, \quad (A + X)B^{-1}B = CB, \quad (A + X)I = CB$$

Expand the left side and then subtract A from both sides:

$$AI + XI = CB, \quad A + X = CB, \quad X = CB - A$$

If a solution exists, it must be $CB - A$. To show that $CB - A$ really *is* a solution, substitute it for X:

$$C^{-1}[A + (CB - A)]B^{-1} = C^{-1}[CB]B^{-1} = C^{-1}CBB^{-1} = II = I.$$

Note: The *Study Guide* suggests that students ask their instructor about how many details to include in their proofs. After some practice with algebra, an expression such as $CC^{-1}(A + X)B^{-1}$ could be simplified directly to $(A + X)B^{-1}$ without first replacing CC^{-1} by I. However, you may wish this detail to be included in the homework for this section.

20. **a**. Left-multiply both sides of $(A - AX)^{-1} = X^{-1}B$ by X to see that B is invertible because it is the product of invertible matrices.

   b. Invert both sides of the original equation and use Theorem 6 about the inverse of a product (which applies because X^{-1} and B are invertible):

$$A - AX = (X^{-1}B)^{-1} = B^{-1}(X^{-1})^{-1} = B^{-1}X$$

   Then $A = AX + B^{-1}X = (A + B^{-1})X$. The product $(A + B^{-1})X$ is invertible because A is invertible. Since X is known to be invertible, so is the other factor, $A + B^{-1}$, by Exercise 16 or by an argument similar to part (a). Finally,

$$(A + B^{-1})^{-1}A = (A + B^{-1})^{-1}(A + B^{-1})X = X$$

Note: This exercise is difficult. The algebra is not trivial, and at this point in the course, most students will not recognize the need to verify that a matrix is invertible.

21. Suppose A is invertible. By Theorem 5, the equation $A\mathbf{x} = \mathbf{0}$ has only one solution, namely, the zero solution. This means that the columns of A are linearly independent, by a remark in Section 1.7.

22. Suppose A is invertible. By Theorem 5, the equation $A\mathbf{x} = \mathbf{b}$ has a solution (in fact, a unique solution) for each $\mathbf{b}$. By Theorem 4 in Section 1.4, the columns of A span $\mathbf{R}^n$.

23. Suppose A is $n \times n$ and the equation $A\mathbf{x} = \mathbf{0}$ has only the trivial solution. Then there are no free variables in this equation, and so A has n pivot columns. Since A is *square* and the n pivot positions must be in different rows, the pivots in an echelon form of A must be on the main diagonal. Hence A is row equivalent to the $n \times n$ identity matrix.

24. If the equation $A\mathbf{x} = \mathbf{b}$ has a solution for each $\mathbf{b}$ in $\mathbf{R}^n$, then A has a pivot position in each row, by Theorem 4 in Section 1.4. Since A is square, the pivots must be on the diagonal of A. It follows that A is row equivalent to I_n. By Theorem 7, A is invertible.

25. Suppose $A = \begin{bmatrix} a & b \\ c & d \end{bmatrix}$ and $ad - bc = 0$. If $a = b = 0$, then examine $\begin{bmatrix} 0 & 0 \\ c & d \end{bmatrix} \begin{bmatrix} x_1 \\ x_2 \end{bmatrix} = \begin{bmatrix} 0 \\ 0 \end{bmatrix}$ This has the

solution $\mathbf{x}_1 = \begin{bmatrix} d \\ -c \end{bmatrix}$. This solution is nonzero, except when $a = b = c = d$. In that case, however, A is the

zero matrix, and $A\mathbf{x} = \mathbf{0}$ for *every* vector $\mathbf{x}$. Finally, if a and b are not both zero, set $\mathbf{x}_2 = \begin{bmatrix} -b \\ a \end{bmatrix}$. Then

$$A\mathbf{x}_2 = \begin{bmatrix} a & b \\ c & d \end{bmatrix} \begin{bmatrix} -b \\ a \end{bmatrix} = \begin{bmatrix} -ab + ba \\ -cb + da \end{bmatrix} = \begin{bmatrix} 0 \\ 0 \end{bmatrix}, \text{ because } -cb + da = 0. \text{ Thus, } \mathbf{x}_2 \text{ is a nontrivial solution of } A\mathbf{x} = \mathbf{0}.$$

So, in all cases, the equation $A\mathbf{x} = \mathbf{0}$ has more than one solution. This is impossible when A is invertible (by Theorem 5), so A is *not* invertible.

26. $\begin{bmatrix} d & -b \\ -c & a \end{bmatrix} \begin{bmatrix} a & b \\ c & d \end{bmatrix} = \begin{bmatrix} da - bc & 0 \\ 0 & -cb + ad \end{bmatrix}$. Divide both sides by $ad - bc$ to get $CA = I$.

$\begin{bmatrix} a & b \\ c & d \end{bmatrix} \begin{bmatrix} d & -b \\ -c & a \end{bmatrix} = \begin{bmatrix} ad - bc & 0 \\ 0 & -cb + da \end{bmatrix}$.

Divide both sides by $ad - bc$. The right side is I. The left side is AC, because

$$\frac{1}{ad - bc} \begin{bmatrix} a & b \\ c & d \end{bmatrix} \begin{bmatrix} d & -b \\ -c & a \end{bmatrix} = \begin{bmatrix} a & b \\ c & d \end{bmatrix} \frac{1}{ad - bc} \begin{bmatrix} d & -b \\ -c & a \end{bmatrix} = AC$$

27. a. Interchange A and B in equation (1) after Example 6 in Section 2.1: $\text{row}_i(BA) = \text{row}_i(B) \cdot A$. Then replace B by the identity matrix: $\text{row}_i(A) = \text{row}_i(IA) = \text{row}_i(I) \cdot A$.

b. Using part (a), when rows 1 and 2 of A are interchanged, write the result as

$$\begin{bmatrix} \text{row}_2(A) \\ \text{row}_1(A) \\ \text{row}_3(A) \end{bmatrix} = \begin{bmatrix} \text{row}_2(I) \cdot A \\ \text{row}_1(I) \cdot A \\ \text{row}_3(I) \cdot A \end{bmatrix} = \begin{bmatrix} \text{row}_2(I) \\ \text{row}_1(I) \\ \text{row}_3(I) \end{bmatrix} A = EA \tag{*}$$

Here, E is obtained by interchanging rows 1 and 2 of I. The second equality in (*) is a consequence of the fact that $\text{row}_i(EA) = \text{row}_i(E) \cdot A$.

c. Using part (a), when row 3 of A is multiplied by 5, write the result as

$$\begin{bmatrix} \text{row}_1(A) \\ \text{row}_2(A) \\ 5 \cdot \text{row}_3(A) \end{bmatrix} = \begin{bmatrix} \text{row}_1(I) \cdot A \\ \text{row}_2(I) \cdot A \\ 5 \cdot \text{row}_3(I) \cdot A \end{bmatrix} = \begin{bmatrix} \text{row}_1(I) \\ \text{row}_2(I) \\ 5 \cdot \text{row}_3(I) \end{bmatrix} A = EA$$

Here, E is obtained by multiplying row 3 of I by 5.

28. When row 3 of A is replaced by $\text{row}_3(A) - 4 \cdot \text{row}_1(A)$, write the result as

$$\begin{bmatrix} \text{row}_1(A) \\ \text{row}_2(A) \\ \text{row}_3(A) - 4 \cdot \text{row}_1(A) \end{bmatrix} = \begin{bmatrix} \text{row}_1(I) \cdot A \\ \text{row}_2(I) \cdot A \\ \text{row}_3(I) \cdot A - 4 \cdot \text{row}_1(I) \cdot A \end{bmatrix}$$

$$= \begin{bmatrix} \text{row}_1(I) \cdot A \\ \text{row}_2(I) \cdot A \\ [\text{row}_3(I) - 4 \cdot \text{row}_1(I)] \cdot A \end{bmatrix} = \begin{bmatrix} \text{row}_1(I) \\ \text{row}_2(I) \\ \text{row}_3(I) - 4 \cdot \text{row}_1(I) \end{bmatrix} A = EA$$

Here, E is obtained by replacing $\text{row}_3(I)$ by $\text{row}_3(I) - 4 \cdot \text{row}_1(I)$.

29. $[A \ \ I] = \begin{bmatrix} 1 & 2 & 1 & 0 \\ 4 & 7 & 0 & 1 \end{bmatrix} \sim \begin{bmatrix} 1 & 2 & 1 & 0 \\ 0 & -1 & -4 & 1 \end{bmatrix} \sim \begin{bmatrix} 1 & 2 & 1 & 0 \\ 0 & 1 & 4 & -1 \end{bmatrix} \sim \begin{bmatrix} 1 & 0 & -7 & 2 \\ 0 & 1 & 4 & -1 \end{bmatrix}$

$A^{-1} = \begin{bmatrix} -7 & 2 \\ 4 & -1 \end{bmatrix}$

30. $[A \ \ I] = \begin{bmatrix} 5 & 10 & 1 & 0 \\ 4 & 7 & 0 & 1 \end{bmatrix} \sim \begin{bmatrix} 1 & 2 & 1/5 & 0 \\ 4 & 7 & 0 & 1 \end{bmatrix} \sim \begin{bmatrix} 1 & 2 & 1/5 & 0 \\ 0 & -1 & -4/5 & 1 \end{bmatrix}$

$\sim \begin{bmatrix} 1 & 2 & 1/5 & 0 \\ 0 & 1 & 4/5 & -1 \end{bmatrix} \sim \begin{bmatrix} 1 & 0 & -7/5 & 2 \\ 0 & 1 & 4/5 & -1 \end{bmatrix}$. $A^{-1} = \begin{bmatrix} -7/5 & 2 \\ 4/5 & -1 \end{bmatrix}$

31. $[A \ \ I] = \begin{bmatrix} 1 & 0 & -2 & 1 & 0 & 0 \\ -3 & 1 & 4 & 0 & 1 & 0 \\ 2 & -3 & 4 & 0 & 0 & 1 \end{bmatrix} \sim \begin{bmatrix} 1 & 0 & -2 & 1 & 0 & 0 \\ 0 & 1 & -2 & 3 & 1 & 0 \\ 0 & -3 & 8 & -2 & 0 & 1 \end{bmatrix}$

$\sim \begin{bmatrix} 1 & 0 & -2 & 1 & 0 & 0 \\ 0 & 1 & -2 & 3 & 1 & 0 \\ 0 & 0 & 2 & 7 & 3 & 1 \end{bmatrix} \sim \begin{bmatrix} 1 & 0 & 0 & 8 & 3 & 1 \\ 0 & 1 & 0 & 10 & 4 & 1 \\ 0 & 0 & 2 & 7 & 3 & 1 \end{bmatrix}$

$\sim \begin{bmatrix} 1 & 0 & 0 & 8 & 3 & 1 \\ 0 & 1 & 0 & 10 & 4 & 1 \\ 0 & 0 & 1 & 7/2 & 3/2 & 1/2 \end{bmatrix}$. $A^{-1} = \begin{bmatrix} 8 & 3 & 1 \\ 10 & 4 & 1 \\ 7/2 & 3/2 & 1/2 \end{bmatrix}$

32. $[A \ \ I] = \begin{bmatrix} 1 & -2 & 1 & 1 & 0 & 0 \\ 4 & -7 & 3 & 0 & 1 & 0 \\ -2 & 6 & -4 & 0 & 0 & 1 \end{bmatrix} \sim \begin{bmatrix} 1 & -2 & 1 & 1 & 0 & 0 \\ 0 & 1 & -1 & -4 & 1 & 0 \\ 0 & 2 & -2 & 2 & 0 & 1 \end{bmatrix}$

$\sim \begin{bmatrix} 1 & -2 & 1 & 1 & 0 & 0 \\ 0 & 1 & -1 & -4 & 1 & 0 \\ 0 & 0 & 0 & 10 & -2 & 1 \end{bmatrix}$. The matrix A is not invertible.

33. Let $B = \begin{bmatrix} 1 & 0 & 0 & \cdots & 0 \\ -1 & 1 & 0 & & 0 \\ 0 & -1 & 1 & & \\ \vdots & & \ddots & \ddots & \vdots \\ 0 & 0 & \cdots & -1 & 1 \end{bmatrix}$, and for $j = 1, \ldots, n$, let $\mathbf{a}_j$, $\mathbf{b}_j$, and $\mathbf{e}_j$ denote the jth columns of A, B,

and I, respectively. Note that for $j = 1, \ldots, n-1$, $\mathbf{a}_j - \mathbf{a}_{j+1} = \mathbf{e}_j$ (because $\mathbf{a}_j$ and $\mathbf{a}_{j+1}$ have the same entries except for the jth row), $\mathbf{b}_j = \mathbf{e}_j - \mathbf{e}_{j+1}$ and $\mathbf{a}_n = \mathbf{b}_n = \mathbf{e}_n$.

To show that $AB = I$, it suffices to show that $A\mathbf{b}_j = \mathbf{e}_j$ for each j. For $j = 1, \ldots, n-1$,

$A\mathbf{b}_j = A(\mathbf{e}_j - \mathbf{e}_{j+1}) = A\mathbf{e}_j - A\mathbf{e}_{j+1} = \mathbf{a}_j - \mathbf{a}_{j+1} = \mathbf{e}_j$

and $A\mathbf{b}_n = A\mathbf{e}_n = \mathbf{a}_n = \mathbf{e}_n$. Next, observe that $\mathbf{a}_j = \mathbf{e}_j + \cdots + \mathbf{e}_n$ for each j. Thus,

$$B\mathbf{a}_j = B(\mathbf{e}_j + \cdots + \mathbf{e}_n) = \mathbf{b}_j + \cdots + \mathbf{b}_n$$
$$= (\mathbf{e}_j - \mathbf{e}_{j+1}) + (\mathbf{e}_{j+1} - \mathbf{e}_{j+2}) + \cdots + (\mathbf{e}_{n-1} - \mathbf{e}_n) + \mathbf{e}_n = \mathbf{e}_j$$

This proves that $BA = I$. Combined with the first part, this proves that $B = A^{-1}$.

Note: Students who do this problem and then do the corresponding exercise in Section 2.4 will appreciate the Invertible Matrix Theorem, partitioned matrix notation, and the power of a proof by induction.

34. Let

$$A = \begin{bmatrix} 1 & 0 & 0 & \cdots & 0 \\ 1 & 2 & 0 & & 0 \\ 1 & 2 & 3 & & 0 \\ \vdots & & & \ddots & \vdots \\ 1 & 2 & 3 & \cdots & n \end{bmatrix}, \text{ and } B = \begin{bmatrix} 1 & 0 & 0 & \cdots & 0 \\ -1/2 & 1/2 & 0 & & \\ 0 & -1/3 & 1/3 & & \\ \vdots & & \ddots & \ddots & \vdots \\ 0 & 0 & & -1/n & 1/n \end{bmatrix}$$

and for $j = 1, \ldots, n$, let $\mathbf{a}_j$, $\mathbf{b}_j$, and $\mathbf{e}_j$ denote the jth columns of A, B, and I, respectively. Note that for $j = 1, \ldots, n-1$, $\mathbf{a}_j = j(\mathbf{e}_j + \cdots + \mathbf{e}_n)$, $\mathbf{b}_j = \dfrac{1}{j}\mathbf{e}_j - \dfrac{1}{j+1}\mathbf{e}_{j+1}$, and $\mathbf{b}_n = \dfrac{1}{n}\mathbf{e}_n$.

To show that $AB = I$, it suffices to show that $A\mathbf{b}_j = \mathbf{e}_j$ for each j. For $j = 1, \ldots, n-1$,

$$A\mathbf{b}_j = A\left(\frac{1}{j}\mathbf{e}_j - \frac{1}{j+1}\mathbf{e}_{j+1}\right) = \frac{1}{j}\mathbf{a}_j - \frac{1}{j+1}\mathbf{a}_{j+1}$$
$$= (\mathbf{e}_j + \cdots + \mathbf{e}_n) - (\mathbf{e}_{j+1} + \cdots + \mathbf{e}_n) = \mathbf{e}_j$$

Also, $A\mathbf{b}_n = A\left(\dfrac{1}{n}\mathbf{e}_n\right) = \dfrac{1}{n}\mathbf{a}_n = \mathbf{e}_n$. Finally, for $j = 1, \ldots, n$, the sum $\mathbf{b}_j + \cdots + \mathbf{b}_n$ is a "telescoping sum" whose value is $\dfrac{1}{j}\mathbf{e}_j$. Thus,

$$B\mathbf{a}_j = j(B\mathbf{e}_j + \cdots + B\mathbf{e}_n) = j(\mathbf{b}_j + \cdots + \mathbf{b}_n) = j\left(\frac{1}{j}\mathbf{e}_j\right) = \mathbf{e}_j$$

which proves that $BA = I$. Combined with the first part, this proves that $B = A^{-1}$.

Note: If you assign Exercise 34, you may wish to supply a hint using the notation from Exercise 33: Express each column of A in terms of the columns $\mathbf{e}_1, \ldots, \mathbf{e}_n$ of the identity matrix. Do the same for B.

35. Row reduce $[A \quad \mathbf{e}_3]$:

$$\begin{bmatrix} -2 & -7 & -9 & 0 \\ 2 & 5 & 6 & 0 \\ 1 & 3 & 4 & 1 \end{bmatrix} \sim \begin{bmatrix} 1 & 3 & 4 & 1 \\ 2 & 5 & 6 & 0 \\ -2 & -7 & -9 & 0 \end{bmatrix} \sim \begin{bmatrix} 1 & 3 & 4 & 1 \\ 0 & -1 & -2 & -2 \\ 0 & -1 & -1 & 2 \end{bmatrix} \sim \begin{bmatrix} 1 & 3 & 4 & 1 \\ 0 & -1 & -2 & -2 \\ 0 & 0 & 1 & 4 \end{bmatrix}$$

$$\sim \begin{bmatrix} 1 & 3 & 0 & -15 \\ 0 & -1 & 0 & 6 \\ 0 & 0 & 1 & 4 \end{bmatrix} \sim \begin{bmatrix} 1 & 3 & 0 & -15 \\ 0 & 1 & 0 & -6 \\ 0 & 0 & 1 & 4 \end{bmatrix} \sim \begin{bmatrix} 1 & 0 & 0 & 3 \\ 0 & 1 & 0 & -6 \\ 0 & 0 & 1 & 4 \end{bmatrix}.$$

Answer: The third column of A^{-1} is $\begin{bmatrix} 3 \\ -6 \\ 4 \end{bmatrix}$.

36. [M] Write $B = [A \quad F]$, where F consists of the last two columns of I_3, and row reduce:

$$B = \begin{bmatrix} -25 & -9 & -27 & 0 & 0 \\ 546 & 180 & 537 & 1 & 0 \\ 154 & 50 & 149 & 0 & 1 \end{bmatrix} \sim \begin{bmatrix} 1 & 0 & 0 & 3/2 & -9/2 \\ 0 & 1 & 0 & -433/6 & 439/2 \\ 0 & 0 & 1 & 68/3 & -69 \end{bmatrix}$$

The last two columns of A^{-1} are $\begin{bmatrix} 1.5000 & -4.5000 \\ -72.1667 & 219.5000 \\ 22.6667 & -69.0000 \end{bmatrix}$

37. There are many possibilities for C, but $C = \begin{bmatrix} 1 & 1 & -1 \\ -1 & 1 & 0 \end{bmatrix}$ is the only one whose entries are 1, –1, and 0.

With only three possibilities for each entry, the construction of C can be done by trial and error. This is probably faster than setting up a system of 4 equations in 6 unknowns. The fact that A cannot be invertible follows from Exercise 25 in Section 2.1, because A is not square.

38. Write $AD = A[\mathbf{d}_1 \quad \mathbf{d}_2] = [A\mathbf{d}_1 \quad A\mathbf{d}_2]$. The structure of A shows that $D = \begin{bmatrix} 1 & 0 \\ 0 & 0 \\ 0 & 0 \\ 0 & 1 \end{bmatrix}$.

[There are 25 possibilities for D if entries of D are allowed to be 1, –1, and 0.] There is *no* 4×2 matrix C such that $CA = I_4$. If this were true, then $CA\mathbf{x}$ would equal $\mathbf{x}$ for all $\mathbf{x}$ in $\mathbf{R}^4$. This cannot happen because the columns of A are linearly dependent and so $A\mathbf{x} = \mathbf{0}$ for some nonzero vector $\mathbf{x}$. For such an $\mathbf{x}$, $CA\mathbf{x} = C(\mathbf{0}) = \mathbf{0}$. An alternate justification would be to cite Exercise 23 or 25 in Section 2.1.

39. $\mathbf{y} = D\mathbf{f} = \begin{bmatrix} .005 & .002 & .001 \\ .002 & .004 & .002 \\ .001 & .002 & .005 \end{bmatrix}\begin{bmatrix} 30 \\ 50 \\ 20 \end{bmatrix} = \begin{bmatrix} .27 \\ .30 \\ .23 \end{bmatrix}$. The deflections are .27 in., .30 in., and .23 in. at points 1, 2, and 3, respectively.

40. [M] The *stiffness matrix* is D^{-1}. Use an "inverse" command to produce

$$D^{-1} = 125\begin{bmatrix} 2 & -1 & 0 \\ -1 & 3 & -1 \\ 0 & -1 & 2 \end{bmatrix}$$

To find the forces (in pounds) required to produce a deflection of .04 cm at point 3, most students will use technology to solve $D\mathbf{f} = (0, 0, .04)$ and obtain $(0, -5, 10)$.

Here is another method, based on the idea suggested in Exercise 42. The first column of D^{-1} lists the forces required to produce a deflection of 1 in. at point 1 (with zero deflection at the other points). Since the transformation $\mathbf{y} \mapsto D^{-1}\mathbf{y}$ is linear, the forces required to produce a deflection of .04 cm at point 3 is given by .04 times the third column of D^{-1}, namely $(.04)(125)$ times $(0, -1, 2)$, or $(0, -5, 10)$ pounds.

41. To determine the forces that produce a deflections of .08, .12, .16, and .12 cm at the four points on the beam, use technology to solve $D\mathbf{f} = \mathbf{y}$, where $\mathbf{y} = (.08, .12, .16, .12)$. The forces at the four points are 12, 1.5, 21.5, and 12 newtons, respectively.

42. **[M]** To determine the forces that produce a deflection of .240 cm at the second point on the beam, use technology to solve $D\mathbf{f} = \mathbf{y}$, where $\mathbf{y} = (0, .24, 0, 0)$. The forces at the four points are -104, 167, -113, and 56.0 newtons, respectively (to three significant digits). These forces are .24 times the entries in the second column of D^{-1}. *Reason*: The transformation $\mathbf{y} \mapsto D^{-1}\mathbf{y}$ is linear, so the forces required to produce a deflection of .24 cm at the second point are .24 times the forces required to produce a deflection of 1 cm at the second point. These forces are listed in the second column of D^{-1}.

Another possible discussion: The solution of $D\mathbf{x} = (0, 1, 0, 0)$ is the second column of D^{-1}. Multiply both sides of this equation by .24 to obtain $D(.24\mathbf{x}) = (0, .24, 0, 0)$. So $.24\mathbf{x}$ is the solution of $D\mathbf{f} = (0, .24, 0, 0)$. (The argument uses linearity, but students may not mention this.)

Note: The *Study Guide* suggests using **gauss**, **swap**, **bgauss**, and **scale** to reduce $[A \quad I]$, because I prefer to postpone the use of **ref** (or **rref**) until later. If you wish to introduce **ref** now, see the *Study Guide*'s technology notes for Sections 2.8 or 4.3. (Recall that Sections 2.8 and 2.9 are only covered when an instructor plans to skip Chapter 4 and get quickly to eigenvalues.)

2.3 SOLUTIONS

Notes: This section ties together most of the concepts studied thus far. With strong encouragement from an instructor, most students can use this opportunity to review and reflect upon what they have learned, and form a solid foundation for future work. Students who fail to do this now usually struggle throughout the rest of the course. Section 2.3 can be used in at least three different ways.

(1) Stop after Example 1 and assign exercises only from among the Practice Problems and Exercises 1 to 28. I do this when teaching "Course 3" described in the text's "Notes to the Instructor. " If you did not cover Theorem 12 in Section 1.9, omit statements (f) and (i) from the Invertible Matrix Theorem.

(2) Include the subsection "Invertible Linear Transformations" in Section 2.3, if you covered Section 1.9. I do this when teaching "Course 1" because our mathematics and computer science majors take this class. Exercises 29–40 support this material.

(3) Skip the linear transformation material here, but discusses the **condition number** and the Numerical Notes. Assign exercises from among 1–28 and 41–45, and perhaps add a computer project on the condition number. (See the projects on our web site.) I do this when teaching "Course 2" for our engineers.

The abbreviation IMT (here and in the *Study Guide*) denotes the Invertible Matrix Theorem (Theorem 8).

1. The columns of the matrix $\begin{bmatrix} 5 & 7 \\ -3 & -6 \end{bmatrix}$ are not multiples, so they are linearly independent. By (e) in the IMT, the matrix is invertible. Also, the matrix is invertible by Theorem 4 in Section 2.2 because the determinant is nonzero.

2. The fact that the columns of $\begin{bmatrix} -4 & 6 \\ 6 & -9 \end{bmatrix}$ are multiples is not so obvious. The fastest check in this case may be the determinant, which is easily seen to be zero. By Theorem 4 in Section 2.2, the matrix is not invertible.

3. Row reduction to echelon form is trivial because there is really no need for arithmetic calculations:

$\begin{bmatrix} 5 & 0 & 0 \\ -3 & -7 & 0 \\ 8 & 5 & -1 \end{bmatrix} \sim \begin{bmatrix} 5 & 0 & 0 \\ 0 & -7 & 0 \\ 0 & 5 & -1 \end{bmatrix} \sim \begin{bmatrix} 5 & 0 & 0 \\ 0 & -7 & 0 \\ 0 & 0 & -1 \end{bmatrix}$ The 3×3 matrix has 3 pivot positions and hence is invertible, by (c) of the IMT. [Another explanation could be given using the transposed matrix. But see the note below that follows the solution of Exercise 14.]

4. The matrix $\begin{bmatrix} -7 & 0 & 4 \\ 3 & 0 & -1 \\ 2 & 0 & 9 \end{bmatrix}$ obviously has linearly dependent columns (because one column is zero), and

so the matrix is not invertible (or singular) by (e) in the IMT.

5. $\begin{bmatrix} 0 & 3 & -5 \\ 1 & 0 & 2 \\ -4 & -9 & 7 \end{bmatrix} \sim \begin{bmatrix} 1 & 0 & 2 \\ 0 & 3 & -5 \\ -4 & -9 & 7 \end{bmatrix} \sim \begin{bmatrix} 1 & 0 & 2 \\ 0 & 3 & -5 \\ 0 & -9 & 15 \end{bmatrix} \sim \begin{bmatrix} 1 & 0 & 2 \\ 0 & 3 & -5 \\ 0 & 0 & 0 \end{bmatrix}$

The matrix is not invertible because it is not row equivalent to the identity matrix.

6. $\begin{bmatrix} 1 & -5 & -4 \\ 0 & 3 & 4 \\ -3 & 6 & 0 \end{bmatrix} \sim \begin{bmatrix} 1 & -5 & -4 \\ 0 & 3 & 4 \\ 0 & -9 & -12 \end{bmatrix} \sim \begin{bmatrix} 1 & -5 & -4 \\ 0 & 3 & 4 \\ 0 & 0 & 0 \end{bmatrix}$

The matrix is not invertible because it is not row equivalent to the identity matrix.

7. $\begin{bmatrix} -1 & -3 & 0 & 1 \\ 3 & 5 & 8 & -3 \\ -2 & -6 & 3 & 2 \\ 0 & -1 & 2 & 1 \end{bmatrix} \sim \begin{bmatrix} -1 & -3 & 0 & 1 \\ 0 & -4 & 8 & 0 \\ 0 & 0 & 3 & 0 \\ 0 & -1 & 2 & 1 \end{bmatrix} \sim \begin{bmatrix} -1 & -3 & 0 & 1 \\ 0 & -4 & 8 & 0 \\ 0 & 0 & 3 & 0 \\ 0 & 0 & 0 & 1 \end{bmatrix}$

The 4×4 matrix has four pivot positions and so is invertible by (c) of the IMT.

8. The 4×4 matrix $\begin{bmatrix} 1 & 3 & 7 & 4 \\ 0 & 5 & 9 & 6 \\ 0 & 0 & 2 & 8 \\ 0 & 0 & 0 & 10 \end{bmatrix}$ is invertible because it has four pivot positions, by (c) of the IMT.

9. [M] $\begin{bmatrix} 4 & 0 & -7 & -7 \\ -6 & 1 & 11 & 9 \\ 7 & -5 & 10 & 19 \\ -1 & 2 & 3 & -1 \end{bmatrix} \sim \begin{bmatrix} -1 & 2 & 3 & -1 \\ -6 & 1 & 11 & 9 \\ 7 & -5 & 10 & 19 \\ 4 & 0 & -7 & -7 \end{bmatrix} \sim \begin{bmatrix} -1 & 2 & 3 & -1 \\ 0 & -11 & -7 & 15 \\ 0 & 9 & 31 & 12 \\ 0 & 8 & 5 & -11 \end{bmatrix}$

$\sim \begin{bmatrix} -1 & 2 & 3 & -1 \\ 0 & 8 & 5 & -11 \\ 0 & 9 & 31 & 12 \\ 0 & -11 & -7 & 15 \end{bmatrix} \sim \begin{bmatrix} -1 & 2 & 3 & -1 \\ 0 & 8 & 5 & -11 \\ 0 & 0 & 25.375 & 24.375 \\ 0 & 0 & -.1250 & -.1250 \end{bmatrix} \sim \begin{bmatrix} -1 & 2 & 3 & -1 \\ 0 & 8 & 5 & -11 \\ 0 & 0 & 25.375 & 24.375 \\ 0 & 0 & 1 & 1 \end{bmatrix}$

$\sim \begin{bmatrix} -1 & 2 & 3 & -1 \\ 0 & 8 & 5 & -11 \\ 0 & 0 & 1 & 1 \\ 0 & 0 & 25.375 & 24.375 \end{bmatrix} \sim \begin{bmatrix} -1 & 2 & 3 & -1 \\ 0 & 8 & 5 & -11 \\ 0 & 0 & 1 & 1 \\ 0 & 0 & 0 & -1 \end{bmatrix}$

The 4×4 matrix is invertible because it has four pivot positions, by (c) of the IMT.

$$\begin{bmatrix} 5 & 3 & 1 & 7 & 9 \\ 6 & 4 & 2 & 8 & -8 \\ 7 & 5 & 3 & 10 & 9 \\ 9 & 6 & 4 & -9 & -5 \\ 8 & 5 & 2 & 11 & 4 \end{bmatrix} \sim \begin{bmatrix} 5 & 3 & 1 & 7 & 9 \\ 0 & .4 & .8 & -.4 & -18.8 \\ 0 & .8 & 1.6 & .2 & -3.6 \\ 0 & .6 & 2.2 & -21.6 & -21.2 \\ 0 & .2 & .4 & -.2 & -10.4 \end{bmatrix}$$

10. [M]

$$\sim \begin{bmatrix} 5 & 3 & 1 & 7 & 9 \\ 0 & .4 & .8 & -.4 & -18.8 \\ 0 & 0 & 0 & 1 & 34 \\ 0 & 0 & 1 & -21 & 7 \\ 0 & 0 & 0 & 0 & -1 \end{bmatrix} \sim \begin{bmatrix} 5 & 3 & 1 & 7 & 9 \\ 0 & .4 & .8 & -.4 & -18.8 \\ 0 & 0 & 1 & -21 & 7 \\ 0 & 0 & 0 & 1 & 34 \\ 0 & 0 & 0 & 0 & -1 \end{bmatrix}$$

The 5×5 matrix is invertible because it has five pivot positions, by (c) of the IMT.

11. **a.** True, by the IMT. If statement (d) of the IMT is true, then so is statement (b).

   b. True. If statement (h) of the IMT is true, then so is statement (e).

   c. False. Statement (g) of the IMT is true only for invertible matrices.

   d. True, by the IMT. If the equation $A\mathbf{x} = \mathbf{0}$ has a nontrivial solution, then statement (d) of the IMT is false. In this case, all the lettered statements in the IMT are false, including statement (c), which means that A must have fewer than n pivot positions.

   e. True, by the IMT. If A^T is not invertible, then statement (1) of the IMT is false, and hence statement (a) must also be false.

12. **a.** True. If statement (k) of the IMT is true, then so is statement (j).

   b. True. If statement (e) of the IMT is true, then so is statement (h).

   c. True. See the remark immediately following the proof of the IMT.

   d. False. The first part of the statement is not part (i) of the IMT. In fact, if A is any $n \times n$ matrix, the linear transformation $\mathbf{x} \mapsto A\mathbf{x}$ maps $\mathbb{R}^n$ into $\mathbb{R}^n$, yet not every such matrix has n pivot positions.

   e. True, by the IMT. If there is a $\mathbf{b}$ in $\mathbb{R}^n$ such that the equation $A\mathbf{x} = \mathbf{b}$ is inconsistent, then statement (g) of the IMT is false, and hence statement (f) is also false. That is, the transformation $\mathbf{x} \mapsto A\mathbf{x}$ cannot be one-to-one.

Note: The solutions below for Exercises 13–30 refer mostly to the IMT. In many cases, however, part or all of an acceptable solution could also be based on various results that were used to establish the IMT.

13. If a square upper triangular $n \times n$ matrix has nonzero diagonal entries, then because it is already in echelon form, the matrix is row equivalent to I_n and hence is invertible, by the IMT. Conversely, if the matrix is invertible, it has n pivots on the diagonal and hence the diagonal entries are nonzero.

14. If A is lower triangular with nonzero entries on the diagonal, then these n diagonal entries can be used as pivots to produce zeros below the diagonal. Thus A has n pivots and so is invertible, by the IMT. If one of the diagonal entries in A is zero, A will have fewer than n pivots and hence be singular.

Notes: For Exercise 14, another correct analysis of the case when A has nonzero diagonal entries is to apply the IMT (or Exercise 13) to A^T. Then use Theorem 6 in Section 2.2 to conclude that since A^T is invertible so is its transpose, A. You might mention this idea in class, but I recommend that you not spend much time discussing A^T and problems related to it, in order to keep from making this section too lengthy. (The transpose is treated infrequently in the text until Chapter 6.)

If you do plan to ask a test question that involves A^T and the IMT, then you should give the students some extra homework that develops skill using A^T. For instance, in Exercise 14 replace "columns" by "rows."

Also, you could ask students to explain why an $n \times n$ matrix with linearly independent columns must also have linearly independent rows.

15. If A has two identical columns then its columns are linearly dependent. Part (e) of the IMT shows that A cannot be invertible.

16. Part (h) of the IMT shows that a 5×5 matrix cannot be invertible when its columns do not span $\mathbf{R}^5$.

17. If A is invertible, so is A^{-1}, by Theorem 6 in Section 2.2. By (e) of the IMT applied to A^{-1}, the columns of A^{-1} are linearly independent.

18. By (g) of the IMT, C is invertible. Hence, each equation $C\mathbf{x} = \mathbf{v}$ has a unique solution, by Theorem 5 in Section 2.2. This fact was pointed out in the paragraph following the proof of the IMT.

19. By (e) of the IMT, D is invertible. Thus the equation $D\mathbf{x} = \mathbf{b}$ has a solution for each $\mathbf{b}$ in $\mathbf{R}^7$, by (g) of the IMT. Even better, the equation $D\mathbf{x} = \mathbf{b}$ has a *unique* solution for each $\mathbf{b}$ in $\mathbf{R}^7$, by Theorem 5 in Section 2.2. (See the paragraph following the proof of the IMT.)

20. By the box following the IMT, E and F are invertible and are inverses. So $FE = I = EF$, and so E and F commute.

21. The matrix G cannot be invertible, by Theorem 5 in Section 2.2 or by the box following the IMT. So (h) of the IMT is false and the columns of G do not span $\mathbf{R}^n$.

22. Statement (g) of the IMT is false for H, so statement (d) is false, too. That is, the equation $H\mathbf{x} = \mathbf{0}$ has a nontrivial solution.

23. Statement (b) of the IMT is false for K, so statements (e) and (h) are also false. That is, the columns of K are linearly *de*pendent and the columns do *not* span $\mathbf{R}^n$.

24. No conclusion about the columns of L may be drawn, because no information about L has been given. The equation $L\mathbf{x} = \mathbf{0}$ *always* has the trivial solution.

25. Suppose that A is square and $AB = I$. Then A is invertible, by the (k) of the IMT. Left-multiplying each side of the equation $AB = I$ by A^{-1}, one has

$$A^{-1}AB = A^{-1}I, \quad IB = A^{-1}, \quad \text{and } B = A^{-1}.$$

By Theorem 6 in Section 2.2, the matrix B (which is A^{-1}) is invertible, and its inverse is $(A^{-1})^{-1}$, which is A.

26. If the columns of A are linearly independent, then since A is square, A is invertible, by the IMT. So A^2, which is the product of invertible matrices, is invertible. By the IMT, the columns of A^2 span $\mathbf{R}^n$.

27. Let W be the inverse of AB. Then $ABW = I$ and $A(BW) = I$. Since A is square, A is invertible, by (k) of the IMT.

Note: The *Study Guide* for Exercise 27 emphasizes here that the equation $A(BW) = I$, *by itself*, does not show that A is invertible. Students are referred to Exercise 38 in Section 2.2 for a counterexample. Although there is an overall assumption that matrices in this section are square, I insist that my students mention this fact when using the IMT. Even so, at the end of the course, I still sometimes find a student who thinks that an equation $AB = I$ implies that A is invertible.

28. Let W be the inverse of AB. Then $WAB = I$ and $(WA)B = I$. By (j) of the IMT applied to B in place of A, the matrix B is invertible.

29. Since the transformation $\mathbf{x} \mapsto A\mathbf{x}$ is not one-to-one, statement (f) of the IMT is false. Then (i) is also false and the transformation $\mathbf{x} \mapsto A\mathbf{x}$ does not map $\mathbf{R}^n$ onto $\mathbf{R}^n$. Also, A is not invertible, which implies that the transformation $\mathbf{x} \mapsto A\mathbf{x}$ is not invertible, by Theorem 9.

30. Since the transformation $\mathbf{x} \mapsto A\mathbf{x}$ is one-to-one, statement (f) of the IMT is true. Then (i) is also true and the transformation $\mathbf{x} \mapsto A\mathbf{x}$ maps $\mathbf{R}^n$ onto $\mathbf{R}^n$. Also, A is invertible, which implies that the transformation $\mathbf{x} \mapsto A\mathbf{x}$ is invertible, by Theorem 9.

31. Since the equation $A\mathbf{x} = \mathbf{b}$ has a solution for each $\mathbf{b}$, the matrix A has a pivot in each row (Theorem 4 in Section 1.4). Since A is square, A has a pivot in each column, and so there are no free variables in the equation $A\mathbf{x} = \mathbf{b}$, which shows that the solution is unique.

Note: The preceding argument shows that the (square) shape of A plays a crucial role. A less revealing proof is to use the "pivot in each row" and the IMT to conclude that A is invertible. Then Theorem 5 in Section 2.2 shows that the solution of $A\mathbf{x} = \mathbf{b}$ is unique.

32. If $A\mathbf{x} = \mathbf{0}$ has only the trivial solution, then A must have a pivot in each of its n columns. Since A is square (and this is the key point), there must be a pivot in each *row* of A. By Theorem 4 in Section 1.4, the equation $A\mathbf{x} = \mathbf{b}$ has a solution for each $\mathbf{b}$ in $\mathbf{R}^n$.

    Another argument: Statement (d) of the IMT is true, so A is invertible. By Theorem 5 in Section 2.2, the equation $A\mathbf{x} = \mathbf{b}$ has a (unique) solution for each $\mathbf{b}$ in $\mathbf{R}^n$.

33. (Solution in *Study Guide*) The standard matrix of T is $A = \begin{bmatrix} -5 & 9 \\ 4 & -7 \end{bmatrix}$, which is invertible because $\det A \neq 0$. By Theorem 9, the transformation T is invertible and the standard matrix of T^{-1} is A^{-1}. From the formula for a 2×2 inverse, $A^{-1} = \begin{bmatrix} 7 & 9 \\ 4 & 5 \end{bmatrix}$. So

$$T^{-1}(x_1, x_2) = \begin{bmatrix} 7 & 9 \\ 4 & 5 \end{bmatrix}\begin{bmatrix} x_1 \\ x_2 \end{bmatrix} = (7x_1 + 9x_2, 4x_1 + 5x_2)$$

34. The standard matrix of T is $A = \begin{bmatrix} 6 & -8 \\ -5 & 7 \end{bmatrix}$, which is invertible because $\det A = 2 \neq 0$. By Theorem 9, T is invertible, and $T^{-1}(\mathbf{x}) = B\mathbf{x}$, where $B = A^{-1} = \dfrac{1}{2}\begin{bmatrix} 7 & 8 \\ 5 & 6 \end{bmatrix}$. Thus

$$T^{-1}(x_1, x_2) = \frac{1}{2}\begin{bmatrix} 7 & 8 \\ 5 & 6 \end{bmatrix}\begin{bmatrix} x_1 \\ x_2 \end{bmatrix} = \left(\frac{7}{2}x_1 + 4x_2, \frac{5}{2}x_1 + 3x_2\right)$$

35. (Solution in *Study Guide*) To show that T is one-to-one, suppose that $T(\mathbf{u}) = T(\mathbf{v})$ for some vectors $\mathbf{u}$ and $\mathbf{v}$ in $\mathbf{R}^n$. Then $S(T(\mathbf{u})) = S(T(\mathbf{v}))$, where S is the inverse of T. By Equation (1), $\mathbf{u} = S(T(\mathbf{u}))$ and $S(T(\mathbf{v})) = \mathbf{v}$, so $\mathbf{u} = \mathbf{v}$. Thus T is one-to-one. To show that T is onto, suppose $\mathbf{y}$ represents an arbitrary vector in $\mathbf{R}^n$ and define $\mathbf{x} = S(\mathbf{y})$. Then, using Equation (2), $T(\mathbf{x}) = T(S(\mathbf{y})) = \mathbf{y}$, which shows that T maps $\mathbf{R}^n$ onto $\mathbf{R}^n$.

    Second proof: By Theorem 9, the standard matrix A of T is invertible. By the IMT, the columns of A are linearly independent and span $\mathbf{R}^n$. By Theorem 12 in Section 1.9, T is one-to-one and maps $\mathbf{R}^n$ onto $\mathbf{R}^n$.

36. If T maps $\mathbf{R}^n$ onto $\mathbf{R}^n$, then the columns of its standard matrix A span $\mathbf{R}^n$, by Theorem 12 in Section 1.9. By the IMT, A is invertible. Hence, by Theorem 9 in Section 2.3, T is invertible, and A^{-1} is the standard matrix of T^{-1}. Since A^{-1} is also invertible, by the IMT, its columns are linearly independent and span $\mathbf{R}^n$. Applying Theorem 12 in Section 1.9 to the transformation T^{-1}, we conclude that T^{-1} is a one-to-one mapping of $\mathbf{R}^n$ onto $\mathbf{R}^n$.

37. Let A and B be the standard matrices of T and U, respectively. Then AB is the standard matrix of the mapping $\mathbf{x} \mapsto T(U(\mathbf{x}))$, because of the way matrix multiplication is defined (in Section 2.1). By hypothesis, this mapping is the identity mapping, so $AB = I$. Since A and B are square, they are invertible, by the IMT, and $B = A^{-1}$. Thus, $BA = I$. This means that the mapping $\mathbf{x} \mapsto U(T(\mathbf{x}))$ is the identity mapping, i.e., $U(T(\mathbf{x})) = \mathbf{x}$ for all $\mathbf{x}$ in $\mathbf{R}^n$.

38. Let A be the standard matrix of T. By hypothesis, T is not a one-to-one mapping. So, by Theorem 12 in Section 1.9, the standard matrix A of T has linearly dependent columns. Since A is square, the columns of A do not span $\mathbf{R}^n$. By Theorem 12, again, T cannot map $\mathbf{R}^n$ onto $\mathbf{R}^n$.

39. Given any $\mathbf{v}$ in $\mathbf{R}^n$, we may write $\mathbf{v} = T(\mathbf{x})$ for some $\mathbf{x}$, because T is an onto mapping. Then, the assumed properties of S and U show that $S(\mathbf{v}) = S(T(\mathbf{x})) = \mathbf{x}$ and $U(\mathbf{v}) = U(T(\mathbf{x})) = \mathbf{x}$. So $S(\mathbf{v})$ and $U(\mathbf{v})$ are equal for each $\mathbf{v}$. That is, S and U are the same function from $\mathbf{R}^n$ into $\mathbf{R}^n$.

40. Given $\mathbf{u}$, $\mathbf{v}$ in $\mathbb{R}^n$, let $\mathbf{x} = S(\mathbf{u})$ and $\mathbf{y} = S(\mathbf{v})$. Then $T(\mathbf{x}) = T(S(\mathbf{u})) = \mathbf{u}$ and $T(\mathbf{y}) = T(S(\mathbf{v})) = \mathbf{v}$, by equation (2). Hence

$$S(\mathbf{u} + \mathbf{v}) = S(T(\mathbf{x}) + T(\mathbf{y}))$$

$$\qquad = S(T(\mathbf{x} + \mathbf{y})) \qquad \text{Because } T \text{ is linear}$$

$$\qquad = \mathbf{x} + \mathbf{y} \qquad \text{By equation (1)}$$

$$\qquad = S(\mathbf{u}) + S(\mathbf{v})$$

So, S preserves sums. For any scalar r,

$$S(r\mathbf{u}) = S(rT(\mathbf{x})) = S(T(r\mathbf{x})) \qquad \text{Because } T \text{ is linear}$$

$$\qquad = r\mathbf{x} \qquad \text{By equation (1)}$$

$$\qquad = rS(\mathbf{u})$$

So S preserves scalar multiples. Thus S ia a linear transformation.

41. **[M] a.** The exact solution of (3) is $x_1 = 3.94$ and $x_2 = .49$. The exact solution of (4) is $x_1 = 2.90$ and $x_2 = 2.00$.

    b. When the solution of (4) is used as an approximation for the solution in (3), the error in using the value of 2.90 for x_1 is about 26%, and the error in using 2.0 for x_2 is about 308%.

    c. The condition number of the coefficient matrix is 3363. The percentage change in the solution from (3) to (4) is about 7700 times the percentage change in the right side of the equation. This is the same order of magnitude as the condition number. The condition number gives a rough measure of how sensitive the solution of $A\mathbf{x} = \mathbf{b}$ can be to changes in $\mathbf{b}$. Further information about the condition number is given at the end of Chapter 6 and in Chapter 7.

Note: See the *Study Guide*'s MATLAB box, or a technology appendix, for information on condition number. Only the TI-83+ and TI-89 lack a command for this.

42. **[M]** MATLAB gives cond(A) = 23683, which is approximately 10^4. If you make several trials with MATLAB, which records 16 digits accurately, you should find that $\mathbf{x}$ and $\mathbf{x}_1$ agree to at least 12 or 13 significant digits. So about 4 significant digits are lost. Here is the result of one experiment. The vectors were all computed to the maximum 16 decimal places but are here displayed with only four decimal places:

$$\mathbf{x} = \text{rand}(4,1) = \begin{bmatrix} .9501 \\ .21311 \\ .6068 \\ .4860 \end{bmatrix}, \mathbf{b} = A\mathbf{x} = \begin{bmatrix} -3.8493 \\ 5.5795 \\ 20.7973 \\ .8467 \end{bmatrix}. \text{ The MATLAB solution is } \mathbf{x}_1 = A\backslash\mathbf{b} = \begin{bmatrix} .9501 \\ .2311 \\ .6068 \\ .4860 \end{bmatrix}.$$

However, $\mathbf{x} - \mathbf{x}_1 = \begin{bmatrix} .0171 \\ .4858 \\ -.2360 \\ .2456 \end{bmatrix} \times 10^{-12}$. The computed solution $\mathbf{x}_1$ is accurate to about

12 decimal places.

43. **[M]** MATLAB gives cond(A) = 68,622. Since this has magnitude between 10^4 and 10^5, the estimated accuracy of a solution of $A\mathbf{x} = \mathbf{b}$ should be to about four or five decimal places *less* than the 16 decimal places that MATLAB usually computes accurately. That is, one should expect the solution to be accurate to only about 11 or 12 decimal places. Here is the result of one experiment. The vectors were all computed to the maximum 16 decimal places but are here displayed with only four decimal places:

$$\mathbf{x} = \text{rand}(5,1) = \begin{bmatrix} .2190 \\ .0470 \\ .6789 \\ .6793 \\ .9347 \end{bmatrix}, \mathbf{b} = A\mathbf{x} = \begin{bmatrix} 15.0821 \\ .8165 \\ 19.0097 \\ -5.8188 \\ 14.5557 \end{bmatrix}. \text{ The MATLAB solution is } \mathbf{x}_1 = A\backslash\mathbf{b} = \begin{bmatrix} .2190 \\ .0470 \\ .6789 \\ .6793 \\ .9347 \end{bmatrix}.$$

However, $\mathbf{x} - \mathbf{x}_1 = \begin{bmatrix} .3165 \\ -.6743 \\ .3343 \\ .0158 \\ -.0005 \end{bmatrix} \times 10^{-11}$. The computed solution $\mathbf{x}_1$ is accurate to about 11 decimal places.

44. **[M]** Solve $A\mathbf{x} = (0, 0, 0, 0, 1)$. MATLAB shows that cond(A) $\approx 4.8 \times 10^5$. Since MATLAB computes numbers accurately to 16 decimal places, the entries in the computed value of $\mathbf{x}$ should be accurate to at least 11 digits. The exact solution is (630, –12600, 56700, –88200, 44100).

45. **[M]** Some versions of MATLAB issue a warning when asked to invert a Hilbert matrix of order 12 or larger using floating-point arithmetic. The product AA^{-1} should have several off-diagonal entries that are far from being zero. If not, try a larger matrix.

Note: All matrix programs supported by the *Study Guide* have data for Exercise 45, but only MATLAB and Maple have a single command to create a Hilbert matrix. The HP-48G data for Exercise 45 contain a program that can be edited to create other Hilbert matrices.

Notes: The *Study Guide* for Section 2.3 organizes the statements of the Invertible Matrix Theorem in a table that imbeds these ideas in a broader discussion of rectangular matrices. The statements are arranged in three columns: statements that are logically equivalent for any $m \times n$ matrix and are related to existence concepts, those that are equivalent only for any $n \times n$ matrix, and those that are equivalent for any $n \times p$ matrix and are related to uniqueness concepts. Four statements are included that are not in the text's official list of statements, to give more symmetry to the three columns. You may or may not wish to comment on them.

   I believe that students cannot fully understand the concepts in the IMT if they do not know the correct wording of each statement. (Of course, this knowledge is not sufficient for understanding.) The *Study Guide*'s Section 2.3 has an example of the type of question I often put on an exam at this point in the course. The section concludes with a discussion of reviewing and reflecting, as important steps to a mastery of linear algebra.

2.4   SOLUTIONS

Notes: Partitioned matrices arise in theoretical discussions in essentially every field that makes use of matrices. The *Study Guide* mentions some examples (with references).

Every student should be exposed to some of the ideas in this section. If time is short, you might omit Example 4 and Theorem 10, and replace Example 5 by a problem similar to one in Exercises 1–10. (A sample replacement is given at the end of these solutions.) Then select homework from Exercises 1–13, 15, and 21–24.

The exercises just mentioned provide a good environment for practicing matrix manipulation. Also, students will be reminded that an equation of the form $AB = I$ does not by itself make A or B invertible. (The matrices must be square and the IMT is required.)

1. Apply the row-column rule as if the matrix entries were numbers, but for each product always write the entry of the left block-matrix on the *left*.

$$\begin{bmatrix} I & 0 \\ E & I \end{bmatrix}\begin{bmatrix} A & B \\ C & D \end{bmatrix} = \begin{bmatrix} IA+0C & IB+0D \\ EA+IC & EB+ID \end{bmatrix} = \begin{bmatrix} A & B \\ EA+C & EB+D \end{bmatrix}$$

2. Apply the row-column rule as if the matrix entries were numbers, but for each product always write the entry of the left block-matrix on the *left*.

$$\begin{bmatrix} E & 0 \\ 0 & F \end{bmatrix}\begin{bmatrix} A & B \\ C & D \end{bmatrix} = \begin{bmatrix} EA+0C & EB+0D \\ 0A+FC & 0B+FD \end{bmatrix} = \begin{bmatrix} EA & EB \\ FC & FD \end{bmatrix}$$

3. Apply the row-column rule as if the matrix entries were numbers, but for each product always write the entry of the left block-matrix on the *left*.

$$\begin{bmatrix} 0 & I \\ I & 0 \end{bmatrix}\begin{bmatrix} W & X \\ Y & Z \end{bmatrix} = \begin{bmatrix} 0W+IY & 0X+IZ \\ IW+0Y & IX+0Z \end{bmatrix} = \begin{bmatrix} Y & Z \\ W & X \end{bmatrix}$$

4. Apply the row-column rule as if the matrix entries were numbers, but for each product always write the entry of the left block-matrix on the *left*.

$$\begin{bmatrix} I & 0 \\ -X & I \end{bmatrix}\begin{bmatrix} A & B \\ C & D \end{bmatrix} = \begin{bmatrix} IA+0C & IB+0D \\ -XA+IC & -XB+ID \end{bmatrix} = \begin{bmatrix} A & B \\ -XA+C & -XB+D \end{bmatrix}$$

5. Compute the left side of the equation:

$$\begin{bmatrix} A & B \\ C & 0 \end{bmatrix}\begin{bmatrix} I & 0 \\ X & Y \end{bmatrix} = \begin{bmatrix} AI+BX & A0+BY \\ CI+0X & C0+0Y \end{bmatrix}$$

Set this equal to the right side of the equation:

$$\begin{bmatrix} A+BX & BY \\ C & 0 \end{bmatrix} = \begin{bmatrix} 0 & I \\ Z & 0 \end{bmatrix} \quad \text{so that} \quad \begin{array}{cc} A+BX=0 & BY=I \\ C=Z & 0=0 \end{array}$$

Since the (2, 1) blocks are equal, $Z = C$. Since the (1, 2) blocks are equal, $BY = I$. To proceed further, assume that B and Y are square. Then the equation $BY =I$ implies that B is invertible, by the IMT, and $Y = B^{-1}$. (See the boxed remark that follows the IMT.) Finally, from the equality of the (1, 1) blocks,

$$BX = -A, \quad B^{-1}BX = B^{-1}(-A), \quad \text{and} \quad X = -B^{-1}A.$$

The order of the factors for X is crucial.

Note: For simplicity, statements (j) and (k) in the Invertible Matrix Theorem involve square matrices C and D. Actually, if A is $n \times n$ and if C is any matrix such that AC is the $n \times n$ identity matrix, then C must be $n \times n$, too. (For AC to be defined, C must have n rows, and the equation $AC = I$ implies that C has n columns.) Similarly, $DA = I$ implies that D is $n \times n$. Rather than discuss this in class, I expect that in Exercises 5–8, when students see an equation such as $BY = I$, they will decide that *both* B and Y should be square in order to use the IMT.

6. Compute the left side of the equation:

$$\begin{bmatrix} X & 0 \\ Y & Z \end{bmatrix} \begin{bmatrix} A & 0 \\ B & C \end{bmatrix} = \begin{bmatrix} XA+0B & X0+0C \\ YA+ZB & Y0+ZC \end{bmatrix} = \begin{bmatrix} XA & 0 \\ YA+ZB & ZC \end{bmatrix}$$

Set this equal to the right side of the equation:

$$\begin{bmatrix} XA & 0 \\ YA+ZB & ZC \end{bmatrix} = \begin{bmatrix} I & 0 \\ 0 & I \end{bmatrix} \quad \text{so that} \quad \begin{array}{cc} XA=I & 0=0 \\ YA+ZB=0 & ZC=I \end{array}$$

To use the equality of the (1, 1) blocks, assume that A and X are square. By the IMT, the equation $XA = I$ implies that A is invertible and $X = A^{-1}$. (See the boxed remark that follows the IMT.) Similarly, if C and Z are assumed to be square, then the equation $ZC = I$ implies that C is invertible, by the IMT, and $Z = C^{-1}$. Finally, use the (2, 1) blocks and right-multiplication by A^{-1}:

$$YA = -ZB = -C^{-1}B, \quad YAA^{-1} = (-C^{-1}B)A^{-1}, \quad \text{and} \quad Y = -C^{-1}BA^{-1}$$

The order of the factors for Y is crucial.

7. Compute the left side of the equation:

$$\begin{bmatrix} X & 0 & 0 \\ Y & 0 & I \end{bmatrix} \begin{bmatrix} A & Z \\ 0 & 0 \\ B & I \end{bmatrix} = \begin{bmatrix} XA+0+0B & XZ+0+0I \\ YA+0+IB & YZ+0+II \end{bmatrix}$$

Set this equal to the right side of the equation:

$$\begin{bmatrix} XA & XZ \\ YA+B & YZ+I \end{bmatrix} = \begin{bmatrix} I & 0 \\ 0 & I \end{bmatrix} \quad \text{so that} \quad \begin{array}{cc} XA=I & XZ=0 \\ YA+B=0 & YZ+I=I \end{array}$$

To use the equality of the (1, 1) blocks, assume that A and X are square. By the IMT, the equation $XA = I$ implies that A is invertible and $X = A^{-1}$. (See the boxed remark that follows the IMT) Also, X is invertible. Since $XZ = 0$, $X^{-1}XZ = X^{-1}0 = 0$, so Z must be 0. Finally, from the equality of the (2, 1) blocks, $YA = -B$. Right-multiplication by A^{-1} shows that $YAA^{-1} = -BA^{-1}$ and $Y = -BA^{-1}$. The order of the factors for Y is crucial.

8. Compute the left side of the equation:

$$\begin{bmatrix} A & B \\ 0 & I \end{bmatrix} \begin{bmatrix} X & Y & Z \\ 0 & 0 & I \end{bmatrix} = \begin{bmatrix} AX+B0 & AY+B0 & AZ+BI \\ 0X+I0 & 0Y+I0 & 0Z+II \end{bmatrix}$$

Set this equal to the right side of the equation:

$$\begin{bmatrix} AX & AY & AZ+B \\ 0 & 0 & I \end{bmatrix} = \begin{bmatrix} I & 0 & 0 \\ 0 & 0 & I \end{bmatrix}$$

To use the equality of the (1, 1) blocks, assume that A and X are square. By the IMT, the equation $XA = I$ implies that A is invertible and $X = A^{-1}$. (See the boxed remark that follows the IMT. Since $AY = 0$, from the equality of the (1, 2) blocks, left-multiplication by A^{-1} gives $A^{-1}AY = A^{-1}0 = 0$, so $Y = 0$. Finally, from the (1, 3) blocks, $AZ = -B$. Left-multiplication by A^{-1} gives $A^{-1}AZ = A^{-1}(-B)$, and $Z = -A^{-1}B$. The order of the factors for Z is crucial.

Note: The *Study Guide* tells students, "Problems such as 5–10 make good exam questions. Remember to mention the IMT when appropriate, and remember that matrix multiplication is generally not commutative." When a problem statement includes a condition that a matrix is square, I expect my students to mention this fact when they apply the IMT.

9. Compute the left side of the equation:

$$\begin{bmatrix} I & 0 & 0 \\ X & I & 0 \\ Y & 0 & I \end{bmatrix}\begin{bmatrix} A_{11} & A_{12} \\ A_{21} & A_{22} \\ A_{31} & A_{32} \end{bmatrix} = \begin{bmatrix} IA_{11}+0A_{21}+0A_{31} & IA_{12}+0A_{22}+0A_{32} \\ XA_{11}+IA_{21}+0A_{31} & XA_{12}+IA_{22}+0A_{32} \\ YA_{11}+0A_{21}+IA_{31} & YA_{12}+0A_{22}+IA_{32} \end{bmatrix}$$

Set this equal to the right side of the equation:

$$\begin{bmatrix} A_{11} & A_{12} \\ XA_{11}+A_{21} & XA_{12}+A_{22} \\ YA_{11}+A_{31} & YA_{12}+A_{32} \end{bmatrix} = \begin{bmatrix} B_{11} & B_{12} \\ 0 & B_{22} \\ 0 & B_{32} \end{bmatrix}$$

$$A_{11} = B_{11} \qquad A_{12} = B_{12}$$

so that $\quad XA_{11}+A_{21}=0 \qquad XA_{12}+A_{22}=B_{22}$

$$YA_{11}+A_{31}=0 \qquad YA_{12}+A_{32}=B_{32}$$

Since the (2,1) blocks are equal, $XA_{11}+A_{21}=0$ and $XA_{11}=-A_{21}$. Since A_{11} is invertible, right multiplication by A_{11}^{-1} gives $X=-A_{21}A_{11}^{-1}$. Likewise since the (3,1) blocks are equal, $YA_{11}+A_{31}=0$ and $YA_{11}=-A_{31}$. Since A_{11} is invertible, right multiplication by A_{11}^{-1} gives $Y=-A_{31}A_{11}^{-1}$. Finally, from the (2,2) entries, $XA_{12}+A_{22}=B_{22}$. Since $X=-A_{21}A_{11}^{-1}, B_{22}=-A_{21}A_{11}^{-1}A_{12}+A_{22}$.

10. Since the two matrices are inverses,

$$\begin{bmatrix} I & 0 & 0 \\ C & I & 0 \\ A & B & I \end{bmatrix}\begin{bmatrix} T & 0 & 0 \\ Z & I & 0 \\ X & Y & I \end{bmatrix} = \begin{bmatrix} I & 0 & 0 \\ 0 & I & 0 \\ 0 & 0 & I \end{bmatrix}$$

Compute the left side of the equation:

$$\begin{bmatrix} I & 0 & 0 \\ C & I & 0 \\ A & B & I \end{bmatrix}\begin{bmatrix} I & 0 & 0 \\ Z & I & 0 \\ X & Y & I \end{bmatrix} = \begin{bmatrix} II+0Z+0X & I0+0I+0Y & I0+00+0I \\ CI+IZ+0X & C0+II+0Y & C0+I0+0I \\ AI+BZ+IX & A0+BI+IY & A0+B0+II \end{bmatrix}$$

Set this equal to the right side of the equation:

$$\begin{bmatrix} I & 0 & 0 \\ C+Z & I & 0 \\ A+BZ+X & B+Y & I \end{bmatrix} = \begin{bmatrix} I & 0 & 0 \\ 0 & I & 0 \\ 0 & 0 & I \end{bmatrix}$$

$$I=I \qquad 0=0 \quad 0=0$$

so that $\qquad C+Z=0 \qquad I=I \quad 0=0$

$$A+BZ+X=0 \quad B+Y=0 \quad I=I$$

Since the (2,1) blocks are equal, $C+Z=0$ and $Z=-C$. Likewise since the (3, 2) blocks are equal, $B+Y=0$ and $Y=-B$. Finally, from the (3,1) entries, $A+BZ+X=0$ and $X=-A-BZ$. Since $Z=-C$, $X=-A-B(-C)=-A+BC$.

11. a. True. See the subsection *Addition and Scalar Multiplication*.

b. False. See the paragraph before Example 3.

12. a. True. See the paragraph before Example 4.

b. False. See the paragraph before Example 3.

13. You are asked to establish an *if and only if* statement. First, supose that A is invertible,

and let $A^{-1} = \begin{bmatrix} D & E \\ F & G \end{bmatrix}$. Then

$$\begin{bmatrix} B & 0 \\ 0 & C \end{bmatrix}\begin{bmatrix} D & E \\ F & G \end{bmatrix} = \begin{bmatrix} BD & BE \\ CF & CG \end{bmatrix} = \begin{bmatrix} I & 0 \\ 0 & I \end{bmatrix}$$

Since B is square, the equation $BD = I$ implies that B is invertible, by the IMT. Similarly, $CG = I$ implies that C is invertible. Also, the equation $BE = 0$ imples that $E = B^{-1}0 = 0$. Similarly $F = 0$. Thus

$$A^{-1} = \begin{bmatrix} B & 0 \\ 0 & C \end{bmatrix}^{-1} = \begin{bmatrix} D & E \\ E & G \end{bmatrix} = \begin{bmatrix} B^{-1} & 0 \\ 0 & C^{-1} \end{bmatrix} \tag{*}$$

This proves that A is invertible *only if* B and C are invertible. For the "*if*" part of the statement, suppose that B and C are invertible. Then (*) provides a likely candidate for A^{-1} which can be used to show that A is invertible. Compute:

$$\begin{bmatrix} B & 0 \\ 0 & C \end{bmatrix}\begin{bmatrix} B^{-1} & 0 \\ 0 & C^{-1} \end{bmatrix} = \begin{bmatrix} BB^{-1} & 0 \\ 0 & CC^{-1} \end{bmatrix} = \begin{bmatrix} I & 0 \\ 0 & I \end{bmatrix}$$

Since A is square, this calculation and the IMT imply that A is invertible. (Don't forget this final sentence. Without it, the argument is incomplete.) Instead of that sentence, you could add the equation:

$$\begin{bmatrix} B^{-1} & 0 \\ 0 & C^{-1} \end{bmatrix}\begin{bmatrix} B & 0 \\ 0 & C \end{bmatrix} = \begin{bmatrix} B^{-1}B & 0 \\ 0 & C^{-1}C \end{bmatrix} = \begin{bmatrix} I & 0 \\ 0 & I \end{bmatrix}$$

14. You are asked to establish an *if and only if* statement. First suppose that A is invertible. Example 5 shows that A_{11} and A_{22} are invertible. This proves that A is invertible *only if* $A_{11} A_{22}$ are invertible. For the *if* part of this statement, suppose that A_{11} and A_{22} are invertible. Then the formula in Example 5 provides a likely candidate for A^{-1} which can be used to show that A is invertible . Compute:

$$\begin{bmatrix} A_{11} & A_{12} \\ 0 & A_{22} \end{bmatrix}\begin{bmatrix} A_{11}^{-1} & -A_{11}^{-1}A_{12}A_{22}^{-1} \\ 0 & A_{22}^{-1} \end{bmatrix} = \begin{bmatrix} A_{11}A_{11}^{-1} + A_{12}0 & A_{11}(-A_{11}^{-1})A_{12}A_{22}^{-1} + A_{12}A_{22}^{-1} \\ 0A_{11}^{-1} + A_{22}0 & 0(-A_{11}^{-1})A_{12}A_{22}^{-1} + A_{22}A_{22}^{-1} \end{bmatrix}$$

$$= \begin{bmatrix} I & -(A_{11}A_{11}^{-1})A_{12}A_{22}^{-1} + A_{12}A_{22}^{-1} \\ 0 & I \end{bmatrix}$$

$$= \begin{bmatrix} I & -A_{12}A_{22}^{-1} + A_{12}A_{22}^{-1} \\ 0 & I \end{bmatrix} = \begin{bmatrix} I & 0 \\ 0 & I \end{bmatrix}$$

Since A is square, this calculation and the IMT imply that A is invertible.

15. Compute the right side of the equation:

$$\begin{bmatrix} I & 0 \\ X & I \end{bmatrix}\begin{bmatrix} A_{11} & 0 \\ 0 & S \end{bmatrix}\begin{bmatrix} I & Y \\ 0 & I \end{bmatrix} = \begin{bmatrix} A_{11} & 0 \\ XA_{11} & S \end{bmatrix}\begin{bmatrix} I & Y \\ 0 & I \end{bmatrix} = \begin{bmatrix} A_{11} & A_{11}Y \\ XA_{11} & XA_{11}Y + S \end{bmatrix}$$

Set this equal to the left side of the equation:

$$\begin{bmatrix} A_{11} & A_{11}Y \\ XA_{11} & XA_{11}Y + S \end{bmatrix} = \begin{bmatrix} A_{11} & A_{12} \\ A_{21} & A_{22} \end{bmatrix} \text{ so that } \begin{array}{ll} A_{11} = A_{11} & A_{11}Y = A_{12} \\ XA_{11} = A_{21} & XA_{11}Y + S = A_{22} \end{array}$$

Since the (1, 2) blocks are equal, $A_{11}Y = A_{12}$. Since A_{11} is invertible, left multiplication by A_{11}^{-1} gives $Y = A_{11}^{-1}A_{12}$. Likewise since the (2,1) blocks are equal, $XA_{11} = A_{21}$. Since A_{11} is invertible, right multiplication by A_{11}^{-1} gives that $X = A_{21}A_{11}^{-1}$. One can check that the matrix S as given in the exercise satisfies the equation $XA_{11}Y + S = A_{22}$ with the calculated values of X and Y given above.

16. Suppose that A and A_{11} are invertible. First note that

$$\begin{bmatrix} I & 0 \\ X & I \end{bmatrix}\begin{bmatrix} I & 0 \\ -X & I \end{bmatrix} = \begin{bmatrix} I & 0 \\ 0 & I \end{bmatrix}$$

and

$$\begin{bmatrix} I & Y \\ 0 & I \end{bmatrix}\begin{bmatrix} I & -Y \\ 0 & I \end{bmatrix} = \begin{bmatrix} I & 0 \\ 0 & I \end{bmatrix}$$

Since the matrices $\begin{bmatrix} I & 0 \\ X & I \end{bmatrix}$ and $\begin{bmatrix} I & Y \\ 0 & I \end{bmatrix}$

are square, they are both invertible by the IMT. Equation (7) may be left multiplied by

$\begin{bmatrix} I & 0 \\ X & I \end{bmatrix}^{-1}$ and right multiplied by $\begin{bmatrix} I & Y \\ 0 & I \end{bmatrix}^{-1}$ to find

$$\begin{bmatrix} A_{11} & 0 \\ 0 & S \end{bmatrix} = \begin{bmatrix} I & 0 \\ X & I \end{bmatrix}^{-1} A \begin{bmatrix} I & Y \\ 0 & I \end{bmatrix}^{-1}$$

Thus by Theorem 6, the matrix $\begin{bmatrix} A_{11} & 0 \\ 0 & S \end{bmatrix}$ is invertible as the product of invertible matrices. Finally,

Exercise 13 above may be used to show that S is invertible.

17. The column-row expansions of G_k and G_{k+1} are:

$$G_k = X_k X_k^T$$
$$= \text{col}_1(X_k)\text{row}_1(X_k^T) + \cdots + \text{col}_k(X_k)\text{row}_k(X_k^T)$$

and

$$G_{k+1} = X_{k+1}X_{k+1}^T$$
$$= \text{col}_1(X_{k+1})\text{row}_1(X_{k+1}^T) + \cdots + \text{col}_k(X_{k+1})\text{row}_k(X_{k+1}^T) + \text{col}_{k+1}(X_{k+1})\text{row}_{k+1}(X_{k+1}^T)$$
$$= \text{col}_1(X_k)\text{row}_1(X_k^T) + \cdots + \text{col}_k(X_k)\text{row}_k(X_k^T) + \text{col}_{k+1}(X_{k+1})\text{row}_{k+1}(X_k^T)$$
$$= G_k + \text{col}_{k+1}(X_{k+1})\text{row}_{k+1}(X_k^T)$$

since the first k columns of X_{k+1} are identical to the first k columns of X_k. Thus to update G_k to produce G_{k+1}, the number $\text{col}_{k+1}(X_{k+1})\text{row}_{k+1}(X_k^T)$ should be added to G_k.

18. Since $W = [X \ \mathbf{x}_0]$,

$$W^TW = \begin{bmatrix} X^T \\ \mathbf{x}_0^T \end{bmatrix}[X \ \mathbf{x}_0] = \begin{bmatrix} X^TX & X^T\mathbf{x}_0 \\ \mathbf{x}_0^TX & \mathbf{x}_0^T\mathbf{x}_0 \end{bmatrix}$$

By applying the formula for S from Exercise 15, S may be computed:

$$S = \mathbf{x}_0^T\mathbf{x}_0 - \mathbf{x}_0^TX(X^TX)^{-1}X^T\mathbf{x}_0$$
$$= \mathbf{x}_0^T(I_m - X(X^TX)^{-1}X^T)\mathbf{x}_0$$
$$= \mathbf{x}_0^TM\mathbf{x}_0$$

19. The matrix equation (8) in the text is equivalent to

$$(A - sI_n)\mathbf{x} + B\mathbf{u} = 0 \quad \text{and} \quad C\mathbf{x} + \mathbf{u} = \mathbf{y}$$

Rewrite the first equation as $(A - sI_n)\mathbf{x} = -B\mathbf{u}$. When $A - sI_n$ is invertible,

$$\mathbf{x} = (A - sI_n)^{-1}(-B\mathbf{u}) = -(A - sI_n)^{-1}B\mathbf{u}$$

Substitute this formula for **x** into the second equation above:

$$C(-(A - sI_n)^{-1}B\mathbf{u}) + \mathbf{u} = \mathbf{y}, \text{ so that } \quad I_m\mathbf{u} - C(A - sI_n)^{-1}B\mathbf{u} = \mathbf{y}$$

Thus $\mathbf{y} = (I_m - C(A - sI_n)^{-1}B)\mathbf{u}$. If $W(s) = I_m - C(A - sI_n)^{-1}B$, then $\mathbf{y} = W(s)\mathbf{u}$. The matrix $W(s)$ is the Schur complement of the matrix $A - sI_n$ in the system matrix in equation (8)

20. The matrix in question is

$$\begin{bmatrix} A - BC - sI_n & B \\ -C & I_m \end{bmatrix}$$

By applying the formula for S from Exercise 15, S may be computed:

$$S = I_m - (-C)(A - BC - sI_m)^{-1}B$$
$$= I_m + C(A - BC - sI_m)^{-1}B$$

21. **a.** $A^2 = \begin{bmatrix} 1 & 0 \\ 3 & -1 \end{bmatrix}\begin{bmatrix} 1 & 0 \\ 3 & -1 \end{bmatrix} = \begin{bmatrix} 1+0 & 0+0 \\ 3-3 & 0+(-1)^2 \end{bmatrix} = \begin{bmatrix} 1 & 0 \\ 0 & 1 \end{bmatrix}$

  b. $M^2 = \begin{bmatrix} A & 0 \\ I & -A \end{bmatrix}\begin{bmatrix} A & 0 \\ I & -A \end{bmatrix} = \begin{bmatrix} A^2+0 & 0+0 \\ A-A & 0+(-A)^2 \end{bmatrix} = \begin{bmatrix} I & 0 \\ 0 & I \end{bmatrix}$

22. Let C be any nonzero 2×3 matrix. Define $A = \begin{bmatrix} I_3 & 0 \\ C & -I_2 \end{bmatrix}$. Then

$$A^2 = \begin{bmatrix} I_3 & 0 \\ C & -I_2 \end{bmatrix}\begin{bmatrix} I_3 & 0 \\ C & -I_2 \end{bmatrix} = \begin{bmatrix} I_3+0 & 0+0 \\ CI_3 - I_2C & 0+(-I_2)^2 \end{bmatrix} = \begin{bmatrix} I_3 & 0 \\ 0 & I_2 \end{bmatrix}$$

23. The product of two 1×1 "lower triangular" matrices is "lower triangular." Suppose that for $n = k$, the product of two $k \times k$ lower triangular matrices is lower triangular, and consider any $(k+1) \times (k+1)$ matrices A_1 and B_1. Partition these matrices as

$$A_1 = \begin{bmatrix} a & \mathbf{0}^T \\ \mathbf{v} & A \end{bmatrix}, \quad B_1 = \begin{bmatrix} b & \mathbf{0}^T \\ \mathbf{w} & B \end{bmatrix}$$

where A and B are $k \times k$ matrices, **v** and **w** are in $\mathbf{R}^k$, and a and b are scalars. Since A_1 and B_1 are lower triangular, so are A and B. Then

$$A_1B_1 = \begin{bmatrix} a & \mathbf{0}^T \\ \mathbf{v} & A \end{bmatrix}\begin{bmatrix} b & \mathbf{0}^T \\ \mathbf{w} & B \end{bmatrix} = \begin{bmatrix} ab + \mathbf{0}^T\mathbf{w} & a\mathbf{0}^T + \mathbf{0}^TB \\ \mathbf{v}b + A\mathbf{w} & \mathbf{v}\mathbf{0}^T + AB \end{bmatrix} = \begin{bmatrix} ab & \mathbf{0}^T \\ b\mathbf{v} + A\mathbf{w} & AB \end{bmatrix}$$

Since A and B are $k \times k$, AB is lower triangular. The form of A_1B_1 shows that it, too, is lower triangular. Thus the statement about lower triangular matrices is true for $n = k+1$ if it is true for $n = k$. By the principle of induction, the statement is true for all $n \geq 1$.

Note: Exercise 23 is good for mathematics and computer science students. The solution of Exercise 23 in the *Study Guide* shows students how to use the principle of induction. The *Study Guide* also has an appendix on "The Principle of Induction," at the end of Section 2.4. The text presents more applications of induction in Section 3.2 and in the Supplementary Exercises for Chapter 3.

24. Let $A_n = \begin{bmatrix} 1 & 0 & 0 & \cdots & 0 \\ 1 & 1 & 0 & & 0 \\ 1 & 1 & 1 & & 0 \\ \vdots & & & \ddots & \\ 1 & 1 & 1 & \cdots & 1 \end{bmatrix}$, $B_n = \begin{bmatrix} 1 & 0 & 0 & \cdots & 0 \\ -1 & 1 & 0 & & 0 \\ 0 & -1 & 1 & & 0 \\ \vdots & & \ddots & \ddots & \\ 0 & & \cdots & -1 & 1 \end{bmatrix}$.

By direct computation $A_2 B_2 = I_2$. Assume that for $n = k$, the matrix $A_k B_k$ is I_k, and write

$$A_{k+1} = \begin{bmatrix} 1 & \mathbf{0}^T \\ \mathbf{v} & A_k \end{bmatrix} \quad \text{and} \quad B_{k+1} = \begin{bmatrix} 1 & \mathbf{0}^T \\ \mathbf{w} & B_k \end{bmatrix}$$

where $\mathbf{v}$ and $\mathbf{w}$ are in $\mathbf{R}^k$, $\mathbf{v}^T = [1 \ 1 \ \cdots \ 1]$, and $\mathbf{w}^T = [-1 \ 0 \ \cdots \ 0]$. Then

$$A_{k+1} B_{k+1} = \begin{bmatrix} 1 & \mathbf{0}^T \\ \mathbf{v} & A_k \end{bmatrix} \begin{bmatrix} 1 & \mathbf{0}^T \\ \mathbf{w} & B_k \end{bmatrix} = \begin{bmatrix} 1 + \mathbf{0}^T \mathbf{w} & \mathbf{0}^T + \mathbf{0}^T B_k \\ \mathbf{v} + A_k \mathbf{w} & \mathbf{v}\mathbf{0}^T + A_k B_k \end{bmatrix} = \begin{bmatrix} 1 & \mathbf{0}^T \\ \mathbf{0} & I_k \end{bmatrix} = I_{k+1}$$

The (2,1)-entry is $\mathbf{0}$ because $\mathbf{v}$ equals the first column of A_k, and $A_k \mathbf{w}$ is -1 times the first column of A_k. By the principle of induction, $A_n B_n = I_n$ for all $n \geq 2$. Since A_n and B_n are square, the IMT shows that these matrices are invertible, and $B_n = A_n^{-1}$.

Note: An induction proof can also be given using partitions with the form shown below. The details are slightly more complicated.

$$A_{k+1} = \begin{bmatrix} A_k & \mathbf{0} \\ \mathbf{v}^T & 1 \end{bmatrix} \quad \text{and} \quad B_{k+1} = \begin{bmatrix} B_k & \mathbf{0} \\ \mathbf{w}^T & 1 \end{bmatrix}$$

$$A_{k+1} B_{k+1} = \begin{bmatrix} A_k & \mathbf{0} \\ \mathbf{v}^T & 1 \end{bmatrix} \begin{bmatrix} B_k & \mathbf{0} \\ \mathbf{w}^T & 1 \end{bmatrix} = \begin{bmatrix} A_k B_k + \mathbf{0}\mathbf{w}^T & A^k \mathbf{0} + \mathbf{0} \\ \mathbf{v}^T B_k + \mathbf{w}^T & \mathbf{v}^T \mathbf{0} + 1 \end{bmatrix} = \begin{bmatrix} I_k & \mathbf{0} \\ \mathbf{0}^T & 1 \end{bmatrix} = I_{k+1}$$

The (2,1)-entry is $\mathbf{0}^T$ because $\mathbf{v}^T$ times a column of B_k equals the sum of the entries in the column, and all of such sums are zero except the last, which is 1. So $\mathbf{v}^T B_k$ is the negative of $\mathbf{w}^T$. By the principle of induction, $A_n B_n = I_n$ for all $n \geq 2$. Since A_n and B_n are square, the IMT shows that these matrices are invertible, and $B_n = A_n^{-1}$.

25. First, visualize a partition of A as a 2×2 block–diagonal matrix, as below, and then visualize the (2,2)-block itself as a block-diagonal matrix. That is,

$$A = \begin{bmatrix} 1 & 2 & 0 & 0 & 0 \\ 3 & 5 & 0 & 0 & 0 \\ 0 & 0 & 2 & 0 & 0 \\ 0 & 0 & 0 & 7 & 8 \\ 0 & 0 & 0 & 5 & 6 \end{bmatrix} = \begin{bmatrix} A_{11} & 0 \\ 0 & A_{22} \end{bmatrix}, \text{ where } A_{22} = \begin{bmatrix} 2 & 0 & 0 \\ 0 & 7 & 8 \\ 0 & 5 & 6 \end{bmatrix} = \begin{bmatrix} 2 & 0 \\ 0 & B \end{bmatrix}$$

Observe that B is invertible and $B^{-1} = \begin{bmatrix} 3 & -4 \\ -2.5 & 3.5 \end{bmatrix}$. By Exercise 13, the block diagonal matrix A_{22} is invertible, and

$$A_{22}^{-1} = \begin{bmatrix} .5 & 0 \\ 0 & \begin{matrix} 3 & -4 \\ -2.5 & 3.5 \end{matrix} \end{bmatrix} = \begin{bmatrix} .5 & 0 & 0 \\ 0 & 3 & -4 \\ 0 & -2.5 & 3.5 \end{bmatrix}$$

Next, observe that A_{11} is also invertible, with inverse $\begin{bmatrix} -5 & 2 \\ 3 & -1 \end{bmatrix}$. By Exercise 13, A itself is invertible, and its inverse is block diagonal:

$$A^{-1} = \begin{bmatrix} A_{11}^{-1} & 0 \\ 0 & A_{22}^{-1} \end{bmatrix} = \begin{bmatrix} \begin{matrix} -5 & 2 \\ 3 & -1 \end{matrix} & 0 \\ 0 & \begin{matrix} .5 & 0 & 0 \\ 0 & 3 & -4 \\ 0 & -2.5 & 3.5 \end{matrix} \end{bmatrix} = \begin{bmatrix} -5 & 2 & 0 & 0 & 0 \\ 3 & -1 & 0 & 0 & 0 \\ 0 & 0 & .5 & 0 & 0 \\ 0 & 0 & 0 & 3 & -4 \\ 0 & 0 & 0 & -2.5 & 3.5 \end{bmatrix}$$

26. **[M]** This exercise and the next, which involve large matrices, are more appropriate for MATLAB, Maple, and Mathematica, than for the graphic calculators.

a. Display the submatrix of A obtained from rows 15 to 20 and columns 5 to 10.

MATLAB: `A(15:20, 5:10)`

Maple: `submatrix(A, 15..20, 5..10)`

Mathematica: `Take[ A, {15,20}, {5,10} ]`

b. Insert a 5×10 matrix B into rows 10 to 14 and columns 20 to 29 of matrix A:

MATLAB: `A(10:14, 20:29) = B ;`   The semicolon suppresses output display.

Maple: `copyinto(B, A, 10, 20):`   The colon suppresses output display.

Mathematica: `For [ i=10, i<=14, i++,`
  `For [ j=20, j<=29, j++,`
   `A[[ i,j ]] = B[[ i-9, j-19 ]] ] ];`   Colon suppresses output.

c. To create $B = \begin{bmatrix} A & 0 \\ 0 & A^T \end{bmatrix}$ with MATLAB, build B out of four blocks:

   `B = [A zeros(30,20); zeros(20,30) A'];`

Another method: first enter `B = A ;` and then enlarge B with the command

   `B(21:50, 31:50) = A';`

This places A^T in the $(2, 2)$ block of the larger B and fills in the $(1, 2)$ and $(2, 1)$ blocks with zeros.

For Maple:

   `B := matrix(50,50,0):`
   `copyinto(A, B, 1, 1):`
   `copyinto( transpose(A), B, 21, 31):`

For Mathematica:

`B = BlockMatrix[ {{A, ZeroMatrix[30,20]}, ZeroMatrix[20,30],`
`Transpose[A]}} ]`

27. a. **[M]** Construct A from four blocks, say C_{11}, C_{12}, C_{21}, and C_{22}, for example with C_{11} a 30×30 matrix and C_{22} a 20×20 matrix.

MATLAB:
```
C11 = A(1:30, 1:30) + B(1:30, 1:30)

C12 = A(1:30, 31:50) + B(1:30, 31:50)

C21 = A(31:50, 1:30)+ B(31:50, 1:30)

C22 = A(31:50, 31:50) + B(31:50, 31:50)

C = [C11 C12; C21 C22]
```

The commands in Maple and Mathematica are analogous, but with different syntax. The first commands are:

Maple:
```
C11 := submatrix(A, 1..30, 1..30) + submatrix(B, 1..30, 1..30)
```
Mathematica:
```
c11 := Take[ A, {1,30}, {1,30} ] + Take[B, {1,30}, {1,30} ]
```

b. The algebra needed comes from block matrix multiplication:

$$AB = \begin{bmatrix} A_{11} & A_{12} \\ A_{21} & A_{22} \end{bmatrix}\begin{bmatrix} B_{11} & B_{12} \\ B_{21} & B_{22} \end{bmatrix} = \begin{bmatrix} A_{11}B_{11} + A_{12}B_{21} & A_{11}B_{12} + A_{12}B_{22} \\ A_{21}B_{11} + A_{22}B_{21} & A_{21}B_{12} + A_{22}B_{22} \end{bmatrix}$$

Partition both A and B, for example with 30×30 (1, 1) blocks and 20×20 (2, 2) blocks. The four necessary submatrix computations use syntax analogous to that shown for (a).

c. The algebra needed comes from the block matrix equation $\begin{bmatrix} A_{11} & 0 \\ A_{21} & A_{22} \end{bmatrix}\begin{bmatrix} \mathbf{x}_1 \\ \mathbf{x}_2 \end{bmatrix} = \begin{bmatrix} \mathbf{b}_1 \\ \mathbf{b}_2 \end{bmatrix}$, where $\mathbf{x}_1$ and $\mathbf{b}_1$ are in $\mathbf{R}^{30}$ and $\mathbf{x}_2$ and $\mathbf{b}_2$ are in $\mathbf{R}^{20}$. Then $A_{11}\mathbf{x}_1 = \mathbf{b}_1$, which can be solved to produce $\mathbf{x}_1$. Once $\mathbf{x}_1$ is found, rewrite the equation $A_{21}\mathbf{x}_1 + A_{22}\mathbf{x}_2 = \mathbf{b}_2$ as $A_{22}\mathbf{x}_2 = \mathbf{c}$, where $\mathbf{c} = \mathbf{b}_2 - A_{21}\mathbf{x}_1$, and solve $A_{22}\mathbf{x}_2 = \mathbf{c}$ for $\mathbf{x}_2$.

Notes: The following may be used in place of Example 5:

Example 5: Use equation (*) to find formulas for X, Y, and Z in terms of A, B, and C. Mention any assumptions you make in order to produce the formulas.

$$\begin{bmatrix} X & 0 \\ Y & Z \end{bmatrix}\begin{bmatrix} I & 0 \\ A & B \end{bmatrix} = \begin{bmatrix} I & 0 \\ C & I \end{bmatrix} \tag{*}$$

Solution:

This matrix equation provides four equations that can be used to find X, Y, and Z:

$X + 0 = I$, $\qquad\qquad\qquad\qquad 0 = 0$

$YI + ZA = C$, $\qquad\qquad\quad Y0 + ZB = I$ $\qquad\qquad$ (Note the order of the factors.)

The first equation says that $X = I$. To solve the fourth equation, $ZB = I$, assume that B and Z are square. In this case, the equation $ZB = I$ implies that B and Z are invertible, by the IMT. (Actually, it suffices to assume either that B is square or that Z is square.) Then, right-multiply each side of $ZB = I$ to get $ZBB^{-1} = IB^{-1}$ and $Z = B^{-1}$. Finally, the third equation is $Y + ZA = C$. So, $Y + B^{-1}A = C$, and $Y = C - B^{-1}A$.

The following counterexample shows that Z need not be square for the equation (*) above to be true.

$$\begin{bmatrix} 1 & 0 & 0 & 0 & 0 \\ 0 & 1 & 0 & 0 & 0 \\ 1 & 2 & 1 & 3 & 1 \\ 3 & 4 & 1 & 0 & -1 \end{bmatrix}\begin{bmatrix} 1 & 0 & 0 & 0 \\ 0 & 1 & 0 & 0 \\ 1 & 1 & 2 & 5 \\ 1 & 1 & -1 & -3 \\ 1 & -1 & 2 & 4 \end{bmatrix} = \begin{bmatrix} 1 & 0 & 0 & 0 \\ 0 & 1 & 0 & 0 \\ 6 & 5 & 1 & 0 \\ 3 & 6 & 0 & 1 \end{bmatrix}$$

Note that Z is not determined by A, B, and C, when B is not square. For instance, another Z that works in this counterexample is $Z = \begin{bmatrix} 3 & 5 & 0 \\ -1 & -2 & 0 \end{bmatrix}$.

2.5   SOLUTIONS

Notes: Modern algorithms in numerical linear algebra are often described using matrix factorizations. For practical work, this section is more important than Sections 4.7 and 5.4, even though matrix factorizations are explained nicely in terms of change of bases. Computational exercises in this section emphasize the use of the LU factorization to solve linear systems. The LU factorization is performed using the algorithm explained in the paragraphs before Example 2, and performed in Example 2. The text discusses how to build L when no interchanges are needed to reduce the given matrix to U. An appendix in the *Study Guide* discusses how to build L in permuted unit lower triangular form when row interchanges are needed. Other factorizations are introduced in Exercises 22–26.

1. $L = \begin{bmatrix} 1 & 0 & 0 \\ -1 & 1 & 0 \\ 2 & -5 & 1 \end{bmatrix}, U = \begin{bmatrix} 3 & -7 & -2 \\ 0 & -2 & -1 \\ 0 & 0 & -1 \end{bmatrix}, \mathbf{b} = \begin{bmatrix} -7 \\ 5 \\ 2 \end{bmatrix}$. First, solve $L\mathbf{y} = \mathbf{b}$.

$$[L \ \ \mathbf{b}] = \begin{bmatrix} 1 & 0 & 0 & -7 \\ -1 & 1 & 0 & 5 \\ 2 & -5 & 1 & 2 \end{bmatrix} \sim \begin{bmatrix} 1 & 0 & 0 & -7 \\ 0 & 1 & 0 & -2 \\ 0 & -5 & 1 & 16 \end{bmatrix} \text{ The only arithmetic is in column 4}$$

$$\sim \begin{bmatrix} 1 & 0 & 0 & -7 \\ 0 & 1 & 0 & -2 \\ 0 & 0 & 1 & 6 \end{bmatrix}, \text{ so } \mathbf{y} = \begin{bmatrix} -7 \\ -2 \\ 6 \end{bmatrix}.$$

Next, solve $U\mathbf{x} = \mathbf{y}$, using back-substitution (with matrix notation).

$$[U \ \ \mathbf{y}] = \begin{bmatrix} 3 & -7 & -2 & -7 \\ 0 & -2 & -1 & -2 \\ 0 & 0 & -1 & 6 \end{bmatrix} \sim \begin{bmatrix} 3 & -7 & -2 & -7 \\ 0 & -2 & -1 & -2 \\ 0 & 0 & 1 & -6 \end{bmatrix} \sim \begin{bmatrix} 3 & -7 & 0 & -19 \\ 0 & -2 & 0 & -8 \\ 0 & 0 & 1 & -6 \end{bmatrix}$$

$$\sim \begin{bmatrix} 3 & -7 & 0 & -19 \\ 0 & 1 & 0 & 4 \\ 0 & 0 & 1 & -6 \end{bmatrix} \sim \begin{bmatrix} 3 & 0 & 0 & 9 \\ 0 & 1 & 0 & 4 \\ 0 & 0 & 1 & -6 \end{bmatrix} \sim \begin{bmatrix} 1 & 0 & 0 & 3 \\ 0 & 1 & 0 & 4 \\ 0 & 0 & 1 & -6 \end{bmatrix}$$

So $\mathbf{x} = (3, 4, -6)$.

To confirm this result, row reduce the matrix $[A \ \mathbf{b}]$:

$$[A \ \ \mathbf{b}] = \begin{bmatrix} 3 & -7 & -2 & -7 \\ -3 & 5 & 1 & 5 \\ 6 & -4 & 0 & 2 \end{bmatrix} \sim \begin{bmatrix} 3 & -7 & -2 & -7 \\ 0 & -2 & -1 & -2 \\ 0 & 10 & 4 & 16 \end{bmatrix} \sim \begin{bmatrix} 3 & -7 & -2 & -7 \\ 0 & -2 & -1 & -2 \\ 0 & 0 & -1 & 6 \end{bmatrix}$$

From this point the row reduction follows that of $[U \ \ \mathbf{y}]$ above, yielding the same result.

2. $L = \begin{bmatrix} 1 & 0 & 0 \\ -1 & 1 & 0 \\ 2 & 0 & 1 \end{bmatrix}, U = \begin{bmatrix} 4 & 3 & -5 \\ 0 & -2 & 2 \\ 0 & 0 & 2 \end{bmatrix}, \mathbf{b} = \begin{bmatrix} 2 \\ -4 \\ 6 \end{bmatrix}$. First, solve $L\mathbf{y} = \mathbf{b}$:

$$[L \ \ \mathbf{b}] = \begin{bmatrix} 1 & 0 & 0 & 2 \\ -1 & 1 & 0 & -4 \\ 2 & 0 & 1 & 6 \end{bmatrix} \sim \begin{bmatrix} 1 & 0 & 0 & 2 \\ 0 & 1 & 0 & -2 \\ 0 & 0 & 1 & 2 \end{bmatrix},$$

so $\mathbf{y} = \begin{bmatrix} 2 \\ -2 \\ 2 \end{bmatrix}$.

Next solve $U\mathbf{x} = \mathbf{y}$, using back-substitution (with matrix notation):

$$[U \ \ \mathbf{y}] = \begin{bmatrix} 4 & 3 & -5 & 2 \\ 0 & -2 & 2 & -2 \\ 0 & 0 & 2 & 2 \end{bmatrix} \sim \begin{bmatrix} 4 & 3 & -5 & 2 \\ 0 & -2 & 2 & -2 \\ 0 & 0 & 1 & 1 \end{bmatrix} \sim \begin{bmatrix} 4 & 3 & 0 & 7 \\ 0 & -2 & 0 & -4 \\ 0 & 0 & 1 & 1 \end{bmatrix}$$

$$\sim \begin{bmatrix} 4 & 3 & 0 & 7 \\ 0 & 1 & 0 & 2 \\ 0 & 0 & 1 & 1 \end{bmatrix} \sim \begin{bmatrix} 4 & 0 & 0 & 1 \\ 0 & 1 & 0 & 2 \\ 0 & 0 & 1 & 1 \end{bmatrix} \sim \begin{bmatrix} 1 & 0 & 0 & 1/4 \\ 0 & 1 & 0 & 2 \\ 0 & 0 & 1 & 1 \end{bmatrix},$$

so $\mathbf{x} = (1/4, 2, 1)$. To confirm this result, row reduce the matrix $[A \ \ \mathbf{b}]$:

$$[A \ \ \mathbf{b}] = \begin{bmatrix} 4 & 3 & -5 & 2 \\ -4 & -5 & 7 & -4 \\ 8 & 6 & -8 & 6 \end{bmatrix} \sim \begin{bmatrix} 4 & 3 & -5 & 2 \\ 0 & -2 & 2 & -2 \\ 0 & 0 & 2 & 2 \end{bmatrix}$$

From this point the row reduction follows that of $[U \ \ \mathbf{y}]$ above, yielding the same result.

3. $L = \begin{bmatrix} 1 & 0 & 0 \\ -3 & 1 & 0 \\ 4 & -1 & 1 \end{bmatrix}, U = \begin{bmatrix} 2 & -1 & 2 \\ 0 & -3 & 4 \\ 0 & 0 & 1 \end{bmatrix}, \mathbf{b} = \begin{bmatrix} 1 \\ 0 \\ 4 \end{bmatrix}$. First, solve $L\mathbf{y} = \mathbf{b}$:

$$[L \ \ \mathbf{b}] = \begin{bmatrix} 1 & 0 & 0 & 1 \\ -3 & 1 & 0 & 0 \\ 4 & -1 & 1 & 4 \end{bmatrix} \sim \begin{bmatrix} 1 & 0 & 0 & 1 \\ 0 & 1 & 0 & 3 \\ 0 & -1 & 1 & 0 \end{bmatrix} \sim \begin{bmatrix} 1 & 0 & 0 & 1 \\ 0 & 1 & 0 & 3 \\ 0 & 0 & 1 & 0 \end{bmatrix},$$

so $\mathbf{y} = \begin{bmatrix} 1 \\ 3 \\ 3 \end{bmatrix}$.

Next solve $U\mathbf{x} = \mathbf{y}$, using back-substitution (with matrix notation):

$$[U \ \ \mathbf{y}] = \begin{bmatrix} 2 & -1 & 2 & 1 \\ 0 & -3 & 4 & 3 \\ 0 & 0 & 1 & 3 \end{bmatrix} \sim \begin{bmatrix} 2 & -1 & 0 & -5 \\ 0 & -3 & 0 & -9 \\ 0 & 0 & 1 & 3 \end{bmatrix} \sim \begin{bmatrix} 2 & -1 & 0 & -5 \\ 0 & 1 & 0 & 3 \\ 0 & 0 & 1 & 3 \end{bmatrix}$$

$$\sim \begin{bmatrix} 2 & 0 & 0 & -2 \\ 0 & 1 & 0 & 3 \\ 0 & 0 & 1 & 3 \end{bmatrix},$$

so $\mathbf{x} = (-1, 3, 3)$.

4. $L = \begin{bmatrix} 1 & 0 & 0 \\ 1/2 & 1 & 0 \\ 3/2 & -5 & 1 \end{bmatrix}, U = \begin{bmatrix} 2 & -2 & 4 \\ 0 & -2 & -1 \\ 0 & 0 & -6 \end{bmatrix}, \mathbf{b} = \begin{bmatrix} 0 \\ -5 \\ 7 \end{bmatrix}$. First, solve $L\mathbf{y} = \mathbf{b}$:

$$[L \quad \mathbf{b}] = \begin{bmatrix} 1 & 0 & 0 & 0 \\ 1/2 & 1 & 0 & -5 \\ 3/2 & -5 & 1 & 7 \end{bmatrix} \sim \begin{bmatrix} 1 & 0 & 0 & 0 \\ 0 & 1 & 0 & -5 \\ 0 & -5 & 1 & 7 \end{bmatrix} \sim \begin{bmatrix} 1 & 0 & 0 & 0 \\ 0 & 1 & 0 & -5 \\ 0 & 0 & 1 & -18 \end{bmatrix},$$

so $\mathbf{y} = \begin{bmatrix} 0 \\ -5 \\ -18 \end{bmatrix}$.

Next solve $U\mathbf{x} = \mathbf{y}$, using back-substitution (with matrix notation):

$$[U \quad \mathbf{y}] = \begin{bmatrix} 2 & -2 & 4 & 0 \\ 0 & -2 & -1 & -5 \\ 0 & 0 & -6 & -18 \end{bmatrix} \sim \begin{bmatrix} 2 & -2 & 4 & 0 \\ 0 & -2 & -1 & -5 \\ 0 & 0 & 1 & 3 \end{bmatrix} \sim \begin{bmatrix} 2 & -2 & 0 & -12 \\ 0 & -2 & 0 & -2 \\ 0 & 0 & 1 & 3 \end{bmatrix}$$

$$\sim \begin{bmatrix} 2 & -2 & 0 & -12 \\ 0 & 1 & 0 & 1 \\ 0 & 0 & 1 & 3 \end{bmatrix} \sim \begin{bmatrix} 2 & 0 & 0 & -10 \\ 0 & 1 & 0 & 1 \\ 0 & 0 & 1 & 3 \end{bmatrix} \sim \begin{bmatrix} 1 & 0 & 0 & -5 \\ 0 & 1 & 0 & 1 \\ 0 & 0 & 1 & 3 \end{bmatrix},$$

so $\mathbf{x} = (-5, 1, 3)$.

5. $L = \begin{bmatrix} 1 & 0 & 0 & 0 \\ 2 & 1 & 0 & 0 \\ -1 & 0 & 1 & 0 \\ -4 & 3 & -5 & 1 \end{bmatrix}, U = \begin{bmatrix} 1 & -2 & -4 & -3 \\ 0 & -3 & 1 & 0 \\ 0 & 0 & 2 & 1 \\ 0 & 0 & 0 & 1 \end{bmatrix}, \mathbf{b} = \begin{bmatrix} 1 \\ 7 \\ 0 \\ 3 \end{bmatrix}$. First solve $L\mathbf{y} = \mathbf{b}$:

$$[L \quad \mathbf{b}] = \begin{bmatrix} 1 & 0 & 0 & 0 & 1 \\ 2 & 1 & 0 & 0 & 7 \\ -1 & 0 & 1 & 0 & 0 \\ -4 & 3 & -5 & 1 & 3 \end{bmatrix} \sim \begin{bmatrix} 1 & 0 & 0 & 0 & 1 \\ 0 & 1 & 0 & 0 & 5 \\ 0 & 0 & 1 & 0 & 1 \\ 0 & 3 & -5 & 1 & 7 \end{bmatrix}$$

$$\sim \begin{bmatrix} 1 & 0 & 0 & 0 & 1 \\ 0 & 1 & 0 & 0 & 5 \\ 0 & 0 & 1 & 0 & 1 \\ 0 & 0 & -5 & 1 & -8 \end{bmatrix} \sim \begin{bmatrix} 1 & 0 & 0 & 0 & 1 \\ 0 & 1 & 0 & 0 & 5 \\ 0 & 0 & 1 & 0 & 1 \\ 0 & 0 & 0 & 1 & -3 \end{bmatrix},$$

so $\mathbf{y} = \begin{bmatrix} 1 \\ 5 \\ 1 \\ -3 \end{bmatrix}$.

Next solve $U\mathbf{x} = \mathbf{y}$, using back-substitution (with matrix notation):

$$[U \quad \mathbf{y}] = \begin{bmatrix} 1 & -2 & -4 & -3 & 1 \\ 0 & -3 & 1 & 0 & 5 \\ 0 & 0 & 2 & 1 & 1 \\ 0 & 0 & 0 & 1 & -3 \end{bmatrix} \sim \begin{bmatrix} 1 & -2 & -4 & 0 & -8 \\ 0 & -3 & 1 & 0 & 5 \\ 0 & 0 & 2 & 0 & 4 \\ 0 & 0 & 0 & 1 & -3 \end{bmatrix}$$

$$
\sim \begin{bmatrix} 1 & -2 & -4 & 0 & -8 \\ 0 & -3 & 1 & 0 & 5 \\ 0 & 0 & 1 & 0 & 2 \\ 0 & 0 & 0 & 1 & -3 \end{bmatrix} \sim \begin{bmatrix} 1 & -2 & 0 & 0 & 0 \\ 0 & -3 & 0 & 0 & 3 \\ 0 & 0 & 1 & 0 & 2 \\ 0 & 0 & 0 & 1 & -3 \end{bmatrix}
$$

$$
\sim \begin{bmatrix} 1 & -2 & 0 & 0 & 0 \\ 0 & 1 & 0 & 0 & -1 \\ 0 & 0 & 1 & 0 & 2 \\ 0 & 0 & 0 & 1 & -3 \end{bmatrix} \sim \begin{bmatrix} 1 & 0 & 0 & 0 & -2 \\ 0 & 1 & 0 & 0 & -1 \\ 0 & 0 & 1 & 0 & 2 \\ 0 & 0 & 0 & 1 & -3 \end{bmatrix},
$$

so $\mathbf{x} = (-2, -1, 2, -3)$.

6. $L = \begin{bmatrix} 1 & 0 & 0 & 0 \\ -3 & 1 & 0 & 0 \\ 3 & -2 & 1 & 0 \\ -5 & 4 & -1 & 1 \end{bmatrix}, U = \begin{bmatrix} 1 & 3 & 4 & 0 \\ 0 & 3 & 5 & 2 \\ 0 & 0 & -2 & 0 \\ 0 & 0 & 0 & 1 \end{bmatrix}, \mathbf{b} = \begin{bmatrix} 1 \\ -2 \\ -1 \\ 2 \end{bmatrix}$. First, solve $L\mathbf{y} = \mathbf{b}$:

$$
[L \quad \mathbf{b}] = \begin{bmatrix} 1 & 0 & 0 & 0 & 1 \\ -3 & 1 & 0 & 0 & -2 \\ 3 & -2 & 1 & 0 & -1 \\ -5 & 4 & -1 & 1 & 2 \end{bmatrix} \sim \begin{bmatrix} 1 & 0 & 0 & 0 & 1 \\ 0 & 1 & 0 & 0 & 1 \\ 0 & -2 & 1 & 0 & -4 \\ 0 & 4 & -1 & 1 & 7 \end{bmatrix}
$$

$$
\sim \begin{bmatrix} 1 & 0 & 0 & 0 & 1 \\ 0 & 1 & 0 & 0 & 1 \\ 0 & 0 & 1 & 0 & -2 \\ 0 & 0 & -1 & 1 & 3 \end{bmatrix} \sim \begin{bmatrix} 1 & 0 & 0 & 0 & 1 \\ 0 & 1 & 0 & 0 & 1 \\ 0 & 0 & 1 & 0 & -2 \\ 0 & 0 & 0 & 1 & 1 \end{bmatrix},
$$

so $\mathbf{y} = \begin{bmatrix} 1 \\ 1 \\ -2 \\ 1 \end{bmatrix}$.

Next solve $U\mathbf{x} = \mathbf{y}$, using back-substitution (with matrix notation):

$$
[U \quad \mathbf{y}] = \begin{bmatrix} 1 & 3 & 4 & 0 & 1 \\ 0 & 3 & 5 & 2 & 1 \\ 0 & 0 & -2 & 0 & -2 \\ 0 & 0 & 0 & 1 & 1 \end{bmatrix} \sim \begin{bmatrix} 1 & 3 & 4 & 0 & 1 \\ 0 & 3 & 5 & 0 & -1 \\ 0 & 0 & -2 & 0 & -2 \\ 0 & 0 & 0 & 1 & 1 \end{bmatrix}
$$

$$
\sim \begin{bmatrix} 1 & 3 & 4 & 0 & 1 \\ 0 & 3 & 5 & 0 & -1 \\ 0 & 0 & 1 & 0 & 1 \\ 0 & 0 & 0 & 1 & 1 \end{bmatrix} \sim \begin{bmatrix} 1 & 3 & 0 & 0 & -3 \\ 0 & 3 & 0 & 0 & -6 \\ 0 & 0 & 1 & 0 & 1 \\ 0 & 0 & 0 & 1 & 1 \end{bmatrix}
$$

$$
\sim \begin{bmatrix} 1 & 3 & 0 & 0 & -3 \\ 0 & 1 & 0 & 0 & -2 \\ 0 & 0 & 1 & 0 & 1 \\ 0 & 0 & 0 & 1 & 1 \end{bmatrix} \sim \begin{bmatrix} 1 & 0 & 0 & 0 & 3 \\ 0 & 1 & 0 & 0 & -2 \\ 0 & 0 & 1 & 0 & 1 \\ 0 & 0 & 0 & 1 & 1 \end{bmatrix},
$$

so $\mathbf{x} = (3, -2, 1, 1)$.

7. Place the first pivot column of $\begin{bmatrix} 2 & 5 \\ -3 & -4 \end{bmatrix}$ into L, after dividing the column by 2 (the pivot), then add

$3/2$ times row 1 to row 2, yielding U.

$$A = \begin{bmatrix} ② & 5 \\ -3 & ⊖4 \end{bmatrix} \sim \begin{bmatrix} 2 & 5 \\ 0 & ⑦/2 \end{bmatrix} = U$$

$$\begin{bmatrix} ② \\ -3 \end{bmatrix} \quad [⑦/2]$$

$$\div 2 \qquad \div 7/2$$

$$\begin{bmatrix} 1 \\ -3/2 & 1 \end{bmatrix}, \ L = \begin{bmatrix} 1 & 0 \\ -3/2 & 1 \end{bmatrix}$$

8. Row reduce A to echelon form using only row replacement operations. Then follow the algorithm in Example 2 to find L.

$$A = \begin{bmatrix} ⑥ & 9 \\ 4 & 5 \end{bmatrix} \sim \begin{bmatrix} 6 & 9 \\ 0 & ⊖1 \end{bmatrix} = U$$

$$\begin{bmatrix} ⑥ \\ 4 \end{bmatrix} \quad [⊖1]$$

$$\div 6 \qquad \div -1$$

$$\begin{bmatrix} 1 \\ 2/3 & 1 \end{bmatrix}, \ L = \begin{bmatrix} 1 & 0 \\ 2/3 & 1 \end{bmatrix}$$

9. $A = \begin{bmatrix} ③ & -1 & 2 \\ -3 & -2 & 10 \\ 9 & -5 & 6 \end{bmatrix} \sim \begin{bmatrix} 3 & -1 & 2 \\ 0 & ⊖3 & 12 \\ 0 & -2 & 0 \end{bmatrix} \sim \begin{bmatrix} 3 & -1 & 2 \\ 0 & -3 & 12 \\ 0 & 0 & ⊖8 \end{bmatrix} = U$

$$\begin{bmatrix} ③ \\ -3 \\ 9 \end{bmatrix} \quad \begin{bmatrix} ⊖3 \\ -2 \end{bmatrix} \quad [⊖8]$$

$$\div 3 \qquad \div -3 \qquad \div -8$$

$$\begin{bmatrix} 1 \\ -1 & 1 \\ 3 & 2/3 & 1 \end{bmatrix}, \ L = \begin{bmatrix} 1 & 0 & 0 \\ -1 & 1 & 0 \\ 3 & 2/3 & 1 \end{bmatrix}$$

10. $A = \begin{bmatrix} -5 & 3 & 4 \\ 10 & -8 & -9 \\ 15 & 1 & 2 \end{bmatrix} \sim \begin{bmatrix} -5 & 3 & 4 \\ 0 & -2 & -1 \\ 0 & 10 & 14 \end{bmatrix} \sim \begin{bmatrix} -5 & 3 & 4 \\ 0 & -2 & -1 \\ 0 & 0 & 9 \end{bmatrix} = U$

$\begin{bmatrix} -5 \\ 10 \\ 15 \end{bmatrix} \begin{bmatrix} -2 \\ 10 \end{bmatrix} [9]$

$\div -5 \quad \div -2 \quad \div 9$

$\begin{bmatrix} 1 & & \\ -2 & 1 & \\ -3 & -5 & 1 \end{bmatrix}, \quad L = \begin{bmatrix} 1 & 0 & 0 \\ -2 & 1 & 0 \\ -3 & -5 & 1 \end{bmatrix}$

11. $A = \begin{bmatrix} 3 & -6 & 3 \\ 6 & -7 & 2 \\ -1 & 7 & 0 \end{bmatrix} \sim \begin{bmatrix} 3 & -6 & 3 \\ 0 & 5 & -4 \\ 0 & 5 & 1 \end{bmatrix} \sim \begin{bmatrix} 3 & -6 & 3 \\ 0 & 5 & -4 \\ 0 & 0 & 5 \end{bmatrix} = U$

$\begin{bmatrix} 3 \\ 6 \\ -1 \end{bmatrix} \begin{bmatrix} 5 \\ 5 \end{bmatrix} [5]$

$\div 3 \quad \div 5 \quad \div 5$

$\begin{bmatrix} 1 & & \\ 2 & 1 & \\ -1/3 & 1 & 1 \end{bmatrix}, \quad L = \begin{bmatrix} 1 & 0 & 0 \\ 2 & 1 & 0 \\ -1/3 & 1 & 1 \end{bmatrix}$

12. Row reduce A to echelon form using only row replacement operations. Then follow the algorithm in Example 2 to find L. Use the last column of I_3 to make L unit lower triangular.

$A = \begin{bmatrix} 2 & -4 & 2 \\ 1 & 5 & -4 \\ -6 & -2 & 4 \end{bmatrix} \sim \begin{bmatrix} 2 & -4 & 2 \\ 0 & 7 & -5 \\ 0 & -14 & 10 \end{bmatrix} \sim \begin{bmatrix} 2 & -4 & 2 \\ 0 & 7 & -5 \\ 0 & 0 & 0 \end{bmatrix} = U$

$\begin{bmatrix} 2 \\ 1 \\ -6 \end{bmatrix} \begin{bmatrix} 7 \\ -14 \end{bmatrix}$

$\div 2 \quad \div 7$

$\begin{bmatrix} 1 & & \\ 1/2 & 1 & \\ -3 & -2 & 1 \end{bmatrix}, \quad L = \begin{bmatrix} 1 & 0 & 0 \\ 1/2 & 1 & 0 \\ -3 & -2 & 1 \end{bmatrix}$

13.

$$\begin{bmatrix} ① & 3 & -5 & -3 \\ -1 & -5 & 8 & 4 \\ 4 & 2 & -5 & -7 \\ -2 & -4 & 7 & 5 \end{bmatrix} \sim \begin{bmatrix} 1 & 3 & -5 & -3 \\ 0 & ⊟2 & 3 & 1 \\ 0 & -10 & 15 & 5 \\ 0 & 2 & -3 & -1 \end{bmatrix} \sim \begin{bmatrix} 1 & 3 & -5 & -3 \\ 0 & -2 & 3 & 1 \\ 0 & 0 & 0 & 0 \\ 0 & 0 & 0 & 0 \end{bmatrix} = U \quad \text{No more pivots!}$$

$$\begin{bmatrix} ① \\ -1 \\ 4 \\ -2 \end{bmatrix} \begin{bmatrix} ⊟2 \\ -10 \\ 2 \end{bmatrix}$$ Use the last two columns of I_4 to make L unit lower triangular.

$\div 1 \quad \div -2$

$$\begin{bmatrix} 1 & & & \\ -1 & 1 & & \\ 4 & 5 & 1 & \\ -2 & -1 & 0 & 1 \end{bmatrix}, \quad L = \begin{bmatrix} 1 & 0 & 0 & 0 \\ -1 & 1 & 0 & 0 \\ 4 & 5 & 1 & 0 \\ -2 & -1 & 0 & 1 \end{bmatrix}$$

14. $A = \begin{bmatrix} ① & 4 & -1 & 5 \\ 3 & 7 & -2 & 9 \\ -2 & -3 & 1 & -4 \\ -1 & 6 & -1 & 7 \end{bmatrix} \sim \begin{bmatrix} 1 & 4 & -1 & 5 \\ 0 & ⊟5 & 1 & -6 \\ 0 & 5 & -1 & 6 \\ 0 & 10 & -2 & 12 \end{bmatrix} \sim \begin{bmatrix} 1 & 4 & -1 & 5 \\ 0 & -5 & 1 & -6 \\ 0 & 0 & 0 & 0 \\ 0 & 0 & 0 & 0 \end{bmatrix} = U$

$$\begin{bmatrix} ① \\ 3 \\ -2 \\ -1 \end{bmatrix} \begin{bmatrix} ⊟5 \\ 5 \\ 10 \end{bmatrix}$$ Use the last two columns of I_4 to make L unit lower triangular.

$\div 1 \quad \div -5$

$$\begin{bmatrix} 1 & & & \\ 3 & 1 & & \\ -2 & -1 & 1 & \\ -1 & -2 & 0 & 1 \end{bmatrix}, \quad L = \begin{bmatrix} 1 & 0 & 0 & 0 \\ 3 & 1 & 0 & 0 \\ -2 & -1 & 1 & 0 \\ -1 & -2 & 0 & 1 \end{bmatrix}$$

15. $A = \begin{bmatrix} ②　 & -4 & 4 & -2 \\ 6 & -9 & 7 & -3 \\ -1 & -4 & 8 & 0 \end{bmatrix} \sim \begin{bmatrix} 2 & -4 & 4 & -2 \\ 0 & ③ & -5 & 3 \\ 0 & -6 & 10 & -1 \end{bmatrix} \sim \begin{bmatrix} 2 & -4 & 4 & -2 \\ 0 & 3 & -5 & 3 \\ 0 & 0 & 0 & ⑤ \end{bmatrix} = U$

$\begin{bmatrix} ② \\ 6 \\ -1 \end{bmatrix} \begin{bmatrix} ③ \\ -6 \end{bmatrix} [⑤]$

$\div 2 \quad \div 3 \quad \div 5$

$\begin{bmatrix} 1 & & \\ 3 & 1 & \\ -1/2 & -2 & 1 \end{bmatrix}, \quad L = \begin{bmatrix} 1 & 0 & 0 \\ 3 & 1 & 0 \\ -1/2 & -2 & 1 \end{bmatrix}$

16. $A = \begin{bmatrix} ② & -6 & 6 \\ -4 & 5 & -7 \\ 3 & 5 & -1 \\ -6 & 4 & -8 \\ 8 & -3 & 9 \end{bmatrix} \sim \begin{bmatrix} 2 & -6 & 6 \\ 0 & ⑦ & 5 \\ 0 & 14 & -10 \\ 0 & -14 & 10 \\ 0 & 21 & -15 \end{bmatrix} \sim \begin{bmatrix} 2 & -6 & 6 \\ 0 & -7 & 5 \\ 0 & 0 & 0 \\ 0 & 0 & 0 \\ 0 & 0 & 0 \end{bmatrix} = U$

$\begin{bmatrix} ② \\ -4 \\ 3 \\ -6 \\ 8 \end{bmatrix} \begin{bmatrix} ⑦ \\ 14 \\ -14 \\ 21 \end{bmatrix}$ Use the last three columns of I_5 to make L unit lower triangular.

$\div 2 \quad \div -7$

$\begin{bmatrix} 1 & & & & \\ -2 & 1 & & & \\ 3/2 & -2 & 1 & & \\ -3 & 2 & 0 & 1 & \\ 4 & -3 & 0 & 0 & 1 \end{bmatrix}, \quad L = \begin{bmatrix} 1 & 0 & 0 & 0 & 0 \\ -2 & 1 & 0 & 0 & 0 \\ 3/2 & -2 & 1 & 0 & 0 \\ -3 & 2 & 0 & 1 & 0 \\ 4 & -3 & 0 & 0 & 1 \end{bmatrix}$

17. $L = \begin{bmatrix} 1 & 0 & 0 \\ -1 & 1 & 0 \\ 2 & 0 & 1 \end{bmatrix}$, $U = \begin{bmatrix} 4 & 3 & -5 \\ 0 & -2 & 2 \\ 0 & 0 & 2 \end{bmatrix}$ To find L^{-1}, use the method of Section 2.2; that is, row reduce $[L \ I]$:

$[L \ I] = \begin{bmatrix} 1 & 0 & 0 & 1 & 0 & 0 \\ -1 & 1 & 0 & 0 & 1 & 0 \\ 2 & 0 & 1 & 0 & 0 & 1 \end{bmatrix} \sim \begin{bmatrix} 1 & 0 & 0 & 1 & 0 & 0 \\ 0 & 1 & 0 & 1 & 1 & 0 \\ 0 & 0 & 1 & -2 & 0 & 1 \end{bmatrix} = [I \ L^{-1}],$

so $L^{-1} = \begin{bmatrix} 1 & 0 & 0 \\ 1 & 1 & 0 \\ -2 & 0 & 1 \end{bmatrix}$. Likewise to find U^{-1}, row reduce $[U\ I]$:

$$[U\ I] = \begin{bmatrix} 4 & 3 & -5 & 1 & 0 & 0 \\ 0 & -2 & 2 & 0 & 1 & 0 \\ 0 & 0 & 2 & 0 & 0 & 1 \end{bmatrix} \sim \begin{bmatrix} 4 & 3 & 0 & 1 & 0 & 5/2 \\ 0 & -2 & 0 & 0 & 1 & -1 \\ 0 & 0 & 2 & 0 & 0 & 1 \end{bmatrix}$$

$$\sim \begin{bmatrix} 4 & 0 & 0 & 1 & 3/2 & 1 \\ 0 & -2 & 0 & 0 & 1 & -1 \\ 0 & 0 & 2 & 0 & 0 & 1 \end{bmatrix} \sim \begin{bmatrix} 1 & 0 & 0 & 1/4 & 3/8 & 1/4 \\ 0 & 1 & 0 & 0 & -1/2 & 1/2 \\ 0 & 0 & 1 & 0 & 0 & 1/2 \end{bmatrix} = [I\ U^{-1}],$$

so $U^{-1} = \begin{bmatrix} 1/4 & 3/8 & 1/4 \\ 0 & -1/2 & 1/2 \\ 0 & 0 & 1/2 \end{bmatrix}$. Thus

$$A^{-1} = U^{-1}L^{-1} = \begin{bmatrix} 1/4 & 3/8 & 1/4 \\ 0 & -1/2 & 1/2 \\ 0 & 0 & 1/2 \end{bmatrix}\begin{bmatrix} 1 & 0 & 0 \\ 1 & 1 & 0 \\ -2 & 0 & 1 \end{bmatrix} = \begin{bmatrix} 1/8 & 3/8 & 1/4 \\ -3/2 & -1/2 & 1/2 \\ -1 & 0 & 1/2 \end{bmatrix}$$

18. $L = \begin{bmatrix} 1 & 0 & 0 \\ -3 & 1 & 0 \\ 4 & -1 & 1 \end{bmatrix}$, $U = \begin{bmatrix} 2 & -1 & 2 \\ 0 & -3 & 4 \\ 0 & 0 & 1 \end{bmatrix}$ To find L^{-1}, row reduce $[L\ I]$:

$$[L\ I] = \begin{bmatrix} 1 & 0 & 0 & 1 & 0 & 0 \\ -3 & 1 & 0 & 0 & 1 & 0 \\ 4 & -1 & 1 & 0 & 0 & 1 \end{bmatrix} \sim \begin{bmatrix} 1 & 0 & 0 & 1 & 0 & 0 \\ 0 & 1 & 0 & 3 & 1 & 0 \\ 0 & -1 & 1 & -4 & 0 & 1 \end{bmatrix}$$

$$\sim \begin{bmatrix} 1 & 0 & 0 & 1 & 0 & 0 \\ 0 & 1 & 0 & 3 & 1 & 0 \\ 0 & 0 & 1 & -1 & 1 & 1 \end{bmatrix} = \begin{bmatrix} I & L^{-1} \end{bmatrix},$$

so $L^{-1} = \begin{bmatrix} 1 & 0 & 0 \\ 3 & 1 & 0 \\ -1 & 1 & 1 \end{bmatrix}$. Likewise to find U^{-1}, row reduce $\begin{bmatrix} U & I \end{bmatrix}$:

$$\begin{bmatrix} U & I \end{bmatrix} = \begin{bmatrix} 2 & -1 & 2 & 1 & 0 & 0 \\ 0 & -3 & 4 & 0 & 1 & 0 \\ 0 & 0 & 1 & 0 & 0 & 1 \end{bmatrix} \sim \begin{bmatrix} 2 & -1 & 0 & 1 & 0 & -2 \\ 0 & -3 & 0 & 0 & 1 & -4 \\ 0 & 0 & 1 & 0 & 0 & 1 \end{bmatrix}$$

$$\sim \begin{bmatrix} 2 & -1 & 0 & 1 & 0 & -2 \\ 0 & 1 & 0 & 0 & -1/3 & 4/3 \\ 0 & 0 & 1 & 0 & 0 & 1 \end{bmatrix} \sim \begin{bmatrix} 2 & 0 & 0 & 1 & -1/3 & -2/3 \\ 0 & 1 & 0 & 0 & -1/3 & 4/3 \\ 0 & 0 & 1 & 0 & 0 & 1 \end{bmatrix}$$

$$\sim \begin{bmatrix} 1 & 0 & 0 & 1/2 & -1/6 & -1/3 \\ 0 & 1 & 0 & 0 & -1/3 & 4/3 \\ 0 & 0 & 1 & 0 & 0 & 1 \end{bmatrix} = [I\ U^{-1}],$$

so $U^{-1} = \begin{bmatrix} 1/2 & -1/6 & -1/3 \\ 0 & -1/3 & 4/3 \\ 0 & 0 & 1 \end{bmatrix}$. Thus

$$A^{-1} = U^{-1}L^{-1} = \begin{bmatrix} 1/2 & -1/6 & -1/3 \\ 0 & -1/3 & 4/3 \\ 0 & 0 & 1 \end{bmatrix} \begin{bmatrix} 1 & 0 & 0 \\ 3 & 1 & 0 \\ -1 & 1 & 1 \end{bmatrix} = \begin{bmatrix} 1/3 & -1/2 & -1/3 \\ -7/3 & 1 & 4/3 \\ -1 & 1 & 1 \end{bmatrix}$$

19. Let A be a lower-triangular $n \times n$ matrix with nonzero entries on the diagonal, and consider the augmented matrix $[A \ \ I]$.

  a. The (1, 1)-entry can be scaled to 1 and the entries below it can be changed to 0 by adding multiples of row 1 to the rows below. This affects only the first column of A and the first column of I. So the (2, 2)-entry in the new matrix is still nonzero and now is the only nonzero entry of row 2 in the first n columns (because A was lower triangular).

  The (2, 2)-entry can be scaled to 1, the entries below it can be changed to 0 by adding multiples of row 2 to the rows below. This affects only columns 2 and $n + 2$ of the augmented matrix. Now the (3, 3) entry in A is the only nonzero entry of the third row in the first n columns, so it can be scaled to 1 and then used as a pivot to zero out entries below it. Continuing in this way, A is eventually reduced to I, by scaling each row with a pivot and then using only row operations that add multiples of the pivot row to rows below.

  b. The row operations just described only add rows to rows below, so the I on the right in $[A \ I]$ changes into a lower triangular matrix. By Theorem 7 in Section 2.2, that matrix is A^{-1}.

20. Let $A = LU$ be an LU factorization for A. Since L is unit lower triangular, it is invertible by Exercise 19. Thus by the Invertible Matrix Theroem, L may be row reduced to I. But L is unit lower triangular, so it can be row reduced to I by adding suitable multiples of a row to the rows below it, beginning with the top row. Note that all of the described row operations done to L are row-replacement operations. If elementary matrices $E_1, E_2, \dots E_p$ implement these row-replacement operations, then

$$E_p \dots E_2 E_1 A = (E_p \dots E_2 E_1)LU = IU = U$$

This shows that A may be row reduced to U using only row-replacement operations.

21. (Solution in *Study Guide*.) Suppose $A = BC$, with B invertible. Then there exist elementary matrices $E_1, \dots, E_p$ corresponding to row operations that reduce B to I, in the sense that $E_p \dots E_1 B = I$. Applying the same sequence of row operations to A amounts to left-multiplying A by the product $E_p \dots E_1$. By associativity of matrix multiplication.

$$E_p \dots E_1 A = E_p \dots E_1 BC = IC = C$$

so the same sequence of row operations reduces A to C.

22. First find an LU factorization for A. Row reduce A to echelon form using only row replacement operations:

$$A = \begin{bmatrix} ② & -4 & -2 & 3 \\ 6 & -9 & -5 & 8 \\ 2 & -7 & -3 & 9 \\ 4 & -2 & -2 & -1 \\ -6 & 3 & 3 & 4 \end{bmatrix} \sim \begin{bmatrix} 2 & -4 & -2 & 3 \\ 0 & ③ & 1 & -1 \\ 0 & -3 & -1 & 6 \\ 0 & 6 & 2 & -7 \\ 0 & -9 & -3 & 13 \end{bmatrix} \sim \begin{bmatrix} 2 & -4 & -2 & 3 \\ 0 & 3 & 1 & -1 \\ 0 & 0 & 0 & ⑤ \\ 0 & 0 & 0 & -5 \\ 0 & 0 & 0 & 10 \end{bmatrix}$$

$$\sim \begin{bmatrix} 2 & -4 & -2 & 3 \\ 0 & 3 & 1 & -1 \\ 0 & 0 & 0 & 5 \\ 0 & 0 & 0 & 0 \\ 0 & 0 & 0 & 0 \end{bmatrix} = U$$

then follow the algorithm in Example 2 to find L. Use the last two columns of I_5 to make L unit lower triangular.

$$\begin{bmatrix} ② \\ 6 \\ 2 \\ 4 \\ -6 \end{bmatrix} \begin{bmatrix} ③ \\ -3 \\ 6 \\ -9 \end{bmatrix} \begin{bmatrix} ⑤ \\ -5 \\ 10 \end{bmatrix}$$
$$\div 2 \quad \div 3 \quad \div 5$$
$$\downarrow \qquad \downarrow \qquad \downarrow$$

$$\begin{bmatrix} 1 & & & & \\ 3 & 1 & & & \\ 1 & -1 & 1 & & \\ 2 & 2 & -1 & 1 & \\ -3 & -3 & 2 & 0 & 1 \end{bmatrix}, \; L = \begin{bmatrix} 1 & 0 & 0 & 0 & 0 \\ 3 & 1 & 0 & 0 & 0 \\ 1 & -1 & 1 & 0 & 0 \\ 2 & 2 & -1 & 1 & 0 \\ -3 & 3 & 2 & 0 & 1 \end{bmatrix}$$

Now notice that the bottom two rows of U contain only zeros. If one uses the row-column method to find LU, the entries in the final two columns of L will not be used, since these entries will be multiplied zeros from the bottom two rows of U. So let B be the first three columns of L and let C be the top three rows of U. That is,

$$B = \begin{bmatrix} 1 & 0 & 0 \\ 3 & 1 & 0 \\ 1 & -1 & 1 \\ 2 & 2 & -1 \\ -3 & 3 & 2 \end{bmatrix}, \; C = \begin{bmatrix} 2 & -4 & -2 & 3 \\ 0 & 3 & 1 & -1 \\ 0 & 0 & 0 & 5 \end{bmatrix}$$

Then B and C have the desired sizes and $BC = LU = A$. We can generalize this process to the case where A in $m \times n$, $A = LU$, and U has only three non-zero rows: let B be the first three columns of L and let C be the top three rows of U.

23. **a.** Express each row of D as the transpose of a column vector. Then use the multiplication rule for partitioned matrices to write

$$A = CD = \begin{bmatrix} \mathbf{c}_1 & \mathbf{c}_2 & \mathbf{c}_3 & \mathbf{c}_4 \end{bmatrix} \begin{bmatrix} \mathbf{d}_1^T \\ \mathbf{d}_2^T \\ \mathbf{d}_3^T \\ \mathbf{d}_4^T \end{bmatrix} = \mathbf{c}_1 \mathbf{d}_1^T + \mathbf{c}_2 \mathbf{d}_2^T + \mathbf{c}_3 \mathbf{d}_3^T + \mathbf{c}_4 \mathbf{d}_4^T$$

which is the sum of four outer products.

b. Since A has $400 \times 100 = 40000$ entries, C has $400 \times 4 = 1600$ entries and D has $4 \times 100 = 400$ entries, to store C and D together requires only 2000 entries, which is 5% of the amount of entries needed to store A directly.

24. Since Q is square and $Q^T Q = I$, Q is invertible by the Invertible Matrix Theorem and $Q^{-1} = Q^T$. Thus A is the product of invertible matrices and hence is invertible. Thus by Theorem 5, the equation $A\mathbf{x} = \mathbf{b}$ has a unique solution for all $\mathbf{b}$. From $A\mathbf{x} = \mathbf{b}$, we have $QR\mathbf{x} = \mathbf{b}$, $Q^T QR\mathbf{x} = Q^T\mathbf{b}$, $R\mathbf{x} = Q^T\mathbf{b}$, and finally $\mathbf{x} = R^{-1}Q^T\mathbf{b}$. A good algorithm for finding $\mathbf{x}$ is to compute $Q^T\mathbf{b}$ and then row reduce the matrix $[\,R \;\; Q^T\mathbf{b}\,]$. See Exercise 11 in Section 2.2 for details on why this process works. The reduction is fast in this case because R is a triangular matrix.

25. $A = UDV^T$. Since U and V^T are square, the equations $U^T U = I$ and $V^T V = I$ imply that U and V^T are invertible, by the IMT, and hence $U^{-1} = U^T$ and $(V^T)^{-1} = V$. Since the diagonal entries $\sigma_1, \dots, \sigma_n$ in D are nonzero, D is invertible, with the inverse of D being the diagonal matrix with $\sigma_1^{-1}, \dots, \sigma_n^{-1}$ on the diagonal. Thus A is a product of invertible matrices. By Theorem 6, A is invertible and $A^{-1} = (UDV^T)^{-1} = (V^T)^{-1}D^{-1}U^{-1} = VD^{-1}U^T$.

26. If $A = PDP^{-1}$, where P is an invertible 3×3 matrix and D is the diagonal matrix

$$D = \begin{bmatrix} 1 & 0 & 0 \\ 0 & 1/2 & 0 \\ 0 & 0 & 1/3 \end{bmatrix}$$

then

$$A^2 = (PDP^{-1})(PDP^{-1}) = PD(P^{-1}P)DP^{-1} = PDIDP^{-1} = PD^2P^{-1}$$

and since

$$D^2 = \begin{bmatrix} 1 & 0 & 0 \\ 0 & 1/2 & 0 \\ 0 & 0 & 1/3 \end{bmatrix}\begin{bmatrix} 1 & 0 & 0 \\ 0 & 1/2 & 0 \\ 0 & 0 & 1/3 \end{bmatrix} = \begin{bmatrix} 1 & 0 & 0 \\ 0 & 1/2^2 & 0 \\ 0 & 0 & 1/3^2 \end{bmatrix} = \begin{bmatrix} 1 & 0 & 0 \\ 0 & 1/4 & 0 \\ 0 & 0 & 1/9 \end{bmatrix}$$

$$A^2 = P\begin{bmatrix} 1 & 0 & 0 \\ 0 & 1/4 & 0 \\ 0 & 0 & 1/9 \end{bmatrix}P^{-1}$$

Likewise, $A^3 = PD^3P^{-1}$, so

$$A^3 = P\begin{bmatrix} 1 & 0 & 0 \\ 0 & 1/2^3 & 0 \\ 0 & 0 & 1/3^3 \end{bmatrix}P^{-1} = P\begin{bmatrix} 1 & 0 & 0 \\ 0 & 1/8 & 0 \\ 0 & 0 & 1/27 \end{bmatrix}P^{-1}$$

In general, $A^k = PD^kP^{-1}$, so

$$A^k = P\begin{bmatrix} 1 & 0 & 0 \\ 0 & 1/2^k & 0 \\ 0 & 0 & 1/3^k \end{bmatrix}P^{-1}$$

27. First consider using a series circuit with resistance R_1 followed by a shunt circuit with resistance R_2 for the network. The transfer matrix for this network is

$$\begin{bmatrix} 1 & 0 \\ -1/R_2 & 1 \end{bmatrix}\begin{bmatrix} 1 & -R_1 \\ 0 & 1 \end{bmatrix} = \begin{bmatrix} 1 & -R_1 \\ -1/R_2 & (R_1 + R_2)/R_2 \end{bmatrix}$$

For an input of 12 volts and 6 amps to produce an output of 9 volts and 4 amps, the transfer matrix must satisfy

$$\begin{bmatrix} 1 & -R_1 \\ -1/R_2 & (R_1+R_2)/R_2 \end{bmatrix}\begin{bmatrix} 12 \\ 6 \end{bmatrix} = \begin{bmatrix} 12-6R_1 \\ (-12+6R_1+6R_2)/R_2 \end{bmatrix} = \begin{bmatrix} 9 \\ 4 \end{bmatrix}$$

Equate the top entries and obtain $R_1 = \frac{1}{2}$ohm. Substitute this value in the bottom entry and solve to obtain $R_2 = \frac{9}{2}$ohms. The ladder network is

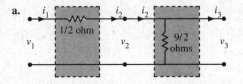

Next consider using a shunt circuit with resistance R_1 followed by a series circuit with resistance R_2 for the network. The transfer matrix for this network is

$$\begin{bmatrix} 1 & -R_2 \\ 0 & 1 \end{bmatrix}\begin{bmatrix} 1 & 0 \\ -1/R_1 & 1 \end{bmatrix} = \begin{bmatrix} (R_1+R_2)/R_1 & -R_2 \\ -1/R_1 & 1 \end{bmatrix}$$

For an input of 12 volts and 6 amps to produce an output of 9 volts and 4 amps, the transfer matrix must satisfy

$$\begin{bmatrix} (R_1+R_2)/R_1 & -R_2 \\ -1/R_1 & 1 \end{bmatrix}\begin{bmatrix} 12 \\ 6 \end{bmatrix} = \begin{bmatrix} (12R_1+12R_2)/R_1 - 6R_2 \\ -12/R_1 + 6 \end{bmatrix} = \begin{bmatrix} 9 \\ 4 \end{bmatrix}$$

Equate the bottom entries and obtain $R_1 = 6$ ohms. Substitute this value in the top entry and solve to obtain $R_2 = \frac{3}{4}$ohms. The ladder network is

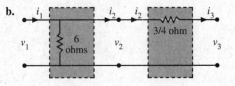

28. The three shunt circuits have transfer matrices

$$\begin{bmatrix} 1 & 0 \\ -1/R_1 & 1 \end{bmatrix}, \begin{bmatrix} 1 & 0 \\ -1/R_2 & 1 \end{bmatrix}, \text{ and } \begin{bmatrix} 1 & 0 \\ -1/R_3 & 1 \end{bmatrix}$$

respectively. To find the transfer matrix for the series of circuits, multiply these matrices

$$\begin{bmatrix} 1 & 0 \\ -1/R_3 & 1 \end{bmatrix}, \begin{bmatrix} 1 & 0 \\ -1/R_2 & 1 \end{bmatrix}, \text{ and } \begin{bmatrix} 1 & 0 \\ -1/R_1 & 1 \end{bmatrix} = \begin{bmatrix} 1 & 0 \\ -(1/R_1+1/R_2+1/R_3) & 1 \end{bmatrix}$$

Thus the resulting network is itself a shunt circuit with resistance $1/R_1 + 1/R_2 + 1/R_3$.

29. a. The first circuit is a shunt circuit with resistance R_1 ohms, so its transfer matrix is $\begin{bmatrix} 1 & 0 \\ -1/R_1 & 1 \end{bmatrix}$.

The second circuit is a series circuit with resistance R_2 ohms, so its transfer matrix is $\begin{bmatrix} 1 & -R_2 \\ 0 & 1 \end{bmatrix}$.

The third circuit is a shunt circuit with resistance R_3 ohms so its transfer matrix is $\begin{bmatrix} 1 & 0 \\ -1/R_3 & 1 \end{bmatrix}$.

The transfer matrix of the network is the product of these matrices, in *right-to-left* order:

$$\begin{bmatrix} 1 & 0 \\ -1/R_3 & 1 \end{bmatrix}\begin{bmatrix} 1 & -R_2 \\ 0 & 1 \end{bmatrix}\begin{bmatrix} 1 & 0 \\ -1/R_1 & 1 \end{bmatrix} = \begin{bmatrix} (R_1 + R_2)/R_1 & -R_2 \\ -(R_1 + R_2 + R_3)/R_3 & (R_2 + R_3)/R_3 \end{bmatrix}$$

b. To find a ladder network with a structure like that in part (a) and with the given transfer matrix A, we must find resistances R_1, R_2, and R_3 such that

$$A = \begin{bmatrix} 4/3 & -12 \\ -1/4 & 3 \end{bmatrix} = \begin{bmatrix} (R_1 + R_2)/R_1 & -R_2 \\ -(R_1 + R_2 + R_3)/R_3 & (R_2 + R_3)/R_3 \end{bmatrix}$$

From the $(1, 2)$ entries, $R_2 = 12$ ohms. The $(1, 1)$ entries now give $(R_1 + 12)/R_1 = 4/3$, which may be solved to obtain $R_1 = 36$ ohms. Likewise the $(2, 2)$ entries give $(R_3 + 12)/R_3 = 3$, which also may be solved to obtain $R_3 = 6$ ohms. Thus the matrix A may be factored as

$$A = \begin{bmatrix} 1 & 0 \\ -1/R_3 & 1 \end{bmatrix}\begin{bmatrix} 1 & -R_2 \\ 0 & 1 \end{bmatrix}\begin{bmatrix} 1 & 0 \\ -1/R_1 & 1 \end{bmatrix}$$

$$= \begin{bmatrix} 1 & 0 \\ -1/6 & 1 \end{bmatrix}\begin{bmatrix} 1 & -12 \\ 0 & 1 \end{bmatrix}\begin{bmatrix} 1 & 0 \\ -1/36 & 1 \end{bmatrix}$$

The ladder network is

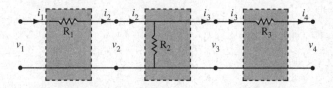

30. Answers may vary. The network below interchanges the series and shunt circuits.

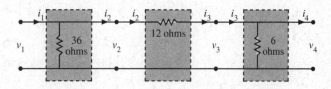

The transfer matrix of this network is the product of the individual transfer matrices, in *right-to-left* order.

$$\begin{bmatrix} 1 & -R_3 \\ 0 & 1 \end{bmatrix}\begin{bmatrix} 1 & 0 \\ -1/R_2 & 1 \end{bmatrix}\begin{bmatrix} 1 & -R_1 \\ 0 & 1 \end{bmatrix} =$$

$$\begin{bmatrix} (R_2 + R_3)/R_2 & -R_3 - R_1(R_2 + R_3)/R_2 \\ -1/R_2 & (R_1 + R_2)/R_2 \end{bmatrix}$$

By setting the matrix A from the previous exercise equal to this matrix, one may find that

$$\begin{bmatrix} (R_2 + R_3)/R_2 & -R_3 - R_1(R_2 + R_3)/R_2 \\ -1/R_2 & (R_1 + R_2)/R_2 \end{bmatrix} = \begin{bmatrix} 4/3 & -12 \\ -1/4 & 3 \end{bmatrix}$$

Set the $(2, 1)$ entries equal and obtain $R_2 = 4$ ohms. Substitute this value for R_2, equating the $(2, 2)$ entries and solving gives $R_1 = 8$ ohms. Likewise equating the $(1, 1)$ entries gives $R_3 = 4/3$ ohms.

The ladder network is

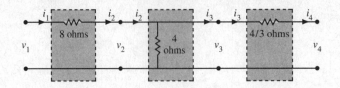

Note: The *Study Guide's* MATLAB box for Section 2.5 suggests that for most LU factorizations in this section, students can use the **gauss** command repeatedly to produce U, and use paper and mental arithmetic to write down the columns of L as the row reduction to U proceeds. This is because for Exercises 7–16 the pivots are integers and other entries are simple fractions. However, for Exercises 31 and 32 this is not reasonable, and students are expected to solve an elementary programming problem. (The *Study Guide* provides no hints.)

31. [M] Store the matrix A in a temporary matrix B and create L initially as the 8×8 identity matrix. The following sequence of MATLAB commands fills in the entries of L below the diagonal, one column at a time, until the first seven columns are filled. (The eighth column is the final column of the identity matrix.)

```
L(2:8, 1) = B(2:8, 1)/B(1, 1)
B = gauss(B, 1)
L(3:8, 2) = B(3:8, 2)/B(2, 2)
B = gauss(B, 2)
⋮
L(8:8, 7) = B(8:8, 7)/B(7, 7)
U = gauss(B,7)
```

Of course, some students may realize that a loop will speed up the process. The **for..end** syntax is illustrated in the MATLAB box for Section 5.6. Here is a MATLAB program that includes the initial setup of B and L:

```
B = A
L = eye(8)
for j=1:7
  L(j+1:8, j) = B(j+1:8, j)/B(j, j)
  B = gauss(B, j)
end
U = B
```

a. To four decimal places, the results of the LU decomposition are

$$L = \begin{bmatrix} 1 & 0 & 0 & 0 & 0 & 0 & 0 & 0 \\ -.25 & 1 & 0 & 0 & 0 & 0 & 0 & 0 \\ -.25 & -.0667 & 1 & 0 & 0 & 0 & 0 & 0 \\ 0 & -.2667 & -.2857 & 1 & 0 & 0 & 0 & 0 \\ 0 & 0 & -.2679 & -.0833 & 1 & 0 & 0 & 0 \\ 0 & 0 & 0 & -.2917 & -.2921 & 1 & 0 & 0 \\ 0 & 0 & 0 & 0 & -.2697 & -.0861 & 1 & 0 \\ 0 & 0 & 0 & 0 & 0 & -.2948 & -.2931 & 1 \end{bmatrix}$$

$$U = \begin{bmatrix} 4 & -1 & -1 & 0 & 0 & 0 & 0 & 0 \\ 0 & 3.75 & -.25 & -1 & 0 & 0 & 0 & 0 \\ 0 & 0 & 3.7333 & -1.0667 & -1 & 0 & 0 & 0 \\ 0 & 0 & 0 & 3.4286 & -.2857 & -1 & 0 & 0 \\ 0 & 0 & 0 & 0 & 3.7083 & -1.0833 & -1 & 0 \\ 0 & 0 & 0 & 0 & 0 & 3.3919 & -.2921 & -1 \\ 0 & 0 & 0 & 0 & 0 & 0 & 3.7052 & -1.0861 \\ 0 & 0 & 0 & 0 & 0 & 0 & 0 & 3.3868 \end{bmatrix}$$

b. The result of solving $L\mathbf{y} = \mathbf{b}$ and then $U\mathbf{x} = \mathbf{y}$ is

$\mathbf{x} = (3.9569, 6.5885, 4.2392, 7.3971, 5.6029, 8.7608, 9.4115, 12.0431)$

c. $A^{-1} = \begin{bmatrix} .2953 & .0866 & .0945 & .0509 & .0318 & .0227 & .0010 & .0082 \\ .0866 & .2953 & .0509 & .0945 & .0227 & .0318 & .0082 & .0100 \\ .0945 & .0509 & .3271 & .1093 & .1045 & .0591 & .0318 & .0227 \\ .0509 & .0945 & .1093 & .3271 & .0591 & .1045 & .0227 & .0318 \\ .0318 & .0227 & .1045 & .0591 & .3271 & .1093 & .0945 & .0509 \\ .0227 & .0318 & .0591 & .1045 & .1093 & .3271 & .0509 & .0945 \\ .0010 & .0082 & .0318 & .0227 & .0945 & .0509 & .2953 & .0866 \\ .0082 & .0100 & .0227 & .0318 & .0509 & .0945 & .0866 & .2953 \end{bmatrix}$

32. [M] $A = \begin{bmatrix} 3 & -1 & 0 & 0 & 0 \\ -1 & 3 & -1 & 0 & 0 \\ 0 & -1 & 3 & -1 & 0 \\ 0 & 0 & -1 & 3 & -1 \\ 0 & 0 & 0 & -1 & 3 \end{bmatrix}$. The commands shown for Exercise 31, but modified for 5×5

matrices, produce

$$L = \begin{bmatrix} 1 & 0 & 0 & 0 & 0 \\ -\frac{1}{3} & 1 & 0 & 0 & 0 \\ 0 & -\frac{3}{8} & 1 & 0 & 0 \\ 0 & 0 & -\frac{8}{21} & 1 & 0 \\ 0 & 0 & 0 & -\frac{21}{55} & 1 \end{bmatrix}$$

$$U = \begin{bmatrix} 3 & -1 & 0 & 0 & 0 \\ 0 & \frac{8}{3} & -1 & 0 & 0 \\ 0 & 0 & \frac{21}{8} & -1 & 0 \\ 0 & 0 & 0 & \frac{55}{21} & -1 \\ 0 & 0 & 0 & 0 & \frac{144}{55} \end{bmatrix}$$

b. Let $\mathbf{s}_{k+1}$ be the solution of $L\mathbf{s}_{k+1} = \mathbf{t}_k$ for $k = 0, 1, 2, \ldots$. Then $\mathbf{t}_{k+1}$ is the solution of $U\mathbf{t}_{k+1} = \mathbf{s}_{k+1}$
for $k = 0, 1, 2, \ldots$. The results are

$$\mathbf{s}_1 = \begin{bmatrix} 10.0000 \\ 15.3333 \\ 17.7500 \\ 18.7619 \\ 17.1636 \end{bmatrix}, \mathbf{t}_1 = \begin{bmatrix} 6.5556 \\ 9.6667 \\ 10.4444 \\ 9.6667 \\ 6.5556 \end{bmatrix}, \mathbf{s}_2 = \begin{bmatrix} 6.5556 \\ 11.8519 \\ 14.8889 \\ 15.3386 \\ 12.4121 \end{bmatrix}, \mathbf{t}_2 = \begin{bmatrix} 4.7407 \\ 7.6667 \\ 8.5926 \\ 7.6667 \\ 4.7407 \end{bmatrix},$$

$$\mathbf{s}_3 = \begin{bmatrix} 4.7407 \\ 9.2469 \\ 12.0602 \\ 12.2610 \\ 9.4222 \end{bmatrix}, \mathbf{t}_3 = \begin{bmatrix} 3.5988 \\ 6.0556 \\ 6.9012 \\ 6.0556 \\ 3.5988 \end{bmatrix}, \mathbf{s}_4 = \begin{bmatrix} 3.5988 \\ 7.2551 \\ 9.6219 \\ 9.7210 \\ 7.3104 \end{bmatrix}, \mathbf{t}_4 = \begin{bmatrix} 2.7922 \\ 4.7778 \\ 5.4856 \\ 4.7778 \\ 2.7922 \end{bmatrix}.$$

2.6   SOLUTIONS

Notes: This section is independent of Section 1.10. The material here makes a good backdrop for the series expansion of $(I–C)^{-1}$ because this formula is actually used in some practical economic work. Exercise 8 gives an interpretation to entries of an inverse matrix that could be stated without the economic context.

1. The answer to this exercise will depend upon the order in which the student chooses to list the sectors. The important fact to remember is that each column is the unit consumption vector for the appropriate sector. If we order the sectors manufacturing, agriculture, and services, then the consumption matrix is

$$C = \begin{bmatrix} .10 & .60 & .60 \\ .30 & .20 & 0 \\ .30 & .10 & .10 \end{bmatrix}$$

The intermediate demands created by the production vector $\mathbf{x}$ are given by $C\mathbf{x}$. Thus in this case the intermediate demand is

$$C\mathbf{x} = \begin{bmatrix} .10 & .60 & .60 \\ .30 & .20 & .00 \\ .30 & .10 & .10 \end{bmatrix} \begin{bmatrix} 0 \\ 100 \\ 0 \end{bmatrix} = \begin{bmatrix} 60 \\ 20 \\ 10 \end{bmatrix}$$

2. Solve the equation $\mathbf{x} = C\mathbf{x} + \mathbf{d}$ for $\mathbf{d}$:

$$\mathbf{d} = \mathbf{x} - C\mathbf{x} = \begin{bmatrix} x_1 \\ x_2 \\ x_3 \end{bmatrix} - \begin{bmatrix} .10 & .60 & .60 \\ .30 & .20 & .00 \\ .30 & .10 & .10 \end{bmatrix} \begin{bmatrix} x_1 \\ x_2 \\ x_3 \end{bmatrix} = \begin{bmatrix} .9x_1 & -.6x_2 & -.6x_3 \\ -.3x_1 & +.8x_2 & \\ -.3x_1 & -.1x_2 & +.9x_3 \end{bmatrix} = \begin{bmatrix} 0 \\ 18 \\ 0 \end{bmatrix}$$

This system of equations has the augmented matrix

$$\begin{bmatrix} -.90 & -.60 & -.60 & 0 \\ -.30 & .80 & .00 & 18 \\ -.30 & -.10 & .90 & 0 \end{bmatrix} \sim \begin{bmatrix} 1 & 0 & 0 & 33.33 \\ 0 & 1 & 0 & 35.00 \\ 0 & 0 & 1 & 15.00 \end{bmatrix}$$

so $\mathbf{x} = (33.33, 35.00, 15.00)$.

3. Solving as in Exercise 2:

$$\mathbf{d} = \mathbf{x} - C\mathbf{x} = \begin{bmatrix} x_1 \\ x_2 \\ x_3 \end{bmatrix} - \begin{bmatrix} .10 & .60 & .60 \\ .30 & .20 & .00 \\ .30 & .10 & .10 \end{bmatrix} \begin{bmatrix} x_1 \\ x_2 \\ x_3 \end{bmatrix} = \begin{bmatrix} .9x_1 & -.6x_2 & -.6x_3 \\ -.3x_1 & +.8x_2 & \\ -.3x_1 & -.1x_2 & +.9x_3 \end{bmatrix} = \begin{bmatrix} 18 \\ 0 \\ 0 \end{bmatrix}$$

This system of equations has the augmented matrix

$$\begin{bmatrix} .90 & -.60 & -.60 & 18 \\ -.30 & .80 & .00 & 0 \\ -.30 & -.10 & .90 & 0 \end{bmatrix} \sim \begin{bmatrix} 1 & 0 & 0 & 40.00 \\ 0 & 1 & 0 & 15.00 \\ 0 & 0 & 1 & 15.00 \end{bmatrix}$$

so $\mathbf{x} = (40.00, 15.00, 15.00)$.

4. Solving as in Exercise 2:

$$\mathbf{d} = \mathbf{x} - C\mathbf{x} = \begin{bmatrix} x_1 \\ x_2 \\ x_3 \end{bmatrix} - \begin{bmatrix} .10 & .60 & .60 \\ .30 & .20 & .00 \\ .30 & .10 & .10 \end{bmatrix} \begin{bmatrix} x_1 \\ x_2 \\ x_3 \end{bmatrix} = \begin{bmatrix} .9x_1 & -.6x_2 & -.6x_3 \\ -.3x_1 & +.8x_2 & \\ -.3x_1 & -.1x_2 & +.9x_3 \end{bmatrix} = \begin{bmatrix} 18 \\ 18 \\ 0 \end{bmatrix}$$

This system of equations has the augmented matrix

$$\begin{bmatrix} -.90 & -.60 & -.60 & 18 \\ -.30 & .80 & .00 & 18 \\ -.30 & -.10 & .90 & 0 \end{bmatrix} \sim \begin{bmatrix} 1 & 0 & 0 & 73.33 \\ 0 & 1 & 0 & 50.00 \\ 0 & 0 & 1 & 30.00 \end{bmatrix}$$

so $\mathbf{x} = (73.33, 50.00, 30.00)$.

Note: Exercises 2–4 may be used by students to discover the linearity of the Leontief model.

5. $\mathbf{x} = (I - C)^{-1}\mathbf{d} = \begin{bmatrix} 1 & -.5 \\ -.6 & .8 \end{bmatrix}^{-1} \begin{bmatrix} 50 \\ 20 \end{bmatrix} = \begin{bmatrix} 1.6 & 1 \\ 1.2 & 2 \end{bmatrix} \begin{bmatrix} 50 \\ 20 \end{bmatrix} = \begin{bmatrix} 110 \\ 120 \end{bmatrix}$

6. $\mathbf{x} = (I - C)^{-1}\mathbf{d} = \begin{bmatrix} .9 & -.6 \\ -.5 & .8 \end{bmatrix}^{-1} \begin{bmatrix} 18 \\ 11 \end{bmatrix} = \begin{bmatrix} 40/21 & 30/21 \\ 25/21 & 45/21 \end{bmatrix} \begin{bmatrix} 18 \\ 11 \end{bmatrix} = \begin{bmatrix} 50 \\ 45 \end{bmatrix}$

7. a. From Exercise 5,

$$(I - C)^{-1} = \begin{bmatrix} 1.6 & 1 \\ 1.2 & 2 \end{bmatrix}$$

so

$$\mathbf{x}_1 = (I - C)^{-1}\mathbf{d}_1 = \begin{bmatrix} 1.6 & 1 \\ 1.2 & 2 \end{bmatrix} \begin{bmatrix} 1 \\ 0 \end{bmatrix} = \begin{bmatrix} 1.6 \\ 1.2 \end{bmatrix}$$

which is the first column of $(I - C)^{-1}$.

b. $\mathbf{x}_2 = (I - C)^{-1}\mathbf{d}_2 = \begin{bmatrix} 1.6 & 1 \\ 1.2 & 2 \end{bmatrix} \begin{bmatrix} 51 \\ 30 \end{bmatrix} = \begin{bmatrix} 111.6 \\ 121.2 \end{bmatrix}$

c. From Exercise 5, the production $\mathbf{x}$ corressponding to $\mathbf{d} = \begin{bmatrix} 50 \\ 20 \end{bmatrix}$ is $\mathbf{x} = \begin{bmatrix} 110 \\ 120 \end{bmatrix}$.

Note that $\mathbf{d}_2 = \mathbf{d} + \mathbf{d}_1$. Thus

$$\begin{aligned} \mathbf{x}_2 &= (I - C)^{-1} \mathbf{d}_2 \\ &= (I - C)^{-1}(\mathbf{d} + \mathbf{d}_1) \\ &= (I - C)^{-1}\mathbf{d} + (I - C)^{-1}\mathbf{d}_1 \\ &= \mathbf{x} + \mathbf{x}_1 \end{aligned}$$

8. **a.** Given $(I - C)\mathbf{x} = \mathbf{d}$ and $(I - C)\Delta\mathbf{x} = \Delta\mathbf{d}$,

$$(I - C)(\mathbf{x} + \Delta\mathbf{x}) = (I - C)\mathbf{x} + (I - C)\Delta\mathbf{x} = \mathbf{d} + \Delta\mathbf{d}$$

Thus $\mathbf{x} + \Delta\mathbf{x}$ is the production level corresponding to a demand of $\mathbf{d} + \Delta\mathbf{d}$.

b. Since $\Delta\mathbf{x} = (I - C)^{-1}\Delta\mathbf{d}$ and $\Delta\mathbf{d}$ is the first column of I, $\Delta\mathbf{x}$ will be the first column of $(I - C)^{-1}$.

9. In this case

$$I - C = \begin{bmatrix} .8 & -.2 & .0 \\ -.3 & .9 & -.3 \\ -.1 & .0 & .8 \end{bmatrix}$$

Row reduce $[I - C \quad \mathbf{d}]$ to find

$$\begin{bmatrix} .8 & -.2 & .0 & 40.0 \\ -.3 & .9 & -.3 & 60.0 \\ -.1 & .0 & .8 & 80.0 \end{bmatrix} \sim \begin{bmatrix} 1 & 0 & 0 & 82.8 \\ 0 & 1 & 0 & 131.0 \\ 0 & 0 & 1 & 110.3 \end{bmatrix}$$

So $\mathbf{x} = (82.8, 131.0, 110.3)$.

10. From Exercise 8, the (i, j) entry in $(I - C)^{-1}$ corresponds to the effect on production of sector i when the final demand for the output of sector j increases by one unit. Since these entries are all positive, an increase in the final demand for any sector will cause the production of all sectors to increase. Thus an increase in the demand for any sector will lead to an increase in the demand for all sectors.

11. (Solution in *study Guide*) Following the hint in the text, compute $\mathbf{p}^T\mathbf{x}$ in two ways. First, take the transpose of both sides of the price equation, $\mathbf{p} = C^T\mathbf{p} + \mathbf{v}$, to obtain

$$\mathbf{p}^T = (C^T\mathbf{p} + \mathbf{v})^T = (C^T\mathbf{p})^T + \mathbf{v}^T = \mathbf{p}^T C + \mathbf{v}^T$$

and right-multiply by $\mathbf{x}$ to get

$$\mathbf{p}^T\mathbf{x} = (\mathbf{p}^T C + \mathbf{v}^T)\mathbf{x} = \mathbf{p}^T C\mathbf{x} + \mathbf{v}^T\mathbf{x}$$

Another way to compute $\mathbf{p}^T\mathbf{x}$ starts with the production equation $\mathbf{x} = C\mathbf{x} + \mathbf{d}$. Left multiply by $\mathbf{p}^T$ to get

$$\mathbf{p}^T\mathbf{x} = \mathbf{p}^T(C\mathbf{x} + \mathbf{d}) = \mathbf{p}^T C\mathbf{x} + \mathbf{p}^T\mathbf{d}$$

The two expression for $\mathbf{p}^T\mathbf{x}$ show that

$$\mathbf{p}^T C\mathbf{x} + \mathbf{v}^T\mathbf{x} = \mathbf{p}^T C\mathbf{x} + \mathbf{p}^T\mathbf{d}$$

so $\mathbf{v}^T\mathbf{x} = \mathbf{p}^T\mathbf{d}$. The *Study Guide* also provides a slightly different solution.

12. Since

$$D_{m+1} = I + C + C^2 + \dots + C^{m+1} = I + C(I + C + \dots + C^m) = I + CD_m$$

D_{m+1} may be found iteratively by $D_{m+1} = I + CD_m$.

13. **[M]** The matrix $I - C$ is

$$\begin{bmatrix} 0.8412 & -0.0064 & -0.0025 & -0.0304 & -0.0014 & -0.0083 & -0.1594 \\ -0.0057 & 0.7355 & -0.0436 & -0.0099 & -0.0083 & -0.0201 & -0.3413 \\ -0.0264 & -0.1506 & 0.6443 & -0.0139 & -0.0142 & -0.0070 & -0.0236 \\ -0.3299 & -0.0565 & -0.0495 & 0.6364 & -0.0204 & -0.0483 & -0.0649 \\ -0.0089 & -0.0081 & -0.0333 & -0.0295 & 0.6588 & -0.0237 & -0.0020 \\ -0.1190 & -0.0901 & -0.0996 & -0.1260 & -0.1722 & 0.7632 & -0.3369 \\ -0.0063 & -0.0126 & -0.0196 & -0.0098 & -0.0064 & -0.0132 & 0.9988 \end{bmatrix}$$

so the augmented matrix $[\,I - C \ \ \mathbf{d}\,]$ may be row reduced to find

$$\begin{bmatrix} 0.8412 & -0.0064 & -0.0025 & -0.0304 & -0.0014 & -0.0083 & -0.1594 & 74000 \\ -0.0057 & 0.7355 & -0.0436 & -0.0099 & -0.0083 & -0.0201 & -0.3413 & 56000 \\ -0.0264 & -0.1506 & 0.6443 & -0.0139 & -0.0142 & -0.0070 & -0.0236 & 10500 \\ -0.3299 & -0.0565 & -0.0495 & 0.6364 & -0.0204 & -0.0483 & -0.0649 & 25000 \\ -0.0089 & -0.0081 & -0.0333 & -0.0295 & 0.6588 & -0.0237 & -0.0020 & 17500 \\ -0.1190 & -0.0901 & -0.0996 & -0.1260 & -0.1722 & 0.7632 & -0.3369 & 196000 \\ -0.0063 & -0.0126 & -0.0196 & -0.0098 & -0.0064 & -0.0132 & 0.9988 & 5000 \end{bmatrix}$$

$$\sim \begin{bmatrix} 1 & 0 & 0 & 0 & 0 & 0 & 0 & 99576 \\ 0 & 1 & 0 & 0 & 0 & 0 & 0 & 97703 \\ 0 & 0 & 1 & 0 & 0 & 0 & 0 & 51231 \\ 0 & 0 & 0 & 1 & 0 & 0 & 0 & 131570 \\ 0 & 0 & 0 & 0 & 1 & 0 & 0 & 49488 \\ 0 & 0 & 0 & 0 & 0 & 1 & 0 & 329554 \\ 0 & 0 & 0 & 0 & 0 & 0 & 1 & 13835 \end{bmatrix}$$

so $\mathbf{x} = (99576, 97703, 51321, 131570, 49488, 329554, 13835)$. Since the entries in $\mathbf{d}$ seem to be accurate to the nearest thousand, a more realistic answer would be $\mathbf{x} = (100000, 98000, 51000, 132000, 49000, 330000, 14000)$.

14. **[M]** The augmented matrix $[\,I - C \ \ \mathbf{d}\,]$ in this case may be row reduced to find

$$\begin{bmatrix} 0.8412 & -0.0064 & -0.0025 & -0.0304 & -0.0014 & -0.0083 & -0.1594 & 99640 \\ -0.0057 & 0.7355 & -0.0436 & -0.0099 & -0.0083 & -0.0201 & -0.3413 & 75548 \\ -0.0264 & -0.1506 & 0.6443 & -0.0139 & -0.0142 & -0.0070 & -0.0236 & 14444 \\ -0.3299 & -0.0565 & -0.0495 & 0.6364 & -0.0204 & -0.0483 & -0.0649 & 33501 \\ -0.0089 & -0.0081 & -0.0333 & -0.0295 & 0.6588 & -0.0237 & -0.0020 & 23527 \\ -0.1190 & -0.0901 & -0.0996 & -0.1260 & -0.1722 & 0.7632 & -0.3369 & 263985 \\ -0.0063 & -0.0126 & -0.0196 & -0.0098 & -0.0064 & -0.0132 & 0.9988 & 6526 \end{bmatrix}$$

$$\sim \begin{bmatrix} 1 & 0 & 0 & 0 & 0 & 0 & 0 & 134034 \\ 0 & 1 & 0 & 0 & 0 & 0 & 0 & 131687 \\ 0 & 0 & 1 & 0 & 0 & 0 & 0 & 69472 \\ 0 & 0 & 0 & 1 & 0 & 0 & 0 & 176912 \\ 0 & 0 & 0 & 0 & 1 & 0 & 0 & 66596 \\ 0 & 0 & 0 & 0 & 0 & 1 & 0 & 443773 \\ 0 & 0 & 0 & 0 & 0 & 0 & 1 & 18431 \end{bmatrix}$$

so $\mathbf{x} = (134034, 131687, 69472, 176912, 66596, 443773, 18431)$. To the nearest thousand, $\mathbf{x} = (134000, 132000, 69000, 177000, 67000, 444000, 18000)$.

15. **[M]** Here are the iterations rounded to the nearest tenth:

$\mathbf{x}^{(0)} = (74000.0, 56000.0, 10500.0, 25000.0, 17500.0, 196000.0, 5000.0)$

$\mathbf{x}^{(1)} = (89344.2, 77730.5, 26708.1, 72334.7, 30325.6, 265158.2, 9327.8)$

$\mathbf{x}^{(2)} = (94681.2, 87714.5, 37577.3, 100520.5, 38598.0, 296563.8, 11480.0)$

$\mathbf{x}^{(3)} = (97091.9, 92573.1, 43867.8, 115457.0, 43491.0, 312319.0, 12598.8)$

$\mathbf{x}^{(4)} = (98291.6, 95033.2, 47314.5, 123202.5, 46247.0, 320502.4, 13185.5)$

$\mathbf{x}^{(5)} = (98907.2, 96305.3, 49160.6, 127213.7, 47756.4, 324796.1, 13493.8)$

$\mathbf{x}^{(6)} = (99226.6, 96969.6, 50139.6, 129296.7, 48569.3, 327053.8, 13655.9)$

$\mathbf{x}^{(7)} = (99393.1, 97317.8, 50656.4, 130381.6, 49002.8, 328240.9, 13741.1)$

$\mathbf{x}^{(8)} = (99480.0, 97500.7, 50928.7, 130948.0, 49232.5, 328864.7, 13785.9)$

$\mathbf{x}^{(9)} = (99525.5, 97596.8, 51071.9, 131244.1, 49353.8, 329192.3, 13809.4)$

$\mathbf{x}^{(10)} = (99549.4, 97647.2, 51147.2, 131399.2, 49417.7, 329364.4, 13821.7)$

$\mathbf{x}^{(11)} = (99561.9, 97673.7, 51186.8, 131480.4, 49451.3, 329454.7, 13828.2)$

$\mathbf{x}^{(12)} = (99568.4, 97687.6, 51207.5, 131523.0, 49469.0, 329502.1, 13831.6)$

so $\mathbf{x}^{(12)}$ is the first vector whose entries are accurate to the nearest thousand. The calculation of $\mathbf{x}^{(12)}$ takes about 1260 flops, while the row reduction above takes about 550 flops. If C is larger than 20×20, then fewer flops are required to compute $\mathbf{x}^{(12)}$ by iteration than by row reduction. The advantage of the iterative method increases with the size of C. The matrix C also becomes more sparse for larger models, so fewer iterations are needed for good accuracy.

2.7   SOLUTIONS

Notes: The content of this section seems to have universal appeal with students. It also provides practice with composition of linear transformations. The case study for Chapter 2 concerns computer graphics – see this case study (available as a project on the website) for more examples of computer graphics in action. The *Study Guide* encourages the student to examine the book by Foley referenced in the text. This section could form the beginning of an independent study on computer graphics with an interested student.

1. Refer to Example 5. The representation in homogenous coordinates can be written as a partitioned matrix of the form $\begin{bmatrix} A & \mathbf{0} \\ \mathbf{0}^T & 1 \end{bmatrix}$, where A is the matrix of the linear transformation. Since in this case

$A = \begin{bmatrix} 1 & .25 \\ 0 & 1 \end{bmatrix}$, the representation of the transformation with respect to homogenous coordinates is

$$\begin{bmatrix} 1 & .25 & 0 \\ 0 & 1 & 0 \\ 0 & 0 & 1 \end{bmatrix}$$

Note: The *Study Guide* shows the student why the action of $\begin{bmatrix} A & \mathbf{0} \\ \mathbf{0}^T & 1 \end{bmatrix}$ on the vector $\begin{bmatrix} \mathbf{x} \\ 1 \end{bmatrix}$ corresponds to the action of A on $\mathbf{x}$.

2. The matrix of the transformation is $A = \begin{bmatrix} -1 & 0 \\ 0 & 1 \end{bmatrix}$, so the transformed data matrix is

$$AD = \begin{bmatrix} -1 & 0 \\ 0 & 1 \end{bmatrix}\begin{bmatrix} 5 & 2 & 4 \\ 0 & 2 & 3 \end{bmatrix} = \begin{bmatrix} -5 & -2 & -4 \\ 0 & 2 & 3 \end{bmatrix}$$

Both the original triangle and the transformed triangle are shown in the following sketch.

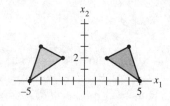

3. Following Examples 4–6,

$$\begin{bmatrix} \sqrt{2}/2 & -\sqrt{2}/2 & 0 \\ \sqrt{2}/2 & \sqrt{2}/2 & 0 \\ 0 & 0 & 1 \end{bmatrix}\begin{bmatrix} 1 & 0 & 3 \\ 0 & 1 & 1 \\ 0 & 0 & 1 \end{bmatrix} = \begin{bmatrix} \sqrt{2}/2 & -\sqrt{2}/2 & \sqrt{2} \\ \sqrt{2}/2 & \sqrt{2}/2 & 2\sqrt{2} \\ 0 & 0 & 1 \end{bmatrix}$$

4. $\begin{bmatrix} .8 & 0 & 0 \\ 0 & 1.2 & 0 \\ 0 & 0 & 1 \end{bmatrix}\begin{bmatrix} 1 & 0 & -2 \\ 0 & 1 & 3 \\ 0 & 0 & 1 \end{bmatrix} = \begin{bmatrix} .8 & 0 & -1.6 \\ 0 & 1.2 & 3.6 \\ 0 & 0 & 1 \end{bmatrix}$

5. $\begin{bmatrix} \sqrt{3}/2 & -1/2 & 0 \\ 1/2 & \sqrt{3}/2 & 0 \\ 0 & 0 & 1 \end{bmatrix}\begin{bmatrix} 1 & 0 & 0 \\ 0 & -1 & 0 \\ 0 & 0 & 1 \end{bmatrix} = \begin{bmatrix} \sqrt{3}/2 & 1/2 & 0 \\ 1/2 & -\sqrt{3}/2 & 0 \\ 0 & 0 & 1 \end{bmatrix}$

6. $\begin{bmatrix} 1 & 0 & 0 \\ 0 & -1 & 0 \\ 0 & 0 & 1 \end{bmatrix}\begin{bmatrix} \sqrt{3}/2 & -1/2 & 0 \\ 1/2 & \sqrt{3}/2 & 0 \\ 0 & 0 & 1 \end{bmatrix} = \begin{bmatrix} \sqrt{3}/2 & -1/2 & 0 \\ -1/2 & -\sqrt{3}/2 & 0 \\ 0 & 0 & 1 \end{bmatrix}$

7. A 60° rotation about the origin is given in homogeneous coordinates by the matrix

$$\begin{bmatrix} 1/2 & -\sqrt{3}/2 & 0 \\ \sqrt{3}/2 & 1/2 & 0 \\ 0 & 0 & 1 \end{bmatrix}.$$ To rotate about the point (6, 8), first translate by (–6, –8), then rotate about the

origin, then translate back by (6, 8) (see the Practice Problem in this section). A 60° rotation about (6, 8) is thus is given in homogeneous coordinates by the matrix

$$\begin{bmatrix} 1 & 0 & 6 \\ 0 & 1 & 8 \\ 0 & 0 & 1 \end{bmatrix} \begin{bmatrix} 1/2 & -\sqrt{3}/2 & 0 \\ \sqrt{3}/2 & 1/2 & 0 \\ 0 & 0 & 1 \end{bmatrix} \begin{bmatrix} 1 & 0 & -6 \\ 0 & 1 & -8 \\ 0 & 0 & 1 \end{bmatrix} = \begin{bmatrix} 1/2 & -\sqrt{3}/2 & 3+4\sqrt{3} \\ \sqrt{3}/2 & 1/2 & 4-3\sqrt{3} \\ 0 & 0 & 1 \end{bmatrix}$$

8. A 45° rotation about the origin is given in homogeneous coordinates by the matrix

$$\begin{bmatrix} \sqrt{2}/2 & -\sqrt{2}/2 & 0 \\ \sqrt{2}/2 & \sqrt{2}/2 & 0 \\ 0 & 0 & 1 \end{bmatrix}.$$ To rotate about the point (3, 7), first translate by (–3, –7), then rotate about the

origin, then translate back by (3, 7) (see the Practice Problem in this section). A 45° rotation about (3, 7) is thus is given in homogeneous coordinates by the matrix

$$\begin{bmatrix} 1 & 0 & 3 \\ 0 & 1 & 7 \\ 0 & 0 & 1 \end{bmatrix} \begin{bmatrix} \sqrt{2}/2 & -\sqrt{2}/2 & 0 \\ \sqrt{2}/2 & \sqrt{2}/2 & 0 \\ 0 & 0 & 1 \end{bmatrix} \begin{bmatrix} 1 & 0 & -3 \\ 0 & 1 & -7 \\ 0 & 0 & 1 \end{bmatrix} = \begin{bmatrix} \sqrt{2}/2 & -\sqrt{2}/2 & 3+2\sqrt{2} \\ \sqrt{2}/2 & \sqrt{2}/2 & 7-5\sqrt{2} \\ 0 & 0 & 1 \end{bmatrix}$$

9. To produce each entry in BD two multiplications are necessary. Since BD is a 2×200 matrix, it will take $2 \times 2 \times 200 = 800$ multiplications to compute BD. By the same reasoning it will take $2 \times 2 \times 200 = 800$ multiplications to compute $A(BD)$. Thus to compute $A(BD)$ from the beginning will take $800 + 800 = 1600$ multiplications.

To compute the 2×2 matrix AB it will take $2 \times 2 \times 2 = 8$ multiplications, and to compute $(AB)D$ it will take $2 \times 2 \times 200 = 800$ multiplications. Thus to compute $(AB)D$ from the beginning will take $8 + 800 = 808$ multiplications.

For computer graphics calculations that require applying multiple transformations to data matrices, it is thus more efficient to compute the product of the transformation matrices before applying the result to the data matrix.

10. Let the transformation matrices in homogeneous coordinates for the dilation, rotation, and translation be called respectively D, and R, and T. Then for some value of s, φ, h, and k,

$$D = \begin{bmatrix} s & 0 & 0 \\ 0 & s & 0 \\ 0 & 0 & 1 \end{bmatrix}, R = \begin{bmatrix} \cos\varphi & -\sin\varphi & 0 \\ \sin\varphi & \cos\varphi & 0 \\ 0 & 0 & 1 \end{bmatrix}, T = \begin{bmatrix} 1 & 0 & h \\ 0 & 1 & k \\ 0 & 0 & 1 \end{bmatrix}$$

Compute the products of these matrices:

$$DR = \begin{bmatrix} s\cos\varphi & -s\sin\varphi & 0 \\ s\sin\varphi & s\cos\varphi & 0 \\ 0 & 0 & 1 \end{bmatrix}, RD = \begin{bmatrix} s\cos\varphi & -s\sin\varphi & 0 \\ s\sin\varphi & s\cos\varphi & 0 \\ 0 & 0 & 1 \end{bmatrix}$$

$$DT = \begin{bmatrix} s & 0 & sh \\ 0 & s & sk \\ 0 & 0 & 1 \end{bmatrix}, TD = \begin{bmatrix} s & 0 & h \\ 0 & s & k \\ 0 & 0 & 1 \end{bmatrix}$$

$$RT = \begin{bmatrix} \cos\varphi & -\sin\varphi & h\cos\varphi - k\sin\varphi \\ \sin\varphi & \cos\varphi & h\sin\varphi + k\cos\varphi \\ 0 & 0 & 1 \end{bmatrix}, TR = \begin{bmatrix} \cos\varphi & -\sin\varphi & h \\ \sin\varphi & \cos\varphi & k \\ 0 & 0 & 1 \end{bmatrix}$$

Since $DR = RD$, $DT \neq TD$ and $RT \neq TR$, D and R commute, D and T do not commute and R and T do not commute.

11. To simplify $A_2 A_1$ completely, the following trigonometric identities will be needed:

1. $-\tan\varphi\cos\varphi = -\frac{\sin\varphi}{\cos\varphi}\cos\varphi = -\sin\varphi$

2. $\sec\varphi - \tan\varphi\sin\varphi = \frac{1}{\cos\varphi} - \frac{\sin\varphi}{\cos\varphi}\sin\varphi = \frac{1-\sin^2\varphi}{\cos\varphi} = \frac{\cos^2\varphi}{\cos\varphi} = \cos\varphi$

Using these identities,

$$A_2 A_1 = \begin{bmatrix} \sec\varphi & -\tan\varphi & 0 \\ 0 & 1 & 0 \\ 0 & 0 & 1 \end{bmatrix}\begin{bmatrix} 1 & 0 & 0 \\ \sin\varphi & \cos\varphi & 0 \\ 0 & 0 & 1 \end{bmatrix}$$

$$= \begin{bmatrix} \sec\varphi - \tan\varphi\sin\varphi & -\tan\varphi\cos\varphi & 0 \\ \sin\varphi & \cos\varphi & 0 \\ 0 & 0 & 1 \end{bmatrix}$$

$$= \begin{bmatrix} \cos\varphi & -\sin\varphi & 0 \\ \sin\varphi & \cos\varphi & 0 \\ 0 & 0 & 1 \end{bmatrix}$$

which is the transformation matrix in homogeneous coordinates for a rotation in $\mathbb{R}^2$.

12. To simplify this product completely, the following trigonometric identity will be needed:

$$\tan\varphi/2 = \frac{1-\cos\varphi}{\sin\varphi} = \frac{\sin\varphi}{1+\cos\varphi}$$

This identity has two important consequences:

$$1 - (\tan\varphi/2)(\sin\varphi) = 1 - \frac{1-\cos\varphi}{\sin\varphi}\sin\varphi = \cos\varphi$$

$$(\cos\varphi)(-\tan\varphi/2) - \tan\varphi/2 = -(\cos\varphi+1)\tan\varphi/2 = -(\cos\varphi+1)\frac{\sin\varphi}{1+\cos\varphi} = -\sin\varphi$$

The product may be computed and simplified using these results:

$$\begin{bmatrix} 1 & -\tan\varphi/2 & 0 \\ 0 & 1 & 0 \\ 0 & 0 & 1 \end{bmatrix}\begin{bmatrix} 1 & 0 & 0 \\ \sin\varphi & 1 & 0 \\ 0 & 0 & 1 \end{bmatrix}\begin{bmatrix} 1 & -\tan\varphi/2 & 0 \\ 0 & 1 & 0 \\ 0 & 0 & 1 \end{bmatrix}$$

$$= \begin{bmatrix} 1-(\tan\varphi/2)(\sin\varphi) & -\tan\varphi/2 & 0 \\ \sin\varphi & 1 & 0 \\ 0 & 0 & 1 \end{bmatrix}\begin{bmatrix} 1 & -\tan\varphi/2 & 0 \\ 0 & 1 & 0 \\ 0 & 0 & 1 \end{bmatrix}$$

$$= \begin{bmatrix} \cos\varphi & -\tan\varphi/2 & 0 \\ \sin\varphi & 1 & 0 \\ 0 & 0 & 1 \end{bmatrix} \begin{bmatrix} 1 & -\tan\varphi/2 & 0 \\ 0 & 1 & 0 \\ 0 & 0 & 1 \end{bmatrix}$$

$$= \begin{bmatrix} \cos\varphi & (\cos\varphi)(-\tan\varphi/2)-\tan\varphi/2 & 0 \\ \sin\varphi & -(\sin\varphi)(\tan\varphi/2)+1 & 0 \\ 0 & 0 & 1 \end{bmatrix}$$

$$= \begin{bmatrix} \cos\varphi & -\sin\varphi & 0 \\ \sin\varphi & \cos\varphi & 0 \\ 0 & 0 & 1 \end{bmatrix}$$

which is the transformation matrix in homogeneous coordinates for a rotation in $\mathbb{R}^2$.

13. Consider first applying the linear transformation on $\mathbb{R}^2$ whose matrix is A, then applying a translation by the vector $\mathbf{p}$ to the result. The matrix representation in homogeneous coordinates of the linear transformation is $\begin{bmatrix} A & \mathbf{0} \\ \mathbf{0}^T & 1 \end{bmatrix}$, while the matrix representation in homogeneous coordinates of the translation is $\begin{bmatrix} I & \mathbf{p} \\ \mathbf{0}^T & 1 \end{bmatrix}$. Applying these transformations in order leads to a transformation whose matrix representation in homogeneous coordinates is

$$\begin{bmatrix} I & \mathbf{p} \\ \mathbf{0}^T & 1 \end{bmatrix} \begin{bmatrix} A & \mathbf{0} \\ \mathbf{0}^T & 1 \end{bmatrix} = \begin{bmatrix} A & \mathbf{p} \\ \mathbf{0}^T & 1 \end{bmatrix}$$

which is the desired matrix.

14. The matrix for the transformation in Exercise 7 was found to be

$$\begin{bmatrix} 1/2 & -\sqrt{3}/2 & 3+4\sqrt{3} \\ \sqrt{3}/2 & 1/2 & 4-3\sqrt{3} \\ 0 & 0 & 1 \end{bmatrix}$$

This matrix is of the form $\begin{bmatrix} A & \mathbf{p} \\ \mathbf{0}^T & 1 \end{bmatrix}$, where

$$A = \begin{bmatrix} 1/2 & -\sqrt{3}/2 \\ \sqrt{3}/2 & 1/2 \end{bmatrix}, \mathbf{p} = \begin{bmatrix} 3+4\sqrt{3} \\ 4-3\sqrt{3} \end{bmatrix}$$

By Exercise 13, this matrix may be written as

$$\begin{bmatrix} I & \mathbf{p} \\ \mathbf{0}^T & 1 \end{bmatrix} \begin{bmatrix} A & \mathbf{0} \\ \mathbf{0}^T & 1 \end{bmatrix}$$

that is, the composition of a linear transformation on $\mathbb{R}^2$ and a translation. The matrix A is the matrix of a rotation about the origin in $\mathbb{R}^2$. Thus the transformation in Exercise 7 is the composition of a rotation about the origin and a translation by $\mathbf{p} = \begin{bmatrix} 3+4\sqrt{3} \\ 4-3\sqrt{3} \end{bmatrix}$.

15. Since $(X, Y, Z, H) = (\frac{1}{2}, -\frac{1}{4}, \frac{1}{8}, \frac{1}{24})$, the corresponding point in $\mathbb{R}^3$ has coordinates

$$(x, y, z) = \left(\frac{X}{H}, \frac{Y}{H}, \frac{Z}{H}\right) = \left(\frac{\frac{1}{2}}{\frac{1}{24}}, \frac{-\frac{1}{4}}{\frac{1}{24}}, \frac{\frac{1}{8}}{\frac{1}{24}}\right) = (12, -6, 3)$$

16. The homogeneous coordinates $(1, -2, 3, 4)$ represent the point
$$(1/4, -2/4, 3/4) = (1/4, -1/2, 3/4)$$

while the homogeneous coordinates $(10, -20, 30, 40)$ represent the point
$$(10/40, -20/40, 30/40) = (1/4, -1/2, 3/4)$$

so the two sets of homogeneous coordinates represent the same point in $\mathbb{R}^3$.

17. Follow Example 7a by first constructing that 3×3 matrix for this rotation. The vector $\mathbf{e}_1$ is not changed by this rotation. The vector $\mathbf{e}_2$ is rotated $60°$ toward the positive z-axis, ending up at the point $(0, \cos 60°, \sin 60°) = (0, 1/2, \sqrt{3}/2)$. The vector $\mathbf{e}_3$ is rotated $60°$ toward the negative y-axis, stopping at the point $(0, \cos 150°, \sin 150°) = (0, -\sqrt{3}/2, 1/2)$. The matrix A for this rotation is thus

$$A = \begin{bmatrix} 1 & 0 & 0 \\ 0 & 1/2 & -\sqrt{3}/2 \\ 0 & \sqrt{3}/2 & 1/2 \end{bmatrix}$$

so in homogeneous coordinates the transformation is represented by the matrix

$$\begin{bmatrix} A & \mathbf{0} \\ \mathbf{0}^T & 1 \end{bmatrix} = \begin{bmatrix} 1 & 0 & 0 & 0 \\ 0 & 1/2 & -\sqrt{3}/2 & 0 \\ 0 & \sqrt{3}/2 & 1/2 & 0 \\ 0 & 0 & 0 & 1 \end{bmatrix}$$

18. First construct the 3×3 matrix for the rotation. The vector $\mathbf{e}_1$ is rotated $30°$ toward the negative y-axis, ending up at the point $(\cos(-30)°, \sin(-30)°, 0) = (\sqrt{3}/2, -1/2, 0)$. The vector $\mathbf{e}_2$ is rotated $60°$ toward the positive x-axis, ending up at the point $(\cos 60°, \sin 60°, 0) = (1/2, \sqrt{3}/2, 0)$. The vector $\mathbf{e}_3$ is not changed by the rotation. The matrix A for the rotation is thus

$$A = \begin{bmatrix} \sqrt{3}/2 & 1/2 & 0 \\ -1/2 & \sqrt{3}/2 & 0 \\ 0 & 0 & 1 \end{bmatrix}$$

so in homogeneous coordinates the rotation is represented by the matrix

$$\begin{bmatrix} A & \mathbf{0} \\ \mathbf{0}^T & 1 \end{bmatrix} = \begin{bmatrix} \sqrt{3}/2 & 1/2 & 0 & 0 \\ -1/2 & \sqrt{3}/2 & 0 & 0 \\ 0 & 0 & 1 & 0 \\ 0 & 0 & 0 & 1 \end{bmatrix}$$

Following Example 7b, in homogeneous coordinates the translation by the vector $(5, -2, 1)$ is represented by the matrix

$$\begin{bmatrix} 1 & 0 & 0 & 5 \\ 0 & 1 & 0 & -2 \\ 0 & 0 & 1 & 1 \\ 0 & 0 & 0 & 1 \end{bmatrix}$$

Thus the complete transformation is represented in homogeneous coordinates by the matrix

$$\begin{bmatrix} 1 & 0 & 0 & 5 \\ 0 & 1 & 0 & -2 \\ 0 & 0 & 1 & 1 \\ 0 & 0 & 0 & 1 \end{bmatrix} \begin{bmatrix} \sqrt{3}/2 & 1/2 & 0 & 0 \\ -1/2 & \sqrt{3}/2 & 0 & 0 \\ 0 & 0 & 1 & 0 \\ 0 & 0 & 0 & 1 \end{bmatrix} = \begin{bmatrix} \sqrt{3}/2 & 1/2 & 0 & 5 \\ -1/2 & \sqrt{3}/2 & 0 & -2 \\ 0 & 0 & 1 & 1 \\ 0 & 0 & 0 & 1 \end{bmatrix}$$

19. Referring to the material preceding Example 8 in the text, we find that the matrix P that performs a perspective projection with center of projection $(0, 0, 10)$ is

$$\begin{bmatrix} 1 & 0 & 0 & 0 \\ 0 & 1 & 0 & 0 \\ 0 & 0 & 0 & 0 \\ 0 & 0 & -.1 & 1 \end{bmatrix}$$

The homogeneous coordinates of the vertices of the triangle may be written as $(4.2, 1.2, 4, 1)$, $(6, 4, 2, 1)$, and $(2, 2, 6, 1)$, so the data matrix for S is

$$\begin{bmatrix} 4.2 & 6 & 2 \\ 1.2 & 4 & 2 \\ 4 & 2 & 6 \\ 1 & 1 & 1 \end{bmatrix}$$

and the data matrix for the transformed triangle is

$$\begin{bmatrix} 1 & 0 & 0 & 0 \\ 0 & 1 & 0 & 0 \\ 0 & 0 & 0 & 0 \\ 0 & 0 & -.1 & 1 \end{bmatrix} \begin{bmatrix} 4.2 & 6 & 2 \\ 1.2 & 4 & 2 \\ 4 & 2 & 6 \\ 1 & 1 & 1 \end{bmatrix} = \begin{bmatrix} 4.2 & 6 & 2 \\ 1.2 & 4 & 2 \\ 0 & 0 & 0 \\ .6 & .8 & .4 \end{bmatrix}$$

Finally, the columns of this matrix may be converted from homogeneous coordinates by dividing by the final coordinate:

$(4.2, 1.2, 0, .6) \rightarrow (4.2/.6, 1.2/.6, 0/.6) = (7, 2, 0)$

$(6, 4, 0, .8) \quad \rightarrow (6/.8, 2/.8, 0/.8) = (7.5, 5, 0)$

$(2, 2, 0, .4) \quad \rightarrow (2/.4, 2/.4, 0/.4) = (5, 5, 0)$

So the coordinates of the vertices of the transformed triangle are $(7, 2, 0)$, $(7.5, 5, 0)$, and $(5, 5, 0)$.

20. As in the previous exercise, the matrix P that performs the perspective projection is

$$\begin{bmatrix} 1 & 0 & 0 & 0 \\ 0 & 1 & 0 & 0 \\ 0 & 0 & 0 & 0 \\ 0 & 0 & -.1 & 1 \end{bmatrix}$$

The homogeneous coordinates of the vertices of the triangle may be written as $(9, 3, -5, 1)$, $(12, 8, 2, 1)$, and $(1.8, 2.7, 1, 1)$, so the data matrix for S is

$$\begin{bmatrix} 9 & 12 & 1.8 \\ 3 & 8 & 2.7 \\ -5 & 2 & 1 \\ 1 & 1 & 1 \end{bmatrix}$$

and the data matrix for the transformed triangle is

$$\begin{bmatrix} 1 & 0 & 0 & 0 \\ 0 & 1 & 0 & 0 \\ 0 & 0 & 0 & 0 \\ 0 & 0 & -.1 & 1 \end{bmatrix} \begin{bmatrix} 9 & 12 & 1.8 \\ 3 & 8 & 2.7 \\ -5 & 2 & 1 \\ 1 & 1 & 1 \end{bmatrix} = \begin{bmatrix} 9 & 12 & 1.8 \\ 3 & 8 & 2.7 \\ 0 & 0 & 0 \\ 1.5 & .8 & .9 \end{bmatrix}$$

Finally, the columns of this matrix may be converted from homogeneous coordinates by dividing by the final coordinate:

$$(9, 3, 0, 1.5) \;\rightarrow (9/1.5, 3/1.5, 0/1.5) = (6, 2, 0)$$

$$(12, 8, 0, .8) \;\;\rightarrow (12/.8, 8/.8, 0/.8) = (15, 10, 0)$$

$$(1.8, 2.7, 0, .9) \rightarrow (1.8/.9, 2.7/.9, 0/.9) = (2, 3, 0)$$

So the coordinates of the vertices of the transformed triangle are $(6, 2, 0)$, $(15, 10, 0)$, and $(2, 3, 0)$.

21. **[M]** Solve the given equation for the vector (R, G, B), giving

$$\begin{bmatrix} R \\ G \\ B \end{bmatrix} = \begin{bmatrix} .61 & .29 & .15 \\ .35 & .59 & .063 \\ .04 & .12 & .787 \end{bmatrix}^{-1} \begin{bmatrix} X \\ Y \\ Z \end{bmatrix} = \begin{bmatrix} 2.2586 & -1.0395 & -.3473 \\ -1.3495 & 2.3441 & .0696 \\ .0910 & -.3046 & 1.2777 \end{bmatrix} \begin{bmatrix} X \\ Y \\ Z \end{bmatrix}$$

22. **[M]** Solve the given equation for the vector (R, G, B), giving

$$\begin{bmatrix} R \\ G \\ B \end{bmatrix} = \begin{bmatrix} .299 & .587 & .114 \\ .596 & -.275 & -.321 \\ .212 & -.528 & .311 \end{bmatrix}^{-1} \begin{bmatrix} Y \\ I \\ Q \end{bmatrix} = \begin{bmatrix} 1.0031 & .9548 & .6179 \\ .9968 & -.2707 & -.6448 \\ 1.0085 & -1.1105 & 1.6996 \end{bmatrix} \begin{bmatrix} Y \\ I \\ Q \end{bmatrix}$$

2.8 SOLUTIONS

Notes: Cover this section only if you plan to skip most or all of Chapter 4. This section and the next cover everything you need from Sections 4.1–4.6 to discuss the topics in Section 4.9 and Chapters 5–7 (except for the general inner product spaces in Sections 6.7 and 6.8). Students may use Section 4.2 for review, particularly the Table near the end of the section. (The final subsection on linear transformations should be omitted.) Example 6 and the associated exercises are critical for work with eigenspaces in Chapters 5 and 7. Exercises 31–36 review the Invertible Matrix Theorem. New statements will be added to this theorem in Section 2.9.

Key Exercises: 5–20 and 23–26.

1. The set is closed under sums but not under multiplication by a negative scalar. A counterexample to the subspace condition is shown at the right.

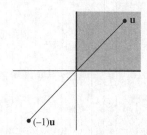

Note: Most students prefer to give a geometric counterexample, but some may choose an algebraic calculation. The four exercises here should help students develop an understanding of subspaces, but they may be insufficient if you want students to be able to analyze an unfamiliar set on an exam. Developing that skill seems more appropriate for classes covering Sections 4.1–4.6.

2. The set is closed under scalar multiples but not sums.
For example, the sum of the vectors **u** and **v** shown
here is not in H.

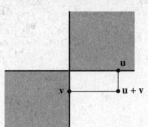

3. No. The set is not closed under sums or scalar multiples. The subset
consisting of the points on the line $x_2 = x_1$ is a subspace, so any
"counterexample" must use at least one point not on this line.
Here are two counterexamples to the subspace conditions:

4. No. The set is closed under sums, but not under multiplication by a
negative scalar.

5. The vector **w** is in the subspace generated by $\mathbf{v}_1$ and $\mathbf{v}_2$ if and only if the vector equation $x_1\mathbf{v}_1 + x_2\mathbf{v}_2 = \mathbf{w}$
is consistent. The row operations below show that **w** is *not* in the subspace generated by $\mathbf{v}_1$ and $\mathbf{v}_2$.

$$[\mathbf{v}_1 \ \ \mathbf{v}_2 \ \ \mathbf{w}] \sim \begin{bmatrix} 2 & -4 & 8 \\ 3 & -5 & 2 \\ -5 & 8 & -9 \end{bmatrix} \sim \begin{bmatrix} 2 & -4 & 8 \\ 0 & 1 & -10 \\ 0 & -2 & 11 \end{bmatrix} \sim \begin{bmatrix} ② & -4 & 8 \\ 0 & ① & -10 \\ 0 & 0 & ⑨ \end{bmatrix}$$

6. The vector **u** is in the subspace generated by $\{\mathbf{v}_1, \mathbf{v}_2, \mathbf{v}_3\}$ if and only if the vector equation $x_1\mathbf{v}_1 + x_2\mathbf{v}_2 +$
$x_3\mathbf{v}_3 = \mathbf{u}$ is consistent. The row operations below show that **u** is *not* in the subspace generated by
$\{\mathbf{v}_1, \mathbf{v}_2, \mathbf{v}_3\}$.

$$[\mathbf{v}_1 \ \ \mathbf{v}_2 \ \ \mathbf{v}_3 \ \ \mathbf{u}] \sim \begin{bmatrix} 1 & 4 & 5 & -4 \\ -2 & -7 & -8 & 10 \\ 4 & 9 & 6 & -7 \\ 3 & 7 & 5 & -5 \end{bmatrix} \sim \begin{bmatrix} 1 & 4 & 5 & -4 \\ 0 & 1 & 2 & 2 \\ 0 & -7 & -14 & 9 \\ 0 & -5 & -10 & 7 \end{bmatrix} \sim \begin{bmatrix} ① & 4 & 5 & -4 \\ 0 & ① & 2 & 2 \\ 0 & 0 & 0 & ㉓ \\ 0 & 0 & 0 & 17 \end{bmatrix}$$

Note: For a quiz, you could use $\mathbf{w} = (1, -3, 11, 8)$, which is *in* Span$\{\mathbf{v}_1, \mathbf{v}_2, \mathbf{v}_3\}$.

7. **a.** There are three vectors: $\mathbf{v}_1$, $\mathbf{v}_2$, and $\mathbf{v}_3$ in the set $\{\mathbf{v}_1, \mathbf{v}_2, \mathbf{v}_3\}$.

   b. There are infinitely many vectors in Span$\{\mathbf{v}_1, \mathbf{v}_2, \mathbf{v}_3\} = $ Col A.

   c. Deciding whether **p** is in Col A requires calculation:

$$[A \ \ \mathbf{p}] \sim \begin{bmatrix} 2 & -3 & -4 & 6 \\ -8 & 8 & 6 & -10 \\ 6 & -7 & -7 & 11 \end{bmatrix} \sim \begin{bmatrix} 2 & -3 & -4 & 6 \\ 0 & -4 & -10 & 14 \\ 0 & 2 & 5 & -7 \end{bmatrix} \sim \begin{bmatrix} ② & -3 & -4 & 6 \\ 0 & ④ & -10 & 14 \\ 0 & 0 & 0 & 0 \end{bmatrix}$$

   The equation $A\mathbf{x} = \mathbf{p}$ has a solution, so **p** is in Col A.

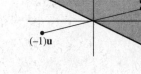

8. $[A \quad \mathbf{p}] = \begin{bmatrix} -3 & -2 & 0 & 1 \\ 0 & 2 & -6 & 14 \\ 6 & 3 & 3 & -9 \end{bmatrix} \sim \begin{bmatrix} -3 & -2 & 0 & 1 \\ 0 & 2 & -6 & 14 \\ 0 & -1 & 3 & -7 \end{bmatrix} \sim \begin{bmatrix} \boxed{-3} & -2 & 0 & 1 \\ 0 & \boxed{2} & -6 & 14 \\ 0 & 0 & 0 & 0 \end{bmatrix}$

Yes, the augmented matrix $[A \quad \mathbf{p}]$ corresponds to a consistent system, so $\mathbf{p}$ is in Col A.

9. To determine whether $\mathbf{p}$ is in Nul A, simply compute $A\mathbf{p}$. Using A and $\mathbf{p}$ as in Exercise 7,

$$A\mathbf{p} = \begin{bmatrix} 2 & -3 & -4 \\ -8 & 8 & 6 \\ 6 & -7 & -7 \end{bmatrix} \begin{bmatrix} 6 \\ -10 \\ 11 \end{bmatrix} = \begin{bmatrix} -2 \\ -62 \\ 29 \end{bmatrix}.$$ Since $A\mathbf{p} \neq \mathbf{0}$, $\mathbf{p}$ is *not* in Nul A.

10. To determine whether $\mathbf{u}$ is in Nul A, simply compute $A\mathbf{u}$. Using A as in Exercise 7 and $\mathbf{u} = (-2, 3, 1)$,

$$A\mathbf{u} = \begin{bmatrix} -3 & -2 & 0 \\ 0 & 2 & -6 \\ 6 & 3 & 3 \end{bmatrix} \begin{bmatrix} -2 \\ 3 \\ 1 \end{bmatrix} = \begin{bmatrix} 0 \\ 0 \\ 0 \end{bmatrix}.$$ Yes, $\mathbf{u}$ is in Nul A.

11. $p = 4$ and $q = 3$. Nul A is a subspace of $\mathbf{R}^4$ because solutions of $A\mathbf{x} = \mathbf{0}$ must have 4 entries, to match the columns of A. Col A is a subspace of $\mathbf{R}^3$ because each column vector has 3 entries.

12. $p = 3$ and $q = 4$. Nul A is a subspace of $\mathbf{R}^3$ because solutions of $A\mathbf{x} = \mathbf{0}$ must have 3 entries, to match the columns of A. Col A is a subspace of $\mathbf{R}^4$ because each column vector has 4 entries.

13. To produce a vector in Col A, select any column of A. For Nul A, solve the equation $A\mathbf{x} = \mathbf{0}$. (Include an augmented column of zeros, to avoid errors.)

$$\begin{bmatrix} 3 & 2 & 1 & -5 & 0 \\ -9 & -4 & 1 & 7 & 0 \\ 9 & 2 & -5 & 1 & 0 \end{bmatrix} \sim \begin{bmatrix} 3 & 2 & 1 & -5 & 0 \\ 0 & 2 & 4 & -8 & 0 \\ 0 & -4 & -8 & 16 & 0 \end{bmatrix} \sim \begin{bmatrix} 3 & 2 & 1 & -5 & 0 \\ 0 & 2 & 4 & -8 & 0 \\ 0 & 0 & 0 & 0 & 0 \end{bmatrix}$$

$$\sim \begin{bmatrix} 3 & 2 & 1 & -5 & 0 \\ 0 & 1 & 2 & -4 & 0 \\ 0 & 0 & 0 & 0 & 0 \end{bmatrix} \sim \begin{bmatrix} \boxed{1} & 0 & -1 & 1 & 0 \\ 0 & \boxed{1} & 2 & -4 & 0 \\ 0 & 0 & 0 & 0 & 0 \end{bmatrix},$$

$\boxed{x_1} \quad - \; x_3 + \; x_4 = 0$
$\boxed{x_2} + 2x_3 - 4x_4 = 0$
$0 = 0$

The general solution is $x_1 = x_3 - x_4$, and $x_2 = -2x_3 + 4x_4$, with x_3 and x_4 free. The general solution in parametric vector form is not needed. All that is required here is one nonzero vector. So choose any values for x_3 and x_4 (not both zero). For instance, set $x_3 = 1$ and $x_4 = 0$ to obtain the vector $(1, -2, 1, 0)$ in Nul A.

Note: Section 2.8 of *Study Guide* introduces the `ref` command (or `rref`, depending on the technology), which produces the reduced echelon form of a matrix. This will greatly speed up homework for students who have a matrix program available.

14. To produce a vector in Col A, select any column of A. For Nul A, solve the equation $A\mathbf{x} = \mathbf{0}$:

$$\begin{bmatrix} 1 & 2 & 3 & 0 \\ 4 & 5 & 7 & 0 \\ -5 & -1 & 0 & 0 \\ 2 & 7 & 11 & 0 \end{bmatrix} \sim \begin{bmatrix} 1 & 2 & 3 & 0 \\ 0 & -3 & -5 & 0 \\ 0 & 9 & 15 & 0 \\ 0 & 3 & 5 & 0 \end{bmatrix} \sim \begin{bmatrix} 1 & 2 & 3 & 0 \\ 0 & 1 & 5/3 & 0 \\ 0 & 0 & 0 & 0 \\ 0 & 0 & 0 & 0 \end{bmatrix} \sim \begin{bmatrix} \boxed{1} & 0 & -1/3 & 0 \\ 0 & \boxed{1} & 5/3 & 0 \\ 0 & 0 & 0 & 0 \\ 0 & 0 & 0 & 0 \end{bmatrix}$$

The general solution is $x_1 = (1/3)x_3$ and $x_2 = (-5/3) x_3$, with x_3 free. The general solution in parametric vector form is not needed. All that is required here is one nonzero vector. So choose any values of x_3 and x_4 (not both zero). For instance, set $x_3 = 3$ to obtain the vector $(1, -5, 3)$ in Nul A.

15. Yes. Let A be the matrix whose columns are the vectors given. Then A is invertible because its determinant is nonzero, and so its columns form a basis for $\mathbf{R}^2$, by the Invertible Matrix Theorem (or by Example 5). (Other reasons for the invertibility of A could be given.)

16. No. One vector is a multiple of the other, so they are linearly dependent and hence cannot be a basis for any subspace.

17. No. Place the three vectors into a 3×3 matrix A and determine whether A is invertible:

$$A = \begin{bmatrix} 0 & 5 & 6 \\ 1 & -7 & 3 \\ -2 & 4 & 5 \end{bmatrix} \sim \begin{bmatrix} 1 & -7 & 3 \\ 0 & 5 & 6 \\ -2 & 4 & 5 \end{bmatrix} \sim \begin{bmatrix} 1 & -7 & 3 \\ 0 & 5 & 6 \\ 0 & -10 & 11 \end{bmatrix} \sim \begin{bmatrix} ① & -7 & 3 \\ 0 & ⑤ & 6 \\ 0 & 0 & ㉓ \end{bmatrix}$$

The matrix A has three pivots, so A is invertible by the IMT and its columns form a basis for $\mathbf{R}^3$ (as pointed out in Example 5).

18. Yes. Place the three vectors into a 3×3 matrix A and determine whether A is invertible:

$$A = \begin{bmatrix} 1 & -5 & 7 \\ 1 & -1 & 0 \\ -2 & 2 & -5 \end{bmatrix} \sim \begin{bmatrix} 1 & -5 & 7 \\ 0 & 4 & -7 \\ 0 & -8 & 9 \end{bmatrix} \sim \begin{bmatrix} ① & -5 & 7 \\ 0 & ④ & -7 \\ 0 & 0 & ⑤ \end{bmatrix}$$

The matrix A has three pivots, so A is invertible by the IMT and its columns form a basis for $\mathbf{R}^3$ (as pointed out in Example 5).

19. No. The vectors cannot be a basis for $\mathbf{R}^3$ because they only span a plan in $\mathbf{R}^3$. Or, point out that the columns of the matrix $\begin{bmatrix} 1 & -5 \\ 1 & -1 \\ -2 & 2 \end{bmatrix}$ cannot possibly span $\mathbf{R}^3$ because the matrix cannot have a pivot in every row. So the columns are not a basis for $\mathbf{R}^3$.

Note: The *Study Guide* warns students not to say that the two vectors here are a basis for $\mathbf{R}^2$.

20. No. The vectors are linearly dependent because there are more vectors in the set than entries in each vector. (Theorem 8 in Section 1.7.) So the vectors cannot be a basis for any subspace.

21. **a.** False. See the definition at the beginning of the section. The critical phrases "for each" are missing.
   b. True. See the paragraph before Example 4.
   c. False. See Theorem 12. The null space is a subspace of $\mathbf{R}^n$, not $\mathbf{R}^m$.
   d. True. See Example 5.
   e. True. See the first part of the solution of Example 8.

22. **a.** False. See the definition at the beginning of the section. The condition about the zero vector is only one of the conditions for a subspace.
   b. True. See Example 3.
   c. True. See Theorem 12.
   d. False. See the paragraph after Example 4.
   e. False. See the Warning that follows Theorem 13.

23. (Solution in *Study Guide*) $A = \begin{bmatrix} 4 & 5 & 9 & -2 \\ 6 & 5 & 1 & 12 \\ 3 & 4 & 8 & -3 \end{bmatrix} \sim \begin{bmatrix} ① & 2 & 6 & -5 \\ 0 & ① & 5 & -6 \\ 0 & 0 & 0 & 0 \end{bmatrix}$. The echelon form identifies

columns 1 and 2 as the pivot columns. A basis for Col A uses columns 1 and 2 of A: $\begin{bmatrix} 4 \\ 6 \\ 3 \end{bmatrix}, \begin{bmatrix} 5 \\ 5 \\ 4 \end{bmatrix}$. This is not

the only choice, but it is the "standard" choice. A *wrong* choice is to select columns 1 and 2 of the echelon form. These columns have zero in the third entry and could not possibly generate the columns displayed in A.

24. For Nul A, obtain the reduced (and augmented) echelon form for $A\mathbf{x} = \mathbf{0}$:

$\begin{bmatrix} ① & 0 & -4 & 7 & 0 \\ 0 & ① & 5 & -6 & 0 \\ 0 & 0 & 0 & 0 & 0 \end{bmatrix}$. This corresponds to: $\quad \begin{aligned} ⓧ_1 \quad - 4x_3 + 7x_4 &= 0 \\ ⓧ_2 + 5x_3 - 6x_4 &= 0. \\ 0 &= 0 \end{aligned}$

Solve for the basic variables and write the solution of $A\mathbf{x} = \mathbf{0}$ in parametric vector form:

$\begin{bmatrix} x_1 \\ x_2 \\ x_3 \\ x_4 \end{bmatrix} = \begin{bmatrix} 4x_3 - 7x_4 \\ -5x_3 + 6x_4 \\ x_3 \\ x_4 \end{bmatrix} = x_3 \begin{bmatrix} 4 \\ -5 \\ 1 \\ 0 \end{bmatrix} + x_4 \begin{bmatrix} -7 \\ 6 \\ 0 \\ 1 \end{bmatrix}$. Basis for Nul A: $\begin{bmatrix} 4 \\ -5 \\ 1 \\ 0 \end{bmatrix}, \begin{bmatrix} -7 \\ 6 \\ 0 \\ 1 \end{bmatrix}$

Notes: (1) A basis is a *set* of vectors. For simplicity, the answers here and in the text list the vectors without enclosing the list inside set brackets. This style is also easier for students. I am careful, however, to distinguish between a matrix and the set or list whose elements are the columns of the matrix.

(2) Recall from Chapter 1 that students are encouraged to use the augmented matrix when solving $A\mathbf{x} = \mathbf{0}$, to avoid the common error of misinterpreting the reduced echelon form of A as itself the augmented matrix for a nonhomogeneous system.

(3) Because the concept of a basis is just being introduced, I insist that my students write the parametric vector form of the solution of $A\mathbf{x} = \mathbf{0}$. They see how the basis vectors span the solution space and are obviously linearly independent. A shortcut, which some instructors might introduce later in the course, is only to solve for the basic variables and to produce each basis vector one at a time. Namely, set all free variables equal to zero except for one free variable, and set that variable equal to a suitable nonzero number.

24. $A = \begin{bmatrix} -3 & 9 & -2 & -7 \\ 2 & -6 & 4 & 8 \\ 3 & -9 & -2 & 2 \end{bmatrix} \sim \begin{bmatrix} ① & -3 & 6 & 9 \\ 0 & 0 & ④ & 5 \\ 0 & 0 & 0 & 0 \end{bmatrix}$. Basis for Col A: $\begin{bmatrix} -3 \\ 2 \\ 3 \end{bmatrix}, \begin{bmatrix} -2 \\ 4 \\ -2 \end{bmatrix}$.

For Nul A, obtain the reduced (and augmented) echelon form for $A\mathbf{x} = \mathbf{0}$:

$\begin{bmatrix} ① & -3 & 0 & 1.50 & 0 \\ 0 & 0 & ① & 1.25 & 0 \\ 0 & 0 & 0 & 0 & 0 \end{bmatrix}$. This corresponds to: $\quad \begin{aligned} ⓧ_1 - 3x_2 \quad + 1.50x_4 &= 0 \\ ⓧ_3 + 1.25x_4 &= 0. \\ 0 &= 0 \end{aligned}$

Solve for the basic variables and write the solution of $A\mathbf{x} = \mathbf{0}$ in parametric vector form:

$\begin{bmatrix} x_1 \\ x_2 \\ x_3 \\ x_4 \end{bmatrix} = \begin{bmatrix} 3x_2 - 1.5x_4 \\ x_2 \\ -1.25x_4 \\ x_4 \end{bmatrix} = x_2 \begin{bmatrix} 3 \\ 1 \\ 0 \\ 0 \end{bmatrix} + x_4 \begin{bmatrix} -1.5 \\ 0 \\ -1.25 \\ 1 \end{bmatrix}$. Basis for Nul A: $\begin{bmatrix} 3 \\ 1 \\ 0 \\ 0 \end{bmatrix}, \begin{bmatrix} -1.5 \\ 0 \\ -1.25 \\ 1 \end{bmatrix}$.

25. $A = \begin{bmatrix} 1 & 4 & 8 & -3 & -7 \\ -1 & 2 & 7 & 3 & 4 \\ -2 & 2 & 9 & 5 & 5 \\ 3 & 6 & 9 & -5 & -2 \end{bmatrix} \sim \begin{bmatrix} ① & 4 & 8 & 0 & 5 \\ 0 & ② & 5 & 0 & -1 \\ 0 & 0 & 0 & ① & 4 \\ 0 & 0 & 0 & 0 & 0 \end{bmatrix}$. Basis for Col A: $\begin{bmatrix} 1 \\ -1 \\ -2 \\ 3 \end{bmatrix}, \begin{bmatrix} 4 \\ 2 \\ 2 \\ 6 \end{bmatrix}, \begin{bmatrix} -3 \\ 3 \\ 5 \\ -5 \end{bmatrix}$.

For Nul A, obtain the reduced (and augmented) echelon form for $A\mathbf{x} = \mathbf{0}$:

$[A \quad \mathbf{0}] \sim \begin{bmatrix} ① & 0 & -2 & 0 & 7 & 0 \\ 0 & ① & 2.5 & 0 & -.5 & 0 \\ 0 & 0 & 0 & ① & 4 & 0 \\ 0 & 0 & 0 & 0 & 0 & 0 \end{bmatrix}$.
$\quad \begin{aligned} ⓧ_1 \quad - \quad 2x_3 \quad + 7x_5 &= 0 \\ ⓧ_2 + 2.5x_3 \quad - .5x_5 &= 0 \\ ⓧ_4 + 4x_5 &= 0 \\ 0 &= 0 \end{aligned}$.

The solution of $A\mathbf{x} = \mathbf{0}$ in parametric vector form : $\begin{bmatrix} x_1 \\ x_2 \\ x_3 \\ x_4 \\ x_5 \end{bmatrix} = \begin{bmatrix} 2x_3 - 7x_5 \\ -2.5x_3 + .5x_5 \\ x_3 \\ -4x_5 \\ x_5 \end{bmatrix} = x_3 \begin{bmatrix} 2 \\ -2.5 \\ 1 \\ 0 \\ 0 \end{bmatrix} + x_5 \begin{bmatrix} -7 \\ .5 \\ 0 \\ -4 \\ 1 \end{bmatrix}$.

$\qquad\qquad\qquad\qquad\qquad\qquad\qquad\qquad\qquad\qquad\qquad\qquad\qquad\quad \mathbf{u} \qquad\quad \mathbf{v}$

Basis for Nul A: $\{\mathbf{u}, \mathbf{v}\}$.

Note: The solution above illustrates how students could write a solution on an exam, when time is precious, namely, describe the basis by giving names to appropriate vectors found in the calculations.

26. $A = \begin{bmatrix} 3 & -1 & 7 & 3 & 9 \\ -2 & 2 & -2 & 7 & 5 \\ -5 & 9 & 3 & 3 & 4 \\ -2 & 6 & 6 & 3 & 7 \end{bmatrix} \sim \begin{bmatrix} ③ & -1 & 7 & 0 & 6 \\ 0 & ② & 4 & 0 & 3 \\ 0 & 0 & 0 & ① & 1 \\ 0 & 0 & 0 & 0 & 0 \end{bmatrix}$. Basis for Col A: $\begin{bmatrix} 3 \\ -2 \\ -5 \\ -2 \end{bmatrix}, \begin{bmatrix} -1 \\ 2 \\ 9 \\ 6 \end{bmatrix}, \begin{bmatrix} 3 \\ 7 \\ 3 \\ 3 \end{bmatrix}$.

For Nul A,

$[A \quad \mathbf{0}] \sim \begin{bmatrix} ① & 0 & 3 & 0 & 2.5 & 0 \\ 0 & ① & 2 & 0 & 1.5 & 0 \\ 0 & 0 & 0 & ① & 1 & 0 \\ 0 & 0 & 0 & 0 & 0 & 0 \end{bmatrix}$.
$\quad \begin{aligned} ⓧ_1 \quad + 3x \quad + 2.5x_5 &= 0 \\ ⓧ_2 + 2x_3 \quad + 1.5x_5 &= 0 \\ ⓧ_4 + \quad x_5 &= 0 \\ 0 &= 0 \end{aligned}$

The solution of $A\mathbf{x} = \mathbf{0}$ in parametric vector form:

$\begin{bmatrix} x_1 \\ x_2 \\ x_3 \\ x_4 \\ x_5 \end{bmatrix} = \begin{bmatrix} -3x_3 - 2.5x_5 \\ -2x_3 - 1.5x_5 \\ x_3 \\ -x_5 \\ x_5 \end{bmatrix} = x_3 \begin{bmatrix} -3 \\ -2 \\ 1 \\ 0 \\ 0 \end{bmatrix} + x_5 \begin{bmatrix} -2.5 \\ -1.5 \\ 0 \\ -1 \\ 1 \end{bmatrix}$. Basis for Nul A: $\{\mathbf{u}, \mathbf{v}\}$.

$\qquad\qquad\qquad\qquad\qquad\qquad\qquad\qquad\qquad\quad \mathbf{u} \qquad\quad \mathbf{v}$

27. Construct a nonzero 3×3 matrix A and construct $\mathbf{b}$ to be almost any convenient linear combination of the columns of A.

28. The easiest construction is to write a 3×3 matrix in echelon form that has only 2 pivots, and let **b** be any vector in $\mathbf{R}^3$ whose third entry is nonzero.

29. (Solution in *Study Guide*) A simple construction is to write any nonzero 3×3 matrix whose columns are obviously linearly dependent, and then make **b** a vector of weights from a linear dependence relation among the columns. For instance, if the first two columns of A are equal, then **b** could be $(1, -1, 0)$.

30. Since Col A is the set of all linear combinations of $\mathbf{a}_1, \ldots, \mathbf{a}_p$, the set $\{\mathbf{a}_1, \ldots, \mathbf{a}_p\}$ spans Col A. Because $\{\mathbf{a}_1, \ldots, \mathbf{a}_p\}$ is also linearly independent, it is a basis for Col A. (There is no need to discuss pivot columns and Theorem 13, though a proof could be given using this information.)

31. If Col $F \neq \mathbf{R}^5$, then the columns of F do not span $\mathbf{R}^5$. Since F is square, the IMT shows that F is not invertible and the equation $F\mathbf{x} = \mathbf{0}$ has a nontrivial solution. That is, Nul F contains a nonzero vector. Another way to describe this is to write Nul $F \neq \{\mathbf{0}\}$.

32. If Nul R contains nonzero vectors, then the equation $R\mathbf{x} = \mathbf{0}$ has nontrivial solutions. Since R is square, the IMT shows that R is not invertible and the columns of R do not span $\mathbf{R}^6$. So Col R is a subspace of $\mathbf{R}^6$, but Col $R \neq \mathbf{R}^6$.

33. If Col $Q = \mathbf{R}^4$, then the columns of Q span $\mathbf{R}^4$. Since Q is square, the IMT shows that Q is invertible and the equation $Q\mathbf{x} = \mathbf{b}$ has a solution for each **b** in $\mathbf{R}^4$. Also, each solution is unique, by Theorem 5 in Section 2.2.

34. If Nul $P = \{\mathbf{0}\}$, then the equation $P\mathbf{x} = \mathbf{0}$ has only the trivial solution. Since P is square, the IMT shows that P is invertible and the equation $P\mathbf{x} = \mathbf{b}$ has a solution for each **b** in $\mathbf{R}^5$. Also, each solution is unique, by Theorem 5 in Section 2.2.

35. If the columns of B are linearly independent, then the equation $B\mathbf{x} = \mathbf{0}$ has only the trivial (zero) solution. That is, Nul $B = \{\mathbf{0}\}$.

36. If the columns of A form a basis, they are linearly independent. This means that A cannot have more columns than rows. Since the columns also span $\mathbf{R}^m$, A must have a pivot in each row, which means that A cannot have more rows than columns. As a result, A must be a square matrix.

37. [M] Use the command that produces the reduced echelon form in one step (**ref** or **rref** depending on the program). See the Section 2.8 in the *Study Guide* for details. By Theorem 13, the pivot columns of A form a basis for Col A.

$$A = \begin{bmatrix} 3 & -5 & 0 & -1 & 3 \\ -7 & 9 & -4 & 9 & -11 \\ -5 & 7 & -2 & 5 & -7 \\ 3 & -7 & -3 & 4 & 0 \end{bmatrix} \sim \begin{bmatrix} ① & 0 & 2.5 & -4.5 & 3.5 \\ 0 & ① & 1.5 & -2.5 & 1.5 \\ 0 & 0 & 0 & 0 & 0 \\ 0 & 0 & 0 & 0 & 0 \end{bmatrix} \quad \text{Basis for Col } A: \begin{bmatrix} 3 \\ -7 \\ -5 \\ 3 \end{bmatrix}, \begin{bmatrix} -5 \\ 9 \\ 7 \\ -7 \end{bmatrix}$$

For Nul A, obtain the solution of $A\mathbf{x} = \mathbf{0}$ in parametric vector form:

$$\widehat{x_1} \quad + 2.5x_3 - 4.5x_4 + 3.5x_5 = 0$$
$$\widehat{x_2} + 1.5x_3 - 2.5x_4 + 1.5x_5 = 0$$

Solution: $\begin{cases} x_1 = -2.5x_3 + 4.5x_4 - 3.5x_5 \\ x_2 = -1.5x_3 + 2.5x_4 - 1.5x_5 \\ x_3, x_4, \text{ and } x_5 \text{ are free} \end{cases}$

$$\mathbf{x} = \begin{bmatrix} x_1 \\ x_2 \\ x_3 \\ x_4 \\ x_5 \end{bmatrix} = \begin{bmatrix} -2.5x_3 + 4.5x_4 - 3.5x_5 \\ -1.5x_3 + 2.5x_4 - 1.5x_5 \\ x_3 \\ x_4 \\ x_5 \end{bmatrix} = x_3 \begin{bmatrix} -2.5 \\ -1.5 \\ 1 \\ 0 \\ 0 \end{bmatrix} + x_4 \begin{bmatrix} 4.5 \\ 2.5 \\ 0 \\ 1 \\ 0 \end{bmatrix} + x_5 \begin{bmatrix} -3.5 \\ -1.5 \\ 0 \\ 0 \\ 1 \end{bmatrix} = x_3\mathbf{u} + x_4\mathbf{v} + x_5\mathbf{w}$$

By the argument in Example 6, a basis for Nul A is $\{\mathbf{u}, \mathbf{v}, \mathbf{w}\}$.

38. **[M]** $A = \begin{bmatrix} 5 & 2 & 0 & -8 & -8 \\ 4 & 1 & 2 & -8 & -9 \\ 5 & 1 & 3 & 5 & 19 \\ -8 & -5 & 6 & 8 & 5 \end{bmatrix} \sim \begin{bmatrix} ① & 0 & 0 & 60 & 122 \\ 0 & ① & 0 & -154 & -309 \\ 0 & 0 & ① & -47 & -94 \\ 0 & 0 & 0 & 0 & 0 \end{bmatrix}.$

The pivot columns of A form a basis for Col A: $\begin{bmatrix} 5 \\ 4 \\ 5 \\ -8 \end{bmatrix}, \begin{bmatrix} 2 \\ 1 \\ 1 \\ -5 \end{bmatrix}, \begin{bmatrix} 0 \\ 2 \\ 3 \\ 6 \end{bmatrix}.$

For Nul A, solve $A\mathbf{x} = \mathbf{0}$:
$$\begin{array}{rcl} ⓧ_1 \qquad\quad + 60x_4 + 122x_5 &=& 0 \\ ⓧ_2 \qquad - 154x_4 - 309x_5 &=& 0 \\ ⓧ_3 - 47x_4 - 94x_5 &=& 0 \end{array}$$

Solution: $\begin{cases} x_1 = -60x_4 - 122x_5 \\ x_2 = 154x_4 + 309x_5 \\ x_3 = 47x_4 + 94x_5 \\ x_4 \text{ and } x_5 \text{ are free} \end{cases}$

$$\mathbf{x} = \begin{bmatrix} x_1 \\ x_2 \\ x_3 \\ x_4 \\ x_5 \end{bmatrix} = \begin{bmatrix} -60x_4 - 122x_5 \\ 154x_4 + 309x_5 \\ 47x_4 + 94x_5 \\ x_4 \\ x_5 \end{bmatrix} = x_4 \begin{bmatrix} -60 \\ 154 \\ 47 \\ 1 \\ 0 \end{bmatrix} + x_5 \begin{bmatrix} -122 \\ 309 \\ 94 \\ 0 \\ 1 \end{bmatrix} = x_4\mathbf{u} + x_5\mathbf{v}$$

By the method of Example 6, a basis for Nul A is $\{\mathbf{u}, \mathbf{v}\}$

Note: The *Study Guide* for Section 2.8 gives directions for students to construct a review sheet for the concept of a subspace and the two main types of subspaces, Col A and Nul A, and a review sheet for the concept of a basis. I encourage you to consider making this an assignment for your class.

2.9   SOLUTIONS

Notes: This section contains the ideas from Sections 4.4–4.6 that are needed for later work in Chapters 5–7. If you have time, you can enrich the geometric content of "coordinate systems" by discussing crystal lattices (Example 3 and Exercises 35 and 36 in Section 4.4.) Some students might profit from reading Examples 1–3 from Section 4.4 and Examples 2, 4, and 5 from Section 4.6. Section 4.5 is probably *not* a good reference for students who have not considered general vector spaces.

Coordinate vectors are important mainly to give an intuitive and geometric feeling for the isomorphism between a k-dimensional subspace and $\mathbf{R}^k$. If you plan to omit Sections 5.4, 5.6, 5.7 and 7.2, you can safely omit Exercises 1–8 here.

Exercises 1–16 may be assigned after students have read as far as Example 2. Exercises 19 and 20 use the Rank Theorem, but they can also be assigned before the Rank Theorem is discussed.

The Rank Theorem in this section omits the nontrivial fact about Row A which is included in the Rank Theorem of Section 4.6, but that is used only in Section 7.4. The row space itself can be introduced in Section 6.2, for use in Chapter 6 and Section 7.4.

Exercises 9–16 include important review of techniques taught in Section 2.8 (and in Sections 1.2 and 2.5). They make good test questions because they require little arithmetic. My students need the practice here. Nearly every time I teach the course and start Chapter 5, I find that at least one or two students cannot find a basis for a two-dimensional eigenspace!

1. If $[\mathbf{x}]_B = \begin{bmatrix} 3 \\ 2 \end{bmatrix}$, then $\mathbf{x}$ is formed from $\mathbf{b}_1$ and $\mathbf{b}_2$ using

weights 3 and 2:

$$\mathbf{x} = 3\mathbf{b}_1 + 2\mathbf{b}_2 = 3\begin{bmatrix} 1 \\ 1 \end{bmatrix} + 2\begin{bmatrix} 2 \\ -1 \end{bmatrix} = \begin{bmatrix} 7 \\ 1 \end{bmatrix}$$

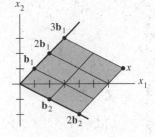

2. If $[\mathbf{x}]_B = \begin{bmatrix} -1 \\ 3 \end{bmatrix}$, then $\mathbf{x}$ is formed from $\mathbf{b}_1$ and $\mathbf{b}_2$ using weights -1 and 3:

$$\mathbf{x} = (-1)\mathbf{b}_1 + 3\mathbf{b}_2 = (-1)\begin{bmatrix} -2 \\ 1 \end{bmatrix} + 3\begin{bmatrix} 3 \\ 1 \end{bmatrix} = \begin{bmatrix} 11 \\ 2 \end{bmatrix}$$

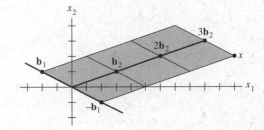

3. To find c_1 and c_2 that satisfy $\mathbf{x} = c_1\mathbf{b}_1 + c_2\mathbf{b}_2$, row reduce the augmented matrix:

$$[\mathbf{b}_1 \ \ \mathbf{b}_2 \ \ \mathbf{x}] = \begin{bmatrix} 1 & -2 & -3 \\ -4 & 7 & 7 \end{bmatrix} \sim \begin{bmatrix} 1 & -2 & -3 \\ 0 & -1 & -5 \end{bmatrix} \sim \begin{bmatrix} 1 & 0 & 7 \\ 0 & 1 & 5 \end{bmatrix}.$$ Or, one can write a matrix equation as

suggested by Exercise 7 and solve using the matrix inverse. In either case,

$$[\mathbf{x}]_B = \begin{bmatrix} c_1 \\ c_2 \end{bmatrix} = \begin{bmatrix} 7 \\ 5 \end{bmatrix}.$$

4. As in Exercise 3, $[\mathbf{b}_1 \ \ \mathbf{b}_2 \ \ \mathbf{x}] = \begin{bmatrix} 1 & -3 & -7 \\ -3 & 5 & 5 \end{bmatrix} \sim \begin{bmatrix} 1 & -3 & -7 \\ 0 & -4 & -16 \end{bmatrix} \sim \begin{bmatrix} 1 & 0 & 5 \\ 0 & 1 & 4 \end{bmatrix}$, and

$$[\mathbf{x}]_B = \begin{bmatrix} c_1 \\ c_2 \end{bmatrix} = \begin{bmatrix} 5 \\ 4 \end{bmatrix}.$$

5. $[\mathbf{b}_1 \ \ \mathbf{b}_2 \ \ \mathbf{x}] = \begin{bmatrix} 1 & -3 & 4 \\ 5 & -7 & 10 \\ -3 & 5 & -7 \end{bmatrix} \sim \begin{bmatrix} 1 & -3 & 4 \\ 0 & 8 & -10 \\ 0 & -4 & 5 \end{bmatrix} \sim \begin{bmatrix} 1 & 0 & 1/4 \\ 0 & 1 & -5/4 \\ 0 & 0 & 0 \end{bmatrix}. [\mathbf{x}]_B = \begin{bmatrix} c_1 \\ c_2 \end{bmatrix} = \begin{bmatrix} 1/4 \\ -5/4 \end{bmatrix}.$

6. $[\mathbf{b}_1 \ \ \mathbf{b}_2 \ \ \mathbf{x}] = \begin{bmatrix} -3 & 7 & 11 \\ 1 & 5 & 0 \\ -4 & -6 & 7 \end{bmatrix} \sim \begin{bmatrix} 1 & 5 & 0 \\ 0 & 22 & 11 \\ 0 & 14 & 7 \end{bmatrix} \sim \begin{bmatrix} 1 & 0 & -5/2 \\ 0 & 1 & 1/2 \\ 0 & 0 & 0 \end{bmatrix}$

$$[\mathbf{x}]_B = \begin{bmatrix} c_1 \\ c_2 \end{bmatrix} = \begin{bmatrix} -5/2 \\ 1/2 \end{bmatrix}.$$

7. Fig. 1 suggests that $\mathbf{w} = 2\mathbf{b}_1 - \mathbf{b}_2$ and $\mathbf{x} = 1.5\mathbf{b}_1 + .5\mathbf{b}_2$, in which case,

$[\mathbf{w}]_B = \begin{bmatrix} 2 \\ -1 \end{bmatrix}$ and $[\mathbf{x}]_B = \begin{bmatrix} 1.5 \\ .5 \end{bmatrix}$. To confirm $[\mathbf{x}]_B$, compute

$$1.5\mathbf{b}_1 + .5\mathbf{b}_2 = 1.5\begin{bmatrix} 3 \\ 0 \end{bmatrix} + .5\begin{bmatrix} -1 \\ 2 \end{bmatrix} = \begin{bmatrix} 4 \\ 1 \end{bmatrix} = \mathbf{x}$$

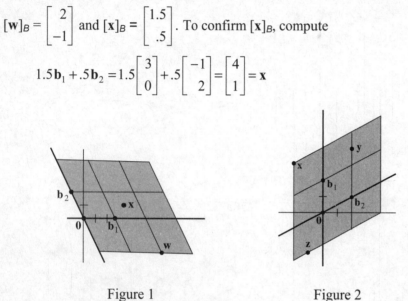

Figure 1   Figure 2

Note: Figures 1 and 2 display what Section 4.4 calls *B*-graph paper.

8. Fig. 2 suggests that $\mathbf{x} = 2\mathbf{b}_1 - \mathbf{b}_2$, $\mathbf{y} = 1.5\mathbf{b}_1 + \mathbf{b}_2$, and $\mathbf{z} = -\mathbf{b}_1 - .5\mathbf{b}_2$. If so, then

$[\mathbf{x}]_B = \begin{bmatrix} 2 \\ -1 \end{bmatrix}$, $[\mathbf{y}]_B = \begin{bmatrix} 1.5 \\ 1.0 \end{bmatrix}$, and $[\mathbf{z}]_B = \begin{bmatrix} -1 \\ -.5 \end{bmatrix}$. To confirm $[\mathbf{y}]_B$ and $[\mathbf{z}]_B$, compute

$$1.5\mathbf{b}_1 + \mathbf{b}_2 = 1.5\begin{bmatrix} 0 \\ 2 \end{bmatrix} + \begin{bmatrix} 2 \\ 1 \end{bmatrix} = \begin{bmatrix} 2 \\ 4 \end{bmatrix} = \mathbf{y} \text{ and } -\mathbf{b}_1 - .5\mathbf{b}_2 = -1\begin{bmatrix} 0 \\ 2 \end{bmatrix} - .5\begin{bmatrix} 2 \\ 1 \end{bmatrix} = \begin{bmatrix} -1 \\ -2.5 \end{bmatrix} = \mathbf{z}.$$

9. The information $A = \begin{bmatrix} 1 & -3 & 2 & -4 \\ -3 & 9 & -1 & 5 \\ 2 & -6 & 4 & -3 \\ -4 & 12 & 2 & 7 \end{bmatrix} \sim \begin{bmatrix} ① & -3 & 2 & -4 \\ 0 & 0 & ⑤ & -7 \\ 0 & 0 & 0 & ⑤ \\ 0 & 0 & 0 & 0 \end{bmatrix}$ is enough to see that columns 1, 3, and 4 of

A form a basis for Col A: $\begin{bmatrix} 1 \\ -3 \\ 2 \\ -4 \end{bmatrix}, \begin{bmatrix} 2 \\ -1 \\ 4 \\ 2 \end{bmatrix}, \begin{bmatrix} -4 \\ 5 \\ -3 \\ 7 \end{bmatrix}$.

Columns 1, 2 and 4, of the echelon form certain cannot span Col A since those vectors all have zero in their fourth entries. For Nul A, use the reduced echelon form, augmented with a zero column to insure that the equation $A\mathbf{x} = \mathbf{0}$ is kept in mind:

$$\begin{bmatrix} ① & -3 & 0 & 0 & 0 \\ 0 & 0 & ① & 0 & 0 \\ 0 & 0 & 0 & ① & 0 \\ 0 & 0 & 0 & 0 & 0 \end{bmatrix}.$$

$$\begin{aligned} Ⓧ_1 - 3x_2 &= 0 \\ Ⓧ_3 &= 0 \\ Ⓧ_4 &= 0 \end{aligned},$$

x_2 is the free variable

$$\mathbf{x} = \begin{bmatrix} x_1 \\ x_2 \\ x_3 \\ x_4 \end{bmatrix} = \begin{bmatrix} 3x_2 \\ x_2 \\ 0 \\ 0 \end{bmatrix} = x_2 \begin{bmatrix} 3 \\ 1 \\ 0 \\ 0 \end{bmatrix}. \text{ So } \begin{bmatrix} 3 \\ 1 \\ 0 \\ 0 \end{bmatrix} \text{ is}$$

a basis for Nul A. From this information, dim Col A = 3 (because A has three pivot columns) and dim Nul A = 1 (because the equation $A\mathbf{x} = \mathbf{0}$ has only one free variable).

10. The information $A = \begin{bmatrix} 1 & -2 & 9 & 5 & 4 \\ 1 & -1 & 6 & 5 & -3 \\ -2 & 0 & -6 & 1 & -2 \\ 4 & 1 & 9 & 1 & -9 \end{bmatrix} \sim \begin{bmatrix} ① & -2 & 9 & 5 & 4 \\ 0 & ① & -3 & 0 & -7 \\ 0 & 0 & 0 & ① & -2 \\ 0 & 0 & 0 & 0 & 0 \end{bmatrix}$ shows that columns 1, 2,

and 4 of A form a basis for Col A: $\begin{bmatrix} 1 \\ 1 \\ -2 \\ 4 \end{bmatrix}, \begin{bmatrix} -2 \\ -1 \\ 0 \\ 1 \end{bmatrix}, \begin{bmatrix} 5 \\ 5 \\ 1 \\ 1 \end{bmatrix}$. For Nul A,

$$[A \ \ \mathbf{0}] \sim \begin{bmatrix} ① & 0 & 3 & 0 & 0 & 0 \\ 0 & ① & -3 & 0 & -7 & 0 \\ 0 & 0 & 0 & ① & -2 & 0 \\ 0 & 0 & 0 & 0 & 0 & 0 \end{bmatrix}.$$

$$\begin{aligned} Ⓧ_1 + 3x_3 &= 0 \\ Ⓧ_2 - 3x_3 - 7x_5 &= 0 \\ Ⓧ_4 - 2x_5 &= 0 \end{aligned}$$

x_3 and x_5 are free variables

$$\mathbf{x} = \begin{bmatrix} x_1 \\ x_2 \\ x_3 \\ x_4 \\ x_5 \end{bmatrix} = \begin{bmatrix} -3x_3 \\ 3x_3 + 7x_5 \\ x_3 \\ 2x_5 \\ x_5 \end{bmatrix} = x_3 \begin{bmatrix} -3 \\ 3 \\ 1 \\ 0 \\ 0 \end{bmatrix} + x_5 \begin{bmatrix} 0 \\ 7 \\ 0 \\ 2 \\ 1 \end{bmatrix}. \text{ Basis for Nul } A: \begin{bmatrix} -3 \\ 3 \\ 1 \\ 0 \\ 0 \end{bmatrix}, \begin{bmatrix} 0 \\ 7 \\ 0 \\ 2 \\ 1 \end{bmatrix}.$$

From this, dim Col A = 3 and dim Nul A = 2.

11. The information $A = \begin{bmatrix} 1 & 2 & -5 & 0 & -1 \\ 2 & 5 & -8 & 4 & 3 \\ -3 & -9 & 9 & -7 & -2 \\ 3 & 10 & -7 & 11 & 7 \end{bmatrix} \sim \begin{bmatrix} ① & 2 & -5 & 0 & -1 \\ 0 & ① & 2 & 4 & 5 \\ 0 & 0 & 0 & ① & 2 \\ 0 & 0 & 0 & 0 & 0 \end{bmatrix}$ shows that columns 1, 2,

and 4 of A form a basis for Col A: $\begin{bmatrix} 1 \\ 2 \\ -3 \\ 3 \end{bmatrix}, \begin{bmatrix} 2 \\ 5 \\ -9 \\ 10 \end{bmatrix}, \begin{bmatrix} 0 \\ 4 \\ -7 \\ 11 \end{bmatrix}$. For Nul A,

$$[A \ \ \mathbf{0}] \sim \begin{bmatrix} ① & 0 & -9 & 0 & 5 & 0 \\ 0 & ① & 2 & 0 & -3 & 0 \\ 0 & 0 & 0 & ① & 2 & 0 \\ 0 & 0 & 0 & 0 & 0 & 0 \end{bmatrix}.$$

$$\begin{aligned} Ⓧ_1 - 9x_3 + 5x_5 &= 0 \\ Ⓧ_2 + 2x_3 - 3x_5 &= 0 \\ Ⓧ_4 + 2x_5 &= 0 \end{aligned}$$

x_3 and x_5 are free variables

$$\mathbf{x} = \begin{bmatrix} x_1 \\ x_2 \\ x_3 \\ x_4 \\ x_5 \end{bmatrix} = \begin{bmatrix} 9x_3 - 5x_5 \\ -2x_3 + 3x_5 \\ x_3 \\ -2x_5 \\ x_5 \end{bmatrix} = x_3 \begin{bmatrix} 9 \\ -2 \\ 1 \\ 0 \\ 0 \end{bmatrix} + x_5 \begin{bmatrix} -5 \\ 3 \\ 0 \\ -2 \\ 1 \end{bmatrix}. \text{ Basis for Nul } A: \begin{bmatrix} 9 \\ -2 \\ 1 \\ 0 \\ 0 \end{bmatrix}, \begin{bmatrix} -5 \\ 3 \\ 0 \\ -2 \\ 1 \end{bmatrix}.$$

From this, dim Col $A = 3$ and dim Nul $A = 2$.

12. The information $A = \begin{bmatrix} 1 & 2 & -4 & 3 & 3 \\ 5 & 10 & -9 & -7 & 8 \\ 4 & 8 & -9 & -2 & 7 \\ -2 & -4 & 5 & 0 & -6 \end{bmatrix} \sim \begin{bmatrix} ① & 2 & -4 & 3 & 3 \\ 0 & 0 & ① & -2 & 0 \\ 0 & 0 & 0 & 0 & ⑤ \\ 0 & 0 & 0 & 0 & 0 \end{bmatrix}$ shows that columns 1, 3,

and 5 of A form a basis for Col A: $\begin{bmatrix} 1 \\ 5 \\ 4 \\ -2 \end{bmatrix}, \begin{bmatrix} -4 \\ -9 \\ -9 \\ 5 \end{bmatrix}, \begin{bmatrix} 3 \\ 8 \\ 7 \\ -6 \end{bmatrix}$. For Nul A

$$[A \quad \mathbf{0}] \sim \begin{bmatrix} ① & 2 & 0 & -5 & 0 & 0 \\ 0 & 0 & ① & -2 & 0 & 0 \\ 0 & 0 & 0 & 0 & ① & 0 \\ 0 & 0 & 0 & 0 & 0 & 0 \end{bmatrix}. \qquad \begin{aligned} ⓧ_1 + 2x_2 \quad - 5x_4 \quad &= 0 \\ ⓧ_3 - 2x_4 \quad &= 0 \\ ⓧ_5 &= 0 \end{aligned}$$

x_2 and x_4 are free variables

$$\mathbf{x} = \begin{bmatrix} x_1 \\ x_2 \\ x_3 \\ x_4 \\ x_5 \end{bmatrix} = \begin{bmatrix} -2x_2 + 5x_4 \\ x_2 \\ 2x_4 \\ x_4 \\ 0 \end{bmatrix} = x_2 \begin{bmatrix} -2 \\ 1 \\ 0 \\ 0 \\ 0 \end{bmatrix} + x_4 \begin{bmatrix} 5 \\ 0 \\ 2 \\ 1 \\ 0 \end{bmatrix}. \text{ Basis for Nul } A: \begin{bmatrix} -2 \\ 1 \\ 0 \\ 0 \\ 0 \end{bmatrix}, \begin{bmatrix} 5 \\ 0 \\ 2 \\ 1 \\ 0 \end{bmatrix}.$$

From this, dim Col $A = 3$ and dim Nul $A = 2$.

13. The four vectors span the column space H of a matrix that can be reduced to echelon form:

$$\begin{bmatrix} 1 & -3 & 2 & -4 \\ -3 & 9 & -1 & 5 \\ 2 & -6 & 4 & -3 \\ -4 & 12 & 2 & 7 \end{bmatrix} \sim \begin{bmatrix} 1 & -3 & 2 & -4 \\ 0 & 0 & 5 & -7 \\ 0 & 0 & 0 & 5 \\ 0 & 0 & 10 & -9 \end{bmatrix} \sim \begin{bmatrix} 1 & -3 & 2 & -4 \\ 0 & 0 & 5 & -7 \\ 0 & 0 & 0 & 5 \\ 0 & 0 & 0 & 5 \end{bmatrix} \sim \begin{bmatrix} ① & -3 & 2 & -4 \\ 0 & 0 & ⑤ & -7 \\ 0 & 0 & 0 & ⑤ \\ 0 & 0 & 0 & 0 \end{bmatrix}$$

Columns 1, 3, and 4 of the original matrix form a basis for H, so dim $H = 3$.

Note: Either Exercise 13 or 14 should be assigned because there are always one or two students who confuse Col A with Nul A. Or, they wrongly connect "set of linear combinations" with "parametric vector form" (of the general solution of $A\mathbf{x} = \mathbf{0}$).

14. The five vectors span the column space H of a matrix that can be reduced to echelon form:

$$\begin{bmatrix} 1 & 2 & 0 & -1 & 3 \\ -1 & -3 & 2 & 4 & -8 \\ -2 & -1 & -6 & -7 & 9 \\ 5 & 6 & 8 & 7 & -5 \end{bmatrix} \sim \begin{bmatrix} 1 & 2 & 0 & -1 & 3 \\ 0 & -1 & 2 & 3 & -5 \\ 0 & 3 & -6 & -9 & 15 \\ 0 & -4 & 8 & 12 & -20 \end{bmatrix} \sim \begin{bmatrix} ① & 2 & 0 & -1 & 3 \\ 0 & ① & 2 & 3 & -5 \\ 0 & 0 & 0 & 0 & 0 \\ 0 & 0 & 0 & 0 & 0 \end{bmatrix}$$

Columns 1 and 2 of the original matrix form a basis for H, so dim $H = 2$.

15. Col $A = \mathbf{R}^3$, because A has a pivot in each row and so the columns of A span $\mathbf{R}^3$. Nul A *cannot* equal $\mathbf{R}^2$, because Nul A is a subspace of $\mathbf{R}^5$. It is true, however, that Nul A is two-dimensional. Reason: the equation $A\mathbf{x} = \mathbf{0}$ has two free variables, because A has five columns and only three of them are pivot columns.

16. Col A *cannot* be $\mathbf{R}^3$ because the columns of A have four entries. (In fact, Col A is a 3-dimensional subspace of $\mathbf{R}^4$, because the 3 pivot columns of A form a basis for Col A.) Since A has 7 columns and 3 pivot columns, the equation $A\mathbf{x} = \mathbf{0}$ has 4 free variables. So, dim Nul $A = 4$.

17. **a.** True. This is the definition of a B-coordinate vector.

 b. False. Dimension is defined only for a subspace. A line must be through the origin in $\mathbf{R}^n$ to be a subspace of $\mathbf{R}^n$.

 c. True. The sentence before Example 1 concludes that the number of pivot columns of A is the rank of A, which is the dimension of Col A by definition.

 d. True. This is equivalent to the Rank Theorem because rank A *is* the dimension of Col A.

 e. True, by the Basis Theorem. In this case, the spanning set is automatically a linearly independent set.

18. **a.** True. This fact is justified in the second paragraph of this section.

 b. True. See the second paragraph after Fig. 1.

 c. False. The dimension of Nul A is the number of *free* variables in the equation $A\mathbf{x} = \mathbf{0}$. See Example 2.

 d. True, by the definition of *rank*.

 e. True, by the Basis Theorem. In this case, the linearly independent set is automatically a spanning set.

19. The fact that the solution space of $A\mathbf{x} = \mathbf{0}$ has a basis of three vectors means that dim Nul $A = 3$. Since a 5×7 matrix A has 7 columns, the Rank Theorem shows that rank $A = 7 - $ dim Nul $A = 4$.

Note: One can solve Exercises 19–22 without explicit reference to the Rank Theorem. For instance, in Exercise 19, if the null space of a matrix A is three-dimensional, then the equation $A\mathbf{x} = \mathbf{0}$ has three free variables, and three of the columns of A are nonpivot columns. Since a 5×7 matrix has seven columns, A must have four pivot columns (which form a basis of Col A). So rank $A = $ dim Col $A = 4$.

20. A 4×5 matrix A has 5 columns. By the Rank Theorem, rank $A = 5 - $ dim Nul A. Since the null space is three-dimensional, rank $A = 2$.

21. A 7×6 matrix has 6 columns. By the Rank Theorem, dim Nul $A = 6 - $ rank A. Since the rank is four, dim Nul $A = 2$. That is, the dimension of the solution space of $A\mathbf{x} = \mathbf{0}$ is two.

22. The wording of this problem was poor in the first printing, because the phrase "it spans a four-dimensional subspace" was never defined. Here is a revision that I will put in later printings of the third edition:

 Show that a set $\{\mathbf{v}_1, \ldots, \mathbf{v}_5\}$ in $\mathbf{R}^n$ is linearly dependent if dim Span$\{\mathbf{v}_1, \ldots, \mathbf{v}_5\} = 4$.

 Solution: Suppose that the subspace $H = $ Span$\{\mathbf{v}_1, \ldots, \mathbf{v}_5\}$ is four-dimensional. If $\{\mathbf{v}_1, \ldots, \mathbf{v}_5\}$ were linearly independent, it would be a basis for H. This is impossible, by the statement just before the definition of *dimension* in Section 2.9, which essentially says that *every* basis of a p-dimensional subspace consists of p vectors. Thus, $\{\mathbf{v}_1, \ldots, \mathbf{v}_5\}$ must be linearly dependent.

23. A 3×4 matrix A with a two-dimensional column space has two pivot columns. The remaining two columns will correspond to free variables in the equation $A\mathbf{x} = \mathbf{0}$. So the desired construction is possible.

There are six possible locations for the two pivot columns, one of which is $\begin{bmatrix} \blacksquare & * & * & * \\ 0 & \blacksquare & * & * \\ 0 & 0 & 0 & 0 \end{bmatrix}$. A simple

construction is to take two vectors in $\mathbf{R}^3$ that are obviously not linearly dependent, and put two copies of these two vectors in any order. The resulting matrix will obviously have a two-dimensional column space. There is no need to worry about whether Nul A has the correct dimension, since this is guaranteed by the Rank Theorem: dim Nul $A = 4 - \text{rank } A$.

24. A rank 1 matrix has a one-dimensional column space. Every column is a multiple of some fixed vector. To construct a 4×3 matrix, choose any nonzero vector in $\mathbf{R}^4$, and use it for one column. Choose any multiples of the vector for the other two columns.

25. The p columns of A span Col A by definition. If dim Col $A = p$, then the spanning set of p columns is automatically a basis for Col A, by the Basis Theorem. In particular, the columns are linearly independent.

26. If columns $\mathbf{a}_1$, $\mathbf{a}_3$, $\mathbf{a}_5$, and $\mathbf{a}_6$ of A are linearly independent and if dim Col $A = 4$, then $\{\mathbf{a}_1, \mathbf{a}_3, \mathbf{a}_5, \mathbf{a}_6\}$ is a linearly independent set in a 4-dimensional column space. By the Basis Theorem, this set of four vectors is a basis for the column space.

27. **a.** Start with $B = [\mathbf{b}_1 \ \cdots \ \mathbf{b}_p]$ and $A = [\mathbf{a}_1 \ \cdots \ \mathbf{a}_q]$, where $q > p$. For $j = 1, \ldots, q$, the vector $\mathbf{a}_j$ is in W. Since the columns of B span W, the vector $\mathbf{a}_j$ is in the column space of B. That is, $\mathbf{a}_j = B\mathbf{c}_j$ for some vector $\mathbf{c}_j$ of weights. Note that $\mathbf{c}_j$ is in $\mathbf{R}^p$ because B has p columns.

b. Let $C = [\mathbf{c}_1 \ \cdots \ \mathbf{c}_q]$. Then C is a $p \times q$ matrix because each of the q columns is in $\mathbf{R}^p$. By hypothesis, q is larger than p, so C has more columns than rows. By a theorem, the columns of C are linearly dependent and there exists a nonzero vector $\mathbf{u}$ in $\mathbf{R}^q$ such that $C\mathbf{u} = \mathbf{0}$.

c. From part (a) and the definition of matrix multiplication

$$A = [\mathbf{a}_1 \ \cdots \ \mathbf{a}_q] = [B\mathbf{c}_1 \ \cdots \ B\mathbf{c}_q] = BC$$

From part (b), $A\mathbf{u} = (BC)\mathbf{u} = B(C\mathbf{u}) = B\mathbf{0} = \mathbf{0}$. Since $\mathbf{u}$ is nonzero, the columns of A are linearly dependent.

28. If A contained more vectors than B, then A would be linearly dependent, by Exercise 27, because B spans W. Repeat the argument with B and A interchanged to conclude that B cannot contain more vectors than A.

29. **[M]** Apply the matrix command **ref** or **rref** to the matrix $[\mathbf{v}_1 \ \mathbf{v}_2 \ \mathbf{x}]$:

$$\begin{bmatrix} 11 & 14 & 19 \\ -5 & -8 & -13 \\ 10 & 13 & 18 \\ 7 & 10 & 15 \end{bmatrix} \sim \begin{bmatrix} ① & 0 & -1.667 \\ 0 & ① & 2.667 \\ 0 & 0 & 0 \\ 0 & 0 & 0 \end{bmatrix}$$

The equation $c_1\mathbf{v}_1 + c_2\mathbf{v}_2 = \mathbf{x}$ is consistent, so $\mathbf{x}$ is in the subspace H. The decimal approximations suggest $c_1 = -5/3$ and $c_2 = 8/3$, and it can be checked that these values are precise. Thus, the B-coordinate of $\mathbf{x}$ is $(-5/3, 8/3)$.

30. **[M]** Apply the matrix command **ref** or **rref** to the matrix $[\mathbf{v}_1 \ \mathbf{v}_2 \ \mathbf{v}_3 \ \mathbf{x}]$:

$$\begin{bmatrix} -6 & 8 & -9 & 4 \\ 4 & -3 & 5 & 7 \\ -9 & 7 & -8 & -8 \\ 4 & -3 & 3 & 3 \end{bmatrix} \sim \begin{bmatrix} ① & 0 & 0 & 3 \\ 0 & ① & 0 & 5 \\ 0 & 0 & ① & 2 \\ 0 & 0 & 0 & 0 \end{bmatrix}$$

The first three columns of $[\mathbf{v}_1 \quad \mathbf{v}_2 \quad \mathbf{v}_3 \quad \mathbf{x}]$ are pivot columns, so $\mathbf{v}_1$, $\mathbf{v}_2$ and $\mathbf{v}_3$ are linearly independent. Thus $\mathbf{v}_1$, $\mathbf{v}_2$ and $\mathbf{v}_3$ form a basis B for the subspace H which they span. View $[\mathbf{v}_1 \quad \mathbf{v}_2 \quad \mathbf{v}_3 \quad \mathbf{x}]$ as an augmented matrix for $c_1\mathbf{v}_1 + c_2\mathbf{v}_2 + c_3\mathbf{v}_3 = \mathbf{x}$. The reduced echelon form shows that $\mathbf{x}$ is in H and

$$[\mathbf{x}]_B = \begin{bmatrix} 3 \\ 5 \\ 2 \end{bmatrix}.$$

Notes: The *Study Guide* for Section 2.9 contains a complete list of the statements in the Invertible Matrix Theorem that have been given so far. The format is the same as that used in Section 2.3, with three columns: statements that are logically equivalent for any $m \times n$ matrix and are related to existence concepts, those that are equivalent only for any $n \times n$ matrix, and those that are equivalent for any $n \times p$ matrix and are related to uniqueness concepts. Four statements are included that are not in the text's official list of statements, to give more symmetry to the three columns.

The *Study Guide* section also contains directions for making a review sheet for "dimension" and "rank."

Chapter 2   SUPPLEMENTARY EXERCISES

1. **a.** True. If A and B are $m \times n$ matrices, then B^T has as many rows as A has columns, so AB^T is defined. Also, A^TB is defined because A^T has m columns and B has m rows.

   b. False. B must have 2 columns. A has as many columns as B has rows.

   c. True. The ith row of A has the form $(0, \ldots, d_i, \ldots, 0)$. So the ith row of AB is $(0, \ldots, d_i, \ldots, 0)B$, which is d_i times the ith row of B.

   d. False. Take the zero matrix for B. Or, construct a matrix B such that the equation $B\mathbf{x} = \mathbf{0}$ has nontrivial solutions, and construct C and D so that $C \neq D$ and the columns of $C - D$ satisfy the equation $B\mathbf{x} = \mathbf{0}$. Then $B(C - D) = 0$ and $BC = BD$.

   e. False. Counterexample: $A = \begin{bmatrix} 1 & 0 \\ 0 & 0 \end{bmatrix}$ and $C = \begin{bmatrix} 0 & 0 \\ 0 & 1 \end{bmatrix}$.

   f. False. $(A + B)(A - B) = A^2 - AB + BA - B^2$. This equals $A^2 - B^2$ if and only if A commutes with B.

   g. True. An $n \times n$ replacement matrix has $n + 1$ nonzero entries. The $n \times n$ scale and interchange matrices have n nonzero entries.

   h. True. The transpose of an elementary matrix is an elementary matrix of the same type.

   i. True. An $n \times n$ elementary matrix is obtained by a row operation on I_n.

   j. False. Elementary matrices are invertible, so a product of such matrices is invertible. But not every square matrix is invertible.

   k. True. If A is 3×3 with three pivot positions, then A is row equivalent to I_3.

   l. False. A must be square in order to conclude from the equation $AB = I$ that A is invertible.

   m. False. AB is invertible, but $(AB)^{-1} = B^{-1}A^{-1}$, and this product is not always equal to $A^{-1}B^{-1}$.

   n. True. Given $AB = BA$, left-multiply by A^{-1} to get $B = A^{-1}BA$, and then right-multiply by A^{-1} to obtain $BA^{-1} = A^{-1}B$.

   o. False. The correct equation is $(rA)^{-1} = r^{-1}A^{-1}$, because

   $$(rA)(r^{-1}A^{-1}) = (rr^{-1})(AA^{-1}) = 1 \cdot I = I.$$

   p. True. If the equation $A\mathbf{x} = \begin{bmatrix} 1 \\ 0 \\ 0 \end{bmatrix}$ has a unique solution, then there are no free variables in this equation, which means that A must have three pivot positions (since A is 3×3). By the Invertible Matrix Theorem, A is invertible.

2. $C = (C^{-1})^{-1} = \dfrac{1}{-2}\begin{bmatrix} 7 & -5 \\ -6 & 4 \end{bmatrix} = \begin{bmatrix} -7/2 & 5/2 \\ 3 & -2 \end{bmatrix}$

3. $A = \begin{bmatrix} 0 & 0 & 0 \\ 1 & 0 & 0 \\ 0 & 1 & 0 \end{bmatrix}$, $A^2 = \begin{bmatrix} 0 & 0 & 0 \\ 1 & 0 & 0 \\ 0 & 1 & 0 \end{bmatrix}\begin{bmatrix} 0 & 0 & 0 \\ 1 & 0 & 0 \\ 0 & 1 & 0 \end{bmatrix} = \begin{bmatrix} 0 & 0 & 0 \\ 0 & 0 & 0 \\ 1 & 0 & 0 \end{bmatrix}$

$A^3 = A \cdot A^2 = \begin{bmatrix} 0 & 0 & 0 \\ 1 & 0 & 0 \\ 0 & 1 & 0 \end{bmatrix}\begin{bmatrix} 0 & 0 & 0 \\ 0 & 0 & 0 \\ 1 & 0 & 0 \end{bmatrix} = \begin{bmatrix} 0 & 0 & 0 \\ 0 & 0 & 0 \\ 0 & 0 & 0 \end{bmatrix}$

Next, $(I - A)(I + A + A^2) = I + A + A^2 - A(I + A + A^2) = I + A + A^2 - A - A^2 - A^3 = I - A^3$.

Since $A^3 = 0$, $(I - A)(I + A + A^2) = I$.

4. From Exercise 3, the inverse of $I - A$ is probably $I + A + A^2 + \cdots + A^{n-1}$. To verify this, compute

$$(I - A)(I + A + \cdots + A^{n-1}) = I + A + \cdots + A^{n-1} - A(I + A + \cdots + A^{n-1}) = I - AA^{n-1} = I - A^n$$

If $A^n = 0$, then the matrix $B = I + A + A^2 + \cdots + A^{n-1}$ satisfies $(I - A)B = I$. Since $I - A$ and B are square, they are invertible by the Invertible Matrix Theorem, and B is the inverse of $I - A$.

5. $A^2 = 2A - I$. Multiply by A: $A^3 = 2A^2 - A$. Substitute $A^2 = 2A - I$: $A^3 = 2(2A - I) - A = 3A - 2I$.
Multiply by A again: $A^4 = A(3A - 2I) = 3A^2 - 2A$. Substitute the identity $A^2 = 2A - I$ again:
Finally, $A^4 = 3(2A - I) - 2A = 4A - 3I$.

6. Let $A = \begin{bmatrix} 1 & 0 \\ 0 & -1 \end{bmatrix}$ and $B = \begin{bmatrix} 0 & 1 \\ 1 & 0 \end{bmatrix}$. By direct computation, $A^2 = I$, $B^2 = I$, and $AB = \begin{bmatrix} 0 & 1 \\ -1 & 0 \end{bmatrix} = -BA$.

7. (Partial answer in *Study Guide*) Since $A^{-1}B$ is the solution of $AX = B$, row reduction of $[A \quad B]$ to $[I \quad X]$ will produce $X = A^{-1}B$. See Exercise 12 in Section 2.2.

$$[A \quad B] = \begin{bmatrix} 1 & 3 & 8 & -3 & 5 \\ 2 & 4 & 11 & 1 & 5 \\ 1 & 2 & 5 & 3 & 4 \end{bmatrix} \sim \begin{bmatrix} 1 & 3 & 8 & -3 & 5 \\ 0 & -2 & -5 & 7 & -5 \\ 0 & -1 & -3 & 6 & -1 \end{bmatrix} \sim \begin{bmatrix} 1 & 3 & 8 & -3 & 5 \\ 0 & 1 & 3 & -6 & 1 \\ 0 & -2 & -5 & 7 & -5 \end{bmatrix}$$

$$\sim \begin{bmatrix} 1 & 3 & 8 & -3 & 5 \\ 0 & 1 & 3 & -6 & 1 \\ 0 & 0 & 1 & -5 & -3 \end{bmatrix} \sim \begin{bmatrix} 1 & 3 & 0 & 37 & 29 \\ 0 & 1 & 0 & 9 & 10 \\ 0 & 0 & 1 & -5 & -3 \end{bmatrix} \sim \begin{bmatrix} 1 & 0 & 0 & 10 & -1 \\ 0 & 1 & 0 & 9 & 10 \\ 0 & 0 & 1 & -5 & -3 \end{bmatrix}$$

Thus, $A^{-1}B = \begin{bmatrix} 10 & -1 \\ 9 & 10 \\ -5 & -3 \end{bmatrix}$.

8. By definition of matrix multiplication, the matrix A satisfies

$$A\begin{bmatrix} 1 & 2 \\ 3 & 7 \end{bmatrix} = \begin{bmatrix} 1 & 3 \\ 1 & 1 \end{bmatrix}$$

Right-multiply both sides by the inverse of $\begin{bmatrix} 1 & 2 \\ 3 & 7 \end{bmatrix}$. The left side becomes A. Thus,

$$A = \begin{bmatrix} 1 & 3 \\ 1 & 1 \end{bmatrix} \begin{bmatrix} 7 & -2 \\ -3 & 1 \end{bmatrix} = \begin{bmatrix} -2 & 1 \\ 4 & -1 \end{bmatrix}$$

9. Given $AB = \begin{bmatrix} 5 & 4 \\ -2 & 3 \end{bmatrix}$ and $B = \begin{bmatrix} 7 & 3 \\ 2 & 1 \end{bmatrix}$, notice that $ABB^{-1} = A$. Since $\det B = 7 - 6 = 1$,

$$B^{-1} = \begin{bmatrix} 1 & -3 \\ -2 & 7 \end{bmatrix} \text{ and } A = (AB)B^{-1} = \begin{bmatrix} 5 & 4 \\ -2 & 3 \end{bmatrix} \begin{bmatrix} 1 & -3 \\ -2 & 7 \end{bmatrix} = \begin{bmatrix} -3 & 13 \\ -8 & 27 \end{bmatrix}$$

Note: Variants of this question make simple exam questions.

10. Since A is invertible, so is A^T, by the Invertible Matrix Theorem. Then $A^T A$ is the product of invertible matrices and so is invertible. Thus, the formula $(A^T A)^{-1} A^T$ makes sense. By Theorem 6 in Section 2.2,

$$(A^T A)^{-1} \cdot A^T = A^{-1}(A^T)^{-1} A^T = A^{-1} I = A^{-1}$$

An alternative calculation: $(A^T A)^{-1} A^T \cdot A = (A^T A)^{-1}(A^T A) = I$. Since A is invertible, this equation shows that its inverse is $(A^T A)^{-1} A^T$.

11. **a.** For $i = 1, \ldots, n$, $p(x_i) = c_0 + c_1 x_i + \cdots + c_{n-1} x_i^{n-1} = \text{row}_i(V) \cdot \begin{bmatrix} c_0 \\ \vdots \\ c_{n-1} \end{bmatrix} = \text{row}_i(V)\mathbf{c}$.

    By a property of matrix multiplication, shown after Example 6 in Section 2.1, and the fact that $\mathbf{c}$ was chosen to satisfy $V\mathbf{c} = \mathbf{y}$,

    $$\text{row}_i(V)\mathbf{c} = \text{row}_i(V\mathbf{c}) = \text{row}_i(\mathbf{y}) = y_i$$

    Thus, $p(x_i) = y_i$. To summarize, the entries in $V\mathbf{c}$ are the values of the polynomial $p(x)$ at $x_1, \ldots, x_n$.

    b. Suppose $x_1, \ldots, x_n$ are distinct, and suppose $V\mathbf{c} = \mathbf{0}$ for some vector $\mathbf{c}$. Then the entries in $\mathbf{c}$ are the coefficients of a polynomial whose value is zero at the distinct points $x_1, \ldots, x_n$. However, a nonzero polynomial of degree $n - 1$ cannot have n zeros, so the polynomial must be identically zero. That is, the entries in $\mathbf{c}$ must all be zero. This shows that the columns of V are linearly independent.

    c. (Solution in *Study Guide*) When $x_1, \ldots, x_n$ are distinct, the columns of V are linearly independent, by (b). By the Invertible Matrix Theorem, V is invertible and its columns span $\mathbf{R}^n$. So, for every $\mathbf{y} = (y_1, \ldots, y_n)$ in $\mathbf{R}^n$, there is a vector $\mathbf{c}$ such that $V\mathbf{c} = \mathbf{y}$. Let p be the polynomial whose coefficients are listed in $\mathbf{c}$. Then, by (a), p is an interpolating polynomial for $(x_1, y_1), \ldots, (x_n, y_n)$.

12. If $A = LU$, then $\text{col}_1(A) = L \cdot \text{col}_1(U)$. Since $\text{col}_1(U)$ has a zero in every entry except possibly the first, $L \cdot \text{col}_1(U)$ is a linear combination of the columns of L in which all weights except possibly the first are zero. So $\text{col}_1(A)$ is a multiple of $\text{col}_1(L)$.

    Similarly, $\text{col}_2(A) = L \cdot \text{col}_2(U)$, which is a linear combination of the columns of L using the first two entries in $\text{col}_2(U)$ as weights, because the other entries in $\text{col}_2(U)$ are zero. Thus $\text{col}_2(A)$ is a linear combination of the first two columns of L.

13. **a.** $P^2 = (\mathbf{u}\mathbf{u}^T)(\mathbf{u}\mathbf{u}^T) = \mathbf{u}(\mathbf{u}^T\mathbf{u})\mathbf{u}^T = \mathbf{u}(1)\mathbf{u}^T = P$, because $\mathbf{u}$ satisfies $\mathbf{u}^T\mathbf{u} = 1$.

    b. $P^T = (\mathbf{u}\mathbf{u}^T)^T = \mathbf{u}^{TT}\mathbf{u}^T = \mathbf{u}\mathbf{u}^T = P$

    c. $Q^2 = (I - 2P)(I - 2P) = I - I(2P) - 2PI + 2P(2P)$
    $$= I - 4P + 4P^2 = I, \text{ because of part (a).}$$

14. Given $\mathbf{u} = \begin{bmatrix} 0 \\ 0 \\ 1 \end{bmatrix}$, define P and Q as in Exercise 13 by

$$P = \mathbf{u}\mathbf{u}^T = \begin{bmatrix} 0 \\ 0 \\ 1 \end{bmatrix}\begin{bmatrix} 0 & 0 & 1 \end{bmatrix} = \begin{bmatrix} 0 & 0 & 0 \\ 0 & 0 & 0 \\ 0 & 0 & 1 \end{bmatrix}, \quad Q = I - 2P = \begin{bmatrix} 1 & 0 & 0 \\ 0 & 1 & 0 \\ 0 & 0 & 1 \end{bmatrix} - 2\begin{bmatrix} 0 & 0 & 0 \\ 0 & 0 & 0 \\ 0 & 0 & 1 \end{bmatrix} = \begin{bmatrix} 1 & 0 & 0 \\ 0 & 1 & 0 \\ 0 & 0 & -1 \end{bmatrix}$$

If $\mathbf{x} = \begin{bmatrix} 1 \\ 5 \\ 3 \end{bmatrix}$, then $P\mathbf{x} = \begin{bmatrix} 0 & 0 & 0 \\ 0 & 0 & 0 \\ 0 & 0 & 1 \end{bmatrix}\begin{bmatrix} 1 \\ 5 \\ 3 \end{bmatrix} = \begin{bmatrix} 0 \\ 0 \\ 3 \end{bmatrix}$ and $Q\mathbf{x} = \begin{bmatrix} 1 & 0 & 0 \\ 0 & 1 & 0 \\ 0 & 0 & -1 \end{bmatrix}\begin{bmatrix} 1 \\ 5 \\ 3 \end{bmatrix} = \begin{bmatrix} 1 \\ 5 \\ -3 \end{bmatrix}$.

15. Left-multiplication by an elementary matrix produces an elementary row operation:

$$B \sim E_1 B \sim E_2 E_1 B \sim E_3 E_2 E_1 B = C$$

so B is row equivalent to C. Since row operations are reversible, C is row equivalent to B. (Alternatively, show C being changed into B by row operations using the inverse of the E_i.)

16. Since A is not invertible, there is a nonzero vector $\mathbf{v}$ in $\mathbf{R}^n$ such that $A\mathbf{v} = \mathbf{0}$. Place n copies of $\mathbf{v}$ into an $n \times n$ matrix B. Then $AB = A[\mathbf{v} \ \cdots \ \mathbf{v}] = [A\mathbf{v} \ \cdots \ A\mathbf{v}] = 0$.

17. Let A be a 6×4 matrix and B a 4×6 matrix. Since B has more columns than rows, its six columns are linearly dependent and there is a nonzero $\mathbf{x}$ such that $B\mathbf{x} = \mathbf{0}$. Thus $AB\mathbf{x} = A\mathbf{0} = \mathbf{0}$. This shows that the matrix AB is not invertible, by the IMT. (Basically the same argument was used to solve Exercise 22 in Section 2.1.)

Note: (In the *Study Guide*) It is possible that BA is invertible. For example, let C be an invertible 4×4 matrix and construct $A = \begin{bmatrix} C \\ 0 \end{bmatrix}$ and $B = [C^{-1} \ 0]$. Then $BA = I_4$, which is invertible.

18. By hypothesis, A is 5×3, C is 3×5, and $AC = I_3$. Suppose $\mathbf{x}$ satisfies $A\mathbf{x} = \mathbf{b}$. Then $CA\mathbf{x} = C\mathbf{b}$. Since $CA = I$, $\mathbf{x}$ must be $C\mathbf{b}$. This shows that $C\mathbf{b}$ is the only solution of $A\mathbf{x} = \mathbf{b}$.

19. **[M]** Let $A = \begin{bmatrix} .4 & .2 & .3 \\ .3 & .6 & .3 \\ .3 & .2 & .4 \end{bmatrix}$. Then $A^2 = \begin{bmatrix} .31 & .26 & .30 \\ .39 & .48 & .39 \\ .30 & .26 & .31 \end{bmatrix}$. Instead of computing A^3 next, speed up the calculations by computing

$$A^4 = A^2 A^2 = \begin{bmatrix} .2875 & .2834 & .2874 \\ .4251 & .4332 & .4251 \\ .2874 & .2834 & .2875 \end{bmatrix}, \quad A^8 = A^4 A^4 = \begin{bmatrix} .2857 & .2857 & .2857 \\ .4285 & .4286 & .4285 \\ .2857 & .2857 & .2857 \end{bmatrix}$$

To four decimal places, as k increases,

$$A^k \to \begin{bmatrix} .2857 & .2857 & .2857 \\ .4286 & .4286 & .4286 \\ .2857 & .2857 & .2857 \end{bmatrix}, \text{ or, in rational format, } A^k \to \begin{bmatrix} 2/7 & 2/7 & 2/7 \\ 3/7 & 3/7 & 3/7 \\ 2/7 & 2/7 & 2/7 \end{bmatrix}.$$

If $B = \begin{bmatrix} 0 & .2 & .3 \\ .1 & .6 & .3 \\ .9 & .2 & .4 \end{bmatrix}$, then $B^2 = \begin{bmatrix} .29 & .18 & .18 \\ .33 & .44 & .33 \\ .38 & .38 & .49 \end{bmatrix}$,

$$B^4 = \begin{bmatrix} .2119 & .1998 & .1998 \\ .3663 & .3764 & .3663 \\ .4218 & .4218 & .4339 \end{bmatrix}, \quad B^8 = \begin{bmatrix} .2024 & .2022 & .2022 \\ .3707 & .3709 & .3707 \\ .4269 & .4269 & .4271 \end{bmatrix}$$

To four decimal places, as k increases,

$$B^k \to \begin{bmatrix} .2022 & .2022 & .2022 \\ .3708 & .3708 & .3708 \\ .4270 & .4270 & .4270 \end{bmatrix}, \text{ or, in rational format, } B^k \to \begin{bmatrix} 18/89 & 18/89 & 18/89 \\ 33/89 & 33/89 & 33/89 \\ 38/89 & 38/89 & 38/89 \end{bmatrix}.$$

20. **[M]** The 4×4 matrix A_4 is the 4×4 matrix of ones, minus the 4×4 identity matrix. The MATLAB command is `A4 = ones(4) - eye(4)`. For the inverse, use `inv(A4)`.

$$A_4 = \begin{bmatrix} 0 & 1 & 1 & 1 \\ 1 & 0 & 1 & 1 \\ 1 & 1 & 0 & 1 \\ 1 & 1 & 1 & 0 \end{bmatrix}, \quad A_4^{-1} = \begin{bmatrix} -2/3 & 1/3 & 1/3 & 1/3 \\ 1/3 & -2/3 & 1/3 & 1/3 \\ 1/3 & 1/3 & -2/3 & 1/3 \\ 1/3 & 1/3 & 1/3 & -2/3 \end{bmatrix}$$

$$A_5 = \begin{bmatrix} 0 & 1 & 1 & 1 & 1 \\ 1 & 0 & 1 & 1 & 1 \\ 1 & 1 & 0 & 1 & 1 \\ 1 & 1 & 1 & 0 & 1 \\ 1 & 1 & 1 & 1 & 0 \end{bmatrix}, \quad A_5^{-1} = \begin{bmatrix} -3/4 & 1/4 & 1/4 & 1/4 & 1/4 \\ 1/4 & -3/4 & 1/4 & 1/4 & 1/4 \\ 1/4 & 1/4 & -3/4 & 1/4 & 1/4 \\ 1/4 & 1/4 & 1/4 & -3/4 & 1/4 \\ 1/4 & 1/4 & 1/4 & 1/4 & -3/4 \end{bmatrix}$$

$$A_6 = \begin{bmatrix} 0 & 1 & 1 & 1 & 1 & 1 \\ 1 & 0 & 1 & 1 & 1 & 1 \\ 1 & 1 & 0 & 1 & 1 & 1 \\ 1 & 1 & 1 & 0 & 1 & 1 \\ 1 & 1 & 1 & 1 & 0 & 1 \\ 1 & 1 & 1 & 1 & 1 & 0 \end{bmatrix}, \quad A_6^{-1} = \begin{bmatrix} -4/5 & 1/5 & 1/5 & 1/5 & 1/5 & 1/5 \\ 1/5 & -4/5 & 1/5 & 1/5 & 1/5 & 1/5 \\ 1/5 & 1/5 & -4/5 & 1/5 & 1/5 & 1/5 \\ 1/5 & 1/5 & 1/5 & -4/5 & 1/5 & 1/5 \\ 1/5 & 1/5 & 1/5 & 1/5 & -4/5 & 1/5 \\ 1/5 & 1/5 & 1/5 & 1/5 & 1/5 & -4/5 \end{bmatrix}$$

The construction of A_6 and the appearance of its inverse suggest that the inverse is related to I_6. In fact, $A_6^{-1} + I_6$ is 1/5 times the 6×6 matrix of ones. Let J denotes the $n \times n$ matrix of ones. The conjecture is:

$$A_n = J - I_n \quad \text{and} \quad A_n^{-1} = \frac{1}{n-1} \cdot J - I_n$$

Proof: (Not required) Observe that $J^2 = nJ$ and $A_n J = (J - I)J = J^2 - J = (n-1)J$. Now compute

$$A_n((n-1)^{-1}J - I) = (n-1)^{-1}A_n J - A_n = J - (J-I) = I$$

Since A_n is square, A_n is invertible and its inverse is $(n-1)^{-1}J - I$.

3 Determinants

3.1 SOLUTIONS

Notes: If time is needed for other topics, this chapter may be omitted. Section 5.2 contains enough information about determinants to support the discussion there of the characteristic polynomial of a matrix. In section 5.1, some exercises in this section provide practice in computing determinants, while others allow the student to discover the properties of determinants which will be studied in the next section. Determinants are developed through the cofactor expansion, which is given in Theorem 1. Exercises 33–36 in this section provide the first step in the inductive proof of Theorem 3 in the next section.

A "*Checkpoint*" in the *Study Guide* leads students to discover that if the kth column of the identity matrix is replaced by a vector **x**, then the determinant of the resulting matrix is the kth entry of **x**. This idea is used in the proof of Cramer's Rule, in Section 3.3.

1. Expand across along the first row:

$$\begin{vmatrix} 3 & 0 & 4 \\ 2 & 3 & 2 \\ 0 & 5 & -1 \end{vmatrix} = 3\begin{vmatrix} 3 & 2 \\ 5 & -1 \end{vmatrix} - 0\begin{vmatrix} 2 & 2 \\ 0 & -1 \end{vmatrix} + 4\begin{vmatrix} 2 & 3 \\ 0 & 5 \end{vmatrix} = 3(-13) + 4(10) = 1$$

Expand down the second column:

$$\begin{vmatrix} 3 & 0 & 4 \\ 2 & 3 & 2 \\ 0 & 5 & -1 \end{vmatrix} = (-1)^{1+2} \cdot 0\begin{vmatrix} 2 & 2 \\ 0 & -1 \end{vmatrix} + (-1)^{2+2} \cdot 3\begin{vmatrix} 3 & 4 \\ 0 & -1 \end{vmatrix} + (-1)^{3+2} \cdot 5\begin{vmatrix} 3 & 4 \\ 2 & 2 \end{vmatrix} = 3(-3) - 5(-2) = 1$$

2. Expand across the first row:

$$\begin{vmatrix} 0 & 5 & 1 \\ 4 & -3 & 0 \\ 2 & 4 & 1 \end{vmatrix} = 0\begin{vmatrix} -3 & 0 \\ 4 & 1 \end{vmatrix} - 5\begin{vmatrix} 4 & 0 \\ 2 & 1 \end{vmatrix} + 1\begin{vmatrix} 4 & -3 \\ 2 & 4 \end{vmatrix} = -5(4) + 1(22) = 2$$

Expand down the second column:

$$\begin{vmatrix} 0 & 5 & 1 \\ 4 & -3 & 0 \\ 2 & 4 & 1 \end{vmatrix} = (-1)^{1+2} \cdot 5\begin{vmatrix} 4 & 0 \\ 2 & 1 \end{vmatrix} + (-1)^{2+2} \cdot (-3)\begin{vmatrix} 0 & 1 \\ 2 & 1 \end{vmatrix} + (-1)^{3+2} \cdot 4\begin{vmatrix} 0 & 1 \\ 4 & 0 \end{vmatrix} = -5(4) - 3(-2) - 4(-4) = 2$$

3. Expand across the first row:

$$\begin{vmatrix} 2 & -4 & 3 \\ 3 & 1 & 2 \\ 1 & 4 & -1 \end{vmatrix} = 2\begin{vmatrix} 1 & 2 \\ 4 & -1 \end{vmatrix} - (-4)\begin{vmatrix} 3 & 2 \\ 1 & -1 \end{vmatrix} + 3\begin{vmatrix} 3 & 1 \\ 1 & 4 \end{vmatrix} = 2(-9) + 4(-5) + (3)(11) = -5$$

Expand down the second column:

$$\begin{vmatrix} 2 & -4 & 3 \\ 3 & 1 & 2 \\ 1 & 4 & -1 \end{vmatrix} = (-1)^{1+2} \cdot (-4) \begin{vmatrix} 3 & 2 \\ 1 & -1 \end{vmatrix} + (-1)^{2+2} \cdot 1 \begin{vmatrix} 2 & 3 \\ 1 & -1 \end{vmatrix} + (-1)^{3+2} \cdot 4 \begin{vmatrix} 2 & 3 \\ 3 & 2 \end{vmatrix} = 4(-5) + 1(-5) - 4(-5) = -5$$

4. Expand across the first row:

$$\begin{vmatrix} 1 & 3 & 5 \\ 2 & 1 & 1 \\ 3 & 4 & 2 \end{vmatrix} = 1 \begin{vmatrix} 1 & 1 \\ 4 & 2 \end{vmatrix} - 3 \begin{vmatrix} 2 & 1 \\ 3 & 2 \end{vmatrix} + 5 \begin{vmatrix} 2 & 1 \\ 3 & 4 \end{vmatrix} = 1(-2) - 3(1) + 5(5) = 20$$

Expand down the second column:

$$\begin{vmatrix} 1 & 3 & 5 \\ 2 & 1 & 1 \\ 3 & 4 & 2 \end{vmatrix} = (-1)^{1+2} \cdot 3 \begin{vmatrix} 2 & 1 \\ 3 & 2 \end{vmatrix} + (-1)^{2+2} \cdot 1 \begin{vmatrix} 1 & 5 \\ 3 & 2 \end{vmatrix} + (-1)^{3+2} \cdot 4 \begin{vmatrix} 1 & 5 \\ 2 & 1 \end{vmatrix} = -3(1) + 1(-13) - 4(-9) = 20$$

5. Expand across the first row:

$$\begin{vmatrix} 2 & 3 & -4 \\ 4 & 0 & 5 \\ 5 & 1 & 6 \end{vmatrix} = 2 \begin{vmatrix} 0 & 5 \\ 1 & 6 \end{vmatrix} - 3 \begin{vmatrix} 4 & 5 \\ 5 & 6 \end{vmatrix} + (-4) \begin{vmatrix} 4 & 0 \\ 5 & 1 \end{vmatrix} = 2(-5) - 3(-1) - 4(4) = -23$$

6. Expand across the first row:

$$\begin{vmatrix} 5 & -2 & 4 \\ 0 & 3 & -5 \\ 2 & -4 & 7 \end{vmatrix} = 5 \begin{vmatrix} 3 & -5 \\ -4 & 7 \end{vmatrix} - (-2) \begin{vmatrix} 0 & -5 \\ 2 & 7 \end{vmatrix} + 4 \begin{vmatrix} 0 & 3 \\ 2 & -4 \end{vmatrix} = 5(1) + 2(10) + 4(-6) = 1$$

7. Expand across the first row:

$$\begin{vmatrix} 4 & 3 & 0 \\ 6 & 5 & 2 \\ 9 & 7 & 3 \end{vmatrix} = 4 \begin{vmatrix} 5 & 2 \\ 7 & 3 \end{vmatrix} - 3 \begin{vmatrix} 6 & 2 \\ 9 & 3 \end{vmatrix} + 0 \begin{vmatrix} 6 & 5 \\ 9 & 7 \end{vmatrix} = 4(1) - 3(0) = 4$$

8. Expand across the first row:

$$\begin{vmatrix} 8 & 1 & 6 \\ 4 & 0 & 3 \\ 3 & -2 & 5 \end{vmatrix} = 8 \begin{vmatrix} 0 & 3 \\ -2 & 5 \end{vmatrix} - 1 \begin{vmatrix} 4 & 3 \\ 3 & 5 \end{vmatrix} + 6 \begin{vmatrix} 4 & 0 \\ 3 & -2 \end{vmatrix} = 8(6) - 1(11) + 6(-8) = -11$$

9. First expand across the third row, then expand across the first row of the remaining matrix:

$$\begin{vmatrix} 6 & 0 & 0 & 5 \\ 1 & 7 & 2 & -5 \\ 2 & 0 & 0 & 0 \\ 8 & 3 & 1 & 8 \end{vmatrix} = (-1)^{3+1} \cdot 2 \begin{vmatrix} 0 & 0 & 5 \\ 7 & 2 & -5 \\ 3 & 1 & 8 \end{vmatrix} = 2 \cdot (-1)^{1+3} \cdot 5 \begin{vmatrix} 7 & 2 \\ 3 & 1 \end{vmatrix} = 10(1) = 10$$

10. First expand across the second row, then expand either across the third row or down the second column of the remaining matrix.

$$\begin{vmatrix} 1 & -2 & 5 & 2 \\ 0 & 0 & 3 & 0 \\ 2 & -6 & -7 & 5 \\ 5 & 0 & 4 & 4 \end{vmatrix} = (-1)^{2+3} \cdot 3 \begin{vmatrix} 1 & -2 & 2 \\ 2 & -6 & 5 \\ 5 & 0 & 4 \end{vmatrix}$$

$$= (-3)\left((-1)^{3+1} \cdot 5 \begin{vmatrix} -2 & 2 \\ -6 & 5 \end{vmatrix} + (-1)^{3+3} \cdot 4 \begin{vmatrix} 1 & -2 \\ 2 & -6 \end{vmatrix} \right) = (-3)(5(2) + 4(-2)) = -6$$

or

$$\begin{vmatrix} 1 & -2 & 5 & 2 \\ 0 & 0 & 3 & 0 \\ 2 & -6 & -7 & 5 \\ 5 & 0 & 4 & 4 \end{vmatrix} = (-1)^{2+3} \cdot 3 \begin{vmatrix} 1 & -2 & 2 \\ 2 & -6 & 5 \\ 5 & 0 & 4 \end{vmatrix}$$

$$= (-3)\left((-1)^{1+2} \cdot (-2) \begin{vmatrix} 2 & 5 \\ 5 & 4 \end{vmatrix} + (-1)^{2+2} \cdot (-6) \begin{vmatrix} 1 & 2 \\ 5 & 4 \end{vmatrix} \right) = (-3)(2(-17) - 6(-6)) = -6$$

11. Following the text's instruction, a good strategy is to expand down the first column of the matrix, and repeat the process until the determinant is expressed as the product of the diagonal entries of the original matrix:

$$\begin{vmatrix} 3 & 5 & -8 & 4 \\ 0 & -2 & 3 & -7 \\ 0 & 0 & 1 & 5 \\ 0 & 0 & 0 & 2 \end{vmatrix} = (-1)^{1+1} \cdot 3 \begin{vmatrix} -2 & 3 & -7 \\ 0 & 1 & 5 \\ 0 & 0 & 2 \end{vmatrix} = 3 \cdot (-1)^{1+1} \cdot (-2) \begin{vmatrix} 1 & 5 \\ 0 & 2 \end{vmatrix} = 3(-2)(2) = -12$$

Of course, with Theorem 2 available, the best strategy is to use it and simply compute the product of the diagonal entries in the matrix.

12. Following the text's instruction, a good strategy is to expand along the first row of the matrix, and repeat the process until the determinant is expressed as the product of the diagonal entries of the original matrix:

$$\begin{vmatrix} 4 & 0 & 0 & 0 \\ 7 & -1 & 0 & 0 \\ 2 & 6 & 3 & 0 \\ 5 & -8 & 4 & -3 \end{vmatrix} = (-1)^{1+1} \cdot 4 \begin{vmatrix} -1 & 0 & 0 \\ 6 & 3 & 0 \\ -8 & 4 & -3 \end{vmatrix} = 4 \cdot (-1)^{1+1} \cdot (-1) \begin{vmatrix} 3 & 0 \\ 4 & -3 \end{vmatrix} = 4(-1)(-9) = 36$$

Of course, with Theorem 2 available, the best strategy is to use it and simply compute the product of the diagonal entries in the matrix.

13. First expand either across the second row or down the second column. Using the second row,

$$\begin{vmatrix} 4 & 0 & -7 & 3 & -5 \\ 0 & 0 & 2 & 0 & 0 \\ 7 & 3 & -6 & 4 & -8 \\ 5 & 0 & 5 & 2 & -3 \\ 0 & 0 & 9 & -1 & 2 \end{vmatrix} = (-1)^{2+3} \cdot 2 \begin{vmatrix} 4 & 0 & 3 & -5 \\ 7 & 3 & 4 & -8 \\ 5 & 0 & 2 & -3 \\ 0 & 0 & -1 & 2 \end{vmatrix}$$

Now expand down the second column to find:

$$(-1)^{2+3} \cdot 2 \begin{vmatrix} 4 & 0 & 3 & -5 \\ 7 & 3 & 4 & -8 \\ 5 & 0 & 2 & -3 \\ 0 & 0 & -1 & 2 \end{vmatrix} = -2 \left((-1)^{2+2} \cdot 3 \begin{vmatrix} 4 & 3 & -5 \\ 5 & 2 & -3 \\ 0 & -1 & 2 \end{vmatrix} \right)$$

Now expand either down the first column or across third row. Using the first column,

$$-2 \left((-1)^{2+2} \cdot 3 \begin{vmatrix} 4 & 3 & -5 \\ 5 & 2 & -3 \\ 0 & -1 & 2 \end{vmatrix} \right) = -6 \left((-1)^{1+1} \cdot 4 \begin{vmatrix} 2 & -3 \\ -1 & 2 \end{vmatrix} + (-1)^{2+1} \cdot 5 \begin{vmatrix} 3 & -5 \\ -1 & 2 \end{vmatrix} \right) = (-6)(4(1) - 5(1)) = 6$$

14. First expand either across the fourth row or down the fifth column. Using the fifth column,

$$\begin{vmatrix} 6 & 3 & 2 & 4 & 0 \\ 9 & 0 & -4 & 1 & 0 \\ 8 & -5 & 6 & 7 & 1 \\ 3 & 0 & 0 & 0 & 0 \\ 4 & 2 & 3 & 2 & 0 \end{vmatrix} = (-1)^{3+5} \cdot 1 \begin{vmatrix} 6 & 3 & 2 & 4 \\ 9 & 0 & -4 & 1 \\ 3 & 0 & 0 & 0 \\ 4 & 2 & 3 & 2 \end{vmatrix}$$

Now expand across the third row to find:

$$(-1)^{3+5} \cdot 1 \begin{vmatrix} 6 & 3 & 2 & 4 \\ 9 & 0 & -4 & 1 \\ 3 & 0 & 0 & 0 \\ 4 & 2 & 3 & 2 \end{vmatrix} = 1 \left((-1)^{3+1} \cdot 3 \begin{vmatrix} 3 & 2 & 4 \\ 0 & -4 & 1 \\ 2 & 3 & 2 \end{vmatrix} \right)$$

Finally, expand either down the first column or along second row. Using the first column,

$$1 \left((-1)^{3+1} \cdot 3 \begin{vmatrix} 3 & 2 & 4 \\ 0 & -4 & 1 \\ 2 & 3 & 2 \end{vmatrix} \right) = 3 \left((-1)^{1+1} \cdot 3 \begin{vmatrix} -4 & 1 \\ 3 & 2 \end{vmatrix} + (-1)^{3+1} \cdot 2 \begin{vmatrix} 2 & 4 \\ -4 & 1 \end{vmatrix} \right) = (3)(3(-11) + 2(18)) = 9$$

15. $\begin{vmatrix} 3 & 0 & 4 \\ 2 & 3 & 2 \\ 0 & 5 & -1 \end{vmatrix} = (3)(3)(-1) + (0)(2)(0) + (4)(2)(5) - (0)(3)(4) - (5)(2)(3) - (-1)(2)(0) =$

$$-9 + 0 + 40 - 0 - 30 - 0 = 1$$

16. $\begin{vmatrix} 0 & 5 & 1 \\ 4 & -3 & 0 \\ 2 & 4 & 1 \end{vmatrix} = (0)(-3)(1) + (5)(0)(2) + (1)(4)(4) - (2)(-3)(1) - (4)(0)(0) - (1)(4)(5) =$

$$0 + 0 + 16 - (-6) - 0 - 20 = 2$$

17. $\begin{vmatrix} 2 & -4 & 3 \\ 3 & 1 & 2 \\ 1 & 4 & -1 \end{vmatrix} = (2)(1)(-1) + (-4)(2)(1) + (3)(3)(4) - (1)(1)(3) - (4)(2)(2) - (-1)(3)(-4) =$

$$-2 + (-8) + 36 - 3 - 16 - 12 = -5$$

18. $\begin{vmatrix} 1 & 3 & 5 \\ 2 & 1 & 1 \\ 3 & 4 & 2 \end{vmatrix} = (1)(1)(2) + (3)(1)(3) + (5)(2)(4) - (3)(1)(5) - (4)(1)(1) - (2)(2)(3) =$

$$2 + 9 + 40 - 15 - 4 - 12 = 20$$

19. $\begin{vmatrix} a & b \\ c & d \end{vmatrix} = ad - bc, \quad \begin{vmatrix} c & d \\ a & b \end{vmatrix} = cb - da = -(ad - bc)$

The row operation swaps rows 1 and 2 of the matrix, and the sign of the determinant is reversed.

20. $\begin{vmatrix} a & b \\ c & d \end{vmatrix} = ad - bc, \quad \begin{vmatrix} a & b \\ kc & kd \end{vmatrix} = a(kd) - (kc)b = kad - kbc = k(ad - bc)$

The row operation scales row 2 by k, and the determinant is multiplied by k.

21. $\begin{vmatrix} 3 & 4 \\ 5 & 6 \end{vmatrix} = 18 - 20 = -2, \quad \begin{vmatrix} 3 & 4 \\ 5+3k & 6+4k \end{vmatrix} = 3(6 + 4k) - (5 + 3k)4 = -2$

The row operation replaces row 2 with k times row 1 plus row 2, and the determinant is unchanged.

22. $\begin{vmatrix} a & b \\ c & d \end{vmatrix} = ad - bc, \quad \begin{vmatrix} a+kc & b+kd \\ c & d \end{vmatrix} = (a + kc)d - c(b + kd) = ad + kcd - bc - kcd = ad - bc$

The row operation replaces row 1 with k times row 2 plus row 1, and the determinant is unchanged.

23. $\begin{vmatrix} 1 & 1 & 1 \\ -3 & 8 & -4 \\ 2 & -3 & 2 \end{vmatrix} = 1(4) - 1(2) + 1(-7) = -5, \quad \begin{vmatrix} k & k & k \\ -3 & 8 & -4 \\ 2 & -3 & 2 \end{vmatrix} = k(4) - k(2) + k(-7) = -5k$

The row operation scales row 1 by k, and the determinant is multiplied by k.

24. $\begin{vmatrix} a & b & c \\ 3 & 2 & 2 \\ 6 & 5 & 6 \end{vmatrix} = a(2) - b(6) + c(3) = 2a - 6b + 3c,$

$\begin{vmatrix} 3 & 2 & 2 \\ a & b & c \\ 6 & 5 & 6 \end{vmatrix} = 3(6b - 5c) - 2(6a - 6c) + 2(5a - 6b) = -2a + 6b - 3c$

The row operation swaps rows 1 and 2 of the matrix, and the sign of the determinant is reversed.

25. By Theorem 2, the determinant of a triangular matrix is the product of the diagonal entries:

$\begin{vmatrix} 1 & 0 & 0 \\ 0 & 1 & 0 \\ 0 & k & 1 \end{vmatrix} = (1)(1)(1) = 1$

26. By Theorem 2, the determinant of a triangular matrix is the product of the diagonal entries:

$\begin{vmatrix} 1 & 0 & 0 \\ 0 & 1 & 0 \\ k & 0 & 1 \end{vmatrix} = (1)(1)(1) = 1$

27. By Theorem 2, the determinant of a triangular matrix is the product of the diagonal entries:

$$\begin{vmatrix} k & 0 & 0 \\ 0 & 1 & 0 \\ 0 & 0 & 1 \end{vmatrix} = (k)(1)(1) = k$$

28. By Theorem 2 the determinant of a triangular matrix is the product of the diagonal entries:

$$\begin{vmatrix} 1 & 0 & 0 \\ 0 & k & 0 \\ 0 & 0 & 1 \end{vmatrix} = (1)(k)(1) = k$$

29. A cofactor expansion across row 1 gives

$$\begin{vmatrix} 0 & 1 & 0 \\ 1 & 0 & 0 \\ 0 & 0 & 1 \end{vmatrix} = -1 \begin{vmatrix} 1 & 0 \\ 0 & 1 \end{vmatrix} = -1$$

30. A cofactor expansion across row 1 gives

$$\begin{vmatrix} 0 & 0 & 1 \\ 0 & 1 & 0 \\ 1 & 0 & 0 \end{vmatrix} = 1 \begin{vmatrix} 0 & 1 \\ 1 & 0 \end{vmatrix} = -1$$

31. A 3×3 elementary row replacement matrix looks like one of the six matrices

$$\begin{bmatrix} 1 & 0 & 0 \\ k & 1 & 0 \\ 0 & 0 & 1 \end{bmatrix}, \begin{bmatrix} 1 & 0 & 0 \\ 0 & 1 & 0 \\ k & 0 & 1 \end{bmatrix}, \begin{bmatrix} 1 & 0 & 0 \\ 0 & 1 & 0 \\ 0 & k & 1 \end{bmatrix}, \begin{bmatrix} 1 & 0 & 0 \\ 0 & 1 & k \\ 0 & 0 & 1 \end{bmatrix}, \begin{bmatrix} 1 & 0 & k \\ 0 & 1 & 0 \\ 0 & 0 & 1 \end{bmatrix}, \begin{bmatrix} 1 & k & 0 \\ 0 & 1 & 0 \\ 0 & 0 & 1 \end{bmatrix}$$

In each of these cases, the matrix is triangular and its determinant is the product of its diagonal entries, which is 1. Thus the determinant of a 3×3 elementary row replacement matrix is 1.

32. A 3×3 elementary scaling matrix with k on the diagonal looks like one of the three matrices

$$\begin{bmatrix} k & 0 & 0 \\ 0 & 1 & 0 \\ 0 & 0 & 1 \end{bmatrix}, \begin{bmatrix} 1 & 0 & 0 \\ 0 & k & 0 \\ 0 & 0 & 1 \end{bmatrix}, \begin{bmatrix} 1 & 0 & 0 \\ 0 & 1 & 0 \\ 0 & 0 & k \end{bmatrix}$$

In each of these cases, the matrix is triangular and its determinant is the product of its diagonal entries, which is k. Thus the determinant of a 3×3 elementary scaling matrix with k on the diagonal is k.

33. $E = \begin{bmatrix} 0 & 1 \\ 1 & 0 \end{bmatrix}$, $A = \begin{bmatrix} a & b \\ c & d \end{bmatrix}$, $EA = \begin{bmatrix} c & d \\ a & b \end{bmatrix}$

det $E = -1$, det $A = ad - bc$,
det $EA = cb - da = -1(ad - bc) = (\det E)(\det A)$

34. $E = \begin{bmatrix} 1 & 0 \\ 0 & k \end{bmatrix}$, $A = \begin{bmatrix} a & b \\ c & d \end{bmatrix}$, $EA = \begin{bmatrix} a & b \\ kc & kd \end{bmatrix}$

det $E = k$, det $A = ad - bc$,
det $EA = a(kd) - (kc)b = k(ad - bc) = (\det E)(\det A)$

35. $E = \begin{bmatrix} 1 & k \\ 0 & 1 \end{bmatrix}$, $A = \begin{bmatrix} a & b \\ c & d \end{bmatrix}$, $EA = \begin{bmatrix} a+kc & b+kd \\ c & d \end{bmatrix}$

det $E = 1$, det $A = ad - bc$,
det $EA = (a + kc)d - c(b + kd) = ad + kcd - bc - kcd = 1(ad - bc) = (\det E)(\det A)$

36. $E = \begin{bmatrix} 1 & 0 \\ k & 1 \end{bmatrix}$, $A = \begin{bmatrix} a & b \\ c & d \end{bmatrix}$, $EA = \begin{bmatrix} a & b \\ ka+c & kb+d \end{bmatrix}$

det $E = 1$, det $A = ad - bc$,
det $EA = a(kb + d) - (ka + c)b = kab + ad - kab - bc = 1(ad - bc) = (\det E)(\det A)$

37. $A = \begin{bmatrix} 3 & 1 \\ 4 & 2 \end{bmatrix}$, $5A = \begin{bmatrix} 15 & 5 \\ 20 & 10 \end{bmatrix}$, det $A = 2$, det $5A = 50 \neq 5\det A$

38. $A = \begin{bmatrix} a & b \\ c & d \end{bmatrix}$, $kA = \begin{bmatrix} ka & kb \\ kc & kd \end{bmatrix}$, det $A = ad - bc$,

det $kA = (ka)(kd) - (kb)(kc) = k^2(ad - bc) = k^2\det A$

39. **a.** True. See the paragraph preceding the definition of the determinant.
   b. False. See the definition of cofactor, which precedes Theorem 1.

40. **a.** False. See Theorem 1.
   b. False. See Theorem 2.

41. The area of the parallelogram determined by $\mathbf{u} = \begin{bmatrix} 3 \\ 0 \end{bmatrix}$, $\mathbf{v} = \begin{bmatrix} 1 \\ 2 \end{bmatrix}$, $\mathbf{u} + \mathbf{v}$, and $\mathbf{0}$ is 6, since the base of the

parallelogram has length 3 and the height of the parallelogram is 2. By the same reasoning, the area of

the parallelogram determined by $\mathbf{u} = \begin{bmatrix} 3 \\ 0 \end{bmatrix}$, $\mathbf{x} = \begin{bmatrix} x \\ 2 \end{bmatrix}$, $\mathbf{u} + \mathbf{x}$, and $\mathbf{0}$ is also 6.

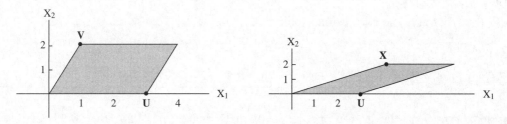

Also note that $\det\begin{bmatrix} \mathbf{u} & \mathbf{v} \end{bmatrix} = \det\begin{bmatrix} 3 & 1 \\ 0 & 2 \end{bmatrix} = 6$, and $\det\begin{bmatrix} \mathbf{u} & \mathbf{x} \end{bmatrix} = \det\begin{bmatrix} 3 & x \\ 0 & 2 \end{bmatrix} = 6$. The determinant of the

matrix whose columns are those vectors which define the sides of the parallelogram adjacent to $\mathbf{0}$ is equal
to the area of the parallelogram.

42. The area of the parallelogram determined by $\mathbf{u} = \begin{bmatrix} a \\ b \end{bmatrix}$, $\mathbf{v} = \begin{bmatrix} c \\ 0 \end{bmatrix}$, $\mathbf{u} + \mathbf{v}$, and $\mathbf{0}$ is cb, since the base of the

parallelogram has length c and the height of the parallelogram is b.

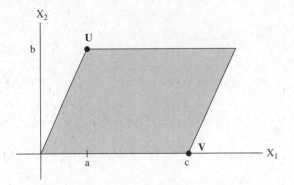

Also note that $\det \begin{bmatrix} \mathbf{u} & \mathbf{v} \end{bmatrix} = \det \begin{bmatrix} a & c \\ b & 0 \end{bmatrix} = -cb$, and $\det \begin{bmatrix} \mathbf{v} & \mathbf{u} \end{bmatrix} = \det \begin{bmatrix} c & a \\ 0 & b \end{bmatrix} = cb$. The determinant of the
matrix whose columns are those vectors which define the sides of the parallelogram adjacent to $\mathbf{0}$ either
is equal to the area of the parallelogram or is equal to the negative of the area of the parallelogram.

43. **[M]** Answers will vary. The conclusion should be that $\det (A + B) \neq \det A + \det B$.

44. **[M]** Answers will vary. The conclusion should be that $\det (AB) = (\det A)(\det B)$.

45. **[M]** Answers will vary. For 4×4 matrices, the conclusions should be that $\det A^T = \det A$, $\det(-A) = \det A$, $\det(2A) = 16\det A$, and $\det(10A) = 10^4 \det A$. For 5×5 matrices, the conclusions should be that $\det A^T = \det A$, $\det(-A) = -\det A$, $\det(2A) = 32\det A$, and $\det(10A) = 10^5 \det A$. For 6×6 matrices, the conclusions should be that $\det A^T = \det A$, $\det(-A) = \det A$, $\det(2A) = 64\det A$, and $\det(10A) = 10^6 \det A$.

46. **[M]** Answers will vary. The conclusion should be that $\det A^{-1} = 1/\det A$.

3.2   SOLUTIONS

Notes: This section presents the main properties of the determinant, including the effects of row operations on the determinant of a matrix. These properties are first studied by examples in Exercises 1–20. The properties are treated in a more theoretical manner in later exercises. An efficient method for computing the determinant using row reduction and selective cofactor expansion is presented in this section and used in Exercises 11–14. Theorems 4 and 6 are used extensively in Chapter 5. The linearity property of the determinant studied in the text is optional, but is used in more advanced courses. Exercises 15-26, 39, and 40 make good test questions because they involve few computations.

   1. Rows 1 and 2 are interchanged, so the determinant changes sign (Theorem 3b.).

   2. The constant 2 may be factored out of the Row 1 (Theorem 3c.).

   3. The row replacement operation does not change the determinant (Theorem 3a.).

   4. The row replacement operation does not change the determinant (Theorem 3a.).

5. $\begin{vmatrix} 1 & 5 & -6 \\ -1 & -4 & 4 \\ -2 & -7 & 9 \end{vmatrix} = \begin{vmatrix} 1 & 5 & -6 \\ 0 & 1 & -2 \\ 0 & 3 & -3 \end{vmatrix} = \begin{vmatrix} 1 & 5 & -6 \\ 0 & 1 & -2 \\ 0 & 0 & 3 \end{vmatrix} = 3$

6. $\begin{vmatrix} 1 & 5 & -3 \\ 3 & -3 & 3 \\ 2 & 13 & -7 \end{vmatrix} = \begin{vmatrix} 1 & 5 & -3 \\ 0 & -18 & 12 \\ 0 & 3 & -1 \end{vmatrix} = 6\begin{vmatrix} 1 & 5 & -3 \\ 0 & -3 & 2 \\ 0 & 3 & -1 \end{vmatrix} = 6\begin{vmatrix} 1 & 5 & -3 \\ 0 & -3 & 2 \\ 0 & 0 & 1 \end{vmatrix} = (6)(-3) = -18$

7. $\begin{vmatrix} 1 & 3 & 0 & 2 \\ -2 & -5 & 7 & 4 \\ 3 & 5 & 2 & 1 \\ 1 & -1 & 2 & -3 \end{vmatrix} = \begin{vmatrix} 1 & 3 & 0 & 2 \\ 0 & 1 & 7 & 8 \\ 0 & -4 & 2 & -5 \\ 0 & -4 & 2 & -5 \end{vmatrix} = \begin{vmatrix} 1 & 3 & 0 & 2 \\ 0 & 1 & 7 & 8 \\ 0 & 0 & 30 & 27 \\ 0 & 0 & 30 & 27 \end{vmatrix} = \begin{vmatrix} 1 & 3 & 0 & 2 \\ 0 & 1 & 7 & 8 \\ 0 & 0 & 30 & 27 \\ 0 & 0 & 0 & 0 \end{vmatrix} = 0$

8. $\begin{vmatrix} 1 & 3 & 3 & -4 \\ 0 & 1 & 2 & -5 \\ 2 & 5 & 4 & -3 \\ -3 & -7 & -5 & 2 \end{vmatrix} = \begin{vmatrix} 1 & 3 & 3 & -4 \\ 0 & 1 & 2 & -5 \\ 0 & -1 & -2 & 5 \\ 0 & 2 & 4 & -10 \end{vmatrix} = \begin{vmatrix} 1 & 3 & 3 & -4 \\ 0 & 1 & 2 & -5 \\ 0 & 0 & 0 & 0 \\ 0 & 0 & 0 & 0 \end{vmatrix} = 0$

9. $\begin{vmatrix} 1 & -1 & -3 & 0 \\ 0 & 1 & 5 & 4 \\ -1 & 2 & 8 & 5 \\ 3 & -1 & -2 & 3 \end{vmatrix} = \begin{vmatrix} 1 & -1 & -3 & 0 \\ 0 & 1 & 5 & 4 \\ 0 & 1 & 5 & 5 \\ 0 & 2 & 7 & 3 \end{vmatrix} = \begin{vmatrix} 1 & -1 & -3 & 0 \\ 0 & 1 & 5 & 4 \\ 0 & 0 & 0 & 1 \\ 0 & 0 & -3 & -5 \end{vmatrix} = -\begin{vmatrix} 1 & -1 & -3 & 0 \\ 0 & 1 & 5 & 4 \\ 0 & 0 & -3 & -5 \\ 0 & 0 & 0 & 1 \end{vmatrix} = -(-3) = 3$

10. $\begin{vmatrix} 1 & 3 & -1 & 0 & -2 \\ 0 & 2 & -4 & -1 & -6 \\ -2 & -6 & 2 & 3 & 9 \\ 3 & 7 & -3 & 8 & -7 \\ 3 & 5 & 5 & 2 & 7 \end{vmatrix} = \begin{vmatrix} 1 & 3 & -1 & 0 & -2 \\ 0 & 2 & -4 & -1 & -6 \\ 0 & 0 & 0 & 3 & 5 \\ 0 & -2 & 0 & 8 & -1 \\ 0 & -4 & 8 & 2 & 13 \end{vmatrix}$

$= \begin{vmatrix} 1 & 3 & -1 & 0 & -2 \\ 0 & 2 & -4 & -1 & -6 \\ 0 & 0 & 0 & 3 & 5 \\ 0 & 0 & -4 & 7 & -7 \\ 0 & 0 & 0 & 0 & 1 \end{vmatrix} = -\begin{vmatrix} 1 & 3 & -1 & 0 & -2 \\ 0 & 2 & -4 & -1 & -6 \\ 0 & 0 & -4 & 7 & -7 \\ 0 & 0 & 0 & 3 & 5 \\ 0 & 0 & 0 & 0 & 1 \end{vmatrix} = -(-24) = 24$

11. First use a row replacement to create zeros in the second column, and then expand down the second column:

$$\begin{vmatrix} 2 & 5 & -3 & -1 \\ 3 & 0 & 1 & -3 \\ -6 & 0 & -4 & 9 \\ 4 & 10 & -4 & -1 \end{vmatrix} = \begin{vmatrix} 2 & 5 & -3 & -1 \\ 3 & 0 & 1 & -3 \\ -6 & 0 & -4 & 9 \\ 0 & 0 & 2 & 1 \end{vmatrix} = -5\begin{vmatrix} 3 & 1 & -3 \\ -6 & -4 & 9 \\ 0 & 2 & 1 \end{vmatrix}$$

Now use a row replacement to create zeros in the first column, and then expand down the first column:

$$-5\begin{vmatrix} 3 & 1 & -3 \\ -6 & -4 & 9 \\ 0 & 2 & 1 \end{vmatrix} = -5\begin{vmatrix} 3 & 1 & -3 \\ 0 & -2 & 3 \\ 0 & 2 & 1 \end{vmatrix} = (-5)(3)\begin{vmatrix} -2 & 3 \\ 2 & 1 \end{vmatrix} = (-5)(3)(-8) = 120$$

12. First use a row replacement to create zeros in the fourth column, and then expand down the fourth column:

$$\begin{vmatrix} -1 & 2 & 3 & 0 \\ 3 & 4 & 3 & 0 \\ 5 & 4 & 6 & 6 \\ 4 & 2 & 4 & 3 \end{vmatrix} = \begin{vmatrix} -1 & 2 & 3 & 0 \\ 3 & 4 & 3 & 0 \\ -3 & 0 & -2 & 0 \\ 4 & 2 & 4 & 3 \end{vmatrix} = 3\begin{vmatrix} -1 & 2 & 3 \\ 3 & 4 & 3 \\ -3 & 0 & -2 \end{vmatrix}$$

Now use a row replacement to create zeros in the first column, and then expand down the first column:

$$3\begin{vmatrix} -1 & 2 & 3 \\ 3 & 4 & 3 \\ -3 & 0 & -2 \end{vmatrix} = 3\begin{vmatrix} -1 & 2 & 3 \\ 0 & 10 & 12 \\ 0 & -6 & -11 \end{vmatrix} = 3(-1)\begin{vmatrix} 10 & 12 \\ -6 & -11 \end{vmatrix} = 3(-1)(-38) = 114$$

13. First use a row replacement to create zeros in the fourth column, and then expand down the fourth column:

$$\begin{vmatrix} 2 & 5 & 4 & 1 \\ 4 & 7 & 6 & 2 \\ 6 & -2 & -4 & 0 \\ -6 & 7 & 7 & 0 \end{vmatrix} = \begin{vmatrix} 2 & 5 & 4 & 1 \\ 0 & -3 & -2 & 0 \\ 6 & -2 & -4 & 0 \\ -6 & 7 & 7 & 0 \end{vmatrix} = -1\begin{vmatrix} 0 & -3 & -2 \\ 6 & -2 & -4 \\ -6 & 7 & 7 \end{vmatrix}$$

Now use a row replacement to create zeros in the first column, and then expand down the first column:

$$-1\begin{vmatrix} 0 & -3 & -2 \\ 6 & -2 & -4 \\ -6 & 7 & 7 \end{vmatrix} = -1\begin{vmatrix} 0 & -3 & -2 \\ 6 & -2 & -4 \\ 0 & 5 & 3 \end{vmatrix} = (-1)(-6)\begin{vmatrix} -3 & -2 \\ 5 & 3 \end{vmatrix} = (-1)(-6)(1) = 6$$

14. First use a row replacement to create zeros in the third column, and then expand down the third column:

$$\begin{vmatrix} -3 & -2 & 1 & -4 \\ 1 & 3 & 0 & -3 \\ -3 & 4 & -2 & 8 \\ 3 & -4 & 0 & 4 \end{vmatrix} = \begin{vmatrix} -3 & -2 & 1 & -4 \\ 1 & 3 & 0 & -3 \\ -9 & 0 & 0 & 0 \\ 3 & -4 & 0 & 4 \end{vmatrix} = 1\begin{vmatrix} 1 & 3 & -3 \\ -9 & 0 & 0 \\ 3 & -4 & 4 \end{vmatrix}$$

Now expand along the second row:

$$1\begin{vmatrix} 1 & 3 & -3 \\ -9 & 0 & 0 \\ 3 & -4 & 4 \end{vmatrix} = 1(-(-9))\begin{vmatrix} 3 & -3 \\ -4 & 4 \end{vmatrix} = (1)(9)(0) = 0$$

15. $\begin{vmatrix} a & b & c \\ d & e & f \\ 5g & 5h & 5i \end{vmatrix} = 5 \begin{vmatrix} a & b & c \\ d & e & f \\ g & h & i \end{vmatrix} = 5(7) = 35$

16. $\begin{vmatrix} a & b & c \\ 3d & 3e & 3f \\ g & h & i \end{vmatrix} = 3 \begin{vmatrix} a & b & c \\ d & e & f \\ g & h & i \end{vmatrix} = 3(7) = 21$

17. $\begin{vmatrix} a & b & c \\ g & h & i \\ d & e & f \end{vmatrix} = - \begin{vmatrix} a & b & c \\ d & e & f \\ g & h & i \end{vmatrix} = -7$

18. $\begin{vmatrix} g & h & i \\ a & b & c \\ d & e & f \end{vmatrix} = - \begin{vmatrix} a & b & c \\ g & h & i \\ d & e & f \end{vmatrix} = - \left(- \begin{vmatrix} a & b & c \\ d & e & f \\ g & h & i \end{vmatrix} \right) = -(-7) = 7$

19. $\begin{vmatrix} a & b & c \\ 2d+a & 2e+b & 2f+c \\ g & h & i \end{vmatrix} = \begin{vmatrix} a & b & c \\ 2d & 2e & 2f \\ g & h & i \end{vmatrix} = 2 \begin{vmatrix} a & b & c \\ d & e & f \\ g & h & i \end{vmatrix} = 2(7) = 14$

20. $\begin{vmatrix} a+d & b+e & c+f \\ d & e & f \\ g & h & i \end{vmatrix} = \begin{vmatrix} a & b & c \\ d & e & f \\ g & h & i \end{vmatrix} = 7$

21. Since $\begin{vmatrix} 2 & 3 & 0 \\ 1 & 3 & 4 \\ 1 & 2 & 1 \end{vmatrix} = -1 \neq 0$, the matrix is invertible.

22. Since $\begin{vmatrix} 5 & 0 & -1 \\ 1 & -3 & -2 \\ 0 & 5 & 3 \end{vmatrix} = 0$, the matrix is not invertible.

23. Since $\begin{vmatrix} 2 & 0 & 0 & 8 \\ 1 & -7 & -5 & 0 \\ 3 & 8 & 6 & 0 \\ 0 & 7 & 5 & 4 \end{vmatrix} = 0$, the matrix is not invertible.

24. Since $\begin{vmatrix} 4 & -7 & -3 \\ 6 & 0 & -5 \\ -7 & 2 & 6 \end{vmatrix} = 11 \neq 0$, the columns of the matrix form a linearly independent set.

25. Since $\begin{vmatrix} 7 & -8 & 7 \\ -4 & 5 & 0 \\ -6 & 7 & -5 \end{vmatrix} = -1 \neq 0$, the columns of the matrix form a linearly independent set.

26. Since $\begin{vmatrix} 3 & 2 & -2 & 0 \\ 5 & -6 & -1 & 0 \\ -6 & 0 & 3 & 0 \\ 4 & 7 & 0 & -3 \end{vmatrix} = 0$, the columns of the matrix form a linearly dependent set.

27. **a.** True. See Theorem 3.
    b. True. See the paragraph following Example 2.
    c. True. See the paragraph following Theorem 4.
    d. False. See the warning following Example 5.

28. **a.** True. See Theorem 3.
    b. False. See the paragraphs following Example 2.
    c. False. See Example 3.
    d. False. See Theorem 5.

29. By Theorem 6, $\det B^5 = (\det B)^5 = (-2)^5 = -32$.

30. Suppose the two rows of a square matrix A are equal. By swapping these two rows, the matrix A is not changed so its determinant should not change. But since swapping rows changes the sign of the determinant, $\det A = - \det A$. This is only possible if $\det A = 0$. The same may be proven true for columns by applying the above result to A^T and using Theorem 5.

31. By Theorem 6, $(\det A)(\det A^{-1}) = \det I = 1$, so $\det A^{-1} = 1/\det A$.

32. By factoring an r out of each of the n rows, $\det(rA) = r^n \det A$.

33. By Theorem 6, $\det AB = (\det A)(\det B) = (\det B)(\det A) = \det BA$.

34. By Theorem 6 and Exercise 31,
$$\det(PAP^{-1}) = (\det P)(\det A)(\det P^{-1}) = (\det P)(\det P^{-1})(\det A)$$
$$= (\det P)\left(\frac{1}{\det P}\right)(\det A) = 1 \det A$$
$$= \det A$$

35. By Theorem 6 and Theorem 5, $\det U^T U = (\det U^T)(\det U) = (\det U)^2$. Since $U^T U = I$,
    $\det U^T U = \det I = 1$, so $(\det U)^2 = 1$. Thus $\det U = \pm 1$.

36. By Theorem 6 $\det A^4 = (\det A)^4$. Since $\det A^4 = 0$, then $(\det A)^4 = 0$. Thus $\det A = 0$, and A is not invertible by Theorem 4.

37. By Theorem 2, $\det A = 3$ and $\det B = 8$, while $AB = \begin{bmatrix} 6 & 0 \\ 17 & 4 \end{bmatrix}$. Thus
    $\det AB = 24 = 3 \times 8 = (\det A)(\det B)$.

38. Compute $\det A = 0$ and $\det B = -2$. Also, $AB = \begin{bmatrix} 6 & 0 \\ -2 & 0 \end{bmatrix}$. Thus $\det AB = 0 =$
    $0 \times -2 = (\det A)(\det B)$.

39. a. By Theorem 6, $\det AB = (\det A)(\det B) = 4 \times -3 = -12$.

   b. By Exercise 32, $\det 5A = 5^3 \det A = 125 \times 4 = 500$.

   c. By Theorem 5, $\det B^T = \det B = -3$.

   d. By Exercise 31, $\det A^{-1} = 1/\det A = 1/4$.

   e. By Theorem 6, $\det A^3 = (\det A)^3 = 4^3 = 64$.

40. a. By Theorem 6, $\det AB = (\det A)(\det B) = -1 \times 2 = -2$.

   b. By Theorem 6, $\det B^5 = (\det B)^5 = 2^5 = 32$.

   c. By Exercise 32, $\det 2A = 2^4 \det A = 16 \times -1 = -16$.

   d. By Theorems 5 and 6, $\det A^T A = (\det A^T)(\det A) = (\det A)(\det A) = -1 \times -1 = 1$.

   e. By Theorem 6 and Exercise 31,
   $$\det B^{-1}AB = (\det B^{-1})(\det A)(\det B) = (1/\det B)(\det A)(\det B) = \det A = -1.$$

41. $\det A = (a+e)d - c(b+f) = ad + ed - bc - cf = (ad - bc) + (ed - cf) = \det B + \det C$.

42. $\det(A+B) = \begin{vmatrix} 1+a & b \\ c & 1+d \end{vmatrix} = (1+a)(1+d) - cb = 1 + a + d + ad - cb = \det A + a + d + \det B$, so

   $\det(A+B) = \det A + \det B$ if and only if $a + d = 0$.

43. Compute $\det A$ by using a cofactor expansion down the third column:

   $$\det A = (u_1 + v_1)\det A_{13} - (u_2 + v_2)\det A_{23} + (u_3 + v_3)\det A_{33}$$
   $$= u_1 \det A_{13} - u_2 \det A_{23} + u_3 \det A_{33} + v_1 \det A_{13} - v_2 \det A_{23} + v_3 \det A_{33}$$
   $$= \det B + \det C$$

44. By Theorem 5, $\det AE = \det(AE)^T$. Since $(AE)^T = E^T A^T$, $\det AE = \det(E^T A^T)$. Now E^T is itself an elementary matrix, so by the proof of Theorem 3, $\det(E^T A^T) = (\det E^T)(\det A^T)$. Thus it is true that $\det AE = (\det E^T)(\det A^T)$, and by applying Theorem 5, $\det AE = (\det E)(\det A)$.

45. [M] Answers will vary, but will show that $\det A^T A$ always equals 0 while $\det AA^T$ should seldom be zero. To see why $A^T A$ should not be invertible (and thus $\det A^T A = 0$), let A be a matrix with more columns than rows. Then the columns of A must be linearly dependent, so the equation $A\mathbf{x} = \mathbf{0}$ must have a non-trivial solution $\mathbf{x}$. Thus $(A^T A)\mathbf{x} = A^T(A\mathbf{x}) = A^T \mathbf{0} = \mathbf{0}$, and the equation $(A^T A)\mathbf{x} = \mathbf{0}$ has a non-trivial solution. Since $A^T A$ is a square matrix, the Invertible Matrix Theorem now says that $A^T A$ is not invertible. Notice that the same argument will not work in general for AA^T, since A^T has more rows than columns, so its columns are not automatically linearly dependent.

46. [M] Compute $\det A = 1$ and $\text{cond } A \approx 23683$. Note that this is the ℓ_2 condition number, which is used in Section 2.3. Since $\det A \neq 0$, it is invertible and

$$A^{-1} = \begin{bmatrix} -19 & -14 & 0 & 7 \\ -549 & -401 & -2 & 196 \\ 267 & 195 & 1 & -95 \\ -278 & -203 & -1 & 99 \end{bmatrix}$$

The determinant is very sensitive to scaling, as $\det 10A = 10^4 \det A = 10,000$ and $\det 0.1A = (0.1)^4 \det A = 0.0001$. The condition number is not changed at all by scaling: $\text{cond}(10A) = \text{cond}(0.1A) = \text{cond}\,A \approx 23683$.

When $A = I_4$, $\det A = 1$ and $\text{cond}\,A = 1$. As before the determinant is sensitive to scaling: $\det 10A = 10^4 \det A = 10,000$ and $\det 0.1A = (0.1)^4 \det A = 0.0001$. Yet the condition number is not changed by scaling: $\text{cond}(10A) = \text{cond}(0.1A) = \text{cond}\,A = 1$.

3.3   SOLUTIONS

Notes: This section features several independent topics from which to choose. The geometric interpretation of the determinant (Theorem 10) provides the key to changes of variables in multiple integrals. Students of economics and engineering are likely to need Cramer's Rule in later courses. Exercises 1–10 concern Cramer's Rule, exercises 11–18 deal with the adjugate, and exercises 19–32 cover the geometric interpretation of the determinant. In particular, Exercise 25 examines students' understanding of linear independence and requires a careful explanation, which is discussed in the *Study Guide*. The *Study Guide* also contains a heuristic proof of Theorem 9 for 2×2 matrices.

1. The system is equivalent to $A\mathbf{x} = \mathbf{b}$, where $A = \begin{bmatrix} 5 & 7 \\ 2 & 4 \end{bmatrix}$ and $\mathbf{b} = \begin{bmatrix} 3 \\ 1 \end{bmatrix}$. Compute

$$A_1(\mathbf{b}) = \begin{bmatrix} 3 & 7 \\ 1 & 4 \end{bmatrix},\ A_2(\mathbf{b}) = \begin{bmatrix} 5 & 3 \\ 2 & 1 \end{bmatrix},\ \det A = 6,\ \det A_1(\mathbf{b}) = 5,\ \det A_2(\mathbf{b}) = -1,$$

$$x_1 = \frac{\det A_1(\mathbf{b})}{\det A} = \frac{5}{6},\ x_2 = \frac{\det A_2(\mathbf{b})}{\det A} = -\frac{1}{6}.$$

2. The system is equivalent to $A\mathbf{x} = \mathbf{b}$, where $A = \begin{bmatrix} 4 & 1 \\ 5 & 2 \end{bmatrix}$ and $\mathbf{b} = \begin{bmatrix} 6 \\ 7 \end{bmatrix}$. Compute

$$A_1(\mathbf{b}) = \begin{bmatrix} 6 & 1 \\ 7 & 2 \end{bmatrix},\ A_2(\mathbf{b}) = \begin{bmatrix} 4 & 6 \\ 5 & 7 \end{bmatrix},\ \det A = 3,\ \det A_1(\mathbf{b}) = 5,\ \det A_2(\mathbf{b}) = -2,$$

$$x_1 = \frac{\det A_1(\mathbf{b})}{\det A} = \frac{5}{3},\ x_2 = \frac{\det A_2(\mathbf{b})}{\det A} = -\frac{2}{3}.$$

3. The system is equivalent to $A\mathbf{x} = \mathbf{b}$, where $A = \begin{bmatrix} 3 & -2 \\ -5 & 6 \end{bmatrix}$ and $\mathbf{b} = \begin{bmatrix} 7 \\ -5 \end{bmatrix}$. Compute

$$A_1(\mathbf{b}) = \begin{bmatrix} 7 & -2 \\ -5 & 6 \end{bmatrix},\ A_2(\mathbf{b}) = \begin{bmatrix} 3 & 7 \\ -5 & -5 \end{bmatrix},\ \det A = 8,\ \det A_1(\mathbf{b}) = 32,\ \det A_2(\mathbf{b}) = 20,$$

$$x_1 = \frac{\det A_1(\mathbf{b})}{\det A} = \frac{32}{8} = 4,\ x_2 = \frac{\det A_2(\mathbf{b})}{\det A} = \frac{20}{8} = \frac{5}{2}.$$

4. The system is equivalent to $A\mathbf{x} = \mathbf{b}$, where $A = \begin{bmatrix} -5 & 3 \\ 3 & -1 \end{bmatrix}$ and $\mathbf{b} = \begin{bmatrix} 9 \\ -5 \end{bmatrix}$. Compute

$$A_1(\mathbf{b}) = \begin{bmatrix} 9 & 3 \\ -5 & -1 \end{bmatrix}, A_2(\mathbf{b}) = \begin{bmatrix} -5 & 9 \\ 3 & -5 \end{bmatrix}, \det A = -4, \det A_1(\mathbf{b}) = 6, \det A_2(\mathbf{b}) = -2,$$

$$x_1 = \frac{\det A_1(\mathbf{b})}{\det A} = \frac{6}{-4} = -\frac{3}{2}, x_2 = \frac{\det A_2(\mathbf{b})}{\det A} = \frac{-2}{-4} = \frac{1}{2}.$$

5. The system is equivalent to $A\mathbf{x} = \mathbf{b}$, where $A = \begin{bmatrix} 2 & 1 & 0 \\ -3 & 0 & 1 \\ 0 & 1 & 2 \end{bmatrix}$ and $\mathbf{b} = \begin{bmatrix} 7 \\ -8 \\ -3 \end{bmatrix}$. Compute

$$A_1(\mathbf{b}) = \begin{bmatrix} 7 & 1 & 0 \\ -8 & 0 & 1 \\ -3 & 1 & 2 \end{bmatrix}, A_2(\mathbf{b}) = \begin{bmatrix} 2 & 7 & 0 \\ -3 & -8 & 1 \\ 0 & -3 & 2 \end{bmatrix}, A_3(\mathbf{b}) = \begin{bmatrix} 2 & 1 & 7 \\ -3 & 0 & -8 \\ 0 & 1 & -3 \end{bmatrix},$$

$$\det A = 4, \det A_1(\mathbf{b}) = 6, \det A_2(\mathbf{b}) = 16, \det A_3(\mathbf{b}) = -14,$$

$$x_1 = \frac{\det A_1(\mathbf{b})}{\det A} = \frac{6}{4} = \frac{3}{2}, x_2 = \frac{\det A_2(\mathbf{b})}{\det A} = \frac{16}{4} = 4, x_3 = \frac{\det A_3(\mathbf{b})}{\det A} = \frac{-14}{4} = -\frac{7}{2}.$$

6. The system is equivalent to $A\mathbf{x} = \mathbf{b}$, where $A = \begin{bmatrix} 2 & 1 & 1 \\ -1 & 0 & 2 \\ 3 & 1 & 3 \end{bmatrix}$ and $\mathbf{b} = \begin{bmatrix} 4 \\ 2 \\ -2 \end{bmatrix}$. Compute

$$A_1(\mathbf{b}) = \begin{bmatrix} 4 & 1 & 1 \\ 2 & 0 & 2 \\ -2 & 1 & 3 \end{bmatrix}, A_2(\mathbf{b}) = \begin{bmatrix} 2 & 4 & 1 \\ -1 & 2 & 2 \\ 3 & -2 & 3 \end{bmatrix}, A_3(\mathbf{b}) = \begin{bmatrix} 2 & 1 & 4 \\ -1 & 0 & 2 \\ 3 & 1 & -2 \end{bmatrix},$$

$$\det A = 4, \det A_1(\mathbf{b}) = -16, \det A_2(\mathbf{b}) = 52, \det A_3(\mathbf{b}) = -4,$$

$$x_1 = \frac{\det A_1(\mathbf{b})}{\det A} = \frac{-16}{4} = -4, x_2 = \frac{\det A_2(\mathbf{b})}{\det A} = \frac{52}{4} = 13, x_3 = \frac{\det A_3(\mathbf{b})}{\det A} = \frac{-4}{4} = -1.$$

7. The system is equivalent to $A\mathbf{x} = \mathbf{b}$, where $A = \begin{bmatrix} 6s & 4 \\ 9 & 2s \end{bmatrix}$ and $\mathbf{b} = \begin{bmatrix} 5 \\ -2 \end{bmatrix}$. Compute

$$A_1(\mathbf{b}) = \begin{bmatrix} 5 & 4 \\ -2 & 2s \end{bmatrix}, A_2(\mathbf{b}) = \begin{bmatrix} 6s & 5 \\ 9 & -2 \end{bmatrix}, \det A_1(\mathbf{b}) = 10s + 8, \det A_2(\mathbf{b}) = -12s - 45.$$

Since $\det A = 12s^2 - 36 = 12(s^2 - 3) \neq 0$ for $s \neq \pm\sqrt{3}$, the system will have a unique solution when $s \neq \pm\sqrt{3}$. For such a system, the solution will be

$$x_1 = \frac{\det A_1(\mathbf{b})}{\det A} = \frac{10s + 8}{12(s^2 - 3)} = \frac{5s + 4}{6(s^2 - 3)}, x_2 = \frac{\det A_2(\mathbf{b})}{\det A} = \frac{-12s - 45}{12(s^2 - 3)} = \frac{-4s - 15}{4(s^2 - 3)}.$$

8. The system is equivalent to $A\mathbf{x} = \mathbf{b}$, where $A = \begin{bmatrix} 3s & -5 \\ 9 & 5s \end{bmatrix}$ and $\mathbf{b} = \begin{bmatrix} 3 \\ 2 \end{bmatrix}$. Compute

$$A_1(\mathbf{b}) = \begin{bmatrix} 3 & -5 \\ 2 & 5s \end{bmatrix}, A_2(\mathbf{b}) = \begin{bmatrix} 3s & 3 \\ 9 & 2 \end{bmatrix}, \det A_1(\mathbf{b}) = 15s + 10, \det A_2(\mathbf{b}) = 6s - 27.$$

Since $\det A = 15s^2 + 45 = 15(s^2 + 3) \neq 0$ for all values of s, the system will have a unique solution for all values of s. For such a system, the solution will be

$$x_1 = \frac{\det A_1(\mathbf{b})}{\det A} = \frac{15s + 10}{15(s^2 + 3)} = \frac{3s + 2}{3(s^2 + 3)}, \ x_2 = \frac{\det A_2(\mathbf{b})}{\det A} = \frac{6s - 27}{15(s^2 + 3)} = \frac{2s - 9}{5(s^2 + 3)}.$$

9. The system is equivalent to $A\mathbf{x} = \mathbf{b}$, where $A = \begin{bmatrix} s & -2s \\ 3 & 6s \end{bmatrix}$ and $\mathbf{b} = \begin{bmatrix} -1 \\ 4 \end{bmatrix}$. Compute

$$A_1(\mathbf{b}) = \begin{bmatrix} -1 & -2s \\ 4 & 6s \end{bmatrix}, \ A_2(\mathbf{b}) = \begin{bmatrix} s & -1 \\ 3 & 4 \end{bmatrix}, \ \det A_1(\mathbf{b}) = 2s, \ \det A_2(\mathbf{b}) = 4s + 3.$$

Since $\det A = 6s^2 + 6s = 6s(s + 1) = 0$ for $s = 0, -1$, the system will have a unique solution when $s \neq 0, -1$. For such a system, the solution will be

$$x_1 = \frac{\det A_1(\mathbf{b})}{\det A} = \frac{2s}{6s(s + 1)} = \frac{1}{3(s + 1)}, \ x_2 = \frac{\det A_2(\mathbf{b})}{\det A} = \frac{4s + 3}{6s(s + 1)}.$$

10. The system is equivalent to $A\mathbf{x} = \mathbf{b}$, where $A = \begin{bmatrix} 2s & 1 \\ 3s & 6s \end{bmatrix}$ and $\mathbf{b} = \begin{bmatrix} 1 \\ 2 \end{bmatrix}$. Compute

$$A_1(\mathbf{b}) = \begin{bmatrix} 1 & 1 \\ 2 & 6s \end{bmatrix}, \ A_2(\mathbf{b}) = \begin{bmatrix} 2s & 1 \\ 3s & 2 \end{bmatrix}, \ \det A_1(\mathbf{b}) = 6s - 2, \ \det A_2(\mathbf{b}) = s.$$

Since $\det A = 12s^2 - 3s = 3s(4s - 1) = 0$ for $s = 0, 1/4$, the system will have a unique solution when $s \neq 0, 1/4$. For such a system, the solution will be

$$x_1 = \frac{\det A_1(\mathbf{b})}{\det A} = \frac{6s - 2}{3s(4s - 1)}, \ x_2 = \frac{\det A_2(\mathbf{b})}{\det A} = \frac{s}{3s(4s - 1)} = \frac{1}{3(4s - 1)}.$$

11. Since $\det A = 3$ and the cofactors of the given matrix are

$$C_{11} = \begin{vmatrix} 0 & 0 \\ 1 & 1 \end{vmatrix} = 0, \qquad C_{12} = -\begin{vmatrix} 3 & 0 \\ -1 & 1 \end{vmatrix} = -3, \quad C_{13} = \begin{vmatrix} 3 & 0 \\ -1 & 1 \end{vmatrix} = 3,$$

$$C_{21} = -\begin{vmatrix} -2 & -1 \\ 1 & 1 \end{vmatrix} = 1, \qquad C_{22} = \begin{vmatrix} 0 & -1 \\ -1 & 1 \end{vmatrix} = -1, \quad C_{23} = -\begin{vmatrix} 0 & -2 \\ -1 & 1 \end{vmatrix} = 2,$$

$$C_{31} = \begin{vmatrix} -2 & -1 \\ 0 & 0 \end{vmatrix} = 0, \qquad C_{32} = -\begin{vmatrix} 0 & -1 \\ 3 & 0 \end{vmatrix} = -3, \quad C_{33} = \begin{vmatrix} 0 & -2 \\ 3 & 0 \end{vmatrix} = 6,$$

$$\text{adj} A = \begin{bmatrix} 0 & 1 & 0 \\ -3 & -1 & -3 \\ 3 & 2 & 6 \end{bmatrix} \text{ and } A^{-1} = \frac{1}{\det A} \text{adj} A = \begin{bmatrix} 0 & 1/3 & 0 \\ -1 & -1/3 & -1 \\ 1 & 2/3 & 2 \end{bmatrix}.$$

12. Since $\det A = 5$ and the cofactors of the given matrix are

$$C_{11} = \begin{vmatrix} -2 & 1 \\ 1 & 0 \end{vmatrix} = -1, \qquad C_{12} = -\begin{vmatrix} 2 & 1 \\ 0 & 0 \end{vmatrix} = 0, \quad C_{13} = \begin{vmatrix} 2 & -2 \\ 0 & 1 \end{vmatrix} = 2,$$

$$C_{21} = -\begin{vmatrix} 1 & 3 \\ 1 & 0 \end{vmatrix} = 3, \qquad C_{22} = \begin{vmatrix} 1 & 3 \\ 0 & 0 \end{vmatrix} = 0, \quad C_{23} = -\begin{vmatrix} 1 & 1 \\ 0 & 1 \end{vmatrix} = -1,$$

$$C_{31} = \begin{vmatrix} 1 & 3 \\ -2 & 1 \end{vmatrix} = 7, \qquad C_{32} = -\begin{vmatrix} 1 & 3 \\ 2 & 1 \end{vmatrix} = 5, \quad C_{33} = \begin{vmatrix} 1 & 1 \\ 2 & -2 \end{vmatrix} = -4,$$

$$\text{adj}\,A = \begin{bmatrix} -1 & 3 & 7 \\ 0 & 0 & 5 \\ 2 & -1 & -4 \end{bmatrix} \text{ and } A^{-1} = \frac{1}{\det A}\,\text{adj}\,A = \begin{bmatrix} -1/5 & 3/5 & 7/5 \\ 0 & 0 & 1 \\ 2/5 & -1/5 & -4/5 \end{bmatrix}.$$

13. Since $\det A = 6$ and the cofactors of the given matrix are

$$C_{11} = \begin{vmatrix} 0 & 1 \\ 1 & 1 \end{vmatrix} = -1, \qquad C_{12} = -\begin{vmatrix} 1 & 1 \\ 2 & 1 \end{vmatrix} = 1, \qquad C_{13} = \begin{vmatrix} 1 & 0 \\ 2 & 1 \end{vmatrix} = 1,$$

$$C_{21} = -\begin{vmatrix} 5 & 4 \\ 1 & 1 \end{vmatrix} = -1, \qquad C_{22} = \begin{vmatrix} 3 & 4 \\ 2 & 1 \end{vmatrix} = -5, \qquad C_{23} = -\begin{vmatrix} 3 & 5 \\ 2 & 1 \end{vmatrix} = 7,$$

$$C_{31} = \begin{vmatrix} 5 & 4 \\ 0 & 1 \end{vmatrix} = 5, \qquad C_{32} = -\begin{vmatrix} 3 & 4 \\ 1 & 1 \end{vmatrix} = 1, \qquad C_{33} = \begin{vmatrix} 3 & 5 \\ 1 & 0 \end{vmatrix} = -5,$$

$$\text{adj}\,A = \begin{bmatrix} -1 & -1 & 5 \\ 1 & -5 & 1 \\ 1 & 7 & -5 \end{bmatrix} \text{ and } A^{-1} = \frac{1}{\det A}\,\text{adj}\,A = \begin{bmatrix} -1/6 & -1/6 & 5/6 \\ 1/6 & -5/6 & 1/6 \\ 1/6 & 7/6 & -5/6 \end{bmatrix}.$$

14. Since $\det A = -1$ and the cofactors of the given matrix are

$$C_{11} = \begin{vmatrix} 2 & 1 \\ 3 & 4 \end{vmatrix} = 5, \qquad C_{12} = -\begin{vmatrix} 0 & 1 \\ 2 & 4 \end{vmatrix} = 2, \qquad C_{13} = \begin{vmatrix} 0 & 2 \\ 2 & 3 \end{vmatrix} = -4,$$

$$C_{21} = -\begin{vmatrix} 6 & 7 \\ 3 & 3 \end{vmatrix} = -3, \qquad C_{22} = \begin{vmatrix} 3 & 7 \\ 2 & 4 \end{vmatrix} = -2, \qquad C_{23} = -\begin{vmatrix} 3 & 6 \\ 2 & 3 \end{vmatrix} = 3,$$

$$C_{31} = \begin{vmatrix} 6 & 7 \\ 2 & 1 \end{vmatrix} = -8, \qquad C_{32} = -\begin{vmatrix} 3 & 7 \\ 0 & 1 \end{vmatrix} = -3, \qquad C_{33} = \begin{vmatrix} 3 & 6 \\ 0 & 2 \end{vmatrix} = 6,$$

$$\text{adj}\,A = \begin{bmatrix} 5 & -3 & -8 \\ 2 & -2 & -3 \\ -4 & 3 & 6 \end{bmatrix} \text{ and } A^{-1} = \frac{1}{\det A}\,\text{adj}\,A = \begin{bmatrix} -5 & 3 & 8 \\ -2 & 2 & 3 \\ 4 & -3 & -6 \end{bmatrix}.$$

15. Since $\det A = 6$ and the cofactors of the given matrix are

$$C_{11} = \begin{vmatrix} 1 & 0 \\ 3 & 2 \end{vmatrix} = 2, \qquad C_{12} = -\begin{vmatrix} -1 & 0 \\ -2 & 2 \end{vmatrix} = 2, \qquad C_{13} = \begin{vmatrix} -1 & 1 \\ -2 & 3 \end{vmatrix} = -1,$$

$$C_{21} = -\begin{vmatrix} 0 & 0 \\ 3 & 2 \end{vmatrix} = 0, \qquad C_{22} = \begin{vmatrix} 3 & 0 \\ -2 & 2 \end{vmatrix} = 6, \qquad C_{23} = -\begin{vmatrix} 3 & 0 \\ -2 & 3 \end{vmatrix} = -9,$$

$$C_{31} = \begin{vmatrix} 0 & 0 \\ 1 & 0 \end{vmatrix} = 0, \qquad C_{31} = \begin{vmatrix} 0 & 0 \\ 1 & 0 \end{vmatrix} = 0, \qquad C_{33} = \begin{vmatrix} 3 & 0 \\ -1 & 1 \end{vmatrix} = 3,$$

$$\text{adj}\,A = \begin{bmatrix} 2 & 0 & 0 \\ 2 & 6 & 0 \\ -1 & -9 & 3 \end{bmatrix} \text{ and } A^{-1} = \frac{1}{\det A}\,\text{adj}\,A = \begin{bmatrix} 1/3 & 0 & 0 \\ 1/3 & 1 & 0 \\ -1/6 & -3/2 & 1/2 \end{bmatrix}.$$

16. Since det $A = -9$ and the cofactors of the given matrix are

$$C_{11} = \begin{vmatrix} -3 & 1 \\ 0 & 3 \end{vmatrix} = -9, \qquad C_{12} = -\begin{vmatrix} 0 & 1 \\ 0 & 3 \end{vmatrix} = 0, \qquad C_{13} = \begin{vmatrix} 0 & -3 \\ 0 & 0 \end{vmatrix} = 0,$$

$$C_{21} = -\begin{vmatrix} 2 & 4 \\ 0 & 3 \end{vmatrix} = -6, \qquad C_{22} = \begin{vmatrix} 1 & 4 \\ 0 & 3 \end{vmatrix} = 3, \qquad C_{23} = -\begin{vmatrix} 1 & 2 \\ 0 & 0 \end{vmatrix} = 0,$$

$$C_{31} = \begin{vmatrix} 2 & 4 \\ -3 & 1 \end{vmatrix} = 14, \qquad C_{32} = -\begin{vmatrix} 1 & 4 \\ 0 & 1 \end{vmatrix} = -1, \qquad C_{33} = \begin{vmatrix} 1 & 2 \\ 0 & -3 \end{vmatrix} = -3,$$

$$\mathrm{adj}\,A = \begin{bmatrix} -9 & -6 & 14 \\ 0 & 3 & -1 \\ 0 & 0 & -3 \end{bmatrix} \text{ and } A^{-1} = \frac{1}{\det A}\mathrm{adj}\,A = \begin{bmatrix} 1 & 2/3 & -14/9 \\ 0 & -1/3 & 1/9 \\ 0 & 0 & 1/3 \end{bmatrix}.$$

17. Let $A = \begin{bmatrix} a & b \\ c & d \end{bmatrix}$. Then the cofactors of A are $C_{11} = |d| = d$, $C_{12} = -|c| = -c$,

$C_{21} = -|b| = -b$, and $C_{22} = |a| = a$. Thus $\mathrm{adj}\,A = \begin{bmatrix} d & -b \\ -c & a \end{bmatrix}$. Since det $A = ad - bc$, Theorem 8 gives that

$A^{-1} = \frac{1}{\det A}\mathrm{adj}\,A = \frac{1}{ad-bc}\begin{bmatrix} d & -b \\ -c & a \end{bmatrix}$. This result is identical to that of Theorem 4 in Section 2.2.

18. Each cofactor of A is an integer since it is a sum of products of entries in A. Hence all entries in adj A will be integers. Since det $A = 1$, the inverse formula in Theorem 8 shows that all the entries in A^{-1} will be integers.

19. The parallelogram is determined by the columns of $A = \begin{bmatrix} 5 & 6 \\ 2 & 4 \end{bmatrix}$, so the area of the parallelogram is

$|\det A| = |8| = 8$.

20. The parallelogram is determined by the columns of $A = \begin{bmatrix} -1 & 4 \\ 3 & -5 \end{bmatrix}$, so the area of the parallelogram is

$|\det A| = |-7| = 7$.

21. First translate one vertex to the origin. For example, subtract $(-1, 0)$ from each vertex to get a new parallelogram with vertices $(0, 0),(1, 5),(2, -4)$, and $(3, 1)$. This parallelogram has the same area as the original, and is determined by the columns of $A = \begin{bmatrix} 1 & 2 \\ 5 & -4 \end{bmatrix}$, so the area of the parallelogram is

$|\det A| = |-14| = 14$.

22. First translate one vertex to the origin. For example, subtract $(0, -2)$ from each vertex to get a new parallelogram with vertices $(0, 0),(6, 1),(-3, 3)$, and $(3, 4)$. This parallelogram has the same area as the original, and is determined by the columns of $A = \begin{bmatrix} 6 & -3 \\ 1 & 3 \end{bmatrix}$, so the area of the parallelogram is

$|\det A| = |21| = 21$.

23. The parallelepiped is determined by the columns of $A = \begin{bmatrix} 1 & 1 & 7 \\ 0 & 2 & 1 \\ -2 & 4 & 0 \end{bmatrix}$, so the volume of the

parallelepiped is $|\det A| = |22| = 22$.

24. The parallelepiped is determined by the columns of $A = \begin{bmatrix} 1 & -2 & -1 \\ 4 & -5 & 2 \\ 0 & 2 & -1 \end{bmatrix}$, so the volume of the

parallelepiped is $|\det A| = |-15| = 15$.

25. The Invertible Matrix Theorem says that a 3×3 matrix A is not invertible if and only if its columns are linearly dependent. This will happen if and only if one of the columns is a linear combination of the others; that is, if one of the vectors is in the plane spanned by the other two vectors. This is equivalent to the condition that the parallelepiped determined by the three vectors has zero volume, which is in turn equivalent to the condition that $\det A = 0$.

26. By definition, $\mathbf{p} + S$ is the set of all vectors of the form $\mathbf{p} + \mathbf{v}$, where $\mathbf{v}$ is in S. Applying T to a typical vector in $\mathbf{p} + S$, we have $T(\mathbf{p} + \mathbf{v}) = T(\mathbf{p}) + T(\mathbf{v})$. This vector is in the set denoted by $T(\mathbf{p}) + T(S)$. This proves that T maps the set $\mathbf{p} + S$ into the set $T(\mathbf{p}) + T(S)$.

Conversely, any vector in $T(\mathbf{p}) + T(S)$ has the form $T(\mathbf{p}) + T(\mathbf{v})$ for some $\mathbf{v}$ in S. This vector may be written as $T(\mathbf{p} + \mathbf{v})$. This shows that every vector in $T(\mathbf{p}) + T(S)$ is the image under T of some point $\mathbf{p} + \mathbf{v}$ in $\mathbf{p} + S$.

27. Since the parallelogram S is determined by the columns of $\begin{bmatrix} -2 & -2 \\ 3 & 5 \end{bmatrix}$, the area of S is

$\left| \det \begin{bmatrix} -2 & -2 \\ 3 & 5 \end{bmatrix} \right| = |-4| = 4$. The matrix A has $\det A = \begin{vmatrix} 6 & -2 \\ -3 & 2 \end{vmatrix} = 6$. By Theorem 10, the area of $T(S)$ is

$|\det A|\{\text{area of } S\} = 6 \cdot 4 = 24$.

Alternatively, one may compute the vectors that determine the image, namely, the columns of

$$A\begin{bmatrix} \mathbf{b}_1 & \mathbf{b}_2 \end{bmatrix} = \begin{bmatrix} 6 & -2 \\ -3 & 2 \end{bmatrix}\begin{bmatrix} -2 & -2 \\ 3 & 5 \end{bmatrix} = \begin{bmatrix} -18 & -22 \\ 12 & 16 \end{bmatrix}$$

The determinant of this matrix is -24, so the area of the image is 24.

28. Since the parallelogram S is determined by the columns of $\begin{bmatrix} 4 & 0 \\ -7 & 1 \end{bmatrix}$, the area of S is

$\left| \det \begin{bmatrix} 4 & 0 \\ -7 & 1 \end{bmatrix} \right| = |4| = 4$. The matrix A has $\det A = \begin{vmatrix} 7 & 2 \\ 1 & 1 \end{vmatrix} = 5$. By Theorem 10, the area of $T(S)$ is

$|\det A|\{\text{area of } S\} = 5 \cdot 4 = 20$.

Alternatively, one may compute the vectors that determine the image, namely, the columns of

$$A\begin{bmatrix} \mathbf{b}_1 & \mathbf{b}_2 \end{bmatrix} = \begin{bmatrix} 7 & 2 \\ 1 & 1 \end{bmatrix}\begin{bmatrix} 4 & 0 \\ -7 & 1 \end{bmatrix} = \begin{bmatrix} 14 & 2 \\ -3 & 1 \end{bmatrix}$$

The determinant of this matrix is 20, so the area of the image is 20.

29. The area of the triangle is one half of the area of the parallelogram determined by $\mathbf{v}_1$ and $\mathbf{v}_2$. By Theorem 9, the area of the triangle is $(1/2)|\det A|$, where $A = \begin{bmatrix} \mathbf{v}_1 & \mathbf{v}_2 \end{bmatrix}$.

30. Translate R to a new triangle of equal area by subtracting (x_3, y_3) from each vertex. The new triangle has vertices $(0, 0)$, $(x_1 - x_3, y_1 - y_3)$, and $(x_2 - x_3, y_2 - y_3)$. By Exercise 29, the area of the triangle is

$$\frac{1}{2}\left|\det\begin{bmatrix} x_1 - x_3 & x_2 - x_3 \\ y_1 - y_3 & y_2 - y_3 \end{bmatrix}\right|.$$

Now consider using row operations and a cofactor expansion to compute the determinant in the formula:

$$\det\begin{bmatrix} x_1 & y_1 & 1 \\ x_2 & y_2 & 1 \\ x_3 & y_3 & 1 \end{bmatrix} = \det\begin{bmatrix} x_1 - x_3 & y_1 - y_3 & 0 \\ x_2 - x_3 & y_2 - y_3 & 0 \\ x_3 & y_3 & 1 \end{bmatrix} = \det\begin{bmatrix} x_1 - x_3 & y_1 - y_3 \\ x_2 - x_3 & y_2 - y_3 \end{bmatrix}$$

By Theorem 5,

$$\det\begin{bmatrix} x_1 - x_3 & y_1 - y_3 \\ x_2 - x_3 & y_2 - y_3 \end{bmatrix} = \det\begin{bmatrix} x_1 - x_3 & x_2 - x_3 \\ y_1 - y_3 & y_2 - y_3 \end{bmatrix}$$

By the observation above, the area of the original triangle is

$$\frac{1}{2}\left|\det\begin{bmatrix} x_1 - x_3 & x_2 - x_3 \\ y_1 - y_3 & y_2 - y_3 \end{bmatrix}\right| = \frac{1}{2}\left|\det\begin{bmatrix} x_1 & y_1 & 1 \\ x_2 & y_2 & 1 \\ x_3 & y_3 & 1 \end{bmatrix}\right|$$

31. a. To show that $T(S)$ is bounded by the ellipsoid with equation $\frac{x_1^2}{a^2} + \frac{x_2^2}{b^2} + \frac{x_3^2}{c^2} = 1$, let $\mathbf{u} = \begin{bmatrix} u_1 \\ u_2 \\ u_3 \end{bmatrix}$ and let

$\mathbf{x} = \begin{bmatrix} x_1 \\ x_2 \\ x_3 \end{bmatrix} = A\mathbf{u}$. Then $u_1 = x_1/a$, $u_2 = x_2/b$, and $u_3 = x_3/c$, and $\mathbf{u}$ lies inside S (or $u_1^2 + u_2^2 + u_3^2 \leq 1$) if

and only if $\mathbf{x}$ lies inside $T(S)$ (or $\frac{x_1^2}{a^2} + \frac{x_2^2}{b^2} + \frac{x_3^2}{c^2} \leq 1$).

b. By the generalization of Theorem 10,

$$\{\text{volume of ellipsoid}\} = \{\text{volume of } T(S)\}$$

$$= |\det A| \cdot \{\text{volume of } S\} = abc\frac{4\pi}{3} = \frac{4\pi abc}{3}$$

32. a. A linear transformation T that maps S onto S' will map $\mathbf{e}_1$ to $\mathbf{v}_1$, $\mathbf{e}_2$ to $\mathbf{v}_2$, and $\mathbf{e}_3$ to $\mathbf{v}_3$; that is, $T(\mathbf{e}_1) = \mathbf{v}_1$, $T(\mathbf{e}_2) = \mathbf{v}_2$, and $T(\mathbf{e}_3) = \mathbf{v}_3$. The standard matrix for this transformation is $A = [T(\mathbf{e}_1)\ T(\mathbf{e}_2)\ T(\mathbf{e}_3)] = [\mathbf{v}_1\ \mathbf{v}_2\ \mathbf{v}_3]$.

b. The area of the base of S is $(1/2)(1)(1) = 1/2$, so the volume of S is $(1/3)(1/2)(1) = 1/6$. By part a. $T(S) = S'$, so the generalization of Theorem 10 gives that the volume of S' is $|\det A|\{\text{volume of } S\} = (1/6)|\det A|$.

33. [M] Answers will vary. In MATLAB, entries in $B - \text{inv}(A)$ are approximately 10^{-15} or smaller.

34. [M] Answers will vary, as will the commands which produce the second entry of $\mathbf{x}$. For example, the MATLAB command is `x2 = det([A(:,1) b A(:,3:4)])/det(A)` while the Mathematica command is `x2 = Det[{Transpose[A][[1]],b,Transpose[A][[3]], Transpose[A][[4]]}]/Det[A]`.

35. [M] MATLAB Student Version 4.0 uses 57,771 flops for inv A and 14,269,045 flops for the inverse formula. The `inv(A)` command requires only about 0.4% of the operations for the inverse formula.

Chapter 3 SUPPLEMENTARY EXERCISES _____

1. **a.** True. The columns of A are linearly dependent.

 b. True. See Exercise 30 in Section 3.2.

 c. False. See Theorem 3(c); in this case $\det 5A = 5^3 \det A$.

 d. False. Consider $A = \begin{bmatrix} 2 & 0 \\ 0 & 1 \end{bmatrix}$, $B = \begin{bmatrix} 1 & 0 \\ 0 & 3 \end{bmatrix}$, and $A + B = \begin{bmatrix} 3 & 0 \\ 0 & 4 \end{bmatrix}$.

 e. False. By Theorem 6, $\det A^3 = 2^3$.

 f. False. See Theorem 3(b).

 g. True. See Theorem 3(c).

 h. True. See Theorem 3(a).

 i. False. See Theorem 5.

 j. False. See Theorem 3(c); this statement is false for $n \times n$ invertible matrices with n an even integer.

 k. True. See Theorems 6 and 5; $\det A^T A = (\det A)^2$.

 l. False. The coefficient matrix must be invertible.

 m. False. The area of the **triangle** is 5.

 n. True. See Theorem 6; $\det A^3 = (\det A)^3$.

 o. False. See Exercise 31 in Section 3.2.

 p. True. See Theorem 6.

2. $\begin{vmatrix} 12 & 13 & 14 \\ 15 & 16 & 17 \\ 18 & 19 & 20 \end{vmatrix} = \begin{vmatrix} 12 & 13 & 14 \\ 3 & 3 & 3 \\ 6 & 6 & 6 \end{vmatrix} = 0$

3. $\begin{vmatrix} 1 & a & b+c \\ 1 & b & a+c \\ 1 & c & a+b \end{vmatrix} = \begin{vmatrix} 1 & a & b+c \\ 0 & b-a & a-b \\ 0 & c-a & a-c \end{vmatrix} = (b-a)(c-a)\begin{vmatrix} 1 & a & b+c \\ 0 & 1 & -1 \\ 0 & 1 & -1 \end{vmatrix} = 0$

4. $\begin{vmatrix} a & b & c \\ a+x & b+x & c+x \\ a+y & b+y & c+y \end{vmatrix} = \begin{vmatrix} a & b & c \\ x & x & x \\ y & y & y \end{vmatrix} = xy\begin{vmatrix} a & b & c \\ 1 & 1 & 1 \\ 1 & 1 & 1 \end{vmatrix} = 0$

5. $\begin{vmatrix} 9 & 1 & 9 & 9 & 9 \\ 9 & 0 & 9 & 9 & 2 \\ 4 & 0 & 0 & 5 & 0 \\ 9 & 0 & 3 & 9 & 0 \\ 6 & 0 & 0 & 7 & 0 \end{vmatrix} = (-1)\begin{vmatrix} 9 & 9 & 9 & 2 \\ 4 & 0 & 5 & 0 \\ 9 & 3 & 9 & 0 \\ 6 & 0 & 7 & 0 \end{vmatrix} = (-1)(-2)\begin{vmatrix} 4 & 0 & 5 \\ 9 & 3 & 9 \\ 6 & 0 & 7 \end{vmatrix}$

$= (-1)(-2)(3)\begin{vmatrix} 4 & 5 \\ 6 & 7 \end{vmatrix} = (-1)(-2)(3)(-2) = -12$

6. $\begin{vmatrix} 4 & 8 & 8 & 8 & 5 \\ 0 & 1 & 0 & 0 & 0 \\ 6 & 8 & 8 & 8 & 7 \\ 0 & 8 & 8 & 3 & 0 \\ 0 & 8 & 2 & 0 & 0 \end{vmatrix} = (1) \begin{vmatrix} 4 & 8 & 8 & 5 \\ 6 & 8 & 8 & 7 \\ 0 & 8 & 3 & 0 \\ 0 & 2 & 0 & 0 \end{vmatrix} = (1)(2) \begin{vmatrix} 4 & 8 & 5 \\ 6 & 8 & 7 \\ 0 & 3 & 0 \end{vmatrix} = (1)(2)(-3) \begin{vmatrix} 4 & 5 \\ 6 & 7 \end{vmatrix} = (1)(2)(-3)(-2) = 12$

7. Expand across the first row to obtain $\begin{vmatrix} 1 & x & y \\ 1 & x_1 & y_1 \\ 1 & x_2 & y_2 \end{vmatrix} = 1 \begin{vmatrix} x_1 & y_1 \\ x_2 & y_2 \end{vmatrix} - x \begin{vmatrix} 1 & y_1 \\ 1 & y_2 \end{vmatrix} + y \begin{vmatrix} 1 & x_1 \\ 1 & x_2 \end{vmatrix} = 0$. This is an

equation of the form $ax + by + c = 0$, and since the points (x_1, y_1) and (x_2, y_2) are distinct, at least one of a and b is not zero. Thus the equation is the equation of a line. The points (x_1, y_1) and (x_2, y_2) are on the line, because when the coordinates of one of the points are substituted for x and y, two rows of the matrix are equal and so the determinant is zero.

8. Expand across the first row to obtain

$\begin{vmatrix} 1 & x & y \\ 1 & x_1 & y_1 \\ 0 & 1 & m \end{vmatrix} = 1 \begin{vmatrix} x_1 & y_1 \\ 1 & m \end{vmatrix} - x \begin{vmatrix} 1 & y_1 \\ 0 & m \end{vmatrix} + y \begin{vmatrix} 1 & x_1 \\ 0 & 1 \end{vmatrix} = 1(mx_1 - y_1) - x(m) + y(1) = 0$. This equation may be

rewritten as $mx_1 - y_1 - mx + y = 0$, or $y - y_1 = m(x - x_1)$.

9. $\det T = \begin{vmatrix} 1 & a & a^2 \\ 1 & b & b^2 \\ 1 & c & c^2 \end{vmatrix} = \begin{vmatrix} 1 & a & a^2 \\ 0 & b-a & b^2-a^2 \\ 0 & c-a & c^2-a^2 \end{vmatrix} = \begin{vmatrix} 1 & a & a^2 \\ 0 & b-a & (b-a)(b+a) \\ 0 & c-a & (c-a)(c+a) \end{vmatrix}$

$= (b-a)(c-a) \begin{vmatrix} 1 & a & a^2 \\ 0 & 1 & b+a \\ 0 & 1 & c+a \end{vmatrix} = (b-a)(c-a) \begin{vmatrix} 1 & a & a^2 \\ 0 & 1 & b+a \\ 0 & 0 & c-b \end{vmatrix} = (b-a)(c-a)(c-b)$

10. Expand across the first row and obtain $f(t) = \det V = c_0 + c_1 t + c_2 t^2 + c_3 t^3$. By Exercise 9,

$c_3 = \begin{vmatrix} 1 & x_1 & x_1^2 \\ 1 & x_2 & x_2^2 \\ 1 & x_3 & x_3^2 \end{vmatrix} = (x_2 - x_1)(x_3 - x_1)(x_3 - x_2) \neq 0$

since x_1, x_2, and x_3 are distinct. Thus $f(t)$ is a cubic polynomial. The points $(x_1, 0)$, $(x_2, 0)$, and $(x_3, 0)$ are on the graph of f, since when any of x_1, x_2 or x_3 are substituted for t, the matrix has two equal rows and thus its determinant (which is $f(t)$) is zero. Thus $f(x_i) = 0$ for $i = 1, 2, 3$.

11. To tell if a quadrilateral determined by four points is a parallelogram, first translate one of the vertices to the origin. If the vertices of this new quadrilateral are $\mathbf{0}$, $\mathbf{v}_1$, $\mathbf{v}_2$, and $\mathbf{v}_3$, then they will be the vertices of a parallelogram if one of $\mathbf{v}_1$, $\mathbf{v}_2$, or $\mathbf{v}_3$ is the sum of the other two. In this exercise, subtract $(1, 4)$ from each vertex to get a new parallelogram with vertices $\mathbf{0} = (0, 0)$, $\mathbf{v}_1 = (-2, 1)$, $\mathbf{v}_2 = (2, 5)$, and $\mathbf{v}_3 = (4, 4)$. Since $\mathbf{v}_2 = \mathbf{v}_3 + \mathbf{v}_1$, the quadrilateral is a parallelogram as stated. The translated parallelogram has the same area as the original, and is determined by the columns of $A = \begin{bmatrix} \mathbf{v}_1 & \mathbf{v}_3 \end{bmatrix} = \begin{bmatrix} -2 & 4 \\ 1 & 4 \end{bmatrix}$, so the area of

the parallelogram is $|\det A| = |-12| = 12$.

12. A 2×2 matrix A is invertible if and only if the parallelogram determined by the columns of A has nonzero area.

13. By Theorem 8, $(\text{adj } A) \cdot \dfrac{1}{\det A} A = A^{-1} A = I$. By the Invertible Matrix Theorem, adj A is invertible and

$(\text{adj } A)^{-1} = \dfrac{1}{\det A} A$.

14. **a**. Consider the matrix $A_k = \begin{bmatrix} A & O \\ O & I_k \end{bmatrix}$, where $1 \le k \le n$ and O is an appropriately sized zero matrix.

Show that $\det A_k = \det A$ for all $1 \le k \le n$ by mathematical induction.

First let $k = 1$. Expand along the last row to obtain

$\det A_1 = \det \begin{bmatrix} A & O \\ O & 1 \end{bmatrix} = (-1)^{(n+1)+(n+1)} \cdot 1 \cdot \det A = \det A$.

Now let $1 < k \le n$ and assume that $\det A_{k-1} = \det A$. Expand across the last row of A_k to obtain

$\det A_k = \det \begin{bmatrix} A & O \\ O & I_k \end{bmatrix} = (-1)^{(n+k)+(n+k)} \cdot 1 \cdot \det A_{k-1} = \det A_{k-1} = \det A$. By induction, $\det A_k = \det A$ for

all k, and the determinant of the matrix in question is $\det A$.

b. Consider the matrix $A_k = \begin{bmatrix} I_k & O \\ C_k & D \end{bmatrix}$, where $1 \le k \le n$, C_k is an $n \times k$ matrix and O is an appropriately

sized zero matrix. Show that $\det A_k = \det D$ for all $1 \le k \le n$ by mathematical induction.

First let $k = 1$. Expand along the first row to obtain

$\det A_1 = \det \begin{bmatrix} 1 & O \\ C_1 & D \end{bmatrix} = (-1)^{1+1} \cdot 1 \cdot \det D = \det D$.

Now let $1 < k \le n$ and assume that $\det A_{k-1} = \det D$. Expand along the first row of A_k to obtain

$\det A_k = \det \begin{bmatrix} I_k & O \\ C_k & D \end{bmatrix} = (-1)^{1+1} \cdot 1 \cdot \det A_{k-1} = \det A_{k-1} = \det D$. By induction, $\det A_k = \det A$ for all k,

and the determinant of the matrix in question is $\det D$.

c. By combining parts (a) and (b),

$\det \begin{bmatrix} A & O \\ C & D \end{bmatrix} = \left(\det \begin{bmatrix} A & O \\ O & I \end{bmatrix} \right) \left(\det \begin{bmatrix} I & O \\ C & D \end{bmatrix} \right) = (\det A)(\det D)$.

From this result and Theorem 5,

$\det \begin{bmatrix} A & B \\ O & D \end{bmatrix} = \det \begin{bmatrix} A & B \\ O & D \end{bmatrix}^T = \det \begin{bmatrix} A^T & O \\ B^T & D^T \end{bmatrix} = (\det A^T)(\det D^T) = (\det A)(\det D)$.

15. a. Compute the right side of the equation. Note: Write XA, not AX.

$$\begin{bmatrix} I & O \\ X & I \end{bmatrix}\begin{bmatrix} A & B \\ O & Y \end{bmatrix} = \begin{bmatrix} A & B \\ XA & XB+Y \end{bmatrix}$$

Set this equal to the left side of the equation:

$$\begin{bmatrix} A & B \\ C & D \end{bmatrix} = \begin{bmatrix} A & B \\ XA & XB+Y \end{bmatrix}$$

so that $XA = C$ and $XB + Y = D$

Since $XA = C$ and A is invertible, $X = CA^{-1}$. Since $XB + Y = D$, $Y = D - XB = D - CA^{-1}B$. Thus by Exercise 14(c),

$$\det\begin{bmatrix} A & B \\ C & D \end{bmatrix} = \det\begin{bmatrix} I & O \\ CA^{-1} & I \end{bmatrix}\det\begin{bmatrix} A & B \\ O & D-CA^{-1}B \end{bmatrix}$$

$$= (\det A)(\det(D - CA^{-1}B))$$

b. From part (a),

$$\det\begin{bmatrix} A & B \\ C & D \end{bmatrix} = (\det A)(\det(D - CA^{-1}B)) = \det[A(D - CA^{-1}B)]$$

$$= \det[AD - ACA^{-1}B] = \det[AD - CAA^{-1}B]$$

$$= \det[AD - CB]$$

16. a. Doing the given operations does not change the determinant of A since the given operations are all row replacement operations. The resulting matrix is

$$\begin{bmatrix} a-b & -a+b & 0 & \dots & 0 \\ 0 & a-b & -a+b & \dots & 0 \\ 0 & 0 & a-b & \dots & 0 \\ \vdots & \vdots & \vdots & \ddots & \vdots \\ b & b & b & \dots & a \end{bmatrix}$$

b. Since column replacement operations are equivalent to row operations on A^T and $\det A^T = \det A$, the given operations do not change the determinant of the matrix. The resulting matrix is

$$\begin{bmatrix} a-b & 0 & 0 & \dots & 0 \\ 0 & a-b & 0 & \dots & 0 \\ 0 & 0 & a-b & \dots & 0 \\ \vdots & \vdots & \vdots & \ddots & \vdots \\ b & 2b & 3b & \dots & a+(n-1)b \end{bmatrix}$$

c. Since the preceding matrix is a triangular matrix with the same determinant as A,

$$\det A = (a-b)^{n-1}(a+(n-1)b).$$

17. First consider the case $n = 2$. In this case

$$\det B = \begin{vmatrix} a-b & b \\ 0 & a \end{vmatrix} = a(a-b), \det C = \begin{vmatrix} b & b \\ b & a \end{vmatrix} = ab - b^2,$$

so $\det A = \det B + \det C = a(a-b) + ab - b^2 = a^2 - b^2 = (a-b)(a+b) = (a-b)^{2-1}(a+(2-1)b)$, and the formula holds for $n = 2$.

Now assume that the formula holds for all $(k-1) \times (k-1)$ matrices, and let A, B, and C be $k \times k$ matrices. By a cofactor expansion down the first column,

$$\det B = (a-b) \begin{vmatrix} a & b & \cdots & b \\ b & a & \cdots & b \\ \vdots & \vdots & \ddots & \vdots \\ b & b & \cdots & a \end{vmatrix} = (a-b)(a-b)^{k-2}(a+(k-2)b) = (a-b)^{k-1}(a+(k-2)b)$$

since the matrix in the above formula is a $(k-1) \times (k-1)$ matrix. We can perform a series of row operations on C to create zeros below each pivot, and produce the following matrix whose determinant is $\det C$:

$$\begin{bmatrix} b & b & \cdots & b \\ 0 & a-b & \cdots & 0 \\ \vdots & \vdots & \ddots & \vdots \\ 0 & 0 & \cdots & a-b \end{bmatrix}.$$

Since this is a triangular matrix, $\det C = b(a-b)^{k-1}$. Thus

$$\det A = \det B + \det C = (a-b)^{k-1}(a+(k-2)b) + b(a-b)^{k-1} = (a-b)^{k-1}(a+(k-1)b),$$

which is what was to be shown. By mathematical induction, this proves the formula.

18. **[M]** Since the first matrix has $a = 3$, $b = 8$, and $n = 4$, its determinant is
$(3-8)^{4-1}(3+(4-1)8) = (-5)^3(3+24) = (-125)(27) = -3375$. Since the second matrix has $a = 8$, $b = 3$, and $n = 5$, its determinant is $(8-3)^{5-1}(8+(5-1)3) = (5)^4(8+12) = (625)(20) = 12{,}500$.

19. **[M]** Compute

$$\begin{vmatrix} 1 & 1 & 1 \\ 1 & 2 & 2 \\ 1 & 2 & 3 \end{vmatrix} = 1, \quad \begin{vmatrix} 1 & 1 & 1 & 1 \\ 1 & 2 & 2 & 2 \\ 1 & 2 & 3 & 3 \\ 1 & 2 & 3 & 4 \end{vmatrix} = 1, \quad \begin{vmatrix} 1 & 1 & 1 & 1 & 1 \\ 1 & 2 & 2 & 2 & 2 \\ 1 & 2 & 3 & 3 & 3 \\ 1 & 2 & 3 & 4 & 4 \\ 1 & 2 & 3 & 4 & 5 \end{vmatrix} = 1.$$

A conjecture is that

$$\begin{vmatrix} 1 & 1 & 1 & \cdots & 1 \\ 1 & 2 & 2 & \cdots & 2 \\ 1 & 2 & 3 & \cdots & 3 \\ \vdots & \vdots & \vdots & \ddots & \vdots \\ 1 & 2 & 3 & \cdots & n \end{vmatrix} = 1.$$

To show this, consider using row replacement operations to create zeros below the first pivot. The resulting matrix is

$$\begin{bmatrix} 1 & 1 & 1 & \cdots & 1 \\ 0 & 1 & 1 & \cdots & 1 \\ 0 & 1 & 2 & \cdots & 2 \\ \vdots & \vdots & \vdots & \ddots & \vdots \\ 0 & 1 & 2 & \cdots & n-1 \end{bmatrix}.$$

4 Vector Spaces

4.1 SOLUTIONS

Notes: This section is designed to avoid the standard exercises in which a student is asked to check ten axioms on an array of sets. Theorem 1 provides the main homework tool in this section for showing that a set is a subspace. Students should be taught how to check the closure axioms. The exercises in this section (and the next few sections) emphasize $\mathbb{R}^n$, to give students time to absorb the abstract concepts. Other vectors do appear later in the chapter: the space $\mathbb{S}$ of signals is used in Section 4.8, and the spaces $\mathbb{P}_n$ of polynomials are used in many sections of Chapters 4 and 6.

1. **a.** If **u** and **v** are in V, then their entries are nonnegative. Since a sum of nonnegative numbers is nonnegative, the vector **u** + **v** has nonnegative entries. Thus **u** + **v** is in V.

    b. *Example:* If $\mathbf{u} = \begin{bmatrix} 2 \\ 2 \end{bmatrix}$ and $c = -1$, then **u** is in V but $c\mathbf{u}$ is not in V.

2. **a.** If $\mathbf{u} = \begin{bmatrix} x \\ y \end{bmatrix}$ is in W, then the vector $c\mathbf{u} = c\begin{bmatrix} x \\ y \end{bmatrix} = \begin{bmatrix} cx \\ cy \end{bmatrix}$ is in W because $(cx)(cy) = c^2(xy) \geq 0$ since $xy \geq 0$.

    b. *Example:* If $\mathbf{u} = \begin{bmatrix} -1 \\ -7 \end{bmatrix}$ and $\mathbf{v} = \begin{bmatrix} 2 \\ 3 \end{bmatrix}$, then **u** and **v** are in W but **u** + **v** is not in W.

3. *Example:* If $\mathbf{u} = \begin{bmatrix} .5 \\ .5 \end{bmatrix}$ and $c = 4$, then **u** is in H but $c\mathbf{u}$ is not in H. Since H is not closed under scalar multiplication, H is not a subspace of $\mathbb{R}^2$.

4. Note that **u** and **v** are on the line L, but **u** + **v** is not.

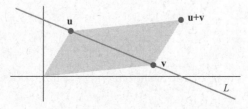

5. Yes. Since the set is $\text{Span}\,\{t^2\}$, the set is a subspace by Theorem 1.

6. No. The zero vector is not in the set.

7. No. The set is not closed under multiplication by scalars which are not integers.

8. Yes. The zero vector is in the set H. If $\mathbf{p}$ and $\mathbf{q}$ are in H, then $(\mathbf{p} + \mathbf{q})(0) = \mathbf{p}(0) + \mathbf{q}(0) = 0 + 0 = 0$, so $\mathbf{p} + \mathbf{q}$ is in H. For any scalar c, $(c\mathbf{p})(0) = c \cdot \mathbf{p}(0) = c \cdot 0 = 0$, so $c\mathbf{p}$ is in H. Thus H is a subspace by Theorem 1.

9. The set $H = \text{Span}\,\{\mathbf{v}\}$, where $\mathbf{v} = \begin{bmatrix} 1 \\ 3 \\ 2 \end{bmatrix}$. Thus H is a subspace of $\mathbb{R}^3$ by Theorem 1.

10. The set $H = \text{Span}\,\{\mathbf{v}\}$, where $\mathbf{v} = \begin{bmatrix} 2 \\ 0 \\ -1 \end{bmatrix}$. Thus H is a subspace of $\mathbb{R}^3$ by Theorem 1.

11. The set $W = \text{Span}\,\{\mathbf{u}, \mathbf{v}\}$, where $\mathbf{u} = \begin{bmatrix} 5 \\ 1 \\ 0 \end{bmatrix}$ and $\mathbf{v} = \begin{bmatrix} 2 \\ 0 \\ 1 \end{bmatrix}$. Thus W is a subspace of $\mathbb{R}^3$ by Theorem 1.

12. The set $W = \text{Span}\,\{\mathbf{u}, \mathbf{v}\}$, where $\mathbf{u} = \begin{bmatrix} 1 \\ 1 \\ 2 \\ 0 \end{bmatrix}$ and $\mathbf{v} = \begin{bmatrix} 3 \\ -1 \\ -1 \\ 4 \end{bmatrix}$. Thus W is a subspace of $\mathbb{R}^4$ by Theorem 1.

13. a. The vector $\mathbf{w}$ is not in the set $\{\mathbf{v}_1, \mathbf{v}_2, \mathbf{v}_3\}$. There are 3 vectors in the set $\{\mathbf{v}_1, \mathbf{v}_2, \mathbf{v}_3\}$.

   b. The set $\text{Span}\{\mathbf{v}_1, \mathbf{v}_2, \mathbf{v}_3\}$ contains infinitely many vectors.

   c. The vector $\mathbf{w}$ is in the subspace spanned by $\{\mathbf{v}_1, \mathbf{v}_2, \mathbf{v}_3\}$ if and only if the equation $x_1\mathbf{v}_1 + x_2\mathbf{v}_2 + x_3\mathbf{v}_3 = \mathbf{w}$ has a solution. Row reducing the augmented matrix for this system of linear equations gives

$$\begin{bmatrix} 1 & 2 & 4 & 3 \\ 0 & 1 & 2 & 1 \\ -1 & 3 & 6 & 2 \end{bmatrix} \sim \begin{bmatrix} 1 & 0 & 0 & 1 \\ 0 & 1 & 2 & 1 \\ 0 & 0 & 0 & 0 \end{bmatrix},$$

so the equation has a solution and $\mathbf{w}$ is in the subspace spanned by $\{\mathbf{v}_1, \mathbf{v}_2, \mathbf{v}_3\}$.

14. The augmented matrix is found as in Exercise 13c. Since

$$\begin{bmatrix} 1 & 2 & 4 & 8 \\ 0 & 1 & 2 & 4 \\ -1 & 3 & 6 & 7 \end{bmatrix} \sim \begin{bmatrix} 1 & 0 & 0 & 0 \\ 0 & 1 & 2 & 0 \\ 0 & 0 & 0 & 1 \end{bmatrix},$$

the equation $x_1\mathbf{v}_1 + x_2\mathbf{v}_2 + x_3\mathbf{v}_3 = \mathbf{w}$ has no solution, and $\mathbf{w}$ is not in the subspace spanned by $\{\mathbf{v}_1, \mathbf{v}_2, \mathbf{v}_3\}$.

15. Since the zero vector is not in W, W is not a vector space.

16. Since the zero vector is not in W, W is not a vector space.

17. Since a vector **w** in W may be written as

$$\mathbf{w} = a\begin{bmatrix} 1 \\ 0 \\ -1 \\ 0 \end{bmatrix} + b\begin{bmatrix} -1 \\ 1 \\ 0 \\ 1 \end{bmatrix} + c\begin{bmatrix} 0 \\ -1 \\ 1 \\ 0 \end{bmatrix}$$

$$S = \left\{ \begin{bmatrix} 1 \\ 0 \\ -1 \\ 0 \end{bmatrix}, \begin{bmatrix} -1 \\ 1 \\ 0 \\ 1 \end{bmatrix}, \begin{bmatrix} 0 \\ -1 \\ 1 \\ 0 \end{bmatrix} \right\}$$

is a set that spans W.

18. Since a vector **w** in W may be written as

$$\mathbf{w} = a\begin{bmatrix} 4 \\ 0 \\ 1 \\ -2 \end{bmatrix} + b\begin{bmatrix} 3 \\ 0 \\ 1 \\ 0 \end{bmatrix} + c\begin{bmatrix} 0 \\ 0 \\ 1 \\ 1 \end{bmatrix}$$

$$S = \left\{ \begin{bmatrix} 4 \\ 0 \\ 1 \\ -2 \end{bmatrix}, \begin{bmatrix} 3 \\ 0 \\ 1 \\ 0 \end{bmatrix}, \begin{bmatrix} 0 \\ 0 \\ 1 \\ 1 \end{bmatrix} \right\}$$

is a set that spans W.

19. Let H be the set of all functions described by $y(t) = c_1 \cos \omega t + c_2 \sin \omega t$. Then H is a subset of the vector space V of all real-valued functions, and may be written as $H = \text{Span}\{\cos \omega t, \sin \omega t\}$. By Theorem 1, H is a subspace of V and is hence a vector space.

20. a. The following facts about continuous functions must be shown.

  1. The constant function $\mathbf{f}(t) = 0$ is continuous.

  2. The sum of two continuous functions is continuous.

  3. A constant multiple of a continuous function is continuous.

  b. Let $H = \{\mathbf{f} \text{ in } C[a, b]: \mathbf{f}(a) = \mathbf{f}(b)\}$.

  1. Let $\mathbf{g}(t) = 0$ for all t in $[a, b]$. Then $\mathbf{g}(a) = \mathbf{g}(b) = 0$, so **g** is in H.

  2. Let **g** and **h** be in H. Then $\mathbf{g}(a) = \mathbf{g}(b)$ and $\mathbf{h}(a) = \mathbf{h}(b)$, and $(\mathbf{g} + \mathbf{h})(a) = \mathbf{g}(a) + \mathbf{h}(a) = \mathbf{g}(b) + \mathbf{h}(b) = (\mathbf{g} + \mathbf{h})(b)$, so $\mathbf{g} + \mathbf{h}$ is in H.

  3. Let **g** be in H. Then $\mathbf{g}(a) = \mathbf{g}(b)$, and $(c\mathbf{g})(a) = c\mathbf{g}(a) = c\mathbf{g}(b) = (c\mathbf{g})(b)$, so $c\mathbf{g}$ is in H.

  Thus H is a subspace of $C[a, b]$.

21. The set H is a subspace of $M_{2\times 2}$. The zero matrix is in H, the sum of two upper triangular matrices is upper triangular, and a scalar multiple of an upper triangular matrix is upper triangular.

22. The set H is a subspace of $M_{2\times 4}$. The 2×4 zero matrix 0 is in H because $F0 = 0$. If A and B are matrices in H, then $F(A + B) = FA + FB = 0 + 0 = 0$, so $A + B$ is in H. If A is in H and c is a scalar, then $F(cA) = c(FA) = c0 = 0$, so cA is in H.

23. **a.** False. The zero vector in V is the function $\mathbf{f}$ whose values $\mathbf{f}(t)$ are zero *for all t* in $\mathbb{R}$.

  b. False. An arrow in three-dimensional space is an example of a vector, but not every arrow is a vector.

  c. False. See Exercises 1, 2, and 3 for examples of subsets which contain the zero vector but are not subspaces.

  d. True. See the paragraph before Example 6.

  e. False. Digital signals are used. See Example 3.

24. **a.** True. See the definition of a vector space.

  b. True. See statement (3) in the box before Example 1.

  c. True. See the paragraph before Example 6.

  d. False. See Example 8.

  e. False. The second and third parts of the conditions are stated incorrectly. For example, part (ii) does not state that $\mathbf{u}$ and $\mathbf{v}$ represent all possible elements of H.

25. 2, 4

26. **a.** 3

  b. 5

  c. 4

27. **a.** 8

  b. 3

  c. 5

  d. 4

28. **a.** 4

  b. 7

  c. 3

  d. 5

  e. 4

29. Consider $\mathbf{u} + (-1)\mathbf{u}$. By Axiom 10, $\mathbf{u} + (-1)\mathbf{u} = 1\mathbf{u} + (-1)\mathbf{u}$. By Axiom 8, $1\mathbf{u} + (-1)\mathbf{u} = (1 + (-1))\mathbf{u} = 0\mathbf{u}$. By Exercise 27, $0\mathbf{u} = \mathbf{0}$. Thus $\mathbf{u} + (-1)\mathbf{u} = \mathbf{0}$, and by Exercise 26 $(-1)\mathbf{u} = -\mathbf{u}$.

30. By Axiom 10 $\mathbf{u} = 1\mathbf{u}$. Since c is nonzero, $c^{-1}c = 1$, and $\mathbf{u} = (c^{-1}c)\mathbf{u}$. By Axiom 9,

$(c^{-1}c)\mathbf{u} = c^{-1}(c\mathbf{u}) = c^{-1}\mathbf{0}$ since $c\mathbf{u} = \mathbf{0}$. Thus $\mathbf{u} = c^{-1}\mathbf{0} = \mathbf{0}$ by Property (2), proven in Exercise 28.

31. Any subspace H that contains $\mathbf{u}$ and $\mathbf{v}$ must also contain all scalar multiples of $\mathbf{u}$ and $\mathbf{v}$, and hence must also contain all sums of scalar multiples of $\mathbf{u}$ and $\mathbf{v}$. Thus H must contain all linear combinations of $\mathbf{u}$ and $\mathbf{v}$, or Span $\{\mathbf{u}, \mathbf{v}\}$.

Note: Exercises 32–34 provide good practice for mathematics majors because these arguments involve simple symbol manipulation typical of mathematical proofs. Most students outside mathematics might profit more from other types of exercises.

32. Both H and K contain the zero vector of V because they are subspaces of V. Thus the zero vector of V is in $H \cap K$. Let $\mathbf{u}$ and $\mathbf{v}$ be in $H \cap K$. Then $\mathbf{u}$ and $\mathbf{v}$ are in H. Since H is a subspace $\mathbf{u} + \mathbf{v}$ is in H. Likewise $\mathbf{u}$ and $\mathbf{v}$ are in K. Since K is a subspace $\mathbf{u} + \mathbf{v}$ is in K. Thus $\mathbf{u} + \mathbf{v}$ is in $H \cap K$. Let $\mathbf{u}$ be in $H \cap K$. Then $\mathbf{u}$ is in H. Since H is a subspace $c\mathbf{u}$ is in H. Likewise $\mathbf{v}$ is in K. Since K is a subspace $c\mathbf{u}$ is in K. Thus $c\mathbf{u}$ is in $H \cap K$ for any scalar c, and $H \cap K$ is a subspace of V.

The union of two subspaces is not in general a subspace. For an example in $\mathbb{R}^2$ let H be the x-axis and let K be the y-axis. Then both H and K are subspaces of $\mathbb{R}^2$, but $H \cup K$ is not closed under vector addition. The subset $H \cup K$ is thus not a subspace of $\mathbb{R}^2$.

33. **a.** Given subspaces H and K of a vector space V, the zero vector of V belongs to $H + K$, because $\mathbf{0}$ is in both H and K (since they are subspaces) and $\mathbf{0} = \mathbf{0} + \mathbf{0}$. Next, take two vectors in $H + K$, say $\mathbf{w}_1 = \mathbf{u}_1 + \mathbf{v}_1$ and $\mathbf{w}_2 = \mathbf{u}_2 + \mathbf{v}_2$ where $\mathbf{u}_1$ and $\mathbf{u}_2$ are in H, and $\mathbf{v}_1$ and $\mathbf{v}_2$ are in K. Then

$$\mathbf{w}_1 + \mathbf{w}_2 = \mathbf{u}_1 + \mathbf{v}_1 + \mathbf{u}_2 + \mathbf{v}_2 = (\mathbf{u}_1 + \mathbf{u}_2) + (\mathbf{v}_1 + \mathbf{v}_2)$$

because vector addition in V is commutative and associative. Now $\mathbf{u}_1 + \mathbf{u}_2$ is in H and $\mathbf{v}_1 + \mathbf{v}_2$ is in K because H and K are subspaces. This shows that $\mathbf{w}_1 + \mathbf{w}_2$ is in $H + K$. Thus $H + K$ is closed under addition of vectors. Finally, for any scalar c,

$$c\mathbf{w}_1 = c(\mathbf{u}_1 + \mathbf{v}_1) = c\mathbf{u}_1 + c\mathbf{v}_1$$

The vector $c\mathbf{u}_1$ belongs to H and $c\mathbf{v}_1$ belongs to K, because H and K are subspaces. Thus, $c\mathbf{w}_1$ belongs to $H + K$, so $H + K$ is closed under multiplication by scalars. These arguments show that $H + K$ satisfies all three conditions necessary to be a subspace of V.

b. Certainly H is a subset of $H + K$ because every vector $\mathbf{u}$ in H may be written as $\mathbf{u} + \mathbf{0}$, where the zero vector $\mathbf{0}$ is in K (and also in H, of course). Since H contains the zero vector of $H + K$, and H is closed under vector addition and multiplication by scalars (because H is a subspace of V), H is a subspace of $H + K$. The same argument applies when H is replaced by K, so K is also a subspace of $H + K$.

34. A proof that $H + K = \text{Span}\{\mathbf{u}_1,\ldots,\mathbf{u}_p,\mathbf{v}_1,\ldots,\mathbf{v}_q\}$ has two parts. First, one must show that $H + K$ is a subset of $\text{Span}\{\mathbf{u}_1,\ldots,\mathbf{u}_p,\mathbf{v}_1,\ldots,\mathbf{v}_q\}$. Second, one must show that $\text{Span}\{\mathbf{u}_1,\ldots,\mathbf{u}_p,\mathbf{v}_1,\ldots,\mathbf{v}_q\}$ is a subset of $H + K$.

(1) A typical vector H has the form $c_1\mathbf{u}_1 + \ldots + c_p\mathbf{u}_p$ and a typical vector in K has the form $d_1\mathbf{v}_1 + \ldots + d_q\mathbf{v}_q$. The sum of these two vectors is a linear combination of $\mathbf{u}_1,\ldots,\mathbf{u}_p,\mathbf{v}_1,\ldots,\mathbf{v}_q$ and so belongs to $\text{Span}\{\mathbf{u}_1,\ldots,\mathbf{u}_p,\mathbf{v}_1,\ldots,\mathbf{v}_q\}$. Thus $H + K$ is a subset of $\text{Span}\{\mathbf{u}_1,\ldots,\mathbf{u}_p,\mathbf{v}_1,\ldots,\mathbf{v}_q\}$.

(2) Each of the vectors $\mathbf{u}_1,\ldots,\mathbf{u}_p,\mathbf{v}_1,\ldots,\mathbf{v}_q$ belongs to $H + K$, by Exercise 33(b), and so any linear combination of these vectors belongs to $H + K$, since $H + K$ is a subspace, by Exercise 33(a). Thus, $\text{Span}\{\mathbf{u}_1,\ldots,\mathbf{u}_p,\mathbf{v}_1,\ldots,\mathbf{v}_q\}$ is a subset of $H + K$.

35. **[M]** Since

$$\begin{bmatrix} 7 & -4 & -9 & -9 \\ -4 & 5 & 4 & 7 \\ -2 & -1 & 4 & 4 \\ 9 & -7 & -7 & 8 \end{bmatrix} \sim \begin{bmatrix} 1 & 0 & 0 & 15/2 \\ 0 & 1 & 0 & 3 \\ 0 & 0 & 1 & 11/2 \\ 0 & 0 & 0 & 0 \end{bmatrix},$$

$\mathbf{w}$ is in the subspace spanned by $\{\mathbf{v}_1,\mathbf{v}_2,\mathbf{v}_3\}$.

36. **[M]** Since

$$[A \quad \mathbf{y}] = \begin{bmatrix} 5 & -5 & -9 & 6 \\ 8 & 8 & -6 & 7 \\ -5 & -9 & 3 & 1 \\ 3 & -2 & -7 & -4 \end{bmatrix} \sim \begin{bmatrix} 1 & 0 & 0 & 11/2 \\ 0 & 1 & 0 & -2 \\ 0 & 0 & 1 & 7/2 \\ 0 & 0 & 0 & 0 \end{bmatrix},$$

$\mathbf{y}$ is in the subspace spanned by the columns of A.

37. **[M]** The graph of **f**(t) is given below. A conjecture is that **f**(t) = cos 4t.

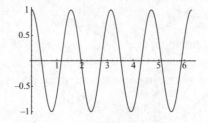

The graph of **g**(t) is given below. A conjecture is that **g**(t) = cos 6t.

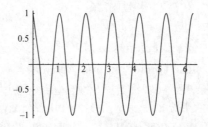

38. **[M]** The graph of **f**(t) is given below. A conjecture is that **f**(t) = sin 3t.

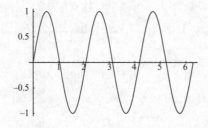

The graph of **g**(t) is given below. A conjecture is that **g**(t) = cos 4t.

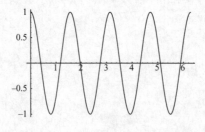

The graph of **h**(t) is given below. A conjecture is that **h**(t) = sin 5t.

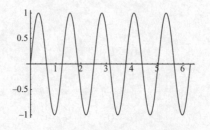

4.2   SOLUTIONS

Notes: This section provides a review of Chapter 1 using the new terminology. Linear tranformations are introduced quickly since students are already comfortable with the idea from $\mathbb{R}^n$. The key exercises are 17–26, which are straightforward but help to solidify the notions of null spaces and column spaces. Exercises 30–36 deal with the kernel and range of a linear transformation and are progressively more advanced theoretically. The idea in Exercises 7–14 is for the student to use Theorems 1, 2, or 3 to determine whether a given set is a subspace.

1. One calculates that

$$A\mathbf{w} = \begin{bmatrix} 3 & -5 & -3 \\ 6 & -2 & 0 \\ -8 & 4 & 1 \end{bmatrix}\begin{bmatrix} 1 \\ 3 \\ -4 \end{bmatrix} = \begin{bmatrix} 0 \\ 0 \\ 0 \end{bmatrix},$$

so $\mathbf{w}$ is in Nul A.

2. One calculates that

$$A\mathbf{w} = \begin{bmatrix} 5 & 21 & 19 \\ 13 & 23 & 2 \\ 8 & 14 & 1 \end{bmatrix}\begin{bmatrix} 5 \\ -3 \\ 2 \end{bmatrix} = \begin{bmatrix} 0 \\ 0 \\ 0 \end{bmatrix},$$

so $\mathbf{w}$ is in Nul A.

3. First find the general solution of $A\mathbf{x} = \mathbf{0}$ in terms of the free variables. Since

$$\begin{bmatrix} A & \mathbf{0} \end{bmatrix} \sim \begin{bmatrix} 1 & 0 & -7 & 6 & 0 \\ 0 & 1 & 4 & -2 & 0 \end{bmatrix},$$

the general solution is $x_1 = 7x_3 - 6x_4$, $x_2 = -4x_3 + 2x_4$, with x_3 and x_4 free. So

$$\mathbf{x} = \begin{bmatrix} x_1 \\ x_2 \\ x_3 \\ x_4 \end{bmatrix} = x_3\begin{bmatrix} 7 \\ -4 \\ 1 \\ 0 \end{bmatrix} + x_4\begin{bmatrix} -6 \\ 2 \\ 0 \\ 1 \end{bmatrix},$$

and a spanning set for Nul A is

$$\left\{ \begin{bmatrix} 7 \\ -4 \\ 1 \\ 0 \end{bmatrix}, \begin{bmatrix} -6 \\ 2 \\ 0 \\ 1 \end{bmatrix} \right\}.$$

4. First find the general solution of $A\mathbf{x} = \mathbf{0}$ in terms of the free variables. Since

$$\begin{bmatrix} A & \mathbf{0} \end{bmatrix} \sim \begin{bmatrix} 1 & -6 & 0 & 0 & 0 \\ 0 & 0 & 1 & 0 & 0 \end{bmatrix},$$

the general solution is $x_1 = 6x_2$, $x_3 = 0$, with x_2 and x_4 free. So

$$\mathbf{x} = \begin{bmatrix} x_1 \\ x_2 \\ x_3 \\ x_4 \end{bmatrix} = x_2\begin{bmatrix} 6 \\ 1 \\ 0 \\ 0 \end{bmatrix} + x_4\begin{bmatrix} 0 \\ 0 \\ 0 \\ 1 \end{bmatrix},$$

and a spanning set for Nul A is

$$\left\{ \begin{bmatrix} 6 \\ 1 \\ 0 \\ 0 \end{bmatrix}, \begin{bmatrix} 0 \\ 0 \\ 0 \\ 1 \end{bmatrix} \right\}.$$

5. First find the general solution of $A\mathbf{x} = \mathbf{0}$ in terms of the free variables. Since

$$\begin{bmatrix} A & \mathbf{0} \end{bmatrix} \sim \begin{bmatrix} 1 & -2 & 0 & 4 & 0 & 0 \\ 0 & 0 & 1 & -9 & 0 & 0 \\ 0 & 0 & 0 & 0 & 1 & 0 \end{bmatrix},$$

the general solution is $x_1 = 2x_2 - 4x_4$, $x_3 = 9x_4$, $x_5 = 0$, with x_2 and x_4 free. So

$$\mathbf{x} = \begin{bmatrix} x_1 \\ x_2 \\ x_3 \\ x_4 \\ x_5 \end{bmatrix} = x_2 \begin{bmatrix} 2 \\ 1 \\ 0 \\ 0 \\ 0 \end{bmatrix} + x_4 \begin{bmatrix} -4 \\ 0 \\ 9 \\ 1 \\ 0 \end{bmatrix},$$

and a spanning set for Nul A is

$$\left\{ \begin{bmatrix} 2 \\ 1 \\ 0 \\ 0 \\ 0 \end{bmatrix}, \begin{bmatrix} -4 \\ 0 \\ 9 \\ 1 \\ 0 \end{bmatrix} \right\}.$$

6. First find the general solution of $A\mathbf{x} = \mathbf{0}$ in terms of the free variables. Since

$$\begin{bmatrix} A & \mathbf{0} \end{bmatrix} \sim \begin{bmatrix} 1 & 0 & 6 & -8 & 1 & 0 \\ 0 & 1 & -2 & 1 & 0 & 0 \\ 0 & 0 & 0 & 0 & 0 & 0 \end{bmatrix},$$

the general solution is $x_1 = -6x_3 + 8x_4 - x_5$, $x_2 = 2x_3 - x_4$, with x_3, x_4, and x_5 free. So

$$\mathbf{x} = \begin{bmatrix} x_1 \\ x_2 \\ x_3 \\ x_4 \\ x_5 \end{bmatrix} = x_3 \begin{bmatrix} -6 \\ 2 \\ 1 \\ 0 \\ 0 \end{bmatrix} + x_4 \begin{bmatrix} 8 \\ -1 \\ 0 \\ 1 \\ 0 \end{bmatrix} + x_5 \begin{bmatrix} -1 \\ 0 \\ 0 \\ 0 \\ 1 \end{bmatrix},$$

and a spanning set for Nul A is

$$\left\{ \begin{bmatrix} -6 \\ 2 \\ 1 \\ 0 \\ 0 \end{bmatrix}, \begin{bmatrix} 8 \\ -1 \\ 0 \\ 1 \\ 0 \end{bmatrix}, \begin{bmatrix} -1 \\ 0 \\ 0 \\ 0 \\ 1 \end{bmatrix} \right\}.$$

7. The set W is a subset of $\mathbb{R}^3$. If W were a vector space (under the standard operations in $\mathbb{R}^3$), then it would be a subspace of $\mathbb{R}^3$. But W is not a subspace of $\mathbb{R}^3$ since the zero vector is not in W. Thus W is not a vector space.

8. The set W is a subset of $\mathbb{R}^3$. If W were a vector space (under the standard operations in $\mathbb{R}^3$), then it would be a subspace of $\mathbb{R}^3$. But W is not a subspace of $\mathbb{R}^3$ since the zero vector is not in W. Thus W is not a vector space.

9. The set W is the set of all solutions to the homogeneous system of equations $a - 2b - 4c = 0$, $2a - c - 3d = 0$. Thus $W = \text{Nul } A$, where $A = \begin{bmatrix} 1 & -2 & -4 & 0 \\ 2 & 0 & -1 & -3 \end{bmatrix}$. Thus W is a subspace of $\mathbb{R}^4$ by Theorem 2, and is a vector space.

10. The set W is the set of all solutions to the homogeneous system of equations $a + 3b - c = 0$, $a + b + c - d = 0$. Thus $W = \text{Nul } A$, where $A = \begin{bmatrix} 1 & 3 & -1 & 0 \\ 1 & 1 & 1 & -1 \end{bmatrix}$. Thus W is a subspace of $\mathbb{R}^4$ by Theorem 2, and is a vector space.

11. The set W is a subset of $\mathbb{R}^4$. If W were a vector space (under the standard operations in $\mathbb{R}^4$), then it would be a subspace of $\mathbb{R}^4$. But W is not a subspace of $\mathbb{R}^4$ since the zero vector is not in W. Thus W is not a vector space.

12. The set W is a subset of $\mathbb{R}^4$. If W were a vector space (under the standard operations in $\mathbb{R}^4$), then it would be a subspace of $\mathbb{R}^4$. But W is not a subspace of $\mathbb{R}^4$ since the zero vector is not in W. Thus W is not a vector space.

13. An element $\mathbf{w}$ on W may be written as

$$\mathbf{w} = c\begin{bmatrix} 1 \\ 0 \\ 1 \end{bmatrix} + d\begin{bmatrix} -6 \\ 1 \\ 0 \end{bmatrix} = \begin{bmatrix} 1 & -6 \\ 0 & 1 \\ 1 & 0 \end{bmatrix}\begin{bmatrix} c \\ d \end{bmatrix}$$

where c and d are any real numbers. So $W = \text{Col } A$ where $A = \begin{bmatrix} 1 & -6 \\ 0 & 1 \\ 1 & 0 \end{bmatrix}$. Thus W is a subspace of $\mathbb{R}^3$ by Theorem 3, and is a vector space.

14. An element $\mathbf{w}$ on W may be written as

$$\mathbf{w} = a\begin{bmatrix} -1 \\ 1 \\ 3 \end{bmatrix} + b\begin{bmatrix} 2 \\ -2 \\ -6 \end{bmatrix} = \begin{bmatrix} -1 & 2 \\ 1 & -2 \\ 3 & -6 \end{bmatrix}\begin{bmatrix} a \\ b \end{bmatrix}$$

where a and b are any real numbers. So $W = \text{Col } A$ where $A = \begin{bmatrix} -1 & 2 \\ 1 & -2 \\ 3 & -6 \end{bmatrix}$. Thus W is a subspace of $\mathbb{R}^3$ by Theorem 3, and is a vector space.

15. An element in this set may be written as

$$r\begin{bmatrix}0\\1\\4\\3\end{bmatrix} + s\begin{bmatrix}2\\1\\1\\-1\end{bmatrix} + t\begin{bmatrix}3\\-2\\0\\-1\end{bmatrix} = \begin{bmatrix}0 & 2 & 3\\1 & 1 & -2\\4 & 1 & 0\\3 & -1 & -1\end{bmatrix}\begin{bmatrix}r\\s\\t\end{bmatrix}$$

where r, s and t are any real numbers. So the set is Col A where $A = \begin{bmatrix}0 & 2 & 3\\1 & 1 & -2\\4 & 1 & 0\\3 & -1 & -1\end{bmatrix}$.

16. An element in this set may be written as

$$b\begin{bmatrix}1\\2\\0\\0\end{bmatrix} + c\begin{bmatrix}-1\\1\\5\\0\end{bmatrix} + d\begin{bmatrix}0\\1\\-4\\1\end{bmatrix} = \begin{bmatrix}1 & -1 & 0\\2 & 1 & 1\\0 & 5 & -4\\0 & 0 & 1\end{bmatrix}\begin{bmatrix}b\\c\\d\end{bmatrix}$$

where b, c and d are any real numbers. So the set is Col A where $A = \begin{bmatrix}1 & -1 & 0\\2 & 1 & 1\\0 & 5 & -4\\0 & 0 & 1\end{bmatrix}$.

17. The matrix A is a 4×2 matrix. Thus
   (a)   Nul A is a subspace of $\mathbb{R}^2$, and
   (b)   Col A is a subspace of $\mathbb{R}^4$.

18. The matrix A is a 4×3 matrix. Thus
   (a)   Nul A is a subspace of $\mathbb{R}^3$, and
   (b)   Col A is a subspace of $\mathbb{R}^4$.

19. The matrix A is a 2×5 matrix. Thus
   (a)   Nul A is a subspace of $\mathbb{R}^5$, and
   (b)   Col A is a subspace of $\mathbb{R}^2$.

20. The matrix A is a 1×5 matrix. Thus
   (a)   Nul A is a subspace of $\mathbb{R}^5$, and
   (b)   Col A is a subspace of $\mathbb{R}^1 = \mathbb{R}$.

21. Either column of A is a nonzero vector in Col A. To find a nonzero vector in Nul A, find the general solution of $A\mathbf{x} = \mathbf{0}$ in terms of the free variables. Since

$$\begin{bmatrix}A & \mathbf{0}\end{bmatrix} \sim \begin{bmatrix}1 & -3 & 0\\0 & 0 & 0\\0 & 0 & 0\\0 & 0 & 0\end{bmatrix},$$

the general solution is $x_1 = 3x_2$, with x_2 free. Letting x_2 be a nonzero value (say $x_2 = 1$) gives the nonzero vector

$$\mathbf{x} = \begin{bmatrix} x_1 \\ x_2 \end{bmatrix} = \begin{bmatrix} 3 \\ 1 \end{bmatrix}$$

which is in Nul A.

22. Any column of A is a nonzero vector in Col A. To find a nonzero vector in Nul A, find the general solution of $A\mathbf{x} = \mathbf{0}$ in terms of the free variables. Since

$$\begin{bmatrix} A & \mathbf{0} \end{bmatrix} \sim \begin{bmatrix} 1 & 0 & -7 & 6 & 0 \\ 0 & 1 & 4 & -2 & 0 \end{bmatrix},$$

the general solution is $x_1 = 7x_3 - 6x_4$, $x_2 = -4x_3 + 2x_4$, with x_3 and x_4 free. Letting x_3 and x_4 be nonzero values (say $x_3 = x_4 = 1$) gives the nonzero vector

$$\mathbf{x} = \begin{bmatrix} x_1 \\ x_2 \\ x_3 \\ x_4 \end{bmatrix} = \begin{bmatrix} 1 \\ -2 \\ 1 \\ 1 \end{bmatrix}$$

which is in Nul A.

23. Consider the system with augmented matrix $\begin{bmatrix} A & \mathbf{w} \end{bmatrix}$. Since

$$\begin{bmatrix} A & \mathbf{w} \end{bmatrix} \sim \begin{bmatrix} 1 & -2 & -1/3 \\ 0 & 0 & 0 \end{bmatrix},$$

the system is consistent and $\mathbf{w}$ is in Col A. Also, since

$$A\mathbf{w} = \begin{bmatrix} -6 & 12 \\ -3 & 6 \end{bmatrix} \begin{bmatrix} 2 \\ 1 \end{bmatrix} = \begin{bmatrix} 0 \\ 0 \end{bmatrix}$$

$\mathbf{w}$ is in Nul A.

24. Consider the system with augmented matrix $\begin{bmatrix} A & \mathbf{w} \end{bmatrix}$. Since

$$\begin{bmatrix} A & \mathbf{w} \end{bmatrix} \sim \begin{bmatrix} 1 & 0 & 1 & -1/2 \\ 0 & 1 & 1/2 & 1 \\ 0 & 0 & 0 & 0 \end{bmatrix},$$

the system is consistent and $\mathbf{w}$ is in Col A. Also, since

$$A\mathbf{w} = \begin{bmatrix} -8 & -2 & -9 \\ 6 & 4 & 8 \\ 4 & 0 & 4 \end{bmatrix} \begin{bmatrix} 2 \\ 1 \\ -2 \end{bmatrix} = \begin{bmatrix} 0 \\ 0 \\ 0 \end{bmatrix}$$

$\mathbf{w}$ is in Nul A.

25. a. True. See the definition before Example 1.

   b. False. See Theorem 2.

   c. True. See the remark just before Example 4.

   d. False. The equation $A\mathbf{x} = \mathbf{b}$ must be consistent *for every* $\mathbf{b}$. See #7 in the table on page 226.

   e. True. See Figure 2.

   f. True. See the remark after Theorem 3.

26. a. True. See Theorem 2.

   b. True. See Theorem 3.

   c. False. See the box after Theorem 3.

   d. True. See the paragraph after the definition of a linear transformation.

   e. True. See Figure 2.

   f. True. See the paragraph before Example 8.

27. Let A be the coefficient matrix of the given homogeneous system of equations. Since $A\mathbf{x} = \mathbf{0}$ for

$$\mathbf{x} = \begin{bmatrix} 3 \\ 2 \\ -1 \end{bmatrix}, \mathbf{x} \text{ is in Nul}A. \text{ Since Nul}A \text{ is a subspace of } \mathbb{R}^3, \text{ it is closed under scalar multiplication. Thus}$$

$$10\mathbf{x} = \begin{bmatrix} 30 \\ 20 \\ -10 \end{bmatrix} \text{ is also in Nul}A, \text{ and } x_1 = 30, x_2 = 20, x_3 = -10 \text{ is also a solution to the system of}$$

equations.

28. Let A be the coefficient matrix of the given systems of equations. Since the first system has a solution,

the constant vector $\mathbf{b} = \begin{bmatrix} 0 \\ 1 \\ 9 \end{bmatrix}$ is in Col$A$. Since Col A is a subspace of $\mathbb{R}^3$, it is closed under scalar

multiplication. Thus $5\mathbf{b} = \begin{bmatrix} 0 \\ 5 \\ 45 \end{bmatrix}$ is also in Col A, and the second system of equations must thus have a

solution.

29. a. Since $A\mathbf{0} = \mathbf{0}$, the zero vector is in Col A.

   b. Since $A\mathbf{x} + A\mathbf{w} = A(\mathbf{x} + \mathbf{w}), A\mathbf{x} + A\mathbf{w}$ is in Col A.

   c. Since $c(A\mathbf{x}) = A(c\mathbf{x}), cA\mathbf{x}$ is in Col A.

30. Since $T(\mathbf{0}_V) = \mathbf{0}_W$, the zero vector $\mathbf{0}_W$ of W is in the range of T. Let $T(\mathbf{x})$ and $T(\mathbf{w})$ be typical elements in the range of T. Then since $T(\mathbf{x}) + T(\mathbf{w}) = T(\mathbf{x} + \mathbf{w}), T(\mathbf{x}) + T(\mathbf{w})$ is in the range of T and the range of T is closed under vector addition. Let c be any scalar. Then since $cT(\mathbf{x}) = T(c\mathbf{x}), cT(\mathbf{x})$ is in the range of T and the range of T is closed under scalar multiplication. Hence the range of T is a subspace of W.

31. a. Let $\mathbf{p}$ and $\mathbf{q}$ be arbitrary polynomials in $\mathbb{P}_2$, and let c be any scalar. Then

$$T(\mathbf{p} + \mathbf{q}) = \begin{bmatrix} (\mathbf{p} + \mathbf{q})(0) \\ (\mathbf{p} + \mathbf{q})(1) \end{bmatrix} = \begin{bmatrix} \mathbf{p}(0) + \mathbf{q}(0) \\ \mathbf{p}(1) + \mathbf{q}(1) \end{bmatrix} = \begin{bmatrix} \mathbf{p}(0) \\ \mathbf{p}(1) \end{bmatrix} + \begin{bmatrix} \mathbf{q}(0) \\ \mathbf{q}(1) \end{bmatrix} = T(\mathbf{p}) + T(\mathbf{q})$$

and

$$T(c\mathbf{p}) = \begin{bmatrix} (c\mathbf{p})(0) \\ (c\mathbf{p})(1) \end{bmatrix} = c\begin{bmatrix} \mathbf{p}(0) \\ \mathbf{p}(1) \end{bmatrix} = cT(\mathbf{p})$$

so T is a linear transformation.

b. Any quadratic polynomial $\mathbf{q}$ for which $\mathbf{q}(0) = 0$ and $\mathbf{q}(1) = 0$ will be in the kernel of T. The polynomial $\mathbf{q}$ must then be a multiple of $\mathbf{p}(t) = t(t-1)$. Given any vector $\begin{bmatrix} x_1 \\ x_2 \end{bmatrix}$ in $\mathbb{R}^2$, the polynomial $\mathbf{p} = x_1 + (x_2 - x_1)t$ has $\mathbf{p}(0) = x_1$ and $\mathbf{p}(1) = x_2$. Thus the range of T is all of $\mathbb{R}^2$.

32. Any quadratic polynomial $\mathbf{q}$ for which $\mathbf{q}(0) = 0$ will be in the kernel of T. The polynomial $\mathbf{q}$ must then be $\mathbf{q} = at + bt^2$. Thus the polynomials $\mathbf{p}_1(t) = t$ and $\mathbf{p}_2(t) = t^2$ span the kernel of T. If a vector is in the range of T, it must be of the form $\begin{bmatrix} a \\ a \end{bmatrix}$. If a vector is of this form, it is the image of the polynomial $\mathbf{p}(t) = a$ in $\mathbb{P}_2$. Thus the range of T is $\left\{ \begin{bmatrix} a \\ a \end{bmatrix} : a \text{ real} \right\}$.

33. a. For any A and B in $M_{2 \times 2}$ and for any scalar c,
$$T(A + B) = (A + B) + (A + B)^T = A + B + A^T + B^T = (A + A^T) + (B + B^T) = T(A) + T(B)$$
and
$$T(cA) = (cA)^T = c(A^T) = cT(A)$$
so T is a linear transformation.

b. Let B be an element of $M_{2 \times 2}$ with $B^T = B$, and let $A = \frac{1}{2}B$. Then
$$T(A) = A + A^T = \frac{1}{2}B + (\frac{1}{2}B)^T = \frac{1}{2}B + \frac{1}{2}B^T = \frac{1}{2}B + \frac{1}{2}B = B$$

c. Part b. showed that the range of T contains the set of all B in $M_{2 \times 2}$ with $B^T = B$. It must also be shown that any B in the range of T has this property. Let B be in the range of T. Then $B = T(A)$ for some A in $M_{2 \times 2}$. Then $B = A + A^T$, and
$$B^T = (A + A^T)^T = A^T + (A^T)^T = A^T + A = A + A^T = B$$
so B has the property that $B^T = B$.

d. Let $A = \begin{bmatrix} a & b \\ c & d \end{bmatrix}$ be in the kernel of T. Then $T(A) = A + A^T = 0$, so
$$A + A^T = \begin{bmatrix} a & b \\ c & d \end{bmatrix} + \begin{bmatrix} a & c \\ b & d \end{bmatrix} = \begin{bmatrix} 2a & c+b \\ b+c & 2d \end{bmatrix} = \begin{bmatrix} 0 & 0 \\ 0 & 0 \end{bmatrix}$$
Solving it is found that $a = d = 0$ and $c = -b$. Thus the kernel of T is $\left\{ \begin{bmatrix} 0 & b \\ -b & 0 \end{bmatrix} : b \text{ real} \right\}$.

34. Let $\mathbf{f}$ and $\mathbf{g}$ be any elements in $C[0, 1]$ and let c be any scalar. Then $T(\mathbf{f})$ is the antiderivative $\mathbf{F}$ of $\mathbf{f}$ with $\mathbf{F}(0) = 0$ and $T(\mathbf{g})$ is the antiderivative $\mathbf{G}$ of $\mathbf{g}$ with $\mathbf{G}(0) = 0$. By the rules for antidifferentiation $\mathbf{F} + \mathbf{G}$ will be an antiderivative of $\mathbf{f} + \mathbf{g}$, and $(\mathbf{F} + \mathbf{G})(0) = \mathbf{F}(0) + \mathbf{G}(0) = 0 + 0 = 0$. Thus $T(\mathbf{f} + \mathbf{g}) = T(\mathbf{f}) + T(\mathbf{g})$. Likewise $c\mathbf{F}$ will be an antiderivative of $c\mathbf{f}$, and $(c\mathbf{F})(0) = c\mathbf{F}(0) = c0 = 0$. Thus $T(c\mathbf{f}) = cT(\mathbf{f})$, and T is a linear transformation. To find the kernel of T, we must find all functions f in $C[0,1]$ with antiderivative equal to the zero function. The only function with this property is the zero function $\mathbf{0}$, so the kernel of T is $\{\mathbf{0}\}$.

35. Since U is a subspace of V, $\mathbf{0}_V$ is in U. Since T is linear, $T(\mathbf{0}_V) = \mathbf{0}_W$. So $\mathbf{0}_W$ is in $T(U)$. Let $T(\mathbf{x})$ and $T(\mathbf{y})$ be typical elements in $T(U)$. Then $\mathbf{x}$ and $\mathbf{y}$ are in U, and since U is a subspace of V, $\mathbf{x}+\mathbf{y}$ is also in U. Since T is linear, $T(\mathbf{x}) + T(\mathbf{y}) = T(\mathbf{x}+\mathbf{y})$. So $T(\mathbf{x})+T(\mathbf{y})$ is in $T(U)$, and $T(U)$ is closed under vector addition. Let c be any scalar. Then since $\mathbf{x}$ is in U and U is a subspace of V, $c\mathbf{x}$ is in U. Since T is linear, $T(c\mathbf{x}) = cT(\mathbf{x})$ and $cT(\mathbf{x})$ is in $T(U)$. Thus $T(U)$ is closed under scalar multiplication, and $T(U)$ is a subspace of W.

36. Since Z is a subspace of W, $\mathbf{0}_W$ is in Z. Since T is linear, $T(\mathbf{0}_V) = \mathbf{0}_W$. So $\mathbf{0}_V$ is in U. Let $\mathbf{x}$ and $\mathbf{y}$ be typical elements in U. Then $T(\mathbf{x})$ and $T(\mathbf{y})$ are in Z, and since Z is a subspace of W, $T(\mathbf{x})+T(\mathbf{y})$ is also in Z. Since T is linear, $T(\mathbf{x})+T(\mathbf{y}) = T(\mathbf{x}+\mathbf{y})$. So $T(\mathbf{x}+\mathbf{y})$ is in Z, and $\mathbf{x}+\mathbf{y}$ is in U. Thus U is closed under vector addition. Let c be any scalar. Then since $\mathbf{x}$ is in U, $T(\mathbf{x})$ is in Z. Since Z is a subspace of W, $cT(\mathbf{x})$ is also in Z. Since T is linear, $cT(\mathbf{x}) = T(c\mathbf{x})$ and $T(c\mathbf{x})$ is in $T(U)$. Thus $c\mathbf{x}$ is in U and U is closed under scalar multiplication. Hence U is a subspace of V.

37. **[M]** Consider the system with augmented matrix $\begin{bmatrix} A & \mathbf{w} \end{bmatrix}$. Since

$$\begin{bmatrix} A & \mathbf{w} \end{bmatrix} \sim \begin{bmatrix} 1 & 0 & 0 & -1/95 & 1/95 \\ 0 & 1 & 0 & 39/19 & -20/19 \\ 0 & 0 & 1 & 267/95 & -172/95 \\ 0 & 0 & 0 & 0 & 0 \end{bmatrix},$$

the system is consistent and $\mathbf{w}$ is in Col$A$. Also, since

$$A\mathbf{w} = \begin{bmatrix} 7 & 6 & -4 & 1 \\ -5 & -1 & 0 & -2 \\ 9 & -11 & 7 & -3 \\ 19 & -9 & 7 & 1 \end{bmatrix} \begin{bmatrix} 1 \\ 1 \\ -1 \\ -3 \end{bmatrix} = \begin{bmatrix} 14 \\ 0 \\ 0 \\ 0 \end{bmatrix}$$

$\mathbf{w}$ is not in Nul$A$.

38. **[M]** Consider the system with augmented matrix $\begin{bmatrix} A & \mathbf{w} \end{bmatrix}$. Since

$$\begin{bmatrix} A & \mathbf{w} \end{bmatrix} \sim \begin{bmatrix} 1 & 0 & -1 & 0 & -2 \\ 0 & 1 & -2 & 0 & -3 \\ 0 & 0 & 0 & 1 & 1 \\ 0 & 0 & 0 & 0 & 0 \end{bmatrix},$$

the system is consistent and $\mathbf{w}$ is in Col$A$. Also, since

$$A\mathbf{w} = \begin{bmatrix} -8 & 5 & -2 & 0 \\ -5 & 2 & 1 & -2 \\ 10 & -8 & 6 & -3 \\ 3 & -2 & 1 & 0 \end{bmatrix} \begin{bmatrix} 1 \\ 2 \\ 1 \\ 0 \end{bmatrix} = \begin{bmatrix} 0 \\ 0 \\ 0 \\ 0 \end{bmatrix}$$

$\mathbf{w}$ is in Nul$A$.

39. [M]

a. To show that $\mathbf{a}_3$ and $\mathbf{a}_5$ are in the column space of B, we can row reduce the matrices $\begin{bmatrix} B & \mathbf{a}_3 \end{bmatrix}$ and $\begin{bmatrix} B & \mathbf{a}_3 \end{bmatrix}$:

$$\begin{bmatrix} B & \mathbf{a}_3 \end{bmatrix} \sim \begin{bmatrix} 1 & 0 & 0 & 1/3 \\ 0 & 1 & 0 & 1/3 \\ 0 & 0 & 1 & 0 \\ 0 & 0 & 0 & 0 \end{bmatrix}$$

$$\begin{bmatrix} B & \mathbf{a}_5 \end{bmatrix} \sim \begin{bmatrix} 1 & 0 & 0 & 10/3 \\ 0 & 1 & 0 & -26/3 \\ 0 & 0 & 1 & -4 \\ 0 & 0 & 0 & 0 \end{bmatrix}$$

Since both these systems are consistent, $\mathbf{a}_3$ and $\mathbf{a}_5$ are in the column space of B. Notice that the same conclusions can be drawn by observing the reduced row echelon form for A:

$$A \sim \begin{bmatrix} 1 & 0 & 1/3 & 0 & 10/3 \\ 0 & 1 & 1/3 & 0 & -26/3 \\ 0 & 0 & 0 & 1 & -4 \\ 0 & 0 & 0 & 0 & 0 \end{bmatrix}$$

b. We find the general solution of $A\mathbf{x} = \mathbf{0}$ in terms of the free variables by using the reduced row echelon form of A given above: $x_1 = (-1/3)x_3 - (10/3)x_5$, $x_2 = (-1/3)x_3 + (26/3)x_5$, $x_4 = 4x_5$ with x_3 and x_5 free. So

$$\mathbf{x} = \begin{bmatrix} x_1 \\ x_2 \\ x_3 \\ x_4 \\ x_5 \end{bmatrix} = x_3 \begin{bmatrix} -1/3 \\ -1/3 \\ 1 \\ 0 \\ 0 \end{bmatrix} + x_5 \begin{bmatrix} -10/3 \\ 26/3 \\ 0 \\ 4 \\ 1 \end{bmatrix},$$

and a spanning set for Nul A is

$$\left\{ \begin{bmatrix} -1/3 \\ -1/3 \\ 1 \\ 0 \\ 0 \end{bmatrix}, \begin{bmatrix} -10/3 \\ 26/3 \\ 0 \\ 4 \\ 1 \end{bmatrix} \right\}.$$

c. The reduced row echelon form of A shows that the columns of A are linearly dependent and do not span $\mathbb{R}^4$. Thus by Theorem 12 in Section 1.9, T is neither one-to-one nor onto.

40. [M] Since the line lies both in $H = \text{Span}\{\mathbf{v}_1, \mathbf{v}_2\}$ and in $K = \text{Span}\{\mathbf{v}_3, \mathbf{v}_4\}$, $\mathbf{w}$ can be written both as $c_1\mathbf{v}_1 + c_2\mathbf{v}_2$ and $c_3\mathbf{v}_3 + c_4\mathbf{v}_4$. To find w we must find the c_j's which solve $c_1\mathbf{v}_1 + c_2\mathbf{v}_2 - c_3\mathbf{v}_3 - c_4\mathbf{v}_4 = \mathbf{0}$. Row reduction of $\begin{bmatrix} \mathbf{v}_1 & \mathbf{v}_2 & -\mathbf{v}_3 & -\mathbf{v}_4 & \mathbf{0} \end{bmatrix}$ yields

$$\begin{bmatrix} 5 & 1 & -2 & 0 & 0 \\ 3 & 3 & 1 & 12 & 0 \\ 8 & 4 & -5 & 28 & 0 \end{bmatrix} \sim \begin{bmatrix} 1 & 0 & 0 & -10/3 & 0 \\ 0 & 1 & 0 & 26/3 & 0 \\ 0 & 0 & 1 & -4 & 0 \end{bmatrix},$$

so the vector of c_j's must be a multiple of $(10/3, -26/3, 4, 1)$. One simple choice is $(10, -26, 12, 3)$, which gives $\mathbf{w} = 10\mathbf{v}_1 - 26\mathbf{v}_2 = 12\mathbf{v}_3 + 3\mathbf{v}_4 = (24, -48, -24)$. Another choice for $\mathbf{w}$ is $(1, -2, -1)$.

4.3   SOLUTIONS

Notes: The definition for basis is given initially for subspaces because this emphasizes that the basis elements must be in the subspace. Students often overlook this point when the definition is given for a vector space (see Exercise 25). The subsection on bases for Nul A and Col A is essential for Sections 4.5 and 4.6. The subsection on "Two Views of a Basis" is also fundamental to understanding the interplay between linearly independent sets, spanning sets, and bases. Key exercises in this section are Exercises 21–25, which help to deepen students' understanding of these different subsets of a vector space.

1. Consider the matrix whose columns are the given set of vectors. This 3×3 matrix is in echelon form, and has 3 pivot positions. Thus by the Invertible Matrix Theorem, its columns are linearly independent and span $\mathbb{R}^3$. So the given set of vectors is a basis for $\mathbb{R}^3$.

2. Since the zero vector is a member of the given set of vectors, the set cannot be linearly independent and thus cannot be a basis for $\mathbb{R}^3$. Now consider the matrix whose columns are the given set of vectors. This 3×3 matrix has only 2 pivot positions. Thus by the Invertible Matrix Theorem, its columns do not span $\mathbb{R}^3$.

3. Consider the matrix whose columns are the given set of vectors. The reduced echelon form of this matrix is

$$\begin{bmatrix} 1 & 3 & -3 \\ 0 & 2 & -5 \\ -2 & -4 & 1 \end{bmatrix} \sim \begin{bmatrix} 1 & 0 & 9/2 \\ 0 & 1 & -5/2 \\ 0 & 0 & 0 \end{bmatrix}$$

so the matrix has only two pivot positions. Thus its columns do not form a basis for $\mathbb{R}^3$; the set of vectors is neither linearly independent nor does it span $\mathbb{R}^3$.

4. Consider the matrix whose columns are the given set of vectors. The reduced echelon form of this matrix is

$$\begin{bmatrix} 2 & 1 & -7 \\ -2 & -3 & 5 \\ 1 & 2 & 4 \end{bmatrix} \sim \begin{bmatrix} 1 & 0 & 0 \\ 0 & 1 & 0 \\ 0 & 0 & 1 \end{bmatrix}$$

so the matrix has three pivot positions. Thus its columns form a basis for $\mathbb{R}^3$.

5. Since the zero vector is a member of the given set of vectors, the set cannot be linearly independent and thus cannot be a basis for $\mathbb{R}^3$. Now consider the matrix whose columns are the given set of vectors. The reduced echelon form of this matrix is

$$\begin{bmatrix} 1 & -2 & 0 & 0 \\ -3 & 9 & 0 & -3 \\ 0 & 0 & 0 & 5 \end{bmatrix} \sim \begin{bmatrix} 1 & 0 & 0 & 0 \\ 0 & 1 & 0 & 0 \\ 0 & 0 & 0 & 1 \end{bmatrix}$$

so the matrix has a pivot in each row. Thus the given set of vectors spans $\mathbb{R}^3$.

6. Consider the matrix whose columns are the given set of vectors. Since the matrix cannot have a pivot in each row, its columns cannot span $\mathbb{R}^3$; thus the given set of vectors is not a basis for $\mathbb{R}^3$. The reduced echelon form of the matrix is

$$\begin{bmatrix} 1 & -4 \\ 2 & -5 \\ -3 & 6 \end{bmatrix} \sim \begin{bmatrix} 1 & 0 \\ 0 & 1 \\ 0 & 0 \end{bmatrix}$$

so the matrix has a pivot in each column. Thus the given set of vectors is linearly independent.

7. Consider the matrix whose columns are the given set of vectors. Since the matrix cannot have a pivot in each row, its columns cannot span $\mathbb{R}^3$; thus the given set of vectors is not a basis for $\mathbb{R}^3$. The reduced echelon form of the matrix is

$$\begin{bmatrix} -2 & 6 \\ 3 & -1 \\ 0 & 5 \end{bmatrix} \sim \begin{bmatrix} 1 & 0 \\ 0 & 1 \\ 0 & 0 \end{bmatrix}$$

so the matrix has a pivot in each column. Thus the given set of vectors is linearly independent.

8. Consider the matrix whose columns are the given set of vectors. Since the matrix cannot have a pivot in each column, the set cannot be linearly independent and thus cannot be a basis for $\mathbb{R}^3$. The reduced echelon form of this matrix is

$$\begin{bmatrix} 1 & 0 & 3 & 0 \\ -4 & 3 & -5 & 2 \\ 3 & -1 & 4 & -2 \end{bmatrix} \sim \begin{bmatrix} 1 & 0 & 0 & -3/2 \\ 0 & 1 & 0 & -1/2 \\ 0 & 0 & 1 & 1/2 \end{bmatrix}$$

so the matrix has a pivot in each row. Thus the given set of vectors spans $\mathbb{R}^3$.

9. We find the general solution of $A\mathbf{x} = \mathbf{0}$ in terms of the free variables by using the reduced echelon form of A:

$$\begin{bmatrix} 1 & 0 & -3 & 2 \\ 0 & 1 & -5 & 4 \\ 3 & -2 & 1 & -2 \end{bmatrix} \sim \begin{bmatrix} 1 & 0 & -3 & 2 \\ 0 & 1 & -5 & 4 \\ 0 & 0 & 0 & 0 \end{bmatrix}.$$

So $x_1 = 3x_3 - 2x_4$, $x_2 = 5x_3 - 4x_4$, with x_3 and x_4 free. So

$$\mathbf{x} = \begin{bmatrix} x_1 \\ x_2 \\ x_3 \\ x_4 \end{bmatrix} = x_3 \begin{bmatrix} 3 \\ 5 \\ 1 \\ 0 \end{bmatrix} + x_4 \begin{bmatrix} -2 \\ -4 \\ 0 \\ 1 \end{bmatrix},$$

and a basis for Nul A is

$$\left\{ \begin{bmatrix} 3 \\ 5 \\ 1 \\ 0 \end{bmatrix}, \begin{bmatrix} -2 \\ -4 \\ 0 \\ 1 \end{bmatrix} \right\}.$$

10. We find the general solution of $A\mathbf{x} = \mathbf{0}$ in terms of the free variables by using the reduced echelon form of A:

$$\begin{bmatrix} 1 & 0 & -5 & 1 & 4 \\ -2 & 1 & 6 & -2 & -2 \\ 0 & 2 & -8 & 1 & 9 \end{bmatrix} \sim \begin{bmatrix} 1 & 0 & -5 & 0 & 7 \\ 0 & 1 & -4 & 0 & 6 \\ 0 & 0 & 0 & 1 & -3 \end{bmatrix}.$$

So $x_1 = 5x_3 - 7x_5$, $x_2 = 4x_3 - 6x_5$, $x_4 = 3x_5$, with x_3 and x_5 free. So

$$\mathbf{x} = \begin{bmatrix} x_1 \\ x_2 \\ x_3 \\ x_4 \\ x_5 \end{bmatrix} = x_3 \begin{bmatrix} 5 \\ 4 \\ 1 \\ 0 \\ 0 \end{bmatrix} + x_5 \begin{bmatrix} -7 \\ -6 \\ 0 \\ 3 \\ 1 \end{bmatrix},$$

and a basis for Nul A is

$$\left\{ \begin{bmatrix} 5 \\ 4 \\ 1 \\ 0 \\ 0 \end{bmatrix}, \begin{bmatrix} -7 \\ -6 \\ 0 \\ 3 \\ 1 \end{bmatrix} \right\}.$$

11. Let $A = \begin{bmatrix} 1 & 2 & 1 \end{bmatrix}$. Then we wish to find a basis for Nul A. We find the general solution of $A\mathbf{x} = \mathbf{0}$ in terms of the free variables: $x = -2y - z$ with y and z free. So

$$\mathbf{x} = \begin{bmatrix} x \\ y \\ z \end{bmatrix} = y \begin{bmatrix} -2 \\ 1 \\ 0 \end{bmatrix} + z \begin{bmatrix} -1 \\ 0 \\ 1 \end{bmatrix},$$

and a basis for Nul A is

$$\left\{ \begin{bmatrix} -2 \\ 1 \\ 0 \end{bmatrix}, \begin{bmatrix} -1 \\ 0 \\ 1 \end{bmatrix} \right\}.$$

12. We want to find a basis for the set of vectors in $\mathbb{R}^2$ in the line $5x - y = 0$. Let $A = \begin{bmatrix} 5 & -1 \end{bmatrix}$. Then we wish to find a basis for Nul A. We find the general solution of $A\mathbf{x} = \mathbf{0}$ in terms of the free variables: $y = 5x$ with x free. So

$$\mathbf{x} = \begin{bmatrix} x \\ y \end{bmatrix} = x \begin{bmatrix} 1 \\ 5 \end{bmatrix},$$

and a basis for Nul A is

$$\left\{ \begin{bmatrix} 1 \\ 5 \end{bmatrix} \right\}.$$

13. Since B is a row echelon form of A, we see that the first and second columns of A are its pivot columns. Thus a basis for Col A is

$$\left\{ \begin{bmatrix} -2 \\ 2 \\ -3 \end{bmatrix}, \begin{bmatrix} 4 \\ -6 \\ 8 \end{bmatrix} \right\}.$$

To find a basis for Nul A, we find the general solution of $A\mathbf{x} = \mathbf{0}$ in terms of the free variables: $x_1 = -6x_3 - 5x_4$, $x_2 = (-5/2)x_3 - (3/2)x_4$, with x_3 and x_4 free. So

$$\mathbf{x} = \begin{bmatrix} x_1 \\ x_2 \\ x_3 \\ x_4 \end{bmatrix} = x_3 \begin{bmatrix} -6 \\ -5/2 \\ 1 \\ 0 \end{bmatrix} + x_4 \begin{bmatrix} -5 \\ -3/2 \\ 0 \\ 1 \end{bmatrix},$$

and a basis for Nul A is

$$\left\{ \begin{bmatrix} -6 \\ -5/2 \\ 1 \\ 0 \end{bmatrix}, \begin{bmatrix} -5 \\ -3/2 \\ 0 \\ 1 \end{bmatrix} \right\}.$$

14. Since B is a row echelon form of A, we see that the first, third, and fifth columns of A are its pivot columns. Thus a basis for Col A is

$$\left\{ \begin{bmatrix} 1 \\ 2 \\ 1 \\ 3 \end{bmatrix}, \begin{bmatrix} -5 \\ -5 \\ 0 \\ -5 \end{bmatrix}, \begin{bmatrix} -3 \\ 2 \\ 5 \\ -2 \end{bmatrix} \right\}.$$

To find a basis for Nul A, we find the general solution of $A\mathbf{x} = \mathbf{0}$ in terms of the free variables, mentally completing the row reduction of B to get: $x_1 = -2x_2 - 4x_4$, $x_3 = (7/5)x_4$, $x_5 = 0$, with x_2 and x_4 free. So

$$\mathbf{x} = \begin{bmatrix} x_1 \\ x_2 \\ x_3 \\ x_4 \\ x_5 \end{bmatrix} = x_2 \begin{bmatrix} -2 \\ 1 \\ 0 \\ 0 \\ 0 \end{bmatrix} + x_4 \begin{bmatrix} -4 \\ 0 \\ 7/5 \\ 1 \\ 0 \end{bmatrix},$$

and a basis for Nul A is

$$\left\{ \begin{bmatrix} -2 \\ 1 \\ 0 \\ 0 \\ 0 \end{bmatrix}, \begin{bmatrix} -4 \\ 0 \\ 7/5 \\ 1 \\ 0 \end{bmatrix} \right\}.$$

15. This problem is equivalent to finding a basis for Col A, where $A = \begin{bmatrix} \mathbf{v}_1 & \mathbf{v}_2 & \mathbf{v}_3 & \mathbf{v}_4 & \mathbf{v}_5 \end{bmatrix}$. Since the reduced echelon form of A is

$$\begin{bmatrix} 1 & 0 & -3 & 1 & 2 \\ 0 & 1 & -4 & -3 & 1 \\ -3 & 2 & 1 & -8 & -6 \\ 2 & -3 & 6 & 7 & 9 \end{bmatrix} \sim \begin{bmatrix} 1 & 0 & -3 & 0 & 4 \\ 0 & 1 & -4 & 0 & -5 \\ 0 & 0 & 0 & 1 & -2 \\ 0 & 0 & 0 & 0 & 0 \end{bmatrix},$$

we see that the first, second, and fourth columns of A are its pivot columns. Thus a basis for the space spanned by the given vectors is

$$\left\{ \begin{bmatrix} 1 \\ 0 \\ -3 \\ 2 \end{bmatrix}, \begin{bmatrix} 0 \\ 1 \\ 2 \\ -3 \end{bmatrix}, \begin{bmatrix} 1 \\ -3 \\ -8 \\ 7 \end{bmatrix} \right\}.$$

16. This problem is equivalent to finding a basis for Col A, where $A = \begin{bmatrix} \mathbf{v}_1 & \mathbf{v}_2 & \mathbf{v}_3 & \mathbf{v}_4 & \mathbf{v}_5 \end{bmatrix}$. Since the reduced echelon form of A is

$$\begin{bmatrix} 1 & -2 & 6 & 5 & 0 \\ 0 & 1 & -1 & -3 & 3 \\ 0 & -1 & 2 & 3 & -1 \\ 1 & 1 & -1 & -4 & 1 \end{bmatrix} \sim \begin{bmatrix} 1 & 0 & 0 & -1 & -2 \\ 0 & 1 & 0 & -3 & 5 \\ 0 & 0 & 1 & 0 & 2 \\ 0 & 0 & 0 & 0 & 0 \end{bmatrix},$$

we see that the first, second, and third columns of A are its pivot columns. Thus a basis for the space spanned by the given vectors is

$$\left\{ \begin{bmatrix} 1 \\ 0 \\ 0 \\ 1 \end{bmatrix}, \begin{bmatrix} -2 \\ 1 \\ -1 \\ 1 \end{bmatrix}, \begin{bmatrix} 6 \\ -1 \\ 2 \\ -1 \end{bmatrix} \right\}.$$

17. **[M]** This problem is equivalent to finding a basis for Col A, where $A = \begin{bmatrix} \mathbf{v}_1 & \mathbf{v}_2 & \mathbf{v}_3 & \mathbf{v}_4 & \mathbf{v}_5 \end{bmatrix}$. Since the reduced echelon form of A is

$$\begin{bmatrix} 8 & 4 & -1 & 6 & -1 \\ 9 & 5 & -4 & 8 & 4 \\ -3 & 1 & -9 & 4 & 11 \\ -6 & -4 & 6 & -7 & -8 \\ 0 & 4 & -7 & 10 & -7 \end{bmatrix} \sim \begin{bmatrix} 1 & 0 & 0 & -1/2 & 3 \\ 0 & 1 & 0 & 5/2 & -7 \\ 0 & 0 & 1 & 0 & -3 \\ 0 & 0 & 0 & 0 & 0 \\ 0 & 0 & 0 & 0 & 0 \end{bmatrix},$$

we see that the first, second, and third columns of A are its pivot columns. Thus a basis for the space spanned by the given vectors is

$$\left\{ \begin{bmatrix} 8 \\ 9 \\ -3 \\ -6 \\ 0 \end{bmatrix}, \begin{bmatrix} 4 \\ 5 \\ 1 \\ -4 \\ 4 \end{bmatrix}, \begin{bmatrix} -1 \\ -4 \\ -9 \\ 6 \\ -7 \end{bmatrix} \right\}.$$

18. [M] This problem is equivalent to finding a basis for Col A, where $A = \begin{bmatrix} \mathbf{v}_1 & \mathbf{v}_2 & \mathbf{v}_3 & \mathbf{v}_4 & \mathbf{v}_5 \end{bmatrix}$. Since the reduced echelon form of A is

$$\begin{bmatrix} -8 & 8 & -8 & 1 & -9 \\ 7 & -7 & 7 & 4 & 3 \\ 6 & -9 & 4 & 9 & -4 \\ 5 & -5 & 5 & 6 & -1 \\ -7 & 7 & -7 & -7 & 0 \end{bmatrix} \sim \begin{bmatrix} 1 & 0 & 5/3 & 0 & 4/3 \\ 0 & 1 & 2/3 & 0 & 1/3 \\ 0 & 0 & 0 & 1 & -1 \\ 0 & 0 & 0 & 0 & 0 \\ 0 & 0 & 0 & 0 & 0 \end{bmatrix},$$

we see that the first, second, and fourth columns of A are its pivot columns. Thus a basis for the space spanned by the given vectors is

$$\left\{ \begin{bmatrix} -8 \\ 7 \\ 6 \\ 5 \\ -7 \end{bmatrix}, \begin{bmatrix} 8 \\ -7 \\ -9 \\ -5 \\ 7 \end{bmatrix}, \begin{bmatrix} 1 \\ 4 \\ 9 \\ 6 \\ -7 \end{bmatrix} \right\}.$$

19. Since $4\mathbf{v}_1 + 5\mathbf{v}_2 - 3\mathbf{v}_3 = \mathbf{0}$, we see that each of the vectors is a linear combination of the others. Thus the sets $\{\mathbf{v}_1, \mathbf{v}_2\}$, $\{\mathbf{v}_1, \mathbf{v}_3\}$, and $\{\mathbf{v}_2, \mathbf{v}_3\}$ all span H. Since we may confirm that none of the three vectors is a multiple of any of the others, the sets $\{\mathbf{v}_1, \mathbf{v}_2\}$, $\{\mathbf{v}_1, \mathbf{v}_3\}$, and $\{\mathbf{v}_2, \mathbf{v}_3\}$ are linearly independent and thus each forms a basis for H.

20. Since $\mathbf{v}_1 - 3\mathbf{v}_2 + 5\mathbf{v}_3 = \mathbf{0}$, we see that each of the vectors is a linear combination of the others. Thus the sets $\{\mathbf{v}_1, \mathbf{v}_2\}$, $\{\mathbf{v}_1, \mathbf{v}_3\}$, and $\{\mathbf{v}_2, \mathbf{v}_3\}$ all span H. Since we may confirm that none of the three vectors is a multiple of any of the others, the sets $\{\mathbf{v}_1, \mathbf{v}_2\}$, $\{\mathbf{v}_1, \mathbf{v}_3\}$, and $\{\mathbf{v}_2, \mathbf{v}_3\}$ are linearly independent and thus each forms a basis for H.

21. **a.** False. The zero vector by itself is linearly dependent. See the paragraph preceding Theorem 4.

   b. False. The set $\{\mathbf{b}_1, \ldots, \mathbf{b}_p\}$ must also be linearly independent. See the definition of a basis.

   c. True. See Example 3.

   d. False. See the subsection "Two Views of a Basis."

   e. False. See the box before Example 9.

22. **a.** False. The subspace spanned by the set must also coincide with H. See the definition of a basis.

   b. True. Apply the Spanning Set Theorem to V instead of H. The space V is nonzero because the spanning set uses nonzero vectors.

   c. True. See the subsection "Two Views of a Basis."

   d. False. See the two paragraphs before Example 8.

   e. False. See the warning after Theorem 6.

23. Let $A = \begin{bmatrix} \mathbf{v}_1 & \mathbf{v}_2 & \mathbf{v}_3 & \mathbf{v}_4 \end{bmatrix}$. Then A is square and its columns span $\mathbb{R}^4$ since $\mathbb{R}^4 = \mathrm{Span}\{\mathbf{v}_1, \mathbf{v}_2, \mathbf{v}_3, \mathbf{v}_4\}$. So its columns are linearly independent by the Invertible Matrix Theorem, and $\{\mathbf{v}_1, \mathbf{v}_2, \mathbf{v}_3, \mathbf{v}_4\}$ is a basis for $\mathbb{R}^4$.

24. Let $A = \begin{bmatrix} \mathbf{v}_1 & \cdots & \mathbf{v}_n \end{bmatrix}$. Then A is square and its columns are linearly independent, so its columns span $\mathbb{R}^n$ by the Invertible Matrix Theorem. Thus $\{\mathbf{v}_1, \ldots, \mathbf{v}_n\}$ is a basis for $\mathbb{R}^n$.

25. In order for the set to be a basis for H, $\{\mathbf{v}_1, \mathbf{v}_2, \mathbf{v}_3\}$ must be a spanning set for H; that is, $H = \text{Span}\{\mathbf{v}_1, \mathbf{v}_2, \mathbf{v}_3\}$. The exercise shows that H is a subset of $\text{Span}\{\mathbf{v}_1, \mathbf{v}_2, \mathbf{v}_3\}$. but there are vectors in $\text{Span}\{\mathbf{v}_1, \mathbf{v}_2, \mathbf{v}_3\}$ which are not in H ($\mathbf{v}_1$ and $\mathbf{v}_3$, for example). So $H \neq \text{Span}\{\mathbf{v}_1, \mathbf{v}_2, \mathbf{v}_3\}$, and $\{\mathbf{v}_1, \mathbf{v}_2, \mathbf{v}_3\}$ is not a basis for H.

26. Since $\sin t \cos t = (1/2) \sin 2t$, the set $\{\sin t, \sin 2t\}$ spans the subspace. By inspection we note that this set is linearly independent, so $\{\sin t, \sin 2t\}$ is a basis for the subspace.

27. The set $\{\cos \omega t, \sin \omega t\}$ spans the subspace. By inspection we note that this set is linearly independent, so $\{\cos \omega t, \sin \omega t\}$ is a basis for the subspace.

28. The set $\{e^{-bt}, te^{-bt}\}$ spans the subspace. By inspection we note that this set is linearly independent, so $\{e^{-bt}, te^{-bt}\}$ is a basis for the subspace.

29. Let A be the $n \times k$ matrix $\begin{bmatrix} \mathbf{v}_1 & \dots & \mathbf{v}_k \end{bmatrix}$. Since A has fewer columns than rows, there cannot be a pivot position in each row of A. By Theorem 4 in Section 1.4, the columns of A do not span $\mathbb{R}^n$ and thus are not a basis for $\mathbb{R}^n$.

30. Let A be the $n \times k$ matrix $\begin{bmatrix} \mathbf{v}_1 & \dots & \mathbf{v}_k \end{bmatrix}$. Since A has fewer rows than columns rows, there cannot be a pivot position in each column of A. By Theorem 8 in Section 1.6, the columns of A are not linearly independent and thus are not a basis for $\mathbb{R}^n$.

31. Suppose that $\{\mathbf{v}_1, \dots, \mathbf{v}_p\}$ is linearly dependent. Then there exist scalars $c_1, \dots, c_p$ not all zero with

$$c_1 \mathbf{v}_1 + \dots + c_p \mathbf{v}_p = \mathbf{0}.$$

Since T is linear,

$$T(c_1 \mathbf{v}_1 + \dots + c_p \mathbf{v}_p) = c_1 T(\mathbf{v}_1) + \dots + c_p T(\mathbf{v}_p)$$

and

$$T(c_1 \mathbf{v}_1 + \dots + c_p \mathbf{v}_p) = T(\mathbf{0}) = \mathbf{0}.$$

Thus

$$c_1 T(\mathbf{v}_1) + \dots + c_p T(\mathbf{v}_p) = \mathbf{0}$$

and since not all of the c_i are zero, $\{T(\mathbf{v}_1), \dots, T(\mathbf{v}_p)\}$ is linearly dependent.

32. Suppose that $\{T(\mathbf{v}_1), \dots, T(\mathbf{v}_p)\}$ is linearly dependent. Then there exist scalars $c_1, \dots, c_p$ not all zero with

$$c_1 T(\mathbf{v}_1) + \dots + c_p T(\mathbf{v}_p) = \mathbf{0}.$$

Since T is linear,

$$T(c_1 \mathbf{v}_1 + \dots + c_p \mathbf{v}_p) = c_1 T(\mathbf{v}_1) + \dots + c_p T(\mathbf{v}_p) = \mathbf{0} = T(\mathbf{0})$$

Since T is one-to-one

$$T(c_1 \mathbf{v}_1 + \dots + c_p \mathbf{v}_p) = T(\mathbf{0})$$

implies that

$$c_1 \mathbf{v}_1 + \dots + c_p \mathbf{v}_p = \mathbf{0}.$$

Since not all of the c_i are zero, $\{\mathbf{v}_1, \dots, \mathbf{v}_p\}$ is linearly dependent.

33. Neither polynomial is a multiple of the other polynomial. So $\{\mathbf{p}_1, \mathbf{p}_2\}$ is a linearly independent set in $\mathbb{P}_3$.
Note: $\{\mathbf{p}_1, \mathbf{p}_2\}$ is also a linearly independent set in $\mathbb{P}_2$ since $\mathbf{p}_1$ and $\mathbf{p}_2$ both happen to be in $\mathbb{P}_2$.

34. By inspection, $\mathbf{p}_3 = \mathbf{p}_1 + \mathbf{p}_2$, or $\mathbf{p}_1 + \mathbf{p}_2 - \mathbf{p}_3 = \mathbf{0}$. By the Spanning Set Theorem,
Span $\{\mathbf{p}_1, \mathbf{p}_2, \mathbf{p}_3\} =$ Span $\{\mathbf{p}_1, \mathbf{p}_2\}$. Since neither $\mathbf{p}_1$ nor $\mathbf{p}_2$ is a multiple of the other, they are linearly independent and hence $\{\mathbf{p}_1, \mathbf{p}_2\}$ is a basis for Span $\{\mathbf{p}_1, \mathbf{p}_2, \mathbf{p}_3\}$.

35. Let $\{\mathbf{v}_1, \mathbf{v}_3\}$ be any linearly independent set in a vector space V, and let $\mathbf{v}_2$ and $\mathbf{v}_4$ each be linear combinations of $\mathbf{v}_1$ and $\mathbf{v}_3$. For instance, let $\mathbf{v}_2 = 5\mathbf{v}_1$ and $\mathbf{v}_4 = \mathbf{v}_1 + \mathbf{v}_3$. Then $\{\mathbf{v}_1, \mathbf{v}_3\}$ is a basis for Span $\{\mathbf{v}_1, \mathbf{v}_2, \mathbf{v}_3, \mathbf{v}_4\}$.

36. **[M]** Row reduce the following matrices to identify their pivot columns:

$$\begin{bmatrix} \mathbf{u}_1 & \mathbf{u}_2 & \mathbf{u}_3 \end{bmatrix} = \begin{bmatrix} 1 & 0 & 2 \\ 2 & 2 & 2 \\ 3 & -1 & 7 \\ -1 & 1 & -3 \end{bmatrix} \sim \begin{bmatrix} 1 & 0 & 2 \\ 0 & 1 & -1 \\ 0 & 0 & 0 \\ 0 & 0 & 0 \end{bmatrix}, \text{ so } \{\mathbf{u}_1, \mathbf{u}_2\} \text{ is a basis for } H.$$

$$\begin{bmatrix} \mathbf{v}_1 & \mathbf{v}_2 & \mathbf{v}_3 \end{bmatrix} = \begin{bmatrix} 1 & 2 & -1 \\ 0 & -2 & 4 \\ 8 & 9 & 6 \\ -4 & -5 & -2 \end{bmatrix} \sim \begin{bmatrix} 1 & 0 & 3 \\ 0 & 1 & -2 \\ 0 & 0 & 0 \\ 0 & 0 & 0 \end{bmatrix}, \text{ so } \{\mathbf{v}_1, \mathbf{v}_2\} \text{ is a basis for } K.$$

$$\begin{bmatrix} \mathbf{u}_1 & \mathbf{u}_2 & \mathbf{u}_3 & \mathbf{v}_1 & \mathbf{v}_2 & \mathbf{v}_3 \end{bmatrix} = \begin{bmatrix} 1 & 0 & 2 & 1 & 2 & -1 \\ 2 & 2 & 2 & 0 & -2 & 4 \\ 3 & -1 & 7 & 8 & 9 & 6 \\ -1 & 1 & -3 & -4 & -5 & -2 \end{bmatrix}$$

$$\sim \begin{bmatrix} 1 & 0 & 2 & 0 & 2 & -4 \\ 0 & 1 & -1 & 0 & -3 & 6 \\ 0 & 0 & 0 & 1 & 0 & 3 \\ 0 & 0 & 0 & 0 & 0 & 0 \end{bmatrix}, \text{ so } \{\mathbf{u}_1, \mathbf{u}_2, \mathbf{v}_1\} \text{ is a basis for } H + K.$$

37. **[M]** For example, writing

$$c_1 \cdot t + c_2 \cdot \sin t + c_3 \cos 2t + c_4 \sin t \cos t = 0$$

with $t = 0, .1, .2, .3$ gives the following coefficient matrix A for the homogeneous system $A\mathbf{c} = \mathbf{0}$ (to four decimal places):

$$A = \begin{bmatrix} 0 & \sin 0 & \cos 0 & \sin 0 \cos 0 \\ .1 & \sin .1 & \cos .2 & \sin .1 \cos .1 \\ .2 & \sin .2 & \cos .4 & \sin .2 \cos .2 \\ .3 & \sin .3 & \cos .6 & \sin .3 \cos .3 \end{bmatrix} = \begin{bmatrix} 0 & 0 & 1 & 0 \\ .1 & .0998 & .9801 & .0993 \\ .2 & .1987 & .9211 & .1947 \\ .3 & .2955 & .8253 & .2823 \end{bmatrix}.$$

This matrix is invertible, so the system $A\mathbf{c} = \mathbf{0}$ has only the trivial solution and $\{t, \sin t, \cos 2t, \sin t \cos t\}$ is a linearly independent set of functions.

38. [M] For example, writing

$$c_1 \cdot 1 + c_2 \cdot \cos t + c_3 \cdot \cos^2 t + c_4 \cdot \cos^3 t + c_5 \cdot \cos^4 t + c_6 \cdot \cos^5 t + c_7 \cdot \cos^6 t = 0$$

with $t = 0, .1, .2, .3, .4, .5, .6$ gives the following coefficent matrix A for the homogeneous system $A\mathbf{c} = \mathbf{0}$ (to four decimal places):

$$A = \begin{bmatrix} 1 & \cos 0 & \cos^2 0 & \cos^3 0 & \cos^4 0 & \cos^5 0 & \cos^6 0 \\ 1 & \cos .1 & \cos^2 .1 & \cos^3 .1 & \cos^4 .1 & \cos^5 .1 & \cos^6 .1 \\ 1 & \cos .2 & \cos^2 .2 & \cos^3 .2 & \cos^4 .2 & \cos^5 .2 & \cos^6 .2 \\ 1 & \cos .3 & \cos^2 .3 & \cos^3 .3 & \cos^4 .3 & \cos^5 .3 & \cos^6 .3 \\ 1 & \cos .4 & \cos^2 .4 & \cos^3 .4 & \cos^4 .4 & \cos^5 .4 & \cos^6 .4 \\ 1 & \cos .5 & \cos^2 .5 & \cos^3 .5 & \cos^4 .5 & \cos^5 .5 & \cos^6 .5 \\ 1 & \cos .6 & \cos^2 .6 & \cos^3 .6 & \cos^4 .6 & \cos^5 .6 & \cos^6 .6 \end{bmatrix}$$

$$= \begin{bmatrix} 1 & 1 & 1 & 1 & 1 & 1 & 1 \\ 1 & .9950 & .9900 & .9851 & .9802 & .9753 & .9704 \\ 1 & .9801 & .9605 & .9414 & .9226 & .9042 & .8862 \\ 1 & .9553 & .9127 & .8719 & .8330 & .7958 & .7602 \\ 1 & .9211 & .8484 & .7814 & .7197 & .6629 & .6106 \\ 1 & .8776 & .7702 & .6759 & .5931 & .5205 & .4568 \\ 1 & .8253 & .6812 & .5622 & .4640 & .3830 & .3161 \end{bmatrix}$$

This matrix is invertible, so the system $A\mathbf{c} = 0$ has only the trivial solution and $\{1, \cos t, \cos^2 t, \cos^3 t, \cos^4 t, \cos^5 t, \cos^6 t\}$ is a linearly independent set of functions.

4.4   SOLUTIONS

Notes: Section 4.7 depends heavily on this section, as does Section 5.4. It is possible to cover the $\mathbb{R}^n$ parts of the two later sections, however, if the first half of Section 4.4 (and perhaps Example 7) is covered. The linearity of the coordinate mapping is used in Section 5.4 to find the matrix of a transformation relative to two bases. The change-of-coordinates matrix appears in Section 5.4, Theorem 8 and Exercise 27. The concept of an isomorphism is needed in the proof of Theorem 17 in Section 4.8. Exercise 25 is used in Section 4.7 to show that the change-of-coordinates matrix is invertible.

1. We calculate that

$$\mathbf{x} = 5 \begin{bmatrix} 3 \\ -5 \end{bmatrix} + 3 \begin{bmatrix} -4 \\ 6 \end{bmatrix} = \begin{bmatrix} 3 \\ -7 \end{bmatrix}.$$

2. We calculate that

$$\mathbf{x} = 8 \begin{bmatrix} 4 \\ 5 \end{bmatrix} + (-5) \begin{bmatrix} 6 \\ 7 \end{bmatrix} = \begin{bmatrix} 2 \\ 5 \end{bmatrix}.$$

3. We calculate that

$$\mathbf{x} = 3 \begin{bmatrix} 1 \\ -4 \\ 3 \end{bmatrix} + 0 \begin{bmatrix} 5 \\ 2 \\ -2 \end{bmatrix} + (-1) \begin{bmatrix} 4 \\ -7 \\ 0 \end{bmatrix} = \begin{bmatrix} -1 \\ -5 \\ 9 \end{bmatrix}.$$

4. We calculate that

$$\mathbf{x} = (-4)\begin{bmatrix} -1 \\ 2 \\ 0 \end{bmatrix} + 8\begin{bmatrix} 3 \\ -5 \\ 2 \end{bmatrix} + (-7)\begin{bmatrix} 4 \\ -7 \\ 3 \end{bmatrix} = \begin{bmatrix} 0 \\ 1 \\ -5 \end{bmatrix}.$$

5. The matrix $\begin{bmatrix} \mathbf{b}_1 & \mathbf{b}_2 & \mathbf{x} \end{bmatrix}$ row reduces to $\begin{bmatrix} 1 & 0 & 8 \\ 0 & 1 & -5 \end{bmatrix}$, so $[\mathbf{x}]_B = \begin{bmatrix} 8 \\ -5 \end{bmatrix}$.

6. The matrix $\begin{bmatrix} \mathbf{b}_1 & \mathbf{b}_2 & \mathbf{x} \end{bmatrix}$ row reduces to $\begin{bmatrix} 1 & 0 & -6 \\ 0 & 1 & 2 \end{bmatrix}$, so $[\mathbf{x}]_B = \begin{bmatrix} -6 \\ 2 \end{bmatrix}$.

7. The matrix $\begin{bmatrix} \mathbf{b}_1 & \mathbf{b}_2 & \mathbf{b}_3 & \mathbf{x} \end{bmatrix}$ row reduces to $\begin{bmatrix} 1 & 0 & 0 & -1 \\ 0 & 1 & 0 & -1 \\ 0 & 0 & 1 & 3 \end{bmatrix}$, so $[\mathbf{x}]_B = \begin{bmatrix} -1 \\ -1 \\ 3 \end{bmatrix}$.

8. The matrix $\begin{bmatrix} \mathbf{b}_1 & \mathbf{b}_2 & \mathbf{b}_3 & \mathbf{x} \end{bmatrix}$ row reduces to $\begin{bmatrix} 1 & 0 & 0 & -2 \\ 0 & 1 & 0 & 0 \\ 0 & 0 & 1 & 5 \end{bmatrix}$, so $[\mathbf{x}]_B = \begin{bmatrix} -2 \\ 0 \\ 5 \end{bmatrix}$.

9. The change-of-coordinates matrix from B to the standard basis in $\mathbb{R}^2$ is

$$P_B = \begin{bmatrix} \mathbf{b}_1 & \mathbf{b}_2 \end{bmatrix} = \begin{bmatrix} 2 & 1 \\ -9 & 8 \end{bmatrix}.$$

10. The change-of-coordinates matrix from B to the standard basis in $\mathbb{R}^3$ is

$$P_B = \begin{bmatrix} \mathbf{b}_1 & \mathbf{b}_2 & \mathbf{b}_3 \end{bmatrix} = \begin{bmatrix} 3 & 2 & 8 \\ -1 & 0 & -2 \\ 4 & -5 & 7 \end{bmatrix}.$$

11. Since P_B^{-1} converts $\mathbf{x}$ into its B-coordinate vector, we find that

$$[\mathbf{x}]_B = P_B^{-1}\mathbf{x} = \begin{bmatrix} 3 & -4 \\ -5 & 6 \end{bmatrix}^{-1}\begin{bmatrix} 2 \\ -6 \end{bmatrix} = \begin{bmatrix} -3 & -2 \\ -5/2 & -3/2 \end{bmatrix}\begin{bmatrix} 2 \\ -6 \end{bmatrix} = \begin{bmatrix} 6 \\ 4 \end{bmatrix}.$$

12. Since P_B^{-1} converts $\mathbf{x}$ into its B-coordinate vector, we find that

$$[\mathbf{x}]_B = P_B^{-1}\mathbf{x} = \begin{bmatrix} 4 & 6 \\ 5 & 7 \end{bmatrix}^{-1}\begin{bmatrix} 2 \\ 0 \end{bmatrix} = \begin{bmatrix} -7/2 & 3 \\ 5/2 & -2 \end{bmatrix}\begin{bmatrix} 2 \\ 0 \end{bmatrix} = \begin{bmatrix} -7 \\ 5 \end{bmatrix}.$$

13. We must find c_1, c_2, and c_3 such that

$$c_1(1+t^2) + c_2(t+t^2) + c_3(1+2t+t^2) = \mathbf{p}(t) = 1 + 4t + 7t^2.$$

Equating the coefficients of the two polynomials produces the system of equations

$$
\begin{array}{rcrcrcl}
c_1 & & & + & c_3 & = & 1 \\
 & & c_2 & + & 2c_3 & = & 4 \\
c_1 & + & c_2 & + & c_3 & = & 7
\end{array}
$$

We row reduce the augmented matrix for the system of equations to find

$$\begin{bmatrix} 1 & 0 & 1 & 1 \\ 0 & 1 & 2 & 4 \\ 1 & 1 & 1 & 7 \end{bmatrix} \sim \begin{bmatrix} 1 & 0 & 0 & 2 \\ 0 & 1 & 0 & 6 \\ 0 & 0 & 1 & -1 \end{bmatrix}, \text{ so } [\mathbf{p}]_B = \begin{bmatrix} 2 \\ 6 \\ -1 \end{bmatrix}.$$

One may also solve this problem using the coordinate vectors of the given polynomials relative to the standard basis $\{1, t, t^2\}$; the same system of linear equations results.

14. We must find c_1, c_2, and c_3 such that

$$c_1(1-t^2) + c_2(t-t^2) + c_3(2-2t+t^2) = \mathbf{p}(t) = 3 + t - 6t^2.$$

Equating the coefficients of the two polynomials produces the system of equations

$$\begin{array}{rcrcrcr} c_1 & & & + & 2c_3 & = & 3 \\ & & c_2 & - & 2c_3 & = & 1 \\ -c_1 & - & c_2 & + & c_3 & = & -6 \end{array}$$

We row reduce the augmented matrix for the system of equations to find

$$\begin{bmatrix} 1 & 0 & 2 & 3 \\ 0 & 1 & -2 & 1 \\ -1 & -1 & 1 & -6 \end{bmatrix} \sim \begin{bmatrix} 1 & 0 & 0 & 7 \\ 0 & 1 & 0 & -3 \\ 0 & 0 & 1 & -2 \end{bmatrix}, \text{ so } [\mathbf{p}]_B = \begin{bmatrix} 7 \\ -3 \\ -2 \end{bmatrix}.$$

One may also solve this problem using the coordinate vectors of the given polynomials relative to the standard basis $\{1, t, t^2\}$; the same system of linear equations results.

15. a. True. See the definition of the B-coordinate vector.

   b. False. See Equation (4).

   c. False. $\mathbb{P}_3$ is isomorphic to $\mathbb{R}^4$. See Example 5.

16. a. True. See Example 2.

   b. False. By definition, the coordinate mapping goes in the opposite direction.

   c. True. If the plane passes through the origin, as in Example 7, the plane is isomorphic to $\mathbb{R}^2$.

17. We must solve the vector equation $x_1 \begin{bmatrix} 1 \\ -3 \end{bmatrix} + x_2 \begin{bmatrix} 2 \\ -8 \end{bmatrix} + x_3 \begin{bmatrix} -3 \\ 7 \end{bmatrix} = \begin{bmatrix} 1 \\ 1 \end{bmatrix}$. We row reduce the augmented matrix for the system of equations to find

$$\begin{bmatrix} 1 & 2 & -3 & 1 \\ -3 & -8 & 7 & 1 \end{bmatrix} \sim \begin{bmatrix} 1 & 0 & -5 & 5 \\ 0 & 1 & 1 & -2 \end{bmatrix}.$$

Thus we can let $x_1 = 5 + 5x_3$ and $x_2 = -2 - x_3$, where x_3 can be any real number. Letting $x_3 = 0$ and $x_3 = 1$ produces two different ways to express $\begin{bmatrix} 1 \\ 1 \end{bmatrix}$ as a linear combination of the other vectors:

$5\mathbf{v}_1 - 2\mathbf{v}_2$ and $10\mathbf{v}_1 - 3\mathbf{v}_2 + \mathbf{v}_3$. There are infintely many correct answers to this problem.

18. For each k, $\mathbf{b}_k = 0 \cdot \mathbf{b}_1 + \cdots + 1 \cdot \mathbf{b}_k + \cdots + 0 \cdot \mathbf{b}_n$, so $[\mathbf{b}_k]_B = (0, \ldots, 1, \ldots, 0) = \mathbf{e}_k$.

19. The set S spans V because every $\mathbf{x}$ in V has a representation as a (unique) linear combination of elements in S. To show linear independence, suppose that $S = \{\mathbf{v}_1, \ldots, \mathbf{v}_n\}$ and that $c_1\mathbf{v}_1 + \cdots + c_n\mathbf{v}_n = \mathbf{0}$ for some scalars $c_1, \ldots, c_n$. The case when $c_1 = \cdots = c_n = 0$ is one possibility. By hypothesis, this is the unique (and thus the only) possible representation of the zero vector as a linear combination of the elements in S. So S is linearly independent and is thus a basis for V.

20. For **w** in V there exist scalars k_1, k_2, k_3, and k_4 such that

$$\mathbf{w} = k_1\mathbf{v}_1 + k_2\mathbf{v}_2 + k_3\mathbf{v}_3 + k_4\mathbf{v}_4 \tag{1}$$

because $\{\mathbf{v}_1, \mathbf{v}_2, \mathbf{v}_3, \mathbf{v}_4\}$ spans V. Because the set is linearly dependent, there exist scalars c_1, c_2, c_3, and c_4 not all zero, such that

$$\mathbf{0} = c_1\mathbf{v}_1 + c_2\mathbf{v}_2 + c_3\mathbf{v}_3 + c_4\mathbf{v}_4 \tag{2}$$

Adding (1) and (2) gives

$$\mathbf{w} = \mathbf{w} + \mathbf{0} = (k_1 + c_1)\mathbf{v}_1 + (k_2 + c_2)\mathbf{v}_2 + (k_3 + c_3)\mathbf{v}_3 + (k_4 + c_4)\mathbf{v}_4 \tag{3}$$

At least one of the weights in (3) differs from the corresponding weight in (1) because at least one of the c_i is nonzero. So **w** is expressed in more than one way as a linear combination of $\mathbf{v}_1$, $\mathbf{v}_2$, $\mathbf{v}_3$, and $\mathbf{v}_4$.

21. The matrix of the transformation will be $P_B^{-1} = \begin{bmatrix} 1 & -2 \\ -4 & 9 \end{bmatrix}^{-1} = \begin{bmatrix} 9 & 2 \\ 4 & 1 \end{bmatrix}$.

22. The matrix of the transformation will be $P_B^{-1} = \begin{bmatrix} \mathbf{b}_1 & \cdots & \mathbf{b}_n \end{bmatrix}^{-1}$.

23. Suppose that

$$[\mathbf{u}]_B = [\mathbf{w}]_B = \begin{bmatrix} c_1 \\ \vdots \\ c_n \end{bmatrix}.$$

By definition of coordinate vectors,

$$\mathbf{u} = \mathbf{w} = c_1\mathbf{b}_1 + \cdots + c_n\mathbf{b}_n.$$

Since **u** and **w** were arbitrary elements of V, the coordinate mapping is one-to-one.

24. Given $\mathbf{y} = (y_1, \ldots, y_n)$ in $\mathbb{R}^n$, let $\mathbf{u} = y_1\mathbf{b}_1 + \cdots + y_n\mathbf{b}_n$. Then, by definition, $[\mathbf{u}]_B = \mathbf{y}$. Since **y** was arbitrary, the coordinate mapping is onto $\mathbb{R}^n$.

25. Since the coordinate mapping is one-to-one, the following equations have the same solutions $c_1, \ldots, c_p$:

$$c_1\mathbf{u}_1 + \cdots + c_p\mathbf{u}_p = \mathbf{0} \qquad \text{(the zero vector in } V) \tag{4}$$

$$\left[c_1\mathbf{u}_1 + \cdots + c_p\mathbf{u}_p \right]_B = [\mathbf{0}]_B \qquad \text{(the zero vector in } \mathbb{R}^n) \tag{5}$$

Since the coordinate mapping is linear, (5) is equivalent to

$$c_1[\mathbf{u}_1]_B + \cdots + c_p[\mathbf{u}_p]_B = \begin{bmatrix} 0 \\ \vdots \\ 0 \end{bmatrix} \tag{6}$$

Thus (4) has only the trivial solution if and only if (6) has only the trivial solution. It follows that $\{\mathbf{u}_1, \ldots, \mathbf{u}_p\}$ is linearly independent if and only if $\{[\mathbf{u}_1]_B, \ldots, [\mathbf{u}_p]_B\}$ is linearly independent. This result also follows directly from Exercises 31 and 32 in Section 4.3.

26. By definition, $\mathbf{w}$ is a linear combination of $\mathbf{u}_1,\ldots,\mathbf{u}_p$ if and only if there exist scalars $c_1,\ldots,c_p$ such that

$$\mathbf{w} = c_1\mathbf{u}_1 + \cdots + c_p\mathbf{u}_p \tag{7}$$

Since the coordinate mapping is linear,

$$[\mathbf{w}]_B = c_1[\mathbf{u}_1]_B + \cdots + c_p[\mathbf{u}_p]_B \tag{8}$$

Conversely, (8) implies (7) because the coordinate mapping is one-to-one. Thus $\mathbf{w}$ is a linear combination of $\mathbf{u}_1,\ldots,\mathbf{u}_p$ if and only if $[\mathbf{w}]_B$ is a linear combination of $[\mathbf{u}]_1,\ldots,[\mathbf{u}]_p$.

Note: Students need to be urged to *write* not just to compute in Exercises 27–34. The language in the *Study Guide* solution of Exercise 31 provides a model for the students. In Exercise 32, students may have difficulty distinguishing between the two isomorphic vector spaces, sometimes giving a vector in $\mathbb{R}^3$ as an answer for part (b).

27. The coordinate mapping produces the coordinate vectors $(1, 0, 0, 1)$, $(3, 1, -2, 0)$, and $(0, -1, 3, -1)$ respectively. We test for linear independence of these vectors by writing them as columns of a matrix and row reducing:

$$\begin{bmatrix} 1 & 3 & 0 \\ 0 & 1 & -1 \\ 0 & -2 & 3 \\ 1 & 0 & -1 \end{bmatrix} \sim \begin{bmatrix} 1 & 0 & 0 \\ 0 & 1 & 0 \\ 0 & 0 & 1 \\ 0 & 0 & 0 \end{bmatrix}.$$

Since the matrix has a pivot in each column, its columns (and thus the given polynomials) are linearly independent.

28. The coordinate mapping produces the coordinate vectors $(1, 0, -2, -3)$, $(0, 1, 0, 1)$, and $(1, 3, -2, 0)$ respectively. We test for linear independence of these vectors by writing them as columns of a matrix and row reducing:

$$\begin{bmatrix} 1 & 0 & 1 \\ 0 & 1 & 3 \\ -2 & 0 & -2 \\ -3 & 1 & 0 \end{bmatrix} \sim \begin{bmatrix} 1 & 0 & 1 \\ 0 & 1 & 3 \\ 0 & 0 & 0 \\ 0 & 0 & 0 \end{bmatrix}.$$

Since the matrix does not have a pivot in each column, its columns (and thus the given polynomials) are linearly dependent.

29. The coordinate mapping produces the coordinate vectors $(1, -2, 1, 0)$, $(-2, 0, 0, 1)$, and $(-8, 12, -6, 1)$ respectively. We test for linear independence of these vectors by writing them as columns of a matrix and row reducing:

$$\begin{bmatrix} 1 & -2 & -8 \\ -2 & 0 & 12 \\ 1 & 0 & -6 \\ 0 & 1 & 1 \end{bmatrix} \sim \begin{bmatrix} 1 & 0 & -6 \\ 0 & 1 & 1 \\ 0 & 0 & 0 \\ 0 & 0 & 0 \end{bmatrix}.$$

Since the matrix does not have a pivot in each column, its columns (and thus the given polynomials) are linearly dependent.

30. The coordinate mapping produces the coordinate vectors $(1, -3, 3, -1)$, $(4, -12, 9, 0)$, and $(0, 0, 3, -4)$ respectively. We test for linear independence of these vectors by writing them as columns of a matrix and row reducing:

$$\begin{bmatrix} 1 & 4 & 0 \\ -3 & -12 & 0 \\ 3 & 9 & 3 \\ -1 & 0 & -4 \end{bmatrix} \sim \begin{bmatrix} 1 & 0 & 4 \\ 0 & 1 & -1 \\ 0 & 0 & 0 \\ 0 & 0 & 0 \end{bmatrix}.$$

Since the matrix does not have a pivot in each column, its columns (and thus the given polynomials) are linearly dependent.

31. In each part, place the coordinate vectors of the polynomials into the columns of a matrix and reduce the matrix to echelon form.

a. $\begin{bmatrix} 1 & -3 & -4 & 1 \\ -3 & 5 & 5 & 0 \\ 5 & -7 & -6 & -1 \end{bmatrix} \sim \begin{bmatrix} 1 & -3 & -4 & 1 \\ 0 & -4 & -7 & 3 \\ 0 & 0 & 0 & 0 \end{bmatrix}$

Since there is not a pivot in each row, the original four column vectors do not span $\mathbb{R}^3$. By the isomorphism between $\mathbb{R}^3$ and $\mathbb{P}_2$, the given set of polynomials does not span $\mathbb{P}_2$.

b. $\begin{bmatrix} 0 & 1 & -3 & 2 \\ 5 & -8 & 4 & -3 \\ 1 & -2 & 2 & 0 \end{bmatrix} \sim \begin{bmatrix} 1 & -2 & 2 & 0 \\ 0 & 2 & -6 & -3 \\ 0 & 0 & 0 & 7/2 \end{bmatrix}$

Since there is a pivot in each row, the original four column vectors span $\mathbb{R}^3$. By the isomorphism between $\mathbb{R}^3$ and $\mathbb{P}_2$, the given set of polynomials spans $\mathbb{P}_2$.

32. a. Place the coordinate vectors of the polynomials into the columns of a matrix and reduce the matrix to echelon form: $\begin{bmatrix} 1 & 2 & 1 \\ 0 & -1 & 2 \\ 1 & 3 & -4 \end{bmatrix} \sim \begin{bmatrix} 1 & 2 & 1 \\ 0 & -1 & 2 \\ 0 & 0 & -3 \end{bmatrix}$

The resulting matrix is invertible since it row equivalent to I_3. The original three column vectors form a basis for $\mathbb{R}^3$ by the Invertible Matrix Theorem. By the isomorphism between $\mathbb{R}^3$ and $\mathbb{P}_2$, the corresponding polynomials form a basis for $\mathbb{P}_2$.

b. Since $[\mathbf{q}]_B = (-3, 1, 2)$, $\mathbf{q} = -3\mathbf{p}_1 + \mathbf{p}_2 + 2\mathbf{p}_3$. One might do the algebra in $\mathbb{P}_2$ or choose to compute $\begin{bmatrix} 1 & 2 & 1 \\ 0 & -1 & 2 \\ 1 & 3 & -4 \end{bmatrix} \begin{bmatrix} -3 \\ 1 \\ 2 \end{bmatrix} = \begin{bmatrix} 1 \\ 3 \\ -8 \end{bmatrix}$. This combination of the columns of the matrix corresponds to the same combination of $\mathbf{p}_1$, $\mathbf{p}_2$, and $\mathbf{p}_3$. So $\mathbf{q}(t) = 1 + 3t - 8t^2$.

33. The coordinate mapping produces the coordinate vectors $(3, 7, 0, 0)$, $(5, 1, 0, -2)$, $(0, 1, -2, 0)$ and $(1, 16, -6, 2)$ respectively. To determine whether the set of polynomials is a basis for $\mathbb{P}_3$, we investigate whether the coordinate vectors form a basis for $\mathbb{R}^4$. Writing the vectors as the columns of a matrix and row reducing

$$\begin{bmatrix} 3 & 5 & 0 & 1 \\ 7 & 1 & 1 & 16 \\ 0 & 0 & -2 & -6 \\ 0 & -2 & 0 & 2 \end{bmatrix} \sim \begin{bmatrix} 1 & 0 & 0 & 2 \\ 0 & 1 & 0 & -1 \\ 0 & 0 & 1 & 3 \\ 0 & 0 & 0 & 0 \end{bmatrix},$$

we find that the matrix is not row equivalent to I_4. Thus the coordinate vectors do not form a basis for $\mathbb{R}^4$. By the isomorphism between $\mathbb{R}^4$ and $\mathbb{P}_3$, the given set of polynomials does not form a basis for $\mathbb{P}_3$.

34. The coordinate mapping produces the coordinate vectors $(5, -3, 4, 2)$, $(9, 1, 8, -6)$, $(6, -2, 5, 0)$, and $(0, 0, 0, 1)$ respectively. To determine whether the set of polynomials is a basis for $\mathbb{P}_3$, we investigate whether the coordinate vectors form a basis for $\mathbb{R}^4$. Writing the vectors as the columns of a matrix, and row reducing

$$\begin{bmatrix} 5 & 9 & 6 & 0 \\ -3 & 1 & -2 & 0 \\ 4 & 8 & 5 & 0 \\ 2 & -6 & 0 & 1 \end{bmatrix} \sim \begin{bmatrix} 1 & 0 & 3/4 & 0 \\ 0 & 1 & 1/4 & 0 \\ 0 & 0 & 0 & 1 \\ 0 & 0 & 0 & 0 \end{bmatrix}$$

we find that the matrix is not row equivalent to I_4. Thus the coordinate vectors do not form a basis for $\mathbb{R}^4$. By the isomorphism between $\mathbb{R}^4$ and $\mathbb{P}_3$, the given set of polynomials does not form a basis for $\mathbb{P}_3$.

35. To show that $\mathbf{x}$ is in $H = \text{Span}\{\mathbf{v}_1, \mathbf{v}_2\}$, we must show that the vector equation $x_1\mathbf{v}_1 + x_2\mathbf{v}_2 = \mathbf{x}$ has a solution. The augmented matrix $\begin{bmatrix} \mathbf{v}_1 & \mathbf{v}_2 & \mathbf{x} \end{bmatrix}$ may be row reduced to show

$$\begin{bmatrix} 11 & 14 & 19 \\ -5 & -8 & -13 \\ 10 & 13 & 18 \\ 7 & 10 & 15 \end{bmatrix} \sim \begin{bmatrix} 1 & 0 & -5/3 \\ 0 & 1 & 8/3 \\ 0 & 0 & 0 \\ 0 & 0 & 0 \end{bmatrix}.$$

Since this system has a solution, x is in H. The solution allows us to find the B-coordinate vector for x: since $\mathbf{x} = x_1\mathbf{v}_1 + x_2\mathbf{v}_2 = (-5/3)\mathbf{v}_1 + (8/3)\mathbf{v}_2$, $[\mathbf{x}]_B = \begin{bmatrix} -5/3 \\ 8/3 \end{bmatrix}$.

36. To show that $\mathbf{x}$ is in $H = \text{Span}\{\mathbf{v}_1, \mathbf{v}_2, \mathbf{v}_3\}$, we must show that the vector equation $x_1\mathbf{v}_1 + x_2\mathbf{v}_2 + x_3\mathbf{v}_3 = \mathbf{x}$ has a solution. The augmented matrix $\begin{bmatrix} \mathbf{v}_1 & \mathbf{v}_2 & \mathbf{v}_3 & \mathbf{x} \end{bmatrix}$ may be row reduced to show

$$\begin{bmatrix} -6 & 8 & -9 & 4 \\ 4 & -3 & 5 & 7 \\ -9 & 7 & -8 & -8 \\ 4 & -3 & 3 & 3 \end{bmatrix} \sim \begin{bmatrix} 1 & 0 & 0 & 3 \\ 0 & 1 & 0 & 5 \\ 0 & 0 & 1 & 2 \\ 0 & 0 & 0 & 0 \end{bmatrix}.$$

The first three columns show that B is a basis for H. Moreover, since this system has a solution, $\mathbf{x}$ is in H. The solution allows us to find the B-coordinate vector for $\mathbf{x}$: since

$$\mathbf{x} = x_1\mathbf{v}_1 + x_2\mathbf{v}_2 + x_3\mathbf{v}_3 = 3\mathbf{v}_1 + 5\mathbf{v}_2 + 2\mathbf{v}_3, \quad [\mathbf{x}]_B = \begin{bmatrix} 3 \\ 5 \\ 2 \end{bmatrix}.$$

37. We are given that $[\mathbf{x}]_B = \begin{bmatrix} 1/2 \\ 1/4 \\ 1/6 \end{bmatrix}$, where $B = \left\{ \begin{bmatrix} 2.6 \\ -1.5 \\ 0 \end{bmatrix}, \begin{bmatrix} 0 \\ 3 \\ 0 \end{bmatrix}, \begin{bmatrix} 0 \\ 0 \\ 4.8 \end{bmatrix} \right\}$. To find the coordinates of x relative to the standard basis in $\mathbb{R}^3$, we must find $\mathbf{x}$. We compute that

$$\mathbf{x} = P_B[\mathbf{x}]_B = \begin{bmatrix} 2.6 & 0 & 0 \\ -1.5 & 3 & 0 \\ 0 & 0 & 4.8 \end{bmatrix} \begin{bmatrix} 1/2 \\ 1/4 \\ 1/6 \end{bmatrix} = \begin{bmatrix} 1.3 \\ 0 \\ 0.8 \end{bmatrix}.$$

38. We are given that $[\mathbf{x}]_B = \begin{bmatrix} 1/2 \\ 1/2 \\ 1/3 \end{bmatrix}$, where $B = \left\{ \begin{bmatrix} 2.6 \\ -1.5 \\ 0 \end{bmatrix}, \begin{bmatrix} 0 \\ 3 \\ 0 \end{bmatrix}, \begin{bmatrix} 0 \\ 0 \\ 4.8 \end{bmatrix} \right\}$. To find the coordinates of $\mathbf{x}$ relative

to the standard basis in $\mathbb{R}^3$, we must find $\mathbf{x}$. We compute that

$$\mathbf{x} = P_B[\mathbf{x}]_B = \begin{bmatrix} 2.6 & 0 & 0 \\ -1.5 & 3 & 0 \\ 0 & 0 & 4.8 \end{bmatrix} \begin{bmatrix} 1/2 \\ 1/2 \\ 1/3 \end{bmatrix} = \begin{bmatrix} 1.3 \\ 0.75 \\ 1.6 \end{bmatrix}.$$

4.5 SOLUTIONS

Notes: Theorem 9 is true because a vector space isomorphic to $\mathbb{R}^n$ has the same algebraic properties as $\mathbb{R}^n$; a proof of this result may not be needed to convince the class. The proof of Theorem 9 relies upon the fact that the coordinate mapping is a linear transformation (which is Theorem 8 in Section 4.4). If you have skipped this result, you can prove Theorem 9 as is done in *Introduction to Linear Algebra* by Serge Lang (Springer-Verlag, New York, 1986). There are two separate groups of true-false questions in this section; the second batch is more theoretical in nature. Example 4 is useful to get students to visualize subspaces of different dimensions, and to see the relationships between subspaces of different dimensions. Exercises 31 and 32 investigate the relationship between the dimensions of the domain and the range of a linear transformation; Exercise 32 is mentioned in the proof of Theorem 17 in Section 4.8.

1. This subspace is $H = \mathrm{Span}\{\mathbf{v}_1, \mathbf{v}_2\}$, where $\mathbf{v}_1 = \begin{bmatrix} 1 \\ 1 \\ 0 \end{bmatrix}$ and $\mathbf{v}_2 = \begin{bmatrix} -2 \\ 1 \\ 3 \end{bmatrix}$. Since $\mathbf{v}_1$ and $\mathbf{v}_2$ are not multiples

of each other, $\{\mathbf{v}_1, \mathbf{v}_2\}$ is linearly independent and is thus a basis for H. Hence the dimension of H is 2.

2. This subspace is $H = \mathrm{Span}\{\mathbf{v}_1, \mathbf{v}_2\}$, where $\mathbf{v}_1 = \begin{bmatrix} 4 \\ -3 \\ 0 \end{bmatrix}$ and $\mathbf{v}_2 = \begin{bmatrix} 0 \\ 0 \\ -1 \end{bmatrix}$. Since $\mathbf{v}_1$ and $\mathbf{v}_2$ are not multiples

of each other, $\{\mathbf{v}_1, \mathbf{v}_2\}$ is linearly independent and is thus a basis for H. Hence the dimension of H is 2.

3. This subspace is $H = \mathrm{Span}\{\mathbf{v}_1, \mathbf{v}_2, \mathbf{v}_3\}$, where $\mathbf{v}_1 = \begin{bmatrix} 0 \\ 1 \\ 0 \\ 1 \end{bmatrix}$, $\mathbf{v}_2 = \begin{bmatrix} 0 \\ -1 \\ 1 \\ 2 \end{bmatrix}$, and $\mathbf{v}_3 = \begin{bmatrix} 2 \\ 0 \\ -3 \\ 0 \end{bmatrix}$. Theorem 4 in

Section 4.3 can be used to show that this set is linearly independent: $\mathbf{v}_1 \neq \mathbf{0}$, $\mathbf{v}_2$ is not a multiple of $\mathbf{v}_1$, and (since its first entry is not zero) $\mathbf{v}_3$ is not a linear combination of $\mathbf{v}_1$ and $\mathbf{v}_2$. Thus $\{\mathbf{v}_1, \mathbf{v}_2, \mathbf{v}_3\}$ is linearly independent and is thus a basis for H. Alternatively, one can show that this set is linearly independent by row reducing the matrix $\begin{bmatrix} \mathbf{v}_1 & \mathbf{v}_2 & \mathbf{v}_3 & \mathbf{0} \end{bmatrix}$. Hence the dimension of the subspace is 3.

4. This subspace is $H = \mathrm{Span}\{\mathbf{v}_1, \mathbf{v}_2\}$, where $\mathbf{v}_1 = \begin{bmatrix} 1 \\ 2 \\ 3 \\ 0 \end{bmatrix}$ and $\mathbf{v}_2 = \begin{bmatrix} 1 \\ 0 \\ -1 \\ -1 \end{bmatrix}$. Since $\mathbf{v}_1$ and $\mathbf{v}_2$ are not multiples

of each other, $\{\mathbf{v}_1, \mathbf{v}_2\}$ is linearly independent and is thus a basis for H. Hence the dimension of H is 2.

5. This subspace is $H = \text{Span}\{\mathbf{v}_1, \mathbf{v}_2, \mathbf{v}_3\}$, where $\mathbf{v}_1 = \begin{bmatrix} 1 \\ 2 \\ -1 \\ -3 \end{bmatrix}$, $\mathbf{v}_2 = \begin{bmatrix} -4 \\ 5 \\ 0 \\ 7 \end{bmatrix}$, and $\mathbf{v}_3 = \begin{bmatrix} -2 \\ -4 \\ 2 \\ 6 \end{bmatrix}$. Since $\mathbf{v}_3 = -2\mathbf{v}_1$,

$\{\mathbf{v}_1, \mathbf{v}_2, \mathbf{v}_3\}$ is linearly dependent. By the Spanning Set Theorem, $\mathbf{v}_3$ may be removed from the set with no change in the span of the set, so $H = \text{Span}\{\mathbf{v}_1, \mathbf{v}_2\}$. Since $\mathbf{v}_1$ and $\mathbf{v}_2$ are not multiples of each other, $\{\mathbf{v}_1, \mathbf{v}_2\}$ is linearly independent and is thus a basis for H. Hence the dimension of H is 2.

6. This subspace is $H = \text{Span}\{\mathbf{v}_1, \mathbf{v}_2, \mathbf{v}_3\}$, where $\mathbf{v}_1 = \begin{bmatrix} 3 \\ 6 \\ -9 \\ -3 \end{bmatrix}$, $\mathbf{v}_2 = \begin{bmatrix} 6 \\ -2 \\ 5 \\ 1 \end{bmatrix}$, and $\mathbf{v}_3 = \begin{bmatrix} -1 \\ -2 \\ 3 \\ 1 \end{bmatrix}$. Since

$\mathbf{v}_3 = -(1/3)\mathbf{v}_1$, $\{\mathbf{v}_1, \mathbf{v}_2, \mathbf{v}_3\}$ is linearly dependent. By the Spanning Set Theorem, $\mathbf{v}_3$ may be removed from the set with no change in the span of the set, so $H = \text{Span}\{\mathbf{v}_1, \mathbf{v}_2\}$. Since $\mathbf{v}_1$ and $\mathbf{v}_2$ are not multiples of each other, $\{\mathbf{v}_1, \mathbf{v}_2\}$ is linearly independent and is thus a basis for H. Hence the dimension of H is 2.

7. This subspace is $H = \text{Nul } A$, where $A = \begin{bmatrix} 1 & -3 & 1 \\ 0 & 1 & -2 \\ 0 & 2 & -1 \end{bmatrix}$. Since $\begin{bmatrix} A & \mathbf{0} \end{bmatrix} \sim \begin{bmatrix} 1 & 0 & 0 & 0 \\ 0 & 1 & 0 & 0 \\ 0 & 0 & 1 & 0 \end{bmatrix}$, the

homogeneous system has only the trivial solution. Thus $H = \text{Nul } A = \{\mathbf{0}\}$, and the dimension of H is 0.

8. From the equation $a - 3b + c = 0$, it is seen that $(a, b, c, d) = b(3, 1, 0, 0) + c(-1, 0, 1, 0) + d(0, 0, 0, 1)$. Thus the subspace is $H = \text{Span}\{\mathbf{v}_1, \mathbf{v}_2, \mathbf{v}_3\}$, where $\mathbf{v}_1 = (3, 1, 0, 0)$, $\mathbf{v}_2 = (-1, 0, 1, 0)$, and $\mathbf{v}_3 = (0, 0, 0, 1)$. It is easily checked that this set of vectors is linearly independent, either by appealing to Theorem 4 in Section 4.3, or by row reducing $\begin{bmatrix} \mathbf{v}_1 & \mathbf{v}_2 & \mathbf{v}_3 & \mathbf{0} \end{bmatrix}$. Hence the dimension of the subspace is 3.

9. This subspace is $H = \left\{ \begin{bmatrix} a \\ b \\ a \end{bmatrix} : a, b \text{ in } \mathbb{R} \right\} = \text{Span}\{\mathbf{v}_1, \mathbf{v}_2\}$, where $\mathbf{v}_1 = \begin{bmatrix} 1 \\ 0 \\ 1 \end{bmatrix}$ and $\mathbf{v}_2 = \begin{bmatrix} 0 \\ 1 \\ 0 \end{bmatrix}$. Since $\mathbf{v}_1$ and

$\mathbf{v}_2$ are not multiples of each other, $\{\mathbf{v}_1, \mathbf{v}_2\}$ is linearly independent and is thus a basis for H. Hence the dimension of H is 2.

10. The matrix A with these vectors as its columns row reduces to

$$\begin{bmatrix} 2 & -4 & -3 \\ -5 & 10 & 6 \end{bmatrix} \sim \begin{bmatrix} 1 & -2 & 0 \\ 0 & 0 & 1 \end{bmatrix}.$$

There are two pivot columns, so the dimension of Col A (which is the dimension of H) is 2.

11. The matrix A with these vectors as its columns row reduces to

$$\begin{bmatrix} 1 & 3 & 9 & -7 \\ 0 & 1 & 4 & -3 \\ 2 & 1 & -2 & 1 \end{bmatrix} \sim \begin{bmatrix} 1 & 0 & -3 & 2 \\ 0 & 1 & 4 & -3 \\ 0 & 0 & 0 & 0 \end{bmatrix}.$$

There are two pivot columns, so the dimension of Col A (which is the dimension of the subspace spanned by the vectors) is 2.

12. The matrix A with these vectors as its columns row reduces to

$$\begin{bmatrix} 1 & -3 & -8 & -3 \\ -2 & 4 & 6 & 0 \\ 0 & 1 & 5 & 7 \end{bmatrix} \sim \begin{bmatrix} 1 & 0 & 7 & 0 \\ 0 & 1 & 5 & 0 \\ 0 & 0 & 0 & 1 \end{bmatrix}.$$

There are three pivot columns, so the dimension of Col A (which is the dimension of the subspace spanned by the vectors) is 3.

13. The matrix A is in echelon form. There are three pivot columns, so the dimension of Col A is 3. There are two columns without pivots, so the equation $A\mathbf{x} = \mathbf{0}$ has two free variables. Thus the dimension of Nul A is 2.

14. The matrix A is in echelon form. There are three pivot columns, so the dimension of Col A is 3. There are three columns without pivots, so the equation $A\mathbf{x} = \mathbf{0}$ has three free variables. Thus the dimension of Nul A is 3.

15. The matrix A is in echelon form. There are two pivot columns, so the dimension of Col A is 2. There are two columns without pivots, so the equation $A\mathbf{x} = \mathbf{0}$ has two free variables. Thus the dimension of Nul A is 2.

16. The matrix A row reduces to

$$\begin{bmatrix} 3 & 4 \\ -6 & 10 \end{bmatrix} \sim \begin{bmatrix} 1 & 0 \\ 0 & 1 \end{bmatrix}.$$

There are two pivot columns, so the dimension of Col A is 2. There are no columns without pivots, so the equation $A\mathbf{x} = \mathbf{0}$ has only the trivial solution $\mathbf{0}$. Thus Nul $A = \{\mathbf{0}\}$, and the dimension of Nul A is 0.

17. The matrix A is in echelon form. There are three pivot columns, so the dimension of Col A is 3. There are no columns without pivots, so the equation $A\mathbf{x} = \mathbf{0}$ has only the trivial solution $\mathbf{0}$. Thus Nul $A = \{\mathbf{0}\}$, and the dimension of Nul A is 0.

18. The matrix A is in echelon form. There are two pivot columns, so the dimension of Col A is 2. There is one column without a pivot, so the equation $A\mathbf{x} = \mathbf{0}$ has one free variable. Thus the dimension of Nul A is 1.

19. a. True. See the box before Example 5.

b. False. The plane must pass through the origin; see Example 4.

c. False. The dimension of $\mathbb{P}_n$ is $n + 1$; see Example 1.

d. False. The set S must also have n elements; see Theorem 12.

e. True. See Theorem 9.

20. a. False. The set $\mathbb{R}^2$ is not even a subset of $\mathbb{R}^3$.

b. False. The number of **free** variables is equal to the dimension of Nul A; see the box before Example 5.

c. False. A basis could still have only finitely many elements, which would make the vector space finite-dimensional.

d. False. The set S must also have n elements; see Theorem 12.

e. True. See Example 4.

21. The matrix whose columns are the coordinate vectors of the Hermite polynomials relative to the standard basis $\{1, t, t^2, t^3\}$ of $\mathbb{P}_3$ is

$$A = \begin{bmatrix} 1 & 0 & -2 & 0 \\ 0 & 2 & 0 & -12 \\ 0 & 0 & 4 & 0 \\ 0 & 0 & 0 & 8 \end{bmatrix}.$$

This matrix has 4 pivots, so its columns are linearly independent. Since their coordinate vectors form a linearly independent set, the Hermite polynomials themselves are linearly independent in $\mathbb{P}_3$. Since there are four Hermite polynomials and dim $\mathbb{P}_3 = 4$, the Basis Theorem states that the Hermite polynomials form a basis for $\mathbb{P}_3$.

22. The matrix whose columns are the coordinate vectors of the Laguerre polynomials relative to the standard basis $\{1, t, t^2, t^3\}$ of $\mathbb{P}_3$ is

$$A = \begin{bmatrix} 1 & 1 & 2 & 6 \\ 0 & -1 & -4 & -18 \\ 0 & 0 & 1 & 9 \\ 0 & 0 & 0 & -1 \end{bmatrix}.$$

This matrix has 4 pivots, so its columns are linearly independent. Since their coordinate vectors form a linearly independent set, the Laguerre polynomials themselves are linearly independent in $\mathbb{P}_3$. Since there are four Laguerre polynomials and dim $\mathbb{P}_3 = 4$, the Basis Theorem states that the Laguerre polynomials form a basis for $\mathbb{P}_3$.

23. The coordinates of $\mathbf{p}(t) = 7 - 12t - 8t^2 + 12t^3$ with respect to B satisfy

$$c_1(1) + c_2(2t) + c_3(-2 + 4t^2) + c_4(-12t + 8t^3) = 7 - 12t - 8t^2 + 12t^3$$

Equating coefficients of like powers of t produces the system of equations

$$
\begin{array}{rcrcl}
c_1 & & -\ 2c_3 & & =\quad 7 \\
& 2c_2 & & -\ 12c_4 & =\ -12 \\
& & 4c_3 & & =\ -8 \\
& & & 8c_4 & =\ 12
\end{array}
$$

Solving this system gives $c_1 = 3$, $c_2 = 3$, $c_3 = -2$, $c_4 = 3/2$, and $[\mathbf{p}]_B = \begin{bmatrix} 3 \\ 3 \\ -2 \\ 3/2 \end{bmatrix}$.

24. The coordinates of $\mathbf{p}(t) = 7 - 8t + 3t^2$ with respect to B satisfy

$$c_1(1) + c_2(1 - t) + c_3(2 - 4t + t^2) = 7 - 8t + 3t^2$$

Equating coefficients of like powers of t produces the system of equations

$$
\begin{array}{rcrcrcr}
c_1 & + & c_2 & + & 2c_3 & = & 7 \\
& & -c_2 & - & 4c_3 & = & -8 \\
& & & & c_3 & = & 3
\end{array}
$$

Solving this system gives $c_1 = 5$, $c_2 = -4$, $c_3 = 3$, and $[\mathbf{p}]_B = \begin{bmatrix} 5 \\ -4 \\ 3 \end{bmatrix}$.

25. Note first that $n \geq 1$ since S cannot have fewer than 1 vector. Since $n \geq 1$, $V \neq \mathbf{0}$. Suppose that S spans V and that S contains fewer than n vectors. By the Spanning Set Theorem, some subset S' of S is a basis for V. Since S contains fewer than n vectors, and S' is a subset of S, S' also contains fewer than n vectors. Thus there is a basis S' for V with fewer than n vectors, but this is impossible by Theorem 10 since $\dim V = n$. Thus S cannot span V.

26. If $\dim V = \dim H = 0$, then $V = \{\mathbf{0}\}$ and $H = \{\mathbf{0}\}$, so $H = V$. Suppose that $\dim V = \dim H > 0$. Then H contains a basis S consisting of n vectors. But applying the Basis Theorem to V, S is also a basis for V. Thus $H = V = \text{Span}S$.

27. Suppose that $\dim \mathbb{P} = k < \infty$. Now $\mathbb{P}_n$ is a subspace of $\mathbb{P}$ for all n, and $\dim \mathbb{P}_{k-1} = k$, so $\dim \mathbb{P}_{k-1} = \dim \mathbb{P}$. This would imply that $\mathbb{P}_{k-1} = \mathbb{P}$, which is clearly untrue: for example $\mathbf{p}(t) = t^k$ is in $\mathbb{P}$ but not in $\mathbb{P}_{k-1}$. Thus the dimension of $\mathbb{P}$ cannot be finite.

28. The space $C(\mathbb{R})$ contains $\mathbb{P}$ as a subspace. If $C(\mathbb{R})$ were finite-dimensional, then $\mathbb{P}$ would also be finite-dimensional by Theorem 11. But $\mathbb{P}$ is infinite-dimensional by Exercise 27, so $C(\mathbb{R})$ must also be infinite-dimensional.

29. **a.** True. Apply the Spanning Set Theorem to the set $\{\mathbf{v}_1, \ldots, \mathbf{v}_p\}$ and produce a basis for V. This basis will not have more than p elements in it, so $\dim V \leq p$.

   b. True. By Theorem 11, $\{\mathbf{v}_1, \ldots, \mathbf{v}_p\}$ can be expanded to find a basis for V. This basis will have at least p elements in it, so $\dim V \geq p$.

   c. True. Take any basis (which will contain p vectors) for V and adjoin the zero vector to it.

30. **a.** False. For a counterexample, let $\mathbf{v}$ be a non-zero vector in $\mathbb{R}^3$, and consider the set $\{\mathbf{v}, 2\mathbf{v}\}$. This is a linearly dependent set in $\mathbb{R}^3$, but $\dim \mathbb{R}^3 = 3 > 2$.

   b. True. If $\dim V \leq p$, there is a basis for V with p or fewer vectors. This basis would be a spanning set for V with p or fewer vectors, which contradicts the assumption.

   c. False. For a counterexample, let $\mathbf{v}$ be a non-zero vector in $\mathbb{R}^3$, and consider the set $\{\mathbf{v}, 2\mathbf{v}\}$. This is a linearly dependent set in $\mathbb{R}^3$ with $3 - 1 = 2$ vectors, and $\dim \mathbb{R}^3 = 3$.

31. Since H is a nonzero subspace of a finite-dimensional vector space V, H is finite-dimensional and has a basis. Let $\{\mathbf{u}_1, \ldots, \mathbf{u}_p\}$ be a basis for H. We show that the set $\{T(\mathbf{u}_1), \ldots, T(\mathbf{u}_p)\}$ spans $T(H)$. Let $\mathbf{y}$ be in $T(H)$. Then there is a vector $\mathbf{x}$ in H with $T(\mathbf{x}) = \mathbf{y}$. Since $\mathbf{x}$ is in H and $\{\mathbf{u}_1, \ldots, \mathbf{u}_p\}$ is a basis for H, $\mathbf{x}$ may be written as $\mathbf{x} = c_1\mathbf{u}_1 + \ldots + c_p\mathbf{u}_p$ for some scalars $c_1, \ldots, c_p$. Since the transformation T is linear,

$$\mathbf{y} = T(\mathbf{x}) = T(c_1\mathbf{u}_1 + \ldots + c_p\mathbf{u}_p) = c_1 T(\mathbf{u}_1) + \ldots + c_p T(\mathbf{u}_p)$$

Thus $\mathbf{y}$ is a linear combination of $T(\mathbf{u}_1), \ldots, T(\mathbf{u}_p)$, and $\{T(\mathbf{u}_1), \ldots, T(\mathbf{u}_p)\}$ spans $T(H)$. By the Spanning Set Theorem, this set contains a basis for $T(H)$. This basis then has not more than p vectors, and $\dim T(H) \leq p = \dim H$.

32. Since H is a nonzero subspace of a finite-dimensional vector space V, H is finite-dimensional and has a basis. Let $\{\mathbf{u}_1, \ldots \mathbf{u}_p\}$ be a basis for H. In Exercise 31 above it was shown that $\{T(\mathbf{u}_1), \ldots, T(\mathbf{u}_p)\}$ spans $T(H)$. In Exercise 32 in Section 4.3, it was shown that $\{T(\mathbf{u}_1), \ldots, T(\mathbf{u}_p)\}$ is linearly independent. Thus $\{T(\mathbf{u}_1), \ldots, T(\mathbf{u}_p)\}$ is a basis for $T(H)$, and $\dim T(H) = p = \dim H$.

33. [M]

    a. To find a basis for $\mathbb{R}^5$ which contains the given vectors, we row reduce

$$\begin{bmatrix} -9 & 9 & 6 & 1 & 0 & 0 & 0 & 0 \\ -7 & 4 & 7 & 0 & 1 & 0 & 0 & 0 \\ 8 & 1 & -8 & 0 & 0 & 1 & 0 & 0 \\ -5 & 6 & 5 & 0 & 0 & 0 & 1 & 0 \\ 7 & -7 & -7 & 0 & 0 & 0 & 0 & 1 \end{bmatrix} \sim \begin{bmatrix} 1 & 0 & 0 & -1/3 & 0 & 0 & 1 & 3/7 \\ 0 & 1 & 0 & 0 & 0 & 0 & 1 & 5/7 \\ 0 & 0 & 1 & -1/3 & 0 & 0 & 0 & -3/7 \\ 0 & 0 & 0 & 0 & 1 & 0 & 3 & 22/7 \\ 0 & 0 & 0 & 0 & 0 & 1 & -9 & -53/7 \end{bmatrix}.$$

       The first, second, third, fifth, and sixth columns are pivot columns, so these columns of the original matrix ($\{\mathbf{v}_1, \mathbf{v}_2, \mathbf{v}_3, \mathbf{e}_2, \mathbf{e}_3\}$) form a basis for $\mathbb{R}^5$:

    b. The original vectors are the first k columns of A. Since the set of original vectors is assumed to be linearly independent, these columns of A will be pivot columns and the original set of vectors will be included in the basis. Since the columns of A include all the columns of the identity matrix, Col $A = \mathbb{R}^n$.

34. [M]

    a. The B-coordinate vectors of the vectors in C are the columns of the matrix

$$P = \begin{bmatrix} 1 & 0 & -1 & 0 & 1 & 0 & -1 \\ 0 & 1 & 0 & -3 & 0 & 5 & 0 \\ 0 & 0 & 2 & 0 & -8 & 0 & 18 \\ 0 & 0 & 0 & 4 & 0 & -20 & 0 \\ 0 & 0 & 0 & 0 & 8 & 0 & -48 \\ 0 & 0 & 0 & 0 & 0 & 16 & 0 \\ 0 & 0 & 0 & 0 & 0 & 0 & 32 \end{bmatrix}.$$

       The matrix P is invertible because it is triangular with nonzero entries along its main diagonal. Thus its columns are linearly independent. Since the coordinate mapping is an isomorphism, this shows that the vectors in C are linearly independent.

    b. We know that dim $H = 7$ because B is a basis for H. Now C is a linearly independent set, and the vectors in C lie in H by the trigonometric identities. Thus by the Basis Theorem, C is a basis for H.

4.6   SOLUTIONS

Notes: This section puts together most of the ideas from Chapter 4. The Rank Theorem is the main result in this section. Many students have difficulty with the difference in finding bases for the row space and the column space of a matrix. The first process uses the nonzero rows of an echelon form of the matrix. The second process uses the pivots columns of the original matrix, which are usually found through row reduction. Students may also have problems with the varied effects of row operations on the linear dependence relations among the rows and columns of a matrix. Problems of the type found in Exercises 19–26 make excellent test questions. Figure 1 and Example 4 prepare the way for Theorem 3 in Section 6.1; Exercises 27–29 anticipate Example 6 in Section 7.4.

1. The matrix B is in echelon form. There are two pivot columns, so the dimension of Col A is 2. There are two pivot rows, so the dimension of Row A is 2. There are two columns without pivots, so the equation $A\mathbf{x} = \mathbf{0}$ has two free variables. Thus the dimension of Nul A is 2. A basis for Col A is the pivot columns of A:

$$\left\{ \begin{bmatrix} 1 \\ -1 \\ 5 \end{bmatrix}, \begin{bmatrix} -4 \\ 2 \\ -6 \end{bmatrix} \right\}.$$

A basis for Row A is the pivot rows of B: $\{(1,0,-1,5),(0,-2,5,-6)\}$. To find a basis for Nul A row reduce to reduced echelon form:

$$A \sim \begin{bmatrix} 1 & 0 & -1 & 5 \\ 0 & 1 & -5/2 & 3 \end{bmatrix}.$$

The solution to $A\mathbf{x} = \mathbf{0}$ in terms of free variables is $x_1 = x_3 - 5x_4$, $x_2 = (5/2)x_3 - 3x_4$ with x_3 and x_4 free. Thus a basis for Nul A is

$$\left\{ \begin{bmatrix} 1 \\ 5/2 \\ 1 \\ 0 \end{bmatrix}, \begin{bmatrix} -5 \\ -3 \\ 0 \\ 1 \end{bmatrix} \right\}.$$

2. The matrix B is in echelon form. There are three pivot columns, so the dimension of Col A is 3. There are three pivot rows, so the dimension of Row A is 3. There are two columns without pivots, so the equation $A\mathbf{x} = \mathbf{0}$ has two free variables. Thus the dimension of Nul A is 2. A basis for Col A is the pivot columns of A:

$$\left\{ \begin{bmatrix} 1 \\ -2 \\ -3 \\ 3 \end{bmatrix}, \begin{bmatrix} 4 \\ -6 \\ -6 \\ 4 \end{bmatrix}, \begin{bmatrix} 9 \\ -10 \\ -3 \\ 0 \end{bmatrix} \right\}.$$

A basis for Row A is the pivot rows of B: $\{(1,-3,0,5,-7),(0,0,2,-3,8),(0,0,0,0,5)\}$. To find a basis for Nul A row reduce to reduced echelon form:

$$A \sim \begin{bmatrix} 1 & -3 & 0 & 5 & 0 \\ 0 & 0 & 1 & -3/2 & 0 \\ 0 & 0 & 0 & 0 & 1 \\ 0 & 0 & 0 & 0 & 0 \end{bmatrix}.$$

The solution to $A\mathbf{x} = \mathbf{0}$ in terms of free variables is $x_1 = 3x_2 - 5x_4$, $x_3 = (3/2)x_4$, $x_5 = 0$, with x_2 and x_4 free. Thus a basis for Nul A is

$$\left\{ \begin{bmatrix} 3 \\ 1 \\ 0 \\ 0 \\ 0 \end{bmatrix}, \begin{bmatrix} -5 \\ 0 \\ 3/2 \\ 1 \\ 0 \end{bmatrix} \right\}.$$

3. The matrix B is in echelon form. There are three pivot columns, so the dimension of Col A is 3. There are three pivot rows, so the dimension of Row A is 3. There are two columns without pivots, so the equation $A\mathbf{x} = \mathbf{0}$ has two free variables. Thus the dimension of Nul A is 2. A basis for Col A is the pivot columns of A:

$$\left\{ \begin{bmatrix} 2 \\ -2 \\ 4 \\ -2 \end{bmatrix}, \begin{bmatrix} 6 \\ -3 \\ 9 \\ 3 \end{bmatrix}, \begin{bmatrix} 2 \\ -3 \\ 5 \\ -4 \end{bmatrix} \right\}.$$

A basis for Row A is the pivot rows of B: $\{(2,-3,6,2,5),(0,0,3,-1,1),(0,0,0,1,3)\}$. To find a basis for Nul A row reduce to reduced echelon form:

$$A \sim \begin{bmatrix} 1 & -3/2 & 0 & 0 & -9/2 \\ 0 & 0 & 1 & 0 & 4/3 \\ 0 & 0 & 0 & 1 & 3 \\ 0 & 0 & 0 & 0 & 0 \end{bmatrix}.$$

The solution to $A\mathbf{x} = \mathbf{0}$ in terms of free variables is $x_1 = (3/2)x_2 + (9/2)x_5$, $x_3 = -(4/3)x_5$, $x_4 = -3x_5$, with x_2 and x_5 free. Thus a basis for Nul A is

$$\left\{ \begin{bmatrix} 3/2 \\ 1 \\ 0 \\ 0 \\ 0 \end{bmatrix}, \begin{bmatrix} 9/2 \\ 0 \\ -4/3 \\ -3 \\ 1 \end{bmatrix} \right\}.$$

4. The matrix B is in echelon form. There are three pivot columns, so the dimension of Col A is 3. There are three pivot rows, so the dimension of Row A is 3. There are three columns without pivots, so the equation $A\mathbf{x} = \mathbf{0}$ has three free variables. Thus the dimension of Nul A is 3. A basis for Col A is the pivot columns of A:

$$\left\{ \begin{bmatrix} 1 \\ 1 \\ 1 \\ 1 \\ 1 \end{bmatrix}, \begin{bmatrix} 1 \\ 2 \\ -1 \\ -3 \\ -2 \end{bmatrix}, \begin{bmatrix} 7 \\ 10 \\ 1 \\ -5 \\ 0 \end{bmatrix} \right\}.$$

A basis for Row A is the pivot rows of B:

$$\{(1,1,-3,7,9,-9),(0,1,-1,3,4,-3),(0,0,0,1,-1,-2)\}.$$

To find a basis for Nul A row reduce to reduced echelon form:

$$A \sim \begin{bmatrix} 1 & 0 & -2 & 0 & 9 & 2 \\ 0 & 1 & -1 & 0 & 7 & 3 \\ 0 & 0 & 0 & 1 & -1 & -2 \\ 0 & 0 & 0 & 0 & 0 & 0 \\ 0 & 0 & 0 & 0 & 0 & 0 \end{bmatrix}.$$

The solution to $A\mathbf{x} = \mathbf{0}$ in terms of free variables is $x_1 = 2x_3 - 9x_5 - 2x_6$, $x_2 = x_3 - 7x_5 - 3x_6$, $x_4 = x_5 + 2x_6$, with x_3, x_5, and x_6 free. Thus a basis for Nul A is

$$\left\{ \begin{bmatrix} 2 \\ 1 \\ 1 \\ 0 \\ 0 \\ 0 \end{bmatrix}, \begin{bmatrix} -9 \\ -7 \\ 0 \\ 1 \\ 1 \\ 0 \end{bmatrix}, \begin{bmatrix} -2 \\ -3 \\ 0 \\ 2 \\ 0 \\ 1 \end{bmatrix} \right\}.$$

5. By the Rank Theorem, dimNul $A = 8 - $ rank $A = 8 - 3 = 5$. Since dimRow $A = $ rank A, dimRow $A = 3$. Since rank $A^T = $ dimCol $A^T = $ dimRow A, rank$A^T = 3$.

6. By the Rank Theorem, dimNul $A = 3 - $ rank $A = 3 - 3 = 0$. Since dimRow $A = $ rank A, dimRow $A = 3$. Since rank $A^T = $ dimCol $A^T = $ dimRow A, rank $A^T = 3$.

7. Yes, Col $A = \mathbb{R}^4$. Since A has four pivot columns, dimCol $A = 4$. Thus Col A is a four-dimensional subspace of $\mathbb{R}^4$, and Col $A = \mathbb{R}^4$.
   No, Nul $A \neq \mathbb{R}^3$. It is true that dimNul $A = 3$, but Nul A is a subspace of $\mathbb{R}^7$.

8. Since A has four pivot columns, rank $A = 4$, and dimNul $A = 6 - $ rank $A = 6 - 4 = 2$.
   No. Col $A \neq \mathbb{R}^4$. It is true that dimCol $A = $ rank $A = 4$, but Col A is a subspace of $\mathbb{R}^5$.

9. Since dimNul $A = 4$, rank $A = 6 - $ dimNul $A = 6 - 4 = 2$. So dimCol $A = $ rank $A = 2$.

10. Since dimNul $A = 5$, rank $A = 6 - $ dimNul $A = 6 - 5 = 1$. So dimCol $A = $ rank $A = 1$.

11. Since dimNul $A = 2$, rank $A = 5 - $ dimNul $A = 5 - 2 = 3$. So dimRow $A = $ dimCol $A = $ rank $A = 3$.

12. Since dimNul $A = 4$, rank $A = 6 - $ dimNul $A = 6 - 4 = 2$. So dimRow $A = $ dimCol $A = $ rank $A = 2$.

13. The rank of a matrix A equals the number of pivot positions which the matrix has. If A is either a 7×5 matrix or a 5×7 matrix, the largest number of pivot positions that A could have is 5. Thus the largest possible value for rank A is 5.

14. The dimension of the row space of a matrix A is equal to rank A, which equals the number of pivot positions which the matrix has. If A is either a 4×3 matrix or a 3×4 matrix, the largest number of pivot positions that A could have is 3. Thus the largest possible value for dimRow A is 3.

15. Since the rank of A equals the number of pivot positions which the matrix has, and A could have at most 6 pivot positions, rank $A \leq 6$. Thus dimNul $A = 8 - $ rank $A \geq 8 - 6 = 2$.

16. Since the rank of A equals the number of pivot positions which the matrix has, and A could have at most 4 pivot positions, rank $A \leq 4$. Thus dimNul $A = 4 - $ rank $A \geq 4 - 4 = 0$.

17. **a.** True. The rows of A are identified with the columns of A^T. See the paragraph before Example 1.
    b. False. See the warning after Example 2.
    c. True. See the Rank Theorem.
    d. False. See the Rank Theorem.
    e. True. See the Numerical Note before the Practice Problem.

18. **a**. False. Review the warning after Theorem 6 in Section 4.3.

   b. False. See the warning after Example 2.

   c. True. See the remark in the proof of the Rank Theorem.

   d. True. This fact was noted in the paragraph before Example 4. It also follows from the fact that the rows of A^T are the columns of $(A^T)^T = A$.

   e. True. See Theorem 13.

19. Yes. Consider the system as $A\mathbf{x} = \mathbf{0}$, where A is a 5×6 matrix. The problem states that $\dim \text{Nul} A = 1$. By the Rank Theorem, rank $A = 6 - \dim \text{Nul } A = 5$. Thus $\dim \text{Col } A = \text{rank } A = 5$, and since Col A is a subspace of $\mathbb{R}^5$, Col $A = \mathbb{R}^5$ So every vector **b** in $\mathbb{R}^5$ is also in Col A, and $A\mathbf{x} = \mathbf{b}$, has a solution for all **b**.

20. No. Consider the system as $A\mathbf{x} = \mathbf{b}$, where A is a 6×8 matrix. The problem states that $\dim \text{Nul } A = 2$. By the Rank Theorem, rank $A = 8 - \dim \text{Nul } A = 6$. Thus $\dim \text{Col } A = \text{rank } A = 6$, and since Col A is a subspace of $\mathbb{R}^6$, Col $A = \mathbb{R}^6$ So every vector **b** in $\mathbb{R}^6$ is also in Col A, and $A\mathbf{x} = \mathbf{b}$ has a solution for all **b**. Thus it is impossible to change the entries in **b** to make $A\mathbf{x} = \mathbf{b}$ into an inconsistent system.

21. No. Consider the system as $A\mathbf{x} = \mathbf{b}$, where A is a 9×10 matrix. Since the system has a solution for all **b** in $\mathbb{R}^9$, A must have a pivot in each row, and so rank$A = 9$. By the Rank Theorem, $\dim \text{Nul} A = 10 - 9 = 1$. Thus it is impossible to find two linearly independent vectors in Nul A.

22. No. Consider the system as $A\mathbf{x} = \mathbf{0}$, where A is a 10×12 matrix. Since A has at most 10 pivot positions, rank$A \le 10$. By the Rank Theorem, $\dim \text{Nul} A = 12 - \text{rank} A \ge 2$. Thus it is impossible to find a single vector in Nul A which spans Nul A.

23. Yes, six equations are sufficient. Consider the system as $A\mathbf{x} = \mathbf{0}$, where A is a 12×8 matrix. The problem states that $\dim \text{Nul } A = 2$. By the Rank Theorem, rank $A = 8 - \dim \text{Nul } A = 6$. Thus $\dim \text{Col } A = \text{rank } A = 6$. So the system $A\mathbf{x} = \mathbf{0}$ is equivalent to the system $B\mathbf{x} = \mathbf{0}$, where B is an echelon form of A with 6 nonzero rows. So the six equations in this system are sufficient to describe the solution set of $A\mathbf{x} = \mathbf{0}$.

24. Yes, No. Consider the system as $A\mathbf{x} = \mathbf{b}$, where A is a 7×6 matrix. Since A has at most 6 pivot positions, rank $A \le 6$. By the Rank Theorem, $\dim \text{Nul } A = 6 - \text{rank } A \ge 0$. If $\dim \text{Nul } A = 0$, then the system $A\mathbf{x} = \mathbf{b}$ will have no free variables. The solution to $A\mathbf{x} = \mathbf{b}$, if it exists, would thus have to be unique. Since rank $A \le 6$, Col A will be a proper subspace of $\mathbb{R}^7$. Thus there exists a **b** in $\mathbb{R}^7$ for which the system $A\mathbf{x} = \mathbf{b}$ is inconsistent, and the system $A\mathbf{x} = \mathbf{b}$ cannot have a unique solution for all **b**.

25. No. Consider the system as $A\mathbf{x} = \mathbf{b}$, where A is a 10×12 matrix. The problem states that $\dim \text{Nul} A = 3$. By the Rank Theorem, $\dim \text{Col } A = \text{rank } A = 12 - \dim \text{Nul } A = 9$. Thus Col A will be a proper subspace of $\mathbb{R}^{10}$ Thus there exists a **b** in $\mathbb{R}^{10}$ for which the system $A\mathbf{x} = \mathbf{b}$ is inconsistent, and the system $A\mathbf{x} = \mathbf{b}$ cannot have a solution for all **b**.

26. Consider the system $A\mathbf{x} = \mathbf{0}$, where A is a $m \times n$ matrix with $m > n$. Since the rank of A is the number of pivot positions that A has and A is assumed to have full rank, rank $A = n$. By the Rank Theorem, $\dim \text{Nul} A = n - \text{rank } A = 0$. So Nul $A = \{\mathbf{0}\}$, and the system $A\mathbf{x} = \mathbf{0}$ has only the trivial solution. This happens if and only if the columns of A are linearly independent.

27. Since A is an $m \times n$ matrix, Row A is a subspace of $\mathbb{R}^n$, Col A is a subspace of $\mathbb{R}^m$, and Nul A is a subspace of $\mathbb{R}^n$. Likewise since A^T is an $n \times m$ matrix, Row A^T is a subspace of $\mathbb{R}^m$, Col A^T is a

subspace of $\mathbb{R}^n$, and Nul A^T is a subspace of $\mathbb{R}^m$. Since Row $A = $ Col A^T and Col $A = $ Row A^T, there are four dinstict subspaces in the list: Row A, Col A, Nul A, and Nul A^T.

28. **a.** Since A is an $m \times n$ matrix and dimRow $A = $ rank A,

   dimRow $A + $ dimNul $A = $ rank $A + $ dimNul $A = n$.

   b. Since A^T is an $n \times m$ matrix and dimCol $A = $ dimRow $A = $ dimCol $A^T = $ rank A^T,

   dimCol $A + $ dimNul $A^T = $ rank $A^T + $ dimNul $A^T = m$.

29. Let A be an $m \times n$ matrix. The system $A\mathbf{x} = \mathbf{b}$ will have a solution for all $\mathbf{b}$ in $\mathbb{R}^m$ if and only if A has a pivot position in each row, which happens if and only if dimCol $A = m$. By Exercise 28 b., dimCol $A = m$ if and only if dimNul $A^T = m - m = 0$, or Nul $A^T = \{\mathbf{0}\}$. Finally, Nul $A^T = \{\mathbf{0}\}$ if and only if the equation $A^T \mathbf{x} = \mathbf{0}$ has only the trivial solution.

30. The equation $A\mathbf{x} = \mathbf{b}$ is consistent if and only if rank $\begin{bmatrix} A & \mathbf{b} \end{bmatrix} = $ rank A because the two ranks will be equal if and only if $\mathbf{b}$ is not a pivot column of $\begin{bmatrix} A & \mathbf{b} \end{bmatrix}$. The result then follows from Theorem 2 in Section 1.2.

31. Compute that $\mathbf{u}\mathbf{v}^T = \begin{bmatrix} 2 \\ -3 \\ 5 \end{bmatrix} \begin{bmatrix} a & b & c \end{bmatrix} = \begin{bmatrix} 2a & 2b & 2c \\ -3a & -3b & -3c \\ 5a & 5b & 5c \end{bmatrix}$. Each column of $\mathbf{u}\mathbf{v}^T$ is a multiple of $\mathbf{u}$, so dimCol $\mathbf{u}\mathbf{v}^T = 1$, unless $a = b = c = 0$, in which case $\mathbf{u}\mathbf{v}^T$ is the 3×3 zero matrix and dimCol $\mathbf{u}\mathbf{v}^T = 0$. In any case, rank $\mathbf{u}\mathbf{v}^T = $ dimCol $\mathbf{u}\mathbf{v}^T \leq 1$

32. Note that the second row of the matrix is twice the first row. Thus if $\mathbf{v} = (1, -3, 4)$, which is the first row of the matrix,

$$\mathbf{u}\mathbf{v}^T = \begin{bmatrix} 1 \\ 2 \end{bmatrix} \begin{bmatrix} 1 & -3 & 4 \end{bmatrix} = \begin{bmatrix} 1 & -3 & 4 \\ 2 & -6 & 8 \end{bmatrix}.$$

33. Let $A = \begin{bmatrix} \mathbf{u}_1 & \mathbf{u}_2 & \mathbf{u}_3 \end{bmatrix}$, and assume that rank $A = 1$. Suppose that $\mathbf{u}_1 \neq \mathbf{0}$. Then $\{\mathbf{u}_1\}$ is basis for Col A, since Col A is assumed to be one-dimensional. Thus there are scalars x and y with $\mathbf{u}_2 = x\mathbf{u}_1$ and

$\mathbf{u}_3 = y\mathbf{u}_1$, and $A = \mathbf{u}_1\mathbf{v}^T$, where $\mathbf{v} = \begin{bmatrix} 1 \\ x \\ y \end{bmatrix}$.

If $\mathbf{u}_1 = \mathbf{0}$ but $\mathbf{u}_2 \neq \mathbf{0}$, then similarly $\{\mathbf{u}_2\}$ is basis for Col A, since Col A is assumed to be one-

dimensional. Thus there is a scalar x with $\mathbf{u}_3 = x\mathbf{u}_2$, and $A = \mathbf{u}_2\mathbf{v}^T$, where $\mathbf{v} = \begin{bmatrix} 0 \\ 1 \\ x \end{bmatrix}$.

If $\mathbf{u}_1 = \mathbf{u}_2 = \mathbf{0}$ but $\mathbf{u}_3 \neq \mathbf{0}$, then $A = \mathbf{u}_3\mathbf{v}^T$, where $\mathbf{v} = \begin{bmatrix} 0 \\ 0 \\ 1 \end{bmatrix}$.

34. Let A be an $m \times n$ matrix with of rank $r > 0$, and let U be an echelon form of A. Since A can be reduced to U by row operations, there exist invertible elementary matrices $E_1, \ldots, E_p$ with $(E_p \cdots E_1)A = U$. Thus

$A = (E_p \cdots E_1)^{-1} U$, since the product of invertible matrices is invertible. Let $E = (E_p \cdots E_1)^{-1}$; then $A = EU$. Let the columns of E be denoted by $\mathbf{c}_1, \ldots, \mathbf{c}_m$. Since the rank of A is r, U has r nonzero rows, which can be denoted $\mathbf{d}_1^T, \ldots, \mathbf{d}_r^T$. By the column-row expansion of A (Theorem 10 in Section 2.4):

$$A = EU = \begin{bmatrix} \mathbf{c}_1 & \cdots & \mathbf{c}_m \end{bmatrix} \begin{bmatrix} \mathbf{d}_1^T \\ \vdots \\ \mathbf{d}_r^T \\ \mathbf{0} \\ \vdots \\ \mathbf{0} \end{bmatrix} = \mathbf{c}_1 \mathbf{d}_1^T + \ldots + \mathbf{c}_r \mathbf{d}_r^T,$$

which is the sum of r rank 1 matrices.

35. **[M]**

    a. Begin by reducing A to reduced echelon form:

$$A \sim \begin{bmatrix} 1 & 0 & 13/2 & 0 & 5 & 0 & -3 \\ 0 & 1 & 11/2 & 0 & 1/2 & 0 & 2 \\ 0 & 0 & 0 & 1 & -11/2 & 0 & 7 \\ 0 & 0 & 0 & 0 & 0 & 1 & 1 \\ 0 & 0 & 0 & 0 & 0 & 0 & 0 \end{bmatrix}.$$

A basis for Col A is the pivot columns of A, so matrix C contains these columns:

$$C = \begin{bmatrix} 7 & -9 & 5 & -3 \\ -4 & 6 & -2 & -5 \\ 5 & -7 & 5 & 2 \\ -3 & 5 & -1 & -4 \\ 6 & -8 & 4 & 9 \end{bmatrix}.$$

A basis for Row A is the pivot rows of the reduced echelon form of A, so matrix R contains these rows:

$$R = \begin{bmatrix} 1 & 0 & 13/2 & 0 & 5 & 0 & -3 \\ 0 & 1 & 11/2 & 0 & 1/2 & 0 & 2 \\ 0 & 0 & 0 & 1 & -11/2 & 0 & 7 \\ 0 & 0 & 0 & 0 & 0 & 1 & 1 \end{bmatrix}.$$

To find a basis for Nul A row reduce to reduced echelon form, note that the solution to $A\mathbf{x} = \mathbf{0}$ in terms of free variables is $x_1 = -(13/2)x_3 - 5x_5 + 3x_7$, $x_2 = -(11/2)x_3 - (1/2)x_5 - 2x_7$, $x_4 = (11/2)x_5 - 7x_7$, $x_6 = -x_7$, with x_3, x_5, and x_7 free. Thus matrix N is

$$N = \begin{bmatrix} -13/2 & -5 & 3 \\ -11/2 & -1/2 & -2 \\ 1 & 0 & 0 \\ 0 & 11/2 & -7 \\ 0 & 1 & 0 \\ 0 & 0 & -1 \\ 0 & 0 & 1 \end{bmatrix}.$$

b. The reduced echelon form of A^T is

$$A^T \sim \begin{bmatrix} 1 & 0 & 0 & 0 & -2/11 \\ 0 & 1 & 0 & 0 & -41/11 \\ 0 & 0 & 1 & 0 & 0 \\ 0 & 0 & 0 & 1 & 28/11 \\ 0 & 0 & 0 & 0 & 0 \\ 0 & 0 & 0 & 0 & 0 \\ 0 & 0 & 0 & 0 & 0 \end{bmatrix},$$

so the solution to $A^T \mathbf{x} = \mathbf{0}$ in terms of free variables is $x_1 = (2/11)x_5$, $x_2 = (41/11)x_5$, $x_3 = 0$, $x_4 = -(28/11)x_5$, with x_5 free. Thus matrix M is

$$M = \begin{bmatrix} 2/11 \\ 41/11 \\ 0 \\ -28/11 \\ 1 \end{bmatrix}.$$

The matrix $S = \begin{bmatrix} R^T & N \end{bmatrix}$ is 7×7 because the columns of R^T and N are in $\mathbb{R}^7$ and dimRow A + dimNul $A = 7$. The matrix $T = \begin{bmatrix} C & M \end{bmatrix}$ is 5×5 because the columns of C and M are in $\mathbb{R}^5$ and dimCol A + dimNul $A^T = 5$. Both S and T are invertible because their columns are linearly independent. This fact will be proven in general in Theorem 3 of Section 6.1.

36. **[M]** Answers will vary, but in most cases C will be 6×4, and will be constructed from the first 4 columns of A. In most cases R will be 4×7, N will be 7×3, and M will be 6×2.

37. **[M]** The C and R from Exercise 35 work here, and $A = CR$.

38. **[M]** If A is nonzero, then $A = CR$. Note that $CR = \begin{bmatrix} C\mathbf{r}_1 & C\mathbf{r}_2 & \dots & C\mathbf{r}_n \end{bmatrix}$, where $\mathbf{r}_1, \dots, \mathbf{r}_n$ are the columns of R. The columns of R are either pivot columns of R or are not pivot columns of R.

Consider first the pivot columns of R. The ith pivot column of R is $\mathbf{e}_i$, the ith column in the identity matrix, so $C\mathbf{e}_i$ is the ith pivot column of A. Since A and R have pivot columns in the same locations, when C multiplies a pivot column of R, the result is the corresponding pivot column of A in its proper location.

Suppose $\mathbf{r}_j$ is a nonpivot column of R. Then $\mathbf{r}_j$ contains the weights needed to construct the jth column of A from the pivot columns of A, as is discussed in Example 9 of Section 4.3 and in the paragraph preceding that example. Thus $\mathbf{r}_j$ contains the weights needed to construct the jth column of A from the columns of C, and $C\mathbf{r}_j = \mathbf{a}_j$.

4.7   SOLUTIONS

Notes: This section depends heavily on the coordinate systems introduced in Section 4.4. The row reduction algorithm that produces $\underset{c \leftarrow B}{P}$ can also be deduced from Exercise 12 in Section 2.2, by row reducing $\begin{bmatrix} P_C \mid P_B \end{bmatrix}$. to $\begin{bmatrix} I \mid P_C^{-1} P_B \end{bmatrix}$. The change-of-coordinates matrix here is interpreted in Section 5.4 as the matrix of the identity transformation relative to two bases.

1. a. Since $\mathbf{b}_1 = 6\mathbf{c}_1 - 2\mathbf{c}_2$ and $\mathbf{b}_2 = 9\mathbf{c}_1 - 4\mathbf{c}_2$, $[\mathbf{b}_1]_C = \begin{bmatrix} 6 \\ -2 \end{bmatrix}$, $[\mathbf{b}_2]_C = \begin{bmatrix} 9 \\ -4 \end{bmatrix}$, and $\underset{C \leftarrow B}{P} = \begin{bmatrix} 6 & 9 \\ -2 & -4 \end{bmatrix}$.

b. Since $\mathbf{x} = -3\mathbf{b}_1 + 2\mathbf{b}_2$, $[\mathbf{x}]_B = \begin{bmatrix} -3 \\ 2 \end{bmatrix}$ and

$$[\mathbf{x}]_C = \underset{C \leftarrow B}{P}[x]_B = \begin{bmatrix} 6 & 9 \\ -2 & -4 \end{bmatrix} \begin{bmatrix} -3 \\ 2 \end{bmatrix} = \begin{bmatrix} 0 \\ -2 \end{bmatrix}$$

2. a. Since $\mathbf{b}_1 = -\mathbf{c}_1 + 4\mathbf{c}_2$ and $\mathbf{b}_2 = 5\mathbf{c}_1 - 3\mathbf{c}_2$, $[\mathbf{b}_1]_C = \begin{bmatrix} -1 \\ 4 \end{bmatrix}$, $[\mathbf{b}_2]_C = \begin{bmatrix} 5 \\ -3 \end{bmatrix}$, and $\underset{C \leftarrow B}{P} = \begin{bmatrix} -1 & 5 \\ 4 & -3 \end{bmatrix}$.

b. Since $\mathbf{x} = 5\mathbf{b}_1 + 3\mathbf{b}_2$, $[\mathbf{x}]_B = \begin{bmatrix} 5 \\ 3 \end{bmatrix}$ and

$$[\mathbf{x}]_C = \underset{C \leftarrow B}{P}[\mathbf{x}]_B = \begin{bmatrix} -1 & 5 \\ 4 & -3 \end{bmatrix} \begin{bmatrix} 5 \\ 3 \end{bmatrix} = \begin{bmatrix} 10 \\ 11 \end{bmatrix}$$

3. Equation (ii) is satisfied by P for all $\mathbf{x}$ in V.

4. Equation (i) is satisfied by P for all $\mathbf{x}$ in V.

5. a. Since $\mathbf{a}_1 = 4\mathbf{b}_1 - \mathbf{b}_2$, $\mathbf{a}_2 = -\mathbf{b}_1 + \mathbf{b}_2 + \mathbf{b}_3$, and $\mathbf{a}_3 = \mathbf{b}_2 - 2\mathbf{b}_3$, $[\mathbf{a}_1]_B = \begin{bmatrix} 4 \\ -1 \\ 0 \end{bmatrix}$, $[\mathbf{a}_2]_B = \begin{bmatrix} -1 \\ 1 \\ 1 \end{bmatrix}$,

$[\mathbf{a}_3]_B = \begin{bmatrix} 0 \\ 1 \\ -2 \end{bmatrix}$, and $\underset{B \leftarrow A}{P} = \begin{bmatrix} 4 & -1 & 0 \\ -1 & 1 & 1 \\ 0 & 1 & -2 \end{bmatrix}$.

b. Since $\mathbf{x} = 3\mathbf{a}_1 + 4\mathbf{a}_2 + \mathbf{a}_3$, $[\mathbf{x}]_A = \begin{bmatrix} 3 \\ 4 \\ 1 \end{bmatrix}$ and

$$[\mathbf{x}]_B = \underset{B \leftarrow A}{P} = \begin{bmatrix} 4 & -1 & 0 \\ -1 & 1 & 1 \\ 0 & 1 & -2 \end{bmatrix} \begin{bmatrix} 3 \\ 4 \\ 1 \end{bmatrix} = \begin{bmatrix} 8 \\ 2 \\ 2 \end{bmatrix}$$

6. a. Since $\mathbf{f}_1 = 2\mathbf{d}_1 - \mathbf{d}_2 + \mathbf{d}_3$, $\mathbf{f}_2 = 3\mathbf{d}_2 + \mathbf{d}_3$, and $\mathbf{f}_3 = -3\mathbf{d}_1 + 2\mathbf{d}_3$, $[\mathbf{f}_1]_D = \begin{bmatrix} 2 \\ -1 \\ 1 \end{bmatrix}$, $[\mathbf{f}_2]_D = \begin{bmatrix} 0 \\ 3 \\ 1 \end{bmatrix}$, $[\mathbf{f}_3]_D = \begin{bmatrix} -3 \\ 0 \\ 2 \end{bmatrix}$,

and $\underset{D \leftarrow F}{P} = \begin{bmatrix} 2 & 0 & -3 \\ -1 & 3 & 0 \\ 1 & 1 & 2 \end{bmatrix}$.

b. Since $\mathbf{x} = \mathbf{f}_1 - 2\mathbf{f}_2 + 2\mathbf{f}_3$, $[\mathbf{x}]_F = \begin{bmatrix} 1 \\ -2 \\ 2 \end{bmatrix}$ and

$$[\mathbf{x}]_D = \underset{D \leftarrow F}{P} [\mathbf{x}]_F = \begin{bmatrix} 2 & 0 & -3 \\ -1 & 3 & 0 \\ 1 & 1 & 2 \end{bmatrix} \begin{bmatrix} 1 \\ -2 \\ 2 \end{bmatrix} = \begin{bmatrix} -4 \\ -7 \\ 3 \end{bmatrix}$$

7. To find $\underset{C \leftarrow B}{P}$, row reduce the matrix $\begin{bmatrix} \mathbf{c}_1 & \mathbf{c}_2 & \mathbf{b}_1 & \mathbf{b}_2 \end{bmatrix}$:

$$\begin{bmatrix} \mathbf{c}_1 & \mathbf{c}_2 & \mathbf{b}_1 & \mathbf{b}_2 \end{bmatrix} \sim \begin{bmatrix} 1 & 0 & -3 & 1 \\ 0 & 1 & -5 & 2 \end{bmatrix}.$$

Thus $\underset{C \leftarrow B}{P} = \begin{bmatrix} -3 & 1 \\ -5 & 2 \end{bmatrix}$, and $\underset{B \leftarrow C}{P} = \underset{C \leftarrow B}{P}^{-1} = \begin{bmatrix} -2 & 1 \\ -5 & 3 \end{bmatrix}$.

8. To find $\underset{C \leftarrow B}{P}$, row reduce the matrix $\begin{bmatrix} \mathbf{c}_1 & \mathbf{c}_2 & \mathbf{b}_1 & \mathbf{b}_2 \end{bmatrix}$:

$$\begin{bmatrix} \mathbf{c}_1 & \mathbf{c}_2 & \mathbf{b}_1 & \mathbf{b}_2 \end{bmatrix} \sim \begin{bmatrix} 1 & 0 & 3 & -2 \\ 0 & 1 & -4 & 3 \end{bmatrix}.$$

Thus $\underset{C \leftarrow B}{P} = \begin{bmatrix} 3 & -2 \\ -4 & 3 \end{bmatrix}$, and $\underset{B \leftarrow C}{P} = \underset{C \leftarrow B}{P}^{-1} = \begin{bmatrix} 3 & 2 \\ 4 & 3 \end{bmatrix}$.

9. To find $\underset{C \leftarrow B}{P}$, row reduce the matrix $\begin{bmatrix} \mathbf{c}_1 & \mathbf{c}_2 & \mathbf{b}_1 & \mathbf{b}_2 \end{bmatrix}$:

$$\begin{bmatrix} \mathbf{c}_1 & \mathbf{c}_2 & \mathbf{b}_1 & \mathbf{b}_2 \end{bmatrix} \sim \begin{bmatrix} 1 & 0 & 9 & -2 \\ 0 & 1 & -4 & 1 \end{bmatrix}.$$

Thus $\underset{C \leftarrow B}{P} = \begin{bmatrix} 9 & -2 \\ -4 & 1 \end{bmatrix}$, and $\underset{B \leftarrow C}{P} = \underset{C \leftarrow B}{P}^{-1} = \begin{bmatrix} 1 & 2 \\ 4 & 9 \end{bmatrix}$.

10. To find $\underset{C \leftarrow B}{P}$, row reduce the matrix $\begin{bmatrix} \mathbf{c}_1 & \mathbf{c}_2 & \mathbf{b}_1 & \mathbf{b}_2 \end{bmatrix}$:

$$\begin{bmatrix} \mathbf{c}_1 & \mathbf{c}_2 & \mathbf{b}_1 & \mathbf{b}_2 \end{bmatrix} \sim \begin{bmatrix} 1 & 0 & 8 & 3 \\ 0 & 1 & -5 & -2 \end{bmatrix}.$$

Thus $\underset{C \leftarrow B}{P} = \begin{bmatrix} 8 & 3 \\ -5 & -2 \end{bmatrix}$, and $\underset{B \leftarrow C}{P} = \underset{C \leftarrow B}{P}^{-1} = \begin{bmatrix} 2 & 3 \\ -5 & -8 \end{bmatrix}$.

11. a. False. See Theorem 15.

b. True. See the first paragraph in the subsection "Change of Basis in $\mathbb{R}^n$."

12. a. True. The columns of $\underset{C\leftarrow B}{P}$ are coordinate vectors of the linearly independent set B. See the second paragraph after Theorem 15.

    b. False. The row reduction is discussed after Example 2. The matrix P obtained there satisfies $[\mathbf{x}]_C = P[\mathbf{x}]_B$

13. Let $B = \{\mathbf{b}_1, \mathbf{b}_2, \mathbf{b}_3\} = \{1 - 2t + t^2, 3 - 5t + 4t^2, 2t + 3t^2\}$ and let $C = \{\mathbf{c}_1, \mathbf{c}_2, \mathbf{c}_3\} = \{1, t, t^2\}$. The C-coordinate vectors of $\mathbf{b}_1$, $\mathbf{b}_2$, and $\mathbf{b}_3$ are

$$[\mathbf{b}_1]_C = \begin{bmatrix} 1 \\ -2 \\ 1 \end{bmatrix}, [\mathbf{b}_2]_C = \begin{bmatrix} 3 \\ -5 \\ 4 \end{bmatrix}, [\mathbf{b}_3]_C = \begin{bmatrix} 0 \\ 2 \\ 3 \end{bmatrix}$$

So

$$\underset{C\leftarrow B}{P} = \begin{bmatrix} 1 & 3 & 0 \\ -2 & -5 & 2 \\ 1 & 4 & 3 \end{bmatrix}$$

Let $\mathbf{x} = -1 + 2t$. Then the coordinate vector $[\mathbf{x}]_B$ satisfies

$$\underset{C\leftarrow B}{P}[\mathbf{x}]_B = [\mathbf{x}]_C = \begin{bmatrix} -1 \\ 2 \\ 0 \end{bmatrix}$$

This system may be solved by row reducing its augmented matrix:

$$\begin{bmatrix} 1 & 3 & 0 & -1 \\ -2 & -5 & 2 & 2 \\ 1 & 4 & 3 & 0 \end{bmatrix} \sim \begin{bmatrix} 1 & 0 & 0 & 5 \\ 0 & 1 & 0 & -2 \\ 0 & 0 & 0 & 1 \end{bmatrix}, \text{ so } [\mathbf{x}]_B = \begin{bmatrix} 5 \\ -2 \\ 1 \end{bmatrix}$$

14. Let $B = \{\mathbf{b}_1, \mathbf{b}_2, \mathbf{b}_3\} = \{1 - 3t^2, 2 + t - 5t^2, 1 + 2t\}$ and let $C = \{\mathbf{c}_1, \mathbf{c}_2, \mathbf{c}_3\} = \{1, t, t^2\}$. The C-coordinate vectors of $\mathbf{b}_1$, $\mathbf{b}_2$, and $\mathbf{b}_3$ are

$$[\mathbf{b}_1]_C = \begin{bmatrix} 1 \\ 0 \\ -3 \end{bmatrix}, [\mathbf{b}_2]_C = \begin{bmatrix} 2 \\ 1 \\ -5 \end{bmatrix}, [\mathbf{b}_3]_C = \begin{bmatrix} 1 \\ 2 \\ 0 \end{bmatrix}$$

So

$$\underset{C\leftarrow B}{P} = \begin{bmatrix} 1 & 2 & 1 \\ 0 & 1 & 2 \\ -3 & -5 & 0 \end{bmatrix}$$

Let $\mathbf{x} = t^2$. Then the coordinate vector $[\mathbf{x}]_B$ satisfies

$$\underset{C\leftarrow B}{P}[\mathbf{x}]_B = [\mathbf{x}]_C = \begin{bmatrix} 0 \\ 0 \\ 1 \end{bmatrix}$$

This system may be solved by row reducing its augmented matrix:

$$\begin{bmatrix} 1 & 2 & 1 & 0 \\ 0 & 1 & 2 & 0 \\ -3 & -5 & 0 & 1 \end{bmatrix} \sim \begin{bmatrix} 1 & 0 & 0 & 3 \\ 0 & 1 & 0 & -2 \\ 0 & 0 & 0 & 1 \end{bmatrix}, \text{ so } [\mathbf{x}]_B = \begin{bmatrix} 3 \\ -2 \\ 1 \end{bmatrix}$$

and $t^2 = 3(1 - 3t^2) - 2(2 + t - 5t^2) + (1 + 2t)$.

15. (a) B is a basis for V

    (b) the coordinate mapping is a linear transformation

    (c) of the product of a matrix and a vector

    (d) the coordinate vector of $\mathbf{v}$ relative to B

16. (a) $[\mathbf{b}_1]_C = Q[\mathbf{b}_1]_B = Q \begin{bmatrix} 1 \\ 0 \\ \vdots \\ 0 \end{bmatrix} = Q\mathbf{e}_1$

    (b) $[\mathbf{b}_k]_C$

    (c) $[\mathbf{b}_k]_C = Q[\mathbf{b}_k]_B = Q\mathbf{e}_k$

17. **[M]**

    a. Since we found P in Exercise 34 of Section 4.5, we can calculate that

    $$P^{-1} = \frac{1}{32} \begin{bmatrix} 32 & 0 & 16 & 0 & 12 & 0 & 10 \\ 0 & 32 & 0 & 24 & 0 & 20 & 0 \\ 0 & 0 & 16 & 0 & 16 & 0 & 15 \\ 0 & 0 & 0 & 8 & 0 & 10 & 0 \\ 0 & 0 & 0 & 0 & 4 & 0 & 6 \\ 0 & 0 & 0 & 0 & 0 & 2 & 0 \\ 0 & 0 & 0 & 0 & 0 & 0 & 1 \end{bmatrix}.$$

    b. Since P is the change-of-coordinates matrix from C to B, P^{-1} will be the change-of-coordinates matrix from B to C. By Theorem 15, the columns of P^{-1} will be the C-coordinate vectors of the basis vectors in B. Thus

    $$\cos^2 t = \frac{1}{2}(1 + \cos 2t)$$

    $$\cos^3 t = \frac{1}{4}(3\cos t + \cos 3t)$$

    $$\cos^4 t = \frac{1}{8}(3 + 4\cos 2t + \cos 4t)$$

    $$\cos^5 t = \frac{1}{16}(10\cos t + 5\cos 3t + \cos 5t)$$

    $$\cos^6 t = \frac{1}{32}(10 + 15\cos 2t + 6\cos 4t + \cos 6t)$$

18. [M] The C-coordinate vector of the integrand is $(0, 0, 0, 5, -6, 5, -12)$. Using P^{-1} from the previous exercise, the B- coordinate vector of the integrand will be

$$P^{-1}(0, 0, 0, 5, -6, 5, -12) = (-6, 55/8, -69/8, 45/16, -3, 5/16, -3/8)$$

Thus the integral may be rewritten as

$$\int -6 + \frac{55}{8}\cos t - \frac{69}{8}\cos 2t + \frac{45}{16}\cos 3t - 3\cos 4t + \frac{5}{16}\cos 5t - \frac{3}{8}\cos 6t\, dt,$$

which equals

$$-6t + \frac{55}{8}\sin t - \frac{69}{16}\sin 2t + \frac{15}{16}\sin 3t - \frac{3}{4}\sin 4t + \frac{1}{16}\sin 5t - \frac{1}{16}\sin 6t + C.$$

19. [M]

   a. If C is the basis $\{\mathbf{v}_1, \mathbf{v}_2, \mathbf{v}_3\}$, then the columns of P are $[\mathbf{u}_1]_C$, $[\mathbf{u}_2]_C$, and $[\mathbf{u}_3]_C$. So $\mathbf{u}_j = [\mathbf{v}_1 \ \mathbf{v}_2 \ \mathbf{v}_3][\mathbf{u}_1]_C$, and $[\mathbf{u}_1 \ \mathbf{u}_2 \ \mathbf{u}_3] = [\mathbf{v}_1 \ \mathbf{v}_2 \ \mathbf{v}_3]P$. In the current exercise,

$$[\mathbf{u}_1 \ \ \mathbf{u}_2 \ \ \mathbf{u}_3] = \begin{bmatrix} -2 & -8 & -7 \\ 2 & 5 & 2 \\ 3 & 2 & 6 \end{bmatrix} \begin{bmatrix} 1 & 2 & -1 \\ -3 & -5 & 0 \\ 4 & 6 & 1 \end{bmatrix} = \begin{bmatrix} -6 & -6 & -5 \\ -5 & -9 & 0 \\ 21 & 32 & 3 \end{bmatrix}.$$

   b. Analogously to part a., $[\mathbf{v}_1 \ \mathbf{v}_2 \ \mathbf{v}_3] = [\mathbf{w}_1 \ \mathbf{w}_2 \ \mathbf{w}_3]P$, so $[\mathbf{w}_1 \ \mathbf{w}_2 \ \mathbf{w}_3] = [\mathbf{v}_1 \ \mathbf{v}_2 \ \mathbf{v}_3]P^{-1}$. In the current exercise,

$$[\mathbf{w}_1 \ \ \mathbf{w}_2 \ \ \mathbf{w}_3] = \begin{bmatrix} -2 & -8 & -7 \\ 2 & 5 & 2 \\ 3 & 2 & 6 \end{bmatrix} \begin{bmatrix} 1 & 2 & -1 \\ -3 & -5 & 0 \\ 4 & 6 & 1 \end{bmatrix}^{-1}$$

$$= \begin{bmatrix} -2 & -8 & -7 \\ 2 & 5 & 2 \\ 3 & 2 & 6 \end{bmatrix} \begin{bmatrix} 5 & 8 & 5 \\ -3 & -5 & -3 \\ -2 & -2 & -1 \end{bmatrix} = \begin{bmatrix} 28 & 38 & 21 \\ -9 & -13 & -7 \\ -3 & 2 & 3 \end{bmatrix}.$$

20. a. $\underset{D \leftarrow B}{P} = \underset{D \leftarrow C}{P}\ \underset{C \leftarrow B}{P}$

Let $\mathbf{x}$ be any vector in the two-dimensional vector space. Since $\underset{C \leftarrow B}{P}$ is the change-of-coordinates matrix from B to C and $\underset{D \leftarrow C}{P}$ is the change-of-coordinates matrix from C to D,

$$[\mathbf{x}]_C = \underset{C \leftarrow B}{P}[\mathbf{x}]_B \text{ and } [\mathbf{x}]_D = \underset{D \leftarrow C}{P}[\mathbf{x}]_C = \underset{D \leftarrow C}{P}\ \underset{C \leftarrow B}{P}[\mathbf{x}]_B$$

But since $\underset{D \leftarrow B}{P}$ is the change-of-coordinates matrix from B to D,

$$[\mathbf{x}]_D = \underset{D \leftarrow B}{P}[\mathbf{x}]_B$$

Thus

$$\underset{D \leftarrow B}{P}[\mathbf{x}]_B = \underset{D \leftarrow C}{P}\ \underset{C \leftarrow B}{P}[\mathbf{x}]_B$$

for any vector $[\mathbf{x}]_B$ in $\mathbb{R}^2$, and

$$\underset{D \leftarrow B}{P} = \underset{D \leftarrow C}{P}\ \underset{C \leftarrow B}{P}$$

b. [M] For example, let $B = \left\{ \begin{bmatrix} 7 \\ 5 \end{bmatrix}, \begin{bmatrix} -3 \\ -1 \end{bmatrix} \right\}$, $C = \left\{ \begin{bmatrix} 1 \\ -5 \end{bmatrix}, \begin{bmatrix} -2 \\ 2 \end{bmatrix} \right\}$, and $D = \left\{ \begin{bmatrix} -1 \\ 8 \end{bmatrix}, \begin{bmatrix} 1 \\ -5 \end{bmatrix} \right\}$. Then we

can calculate the change-of-coordinates matrices:

$$\begin{bmatrix} 1 & -2 & 7 & -3 \\ -5 & 2 & 5 & -1 \end{bmatrix} \sim \begin{bmatrix} 1 & 0 & -3 & 1 \\ 0 & 1 & -5 & 2 \end{bmatrix} \Rightarrow \underset{C \leftarrow B}{P} = \begin{bmatrix} -3 & 1 \\ -5 & 2 \end{bmatrix}$$

$$\begin{bmatrix} -1 & 1 & 1 & -2 \\ 8 & -5 & -5 & 2 \end{bmatrix} \sim \begin{bmatrix} 1 & 0 & 0 & -8/3 \\ 0 & 1 & 1 & -14/3 \end{bmatrix} \Rightarrow \underset{D \leftarrow C}{P} = \begin{bmatrix} 0 & -8/3 \\ 1 & -14/3 \end{bmatrix}$$

$$\begin{bmatrix} -1 & 1 & 7 & -3 \\ 8 & -5 & 5 & -1 \end{bmatrix} \sim \begin{bmatrix} 1 & 0 & 40/3 & -16/3 \\ 0 & 1 & 61/3 & -25/3 \end{bmatrix} \Rightarrow \underset{D \leftarrow B}{P} = \begin{bmatrix} 40/3 & -16/3 \\ 61/3 & -25/3 \end{bmatrix}$$

One confirms easily that

$$\underset{D \leftarrow B}{P} = \begin{bmatrix} 40/3 & -16/3 \\ 61/3 & -25/3 \end{bmatrix} = \begin{bmatrix} 0 & -8/3 \\ 1 & -14/3 \end{bmatrix} \begin{bmatrix} -3 & 1 \\ -5 & 2 \end{bmatrix} = \underset{D \leftarrow C}{P} \underset{C \leftarrow B}{P}$$

4.8   SOLUTIONS

Notes: This is an important section for engineering students and worth extra class time. To spend only one lecture on this section, you could cover through Example 5, but assign the somewhat lengthy Example 3 for reading. Finding a spanning set for the solution space of a difference equation uses the Basis Theorem (Section 4.5) and Theorem 17 in this section, and demonstrates the power of the theory of Chapter 4 in helping to solve applied problems. This section anticipates Section 5.7 on differential equations. The reduction of an nth order difference equation to a linear system of first order difference equations was introduced in Section 1.10, and is revisited in Sections 4.9 and 5.6. Example 3 is the background for Exercise 26 in Section 6.5.

1. Let $y_k = 2^k$. Then

$$y_{k+2} + 2y_{k+1} - 8y_k = 2^{k+2} + 2(2^{k+1}) - 8(2^k)$$
$$= 2^k (2^2 + 2^2 - 8)$$
$$= 2^k (0) = 0 \text{ for all } k$$

Since the difference equation holds for all k, 2^k is a solution.

Let $y_k = (-4)^k$. Then

$$y_{k+2} + 2y_{k+1} - 8y_k = (-4)^{k+2} + 2(-4)^{k+1} - 8(-4)^k$$
$$= (-4)^k ((-4)^2 + 2(-4) - 8)$$
$$= (-4)^k (0) = 0 \text{ for all } k$$

Since the difference equation holds for all k, $(-4)^k$ is a solution.

2. Let $y_k = 3^k$. Then

$$y_{k+2} - 9y_k = 3^{k+2} - 9(3^k)$$
$$= 3^k (3^2 - 9)$$
$$= 3^k (0) = 0 \text{ for all } k$$

Since the difference equation holds for all k, 3^k is a solution.

Let $y_k = (-3)^k$. Then

$$y_{k+2} - 9y_k = (-3)^{k+2} - 9(-3)^k$$
$$= (-3)^k((-3)^2 - 9)$$
$$= (-3)^k(0) = 0 \text{ for all } k$$

Since the difference equation holds for all k, $(-3)^k$ is a solution.

3. The signals 2^k and $(-4)^k$ are linearly independent because neither is a multiple of the other; that is, there is no scalar c such that $2^k = c(-4)^k$ for all k. By Theorem 17, the solution set H of the difference equation $y_{k+2} + 2y_{k+1} - 8y_k = 0$ is two-dimensional. By the Basis Theorem, the two linearly independent signals 2^k and $(-4)^k$ form a basis for H.

4. The signals 3^k and $(-3)^k$ are linearly independent because neither is a multiple of the other; that is, there is no scalar c such that $3^k = c(-3)^k$ for all k. By Theorem 17, the solution set H of the difference equation $y_{k+2} - 9y_k = 0$ is two-dimensional. By the Basis Theorem, the two linearly independent signals 3^k and $(-3)^k$ form a basis for H.

5. Let $y_k = (-3)^k$. Then

$$y_{k+2} + 6y_{k+1} + 9y_k = (-3)^{k+2} + 6(-3)^{k+1} + 9(-3)^k$$
$$= (-3)^k((-3)^2 + 6(-3) + 9)$$
$$= (-3)^k(0) = 0 \text{ for all } k$$

Since the difference equation holds for all k, $(-3)^k$ is in the solution set H.

Let $y_k = k(-3)^k$. Then

$$y_{k+2} + 6y_{k+1} + 9y_k = (k+2)(-3)^{k+2} + 6(k+1)(-3)^{k+1} + 9k(-3)^k$$
$$= (-3)^k((k+2)(-3)^2 + 6(k+1)(-3) + 9k)$$
$$= (-3)^k(9k + 18 - 18k - 18 + 9k)$$
$$= (-3)^k(0) = 0 \text{ for all } k$$

Since the difference equation holds for all k, $k(-3)^k$ is in the solution set H.

The signals $(-3)^k$ and $k(-3)^k$ are linearly independent because neither is a multiple of the other; that is, there is no scalar c such that $(-3)^k = ck(-3)^k$ for all k and there is no scalar c such that $c(-3)^k = k(-3)^k$ for all k. By Theorem 17, dim $H = 2$, so the two linearly independent signals 3^k and $(-3)^k$ form a basis for H by the Basis Theorem.

6. Let $y_k = 5^k \cos\frac{k\pi}{2}$. Then

$$y_{k+2} + 25y_k = 5^{k+2}\cos\frac{(k+2)\pi}{2} + 25\left(5^k\cos\frac{k\pi}{2}\right)$$

$$= 5^k\left(5^2\cos\frac{(k+2)\pi}{2} + 25\cos\frac{k\pi}{2}\right)$$

$$= 25\cdot 5^k\left(\cos\left(\frac{k\pi}{2}+\pi\right) + \cos\frac{k\pi}{2}\right)$$

$$= 25\cdot 5^k(0) = 0 \text{ for all } k$$

since $\cos(t+\pi) = -\cos t$ for all t. Since the difference equation holds for all k, $5^k\cos\frac{k\pi}{2}$ is in the solution set H.

Let $y_k = 5^k\sin\frac{k\pi}{2}$. Then

$$y_{k+2} + 25y_k = 5^{k+2}\sin\frac{(k+2)\pi}{2} + 25\left(5^k\sin\frac{k\pi}{2}\right)$$

$$= 5^k\left(5^2\sin\frac{(k+2)\pi}{2} + 25\sin\frac{k\pi}{2}\right)$$

$$= 25\cdot 5^k\left(\sin\left(\frac{k\pi}{2}+\pi\right) + \sin\frac{k\pi}{2}\right)$$

$$= 25\cdot 5^k(0) = 0 \text{ for all } k$$

since $\sin(t+\pi) = -\sin t$ for all t. Since the difference equation holds for all k, $5^k\sin\frac{k\pi}{2}$ is in the solution set H.

The signals $5^k\cos\frac{k\pi}{2}$ and $5^k\sin\frac{k\pi}{2}$ are linearly independent because neither is a multiple of the other. By Theorem 17, dim $H = 2$, so the two linearly independent signals $5^k\cos\frac{k\pi}{2}$ and $5^k\sin\frac{k\pi}{2}$ form a basis for H by the Basis Theorem.

7. Compute and row reduce the Casorati matrix for the signals 1^k, 2^k, and $(-2)^k$, setting $k = 0$ for convenience:

$$\begin{bmatrix} 1^0 & 2^0 & (-2)^0 \\ 1^1 & 2^1 & (-2)^1 \\ 1^2 & 2^2 & (-2)^2 \end{bmatrix} \sim \begin{bmatrix} 1 & 0 & 0 \\ 0 & 1 & 0 \\ 0 & 0 & 1 \end{bmatrix}$$

This Casorati matrix is row equivalent to the identity matrix, thus is invertible by the IMT. Hence the set of signals $\{1^k, 2^k, (-2)^k\}$ is linearly independent in $\mathbb{S}$. The exercise states that these signals are in the solution set H of a third-order difference equation. By Theorem 17, dim $H = 3$, so the three linearly independent signals 1^k, 2^k, $(-2)^k$ form a basis for H by the Basis Theorem.

8. Compute and row reduce the Casorati matrix for the signals 2^k, 4^k, and $(-5)^k$, setting $k = 0$ for convenience:

$$\begin{bmatrix} 2^0 & 4^0 & (-5)^0 \\ 2^1 & 4^1 & (-5)^1 \\ 2^2 & 4^2 & (-5)^2 \end{bmatrix} \sim \begin{bmatrix} 1 & 0 & 0 \\ 0 & 1 & 0 \\ 0 & 0 & 1 \end{bmatrix}$$

This Casorati matrix is row equivalent to the identity matrix, thus is invertible by the IMT. Hence the set of signals $\{2^k, 4^k, (-5)^k\}$ is linearly independent in $\mathbb{S}$. The exercise states that these signals are in the solution set H of a third-order difference equation. By Theorem 17, dim $H = 3$, so the three linearly independent signals 2^k, 4^k, $(-5)^k$ form a basis for H by the Basis Theorem.

9. Compute and row reduce the Casorati matrix for the signals 1^k, $3^k \cos \frac{k\pi}{2}$, and $3^k \sin \frac{k\pi}{2}$, setting $k = 0$ for convenience:

$$\begin{bmatrix} 1^0 & 3^0 \cos 0 & 3^0 \sin 0 \\ 1^1 & 3^1 \cos \frac{\pi}{2} & 3^1 \sin \frac{\pi}{2} \\ 1^2 & 3^2 \cos \pi & 3^2 \sin \pi \end{bmatrix} \sim \begin{bmatrix} 1 & 0 & 0 \\ 0 & 1 & 0 \\ 0 & 0 & 1 \end{bmatrix}$$

This Casorati matrix is row equivalent to the identity matrix, thus is invertible by the IMT. Hence the set of signals $\{1^k, 3^k \cos \frac{k\pi}{2}, 3^k \sin \frac{k\pi}{2}\}$ is linearly independent in $\mathbb{S}$. The exercise states that these signals are in the solution set H of a third-order difference equation. By Theorem 17, dim $H = 3$, so the three linearly independent signals 1^k, $3^k \cos \frac{k\pi}{2}$, and $3^k \sin \frac{k\pi}{2}$, form a basis for H by the Basis Theorem.

10. Compute and row reduce the Casorati matrix for the signals $(-1)^k$, $k(-1)^k$, and 5^k, setting $k = 0$ for convenience:

$$\begin{bmatrix} (-1)^0 & 0(-1)^0 & 5^0 \\ (-1)^1 & 1(-1)^1 & 5^1 \\ (-1)^2 & 2(-1)^2 & 5^2 \end{bmatrix} \sim \begin{bmatrix} 1 & 0 & 0 \\ 0 & 1 & 0 \\ 0 & 0 & 1 \end{bmatrix}$$

This Casorati matrix is row equivalent to the identity matrix, thus is invertible by the IMT. Hence the set of signals $\{(-1)^k, k(-1)^k, 5^k\}$ is linearly independent in $\mathbb{S}$. The exercise states that these signals are in the solution set H of a third-order difference equation. By Theorem 17, dim $H = 3$, so the three linearly independent signals $(-1)^k$, $k(-1)^k$, and 5^k form a basis for H by the Basis Theorem.

11. The solution set H of this third-order difference equation has dim $H = 3$ by Theorem 17. The two signals $(-1)^k$ and 3^k cannot possibly span a three-dimensional space, and so cannot be a basis for H.

12. The solution set H of this fourth-order difference equation has dim $H = 4$ by Theorem 17. The two signals 1^k and $(-1)^k$ cannot possibly span a four-dimensional space, and so cannot be a basis for H.

13. The auxiliary equation for this difference equation is $r^2 - r + 2/9 = 0$. By the quadratic formula (or factoring), $r = 2/3$ or $r = 1/3$, so two solutions of the difference equation are $(2/3)^k$ and $(1/3)^k$. The signals $(2/3)^k$ and $(1/3)^k$ are linearly independent because neither is a multiple of the other.

By Theorem 17, the solution space is two-dimensional, so the two linearly independent signals $(2/3)^k$ and $(1/3)^k$ form a basis for the solution space by the Basis Theorem.

14. The auxiliary equation for this difference equation is $r^2 - 7r + 12 = 0$. By the quadratic formula (or factoring), $r = 3$ or $r = 4$, so two solutions of the difference equation are 3^k and 4^k. The signals 3^k and 4^k are linearly independent because neither is a multiple of the other. By Theorem 17, the solution space is two-dimensional, so the two linearly independent signals 3^k and 4^k form a basis for the solution space by the Basis Theorem.

15. The auxiliary equation for this difference equation is $r^2 - 25 = 0$. By the quadratic formula (or factoring), $r = 5$ or $r = -5$, so two solutions of the difference equation are 5^k and $(-5)^k$. The signals 5^k and $(-5)^k$ are linearly independent because neither is a multiple of the other. By Theorem 17, the solution space is two-dimensional, so the two linearly independent signals 5^k and $(-5)^k$ form a basis for the solution space by the Basis Theorem.

16. The auxiliary equation for this difference equation is $16r^2 + 8r - 3 = 0$. By the quadratic formula (or factoring), $r = 1/4$ or $r = -3/4$, so two solutions of the difference equation are $(1/4)^k$ and $(-3/4)^k$. The signals $(1/4)^k$ and $(-3/4)^k$ are linearly independent because neither is a multiple of the other. By Theorem 17, the solution space is two-dimensional, so the two linearly independent signals $(1/4)^k$ and $(-3/4)^k$ form a basis for the solution space by the Basis Theorem.

17. Letting $a = .9$ and $b = 4/9$ gives the difference equation $Y_{k+2} - 1.3Y_{k+1} + .4Y_k = 1$. First we find a particular solution $Y_k = T$ of this equation, where T is a constant. The solution of the equation $T - 1.3T + .4T = 1$ is $T = 10$, so 10 is a particular solution to $Y_{k+2} - 1.3Y_{k+1} + .4Y_k = 1$. Next we solve the homogeneous difference equation $Y_{k+2} - 1.3Y_{k+1} + .4Y_k = 0$. The auxiliary equation for this difference equation is $r^2 - 1.3r + .4 = 0$. By the quadratic formula (or factoring), $r = .8$ or $r = .5$, so two solutions of the homogeneous difference equation are $.8^k$ and $.5^k$. The signals $(.8)^k$ and $(.5)^k$ are linearly independent because neither is a multiple of the other. By Theorem 17, the solution space is two-dimensional, so the two linearly independent signals $(.8)^k$ and $(.5)^k$ form a basis for the solution space of the homogeneous difference equation by the Basis Theorem. Translating the solution space of the homogeneous difference equation by the particular solution 10 of the nonhomogeneous difference equation gives us the general solution of $Y_{k+2} - 1.3Y_{k+1} + .4Y_k = 1$: $Y_k = c_1(.8)^k + c_2(.5)^k + 10$. As k increases the first two terms in the solution approach 0, so Y_k approaches 10.

18. Letting $a = .9$ and $b = .5$ gives the difference equation $Y_{k+2} - 1.35Y_{k+1} + .45Y_k = 1$. First we find a particular solution $Y_k = T$ of this equation, where T is a constant. The solution of the equation $T - 1.35T + .45T = 1$ is $T = 10$, so 10 is a particular solution to $Y_{k+2} - 1.3Y_{k+1} + .4Y_k = 1$. Next we solve the homogeneous difference equation $Y_{k+2} - 1.35Y_{k+1} + .45Y_k = 0$. The auxiliary equation for this difference equation is $r^2 - 1.35r + .45 = 0$. By the quadratic formula (or factoring), $r = .6$ or $r = .75$, so two solutions of the homogeneous difference equation are $.6^k$ and $.75^k$. The signals $(.6)^k$ and $(.75)^k$ are linearly independent because neither is a multiple of the other. By Theorem 17, the solution space is two-dimensional, so the two linearly independent signals $(.6)^k$ and $(.75)^k$ form a basis for the solution space of the homogeneous difference equation by the Basis Theorem. Translating the solution space of the

homogeneous difference equation by the particular solution 10 of the nonhomogeneous difference equation gives us the general solution of $Y_{k+2} - 1.35Y_{k+1} + .45Y_k = 1$: $Y_k = c_1(.6)^k + c_2(.75)^k + 10$.

19. The auxiliary equation for this difference equation is $r^2 + 4r + 1 = 0$. By the quadratic formula, $r = -2 + \sqrt{3}$ or $r = -2 - \sqrt{3}$, so two solutions of the difference equation are $(-2 + \sqrt{3})^k$ and $(-2 - \sqrt{3})^k$. The signals $(-2 + \sqrt{3})^k$ and $(-2 - \sqrt{3})^k$ are linearly independent because neither is a multiple of the other. By Theorem 17, the solution space is two-dimensional, so the two linearly independent signals $(-2 + \sqrt{3})^k$ and $(-2 - \sqrt{3})^k$ form a basis for the solution space by the Basis Theorem. Thus a general solution to this difference equation is $y_k = c_1(-2 + \sqrt{3})^k + c_2(-2 - \sqrt{3})^k$.

20. Let $a = -2 + \sqrt{3}$ and $b = -2 - \sqrt{3}$. Using the solution from the previous exercise, we find that $y_1 = c_1 a + c_2 b = 5000$ and $y_N = c_1 a^N + c_2 b^N = 0$. This is a system of linear equations with variables c_1 and c_2 whose augmented matrix may be row reduced:

$$\begin{bmatrix} a & b & 5000 \\ a^N & b^N & 0 \end{bmatrix} \sim \begin{bmatrix} 1 & 0 & \dfrac{5000b^N}{b^N a - a^N b} \\ 0 & 1 & \dfrac{5000a^N}{b^N a - a^N b} \end{bmatrix}$$

so

$$c_1 = \frac{5000b^N}{b^N a - a^N b}, c_2 = \frac{5000a^N}{b^N a - a^N b}$$

(Alternatively, Cramer's Rule may be applied to get the same solution). Thus

$$y_k = c_1 a^k + c_2 b^k$$
$$= \frac{5000(a^k b^N - a^N b^k)}{b^N a - a^N b}$$

21. The smoothed signal z_k has the following values: $z_1 = (9 + 5 + 7)/3 = 7$, $z_2 = (5 + 7 + 3)/3 = 5$, $z_3 = (7 + 3 + 2)/3 = 4$, $z_4 = (3 + 2 + 4)/3 = 3$, $z_5 = (2 + 4 + 6)/3 = 4$, $z_6 = (4 + 6 + 5)/3 = 5$, $z_7 = (6 + 5 + 7)/3 = 6$, $z_8 = (5 + 7 + 6)/3 = 6$, $z_9 = (7 + 6 + 8)/3 = 7$, $z_{10} = (6 + 8 + 10)/3 = 8$, $z_{11} = (8 + 10 + 9)/3 = 9$, $z_{12} = (10 + 9 + 5)/3 = 8$, $z_{13} = (9 + 5 + 7)/3 = 7$.

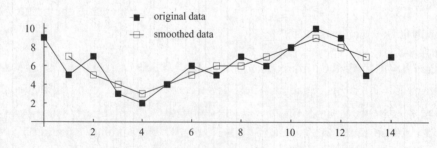

22. **a.** The smoothed signal z_k has the following values:

$$z_0 = .35y_2 + .5y_1 + .35y_0 = .35(0) + .5(.7) + .35(3) = 1.4,$$
$$z_1 = .35y_3 + .5y_2 + .35y_1 = .35(-.7) + .5(0) + .35(.7) = 0,$$
$$z_2 = .35y_4 + .5y_3 + .35y_2 = .35(-.3) + .5(-.7) + .35(0) = -1.4,$$
$$z_3 = .35y_5 + .5y_4 + .35y_3 = .35(-.7) + .5(-.3) + .35(-.7) = -2,$$

$$z_4 = .35y_6 + .5y_5 + .35y_4 = .35(0) + .5(-.7) + .35(-.3) = -1.4,$$

$$z_5 = .35y_7 + .5y_6 + .35y_5 = .35(.7) + .5(0) + .35(-.7) = 0,$$

$$z_6 = .35y_8 + .5y_7 + .35y_6 = .35(3) + .5(.7) + .35(0) = 1.4,$$

$$z_7 = .35y_9 + .5y_8 + .35y_7 = .35(.7) + .5(3) + .35(.7) = 2,$$

$$z_8 = .35y_{10} + .5y_9 + .35y_8 = .35(0) + .5(.7) + .35(3) = 1.4,\ldots$$

b. This signal is two times the signal output by the filter when the input (in Example 3) was $y = \cos(\pi/4)$. This is expected because the filter is linear. The output from the input $2\cos(\pi/4) + \cos(3\pi/4)$ should be two times the output from $\cos(\pi/4)$ plus the output from $\cos(3\pi/4)$ (which is zero).

23. a. $y_{k+1} - 1.01y_k = -450, \ y_0 = 10,000.$

b. **[M]** MATLAB code to create the table:

```
pay = 450, y = 10000, m = 0, table = [0;y]
while y>450
    y = 1.01*y-pay
    m = m+1
    table = [table [m;y]]
end
m,y
```

Mathematica code to create the table:

```
pay = 450; y = 10000; m = 0; balancetable = {{0, y}};
While[y > 450, {y = 1.01*y - pay; m = m + 1,
    AppendTo[balancetable, {m, y}]}];
m
y
```

c. **[M]** At month 26, the last payment is $114.88. The total paid by the borrower is $11,364.88.

24. a. $y_{k+1} - 1.005y_k = 200, \ y_0 = 1,000.$

b. **[M]** MATLAB code to create the table:

```
pay = 200, y = 1000, m = 0, table = [0;y]
for m = 1: 60
    y = 1.005*y+pay
    table = [table [m;y]]
end
interest = y-60*pay-1000
```

Mathematica code to create the table:

```
pay = 200; y = 1000; amounttable = {{0, y}};
Do[{y = 1.005*y + pay;
    AppendTo[amounttable, {m, y}]}, {m,1,60}];
interest = y-60*pay-1000
```

   c. **[M]** The total is \$6213.55 at $k = 24$, \$12,090.06 at $k = 48$, and \$15,302.86 at $k = 60$. When $k = 60$, the interest earned is \$2302.86.

25. To show that $y_k = k^2$ is a solution of $y_{k+2} + 3_{k+1} - 4y_k = 10k + 7$, substitute $y_k = k^2$, $y_{k+1} = (k+1)^2$, and $y_{k+2} = (k+2)^2$:

$$y_{k+2} + 3_{k+1} - 4y_k = (k+2)^2 + 3(k+1)^2 - 4k^2$$
$$= (k^2 + 4k + 4) + 3(k^2 + 2k + 1) - 4k^2$$
$$= k^2 + 4k + 4 + 3k^2 + 6k + 3 - 4k^2$$
$$= 10k + 7 \text{ for all } k$$

The auxiliary equation for the homogeneous difference equation $y_{k+2} + 3y_{k+1} - 4y_k = 0$ is $r^2 + 3r - 4 = 0$. By the quadratic formula (or factoring), $r = -4$ or $r = 1$, so two solutions of the difference equation are $(-4)^k$ and 1^k. The signals $(-4)^k$ and 1^k are linearly independent because neither is a multiple of the other. By Theorem 17, the solution space is two-dimensional, so the two linearly independent signals $(-4)^k$ and 1^k form a basis for the solution space of the homogeneous difference equation by the Basis Theorem. The general solution to the homogeneous difference equation is thus $c_1(-4)^k + c_2 \cdot 1^k = c_1(-4)^k + c_2$. Adding the particular solution k^2 of the nonhomogeneous difference equation, we find that the general solution of the difference equation $y_{k+2} + 3y_{k+1} - 4y_k = 10k + 7$ is $y_k = k^2 + c_1(-4)^k + c_2$.

26. To show that $y_k = 1 + k$ is a solution of $y_{k+2} - 8y_{k+1} + 15y_k = 8k + 2$, substitute $y_k = 1 + k$, $y_{k+1} = 1 + (k+1) = 2 + k$, and $y_{k+2} = 1 + (k+2) = 3 + k$:

$$y_{k+2} - 8y_{k+1} + 15y_k = (3+k) - 8(2+k) + 15(1+k)$$
$$= 3 + k - 16 - 8k + 15 + 15k$$
$$= 8k + 2 \text{ for all } k$$

The auxiliary equation for the homogeneous difference equation $y_{k+2} - 8y_{k+1} + 15y_k = 0$ is $r^2 - 8r + 15 = 0$. By the quadratic formula (or factoring), $r = 5$ or $r = 3$, so two solutions of the difference equation are 5^k and 3^k. The signals 5^k and 3^k are linearly independent because neither is a multiple of the other. By Theorem 17, the solution space is two-dimensional, so the two linearly independent signals 5^k and 3^k form a basis for the solution space of the homogeneous difference equation by the Basis Theorem. The general solution to the homogeneous difference equation is thus $c_1 \cdot 5^k + c_2 \cdot 3^k$. Adding the particular solution $1 + k$ of the nonhomogeneous difference equation, we find that the general solution of the difference equation $y_{k+2} - 8y_{k+1} + 15y_k = 8k + 2$ is $y_k = 1 + k + c_1 \cdot 5^k + c_2 \cdot 3^k$.

27. To show that $y_k = 2 - 2k$ is a solution of $y_{k+2} - (9/2)y_{k+1} + 2y_k = 3k + 2$, substitute $y_k = 2 - 2k$, $y_{k+1} = 2 - 2(k+1) = -2k$, and $y_{k+2} = 2 - 2(k+2) = -2 - 2k$:

$$y_{k+2} - (9/2)y_{k+1} + 2y_k = (-2 - 2k) - (9/2)(-2k) + 2(2 - 2k)$$
$$= -2 - 2k + 9k + 4 - 4k$$
$$= 3k + 2 \text{ for all } k$$

The auxiliary equation for the homogeneous difference equation $y_{k+2} - (9/2)y_{k+1} + 2y_k = 0$ is $r^2 - (9/2)r + 2 = 0$. By the quadratic formula (or factoring), $r = 4$ or $r = 1/2$, so two solutions of the difference equation are 4^k and $(1/2)^k$. The signals 4^k and $(1/2)^k$ are linearly independent because neither is a multiple of the other. By Theorem 17, the solution space is two-dimensional, so the two linearly independent signals 4^k and $(1/2)^k$ form a basis for the solution space of the homogeneous difference equation by the Basis Theorem. The general solution to the homogeneous difference equation is thus $c_1 \cdot 4^k + c_2 \cdot (1/2)^k = c_1 \cdot 4^k + c_2 \cdot 2^{-k}$. Adding the particular solution $2 - 2k$ of the nonhomogeneous difference equation, we find that the general solution of the difference equation $y_{k+2} - (9/2)y_{k+1} + 2y_k = 3k + 2$ is $y_k = 2 - 2k + c_1 \cdot 4^k + c_2 \cdot 2^{-k}$.

28. To show that $y_k = 2k - 4$ is a solution of $y_{k+2} + (3/2)y_{k+1} - y_k = 1 + 3k$, substitute $y_k = 2k - 4$, $y_{k+1} = 2(k+1) - 4 = 2k - 2$, and $y_{k+2} = 2(k+2) - 4 = 2k$:

$$y_{k+2} + (3/2)y_{k+1} - y_k = 2k + (3/2)(2k-2) - (2k-4)$$
$$= 2k + 3k - 3 - 2k + 4$$
$$= 1 + 3k \text{ for all } k$$

The auxiliary equation for the homogeneous difference equation $y_{k+2} + (3/2)y_{k+1} - y_k = 0$ is $r^2 + (3/2)r - 1 = 0$. By the quadratic formula (or factoring), $r = -2$ or $r = 1/2$, so two solutions of the difference equation are $(-2)^k$ and $(1/2)^k$. The signals $(-2)^k$ and $(1/2)^k$ are linearly independent because neither is a multiple of the other. By Theorem 17, the solution space is two-dimensional, so the two linearly independent signals $(-2)^k$ and $(1/2)^k$ form a basis for the solution space of the homogeneous difference equation by the Basis Theorem. The general solution to the homogeneous difference equation is thus $c_1 \cdot (-2)^k + c_2 \cdot (1/2)^k = c_1 \cdot (-2)^k + c_2 \cdot 2^{-k}$. Adding the particular solution $2k - 4$ of the nonhomogeneous difference equation, we find that the general solution of the difference equation $y_{k+2} + (3/2)y_{k+1} - y_k = 1 + 3k$ is $y_k = 2k - 4 + c_1 \cdot (-2)^k + c_2 \cdot 2^{-k}$.

29. Let $\mathbf{x}_k = \begin{bmatrix} y_k \\ y_{k+1} \\ y_{k+2} \\ y_{k+3} \end{bmatrix}$. Then $\mathbf{x}_{k+1} = \begin{bmatrix} y_{k+1} \\ y_{k+2} \\ y_{k+3} \\ y_{k+4} \end{bmatrix} = \begin{bmatrix} 0 & 1 & 0 & 0 \\ 0 & 0 & 1 & 0 \\ 0 & 0 & 0 & 1 \\ 9 & -6 & -8 & 6 \end{bmatrix} \begin{bmatrix} y_k \\ y_{k+1} \\ y_{k+2} \\ y_{k+3} \end{bmatrix} = A\mathbf{x}_k$.

30. Let $\mathbf{x}_k = \begin{bmatrix} y_k \\ y_{k+1} \\ y_{k+2} \end{bmatrix}$. Then $\mathbf{x}_{k+1} = \begin{bmatrix} y_{k+1} \\ y_{k+2} \\ y_{k+3} \end{bmatrix} = \begin{bmatrix} 0 & 1 & 0 \\ 0 & 0 & 1 \\ -1/16 & 0 & 3/4 \end{bmatrix} \begin{bmatrix} y_k \\ y_{k+1} \\ y_{k+2} \end{bmatrix} = A\mathbf{x}_k$.

31. The difference equation is of order 2. Since the equation $y_{k+3} + 5y_{k+2} + 6y_{k+1} = 0$ holds for all k, it holds if k is replaced by $k - 1$. Performing this replacement transforms the equation into $y_{k+2} + 5y_{k+1} + 6y_k = 0$, which is also true for all k. The transformed equation has order 2.

32. The order of the difference equation depends on the values of a_1, a_2, and a_3. If $a_3 \neq 0$, then the order is 3. If $a_3 = 0$ and $a_2 \neq 0$, then the order is 2. If $a_3 = a_2 = 0$ and $a_1 \neq 0$, then the order is 1. If $a_3 = a_2 = a_1 = 0$, then the order is 0, and the equation has only the zero signal for a solution.

33. The Casorati matrix $C(k)$ is

$$C(k) = \begin{bmatrix} y_k & z_k \\ y_{k+1} & z_{k+1} \end{bmatrix} = \begin{bmatrix} k^2 & 2k\,|k| \\ (k+1)^2 & 2(k+1)\,|k+1| \end{bmatrix}$$

In particular,

$$C(0) = \begin{bmatrix} 0 & 0 \\ 1 & 2 \end{bmatrix}, C(-1) = \begin{bmatrix} 1 & -2 \\ 0 & 0 \end{bmatrix}, \text{ and } C(-2) = \begin{bmatrix} 4 & -8 \\ 1 & -2 \end{bmatrix}$$

none of which are invertible. In fact, $C(k)$ is not invertible for all k, since

$$\det C(k) = 2k^2(k+1)|k+1| - 2(k+1)^2 k|k| = 2k(k+1)\big(k|k+1| - (k+1)|k|\big)$$

If $k = 0$ or $k = -1$, $\det C(k) = 0$. If $k > 0$, then $k + 1 > 0$ and $k|k+1| - (k+1)|k| = k(k+1) - (k+1)k = 0$, so $\det C(k) = 0$. If $k < -1$, then $k + 1 < 0$ and $k|k+1| - (k+1)|k| = -k(k+1) + (k+1)k = 0$, so $\det C(k) = 0$. Thus $\det C(k) = 0$ for all k, and $C(k)$ is not invertible for all k. Since $C(k)$ is not invertible for all k, it provides no information about whether the signals $\{y_k\}$ and $\{z_k\}$ are linearly dependent or linearly independent. In fact, neither signal is a multiple of the other, so the signals $\{y_k\}$ and $\{z_k\}$ are linearly independent.

34. No, the signals could be linearly dependent, since the vector space V of functions considered on the entire real line is not the vector space $\mathbb{S}$ of signals. For example, consider the functions $f(t) = \sin \pi t$, $g(t) = \sin 2\pi t$, and $h(t) = \sin 3\pi t$. The functions f, g, and h are linearly independent in V since they have different periods and thus no function could be a linear combination of the other two. However, sampling the functions at any integer n gives $f(n) = g(n) = h(n) = 0$, so the signals are linearly dependent in $\mathbb{S}$.

35. Let $\{y_k\}$ and $\{z_k\}$ be in $\mathbb{S}$, and let r be any scalar. The kth term of $\{y_k\} + \{z_k\}$ is $y_k + z_k$, while the kth term of $r\{y_k\}$ is ry_k. Thus

$$T(\{y_k\} + \{z_k\}) = T\{y_k + z_k\}$$
$$= (y_{k+2} + z_{k+2}) + a(y_{k+1} + z_{k+1}) + b(y_k + z_k)$$
$$= (y_{k+2} + ay_{k+1} + by_k) + (z_{k+2} + az_{k+1} + bz_k)$$
$$= T\{y_k\} + T\{z_k\}, \text{and}$$
$$T(r\{y_k\}) = T\{ry_k\}$$
$$= ry_{k+2} + a(ry_{k+1}) + b(ry_k)$$
$$= r(y_{k+2} + ay_{k+1} + by_k)$$
$$= rT\{y_k\}$$

so T has the two properties that define a linear transformation.

36. Let $\mathbf{z}$ be in V, and suppose that $\mathbf{x}_p$ in V satisfies $T(\mathbf{x}_p) = \mathbf{z}$. Let $\mathbf{u}$ be in the kernel of T; then $T(\mathbf{u}) = \mathbf{0}$. Since T is a linear transformation, $T(\mathbf{u} + \mathbf{x}_p) = T(\mathbf{u}) + T(\mathbf{x}_p) = \mathbf{0} + \mathbf{z} = \mathbf{z}$, so the vector $\mathbf{x} = \mathbf{u} + \mathbf{x}_p$ satisfies the nonhomogeneous equation $T(\mathbf{x}) = \mathbf{z}$.

37. We compute that

$$(TD)(y_0, y_1, y_2, \ldots) = T(D(y_0, y_1, y_2, \ldots)) = T(0, y_0, y_1, y_2, \ldots) = (y_0, y_1, y_2, \ldots)$$

while

$$(DT)(y_0, y_1, y_2, \ldots) = D(T(y_0, y_1, y_2, \ldots)) = D(y_1, y_2, y_3, \ldots) = (0, y_1, y_2, y_3, \ldots)$$

Thus $TD = I$ (the identity transformation on $\mathbb{S}_0$), while $DT \neq I$.

4.9   SOLUTIONS

Notes: This section builds on the population movement example in Section 1.10. The migration matrix is examined again in Section 5.2, where an eigenvector decomposition shows explicitly why the sequence of state vectors $\mathbf{x}_k$ tends to a steady state vector. The discussion in Section 5.2 does not depend on prior knowledge of this section.

1. **a.** Let N stand for "News" and M stand for "Music." Then the listeners' behavior is given by the table

From:

N	M	To:
.7	.6	N
.3	.4	M

so the stochastic matrix is $P = \begin{bmatrix} .7 & .6 \\ .3 & .4 \end{bmatrix}$.

b. Since 100% of the listeners are listening to news at 8: 15, the initial state vector is $\mathbf{x}_0 = \begin{bmatrix} 1 \\ 0 \end{bmatrix}$.

c. There are two breaks between 8: 15 and 9: 25, so we calculate $\mathbf{x}_2$:

$$\mathbf{x}_1 = P\mathbf{x}_0 = \begin{bmatrix} .7 & .6 \\ .3 & .4 \end{bmatrix}\begin{bmatrix} 1 \\ 0 \end{bmatrix} = \begin{bmatrix} .7 \\ .3 \end{bmatrix}$$

$$\mathbf{x}_2 = P\mathbf{x}_1 = \begin{bmatrix} .7 & .6 \\ .3 & .4 \end{bmatrix}\begin{bmatrix} .7 \\ .3 \end{bmatrix} = \begin{bmatrix} .67 \\ .33 \end{bmatrix}$$

Thus 33% of the listeners are listening to news at 9: 25.

2. **a.** Let the foods be labelled "1," "2," and "3." Then the animals' behavior is given by the table

From:

1	2	3	To:
.5	.25	.25	1
.25	.5	.25	2
.25	.25	.5	3

so the stochastic matrix is $P = \begin{bmatrix} .5 & .25 & .25 \\ .25 & .5 & .25 \\ .25 & .25 & .5 \end{bmatrix}$.

b. There are two trials after the initial trial, so we calculate $\mathbf{x}_2$. The initial state vector is $\begin{bmatrix} 1 \\ 0 \\ 0 \end{bmatrix}$.

$$\mathbf{x}_1 = P\mathbf{x}_0 = \begin{bmatrix} .5 & .25 & .25 \\ .25 & .5 & .25 \\ .25 & .25 & .5 \end{bmatrix}\begin{bmatrix} 1 \\ 0 \\ 0 \end{bmatrix} = \begin{bmatrix} .5 \\ .25 \\ .25 \end{bmatrix}$$

$$\mathbf{x}_2 = P\mathbf{x}_1 = \begin{bmatrix} .5 & .25 & .25 \\ .25 & .5 & .25 \\ .25 & .25 & .5 \end{bmatrix}\begin{bmatrix} .5 \\ .25 \\ .25 \end{bmatrix} = \begin{bmatrix} .375 \\ .3125 \\ .3125 \end{bmatrix}$$

Thus the probability that the animal will choose food #2 is .3125.

3. a. Let H stand for "Healthy" and I stand for "Ill." Then the students' conditions are given by the table

	From:		To:
	H	I	
	.95	.45	H
	.05	.55	I

so the stochastic matrix is $P = \begin{bmatrix} .95 & .45 \\ .05 & .55 \end{bmatrix}$.

b. Since 20% of the students are ill on Monday, the initial state vector is $\mathbf{x}_0 = \begin{bmatrix} .8 \\ .2 \end{bmatrix}$. For Tuesday's

percentages, we calculate $\mathbf{x}_1$; for Wednesday's percentages, we calculate $\mathbf{x}_2$:

$$\mathbf{x}_1 = P\mathbf{x}_0 = \begin{bmatrix} .95 & .45 \\ .05 & .55 \end{bmatrix}\begin{bmatrix} .8 \\ .2 \end{bmatrix} = \begin{bmatrix} .85 \\ .15 \end{bmatrix}$$

$$\mathbf{x}_2 = P\mathbf{x}_1 = \begin{bmatrix} .95 & .45 \\ .05 & .55 \end{bmatrix}\begin{bmatrix} .85 \\ .15 \end{bmatrix} = \begin{bmatrix} .875 \\ .125 \end{bmatrix}$$

Thus 15% of the students are ill on Tuesday, and 12.5% are ill on Wednesday.

c. Since the student is well today, the initial state vector is $\mathbf{x}_0 = \begin{bmatrix} 1 \\ 0 \end{bmatrix}$. We calculate $\mathbf{x}_2$:

$$\mathbf{x}_1 = P\mathbf{x}_0 = \begin{bmatrix} .95 & .45 \\ .05 & .55 \end{bmatrix}\begin{bmatrix} 1 \\ 0 \end{bmatrix} = \begin{bmatrix} .95 \\ .05 \end{bmatrix}$$

$$\mathbf{x}_2 = P\mathbf{x}_1 = \begin{bmatrix} .95 & .45 \\ .05 & .55 \end{bmatrix}\begin{bmatrix} .95 \\ .05 \end{bmatrix} = \begin{bmatrix} .925 \\ .075 \end{bmatrix}$$

Thus the probability that the student is well two days from now is .925.

4. a. Let G stand for good weather, I for indifferent weather, and B for bad weather. Then the change in the weather is given by the table

	From:			To:
	G	I	B	
	.6	.4	.4	G
	.3	.3	.5	I
	.1	.3	.1	B

so the stochastic matrix is $P = \begin{bmatrix} .6 & .4 & .4 \\ .3 & .3 & .5 \\ .1 & .3 & .1 \end{bmatrix}$.

b. The initial state vector is $\begin{bmatrix} .5 \\ .5 \\ 0 \end{bmatrix}$. We calculate $\mathbf{x}_1$:

$$\mathbf{x}_1 = P\mathbf{x}_0 = \begin{bmatrix} .6 & .4 & .4 \\ .3 & .3 & .5 \\ .1 & .3 & .1 \end{bmatrix}\begin{bmatrix} .5 \\ .5 \\ 0 \end{bmatrix} = \begin{bmatrix} .5 \\ .3 \\ .2 \end{bmatrix}$$

Thus the chance of bad weather tomorrow is 20%.

c. The initial state vector is $\mathbf{x}_0 = \begin{bmatrix} 0 \\ .4 \\ .6 \end{bmatrix}$. We calculate $\mathbf{x}_2$:

$$\mathbf{x}_1 = P\mathbf{x}_0 = \begin{bmatrix} .6 & .4 & .4 \\ .3 & .3 & .5 \\ .1 & .3 & .1 \end{bmatrix} \begin{bmatrix} 0 \\ .4 \\ .6 \end{bmatrix} = \begin{bmatrix} .4 \\ .42 \\ .18 \end{bmatrix}$$

$$\mathbf{x}_2 = P\mathbf{x}_1 = \begin{bmatrix} .6 & .4 & .4 \\ .3 & .3 & .5 \\ .1 & .3 & .1 \end{bmatrix} \begin{bmatrix} .4 \\ .42 \\ .18 \end{bmatrix} = \begin{bmatrix} .48 \\ .336 \\ .184 \end{bmatrix}$$

Thus the chance of good weather on Wednesday is 48%.

5. We solve $P\mathbf{x} = \mathbf{x}$ by rewriting the equation as $(P - I)\mathbf{x} = \mathbf{0}$, where $P - I = \begin{bmatrix} -.9 & .6 \\ .9 & -.6 \end{bmatrix}$. Row reducing the augmented matrix for the homogeneous system $(P - I)\mathbf{x} = \mathbf{0}$ gives

$$\begin{bmatrix} -.9 & .6 & 0 \\ .9 & -.6 & 0 \end{bmatrix} \sim \begin{bmatrix} 1 & -2/3 & 0 \\ 0 & 0 & 0 \end{bmatrix}$$

Thus $\mathbf{x} = \begin{bmatrix} x_1 \\ x_2 \end{bmatrix} = x_2 \begin{bmatrix} 2/3 \\ 1 \end{bmatrix}$, and one solution is $\begin{bmatrix} 2 \\ 3 \end{bmatrix}$. Since the entries in $\begin{bmatrix} 2 \\ 3 \end{bmatrix}$ sum to 5, multiply by 1/5 to obtain the steady-state vector $\mathbf{q} = \begin{bmatrix} 2/5 \\ 3/5 \end{bmatrix} = \begin{bmatrix} .4 \\ .6 \end{bmatrix}$.

6. We solve $P\mathbf{x} = \mathbf{x}$ by rewriting the equation as $(P - I)\mathbf{x} = \mathbf{0}$, where $P - I = \begin{bmatrix} -.2 & .5 \\ .2 & -.5 \end{bmatrix}$. Row reducing the augmented matrix for the homogeneous system $(P - I)\mathbf{x} = \mathbf{0}$ gives

$$\begin{bmatrix} -.2 & .5 & 0 \\ .2 & -.5 & 0 \end{bmatrix} \sim \begin{bmatrix} 1 & -5/2 & 0 \\ 0 & 0 & 0 \end{bmatrix}$$

Thus $\mathbf{x} = \begin{bmatrix} x_1 \\ x_2 \end{bmatrix} = x_2 \begin{bmatrix} 5/2 \\ 1 \end{bmatrix}$, and one solution is $\begin{bmatrix} 5 \\ 2 \end{bmatrix}$. Since the entries in $\begin{bmatrix} 5 \\ 2 \end{bmatrix}$ sum to 7, multiply by 1/7 to obtain the steady-state vector $\mathbf{q} = \begin{bmatrix} 5/7 \\ 2/7 \end{bmatrix} \approx \begin{bmatrix} .714 \\ .286 \end{bmatrix}$.

7. We solve $P\mathbf{x} = \mathbf{x}$ by rewriting the equation as $(P - I)\mathbf{x} = \mathbf{0}$, where $P - I = \begin{bmatrix} -.3 & .1 & .1 \\ .2 & -.2 & .2 \\ .1 & .1 & -.3 \end{bmatrix}$. Row reducing the augmented matrix for the homogeneous system $(P - I)\mathbf{x} = \mathbf{0}$ gives

$$\begin{bmatrix} -.3 & .1 & .1 & 0 \\ .2 & -.2 & .2 & 0 \\ .1 & .1 & -.3 & 0 \end{bmatrix} \sim \begin{bmatrix} 1 & 0 & -1 & 0 \\ 0 & 1 & -2 & 0 \\ 0 & 0 & 0 & 0 \end{bmatrix}$$

Thus $\mathbf{x} = \begin{bmatrix} x_1 \\ x_2 \\ x_3 \end{bmatrix} = x_3 \begin{bmatrix} 1 \\ 2 \\ 1 \end{bmatrix}$, and one solution is $\begin{bmatrix} 1 \\ 2 \\ 1 \end{bmatrix}$. Since the entries in $\begin{bmatrix} 1 \\ 2 \\ 1 \end{bmatrix}$ sum to 4, multiply by 1/4 to

obtain the steady-state vector $\mathbf{q} = \begin{bmatrix} 1/4 \\ 1/2 \\ 1/4 \end{bmatrix} = \begin{bmatrix} .25 \\ .5 \\ .25 \end{bmatrix}$.

8. We solve $P\mathbf{x} = \mathbf{x}$ by rewriting the equation as $(P - I)\mathbf{x} = \mathbf{0}$, where $P - I = \begin{bmatrix} -.3 & .2 & .2 \\ 0 & -.8 & .4 \\ .3 & .6 & -.6 \end{bmatrix}$. Row

reducing the augmented matrix for the homogeneous system $(P - I)\mathbf{x} = \mathbf{0}$ gives

$$\begin{bmatrix} -.3 & .2 & .2 & 0 \\ 0 & -.8 & .4 & 0 \\ .3 & .6 & -.6 & 0 \end{bmatrix} \sim \begin{bmatrix} 1 & 0 & -1 & 0 \\ 0 & 1 & -1/2 & 0 \\ 0 & 0 & 0 & 0 \end{bmatrix}$$

Thus $\mathbf{x} = \begin{bmatrix} x_1 \\ x_2 \\ x_3 \end{bmatrix} = x_3 \begin{bmatrix} 1 \\ 1/2 \\ 1 \end{bmatrix}$, and one solution is $\begin{bmatrix} 2 \\ 1 \\ 2 \end{bmatrix}$. Since the entries in $\begin{bmatrix} 2 \\ 1 \\ 2 \end{bmatrix}$ sum to 5, multiply by 1/5 to

obtain the steady-state vector $\mathbf{q} = \begin{bmatrix} 2/5 \\ 1/5 \\ 2/5 \end{bmatrix} = \begin{bmatrix} .4 \\ .2 \\ .4 \end{bmatrix}$.

9. Since $P^2 = \begin{bmatrix} .84 & .2 \\ .16 & .8 \end{bmatrix}$ has all positive entries, P is a regular stochastic matrix.

10. Since $P^k = \begin{bmatrix} 1 & 1-.8^k \\ 0 & .8^k \end{bmatrix}$ will have a zero as its (2,1) entry for all k, so P is not a regular

stochastic matrix.

11. From Exercise 1, $P = \begin{bmatrix} .7 & .6 \\ .3 & .4 \end{bmatrix}$, so $P - I = \begin{bmatrix} -.3 & .6 \\ .3 & -.6 \end{bmatrix}$. Solving $(P - I)\mathbf{x} = \mathbf{0}$ by row reducing the

augmented matrix gives

$$\begin{bmatrix} -.3 & .6 & 0 \\ .3 & -.6 & 0 \end{bmatrix} \sim \begin{bmatrix} 1 & -2 & 0 \\ 0 & 0 & 0 \end{bmatrix}$$

Thus $\mathbf{x} = \begin{bmatrix} x_1 \\ x_2 \end{bmatrix} = x_2 \begin{bmatrix} 2 \\ 1 \end{bmatrix}$, and one solution is $\begin{bmatrix} 2 \\ 1 \end{bmatrix}$. Since the entries in $\begin{bmatrix} 2 \\ 1 \end{bmatrix}$ sum to 3, multiply by 1/3 to

obtain the steady-state vector $\mathbf{q} = \begin{bmatrix} 2/3 \\ 1/3 \end{bmatrix} \approx \begin{bmatrix} .667 \\ .333 \end{bmatrix}$.

12. From Exercise 2, $P = \begin{bmatrix} .5 & .25 & .25 \\ .25 & .5 & .25 \\ .25 & .25 & .5 \end{bmatrix}$, so $P - I = \begin{bmatrix} -.5 & .25 & .25 \\ .25 & -.5 & .25 \\ .25 & .25 & -.5 \end{bmatrix}$. Solving $(P - I)\mathbf{x} = \mathbf{0}$ by row

reducing the augmented matrix gives

$$\begin{bmatrix} -.5 & .25 & .25 & 0 \\ .25 & -.5 & .25 & 0 \\ .25 & .25 & -.5 & 0 \end{bmatrix} \sim \begin{bmatrix} 1 & 0 & -1 & 0 \\ 0 & 1 & -1 & 0 \\ 0 & 0 & 0 & 0 \end{bmatrix}$$

Thus $\mathbf{x} = \begin{bmatrix} x_1 \\ x_2 \\ x_3 \end{bmatrix} = x_3 \begin{bmatrix} 1 \\ 1 \\ 1 \end{bmatrix}$, and one solution is $\begin{bmatrix} 1 \\ 1 \\ 1 \end{bmatrix}$. Since the entries in $\begin{bmatrix} 1 \\ 1 \\ 1 \end{bmatrix}$ sum to 3, multiply by 1/3 to

obtain the steady-state vector $\mathbf{q} = \begin{bmatrix} 1/3 \\ 1/3 \\ 1/3 \end{bmatrix} \approx \begin{bmatrix} .333 \\ .333 \\ .333 \end{bmatrix}$. Thus in the long run each food will be preferred

equally.

13. a. From Exercise 3, $P = \begin{bmatrix} .95 & .45 \\ .05 & .55 \end{bmatrix}$, so $P - I = \begin{bmatrix} -.05 & .45 \\ .05 & -.45 \end{bmatrix}$. Solving $(P - I)\mathbf{x} = \mathbf{0}$ by row reducing

the augmented matrix gives

$$\begin{bmatrix} -.05 & .45 & 0 \\ .05 & -.45 & 0 \end{bmatrix} \sim \begin{bmatrix} 1 & -9 & 0 \\ 0 & 0 & 0 \end{bmatrix}$$

Thus $\mathbf{x} = \begin{bmatrix} x_1 \\ x_2 \end{bmatrix} = x_2 \begin{bmatrix} 9 \\ 1 \end{bmatrix}$, and one solution is $\begin{bmatrix} 9 \\ 1 \end{bmatrix}$. Since the entries in $\begin{bmatrix} 9 \\ 1 \end{bmatrix}$ sum to 10, multiply by 1/10

to obtain the steady-state vector $\mathbf{q} = \begin{bmatrix} 9/10 \\ 1/10 \end{bmatrix} = \begin{bmatrix} .9 \\ .1 \end{bmatrix}$.

b. After many days, a specific student is ill with probability .1, and it does not matter whether that student is ill today or not.

14. From Exercise 4, $P = \begin{bmatrix} .6 & .4 & .4 \\ .3 & .3 & .5 \\ .1 & .3 & .1 \end{bmatrix}$, so $P - I = \begin{bmatrix} -.4 & .4 & .4 \\ .3 & -.7 & .5 \\ .1 & .3 & -.9 \end{bmatrix}$. Solving $(P - I)\mathbf{x} = \mathbf{0}$ by row reducing

the augmented matrix gives

$$\begin{bmatrix} -.4 & .4 & .4 & 0 \\ .3 & -.7 & .5 & 0 \\ .1 & .3 & -.9 & 0 \end{bmatrix} \sim \begin{bmatrix} 1 & 0 & -3 & 0 \\ 0 & 1 & -2 & 0 \\ 0 & 0 & 0 & 0 \end{bmatrix}$$

Thus $\mathbf{x} = \begin{bmatrix} x_1 \\ x_2 \\ x_3 \end{bmatrix} = x_3 \begin{bmatrix} 3 \\ 2 \\ 1 \end{bmatrix}$, and one solution is $\begin{bmatrix} 3 \\ 2 \\ 1 \end{bmatrix}$. Since the entries in $\begin{bmatrix} 3 \\ 2 \\ 1 \end{bmatrix}$ sum to 6, multiply by 1/6 to

obtain the steady-state vector $\mathbf{q} = \begin{bmatrix} 1/2 \\ 1/3 \\ 1/6 \end{bmatrix} \approx \begin{bmatrix} .5 \\ .333 \\ .167 \end{bmatrix}$. Thus in the long run the chance that a day has good

weather is 50%.

15. [M] Let $P = \begin{bmatrix} .9821 & .0029 \\ .0179 & .9971 \end{bmatrix}$, so $P - I = \begin{bmatrix} -.0179 & .0029 \\ .0179 & -.0029 \end{bmatrix}$. Solving $(P - I)\mathbf{x} = \mathbf{0}$ by row reducing the augmented matrix gives

$$\begin{bmatrix} -.0179 & .0029 & 0 \\ .0179 & -.0029 & 0 \end{bmatrix} \sim \begin{bmatrix} 1 & -.162011 & 0 \\ 0 & 0 & 0 \end{bmatrix}$$

Thus $\mathbf{x} = \begin{bmatrix} x_1 \\ x_2 \end{bmatrix} = x_2 \begin{bmatrix} .162011 \\ 1 \end{bmatrix}$, and one solution is $\begin{bmatrix} .162011 \\ 1 \end{bmatrix}$. Since the entries in $\begin{bmatrix} .162011 \\ 1 \end{bmatrix}$ sum to

1.162011, multiply by 1/1.162011 to obtain the steady-state vector $\mathbf{q} = \begin{bmatrix} .139423 \\ .860577 \end{bmatrix}$. Thus about 13.9% of

the total U.S. population would eventually live in California.

16. [M] Let $P = \begin{bmatrix} .90 & .01 & .09 \\ .01 & .90 & .01 \\ .09 & .09 & .90 \end{bmatrix}$, so $P - I = \begin{bmatrix} -.10 & .01 & .09 \\ .01 & -.10 & .01 \\ .09 & .09 & -.1 \end{bmatrix}$. Solving $(P - I)\mathbf{x} = \mathbf{0}$ by row reducing the

augmented matrix gives

$$\begin{bmatrix} -.10 & .01 & .09 & 0 \\ .01 & -.10 & .01 & 0 \\ .09 & .09 & -.1 & 0 \end{bmatrix} \sim \begin{bmatrix} 1 & 0 & -.919192 & 0 \\ 0 & 1 & -.191919 & 0 \\ 0 & 0 & 0 & 0 \end{bmatrix}$$

Thus $\mathbf{x} = \begin{bmatrix} x_1 \\ x_2 \\ x_3 \end{bmatrix} = x_3 \begin{bmatrix} .919192 \\ .191919 \\ 1 \end{bmatrix}$, and one solution is $\begin{bmatrix} .919192 \\ .191919 \\ 1 \end{bmatrix}$. Since the entries in $\begin{bmatrix} .919192 \\ .191919 \\ 1 \end{bmatrix}$ sum to

2.111111, multiply by 1/2.111111 to obtain the steady-state vector $\mathbf{q} = \begin{bmatrix} .435407 \\ .090909 \\ .473684 \end{bmatrix}$. Thus on a typical day,

about $(.090909)(2000) = 182$ cars will be rented or available from the downtown location.

17. a. The entries in each column of P sum to 1. Each column in the matrix $P - I$ has the same entries as in P except one of the entries is decreased by 1. Thus the entries in each column of $P - I$ sum to 0, and adding all of the other rows of $P - I$ to its bottom row produces a row of zeros.

b. By part a., the bottom row of $P - I$ is the negative of the sum of the other rows, so the rows of $P - I$ are linearly dependent.

c. By part b. and the Spanning Set Theorem, the bottom row of $P - I$ can be removed and the remaining $(n - 1)$ rows will still span the row space of $P - I$. Thus the dimension of the row space of $P - I$ is less than n. Alternatively, let A be the matrix obtained from $P - I$ by adding to the bottom row all the other rows. These row operations did not change the row space, so the row space of $P - I$ is spanned by the nonzero rows of A. By part a., the bottom row of A is a zero row, so the row space of $P - I$ is spanned by the first $(n - 1)$ rows of A.

d. By part c., the rank of $P - I$ is less than n, so the Rank Theorem may be used to show that $\dim \mathrm{Nul}(P - I) = n - \mathrm{rank}(P - I) > 0$. Alternatively the Invertible Martix Theorem may be used since $P - I$ is a square matrix.

18. If $\alpha = \beta = 0$ then $P = \begin{bmatrix} 1 & 0 \\ 0 & 1 \end{bmatrix}$. Notice that $P\mathbf{x} = \mathbf{x}$ for any vector $\mathbf{x}$ in $\mathbb{R}^2$, and that $\begin{bmatrix} 1 \\ 0 \end{bmatrix}$ and $\begin{bmatrix} 0 \\ 1 \end{bmatrix}$ are two linearly independent steady-state vectors in this case.

If $\alpha \neq 0$ or $\beta \neq 0$, we solve $(P - I)\mathbf{x} = \mathbf{0}$ where $P - I = \begin{bmatrix} -\alpha & \beta \\ \alpha & -\beta \end{bmatrix}$. Row reducing the augmented matrix gives

$$\begin{bmatrix} -\alpha & \beta & 0 \\ \alpha & -\beta & 0 \end{bmatrix} \sim \begin{bmatrix} \alpha & -\beta & 0 \\ 0 & 0 & 0 \end{bmatrix}$$

So $\alpha x_1 = \beta x_2$, and one possible solution is to let $x_1 = \beta$, $x_2 = \alpha$. Thus $\mathbf{x} = \begin{bmatrix} x_1 \\ x_2 \end{bmatrix} = \begin{bmatrix} \beta \\ \alpha \end{bmatrix}$. Since the entries in $\begin{bmatrix} \beta \\ \alpha \end{bmatrix}$ sum to $\alpha + \beta$, multiply by $1/(\alpha + \beta)$ to obtain the steady-state vector $\mathbf{q} = \dfrac{1}{\alpha + \beta} \begin{bmatrix} \beta \\ \alpha \end{bmatrix}$.

19. a. The product $S\mathbf{x}$ equals the sum of the entries in $\mathbf{x}$. Thus $\mathbf{x}$ is a probability vector if and only if its entries are nonnegative and $S\mathbf{x} = 1$.

b. Let $P = \begin{bmatrix} \mathbf{p}_1 & \mathbf{p}_2 & \dots & \mathbf{p}_n \end{bmatrix}$, where $\mathbf{p}_1, \mathbf{p}_2, \dots, \mathbf{p}_n$ are probability vectors. By part a.,

$$SP = \begin{bmatrix} S\mathbf{p}_1 & S\mathbf{p}_2 & \dots & S\mathbf{p}_n \end{bmatrix} = \begin{bmatrix} 1 & 1 & \dots & 1 \end{bmatrix} = S$$

c. By part b., $S(P\mathbf{x}) = (SP)\mathbf{x} = S\mathbf{x} = 1$. The entries in $P\mathbf{x}$ are nonnegative since P and $\mathbf{x}$ have only nonnegative entries. By part a., the condition $S(P\mathbf{x}) = 1$ shows that $P\mathbf{x}$ is a probability vector.

20. Let $P = \begin{bmatrix} \mathbf{p}_1 & \mathbf{p}_2 & \dots & \mathbf{p}_n \end{bmatrix}$, so $P^2 = PP = \begin{bmatrix} P\mathbf{p}_1 & P\mathbf{p}_2 & \dots & P\mathbf{p}_n \end{bmatrix}$. By Exercise 19c., the columns of P^2 are probability vectors, so P^2 is a stochastic matrix.

Alternatively, $SP = S$ by Exercise 19b., since P is a stochastic matrix. Right multiplication by P gives $SP^2 = SP$, so $SP = S$ implies that $SP^2 = S$. Since the entries in P are nonnegative, so are the entries in P^2, and P^2 is stochastic matrix.

21. [M]

a. To four decimal places,

$$P^2 = \begin{bmatrix} .2779 & .2780 & .2803 & .2941 \\ .3368 & .3355 & .3357 & .3335 \\ .1847 & .1861 & .1833 & .1697 \\ .2005 & .2004 & .2007 & .2027 \end{bmatrix}, P^3 = \begin{bmatrix} .2817 & .2817 & .2817 & .2814 \\ .3356 & .3356 & .3355 & .3352 \\ .1817 & .1817 & .1819 & .1825 \\ .2010 & .2010 & .2010 & .2009 \end{bmatrix},$$

$$P^4 = P^5 = \begin{bmatrix} .2816 & .2816 & .2816 & .2816 \\ .3355 & .3355 & .3355 & .3355 \\ .1819 & .1819 & .1819 & .1819 \\ .2009 & .2009 & .2009 & .2009 \end{bmatrix}$$

The columns of P^k are converging to a common vector as k increases. The steady state vector $\mathbf{q}$

for P is $\mathbf{q} = \begin{bmatrix} .2816 \\ .3355 \\ .1819 \\ .2009 \end{bmatrix}$, which is the vector to which the columns of P^k are converging.

b. To four decimal places,

$$Q^{10} = \begin{bmatrix} .8222 & .4044 & .5385 \\ .0324 & .3966 & .1666 \\ .1453 & .1990 & .2949 \end{bmatrix}, Q^{20} = \begin{bmatrix} .7674 & .6000 & .6690 \\ .0637 & .2036 & .1326 \\ .1688 & .1964 & .1984 \end{bmatrix},$$

$$Q^{30} = \begin{bmatrix} .7477 & .6815 & .7105 \\ .0783 & .1329 & .1074 \\ .1740 & .1856 & .1821 \end{bmatrix}, Q^{40} = \begin{bmatrix} .7401 & .7140 & .7257 \\ .0843 & .1057 & .0960 \\ .1756 & .1802 & .1783 \end{bmatrix},$$

$$Q^{50} = \begin{bmatrix} .7372 & .7269 & .7315 \\ .0867 & .0951 & .0913 \\ .1761 & .1780 & .1772 \end{bmatrix}, Q^{60} = \begin{bmatrix} .7360 & .7320 & .7338 \\ .0876 & .0909 & .0894 \\ .1763 & .1771 & .1767 \end{bmatrix},$$

$$Q^{70} = \begin{bmatrix} .7356 & .7340 & .7347 \\ .0880 & .0893 & .0887 \\ .1764 & .1767 & .1766 \end{bmatrix}, Q^{80} = \begin{bmatrix} .7354 & .7348 & .7351 \\ .0881 & .0887 & .0884 \\ .1764 & .1766 & .1765 \end{bmatrix},$$

$$Q^{116} = Q^{117} = \begin{bmatrix} .7353 & .7353 & .7353 \\ .0882 & .0882 & .0882 \\ .1765 & .1765 & .1765 \end{bmatrix}$$

The steady state vector $\mathbf{q}$ for Q is $\mathbf{q} = \begin{bmatrix} .7353 \\ .0882 \\ .1765 \end{bmatrix}$ Conjecture: the columns of P^k, where P is a regular stochastic matrix, converge to the steady state vector for P as k increases.

c. Let P be an $n \times n$ regular stochastic matrix, $\mathbf{q}$ the steady state vector of P, and $\mathbf{e}_j$ the jth column of the $n \times n$ identity matrix. Consider the Markov chain $\{\mathbf{x}_k\}$ where $\mathbf{x}_{k+1} = P\mathbf{x}_k$ and $\mathbf{x}_0 = e_j$. By Theorem 18, $\mathbf{x}_k = P^k\mathbf{x}_0$ converges to $\mathbf{q}$ as $k \to \infty$. But $P^k\mathbf{x}_0 = P^k\mathbf{e}_j$, which is the jth column of P^k. Thus the jth column of P^k converges to $\mathbf{q}$ as $k \to \infty$; that is, $P^k \to \begin{bmatrix} \mathbf{q} & \mathbf{q} & \cdots & \mathbf{q} \end{bmatrix}$.

22. **[M]** Answers will vary.

MATLAB Student Version 4.0 code for Method (1):

```
A=randstoc(32); flops(0);
tic, x=nulbasis(A-eye(32));
q=x/sum(x); toc, flops
```

MATLAB Student Version 4.0 code for Method (2):

```
A=randstoc(32); flops(0);
tic, B=A^100; q=B(: ,1); toc, flops
```

Chapter 4 SUPPLEMENTARY EXERCISES _____

1. **a.** True. This set is $\text{Span}\{\mathbf{v}_1, \ldots \mathbf{v}_p\}$, and every subspace is itself a vector space.

   b. True. Any linear combination of $\mathbf{v}_1, \ldots, \mathbf{v}_{p-1}$ is also a linear combination of $\mathbf{v}_1, \ldots, \mathbf{v}_{p-1}, \mathbf{v}_p$ using the zero weight on $\mathbf{v}_p$.

   c. False. Counterexample: Take $\mathbf{v}_p = 2\mathbf{v}_1$. Then $\{\mathbf{v}_1, \ldots \mathbf{v}_p\}$ is linearly dependent.

   d. False. Counterexample: Let $\{\mathbf{e}_1, \mathbf{e}_2, \mathbf{e}_3\}$ be the standard basis for $\mathbb{R}^3$. Then $\{\mathbf{e}_1, \mathbf{e}_2\}$ is a linearly independent set but is not a basis for $\mathbb{R}^3$.

   e. True. See the Spanning Set Theorem (Section 4.3).

   f. True. By the Basis Theorem, S is a basis for V because S spans V and has exactly p elements. So S must be linearly independent.

   g. False. The plane must pass through the origin to be a subspace.

   h. False. Counterexample: $\begin{bmatrix} 2 & 5 & -2 & 0 \\ 0 & 0 & 7 & 3 \\ 0 & 0 & 0 & 0 \end{bmatrix}$.

   i. True. This statement appears before Theorem 13 in Section 4.6.

   j. False. Row operations on A do not change the solutions of $A\mathbf{x} = \mathbf{0}$.

   k. False. Counterexample: $A = \begin{bmatrix} 1 & 2 \\ 3 & 6 \end{bmatrix}$; A has two nonzero rows but the rank of A is 1.

   l. False. If U has k nonzero rows, then rank $A = k$ and dimNul $A = n - k$ by the Rank Theorem.

   m. True. Row equivalent matrices have the same number of pivot columns.

   n. False. The nonzero rows of A span Row A but they may not be linearly independent.

   o. True. The nonzero rows of the reduced echelon form E form a basis for the row space of each matrix that is row equivalent to E.

   p. True. If H is the zero subspace, let A be the 3×3 zero matrix. If dim $H = 1$, let $\{\mathbf{v}\}$ be a basis for H and set $A = \begin{bmatrix} \mathbf{v} & \mathbf{v} & \mathbf{v} \end{bmatrix}$. If dim $H = 2$, let $\{\mathbf{u}, \mathbf{v}\}$ be a basis for H and set $A = \begin{bmatrix} \mathbf{u} & \mathbf{v} & \mathbf{v} \end{bmatrix}$, for example. If dim $H = 3$, then $H = \mathbb{R}^3$, so A can be any 3×3 invertible matrix. Or, let $\{\mathbf{u}, \mathbf{v}, \mathbf{w}\}$ be a basis for H and set $A = \begin{bmatrix} \mathbf{u} & \mathbf{v} & \mathbf{w} \end{bmatrix}$.

   q. False. Counterexample: $A = \begin{bmatrix} 1 & 0 & 0 \\ 0 & 1 & 0 \end{bmatrix}$. If rank $A = n$ (the number of *columns* in A), then the transformation $\mathbf{x} \mapsto A\mathbf{x}$ is one-to-one.

   r. True. If $\mathbf{x} \mapsto A\mathbf{x}$ is onto, then Col $A = \mathbb{R}^m$ and rank $A = m$. See Theorem 12(a) in Section 1.9.

   s. True. See the second paragraph after Theorem 15 in Section 4.7.

   t. False. The jth column of $\underset{C \leftarrow B}{P}$ is $\begin{bmatrix} \mathbf{b}_j \end{bmatrix}_C$.

2. The set is Span S, where $S = \left\{ \begin{bmatrix} 1 \\ 2 \\ -1 \\ 3 \end{bmatrix}, \begin{bmatrix} -2 \\ 5 \\ -4 \\ 1 \end{bmatrix}, \begin{bmatrix} 5 \\ -8 \\ 7 \\ 1 \end{bmatrix} \right\}$. Note that S is a linearly dependent set, but each pair

   of vectors in S forms a linearly independent set. Thus any two of the three vectors $\begin{bmatrix} 1 \\ 2 \\ -1 \\ 3 \end{bmatrix}, \begin{bmatrix} -2 \\ 5 \\ -4 \\ 1 \end{bmatrix}, \begin{bmatrix} 5 \\ -8 \\ 7 \\ 1 \end{bmatrix}$

   will be a basis for Span S.

3. The vector $\mathbf{b}$ will be in $W = \text{Span}\{\mathbf{u}_1, \mathbf{u}_2\}$ if and only if there exist constants c_1 and c_2 with
   $c_1\mathbf{u}_1 + c_2\mathbf{u}_2 = \mathbf{b}$. Row reducing the augmented matrix gives

   $$\begin{bmatrix} -2 & 1 & b_1 \\ 4 & 2 & b_2 \\ -6 & -5 & b_3 \end{bmatrix} \sim \begin{bmatrix} -2 & 1 & b_1 \\ 0 & 4 & 2b_1 + b_2 \\ 0 & 0 & b_1 + 2b_2 + b_3 \end{bmatrix}$$

   so $W = \text{Span}\{\mathbf{u}_1, \mathbf{u}_2\}$ is the set of all (b_1, b_2, b_3) satisfying $b_1 + 2b_2 + b_3 = 0$.

4. The vector $\mathbf{g}$ is not a scalar multiple of the vector $\mathbf{f}$, and $\mathbf{f}$ is not a scalar multiple of $\mathbf{g}$, so the set $\{\mathbf{f}, \mathbf{g}\}$ is
   linearly independent. Even though the *number* $\mathbf{g}(t)$ is a scalar multiple of $\mathbf{f}(t)$ for each t, the scalar
   depends on t.

5. The vector $\mathbf{p}_1$ is not zero, and $\mathbf{p}_2$ is not a multiple of $\mathbf{p}_1$. However, $\mathbf{p}_3$ is $2\mathbf{p}_1 + 2\mathbf{p}_2$, so $\mathbf{p}_3$ is discarded.
   The vector $\mathbf{p}_4$ cannot be a linear combination of $\mathbf{p}_1$ and $\mathbf{p}_2$ since $\mathbf{p}_4$ involves t^2 but $\mathbf{p}_1$ and $\mathbf{p}_2$ do not
   involve t^2. The vector $\mathbf{p}_5$ is $(3/2)\mathbf{p}_1 - (1/2)\mathbf{p}_2 + \mathbf{p}_4$ (which may not be so easy to see at first.) Thus $\mathbf{p}_5$
   is a linear combination of $\mathbf{p}_1$, $\mathbf{p}_2$, and $\mathbf{p}_4$, so $\mathbf{p}_5$ is discarded. So the resulting basis is $\{\mathbf{p}_1, \mathbf{p}_2, \mathbf{p}_4\}$.

6. Find two polynomials from the set $\{\mathbf{p}_1, \ldots, \mathbf{p}_4\}$ that are not multiples of one another. This is easy,
   because one compares only two polynomials at a time. Since these two polynomials form a linearly
   independent set in a two-dimensional space, they form a basis for H by the Basis Theorem.

7. You would have to know that the solution set of the homogeneous system is spanned by two solutions. In
   this case, the null space of the 18×20 coefficient matrix A is at most two-dimensional. By the Rank
   Theorem, dimCol $A = 20 - \text{dimNul } A \geq 20 - 2 = 18$. Since Col A is a subspace of $\mathbb{R}^{18}$, Col $A = \mathbb{R}^{18}$. Thus
   $A\mathbf{x} = \mathbf{b}$ has a solution for every $\mathbf{b}$ in $\mathbb{R}^{18}$.

8. If $n = 0$, then H and V are both the zero subspace, and $H = V$. If $n > 0$, then a basis for H consists of n
   linearly independent vectors $\mathbf{u}_1, \ldots, \mathbf{u}_n$. These vectors are also linearly independent as elements of V.
   But since dim$V = n$, any set of n linearly independent vectors in V must be a basis for V by the Basis
   Theorem. So $\mathbf{u}_1, \ldots, \mathbf{u}_n$ span V, and $H = \text{Span}\{\mathbf{u}_1, \ldots, \mathbf{u}_n\} = V$.

9. Let T: $\mathbb{R}^n \longrightarrow \mathbb{R}^m$ be a linear transformation, and let A be the $m \times n$ standard matrix of T.

   a. If T is one-to-one, then the columns of A are linearly independent by Theoerm 12 in Section 1.9,
      so dimNul $A = 0$. By the Rank Theorem, dimCol $A = n - 0 = n$, which is the number of columns of A.
      As noted in Section 4.2, the range of T is Col A, so the dimension of the range of T is n.

b. If T maps $\mathbb{R}^n$ onto $\mathbb{R}^m$, then the columns of A span $\mathbb{R}^m$ by Theoerm 12 in Section 1.9, so dimCol $A = m$. By the Rank Theorem, dimNul $A = n - m$. As noted in Section 4.2, the kernel of T is Nul A, so the dimension of the kernel of T is $n - m$. Note that $n - m$ must be nonnegative in this case: since A must have a pivot in each row, $n \geq m$.

10. Let $S = \{\mathbf{v}_1, \ldots, \mathbf{v}_p\}$. If S were linearly independent and not a basis for V, then S would not span V. In this case, there would be a vector $\mathbf{v}_{p+1}$ in V that is not in $\text{Span}\{\mathbf{v}_1, \ldots, \mathbf{v}_p\}$. Let $S' = \{\mathbf{v}_1, \ldots, \mathbf{v}_p, \mathbf{v}_{p+1}\}$. Then S' is linearly independent since none of the vectors in S' is a linear combination of vectors that precede it. Since S' has more elements than S, this would contradict the maximality of S. Hence S must be a basis for V.

11. If S is a finite spanning set for V, then a subset of S is a basis for V. Denote this subset of S by S'. Since S' is a basis for V, S' must span V. Since S is a minimal spanning set, S' cannot be a proper subset of S. Thus $S' = S$, and S is a basis for V.

12. **a.** Let $\mathbf{y}$ be in Col AB. Then $\mathbf{y} = AB\mathbf{x}$ for some $\mathbf{x}$. But $AB\mathbf{x} = A(B\mathbf{x})$, so $\mathbf{y} = A(B\mathbf{x})$, and $\mathbf{y}$ is in Col A. Thus Col AB is a subspace of Col A, so rank $AB = \text{dimCol } AB \leq \text{dimCol } A = \text{rank } A$ by Theorem 11 in Section 4.5.

   b. By the Rank Theorem and part a.:
   $$\text{rank } AB = \text{rank}(AB)^T = \text{rank } B^T A^T \leq \text{rank } B^T = \text{rank } B$$

13. By Exercise 12, rank $PA \leq \text{rank } A$, and rank $A = \text{rank}(P^{-1}P)A = \text{rank } P^{-1}(PA) \leq \text{rank } PA$, so rank $PA = \text{rank } A$.

14. Note that $(AQ)^T = Q^T A^T$. Since Q^T is invertible, we can use Exercise 13 to conclude that rank$(AQ)^T = \text{rank } Q^T A^T = \text{rank } A^T$. Since the ranks of a matrix and its transpose are equal (by the Rank Theorem), rank $AQ = \text{rank } A$.

15. The equation $AB = O$ shows that each column of B is in Nul A. Since Nul A is a subspace of $\mathbb{R}^n$, all linear combinations of the columns of B are in Nul A. That is, Col B is a subspace of Nul A. By Theorem 11 in Section 4.5, rank $B = \text{dimCol } B \leq \text{dimNul } A$. By this inequality and the Rank Theorem applied to A,
   $$n = \text{rank } A + \text{dimNul } A \geq \text{rank } A + \text{rank } B$$

16. Suppose that rank $A = r_1$ and rank $B = r_2$. Then there are rank factorizations $A = C_1 R_1$ and $B = C_2 R_2$ of A and B, where C_1 is $m \times r_1$ with rank r_1, C_2 is $m \times r_2$ with rank r_2, R_1 is $r_1 \times n$ with rank r_1, and R_2 is $r_2 \times n$ with rank r_2. Create an $m \times (r_1 + r_2)$ matrix $C = \begin{bmatrix} C_1 & C_2 \end{bmatrix}$ and an $(r_1 + r_2) \times n$ matrix R by stacking R_1 over R_2. Then

$$A + B = C_1 R_1 + C_2 R_2 = \begin{bmatrix} C_1 & C_2 \end{bmatrix} \begin{bmatrix} R_1 \\ R_2 \end{bmatrix} = CR$$

Since the matrix CR is a product, its rank cannot exceed the rank of either of its factors by Exercise 12. Since C has $r_1 + r_2$ columns, the rank of C cannot exceed $r_1 + r_2$. Likewise R has $r_1 + r_2$ rows, so the rank of R cannot exceed $r_1 + r_2$. Thus the rank of $A + B$ cannot exceed $r_1 + r_2 = \text{rank } A + \text{rank } B$, or rank $(A + B) \leq \text{rank } A + \text{rank } B$.

17. Let A be an $m \times n$ matrix with rank r.

  (a) Let A_1 consist of the r pivot columns of A. The columns of A_1 are linearly independent, so A_1 is an $m \times r$ matrix with rank r.

  (b) By the Rank Theorem applied to A_1, the dimension of RowA_1 is r, so A_1 has r linearly independent rows. Let A_2 consist of the r linearly independent rows of A_1. Then A_2 is an $r \times r$ matrix with linearly independent rows. By the Invertible Matrix Theorem, A_2 is invertible.

18. Let A be a 4×4 matrix and B be a 4×2 matrix, and let $\mathbf{u}_0, \ldots, \mathbf{u}_3$ be a sequence of input vectors in $\mathbb{R}^2$.

  a. Use the equation $\mathbf{x}_{k+1} = A\mathbf{x}_k + B\mathbf{u}_k$ for $k = 0, \ldots, 4$, $k = 0, \ldots, 4$, with $\mathbf{x}_0 = \mathbf{0}$.

  $$\mathbf{x}_1 = A\mathbf{x}_0 + B\mathbf{u}_0 = B\mathbf{u}_0$$

  $$\mathbf{x}_2 = A\mathbf{x}_1 + B\mathbf{u}_1 = AB\mathbf{u}_0 + B\mathbf{u}_1$$

  $$\mathbf{x}_3 = A\mathbf{x}_2 + B\mathbf{u}_2 = A(AB\mathbf{u}_0 + B\mathbf{u}_1) + B\mathbf{u}_2 = A^2B\mathbf{u}_0 + AB\mathbf{u}_1 + B\mathbf{u}_2$$

  $$\mathbf{x}_4 = A\mathbf{x}_3 + B\mathbf{u}_3 = A(A^2B\mathbf{u}_0 + AB\mathbf{u}_1 + B\mathbf{u}_2) + B\mathbf{u}_3$$

  $$= A^3B\mathbf{u}_0 + A^2B\mathbf{u}_1 + AB\mathbf{u}_2 + B\mathbf{u}_3$$

  $$= \begin{bmatrix} B & AB & A^2B & A^3B \end{bmatrix} \begin{bmatrix} \mathbf{u}_3 \\ \mathbf{u}_2 \\ \mathbf{u}_1 \\ \mathbf{u}_0 \end{bmatrix} = M\mathbf{u}$$

  Note that M has 4 rows because B does, and that M has 8 columns because B and each of the matrices A^kB have 2 columns. The vector $\mathbf{u}$ in the final equation is in $\mathbb{R}^8$, because each $\mathbf{u}_k$ is in $\mathbb{R}^2$.

  b. If (A, B) is controllable, then the controlability matrix has rank 4, with a pivot in each row, and the columns of M span $\mathbb{R}^4$. Therefore, for any vector $\mathbf{v}$ in $\mathbb{R}^4$, there is a vector $\mathbf{u}$ in $\mathbb{R}^8$ such that $\mathbf{v} = M\mathbf{u}$. However, from part a. we know that $\mathbf{x}_4 = M\mathbf{u}$ when $\mathbf{u}$ is partitioned into a control sequence $\mathbf{u}_0, \ldots, \mathbf{u}_3$. This particular control sequence makes $\mathbf{x}_4 = \mathbf{v}$.

19. To determine if the matrix pair (A, B) is controllable, we compute the rank of the matrix $\begin{bmatrix} B & AB & A^2B \end{bmatrix}$. To find the rank, we row reduce:

  $$\begin{bmatrix} B & AB & A^2B \end{bmatrix} = \begin{bmatrix} 0 & 1 & 0 \\ 1 & -.9 & .81 \\ 1 & .5 & .25 \end{bmatrix} \sim \begin{bmatrix} 1 & 0 & 0 \\ 0 & 1 & 0 \\ 0 & 0 & 1 \end{bmatrix}.$$

The rank of the matrix is 3, and the pair (A, B) is controllable.

20. To determine if the matrix pair (A, B) is controllable, we compute the rank of the matrix $\begin{bmatrix} B & AB & A^2B \end{bmatrix}$. To find the rank, we note that :

  $$\begin{bmatrix} B & AB & A^2B \end{bmatrix} = \begin{bmatrix} 1 & .5 & .19 \\ 1 & .7 & .45 \\ 0 & 0 & 0 \end{bmatrix}.$$

The rank of the matrix must be less than 3, and the pair (A, B) is not controllable.

21. [M] To determine if the matrix pair (A, B) is controllable, we compute the rank of the matrix $\begin{bmatrix} B & AB & A^2B & A^3B \end{bmatrix}$. To find the rank, we row reduce:

$$\begin{bmatrix} B & AB & A^2B & A^3B \end{bmatrix} = \begin{bmatrix} 1 & 0 & 0 & -1 \\ 0 & 0 & -1 & 1.6 \\ 0 & -1 & 1.6 & -.96 \\ -1 & 1.6 & -.96 & -.024 \end{bmatrix} \sim \begin{bmatrix} 1 & 0 & 0 & -1 \\ 0 & 1 & 0 & -1.6 \\ 0 & 0 & 1 & -1.6 \\ 0 & 0 & 0 & 0 \end{bmatrix}.$$

The rank of the matrix is 3, and the pair (A, B) is not controllable.

22. [M] To determine if the matrix pair (A, B) is controllable, we compute the rank of the matrix $\begin{bmatrix} B & AB & A^2B & A^3B \end{bmatrix}$. To find the rank, we row reduce:

$$\begin{bmatrix} B & AB & A^2B & A^3B \end{bmatrix} = \begin{bmatrix} 1 & 0 & 0 & -1 \\ 0 & 0 & -1 & .5 \\ 0 & -1 & .5 & 11.45 \\ -1 & .5 & 11.45 & -10.275 \end{bmatrix} \sim \begin{bmatrix} 1 & 0 & 0 & 0 \\ 0 & 1 & 0 & 0 \\ 0 & 0 & 1 & 0 \\ 0 & 0 & 0 & 1 \end{bmatrix}.$$

The rank of the matrix is 4, and the pair (A, B) is controllable.

5 Eigenvalues and Eigenvectors

5.1 SOLUTIONS

Notes: Exercises 1–6 reinforce the definitions of eigenvalues and eigenvectors. The subsection on eigenvectors and difference equations, along with Exercises 33 and 34, refers to the chapter introductory example and anticipates discussions of dynamical systems in Sections 5.2 and 5.6.

1. The number 2 is an eigenvalue of A if and only if the equation $A\mathbf{x} = 2\mathbf{x}$ has a nontrivial solution. This equation is equivalent to $(A - 2I)\mathbf{x} = 0$. Compute

$$A - 2I = \begin{bmatrix} 3 & 2 \\ 3 & 8 \end{bmatrix} - \begin{bmatrix} 2 & 0 \\ 0 & 2 \end{bmatrix} = \begin{bmatrix} 1 & 2 \\ 3 & 6 \end{bmatrix}$$

   The columns of A are obviously linearly dependent, so $(A - 2I)\mathbf{x} = 0$ has a nontrivial solution, and so 2 is an eigenvalue of A.

2. The number -2 is an eigenvalue of A if and only if the equation $A\mathbf{x} = -2\mathbf{x}$ has a nontrivial solution. This equation is equivalent to $(A + 2I)\mathbf{x} = 0$. Compute

$$A + 2I = \begin{bmatrix} 7 & 3 \\ 3 & -1 \end{bmatrix} + \begin{bmatrix} 2 & 0 \\ 0 & 2 \end{bmatrix} = \begin{bmatrix} 9 & 3 \\ 3 & 1 \end{bmatrix}$$

   The columns of A are obviously linearly dependent, so $(A + 2I)\mathbf{x} = 0$ has a nontrivial solution, and so -2 is an eigenvalue of A.

3. Is $A\mathbf{x}$ a multiple of $\mathbf{x}$? Compute $\begin{bmatrix} -3 & 1 \\ -3 & 8 \end{bmatrix}\begin{bmatrix} 1 \\ 4 \end{bmatrix} = \begin{bmatrix} 1 \\ 29 \end{bmatrix} \neq \lambda\begin{bmatrix} 1 \\ 4 \end{bmatrix}$. So $\begin{bmatrix} 1 \\ 4 \end{bmatrix}$ is *not* an eigenvector of A.

4. Is $A\mathbf{x}$ a multiple of $\mathbf{x}$? Compute $\begin{bmatrix} 2 & 1 \\ 1 & 4 \end{bmatrix}\begin{bmatrix} -1+\sqrt{2} \\ 1 \end{bmatrix} = \begin{bmatrix} -1+2\sqrt{2} \\ 3+\sqrt{2} \end{bmatrix}$ The second entries of $\mathbf{x}$ and $A\mathbf{x}$ shows

   that if $A\mathbf{x}$ is a multiple of $\mathbf{x}$, then that multiple must be $3+\sqrt{2}$. Check $3+\sqrt{2}$ times the first entry of $\mathbf{x}$:

$$(3+\sqrt{2})(-1+\sqrt{2}) = -3 + \left(\sqrt{2}\right)^2 + 2\sqrt{2} = -1 + 2\sqrt{2}$$

   This matches the first entry of $A\mathbf{x}$, so $\begin{bmatrix} -1+\sqrt{2} \\ 1 \end{bmatrix}$ is an eigenvector of A, and the corresponding

   eigenvalue is $3+\sqrt{2}$.

5. Is $A\mathbf{x}$ a multiple of $\mathbf{x}$? Compute $\begin{bmatrix} 3 & 7 & 9 \\ -4 & -5 & 1 \\ 2 & 4 & 4 \end{bmatrix}\begin{bmatrix} 4 \\ -3 \\ 1 \end{bmatrix} = \begin{bmatrix} 0 \\ 0 \\ 0 \end{bmatrix}$. So $\begin{bmatrix} 4 \\ -3 \\ 1 \end{bmatrix}$ is an eigenvector of A for the

eigenvalue 0.

6. Is $A\mathbf{x}$ a multiple of $\mathbf{x}$? Compute $\begin{bmatrix} 3 & 6 & 7 \\ 3 & 3 & 7 \\ 5 & 6 & 5 \end{bmatrix}\begin{bmatrix} 1 \\ -2 \\ 1 \end{bmatrix} = \begin{bmatrix} -2 \\ 4 \\ -2 \end{bmatrix} = (-2)\begin{bmatrix} 1 \\ -2 \\ 1 \end{bmatrix}$ So $\begin{bmatrix} 1 \\ -2 \\ 1 \end{bmatrix}$ is an eigenvector of

A for the eigenvalue -2.

7. To determine if 4 is an eigenvalue of A, decide if the matrix $A - 4I$ is invertible.

$$A - 4I = \begin{bmatrix} 3 & 0 & -1 \\ 2 & 3 & 1 \\ -3 & 4 & 5 \end{bmatrix} - \begin{bmatrix} 4 & 0 & 0 \\ 0 & 4 & 0 \\ 0 & 0 & 4 \end{bmatrix} = \begin{bmatrix} -1 & 0 & -1 \\ 2 & -1 & 1 \\ -3 & 4 & 1 \end{bmatrix}$$

Invertibility can be checked in several ways, but since an eigenvector is needed in the event that one exists, the best strategy is to row reduce the augmented matrix for $(A - 4I)\mathbf{x} = \mathbf{0}$:

$$\begin{bmatrix} -1 & 0 & -1 & 0 \\ 2 & -1 & 1 & 0 \\ -3 & 4 & 1 & 0 \end{bmatrix} \sim \begin{bmatrix} -1 & 0 & -1 & 0 \\ 0 & -1 & -1 & 0 \\ 0 & 4 & 4 & 0 \end{bmatrix} \sim \begin{bmatrix} 1 & 0 & 1 & 0 \\ 0 & -1 & -1 & 0 \\ 0 & 0 & 0 & 0 \end{bmatrix}$$

The equation $(A - 4I)\mathbf{x} = \mathbf{0}$ has a nontrivial solution, so 4 is an eigenvalue. Any nonzero solution of $(A - 4I)\mathbf{x} = \mathbf{0}$ is a corresponding eigenvector. The entries in a solution satisfy $x_1 + x_3 = 0$ and $-x_2 - x_3 = 0$, with x_3 free. The general solution is *not* requested, so to save time, simply take any nonzero value for x_3 to produce an eigenvector. If $x_3 = 1$, then $\mathbf{x} = (-1, -1, 1)$.

Note: The answer in the text is $(1, 1, -1)$, written in this form to make the students wonder whether the more common answer given above is also correct. This may initiate a class discussion of what answers are "correct."

8. To determine if 3 is an eigenvalue of A, decide if the matrix $A - 3I$ is invertible.

$$A - 3I = \begin{bmatrix} 1 & 2 & 2 \\ 3 & -2 & 1 \\ 0 & 1 & 1 \end{bmatrix} - \begin{bmatrix} 3 & 0 & 0 \\ 0 & 3 & 0 \\ 0 & 0 & 3 \end{bmatrix} = \begin{bmatrix} -2 & 2 & 2 \\ 3 & -5 & 1 \\ 0 & 1 & -2 \end{bmatrix}$$

Row reducing the augmented matrix $[(A - 3I) \quad \mathbf{0}]$ yields:

$$\begin{bmatrix} -2 & 2 & 2 & 0 \\ 3 & -5 & 1 & 0 \\ 0 & 1 & -2 & 0 \end{bmatrix} \sim \begin{bmatrix} 1 & -1 & -1 & 0 \\ 0 & 1 & -2 & 0 \\ 0 & -2 & 4 & 0 \end{bmatrix} \sim \begin{bmatrix} 1 & 0 & -3 & 0 \\ 0 & 1 & -2 & 0 \\ 0 & 0 & 0 & 0 \end{bmatrix}$$

The equation $(A - 3I)\mathbf{x} = \mathbf{0}$ has a nontrivial solution, so 3 is an eigenvalue. Any nonzero solution of $(A - 3I)\mathbf{x} = \mathbf{0}$ is a corresponding eigenvector. The entries in a solution satisfy $x_1 - 3x_3 = 0$ and $x_2 - 2x_3 = 0$, with x_3 free. The general solution is *not* requested, so to save time, simply take any nonzero value for x_3 to produce an eigenvector. If $x_3 = 1$, then $\mathbf{x} = (3, 2, 1)$.

9. For $\lambda = 1$: $A - 1I = \begin{bmatrix} 5 & 0 \\ 2 & 1 \end{bmatrix} - \begin{bmatrix} 1 & 0 \\ 0 & 1 \end{bmatrix} = \begin{bmatrix} 4 & 0 \\ 2 & 0 \end{bmatrix}$

The augmented matrix for $(A - I)\mathbf{x} = \mathbf{0}$ is $\begin{bmatrix} 4 & 0 & 0 \\ 2 & 0 & 0 \end{bmatrix}$. Thus $x_1 = 0$ and x_2 is free. The general solution

of $(A - I)\mathbf{x} = \mathbf{0}$ is $x_2\mathbf{e}_2$, where $\mathbf{e}_2 = \begin{bmatrix} 0 \\ 1 \end{bmatrix}$, and so $\mathbf{e}_2$ is a basis for the eigenspace corresponding to the

eigenvalue 1.

For $\lambda = 5$: $A - 5I = \begin{bmatrix} 5 & 0 \\ 2 & 1 \end{bmatrix} - \begin{bmatrix} 5 & 0 \\ 0 & 5 \end{bmatrix} = \begin{bmatrix} 0 & 0 \\ 2 & -4 \end{bmatrix}$

The equation $(A - 5I)\mathbf{x} = \mathbf{0}$ leads to $2x_1 - 4x_2 = 0$, so that $x_1 = 2x_2$ and x_2 is free. The general solution

is $\begin{bmatrix} x_1 \\ x_2 \end{bmatrix} = \begin{bmatrix} 2x_2 \\ x_2 \end{bmatrix} = x_2\begin{bmatrix} 2 \\ 1 \end{bmatrix}$. So $\begin{bmatrix} 2 \\ 1 \end{bmatrix}$ is a basis for the eigenspace.

10. For $\lambda = 4$: $A - 4I = \begin{bmatrix} 10 & -9 \\ 4 & -2 \end{bmatrix} - \begin{bmatrix} 4 & 0 \\ 0 & 4 \end{bmatrix} = \begin{bmatrix} 6 & -9 \\ 4 & -6 \end{bmatrix}$.

The augmented matrix for $(A - 4I)\mathbf{x} = \mathbf{0}$ is $\begin{bmatrix} 6 & -9 & 0 \\ 4 & -6 & 0 \end{bmatrix} \sim \begin{bmatrix} 1 & -9/6 & 0 \\ 0 & 0 & 0 \end{bmatrix}$. Thus $x_1 = (3/2)x_2$ and

x_2 is free. The general solution is $\begin{bmatrix} x_1 \\ x_2 \end{bmatrix} = \begin{bmatrix} (3/2)x_2 \\ x_2 \end{bmatrix} = x_2\begin{bmatrix} 3/2 \\ 1 \end{bmatrix}$. A basis for the eigenspace corresponding

to 4 is $\begin{bmatrix} 3/2 \\ 1 \end{bmatrix}$. Another choice is $\begin{bmatrix} 3 \\ 2 \end{bmatrix}$.

11. $A - 10I = \begin{bmatrix} 4 & -2 \\ -3 & 9 \end{bmatrix} - \begin{bmatrix} 10 & 0 \\ 0 & 10 \end{bmatrix} = \begin{bmatrix} -6 & -2 \\ -3 & -1 \end{bmatrix}$

The augmented matrix for $(A - 10I)\mathbf{x} = \mathbf{0}$ is $\begin{bmatrix} -6 & -2 & 0 \\ -3 & -1 & 0 \end{bmatrix} \sim \begin{bmatrix} 1 & 1/3 & 0 \\ 0 & 0 & 0 \end{bmatrix}$. Thus $x_1 = (-1/3)x_2$ and

x_2 is free. The general solution is $\begin{bmatrix} x_1 \\ x_2 \end{bmatrix} = \begin{bmatrix} -(1/3)x_2 \\ x_2 \end{bmatrix} = x_2\begin{bmatrix} -1/3 \\ 1 \end{bmatrix}$. A basis for the eigenspace

corresponding to 10 is $\begin{bmatrix} -1/3 \\ 1 \end{bmatrix}$. Another choice is $\begin{bmatrix} -1 \\ 3 \end{bmatrix}$.

12. For $\lambda = 1$: $A - I = \begin{bmatrix} 7 & 4 \\ -3 & -1 \end{bmatrix} - \begin{bmatrix} 1 & 0 \\ 0 & 1 \end{bmatrix} = \begin{bmatrix} 6 & 4 \\ -3 & -2 \end{bmatrix}$

The augmented matrix for $(A - I)\mathbf{x} = \mathbf{0}$ is $\begin{bmatrix} 6 & 4 & 0 \\ -3 & -2 & 0 \end{bmatrix} \sim \begin{bmatrix} 1 & 2/3 & 0 \\ 0 & 0 & 0 \end{bmatrix}$. Thus $x_1 = (-2/3)x_2$ and

x_2 is free. A basis for the eigenspace corresponding to 1 is $\begin{bmatrix} -2/3 \\ 1 \end{bmatrix}$. Another choice is $\begin{bmatrix} -2 \\ 3 \end{bmatrix}$.

For $\lambda = 5$: $A - 5I = \begin{bmatrix} 7 & 4 \\ -3 & -1 \end{bmatrix} - \begin{bmatrix} 5 & 0 \\ 0 & 5 \end{bmatrix} = \begin{bmatrix} 2 & 4 \\ -3 & -6 \end{bmatrix}$.

The augmented matrix for $(A - 5I)\mathbf{x} = \mathbf{0}$ is $\begin{bmatrix} 2 & 4 & 0 \\ -3 & -6 & 0 \end{bmatrix} \sim \begin{bmatrix} 1 & 2 & 0 \\ 0 & 0 & 0 \end{bmatrix}$. Thus $x_1 = 2x_2$ and x_2 is free.

The general solution is $\begin{bmatrix} x_1 \\ x_2 \end{bmatrix} = \begin{bmatrix} -2x_2 \\ x_2 \end{bmatrix} = x_2 \begin{bmatrix} -2 \\ 1 \end{bmatrix}$. A basis for the eigenspace is $\begin{bmatrix} -2 \\ 1 \end{bmatrix}$.

13. For $\lambda = 1$:

$$A - 1I = \begin{bmatrix} 4 & 0 & 1 \\ -2 & 1 & 0 \\ -2 & 0 & 1 \end{bmatrix} - \begin{bmatrix} 1 & 0 & 0 \\ 0 & 1 & 0 \\ 0 & 0 & 1 \end{bmatrix} = \begin{bmatrix} 3 & 0 & 1 \\ -2 & 0 & 0 \\ -2 & 0 & 0 \end{bmatrix}$$

The equations for $(A - I)\mathbf{x} = \mathbf{0}$ are easy to solve: $\left\{ \begin{array}{l} 3x_1 + x_3 = 0 \\ -2x_1 \quad\;\; = 0 \end{array} \right\}$

Row operations hardly seem necessary. Obviously x_1 is zero, and hence x_3 is also zero. There are three-variables, so x_2 is free. The general solution of $(A - I)\mathbf{x} = \mathbf{0}$ is $x_2 \mathbf{e}_2$, where $\mathbf{e}_2 = (0,1,0)$, and so $\mathbf{e}_2$ provides a basis for the eigenspace.

For $\lambda = 2$:

$$A - 2I = \begin{bmatrix} 4 & 0 & 1 \\ -2 & 1 & 0 \\ -2 & 0 & 1 \end{bmatrix} - \begin{bmatrix} 2 & 0 & 0 \\ 0 & 2 & 0 \\ 0 & 0 & 2 \end{bmatrix} = \begin{bmatrix} 2 & 0 & 1 \\ -2 & -1 & 0 \\ -2 & 0 & 1 \end{bmatrix}$$

$$[(A - 2I)\ \mathbf{0}] = \begin{bmatrix} 2 & 0 & 1 & 0 \\ -2 & -1 & 0 & 0 \\ -2 & 0 & -1 & 0 \end{bmatrix} \sim \begin{bmatrix} 2 & 0 & 1 & 0 \\ 0 & -1 & 1 & 0 \\ 0 & 0 & 0 & 0 \end{bmatrix} \sim \begin{bmatrix} ① & 0 & 1/2 & 0 \\ 0 & ① & -1 & 0 \\ 0 & 0 & 0 & 0 \end{bmatrix}$$

So $x_1 = -(1/2)x_3, x_2 = x_3$, with x_3 free. The general solution of $(A - 2I)\mathbf{x} = \mathbf{0}$ is $x_3 \begin{bmatrix} -1/2 \\ 1 \\ 1 \end{bmatrix}$. A nice basis

vector for the eigenspace is $\begin{bmatrix} -1 \\ 2 \\ 2 \end{bmatrix}$.

For $\lambda = 3$:

$$A - 3I = \begin{bmatrix} 4 & 0 & 1 \\ -2 & 1 & 0 \\ -2 & 0 & 1 \end{bmatrix} - \begin{bmatrix} 3 & 0 & 0 \\ 0 & 3 & 0 \\ 0 & 0 & 3 \end{bmatrix} = \begin{bmatrix} 1 & 0 & 1 \\ -2 & -2 & 0 \\ -2 & 0 & -2 \end{bmatrix}$$

$$[(A - 3I)\ \mathbf{0}] = \begin{bmatrix} 1 & 0 & 1 & 0 \\ -2 & -2 & 0 & 0 \\ -2 & 0 & -2 & 0 \end{bmatrix} \sim \begin{bmatrix} 1 & 0 & 1 & 0 \\ 0 & -2 & 2 & 0 \\ 0 & 0 & 0 & 0 \end{bmatrix} \sim \begin{bmatrix} ① & 0 & 1 & 0 \\ 0 & ① & -1 & 0 \\ 0 & 0 & 0 & 0 \end{bmatrix}$$

So $x_1 = -x_3, x_2 = x_3$, with x_3 free. A basis vector for the eigenspace is $\begin{bmatrix} -1 \\ 1 \\ 1 \end{bmatrix}$.

14. For $\lambda = -2$: $A - (-2I) = A + 2I = \begin{bmatrix} 1 & 0 & -1 \\ 1 & -3 & 0 \\ 4 & -13 & 1 \end{bmatrix} + \begin{bmatrix} 2 & 0 & 0 \\ 0 & 2 & 0 \\ 0 & 0 & 2 \end{bmatrix} = \begin{bmatrix} 3 & 0 & -1 \\ 1 & -1 & 0 \\ 4 & -13 & 3 \end{bmatrix}$.

The augmented matrix for $[A - (-2)I]\mathbf{x} = \mathbf{0}$, or $(A + 2I)\mathbf{x} = \mathbf{0}$, is

$$[(A + 2I) \quad \mathbf{0}] = \begin{bmatrix} 3 & 0 & -1 & 0 \\ 1 & -1 & 0 & 0 \\ 4 & -13 & 3 & 0 \end{bmatrix} \sim \begin{bmatrix} 1 & 0 & -1/3 & 0 \\ 0 & 1 & -1/3 & 0 \\ 0 & -13 & 13/3 & 0 \end{bmatrix} \sim \begin{bmatrix} 1 & 0 & -1/3 & 0 \\ 0 & 1 & -1/3 & 0 \\ 0 & 0 & 0 & 0 \end{bmatrix}$$

Thus $x_1 = (1/3)x_3, x_2 = (1/3)x_3$, with x_3 free. The general solution of $(A + 2I)\mathbf{x} = \mathbf{0}$ is $x_3 \begin{bmatrix} 1/3 \\ 1/3 \\ 1 \end{bmatrix}$.

A basis for the eigenspace corresponding to -2 is $\begin{bmatrix} 1/3 \\ 1/3 \\ 1 \end{bmatrix}$; another is $\begin{bmatrix} 1 \\ 1 \\ 3 \end{bmatrix}$.

15. For $\lambda = 3$: $[(A - 3I) \quad \mathbf{0}] = \begin{bmatrix} 1 & 2 & 3 & 0 \\ -1 & -2 & -3 & 0 \\ 2 & 4 & 6 & 0 \end{bmatrix} \sim \begin{bmatrix} 1 & 2 & 3 & 0 \\ 0 & 0 & 0 & 0 \\ 0 & 0 & 0 & 0 \end{bmatrix}$. Thus $x_1 + 2x_2 + 3x_3 = 0$, with x_2 and

x_3 free. The general solution of $(A - 3I)\mathbf{x} = \mathbf{0}$, is

$$\mathbf{x} = \begin{bmatrix} -2x_2 - 3x_3 \\ x_2 \\ x_3 \end{bmatrix} = x_2 \begin{bmatrix} -2 \\ 1 \\ 0 \end{bmatrix} + x_3 \begin{bmatrix} -3 \\ 0 \\ 1 \end{bmatrix}. \text{ Basis for the eigenspace}: \left\{ \begin{bmatrix} -2 \\ 1 \\ 0 \end{bmatrix}, \begin{bmatrix} -3 \\ 0 \\ 1 \end{bmatrix} \right\}$$

Note: For simplicity, the text answer omits the set brackets. I permit my students to list a basis without the set brackets. Some instructors may prefer to include brackets.

16. For $\lambda = 4$: $A - 4I = \begin{bmatrix} 3 & 0 & 2 & 0 \\ 1 & 3 & 1 & 0 \\ 0 & 1 & 1 & 0 \\ 0 & 0 & 0 & 4 \end{bmatrix} - \begin{bmatrix} 4 & 0 & 0 & 0 \\ 0 & 4 & 0 & 0 \\ 0 & 0 & 4 & 0 \\ 0 & 0 & 0 & 4 \end{bmatrix} = \begin{bmatrix} -1 & 0 & 2 & 0 \\ 1 & -1 & 1 & 0 \\ 0 & 1 & -3 & 0 \\ 0 & 0 & 0 & 0 \end{bmatrix}$.

$$[(A - 4I) \quad \mathbf{0}] = \begin{bmatrix} -1 & 0 & 2 & 0 & 0 \\ 1 & -1 & 1 & 0 & 0 \\ 0 & 1 & -3 & 0 & 0 \\ 0 & 0 & 0 & 0 & 0 \end{bmatrix} \sim \begin{bmatrix} 1 & 0 & -2 & 0 & 0 \\ 0 & 1 & -3 & 0 & 0 \\ 0 & 0 & 0 & 0 & 0 \\ 0 & 0 & 0 & 0 & 0 \end{bmatrix}. \text{ So } x_1 = 2x_3, x_2 = 3x_3, \text{ with } x_3 \text{ and } x_4$$

free variables. The general solution of $(A - 4I)\mathbf{x} = \mathbf{0}$ is

$$\mathbf{x} = \begin{bmatrix} x_1 \\ x_2 \\ x_3 \\ x_4 \end{bmatrix} = \begin{bmatrix} 2x_3 \\ 3x_3 \\ x_3 \\ x_4 \end{bmatrix} = x_3 \begin{bmatrix} 2 \\ 3 \\ 1 \\ 0 \end{bmatrix} + x_4 \begin{bmatrix} 0 \\ 0 \\ 0 \\ 1 \end{bmatrix}. \text{ Basis for the eigenspace}: \left\{ \begin{bmatrix} 2 \\ 3 \\ 1 \\ 0 \end{bmatrix}, \begin{bmatrix} 0 \\ 0 \\ 0 \\ 1 \end{bmatrix} \right\}$$

Note: I urge my students always to include the extra column of zeros when solving a homogeneous system. Exercise 16 provides a situation in which *failing* to add the column is likely to create problems for a student, because the matrix $A - 4I$ itself has a column of zeros.

17. The eigenvalues of $\begin{bmatrix} 0 & 0 & 0 \\ 0 & 2 & 5 \\ 0 & 0 & -1 \end{bmatrix}$ are 0, 2, and −1, on the main diagonal, by Theorem 1.

18. The eigenvalues of $\begin{bmatrix} 4 & 0 & 0 \\ 0 & 0 & 0 \\ 1 & 0 & -3 \end{bmatrix}$ are 4, 0, and −3, on the main diagonal, by Theorem 1.

19. The matrix $\begin{bmatrix} 1 & 2 & 3 \\ 1 & 2 & 3 \\ 1 & 2 & 3 \end{bmatrix}$ is not invertible because its columns are linearly dependent. So the number 0 is

an eigenvalue of the matrix. See the discussion following Example 5.

20. The matrix $A = \begin{bmatrix} 5 & 5 & 5 \\ 5 & 5 & 5 \\ 5 & 5 & 5 \end{bmatrix}$ is not invertible because its columns are linearly dependent. So the number 0

is an eigenvalue of A. Eigenvectors for the eigenvalue 0 are solutions of $A\mathbf{x} = \mathbf{0}$ and therefore have entries that produce a linear dependence relation among the columns of A. Any nonzero vector (in $\mathbf{R}^3$) whose entries sum to 0 will work. Find any two such vectors that are not multiples; for instance, $(1, 1, -2)$ and $(1, -1, 0)$.

21.   **a**. False. The equation $A\mathbf{x} = \lambda\mathbf{x}$ must have a *nontrivial* solution.

  b. True. See the paragraph after Example 5.

  c. True. See the discussion of equation (3).

  d. True. See Example 2 and the paragraph preceding it. Also, see the Numerical Note.

  e. False. See the warning after Example 3.

22.   **a**. False. The vector **x** in $A\mathbf{x} = \lambda\mathbf{x}$ must be *nonzero*.

  b. False. See Example 4 for a two-dimensional eigenspace, which contains two linearly independent eigenvectors corresponding to the same eigenvalue. The statement given is not at all the same as Theorem 2. In fact, it is the *converse* of Theorem 2 (for the case $r = 2$).

  c. True. See the paragraph after Example 1.

  d. False. Theorem 1 concerns a *triangular* matrix. See Examples 3 and 4 for counterexamples.

  e. True. See the paragraph following Example 3. The eigenspace of A corresponding to λ is the null space of the matrix $A - \lambda I$.

23. If a 2×2 matrix A were to have three distinct eigenvalues, then by Theorem 2 there would correspond three linearly independent eigenvectors (one for each eigenvalue). This is impossible because the vectors all belong to a two-dimensional vector space, in which any set of three vectors is linearly dependent. See Theorem 8 in Section 1.7. In general, if an $n \times n$ matrix has p distinct eigenvalues, then by Theorem 2 there would be a linearly independent set of p eigenvectors (one for each eigenvalue). Since these vectors belong to an n-dimensional vector space, p cannot exceed n.

24. A simple example of a 2×2 matrix with only one distinct eigenvalue is a triangular matrix with the same number on the diagonal. By experimentation, one finds that if such a matrix is actually a diagonal matrix then the eigenspace is two dimensional, and otherwise the eigenspace is only one dimensional.

Examples: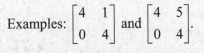

25. If λ is an eigenvalue of A, then there is a nonzero vector $\mathbf{x}$ such that $A\mathbf{x} = \lambda\mathbf{x}$. Since A is invertible, $A^{-1}A\mathbf{x} = A^{-1}(\lambda\mathbf{x})$, and so $\mathbf{x} = \lambda(A^{-1}\mathbf{x})$. Since $\mathbf{x} \neq \mathbf{0}$ (and since A is invertible), λ cannot be zero. Then $\lambda^{-1}\mathbf{x} = A^{-1}\mathbf{x}$, which shows that λ^{-1} is an eigenvalue of A^{-1}.

Note: The *Study Guide* points out here that the relation between the eigenvalues of A and A^{-1} is important in the so-called *inverse power method* for estimating an eigenvalue of a matrix. See Section 5.8.

26. Suppose that A^2 is the zero matrix. If $A\mathbf{x} = \lambda\mathbf{x}$ for some $\mathbf{x} \neq \mathbf{0}$, then $A^2\mathbf{x} = A(A\mathbf{x}) = A(\lambda\mathbf{x}) = \lambda A\mathbf{x} = \lambda^2\mathbf{x}$. Since $\mathbf{x}$ is nonzero, λ must be nonzero. Thus each eigenvalue of A is zero.

27. Use the *Hint* in the text to write, for any $\lambda, (A - \lambda I)^T = A^T - (\lambda I)^T = A^T - \lambda I$. Since $(A - \lambda I)^T$ is invertible if and only if $A - \lambda I$ is invertible (by Theorem 6(c) in Section 2.2), it follows that $A^T - \lambda I$ is *not* invertible if and only if $A - \lambda I$ is *not* invertible. That is, λ is an eigenvalue of A^T if and only if λ is an eigenvalue of A.

Note: If you discuss Exercise 27, you might ask students on a test to show that A and A^T have the same characteristic polynomial (discussed in Section 5.2). Since $\det A = \det A^T$, for any square matrix A,

$$\det(A - \lambda I) = \det(A - \lambda I)^T = \det(A^T - (\lambda I)^T) = \det(A^T - \lambda I).$$

28. If A is lower triangular, then A^T is upper triangular and has the same diagonal entries as A. Hence, by the part of Theorem 1 already proved in the text, these diagonal entries are eigenvalues of A^T. By Exercise 27, they are also eigenvalues of A.

29. Let $\mathbf{v}$ be the vector in $\mathbf{R}^n$ whose entries are all ones. Then $A\mathbf{v} = s\mathbf{v}$.

30. Suppose the column sums of an $n \times n$ matrix A all equal the same number s. By Exercise 29 applied to A^T in place of A, the number s is an eigenvalue of A^T. By Exercise 27, s is an eigenvalue of A.

31. Suppose T reflects points across (or through) a line that passes through the origin. That line consists of all multiples of some nonzero vector $\mathbf{v}$. The points on this line do not move under the action of A. So $T(\mathbf{v}) = \mathbf{v}$. If A is the standard matrix of T, then $A\mathbf{v} = \mathbf{v}$. Thus $\mathbf{v}$ is an eigenvector of A corresponding to the eigenvalue 1. The eigenspace is Span $\{\mathbf{v}\}$. Another eigenspace is generated by any nonzero vector $\mathbf{u}$ that is perpendicular to the given line. (Perpendicularity in $\mathbf{R}^2$ should be a familiar concept even though orthogonality in $\mathbf{R}^n$ has not been discussed yet.) Each vector $\mathbf{x}$ on the line through $\mathbf{u}$ is transformed into the vector $-\mathbf{x}$. The eigenvalue is -1.

33. (The solution is given in the text.)

   a. Replace k by $k+1$ in the definition of $\mathbf{x}_k$, and obtain $\mathbf{x}_{k+1} = c_1\lambda^{k+1}\mathbf{u} + c_2\mu^{k+1}\mathbf{v}$.

   b. $A\mathbf{x}_k = A(c_1\lambda^k\mathbf{u} + c_2\mu^k\mathbf{v})$
   $= c_1\lambda^k A\mathbf{u} + c_2\mu^k A\mathbf{v}$ by linearity
   $= c_1\lambda^k \lambda\mathbf{u} + c_2\mu^k \mu\mathbf{v}$ since $\mathbf{u}$ and $\mathbf{v}$ are eigenvectors
   $= \mathbf{x}_{k+1}$

34. You could try to write $\mathbf{x}_0$ as linear combination of eigenvectors, $\mathbf{v}_1, \ldots, \mathbf{v}_p$. If $\lambda_1, \ldots, \lambda_p$ are corresponding eigenvalues, and if $\mathbf{x}_0 = c_1 \mathbf{v}_1 + \cdots + c_p \mathbf{v}_p$, then you could *define*

$$\mathbf{x}_k = c_1 \lambda_1^k \mathbf{v}_1 + \cdots + c_p \lambda_p^k \mathbf{v}_p$$

In this case, for $k = 0, 1, 2, \ldots$,

$$
\begin{aligned}
A\mathbf{x}_k &= A(c_1 \lambda_1^k \mathbf{v}_1 + \cdots + c_p \lambda_p^k \mathbf{v}_p) \\
&= c_1 \lambda_1^k A\mathbf{v}_1 + \cdots + c_p \lambda_p^k A\mathbf{v}_p \quad \text{Linearity} \\
&= c_1 \lambda_1^{k+1} \mathbf{v}_1 + \cdots + c_p \lambda_p^{k+1} \mathbf{v}_p \quad \text{The } \mathbf{v}_i \text{ are eigenvectors.} \\
&= \mathbf{x}_{k+1}
\end{aligned}
$$

35. Using the figure in the exercise, plot $T(\mathbf{u})$ as $2\mathbf{u}$, because $\mathbf{u}$ is an eigenvector for the eigenvalue 2 of the standard matrix A. Likewise, plot $T(\mathbf{v})$ as $3\mathbf{v}$, because $\mathbf{v}$ is an eigenvector for the eigenvalue 3. Since T is linear, the image of $\mathbf{w}$ is $T(\mathbf{w}) = T(\mathbf{u} + \mathbf{v}) = T(\mathbf{u}) + T(\mathbf{v})$.

36. As in Exercise 35, $T(\mathbf{u}) = -\mathbf{u}$ and $T(\mathbf{v}) = 3\mathbf{v}$ because $\mathbf{u}$ and $\mathbf{v}$ are eigenvectors for the eigenvalues -1 and 3, respectively, of the standard matrix A. Since T is linear, the image of $\mathbf{w}$ is $T(\mathbf{w}) = T(\mathbf{u} + \mathbf{v}) = T(\mathbf{u}) + T(\mathbf{v})$.

Note: The matrix programs supported by this text all have an eigenvalue command. In some cases, such as MATLAB, the command can be structured so it provides eigenvectors as well as a list of the eigenvalues. At this point in the course, students should *not* use the extra power that produces eigenvectors. Students need to be reminded frequently that eigenvectors of A are null vectors of a translate of A. That is why the instructions for Exercises 35–38 tell students to use the method of Example 4.

It is my experience that nearly all students need manual practice finding eigenvectors by the method of Example 4, at least in this section if not also in Sections 5.2 and 5.3. However, [M] exercises do create a burden if eigenvectors must be found manually. For this reason, the data files for the text include a special command, nulbasis for each matrix program (MATLAB, Maple, etc.). The output of nulbasis (A) is a matrix whose columns provide a basis for the null space of A, and these columns are identical to the ones a student would find by row reducing the augmented matrix [A **0**]. With nulbasis, student answers will be the same (up to multiples) as those in the text. I encourage my students to use technology to speed up all numerical homework here, not just the [M] exercises,

37. [M] Let A be the given matrix. Use the MATLAB commands eig and nulbasis (or equivalent commands). The command ev = eig(A) computes the three eigenvalues of A and stores them in a vector ev. In this exercise, ev = $(3, 13, 13)$. The eigenspace for the eigenvalue 3 is the null space of $A - 3I$. Use nulbasis to produce a basis for each null space. If the format is set for rational display, the result is

$$\text{nulbasis}(A - \text{ev}(1) * \text{eye}(3)) = \begin{bmatrix} 5/9 \\ -2/9 \\ 1 \end{bmatrix}.$$

For simplicity, scale the entries by 9. A basis for the eigenspace for $\lambda = 3$: $\begin{bmatrix} 5 \\ -2 \\ 9 \end{bmatrix}$

For the next eigenvalue, 13, compute $\texttt{nulbasis(A - ev(2)*eye(3))} = \begin{bmatrix} -2 & -1 \\ 1 & 0 \\ 0 & 1 \end{bmatrix}$.

Basis for eigenspace for $\lambda = 13$: $\left\{ \begin{bmatrix} -2 \\ 1 \\ 0 \end{bmatrix}, \begin{bmatrix} -1 \\ 0 \\ 1 \end{bmatrix} \right\}$

There is no need to use $\texttt{ev(3)}$ because it is the same as $\texttt{ev(2)}$.

38. **[M]** $\texttt{ev = eig(A)} = (13, -12, -12, 13)$. For $\lambda = 13$:

$$\texttt{nulbasis (A - ev(1)*eye(4))} = \begin{bmatrix} -1/2 & 1/3 \\ 0 & -4/3 \\ 1 & 0 \\ 0 & 1 \end{bmatrix}. \text{ Basis for eigenspace}: \left\{ \begin{bmatrix} -1 \\ 0 \\ 2 \\ 0 \end{bmatrix}, \begin{bmatrix} 1 \\ -4 \\ 0 \\ 3 \end{bmatrix} \right\}$$

For $\lambda = -12$: $\texttt{nulbasis(A - ev(2)*eye(4))} = \begin{bmatrix} 2/7 & 0 \\ 1 & -1 \\ 1 & 0 \\ 0 & 1 \end{bmatrix}. \text{ Basis}: \left\{ \begin{bmatrix} 2 \\ 7 \\ 7 \\ 0 \end{bmatrix}, \begin{bmatrix} 0 \\ -1 \\ 0 \\ 1 \end{bmatrix} \right\}$

39. **[M]** For $\lambda = 5$, basis: $\left\{ \begin{bmatrix} 2 \\ -1 \\ 1 \\ 0 \\ 0 \end{bmatrix}, \begin{bmatrix} -1 \\ 1 \\ 0 \\ 1 \\ 0 \end{bmatrix}, \begin{bmatrix} 2 \\ 0 \\ 0 \\ 0 \\ 1 \end{bmatrix} \right\}$. For $\lambda = -2$, basis: $\left\{ \begin{bmatrix} -2 \\ 7 \\ -5 \\ 5 \\ 0 \end{bmatrix}, \begin{bmatrix} 3 \\ 7 \\ -5 \\ 0 \\ 5 \end{bmatrix} \right\}$

40. **[M]** $\texttt{ev = eig(A)} = (21.68984106239549, -16.68984106239549, 3, 2, 2)$. The first two eigenvalues are the roots of $\lambda^2 - 5\lambda - 362 = 0$.

Basis for $\lambda = \texttt{ev(1)}$: $\begin{bmatrix} -0.33333333333333 \\ 2.39082008853296 \\ 0.33333333333333 \\ 0.58333333333333 \\ 1.000000000000000 \end{bmatrix}$, for $\lambda = \texttt{ev(2)}$: $\begin{bmatrix} -0.33333333333333 \\ -0.80748675519962 \\ 0.33333333333333 \\ 0.58333333333333 \\ 1.00000000000000 \end{bmatrix}$.

For the eigenvalues 3 and 2, the eigenbases are $\begin{bmatrix} 0 \\ -2 \\ 0 \\ 1 \\ 0 \end{bmatrix}$, and $\left\{ \begin{bmatrix} -2 \\ 1 \\ 0 \\ 1 \\ 0 \end{bmatrix}, \begin{bmatrix} -.5 \\ .5 \\ 0 \\ 0 \\ 1 \end{bmatrix} \right\}$, respectively.

Note: Since so many eigenvalues in text problems are small integers, it is easy for students to form a habit of entering a value for λ in $\texttt{nulbasis (A - }\lambda\texttt{I)}$ based on a *visual examination* of the eigenvalues produced by $\texttt{eig(A)}$ when only a few decimal places for λ are displayed. Exercise 40 may help your students discover the dangers of this approach.

5.2   SOLUTIONS

Notes: Exercises 9–14 can be omitted, unless you want your students to have some facility with determinants of 3×3 matrices. In later sections, the text will provide eigenvalues when they are needed for matrices larger than 2×2. If you discussed partitioned matrices in Section 2.4, you might wish to bring in Supplementary Exercises 12–14 in Chapter 5. (Also, see Exercise 14 of Section 2.4.)

Exercises 25 and 27 support the subsection on dynamical systems. The calculations in these exercises and Example 5 prepare for the discussion in Section 5.6 about eigenvector decompositions.

1. $A = \begin{bmatrix} 2 & 7 \\ 7 & 2 \end{bmatrix}$, $A - \lambda I = \begin{bmatrix} 2 & 7 \\ 7 & 2 \end{bmatrix} - \begin{bmatrix} \lambda & 0 \\ 0 & \lambda \end{bmatrix} = \begin{bmatrix} 2-\lambda & 7 \\ 7 & 2-\lambda \end{bmatrix}$. The characteristic polynomial is

$$\det(A - \lambda I) = (2-\lambda)^2 - 7^2 = 4 - 4\lambda + \lambda^2 - 49 = \lambda^2 - 4\lambda - 45$$

In factored form, the characteristic equation is $(\lambda - 9)(\lambda + 5) = 0$, so the eigenvalues of A are 9 and −5.

2. $A = \begin{bmatrix} 5 & 3 \\ 3 & 5 \end{bmatrix}$, $A - \lambda I = \begin{bmatrix} 5-\lambda & 3 \\ 3 & 5-\lambda \end{bmatrix}$. The characteristic polynomial is

$$\det(A - \lambda I) = (5-\lambda)(5-\lambda) - 3 \cdot 3 = \lambda^2 - 10\lambda + 16$$

Since $\lambda^2 - 10\lambda + 16 = (\lambda - 8)(\lambda - 2)$, the eigenvalues of A are 8 and 2.

3. $A = \begin{bmatrix} 3 & -2 \\ 1 & -1 \end{bmatrix}$, $A - \lambda I = \begin{bmatrix} 3-\lambda & -2 \\ 1 & -1-\lambda \end{bmatrix}$. The characteristic polynomial is

$$\det(A - \lambda I) = (3-\lambda)(-1-\lambda) - (-2)(1) = \lambda^2 - 2\lambda - 1$$

Use the quadratic formula to solve the characteristic equation and find the eigenvalues:

$$\lambda = \frac{-b \pm \sqrt{b^2 - 4ac}}{2a} = \frac{2 \pm \sqrt{4+4}}{2} = 1 \pm \sqrt{2}$$

4. $A = \begin{bmatrix} 5 & -3 \\ -4 & 3 \end{bmatrix}$, $A - \lambda I = \begin{bmatrix} 5-\lambda & -3 \\ -4 & 3-\lambda \end{bmatrix}$. The characteristic polynomial of A is

$$\det(A - \lambda I) = (5-\lambda)(3-\lambda) - (-3)(-4) = \lambda^2 - 8\lambda + 3$$

Use the quadratic formula to solve the characteristic equation and find the eigenvalues:

$$\lambda = \frac{8 \pm \sqrt{64 - 4(3)}}{2} = \frac{8 \pm 2\sqrt{13}}{2} = 4 \pm \sqrt{13}$$

5. $A = \begin{bmatrix} 2 & 1 \\ -1 & 4 \end{bmatrix}$, $A - \lambda I = \begin{bmatrix} 2-\lambda & 1 \\ -1 & 4-\lambda \end{bmatrix}$. The characteristic polynomial of A is

$$\det(A - \lambda I) = (2-\lambda)(4-\lambda) - (1)(-1) = \lambda^2 - 6\lambda + 9 = (\lambda - 3)^2$$

Thus, A has only one eigenvalue 3, with multiplicity 2.

6. $A = \begin{bmatrix} 3 & -4 \\ 4 & 8 \end{bmatrix}$, $A - \lambda I = \begin{bmatrix} 3-\lambda & -4 \\ 4 & 8-\lambda \end{bmatrix}$. The characteristic polynomial is

$$\det(A - \lambda I) = (3-\lambda)(8-\lambda) - (-4)(4) = \lambda^2 - 11\lambda + 40$$

Use the quadratic formula to solve det $(A - \lambda I) = 0$:

$$\lambda = \frac{-11 \pm \sqrt{121 - 4(40)}}{2} = \frac{-11 \pm \sqrt{-39}}{2}$$

These values are complex numbers, not real numbers, so A has no real eigenvalues. There is no nonzero vector $\mathbf{x}$ in $\mathbf{R}^2$ such that $A\mathbf{x} = \lambda\mathbf{x}$, because a real vector $A\mathbf{x}$ cannot equal a complex multiple of $\mathbf{x}$.

7. $A = \begin{bmatrix} 5 & 3 \\ -4 & 4 \end{bmatrix}$, $A - \lambda I = \begin{bmatrix} 5 - \lambda & 3 \\ -4 & 4 - \lambda \end{bmatrix}$. The characteristic polynomial is

$$\det(A - \lambda I) = (5 - \lambda)(4 - \lambda) - (3)(-4) = \lambda^2 - 9\lambda + 32$$

Use the quadratic formula to solve det $(A - \lambda I) = 0$:

$$\lambda = \frac{9 \pm \sqrt{81 - 4(32)}}{2} = \frac{9 \pm \sqrt{-47}}{2}$$

These values are complex numbers, not real numbers, so A has no real eigenvalues. There is no nonzero vector $\mathbf{x}$ in $\mathbf{R}^2$ such that $A\mathbf{x} = \lambda\mathbf{x}$, because a real vector $A\mathbf{x}$ cannot equal a complex multiple of $\mathbf{x}$.

8. $A = \begin{bmatrix} 7 & -2 \\ 2 & 3 \end{bmatrix}$, $A - \lambda I = \begin{bmatrix} 7 - \lambda & -2 \\ 2 & 3 - \lambda \end{bmatrix}$. The characteristic polynomial is

$$\det(A - \lambda I) = (7 - \lambda)(3 - \lambda) - (-2)(2) = \lambda^2 - 10\lambda + 25$$

Since $\lambda^2 - 10\lambda + 25 = (\lambda - 5)^2$, the only eigenvalue is 5, with multiplicity 2.

9. $\det(A - \lambda I) = \det \begin{bmatrix} 1 - \lambda & 0 & -1 \\ 2 & 3 - \lambda & -1 \\ 0 & 6 & 0 - \lambda \end{bmatrix}$. From the special formula for 3×3 determinants, the

characteristic polynomial is

$$\begin{aligned} \det(A - \lambda I) &= (1 - \lambda)(3 - \lambda)(-\lambda) + 0 + (-1)(2)(6) - 0 - (6)(-1)(1 - \lambda) - 0 \\ &= (\lambda^2 - 4\lambda + 3)(-\lambda) - 12 + 6(1 - \lambda) \\ &= -\lambda^3 + 4\lambda^2 - 3\lambda - 12 + 6 - 6\lambda \\ &= -\lambda^3 + 4\lambda^2 - 9\lambda - 6 \end{aligned}$$

(This polynomial has one irrational zero and two imaginary zeros.) Another way to evaluate the determinant is to interchange rows 1 and 2 (which reverses the sign of the determinant) and then make one row replacement:

$$\det \begin{bmatrix} 1 - \lambda & 0 & -1 \\ 2 & 3 - \lambda & -1 \\ 0 & 6 & 0 - \lambda \end{bmatrix} = -\det \begin{bmatrix} 2 & 3 - \lambda & -1 \\ 1 - \lambda & 0 & -1 \\ 0 & 6 & 0 - \lambda \end{bmatrix}$$

$$= -\det \begin{bmatrix} 2 & 3 - \lambda & -1 \\ 0 & 0 + (.5\lambda - .5)(3 - \lambda) & -1 + (.5\lambda - .5)(-1) \\ 0 & 6 & 0 - \lambda \end{bmatrix}$$

Next, expand by cofactors down the first column. The quantity above equals

$$-2\det \begin{bmatrix} (.5\lambda - .5)(3 - \lambda) & -.5 - .5\lambda \\ 6 & -\lambda \end{bmatrix} = -2[(.5\lambda - .5)(3 - \lambda)(-\lambda) - (-.5 - .5\lambda)(6)]$$

$$= (1 - \lambda)(3 - \lambda)(-\lambda) - (1 + \lambda)(6) = (\lambda^2 - 4\lambda + 3)(-\lambda) - 6 - 6\lambda = -\lambda^3 + 4\lambda^2 - 9\lambda - 6$$

10. $\det(A - \lambda I) = \det \begin{bmatrix} 0-\lambda & 3 & 1 \\ 3 & 0-\lambda & 2 \\ 1 & 2 & 0-\lambda \end{bmatrix}$. From the special formula for 3×3 determinants, the

characteristic polynomial is

$$\det(A - \lambda I) = (-\lambda)(-\lambda)(-\lambda) + 3 \cdot 2 \cdot 1 + 1 \cdot 3 \cdot 2 - 1 \cdot (-\lambda) \cdot 1 - 2 \cdot 2 \cdot (-\lambda) - (-\lambda) \cdot 3 \cdot 3$$

$$= -\lambda^3 + 6 + 6 + \lambda + 4\lambda + 9\lambda = -\lambda^3 + 14\lambda + 12$$

11. The special arrangements of zeros in A makes a cofactor expansion along the first row highly effective.

$$\det(A - \lambda I) = \det \begin{bmatrix} 4-\lambda & 0 & 0 \\ 5 & 3-\lambda & 2 \\ -2 & 0 & 2-\lambda \end{bmatrix} = (4-\lambda)\det \begin{bmatrix} 3-\lambda & 2 \\ 0 & 2-\lambda \end{bmatrix}$$

$$= (4-\lambda)(3-\lambda)(2-\lambda) = (4-\lambda)(\lambda^2 - 5\lambda + 6) = -\lambda^3 + 9\lambda^2 - 26\lambda + 24$$

If only the eigenvalues were required, there would be no need here to write the characteristic polynomial in expanded form.

12. Make a cofactor expansion along the third row:

$$\det(A - \lambda I) = \det \begin{bmatrix} -1-\lambda & 0 & 1 \\ -3 & 4-\lambda & 1 \\ 0 & 0 & 2-\lambda \end{bmatrix} = (2-\lambda) \cdot \det \begin{bmatrix} -1-\lambda & 0 \\ -3 & 4-\lambda \end{bmatrix}$$

$$= (2-\lambda)(-1-\lambda)(4-\lambda) = -\lambda^3 + 5\lambda^2 - 2\lambda - 8$$

13. Make a cofactor expansion down the third column:

$$\det(A - \lambda I) = \det \begin{bmatrix} 6-\lambda & -2 & 0 \\ -2 & 9-\lambda & 0 \\ 5 & 8 & 3-\lambda \end{bmatrix} = (3-\lambda) \cdot \det \begin{bmatrix} 6-\lambda & -2 \\ -2 & 9-\lambda \end{bmatrix}$$

$$= (3-\lambda)[(6-\lambda)(9-\lambda) - (-2)(-2)] = (3-\lambda)(\lambda^2 - 15\lambda + 50)$$

$$= -\lambda^3 + 18\lambda^2 - 95\lambda + 150 \text{ or } (3-\lambda)(\lambda-5)(\lambda-10)$$

14. Make a cofactor expansion along the second row:

$$\det(A - \lambda I) = \det \begin{bmatrix} 5-\lambda & -2 & 3 \\ 0 & 1-\lambda & 0 \\ 6 & 7 & -2-\lambda \end{bmatrix} = (1-\lambda) \cdot \det \begin{bmatrix} 5-\lambda & 3 \\ 6 & -2-\lambda \end{bmatrix}$$

$$= (1-\lambda) \cdot [(5-\lambda)(-2-\lambda) - 3 \cdot 6] = (1-\lambda)(\lambda^2 - 3\lambda - 28)$$

$$= -\lambda^3 + 4\lambda^2 + 25\lambda - 28 \text{ or } (1-\lambda)(\lambda-7)(\lambda+4)$$

15. Use the fact that the determinant of a triangular matrix is the product of the diagonal entries:

$$\det(A - \lambda I) = \det \begin{bmatrix} 4-\lambda & -7 & 0 & 2 \\ 0 & 3-\lambda & -4 & 6 \\ 0 & 0 & 3-\lambda & -8 \\ 0 & 0 & 0 & 1-\lambda \end{bmatrix} = (4-\lambda)(3-\lambda)^2(1-\lambda)$$

The eigenvalues are 4, 3, 3, and 1.

16. The determinant of a triangular matrix is the product of its diagonal entries:

$$\det(A - \lambda I) = \det \begin{bmatrix} 5-\lambda & 0 & 0 & 0 \\ 8 & -4-\lambda & 0 & 0 \\ 0 & 7 & 1-\lambda & 0 \\ 1 & -5 & 2 & 1-\lambda \end{bmatrix} = (5-\lambda)(-4-\lambda)(1-\lambda)^2$$

The eigenvalues are 5, 1, 1, and –4.

17. The determinant of a triangular matrix is the product of its diagonal entries:

$$\begin{bmatrix} 3-\lambda & 0 & 0 & 0 & 0 \\ -5 & 1-\lambda & 0 & 0 & 0 \\ 3 & 8 & 0-\lambda & 0 & 0 \\ 0 & -7 & 2 & 1-\lambda & 0 \\ -4 & 1 & 9 & -2 & 3-\lambda \end{bmatrix} = (3-\lambda)^2(1-\lambda)^2(-\lambda)$$

The eigenvalues are 3, 3, 1, 1, and 0.

18. Row reduce the augmented matrix for the equation $(A - 5I)\mathbf{x} = \mathbf{0}$:

$$\begin{bmatrix} 0 & -2 & 6 & -1 & 0 \\ 0 & -2 & h & 0 & 0 \\ 0 & 0 & 0 & 4 & 0 \\ 0 & 0 & 0 & -4 & 0 \end{bmatrix} \sim \begin{bmatrix} 0 & -2 & 6 & -1 & 0 \\ 0 & 0 & h-6 & 1 & 0 \\ 0 & 0 & 0 & 4 & 0 \\ 0 & 0 & 0 & 4 & 0 \end{bmatrix} \sim \begin{bmatrix} 0 & 1 & -3 & 0 & 0 \\ 0 & 0 & h-6 & 0 & 0 \\ 0 & 0 & 0 & 1 & 0 \\ 0 & 0 & 0 & 0 & 0 \end{bmatrix}$$

For a two-dimensional eigenspace, the system above needs two free variables. This happens if and only if $h = 6$.

19. Since the equation $\det(A - \lambda I) = (\lambda_1 - \lambda)(\lambda_2 - \lambda) \cdots (\lambda_n - \lambda)$ holds for all λ, set $\lambda = 0$ and conclude that $\det A = \lambda_1 \lambda_2 \cdots \lambda_n$.

20. $\det(A^T - \lambda I) = \det(A^T - \lambda I^T)$

$\qquad\qquad = \det(A - \lambda I)^T \qquad$ Transpose property

$\qquad\qquad = \det(A - \lambda I) \qquad$ Theorem 3(c)

21. **a**. False. See Example 1.

　　b. False. See Theorem 3.

　　c. True. See Theorem 3.

　　d. False. See the solution of Example 4.

22. **a**. False. See the paragraph before Theorem 3.

　　b. False. See Theorem 3.

　　c. True. See the paragraph before Example 4.

　　d. False. See the warning after Theorem 4.

23. If $A = QR$, with Q invertible, and if $A_1 = RQ$, then write $A_1 = Q^{-1}QRQ = Q^{-1}AQ$, which shows that A_1 is similar to A.

24. First, observe that if P is invertible, then Theorem 3(b) shows that

$$1 = \det I = \det(PP^{-1}) = (\det P)(\det P^{-1})$$

Use Theorem 3(b) again when $A = PBP^{-1}$,

$$\det A = \det(PBP^{-1}) = (\det P)(\det B)(\det P^{-1}) = (\det B)(\det P)(\det P^{-1}) = \det B$$

25. Example 5 of Section 4.9 showed that $A\mathbf{v}_1 = \mathbf{v}_1$, which means that $\mathbf{v}_1$ is an eigenvector of A corresponding to the eigenvalue 1.

a. Since A is a 2×2 matrix, the eigenvalues are easy to find, and factoring the characteristic polynomial is easy when one of the two factors is known.

$$\det \begin{bmatrix} .6 - \lambda & .3 \\ .4 & .7 - \lambda \end{bmatrix} = (.6 - \lambda)(.7 - \lambda) - (.3)(.4) = \lambda^2 - 1.3\lambda + .3 = (\lambda - 1)(\lambda - .3)$$

The eigenvalues are 1 and .3. For the eigenvalue .3, solve $(A - .3I)\mathbf{x} = \mathbf{0}$:

$$\begin{bmatrix} .6 - .3 & .3 & 0 \\ .4 & .7 - .3 & 0 \end{bmatrix} = \begin{bmatrix} .3 & .3 & 0 \\ .4 & .4 & 0 \end{bmatrix} \sim \begin{bmatrix} 1 & 1 & 0 \\ 0 & 0 & 0 \end{bmatrix}$$

Here $x_1 - x_2 = 0$, with x_2 free. The general solution is not needed. Set $x_2 = 1$ to find an eigenvector $\mathbf{v}_2 = \begin{bmatrix} -1 \\ 1 \end{bmatrix}$. A suitable basis for $\mathbf{R}^2$ is $\{\mathbf{v}_1, \mathbf{v}_2\}$.

b. Write $\mathbf{x}_0 = \mathbf{v}_1 + c\mathbf{v}_2$: $\begin{bmatrix} 1/2 \\ 1/2 \end{bmatrix} = \begin{bmatrix} 3/7 \\ 4/7 \end{bmatrix} + c\begin{bmatrix} -1 \\ 1 \end{bmatrix}$. By inspection, c is $-1/14$. (The value of c depends on how $\mathbf{v}_2$ is scaled.)

c. For $k = 1, 2, ...$, define $\mathbf{x}_k = A^k\mathbf{x}_0$. Then $\mathbf{x}_1 = A(\mathbf{v}_1 + c\mathbf{v}_2) = A\mathbf{v}_1 + cA\mathbf{v}_2 = \mathbf{v}_1 + c(.3)\mathbf{v}_2$, because $\mathbf{v}_1$ and $\mathbf{v}_2$ are eigenvectors. Again

$$\mathbf{x}_2 = A\mathbf{x}_1 = A(\mathbf{v}_1 + c(.3)\mathbf{v}_2) = A\mathbf{v}_1 + c(.3)A\mathbf{v}_2 = \mathbf{v}_1 + c(.3)(.3)\mathbf{v}_2.$$

Continuing, the general pattern is $\mathbf{x}_k = \mathbf{v}_1 + c(.3)^k\mathbf{v}_2$. As k increases, the second term tends to $\mathbf{0}$ and so $\mathbf{x}_k$ tends to $\mathbf{v}_1$.

26. If $a \neq 0$, then $A = \begin{bmatrix} a & b \\ c & d \end{bmatrix} \sim \begin{bmatrix} a & b \\ 0 & d - ca^{-1}b \end{bmatrix} = U$, and $\det A = (a)(d - ca^{-1}b) = ad - bc$. If $a = 0$, then

$A = \begin{bmatrix} 0 & b \\ c & d \end{bmatrix} \sim \begin{bmatrix} c & d \\ 0 & b \end{bmatrix} = U$ (with one interchange), so $\det A = (-1)^1(cb) = 0 - bc = ad - bc$.

27. a. $A\mathbf{v}_1 = \mathbf{v}_1$, $A\mathbf{v}_2 = .5\mathbf{v}_2$, $A\mathbf{v}_3 = .2\mathbf{v}_3$.

b. The set $\{\mathbf{v}_1, \mathbf{v}_2, \mathbf{v}_3\}$ is linearly independent because the eigenvectors correspond to different eigenvalues (Theorem 2). Since there are three vectors in the set, the set is a basis for $\mathbb{R}^3$. So there exist unique constants such that $\mathbf{x}_0 = c_1\mathbf{v}_1 + c_2\mathbf{v}_2 + c_3\mathbf{v}_3$, and $\mathbf{w}^T\mathbf{x}_0 = c_1\mathbf{w}^T\mathbf{v}_1 + c_2\mathbf{w}^T\mathbf{v}_2 + c_3\mathbf{w}^T\mathbf{v}_3$. Since $\mathbf{x}_0$ and $\mathbf{v}_1$ are probability vectors and since the entries in $\mathbf{v}_2$ and $\mathbf{v}_3$ sum to 0, the above equation shows that $c_1 = 1$.

c. By (b), $\mathbf{x}_0 = c_1\mathbf{v}_1 + c_2\mathbf{v}_2 + c_3\mathbf{v}_3$. Using (a),

$$\mathbf{x}_k = A^k\mathbf{x}_0 = c_1A^k\mathbf{v}_1 + c_2A^k\mathbf{v}_2 + c_3A^k\mathbf{v}_3 = \mathbf{v}_1 + c_2(.5)^k\mathbf{v}_2 + c_3(.2)^k\mathbf{v}_3 \to \mathbf{v}_1 \text{ as } k \to \infty$$

28. [M]

Answers will vary, but should show that the eigenvectors of A are not the same as the eigenvectors of A^T, unless, of course, $A^T = A$.

29. [M]   Answers will vary. The product of the eigenvalues of A should equal det A.

30. [M]   The characteristic polynomials and the eigenvalues for the various values of a are given in the following table:

a	Characteristic Polynomial	Eigenvalues
31.8	$-.4 - 2.6t + 4t^2 - t^3$	$3.1279, 1, -.1279$
31.9	$.8 - 3.8t + 4t^2 - t^3$	$2.7042, 1, .2958$
32.0	$2 - 5t + 4t^2 - t^3$	$2, 1, 1$
32.1	$3.2 - 6.2t + 4t^2 - t^3$	$1.5 \pm .9747i, 1$
32.2	$4.4 - 7.4t + 4t^2 - t^3$	$1.5 \pm 1.4663i, 1$

The graphs of the characteristic polynomials are:

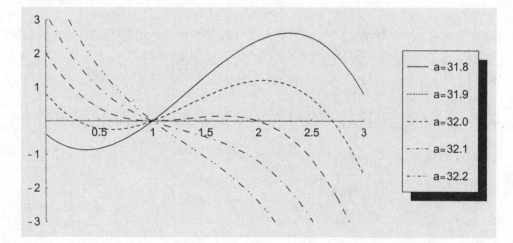

Notes: An appendix in Section 5.3 of the *Study Guide* gives an example of factoring a cubic polynomial with integer coefficients, in case you want your students to find integer eigenvalues of simple 3×3 or perhaps 4×4 matrices.

The MATLAB box for Section 5.3 introduces the command `poly (A)`, which lists the coefficients of the characteristic polynomial of the matrix A, and it gives MATLAB code that will produce a graph of the characteristic polynomial. (This is needed for Exercise 30.) The Maple and Mathematica appendices have corresponding information. The appendices for the TI and HP calculators contain only the commands that list the coefficients of the characteristic polynomial.

5.3   SOLUTIONS

1. $P = \begin{bmatrix} 5 & 7 \\ 2 & 3 \end{bmatrix}, D = \begin{bmatrix} 2 & 0 \\ 0 & 1 \end{bmatrix}, A = PDP^{-1}$, and $A^4 = PD^4P^{-1}$. We compute $P^{-1} = \begin{bmatrix} 3 & -7 \\ -2 & 5 \end{bmatrix}, D^4 = \begin{bmatrix} 16 & 0 \\ 0 & 1 \end{bmatrix}$,

and $A^4 = \begin{bmatrix} 5 & 7 \\ 2 & 3 \end{bmatrix}\begin{bmatrix} 16 & 0 \\ 0 & 1 \end{bmatrix}\begin{bmatrix} 3 & -7 \\ -2 & 5 \end{bmatrix} = \begin{bmatrix} 226 & -525 \\ 90 & -209 \end{bmatrix}$

2. $P = \begin{bmatrix} 2 & -3 \\ -3 & 5 \end{bmatrix}, D = \begin{bmatrix} 1 & 0 \\ 0 & 1/2 \end{bmatrix}, A = PDP^{-1}$, and $A^4 = PD^4P^{-1}$. We compute

$P^{-1} = \begin{bmatrix} 5 & 3 \\ 3 & 2 \end{bmatrix}, D^4 = \begin{bmatrix} 1 & 0 \\ 0 & 1/16 \end{bmatrix}$, and $A^4 = \begin{bmatrix} 2 & -3 \\ -3 & 5 \end{bmatrix}\begin{bmatrix} 1 & 0 \\ 0 & 1/16 \end{bmatrix}\begin{bmatrix} 5 & 3 \\ 3 & 2 \end{bmatrix} = \frac{1}{16}\begin{bmatrix} 151 & 90 \\ -225 & -134 \end{bmatrix}$

3. $A^k = PD^kP^{-1} = \begin{bmatrix} 1 & 0 \\ 3 & 1 \end{bmatrix}\begin{bmatrix} a^k & 0 \\ 0 & b^k \end{bmatrix}\begin{bmatrix} 1 & 0 \\ -3 & 1 \end{bmatrix} = \begin{bmatrix} a^k & 0 \\ 3a^k - 3b^k & b^k \end{bmatrix}$.

4. $A^k = PD^kP^{-1} = \begin{bmatrix} 3 & 4 \\ 1 & 1 \end{bmatrix}\begin{bmatrix} 2^k & 0 \\ 0 & 1^k \end{bmatrix}\begin{bmatrix} -1 & 4 \\ 1 & -3 \end{bmatrix} = \begin{bmatrix} 4 - 3 \cdot 2^k & 12 \cdot 2^k - 12 \\ 1 - 2^k & 4 \cdot 2^k - 3 \end{bmatrix}$.

5. By the Diagonalization Theorem, eigenvectors form the columns of the left factor, and they correspond respectively to the eigenvalues on the diagonal of the middle factor.

$$\lambda = 5: \begin{bmatrix} 1 \\ 1 \\ 1 \end{bmatrix}; \lambda = 1: \begin{bmatrix} 1 \\ 0 \\ -1 \end{bmatrix}, \begin{bmatrix} 2 \\ -1 \\ 0 \end{bmatrix}$$

6. As in Exercise 5, inspection of the factorization gives:

$$\lambda = 4: \begin{bmatrix} -1 \\ 2 \\ 0 \end{bmatrix}; \lambda = 5: \begin{bmatrix} -2 \\ 0 \\ 1 \end{bmatrix}, \begin{bmatrix} 0 \\ 1 \\ 0 \end{bmatrix}$$

7. Since A is triangular, its eigenvalues are obviously ± 1.

For $\lambda = 1$: $A - 1I = \begin{bmatrix} 0 & 0 \\ 6 & -2 \end{bmatrix}$. The equation $(A - 1I)\mathbf{x} = \mathbf{0}$ amounts to $6x_1 - 2x_2 = 0$, so $x_1 = (1/3)x_2$ with

x_2 free. The general solution is $x_2 \begin{bmatrix} 1/3 \\ 1 \end{bmatrix}$, and a nice basis vector for the eigenspace is $\mathbf{v}_1 = \begin{bmatrix} 1 \\ 3 \end{bmatrix}$.

For $\lambda = -1$: $A + 1I = \begin{bmatrix} 2 & 0 \\ 6 & 0 \end{bmatrix}$. The equation $(A + 1I)\mathbf{x} = \mathbf{0}$ amounts to $2x_1 = 0$, so $x_1 = 0$ with x_2 free.

The general solution is $x_2 \begin{bmatrix} 0 \\ 1 \end{bmatrix}$, and a basis vector for the eigenspace is $\mathbf{v}_2 = \begin{bmatrix} 0 \\ 1 \end{bmatrix}$.

From $\mathbf{v}_1$ and $\mathbf{v}_2$ construct $P = \begin{bmatrix} \mathbf{v}_1 & \mathbf{v}_2 \end{bmatrix} = \begin{bmatrix} 1 & 0 \\ 3 & 1 \end{bmatrix}$. Then set $D = \begin{bmatrix} 1 & 0 \\ 0 & -1 \end{bmatrix}$, where the eigenvalues in D

correspond to $\mathbf{v}_1$ and $\mathbf{v}_2$ respectively.

8. Since A is triangular, its only eigenvalue is obviously 5.

For $\lambda = 5$: $A - 5I = \begin{bmatrix} 0 & 1 \\ 0 & 0 \end{bmatrix}$. The equation $(A - 5I)\mathbf{x} = \mathbf{0}$ amounts to $x_2 = 0$, so $x_2 = 0$ with x_1 free. The

general solution is $x_1 \begin{bmatrix} 1 \\ 0 \end{bmatrix}$. Since we cannot generate an eigenvector basis for $\mathbb{R}^2$, A is not diagonalizable.

9. To find the eigenvalues of A, compute its characteristic polynomial:

$$\det(A - \lambda I) = \det \begin{bmatrix} 3 - \lambda & -1 \\ 1 & 5 - \lambda \end{bmatrix} = (3 - \lambda)(5 - \lambda) - (-1)(1) = \lambda^2 - 8\lambda + 16 = (\lambda - 4)^2$$

Thus the only eigenvalue of A is 4.

For $\lambda = 4$: $A - 4I = \begin{bmatrix} -1 & -1 \\ 1 & 1 \end{bmatrix}$. The equation $(A - 4I)\mathbf{x} = \mathbf{0}$ amounts to $x_1 + x_2 = 0$, so $x_1 = -x_2$ with x_2

free. The general solution is $x_2 \begin{bmatrix} -1 \\ 1 \end{bmatrix}$. Since we cannot generate an eigenvector basis for $\mathbb{R}^2$, A is not

diagonalizable.

10. To find the eigenvalues of A, compute its characteristic polynomial:

$$\det(A - \lambda I) = \det \begin{bmatrix} 2 - \lambda & 3 \\ 4 & 1 - \lambda \end{bmatrix} = (2 - \lambda)(1 - \lambda) - (3)(4) = \lambda^2 - 3\lambda - 10 = (\lambda - 5)(\lambda + 2)$$

Thus the eigenvalues of A are 5 and -2.

For $\lambda = 5$: $A - 5I = \begin{bmatrix} -3 & 3 \\ 4 & -4 \end{bmatrix}$. The equation $(A - 5I)\mathbf{x} = \mathbf{0}$ amounts to $x_1 - x_2 = 0$, so $x_1 = x_2$ with x_2

free. The general solution is $x_2 \begin{bmatrix} 1 \\ 1 \end{bmatrix}$, and a basis vector for the eigenspace is $\mathbf{v}_1 = \begin{bmatrix} 1 \\ 1 \end{bmatrix}$.

For $\lambda = -2$: $A + 2I = \begin{bmatrix} 4 & 3 \\ 4 & 3 \end{bmatrix}$. The equation $(A + 1I)\mathbf{x} = \mathbf{0}$ amounts to $4x_1 + 3x_2 = 0$, so $x_1 = (-3/4)x_2$

with x_2 free. The general solution is $x_2 \begin{bmatrix} -3/4 \\ 1 \end{bmatrix}$, and a nice basis vector for the eigenspace is $\mathbf{v}_2 = \begin{bmatrix} -3 \\ 4 \end{bmatrix}$.

From $\mathbf{v}_1$ and $\mathbf{v}_2$ construct $P = \begin{bmatrix} \mathbf{v}_1 & \mathbf{v}_2 \end{bmatrix} = \begin{bmatrix} 1 & -3 \\ 1 & 4 \end{bmatrix}$. Then set $D = \begin{bmatrix} 5 & 0 \\ 0 & -2 \end{bmatrix}$, where the eigenvalues in

D correspond to $\mathbf{v}_1$ and $\mathbf{v}_2$ respectively.

11. The eigenvalues of A are given to be 1, 2, and 3.

For $\lambda = 3$: $A - 3I = \begin{bmatrix} -4 & 4 & -2 \\ -3 & 1 & 0 \\ -3 & 1 & 0 \end{bmatrix}$, and row reducing $\begin{bmatrix} A - 3I & \mathbf{0} \end{bmatrix}$ yields $\begin{bmatrix} 1 & 0 & -1/4 & 0 \\ 0 & 1 & -3/4 & 0 \\ 0 & 0 & 0 & 0 \end{bmatrix}$. The

general solution is $x_3 \begin{bmatrix} 1/4 \\ 3/4 \\ 1 \end{bmatrix}$, and a nice basis vector for the eigenspace is $\mathbf{v}_1 = \begin{bmatrix} 1 \\ 3 \\ 4 \end{bmatrix}$.

For $\lambda = 2$: $A - 2I = \begin{bmatrix} -3 & 4 & -2 \\ -3 & 2 & 0 \\ -3 & 1 & 1 \end{bmatrix}$, and row reducing $\begin{bmatrix} A - 2I & \mathbf{0} \end{bmatrix}$ yields $\begin{bmatrix} 1 & 0 & -2/3 & 0 \\ 0 & 1 & -1 & 0 \\ 0 & 0 & 0 & 0 \end{bmatrix}$. The

general solution is $x_3 \begin{bmatrix} 2/3 \\ 1 \\ 1 \end{bmatrix}$, and a nice basis vector for the eigenspace is $\mathbf{v}_2 = \begin{bmatrix} 2 \\ 3 \\ 3 \end{bmatrix}$.

For $\lambda = 1$: $A - I = \begin{bmatrix} -2 & 4 & -2 \\ -3 & 3 & 0 \\ -3 & 1 & 2 \end{bmatrix}$, and row reducing $\begin{bmatrix} A - 1I & \mathbf{0} \end{bmatrix}$ yields $\begin{bmatrix} 1 & 0 & -1 & 0 \\ 0 & 1 & -1 & 0 \\ 0 & 0 & 0 & 0 \end{bmatrix}$. The general

solution is $x_3 \begin{bmatrix} 1 \\ 1 \\ 1 \end{bmatrix}$, and a basis vector for the eigenspace is $\mathbf{v}_3 = \begin{bmatrix} 1 \\ 1 \\ 1 \end{bmatrix}$.

From $\mathbf{v}_1, \mathbf{v}_2$ and $\mathbf{v}_3$ construct $P = \begin{bmatrix} \mathbf{v}_1 & \mathbf{v}_2 & \mathbf{v}_3 \end{bmatrix} = \begin{bmatrix} 1 & 2 & 1 \\ 3 & 3 & 1 \\ 4 & 3 & 1 \end{bmatrix}$. Then set $D = \begin{bmatrix} 3 & 0 & 0 \\ 0 & 2 & 0 \\ 0 & 0 & 1 \end{bmatrix}$, where the

eigenvalues in D correspond to $\mathbf{v}_1, \mathbf{v}_2$ and $\mathbf{v}_3$ respectively.

12. The eigenvalues of A are given to be 2 and 8.

For $\lambda = 8$: $A - 8I = \begin{bmatrix} -4 & 2 & 2 \\ 2 & -4 & 2 \\ 2 & 2 & -4 \end{bmatrix}$, and row reducing $\begin{bmatrix} A - 8I & \mathbf{0} \end{bmatrix}$ yields $\begin{bmatrix} 1 & 0 & -1 & 0 \\ 0 & 1 & -1 & 0 \\ 0 & 0 & 0 & 0 \end{bmatrix}$. The

general solution is $x_3 \begin{bmatrix} 1 \\ 1 \\ 1 \end{bmatrix}$, and a basis vector for the eigenspace is $\mathbf{v}_1 = \begin{bmatrix} 1 \\ 1 \\ 1 \end{bmatrix}$.

For $\lambda = 2$: $A - 2I = \begin{bmatrix} 2 & 2 & 2 \\ 2 & 2 & 2 \\ 2 & 2 & 2 \end{bmatrix}$, and row reducing $\begin{bmatrix} A - 2I & \mathbf{0} \end{bmatrix}$ yields $\begin{bmatrix} 1 & 1 & 1 & 0 \\ 0 & 0 & 0 & 0 \\ 0 & 0 & 0 & 0 \end{bmatrix}$. The general

solution is $x_2 \begin{bmatrix} -1 \\ 1 \\ 0 \end{bmatrix} + x_3 \begin{bmatrix} -1 \\ 0 \\ 1 \end{bmatrix}$, and a basis for the eigenspace is $\{\mathbf{v}_2, \mathbf{v}_3\} = \left\{ \begin{bmatrix} -1 \\ 1 \\ 0 \end{bmatrix}, \begin{bmatrix} -1 \\ 0 \\ 1 \end{bmatrix} \right\}$.

From $\mathbf{v}_1, \mathbf{v}_2$ and $\mathbf{v}_3$ construct $P = \begin{bmatrix} \mathbf{v}_1 & \mathbf{v}_2 & \mathbf{v}_3 \end{bmatrix} = \begin{bmatrix} 1 & -1 & -1 \\ 1 & 1 & 0 \\ 1 & 0 & 1 \end{bmatrix}$. Then set $D = \begin{bmatrix} 8 & 0 & 0 \\ 0 & 2 & 0 \\ 0 & 0 & 2 \end{bmatrix}$, where the

eigenvalues in D correspond to $\mathbf{v}_1, \mathbf{v}_2$ and $\mathbf{v}_3$ respectively.

13. The eigenvalues of A are given to be 5 and 1.

For $\lambda = 5$: $A - 5I = \begin{bmatrix} -3 & 2 & -1 \\ 1 & -2 & -1 \\ -1 & -2 & -3 \end{bmatrix}$, and row reducing $\begin{bmatrix} A - 5I & \mathbf{0} \end{bmatrix}$ yields $\begin{bmatrix} 1 & 0 & 1 & 0 \\ 0 & 1 & 1 & 0 \\ 0 & 0 & 0 & 0 \end{bmatrix}$. The general

solution is $x_3 \begin{bmatrix} -1 \\ -1 \\ 1 \end{bmatrix}$, and a basis for the eigenspace is $\mathbf{v}_1 = \begin{bmatrix} -1 \\ -1 \\ 1 \end{bmatrix}$.

For $\lambda = 1$: $A - 1I = \begin{bmatrix} 1 & 2 & -1 \\ 1 & 2 & -1 \\ -1 & -2 & 1 \end{bmatrix}$, and row reducing $\begin{bmatrix} A - I & \mathbf{0} \end{bmatrix}$ yields $\begin{bmatrix} 1 & 2 & -1 & 0 \\ 0 & 0 & 0 & 0 \\ 0 & 0 & 0 & 0 \end{bmatrix}$. The general

solution is $x_2 \begin{bmatrix} -2 \\ 1 \\ 0 \end{bmatrix} + x_3 \begin{bmatrix} 1 \\ 0 \\ 1 \end{bmatrix}$, and a basis for the eigenspace is $\{\mathbf{v}_2, \mathbf{v}_3\} = \left\{ \begin{bmatrix} -2 \\ 1 \\ 0 \end{bmatrix}, \begin{bmatrix} 1 \\ 0 \\ 1 \end{bmatrix} \right\}$.

From $\mathbf{v}_1, \mathbf{v}_2$ and $\mathbf{v}_3$ construct $P = \begin{bmatrix} \mathbf{v}_1 & \mathbf{v}_2 & \mathbf{v}_3 \end{bmatrix} = \begin{bmatrix} -1 & -2 & 1 \\ -1 & 1 & 0 \\ 1 & 0 & 1 \end{bmatrix}$. Then set $D = \begin{bmatrix} 5 & 0 & 0 \\ 0 & 1 & 0 \\ 0 & 0 & 1 \end{bmatrix}$, where the

eigenvalues in D correspond to $\mathbf{v}_1, \mathbf{v}_2$ and $\mathbf{v}_3$ respectively.

14. The eigenvalues of A are given to be 5 and 4.

For $\lambda = 5$: $A - 5I = \begin{bmatrix} -1 & 0 & -2 \\ 2 & 0 & 4 \\ 0 & 0 & 0 \end{bmatrix}$, and row reducing $\begin{bmatrix} A - 5I & \mathbf{0} \end{bmatrix}$ yields $\begin{bmatrix} 1 & 0 & 2 & 0 \\ 0 & 0 & 0 & 0 \\ 0 & 0 & 0 & 0 \end{bmatrix}$. The general

solution is $x_2 \begin{bmatrix} 0 \\ 1 \\ 0 \end{bmatrix} + x_3 \begin{bmatrix} -2 \\ 0 \\ 1 \end{bmatrix}$, and a basis for the eigenspace is $\{\mathbf{v}_1, \mathbf{v}_2\} = \left\{ \begin{bmatrix} -2 \\ 0 \\ 1 \end{bmatrix}, \begin{bmatrix} 0 \\ 1 \\ 0 \end{bmatrix} \right\}$.

For $\lambda = 4$: $A - 4I = \begin{bmatrix} 0 & 0 & -2 \\ 2 & 1 & 4 \\ 0 & 0 & 1 \end{bmatrix}$, and row reducing $\begin{bmatrix} A - 4I & \mathbf{0} \end{bmatrix}$ yields $\begin{bmatrix} 1 & 1/2 & 0 & 0 \\ 0 & 0 & 1 & 0 \\ 0 & 0 & 0 & 0 \end{bmatrix}$. The general

solution is $x_3 \begin{bmatrix} -1/2 \\ 1 \\ 0 \end{bmatrix}$, and a nice basis vector for the eigenspace is $\mathbf{v}_3 = \begin{bmatrix} -1 \\ 2 \\ 0 \end{bmatrix}$.

From $\mathbf{v}_1, \mathbf{v}_2$ and $\mathbf{v}_3$ construct $P = \begin{bmatrix} \mathbf{v}_1 & \mathbf{v}_2 & \mathbf{v}_3 \end{bmatrix} = \begin{bmatrix} -2 & 0 & -1 \\ 0 & 1 & 2 \\ 1 & 0 & 0 \end{bmatrix}$. Then set $D = \begin{bmatrix} 5 & 0 & 0 \\ 0 & 5 & 0 \\ 0 & 0 & 4 \end{bmatrix}$, where the

eigenvalues in D correspond to $\mathbf{v}_1, \mathbf{v}_2$ and $\mathbf{v}_3$ respectively.

15. The eigenvalues of A are given to be 3 and 1.

For $\lambda = 3$: $A - 3I = \begin{bmatrix} 4 & 4 & 16 \\ 2 & 2 & 8 \\ -2 & -2 & -8 \end{bmatrix}$, and row reducing $\begin{bmatrix} A - 3I & \mathbf{0} \end{bmatrix}$ yields $\begin{bmatrix} 1 & 1 & 4 & 0 \\ 0 & 0 & 0 & 0 \\ 0 & 0 & 0 & 0 \end{bmatrix}$. The general

solution is $x_2 \begin{bmatrix} -1 \\ 1 \\ 0 \end{bmatrix} + x_3 \begin{bmatrix} -4 \\ 0 \\ 1 \end{bmatrix}$, and a basis for the eigenspace is $\{\mathbf{v}_1, \mathbf{v}_2\} = \left\{ \begin{bmatrix} -1 \\ 1 \\ 0 \end{bmatrix}, \begin{bmatrix} -4 \\ 0 \\ 1 \end{bmatrix} \right\}$

For $\lambda = 1$: $A - I = \begin{bmatrix} 6 & 4 & 16 \\ 2 & 4 & 8 \\ -2 & -2 & -6 \end{bmatrix}$, and row reducing $\begin{bmatrix} A - I & \mathbf{0} \end{bmatrix}$ yields $\begin{bmatrix} 1 & 0 & 2 & 0 \\ 0 & 1 & 1 & 0 \\ 0 & 0 & 0 & 0 \end{bmatrix}$. The general

solution is $x_3 \begin{bmatrix} -2 \\ -1 \\ 1 \end{bmatrix}$, and a basis for the eigenspace is $\mathbf{v}_3 = \begin{bmatrix} -2 \\ -1 \\ 1 \end{bmatrix}$.

From $\mathbf{v}_1, \mathbf{v}_2$ and $\mathbf{v}_3$ construct $P = \begin{bmatrix} \mathbf{v}_1 & \mathbf{v}_2 & \mathbf{v}_3 \end{bmatrix} = \begin{bmatrix} -1 & -4 & -2 \\ 1 & 0 & -1 \\ 0 & 1 & 1 \end{bmatrix}$. Then set $D = \begin{bmatrix} 3 & 0 & 0 \\ 0 & 3 & 0 \\ 0 & 0 & 1 \end{bmatrix}$, where

the eigenvalues in D correspond to $\mathbf{v}_1, \mathbf{v}_2$ and $\mathbf{v}_3$ respectively.

16. The eigenvalues of A are given to be 2 and 1.

For $\lambda = 2$: $A - 2I = \begin{bmatrix} -2 & -4 & -6 \\ -1 & -2 & -3 \\ 1 & 2 & 3 \end{bmatrix}$, and row reducing $\begin{bmatrix} A - 2I & \mathbf{0} \end{bmatrix}$ yields $\begin{bmatrix} 1 & 2 & 3 & 0 \\ 0 & 0 & 0 & 0 \\ 0 & 0 & 0 & 0 \end{bmatrix}$. The general

solution is $x_2 \begin{bmatrix} -2 \\ 1 \\ 0 \end{bmatrix} + x_3 \begin{bmatrix} -3 \\ 0 \\ 1 \end{bmatrix}$, and a basis for the eigenspace is $\{\mathbf{v}_1, \mathbf{v}_2\} = \left\{ \begin{bmatrix} -2 \\ 1 \\ 0 \end{bmatrix}, \begin{bmatrix} -3 \\ 0 \\ 1 \end{bmatrix} \right\}$.

For $\lambda = 1$: $A - I = \begin{bmatrix} -1 & -4 & -6 \\ -1 & -1 & -3 \\ 1 & 2 & 4 \end{bmatrix}$, and row reducing $\begin{bmatrix} A - I & \mathbf{0} \end{bmatrix}$ yields $\begin{bmatrix} 1 & 0 & 2 & 0 \\ 0 & 1 & 1 & 0 \\ 0 & 0 & 0 & 0 \end{bmatrix}$. The general

solution is $x_3 \begin{bmatrix} -2 \\ -1 \\ 1 \end{bmatrix}$, and a basis for the eigenspace is $\mathbf{v}_3 = \begin{bmatrix} -2 \\ -1 \\ 1 \end{bmatrix}$.

From $\mathbf{v}_1, \mathbf{v}_2$ and $\mathbf{v}_3$ construct $P = \begin{bmatrix} \mathbf{v}_1 & \mathbf{v}_2 & \mathbf{v}_3 \end{bmatrix} = \begin{bmatrix} -2 & -3 & -2 \\ 1 & 0 & -1 \\ 0 & 1 & 1 \end{bmatrix}$. Then set $D = \begin{bmatrix} 2 & 0 & 0 \\ 0 & 2 & 0 \\ 0 & 0 & 1 \end{bmatrix}$, where

the eigenvalues in D correspond to $\mathbf{v}_1, \mathbf{v}_2$ and $\mathbf{v}_3$ respectively.

17. Since A is triangular, its eigenvalues are obviously 4 and 5.

For $\lambda = 4$: $A - 4I = \begin{bmatrix} 0 & 0 & 0 \\ 1 & 0 & 0 \\ 0 & 0 & 1 \end{bmatrix}$, and row reducing $\begin{bmatrix} A - 4I & \mathbf{0} \end{bmatrix}$ yields $\begin{bmatrix} 1 & 0 & 0 & 0 \\ 0 & 0 & 1 & 0 \\ 0 & 0 & 0 & 0 \end{bmatrix}$. The general

solution is $x_2 \begin{bmatrix} 0 \\ 1 \\ 0 \end{bmatrix}$, and a basis for the eigenspace is $\mathbf{v}_1 = \begin{bmatrix} 0 \\ 1 \\ 0 \end{bmatrix}$.

Since $\lambda = 5$ must have only a one-dimensional eigenspace, we can find at most 2 linearly independent eigenvectors for A, so A is not diagonalizable.

18. An eigenvalue of A is given to be 5; an eigenvector $\mathbf{v}_1 = \begin{bmatrix} -2 \\ 1 \\ 2 \end{bmatrix}$ is also given. To find the eigenvalue

corresponding to $\mathbf{v}_1$, compute $A\mathbf{v}_1 = \begin{bmatrix} -7 & -16 & 4 \\ 6 & 13 & -2 \\ 12 & 16 & 1 \end{bmatrix}\begin{bmatrix} -2 \\ 1 \\ 2 \end{bmatrix} = \begin{bmatrix} 6 \\ -3 \\ 6 \end{bmatrix} = -3\mathbf{v}_1$. Thus the eigenvalue in

question is -3.

For $\lambda = 5$: $A - 5I = \begin{bmatrix} -12 & -16 & 4 \\ 6 & 8 & -2 \\ 12 & 16 & -4 \end{bmatrix}$, and row reducing $\begin{bmatrix} A - 5I & \mathbf{0} \end{bmatrix}$ yields $\begin{bmatrix} 1 & 4/3 & -1/3 & 0 \\ 0 & 0 & 0 & 0 \\ 0 & 0 & 0 & 0 \end{bmatrix}$.

The general solution is $x_2 \begin{bmatrix} -4/3 \\ 1 \\ 0 \end{bmatrix} + x_3 \begin{bmatrix} 1/3 \\ 0 \\ 1 \end{bmatrix}$, and a nice basis for the eigenspace is

$\{\mathbf{v}_2, \mathbf{v}_3\} = \left\{ \begin{bmatrix} -4 \\ 3 \\ 0 \end{bmatrix}, \begin{bmatrix} 1 \\ 0 \\ 3 \end{bmatrix} \right\}$.

From $\mathbf{v}_1, \mathbf{v}_2$ and $\mathbf{v}_3$ construct $P = \begin{bmatrix} \mathbf{v}_1 & \mathbf{v}_2 & \mathbf{v}_3 \end{bmatrix} = \begin{bmatrix} -2 & -4 & 1 \\ 1 & 3 & 0 \\ 2 & 0 & 3 \end{bmatrix}$. Then set $D = \begin{bmatrix} -3 & 0 & 0 \\ 0 & 5 & 0 \\ 0 & 0 & 5 \end{bmatrix}$, where the

eigenvalues in D correspond to $\mathbf{v}_1, \mathbf{v}_2$ and $\mathbf{v}_3$ respectively. Note that this answer differs from the text. There, $P = \begin{bmatrix} \mathbf{v}_2 & \mathbf{v}_3 & \mathbf{v}_1 \end{bmatrix}$ and the entries in D are rearranged to match the new order of the eigenvectors. According to the Diagonalization Theorem, both answers are correct.

19. Since A is triangular, its eigenvalues are obviously 2, 3, and 5.

For $\lambda = 2$: $A - 2I = \begin{bmatrix} 3 & -3 & 0 & 9 \\ 0 & 1 & 1 & -2 \\ 0 & 0 & 0 & 0 \\ 0 & 0 & 0 & 0 \end{bmatrix}$, and row reducing $\begin{bmatrix} A - 2I & \mathbf{0} \end{bmatrix}$ yields $\begin{bmatrix} 1 & 0 & 1 & 1 & 0 \\ 0 & 1 & 1 & -2 & 0 \\ 0 & 0 & 0 & 0 & 0 \\ 0 & 0 & 0 & 0 & 0 \end{bmatrix}$. The

general solution is $x_3 \begin{bmatrix} -1 \\ -1 \\ 1 \\ 0 \end{bmatrix} + x_4 \begin{bmatrix} -1 \\ 2 \\ 0 \\ 1 \end{bmatrix}$, and a nice basis for the eigenspace is $\{\mathbf{v}_1, \mathbf{v}_2\} = \left\{ \begin{bmatrix} -1 \\ -1 \\ 1 \\ 0 \end{bmatrix}, \begin{bmatrix} -1 \\ 2 \\ 0 \\ 1 \end{bmatrix} \right\}$.

For $\lambda = 3$: $A - 3I = \begin{bmatrix} 2 & -3 & 0 & 9 \\ 0 & 0 & 1 & -2 \\ 0 & 0 & -1 & 0 \\ 0 & 0 & 0 & -1 \end{bmatrix}$, and row reducing $\begin{bmatrix} A - 3I & \mathbf{0} \end{bmatrix}$ yields $\begin{bmatrix} 1 & -3/2 & 0 & 0 & 0 \\ 0 & 0 & 1 & 0 & 0 \\ 0 & 0 & 0 & 1 & 0 \\ 0 & 0 & 0 & 0 & 0 \end{bmatrix}$.

The general solution is $x_2 \begin{bmatrix} 3/2 \\ 1 \\ 0 \\ 0 \end{bmatrix}$, and a nice basis for the eigenspace is $\mathbf{v}_3 = \begin{bmatrix} 3 \\ 2 \\ 0 \\ 0 \end{bmatrix}$.

For $\lambda = 5$: $A - 5I = \begin{bmatrix} 0 & -3 & 0 & 9 \\ 0 & -2 & 1 & -2 \\ 0 & 0 & -3 & 0 \\ 0 & 0 & 0 & -3 \end{bmatrix}$, and row reducing $\begin{bmatrix} A - 5I & \mathbf{0} \end{bmatrix}$ yields $\begin{bmatrix} 0 & 1 & 0 & 0 & 0 \\ 0 & 0 & 1 & 0 & 0 \\ 0 & 0 & 0 & 1 & 0 \\ 0 & 0 & 0 & 0 & 0 \end{bmatrix}$. The

general solution is $x_1 \begin{bmatrix} 1 \\ 0 \\ 0 \\ 0 \end{bmatrix}$, and a basis for the eigenspace is $\mathbf{v}_4 = \begin{bmatrix} 1 \\ 0 \\ 0 \\ 0 \end{bmatrix}$.

From $\mathbf{v}_1, \mathbf{v}_2, \mathbf{v}_3$ and $\mathbf{v}_4$ construct $P = \begin{bmatrix} \mathbf{v}_1 & \mathbf{v}_2 & \mathbf{v}_3 & \mathbf{v}_4 \end{bmatrix} = \begin{bmatrix} -1 & -1 & 3 & 1 \\ -1 & 2 & 2 & 0 \\ 1 & 0 & 0 & 0 \\ 0 & 1 & 0 & 0 \end{bmatrix}$. Then set $D = \begin{bmatrix} 2 & 0 & 0 & 0 \\ 0 & 2 & 0 & 0 \\ 0 & 0 & 3 & 0 \\ 0 & 0 & 0 & 5 \end{bmatrix}$,

where the eigenvalues in D correspond to $\mathbf{v}_1, \mathbf{v}_2$ and $\mathbf{v}_3$ respectively. Note that this answer differs from the text. There, $P = \begin{bmatrix} \mathbf{v}_4 & \mathbf{v}_3 & \mathbf{v}_1 & \mathbf{v}_2 \end{bmatrix}$ and the entries in D are rearranged to match the new order of the eigenvectors. According to the Diagonalization Theorem, both answers are correct.

20. Since A is triangular, its eigenvalues are obviously 4 and 2.

For $\lambda = 4$: $A - 4I = \begin{bmatrix} 0 & 0 & 0 & 0 \\ 0 & 0 & 0 & 0 \\ 0 & 0 & -2 & 0 \\ 1 & 0 & 0 & -2 \end{bmatrix}$, and row reducing $\begin{bmatrix} A - 4I & \mathbf{0} \end{bmatrix}$ yields $\begin{bmatrix} 1 & 0 & 0 & -2 & 0 \\ 0 & 0 & 1 & 0 & 0 \\ 0 & 0 & 0 & 0 & 0 \\ 0 & 0 & 0 & 0 & 0 \end{bmatrix}$. The

general solution is $x_2 \begin{bmatrix} 0 \\ 1 \\ 0 \\ 0 \end{bmatrix} + x_4 \begin{bmatrix} 2 \\ 0 \\ 0 \\ 1 \end{bmatrix}$, and a basis for the eigenspace is $\{\mathbf{v}_1, \mathbf{v}_2\} = \left\{ \begin{bmatrix} 0 \\ 1 \\ 0 \\ 0 \end{bmatrix}, \begin{bmatrix} 2 \\ 0 \\ 0 \\ 1 \end{bmatrix} \right\}$.

For $\lambda = 2$: $A - 2I = \begin{bmatrix} 2 & 0 & 0 & 0 \\ 0 & 2 & 0 & 0 \\ 0 & 0 & 0 & 0 \\ 1 & 0 & 0 & 0 \end{bmatrix}$, and row reducing $\begin{bmatrix} A - 2I & \mathbf{0} \end{bmatrix}$ yields $\begin{bmatrix} 1 & 0 & 0 & 0 & 0 \\ 0 & 1 & 0 & 0 & 0 \\ 0 & 0 & 0 & 0 & 0 \\ 0 & 0 & 0 & 0 & 0 \end{bmatrix}$. The

general solution is $x_3 \begin{bmatrix} 0 \\ 0 \\ 1 \\ 0 \end{bmatrix} + x_4 \begin{bmatrix} 0 \\ 0 \\ 0 \\ 1 \end{bmatrix}$, and a basis for the eigenspace is $\{\mathbf{v}_3, \mathbf{v}_4\} = \left\{ \begin{bmatrix} 0 \\ 0 \\ 1 \\ 0 \end{bmatrix}, \begin{bmatrix} 0 \\ 0 \\ 0 \\ 1 \end{bmatrix} \right\}$.

From $\mathbf{v}_1, \mathbf{v}_2, \mathbf{v}_3$ and $\mathbf{v}_4$ construct $P = [\mathbf{v}_1\ \mathbf{v}_2\ \mathbf{v}_3\ \mathbf{v}_4] = \begin{bmatrix} 0 & 2 & 0 & 0 \\ 1 & 0 & 0 & 0 \\ 0 & 0 & 1 & 0 \\ 0 & 1 & 0 & 1 \end{bmatrix}$. Then set $D = \begin{bmatrix} 4 & 0 & 0 & 0 \\ 0 & 4 & 0 & 0 \\ 0 & 0 & 2 & 0 \\ 0 & 0 & 0 & 2 \end{bmatrix}$,

where the eigenvalues in D correspond to $\mathbf{v}_1, \mathbf{v}_2$ and $\mathbf{v}_3$ respectively.

21. **a**. False. The symbol D does not automatically denote a diagonal matrix.

   b. True. See the remark after the statement of the Diagonalization Theorem.

   c. False. The 3×3 matrix in Example 4 has 3 eigenvalues, counting multiplicities, but it is not diagonalizable.

   d. False. Invertibility depends on 0 not being an eigenvalue. (See the Invertible Matrix Theorem.) A diagonalizable matrix may or may not have 0 as an eigenvalue. See Examples 3 and 5 for both possibilities.

22. **a**. False. The n eigenvectors must be linearly independent. See the Diagonalization Theorem.

   b. False. The matrix in Example 3 is diagonalizable, but it has only 2 distinct eigenvalues. (The statement given is the *converse* of Theorem 6.)

   c. True. This follows from $AP = PD$ and formulas (1) and (2) in the proof of the Diagonalization Theorem.

   d. False. See Example 4. The matrix there is invertible because 0 is not an eigenvalue, but the matrix is not diagonalizable.

23. A is diagonalizable because you know that five linearly independent eigenvectors exist: three in the three-dimensional eigenspace and two in the two-dimensional eigenspace. Theorem 7 guarantees that the set of all five eigenvectors is linearly independent.

24. No, by Theorem 7(b). Here is an explanation that does not appeal to Theorem 7: Let $\mathbf{v}_1$ and $\mathbf{v}_2$ be eigenvectors that span the two one-dimensional eigenspaces. If $\mathbf{v}$ is any other eigenvector, then it belongs to one of the eigenspaces and hence is a multiple of either $\mathbf{v}_1$ or $\mathbf{v}_2$. So there cannot exist three linearly independent eigenvectors. By the Diagonalization Theorem, A cannot be diagonalizable.

25. Let $\{\mathbf{v}_1\}$ be a basis for the one-dimensional eigenspace, let $\mathbf{v}_2$ and $\mathbf{v}_3$ form a basis for the two-dimensional eigenspace, and let $\mathbf{v}_4$ be any eigenvector in the remaining eigenspace. By Theorem 7, $\{\mathbf{v}_1, \mathbf{v}_2, \mathbf{v}_3, \mathbf{v}_4\}$ is linearly independent. Since A is 4×4, the Diagonalization Theorem shows that A is diagonalizable.

26. Yes, if the third eigenspace is only one-dimensional. In this case, the sum of the dimensions of the eigenspaces will be six, whereas the matrix is 7×7. See Theorem 7(b). An argument similar to that for Exercise 24 can also be given.

27. If A is diagonalizable, then $A = PDP^{-1}$ for some invertible P and diagonal D. Since A is invertible, 0 is not an eigenvalue of A. So the diagonal entries in D (which are eigenvalues of A) are not zero, and D is invertible. By the theorem on the inverse of a product,

$$A^{-1} = (PDP^{-1})^{-1} = (P^{-1})^{-1} D^{-1} P^{-1} = PD^{-1}P^{-1}$$

Since D^{-1} is obviously diagonal, A^{-1} is diagonalizable.

28. If A has n linearly independent eigenvectors, then by the Diagonalization Theorem, $A = PDP^{-1}$ for some invertible P and diagonal D. Using properties of transposes,

$$A^T = (PDP^{-1})^T = (P^{-1})^T D^T P^T$$
$$= (P^T)^{-1} D P^T = QDQ^{-1}$$

where $Q = (P^T)^{-1}$. Thus A^T is diagonalizable. By the Diagonalization Theorem, the columns of Q are n linearly independent eigenvectors of A^T.

29. The diagonal entries in D_1 are reversed from those in D. So interchange the (eigenvector) columns of P to make them correspond properly to the eigenvalues in D_1. In this case,

$$P_1 = \begin{bmatrix} 1 & 1 \\ -2 & -1 \end{bmatrix} \text{ and } D_1 = \begin{bmatrix} 3 & 0 \\ 0 & 5 \end{bmatrix}$$

Although the first column of P must be an eigenvector corresponding to the eigenvalue 3, there is nothing to prevent us from selecting some multiple of $\begin{bmatrix} 1 \\ -2 \end{bmatrix}$, say $\begin{bmatrix} -3 \\ 6 \end{bmatrix}$, and letting $P_2 = \begin{bmatrix} -3 & 1 \\ 6 & -1 \end{bmatrix}$. We now have three different factorizations or "diagonalizations" of A:

$$A = PDP^{-1} = P_1 D_1 P_1^{-1} = P_2 D_1 P_2^{-1}$$

30. A nonzero multiple of an eigenvector is another eigenvector. To produce P_2, simply multiply one or both columns of P by a nonzero scalar unequal to 1.

31. For a 2×2 matrix A to be invertible, its eigenvalues must be nonzero. A first attempt at a construction might be something such as $\begin{bmatrix} 2 & 3 \\ 0 & 4 \end{bmatrix}$, whose eigenvalues are 2 and 4. Unfortunately, a 2×2 matrix with two distinct eigenvalues is diagonalizable (Theorem 6). So, adjust the construction to $\begin{bmatrix} 2 & 3 \\ 0 & 2 \end{bmatrix}$, which works. In fact, any matrix of the form $\begin{bmatrix} a & b \\ 0 & a \end{bmatrix}$ has the desired properties when a and b are nonzero. The eigenspace for the eigenvalue a is one-dimensional, as a simple calculation shows, and there is no other eigenvalue to produce a second eigenvector.

32. Any 2×2 matrix with two distinct eigenvalues is diagonalizable, by Theorem 6. If one of those eigenvalues is zero, then the matrix will not be invertible. Any matrix of the form $\begin{bmatrix} a & b \\ 0 & 0 \end{bmatrix}$ has the desired properties when a and b are nonzero. The number a must be nonzero to make the matrix diagonalizable; b must be nonzero to make the matrix not diagonal. Other solutions are $\begin{bmatrix} 0 & 0 \\ a & b \end{bmatrix}$ and $\begin{bmatrix} 0 & a \\ 0 & b \end{bmatrix}$.

33. $A = \begin{bmatrix} -6 & 4 & 0 & 9 \\ -3 & 0 & 1 & 6 \\ -1 & -2 & 1 & 0 \\ -4 & 4 & 0 & 7 \end{bmatrix}$,

ev = eig(A) = (5,1,-2,-2)

nulbasis(A-ev(1)*eye(4)) = $\begin{bmatrix} 1.0000 \\ 0.5000 \\ -0.5000 \\ 1.0000 \end{bmatrix}$

A basis for the eigenspace of $\lambda = 5$ is $\begin{bmatrix} 2 \\ 1 \\ -1 \\ 2 \end{bmatrix}$.

nulbasis(A-ev(2)*eye(4)) = $\begin{bmatrix} 1.0000 \\ -0.5000 \\ -3.5000 \\ 1.0000 \end{bmatrix}$

A basis for the eigenspace of $\lambda = 1$ is $\begin{bmatrix} 2 \\ -1 \\ -7 \\ 2 \end{bmatrix}$.

nulbasis(A-ev(3)*eye(4)) = $\begin{bmatrix} 1.0000 \\ 1.0000 \\ 1.0000 \\ 0 \end{bmatrix}, \begin{bmatrix} 1.5000 \\ -0.7500 \\ 0 \\ 1.0000 \end{bmatrix}$

A basis for the eigenspace of $\lambda = -2$ is $\begin{bmatrix} 1 \\ 1 \\ 1 \\ 0 \end{bmatrix}, \begin{bmatrix} 6 \\ -3 \\ 0 \\ 4 \end{bmatrix}$.

Thus we construct $P = \begin{bmatrix} 2 & 2 & 1 & 6 \\ 1 & -1 & 1 & -3 \\ -1 & -7 & 1 & 0 \\ 2 & 2 & 0 & 4 \end{bmatrix}$ and $D = \begin{bmatrix} 5 & 0 & 0 & 0 \\ 0 & 1 & 0 & 0 \\ 0 & 0 & -2 & 0 \\ 0 & 0 & 0 & -2 \end{bmatrix}$.

34. $A = \begin{bmatrix} 0 & 13 & 8 & 4 \\ 4 & 9 & 8 & 4 \\ 8 & 6 & 12 & 8 \\ 0 & 5 & 0 & -4 \end{bmatrix}$,

ev = eig(A) = (-4,24,1,-4)

$$\texttt{nulbasis(A-ev(1)*eye(4))} = \begin{bmatrix} -2 \\ 0 \\ 1 \\ 0 \end{bmatrix}, \begin{bmatrix} -1 \\ 0 \\ 0 \\ 1 \end{bmatrix}$$

A basis for the eigenspace of $\lambda = -4$ is $\begin{bmatrix} -2 \\ 0 \\ 1 \\ 0 \end{bmatrix}, \begin{bmatrix} -1 \\ 0 \\ 0 \\ 1 \end{bmatrix}$.

$$\texttt{nulbasis(A-ev(2)*eye(4))} = \begin{bmatrix} 5.6000 \\ 5.6000 \\ 7.2000 \\ 1.0000 \end{bmatrix}$$

A basis for the eigenspace of $\lambda = 24$ is $\begin{bmatrix} 28 \\ 28 \\ 36 \\ 5 \end{bmatrix}$.

$$\texttt{nulbasis(A-ev(3)*eye(4))} = \begin{bmatrix} 1.0000 \\ 1.0000 \\ -2.0000 \\ 1.0000 \end{bmatrix}$$

A basis for the eigenspace of $\lambda = 1$ is $\begin{bmatrix} 1 \\ 1 \\ -2 \\ 1 \end{bmatrix}$.

Thus we construct $P = \begin{bmatrix} -2 & -1 & 28 & 1 \\ 0 & 0 & 28 & 1 \\ 1 & 0 & 36 & -2 \\ 0 & 1 & 5 & 1 \end{bmatrix}$ and $D = \begin{bmatrix} -4 & 0 & 0 & 0 \\ 0 & -4 & 0 & 0 \\ 0 & 0 & 24 & 0 \\ 0 & 0 & 0 & 1 \end{bmatrix}$.

35. $A = \begin{bmatrix} 11 & -6 & 4 & -10 & -4 \\ -3 & 5 & -2 & 4 & 1 \\ -8 & 12 & -3 & 12 & 4 \\ 1 & 6 & -2 & 3 & -1 \\ 8 & -18 & 8 & -14 & -1 \end{bmatrix}$,

$\texttt{ev = eig(A)} = (5,1,3,5,1)$

$$\texttt{nulbasis(A-ev(1)*eye(5))} = \begin{bmatrix} 2.0000 \\ -0.3333 \\ -1.0000 \\ 1.0000 \\ 0 \end{bmatrix}, \begin{bmatrix} 1.0000 \\ -0.3333 \\ -1.0000 \\ 0 \\ 1.0000 \end{bmatrix}$$

A basis for the eigenspace of $\lambda = 5$ is $\begin{bmatrix} 6 \\ -1 \\ -3 \\ 3 \\ 0 \end{bmatrix}, \begin{bmatrix} 3 \\ -1 \\ -3 \\ 0 \\ 3 \end{bmatrix}$.

$\texttt{nulbasis(A-ev(2)*eye(5))} = \begin{bmatrix} 0.8000 \\ -0.6000 \\ -0.4000 \\ 1.0000 \\ 0 \end{bmatrix}, \begin{bmatrix} 0.6000 \\ -0.2000 \\ -0.8000 \\ 0 \\ 1.0000 \end{bmatrix}$

A basis for the eigenspace of $\lambda = 1$ is $\begin{bmatrix} 4 \\ -3 \\ -2 \\ 5 \\ 0 \end{bmatrix}, \begin{bmatrix} 3 \\ -1 \\ -4 \\ 0 \\ 5 \end{bmatrix}$.

$\texttt{nulbasis(A-ev(3)*eye(5))} = \begin{bmatrix} 0.5000 \\ -0.2500 \\ -1.0000 \\ -0.2500 \\ 1.0000 \end{bmatrix}$

A basis for the eigenspace of $\lambda = 3$ is $\begin{bmatrix} 2 \\ -1 \\ -4 \\ -1 \\ 4 \end{bmatrix}$.

Thus we construct $P = \begin{bmatrix} 6 & 3 & 4 & 3 & 2 \\ -1 & -1 & -3 & -1 & -1 \\ -3 & -3 & -2 & -4 & -4 \\ 3 & 0 & 5 & 0 & -1 \\ 0 & 3 & 0 & 5 & 4 \end{bmatrix}$ and $D = \begin{bmatrix} 5 & 0 & 0 & 0 & 0 \\ 0 & 5 & 0 & 0 & 0 \\ 0 & 0 & 1 & 0 & 0 \\ 0 & 0 & 0 & 1 & 0 \\ 0 & 0 & 0 & 0 & 3 \end{bmatrix}$.

36. $A = \begin{bmatrix} 4 & 4 & 2 & 3 & -2 \\ 0 & 1 & -2 & -2 & 2 \\ 6 & 12 & 11 & 2 & -4 \\ 9 & 20 & 10 & 10 & -6 \\ 15 & 28 & 14 & 5 & -3 \end{bmatrix}$,

$\texttt{ev = eig(A) = (3,5,7,5,3)}$

$$\texttt{nulbasis(A-ev(1)*eye(5))} = \begin{bmatrix} 2.0000 \\ -1.5000 \\ 0.5000 \\ 1.0000 \\ 0 \end{bmatrix}, \begin{bmatrix} -1.0000 \\ 0.5000 \\ 0.5000 \\ 0 \\ 1.0000 \end{bmatrix}$$

A basis for the eigenspace of $\lambda = 3$ is $\begin{bmatrix} 4 \\ -3 \\ 1 \\ 2 \\ 0 \end{bmatrix}, \begin{bmatrix} -2 \\ 1 \\ 1 \\ 0 \\ 2 \end{bmatrix}$.

$$\texttt{nulbasis(A-ev(2)*eye(5))} = \begin{bmatrix} 0 \\ -0.5000 \\ 1.0000 \\ 0 \\ 0 \end{bmatrix}, \begin{bmatrix} -1.0000 \\ 1.0000 \\ 0 \\ -1.0000 \\ 1.0000 \end{bmatrix}$$

A basis for the eigenspace of $\lambda = 5$ is $\begin{bmatrix} 0 \\ -1 \\ 2 \\ 0 \\ 0 \end{bmatrix}, \begin{bmatrix} -1 \\ 1 \\ 0 \\ -1 \\ 1 \end{bmatrix}$.

$$\texttt{nulbasis(A-ev(3)*eye(5))} = \begin{bmatrix} 0.3333 \\ 0.0000 \\ 0.0000 \\ 1.0000 \\ 1.0000 \end{bmatrix}$$

A basis for the eigenspace of $\lambda = 7$ is $\begin{bmatrix} 1 \\ 0 \\ 0 \\ 3 \\ 3 \end{bmatrix}$.

Thus we construct $P = \begin{bmatrix} 4 & -2 & 0 & -1 & 1 \\ -3 & 1 & -1 & 1 & 0 \\ 1 & 1 & 2 & 0 & 0 \\ 2 & 0 & 0 & -1 & 3 \\ 0 & 2 & 0 & 1 & 3 \end{bmatrix}$ and $D = \begin{bmatrix} 3 & 0 & 0 & 0 & 0 \\ 0 & 3 & 0 & 0 & 0 \\ 0 & 0 & 5 & 0 & 0 \\ 0 & 0 & 0 & 5 & 0 \\ 0 & 0 & 0 & 0 & 7 \end{bmatrix}$.

Notes: For your use, here is another matrix with five distinct real eigenvalues. To four decimal places, they are 11.0654, 9.8785, 3.8238, −3.7332, and −6.0345.

$$\begin{bmatrix} 6 & -8 & 5 & -3 & 0 \\ -7 & 3 & -5 & 3 & 0 \\ -3 & -7 & 5 & -3 & 5 \\ 0 & -4 & 1 & -7 & 5 \\ -5 & -3 & -2 & 0 & 8 \end{bmatrix}$$

The MATLAB box in the *Study Guide* encourages students to use eig (A) and nulbasis to practice the diagonalization procedure in this section. It also remarks that in later work, a student may automate the process, using the command [P D]= eig (A). You may wish to permit students to use the full power of eig in some problems in Sections 5.5 and 5.7.

5.4   SOLUTIONS

1. Since $T(\mathbf{b}_1) = 3\mathbf{d}_1 - 5\mathbf{d}_2, [T(\mathbf{b}_1)]_D = \begin{bmatrix} 3 \\ -5 \end{bmatrix}$. Likewise $T(\mathbf{b}_2) = -\mathbf{d}_1 + 6\mathbf{d}_2$ implies that $[T(\mathbf{b}_2)]_D = \begin{bmatrix} -1 \\ 6 \end{bmatrix}$ and

$T(\mathbf{b}_3) = 4\mathbf{d}_2$ implies that $[T(\mathbf{b}_3)]_D = \begin{bmatrix} 0 \\ 4 \end{bmatrix}$. Thus the matrix for T relative to B and

D is $\left[[T(\mathbf{b}_1)]_D [T(\mathbf{b}_2)]_D [T(\mathbf{b}_3)]_D \right] = \begin{bmatrix} 3 & -1 & 0 \\ -5 & 6 & 4 \end{bmatrix}$.

2. Since $T(\mathbf{d}_1) = 2\mathbf{b}_1 - 3\mathbf{b}_2, [T(\mathbf{d}_1)]_B = \begin{bmatrix} 2 \\ -3 \end{bmatrix}$. Likewise $T(\mathbf{d}_2) = -4\mathbf{b}_1 + 5\mathbf{b}_2$ implies that $[T(\mathbf{d}_2)]_B = \begin{bmatrix} -4 \\ 5 \end{bmatrix}$.

Thus the matrix for T relative to D and B is $\left[[T(\mathbf{d}_1)]_B [T(\mathbf{d}_2)]_B \right] = \begin{bmatrix} 2 & -4 \\ -3 & 5 \end{bmatrix}$.

3. a. $T(\mathbf{e}_1) = 0\mathbf{b}_1 - 1\mathbf{b}_2 + \mathbf{b}_3, T(\mathbf{e}_2) = -1\mathbf{b}_1 - 0\mathbf{b}_2 - 1\mathbf{b}_3, T(\mathbf{e}_3) = 1\mathbf{b}_1 - 1\mathbf{b}_2 + 0\mathbf{b}_3$

b. $[T(\mathbf{e}_1)]_B = \begin{bmatrix} 0 \\ -1 \\ 1 \end{bmatrix}, [T(\mathbf{e}_2)]_B = \begin{bmatrix} -1 \\ 0 \\ -1 \end{bmatrix}, [T(\mathbf{e}_3)]_B = \begin{bmatrix} 1 \\ -1 \\ 0 \end{bmatrix}$

c. The matrix for T relative to $\mathcal{E}$ and B is $[[T(\mathbf{e}_1)]_B \ [T(\mathbf{e}_2)]_B \ [T(\mathbf{e}_3)]_B] = \begin{bmatrix} 0 & -1 & 1 \\ -1 & 0 & -1 \\ 1 & -1 & 0 \end{bmatrix}$.

4. Let $\mathcal{E} = \{\mathbf{e}_1, \mathbf{e}_2\}$ be the standard basis for $\mathbb{R}^2$. Since $[T(\mathbf{b}_1)]_\mathcal{E} = T(\mathbf{b}_1) = \begin{bmatrix} 2 \\ 0 \end{bmatrix}, [T(\mathbf{b}_2)]_\mathcal{E} = T(\mathbf{b}_2) = \begin{bmatrix} -4 \\ -1 \end{bmatrix}$,

and $[T(\mathbf{b}_3)]_\mathcal{E} = T(\mathbf{b}_3) = \begin{bmatrix} 5 \\ 3 \end{bmatrix}$, the matrix for T relative to B and $\mathcal{E}$ is $[[T(\mathbf{b}_1)]_\mathcal{E} \ [T(\mathbf{b}_2)]_\mathcal{E} \ [T(\mathbf{b}_3)]_\mathcal{E}] = $

$\begin{bmatrix} 2 & -4 & 5 \\ 0 & -1 & 3 \end{bmatrix}$.

5. a. $T(\mathbf{p}) = (t+5)(2-t+t^2) = 10 - 3t + 4t^2 + t^3$

b. Let $\mathbf{p}$ and $\mathbf{q}$ be polynomials in $\mathbb{P}_2$, and let c be any scalar. Then

$$T(\mathbf{p}(t) + \mathbf{q}(t)) = (t+5)[\mathbf{p}(t) + \mathbf{q}(t)] = (t+5)\mathbf{p}(t) + (t+5)\mathbf{q}(t)$$
$$= T(\mathbf{p}(t)) + T(\mathbf{q}(t))$$
$$T(c \cdot \mathbf{p}(t)) = (t+5)[c \cdot \mathbf{p}(t)] = c \cdot (t+5)\mathbf{p}(t)$$
$$= c \cdot T[\mathbf{p}(t)]$$

and T is a linear transformation.

c. Let $B = \{1, t, t^2\}$ and $C = \{1, t, t^2, t^3\}$. Since $T(\mathbf{b}_1) = T(1) = (t+5)(1) = t+5$, $[T(\mathbf{b}_1)]_C = \begin{bmatrix} 5 \\ 1 \\ 0 \\ 0 \end{bmatrix}$. Likewise

since $T(\mathbf{b}_2) = T(t) = (t+5)(t) = t^2 + 5t$, $[T(\mathbf{b}_2)]_C = \begin{bmatrix} 0 \\ 5 \\ 1 \\ 0 \end{bmatrix}$, and since

$T(\mathbf{b}_3) = T(t^2) = (t+5)(t^2) = t^3 + 5t^2$, $[T(\mathbf{b}_3)]_C = \begin{bmatrix} 0 \\ 0 \\ 5 \\ 1 \end{bmatrix}$. Thus the matrix for T relative to B and

C is $[\,[T(\mathbf{b}_1)]_C \;\; [T(\mathbf{b}_2)]_C \;\; [T(\mathbf{b}_3)]_C\,] = \begin{bmatrix} 5 & 0 & 0 \\ 1 & 5 & 0 \\ 0 & 1 & 5 \\ 0 & 0 & 1 \end{bmatrix}$.

6. a. $T(\mathbf{p}) = (2-t+t^2) + t^2(2-t+t^2) = 2 - t + 3t^2 - t^3 + t^4$

b. Let $\mathbf{p}$ and $\mathbf{q}$ be polynomials in $\mathbb{P}_2$, and let c be any scalar. Then

$$T(\mathbf{p}(t) + \mathbf{q}(t)) = [\mathbf{p}(t) + \mathbf{q}(t)] + t^2[\mathbf{p}(t) + \mathbf{q}(t)]$$
$$= [\mathbf{p}(t) + t^2\mathbf{p}(t)] + [\mathbf{q}(t) + t^2\mathbf{q}(t)]$$
$$= T(\mathbf{p}(t)) + T(\mathbf{q}(t))$$
$$T(c \cdot \mathbf{p}(t)) = [c \cdot \mathbf{p}(t)] + t^2[c \cdot \mathbf{p}(t)]$$
$$= c \cdot [\mathbf{p}(t) + t^2\mathbf{p}(t)]$$
$$= c \cdot T[\mathbf{p}(t)]$$

and T is a linear transformation.

c. Let $B = \{1, t, t^2\}$ and $C = \{1, t, t^2, t^3, t^4\}$. Since $T(\mathbf{b}_1) = T(1) = 1 + t^2(1) = t^2 + 1, [T(\mathbf{b}_1)]_C = \begin{bmatrix} 1 \\ 0 \\ 1 \\ 0 \\ 0 \end{bmatrix}$.

Likewise since $T(\mathbf{b}_2) = T(t) = t + (t^2)(t) = t^3 + t, [T(\mathbf{b}_2)]_C = \begin{bmatrix} 0 \\ 1 \\ 0 \\ 1 \\ 0 \end{bmatrix}$, and

since $T(\mathbf{b}_3) = T(t^2) = t^2 + (t^2)(t^2) = t^4 + t^2, [T(\mathbf{b}_3)]_C = \begin{bmatrix} 0 \\ 0 \\ 1 \\ 0 \\ 1 \end{bmatrix}$. Thus the matrix for T relative to

B and C is $[\ [T(\mathbf{b}_1)]_C \quad [T(\mathbf{b}_2)]_C \quad [T(\mathbf{b}_3)]_C\ ] = \begin{bmatrix} 1 & 0 & 0 \\ 0 & 1 & 0 \\ 1 & 0 & 1 \\ 0 & 1 & 0 \\ 0 & 0 & 1 \end{bmatrix}$.

7. Since $T(\mathbf{b}_1) = T(1) = 3 + 5t, [T(\mathbf{b}_1)]_B = \begin{bmatrix} 3 \\ 5 \\ 0 \end{bmatrix}$. Likewise since $T(\mathbf{b}_2) = T(t) = -2t + 4t^2, [T(\mathbf{b}_2)]_B = \begin{bmatrix} 0 \\ -2 \\ 4 \end{bmatrix}$,

and since $T(\mathbf{b}_3) = T(t^2) = t^2, [T(\mathbf{b}_3)]_B = \begin{bmatrix} 0 \\ 0 \\ 1 \end{bmatrix}$. Thus the matrix representation of T relative to the basis

B is $\left[[T(\mathbf{b}_1)]_B \quad [T(\mathbf{b}_2)]_B \quad [T(\mathbf{b}_3)]_B \right] = \begin{bmatrix} 3 & 0 & 0 \\ 5 & -2 & 0 \\ 0 & 4 & 1 \end{bmatrix}$. Perhaps a faster way is to realize that the

information given provides the general form of $T(\mathbf{p})$ as shown in the figure below:

$$a_0 + a_1 t + a_2 t^2 \xrightarrow{\quad T \quad} 3a_0 + (5a_0 - 2a_1)t + (4a_1 + a_2)t^2$$

coordinate mapping $\downarrow$ coordinate mapping $\downarrow$

$$\begin{bmatrix} a_0 \\ a_1 \\ a_2 \end{bmatrix} \xrightarrow[\text{by}[T]_B]{\text{multiplication}} \begin{bmatrix} 3a_0 \\ 5a_0 - 2a_1 \\ 4a_1 + a_2 \end{bmatrix}$$

The matrix that implements the multiplication along the bottom of the figure is easily filled in by inspection:

$$\begin{bmatrix} ? & ? & ? \\ ? & ? & ? \\ ? & ? & ? \end{bmatrix}\begin{bmatrix} a_0 \\ a_1 \\ a_2 \end{bmatrix} = \begin{bmatrix} 3a_0 \\ 5a_0 - 2a_1 \\ 4a_1 + a_2 \end{bmatrix} \text{ implies that } [T]_B = \begin{bmatrix} 3 & 0 & 0 \\ 5 & -2 & 0 \\ 0 & 4 & 1 \end{bmatrix}$$

8. Since $[3\mathbf{b}_1 - 4\mathbf{b}_2]_B = \begin{bmatrix} 3 \\ -4 \\ 0 \end{bmatrix}$, $[T(3\mathbf{b}_1 - 4\mathbf{b}_2)]_B = [T]_B[3\mathbf{b}_1 - 4\mathbf{b}_2]_B = \begin{bmatrix} 0 & -6 & 1 \\ 0 & 5 & -1 \\ 1 & -2 & 7 \end{bmatrix}\begin{bmatrix} 3 \\ -4 \\ 0 \end{bmatrix} = \begin{bmatrix} 24 \\ -20 \\ 11 \end{bmatrix}$

and $T(3\mathbf{b}_1 - 4\mathbf{b}_2) = 24\mathbf{b}_1 - 20\mathbf{b}_2 + 11\mathbf{b}_3$.

9. **a.** $T(\mathbf{p}) = \begin{bmatrix} 5 + 3(-1) \\ 5 + 3(0) \\ 5 + 3(1) \end{bmatrix} = \begin{bmatrix} 2 \\ 5 \\ 8 \end{bmatrix}$

b. Let $\mathbf{p}$ and $\mathbf{q}$ be polynomials in $\mathbb{P}_2$, and let c be any scalar. Then

$$T(\mathbf{p} + \mathbf{q}) = \begin{bmatrix} (\mathbf{p} + \mathbf{q})(-1) \\ (\mathbf{p} + \mathbf{q})(0) \\ (\mathbf{p} + \mathbf{q})(1) \end{bmatrix} = \begin{bmatrix} \mathbf{p}(-1) + \mathbf{q}(-1) \\ \mathbf{p}(0) + \mathbf{q}(0) \\ \mathbf{p}(1) + \mathbf{q}(1) \end{bmatrix} = \begin{bmatrix} \mathbf{p}(-1) \\ \mathbf{p}(0) \\ \mathbf{p}(1) \end{bmatrix} + \begin{bmatrix} \mathbf{q}(-1) \\ \mathbf{q}(0) \\ \mathbf{q}(1) \end{bmatrix} = T(\mathbf{p}) + T(\mathbf{q})$$

$$T(c \cdot \mathbf{p}) = \begin{bmatrix} (c \cdot \mathbf{p})(-1) \\ (c \cdot \mathbf{p})(0) \\ (c \cdot \mathbf{p})(1) \end{bmatrix} = \begin{bmatrix} c \cdot (\mathbf{p}(-1)) \\ c \cdot (\mathbf{p}(0)) \\ c \cdot (\mathbf{p}(1)) \end{bmatrix} = c \cdot \begin{bmatrix} \mathbf{p}(-1) \\ \mathbf{p}(0) \\ \mathbf{p}(1) \end{bmatrix} = c \cdot T(\mathbf{p})$$

and T is a linear transformation.

c. Let $B = \{1, t, t^2\}$ and $\mathcal{E} = \{\mathbf{e}_1, \mathbf{e}_2, \mathbf{e}_3\}$ be the standard basis for $\mathbb{R}^3$. Since

$$[T(\mathbf{b}_1)]_\mathcal{E} = T(\mathbf{b}_1) = T(1) = \begin{bmatrix} 1 \\ 1 \\ 1 \end{bmatrix}, \; [T(\mathbf{b}_2)]_\mathcal{E} = T(\mathbf{b}_2) = T(t) = \begin{bmatrix} -1 \\ 0 \\ 1 \end{bmatrix}, \text{ and } [T(\mathbf{b}_3)]_\mathcal{E} = T(\mathbf{b}_3) = T(t^2) = \begin{bmatrix} 1 \\ 0 \\ 1 \end{bmatrix},$$

the matrix for T relative to B and $\mathcal{E}$ is $\begin{bmatrix} [T(\mathbf{b}_1)]_\mathcal{E} & [T(\mathbf{b}_2)]_\mathcal{E} & [T(\mathbf{b}_3)]_\mathcal{E} \end{bmatrix} = \begin{bmatrix} 1 & -1 & 1 \\ 1 & 0 & 0 \\ 1 & 1 & 1 \end{bmatrix}$.

10. **a**. Let $\mathbf{p}$ and $\mathbf{q}$ be polynomials in $\mathbb{P}_3$, and let c be any scalar. Then

$$T(\mathbf{p} + \mathbf{q}) = \begin{bmatrix} (\mathbf{p} + \mathbf{q})(-3) \\ (\mathbf{p} + \mathbf{q})(-1) \\ (\mathbf{p} + \mathbf{q})(1) \\ (\mathbf{p} + \mathbf{q})(3) \end{bmatrix} = \begin{bmatrix} \mathbf{p}(-3) + \mathbf{q}(-3) \\ \mathbf{p}(-1) + \mathbf{q}(-1) \\ \mathbf{p}(1) + \mathbf{q}(1) \\ \mathbf{p}(3) + \mathbf{q}(3) \end{bmatrix} = \begin{bmatrix} \mathbf{p}(-3) \\ \mathbf{p}(-1) \\ \mathbf{p}(1) \\ \mathbf{p}(3) \end{bmatrix} + \begin{bmatrix} \mathbf{q}(-3) \\ \mathbf{q}(-1) \\ \mathbf{q}(1) \\ \mathbf{q}(3) \end{bmatrix} = T(\mathbf{p}) + T(\mathbf{q})$$

$$T(c \cdot \mathbf{p}) = \begin{bmatrix} (c \cdot \mathbf{p})(-3) \\ (c \cdot \mathbf{p})(-1) \\ (c \cdot \mathbf{p})(1) \\ (c \cdot \mathbf{p})(3) \end{bmatrix} = \begin{bmatrix} c \cdot (\mathbf{p}(-3)) \\ c \cdot (\mathbf{p}(-1)) \\ c \cdot (\mathbf{p}(1)) \\ c \cdot (\mathbf{p}(3)) \end{bmatrix} = c \cdot \begin{bmatrix} \mathbf{p}(-3) \\ \mathbf{p}(-1) \\ \mathbf{p}(1) \\ \mathbf{p}(3) \end{bmatrix} = c \cdot T(\mathbf{p})$$

and T is a linear transformation.

b. Let $B = \{1, t, t^2, t^3\}$ and $\mathcal{E} = \{\mathbf{e}_1, \mathbf{e}_2, \mathbf{e}_3, \mathbf{e}_4\}$ be the standard basis for $\mathbb{R}^3$. Since

$$[T(\mathbf{b}_1)]_{\mathcal{E}} = T(\mathbf{b}_1) = T(1) = \begin{bmatrix} 1 \\ 1 \\ 1 \\ 1 \end{bmatrix}, \; [T(\mathbf{b}_2)]_{\mathcal{E}} = T(\mathbf{b}_2) = T(t) = \begin{bmatrix} -3 \\ -1 \\ 1 \\ 3 \end{bmatrix}, \; [T(\mathbf{b}_3)]_{\mathcal{E}} = T(\mathbf{b}_3) = T(t^2) = \begin{bmatrix} 9 \\ 1 \\ 1 \\ 9 \end{bmatrix}, \text{ and}$$

$$[T(\mathbf{b}_4)]_{\mathcal{E}} = T(\mathbf{b}_4) = T(t^3) = \begin{bmatrix} -27 \\ -1 \\ 1 \\ 27 \end{bmatrix}, \text{ the matrix for } T \text{ relative to } B \text{ and } \mathcal{E} \text{ is}$$

$$\begin{bmatrix} [T(\mathbf{b}_1)]_{\mathcal{E}} & [T(\mathbf{b}_2)]_{\mathcal{E}} & [T(\mathbf{b}_3)]_{\mathcal{E}} & [T(\mathbf{b}_4)]_{\mathcal{E}} \end{bmatrix} = \begin{bmatrix} 1 & -3 & 9 & -27 \\ 1 & -1 & 1 & -1 \\ 1 & 1 & 1 & 1 \\ 1 & 3 & 9 & 27 \end{bmatrix}.$$

11. Following Example 4, if $P = \begin{bmatrix} \mathbf{b}_1 & \mathbf{b}_2 \end{bmatrix} = \begin{bmatrix} 2 & 1 \\ -1 & 2 \end{bmatrix}$, then the B-matrix is

$$P^{-1}AP = \frac{1}{5} \begin{bmatrix} 2 & -1 \\ 1 & 2 \end{bmatrix} \begin{bmatrix} 3 & 4 \\ -1 & -1 \end{bmatrix} \begin{bmatrix} 2 & 1 \\ -1 & 2 \end{bmatrix} = \begin{bmatrix} 1 & 5 \\ 0 & 1 \end{bmatrix}$$

12. Following Example 4, if $P = \begin{bmatrix} \mathbf{b}_1 & \mathbf{b}_2 \end{bmatrix} = \begin{bmatrix} 3 & -1 \\ 2 & 1 \end{bmatrix}$, then the B-matrix is

$$P^{-1}AP = \frac{1}{5} \begin{bmatrix} 1 & 1 \\ -2 & 3 \end{bmatrix} \begin{bmatrix} -1 & 4 \\ -2 & 3 \end{bmatrix} \begin{bmatrix} 3 & -1 \\ 2 & 1 \end{bmatrix} = \begin{bmatrix} 1 & 2 \\ -2 & 1 \end{bmatrix}$$

13. Start by diagonalizing A. The characteristic polynomial is $\lambda^2 - 4\lambda + 3 = (\lambda - 1)(\lambda - 3)$, so the eigenvalues of A are 1 and 3.

For $\lambda = 1$: $A - I = \begin{bmatrix} -1 & 1 \\ -3 & 3 \end{bmatrix}$. The equation $(A - I)\mathbf{x} = \mathbf{0}$ amounts to $-x_1 + x_2 = 0$, so $x_1 = x_2$ with x_2

free. A basis vector for the eigenspace is thus $\mathbf{v}_1 = \begin{bmatrix} 1 \\ 1 \end{bmatrix}$.

For $\lambda = 3$: $A - 3I = \begin{bmatrix} -3 & 1 \\ -3 & 1 \end{bmatrix}$. The equation $(A - 3I)\mathbf{x} = \mathbf{0}$ amounts to $-3x_1 + x_2 = 0$, so $x_1 = (1/3)x_2$ with

x_2 free. A nice basis vector for the eigenspace is thus $\mathbf{v}_2 = \begin{bmatrix} 1 \\ 3 \end{bmatrix}$.

From $\mathbf{v}_1$ and $\mathbf{v}_2$ we may construct $P = \begin{bmatrix} \mathbf{v}_1 & \mathbf{v}_2 \end{bmatrix} = \begin{bmatrix} 1 & 1 \\ 1 & 3 \end{bmatrix}$ which diagonalizes A. By Theorem 8, the

basis $B = \{\mathbf{v}_1, \mathbf{v}_2\}$ has the property that the B-matrix of the transformation $\mathbf{x} \mapsto A\mathbf{x}$ is a diagonal matrix.

14. Start by diagonalizing A. The characteristic polynomial is $\lambda^2 - 6\lambda - 16 = (\lambda - 8)(\lambda + 2)$, so the eigenvalues of A are 8 and -2.

For $\lambda = 8$: $A - 8I = \begin{bmatrix} -3 & -3 \\ -7 & -7 \end{bmatrix}$. The equation $(A - 8I)\mathbf{x} = \mathbf{0}$ amounts to $x_1 + x_2 = 0$, so $x_1 = -x_2$ with x_2 free. A basis vector for the eigenspace is thus $\mathbf{v}_1 = \begin{bmatrix} -1 \\ 1 \end{bmatrix}$.

For $\lambda = 2$: $A + 2I = \begin{bmatrix} 7 & -3 \\ -7 & 3 \end{bmatrix}$. The equation $(A - 2I)\mathbf{x} = \mathbf{0}$ amounts to $7x_1 - 3x_2 = 0$, so $x_1 = (3/7)x_2$ with x_2 free. A nice basis vector for the eigenspace is thus $\mathbf{v}_2 = \begin{bmatrix} 3 \\ 7 \end{bmatrix}$.

From $\mathbf{v}_1$ and $\mathbf{v}_2$ we may construct $P = \begin{bmatrix} \mathbf{v}_1 & \mathbf{v}_2 \end{bmatrix} = \begin{bmatrix} -1 & 3 \\ 1 & 7 \end{bmatrix}$ which diagonalizes A. By Theorem 8, the basis $B = \{\mathbf{v}_1, \mathbf{v}_2\}$ has the property that the B-matrix of the transformation $\mathbf{x} \mapsto A\mathbf{x}$ is a diagonal matrix.

15. Start by diagonalizing A. The characteristic polynomial is $\lambda^2 - 7\lambda + 10 = (\lambda - 5)(\lambda - 2)$, so the eigenvalues of A are 5 and 2.

For $\lambda = 5$: $A - 5I = \begin{bmatrix} -1 & -2 \\ -1 & -2 \end{bmatrix}$. The equation $(A - 5I)\mathbf{x} = \mathbf{0}$ amounts to $x_1 + 2x_2 = 0$, so $x_1 = -2x_2$ with x_2 free. A basis vector for the eigenspace is thus $\mathbf{v}_1 = \begin{bmatrix} -2 \\ 1 \end{bmatrix}$.

For $\lambda = 2$: $A - 2I = \begin{bmatrix} 2 & -2 \\ -1 & 1 \end{bmatrix}$. The equation $(A - 2I)\mathbf{x} = \mathbf{0}$ amounts to $x_1 - x_2 = 0$, so $x_1 = x_2$ with x_2 free. A basis vector for the eigenspace is thus $\mathbf{v}_2 = \begin{bmatrix} 1 \\ 1 \end{bmatrix}$.

From $\mathbf{v}_1$ and $\mathbf{v}_2$ we may construct $P = \begin{bmatrix} \mathbf{v}_1 & \mathbf{v}_2 \end{bmatrix} = \begin{bmatrix} -2 & 1 \\ 1 & 1 \end{bmatrix}$ which diagonalizes A. By Theorem 8, the basis $B = \{\mathbf{v}_1, \mathbf{v}_2\}$ has the property that the B-matrix of the transformation $\mathbf{x} \mapsto A\mathbf{x}$ is a diagonal matrix.

16. Start by diagonalizing A. The characteristic polynomial is $\lambda^2 - 5\lambda = \lambda(\lambda - 5)$, so the eigenvalues of A are 5 and 0.

For $\lambda = 5$: $A - 5I = \begin{bmatrix} -3 & -6 \\ -1 & -2 \end{bmatrix}$. The equation $(A - 5I)\mathbf{x} = \mathbf{0}$ amounts to $x_1 + 2x_2 = 0$, so $x_1 = -2x_2$ with x_2 free. A basis vector for the eigenspace is thus $\mathbf{v}_1 = \begin{bmatrix} -2 \\ 1 \end{bmatrix}$.

For $\lambda = 0$: $A - 0I = \begin{bmatrix} 2 & -6 \\ -1 & 3 \end{bmatrix}$. The equation $(A - 0I)\mathbf{x} = \mathbf{0}$ amounts to $x_1 - 3x_2 = 0$, so $x_1 = 3x_2$ with x_2 free. A basis vector for the eigenspace is thus $\mathbf{v}_2 = \begin{bmatrix} 3 \\ 1 \end{bmatrix}$.

From $\mathbf{v}_1$ and $\mathbf{v}_2$ we may construct $P = \begin{bmatrix} \mathbf{v}_1 & \mathbf{v}_2 \end{bmatrix} = \begin{bmatrix} -2 & 3 \\ 1 & 1 \end{bmatrix}$ which diagonalizes A. By Theorem 8, the basis $B = \{\mathbf{v}_1, \mathbf{v}_2\}$ has the property that the B-matrix of the transformation $\mathbf{x} \mapsto A\mathbf{x}$ is a diagonal matrix.

17. **a.** We compute that

$$A\mathbf{b}_1 = \begin{bmatrix} 1 & 1 \\ -1 & 3 \end{bmatrix}\begin{bmatrix} 1 \\ 1 \end{bmatrix} = \begin{bmatrix} 2 \\ 2 \end{bmatrix} = 2\mathbf{b}_1$$

so $\mathbf{b}_1$ is an eigenvector of A corresponding to the eigenvalue 2. The characteristic polynomial of A is $\lambda^2 - 4\lambda + 4 = (\lambda - 2)^2$, so 2 is the only eigenvalue for A. Now $A - 2I = \begin{bmatrix} -1 & 1 \\ -1 & 1 \end{bmatrix}$, which implies that the eigenspace corresponding to the eigenvalue 2 is one-dimensional. Thus the matrix A is not diagonalizable.

b. Following Example 4, if $P = \begin{bmatrix} \mathbf{b}_1 & \mathbf{b}_2 \end{bmatrix}$, then the B-matrix for T is

$$P^{-1}AP = \begin{bmatrix} -4 & 5 \\ 1 & -1 \end{bmatrix}\begin{bmatrix} 1 & 1 \\ -1 & 3 \end{bmatrix}\begin{bmatrix} 1 & 1 \\ -1 & 3 \end{bmatrix} = \begin{bmatrix} 1 & 5 \\ 1 & 4 \end{bmatrix} = \begin{bmatrix} 2 & -1 \\ 0 & 2 \end{bmatrix}$$

18. If there is a basis B such that $[T]_B$ is diagonal, then A is similar to a diagonal matrix, by the second paragraph following Example 3. In this case, A would have three linearly independent eigenvectors. However, this is not necessarily the case, because A has only two distinct eigenvalues.

19. If A is similar to B, then there exists an invertible matrix P such that $P^{-1}AP = B$. Thus B is invertible because it is the product of invertible matrices. By a theorem about inverses of products, $B^{-1} = P^{-1}A^{-1}(P^{-1})^{-1} = P^{-1}A^{-1}P$, which shows that A^{-1} is similar to B^{-1}.

20. If $A = PBP^{-1}$, then $A^2 = (PBP^{-1})(PBP^{-1}) = PB(P^{-1}P)BP^{-1} = PB \cdot I \cdot BP^{-1} = PB^2P^{-1}$. So A^2 is similar to B^2.

21. By hypothesis, there exist invertible P and Q such that $P^{-1}BP = A$ and $Q^{-1}CQ = A$. Then $P^{-1}BP = Q^{-1}CQ$. Left-multiply by Q and right-multiply by Q^{-1} to obtain $QP^{-1}BPQ^{-1} = QQ^{-1}CQQ^{-1}$. So $C = QP^{-1}BPQ^{-1} = (PQ^{-1})^{-1}B(PQ^{-1})$, which shows that B is similar to C.

22. If A is diagonalizable, then $A = PDP^{-1}$ for some P. Also, if B is similar to A, then $B = QAQ^{-1}$ for some Q. Then $B = Q(PDP^{-1})Q^{-1} = (QP)D(P^{-1}Q^{-1}) = (QP)D(QP)^{-1}$

So B is diagonalizable.

23. If $A\mathbf{x} = \lambda\mathbf{x}, \mathbf{x} \neq \mathbf{0}$, then $P^{-1}A\mathbf{x} = \lambda P^{-1}\mathbf{x}$. If $B = P^{-1}AP$, then

$$B(P^{-1}\mathbf{x}) = P^{-1}AP(P^{-1}\mathbf{x}) = P^{-1}A\mathbf{x} = \lambda P^{-1}\mathbf{x} \tag{*}$$

by the first calculation. Note that $P^{-1}\mathbf{x} \neq \mathbf{0}$, because $\mathbf{x} \neq \mathbf{0}$ and P^{-1} is invertible. Hence (*) shows that $P^{-1}\mathbf{x}$ is an eigenvector of B corresponding to λ. (Of course, λ is an eigenvalue of both A and B because the matrices are similar, by Theorem 4 in Section 5.2.)

24. If $A = PBP^{-1}$, then rank $A = $ rank $P(BP^{-1}) = $ rank BP^{-1}, by Supplementary Exercise 13 in Chapter 4. Also, rank $BP^{-1} = $ rank B, by Supplementary Exercise 14 in Chapter 4, since P^{-1} is invertible. Thus rank $A = $ rank B.

25. If $A = PBP^{-1}$, then

$$\operatorname{tr}(A) = \operatorname{tr}((PB)P^{-1}) = \operatorname{tr}(P^{-1}(PB)) \qquad \text{By the trace property}$$
$$= \operatorname{tr}(P^{-1}PB) = \operatorname{tr}(IB) = \operatorname{tr}(B)$$

If B is diagonal, then the diagonal entries of B must be the eigenvalues of A, by the Diagonalization Theorem (Theorem 5 in Section 5.3). So $\operatorname{tr} A = \operatorname{tr} B = \{\text{sum of the eigenvalues of } A\}$.

26. If $A = PDP^{-1}$ for some P, then the general trace property from Exercise 25 shows that $\operatorname{tr} A = \operatorname{tr}[(PD)P^{-1}] = \operatorname{tr}[P^{-1}PD] = \operatorname{tr} D$. (Or, one can use the result of Exercise 25 that since A is similar to D, $\operatorname{tr} A = \operatorname{tr} D$.) Since the eigenvalues of A are on the main diagonal of D, $\operatorname{tr} D$ is the sum of the eigenvalues of A.

27. For each j, $I(\mathbf{b}_j) = \mathbf{b}_j$. Since the standard coordinate vector of any vector in $\mathbb{R}^n$ is just the vector itself, $[I(\mathbf{b}_j)]_{\varepsilon} = \mathbf{b}_j$. Thus the matrix for I relative to B and the standard basis $\mathcal{E}$ is simply $\begin{bmatrix} \mathbf{b}_1 & \mathbf{b}_2 & \dots & \mathbf{b}_n \end{bmatrix}$. This matrix is precisely the *change-of-coordinates* matrix P_B defined in Section 4.4.

28. For each j, $I(\mathbf{b}_j) = \mathbf{b}_j$, and $[I(\mathbf{b}_j)]_C = [\mathbf{b}_j]_C$. By formula (4), the matrix for I relative to the bases B and C is

$$M = \begin{bmatrix} [\mathbf{b}_1]_C & [\mathbf{b}_2]_C & \dots & [\mathbf{b}_n]_C \end{bmatrix}$$

In Theorem 15 of Section 4.7, this matrix was denoted by $\underset{C \leftarrow B}{P}$ and was called the *change-of-coordinates matrix from B to C*.

29. If $B = \{\mathbf{b}_1, \dots, \mathbf{b}_n\}$, then the B-coordinate vector of $\mathbf{b}_j$ is $\mathbf{e}_j$, the standard basis vector for $\mathbb{R}^n$. For instance,

$$\mathbf{b}_1 = 1 \cdot \mathbf{b}_1 + 0 \cdot \mathbf{b}_2 + \dots + 0 \cdot \mathbf{b}_n$$

Thus $[I(\mathbf{b}_j)]_B = [\mathbf{b}_j]_B = \mathbf{e}_j$, and

$$[I]_B = \begin{bmatrix} [I(\mathbf{b}_1)]_B & \cdots & [I(\mathbf{b}_n)]_B \end{bmatrix} = [\mathbf{e}_1 \cdots \mathbf{e}_n] = I$$

30. **[M]** If P is the matrix whose columns come from B, then the B-matrix of the transformation $\mathbf{x} \mapsto A\mathbf{x}$ is $D = P^{-1}AP$. From the data in the text,

$$A = \begin{bmatrix} -14 & 4 & -14 \\ -33 & 9 & -31 \\ 11 & -4 & 11 \end{bmatrix}, P = \begin{bmatrix} \mathbf{b}_1 & \mathbf{b}_2 & \mathbf{b}_3 \end{bmatrix} = \begin{bmatrix} -1 & -1 & -1 \\ -2 & -1 & -2 \\ 1 & 1 & 0 \end{bmatrix},$$

$$D = \begin{bmatrix} 2 & -1 & 1 \\ -2 & 1 & 0 \\ -1 & 0 & -1 \end{bmatrix} \begin{bmatrix} -14 & 4 & -14 \\ -33 & 9 & -31 \\ 11 & -4 & 11 \end{bmatrix} \begin{bmatrix} -1 & -1 & -1 \\ -2 & -1 & -2 \\ 1 & 1 & 0 \end{bmatrix} = \begin{bmatrix} 8 & 3 & -6 \\ 0 & 1 & 3 \\ 0 & 0 & -3 \end{bmatrix}$$

31. [M] If P is the matrix whose columns come from B, then the B-matrix of the transformation $\mathbf{x} \mapsto A\mathbf{x}$ is $D = P^{-1}AP$. From the data in the text,

$$A = \begin{bmatrix} -7 & -48 & -16 \\ 1 & 14 & 6 \\ -3 & -45 & -19 \end{bmatrix}, P = \begin{bmatrix} \mathbf{b}_1 & \mathbf{b}_2 & \mathbf{b}_3 \end{bmatrix} = \begin{bmatrix} -3 & -2 & 3 \\ 1 & 1 & -1 \\ -3 & -3 & 0 \end{bmatrix},$$

$$D = \begin{bmatrix} -1 & -3 & -1/3 \\ 1 & 3 & 0 \\ 0 & -1 & -1/3 \end{bmatrix}\begin{bmatrix} -7 & -48 & -16 \\ 1 & 14 & 6 \\ -3 & -45 & -19 \end{bmatrix}\begin{bmatrix} -3 & -2 & 3 \\ 1 & 1 & -1 \\ -3 & -3 & 0 \end{bmatrix} = \begin{bmatrix} -7 & -2 & -6 \\ 0 & -4 & -6 \\ 0 & 0 & -1 \end{bmatrix}$$

32. [M] $A = \begin{bmatrix} 15 & -66 & -44 & -33 \\ 0 & 13 & 21 & -15 \\ 1 & -15 & -21 & 12 \\ 2 & -18 & -22 & 8 \end{bmatrix}$,

$\mathtt{ev=eig(A)=(2, 4, 4, 5)}$

$\mathtt{nulbasis(A-ev(1)*eye(4))} = \begin{bmatrix} 0.0000 \\ -1.5000 \\ 1.5000 \\ 1.0000 \end{bmatrix}$

A basis for the eigenspace of $\lambda = 2$ is $\mathbf{b}_1 = \begin{bmatrix} 0 \\ -3 \\ 3 \\ 2 \end{bmatrix}$.

$\mathtt{nulbasis(A-ev(2)*eye(4))} = \begin{bmatrix} -10.0000 \\ -2.3333 \\ 1.0000 \\ 0 \end{bmatrix}, \begin{bmatrix} 13.0000 \\ 1.6667 \\ 0 \\ 1.0000 \end{bmatrix}$

A basis for the eigenspace of $\lambda = 4$ is $\{\mathbf{b}_2, \mathbf{b}_3\} = \left\{ \begin{bmatrix} -30 \\ -7 \\ 3 \\ 0 \end{bmatrix}, \begin{bmatrix} 39 \\ 5 \\ 0 \\ 3 \end{bmatrix} \right\}$.

$\mathtt{nulbasis(A-ev(4)*eye(4))} = \begin{bmatrix} 2.7500 \\ -0.7500 \\ 1.0000 \\ 1.0000 \end{bmatrix}$

A basis for the eigenspace of $\lambda = 5$ is $\mathbf{b}_4 = \begin{bmatrix} 11 \\ -3 \\ 4 \\ 4 \end{bmatrix}$.

The basis $B = \{\mathbf{b}_1, \mathbf{b}_2, \mathbf{b}_3, \mathbf{b}_4\}$ is a basis for $\mathbb{R}^4$ with the property that $[T]_B$ is diagonal.

Note: The *Study Guide* comments on Exercise 25 and tells students that the trace of *any* square matrix A equals the sum of the eigenvalues of A, counted according to multiplicities. This provides a quick check on the accuracy of an eigenvalue calculation. You could also refer students to the property of the determinant described in Exercise 19 of Section 5.2.

5.5   SOLUTIONS

1. $A = \begin{bmatrix} 1 & -2 \\ 1 & 3 \end{bmatrix}, A - \lambda I = \begin{bmatrix} 1 - \lambda & -2 \\ 1 & 3 - \lambda \end{bmatrix}$

$$\det(A - \lambda I) = (1 - \lambda)(3 - \lambda) - (-2) = \lambda^2 - 4\lambda + 5$$

Use the quadratic formula to find the eigenvalues: $\lambda = \dfrac{4 \pm \sqrt{16 - 20}}{2} = 2 \pm i$. Example 2 gives a shortcut for finding one eigenvector, and Example 5 shows how to write the other eigenvector with no effort.

For $\lambda = 2 + i$: $A - (2 + i)I = \begin{bmatrix} -1 - i & -2 \\ 1 & 1 - i \end{bmatrix}$. The equation $(A - \lambda I)\mathbf{x} = \mathbf{0}$ gives

$$(-1 - i)x_1 - 2x_2 = 0$$
$$x_1 + (1 - i)x_2 = 0$$

As in Example 2, the two equations are equivalent—each determines the same relation between x_1 and x_2. So use the second equation to obtain $x_1 = -(1 - i)x_2$, with x_2 free. The general solution is $x_2 \begin{bmatrix} -1 + i \\ 1 \end{bmatrix}$, and the vector $\mathbf{v}_1 = \begin{bmatrix} -1 + i \\ 1 \end{bmatrix}$ provides a basis for the eigenspace.

For $\sim\lambda = 2 - i$:   Let $\mathbf{v}_2 = \overline{\mathbf{v}}_1 = \begin{bmatrix} -1 - i \\ 1 \end{bmatrix}$. The remark prior to Example 5 shows that $\mathbf{v}_2$ is automatically an eigenvector for $\overline{2 + i}$. In fact, calculations similar to those above would show that $\{\mathbf{v}_2\}$ is a basis for the eigenspace. (In general, for a real matrix A, it can be shown that the set of complex conjugates of the vectors in a basis of the eigenspace for λ is a basis of the eigenspace for $\overline{\lambda}$.)

2. $A = \begin{bmatrix} 5 & -5 \\ 1 & 1 \end{bmatrix}$. The characteristic polynomial is $\lambda^2 - 6\lambda + 10$, so the eigenvalues of A are

$$\lambda = \frac{6 \pm \sqrt{36 - 40}}{2} = 3 \pm i.$$

For $\lambda = 3 + i$: $A - (3 + i)I = \begin{bmatrix} 2 - i & -5 \\ 1 & -2 - i \end{bmatrix}$. The equation $(A - (3 + i)I)\mathbf{x} = \mathbf{0}$ amounts to

$x_1 + (-2 - i)x_2 = 0$, so $x_1 = (2 + i)x_2$ with x_2 free. A basis vector for the eigenspace is thus $\mathbf{v}_1 = \begin{bmatrix} 2 + i \\ 1 \end{bmatrix}$.

For $\lambda = 3 - i$:   A basis vector for the eigenspace is $\mathbf{v}_2 = \overline{\mathbf{v}}_1 = \begin{bmatrix} 2 - i \\ 1 \end{bmatrix}$.

3. $A = \begin{bmatrix} 1 & 5 \\ -2 & 3 \end{bmatrix}$. The characteristic polynomial is $\lambda^2 - 4\lambda + 13$, so the eigenvalues of A are

$$\lambda = \frac{4 \pm \sqrt{-36}}{2} = 2 \pm 3i.$$

For $\lambda = 2 + 3i$: $A - (2+3i)I = \begin{bmatrix} -1-3i & 5 \\ -2 & 1-3i \end{bmatrix}$. The equation $(A-(2+3i)I)\mathbf{x} = \mathbf{0}$ amounts to

$-2x_1 + (1-3i)x_2 = 0$, so $x_1 = \dfrac{1-3i}{2}x_2$ with x_2 free. A nice basis vector for the eigenspace is thus

$\mathbf{v}_1 = \begin{bmatrix} 1-3i \\ 2 \end{bmatrix}$.

For $\lambda = 2 - 3i$:   A basis vector for the eigenspace is $\mathbf{v}_2 = \overline{\mathbf{v}}_1 = \begin{bmatrix} 1+3i \\ 2 \end{bmatrix}$.

4. $A = \begin{bmatrix} 5 & -2 \\ 1 & 3 \end{bmatrix}$. The characteristic polynomial is $\lambda^2 - 8\lambda + 17$, so the eigenvalues of A are

$$\lambda = \frac{8 \pm \sqrt{-4}}{2} = 4 \pm i.$$

For $\lambda = 4 + i$: $A - (4+i)I = \begin{bmatrix} 1-i & -2 \\ 1 & -1-i \end{bmatrix}$. The equation $(A-(4+i)I)\mathbf{x} = \mathbf{0}$ amounts to

$x_1 + (-1-i)x_2 = 0$, so $x_1 = (1+i)x_2$ with x_2 free. A basis vector for the eigenspace is thus $\mathbf{v}_1 = \begin{bmatrix} 1+i \\ 1 \end{bmatrix}$.

For $\lambda = 4 - i$:   A basis vector for the eigenspace is $\mathbf{v}_2 = \overline{\mathbf{v}}_1 = \begin{bmatrix} 1-i \\ 1 \end{bmatrix}$.

5. $A = \begin{bmatrix} 0 & 1 \\ -8 & 4 \end{bmatrix}$. The characteristic polynomial is $\lambda^2 - 4\lambda + 8$, so the eigenvalues of A are

$$\lambda = \frac{4 \pm \sqrt{-16}}{2} = 2 \pm 2i.$$

For $\lambda = 2 + 2i$: $A - (2+2i)I = \begin{bmatrix} -2-2i & 1 \\ -8 & 2-2i \end{bmatrix}$. The equation $(A-(2+2i)I)\mathbf{x} = \mathbf{0}$ amounts to

$(-2-2i)x_1 + x_2 = 0$, so $x_2 = (2+2i)x_1$ with x_1 free. A basis vector for the eigenspace is thus

$\mathbf{v}_1 = \begin{bmatrix} 1 \\ 2+2i \end{bmatrix}$.

For $\lambda = 2 - 2i$:   A basis vector for the eigenspace is $\mathbf{v}_2 = \overline{\mathbf{v}}_1 = \begin{bmatrix} 1 \\ 2-2i \end{bmatrix}$.

6. $A = \begin{bmatrix} 4 & 3 \\ -3 & 4 \end{bmatrix}$. The characteristic polynomial is $\lambda^2 - 8\lambda + 25$, so the eigenvalues of A are

$$\lambda = \frac{8 \pm \sqrt{-36}}{2} = 4 \pm 3i.$$

For $\lambda = 4 + 3i$: $A - (4 + 3i)I = \begin{bmatrix} -3i & 3 \\ -3 & -3i \end{bmatrix}$. The equation $(A - (4 + 3i)I)\mathbf{x} = \mathbf{0}$ amounts to $x_1 + ix_2 = 0$, so

$x_1 = -ix_2$ with x_2 free. A basis vector for the eigenspace is thus $\mathbf{v}_1 = \begin{bmatrix} -i \\ 1 \end{bmatrix}$.

For $\lambda = 4 - 3i$:   A basis vector for the eigenspace is $\mathbf{v}_2 = \bar{\mathbf{v}}_1 = \begin{bmatrix} i \\ 1 \end{bmatrix}$.

7. $A = \begin{bmatrix} \sqrt{3} & -1 \\ 1 & \sqrt{3} \end{bmatrix}$. From Example 6, the eigenvalues are $\sqrt{3} \pm i$. The scale factor for the transformation

$\mathbf{x} \mapsto A\mathbf{x}$ is $r = |\lambda| = \sqrt{(\sqrt{3})^2 + 1^2} = 2$. For the angle of rotation, plot the point $(a,b) = (\sqrt{3}, 1)$ in the
xy-plane and use trigonometry:

$$\varphi = \arctan(b/a) = \arctan(1/\sqrt{3}) = \pi/6 \text{ radians.}$$

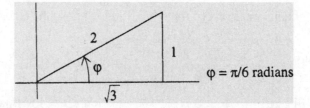

Note: Your students will want to know whether you permit them on an exam to omit calculations for a matrix

of the form $\begin{bmatrix} a & -b \\ b & a \end{bmatrix}$ and simply write the eigenvalues $a \pm bi$. A similar question may arise about the

corresponding eigenvectors, $\begin{bmatrix} 1 \\ -i \end{bmatrix}$ and $\begin{bmatrix} 1 \\ i \end{bmatrix}$, which are announced in the Practice Problem. Students may have

trouble keeping track of the correspondence between eigenvalues and eigenvectors.

8. $A = \begin{bmatrix} \sqrt{3} & 3 \\ -3 & \sqrt{3} \end{bmatrix}$. From Example 6, the eigenvalues are $\sqrt{3} \pm 3i$. The scale factor for the transformation

$\mathbf{x} \mapsto A\mathbf{x}$ is $r = |\lambda| = \sqrt{(\sqrt{3})^2 + 3^2} = 2\sqrt{3}$. From trigonometry, the angle of rotation φ is $\arctan(b/a) = $
$\arctan(-3/\sqrt{3}) = -\pi/3$ radians.

9. $A = \begin{bmatrix} -\sqrt{3}/2 & 1/2 \\ -1/2 & -\sqrt{3}/2 \end{bmatrix}$. From Example 6, the eigenvalues are $-\sqrt{3}/2 \pm (1/2)i$. The scale factor for the

transformation $\mathbf{x} \mapsto A\mathbf{x}$ is $r = |\lambda| = \sqrt{(-\sqrt{3}/2)^2 + (1/2)^2} = 1$. From trigonometry, the angle of rotation φ
is $\arctan(b/a) = \arctan((-1/2)/(-\sqrt{3}/2)) = -5\pi/6$ radians.

10. $A = \begin{bmatrix} -5 & -5 \\ 5 & -5 \end{bmatrix}$. From Example 6, the eigenvalues are $-5 \pm 5i$. The scale factor for the transformation

$\mathbf{x} \mapsto A\mathbf{x}$ is $r = |\lambda| = \sqrt{(-5)^2 + 5^2} = 5\sqrt{2}$. From trigonometry, the angle of rotation φ is

$\arctan(b/a) = \arctan(5/(-5)) = 3\pi/4$ radians.

11. $A = \begin{bmatrix} .1 & .1 \\ -.1 & .1 \end{bmatrix}$. From Example 6, the eigenvalues are $.1 \pm .1i$. The scale factor for the transformation

$\mathbf{x} \mapsto A\mathbf{x}$ is $r = |\lambda| = \sqrt{(.1)^2 + (.1)^2} = \sqrt{2}/10$. From trigonometry, the angle of rotation φ is $\arctan(b/a) = \arctan(-.1/.1) = -\pi/4$ radians.

12. $A = \begin{bmatrix} 0 & .3 \\ -.3 & 0 \end{bmatrix}$. From Example 6, the eigenvalues are $0 \pm .3i$. The scale factor for the transformation

$\mathbf{x} \mapsto A\mathbf{x}$ is $r = |\lambda| = \sqrt{0^2 + (.3)^2} = .3$. From trigonometry, the angle of rotation φ is $\arctan(b/a) = \arctan(-\infty) = -\pi/2$ radians.

13. From Exercise 1, $\lambda = 2 \pm i$, and the eigenvector $\mathbf{v} = \begin{bmatrix} -1-i \\ 1 \end{bmatrix}$ corresponds to $\lambda = 2 - i$. Since Re $\mathbf{v} = \begin{bmatrix} -1 \\ 1 \end{bmatrix}$

and Im $\mathbf{v} = \begin{bmatrix} -1 \\ 0 \end{bmatrix}$, take $P = \begin{bmatrix} -1 & -1 \\ 1 & 0 \end{bmatrix}$. Then compute

$$C = P^{-1}AP = \begin{bmatrix} 0 & 1 \\ -1 & -1 \end{bmatrix}\begin{bmatrix} 1 & -2 \\ 1 & 3 \end{bmatrix}\begin{bmatrix} -1 & -1 \\ 1 & 0 \end{bmatrix} = \begin{bmatrix} 0 & 1 \\ -1 & -1 \end{bmatrix}\begin{bmatrix} -3 & -1 \\ 2 & -1 \end{bmatrix} = \begin{bmatrix} 2 & -1 \\ 1 & 2 \end{bmatrix}$$

Actually, Theorem 9 gives the formula for C. Note that the eigenvector $\mathbf{v}$ corresponds to $a - bi$ instead

of $a + bi$. If, for instance, you use the eigenvector for $2 + i$, your C will be $\begin{bmatrix} 2 & 1 \\ -1 & 2 \end{bmatrix}$.

Notes: The *Study Guide* points out that the matrix C is described in Theorem 9 and the first column of C is the real part of the eigenvector corresponding to $a - bi$, not $a + bi$, as one might expect. Since students may forget this, they are encouraged to compute C from the formula $C = P^{-1}AP$, as in the solution above.

The *Study Guide* also comments that because there are two possibilities for C in the factorization of a 2×2 matrix as in Exercise 13, the measure of rotation of the angle associated with the transformation $\mathbf{x} \mapsto A\mathbf{x}$ is determined only up to a change of sign. The "orientation" of the angle is determined by the change of variable $\mathbf{x} = P\mathbf{u}$. See Figure 4 in the text.

14. $A = \begin{bmatrix} 5 & -5 \\ 1 & 1 \end{bmatrix}$. From Exercise 2, the eigenvalues of A are $\lambda = 3 \pm i$, and the eigenvector

$\mathbf{v} = \begin{bmatrix} 2-i \\ 1 \end{bmatrix}$ corresponds to $\lambda = 3 - i$. By Theorem 9, $P = [\text{Re } \mathbf{v} \ \ \text{Im } \mathbf{v}] = \begin{bmatrix} 2 & -1 \\ 1 & 0 \end{bmatrix}$ and

$$C = P^{-1}AP = \begin{bmatrix} 0 & 1 \\ -1 & 2 \end{bmatrix}\begin{bmatrix} 5 & -5 \\ 1 & 1 \end{bmatrix}\begin{bmatrix} 2 & -1 \\ 1 & 0 \end{bmatrix} = \begin{bmatrix} 3 & -1 \\ 1 & 3 \end{bmatrix}$$

15. $A = \begin{bmatrix} 1 & 5 \\ -2 & 3 \end{bmatrix}$. From Exercise 3, the eigenvalues of A are $\lambda = 2 \pm 3i$, and the eigenvector

$\mathbf{v} = \begin{bmatrix} 1+3i \\ 2 \end{bmatrix}$ corresponds to $\lambda = 2 - 3i$. By Theorem 9, $P = [\text{Re } \mathbf{v} \ \ \text{Im } \mathbf{v}] = \begin{bmatrix} 1 & 3 \\ 2 & 0 \end{bmatrix}$ and

$$C = P^{-1}AP = \frac{1}{6}\begin{bmatrix} 0 & -3 \\ -2 & 1 \end{bmatrix}\begin{bmatrix} 1 & 5 \\ -2 & 3 \end{bmatrix}\begin{bmatrix} 1 & 3 \\ 2 & 0 \end{bmatrix} = \begin{bmatrix} 2 & -3 \\ 3 & 2 \end{bmatrix}$$

16. $A = \begin{bmatrix} 5 & -2 \\ 1 & 3 \end{bmatrix}$. From Exercise 4, the eigenvalues of A are $\lambda = 4 \pm i$, and the eigenvector

$\mathbf{v} = \begin{bmatrix} 1-i \\ 1 \end{bmatrix}$ corresponds to $\lambda = 4 - i$. By Theorem 9, $P = [\text{Re } \mathbf{v} \ \ \text{Im } \mathbf{v}] = \begin{bmatrix} 1 & -1 \\ 1 & 0 \end{bmatrix}$ and

$$C = P^{-1}AP = \begin{bmatrix} 0 & 1 \\ -1 & 1 \end{bmatrix}\begin{bmatrix} 5 & -2 \\ 1 & 3 \end{bmatrix}\begin{bmatrix} 1 & -1 \\ 1 & 0 \end{bmatrix} = \begin{bmatrix} 4 & -1 \\ 1 & 4 \end{bmatrix}$$

17. $A = \begin{bmatrix} 1 & -.8 \\ 4 & -2.2 \end{bmatrix}$. The characteristic polynomial is $\lambda^2 + 1.2\lambda + 1$, so the eigenvalues of A are $\lambda = -.6 \pm .8i$.

To find an eigenvector corresponding to $-.6 - .8i$, we compute

$$A - (-.6 - .8i)I = \begin{bmatrix} 1.6 + .8i & -.8 \\ 4 & -1.6 + .8i \end{bmatrix}$$

The equation $(A - (-.6 - .8i)I)\mathbf{x} = \mathbf{0}$ amounts to $4x_1 + (-1.6 + .8i)x_2 = 0$, so $x_1 = ((2 - i)/5)x_2$

with x_2 free. A nice eigenvector corresponding to $-.6 - .8i$ is thus $\mathbf{v} = \begin{bmatrix} 2-i \\ 5 \end{bmatrix}$. By Theorem 9,

$$P = [\text{Re } \mathbf{v} \ \ \text{Im } \mathbf{v}] = \begin{bmatrix} 2 & -1 \\ 5 & 0 \end{bmatrix} \text{ and } C = P^{-1}AP = \frac{1}{5}\begin{bmatrix} 0 & 1 \\ -5 & 1 \end{bmatrix}\begin{bmatrix} 1 & -.8 \\ 4 & -2.2 \end{bmatrix}\begin{bmatrix} 2 & -1 \\ 5 & 0 \end{bmatrix} = \begin{bmatrix} -.6 & -.8 \\ .8 & -.6 \end{bmatrix}$$

18. $A = \begin{bmatrix} 1 & -1 \\ .4 & .6 \end{bmatrix}$. The characteristic polynomial is $\lambda^2 - 1.6\lambda + 1$, so the eigenvalues of A are $\lambda = .8 \pm .6i$. To

find an eigenvector corresponding to $.8 - .6i$, we compute

$$A - (.8 - .6i)I = \begin{bmatrix} .2 + .6i & -1 \\ .4 & -.2 + .6i \end{bmatrix}$$

The equation $(A - (.8 - .6i)I)\mathbf{x} = \mathbf{0}$ amounts to $.4x_1 + (-.2 + .6i)x_2 = 0$, so $x_1 = ((1 - 3i)/2)x_2$ with x_2 free.

A nice eigenvector corresponding to $.8 - .6i$ is thus $\mathbf{v} = \begin{bmatrix} 1-3i \\ 2 \end{bmatrix}$. By Theorem 9,

$$P = [\text{Re } \mathbf{v} \ \ \text{Im } \mathbf{v}] = \begin{bmatrix} 1 & -3 \\ 2 & 0 \end{bmatrix} \text{ and } C = P^{-1}AP = \frac{1}{6}\begin{bmatrix} 0 & 3 \\ -2 & 1 \end{bmatrix}\begin{bmatrix} 1 & -1 \\ .4 & .6 \end{bmatrix}\begin{bmatrix} 1 & -3 \\ 2 & 0 \end{bmatrix} = \begin{bmatrix} .8 & -.6 \\ .6 & .8 \end{bmatrix}$$

19. $A = \begin{bmatrix} 1.52 & -.7 \\ .56 & .4 \end{bmatrix}$. The characteristic polynomial is $\lambda^2 - 1.92\lambda + 1$, so the eigenvalues of A are

$\lambda = .96 \pm .28i$. To find an eigenvector corresponding to $.96 - .28i$, we compute

$$A - (.96 - .28i)I = \begin{bmatrix} .56 + .28i & -.7 \\ .56 & -.56 + .28i \end{bmatrix}$$

The equation $(A - (.96 - .28i)I)\mathbf{x} = \mathbf{0}$ amounts to $.56x_1 + (-.56 + .28i)x_2 = 0$, so $x_1 = ((2-i)/2)x_2$ with

x_2 free. A nice eigenvector corresponding to $.96 - .28i$ is thus $\mathbf{v} = \begin{bmatrix} 2-i \\ 2 \end{bmatrix}$. By Theorem 9,

$$P = \begin{bmatrix} \text{Re } \mathbf{v} & \text{Im } \mathbf{v} \end{bmatrix} = \begin{bmatrix} 2 & -1 \\ 2 & 0 \end{bmatrix} \text{ and } C = P^{-1}AP = \frac{1}{2}\begin{bmatrix} 0 & 1 \\ -2 & 2 \end{bmatrix}\begin{bmatrix} 1.52 & -.7 \\ .56 & .4 \end{bmatrix}\begin{bmatrix} 2 & -1 \\ 2 & 0 \end{bmatrix} = \begin{bmatrix} .96 & -.28 \\ .28 & .96 \end{bmatrix}$$

20. $A = \begin{bmatrix} -1.64 & -2.4 \\ 1.92 & 2.2 \end{bmatrix}$. The characteristic polynomial is $\lambda^2 - .56\lambda + 1$, so the eigenvalues of A are

$\lambda = .28 \pm .96i$. To find an eigenvector corresponding to $.28 - .96i$, we compute

$$A - (.28 - .96i)I = \begin{bmatrix} -1.92 + .96i & -2.4 \\ 1.92 & 1.92 + .96i \end{bmatrix}$$

The equation $(A - (.28 - .96i)I)\mathbf{x} = \mathbf{0}$ amounts to $1.92x_1 + (1.92 + .96i)x_2 = 0$, so $x_1 = ((-2-i)/2)x_2$ with

x_2 free. A nice eigenvector corresponding to $.28 - .96i$ is thus $\mathbf{v} = \begin{bmatrix} -2-i \\ 2 \end{bmatrix}$. By Theorem 9,

$$P = \begin{bmatrix} \text{Re } \mathbf{v} & \text{Im } \mathbf{v} \end{bmatrix} = \begin{bmatrix} -2 & -1 \\ 2 & 0 \end{bmatrix} \text{ and } C = P^{-1}AP = \frac{1}{2}\begin{bmatrix} 0 & 1 \\ -2 & -2 \end{bmatrix}\begin{bmatrix} -1.64 & -2.4 \\ 1.92 & 2.2 \end{bmatrix}\begin{bmatrix} -2 & -1 \\ 2 & 0 \end{bmatrix} = \begin{bmatrix} .28 & -.96 \\ .96 & .28 \end{bmatrix}.$$

21. The first equation in (2) is $(-.3 + .6i)x_1 - .6x_2 = 0$. We solve this for x_2 to find that

$x_2 = ((-.3 + .6i)/.6)x_1 = ((-1 + 2i)/2)x_1$. Letting $x_1 = 2$, we find that $\mathbf{y} = \begin{bmatrix} 2 \\ -1 + 2i \end{bmatrix}$ is an eigenvector for

the matrix A. Since $\mathbf{y} = \begin{bmatrix} 2 \\ -1 + 2i \end{bmatrix} = \frac{-1 + 2i}{5}\begin{bmatrix} -2 - 4i \\ 5 \end{bmatrix} = \frac{-1 + 2i}{5}\mathbf{v}_1$ the vector $\mathbf{y}$ is a complex multiple of the

vector $\mathbf{v}_1$ used in Example 2.

22. Since $A(\mu\mathbf{x}) = \mu(A\mathbf{x}) = \mu(\lambda\mathbf{x}) = \lambda(\mu\mathbf{x}), \mu\mathbf{x}$ is an eigenvector of A.

23. (a) properties of conjugates and the fact that $\overline{\mathbf{x}}^T = \overline{\mathbf{x}^T}$

(b) $\overline{A\mathbf{x}} = A\overline{\mathbf{x}}$ and A is real

(c) $\mathbf{x}^T A\overline{\mathbf{x}}$ is a scalar and hence may be viewed as a 1×1 matrix

(d) properties of transposes

(e) $A^T = A$ and the definition of q

24. $\overline{\mathbf{x}}^T A\mathbf{x} = \overline{\mathbf{x}}^T(\lambda\mathbf{x}) = \lambda \cdot \overline{\mathbf{x}}^T\mathbf{x}$ because $\mathbf{x}$ is an eigenvector. It is easy to see that $\overline{\mathbf{x}}^T\mathbf{x}$ is real (and positive)

because $\overline{z}z$ is nonnegative for every complex number z. Since $\overline{\mathbf{x}}^T A\mathbf{x}$ is real, by Exercise 23, so is λ.

Next, write $\mathbf{x} = \mathbf{u} + i\mathbf{v}$, where $\mathbf{u}$ and $\mathbf{v}$ are real vectors. Then

$A\mathbf{x} = A(\mathbf{u} + i\mathbf{v}) = A\mathbf{u} + iA\mathbf{v}$ and $\lambda\mathbf{x} = \lambda\mathbf{u} + i\lambda\mathbf{v}$

The real part of $A\mathbf{x}$ is $A\mathbf{u}$ because the entries in A, $\mathbf{u}$, and $\mathbf{v}$ are all real. The real part of $\lambda\mathbf{x}$ is $\lambda\mathbf{u}$ because λ and the entries in $\mathbf{u}$ and $\mathbf{v}$ are real. Since $A\mathbf{x}$ and $\lambda\mathbf{x}$ are equal, their real parts are equal, too. (Apply the corresponding statement about complex numbers to each entry of $A\mathbf{x}$.) Thus $A\mathbf{u} = \lambda\mathbf{u}$, which shows that the real part of $\mathbf{x}$ is an eigenvector of A.

25. Write $\mathbf{x} = \operatorname{Re}\mathbf{x} + i(\operatorname{Im}\mathbf{x})$, so that $A\mathbf{x} = A(\operatorname{Re}\mathbf{x}) + iA(\operatorname{Im}\mathbf{x})$. Since A is real, so are $A(\operatorname{Re}\mathbf{x})$ and $A(\operatorname{Im}\mathbf{x})$. Thus $A(\operatorname{Re}\mathbf{x})$ is the real part of $A\mathbf{x}$ and $A(\operatorname{Im}\mathbf{x})$ is the imaginary part of $A\mathbf{x}$.

26. a. If $\lambda = a - bi$, then

$$A\mathbf{v} = \lambda\mathbf{v} = (a - bi)(\operatorname{Re}\mathbf{v} + i\operatorname{Im}\mathbf{v})$$
$$= \underbrace{(a\operatorname{Re}\mathbf{v} + b\operatorname{Im}\mathbf{v})}_{\operatorname{Re}A\mathbf{v}} + i\underbrace{(a\operatorname{Im}\mathbf{v} - b\operatorname{Re}\mathbf{v})}_{\operatorname{Im}A\mathbf{v}}$$

By Exercise 25,

$$A(\operatorname{Re}\mathbf{v}) = \operatorname{Re}A\mathbf{v} = a\operatorname{Re}\mathbf{v} + b\operatorname{Im}\mathbf{v}$$
$$A(\operatorname{Im}\mathbf{v}) = \operatorname{Im}A\mathbf{v} = -b\operatorname{Re}\mathbf{v} + a\operatorname{Im}\mathbf{v}$$

b. Let $P = [\operatorname{Re}\mathbf{v} \quad \operatorname{Im}\mathbf{v}]$. By (a),

$$A(\operatorname{Re}\mathbf{v}) = P\begin{bmatrix} a \\ b \end{bmatrix}, \, A(\operatorname{Im}\mathbf{v}) = P\begin{bmatrix} -b \\ a \end{bmatrix}$$

So

$$AP = [A(\operatorname{Re}\mathbf{v}) \quad A(\operatorname{Im}\mathbf{v})]$$
$$= \left[P\begin{bmatrix} a \\ b \end{bmatrix} P\begin{bmatrix} -b \\ a \end{bmatrix} \right] = P\begin{bmatrix} a & -b \\ b & a \end{bmatrix} = PC$$

27. [M] $A = \begin{bmatrix} .7 & 1.1 & 2.0 & 1.7 \\ -2.0 & -4.0 & -8.6 & -7.4 \\ 0 & -.5 & -1.0 & -1.0 \\ 1.0 & 2.8 & 6.0 & 5.3 \end{bmatrix}$

`ev=eig(A) =(.2+.5i,.2-.5i,.3+.1i,.3-.1i)`

For $\lambda = .2 - .5i$, an eigenvector is

`nulbasis(A-ev(2)*eye(4)) =`

```
 0.5000 -  0.5000i
-2.0000 +  0.0000i
 0.0000 -  0.0000i
 1.0000
```

so that $\mathbf{v}_1 = \begin{bmatrix} .5 - .5i \\ -2 \\ 0 \\ 1 \end{bmatrix}$

For $\lambda = .3 - .1i$, an eigenvector is

`nulbasis(A-ev(4)*eye(4))=`

```
-0.5000 -  0.0000i
 0.0000 +  0.5000i
```

```
-0.7500 - 0.2500i
 1.0000
```

so that $\mathbf{v}_2 = \begin{bmatrix} -.5 \\ .5i \\ -.75 - .25i \\ 1 \end{bmatrix}$

Hence by Theorem 9, $P = \begin{bmatrix} \text{Re } \mathbf{v}_1 & \text{Im } \mathbf{v}_1 & \text{Re } \mathbf{v}_2 & \text{Im } \mathbf{v}_2 \end{bmatrix} = \begin{bmatrix} .5 & -.5 & -.5 & 0 \\ -2 & 0 & 0 & .5 \\ 0 & 0 & -.75 & -.25 \\ 1 & 0 & 1 & 0 \end{bmatrix}$ and

$C = \begin{bmatrix} .2 & -.5 & 0 & 0 \\ .5 & .2 & 0 & 0 \\ 0 & 0 & .3 & -.1 \\ 0 & 0 & .1 & .3 \end{bmatrix}$. Other choices are possible, but C must equal $P^{-1}AP$.

28. **[M]** $A = \begin{bmatrix} -1.4 & -2.0 & -2.0 & -2.0 \\ -1.3 & -.8 & -.1 & -.6 \\ .3 & -1.9 & -1.6 & -1.4 \\ 2.0 & 3.3 & 2.3 & 2.6 \end{bmatrix}$

```
ev = eig(A) = (-.4+i,-.4-i,-.2+.5i,-.2-.5i)
```

For $\lambda = -.4 - i$, an eigenvector is

```
nulbasis(A-ev(2)*eye(4)) =
-1.0000 -  1.0000i
-1.0000 +  1.0000i
 1.0000 -  1.0000i
 1.0000
```

so that $\mathbf{v}_1 = \begin{bmatrix} -1-i \\ -1+i \\ 1-i \\ 1 \end{bmatrix}$

For $\lambda = -.2 - .5i$, an eigenvector is

```
nulbasis(A-ev(4)*eye(4)) =
 0.0000 -  0.0000i
-0.5000 -  0.5000i
-0.5000 +  0.5000i
 1.0000
```

so that $\mathbf{v}_2 = \begin{bmatrix} 0 \\ -1-i \\ -1+i \\ 2 \end{bmatrix}$

Hence by Theorem 9, $P = \begin{bmatrix} \text{Re } \mathbf{v}_1 & \text{Im } \mathbf{v}_1 & \text{Re } \mathbf{v}_2 & \text{Im } \mathbf{v}_2 \end{bmatrix} = \begin{bmatrix} -1 & -1 & 0 & 0 \\ -1 & 1 & -1 & -1 \\ 1 & -1 & -1 & 1 \\ 1 & 0 & 2 & 0 \end{bmatrix}$ and

$C = \begin{bmatrix} -.4 & -1 & 0 & 0 \\ 1 & -.4 & 0 & 0 \\ 0 & 0 & -.2 & -.5 \\ 0 & 0 & .5 & -.2 \end{bmatrix}$. Other choices are possible, but C must equal $P^{-1}AP$.

5.6   SOLUTIONS

1. The exercise does not specify the matrix A, but only lists the eigenvalues 3 and 1/3, and the
   corresponding eigenvectors $\mathbf{v}_1 = \begin{bmatrix} 1 \\ 1 \end{bmatrix}$ and $\mathbf{v}_2 = \begin{bmatrix} -1 \\ 1 \end{bmatrix}$. Also, $\mathbf{x}_0 = \begin{bmatrix} 9 \\ 1 \end{bmatrix}$.

   a. To find the action of A on $\mathbf{x}_0$, express $\mathbf{x}_0$ in terms of $\mathbf{v}_1$ and $\mathbf{v}_2$. That is, find c_1 and c_2 such that
   $\mathbf{x}_0 = c_1\mathbf{v}_1 + c_2\mathbf{v}_2$. This is certainly possible because the eigenvectors $\mathbf{v}_1$ and $\mathbf{v}_2$ are linearly
   independent (by inspection and also because they correspond to distinct eigenvalues) and hence form
   a basis for $\mathbf{R}^2$. (Two linearly independent vectors in $\mathbf{R}^2$ automatically span $\mathbf{R}^2$.) The row reduction
   $\begin{bmatrix} \mathbf{v}_1 & \mathbf{v}_2 & \mathbf{x}_0 \end{bmatrix} = \begin{bmatrix} 1 & -1 & 9 \\ 1 & 1 & 1 \end{bmatrix} \sim \begin{bmatrix} 1 & 0 & 5 \\ 0 & 1 & -4 \end{bmatrix}$ shows that $\mathbf{x}_0 = 5\mathbf{v}_1 - 4\mathbf{v}_2$. Since $\mathbf{v}_1$ and $\mathbf{v}_2$ are
   eigenvectors (for the eigenvalues 3 and 1/3):
   $$\mathbf{x}_1 = A\mathbf{x}_0 = 5A\mathbf{v}_1 - 4A\mathbf{v}_2 = 5 \cdot 3\mathbf{v}_1 - 4 \cdot (1/3)\mathbf{v}_2 = \begin{bmatrix} 15 \\ 15 \end{bmatrix} - \begin{bmatrix} -4/3 \\ 4/3 \end{bmatrix} = \begin{bmatrix} 49/3 \\ 41/3 \end{bmatrix}$$

   b. Each time A acts on a linear combination of $\mathbf{v}_1$ and $\mathbf{v}_2$, the $\mathbf{v}_1$ term is multiplied by the eigenvalue
   3 and the $\mathbf{v}_2$ term is multiplied by the eigenvalue 1/3:
   $$\mathbf{x}_2 = A\mathbf{x}_1 = A[5 \cdot 3\mathbf{v}_1 - 4(1/3)\mathbf{v}_2] = 5(3)^2\mathbf{v}_1 - 4(1/3)^2\mathbf{v}_2$$
   In general, $\mathbf{x}_k = 5(3)^k\mathbf{v}_1 - 4(1/3)^k\mathbf{v}_2$, for $k \geq 0$.

2. The vectors $\mathbf{v}_1 = \begin{bmatrix} 1 \\ 0 \\ -3 \end{bmatrix}, \mathbf{v}_2 = \begin{bmatrix} 2 \\ 1 \\ -5 \end{bmatrix}, \mathbf{v}_3 = \begin{bmatrix} -3 \\ -3 \\ 7 \end{bmatrix}$ are eigenvectors of a 3×3 matrix A, corresponding to

   eigenvalues 3, 4/5, and 3/5, respectively. Also, $\mathbf{x}_0 = \begin{bmatrix} -2 \\ -5 \\ 3 \end{bmatrix}$. To describe the solution of the equation

   $\mathbf{x}_{k+1} = A\mathbf{x}_k (k = 1, 2, ...)$, first write $\mathbf{x}_0$ in terms of the eigenvectors.
   $$\begin{bmatrix} \mathbf{v}_1 & \mathbf{v}_2 & \mathbf{v}_3 & \mathbf{x}_0 \end{bmatrix} = \begin{bmatrix} 1 & 2 & -3 & -2 \\ 0 & 1 & -3 & -5 \\ -3 & -5 & 7 & 3 \end{bmatrix} \sim \begin{bmatrix} 1 & 0 & 0 & 2 \\ 0 & 1 & 0 & 1 \\ 0 & 0 & 0 & 2 \end{bmatrix} \Rightarrow \mathbf{x}_0 = 2\mathbf{v}_1 + \mathbf{v}_2 + 2\mathbf{v}_3$$

Then, $\mathbf{x}_1 = A(2\mathbf{v}_1 + \mathbf{v}_2 + 2\mathbf{v}_3) = 2A\mathbf{v}_1 + A\mathbf{v}_2 + 2A\mathbf{v}_3 = 2\cdot 3\mathbf{v}_1 + (4/5)\mathbf{v}_2 + 2\cdot(3/5)\mathbf{v}_3$. In general,

$\mathbf{x}_k = 2\cdot 3^k \mathbf{v}_1 + (4/5)^k \mathbf{v}_2 + 2\cdot(3/5)^k \mathbf{v}_3$. For all k sufficiently large,

$$\mathbf{x}_k \approx 2\cdot 3^k \mathbf{v}_1 = 2\cdot 3^k \begin{bmatrix} 1 \\ 0 \\ -3 \end{bmatrix}$$

3. $A = \begin{bmatrix} .5 & .4 \\ -.2 & 1.1 \end{bmatrix}$, $\det(A - \lambda I) = (.5 - \lambda)(1.1 - \lambda) + .08 = \lambda^2 - 1.6\lambda + .63$. This characteristic polynomial

factors as $(\lambda - .9)(\lambda - .7)$, so the eigenvalues are .9 and .7. If $\mathbf{v}_1$ and $\mathbf{v}_2$ denote corresponding

eigenvectors, and if $\mathbf{x}_0 = c_1\mathbf{v}_1 + c_2\mathbf{v}_2$, then

$$\mathbf{x}_1 = A(c_1\mathbf{v}_1 + c_2\mathbf{v}_2) = c_1 A\mathbf{v}_1 + c_2 A\mathbf{v}_2 = c_1(.9)\mathbf{v}_1 + c_2(.7)\mathbf{v}_2$$

and for $k \geq 1$,

$$\mathbf{x}_k = c_1(.9)^k \mathbf{v}_1 + c_2(.7)^k \mathbf{v}_2$$

For any choices of c_1 and c_2, both the owl and wood rat populations decline over time.

4. $A = \begin{bmatrix} .5 & .4 \\ -.125 & 1.1 \end{bmatrix}$, $\det(A - \lambda I) = (.5 - \lambda)(1.1 - \lambda) - (.4)(.125) = \lambda^2 - 1.6\lambda + .6$. This characteristic

polynomial factors as $(\lambda - 1)(\lambda - .6)$, so the eigenvalues are 1 and .6. For the eigenvalue 1, solve

$(A - I)\mathbf{x} = 0$: $\begin{bmatrix} -.5 & .4 & 0 \\ -.125 & .1 & 0 \end{bmatrix} \sim \begin{bmatrix} -5 & 4 & 0 \\ 0 & 0 & 0 \end{bmatrix}$. A basis for the eigenspace is $\mathbf{v}_1 = \begin{bmatrix} 4 \\ 5 \end{bmatrix}$. Let $\mathbf{v}_2$ be an

eigenvector for the eigenvalue .6. (The entries in $\mathbf{v}_2$ are not important for the long-term behavior of the

system.) If $\mathbf{x}_0 = c_1\mathbf{v}_1 + c_2\mathbf{v}_2$, then $\mathbf{x}_1 = c_1 A\mathbf{v}_1 + c_2 A\mathbf{v}_2 = c_1\mathbf{v}_1 + c_2(.6)\mathbf{v}_2$, and for k sufficiently large,

$$\mathbf{x}_k = c_1\begin{bmatrix} 4 \\ 5 \end{bmatrix} + c_2(.6)^k \mathbf{v}_2 \approx c_1\begin{bmatrix} 4 \\ 5 \end{bmatrix}$$

Provided that $c_1 \neq 0$, the owl and wood rat populations each stabilize in size, and eventually the
populations are in the ratio of 4 owls for each 5 thousand rats. If some aspect of the model were to
change slightly, the characteristic equation would change slightly and the perturbed matrix A might not
have 1 as an eigenvalue. If the eigenvalue becomes slightly large than 1, the two populations will grow;
if the eigenvalue becomes slightly less than 1, both populations will decline.

5. $A = \begin{bmatrix} .4 & .3 \\ -.325 & 1.2 \end{bmatrix}$, $\det(A - \lambda I) = \lambda^2 - 1.6\lambda + .5775$. The quadratic formula provides the roots of the

characteristic equation:

$$\lambda = \frac{1.6 \pm \sqrt{1.6^2 - 4(.5775)}}{2} = \frac{1.6 \pm \sqrt{.25}}{2} = 1.05 \text{ and } .55$$

Because one eigenvalue is larger than one, both populations grow in size. Their relative sizes are
determined eventually by the entries in the eigenvector corresponding to 1.05. Solve $(A - 1.05I)\mathbf{x} = 0$:

$$\begin{bmatrix} -.65 & .3 & 0 \\ -.325 & .15 & 0 \end{bmatrix} \sim \begin{bmatrix} -13 & 6 & 0 \\ 0 & 0 & 0 \end{bmatrix}.$$ An eigenvector is $\mathbf{v}_1 = \begin{bmatrix} 6 \\ 13 \end{bmatrix}$.

Eventually, there will be about 6 spotted owls for every 13 (thousand) flying squirrels.

6. When $p = .5$, $A = \begin{bmatrix} .4 & .3 \\ -.5 & 1.2 \end{bmatrix}$, and $\det(A - \lambda I) = \lambda^2 - 1.6\lambda + .63 = (\lambda - .9)(\lambda - .7)$.

The eigenvalues of A are .9 and .7, both less than 1 in magnitude. The origin is an attractor for the dynamical system and each trajectory tends toward **0**. So both populations of owls and squirrels eventually perish.

The calculations in Exercise 4 (as well as those in Exercises 35 and 27 in Section 5.1) show that if the largest eigenvalue of A is 1, then in most cases the population vector $\mathbf{x}_k$ will tend toward a multiple of the eigenvector corresponding to the eigenvalue 1. [If $\mathbf{v}_1$ and $\mathbf{v}_2$ are eigenvectors, with $\mathbf{v}_1$ corresponding to $\lambda = 1$, and if $\mathbf{x}_0 = c_1\mathbf{v}_1 + c_2\mathbf{v}_2$, then $\mathbf{x}_k$ tends toward $c_1\mathbf{v}_1$, provided c_1 is not zero.] So the problem here is to determine the value of the predation parameter p such that the largest eigenvalue of A is 1. Compute the characteristic polynomial:

$$\det\begin{bmatrix} .4 - \lambda & .3 \\ -p & 1.2 - \lambda \end{bmatrix} = (.4 - \lambda)(1.2 - \lambda) + .3p = \lambda^2 - 1.6\lambda + (.48 + .3p)$$

By the quadratic formula,

$$\lambda = \frac{1.6 \pm \sqrt{1.6^2 - 4(.48 + .3p)}}{2}$$

The larger eigenvalue is 1 when

$$1.6 + \sqrt{1.6^2 - 4(.48 + .3p)} = 2 \text{ and } \sqrt{2.56 - 1.92 - 1.2p} = .4$$

In this case, $.64 - 1.2p = .16$, and $p = .4$.

7. a. The matrix A in Exercise 1 has eigenvalues 3 and 1/3. Since $|3| > 1$ and $|1/3| < 1$, the origin is a saddle point.

  b. The direction of greatest attraction is determined by $\mathbf{v}_2 = \begin{bmatrix} -1 \\ 1 \end{bmatrix}$, the eigenvector corresponding to the eigenvalue with absolute value less than 1. The direction of greatest repulsion is determined by $\mathbf{v}_1 = \begin{bmatrix} 1 \\ 1 \end{bmatrix}$, the eigenvector corresponding to the eigenvalue greater than 1.

  c. The drawing below shows: (1) lines through the eigenvectors and the origin, (2) arrows toward the origin (showing attraction) on the line through $\mathbf{v}_2$ and arrows away from the origin (showing repulsion) on the line through $\mathbf{v}_1$, (3) several typical trajectories (with arrows) that show the general flow of points. No specific points other than $\mathbf{v}_1$ and $\mathbf{v}_2$ were computed. This type of drawing is about all that one can make without using a computer to plot points.

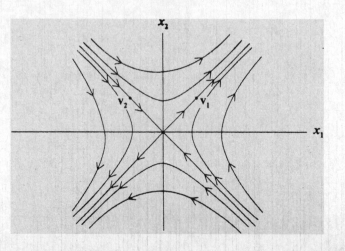

Note: If you wish your class to sketch trajectories for anything except saddle points, you will need to go beyond the discussion in the text. The following remarks from the *Study Guide* are relevant.

Sketching trajectories for a dynamical system in which the origin is an attractor or a repellor is more difficult than the sketch in Exercise 7. There has been no discussion of the direction in which the trajectories "bend" as they move toward or away from the origin. For instance, if you rotate Figure 1 of Section 5.6 through a quarter-turn and relabel the axes so that x_1 is on the horizontal axis, then the new figure corresponds to the matrix A with the diagonal entries .8 and .64 interchanged. In general, if A is a diagonal matrix, with positive diagonal entries a and d, unequal to 1, then the trajectories lie on the axes or on curves whose equations have the form $x_2 = r(x_1)^s$, where $s = (\ln d)/(\ln a)$ and r depends on the initial point $\mathbf{x}_0$. (See *Encounters with Chaos*, by Denny Gulick, New York: McGraw-Hill, 1992, pp. 147–150.)

8. The matrix from Exercise 2 has eigenvalues 3, 4/5, and 3/5. Since one eigenvalue is greater than 1 and the others are less than one in magnitude, the origin is a saddle point. The direction of greatest repulsion is the line through the origin and the eigenvector $(1, 0, -3)$ for the eigenvalue 3. The direction of greatest attraction is the line through the origin and the eigenvector $(-3, -3, 7)$ for the smallest eigenvalue 3/5.

9. $A = \begin{bmatrix} 1.7 & -.3 \\ -1.2 & .8 \end{bmatrix}$, $\det(A - \lambda I) = \lambda^2 - 2.5\lambda + 1 = 0$

$$\lambda = \frac{2.5 \pm \sqrt{2.5^2 - 4(1)}}{2} = \frac{2.5 \pm \sqrt{2.25}}{2} = \frac{2.5 \pm 1.5}{2} = 2 \text{ and } .5$$

The origin is a saddle point because one eigenvalue is greater than 1 and the other eigenvalue is less than 1 in magnitude. The direction of greatest repulsion is through the origin and the eigenvector $\mathbf{v}_1$ found below. Solve $(A - 2I)\mathbf{x} = \mathbf{0}$: $\begin{bmatrix} -.3 & -.3 & 0 \\ -1.2 & -1.2 & 0 \end{bmatrix} \sim \begin{bmatrix} 1 & 1 & 0 \\ 0 & 0 & 0 \end{bmatrix}$, so $x_1 = -x_2$, and x_2 is free. Take $\mathbf{v}_1 = \begin{bmatrix} -1 \\ 1 \end{bmatrix}$.

The direction of greatest attraction is through the origin and the eigenvector $\mathbf{v}_2$ found below. Solve $(A - .5I)\mathbf{x} = \mathbf{0}$: $\begin{bmatrix} 1.2 & -.3 & 0 \\ -1.2 & .3 & 0 \end{bmatrix} \sim \begin{bmatrix} 1 & -.25 & 0 \\ 0 & 0 & 0 \end{bmatrix}$, so $x_1 = -.25x_2$, and x_2 is free. Take $\mathbf{v}_2 = \begin{bmatrix} 1 \\ 4 \end{bmatrix}$.

10. $A = \begin{bmatrix} .3 & .4 \\ -.3 & 1.1 \end{bmatrix}$, $\det(A - \lambda I) = \lambda^2 - 1.4\lambda + .45 = 0$

$$\lambda = \frac{1.4 \pm \sqrt{1.4^2 - 4(.45)}}{2} = \frac{1.4 \pm \sqrt{.16}}{2} = \frac{1.4 \pm .4}{2} = .5 \text{ and } .9$$

The origin is an attractor because both eigenvalues are less than 1 in magnitude. The direction of greatest attraction is through the origin and the eigenvector $\mathbf{v}_1$ found below. Solve $(A - .5I)\mathbf{x} = \mathbf{0}$: $\begin{bmatrix} -.2 & .4 & 0 \\ -.3 & .6 & 0 \end{bmatrix} \sim \begin{bmatrix} 1 & -2 & 0 \\ 0 & 0 & 0 \end{bmatrix}$, so $x_1 = 2x_2$, and x_2 is free. Take $\mathbf{v}_1 = \begin{bmatrix} 2 \\ 1 \end{bmatrix}$.

11. $A = \begin{bmatrix} .4 & .5 \\ -.4 & 1.3 \end{bmatrix}$, $\det(A - \lambda I) = \lambda^2 - 1.7\lambda + .72 = 0$

$$\lambda = \frac{1.7 \pm \sqrt{1.7^2 - 4(.72)}}{2} = \frac{1.7 \pm \sqrt{.01}}{2} = \frac{1.7 \pm .1}{2} = .8 \text{ and } .9$$

The origin is an attractor because both eigenvalues are less than 1 in magnitude. The direction of greatest attraction is through the origin and the eigenvector $\mathbf{v}_1$ found below. Solve $(A - .8I)\mathbf{x} = \mathbf{0}$: $\begin{bmatrix} -.4 & .5 & 0 \\ -.4 & .5 & 0 \end{bmatrix} \sim \begin{bmatrix} 1 & -1.25 & 0 \\ 0 & 0 & 0 \end{bmatrix}$, so $x_1 = 1.25x_2$, and x_2 is free. Take $\mathbf{v}_1 = \begin{bmatrix} 5 \\ 4 \end{bmatrix}$.

12. $A = \begin{bmatrix} .5 & .6 \\ -.3 & 1.4 \end{bmatrix}$, $\det(A - \lambda I) = \lambda^2 - 1.9\lambda + .88 = 0$

$$\lambda = \frac{1.9 \pm \sqrt{1.9^2 - 4(.88)}}{2} = \frac{1.9 \pm \sqrt{.09}}{2} = \frac{1.9 \pm .3}{2} = .8 \text{ and } 1.1$$

The origin is a saddle point because one eigenvalue is greater than 1 and the other eigenvalue is less than 1 in magnitude. The direction of greatest repulsion is through the origin and the eigenvector $\mathbf{v}_1$ found below. Solve $(A - 1.1I)\mathbf{x} = \mathbf{0}$: $\begin{bmatrix} -.6 & .6 & 0 \\ -.3 & .3 & 0 \end{bmatrix} \sim \begin{bmatrix} 1 & -1 & 0 \\ 0 & 0 & 0 \end{bmatrix}$, so $x_1 = x_2$, and x_2 is free. Take $\mathbf{v}_1 = \begin{bmatrix} 1 \\ 1 \end{bmatrix}$.

The direction of greatest attraction is through the origin and the eigenvector $\mathbf{v}_2$ found below. Solve $(A - .8I)\mathbf{x} = \mathbf{0}$: $\begin{bmatrix} -.3 & .6 & 0 \\ -.3 & .6 & 0 \end{bmatrix} \sim \begin{bmatrix} 1 & -2 & 0 \\ 0 & 0 & 0 \end{bmatrix}$, so $x_1 = 2x_2$, and x_2 is free. Take $\mathbf{v}_2 = \begin{bmatrix} 2 \\ 1 \end{bmatrix}$.

13. $A = \begin{bmatrix} .8 & .3 \\ -.4 & 1.5 \end{bmatrix}$, $\det(A - \lambda I) = \lambda^2 - 2.3\lambda + 1.32 = 0$

$$\lambda = \frac{2.3 \pm \sqrt{2.3^2 - 4(1.32)}}{2} = \frac{2.3 \pm \sqrt{.01}}{2} = \frac{2.3 \pm .1}{2} = 1.1 \text{ and } 1.2$$

The origin is a repellor because both eigenvalues are greater than 1 in magnitude. The direction of greatest repulsion is through the origin and the eigenvector $\mathbf{v}_1$ found below. Solve $(A - 1.2I)\mathbf{x} = \mathbf{0}$: $\begin{bmatrix} -.4 & .3 & 0 \\ -.4 & .3 & 0 \end{bmatrix} \sim \begin{bmatrix} 1 & -.75 & 0 \\ 0 & 0 & 0 \end{bmatrix}$, so $x_1 = .75x_2$, and x_2 is free. Take $\mathbf{v}_1 = \begin{bmatrix} 3 \\ 4 \end{bmatrix}$.

14. $A = \begin{bmatrix} 1.7 & .6 \\ -.4 & .7 \end{bmatrix}$, $\det(A - \lambda I) = \lambda^2 - 2.4\lambda + 1.43 = 0$

$$\lambda = \frac{2.4 \pm \sqrt{2.4^2 - 4(1.43)}}{2} = \frac{2.4 \pm \sqrt{.04}}{2} = \frac{2.4 \pm .2}{2} = 1.1 \text{ and } 1.3$$

The origin is a repellor because both eigenvalues are greater than 1 in magnitude. The direction of greatest repulsion is through the origin and the eigenvector $\mathbf{v}_1$ found below. Solve $(A - 1.3I)\mathbf{x} = \mathbf{0}$: $\begin{bmatrix} .4 & .6 & 0 \\ -.4 & -.6 & 0 \end{bmatrix} \sim \begin{bmatrix} 1 & 1.5 & 0 \\ 0 & 0 & 0 \end{bmatrix}$, so $x_1 = -1.5x_2$, and x_2 is free. Take $\mathbf{v}_1 = \begin{bmatrix} -3 \\ 2 \end{bmatrix}$.

15. $A = \begin{bmatrix} .4 & 0 & .2 \\ .3 & .8 & .3 \\ .3 & .2 & .5 \end{bmatrix}$. Given eigenvector $\mathbf{v}_1 = \begin{bmatrix} .1 \\ .6 \\ .3 \end{bmatrix}$ and eigenvalues .5 and .2. To find the eigenvalue for $\mathbf{v}_1$, compute

$$A\mathbf{v}_1 = \begin{bmatrix} .4 & 0 & .2 \\ .3 & .8 & .3 \\ .3 & .2 & .5 \end{bmatrix} \begin{bmatrix} .1 \\ .6 \\ .3 \end{bmatrix} = \begin{bmatrix} .1 \\ .6 \\ .3 \end{bmatrix} = 1 \cdot \mathbf{v}_1 \quad \text{Thus } \mathbf{v}_1 \text{ is an eigenvector for } \lambda = 1.$$

For $\lambda = .5$: $\begin{bmatrix} -.1 & 0 & .2 & 0 \\ .3 & .3 & .3 & 0 \\ .3 & .2 & 0 & 0 \end{bmatrix} \sim \begin{bmatrix} 1 & 0 & -2 & 0 \\ 0 & 1 & 3 & 0 \\ 0 & 0 & 0 & 0 \end{bmatrix}$, $\begin{matrix} x_1 = 2x_3 \\ x_2 = -3x_3 \\ x_3 \text{ is free} \end{matrix}$. Set $\mathbf{v}_2 = \begin{bmatrix} 2 \\ -3 \\ 1 \end{bmatrix}$.

For $\lambda = .2$: $\begin{bmatrix} .2 & 0 & .2 & 0 \\ .3 & .6 & .3 & 0 \\ .3 & .2 & .3 & 0 \end{bmatrix} \sim \begin{bmatrix} 1 & 0 & 1 & 0 \\ 0 & 1 & 0 & 0 \\ 0 & 0 & 0 & 0 \end{bmatrix}$, $\begin{matrix} x_1 = -x_3 \\ x_2 = 0 \\ x_3 \text{ is free} \end{matrix}$. Set $\mathbf{v}_3 = \begin{bmatrix} -1 \\ 0 \\ 1 \end{bmatrix}$

Given $\mathbf{x}_0 = (0, .3, .7)$, find weights such that $\mathbf{x}_0 = c_1\mathbf{v}_1 + c\mathbf{v}_2 + c_3\mathbf{v}_3$.

$$\begin{bmatrix} \mathbf{v}_1 & \mathbf{v}_2 & \mathbf{v}_3 & \mathbf{x}_0 \end{bmatrix} = \begin{bmatrix} .1 & 2 & -1 & 0 \\ .6 & -3 & 0 & .3 \\ .3 & 1 & 1 & .7 \end{bmatrix} \sim \begin{bmatrix} 1 & 0 & 0 & 1 \\ 0 & 1 & 0 & .1 \\ 0 & 0 & 0 & .3 \end{bmatrix}.$$

$\mathbf{x}_0 = \mathbf{v}_1 + .1\mathbf{v}_2 + .3\mathbf{v}_3$

$\mathbf{x}_1 = A\mathbf{v}_1 + .1A\mathbf{v}_2 + .3A\mathbf{v}_3 = \mathbf{v}_1 + .1(.5)\mathbf{v}_2 + .3(.2)\mathbf{v}_3$, and

$\mathbf{x}_k = \mathbf{v}_1 + .1(.5)^k\mathbf{v}_2 + .3(.2)^k\mathbf{v}_3$. As k increases, $\mathbf{x}_k$ approaches $\mathbf{v}_1$.

16. [M]

$$A = \begin{bmatrix} .90 & .01 & .09 \\ .01 & .90 & .01 \\ .09 & .09 & .90 \end{bmatrix} \cdot \text{ev} = \text{eig}(A) = \begin{bmatrix} 1.0000 \\ 0.8900 \\ .8100 \end{bmatrix}.$$ To four decimal places,

$$\mathbf{v}_1 = \text{nulbasis}(A - \text{eye}(3)) = \begin{bmatrix} 0.9192 \\ 0.1919 \\ 1.0000 \end{bmatrix}. \text{ Exact}: \begin{bmatrix} 91/99 \\ 19/99 \\ 1 \end{bmatrix}$$

$$\mathbf{v}_2 = \text{nulbasis}(A - \text{ev}(2) * \text{eye}(3)) = \begin{bmatrix} -1 \\ 1 \\ 0 \end{bmatrix}$$

$$\mathbf{v}_3 = \text{nulbasis}(A - \text{ev}(3) * \text{eye}(3)) = \begin{bmatrix} -1 \\ 0 \\ 1 \end{bmatrix}$$

The general solution of the dynamical system is $\mathbf{x}_k = c_1\mathbf{v}_1 + c_2(.89)^k\mathbf{v}_2 + c_3(.81)^k\mathbf{v}_3$.

Note: When working with stochastic matrices and starting with a probability vector (having nonnegative entries whose sum is 1), it helps to scale $\mathbf{v}_1$ to make its entries sum to 1. If $\mathbf{v}_1 = (91/209, 19/209, 99/209)$, or $(.435, .091, .474)$ to three decimal places, then the weight c_1 above turns out to be 1. See the text's discussion of Exercise 27 in Section 5.2.

17. a. $A = \begin{bmatrix} 0 & 1.6 \\ .3 & .8 \end{bmatrix}$

b. $\det \begin{bmatrix} -\lambda & 1.6 \\ .3 & .8 - \lambda \end{bmatrix} = \lambda^2 - .8\lambda - .48 = 0$. The eigenvalues of A are given by

$$\lambda = \frac{.8 \pm \sqrt{(-.8)^2 - 4(-.48)}}{2} = \frac{.8 \pm \sqrt{2.56}}{2} = \frac{.8 \pm 1.6}{2} = 1.2 \text{ and } -.4$$

The numbers of juveniles and adults are increasing because the largest eigenvalue is greater than 1. The eventual growth rate of each age class is 1.2, which is 20% per year.

To find the eventual relative population sizes, solve $(A - 1.2I)\mathbf{x} = \mathbf{0}$:

$$\begin{bmatrix} -1.2 & 1.6 & 0 \\ .3 & -.4 & 0 \end{bmatrix} \sim \begin{bmatrix} 1 & -4/3 & 0 \\ 0 & 0 & 0 \end{bmatrix}. \quad \begin{array}{l} x_1 = (4/3)x_2 \\ x_2 \text{ is free} \end{array} \quad \text{Set } \mathbf{v}_1 = \begin{bmatrix} 4 \\ 3 \end{bmatrix}.$$

Eventually, there will be about 4 juveniles for every 3 adults.

c. **[M]** Suppose that the initial populations are given by $\mathbf{x}_0 = (15, 10)$. The *Study Guide* describes how to generate the trajectory for as many years as desired and then to plot the values for each population. Let $\mathbf{x}_k = (j_k, a_k)$. Then we need to plot the sequences $\{j_k\}$, $\{a_k\}$, $\{j_k + a_k\}$, and $\{j_k/a_k\}$. Adjacent points in a sequence can be connected with a line segment. When a sequence is plotted, the resulting graph can be captured on the screen and printed (if done on a computer) or copied by hand onto paper (if working with a graphics calculator).

18. a. $A = \begin{bmatrix} 0 & 0 & .42 \\ .6 & 0 & 0 \\ 0 & .75 & .95 \end{bmatrix}$

b. $\text{ev} = \text{eig}(A) = \begin{bmatrix} 0.0774 + 0.4063i \\ 0.0774 - 0.4063i \\ 1.1048 \end{bmatrix}$

The long-term growth rate is 1.105, about 10.5 % per year.

$$v = \text{nulbasis}(A - \text{ev}(3) * \text{eye}(3)) = \begin{bmatrix} 0.3801 \\ 0.2064 \\ 1.0000 \end{bmatrix}$$

For each 100 adults, there will be approximately 38 calves and 21 yearlings.

Note: The MATLAB box in the *Study Guide* and the various technology appendices all give directions for generating the sequence of points in a trajectory of a dynamical system. Details for producing a graphical representation of a trajectory are also given, with several options available in MATLAB, Maple, and Mathematica.

5.7   SOLUTIONS

1. From the "eigendata" (eigenvalues and corresponding eigenvectors) given, the eigenfunctions for the differential equation $\mathbf{x}' = A\mathbf{x}$ are $\mathbf{v}_1 e^{4t}$ and $\mathbf{v}_2 e^{2t}$. The general solution of $\mathbf{x}' = A\mathbf{x}$ has the form

$$c_1 \begin{bmatrix} -3 \\ 1 \end{bmatrix} e^{4t} + c_2 \begin{bmatrix} -1 \\ 1 \end{bmatrix} e^{2t}$$

The initial condition $\mathbf{x}(0) = \begin{bmatrix} -6 \\ 1 \end{bmatrix}$ determines c_1 and c_2:

$$c_1 \begin{bmatrix} -3 \\ 1 \end{bmatrix} e^{4(0)} + c_2 \begin{bmatrix} -1 \\ 1 \end{bmatrix} e^{2(0)} = \begin{bmatrix} -6 \\ 1 \end{bmatrix}$$

$$\begin{bmatrix} -3 & -1 & -6 \\ 1 & 1 & 1 \end{bmatrix} \sim \begin{bmatrix} 1 & 0 & 5/2 \\ 0 & 1 & -3/2 \end{bmatrix}$$

Thus $c_1 = 5/2$, $c_2 = -3/2$, and $\mathbf{x}(t) = \dfrac{5}{2} \begin{bmatrix} -3 \\ 1 \end{bmatrix} e^{4t} - \dfrac{3}{2} \begin{bmatrix} -1 \\ 1 \end{bmatrix} e^{2t}$.

2. From the eigendata given, the eigenfunctions for the differential equation $x' = Ax$ are $v_1 e^{-3t}$ and $v_2 e^{-1t}$. The general solution of $x' = Ax$ has the form

$$c_1 \begin{bmatrix} -1 \\ 1 \end{bmatrix} e^{-3t} + c_2 \begin{bmatrix} 1 \\ 1 \end{bmatrix} e^{-1t}$$

The initial condition $x(0) = \begin{bmatrix} 2 \\ 3 \end{bmatrix}$ determines c_1 and c_2:

$$c_1 \begin{bmatrix} -1 \\ 1 \end{bmatrix} e^{-3(0)} + c_2 \begin{bmatrix} 1 \\ 1 \end{bmatrix} e^{-1(0)} = \begin{bmatrix} 2 \\ 3 \end{bmatrix}$$

$$\begin{bmatrix} -1 & 1 & 2 \\ 1 & 1 & 3 \end{bmatrix} \sim \begin{bmatrix} 1 & 0 & 1/2 \\ 0 & 1 & 5/2 \end{bmatrix}$$

Thus $c_1 = 1/2, c_2 = 5/2$, and $x(t) = \dfrac{1}{2} \begin{bmatrix} -1 \\ 1 \end{bmatrix} e^{-3t} + \dfrac{5}{2} \begin{bmatrix} 1 \\ 1 \end{bmatrix} e^{-t}$.

3. $A = \begin{bmatrix} 2 & 3 \\ -1 & -2 \end{bmatrix}$, $\det(A - \lambda I) = \lambda^2 - 1 = (\lambda - 1)(\lambda + 1) = 0$. Eigenvalues: 1 and -1.

<u>For $\lambda = 1$:</u> $\begin{bmatrix} 1 & 3 & 0 \\ -1 & -3 & 0 \end{bmatrix} \sim \begin{bmatrix} 1 & 3 & 0 \\ 0 & 0 & 0 \end{bmatrix}$, so $x_1 = -3x_2$ with x_2 free. Take $x_2 = 1$ and $v_1 = \begin{bmatrix} -3 \\ 1 \end{bmatrix}$.

<u>For $\lambda = -1$:</u> $\begin{bmatrix} 3 & 3 & 0 \\ -1 & -1 & 0 \end{bmatrix} \sim \begin{bmatrix} 1 & 1 & 0 \\ 0 & 0 & 0 \end{bmatrix}$, so $x_1 = -x_2$ with x_2 free. Take $x_2 = 1$ and $v_2 = \begin{bmatrix} -1 \\ 1 \end{bmatrix}$.

For the initial condition $x(0) = \begin{bmatrix} 3 \\ 2 \end{bmatrix}$, find c_1 and c_2 such that $c_1 v_1 + c_2 v_2 = x(0)$:

$$\begin{bmatrix} v_1 & v_2 & x(0) \end{bmatrix} = \begin{bmatrix} -3 & -1 & 3 \\ 1 & 1 & 2 \end{bmatrix} \sim \begin{bmatrix} 1 & 0 & -5/2 \\ 0 & 1 & 9/2 \end{bmatrix}$$

Thus $c_1 = -5/2, c_2 = 9/2$, and $x(t) = -\dfrac{5}{2} \begin{bmatrix} -3 \\ 1 \end{bmatrix} e^{t} + \dfrac{9}{2} \begin{bmatrix} -1 \\ 1 \end{bmatrix} e^{-t}$.

Since one eigenvalue is positive and the other is negative, the origin is a saddle point of the dynamical system described by $x' = Ax$. The direction of greatest attraction is the line through v_2 and the origin. The direction of greatest repulsion is the line through v_1 and the origin.

4. $A = \begin{bmatrix} -2 & -5 \\ 1 & 4 \end{bmatrix}$, $\det(A - \lambda I) = \lambda^2 - 2\lambda - 3 = (\lambda + 1)(\lambda - 3) = 0$. Eigenvalues: -1 and 3.

<u>For $\lambda = 3$:</u> $\begin{bmatrix} -5 & -5 & 0 \\ 1 & 1 & 0 \end{bmatrix} \sim \begin{bmatrix} 1 & 1 & 0 \\ 0 & 0 & 0 \end{bmatrix}$, so $x_1 = -x_2$ with x_2 free. Take $x_2 = 1$ and $v_1 = \begin{bmatrix} -1 \\ 1 \end{bmatrix}$.

<u>For $\lambda = -1$:</u> $\begin{bmatrix} -1 & -5 & 0 \\ 1 & 5 & 0 \end{bmatrix} \sim \begin{bmatrix} 1 & 5 & 0 \\ 0 & 0 & 0 \end{bmatrix}$, so $x_1 = -5x_2$ with x_2 free. Take $x_2 = 1$ and $v_2 = \begin{bmatrix} -5 \\ 1 \end{bmatrix}$.

For the initial condition $\mathbf{x}(0) = \begin{bmatrix} 3 \\ 2 \end{bmatrix}$, find c_1 and c_2 such that $c_1\mathbf{v}_1 + c_2\mathbf{v}_2 = \mathbf{x}(0)$:

$$\begin{bmatrix} \mathbf{v}_1 & \mathbf{v}_2 & \mathbf{x}(0) \end{bmatrix} = \begin{bmatrix} -1 & -5 & 3 \\ 1 & 1 & 2 \end{bmatrix} \sim \begin{bmatrix} 1 & 0 & 13/4 \\ 0 & 1 & -5/4 \end{bmatrix}$$

Thus $c_1 = 13/4, c_2 = -5/4$, and $\mathbf{x}(t) = \dfrac{13}{4}\begin{bmatrix} -1 \\ 1 \end{bmatrix}e^{3t} - \dfrac{5}{4}\begin{bmatrix} -5 \\ 1 \end{bmatrix}e^{-t}$.

Since one eigenvalue is positive and the other is negative, the origin is a saddle point of the dynamical system described by $\mathbf{x}' = A\mathbf{x}$. The direction of greatest attraction is the line through $\mathbf{v}_2$ and the origin. The direction of greatest repulsion is the line through $\mathbf{v}_1$ and the origin.

5. $A = \begin{bmatrix} 7 & -1 \\ 3 & 3 \end{bmatrix}$, $\det (A - \lambda I) = \lambda^2 - 10\lambda + 24 = (\lambda - 4)(\lambda - 6) = 0$. Eigenvalues: 4 and 6.

For $\lambda = 4$: $\begin{bmatrix} 3 & -1 & 0 \\ 3 & -1 & 0 \end{bmatrix} \sim \begin{bmatrix} 1 & -1/3 & 0 \\ 0 & 0 & 0 \end{bmatrix}$, so $x_1 = (1/3)x_2$ with x_2 free. Take $x_2 = 3$ and $\mathbf{v}_1 = \begin{bmatrix} 1 \\ 3 \end{bmatrix}$.

For $\lambda = 6$: $\begin{bmatrix} 1 & -1 & 0 \\ 3 & -3 & 0 \end{bmatrix} \sim \begin{bmatrix} 1 & -1 & 0 \\ 0 & 0 & 0 \end{bmatrix}$, so $x_1 = x_2$ with x_2 free. Take $x_2 = 1$ and $\mathbf{v}_2 = \begin{bmatrix} 1 \\ 1 \end{bmatrix}$.

For the initial condition $\mathbf{x}(0) = \begin{bmatrix} 3 \\ 2 \end{bmatrix}$, find c_1 and c_2 such that $c_1\mathbf{v}_1 + c_2\mathbf{v}_2 = \mathbf{x}(0)$:

$$\begin{bmatrix} \mathbf{v}_1 & \mathbf{v}_2 & \mathbf{x}(0) \end{bmatrix} = \begin{bmatrix} 1 & 1 & 3 \\ 3 & 1 & 2 \end{bmatrix} \sim \begin{bmatrix} 1 & 0 & -1/2 \\ 0 & 1 & 7/2 \end{bmatrix}$$

Thus $c_1 = -1/2, c_2 = 7/2$, and $\mathbf{x}(t) = -\dfrac{1}{2}\begin{bmatrix} 1 \\ 3 \end{bmatrix}e^{4t} + \dfrac{7}{2}\begin{bmatrix} 1 \\ 1 \end{bmatrix}e^{6t}$.

Since both eigenvalues are positive, the origin is a repellor of the dynamical system described by $\mathbf{x}' = A\mathbf{x}$. The direction of greatest repulsion is the line through $\mathbf{v}_2$ and the origin.

6. $A = \begin{bmatrix} 1 & -2 \\ 3 & -4 \end{bmatrix}$, $\det (A - \lambda I) = \lambda^2 + 3\lambda + 2 = (\lambda + 1)(\lambda + 2) = 0$. Eigenvalues: -1 and -2.

For $\lambda = -2$: $\begin{bmatrix} 3 & -2 & 0 \\ 3 & -2 & 0 \end{bmatrix} \sim \begin{bmatrix} 1 & -2/3 & 0 \\ 0 & 0 & 0 \end{bmatrix}$, so $x_1 = (2/3)x_2$ with x_2 free. Take $x_2 = 3$ and $\mathbf{v}_1 = \begin{bmatrix} 2 \\ 3 \end{bmatrix}$.

For $\lambda = -1$: $\begin{bmatrix} 2 & -2 & 0 \\ 3 & -3 & 0 \end{bmatrix} \sim \begin{bmatrix} 1 & -1 & 0 \\ 0 & 0 & 0 \end{bmatrix}$, so $x_1 = x_2$ with x_2 free. Take $x_2 = 1$ and $\mathbf{v}_2 = \begin{bmatrix} 1 \\ 1 \end{bmatrix}$.

For the initial condition $\mathbf{x}(0) = \begin{bmatrix} 3 \\ 2 \end{bmatrix}$, find c_1 and c_2 such that $c_1\mathbf{v}_1 + c_2\mathbf{v}_2 = \mathbf{x}(0)$:

$$\begin{bmatrix} \mathbf{v}_1 & \mathbf{v}_2 & \mathbf{x}(0) \end{bmatrix} = \begin{bmatrix} 2 & 1 & 3 \\ 3 & 1 & 2 \end{bmatrix} \sim \begin{bmatrix} 1 & 0 & -1 \\ 0 & 1 & 5 \end{bmatrix}$$

Thus $c_1 = -1, c_2 = 5$, and $\mathbf{x}(t) = -\begin{bmatrix} 2 \\ 3 \end{bmatrix}e^{-2t} + 5\begin{bmatrix} 1 \\ 1 \end{bmatrix}e^{-t}$.

Since both eigenvalues are negative, the origin is an attractor of the dynamical system described by $\mathbf{x}' = A\mathbf{x}$. The direction of greatest attraction is the line through $\mathbf{v}_1$ and the origin.

7. From Exercise 5, $A = \begin{bmatrix} 7 & -1 \\ 3 & 3 \end{bmatrix}$, with eigenvectors $\mathbf{v}_1 = \begin{bmatrix} 1 \\ 3 \end{bmatrix}$ and $\mathbf{v}_2 = \begin{bmatrix} 1 \\ 1 \end{bmatrix}$ corresponding to eigenvalues

4 and 6 respectively. To decouple the equation $\mathbf{x}' = A\mathbf{x}$, set $P = [\mathbf{v}_1 \ \mathbf{v}_2] = \begin{bmatrix} 1 & 1 \\ 3 & 1 \end{bmatrix}$ and let $D = \begin{bmatrix} 4 & 0 \\ 0 & 6 \end{bmatrix}$,

so that $A = PDP^{-1}$ and $D = P^{-1}AP$. Substituting $\mathbf{x}(t) = P\mathbf{y}(t)$ into $\mathbf{x}' = A\mathbf{x}$ we have

$$\frac{d}{dt}(P\mathbf{y}) = A(P\mathbf{y}) = PDP^{-1}(P\mathbf{y}) = PD\mathbf{y}$$

Since P has constant entries, $\frac{d}{dt}(P\mathbf{y}) = P(\frac{d}{dt}(\mathbf{y}))$, so that left-multiplying the equality $P(\frac{d}{dt}(\mathbf{y})) = PD\mathbf{y}$ by

P^{-1} yields $\mathbf{y}' = D\mathbf{y}$, or

$$\begin{bmatrix} y_1'(t) \\ y_2'(t) \end{bmatrix} = \begin{bmatrix} 4 & 0 \\ 0 & 6 \end{bmatrix} \begin{bmatrix} y_1(t) \\ y_2(t) \end{bmatrix}$$

8. From Exercise 6, $A = \begin{bmatrix} 1 & -2 \\ 3 & -4 \end{bmatrix}$, with eigenvectors $\mathbf{v}_1 = \begin{bmatrix} 2 \\ 3 \end{bmatrix}$ and $\mathbf{v}_2 = \begin{bmatrix} 1 \\ 1 \end{bmatrix}$ corresponding to eigenvalues

-2 and -1 respectively. To decouple the equation $\mathbf{x}' = A\mathbf{x}$, set $P = \begin{bmatrix} \mathbf{v}_1 & \mathbf{v}_2 \end{bmatrix} = \begin{bmatrix} 2 & 1 \\ 3 & 1 \end{bmatrix}$ and let

$D = \begin{bmatrix} -2 & 0 \\ 0 & -1 \end{bmatrix}$, so that $A = PDP^{-1}$ and $D = P^{-1}AP$. Substituting $\mathbf{x}(t) = P\mathbf{y}(t)$ into $\mathbf{x}' = A\mathbf{x}$ we have

$$\frac{d}{dt}(P\mathbf{y}) = A(P\mathbf{y}) = PDP^{-1}(P\mathbf{y}) = PD\mathbf{y}$$

Since P has constant entries, $\frac{d}{dt}(P\mathbf{y}) = P(\frac{d}{dt}(\mathbf{y}))$, so that left-multiplying the equality $P(\frac{d}{dt}(\mathbf{y})) = PD\mathbf{y}$

by P^{-1} yields $\mathbf{y}' = D\mathbf{y}$, or

$$\begin{bmatrix} y_1'(t) \\ y_2'(t) \end{bmatrix} = \begin{bmatrix} -2 & 0 \\ 0 & -1 \end{bmatrix} \begin{bmatrix} y_1(t) \\ y_2(t) \end{bmatrix}$$

9. $A = \begin{bmatrix} -3 & 2 \\ -1 & -1 \end{bmatrix}$. An eigenvalue of A is $-2 + i$ with corresponding eigenvector $\mathbf{v} = \begin{bmatrix} 1 - i \\ 1 \end{bmatrix}$. The complex

eigenfunctions $\mathbf{v}e^{\lambda t}$ and $\overline{\mathbf{v}}e^{\overline{\lambda}t}$ form a basis for the set of all complex solutions to $\mathbf{x}' = A\mathbf{x}$. The general complex solution is

$$c_1 \begin{bmatrix} 1 - i \\ 1 \end{bmatrix} e^{(-2+i)t} + c_2 \begin{bmatrix} 1 + i \\ 1 \end{bmatrix} e^{(-2-i)t}$$

where c_1 and c_2 are arbitrary complex numbers. To build the general real solution, rewrite $\mathbf{v}e^{(-2+i)t}$ as:

$$\mathbf{v}e^{(-2+i)t} = \begin{bmatrix} 1 - i \\ 1 \end{bmatrix} e^{-2t} e^{it} = \begin{bmatrix} 1 - i \\ 1 \end{bmatrix} e^{-2t}(\cos t + i\sin t)$$

$$= \begin{bmatrix} \cos t - i\cos t + i\sin t - i^2 \sin t \\ \cos t + i\sin t \end{bmatrix} e^{-2t}$$

$$= \begin{bmatrix} \cos t + \sin t \\ \cos t \end{bmatrix} e^{-2t} + i \begin{bmatrix} \sin t - \cos t \\ \sin t \end{bmatrix} e^{-2t}$$

The general real solution has the form

$$c_1 \begin{bmatrix} \cos t + \sin t \\ \cos t \end{bmatrix} e^{-2t} + c_2 \begin{bmatrix} \sin t - \cos t \\ \sin t \end{bmatrix} e^{-2t}$$

where c_1 and c_2 now are real numbers. The trajectories are spirals because the eigenvalues are complex. The spirals tend toward the origin because the real parts of the eigenvalues are negative.

10. $A = \begin{bmatrix} 3 & 1 \\ -2 & 1 \end{bmatrix}$. An eigenvalue of A is $2+i$ with corresponding eigenvector $\mathbf{v} = \begin{bmatrix} 1+i \\ -2 \end{bmatrix}$. The complex eigenfunctions $\mathbf{v}e^{\lambda t}$ and $\overline{\mathbf{v}}e^{\overline{\lambda}t}$ form a basis for the set of all complex solutions to $\mathbf{x}' = A\mathbf{x}$. The general complex solution is

$$c_1 \begin{bmatrix} 1+i \\ -2 \end{bmatrix} e^{(2+i)t} + c_2 \begin{bmatrix} 1-i \\ -2 \end{bmatrix} e^{(2-i)t}$$

where c_1 and c_2 are arbitrary complex numbers. To build the general real solution, rewrite $\mathbf{v}e^{(2+i)t}$ as:

$$\mathbf{v}e^{(2+i)t} = \begin{bmatrix} 1+i \\ -2 \end{bmatrix} e^{2t} e^{it} = \begin{bmatrix} 1+i \\ -2 \end{bmatrix} e^{2t} (\cos t + i\sin t)$$

$$= \begin{bmatrix} \cos t + i\cos t + i\sin t + i^2 \sin t \\ -2\cos t - 2i\sin t \end{bmatrix} e^{2t}$$

$$= \begin{bmatrix} \cos t - \sin t \\ -2\cos t \end{bmatrix} e^{2t} + i \begin{bmatrix} \sin t + \cos t \\ -2\sin t \end{bmatrix} e^{2t}$$

The general real solution has the form

$$c_1 \begin{bmatrix} \cos t - \sin t \\ -2\cos t \end{bmatrix} e^{2t} + c_2 \begin{bmatrix} \sin t + \cos t \\ -2\sin t \end{bmatrix} e^{2t}$$

where c_1 and c_2 now are real numbers. The trajectories are spirals because the eigenvalues are complex. The spirals tend away from the origin because the real parts of the eigenvalues are positive.

11. $A = \begin{bmatrix} -3 & -9 \\ 2 & 3 \end{bmatrix}$. An eigenvalue of A is $3i$ with corresponding eigenvector $\mathbf{v} = \begin{bmatrix} -3+3i \\ 2 \end{bmatrix}$. The complex eigenfunctions $\mathbf{v}e^{\lambda t}$ and $\overline{\mathbf{v}}e^{\overline{\lambda}t}$ form a basis for the set of all complex solutions to $\mathbf{x}' = A\mathbf{x}$. The general complex solution is

$$c_1 \begin{bmatrix} -3+3i \\ 2 \end{bmatrix} e^{(3i)t} + c_2 \begin{bmatrix} -3-3i \\ 2 \end{bmatrix} e^{(-3i)t}$$

where c_1 and c_2 are arbitrary complex numbers. To build the general real solution, rewrite $\mathbf{v}e^{(3i)t}$ as:

$$\mathbf{v}e^{(3i)t} = \begin{bmatrix} -3+3i \\ 2 \end{bmatrix} (\cos 3t + i\sin 3t)$$

$$= \begin{bmatrix} -3\cos 3t - 3\sin 3t \\ 2\cos 3t \end{bmatrix} + i \begin{bmatrix} -3\sin 3t + 3\cos 3t \\ 2\sin 3t \end{bmatrix}$$

The general real solution has the form

$$c_1 \begin{bmatrix} -3\cos 3t - 3\sin 3t \\ 2\cos 3t \end{bmatrix} + c_2 \begin{bmatrix} -3\sin 3t + 3\cos 3t \\ 2\sin 3t \end{bmatrix}$$

where c_1 and c_2 now are real numbers. The trajectories are ellipses about the origin because the real parts of the eigenvalues are zero.

12. $A = \begin{bmatrix} -7 & 10 \\ -4 & 5 \end{bmatrix}$. An eigenvalue of A is $-1+2i$ with corresponding eigenvector $\mathbf{v} = \begin{bmatrix} 3-i \\ 2 \end{bmatrix}$. The complex

eigenfunctions $\mathbf{v}e^{\lambda t}$ and $\overline{\mathbf{v}}e^{\overline{\lambda}t}$ form a basis for the set of all complex solutions to $\mathbf{x}' = A\mathbf{x}$. The general complex solution is

$$c_1 \begin{bmatrix} 3-i \\ 2 \end{bmatrix} e^{(-1+2i)t} + c_2 \begin{bmatrix} 3+i \\ 1 \end{bmatrix} e^{(-1-2i)t}$$

where c_1 and c_2 are arbitrary complex numbers. To build the general real solution, rewrite $\mathbf{v}e^{(-1+2i)t}$ as:

$$\mathbf{v}e^{(-1+2i)t} = \begin{bmatrix} 3-i \\ 2 \end{bmatrix} e^{-t}(\cos 2t + i\sin 2t)$$

$$= \begin{bmatrix} 3\cos 2t + \sin 2t \\ 2\cos 2t \end{bmatrix} e^{-t} + i \begin{bmatrix} 3\sin 2t - \cos 2t \\ 2\sin 2t \end{bmatrix} e^{-t}$$

The general real solution has the form

$$c_1 \begin{bmatrix} 3\cos 2t + \sin 2t \\ 2\cos 2t \end{bmatrix} e^{-t} + c_2 \begin{bmatrix} 3\sin 2t - \cos 2t \\ 2\sin 2t \end{bmatrix} e^{-t}$$

where c_1 and c_2 now are real numbers. The trajectories are spirals because the eigenvalues are complex. The spirals tend toward the origin because the real parts of the eigenvalues are negative.

13. $A = \begin{bmatrix} 4 & -3 \\ 6 & -2 \end{bmatrix}$. An eigenvalue of A is $1+3i$ with corresponding eigenvector $\mathbf{v} = \begin{bmatrix} 1+i \\ 2 \end{bmatrix}$. The complex

eigenfunctions $\mathbf{v}e^{\lambda t}$ and $\overline{\mathbf{v}}e^{\overline{\lambda}t}$ form a basis for the set of all complex solutions to $\mathbf{x}' = A\mathbf{x}$. The general complex solution is

$$c_1 \begin{bmatrix} 1+i \\ 2 \end{bmatrix} e^{(1+3i)t} + c_2 \begin{bmatrix} 1-i \\ 1 \end{bmatrix} e^{(1-3i)t}$$

where c_1 and c_2 are arbitrary complex numbers. To build the general real solution, rewrite $\mathbf{v}e^{(1+3i)t}$ as:

$$\mathbf{v}e^{(1+3i)t} = \begin{bmatrix} 1+i \\ 2 \end{bmatrix} e^{t}(\cos 3t + i\sin 3t)$$

$$= \begin{bmatrix} \cos 3t - \sin 3t \\ 2\cos 3t \end{bmatrix} e^{t} + i \begin{bmatrix} \sin 3t + \cos 3t \\ 2\sin 3t \end{bmatrix} e^{t}$$

The general real solution has the form

$$c_1 \begin{bmatrix} \cos 3t - \sin 3t \\ 2\cos 3t \end{bmatrix} e^{t} + c_2 \begin{bmatrix} \sin 3t + \cos 3t \\ 2\sin 3t \end{bmatrix} e^{t}$$

where c_1 and c_2 now are real numbers. The trajectories are spirals because the eigenvalues are complex. The spirals tend away from the origin because the real parts of the eigenvalues are positive.

14. $A = \begin{bmatrix} -2 & 1 \\ -8 & 2 \end{bmatrix}$. An eigenvalue of A is $2i$ with corresponding eigenvector $\mathbf{v} = \begin{bmatrix} 1-i \\ 4 \end{bmatrix}$. The complex

eigenfunctions $\mathbf{v}e^{\lambda t}$ and $\overline{\mathbf{v}}e^{\overline{\lambda}t}$ form a basis for the set of all complex solutions to $\mathbf{x}' = A\mathbf{x}$. The general complex solution is

$$c_1 \begin{bmatrix} 1-i \\ 4 \end{bmatrix} e^{(2i)t} + c_2 \begin{bmatrix} 1+i \\ 4 \end{bmatrix} e^{(-2i)t}$$

where c_1 and c_2 are arbitrary complex numbers. To build the general real solution, rewrite $\mathbf{v}e^{(2i)t}$ as:

$$\mathbf{v}e^{(2i)t} = \begin{bmatrix} 1-i \\ 4 \end{bmatrix}(\cos 2t + i\sin 2t)$$

$$= \begin{bmatrix} \cos 2t + \sin 2t \\ 4\cos 2t \end{bmatrix} + i\begin{bmatrix} \sin 2t - \cos 2t \\ 4\sin 2t \end{bmatrix}$$

The general real solution has the form

$$c_1\begin{bmatrix} \cos 2t + \sin 2t \\ 4\cos 2t \end{bmatrix} + c_2\begin{bmatrix} \sin 2t - \cos 2t \\ 4\sin 2t \end{bmatrix}$$

where c_1 and c_2 now are real numbers. The trajectories are ellipses about the origin because the real parts of the eigenvalues are zero.

15. **[M]** $A = \begin{bmatrix} -8 & -12 & -6 \\ 2 & 1 & 2 \\ 7 & 12 & 5 \end{bmatrix}$. The eigenvalues of A are:

```
ev = eig(A) =
  1.0000
 -1.0000
 -2.0000
nulbasis(A-ev(1)*eye(3)) =
 -1.0000
  0.2500
  1.0000
```

so that $\mathbf{v}_1 = \begin{bmatrix} -4 \\ 1 \\ 4 \end{bmatrix}$

```
nulbasis(A-ev(2)*eye(3)) =
 -1.2000
  0.2000
  1.0000
```

so that $\mathbf{v}_2 = \begin{bmatrix} -6 \\ 1 \\ 5 \end{bmatrix}$

```
nulbasis (A-ev(3)*eye(3)) =
 -1.0000
  0.0000
  1.0000
```

so that $\mathbf{v}_3 = \begin{bmatrix} -1 \\ 0 \\ 1 \end{bmatrix}$

Hence the general solution is $\mathbf{x}(t) = c_1 \begin{bmatrix} -4 \\ 1 \\ 4 \end{bmatrix} e^t + c_2 \begin{bmatrix} -6 \\ 1 \\ 5 \end{bmatrix} e^{-t} + c_3 \begin{bmatrix} -1 \\ 0 \\ 1 \end{bmatrix} e^{-2t}$. The origin is a saddle point.

A solution with $c_1 = 0$ is attracted to the origin while a solution with $c_2 = c_3 = 0$ is repelled.

16. **[M]** $A = \begin{bmatrix} -6 & -11 & 16 \\ 2 & 5 & -4 \\ -4 & -5 & 10 \end{bmatrix}$. The eigenvalues of A are:

ev = eig(A) =

4.0000

3.0000

2.0000

nulbasis(A-ev(1)*eye(3)) =

 2.3333

-0.6667

 1.0000

so that $\mathbf{v}_1 = \begin{bmatrix} 7 \\ -2 \\ 3 \end{bmatrix}$

nulbasis(A-ev(2)*eye(3)) =

 3.0000

-1.0000

 1.0000

so that $\mathbf{v}_2 = \begin{bmatrix} 3 \\ -1 \\ 1 \end{bmatrix}$

nulbasis(A-ev(3)*eye(3)) =

2.0000

0.0000

1.0000

so that $\mathbf{v}_3 = \begin{bmatrix} 2 \\ 0 \\ 1 \end{bmatrix}$

Hence the general solution is $\mathbf{x}(t) = c_1 \begin{bmatrix} 7 \\ -2 \\ 3 \end{bmatrix} e^{4t} + c_2 \begin{bmatrix} 3 \\ -1 \\ 1 \end{bmatrix} e^{3t} + c_3 \begin{bmatrix} 2 \\ 0 \\ 1 \end{bmatrix} e^{2t}$. The origin is a repellor, because

all eigenvalues are positive. All trajectories tend away from the origin.

17. **[M]** $A = \begin{bmatrix} 30 & 64 & 23 \\ -11 & -23 & -9 \\ 6 & 15 & 4 \end{bmatrix}$. The eigenvalues of A are:

$\text{ev} = \text{eig}(A) =$

$5.0000 + 2.0000i$

$5.0000 - 2.0000i$

1.0000

$\text{nulbasis}(A-\text{ev}(1)*\text{eye}(3)) =$

$7.6667 - 11.3333i$

$-3.0000 + 4.6667i$

1.0000

so that $\mathbf{v}_1 = \begin{bmatrix} 23-34i \\ -9+14i \\ 3 \end{bmatrix}$

$\text{nulbasis}(A-\text{ev}(2)*\text{eye}(3)) =$

$7.6667 + 11.3333i$

$-3.0000 - 4.6667i$

1.0000

so that $\mathbf{v}_2 = \begin{bmatrix} 23+34i \\ -9-14i \\ 3 \end{bmatrix}$

$\text{nulbasis}(A-\text{ev}(3)*\text{eye}(3)) =$

-3.0000

1.0000

1.0000

so that $\mathbf{v}_3 = \begin{bmatrix} -3 \\ 1 \\ 1 \end{bmatrix}$

Hence the general complex solution is

$$\mathbf{x}(t) = c_1 \begin{bmatrix} 23-34i \\ -9+14i \\ 3 \end{bmatrix} e^{(5+2i)t} + c_2 \begin{bmatrix} 23+34i \\ -9-14i \\ 3 \end{bmatrix} e^{(5-2i)t} + c_3 \begin{bmatrix} -3 \\ 1 \\ 1 \end{bmatrix} e^t$$

Rewriting the first eigenfunction yields

$$\begin{bmatrix} 23-34i \\ -9+14i \\ 3 \end{bmatrix} e^{5t}(\cos 2t + i\sin 2t) = \begin{bmatrix} 23\cos 2t + 34\sin 2t \\ -9\cos 2t - 14\sin 2t \\ 3\cos 2t \end{bmatrix} e^{5t} + i \begin{bmatrix} 23\sin 2t - 34\cos 2t \\ -9\sin 2t + 14\cos 2t \\ 3\sin 2t \end{bmatrix} e^{5t}$$

Hence the general real solution is

$$\mathbf{x}(t) = c_1 \begin{bmatrix} 23\cos 2t + 34\sin 2t \\ -9\cos 2t - 14\sin 2t \\ 3\cos 2t \end{bmatrix} e^{5t} + c_2 \begin{bmatrix} 23\sin 2t - 34\cos 2t \\ -9\sin 2t + 14\cos 2t \\ 3\sin 2t \end{bmatrix} e^{5t} + c_3 \begin{bmatrix} -3 \\ 1 \\ 1 \end{bmatrix} e^{t}$$

where $c_1, c_2,$ and c_3 are real. The origin is a repellor, because the real parts of all eigenvalues are positive. All trajectories spiral away from the origin.

18. **[M]** $A = \begin{bmatrix} 53 & -30 & -2 \\ 90 & -52 & -3 \\ 20 & -10 & 2 \end{bmatrix}$. The eigenvalues of A are:

```
ev = eig(A) =
```
```
-7.0000
 5.0000 + 1.0000i
 5.0000 - 1.0000i
```
```
nulbasis(A-ev(1)*eye(3)) =
```
```
0.5000
1.0000
0.0000
```

so that $\mathbf{v}_1 = \begin{bmatrix} 1 \\ 2 \\ 0 \end{bmatrix}$

```
nulbasis(A-ev(2)*eye(3)) =
```
```
0.6000 + 0.2000i
0.9000 + 0.3000i
1.0000
```

so that $\mathbf{v}_2 = \begin{bmatrix} 6+2i \\ 9+3i \\ 10 \end{bmatrix}$

```
nulbasis(A-ev(3)*eye(3)) =
```
```
0.6000 - 0.20000
0.9000 - 0.3000i
1.0000
```

so that $\mathbf{v}_3 = \begin{bmatrix} 6-2i \\ 9-3i \\ 10 \end{bmatrix}$

Hence the general complex solution is

$$\mathbf{x}(t) = c_1 \begin{bmatrix} 1 \\ 2 \\ 0 \end{bmatrix} e^{-7t} + c_2 \begin{bmatrix} 6+2i \\ 9+3i \\ 10 \end{bmatrix} e^{(5+i)t} + c_3 \begin{bmatrix} 6-2i \\ 9-3i \\ 10 \end{bmatrix} e^{(5-i)t}$$

Rewriting the second eigenfunction yields

$$\begin{bmatrix} 6+2i \\ 9+3i \\ 10 \end{bmatrix} e^{5t}(\cos t + i\sin t) = \begin{bmatrix} 6\cos t - 2\sin t \\ 9\cos t - 3\sin t \\ 10\cos t \end{bmatrix} e^{5t} + i \begin{bmatrix} 6\sin t + 2\cos t \\ 9\sin t + 3\cos t \\ 10\sin t \end{bmatrix} e^{5t}$$

Hence the general real solution is

$$\mathbf{x}(t) = c_1 \begin{bmatrix} 1 \\ 2 \\ 0 \end{bmatrix} e^{-7t} + c_2 \begin{bmatrix} 6\cos t - 2\sin t \\ 9\cos t - 3\sin t \\ 10\cos t \end{bmatrix} e^{5t} + c_3 \begin{bmatrix} 6\sin t + 2\cos t \\ 9\sin t + 3\cos t \\ 10\sin t \end{bmatrix} e^{5t}$$

where c_1, c_2, and c_3 are real. When $c_2 = c_3 = 0$ the trajectories tend toward the origin, and in other cases the trajectories spiral away from the origin.

19. **[M]** Substitute $R_1 = 1/5$, $R_2 = 1/3$, $C_1 = 4$, and $C_2 = 3$ into the formula for A given in Example 1, and use a matrix program to find the eigenvalues and eigenvectors:

$$A = \begin{bmatrix} -2 & 3/4 \\ 1 & -1 \end{bmatrix}, \quad \lambda_1 = -.5 : \mathbf{v}_1 = \begin{bmatrix} 1 \\ 2 \end{bmatrix}, \quad \lambda_2 = -2.5 : \mathbf{v}_1 = \begin{bmatrix} -3 \\ 2 \end{bmatrix}$$

The general solution is thus $\mathbf{x}(t) = c_1 \begin{bmatrix} 1 \\ 2 \end{bmatrix} e^{-.5t} + c_2 \begin{bmatrix} -3 \\ 2 \end{bmatrix} e^{-2.5t}$. The condition $\mathbf{x}(0) = \begin{bmatrix} 4 \\ 4 \end{bmatrix}$ implies

that $\begin{bmatrix} 1 & -3 \\ 2 & 2 \end{bmatrix} \begin{bmatrix} c_1 \\ c_2 \end{bmatrix} = \begin{bmatrix} 4 \\ 4 \end{bmatrix}$. By a matrix program, $c_1 = 5/2$ and $c_2 = -1/2$, so that

$$\begin{bmatrix} v_1(t) \\ v_2(t) \end{bmatrix} = \mathbf{x}(t) = \frac{5}{2} \begin{bmatrix} 1 \\ 2 \end{bmatrix} e^{-.5t} - \frac{1}{2} \begin{bmatrix} -3 \\ 2 \end{bmatrix} e^{-2.5t}$$

20. **[M]** Substitute $R_1 = 1/15$, $R_2 = 1/3$, $C_1 = 4$, and $C_2 = 2$ into the formula for A given in Example 1, and use a matrix program to find the eigenvalues and eigenvectors:

$$A = \begin{bmatrix} -2 & 1/3 \\ 3/2 & -3/2 \end{bmatrix}, \quad \lambda_1 = -1 : \mathbf{v}_1 = \begin{bmatrix} 1 \\ 3 \end{bmatrix}, \quad \lambda_2 = -2.5 : \mathbf{v}_2 = \begin{bmatrix} -2 \\ 3 \end{bmatrix}$$

The general solution is thus $\mathbf{x}(t) = c_1 \begin{bmatrix} 1 \\ 3 \end{bmatrix} e^{-t} + c_2 \begin{bmatrix} -2 \\ 3 \end{bmatrix} e^{-2.5t}$. The condition $\mathbf{x}(0) = \begin{bmatrix} 3 \\ 3 \end{bmatrix}$ implies

that $\begin{bmatrix} 1 & -2 \\ 3 & 3 \end{bmatrix} \begin{bmatrix} c_1 \\ c_2 \end{bmatrix} = \begin{bmatrix} 3 \\ 3 \end{bmatrix}$. By a matrix program, $c_1 = 5/3$ and $c_2 = -2/3$, so that

$$\begin{bmatrix} v_1(t) \\ v_2(t) \end{bmatrix} = \mathbf{x}(t) = \frac{5}{3} \begin{bmatrix} 1 \\ 3 \end{bmatrix} e^{-t} - \frac{2}{3} \begin{bmatrix} -2 \\ 3 \end{bmatrix} e^{-2.5t}$$

21. **[M]** $A = \begin{bmatrix} -1 & -8 \\ 5 & -5 \end{bmatrix}$. Using a matrix program we find that an eigenvalue of A is $-3+6i$ with

corresponding eigenvector $\mathbf{v} = \begin{bmatrix} 2+6i \\ 5 \end{bmatrix}$. The conjugates of these form the second

eigenvalue-eigenvector pair. The general complex solution is

$$\mathbf{x}(t) = c_1 \begin{bmatrix} 2+6i \\ 5 \end{bmatrix} e^{(-3+6i)t} + c_2 \begin{bmatrix} 2-6i \\ 5 \end{bmatrix} e^{(-3-6i)t}$$

where c_1 and c_2 are arbitrary complex numbers. Rewriting the first eigenfunction and taking its real and imaginary parts, we have

$$\mathbf{v}e^{(-3+6i)t} = \begin{bmatrix} 2+6i \\ 5 \end{bmatrix} e^{-3t}(\cos 6t + i\sin 6t)$$

$$= \begin{bmatrix} 2\cos 6t - 6\sin 6t \\ 5\cos 6t \end{bmatrix} e^{-3t} + i\begin{bmatrix} 2\sin 6t + 6\cos 6t \\ 5\sin 6t \end{bmatrix} e^{-3t}$$

The general real solution has the form

$$\mathbf{x}(t) = c_1 \begin{bmatrix} 2\cos 6t - 6\sin 6t \\ 5\cos 6t \end{bmatrix} e^{-3t} + c_2 \begin{bmatrix} 2\sin 6t + 6\cos 6t \\ 5\sin 6t \end{bmatrix} e^{-3t}$$

where c_1 and c_2 now are real numbers. To satisfy the initial condition $\mathbf{x}(0) = \begin{bmatrix} 0 \\ 15 \end{bmatrix}$, we solve

$$c_1 \begin{bmatrix} 2 \\ 5 \end{bmatrix} + c_2 \begin{bmatrix} 6 \\ 0 \end{bmatrix} = \begin{bmatrix} 0 \\ 15 \end{bmatrix}$$ to get $c_1 = 3, c_2 = -1$. We now have

$$\begin{bmatrix} i_L(t) \\ v_C(t) \end{bmatrix} = \mathbf{x}(t) = 3\begin{bmatrix} 2\cos 6t - 6\sin 6t \\ 5\cos 6t \end{bmatrix} e^{-3t} - \begin{bmatrix} 2\sin 6t + 6\cos 6t \\ 5\sin 6t \end{bmatrix} e^{-3t} = \begin{bmatrix} -20\sin 6t \\ 15\cos 6t - 5\sin 6t \end{bmatrix} e^{-3t}$$

22. **[M]** $A = \begin{bmatrix} 0 & 2 \\ -.4 & -.8 \end{bmatrix}$. Using a matrix program we find that an eigenvalue of A is $-.4 + .8i$ with

corresponding eigenvector $\mathbf{v} = \begin{bmatrix} -1-2i \\ 1 \end{bmatrix}$. The conjugates of these form the second eigenvalue-

eigenvector pair. The general complex solution is

$$\mathbf{x}(t) = c_1 \begin{bmatrix} -1-2i \\ 1 \end{bmatrix} e^{(-.4+.8i)t} + c_2 \begin{bmatrix} -1+2i \\ 1 \end{bmatrix} e^{(-.4-.8i)t}$$

where c_1 and c_2 are arbitrary complex numbers. Rewriting the first eigenfunction and taking its real and imaginary parts, we have

$$\mathbf{v}e^{(-.4+.8i)t} = \begin{bmatrix} -1-2i \\ 1 \end{bmatrix} e^{-.4t}(\cos .8t + i\sin .8t)$$

$$= \begin{bmatrix} -\cos .8t + 2\sin .8t \\ \cos .8t \end{bmatrix} e^{-.4t} + i\begin{bmatrix} -\sin .8t - 2\cos .8t \\ \sin .8t \end{bmatrix} e^{-.4t}$$

The general real solution has the form

$$\mathbf{x}(t) = c_1 \begin{bmatrix} -\cos .8t + 2\sin .8t \\ \cos .8t \end{bmatrix} e^{-.4t} + c_2 \begin{bmatrix} -\sin .8t - 2\cos .8t \\ \sin .8t \end{bmatrix} e^{-.4t}$$

where c_1 and c_2 now are real numbers. To satisfy the initial condition $\mathbf{x}(0) = \begin{bmatrix} 0 \\ 12 \end{bmatrix}$, we solve

$$c_1 \begin{bmatrix} -1 \\ 1 \end{bmatrix} + c_2 \begin{bmatrix} -2 \\ 0 \end{bmatrix} = \begin{bmatrix} 0 \\ 12 \end{bmatrix}$$ to get $c_1 = 12, c_2 = -6$. We now have

$$\begin{bmatrix} i_L(t) \\ v_C(t) \end{bmatrix} = \mathbf{x}(t) = 12\begin{bmatrix} -\cos .8t + 2\sin .8t \\ \cos .8t \end{bmatrix} e^{-.4t} - 6\begin{bmatrix} -\sin .8t - 2\cos .8t \\ \sin .8t \end{bmatrix} e^{-.4t} = \begin{bmatrix} 30\sin .8t \\ 12\cos .8t - 6\sin .8t \end{bmatrix} e^{-.4t}$$

5.8   SOLUTIONS

1. The vectors in the given sequence approach an eigenvector $\mathbf{v}_1$. The last vector in the sequence,

$\mathbf{x}_4 = \begin{bmatrix} 1 \\ .3326 \end{bmatrix}$, is probably the best estimate for $\mathbf{v}_1$. To compute an estimate for λ_1, examine

$A\mathbf{x}_4 = \begin{bmatrix} 4.9978 \\ 1.6652 \end{bmatrix}$. This vector is approximately $\lambda_1 \mathbf{v}_1$. From the first entry in this vector, an estimate

of λ_1 is 4.9978.

2. The vectors in the given sequence approach an eigenvector $\mathbf{v}_1$. The last vector in the sequence,

$\mathbf{x}_4 = \begin{bmatrix} -.2520 \\ 1 \end{bmatrix}$, is probably the best estimate for $\mathbf{v}_1$. To compute an estimate for λ_1, examine

$A\mathbf{x}_4 = \begin{bmatrix} -1.2536 \\ 5.0064 \end{bmatrix}$. This vector is approximately $\lambda_1 \mathbf{v}_1$. From the second entry in this vector, an estimate

of λ_1 is 5.0064.

3. The vectors in the given sequence approach an eigenvector $\mathbf{v}_1$. The last vector in the sequence,

$\mathbf{x}_4 = \begin{bmatrix} .5188 \\ 1 \end{bmatrix}$, is probably the best estimate for $\mathbf{v}_1$. To compute an estimate for λ_1, examine

$A\mathbf{x}_4 = \begin{bmatrix} .4594 \\ .9075 \end{bmatrix}$. This vector is approximately $\lambda_1 \mathbf{v}_1$. From the second entry in this vector, an estimate of

λ_1 is .9075.

4. The vectors in the given sequence approach an eigenvector $\mathbf{v}_1$. The last vector in the sequence,

$\mathbf{x}_4 = \begin{bmatrix} 1 \\ .7502 \end{bmatrix}$, is probably the best estimate for $\mathbf{v}_1$. To compute an estimate for λ_1, examine

$A\mathbf{x}_4 = \begin{bmatrix} -.4012 \\ -.3009 \end{bmatrix}$. This vector is approximately $\lambda_1 \mathbf{v}_1$. From the first entry in this vector, an estimate of λ_1

is $-.4012$.

5. Since $A^5 \mathbf{x} = \begin{bmatrix} 24991 \\ -31241 \end{bmatrix}$ is an estimate for an eigenvector, the vector $\mathbf{v} = -\dfrac{1}{31241}\begin{bmatrix} 24991 \\ -31241 \end{bmatrix} = \begin{bmatrix} -.7999 \\ 1 \end{bmatrix}$ is

a vector with a 1 in its second entry that is close to an eigenvector of A. To estimate the dominant

eigenvalue λ_1 of A, compute $A\mathbf{v} = \begin{bmatrix} 4.0015 \\ -5.0020 \end{bmatrix}$. From the second entry in this vector, an estimate of λ_1

is -5.0020.

6. Since $A^5 \mathbf{x} = \begin{bmatrix} -2045 \\ 4093 \end{bmatrix}$ is an estimate for an eigenvector, the vector $\mathbf{v} = \dfrac{1}{4093}\begin{bmatrix} -2045 \\ 4093 \end{bmatrix} = \begin{bmatrix} -.4996 \\ 1 \end{bmatrix}$ is

a vector with a 1 in its second entry that is close to an eigenvector of A. To estimate the dominant

eigenvalue λ_1 of A, compute $A\mathbf{v} = \begin{bmatrix} -2.0008 \\ 4.0024 \end{bmatrix}$. From the second entry in this vector, an estimate of λ_1

is 4.0024.

7. **[M]** $A = \begin{bmatrix} 6 & 7 \\ 8 & 5 \end{bmatrix}$, $\mathbf{x}_0 = \begin{bmatrix} 1 \\ 0 \end{bmatrix}$. The data in the table below was calculated using Mathematica, which carried more digits than shown here.

k	0	1	2	3	4	5
$\mathbf{x}_k$	$\begin{bmatrix} 1 \\ 0 \end{bmatrix}$	$\begin{bmatrix} .75 \\ 1 \end{bmatrix}$	$\begin{bmatrix} 1 \\ .9565 \end{bmatrix}$	$\begin{bmatrix} .9932 \\ 1 \end{bmatrix}$	$\begin{bmatrix} 1 \\ .9990 \end{bmatrix}$	$\begin{bmatrix} .9998 \\ 1 \end{bmatrix}$
$A\mathbf{x}_k$	$\begin{bmatrix} 6 \\ 8 \end{bmatrix}$	$\begin{bmatrix} 11.5 \\ 11.0 \end{bmatrix}$	$\begin{bmatrix} 12.6957 \\ 12.7826 \end{bmatrix}$	$\begin{bmatrix} 12.9592 \\ 12.9456 \end{bmatrix}$	$\begin{bmatrix} 12.9927 \\ 12.9948 \end{bmatrix}$	$\begin{bmatrix} 12.9990 \\ 12.9987 \end{bmatrix}$
μ_k	8	11.5	12.7826	12.9592	12.9948	12.9990

The actual eigenvalue is 13.

8. **[M]** $A = \begin{bmatrix} 2 & 1 \\ 4 & 5 \end{bmatrix}$, $\mathbf{x}_0 = \begin{bmatrix} 1 \\ 0 \end{bmatrix}$. The data in the table below was calculated using Mathematica, which carried more digits than shown here.

k	0	1	2	3	4	5
$\mathbf{x}_k$	$\begin{bmatrix} 1 \\ 0 \end{bmatrix}$	$\begin{bmatrix} .5 \\ 1 \end{bmatrix}$	$\begin{bmatrix} .2857 \\ 1 \end{bmatrix}$	$\begin{bmatrix} .2558 \\ 1 \end{bmatrix}$	$\begin{bmatrix} .2510 \\ 1 \end{bmatrix}$	$\begin{bmatrix} .2502 \\ 1 \end{bmatrix}$
$A\mathbf{x}_k$	$\begin{bmatrix} 2 \\ 4 \end{bmatrix}$	$\begin{bmatrix} 2 \\ 7 \end{bmatrix}$	$\begin{bmatrix} 1.5714 \\ 6.1429 \end{bmatrix}$	$\begin{bmatrix} 1.5116 \\ 6.0233 \end{bmatrix}$	$\begin{bmatrix} 1.5019 \\ 6.0039 \end{bmatrix}$	$\begin{bmatrix} 1.5003 \\ 6.0006 \end{bmatrix}$
μ_k	4	7	6.1429	6.0233	6.0039	6.0006

The actual eigenvalue is 6.

9. **[M]** $A = \begin{bmatrix} 8 & 0 & 12 \\ 1 & -2 & 1 \\ 0 & 3 & 0 \end{bmatrix}$, $\mathbf{x}_0 = \begin{bmatrix} 1 \\ 0 \\ 0 \end{bmatrix}$. The data in the table below was calculated using Mathematica, which carried more digits than shown here.

k	0	1	2	3	4	5	6
$\mathbf{x}_k$	$\begin{bmatrix} 1 \\ 0 \\ 0 \end{bmatrix}$	$\begin{bmatrix} 1 \\ .125 \\ 0 \end{bmatrix}$	$\begin{bmatrix} 1 \\ .0938 \\ .0469 \end{bmatrix}$	$\begin{bmatrix} 1 \\ .1004 \\ .0328 \end{bmatrix}$	$\begin{bmatrix} 1 \\ .0991 \\ .0359 \end{bmatrix}$	$\begin{bmatrix} 1 \\ .0994 \\ .0353 \end{bmatrix}$	$\begin{bmatrix} 1 \\ .0993 \\ .0354 \end{bmatrix}$
$A\mathbf{x}_k$	$\begin{bmatrix} 8 \\ 1 \\ 0 \end{bmatrix}$	$\begin{bmatrix} 8 \\ .75 \\ .375 \end{bmatrix}$	$\begin{bmatrix} 8.5625 \\ .8594 \\ .2812 \end{bmatrix}$	$\begin{bmatrix} 8.3942 \\ .8321 \\ .3011 \end{bmatrix}$	$\begin{bmatrix} 8.4304 \\ .8376 \\ .2974 \end{bmatrix}$	$\begin{bmatrix} 8.4233 \\ .8366 \\ .2981 \end{bmatrix}$	$\begin{bmatrix} 8.4246 \\ .8368 \\ .2979 \end{bmatrix}$
μ_k	8	8	8.5625	8.3942	8.4304	8.4233	8.4246

Thus $\mu_5 = 8.4233$ and $\mu_6 = 8.4246$. The actual eigenvalue is $(7 + \sqrt{97})/2$, or 8.42443 to five decimal places.

10. [M] $A = \begin{bmatrix} 1 & 2 & -2 \\ 1 & 1 & 9 \\ 0 & 1 & 9 \end{bmatrix}$, $\mathbf{x}_0 = \begin{bmatrix} 1 \\ 0 \\ 0 \end{bmatrix}$. The data in the table below was calculated using Mathematica, which carried more digits than shown here.

k	0	1	2	3	4	5	6
$\mathbf{x}_k$	$\begin{bmatrix} 1 \\ 0 \\ 0 \end{bmatrix}$	$\begin{bmatrix} 1 \\ 1 \\ 0 \end{bmatrix}$	$\begin{bmatrix} 1 \\ .6667 \\ .3333 \end{bmatrix}$	$\begin{bmatrix} .3571 \\ 1 \\ .7857 \end{bmatrix}$	$\begin{bmatrix} .0932 \\ 1 \\ .9576 \end{bmatrix}$	$\begin{bmatrix} .0183 \\ 1 \\ .9904 \end{bmatrix}$	$\begin{bmatrix} .0038 \\ 1 \\ .9982 \end{bmatrix}$
$A\mathbf{x}_k$	$\begin{bmatrix} 1 \\ 1 \\ 0 \end{bmatrix}$	$\begin{bmatrix} 3 \\ 2 \\ 1 \end{bmatrix}$	$\begin{bmatrix} 1.6667 \\ 4.6667 \\ 3.6667 \end{bmatrix}$	$\begin{bmatrix} .7857 \\ 8.4286 \\ 8.0714 \end{bmatrix}$	$\begin{bmatrix} .1780 \\ 9.7119 \\ 9.6186 \end{bmatrix}$	$\begin{bmatrix} .0375 \\ 9.9319 \\ 9.9136 \end{bmatrix}$	$\begin{bmatrix} .0075 \\ 9.9872 \\ 9.9834 \end{bmatrix}$
μ_k	1	3	4.6667	8.4286	9.7119	9.9319	9.9872

Thus $\mu_5 = 9.9319$ and $\mu_6 = 9.9872$. The actual eigenvalue is 10.

11. [M] $A = \begin{bmatrix} 5 & 2 \\ 2 & 2 \end{bmatrix}$, $\mathbf{x}_0 = \begin{bmatrix} 1 \\ 0 \end{bmatrix}$. The data in the table below was calculated using Mathematica, which carried more digits than shown here.

k	0	1	2	3	4
$\mathbf{x}_k$	$\begin{bmatrix} 1 \\ 0 \end{bmatrix}$	$\begin{bmatrix} 1 \\ .4 \end{bmatrix}$	$\begin{bmatrix} 1 \\ .4828 \end{bmatrix}$	$\begin{bmatrix} 1 \\ .4971 \end{bmatrix}$	$\begin{bmatrix} 1 \\ .4995 \end{bmatrix}$
$A\mathbf{x}_k$	$\begin{bmatrix} 5 \\ 2 \end{bmatrix}$	$\begin{bmatrix} 5.8 \\ 2.8 \end{bmatrix}$	$\begin{bmatrix} 5.9655 \\ 2.9655 \end{bmatrix}$	$\begin{bmatrix} 5.9942 \\ 2.9942 \end{bmatrix}$	$\begin{bmatrix} 5.9990 \\ 2.9990 \end{bmatrix}$
μ_k	5	5.8	5.9655	5.9942	5.9990
$R(\mathbf{x}_k)$	5	5.9655	5.9990	5.99997	5.9999993

The actual eigenvalue is 6. The bottom two columns of the table show that $R(\mathbf{x}_k)$ estimates the eigenvalue more accurately than μ_k.

12. [M] $A = \begin{bmatrix} -3 & 2 \\ 2 & 2 \end{bmatrix}$, $\mathbf{x}_0 = \begin{bmatrix} 1 \\ 0 \end{bmatrix}$. The data in the table below was calculated using Mathematica, which carried more digits than shown here.

k	0	1	2	3	4
$\mathbf{x}_k$	$\begin{bmatrix} 1 \\ 0 \end{bmatrix}$	$\begin{bmatrix} -1 \\ .6667 \end{bmatrix}$	$\begin{bmatrix} 1 \\ -.4615 \end{bmatrix}$	$\begin{bmatrix} -1 \\ .5098 \end{bmatrix}$	$\begin{bmatrix} 1 \\ -.4976 \end{bmatrix}$
$A\mathbf{x}_k$	$\begin{bmatrix} -3 \\ 2 \end{bmatrix}$	$\begin{bmatrix} 4.3333 \\ -2.0000 \end{bmatrix}$	$\begin{bmatrix} -3.9231 \\ 2.0000 \end{bmatrix}$	$\begin{bmatrix} 4.0196 \\ -2.0000 \end{bmatrix}$	$\begin{bmatrix} -3.9951 \\ 2.0000 \end{bmatrix}$
μ_k	-3	-4.3333	-3.9231	-4.0196	-3.9951
$R(\mathbf{x}_k)$	-3	-3.9231	-3.9951	-3.9997	-3.99998

The actual eigenvalue is −4. The bottom two columns of the table show that $R(\mathbf{x}_k)$ estimates the eigenvalue more accurately than μ_k.

13. If the eigenvalues close to 4 and −4 have different absolute values, then one of these is a strictly dominant eigenvalue, so the power method will work. But the power method depends on powers of the quotients λ_2/λ_1 and λ_3/λ_1 going to zero. If $|\lambda_2/\lambda_1|$ is close to 1, its powers will go to zero slowly, and the power method will converge slowly.

14. If the eigenvalues close to 4 and −4 have the same absolute value, then neither of these is a strictly dominant eigenvalue, so the power method will not work. However, the inverse power method may still be used. If the initial estimate is chosen near the eigenvalue close to 4, then the inverse power method should produce a sequence that estimates the eigenvalue close to 4.

15. Suppose $A\mathbf{x} = \lambda\mathbf{x}$, with $\mathbf{x} \neq 0$. For any α, $A\mathbf{x} - \alpha I\mathbf{x} = (\lambda - \alpha)\mathbf{x}$. If α is *not* an eigenvalue of A, then $A - \alpha I$ is invertible and $\lambda - \alpha$ is not 0; hence

$$\mathbf{x} = (A - \alpha I)^{-1}(\lambda - \alpha)\mathbf{x} \text{ and } (\lambda - \alpha)^{-1}\mathbf{x} = (A - \alpha I)^{-1}\mathbf{x}$$

This last equation shows that $\mathbf{x}$ is an eigenvector of $(A - \alpha I)^{-1}$ corresponding to the eigenvalue $(\lambda - \alpha)^{-1}$.

16. Suppose that μ is an eigenvalue of $(A - \alpha I)^{-1}$ with corresponding eigenvector $\mathbf{x}$. Since $(A - \alpha I)^{-1}\mathbf{x} = \mu\mathbf{x}$,

$$\mathbf{x} = (A - \alpha I)(\mu\mathbf{x}) = A(\mu\mathbf{x}) - (\alpha I)(\mu\mathbf{x}) = \mu(A\mathbf{x}) - \alpha\mu\mathbf{x}$$

Solving this equation for $A\mathbf{x}$, we find that

$$A\mathbf{x} = \left(\frac{1}{\mu}\right)(\alpha\mu\mathbf{x} + \mathbf{x}) = \left(\alpha + \frac{1}{\mu}\right)\mathbf{x}$$

Thus $\lambda = \alpha + (1/\mu)$ is an eigenvalue of A with corresponding eigenvector $\mathbf{x}$.

17. [M] $A = \begin{bmatrix} 10 & -8 & -4 \\ -8 & 13 & 4 \\ -4 & 5 & 4 \end{bmatrix}$, $\mathbf{x}_0 = \begin{bmatrix} 1 \\ 0 \\ 0 \end{bmatrix}$, $\alpha = 3.3$. The data in the table below was calculated using Mathematica, which carried more digits than shown here.

k	0	1	2
$\mathbf{x}_k$	$\begin{bmatrix} 1 \\ 0 \\ 0 \end{bmatrix}$	$\begin{bmatrix} 1 \\ .7873 \\ .0908 \end{bmatrix}$	$\begin{bmatrix} 1 \\ .7870 \\ .0957 \end{bmatrix}$
$\mathbf{y}_k$	$\begin{bmatrix} 26.0552 \\ 20.5128 \\ 2.3669 \end{bmatrix}$	$\begin{bmatrix} 47.1975 \\ 37.1436 \\ 4.5187 \end{bmatrix}$	$\begin{bmatrix} 47.1233 \\ 37.0866 \\ 4.5083 \end{bmatrix}$
μ_k	26.0552	47.1975	47.1233
ν_k	3.3384	3.32119	3.3212209

Thus an estimate for the eigenvalue to four decimal places is 3.3212. The actual eigenvalue is $(25 - \sqrt{337})/2$, or 3.3212201 to seven decimal places.

18. [M] $A = \begin{bmatrix} 8 & 0 & 12 \\ 1 & -2 & 1 \\ 0 & 3 & 0 \end{bmatrix}$, $\mathbf{x}_0 = \begin{bmatrix} 1 \\ 0 \\ 0 \end{bmatrix}$, $\alpha = -1.4$. The data in the table below was calculated using

Mathematica, which carried more digits than shown here.

k	0	1	2	3	4
$\mathbf{x}_k$	$\begin{bmatrix} 1 \\ 0 \\ 0 \end{bmatrix}$	$\begin{bmatrix} 1 \\ .3646 \\ -.7813 \end{bmatrix}$	$\begin{bmatrix} 1 \\ .3734 \\ -.7854 \end{bmatrix}$	$\begin{bmatrix} 1 \\ .3729 \\ -.7854 \end{bmatrix}$	$\begin{bmatrix} 1 \\ .3729 \\ -.7854 \end{bmatrix}$
$\mathbf{y}_k$	$\begin{bmatrix} 40 \\ 14.5833 \\ -31.25 \end{bmatrix}$	$\begin{bmatrix} -38.125 \\ -14.2361 \\ 29.9479 \end{bmatrix}$	$\begin{bmatrix} -41.1134 \\ -15.3300 \\ 32.2888 \end{bmatrix}$	$\begin{bmatrix} -40.9243 \\ -15.2608 \\ 32.1407 \end{bmatrix}$	$\begin{bmatrix} -40.9358 \\ -15.2650 \\ 32.1497 \end{bmatrix}$
μ_k	40	-38.125	-41.1134	-40.9243	-40.9358
ν_k	-1.375	-1.42623	-1.42432	-1.42444	-1.42443

Thus an estimate for the eigenvalue to four decimal places is -1.4244. The actual eigenvalue is $(7 - \sqrt{97})/2$, or -1.424429 to six decimal places.

19. [M] $A = \begin{bmatrix} 10 & 7 & 8 & 7 \\ 7 & 5 & 6 & 5 \\ 8 & 6 & 10 & 9 \\ 7 & 5 & 9 & 10 \end{bmatrix}$, $\mathbf{x}_0 = \begin{bmatrix} 1 \\ 0 \\ 0 \\ 0 \end{bmatrix}$.

(a) The data in the table below was calculated using Mathematica, which carried more digits than shown here.

k	0	1	2	3
$\mathbf{x}_k$	$\begin{bmatrix} 1 \\ 0 \\ 0 \\ 0 \end{bmatrix}$	$\begin{bmatrix} 1 \\ .7 \\ .8 \\ .7 \end{bmatrix}$	$\begin{bmatrix} .988679 \\ .709434 \\ 1 \\ .932075 \end{bmatrix}$	$\begin{bmatrix} .961467 \\ .691491 \\ 1 \\ .942201 \end{bmatrix}$
$A\mathbf{x}_k$	$\begin{bmatrix} 10 \\ 7 \\ 8 \\ 7 \end{bmatrix}$	$\begin{bmatrix} 26.2 \\ 18.8 \\ 26.5 \\ 24.7 \end{bmatrix}$	$\begin{bmatrix} 29.3774 \\ 21.1283 \\ 30.5547 \\ 28.7887 \end{bmatrix}$	$\begin{bmatrix} 29.0505 \\ 20.8987 \\ 30.3205 \\ 28.6097 \end{bmatrix}$
μ_k	10	26.5	30.5547	30.3205

k	4	5	6	7
$\mathbf{x}_k$	$\begin{bmatrix} .958115 \\ .689261 \\ 1 \\ .943578 \end{bmatrix}$	$\begin{bmatrix} .957691 \\ .688978 \\ 1 \\ .943755 \end{bmatrix}$	$\begin{bmatrix} .957637 \\ .688942 \\ 1 \\ .943778 \end{bmatrix}$	$\begin{bmatrix} .957630 \\ .688938 \\ 1 \\ .943781 \end{bmatrix}$
$A\mathbf{x}_k$	$\begin{bmatrix} 29.0110 \\ 20.8710 \\ 30.2927 \\ 28.5889 \end{bmatrix}$	$\begin{bmatrix} 29.0060 \\ 20.8675 \\ 30.2892 \\ 28.5863 \end{bmatrix}$	$\begin{bmatrix} 29.0054 \\ 20.8671 \\ 30.2887 \\ 28.5859 \end{bmatrix}$	$\begin{bmatrix} 29.0053 \\ 20.8670 \\ 30.2887 \\ 28.5859 \end{bmatrix}$
μ_k	30.2927	30.2892	30.2887	30.2887

Thus an estimate for the eigenvalue to four decimal places is 30.2887. The actual eigenvalue is 30.2886853 to seven decimal places. An estimate for the corresponding eigenvector is $\begin{bmatrix} .957630 \\ .688938 \\ 1 \\ .943781 \end{bmatrix}$.

(b) The data in the table below was calculated using Mathematica, which carried more digits than shown here.

k	0	1	2	3	4
$\mathbf{x}_k$	$\begin{bmatrix} 1 \\ 0 \\ 0 \\ 0 \end{bmatrix}$	$\begin{bmatrix} -.609756 \\ 1 \\ -.243902 \\ .146341 \end{bmatrix}$	$\begin{bmatrix} -.604007 \\ 1 \\ -.251051 \\ .148899 \end{bmatrix}$	$\begin{bmatrix} -.603973 \\ 1 \\ -.251134 \\ .148953 \end{bmatrix}$	$\begin{bmatrix} -.603972 \\ 1 \\ -.251135 \\ .148953 \end{bmatrix}$
$\mathbf{y}_k$	$\begin{bmatrix} 25 \\ -41 \\ 10 \\ -6 \end{bmatrix}$	$\begin{bmatrix} -59.5610 \\ 98.6098 \\ -24.7561 \\ 14.6829 \end{bmatrix}$	$\begin{bmatrix} -59.5041 \\ 98.5211 \\ -24.7420 \\ 14.6750 \end{bmatrix}$	$\begin{bmatrix} -59.5044 \\ 98.5217 \\ -24.7423 \\ 14.6751 \end{bmatrix}$	$\begin{bmatrix} -59.5044 \\ 98.5217 \\ -24.7423 \\ 14.6751 \end{bmatrix}$
μ_k	-41	98.6098	98.5211	98.5217	98.5217
ν_k	-.0243902	.0101410	.0101501	.0101500	.0101500

Thus an estimate for the eigenvalue to five decimal places is .01015. The actual eigenvalue is .01015005 to eight decimal places. An estimate for the corresponding eigenvector is $\begin{bmatrix} -.603972 \\ 1 \\ -.251135 \\ .148953 \end{bmatrix}$.

20. [M] $A = \begin{bmatrix} 1 & 2 & 3 & 2 \\ 2 & 12 & 13 & 11 \\ -2 & 3 & 0 & 2 \\ 4 & 5 & 7 & 2 \end{bmatrix}, \mathbf{x}_0 = \begin{bmatrix} 1 \\ 0 \\ 0 \\ 0 \end{bmatrix}.$

(a)   The data in the table below was calculated using Mathematica, which carried more digits than shown here.

k	0	1	2	3	4
$\mathbf{x}_k$	$\begin{bmatrix} 1 \\ 0 \\ 0 \\ 0 \end{bmatrix}$	$\begin{bmatrix} .25 \\ .5 \\ -.5 \\ 1 \end{bmatrix}$	$\begin{bmatrix} .159091 \\ 1 \\ .272727 \\ .181818 \end{bmatrix}$	$\begin{bmatrix} .187023 \\ 1 \\ .170483 \\ .442748 \end{bmatrix}$	$\begin{bmatrix} .184166 \\ 1 \\ .180439 \\ .402197 \end{bmatrix}$
$A\mathbf{x}_k$	$\begin{bmatrix} 1 \\ 2 \\ -2 \\ 4 \end{bmatrix}$	$\begin{bmatrix} 1.75 \\ 11 \\ 3 \\ 2 \end{bmatrix}$	$\begin{bmatrix} 3.34091 \\ 17.8636 \\ 3.04545 \\ 7.90909 \end{bmatrix}$	$\begin{bmatrix} 3.58397 \\ 19.4606 \\ 3.51145 \\ 7.82697 \end{bmatrix}$	$\begin{bmatrix} 3.52988 \\ 19.1382 \\ 3.43606 \\ 7.80413 \end{bmatrix}$
μ_k	4	11	17.8636	19.4606	19.1382

k	5	6	7	8	9
$\mathbf{x}_k$	$\begin{bmatrix} .184441 \\ 1 \\ .179539 \\ .407778 \end{bmatrix}$	$\begin{bmatrix} .184414 \\ 1 \\ .179622 \\ .407021 \end{bmatrix}$	$\begin{bmatrix} .184417 \\ 1 \\ .179615 \\ .407121 \end{bmatrix}$	$\begin{bmatrix} .184416 \\ 1 \\ .179615 \\ .407108 \end{bmatrix}$	$\begin{bmatrix} .184416 \\ 1 \\ .179615 \\ .407110 \end{bmatrix}$
$A\mathbf{x}_k$	$\begin{bmatrix} 3.53861 \\ 19.1884 \\ 3.44667 \\ 7.81010 \end{bmatrix}$	$\begin{bmatrix} 3.53732 \\ 19.1811 \\ 3.44521 \\ 7.80905 \end{bmatrix}$	$\begin{bmatrix} 3.53750 \\ 19.1822 \\ 3.44541 \\ 7.80921 \end{bmatrix}$	$\begin{bmatrix} 3.53748 \\ 19.1820 \\ 3.44538 \\ 7.80919 \end{bmatrix}$	$\begin{bmatrix} 3.53748 \\ 19.1811 \\ 3.44539 \\ 7.80919 \end{bmatrix}$
μ_k	19.1884	19.1811	19.1822	19.1820	19.1820

Thus an estimate for the eigenvalue to four decimal places is 19.1820. The actual eigenvalue is 19.1820368 to seven decimal places. An estimate for the corresponding eigenvector is $\begin{bmatrix} .184416 \\ 1 \\ .179615 \\ .407110 \end{bmatrix}$.

(b) The data in the table below was calculated using Mathematica, which carried more digits than shown here.

k	0	1	2
$\mathbf{x}_k$	$\begin{bmatrix} 1 \\ 0 \\ 0 \\ 0 \end{bmatrix}$	$\begin{bmatrix} 1 \\ .226087 \\ -.921739 \\ .660870 \end{bmatrix}$	$\begin{bmatrix} 1 \\ .222577 \\ -.917970 \\ .660496 \end{bmatrix}$
$\mathbf{y}_k$	$\begin{bmatrix} 115 \\ 26 \\ -106 \\ 76 \end{bmatrix}$	$\begin{bmatrix} 81.7304 \\ 18.1913 \\ -75.0261 \\ 53.9826 \end{bmatrix}$	$\begin{bmatrix} 81.9314 \\ 18.2387 \\ -75.2125 \\ 54.1143 \end{bmatrix}$
μ_k	115	81.7304	81.9314
ν_k	.00869565	.0122353	.0122053

Thus an estimate for the eigenvalue to four decimal places is .0122. The actual eigenvalue is .01220556 to eight decimal places. An estimate for the corresponding eigenvector is $\begin{bmatrix} 1 \\ .222577 \\ -.917970 \\ .660496 \end{bmatrix}$.

21. a. $A = \begin{bmatrix} .8 & 0 \\ 0 & .2 \end{bmatrix}$, $\mathbf{x} = \begin{bmatrix} .5 \\ .5 \end{bmatrix}$. Here is the sequence $A^k\mathbf{x}$ for $k = 1, \dots 5$:

$$\begin{bmatrix} .4 \\ .1 \end{bmatrix}, \begin{bmatrix} .32 \\ .02 \end{bmatrix}, \begin{bmatrix} .256 \\ .004 \end{bmatrix}, \begin{bmatrix} .2048 \\ .0008 \end{bmatrix}, \begin{bmatrix} .16384 \\ .00016 \end{bmatrix}$$

Notice that $A^5\mathbf{x}$ is approximately $.8(A^4\mathbf{x})$.

Conclusion: If the eigenvalues of A are all less than 1 in magnitude, and if $\mathbf{x} \neq 0$, then $A^k\mathbf{x}$ is approximately an eigenvector for large k.

b. $A = \begin{bmatrix} 1 & 0 \\ 0 & .8 \end{bmatrix}$, $\mathbf{x} = \begin{bmatrix} .5 \\ .5 \end{bmatrix}$. Here is the sequence $A^k\mathbf{x}$ for $k = 1, \dots 5$:

$$\begin{bmatrix} .5 \\ .4 \end{bmatrix}, \begin{bmatrix} .5 \\ .32 \end{bmatrix}, \begin{bmatrix} .5 \\ .256 \end{bmatrix}, \begin{bmatrix} .5 \\ .2048 \end{bmatrix}, \begin{bmatrix} .5 \\ .16384 \end{bmatrix}$$

Notice that $A^k\mathbf{x}$ seems to be converging to $\begin{bmatrix} .5 \\ 0 \end{bmatrix}$.

Conclusion: If the strictly dominant eigenvalue of A is 1, and if $\mathbf{x}$ has a component in the direction of the corresponding eigenvector, then $\{A^k\mathbf{x}\}$ will converge to a multiple of that eigenvector.

c. $A = \begin{bmatrix} 8 & 0 \\ 0 & 2 \end{bmatrix}$, $\mathbf{x} = \begin{bmatrix} .5 \\ .5 \end{bmatrix}$. Here is the sequence $A^k\mathbf{x}$ for $k = 1, \dots 5$:

$$\begin{bmatrix} 4 \\ 1 \end{bmatrix}, \begin{bmatrix} 32 \\ 2 \end{bmatrix}, \begin{bmatrix} 256 \\ 4 \end{bmatrix}, \begin{bmatrix} 2048 \\ 8 \end{bmatrix}, \begin{bmatrix} 16384 \\ 16 \end{bmatrix}$$

Notice that the distance of $A^k \mathbf{x}$ from either eigenvector of A is increasing rapidly as k increases.

Conclusion: If the eigenvalues of A are all greater than 1 in magnitude, and if $\mathbf{x}$ is not an eigenvector, then the distance from $A^k \mathbf{x}$ to the nearest eigenvector will *increase* as $k \rightarrow \infty$.

Chapter 5   SUPPLEMENTARY EXERCISES _____

1. **a.** True. If A is invertible and if $A\mathbf{x} = 1 \cdot \mathbf{x}$ for some nonzero $\mathbf{x}$, then left-multiply by A^{-1} to obtain $\mathbf{x} = A^{-1}\mathbf{x}$, which may be rewritten as $A^{-1}\mathbf{x} = 1 \cdot \mathbf{x}$. Since $\mathbf{x}$ is nonzero, this shows 1 is an eigenvalue of A^{-1}.

   b. False. If A is row equivalent to the identity matrix, then A is invertible. The matrix in Example 4 of Section 5.3 shows that an invertible matrix need not be diagonalizable. Also, see Exercise 31 in Section 5.3.

   c. True. If A contains a row or column of zeros, then A is not row equivalent to the identity matrix and thus is not invertible. By the Invertible Matrix Theorem (as stated in Section 5.2), 0 is an eigenvalue of A.

   d. False. Consider a diagonal matrix D whose eigenvalues are 1 and 3, that is, its diagonal entries are 1 and 3. Then D^2 is a diagonal matrix whose eigenvalues (diagonal entries) are 1 and 9. In general, the eigenvalues of A^2 are the *squares* of the eigenvalues of A.

   e. True. Suppose a nonzero vector $\mathbf{x}$ satisfies $A\mathbf{x} = \lambda\mathbf{x}$, then

   $$A^2\mathbf{x} = A(A\mathbf{x}) = A(\lambda\mathbf{x}) = \lambda A\mathbf{x} = \lambda^2\mathbf{x}$$

   This shows that $\mathbf{x}$ is also an eigenvector for A^2

   f. True. Suppose a nonzero vector $\mathbf{x}$ satisfies $A\mathbf{x} = \lambda\mathbf{x}$, then left-multiply by A^{-1} to obtain $\mathbf{x} = A^{-1}(\lambda\mathbf{x}) = \lambda A^{-1}\mathbf{x}$. Since A is invertible, the eigenvalue λ is not zero. So $\lambda^{-1}\mathbf{x} = A^{-1}\mathbf{x}$, which shows that $\mathbf{x}$ is also an eigenvector of A^{-1}.

   g. False. Zero is an eigenvalue of each singular square matrix.

   h. True. By definition, an eigenvector must be nonzero.

   i. False. Let $\mathbf{v}$ be an eigenvector for A. Then $\mathbf{v}$ and $2\mathbf{v}$ are distinct eigenvectors for the same eigenvalue (because the eigenspace is a subspace), but $\mathbf{v}$ and $2\mathbf{v}$ are linearly dependent.

   j. True. This follows from Theorem 4 in Section 5.2

   k. False. Let A be the 3×3 matrix in Example 3 of Section 5.3. Then A is similar to a diagonal matrix D. The eigenvectors of D are the columns of I_3, but the eigenvectors of A are entirely different.

   l. False. Let $A = \begin{bmatrix} 2 & 0 \\ 0 & 3 \end{bmatrix}$. Then $\mathbf{e}_1 = \begin{bmatrix} 1 \\ 0 \end{bmatrix}$ and $\mathbf{e}_2 = \begin{bmatrix} 0 \\ 1 \end{bmatrix}$ are eigenvectors of A, but $\mathbf{e}_1 + \mathbf{e}_2$ is not.

   (Actually, it can be shown that if two eigenvectors of A correspond to distinct eigenvalues, then their sum cannot be an eigenvector.)

   m. False. *All* the diagonal entries of an upper triangular matrix are the eigenvalues of the matrix (Theorem 1 in Section 5.1). A diagonal entry may be zero.

   n. True. Matrices A and A^T have the same characteristic polynomial, because $\det(A^T - \lambda I) = \det(A - \lambda I)^T = \det(A - \lambda I)$, by the determinant transpose property.

   o. False. Counterexample: Let A be the 5×5 identity matrix.

   p. True. For example, let A be the matrix that rotates vectors through $\pi/2$ radians about the origin. Then $A\mathbf{x}$ is not a multiple of $\mathbf{x}$ when $\mathbf{x}$ is nonzero.

q. False. If A is a diagonal matrix with 0 on the diagonal, then the columns of A are not linearly independent.

r. True. If $A\mathbf{x} = \lambda_1\mathbf{x}$ and $A\mathbf{x} = \lambda_2\mathbf{x}$, then $\lambda_1\mathbf{x} = \lambda_2\mathbf{x}$ and $(\lambda_1 - \lambda_2)\mathbf{x} = \mathbf{0}$. If $\mathbf{x} \neq \mathbf{0}$, then λ_1 must equal λ_2.

s. False. Let A be a singular matrix that is diagonalizable. (For instance, let A be a diagonal matrix with 0 on the diagonal.) Then, by Theorem 8 in Section 5.4, the transformation $\mathbf{x} \mapsto A\mathbf{x}$ is represented by a diagonal matrix relative to a coordinate system determined by eigenvectors of A.

t. True. By definition of matrix multiplication,
$$A = AI = A[\mathbf{e}_1 \quad \mathbf{e}_2 \quad \cdots \quad \mathbf{e}_n] = [A\mathbf{e}_1 \quad A\mathbf{e}_2 \quad \cdots \quad A\mathbf{e}_n]$$
If $A\mathbf{e}_j = d_j\mathbf{e}_j$ for $j = 1, ..., n$, then A is a diagonal matrix with diagonal entries $d_1, ..., d_n$.

u. True. If $B = PDP^{-1}$, where D is a diagonal matrix, and if $A = QBQ^{-1}$, then
$A = Q(PDP^{-1})Q^{-1} = (QP)D(PQ)^{-1}$, which shows that A is diagonalizable.

v. True. Since B is invertible, AB is similar to $B(AB)B^{-1}$, which equals BA.

w. False. Having n linearly independent eigenvectors makes an $n \times n$ matrix diagonalizable (by the Diagonalization Theorem 5 in Section 5.3), but not necessarily invertible. One of the eigenvalues of the matrix could be zero.

x. True. If A is diagonalizable, then by the Diagonalization Theorem, A has n linearly independent eigenvectors $\mathbf{v}_1, ..., \mathbf{v}_n$ in $\mathbf{R}^n$. By the Basis Theorem, $\{\mathbf{v}_1, ..., \mathbf{v}_n\}$ spans $\mathbf{R}^n$. This means that each vector in $\mathbf{R}^n$ can be written as a linear combination of $\mathbf{v}_1, ..., \mathbf{v}_n$.

2. Suppose $B\mathbf{x} \neq \mathbf{0}$ and $AB\mathbf{x} = \lambda\mathbf{x}$ for some λ. Then $A(B\mathbf{x}) = \lambda\mathbf{x}$. Left-multiply each side by B and obtain $BA(B\mathbf{x}) = B(\lambda\mathbf{x}) = \lambda(B\mathbf{x})$. This equation says that $B\mathbf{x}$ is an eigenvector of BA, because $B\mathbf{x} \neq \mathbf{0}$.

3. a. Suppose $A\mathbf{x} = \lambda\mathbf{x}$, with $\mathbf{x} \neq \mathbf{0}$. Then $(5I - A)\mathbf{x} = 5\mathbf{x} - A\mathbf{x} = 5\mathbf{x} - \lambda\mathbf{x} = (5 - \lambda)\mathbf{x}$. The eigenvalue is $5 - \lambda$.

b. $(5I - 3A + A^2)\mathbf{x} = 5\mathbf{x} - 3A\mathbf{x} + A(A\mathbf{x}) = 5\mathbf{x} - 3(\lambda\mathbf{x}) + \lambda^2\mathbf{x} = (5 - 3\lambda + \lambda^2)\mathbf{x}$. The eigenvalue is $5 - 3\lambda + \lambda^2$.

4. Assume that $A\mathbf{x} = \lambda\mathbf{x}$ for some nonzero vector $\mathbf{x}$. The desired statement is true for $m = 1$, by the assumption about λ. Suppose that for some $k \geq 1$, the statement holds when $m = k$. That is, suppose that $A^k\mathbf{x} = \lambda^k\mathbf{x}$. Then $A^{k+1}\mathbf{x} = A(A^k\mathbf{x}) = A(\lambda^k\mathbf{x})$ by the induction hypothesis. Continuing,
$A^{k+1}\mathbf{x} = \lambda^k A\mathbf{x} = \lambda^{k+1}\mathbf{x}$, because $\mathbf{x}$ is an eigenvector of A corresponding to A. Since $\mathbf{x}$ is nonzero, this equation shows that λ^{k+1} is an eigenvalue of A^{k+1}, with corresponding eigenvector $\mathbf{x}$. Thus the desired statement is true when $m = k + 1$. By the principle of induction, the statement is true for each positive integer m.

5. Suppose $A\mathbf{x} = \lambda\mathbf{x}$, with $\mathbf{x} \neq \mathbf{0}$. Then
$$p(A)\mathbf{x} = (c_0 I + c_1 A + c_2 A^2 + ... + c_n A^n)\mathbf{x}$$
$$= c_0\mathbf{x} + c_1 A\mathbf{x} + c_2 A^2\mathbf{x} + ... + c_n A^n\mathbf{x}$$
$$= c_0\mathbf{x} + c_1\lambda\mathbf{x} + c_2\lambda^2\mathbf{x} + ... + c_n\lambda^n\mathbf{x} = p(\lambda)\mathbf{x}$$
So $p(\lambda)$ is an eigenvalue of $p(A)$.

6. a. If $A = PDP^{-1}$, then $A^k = PD^k P^{-1}$, and

$$B = 5I - 3A + A^2 = 5PIP^{-1} - 3PDP^{-1} + PD^2 P^{-1}$$
$$= P(5I - 3D + D^2)P^{-1}$$

Since D is diagonal, so is $5I - 3D + D^2$. Thus B is similar to a diagonal matrix.

b. $p(A) = c_0 I + c_1 PDP^{-1} + c_2 PD^2 P^{-1} + \cdots + c_n PD^n P^{-1}$

$$= P(c_0 I + c_1 D + c_2 D^2 + \cdots + c_n D^n)P^{-1}$$
$$= Pp(D)P^{-1}$$

This shows that $p(A)$ is diagonalizable, because $p(D)$ is a linear combination of diagonal matrices and hence is diagonal. In fact, because D is diagonal, it is easy to see that

$$p(D) = \begin{bmatrix} p(2) & 0 \\ 0 & p(7) \end{bmatrix}$$

7. If $A = PDP^{-1}$, then $p(A) = Pp(D)P^{-1}$, as shown in Exercise 6. If the (j, j) entry in D is λ, then the (j, j) entry in D^k is λ^k, and so the (j, j) entry in $p(D)$ is $p(\lambda)$. If p is the characteristic polynomial of A, then $p(\lambda) = 0$ for each diagonal entry of D, because these entries in D are the eigenvalues of A. Thus $p(D)$ is the zero matrix. Thus $p(A) = P \cdot 0 \cdot P^{-1} = 0$.

8. a. If λ is an eigenvalue of an $n \times n$ diagonalizable matrix A, then $A = PDP^{-1}$ for an invertible matrix P and an $n \times n$ diagonal matrix D whose diagonal entries are the eigenvalues of A. If the multiplicity of λ is n, then λ must appear in every diagonal entry of D. That is, $D = \lambda I$. In this case, $A = P(\lambda I)P^{-1} = \lambda PIP^{-1} = \lambda PP^{-1} = \lambda I$.

b. Since the matrix $A = \begin{bmatrix} 3 & 1 \\ 0 & 3 \end{bmatrix}$ is triangular, its eigenvalues are on the diagonal. Thus 3 is an eigenvalue with multiplicity 2. If the 2×2 matrix A were diagonalizable, then A would be $3I$, by part (a). This is not the case, so A is not diagonalizable.

9. If $I - A$ were not invertible, then the equation $(I - A)\mathbf{x} = \mathbf{0}$ would have a nontrivial solution $\mathbf{x}$. Then $\mathbf{x} - A\mathbf{x} = \mathbf{0}$ and $A\mathbf{x} = 1 \cdot \mathbf{x}$, which shows that A would have 1 as an eigenvalue. This cannot happen if all the eigenvalues are less than 1 in magnitude. So $I - A$ must be invertible.

10. To show that A^k tends to the zero matrix, it suffices to show that each column of A^k can be made as close to the zero vector as desired by taking k sufficiently large. The jth column of A is $A\mathbf{e}_j$, where $\mathbf{e}_j$ is the jth column of the identity matrix. Since A is diagonalizable, there is a basis for $\mathbb{R}^n$ consisting of eigenvectors $\mathbf{v}_1, \ldots, \mathbf{v}_n$, corresponding to eigenvalues $\lambda_1, \ldots, \lambda_n$. So there exist scalars $c_1, \ldots, c_n$, such that

$$\mathbf{e}_j = c_1 \mathbf{v}_1 + \cdots + c_n \mathbf{v}_n \quad \text{(an eigenvector decomposition of } \mathbf{e}_j\text{)}$$

Then, for $k = 1, 2, \ldots$,

$$A^k \mathbf{e}_j = c_1 (\lambda_1)^k \mathbf{v}_1 + \cdots + c_n (\lambda_n)^k \mathbf{v}_n \quad (*)$$

If the eigenvalues are all less than 1 in absolute value, then their kth powers all tend to zero. So $(*)$ shows that $A^k \mathbf{e}_j$ tends to the zero vector, as desired.

11. a. Take $\mathbf{x}$ in H. Then $\mathbf{x} = c\mathbf{u}$ for some scalar c. So $A\mathbf{x} = A(c\mathbf{u}) = c(A\mathbf{u}) = c(\lambda\mathbf{u}) = (c\lambda)\mathbf{u}$, which shows that $A\mathbf{x}$ is in H.

b. Let $\mathbf{x}$ be a nonzero vector in K. Since K is one-dimensional, K must be the set of all scalar multiples of $\mathbf{x}$. If K is invariant under A, then $A\mathbf{x}$ is in K and hence $A\mathbf{x}$ is a multiple of $\mathbf{x}$. Thus $\mathbf{x}$ is an eigenvector of A.

12. Let U and V be echelon forms of A and B, obtained with r and s row interchanges, respectively, and no scaling. Then $\det A = (-1)^r \det U$ and $\det B = (-1)^s \det V$

Using first the row operations that reduce A to U, we can reduce G to a matrix of the form $G' = \begin{bmatrix} U & Y \\ 0 & B \end{bmatrix}$.

Then, using the row operations that reduce B to V, we can further reduce G' to $G'' = \begin{bmatrix} U & Y \\ 0 & V \end{bmatrix}$. There

will be $r + s$ row interchanges, and so $\det G = \det \begin{bmatrix} A & X \\ 0 & B \end{bmatrix} = (-1)^{r+s} \det \begin{bmatrix} U & Y \\ 0 & V \end{bmatrix}$ Since $\begin{bmatrix} U & Y \\ 0 & V \end{bmatrix}$ is

upper triangular, its determinant equals the product of the diagonal entries, and since U and V are upper triangular, this product also equals $(\det U)(\det V)$. Thus

$\det G = (-1)^{r+s}(\det U)(\det V) = (\det A)(\det B)$

For any scalar λ, the matrix $G - \lambda I$ has the same partitioned form as G, with $A - \lambda I$ and $B - \lambda I$ as its diagonal blocks. (Here I represents various identity matrices of appropriate sizes.) Hence the result about $\det G$ shows that $\det(G - \lambda I) = \det(A - \lambda I) \cdot \det(B - \lambda I)$

13. By Exercise 12, the eigenvalues of A are the eigenvalues of the matrix $[3]$ together with the eigenvalues

of $\begin{bmatrix} 5 & -2 \\ -4 & 3 \end{bmatrix}$. The only eigenvalue of $[3]$ is 3, while the eigenvalues of $\begin{bmatrix} 5 & -2 \\ -4 & 3 \end{bmatrix}$ are 1 and 7. Thus the

eigenvalues of A are 1, 3, and 7.

14. By Exercise 12, the eigenvalues of A are the eigenvalues of the matrix $\begin{bmatrix} 1 & 5 \\ 2 & 4 \end{bmatrix}$ together with the

eigenvalues of $\begin{bmatrix} -7 & -4 \\ 3 & 1 \end{bmatrix}$. The eigenvalues of $\begin{bmatrix} 1 & 5 \\ 2 & 4 \end{bmatrix}$ are -1 and 6, while the eigenvalues of

$\begin{bmatrix} -7 & -4 \\ 3 & 1 \end{bmatrix}$ are -5 and -1. Thus the eigenvalues of A are $-1, -5,$ and 6, and the eigenvalue -1 has

multiplicity 2.

15. Replace A by $A - \lambda$ in the determinant formula from Exercise 16 in Chapter 3 Supplementary Exercises.

$\det(A - \lambda I) = (a - b - \lambda)^{n-1}[a - \lambda + (n-1)b]$

This determinant is zero only if $a - b - \lambda = 0$ or $a - \lambda + (n-1)b = 0$. Thus λ is an eigenvalue of A if and only if $\lambda = a - b$ or $\lambda = a + (n-1)$. From the formula for $\det(A - \lambda I)$ above, the algebraic multiplicity is $n - 1$ for $a - b$ and 1 for $a + (n-1)b$.

16. The 3×3 matrix has eigenvalues $1 - 2$ and $1 + (2)(2)$, that is, -1 and 5. The eigenvalues of the 5×5 matrix are $7 - 3$ and $7 + (4)(3)$, that is 4 and 19.

17. Note that $\det(A - \lambda I) = (a_{11} - \lambda)(a_{22} - \lambda) - a_{12}a_{21} = \lambda^2 - (a_{11} + a_{22})\lambda + (a_{11}a_{22} - a_{12}a_{21})$

$= \lambda^2 - (\text{tr } A)\lambda + \det A,$ and use the quadratic formula to solve the characteristic equation:

$$\lambda = \frac{\text{tr } A \pm \sqrt{(\text{tr } A)^2 - 4\det A}}{2}$$

The eigenvalues are both real if and only if the discriminant is nonnegative, that is, $(\text{tr } A)^2 - 4\det A \geq 0$.

This inequality simplifies to $(\text{tr } A)^2 \geq 4\det A$ and $\left(\dfrac{trA}{2}\right)^2 \geq \det A$.

18. The eigenvalues of A are 1 and .6. Use this to factor A and A^k.

$$A = \begin{bmatrix} -1 & -3 \\ 2 & 2 \end{bmatrix}\begin{bmatrix} 1 & 0 \\ 0 & .6 \end{bmatrix}\frac{1}{4}\begin{bmatrix} 2 & 3 \\ -2 & -1 \end{bmatrix}$$

$$A^k = \begin{bmatrix} -1 & -3 \\ 2 & 2 \end{bmatrix}\begin{bmatrix} 1^k & 0 \\ 0 & .6^k \end{bmatrix}\cdot\frac{1}{4}\begin{bmatrix} 2 & 3 \\ -2 & -1 \end{bmatrix}$$

$$= \frac{1}{4}\begin{bmatrix} -1 & -3 \\ 2 & 2 \end{bmatrix}\begin{bmatrix} 2 & 3 \\ -2\cdot(.6)^k & -(.6)^k \end{bmatrix}$$

$$= \frac{1}{4}\begin{bmatrix} -2+6(.6)^k & -3+3(.6)^k \\ 4-4(.6)^k & 6-2(.6)^k \end{bmatrix}$$

$$\rightarrow \frac{1}{4}\begin{bmatrix} -2 & -3 \\ 4 & 6 \end{bmatrix} \text{ as } k \rightarrow \infty$$

19. $C_p = \begin{bmatrix} 0 & 1 \\ -6 & 5 \end{bmatrix}; \det(C_p - \lambda I) = 6 - 5\lambda + \lambda^2 = p(\lambda)$

20. $C_p = \begin{bmatrix} 0 & 1 & 0 \\ 0 & 0 & 1 \\ 24 & -26 & 9 \end{bmatrix};$

$\det(C_p - \lambda I) = 24 - 26\lambda + 9\lambda^2 - \lambda^3 = p(\lambda)$

21. If p is a polynomial of order 2, then a calculation such as in Exercise 19 shows that the characteristic polynomial of C_p is $p(\lambda) = (-1)^2 p(\lambda)$, so the result is true for $n = 2$. Suppose the result is true for $n = k$ for some $k \geq 2$, and consider a polynomial p of degree $k+1$. Then expanding $\det(C_p - \lambda I)$ by cofactors down the first column, the determinant of $C_p - \lambda I$ equals

$$(-\lambda)\det\begin{bmatrix} -\lambda & 1 & \cdots & 0 \\ \vdots & & & \vdots \\ 0 & & & 1 \\ -a_1 & -a_2 & \cdots & -a_k - \lambda \end{bmatrix} + (-1)^{k+1}a_0$$

The $k \times k$ matrix shown is $C_q - \lambda I$, where $q(t) = a_1 + a_2 t + \cdots + a_k t^{k-1} + t^k$. By the induction assumption, the determinant of $C_q - \lambda I$ is $(-1)^k q(\lambda)$. Thus

$$\det(C_p - \lambda I) = (-1)^{k+1} a_0 + (-\lambda)(-1)^k q(\lambda)$$
$$= (-1)^{k+1} [a_0 + \lambda(a_1 + \cdots + a_k \lambda^{k-1} + \lambda^k)]$$
$$= (-1)^{k+1} p(\lambda)$$

So the formula holds for $n = k + 1$ when it holds for $n = k$. By the principle of induction, the formula for $\det(C_p - \lambda I)$ is true for all $n \geq 2$.

22. **a.** $C_p = \begin{bmatrix} 0 & 1 & 0 \\ 0 & 0 & 1 \\ -a_0 & -a_1 & -a_2 \end{bmatrix}$

b. Since λ is a zero of p, $a_0 + a_1\lambda + a_2\lambda^2 + \lambda^3 = 0$ and $-a_0 - a_1\lambda - a_2\lambda^2 = \lambda^3$. Thus

$$C_p \begin{bmatrix} 1 \\ \lambda \\ \lambda^2 \end{bmatrix} = \begin{bmatrix} \lambda \\ \lambda^2 \\ -a_0 - a_1\lambda - a_2\lambda^2 \end{bmatrix} = \begin{bmatrix} \lambda \\ \lambda^2 \\ \lambda^3 \end{bmatrix}$$

That is, $C_p(1, \lambda, \lambda^2) = \lambda(1, \lambda, \lambda^2)$, which shows that $(1, \lambda, \lambda^2)$ is an eigenvector of C_p corresponding to the eigenvalue λ.

23. From Exercise 22, the columns of the Vandermonde matrix V are eigenvectors of C_p, corresponding to the eigenvalues $\lambda_1, \lambda_2, \lambda_3$ (the roots of the polynomial p). Since these eigenvalues are distinct, the eigenvectors from a linearly independent set, by Theorem 2 in Section 5.1. Thus V has linearly independent columns and hence is invertible, by the Invertible Matrix Theorem. Finally, since the columns of V are eigenvectors of C_p, the Diagonalization Theorem (Theorem 5 in Section 5.3) shows that $V^{-1} C_p V$ is diagonal.

24. **[M]** The MATLAB command `roots (p)` requires as input a row vector p whose entries are the coefficients of a polynomial, with the highest order coefficient listed first. MATLAB constructs a companion matrix C_p whose characteristic polynomial is p, so the roots of p are the eigenvalues of C_p. The numerical values of the eigenvalues (roots) are found by the same QR algorithm used by the command `eig(A)`.

25. **[M]** The MATLAB command `[P  D] = eig(A)` produces a matrix P, whose condition number is 1.6×10^8, and a diagonal matrix D, whose entries are *almost* 2, 2, 1. However, the exact eigenvalues of A are 2, 2, 1, and A is not diagonalizable.

26. **[M]** This matrix may cause the same sort of trouble as the matrix in Exercise 25. A matrix program that computes eigenvalues by an interative process may indicate that A has four distinct eigenvalues, all close to zero. However, the only eigenvalue is 0, with multiplicity 4, because $A^4 = 0$.

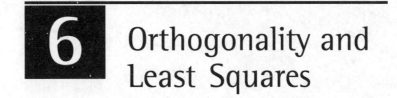

6 Orthogonality and Least Squares

6.1 SOLUTIONS

Notes: The first half of this section is computational and is easily learned. The second half concerns the concepts of orthogonality and orthogonal complements, which are essential for later work. Theorem 3 is an important general fact, but is needed only for Supplementary Exercise 13 at the end of the chapter and in Section 7.4. The optional material on angles is not used later. Exercises 27–31 concern facts used later.

1. Since $\mathbf{u} = \begin{bmatrix} -1 \\ 2 \end{bmatrix}$ and $\mathbf{v} = \begin{bmatrix} 4 \\ 6 \end{bmatrix}$, $\mathbf{u} \cdot \mathbf{u} = (-1)^2 + 2^2 = 5$, $\mathbf{v} \cdot \mathbf{u} = 4(-1) + 6(2) = 8$, and $\dfrac{\mathbf{v} \cdot \mathbf{u}}{\mathbf{u} \cdot \mathbf{u}} = \dfrac{8}{5}$.

2. Since $\mathbf{w} = \begin{bmatrix} 3 \\ -1 \\ -5 \end{bmatrix}$ and $\mathbf{x} = \begin{bmatrix} 6 \\ -2 \\ 3 \end{bmatrix}$, $\mathbf{w} \cdot \mathbf{w} = 3^2 + (-1)^2 + (-5)^2 = 35$, $\mathbf{x} \cdot \mathbf{w} = 6(3) + (-2)(-1) + 3(-5) = 5$, and

   $\dfrac{\mathbf{x} \cdot \mathbf{w}}{\mathbf{w} \cdot \mathbf{w}} = \dfrac{5}{35} = \dfrac{1}{7}$.

3. Since $\mathbf{w} = \begin{bmatrix} 3 \\ -1 \\ -5 \end{bmatrix}$, $\mathbf{w} \cdot \mathbf{w} = 3^2 + (-1)^2 + (-5)^2 = 35$, and $\dfrac{1}{\mathbf{w} \cdot \mathbf{w}} \mathbf{w} = \begin{bmatrix} 3/35 \\ -1/35 \\ -1/7 \end{bmatrix}$.

4. Since $\mathbf{u} = \begin{bmatrix} -1 \\ 2 \end{bmatrix}$, $\mathbf{u} \cdot \mathbf{u} = (-1)^2 + 2^2 = 5$ and $\dfrac{1}{\mathbf{u} \cdot \mathbf{u}} \mathbf{u} = \begin{bmatrix} -1/5 \\ 2/5 \end{bmatrix}$.

5. Since $\mathbf{u} = \begin{bmatrix} -1 \\ 2 \end{bmatrix}$ and $\mathbf{v} = \begin{bmatrix} 4 \\ 6 \end{bmatrix}$, $\mathbf{u} \cdot \mathbf{v} = (-1)(4) + 2(6) = 8$, $\mathbf{v} \cdot \mathbf{v} = 4^2 + 6^2 = 52$, and

   $\left(\dfrac{\mathbf{u} \cdot \mathbf{v}}{\mathbf{v} \cdot \mathbf{v}} \right) \mathbf{v} = \dfrac{2}{13} \begin{bmatrix} 4 \\ 6 \end{bmatrix} = \begin{bmatrix} 8/13 \\ 12/13 \end{bmatrix}$.

6. Since $\mathbf{x} = \begin{bmatrix} 6 \\ -2 \\ 3 \end{bmatrix}$ and $\mathbf{w} = \begin{bmatrix} 3 \\ -1 \\ -5 \end{bmatrix}$, $\mathbf{x} \cdot \mathbf{w} = 6(3) + (-2)(-1) + 3(-5) = 5$, $\mathbf{x} \cdot \mathbf{x} = 6^2 + (-2)^2 + 3^2 = 49$, and

   $\left(\dfrac{\mathbf{x} \cdot \mathbf{w}}{\mathbf{x} \cdot \mathbf{x}} \right) \mathbf{x} = \dfrac{5}{49} \begin{bmatrix} 6 \\ -2 \\ 3 \end{bmatrix} = \begin{bmatrix} 30/49 \\ -10/49 \\ 15/49 \end{bmatrix}$.

7. Since $\mathbf{w} = \begin{bmatrix} 3 \\ -1 \\ -5 \end{bmatrix}$, $\|\mathbf{w}\| = \sqrt{\mathbf{w} \cdot \mathbf{w}} = \sqrt{3^2 + (-1)^2 + (-5)^2} = \sqrt{35}$.

8. Since $\mathbf{x} = \begin{bmatrix} 6 \\ -2 \\ 3 \end{bmatrix}$, $\|\mathbf{x}\| = \sqrt{\mathbf{x} \cdot \mathbf{x}} = \sqrt{6^2 + (-2)^2 + 3^2} = \sqrt{49} = 7$.

9. A unit vector in the direction of the given vector is

$$\frac{1}{\sqrt{(-30)^2 + 40^2}} \begin{bmatrix} -30 \\ 40 \end{bmatrix} = \frac{1}{50} \begin{bmatrix} -30 \\ 40 \end{bmatrix} = \begin{bmatrix} -3/5 \\ 4/5 \end{bmatrix}$$

10. A unit vector in the direction of the given vector is

$$\frac{1}{\sqrt{(-6)^2 + 4^2 + (-3)^2}} \begin{bmatrix} -6 \\ 4 \\ -3 \end{bmatrix} = \frac{1}{\sqrt{61}} \begin{bmatrix} -6 \\ 4 \\ -3 \end{bmatrix} = \begin{bmatrix} -6/\sqrt{61} \\ 4/\sqrt{61} \\ -3\sqrt{61} \end{bmatrix}$$

11. A unit vector in the direction of the given vector is

$$\frac{1}{\sqrt{(7/4)^2 + (1/2)^2 + 1^2}} \begin{bmatrix} 7/4 \\ 1/2 \\ 1 \end{bmatrix} = \frac{1}{\sqrt{69/16}} \begin{bmatrix} 7/4 \\ 1/2 \\ 1 \end{bmatrix} = \begin{bmatrix} 7/\sqrt{69} \\ 2/\sqrt{69} \\ 4/\sqrt{69} \end{bmatrix}$$

12. A unit vector in the direction of the given vector is

$$\frac{1}{\sqrt{(8/3)^2 + 2^2}} \begin{bmatrix} 8/3 \\ 2 \end{bmatrix} = \frac{1}{\sqrt{100/9}} \begin{bmatrix} 8/3 \\ 2 \end{bmatrix} = \begin{bmatrix} 4/5 \\ 3/5 \end{bmatrix}$$

13. Since $\mathbf{x} = \begin{bmatrix} 10 \\ -3 \end{bmatrix}$ and $\mathbf{y} = \begin{bmatrix} -1 \\ -5 \end{bmatrix}$, $\|\mathbf{x} - \mathbf{y}\|^2 = [10 - (-1)]^2 + [-3 - (-5)]^2 = 125$ and $\text{dist}(\mathbf{x}, \mathbf{y}) = \sqrt{125} = 5\sqrt{5}$.

14. Since $\mathbf{u} = \begin{bmatrix} 0 \\ -5 \\ 2 \end{bmatrix}$ and $\mathbf{z} = \begin{bmatrix} -4 \\ -1 \\ 8 \end{bmatrix}$, $\|\mathbf{u} - \mathbf{z}\|^2 = [0 - (-4)]^2 + [-5 - (-1)]^2 + [2 - 8]^2 = 68$ and

$\text{dist}(\mathbf{u}, \mathbf{z}) = \sqrt{68} = 2\sqrt{17}$.

15. Since $\mathbf{a} \cdot \mathbf{b} = 8(-2) + (-5)(-3) = -1 \neq 0$, $\mathbf{a}$ and $\mathbf{b}$ are not orthogonal.

16. Since $\mathbf{u} \cdot \mathbf{v} = 12(2) + (3)(-3) + (-5)(3) = 0$, $\mathbf{u}$ and $\mathbf{v}$ are orthogonal.

17. Since $\mathbf{u} \cdot \mathbf{v} = 3(-4) + 2(1) + (-5)(-2) + 0(6) = 0$, $\mathbf{u}$ and $\mathbf{v}$ are orthogonal.

18. Since $\mathbf{y} \cdot \mathbf{z} = (-3)(1) + 7(-8) + 4(15) + 0(-7) = 1 \neq 0$, $\mathbf{y}$ and $\mathbf{z}$ are not orthogonal.

19. **a.** True. See the definition of $\|\mathbf{v}\|$.

   b. True. See Theorem 1(c).

   c. True. See the discussion of Figure 5.

d. False. Counterexample: $\begin{bmatrix} 1 & 1 \\ 0 & 0 \end{bmatrix}$.

e. True. See the box following Example 6.

20. **a**. True. See Example 1 and Theorem 1(a).

b. False. The absolute value sign is missing. See the box before Example 2.

c. True. See the defintion of orthogonal complement.

d. True. See the Pythagorean Theorem.

e. True. See Theorem 3.

21. Theorem 1(b):

$$(\mathbf{u} + \mathbf{v}) \cdot \mathbf{w} = (\mathbf{u} + \mathbf{v})^T \mathbf{w} = (\mathbf{u}^T + \mathbf{v}^T)\mathbf{w} = \mathbf{u}^T\mathbf{w} + \mathbf{v}^T\mathbf{w} = \mathbf{u} \cdot \mathbf{w} + \mathbf{v} \cdot \mathbf{w}$$

The second and third equalities used Theorems 3(b) and 2(c), respectively, from Section 2.1.

Theorem 1(c):

$$(c\mathbf{u}) \cdot \mathbf{v} = (c\mathbf{u})^T \mathbf{v} = c(\mathbf{u}^T \mathbf{v}) = c(\mathbf{u} \cdot \mathbf{v})$$

The second and third equalities used Theorems 3(c) and 2(d), respectively, from Section 2.1.

22. Since $\mathbf{u} \cdot \mathbf{u}$ is the sum of the squares of the entries in $\mathbf{u}$, $\mathbf{u} \cdot \mathbf{u} \geq 0$. The sum of squares of numbers is zero if and only if all the numbers are themselves zero.

23. One computes that $\mathbf{u} \cdot \mathbf{v} = 2(-7) + (-5)(-4) + (-1)6 = 0$, $\|\mathbf{u}\|^2 = \mathbf{u} \cdot \mathbf{u} = 2^2 + (-5)^2 + (-1)^2 = 30$, $\|\mathbf{v}\|^2 = \mathbf{v} \cdot \mathbf{v} = (-7)^2 + (-4)^2 + 6^2 = 101$, and $\|\mathbf{u} + \mathbf{v}\|^2 = (\mathbf{u} + \mathbf{v}) \cdot (\mathbf{u} + \mathbf{v}) = (2 + (-7))^2 + (-5 + (-4))^2 + (-1 + 6)^2 = 131$.

24. One computes that

$$\|\mathbf{u} + \mathbf{v}\|^2 = (\mathbf{u} + \mathbf{v}) \cdot (\mathbf{u} + \mathbf{v}) = \mathbf{u} \cdot \mathbf{u} + 2\mathbf{u} \cdot \mathbf{v} + \mathbf{v} \cdot \mathbf{v} = \|\mathbf{u}\|^2 + 2\mathbf{u} \cdot \mathbf{v} + \|\mathbf{v}\|^2$$

and

$$\|\mathbf{u} - \mathbf{v}\|^2 = (\mathbf{u} - \mathbf{v}) \cdot (\mathbf{u} - \mathbf{v}) = \mathbf{u} \cdot \mathbf{u} - 2\mathbf{u} \cdot \mathbf{v} + \mathbf{v} \cdot \mathbf{v} = \|\mathbf{u}\|^2 - 2\mathbf{u} \cdot \mathbf{v} + \|\mathbf{v}\|^2$$

so

$$\|\mathbf{u} + \mathbf{v}\|^2 + \|\mathbf{u} - \mathbf{v}\|^2 = \|\mathbf{u}\|^2 + 2\mathbf{u} \cdot \mathbf{v} + \|\mathbf{v}\|^2 + \|\mathbf{u}\|^2 - 2\mathbf{u} \cdot \mathbf{v} + \|\mathbf{v}\|^2 = 2\|\mathbf{u}\|^2 + 2\|\mathbf{v}\|^2$$

25. When $\mathbf{v} = \begin{bmatrix} a \\ b \end{bmatrix}$, the set H of all vectors $\begin{bmatrix} x \\ y \end{bmatrix}$ that are orthogonal to $\mathbf{v}$ is the subspace of vectors whose entries satisfy $ax + by = 0$. If $a \neq 0$, then $x = -(b/a)y$ with y a free variable, and H is a line through the origin. A natural choice for a basis for H in this case is $\left\{ \begin{bmatrix} -b \\ a \end{bmatrix} \right\}$. If $a = 0$ and $b \neq 0$, then $by = 0$. Since $b \neq 0$, $y = 0$ and x is a free variable. The subspace H is again a line through the origin. A natural choice for a basis for H in this case is $\left\{ \begin{bmatrix} 1 \\ 0 \end{bmatrix} \right\}$, but $\left\{ \begin{bmatrix} -b \\ a \end{bmatrix} \right\}$ is still a basis for H since $a = 0$ and $b \neq 0$. If $a = 0$ and $b = 0$, then $H = \mathbb{R}^2$ since the equation $0x + 0y = 0$ places no restrictions on x or y.

26. Theorem 2 in Chapter 4 may be used to show that W is a subspace of $\mathbb{R}^3$, because W is the null space of the 1×3 matrix $\mathbf{u}^T$. Geometrically, W is a plane through the origin.

27. If $\mathbf{y}$ is orthogonal to $\mathbf{u}$ and $\mathbf{v}$, then $\mathbf{y} \cdot \mathbf{u} = \mathbf{y} \cdot \mathbf{v} = 0$, and hence by a property of the inner product, $\mathbf{y} \cdot (\mathbf{u} + \mathbf{v}) = \mathbf{y} \cdot \mathbf{u} + \mathbf{y} \cdot \mathbf{v} = 0 + 0 = 0$. Thus $\mathbf{y}$ is orthogonal to $\mathbf{u} + \mathbf{v}$.

28. An arbitrary $\mathbf{w}$ in Span$\{\mathbf{u}, \mathbf{v}\}$ has the form $\mathbf{w} = c_1\mathbf{u} + c_2\mathbf{v}$. If $\mathbf{y}$ is orthogonal to $\mathbf{u}$ and $\mathbf{v}$, then $\mathbf{u} \cdot \mathbf{y} = \mathbf{v} \cdot \mathbf{y} = 0$. By Theorem 1(b) and 1(c),
$$\mathbf{w} \cdot \mathbf{y} = (c_1\mathbf{u} + c_2\mathbf{v}) \cdot \mathbf{y} = c_1(\mathbf{u} \cdot \mathbf{y}) + c_2(\mathbf{v} \cdot \mathbf{y}) = 0 + 0 = 0$$

29. A typical vector in W has the form $\mathbf{w} = c_1\mathbf{v}_1 + \ldots + c_p\mathbf{v}_p$. If $\mathbf{x}$ is orthogonal to each $\mathbf{v}_j$, then by Theorems 1(b) and 1(c),
$$\mathbf{w} \cdot \mathbf{x} = (c_1\mathbf{v}_1 + \ldots + c_p\mathbf{v}_p) \cdot \mathbf{y} = c_1(\mathbf{v}_1 \cdot \mathbf{x}) + \ldots + c_p(\mathbf{v}_p \cdot \mathbf{x}) = 0$$

So $\mathbf{x}$ is orthogonal to each $\mathbf{w}$ in W.

30. a. If $\mathbf{z}$ is in $W^{\perp}$, $\mathbf{u}$ is in W, and c is any scalar, then $(c\mathbf{z}) \cdot \mathbf{u} = c(\mathbf{z} \cdot \mathbf{u}) - c0 = 0$. Since $\mathbf{u}$ is any element of W, $c\mathbf{z}$ is in $W^{\perp}$.

b. Let $\mathbf{z}_1$ and $\mathbf{z}_2$ be in $W^{\perp}$. Then for any $\mathbf{u}$ in W, $(\mathbf{z}_1 + \mathbf{z}_2) \cdot \mathbf{u} = \mathbf{z}_1 \cdot \mathbf{u} + \mathbf{z}_2 \cdot \mathbf{u} = 0 + 0 = 0$. Thus $\mathbf{z}_1 + \mathbf{z}_2$ is in $W^{\perp}$.

c. Since $\mathbf{0}$ is orthogonal to every vector, $\mathbf{0}$ is in $W^{\perp}$. Thus $W^{\perp}$ is a subspace.

31. Suppose that $\mathbf{x}$ is in W and $W^{\perp}$. Since $\mathbf{x}$ is in $W^{\perp}$, $\mathbf{x}$ is orthogonal to every vector in W, including $\mathbf{x}$ itself. So $\mathbf{x} \cdot \mathbf{x} = 0$, which happens only when $\mathbf{x} = \mathbf{0}$.

32. [M]

a. One computes that $\|\mathbf{a}_1\| = \|\mathbf{a}_2\| = \|\mathbf{a}_3\| = \|\mathbf{a}_4\| = 1$ and that $\mathbf{a}_i \cdot \mathbf{a}_j = 0$ for $i \neq j$.

b. Answers will vary, but it should be that $\|A\mathbf{u}\| = \|\mathbf{u}\|$ and $\|A\mathbf{v}\| = \|\mathbf{v}\|$.

c. Answers will again vary, but the cosines should be equal.

d. A conjecture is that multiplying by A does not change the lengths of vectors or the angles between vectors.

33. [M] Answers to the calculations will vary, but will demonstrate that the mapping $\mathbf{x} \mapsto T(\mathbf{x}) = \left(\dfrac{\mathbf{x} \cdot \mathbf{v}}{\mathbf{v} \cdot \mathbf{v}} \right) \mathbf{v}$

(for $\mathbf{v} \neq \mathbf{0}$) is a linear transformation. To confirm this, let $\mathbf{x}$ and $\mathbf{y}$ be in $\mathbb{R}^n$, and let c be any scalar. Then
$$T(\mathbf{x} + \mathbf{y}) = \left(\frac{(\mathbf{x} + \mathbf{y}) \cdot \mathbf{v}}{\mathbf{v} \cdot \mathbf{v}} \right) \mathbf{v} = \left(\frac{(\mathbf{x} \cdot \mathbf{v}) + (\mathbf{y} \cdot \mathbf{v})}{\mathbf{v} \cdot \mathbf{v}} \right) \mathbf{v} = \left(\frac{\mathbf{x} \cdot \mathbf{v}}{\mathbf{v} \cdot \mathbf{v}} \right) \mathbf{v} + \left(\frac{\mathbf{y} \cdot \mathbf{v}}{\mathbf{v} \cdot \mathbf{v}} \right) \mathbf{v} = T(\mathbf{x}) + T(\mathbf{y})$$

and
$$T(c\mathbf{x}) = \left(\frac{(c\mathbf{x}) \cdot \mathbf{v}}{\mathbf{v} \cdot \mathbf{v}} \right) \mathbf{v} = \left(\frac{c(\mathbf{x} \cdot \mathbf{v})}{\mathbf{v} \cdot \mathbf{v}} \right) \mathbf{v} = c \left(\frac{\mathbf{x} \cdot \mathbf{v}}{\mathbf{v} \cdot \mathbf{v}} \right) \mathbf{v} = cT(\mathbf{x})$$

34. [M] One finds that
$$N = \begin{bmatrix} -5 & 1 \\ -1 & 4 \\ 1 & 0 \\ 0 & -1 \\ 0 & 3 \end{bmatrix}, R = \begin{bmatrix} 1 & 0 & 5 & 0 & -1/3 \\ 0 & 1 & 1 & 0 & -4/3 \\ 0 & 0 & 0 & 1 & 1/3 \end{bmatrix}$$

The row-column rule for computing RN produces the 3×2 zero matrix, which shows that the rows of R are orthogonal to the columns of N. This is expected by Theorem 3 since each row of R is in Row A and each column of N is in Nul A.

6.2   SOLUTIONS

Notes: The nonsquare matrices in Theorems 6 and 7 are needed for the QR factorizarion in Section 6.4. It is important to emphasize that the term *orthogonal matrix* applies only to certain *square* matrices. The subsection on orthogonal projections not only sets the stage for the general case in Section 6.3, it also provides what is needed for the orthogonal diagonalization exercises in Section 7.1, because none of the eigenspaces there have dimension greater than 2. For this reason, the Gram-Schmidt process (Section 6.4) is not really needed in Chapter 7. Exercises 13 and 14 prepare for Section 6.3.

1. Since $\begin{bmatrix} -1 \\ 4 \\ -3 \end{bmatrix} \cdot \begin{bmatrix} 3 \\ -4 \\ -7 \end{bmatrix} = 2 \neq 0$, the set is not orthogonal.

2. Since $\begin{bmatrix} 1 \\ -2 \\ 1 \end{bmatrix} \cdot \begin{bmatrix} 0 \\ 1 \\ 2 \end{bmatrix} = \begin{bmatrix} 1 \\ -2 \\ 1 \end{bmatrix} \cdot \begin{bmatrix} -5 \\ -2 \\ 1 \end{bmatrix} = \begin{bmatrix} 0 \\ 1 \\ 2 \end{bmatrix} \cdot \begin{bmatrix} -5 \\ -2 \\ 1 \end{bmatrix} = 0$, the set is orthogonal.

3. Since $\begin{bmatrix} -6 \\ -3 \\ 9 \end{bmatrix} \cdot \begin{bmatrix} 3 \\ 1 \\ -1 \end{bmatrix} = -30 \neq 0$, the set is not orthogonal.

4. Since $\begin{bmatrix} 2 \\ -5 \\ -3 \end{bmatrix} \cdot \begin{bmatrix} 0 \\ 0 \\ 0 \end{bmatrix} = \begin{bmatrix} 2 \\ -5 \\ -3 \end{bmatrix} \cdot \begin{bmatrix} 4 \\ -2 \\ 6 \end{bmatrix} = \begin{bmatrix} 0 \\ 0 \\ 0 \end{bmatrix} \cdot \begin{bmatrix} 4 \\ -2 \\ 6 \end{bmatrix} = 0$, the set is orthogonal.

5. Since $\begin{bmatrix} 3 \\ -2 \\ 1 \\ 3 \end{bmatrix} \cdot \begin{bmatrix} -1 \\ 3 \\ -3 \\ 4 \end{bmatrix} = \begin{bmatrix} 3 \\ -2 \\ 1 \\ 3 \end{bmatrix} \cdot \begin{bmatrix} 3 \\ 8 \\ 7 \\ 0 \end{bmatrix} = \begin{bmatrix} -1 \\ 3 \\ -3 \\ 4 \end{bmatrix} \cdot \begin{bmatrix} 3 \\ 8 \\ 7 \\ 0 \end{bmatrix} = 0$, the set is orthogonal.

6. Since $\begin{bmatrix} -4 \\ 1 \\ -3 \\ 8 \end{bmatrix} \cdot \begin{bmatrix} 3 \\ 3 \\ 5 \\ -1 \end{bmatrix} = -32 \neq 0$, the set is not orthogonal.

7. Since $\mathbf{u}_1 \cdot \mathbf{u}_2 = 12 - 12 = 0$, $\{\mathbf{u}_1, \mathbf{u}_2\}$ is an orthogonal set. Since the vectors are non-zero, $\mathbf{u}_1$ and $\mathbf{u}_2$ are linearly independent by Theorem 4. Two such vectors in $\mathbb{R}^2$ automatically form a basis for $\mathbb{R}^2$. So $\{\mathbf{u}_1, \mathbf{u}_2\}$ is an orthogonal basis for $\mathbb{R}^2$. By Theorem 5,

$$\mathbf{x} = \frac{\mathbf{x} \cdot \mathbf{u}_1}{\mathbf{u}_1 \cdot \mathbf{u}_1} \mathbf{u}_1 + \frac{\mathbf{x} \cdot \mathbf{u}_2}{\mathbf{u}_2 \cdot \mathbf{u}_2} \mathbf{u}_2 = 3\mathbf{u}_1 + \frac{1}{2} \mathbf{u}_2$$

8. Since $\mathbf{u}_1 \cdot \mathbf{u}_2 = -6 + 6 = 0$, $\{\mathbf{u}_1, \mathbf{u}_2\}$ is an orthogonal set. Since the vectors are non-zero, $\mathbf{u}_1$ and $\mathbf{u}_2$ are linearly independent by Theorem 4. Two such vectors in $\mathbb{R}^2$ automatically form a basis for $\mathbb{R}^2$. So $\{\mathbf{u}_1, \mathbf{u}_2\}$ is an orthogonal basis for $\mathbb{R}^2$. By Theorem 5,

$$\mathbf{x} = \frac{\mathbf{x} \cdot \mathbf{u}_1}{\mathbf{u}_1 \cdot \mathbf{u}_1}\mathbf{u}_1 + \frac{\mathbf{x} \cdot \mathbf{u}_2}{\mathbf{u}_2 \cdot \mathbf{u}_2}\mathbf{u}_2 = -\frac{3}{2}\mathbf{u}_1 + \frac{3}{4}\mathbf{u}_2$$

9. Since $\mathbf{u}_1 \cdot \mathbf{u}_2 = \mathbf{u}_1 \cdot \mathbf{u}_3 = \mathbf{u}_2 \cdot \mathbf{u}_3 = 0$, $\{\mathbf{u}_1, \mathbf{u}_2, \mathbf{u}_3\}$ is an orthogonal set. Since the vectors are non-zero, $\mathbf{u}_1$, $\mathbf{u}_2$, and $\mathbf{u}_3$ are linearly independent by Theorem 4. Three such vectors in $\mathbb{R}^3$ automatically form a basis for $\mathbb{R}^3$. So $\{\mathbf{u}_1, \mathbf{u}_2, \mathbf{u}_3\}$ is an orthogonal basis for $\mathbb{R}^3$. By Theorem 5,

$$\mathbf{x} = \frac{\mathbf{x} \cdot \mathbf{u}_1}{\mathbf{u}_1 \cdot \mathbf{u}_1}\mathbf{u}_1 + \frac{\mathbf{x} \cdot \mathbf{u}_2}{\mathbf{u}_2 \cdot \mathbf{u}_2}\mathbf{u}_2 + \frac{\mathbf{x} \cdot \mathbf{u}_3}{\mathbf{u}_3 \cdot \mathbf{u}_3}\mathbf{u}_3 = \frac{5}{2}\mathbf{u}_1 - \frac{3}{2}\mathbf{u}_2 + 2\mathbf{u}_3$$

10. Since $\mathbf{u}_1 \cdot \mathbf{u}_2 = \mathbf{u}_1 \cdot \mathbf{u}_3 = \mathbf{u}_2 \cdot \mathbf{u}_3 = 0$, $\{\mathbf{u}_1, \mathbf{u}_2, \mathbf{u}_3\}$ is an orthogonal set. Since the vectors are non-zero, $\mathbf{u}_1$, $\mathbf{u}_2$, and $\mathbf{u}_3$ are linearly independent by Theorem 4. Three such vectors in $\mathbb{R}^3$ automatically form a basis for $\mathbb{R}^3$. So $\{\mathbf{u}_1, \mathbf{u}_2, \mathbf{u}_3\}$ is an orthogonal basis for $\mathbb{R}^3$. By Theorem 5,

$$\mathbf{x} = \frac{\mathbf{x} \cdot \mathbf{u}_1}{\mathbf{u}_1 \cdot \mathbf{u}_1}\mathbf{u}_1 + \frac{\mathbf{x} \cdot \mathbf{u}_2}{\mathbf{u}_2 \cdot \mathbf{u}_2}\mathbf{u}_2 + \frac{\mathbf{x} \cdot \mathbf{u}_3}{\mathbf{u}_3 \cdot \mathbf{u}_3}\mathbf{u}_3 = \frac{4}{3}\mathbf{u}_1 + \frac{1}{3}\mathbf{u}_2 + \frac{1}{3}\mathbf{u}_3$$

11. Let $\mathbf{y} = \begin{bmatrix} 1 \\ 7 \end{bmatrix}$ and $\mathbf{u} = \begin{bmatrix} -4 \\ 2 \end{bmatrix}$. The orthogonal projection of $\mathbf{y}$ onto the line through $\mathbf{u}$ and the origin is the orthogonal projection of $\mathbf{y}$ onto $\mathbf{u}$, and this vector is

$$\hat{\mathbf{y}} = \frac{\mathbf{y} \cdot \mathbf{u}}{\mathbf{u} \cdot \mathbf{u}}\mathbf{u} = \frac{1}{2}\mathbf{u} = \begin{bmatrix} 2 \\ -1 \end{bmatrix}$$

12. Let $\mathbf{y} = \begin{bmatrix} 1 \\ -1 \end{bmatrix}$ and $\mathbf{u} = \begin{bmatrix} -1 \\ 3 \end{bmatrix}$. The orthogonal projection of $\mathbf{y}$ onto the line through $\mathbf{u}$ and the origin is the orthogonal projection of $\mathbf{y}$ onto $\mathbf{u}$, and this vector is

$$\hat{\mathbf{y}} = \frac{\mathbf{y} \cdot \mathbf{u}}{\mathbf{u} \cdot \mathbf{u}}\mathbf{u} = -\frac{2}{5}\mathbf{u} = \begin{bmatrix} 2/5 \\ -6/5 \end{bmatrix}$$

13. The orthogonal projection of $\mathbf{y}$ onto $\mathbf{u}$ is

$$\hat{\mathbf{y}} = \frac{\mathbf{y} \cdot \mathbf{u}}{\mathbf{u} \cdot \mathbf{u}}\mathbf{u} = -\frac{13}{65}\mathbf{u} = \begin{bmatrix} -4/5 \\ 7/5 \end{bmatrix}$$

The component of $\mathbf{y}$ orthogonal to $\mathbf{u}$ is

$$\mathbf{y} - \hat{\mathbf{y}} = \begin{bmatrix} 14/5 \\ 8/5 \end{bmatrix}$$

Thus $\mathbf{y} = \hat{\mathbf{y}} + (\mathbf{y} - \hat{\mathbf{y}}) = \begin{bmatrix} -4/5 \\ 7/5 \end{bmatrix} + \begin{bmatrix} 14/5 \\ 8/5 \end{bmatrix}$.

14. The orthogonal projection of $\mathbf{y}$ onto $\mathbf{u}$ is

$$\hat{\mathbf{y}} = \frac{\mathbf{y} \cdot \mathbf{u}}{\mathbf{u} \cdot \mathbf{u}}\mathbf{u} = \frac{2}{5}\mathbf{u} = \begin{bmatrix} 14/5 \\ 2/5 \end{bmatrix}$$

The component of **y** orthogonal to **u** is

$$\mathbf{y} - \hat{\mathbf{y}} = \begin{bmatrix} -4/5 \\ 28/5 \end{bmatrix}$$

Thus $\mathbf{y} = \hat{\mathbf{y}} + (\mathbf{y} - \hat{\mathbf{y}}) = \begin{bmatrix} 14/5 \\ 2/5 \end{bmatrix} + \begin{bmatrix} -4/5 \\ 28/5 \end{bmatrix}$.

15. The distance from **y** to the line through **u** and the origin is $\|\mathbf{y} - \hat{\mathbf{y}}\|$. One computes that

$$\mathbf{y} - \hat{\mathbf{y}} = \mathbf{y} - \frac{\mathbf{y} \cdot \mathbf{u}}{\mathbf{u} \cdot \mathbf{u}}\mathbf{u} = \begin{bmatrix} 3 \\ 1 \end{bmatrix} - \frac{3}{10}\begin{bmatrix} 8 \\ 6 \end{bmatrix} = \begin{bmatrix} 3/5 \\ -4/5 \end{bmatrix}$$

so $\|\mathbf{y} - \hat{\mathbf{y}}\| = \sqrt{9/25 + 16/25} = 1$ is the desired distance.

16. The distance from **y** to the line through **u** and the origin is $\|\mathbf{y} - \hat{\mathbf{y}}\|$. One computes that

$$\mathbf{y} - \hat{\mathbf{y}} = \mathbf{y} - \frac{\mathbf{y} \cdot \mathbf{u}}{\mathbf{u} \cdot \mathbf{u}}\mathbf{u} = \begin{bmatrix} -3 \\ 9 \end{bmatrix} - 3\begin{bmatrix} 1 \\ 2 \end{bmatrix} = \begin{bmatrix} -6 \\ 3 \end{bmatrix}$$

so $\|\mathbf{y} - \hat{\mathbf{y}}\| = \sqrt{36 + 9} = 3\sqrt{5}$ is the desired distance.

17. Let $\mathbf{u} = \begin{bmatrix} 1/3 \\ 1/3 \\ 1/3 \end{bmatrix}$, $\mathbf{v} = \begin{bmatrix} -1/2 \\ 0 \\ 1/2 \end{bmatrix}$. Since $\mathbf{u} \cdot \mathbf{v} = 0$, {**u**, **v**} is an orthogonal set. However, $\|\mathbf{u}\|^2 = \mathbf{u} \cdot \mathbf{u} = 1/3$ and

$\|\mathbf{v}\|^2 = \mathbf{v} \cdot \mathbf{v} = 1/2$, so {**u**, **v**} is not an orthonormal set. The vectors **u** and **v** may be normalized to form the orthonormal set

$$\left\{ \frac{\mathbf{u}}{\|\mathbf{u}\|}, \frac{\mathbf{v}}{\|\mathbf{v}\|} \right\} = \left\{ \begin{bmatrix} \sqrt{3}/3 \\ \sqrt{3}/3 \\ \sqrt{3}/3 \end{bmatrix}, \begin{bmatrix} -\sqrt{2}/2 \\ 0 \\ \sqrt{2}/2 \end{bmatrix} \right\}$$

18. Let $\mathbf{u} = \begin{bmatrix} 0 \\ 1 \\ 0 \end{bmatrix}$, $\mathbf{v} = \begin{bmatrix} 0 \\ -1 \\ 0 \end{bmatrix}$. Since $\mathbf{u} \cdot \mathbf{v} = -1 \neq 0$, {**u**, **v**} is not an orthogonal set.

19. Let $\mathbf{u} = \begin{bmatrix} -.6 \\ .8 \end{bmatrix}$, $\mathbf{v} = \begin{bmatrix} .8 \\ .6 \end{bmatrix}$. Since $\mathbf{u} \cdot \mathbf{v} = 0$, {**u**, **v**} is an orthogonal set. Also, $\|\mathbf{u}\|^2 = \mathbf{u} \cdot \mathbf{u} = 1$ and

$\|\mathbf{v}\|^2 = \mathbf{v} \cdot \mathbf{v} = 1$, so {**u**, **v**} is an orthonormal set.

20. Let $\mathbf{u} = \begin{bmatrix} -2/3 \\ 1/3 \\ 2/3 \end{bmatrix}$, $\mathbf{v} = \begin{bmatrix} 1/3 \\ 2/3 \\ 0 \end{bmatrix}$. Since $\mathbf{u} \cdot \mathbf{v} = 0$, {**u**, **v**} is an orthogonal set. However, $\|\mathbf{u}\|^2 = \mathbf{u} \cdot \mathbf{u} = 1$ and

$\|\mathbf{v}\|^2 = \mathbf{v} \cdot \mathbf{v} = 5/9$, so {**u**, **v**} is not an orthonormal set. The vectors **u** and **v** may be normalized to form the orthonormal set

$$\left\{ \frac{\mathbf{u}}{\|\mathbf{u}\|}, \frac{\mathbf{v}}{\|\mathbf{v}\|} \right\} = \left\{ \begin{bmatrix} -2/3 \\ 1/3 \\ 2/3 \end{bmatrix}, \begin{bmatrix} 1/\sqrt{5} \\ 2/\sqrt{5} \\ 0 \end{bmatrix} \right\}$$

21. Let $\mathbf{u} = \begin{bmatrix} 1/\sqrt{10} \\ 3/\sqrt{20} \\ 3/\sqrt{20} \end{bmatrix}$, $\mathbf{v} = \begin{bmatrix} 3/\sqrt{10} \\ -1/\sqrt{20} \\ -1/\sqrt{20} \end{bmatrix}$, and $\mathbf{w} = \begin{bmatrix} 0 \\ -1/\sqrt{2} \\ 1/\sqrt{2} \end{bmatrix}$. Since $\mathbf{u} \cdot \mathbf{v} = \mathbf{u} \cdot \mathbf{w} = \mathbf{v} \cdot \mathbf{w} = 0$, $\{\mathbf{u}, \mathbf{v}, \mathbf{w}\}$ is an

orthogonal set. Also, $\|\mathbf{u}\|^2 = \mathbf{u} \cdot \mathbf{u} = 1$, $\|\mathbf{v}\|^2 = \mathbf{v} \cdot \mathbf{v} = 1$, and $\|\mathbf{w}\|^2 = \mathbf{w} \cdot \mathbf{w} = 1$, so $\{\mathbf{u}, \mathbf{v}, \mathbf{w}\}$ is an orthonormal set.

22. Let $\mathbf{u} = \begin{bmatrix} 1/\sqrt{18} \\ 4/\sqrt{18} \\ 1/\sqrt{18} \end{bmatrix}$, $\mathbf{v} = \begin{bmatrix} 1/\sqrt{2} \\ 0 \\ -1/\sqrt{2} \end{bmatrix}$, and $\mathbf{w} = \begin{bmatrix} -2/3 \\ 1/3 \\ -2/3 \end{bmatrix}$. Since $\mathbf{u} \cdot \mathbf{v} = \mathbf{u} \cdot \mathbf{w} = \mathbf{v} \cdot \mathbf{w} = 0$, $\{\mathbf{u}, \mathbf{v}, \mathbf{w}\}$ is an

orthogonal set. Also, $\|\mathbf{u}\|^2 = \mathbf{u} \cdot \mathbf{u} = 1$, $\|\mathbf{v}\|^2 = \mathbf{v} \cdot \mathbf{v} = 1$, and $\|\mathbf{w}\|^2 = \mathbf{w} \cdot \mathbf{w} = 1$, so $\{\mathbf{u}, \mathbf{v}, \mathbf{w}\}$ is an orthonormal set.

23. a. True. For example, the vectors $\mathbf{u}$ and $\mathbf{y}$ in Example 3 are linearly independent but not orthogonal.

   b. True. The formulas for the weights are given in Theorem 5.

   c. False. See the paragraph following Example 5.

   d. False. The matrix must also be square. See the paragraph before Example 7.

   e. False. See Example 4. The distance is $\|\mathbf{y} - \hat{\mathbf{y}}\|$.

24. a. True. But every orthogonal set of *nonzero vectors* is linearly independent. See Theorem 4.

   b. False. To be orthonormal, the vectors is S must be unit vectors as well as being orthogonal to each other.

   c. True. See Theorem 7(a).

   d. True. See the paragraph before Example 3.

   e. True. See the paragraph before Example 7.

25. To prove part (b), note that

$$(U\mathbf{x}) \cdot (U\mathbf{y}) = (U\mathbf{x})^T (U\mathbf{y}) = \mathbf{x}^T U^T U \mathbf{y} = \mathbf{x}^T \mathbf{y} = \mathbf{x} \cdot \mathbf{y}$$

because $U^T U = I$. If $\mathbf{y} = \mathbf{x}$ in part (b), $(U\mathbf{x}) \cdot (U\mathbf{x}) = \mathbf{x} \cdot \mathbf{x}$, which implies part (a). Part (c) of the Theorem follows immediately fom part (b).

26. A set of n nonzero orthogonal vectors must be linearly independent by Theorem 4, so if such a set spans W it is a basis for W. Thus W is an n-dimensional subspace of $\mathbb{R}^n$, and $W = \mathbb{R}^n$.

27. If U has orthonormal columns, then $U^T U = I$ by Theorem 6. If U is also a square matrix, then the equation $U^T U = I$ implies that U is invertible by the Invertible Matrix Theorem.

28. If U is an $n \times n$ orthogonal matrix, then $I = UU^{-1} = UU^T$. Since U is the transpose of U^T, Theorem 6 applied to U^T says that U^T has orthogonal columns. In particular, the columns of U^T are linearly independent and hence form a basis for $\mathbb{R}^n$ by the Invertible Matrix Theorem. That is, the rows of U form a basis (an orthonormal basis) for $\mathbb{R}^n$.

29. Since U and V are orthogonal, each is invertible. By Theorem 6 in Section 2.2, UV is invertible and $(UV)^{-1} = V^{-1}U^{-1} = V^T U^T = (UV)^T$, where the final equality holds by Theorem 3 in Section 2.1. Thus UV is an orthogonal matrix.

30. If U is an orthogonal matrix, its columns are orthonormal. Interchanging the columns does not change their orthonormality, so the new matrix – say, V – still has orthonormal columns. By Theorem 6, $V^T V = I$. Since V is square, $V^T = V^{-1}$ by the Invertible Matrix Theorem.

31. Suppose that $\hat{\mathbf{y}} = \dfrac{\mathbf{y} \cdot \mathbf{u}}{\mathbf{u} \cdot \mathbf{u}} \mathbf{u}$. Replacing $\mathbf{u}$ by $c\mathbf{u}$ with $c \neq 0$ gives

$$\frac{\mathbf{y} \cdot (c\mathbf{u})}{(c\mathbf{u}) \cdot (c\mathbf{u})}(c\mathbf{u}) = \frac{c(\mathbf{y} \cdot \mathbf{u})}{c^2(\mathbf{u} \cdot \mathbf{u})}(c)\mathbf{u} = \frac{c^2(\mathbf{y} \cdot \mathbf{u})}{c^2(\mathbf{u} \cdot \mathbf{u})}\mathbf{u} = \frac{\mathbf{y} \cdot \mathbf{u}}{\mathbf{u} \cdot \mathbf{u}}\mathbf{u} = \hat{\mathbf{y}}$$

So $\hat{\mathbf{y}}$ does not depend on the choice of a nonzero $\mathbf{u}$ in the line L used in the formula.

32. If $\mathbf{v}_1 \cdot \mathbf{v}_2 = 0$, then by Theorem 1(c) in Section 6.1,

$$(c_1 \mathbf{v}_1) \cdot (c_2 \mathbf{v}_2) = c_1[\mathbf{v}_1 \cdot (c_2 \mathbf{v}_2)] = c_1 c_2 (\mathbf{v}_1 \cdot \mathbf{v}_2) = c_1 c_2 0 = 0$$

33. Let $L = \text{Span}\{\mathbf{u}\}$, where $\mathbf{u}$ is nonzero, and let $T(\mathbf{x}) = \dfrac{\mathbf{x} \cdot \mathbf{u}}{\mathbf{u} \cdot \mathbf{u}}\mathbf{u}$. For any vectors $\mathbf{x}$ and $\mathbf{y}$ in $\mathbb{R}^n$ and any scalars c and d, the properties of the inner product (Theorem 1) show that

$$T(c\mathbf{x} + d\mathbf{y}) = \frac{(c\mathbf{x} + d\mathbf{y}) \cdot \mathbf{u}}{\mathbf{u} \cdot \mathbf{u}}\mathbf{u}$$

$$= \frac{c\mathbf{x} \cdot \mathbf{u} + d\mathbf{y} \cdot \mathbf{u}}{\mathbf{u} \cdot \mathbf{u}}\mathbf{u}$$

$$= \frac{c\mathbf{x} \cdot \mathbf{u}}{\mathbf{u} \cdot \mathbf{u}}\mathbf{u} + \frac{d\mathbf{y} \cdot \mathbf{u}}{\mathbf{u} \cdot \mathbf{u}}\mathbf{u}$$

$$= cT(\mathbf{x}) + dT(\mathbf{y})$$

Thus T is a linear transformation. Another approach is to view T as the composition of the following three linear mappings: $\mathbf{x} \mapsto a = \mathbf{x} \cdot \mathbf{v}$, $a \mapsto b = a / \mathbf{v} \cdot \mathbf{v}$, and $b \mapsto b\mathbf{v}$.

34. Let $L = \text{Span}\{\mathbf{u}\}$, where $\mathbf{u}$ is nonzero, and let $T(\mathbf{x}) = \text{refl}_L \mathbf{y} = 2\text{proj}_L \mathbf{y} - \mathbf{y}$. By Exercise 33, the mapping $\mathbf{y} \mapsto \text{proj}_L \mathbf{y}$ is linear. Thus for any vectors $\mathbf{y}$ and $\mathbf{z}$ in $\mathbb{R}^n$ and any scalars c and d,

$$T(c\mathbf{y} + d\mathbf{z}) = 2\,\text{proj}_L(c\mathbf{y} + d\mathbf{z}) - (c\mathbf{y} + d\mathbf{z})$$

$$= 2(c\,\text{proj}_L \mathbf{y} + d\,\text{proj}_L \mathbf{z}) - c\mathbf{y} - d\mathbf{z}$$

$$= 2c\,\text{proj}_L \mathbf{y} - c\mathbf{y} + 2d\,\text{proj}_L \mathbf{z} - d\mathbf{z}$$

$$= c(2\,\text{proj}_L \mathbf{y} - \mathbf{y}) + d(2\,\text{proj}_L \mathbf{z} - \mathbf{z})$$

$$= cT(\mathbf{y}) + dT(\mathbf{z})$$

Thus T is a linear transformation.

35. **[M]** One can compute that $A^T A = 100I_4$. Since the off-diagonal entries in $A^T A$ are zero, the columns of A are orthogonal.

36. [M]

  a. One computes that $U^T U = I_4$, while

$$UU^T = \left(\frac{1}{100}\right)\begin{bmatrix} 82 & 0 & -20 & 8 & 6 & 20 & 24 & 0 \\ 0 & 42 & 24 & 0 & -20 & 6 & 20 & -32 \\ -20 & 24 & 58 & 20 & 0 & 32 & 0 & 6 \\ 8 & 0 & 20 & 82 & 24 & -20 & 6 & 0 \\ 6 & -20 & 0 & 24 & 18 & 0 & -8 & 20 \\ 20 & 6 & 32 & -20 & 0 & 58 & 0 & 24 \\ 24 & 20 & 0 & 6 & -8 & 0 & 18 & -20 \\ 0 & -32 & 6 & 0 & 20 & 24 & -20 & 42 \end{bmatrix}$$

  The matrices $U^T U$ and UU^T are of different sizes and look nothing like each other.

  b. Answers will vary. The vector $\mathbf{p} = UU^T\mathbf{y}$ is in $\text{Col } U$ because $\mathbf{p} = U(U^T\mathbf{y})$. Since the columns of U are simply scaled versions of the columns of A, $\text{Col } U = \text{Col} A$. Thus each $\mathbf{p}$ is in $\text{Col } A$.

  c. One computes that $U^T\mathbf{z} = \mathbf{0}$.

  d. From (c), $\mathbf{z}$ is orthogonal to each column of A. By Exercise 29 in Section 6.1, $\mathbf{z}$ must be orthogonal to every vector in $\text{Col } A$; that is, $\mathbf{z}$ is in $(\text{Col } A)^{\perp}$.

6.3   SOLUTIONS

Notes: Example 1 seems to help students understand Theorem 8. Theorem 8 is needed for the Gram-Schmidt process (but only for a subspace that itself has an orthogonal basis). Theorems 8 and 9 are needed for the discussions of least squares in Sections 6.5 and 6.6. Theorem 10 is used with the QR factorization to provide a good numerical method for solving least squares problems, in Section 6.5. Exercises 19 and 20 lead naturally into consideration of the Gram-Schmidt process.

  1. The vector in $\text{Span}\{\mathbf{u}_4\}$ is

$$\frac{\mathbf{x}\cdot\mathbf{u}_4}{\mathbf{u}_4\cdot\mathbf{u}_4}\mathbf{u}_4 = \frac{72}{36}\mathbf{u}_4 = 2\mathbf{u}_4 = \begin{bmatrix} 10 \\ -6 \\ -2 \\ 2 \end{bmatrix}$$

  Since $\mathbf{x} = c_1\mathbf{u}_1 + c_2\mathbf{u}_2 + c_3\mathbf{u}_3 + \dfrac{\mathbf{x}\cdot\mathbf{u}_4}{\mathbf{u}_4\cdot\mathbf{u}_4}\mathbf{u}_4$, the vector

$$\mathbf{x} - \frac{\mathbf{x}\cdot\mathbf{u}_4}{\mathbf{u}_4\cdot\mathbf{u}_4}\mathbf{u}_4 = \begin{bmatrix} 10 \\ -8 \\ 2 \\ 0 \end{bmatrix} - \begin{bmatrix} 10 \\ -6 \\ -2 \\ 2 \end{bmatrix} = \begin{bmatrix} 0 \\ -2 \\ 4 \\ -2 \end{bmatrix}$$

  is in $\text{Span}\{\mathbf{u}_1, \mathbf{u}_2, \mathbf{u}_3\}$.

2. The vector in Span$\{\mathbf{u}_1\}$ is

$$\frac{\mathbf{v} \cdot \mathbf{u}_1}{\mathbf{u}_1 \cdot \mathbf{u}_1}\mathbf{u}_1 = \frac{14}{7}\mathbf{u}_1 = 2\mathbf{u}_1 = \begin{bmatrix} 2 \\ 4 \\ 2 \\ 2 \end{bmatrix}$$

Since $\mathbf{x} = \dfrac{\mathbf{v} \cdot \mathbf{u}_1}{\mathbf{u}_1 \cdot \mathbf{u}_1}\mathbf{u}_1 + c_2\mathbf{u}_2 + c_3\mathbf{u}_3 + c_4\mathbf{u}_4$, the vector

$$\mathbf{v} - \frac{\mathbf{v} \cdot \mathbf{u}_1}{\mathbf{u}_1 \cdot \mathbf{u}_1}\mathbf{u}_1 = \begin{bmatrix} 4 \\ 5 \\ -3 \\ 3 \end{bmatrix} - \begin{bmatrix} 2 \\ 4 \\ 2 \\ 2 \end{bmatrix} = \begin{bmatrix} 2 \\ 1 \\ -5 \\ 1 \end{bmatrix}$$

is in Span$\{\mathbf{u}_2, \mathbf{u}_3, \mathbf{u}_4\}$.

3. Since $\mathbf{u}_1 \cdot \mathbf{u}_2 = -1 + 1 + 0 = 0$, $\{\mathbf{u}_1, \mathbf{u}_2\}$ is an orthogonal set. The orthogonal projection of $\mathbf{y}$ onto Span$\{\mathbf{u}_1, \mathbf{u}_2\}$ is

$$\hat{\mathbf{y}} = \frac{\mathbf{y} \cdot \mathbf{u}_1}{\mathbf{u}_1 \cdot \mathbf{u}_1}\mathbf{u}_1 + \frac{\mathbf{y} \cdot \mathbf{u}_2}{\mathbf{u}_2 \cdot \mathbf{u}_2}\mathbf{u}_2 = \frac{3}{2}\mathbf{u}_1 + \frac{5}{2}\mathbf{u}_2 = \frac{3}{2}\begin{bmatrix} 1 \\ 1 \\ 0 \end{bmatrix} + \frac{5}{2}\begin{bmatrix} -1 \\ 1 \\ 0 \end{bmatrix} = \begin{bmatrix} -1 \\ 4 \\ 0 \end{bmatrix}$$

4. Since $\mathbf{u}_1 \cdot \mathbf{u}_2 = -12 + 12 + 0 = 0$, $\{\mathbf{u}_1, \mathbf{u}_2\}$ is an orthogonal set. The orthogonal projection of $\mathbf{y}$ onto Span$\{\mathbf{u}_1, \mathbf{u}_2\}$ is

$$\hat{\mathbf{y}} = \frac{\mathbf{y} \cdot \mathbf{u}_1}{\mathbf{u}_1 \cdot \mathbf{u}_1}\mathbf{u}_1 + \frac{\mathbf{y} \cdot \mathbf{u}_2}{\mathbf{u}_2 \cdot \mathbf{u}_2}\mathbf{u}_2 = \frac{30}{25}\mathbf{u}_1 - \frac{15}{25}\mathbf{u}_2 = \frac{6}{5}\begin{bmatrix} 3 \\ 4 \\ 0 \end{bmatrix} - \frac{3}{5}\begin{bmatrix} -4 \\ 3 \\ 0 \end{bmatrix} = \begin{bmatrix} 6 \\ 3 \\ 0 \end{bmatrix}$$

5. Since $\mathbf{u}_1 \cdot \mathbf{u}_2 = 3 + 1 - 4 = 0$, $\{\mathbf{u}_1, \mathbf{u}_2\}$ is an orthogonal set. The orthogonal projection of $\mathbf{y}$ onto Span$\{\mathbf{u}_1, \mathbf{u}_2\}$ is

$$\hat{\mathbf{y}} = \frac{\mathbf{y} \cdot \mathbf{u}_1}{\mathbf{u}_1 \cdot \mathbf{u}_1}\mathbf{u}_1 + \frac{\mathbf{y} \cdot \mathbf{u}_2}{\mathbf{u}_2 \cdot \mathbf{u}_2}\mathbf{u}_2 = \frac{7}{14}\mathbf{u}_1 - \frac{15}{6}\mathbf{u}_2 = \frac{1}{2}\begin{bmatrix} 3 \\ -1 \\ 2 \end{bmatrix} - \frac{5}{2}\begin{bmatrix} 1 \\ -1 \\ 2 \end{bmatrix} = \begin{bmatrix} -1 \\ 2 \\ 6 \end{bmatrix}$$

6. Since $\mathbf{u}_1 \cdot \mathbf{u}_2 = 0 - 1 + 1 = 0$, $\{\mathbf{u}_1, \mathbf{u}_2\}$ is an orthogonal set. The orthogonal projection of $\mathbf{y}$ onto Span$\{\mathbf{u}_1, \mathbf{u}_2\}$ is

$$\hat{\mathbf{y}} = \frac{\mathbf{y} \cdot \mathbf{u}_1}{\mathbf{u}_1 \cdot \mathbf{u}_1}\mathbf{u}_1 + \frac{\mathbf{y} \cdot \mathbf{u}_2}{\mathbf{u}_2 \cdot \mathbf{u}_2}\mathbf{u}_2 = -\frac{27}{18}\mathbf{u}_1 + \frac{5}{2}\mathbf{u}_2 = -\frac{3}{2}\begin{bmatrix} -4 \\ -1 \\ 1 \end{bmatrix} + \frac{5}{2}\begin{bmatrix} 0 \\ 1 \\ 1 \end{bmatrix} = \begin{bmatrix} 6 \\ 4 \\ 1 \end{bmatrix}$$

7. Since $\mathbf{u}_1 \cdot \mathbf{u}_2 = 5 + 3 - 8 = 0$, $\{\mathbf{u}_1, \mathbf{u}_2\}$ is an orthogonal set. By the Orthogonal Decomposition Theorem,

$$\hat{\mathbf{y}} = \frac{\mathbf{y} \cdot \mathbf{u}_1}{\mathbf{u}_1 \cdot \mathbf{u}_1}\mathbf{u}_1 + \frac{\mathbf{y} \cdot \mathbf{u}_2}{\mathbf{u}_2 \cdot \mathbf{u}_2}\mathbf{u}_2 = 0\mathbf{u}_1 + \frac{2}{3}\mathbf{u}_2 = \begin{bmatrix} 10/3 \\ 2/3 \\ 8/3 \end{bmatrix}, \mathbf{z} = \mathbf{y} - \hat{\mathbf{y}} = \begin{bmatrix} -7/3 \\ 7/3 \\ 7/3 \end{bmatrix}$$

and $\mathbf{y} = \hat{\mathbf{y}} + \mathbf{z}$, where $\hat{\mathbf{y}}$ is in W and $\mathbf{z}$ is in $W^\perp$.

8. Since $\mathbf{u}_1 \cdot \mathbf{u}_2 = -1 + 3 - 2 = 0$, $\{\mathbf{u}_1, \mathbf{u}_2\}$ is an orthogonal set. By the Orthogonal Decomposition Theorem,

$$\hat{\mathbf{y}} = \frac{\mathbf{y} \cdot \mathbf{u}_1}{\mathbf{u}_1 \cdot \mathbf{u}_1}\mathbf{u}_1 + \frac{\mathbf{y} \cdot \mathbf{u}_2}{\mathbf{u}_2 \cdot \mathbf{u}_2}\mathbf{u}_2 = 2\mathbf{u}_1 + \frac{1}{2}\mathbf{u}_2 = \begin{bmatrix} 3/2 \\ 7/2 \\ 1 \end{bmatrix}, \mathbf{z} = \mathbf{y} - \hat{\mathbf{y}} = \begin{bmatrix} -5/2 \\ 1/2 \\ 2 \end{bmatrix}$$

and $\mathbf{y} = \hat{\mathbf{y}} + \mathbf{z}$, where $\hat{\mathbf{y}}$ is in W and $\mathbf{z}$ is in $W^\perp$.

9. Since $\mathbf{u}_1 \cdot \mathbf{u}_2 = \mathbf{u}_1 \cdot \mathbf{u}_3 = \mathbf{u}_2 \cdot \mathbf{u}_3 = 0$, $\{\mathbf{u}_1, \mathbf{u}_2, \mathbf{u}_3\}$ is an orthogonal set. By the Orthogonal Decomposition Theorem,

$$\hat{\mathbf{y}} = \frac{\mathbf{y} \cdot \mathbf{u}_1}{\mathbf{u}_1 \cdot \mathbf{u}_1}\mathbf{u}_1 + \frac{\mathbf{y} \cdot \mathbf{u}_2}{\mathbf{u}_2 \cdot \mathbf{u}_2}\mathbf{u}_2 + \frac{\mathbf{y} \cdot \mathbf{u}_3}{\mathbf{u}_3 \cdot \mathbf{u}_3}\mathbf{u}_3 = 2\mathbf{u}_1 + \frac{2}{3}\mathbf{u}_2 - \frac{2}{3}\mathbf{u}_3 = \begin{bmatrix} 2 \\ 4 \\ 0 \\ 0 \end{bmatrix}, \mathbf{z} = \mathbf{y} - \hat{\mathbf{y}} = \begin{bmatrix} 2 \\ -1 \\ 3 \\ -1 \end{bmatrix}$$

and $\mathbf{y} = \hat{\mathbf{y}} + \mathbf{z}$, where $\hat{\mathbf{y}}$ is in W and $\mathbf{z}$ is in $W^\perp$.

10. Since $\mathbf{u}_1 \cdot \mathbf{u}_2 = \mathbf{u}_1 \cdot \mathbf{u}_3 = \mathbf{u}_2 \cdot \mathbf{u}_3 = 0$, $\{\mathbf{u}_1, \mathbf{u}_2, \mathbf{u}_3\}$ is an orthogonal set. By the Orthogonal Decomposition Theorem,

$$\hat{\mathbf{y}} = \frac{\mathbf{y} \cdot \mathbf{u}_1}{\mathbf{u}_1 \cdot \mathbf{u}_1}\mathbf{u}_1 + \frac{\mathbf{y} \cdot \mathbf{u}_2}{\mathbf{u}_2 \cdot \mathbf{u}_2}\mathbf{u}_2 + \frac{\mathbf{y} \cdot \mathbf{u}_3}{\mathbf{u}_3 \cdot \mathbf{u}_3}\mathbf{u}_3 = \frac{1}{3}\mathbf{u}_1 + \frac{14}{3}\mathbf{u}_2 - \frac{5}{3}\mathbf{u}_3 = \begin{bmatrix} 5 \\ 2 \\ 3 \\ 6 \end{bmatrix}, \mathbf{z} = \mathbf{y} - \hat{\mathbf{y}} = \begin{bmatrix} -2 \\ 2 \\ 2 \\ 0 \end{bmatrix}$$

and $\mathbf{y} = \hat{\mathbf{y}} + \mathbf{z}$, where $\hat{\mathbf{y}}$ is in W and $\mathbf{z}$ is in $W^\perp$.

11. Note that $\mathbf{v}_1$ and $\mathbf{v}_2$ are orthogonal. The Best Approximation Theorem says that $\hat{\mathbf{y}}$, which is the orthogonal projection of $\mathbf{y}$ onto $W = \text{Span}\{\mathbf{v}_1, \mathbf{v}_2\}$, is the closest point to $\mathbf{y}$ in W. This vector is

$$\hat{\mathbf{y}} = \frac{\mathbf{y} \cdot \mathbf{v}_1}{\mathbf{v}_1 \cdot \mathbf{v}_1}\mathbf{v}_1 + \frac{\mathbf{y} \cdot \mathbf{v}_2}{\mathbf{v}_2 \cdot \mathbf{v}_2}\mathbf{v}_2 = \frac{1}{2}\mathbf{v}_1 + \frac{3}{2}\mathbf{v}_2 = \begin{bmatrix} 3 \\ -1 \\ 1 \\ -1 \end{bmatrix}$$

12. Note that $\mathbf{v}_1$ and $\mathbf{v}_2$ are orthogonal. The Best Approximation Theorem says that $\hat{\mathbf{y}}$, which is the orthogonal projection of y onto $W = \text{Span}\{\mathbf{v}_1, \mathbf{v}_2\}$, is the closest point to $\mathbf{y}$ in W. This vector is

$$\hat{\mathbf{y}} = \frac{\mathbf{y} \cdot \mathbf{v}_1}{\mathbf{v}_1 \cdot \mathbf{v}_1}\mathbf{v}_1 + \frac{\mathbf{y} \cdot \mathbf{v}_2}{\mathbf{v}_2 \cdot \mathbf{v}_2}\mathbf{v}_2 = 3\mathbf{v}_1 + 1\mathbf{v}_2 = \begin{bmatrix} -1 \\ -5 \\ -3 \\ 9 \end{bmatrix}$$

13. Note that $\mathbf{v}_1$ and $\mathbf{v}_2$ are orthogonal. By the Best Approximation Theorem, the closest point in $\text{Span}\{\mathbf{v}_1, \mathbf{v}_2\}$ to $\mathbf{z}$ is

$$\hat{\mathbf{z}} = \frac{\mathbf{z} \cdot \mathbf{v}_1}{\mathbf{v}_1 \cdot \mathbf{v}_1}\mathbf{v}_1 + \frac{\mathbf{z} \cdot \mathbf{v}_2}{\mathbf{v}_2 \cdot \mathbf{v}_2}\mathbf{v}_2 = \frac{2}{3}\mathbf{v}_1 - \frac{7}{3}\mathbf{v}_2 = \begin{bmatrix} -1 \\ -3 \\ -2 \\ 3 \end{bmatrix}$$

14. Note that $\mathbf{v}_1$ and $\mathbf{v}_2$ are orthogonal. By the Best Approximation Theorem, the closest point in $\text{Span}\{\mathbf{v}_1, \mathbf{v}_2\}$ to $\mathbf{z}$ is

$$\hat{\mathbf{z}} = \frac{\mathbf{z} \cdot \mathbf{v}_1}{\mathbf{v}_1 \cdot \mathbf{v}_1}\mathbf{v}_1 + \frac{\mathbf{z} \cdot \mathbf{v}_2}{\mathbf{v}_2 \cdot \mathbf{v}_2}\mathbf{v}_2 = \frac{1}{2}\mathbf{v}_1 + 0\mathbf{v}_2 = \begin{bmatrix} 1 \\ 0 \\ -1/2 \\ -3/2 \end{bmatrix}$$

15. The distance from the point $\mathbf{y}$ in $\mathbb{R}^3$ to a subspace W is defined as the distance from $\mathbf{y}$ to the closest point in W. Since the closest point in W to $\mathbf{y}$ is $\hat{\mathbf{y}} = \text{proj}_W \mathbf{y}$, the desired distance is $\| \mathbf{y} - \hat{\mathbf{y}} \|$. One computes that

$$\hat{\mathbf{y}} = \begin{bmatrix} 3 \\ -9 \\ -1 \end{bmatrix}, \mathbf{y} - \hat{\mathbf{y}} = \begin{bmatrix} 2 \\ 0 \\ 6 \end{bmatrix}, \text{ and } \| \mathbf{y} - \hat{\mathbf{y}} \| = \sqrt{40} = 2\sqrt{10}.$$

16. The distance from the point $\mathbf{y}$ in $\mathbb{R}^4$ to a subspace W is defined as the distance from $\mathbf{y}$ to the closest point in W. Since the closest point in W to $\mathbf{y}$ is $\hat{\mathbf{y}} = \text{proj}_W \mathbf{y}$, the desired distance is $\| \mathbf{y} - \hat{\mathbf{y}} \|$. One computes that

$$\hat{\mathbf{y}} = \begin{bmatrix} -1 \\ -5 \\ -3 \\ 9 \end{bmatrix}, \mathbf{y} - \hat{\mathbf{y}} = \begin{bmatrix} 4 \\ 4 \\ 4 \\ 4 \end{bmatrix}, \text{ and } \| \mathbf{y} - \hat{\mathbf{y}} \| = 8.$$

17. a. $U^T U = \begin{bmatrix} 1 & 0 \\ 0 & 1 \end{bmatrix}, UU^T = \begin{bmatrix} 8/9 & -2/9 & 2/9 \\ -2/9 & 5/9 & 4/9 \\ 2/9 & 4/9 & 5/9 \end{bmatrix}$

b. Since $U^T U = I_2$, the columns of U form an orthonormal basis for W, and by Theorem 10

$$\text{proj}_W \mathbf{y} = UU^T \mathbf{y} = \begin{bmatrix} 8/9 & -2/9 & 2/9 \\ -2/9 & 5/9 & 4/9 \\ 2/9 & 4/9 & 5/9 \end{bmatrix} \begin{bmatrix} 4 \\ 8 \\ 1 \end{bmatrix} = \begin{bmatrix} 2 \\ 4 \\ 5 \end{bmatrix}.$$

18. a. $U^T U = [1] = 1, UU^T = \begin{bmatrix} 1/10 & -3/10 \\ -3/10 & 9/10 \end{bmatrix}$

b. Since $U^T U = 1$, $\{\mathbf{u}_1\}$ forms an orthonormal basis for W, and by Theorem 10

$$\text{proj}_W \mathbf{y} = UU^T \mathbf{y} = \begin{bmatrix} 1/10 & -3/10 \\ -3/10 & 9/10 \end{bmatrix} \begin{bmatrix} 7 \\ 9 \end{bmatrix} = \begin{bmatrix} -2 \\ 6 \end{bmatrix}.$$

19. By the Orthogonal Decomposition Theorem, $\mathbf{u}_3$ is the sum of a vector in $W = \text{Span}\{\mathbf{u}_1, \mathbf{u}_2\}$ and a vector $\mathbf{v}$ orthogonal to W. This exercise asks for the vector $\mathbf{v}$:

$$\mathbf{v} = \mathbf{u}_3 - \text{proj}_W \mathbf{u}_3 = \mathbf{u}_3 - \left(-\frac{1}{3}\mathbf{u}_1 + \frac{1}{15}\mathbf{u}_2\right) = \begin{bmatrix} 0 \\ 0 \\ 1 \end{bmatrix} - \begin{bmatrix} 0 \\ -2/5 \\ 4/5 \end{bmatrix} = \begin{bmatrix} 0 \\ 2/5 \\ 1/5 \end{bmatrix}$$

Any multiple of the vector $\mathbf{v}$ will also be in $W^\perp$.

20. By the Orthogonal Decomposition Theorem, $\mathbf{u}_4$ is the sum of a vector in $W = \text{Span}\{\mathbf{u}_1, \mathbf{u}_2\}$ and a vector $\mathbf{v}$ orthogonal to W. This exercise asks for the vector $\mathbf{v}$:

$$\mathbf{v} = \mathbf{u}_4 - \text{proj}_W \mathbf{u}_4 = \mathbf{u}_4 - \left(\frac{1}{6}\mathbf{u}_1 - \frac{1}{30}\mathbf{u}_2\right) = \begin{bmatrix} 0 \\ 1 \\ 0 \end{bmatrix} - \begin{bmatrix} 0 \\ 1/5 \\ -2/5 \end{bmatrix} = \begin{bmatrix} 0 \\ 4/5 \\ 2/5 \end{bmatrix}$$

Any multiple of the vector $\mathbf{v}$ will also be in $W^{\perp}$.

21. **a.** True. See the calculations for $\mathbf{z}_2$ in Example 1 or the box after Example 6 in Section 6.1.

   b. True. See the Orthogonal Decomposition Theorem.

   c. False. See the last paragraph in the proof of Theorem 8, or see the second paragraph after the statement of Theorem 9.

   d. True. See the box before the Best Approximation Theorem.

   e. True. Theorem 10 applies to the column space W of U because the columns of U are linearly independent and hence form a basis for W.

22. **a.** True. See the proof of the Orthogonal Decomposition Theorem.

   b. True. See the subsection "A Geometric Interpretation of the Orthogonal Projection."

   c. True. The orthgonal decomposition in Theorem 8 is unique.

   d. False. The Best Approximation Theorem says that the best approximation to $\mathbf{y}$ is $\text{proj}_W \mathbf{y}$.

   e. False. This statement is only true if $\mathbf{x}$ is in the column space of U. If $n > p$, then the column space of U will not be all of $\mathbb{R}^n$, so the statement cannot be true for all $\mathbf{x}$ in $\mathbb{R}^n$.

23. By the Orthogonal Decomposition Theorem, each $\mathbf{x}$ in $\mathbb{R}^n$ can be written uniquely as $\mathbf{x} = \mathbf{p} + \mathbf{u}$, with $\mathbf{p}$ in Row A and $\mathbf{u}$ in $(\text{Row } A)^{\perp}$. By Theorem 3 in Section 6.1, $(\text{Row } A)^{\perp} = \text{Nul } A$, so $\mathbf{u}$ is in Nul$A$.

Next, suppose $A\mathbf{x} = \mathbf{b}$ is consistent. Let $\mathbf{x}$ be a solution and write $\mathbf{x} = \mathbf{p} + \mathbf{u}$ as above. Then $A\mathbf{p} = A(\mathbf{x} - \mathbf{u}) = A\mathbf{x} - A\mathbf{u} = \mathbf{b} - \mathbf{0} = \mathbf{b}$, so the equation $A\mathbf{x} = \mathbf{b}$ has at least one solution $\mathbf{p}$ in Row A. Finally, suppose that $\mathbf{p}$ and $\mathbf{p}_1$ are both in Row$A$ and both satisfy $A\mathbf{x} = \mathbf{b}$. Then $\mathbf{p} - \mathbf{p}_1$ is in Nul$A = (\text{Row } A)^{\perp}$, since $A(\mathbf{p} - \mathbf{p}_1) = A\mathbf{p} - A\mathbf{p}_1 = \mathbf{b} - \mathbf{b} = \mathbf{0}$. The equations $\mathbf{p} = \mathbf{p}_1 + (\mathbf{p} - \mathbf{p}_1)$ and $\mathbf{p} = \mathbf{p} + \mathbf{0}$ both then decompose $\mathbf{p}$ as the sum of a vector in Row$A$ and a vector in $(\text{Row } A)^{\perp}$. By the uniqueness of the orthogonal decomposition (Theorem 8), $\mathbf{p} = \mathbf{p}_1$, and $\mathbf{p}$ is unique.

24. **a.** By hypothesis, the vectors $\mathbf{w}_1, \ldots, \mathbf{w}_p$ are pairwise orthogonal, and the vectors $\mathbf{v}_1, \ldots, \mathbf{v}_q$ are pairwise orthogonal. Since $\mathbf{w}_i$ is in W for any i and $\mathbf{v}_j$ is in $W^{\perp}$ for any j, $\mathbf{w}_i \cdot \mathbf{v}_j = 0$ for any i and j. Thus $\{\mathbf{w}_1, \ldots, \mathbf{w}_p, \mathbf{v}_1, \ldots, \mathbf{v}_q\}$ forms an orthogonal set.

   b. For any $\mathbf{y}$ in $\mathbb{R}^n$, write $\mathbf{y} = \hat{\mathbf{y}} + \mathbf{z}$ as in the Orthogonal Decomposition Theorem, with $\hat{\mathbf{y}}$ in W and $\mathbf{z}$ in $W^{\perp}$. Then there exist scalars $c_1, \ldots, c_p$ and $d_1, \ldots, d_q$ such that $\mathbf{y} = \hat{\mathbf{y}} + \mathbf{z} = c_1\mathbf{w}_1 + \ldots + c_p\mathbf{w}_p + d_1\mathbf{v}_1 + \ldots + d_q\mathbf{v}_q$. Thus the set $\{\mathbf{w}_1, \ldots, \mathbf{w}_p, \mathbf{v}_1, \ldots, \mathbf{v}_q\}$ spans $\mathbb{R}^n$.

   c. The set $\{\mathbf{w}_1, \ldots, \mathbf{w}_p, \mathbf{v}_1, \ldots, \mathbf{v}_q\}$ is linearly independent by (a) and spans $\mathbb{R}^n$ by (b), and is thus a basis for $\mathbb{R}^n$. Hence $\dim W + \dim W^{\perp} = p + q = \dim \mathbb{R}^n$.

25. [M] Since $U^T U = I_4$, U has orthonormal columns by Theorem 6 in Section 6.2. The closest point to $\mathbf{y}$ in Col U is the orthogonal projection $\hat{\mathbf{y}}$ of $\mathbf{y}$ onto Col U. From Theorem 10,

$$\hat{\mathbf{y}} = UU^T\mathbf{y} = \begin{bmatrix} 1.2 \\ .4 \\ 1.2 \\ 1.2 \\ .4 \\ 1.2 \\ .4 \\ .4 \end{bmatrix}$$

26. [M] The distance from $\mathbf{b}$ to Col U is $\| \mathbf{b} - \hat{\mathbf{b}} \|$, where $\hat{\mathbf{b}} = UU^T\mathbf{b}$. One computes that

$$\hat{\mathbf{b}} = UU^T\mathbf{b} = \begin{bmatrix} .2 \\ .92 \\ .44 \\ 1 \\ -.2 \\ -.44 \\ .6 \\ -.92 \end{bmatrix}, \mathbf{b} - \hat{\mathbf{b}} = \begin{bmatrix} .8 \\ .08 \\ .56 \\ 0 \\ -.8 \\ -.56 \\ -1.6 \\ -.08 \end{bmatrix}, \| \mathbf{b} - \hat{\mathbf{b}} \| = \frac{\sqrt{112}}{5}$$

which is 2.1166 to four decimal places.

6.4   SOLUTIONS

Notes: The QR factorization encapsulates the essential outcome of the Gram-Schmidt process, just as the LU factorization describes the result of a row reduction process. For practical use of linear algebra, the factorizations are more important than the algorithms that produce them. In fact, the Gram-Schmidt process is *not* the appropriate way to compute the QR factorization. For that reason, one should consider deemphasizing the hand calculation of the Gram-Schmidt process, even though it provides easy exam questions.

The Gram-Schmidt process is used in Sections 6.7 and 6.8, in connection with various sets of orthogonal polynomials. The process is mentioned in Sections 7.1 and 7.4, but the one-dimensional projection constructed in Section 6.2 will suffice. The QR factorization is used in an optional subsection of Section 6.5, and it is needed in Supplementary Exercise 7 of Chapter 7 to produce the Cholesky factorization of a positive definite matrix.

1. Set $\mathbf{v}_1 = \mathbf{x}_1$ and compute that $\mathbf{v}_2 = \mathbf{x}_2 - \dfrac{\mathbf{x}_2 \cdot \mathbf{v}_1}{\mathbf{v}_1 \cdot \mathbf{v}_1}\mathbf{v}_1 = \mathbf{x}_2 - 3\mathbf{v}_1 = \begin{bmatrix} -1 \\ 5 \\ -3 \end{bmatrix}$. Thus an orthogonal basis for W is

$$\left\{ \begin{bmatrix} 3 \\ 0 \\ -1 \end{bmatrix}, \begin{bmatrix} -1 \\ 5 \\ -3 \end{bmatrix} \right\}.$$

2. Set $\mathbf{v}_1 = \mathbf{x}_1$ and compute that $\mathbf{v}_2 = \mathbf{x}_2 - \dfrac{\mathbf{x}_2 \cdot \mathbf{v}_1}{\mathbf{v}_1 \cdot \mathbf{v}_1} \mathbf{v}_1 = \mathbf{x}_2 - \dfrac{1}{2} \mathbf{v}_1 = \begin{bmatrix} 5 \\ 4 \\ -8 \end{bmatrix}$. Thus an orthogonal basis for W is

$$\left\{ \begin{bmatrix} 0 \\ 4 \\ 2 \end{bmatrix}, \begin{bmatrix} 5 \\ 4 \\ -8 \end{bmatrix} \right\}.$$

3. Set $\mathbf{v}_1 = \mathbf{x}_1$ and compute that $\mathbf{v}_2 = \mathbf{x}_2 - \dfrac{\mathbf{x}_2 \cdot \mathbf{v}_1}{\mathbf{v}_1 \cdot \mathbf{v}_1} \mathbf{v}_1 = \mathbf{x}_2 - \dfrac{1}{2} \mathbf{v}_1 = \begin{bmatrix} 3 \\ 3/2 \\ 3/2 \end{bmatrix}$. Thus an orthogonal basis for W is

$$\left\{ \begin{bmatrix} 2 \\ -5 \\ 1 \end{bmatrix}, \begin{bmatrix} 3 \\ 3/2 \\ 3/2 \end{bmatrix} \right\}.$$

4. Set $\mathbf{v}_1 = \mathbf{x}_1$ and compute that $\mathbf{v}_2 = \mathbf{x}_2 - \dfrac{\mathbf{x}_2 \cdot \mathbf{v}_1}{\mathbf{v}_1 \cdot \mathbf{v}_1} \mathbf{v}_1 = \mathbf{x}_2 - (-2)\mathbf{v}_1 = \begin{bmatrix} 3 \\ 6 \\ 3 \end{bmatrix}$. Thus an orthogonal basis for W is

$$\left\{ \begin{bmatrix} 3 \\ -4 \\ 5 \end{bmatrix}, \begin{bmatrix} 3 \\ 6 \\ 3 \end{bmatrix} \right\}.$$

5. Set $\mathbf{v}_1 = \mathbf{x}_1$ and compute that $\mathbf{v}_2 = \mathbf{x}_2 - \dfrac{\mathbf{x}_2 \cdot \mathbf{v}_1}{\mathbf{v}_1 \cdot \mathbf{v}_1} \mathbf{v}_1 = \mathbf{x}_2 - 2\mathbf{v}_1 = \begin{bmatrix} 5 \\ 1 \\ -4 \\ -1 \end{bmatrix}$. Thus an orthogonal basis for W is

$$\left\{ \begin{bmatrix} 1 \\ -4 \\ 0 \\ 1 \end{bmatrix}, \begin{bmatrix} 5 \\ 1 \\ -4 \\ -1 \end{bmatrix} \right\}.$$

6. Set $\mathbf{v}_1 = \mathbf{x}_1$ and compute that $\mathbf{v}_2 = \mathbf{x}_2 - \dfrac{\mathbf{x}_2 \cdot \mathbf{v}_1}{\mathbf{v}_1 \cdot \mathbf{v}_1} \mathbf{v}_1 = \mathbf{x}_2 - (-3)\mathbf{v}_1 = \begin{bmatrix} 4 \\ 6 \\ -3 \\ 0 \end{bmatrix}$. Thus an orthogonal basis for W is

$$\left\{ \begin{bmatrix} 3 \\ -1 \\ 2 \\ -1 \end{bmatrix}, \begin{bmatrix} 4 \\ 6 \\ -3 \\ 0 \end{bmatrix} \right\}.$$

7. Since $\| \mathbf{v}_1 \| = \sqrt{30}$ and $\| \mathbf{v}_2 \| = \sqrt{27/2} = 3\sqrt{6}/2$, an orthonormal basis for W is

$$\left\{ \frac{\mathbf{v}_1}{\| \mathbf{v}_1 \|}, \frac{\mathbf{v}_2}{\| \mathbf{v}_2 \|} \right\} = \left\{ \begin{bmatrix} 2/\sqrt{30} \\ -5/\sqrt{30} \\ 1/\sqrt{30} \end{bmatrix}, \begin{bmatrix} 2/\sqrt{6} \\ 1/\sqrt{6} \\ 1/\sqrt{6} \end{bmatrix} \right\}.$$

8. Since $\| \mathbf{v}_1 \| = \sqrt{50}$ and $\| \mathbf{v}_2 \| = \sqrt{54} = 3\sqrt{6}$, an orthonormal basis for W is

$$\left\{ \frac{\mathbf{v}_1}{\| \mathbf{v}_1 \|}, \frac{\mathbf{v}_2}{\| \mathbf{v}_2 \|} \right\} = \left\{ \begin{bmatrix} 3/\sqrt{50} \\ -4/\sqrt{50} \\ 5/\sqrt{50} \end{bmatrix}, \begin{bmatrix} 1/\sqrt{6} \\ 2/\sqrt{6} \\ 1/\sqrt{6} \end{bmatrix} \right\}.$$

9. Call the columns of the matrix $\mathbf{x}_1$, $\mathbf{x}_2$, and $\mathbf{x}_3$ and perform the Gram-Schmidt process on these vectors:

$$\mathbf{v}_1 = \mathbf{x}_1$$

$$\mathbf{v}_2 = \mathbf{x}_2 - \frac{\mathbf{x}_2 \cdot \mathbf{v}_1}{\mathbf{v}_1 \cdot \mathbf{v}_1} \mathbf{v}_1 = \mathbf{x}_2 - (-2)\mathbf{v}_1 = \begin{bmatrix} 1 \\ 3 \\ 3 \\ -1 \end{bmatrix}$$

$$\mathbf{v}_3 = \mathbf{x}_3 - \frac{\mathbf{x}_3 \cdot \mathbf{v}_1}{\mathbf{v}_1 \cdot \mathbf{v}_1} \mathbf{v}_1 - \frac{\mathbf{x}_3 \cdot \mathbf{v}_2}{\mathbf{v}_2 \cdot \mathbf{v}_2} \mathbf{v}_2 = \mathbf{x}_3 - \frac{3}{2}\mathbf{v}_1 - \left(-\frac{1}{2}\right)\mathbf{v}_2 = \begin{bmatrix} -3 \\ 1 \\ 1 \\ 3 \end{bmatrix}$$

Thus an orthogonal basis for W is $\left\{ \begin{bmatrix} 3 \\ 1 \\ -1 \\ 3 \end{bmatrix}, \begin{bmatrix} 1 \\ 3 \\ 3 \\ -1 \end{bmatrix}, \begin{bmatrix} -3 \\ 1 \\ 1 \\ 3 \end{bmatrix} \right\}.$

10. Call the columns of the matrix $\mathbf{x}_1$, $\mathbf{x}_2$, and $\mathbf{x}_3$ and perform the Gram-Schmidt process on these vectors:

$$\mathbf{v}_1 = \mathbf{x}_1$$

$$\mathbf{v}_2 = \mathbf{x}_2 - \frac{\mathbf{x}_2 \cdot \mathbf{v}_1}{\mathbf{v}_1 \cdot \mathbf{v}_1} \mathbf{v}_1 = \mathbf{x}_2 - (-3)\mathbf{v}_1 = \begin{bmatrix} 3 \\ 1 \\ 1 \\ -1 \end{bmatrix}$$

$$\mathbf{v}_3 = \mathbf{x}_3 - \frac{\mathbf{x}_3 \cdot \mathbf{v}_1}{\mathbf{v}_1 \cdot \mathbf{v}_1} \mathbf{v}_1 - \frac{\mathbf{x}_3 \cdot \mathbf{v}_2}{\mathbf{v}_2 \cdot \mathbf{v}_2} \mathbf{v}_2 = \mathbf{x}_3 - \frac{1}{2}\mathbf{v}_1 - \frac{5}{2}\mathbf{v}_2 = \begin{bmatrix} -1 \\ -1 \\ 3 \\ -1 \end{bmatrix}$$

Thus an orthogonal basis for W is $\left\{ \begin{bmatrix} -1 \\ 3 \\ 1 \\ 1 \end{bmatrix}, \begin{bmatrix} 3 \\ 1 \\ 1 \\ -1 \end{bmatrix}, \begin{bmatrix} -1 \\ -1 \\ 3 \\ -1 \end{bmatrix} \right\}.$

11. Call the columns of the matrix $\mathbf{x}_1$, $\mathbf{x}_2$, and $\mathbf{x}_3$ and perform the Gram-Schmidt process on these vectors:

$$\mathbf{v}_1 = \mathbf{x}_1$$

$$\mathbf{v}_2 = \mathbf{x}_2 - \frac{\mathbf{x}_2 \cdot \mathbf{v}_1}{\mathbf{v}_1 \cdot \mathbf{v}_1}\,\mathbf{v}_1 = \mathbf{x}_2 - (-1)\mathbf{v}_1 = \begin{bmatrix} 3 \\ 0 \\ 3 \\ -3 \\ 3 \end{bmatrix}$$

$$\mathbf{v}_3 = \mathbf{x}_3 - \frac{\mathbf{x}_3 \cdot \mathbf{v}_1}{\mathbf{v}_1 \cdot \mathbf{v}_1}\,\mathbf{v}_1 - \frac{\mathbf{x}_3 \cdot \mathbf{v}_2}{\mathbf{v}_2 \cdot \mathbf{v}_2}\,\mathbf{v}_2 = \mathbf{x}_3 - 4\mathbf{v}_1 - \left(-\frac{1}{3}\right)\mathbf{v}_2 = \begin{bmatrix} 2 \\ 0 \\ 2 \\ 2 \\ -2 \end{bmatrix}$$

Thus an orthogonal basis for W is $\left\{ \begin{bmatrix} 1 \\ -1 \\ -1 \\ 1 \\ 1 \end{bmatrix}, \begin{bmatrix} 3 \\ 0 \\ 3 \\ -3 \\ 3 \end{bmatrix}, \begin{bmatrix} 2 \\ 0 \\ 2 \\ 2 \\ -2 \end{bmatrix} \right\}$.

12. Call the columns of the matrix $\mathbf{x}_1$, $\mathbf{x}_2$, and $\mathbf{x}_3$ and perform the Gram-Schmidt process on these vectors:

$$\mathbf{v}_1 = \mathbf{x}_1$$

$$\mathbf{v}_2 = \mathbf{x}_2 - \frac{\mathbf{x}_2 \cdot \mathbf{v}_1}{\mathbf{v}_1 \cdot \mathbf{v}_1}\,\mathbf{v}_1 = \mathbf{x}_2 - 4\mathbf{v}_1 = \begin{bmatrix} -1 \\ 1 \\ 2 \\ 1 \\ 1 \end{bmatrix}$$

$$\mathbf{v}_3 = \mathbf{x}_3 - \frac{\mathbf{x}_3 \cdot \mathbf{v}_1}{\mathbf{v}_1 \cdot \mathbf{v}_1}\,\mathbf{v}_1 - \frac{\mathbf{x}_3 \cdot \mathbf{v}_2}{\mathbf{v}_2 \cdot \mathbf{v}_2}\,\mathbf{v}_2 = \mathbf{x}_3 - \frac{7}{2}\mathbf{v}_1 - \frac{3}{2}\mathbf{v}_2 = \begin{bmatrix} 3 \\ 3 \\ 0 \\ -3 \\ -3 \end{bmatrix}$$

Thus an orthogonal basis for W is $\left\{ \begin{bmatrix} 1 \\ -1 \\ 0 \\ 1 \\ 1 \end{bmatrix}, \begin{bmatrix} -1 \\ 1 \\ 2 \\ 1 \\ 1 \end{bmatrix}, \begin{bmatrix} 3 \\ 3 \\ 0 \\ -3 \\ -3 \end{bmatrix} \right\}$.

13. Since A and Q are given,

$$R = Q^T A = \begin{bmatrix} 5/6 & 1/6 & -3/6 & 1/6 \\ -1/6 & 5/6 & 1/6 & 3/6 \end{bmatrix} \begin{bmatrix} 5 & 9 \\ 1 & 7 \\ -3 & -5 \\ 1 & 5 \end{bmatrix} = \begin{bmatrix} 6 & 12 \\ 0 & 6 \end{bmatrix}$$

14. Since A and Q are given,

$$R = Q^T A = \begin{bmatrix} -2/7 & 5/7 & 2/7 & 4/7 \\ 5/7 & 2/7 & -4/7 & 2/7 \end{bmatrix} \begin{bmatrix} -2 & 3 \\ 5 & 7 \\ 2 & -2 \\ 4 & 6 \end{bmatrix} = \begin{bmatrix} 7 & 7 \\ 0 & 7 \end{bmatrix}$$

15. The columns of Q will be normalized versions of the vectors $\mathbf{v}_1$, $\mathbf{v}_2$, and $\mathbf{v}_3$ found in Exercise 11. Thus

$$Q = \begin{bmatrix} 1/\sqrt{5} & 1/2 & 1/2 \\ -1/\sqrt{5} & 0 & 0 \\ -1/\sqrt{5} & 1/2 & 1/2 \\ 1/\sqrt{5} & -1/2 & 1/2 \\ 1/\sqrt{5} & 1/2 & -1/2 \end{bmatrix}, R = Q^T A = \begin{bmatrix} \sqrt{5} & -\sqrt{5} & 4\sqrt{5} \\ 0 & 6 & -2 \\ 0 & 0 & 4 \end{bmatrix}$$

16. The columns of Q will be normalized versions of the vectors $\mathbf{v}_1$, $\mathbf{v}_2$, and $\mathbf{v}_3$ found in Exercise 12. Thus

$$Q = \begin{bmatrix} 1/2 & -1/2\sqrt{2} & 1/2 \\ -1/2 & 1/2\sqrt{2} & 1/2 \\ 0 & 1/\sqrt{2} & 0 \\ 1/2 & 1/2\sqrt{2} & -1/2 \\ 1/2 & 1/2\sqrt{2} & 1/2 \end{bmatrix}, R = Q^T A = \begin{bmatrix} 2 & 8 & 7 \\ 0 & 2\sqrt{2} & 3\sqrt{2} \\ 0 & 0 & 6 \end{bmatrix}$$

17. **a.** False. Scaling was used in Example 2, but the scale factor was nonzero.

    b. True. See (1) in the statement of Theorem 11.

    c. True. See the solution of Example 4.

18. **a.** False. The three orthogonal vectors must be *nonzero* to be a basis for a three-dimensional subspace. (This was the case in Step 3 of the solution of Example 2.)

    b. True. If $\mathbf{x}$ is not in a subspace $\mathbf{w}$, then $\mathbf{x}$ cannot equal $\text{proj}_W \mathbf{x}$, because $\text{proj}_W \mathbf{x}$ is in W. This idea was used for $\mathbf{v}_{k+1}$ in the proof of Theorem 11.

    c. True. See Theorem 12.

19. Suppose that $\mathbf{x}$ satisfies $R\mathbf{x} = \mathbf{0}$; then $QR\mathbf{x} = Q\mathbf{0} = \mathbf{0}$, and $A\mathbf{x} = \mathbf{0}$. Since the columns of A are linearly independent, $\mathbf{x}$ must be $\mathbf{0}$. This fact, in turn, shows that the columns of R are linearly indepedent. Since R is square, it is invertible by the Invertible Matrix Theorem.

20. If $\mathbf{y}$ is in Col A, then $\mathbf{y} = A\mathbf{x}$ for some $\mathbf{x}$. Then $\mathbf{y} = QR\mathbf{x} = Q(R\mathbf{x})$, which shows that $\mathbf{y}$ is a linear combination of the columns of Q using the entries in $R\mathbf{x}$ as weights. Conversely, suppose that $\mathbf{y} = Q\mathbf{x}$ for some $\mathbf{x}$. Since R is invertible, the equation $A = QR$ implies that $Q = AR^{-1}$. So $\mathbf{y} = AR^{-1}\mathbf{x} = A(R^{-1}\mathbf{x})$, which shows that $\mathbf{y}$ is in Col A.

21. Denote the columns of Q by $\{\mathbf{q}_1, \ldots, \mathbf{q}_n\}$. Note that $n \leq m$, because A is $m \times n$ and has linearly independent columns. The columns of Q can be extended to an orthonormal basis for $\mathbb{R}^m$ as follows. Let $\mathbf{f}_1$ be the first vector in the standard basis for $\mathbb{R}^m$ that is *not* in $W_n = \mathrm{Span}\{\mathbf{q}_1, \ldots, \mathbf{q}_n\}$, let $\mathbf{u}_1 = \mathbf{f}_1 - \mathrm{proj}_{W_n}\mathbf{f}_1$, and let $\mathbf{q}_{n+1} = \mathbf{u}_1 / \|\mathbf{u}_1\|$. Then $\{\mathbf{q}_1, \ldots, \mathbf{q}_n, \mathbf{q}_{n+1}\}$ is an orthonormal basis for $W_{n+1} = \mathrm{Span}\{\mathbf{q}_1, \ldots, \mathbf{q}_n, \mathbf{q}_{n+1}\}$. Next let $\mathbf{f}_2$ be the first vector in the standard basis for $\mathbb{R}^m$ that is *not* in W_{n+1}, let $\mathbf{u}_2 = \mathbf{f}_2 - \mathrm{proj}_{W_{n+1}}\mathbf{f}_2$, and let $\mathbf{q}_{n+2} = \mathbf{u}_2 / \|\mathbf{u}_2\|$. Then $\{\mathbf{q}_1, \ldots, \mathbf{q}_n, \mathbf{q}_{n+1}, \mathbf{q}_{n+2}\}$ is an orthogonal basis for $W_{n+2} = \mathrm{Span}\{\mathbf{q}_1, \ldots, \mathbf{q}_n, \mathbf{q}_{n+1}, \mathbf{q}_{n+2}\}$. This process will continue until $m - n$ vectors have been added to the original n vectors, and $\{\mathbf{q}_1, \ldots, \mathbf{q}_n, \mathbf{q}_{n+1}, \ldots, \mathbf{q}_m\}$ is an orthonormal basis for $\mathbb{R}^m$. Let $Q_0 = \begin{bmatrix} \mathbf{q}_{n+1} & \cdots & \mathbf{q}_m \end{bmatrix}$ and $Q_1 = \begin{bmatrix} Q & Q_0 \end{bmatrix}$. Then, using partitioned matrix multiplication,

$$Q_1 \begin{bmatrix} R \\ O \end{bmatrix} = QR = A.$$

22. We may assume that $\{\mathbf{u}_1, \ldots, \mathbf{u}_p\}$ is an orthonormal basis for W, by normalizing the vectors in the original basis given for W, if necessary. Let U be the matrix whose columns are $\mathbf{u}_1, \ldots, \mathbf{u}_p$. Then, by Theorem 10 in Section 6.3, $T(\mathbf{x}) = \mathrm{proj}_W \mathbf{x} = (UU^T)\mathbf{x}$ for $\mathbf{x}$ in $\mathbb{R}^n$. Thus T is a matrix transformation and hence is a linear transformation, as was shown in Section 1.8.

23. Given $A = QR$, partition $A = \begin{bmatrix} A_1 & A_2 \end{bmatrix}$, where A_1 has p columns. Partition Q as $Q = \begin{bmatrix} Q_1 & Q_2 \end{bmatrix}$ where Q_1 has p columns, and partition R as $R = \begin{bmatrix} R_{11} & R_{12} \\ O & R_{22} \end{bmatrix}$, where R_{11} is a $p \times p$ matrix. Then

$$A = \begin{bmatrix} A_1 & A_2 \end{bmatrix} = QR = \begin{bmatrix} Q_1 & Q_2 \end{bmatrix} \begin{bmatrix} R_{11} & R_{12} \\ O & R_{22} \end{bmatrix} = \begin{bmatrix} Q_1 R_{11} & Q_1 R_{12} + Q_2 R_{22} \end{bmatrix}$$

Thus $A_1 = Q_1 R_{11}$. The matrix Q_1 has orthonormal columns because its columns come from Q. The matrix R_{11} is square and upper triangular due to its position within the upper triangular matrix R. The diagonal entries of R_{11} are positive because they are diagonal entries of R. Thus $Q_1 R_{11}$ is a QR factorization of A_1.

24. [M] Call the columns of the matrix $\mathbf{x}_1$, $\mathbf{x}_2$, $\mathbf{x}_3$, and $\mathbf{x}_4$ and perform the Gram-Schmidt process on these vectors:

$$\mathbf{v}_1 = \mathbf{x}_1$$

$$\mathbf{v}_2 = \mathbf{x}_2 - \frac{\mathbf{x}_2 \cdot \mathbf{v}_1}{\mathbf{v}_1 \cdot \mathbf{v}_1}\mathbf{v}_1 = \mathbf{x}_2 - (-1)\mathbf{v}_1 = \begin{bmatrix} 3 \\ 3 \\ -3 \\ 0 \\ 3 \end{bmatrix}$$

$$\mathbf{v}_3 = \mathbf{x}_3 - \frac{\mathbf{x}_3 \cdot \mathbf{v}_1}{\mathbf{v}_1 \cdot \mathbf{v}_1}\mathbf{v}_1 - \frac{\mathbf{x}_3 \cdot \mathbf{v}_2}{\mathbf{v}_2 \cdot \mathbf{v}_2}\mathbf{v}_2 = \mathbf{x}_3 - \left(-\frac{1}{2}\right)\mathbf{v}_1 - \left(-\frac{4}{3}\right)\mathbf{v}_2 = \begin{bmatrix} 6 \\ 0 \\ 6 \\ 6 \\ 0 \end{bmatrix}$$

$$\mathbf{v}_4 = \mathbf{x}_4 - \frac{\mathbf{x}_4 \cdot \mathbf{v}_1}{\mathbf{v}_1 \cdot \mathbf{v}_1}\mathbf{v}_1 - \frac{\mathbf{x}_4 \cdot \mathbf{v}_2}{\mathbf{v}_2 \cdot \mathbf{v}_2}\mathbf{v}_2 - \frac{\mathbf{x}_4 \cdot \mathbf{v}_3}{\mathbf{v}_3 \cdot \mathbf{v}_3}\mathbf{v}_3 = \mathbf{x}_4 - \frac{1}{2}\mathbf{v}_1 - (-1)\mathbf{v}_2 - \left(-\frac{1}{2}\right)\mathbf{v}_3 = \begin{bmatrix} 0 \\ 5 \\ 0 \\ 0 \\ -5 \end{bmatrix}$$

Thus an orthogonal basis for W is $\left\{ \begin{bmatrix} -10 \\ 2 \\ -6 \\ 16 \\ 2 \end{bmatrix}, \begin{bmatrix} 3 \\ 3 \\ -3 \\ 0 \\ 3 \end{bmatrix}, \begin{bmatrix} 6 \\ 0 \\ 6 \\ 6 \\ 0 \end{bmatrix}, \begin{bmatrix} 0 \\ 5 \\ 0 \\ 0 \\ -5 \end{bmatrix} \right\}$.

25. **[M]** The columns of Q will be normalized versions of the vectors $\mathbf{v}_1$, $\mathbf{v}_2$, and $\mathbf{v}_3$ found in Exercise 24. Thus

$$Q = \begin{bmatrix} -1/2 & 1/2 & 1/\sqrt{3} & 0 \\ 1/10 & 1/2 & 0 & 1/\sqrt{2} \\ -3/10 & -1/2 & 1/\sqrt{3} & 0 \\ 4/5 & 0 & 1/\sqrt{3} & 0 \\ 1/10 & 1/2 & 0 & -1/\sqrt{2} \end{bmatrix}, R = Q^T A = \begin{bmatrix} 20 & -20 & -10 & 10 \\ 0 & 6 & -8 & -6 \\ 0 & 0 & 6\sqrt{3} & -3\sqrt{3} \\ 0 & 0 & 0 & 5\sqrt{2} \end{bmatrix}$$

26. **[M]** In MATLAB, when A has n columns, suitable commands are

```
Q = A(:,1)/norm(A(:,1))
   %  The first column of Q
   for j=2: n
      v=A(:,j) - Q*(Q'*A(:,j))
      Q(:,j)=v/norm(v)
      % Add a new column to Q
   end
```

6.5 SOLUTIONS

Notes: This is a core section – the basic geometric principles in this section provide the foundation for all the applications in Sections 6.6–6.8. Yet this section need not take a full day. Each example provides a stopping place. Theorem 13 and Example 1 are all that is needed for Section 6.6. Theorem 15, however, gives an illustration of why the QR factorization is important. Example 4 is related to Exercise 17 in Section 6.6.

1. To find the normal equations and to find $\hat{\mathbf{x}}$, compute

$$A^T A = \begin{bmatrix} -1 & 2 & -1 \\ 2 & -3 & 3 \end{bmatrix} \begin{bmatrix} -1 & 2 \\ 2 & -3 \\ -1 & 3 \end{bmatrix} = \begin{bmatrix} 6 & -11 \\ -11 & 22 \end{bmatrix}$$

$$A^T \mathbf{b} = \begin{bmatrix} -1 & 2 & -1 \\ 2 & -3 & 3 \end{bmatrix} \begin{bmatrix} 4 \\ 1 \\ 2 \end{bmatrix} = \begin{bmatrix} -4 \\ 11 \end{bmatrix}$$

a. The normal equations are $(A^T A)\mathbf{x} = A^T \mathbf{b}$: $\begin{bmatrix} 6 & -11 \\ -11 & 22 \end{bmatrix} \begin{bmatrix} x_1 \\ x_2 \end{bmatrix} = \begin{bmatrix} -4 \\ 11 \end{bmatrix}$.

b. Compute

$$\hat{\mathbf{x}} = (A^T A)^{-1} A^T \mathbf{b} = \begin{bmatrix} 6 & -11 \\ -11 & 22 \end{bmatrix}^{-1} \begin{bmatrix} -4 \\ 11 \end{bmatrix} = \frac{1}{11} \begin{bmatrix} 22 & 11 \\ 11 & 6 \end{bmatrix} \begin{bmatrix} -4 \\ 11 \end{bmatrix}$$

$$= \frac{1}{11} \begin{bmatrix} 33 \\ 22 \end{bmatrix} = \begin{bmatrix} 3 \\ 2 \end{bmatrix}$$

2. To find the normal equations and to find $\hat{\mathbf{x}}$, compute

$$A^T A = \begin{bmatrix} 2 & -2 & 2 \\ 1 & 0 & 3 \end{bmatrix} \begin{bmatrix} 2 & 1 \\ -2 & 0 \\ 2 & 3 \end{bmatrix} = \begin{bmatrix} 12 & 8 \\ 8 & 10 \end{bmatrix}$$

$$A^T \mathbf{b} = \begin{bmatrix} 2 & -2 & 2 \\ 1 & 0 & 3 \end{bmatrix} \begin{bmatrix} -5 \\ 8 \\ 1 \end{bmatrix} = \begin{bmatrix} -24 \\ -2 \end{bmatrix}$$

a. The normal equations are $(A^T A)\mathbf{x} = A^T \mathbf{b}$: $\begin{bmatrix} 12 & 8 \\ 8 & 10 \end{bmatrix} \begin{bmatrix} x_1 \\ x_2 \end{bmatrix} = \begin{bmatrix} -24 \\ -2 \end{bmatrix}$.

b. Compute

$$\hat{\mathbf{x}} = (A^T A)^{-1} A^T \mathbf{b} = \begin{bmatrix} 12 & 8 \\ 8 & 10 \end{bmatrix}^{-1} \begin{bmatrix} -24 \\ -2 \end{bmatrix} = \frac{1}{56} \begin{bmatrix} 10 & -8 \\ -8 & 12 \end{bmatrix} \begin{bmatrix} -24 \\ -2 \end{bmatrix}$$

$$= \frac{1}{56} \begin{bmatrix} 224 \\ 168 \end{bmatrix} = \begin{bmatrix} -4 \\ 3 \end{bmatrix}$$

3. To find the normal equations and to find $\hat{\mathbf{x}}$, compute

$$A^T A = \begin{bmatrix} 1 & -1 & 0 & 2 \\ -2 & 2 & 3 & 5 \end{bmatrix} \begin{bmatrix} 1 & -2 \\ -1 & 2 \\ 0 & 3 \\ 2 & 5 \end{bmatrix} = \begin{bmatrix} 6 & 6 \\ 6 & 42 \end{bmatrix}$$

$$A^T \mathbf{b} = \begin{bmatrix} 1 & -1 & 0 & 2 \\ -2 & 2 & 3 & 5 \end{bmatrix} \begin{bmatrix} 3 \\ 1 \\ -4 \\ 2 \end{bmatrix} = \begin{bmatrix} 6 \\ -6 \end{bmatrix}$$

a. The normal equations are $(A^T A)\mathbf{x} = A^T\mathbf{b}$: $\begin{bmatrix} 6 & 6 \\ 6 & 42 \end{bmatrix}\begin{bmatrix} x_1 \\ x_2 \end{bmatrix} = \begin{bmatrix} 6 \\ -6 \end{bmatrix}$

b. Compute

$$\hat{\mathbf{x}} = (A^T A)^{-1} A^T\mathbf{b} = \begin{bmatrix} 6 & 6 \\ 6 & 42 \end{bmatrix}^{-1}\begin{bmatrix} 6 \\ -6 \end{bmatrix} = \frac{1}{216}\begin{bmatrix} 42 & -6 \\ -6 & 6 \end{bmatrix}\begin{bmatrix} 6 \\ -6 \end{bmatrix}$$

$$= \frac{1}{216}\begin{bmatrix} 288 \\ -72 \end{bmatrix} = \begin{bmatrix} 4/3 \\ -1/3 \end{bmatrix}$$

4. To find the normal equations and to find $\hat{\mathbf{x}}$, compute

$$A^T A = \begin{bmatrix} 1 & 1 & 1 \\ 3 & -1 & 1 \end{bmatrix}\begin{bmatrix} 1 & 3 \\ 1 & -1 \\ 1 & 1 \end{bmatrix} = \begin{bmatrix} 3 & 3 \\ 3 & 11 \end{bmatrix}$$

$$A^T\mathbf{b} = \begin{bmatrix} 1 & 1 & 1 \\ 3 & -1 & 1 \end{bmatrix}\begin{bmatrix} 5 \\ 1 \\ 0 \end{bmatrix} = \begin{bmatrix} 6 \\ 14 \end{bmatrix}$$

a. The normal equations are $(A^T A)\mathbf{x} = A^T\mathbf{b}$: $\begin{bmatrix} 3 & 3 \\ 3 & 11 \end{bmatrix}\begin{bmatrix} x_1 \\ x_2 \end{bmatrix} = \begin{bmatrix} 6 \\ 14 \end{bmatrix}$

b. Compute

$$\hat{\mathbf{x}} = (A^T A)^{-1} A^T\mathbf{b} = \begin{bmatrix} 3 & 3 \\ 3 & 11 \end{bmatrix}^{-1}\begin{bmatrix} 6 \\ 14 \end{bmatrix} = \frac{1}{24}\begin{bmatrix} 11 & -3 \\ -3 & 3 \end{bmatrix}\begin{bmatrix} 6 \\ 14 \end{bmatrix}$$

$$= \frac{1}{24}\begin{bmatrix} 24 \\ 24 \end{bmatrix} = \begin{bmatrix} 1 \\ 1 \end{bmatrix}$$

5. To find the least squares solutions to $A\mathbf{x} = \mathbf{b}$, compute and row reduce the augmented matrix for the system $A^T A\mathbf{x} = A^T\mathbf{b}$:

$$\begin{bmatrix} A^T A & A^T\mathbf{b} \end{bmatrix} = \begin{bmatrix} 4 & 2 & 2 & 14 \\ 2 & 2 & 0 & 4 \\ 2 & 0 & 2 & 10 \end{bmatrix} \sim \begin{bmatrix} 1 & 0 & 1 & 5 \\ 0 & 1 & -1 & -3 \\ 0 & 0 & 0 & 0 \end{bmatrix}$$

so all vectors of the form $\hat{\mathbf{x}} = \begin{bmatrix} 5 \\ -3 \\ 0 \end{bmatrix} + x_3\begin{bmatrix} -1 \\ 1 \\ 1 \end{bmatrix}$ are the least-squares solutions of $A\mathbf{x} = \mathbf{b}$.

6. To find the least squares solutions to $A\mathbf{x} = \mathbf{b}$, compute and row reduce the augmented matrix for the system $A^T A\mathbf{x} = A^T\mathbf{b}$:

$$\begin{bmatrix} A^T A & A^T\mathbf{b} \end{bmatrix} = \begin{bmatrix} 6 & 3 & 3 & 27 \\ 3 & 3 & 0 & 12 \\ 3 & 0 & 3 & 15 \end{bmatrix} \sim \begin{bmatrix} 1 & 0 & 1 & 5 \\ 0 & 1 & -1 & -1 \\ 0 & 0 & 0 & 0 \end{bmatrix}$$

so all vectors of the form $\hat{\mathbf{x}} = \begin{bmatrix} 5 \\ -1 \\ 0 \end{bmatrix} + x_3\begin{bmatrix} -1 \\ 1 \\ 1 \end{bmatrix}$ are the least-squares solutions of $A\mathbf{x} = \mathbf{b}$.

7. From Exercise 3, $A = \begin{bmatrix} 1 & -2 \\ -1 & 2 \\ 0 & 3 \\ 2 & 5 \end{bmatrix}$, $\mathbf{b} = \begin{bmatrix} 3 \\ 1 \\ -4 \\ 2 \end{bmatrix}$, and $\hat{\mathbf{x}} = \begin{bmatrix} 4/3 \\ -1/3 \end{bmatrix}$. Since

$$A\hat{\mathbf{x}} - \mathbf{b} = \begin{bmatrix} 1 & -2 \\ -1 & 2 \\ 0 & 3 \\ 2 & 5 \end{bmatrix} \begin{bmatrix} 4/3 \\ -1/3 \end{bmatrix} - \begin{bmatrix} 3 \\ 1 \\ -4 \\ 2 \end{bmatrix} = \begin{bmatrix} 2 \\ -2 \\ -1 \\ 1 \end{bmatrix} - \begin{bmatrix} 3 \\ 1 \\ -4 \\ 2 \end{bmatrix} = \begin{bmatrix} -1 \\ -3 \\ 3 \\ -1 \end{bmatrix}$$

the least squares error is $\| A\hat{\mathbf{x}} - \mathbf{b} \| = \sqrt{20} = 2\sqrt{5}$.

8. From Exercise 4, $A = \begin{bmatrix} 1 & 3 \\ 1 & -1 \\ 1 & 1 \end{bmatrix}$, $\mathbf{b} = \begin{bmatrix} 5 \\ 1 \\ 0 \end{bmatrix}$, and $\hat{\mathbf{x}} = \begin{bmatrix} 1 \\ 1 \end{bmatrix}$. Since

$$A\hat{\mathbf{x}} - \mathbf{b} = \begin{bmatrix} 1 & 3 \\ 1 & -1 \\ 1 & 1 \end{bmatrix} \begin{bmatrix} 1 \\ 1 \end{bmatrix} - \begin{bmatrix} 5 \\ 1 \\ 0 \end{bmatrix} = \begin{bmatrix} 4 \\ 0 \\ 2 \end{bmatrix} - \begin{bmatrix} 5 \\ 1 \\ 0 \end{bmatrix} = \begin{bmatrix} -1 \\ -1 \\ 2 \end{bmatrix}$$

the least squares error is $\| A\hat{\mathbf{x}} - \mathbf{b} \| = \sqrt{6}$.

9. (a) Because the columns $\mathbf{a}_1$ and $\mathbf{a}_2$ of A are orthogonal, the method of Example 4 may be used to find $\hat{\mathbf{b}}$, the orthogonal projection of $\mathbf{b}$ onto Col A:

$$\hat{\mathbf{b}} = \frac{\mathbf{b} \cdot \mathbf{a}_1}{\mathbf{a}_1 \cdot \mathbf{a}_1} \mathbf{a}_1 + \frac{\mathbf{b} \cdot \mathbf{a}_2}{\mathbf{a}_2 \cdot \mathbf{a}_2} \mathbf{a}_2 = \frac{2}{7} \mathbf{a}_1 + \frac{1}{7} \mathbf{a}_2 = \frac{2}{7} \begin{bmatrix} 1 \\ 3 \\ -2 \end{bmatrix} + \frac{1}{7} \begin{bmatrix} 5 \\ 1 \\ 4 \end{bmatrix} = \begin{bmatrix} 1 \\ 1 \\ 0 \end{bmatrix}$$

(b) The vector $\hat{\mathbf{x}}$ contains the weights which must be placed on $\mathbf{a}_1$ and $\mathbf{a}_2$ to produce $\hat{\mathbf{b}}$. These weights are easily read from the above equation, so $\hat{\mathbf{x}} = \begin{bmatrix} 2/7 \\ 1/7 \end{bmatrix}$.

10. (a) Because the columns $\mathbf{a}_1$ and $\mathbf{a}_2$ of A are orthogonal, the method of Example 4 may be used to find $\hat{\mathbf{b}}$, the orthogonal projection of $\mathbf{b}$ onto Col A:

$$\hat{\mathbf{b}} = \frac{\mathbf{b} \cdot \mathbf{a}_1}{\mathbf{a}_1 \cdot \mathbf{a}_1} \mathbf{a}_1 + \frac{\mathbf{b} \cdot \mathbf{a}_2}{\mathbf{a}_2 \cdot \mathbf{a}_2} \mathbf{a}_2 = 3\mathbf{a}_1 + \frac{1}{2} \mathbf{a}_2 = 3 \begin{bmatrix} 1 \\ -1 \\ 1 \end{bmatrix} + \frac{1}{2} \begin{bmatrix} 2 \\ 4 \\ 2 \end{bmatrix} = \begin{bmatrix} 4 \\ -1 \\ 4 \end{bmatrix}$$

(b) The vector $\hat{\mathbf{x}}$ contains the weights which must be placed on $\mathbf{a}_1$ and $\mathbf{a}_2$ to produce $\hat{\mathbf{b}}$. These weights are easily read from the above equation, so $\hat{\mathbf{x}} = \begin{bmatrix} 3 \\ 1/2 \end{bmatrix}$.

11. (a) Because the columns $\mathbf{a}_1$, $\mathbf{a}_2$ and $\mathbf{a}_3$ of A are orthogonal, the method of Example 4 may be used to find $\hat{\mathbf{b}}$, the orthogonal projection of $\mathbf{b}$ onto Col A:

$$\hat{\mathbf{b}} = \frac{\mathbf{b} \cdot \mathbf{a}_1}{\mathbf{a}_1 \cdot \mathbf{a}_1}\mathbf{a}_1 + \frac{\mathbf{b} \cdot \mathbf{a}_2}{\mathbf{a}_2 \cdot \mathbf{a}_2}\mathbf{a}_2 + \frac{\mathbf{b} \cdot \mathbf{a}_3}{\mathbf{a}_3 \cdot \mathbf{a}_3}\mathbf{a}_3 = \frac{2}{3}\mathbf{a}_1 + 0\mathbf{a}_2 + \frac{1}{3}\mathbf{a}_3$$

$$= \frac{2}{3}\begin{bmatrix} 4 \\ 1 \\ 6 \\ 1 \end{bmatrix} + 0\begin{bmatrix} 0 \\ -5 \\ 1 \\ -1 \end{bmatrix} + \frac{1}{3}\begin{bmatrix} 1 \\ 1 \\ 0 \\ -5 \end{bmatrix} = \begin{bmatrix} 3 \\ 1 \\ 4 \\ -1 \end{bmatrix}$$

(b) The vector $\hat{\mathbf{x}}$ contains the weights which must be placed on $\mathbf{a}_1$, $\mathbf{a}_2$, and $\mathbf{a}_3$ to produce $\hat{\mathbf{b}}$. These weights are easily read from the above equation, so $\hat{\mathbf{x}} = \begin{bmatrix} 2/3 \\ 0 \\ 1/3 \end{bmatrix}$.

12. (a) Because the columns $\mathbf{a}_1$, $\mathbf{a}_2$ and $\mathbf{a}_3$ of A are orthogonal, the method of Example 4 may be used to find $\hat{\mathbf{b}}$, the orthogonal projection of $\mathbf{b}$ onto Col A:

$$\hat{\mathbf{b}} = \frac{\mathbf{b} \cdot \mathbf{a}_1}{\mathbf{a}_1 \cdot \mathbf{a}_1}\mathbf{a}_1 + \frac{\mathbf{b} \cdot \mathbf{a}_2}{\mathbf{a}_2 \cdot \mathbf{a}_2}\mathbf{a}_2 + \frac{\mathbf{b} \cdot \mathbf{a}_3}{\mathbf{a}_3 \cdot \mathbf{a}_3}\mathbf{a}_3 = \frac{1}{3}\mathbf{a}_1 + \frac{14}{3}\mathbf{a}_2 + \left(-\frac{5}{3}\right)\mathbf{a}_3$$

$$= \frac{1}{3}\begin{bmatrix} 1 \\ 1 \\ 0 \\ -1 \end{bmatrix} + \frac{14}{3}\begin{bmatrix} 1 \\ 0 \\ 1 \\ 1 \end{bmatrix} - \frac{5}{3}\begin{bmatrix} 0 \\ -1 \\ 1 \\ -1 \end{bmatrix} = \begin{bmatrix} 5 \\ 2 \\ 3 \\ 6 \end{bmatrix}$$

(b) The vector $\hat{\mathbf{x}}$ contains the weights which must be placed on $\mathbf{a}_1$, $\mathbf{a}_2$, and $\mathbf{a}_3$ to produce $\hat{\mathbf{b}}$. These weights are easily read from the above equation, so $\hat{\mathbf{x}} = \begin{bmatrix} 1/3 \\ 14/3 \\ -5/3 \end{bmatrix}$.

13. One computes that

$$A\mathbf{u} = \begin{bmatrix} 11 \\ -11 \\ 11 \end{bmatrix}, \mathbf{b} - A\mathbf{u} = \begin{bmatrix} 0 \\ 2 \\ -6 \end{bmatrix}, \| \mathbf{b} - A\mathbf{u} \| = \sqrt{40}$$

$$A\mathbf{v} = \begin{bmatrix} 7 \\ -12 \\ 7 \end{bmatrix}, \mathbf{b} - A\mathbf{v} = \begin{bmatrix} 4 \\ 3 \\ -2 \end{bmatrix}, \| \mathbf{b} - A\mathbf{v} \| = \sqrt{29}$$

Since $A\mathbf{v}$ is closer to $\mathbf{b}$ than $A\mathbf{u}$ is, $A\mathbf{u}$ is not the closest point in Col A to $\mathbf{b}$. Thus $\mathbf{u}$ cannot be a least-squares solution of $A\mathbf{x} = \mathbf{b}$.

14. One computes that

$$Au = \begin{bmatrix} 3 \\ 8 \\ 2 \end{bmatrix}, \mathbf{b} - Au = \begin{bmatrix} 2 \\ -4 \\ 2 \end{bmatrix}, \| \mathbf{b} - Au \| = \sqrt{24}$$

$$Av = \begin{bmatrix} 7 \\ 2 \\ 8 \end{bmatrix}, \mathbf{b} - Av = \begin{bmatrix} -2 \\ 2 \\ -4 \end{bmatrix}, \| \mathbf{b} - Av \| = \sqrt{24}$$

Since Au and Au are equally close to $\mathbf{b}$, and the orthogonal projection is the *unique* closest point in Col A to $\mathbf{b}$, neither Au nor Av can be the closest point in Col A to $\mathbf{b}$. Thus neither $\mathbf{u}$ nor $\mathbf{v}$ can be a least-squares solution of $Ax = \mathbf{b}$.

15. The least squares solution satisfies $R\hat{\mathbf{x}} = Q^T\mathbf{b}$. Since $R = \begin{bmatrix} 3 & 5 \\ 0 & 1 \end{bmatrix}$ and $Q^T\mathbf{b} = \begin{bmatrix} 7 \\ -1 \end{bmatrix}$, the augmented matrix

for the system may be row reduced to find

$$\begin{bmatrix} R & Q^T\mathbf{b} \end{bmatrix} = \begin{bmatrix} 3 & 5 & 7 \\ 0 & 1 & -1 \end{bmatrix} \sim \begin{bmatrix} 1 & 0 & 4 \\ 0 & 1 & -1 \end{bmatrix}$$

and so $\hat{\mathbf{x}} = \begin{bmatrix} 4 \\ -1 \end{bmatrix}$ is the least squares solution of $Ax = \mathbf{b}$.

16. The least squares solution satisfies $R\hat{\mathbf{x}} = Q^T\mathbf{b}$. Since $R = \begin{bmatrix} 2 & 3 \\ 0 & 5 \end{bmatrix}$ and $Q^T\mathbf{b} = \begin{bmatrix} 17/2 \\ 9/2 \end{bmatrix}$, the augmented

matrix for the system may be row reduced to find

$$\begin{bmatrix} R & Q^T\mathbf{b} \end{bmatrix} = \begin{bmatrix} 2 & 3 & 17/2 \\ 0 & 5 & 9/2 \end{bmatrix} \sim \begin{bmatrix} 1 & 0 & 2.9 \\ 0 & 1 & .9 \end{bmatrix}$$

and so $\hat{\mathbf{x}} = \begin{bmatrix} 2.9 \\ .9 \end{bmatrix}$ is the least squares solution of $Ax = \mathbf{b}$.

17. a. True. See the beginning of the section. The distance from Ax to $\mathbf{b}$ is $\| Ax - \mathbf{b} \|$.

b. True. See the comments about equation (1).

c. False. The inequality points in the wrong direction. See the definition of a least-squares solution.

d. True. See Theorem 13.

e. True. See Theorem 14.

18. a. True. See the paragraph following the definition of a least-squares solution.

b. False. If $\hat{\mathbf{x}}$ is the least-squares solution, then $A\hat{\mathbf{x}}$ is the point in the column space of A closest to $\mathbf{b}$. See Figure 1 and the paragraph preceding it.

c. True. See the discussion following equation (1).

d. False. The formula applies only when the columns of A are linearly independent. See Theorem 14.

e. False. See the comments after Example 4.

f. False. See the Numerical Note.

19. a. If $A\mathbf{x} = \mathbf{0}$, then $A^T A\mathbf{x} = A^T \mathbf{0} = \mathbf{0}$. This shows that Nul A is contained in Nul $A^T A$.

b. If $A^T A\mathbf{x} = \mathbf{0}$, then $\mathbf{x}^T A^T A\mathbf{x} = \mathbf{x}^T \mathbf{0} = 0$. So $(A\mathbf{x})^T (A\mathbf{x}) = 0$, which means that $\| A\mathbf{x} \|^2 = 0$, and hence $A\mathbf{x} = \mathbf{0}$. This shows that Nul $A^T A$ is contained in Nul A.

20. Suppose that $A\mathbf{x} = \mathbf{0}$. Then $A^T A\mathbf{x} = A^T \mathbf{0} = \mathbf{0}$. Since $A^T A$ is invertible, $\mathbf{x}$ must be $\mathbf{0}$. Hence the columns of A are linearly independent.

21. a. If A has linearly independent columns, then the equation $A\mathbf{x} = \mathbf{0}$ has only the trivial solution. By Exercise 17, the equation $A^T A\mathbf{x} = \mathbf{0}$ also has only the trivial solution. Since $A^T A$ is a square matrix, it must be invertible by the Invertible Matrix Theorem.

b. Since the n linearly independent columns of A belong to $\mathbb{R}^m$, m could not be less than n.

c. The n linearly independent columns of A form a basis for Col A, so the rank of A is n.

22. Note that $A^T A$ has n columns because A does. Then by the Rank Theorem and Exercise 19,

$$\operatorname{rank} A^T A = n - \dim \operatorname{Nul} A^T A = n - \dim \operatorname{Nul} A = \operatorname{rank} A$$

23. By Theorem 14, $\hat{\mathbf{b}} = A\hat{\mathbf{x}} = A(A^T A)^{-1} A^T \mathbf{b}$. The matrix $A(A^T A)^{-1} A^T$ is sometimes called the *hat-matrix* in statistics.

24. Since in this case $A^T A = I$, the normal equations give $\hat{\mathbf{x}} = A^T \mathbf{b}$.

25. The normal equations are $\begin{bmatrix} 2 & 2 \\ 2 & 2 \end{bmatrix} \begin{bmatrix} x \\ y \end{bmatrix} = \begin{bmatrix} 6 \\ 6 \end{bmatrix}$, whose solution is the set of all (x, y) such that $x + y = 3$.

The solutions correspond to the points on the line midway between the lines $x + y = 2$ and $x + y = 4$.

26. [M] Using .7 as an approximation for $\sqrt{2}/2$, $a_0 = a_2 \approx .353535$ and $a_1 = .5$. Using .707 as an approximation for $\sqrt{2}/2$, $a_0 = a_2 \approx .35355339$, $a_1 = .5$.

6.6   SOLUTIONS

Notes: This section is a valuable reference for any person who works with data that requires statistical analysis. Many graduate fields require such work. Science students in particular will benefit from Example 1. The general linear model and the subsequent examples are aimed at students who may take a multivariate statistics course. That may include more students than one might expect.

1. The design matrix X and the observation vector $\mathbf{y}$ are

$$X = \begin{bmatrix} 1 & 0 \\ 1 & 1 \\ 1 & 2 \\ 1 & 3 \end{bmatrix}, \mathbf{y} = \begin{bmatrix} 1 \\ 1 \\ 2 \\ 2 \end{bmatrix},$$

and one can compute

$$X^T X = \begin{bmatrix} 4 & 6 \\ 6 & 14 \end{bmatrix}, X^T \mathbf{y} = \begin{bmatrix} 6 \\ 11 \end{bmatrix}, \hat{\beta} = (X^T X)^{-1} X^T \mathbf{y} = \begin{bmatrix} .9 \\ .4 \end{bmatrix}$$

The least-squares line $y = \beta_0 + \beta_1 x$ is thus $y = .9 + .4x$.

2. The design matrix X and the observation vector $\mathbf{y}$ are

$$X = \begin{bmatrix} 1 & 1 \\ 1 & 2 \\ 1 & 4 \\ 1 & 5 \end{bmatrix}, \mathbf{y} = \begin{bmatrix} 0 \\ 1 \\ 2 \\ 3 \end{bmatrix},$$

and one can compute

$$X^T X = \begin{bmatrix} 4 & 12 \\ 12 & 46 \end{bmatrix}, X^T \mathbf{y} = \begin{bmatrix} 6 \\ 25 \end{bmatrix}, \hat{\beta} = (X^T X)^{-1} X^T \mathbf{y} = \begin{bmatrix} -.6 \\ .7 \end{bmatrix}$$

The least-squares line $y = \beta_0 + \beta_1 x$ is thus $y = -.6 + .7x$.

3. The design matrix X and the observation vector y are

$$X = \begin{bmatrix} 1 & -1 \\ 1 & 0 \\ 1 & 1 \\ 1 & 2 \end{bmatrix}, \mathbf{y} = \begin{bmatrix} 0 \\ 1 \\ 2 \\ 4 \end{bmatrix},$$

and one can compute

$$X^T X = \begin{bmatrix} 4 & 2 \\ 2 & 6 \end{bmatrix}, X^T \mathbf{y} = \begin{bmatrix} 7 \\ 10 \end{bmatrix}, \hat{\beta} = (X^T X)^{-1} X^T \mathbf{y} = \begin{bmatrix} 1.1 \\ 1.3 \end{bmatrix}$$

The least-squares line $y = \beta_0 + \beta_1 x$ is thus $y = 1.1 + 1.3x$.

4. The design matrix X and the observation vector $\mathbf{y}$ are

$$X = \begin{bmatrix} 1 & 2 \\ 1 & 3 \\ 1 & 5 \\ 1 & 6 \end{bmatrix}, \mathbf{y} = \begin{bmatrix} 3 \\ 2 \\ 1 \\ 0 \end{bmatrix},$$

and one can compute

$$X^T X = \begin{bmatrix} 4 & 16 \\ 16 & 74 \end{bmatrix}, X^T \mathbf{y} = \begin{bmatrix} 6 \\ 17 \end{bmatrix}, \hat{\beta} = (X^T X)^{-1} X^T \mathbf{y} = \begin{bmatrix} 4.3 \\ -.7 \end{bmatrix}$$

The least-squares line $y = \beta_0 + \beta_1 x$ is thus $y = 4.3 - .7x$.

5. If two data points have different x-coordinates, then the two columns of the design matrix X cannot be multiples of each other and hence are linearly independent. By Theorem 14 in Section 6.5, the normal equations have a unique solution.

6. If the columns of X were linearly dependent, then the same dependence relation would hold for the vectors in $\mathbb{R}^3$ formed from the top three entries in each column. That is, the columns of the matrix

$$\begin{bmatrix} 1 & x_1 & x_1^2 \\ 1 & x_2 & x_2^2 \\ 1 & x_3 & x_3^2 \end{bmatrix}$$ would also be linearly dependent, and so this matrix (called a Vandermonde matrix)

would be noninvertible. Note that the determinant of this matrix is $(x_2 - x_1)(x_3 - x_1)(x_3 - x_2) \neq 0$ since x_1, x_2, and x_3 are distinct. Thus this matrix is invertible, which means that the columns of X are in fact linearly independent. By Theorem 14 in Section 6.5, the normal equations have a unique solution.

7. a. The model that produces the correct least-squares fit is $\mathbf{y} = X\beta + \epsilon$, where

$$X = \begin{bmatrix} 1 & 1 \\ 2 & 4 \\ 3 & 9 \\ 4 & 16 \\ 5 & 25 \end{bmatrix}, \mathbf{y} = \begin{bmatrix} 1.8 \\ 2.7 \\ 3.4 \\ 3.8 \\ 3.9 \end{bmatrix}, \beta = \begin{bmatrix} \beta_1 \\ \beta_2 \end{bmatrix}, \text{ and } \epsilon = \begin{bmatrix} \epsilon_1 \\ \epsilon_2 \\ \epsilon_3 \\ \epsilon_4 \\ \epsilon_5 \end{bmatrix}$$

b. [M] One computes that (to two decimal places) $\hat{\beta} = \begin{bmatrix} 1.76 \\ -.20 \end{bmatrix}$, so the desired least-squares equation is

$y = 1.76x - .20x^2$.

8. a. The model that produces the correct least-squares fit is $\mathbf{y} = X\beta + \epsilon$, where

$$X = \begin{bmatrix} x_1 & x_1^2 & x_1^3 \\ \vdots & \vdots & \vdots \\ x_n & x_n^2 & x_n^3 \end{bmatrix}, \mathbf{y} = \begin{bmatrix} y_1 \\ \vdots \\ y_n \end{bmatrix}, \beta = \begin{bmatrix} \beta_1 \\ \beta_2 \\ \beta_3 \end{bmatrix}, \text{ and } \epsilon = \begin{bmatrix} \epsilon_1 \\ \vdots \\ \epsilon_n \end{bmatrix}$$

b. [M] For the given data,

$$X = \begin{bmatrix} 4 & 16 & 64 \\ 6 & 36 & 216 \\ 8 & 64 & 512 \\ 10 & 100 & 1000 \\ 12 & 144 & 1728 \\ 14 & 196 & 2744 \\ 16 & 256 & 4096 \\ 18 & 324 & 5832 \end{bmatrix} \text{ and } \mathbf{y} = \begin{bmatrix} 1.58 \\ 2.08 \\ 2.5 \\ 2.8 \\ 3.1 \\ 3.4 \\ 3.8 \\ 4.32 \end{bmatrix}$$

so $\hat{\beta} = (X^T X)^{-1} X^T \mathbf{y} = \begin{bmatrix} .5132 \\ -.03348 \\ .001016 \end{bmatrix}$, and the least-squares curve is $y = .5132x - .03348x^2 + .001016x^3$.

9. The model that produces the correct least-squares fit is $\mathbf{y} = X\beta + \epsilon$, where

$$X = \begin{bmatrix} \cos 1 & \sin 1 \\ \cos 2 & \sin 2 \\ \cos 3 & \sin 3 \end{bmatrix}, \mathbf{y} = \begin{bmatrix} 7.9 \\ 5.4 \\ -.9 \end{bmatrix}, \beta = \begin{bmatrix} A \\ B \end{bmatrix}, \text{ and } \epsilon = \begin{bmatrix} \epsilon_1 \\ \epsilon_2 \\ \epsilon_3 \end{bmatrix}$$

10. a. The model that produces the correct least-squares fit is $\mathbf{y} = X\beta + \epsilon$, where

$$X = \begin{bmatrix} e^{-.02(10)} & e^{-.07(10)} \\ e^{-.02(11)} & e^{-.07(11)} \\ e^{-.02(12)} & e^{-.07(12)} \\ e^{-.02(14)} & e^{-.07(14)} \\ e^{-.02(15)} & e^{-.07(15)} \end{bmatrix}, \mathbf{y} = \begin{bmatrix} 21.34 \\ 20.68 \\ 20.05 \\ 18.87 \\ 18.30 \end{bmatrix}, \beta = \begin{bmatrix} M_A \\ M_B \end{bmatrix}, \text{ and } \epsilon = \begin{bmatrix} \epsilon_1 \\ \epsilon_2 \\ \epsilon_3 \\ \epsilon_4 \\ \epsilon_5 \end{bmatrix},$$

b. [M] One computes that (to two decimal places) $\hat{\beta} = \begin{bmatrix} 19.94 \\ 10.10 \end{bmatrix}$, so the desired least-squares equation is

$$y = 19.94e^{-.02t} + 10.10e^{-.07t}.$$

11. [M] The model that produces the correct least-squares fit is $\mathbf{y} = X\beta + \boldsymbol{\epsilon}$, where

$$X = \begin{bmatrix} 1 & 3\cos.88 \\ 1 & 2.3\cos1.1 \\ 1 & 1.65\cos1.42 \\ 1 & 1.25\cos1.77 \\ 1 & 1.01\cos2.14 \end{bmatrix}, \mathbf{y} = \begin{bmatrix} 3 \\ 2.3 \\ 1.65 \\ 1.25 \\ 1.01 \end{bmatrix}, \beta = \begin{bmatrix} \beta \\ e \end{bmatrix}, \text{ and } \boldsymbol{\epsilon} = \begin{bmatrix} \epsilon_1 \\ \epsilon_2 \\ \epsilon_3 \\ \epsilon_4 \\ \epsilon_5 \end{bmatrix}$$

One computes that (to two decimal places) $\hat{\beta} = \begin{bmatrix} 1.45 \\ .811 \end{bmatrix}$. Since $e = .811 < 1$ the orbit is an ellipse. The

equation $r = \beta / (1 - e\cos\vartheta)$ produces $r = 1.33$ when $\vartheta = 4.6$.

12. [M] The model that produces the correct least-squares fit is $\mathbf{y} = X\beta + \boldsymbol{\epsilon}$, where

$$X = \begin{bmatrix} 1 & 3.78 \\ 1 & 4.11 \\ 1 & 4.41 \\ 1 & 4.73 \\ 1 & 4.88 \end{bmatrix}, \mathbf{y} = \begin{bmatrix} 91 \\ 98 \\ 103 \\ 110 \\ 112 \end{bmatrix}, \beta = \begin{bmatrix} \beta_0 \\ \beta_1 \end{bmatrix}, \text{ and } \boldsymbol{\epsilon} = \begin{bmatrix} \epsilon_1 \\ \epsilon_2 \\ \epsilon_3 \\ \epsilon_4 \\ \epsilon_5 \end{bmatrix}$$

One computes that (to two decimal places) $\hat{\beta} = \begin{bmatrix} 18.56 \\ 19.24 \end{bmatrix}$, so the desired least-squares equation is

$p = 18.56 + 19.24 \ln w$. When $w = 100$, $p \approx 107$ millimeters of mercury.

13. [M]

a. The model that produces the correct least-squares fit is $\mathbf{y} = X\beta + \boldsymbol{\epsilon}$, where

$$X = \begin{bmatrix} 1 & 0 & 0 & 0 \\ 1 & 1 & 1 & 1 \\ 1 & 2 & 2^2 & 2^3 \\ 1 & 3 & 3^2 & 3^3 \\ 1 & 4 & 4^2 & 4^3 \\ 1 & 5 & 5^2 & 5^3 \\ 1 & 6 & 6^2 & 6^3 \\ 1 & 7 & 7^2 & 7^3 \\ 1 & 8 & 8^2 & 8^3 \\ 1 & 9 & 9^2 & 9^3 \\ 1 & 10 & 10^2 & 10^3 \\ 1 & 11 & 11^2 & 11^3 \\ 1 & 12 & 12^2 & 12^3 \end{bmatrix}, \mathbf{y} = \begin{bmatrix} 0 \\ 8.8 \\ 29.9 \\ 62.0 \\ 104.7 \\ 159.1 \\ 222.0 \\ 294.5 \\ 380.4 \\ 471.1 \\ 571.7 \\ 686.8 \\ 809.2 \end{bmatrix}, \beta = \begin{bmatrix} \beta_0 \\ \beta_1 \\ \beta_2 \\ \beta_3 \end{bmatrix}, \text{ and } \boldsymbol{\epsilon} = \begin{bmatrix} \epsilon_1 \\ \epsilon_2 \\ \epsilon_3 \\ \epsilon_4 \\ \epsilon_5 \\ \epsilon_6 \\ \epsilon_7 \\ \epsilon_8 \\ \epsilon_9 \\ \epsilon_{10} \\ \epsilon_{11} \\ \epsilon_{12} \end{bmatrix}$$

One computes that (to four decimal places) $\hat{\beta} = \begin{bmatrix} -.8558 \\ 4.7025 \\ 5.5554 \\ -.0274 \end{bmatrix}$, so the desired least-squares polynomial is

$$y(t) = -.8558 + 4.7025t + 5.5554t^2 - .0274t^3.$$

b. The velocity $v(t)$ is the derivative of the position function $y(t)$, so $v(t) = 4.7025 + 11.1108t - .0822t^2$, and $v(4.5) = 53.0$ ft/sec.

14. Write the design matrix as $\begin{bmatrix} 1 & \mathbf{x} \end{bmatrix}$. Since the residual vector $\epsilon = \mathbf{y} - X\hat{\beta}$ is orthogonal to Col X,

$$0 = \mathbf{1} \cdot \epsilon = \mathbf{1} \cdot (\mathbf{y} - X\hat{\beta}) = \mathbf{1}^T \mathbf{y} - (\mathbf{1}^T X)\hat{\beta}$$

$$= (y_1 + \ldots + y_n) - \begin{bmatrix} n & \sum x \end{bmatrix} \begin{bmatrix} \hat{\beta}_0 \\ \hat{\beta}_1 \end{bmatrix} = \sum y - n\hat{\beta}_0 - \hat{\beta}_1 \sum x = n\bar{y} - n\hat{\beta}_0 - n\hat{\beta}_1\bar{x}$$

This equation may be solved for $\bar{y}$ to find $\bar{y} = \hat{\beta}_0 + \hat{\beta}_1\bar{x}$.

15. From equation (1) on page 420,

$$X^T X = \begin{bmatrix} 1 & \cdots & 1 \\ x_1 & \cdots & x_n \end{bmatrix} \begin{bmatrix} 1 & x_1 \\ \vdots & \vdots \\ 1 & x_n \end{bmatrix} = \begin{bmatrix} n & \sum x \\ \sum x & \left(\sum x\right)^2 \end{bmatrix}$$

$$X^T \mathbf{y} = \begin{bmatrix} 1 & \cdots & 1 \\ x_1 & \cdots & x_n \end{bmatrix} \begin{bmatrix} y_1 \\ \vdots \\ y_n \end{bmatrix} = \begin{bmatrix} \sum y \\ \sum xy \end{bmatrix}$$

The equations (7) in the text follow immediately from the normal equations $X^T X \beta = X^T \mathbf{y}$.

16. The determinant of the coefficient matrix of the equations in (7) is $n\sum x^2 - \left(\sum x\right)^2$. Using the 2×2 formula for the inverse of the coefficient matrix,

$$\begin{bmatrix} \hat{\beta}_0 \\ \hat{\beta}_1 \end{bmatrix} = \frac{1}{n\sum x^2 - \left(\sum x\right)^2} \begin{bmatrix} \sum x^2 & -\sum x \\ -\sum x & n \end{bmatrix} \begin{bmatrix} \sum y \\ \sum xy \end{bmatrix}$$

Hence

$$\hat{\beta}_0 = \frac{\left(\sum x^2\right)\left(\sum y\right) - \left(\sum x\right)\left(\sum xy\right)}{n\sum x^2 - \left(\sum x\right)^2}, \hat{\beta}_1 = \frac{n\sum xy - \left(\sum x\right)\left(\sum y\right)}{n\sum x^2 - \left(\sum x\right)^2}$$

Note: A simple algebraic calculation shows that $\sum y - \left(\sum x\right)\hat{\beta}_1 = n\hat{\beta}_0$, which provides a simple formula for $\hat{\beta}_0$ once $\hat{\beta}_1$ is known.

17. a. The mean of the data in Example 1 is $\bar{x} = 5.5$, so the data in mean-deviation form are $(-3.5, 1)$,

$(-.5, 2)$, $(1.5, 3)$, $(2.5, 3)$, and the associated design matrix is $X = \begin{bmatrix} 1 & -3.5 \\ 1 & -.5 \\ 1 & 1.5 \\ 1 & 2.5 \end{bmatrix}$. The columns of X are

orthogonal because the entries in the second column sum to 0.

b. The normal equations are $X^T X \beta = X^T \mathbf{y}$, or $\begin{bmatrix} 4 & 0 \\ 0 & 21 \end{bmatrix} \begin{bmatrix} \beta_0 \\ \beta_1 \end{bmatrix} = \begin{bmatrix} 9 \\ 7.5 \end{bmatrix}$. One computes that $\hat{\beta} = \begin{bmatrix} 9/4 \\ 5/14 \end{bmatrix}$,

so the desired least-squares line is $y = (9/4) + (5/14)x^* = (9/4) + (5/14)(x - 5.5)$.

18. Since

$$X^T X = \begin{bmatrix} 1 & \cdots & 1 \\ x_1 & \cdots & x_n \end{bmatrix} \begin{bmatrix} 1 & x_1 \\ \vdots & \vdots \\ 1 & x_n \end{bmatrix} = \begin{bmatrix} n & \sum x \\ \sum x & \left(\sum x \right)^2 \end{bmatrix}$$

$X^T X$ is a diagonal matrix when $\sum x = 0$.

19. The residual vector $\boldsymbol{\epsilon} = \mathbf{y} - X\hat{\beta}$ is orthogonal to Col X, while $\hat{\mathbf{y}} = X\hat{\beta}$ is in Col X. Since $\boldsymbol{\epsilon}$ and $\hat{\mathbf{y}}$ are thus orthogonal, apply the Pythagorean Theorem to these vectors to obtain

$$\mathrm{SS(T)} = \| \mathbf{y} \|^2 = \| \hat{\mathbf{y}} + \boldsymbol{\epsilon} \|^2 = \| \hat{\mathbf{y}} \|^2 + \| \boldsymbol{\epsilon} \|^2 = \| X\hat{\beta} \|^2 + \| \mathbf{y} - X\hat{\beta} \|^2 = \mathrm{SS(R)} + \mathrm{SS(E)}$$

20. Since $\hat{\beta}$ satisfies the normal equations, $X^T X \hat{\beta} = X^T \mathbf{y}$, and

$$\| X\hat{\beta} \|^2 = (X\hat{\beta})^T (X\hat{\beta}) = \hat{\beta}^T X^T X \hat{\beta} = \hat{\beta}^T X^T \mathbf{y}$$

Since $\| X\hat{\beta} \|^2 = \mathrm{SS(R)}$ and $\mathbf{y}^T \mathbf{y} = \| \mathbf{y} \|^2 = \mathrm{SS(T)}$, Exercise 19 shows that

$$\mathrm{SS(E)} = \mathrm{SS(T)} - \mathrm{SS(R)} = \mathbf{y}^T \mathbf{y} - \hat{\beta}^T X^T \mathbf{y}$$

6.7   SOLUTIONS

Notes: The three types of inner products described here (in Examples 1, 2, and 7) are matched by examples in Section 6.8. It is possible to spend just one day on selected portions of both sections. Example 1 matches the weighted least squares in Section 6.8. Examples 2–6 are applied to trend analysis in Seciton 6.8. This material is aimed at students who have not had much calculus or who intend to take more than one course in statistics.

For students who have seen some calculus, Example 7 is needed to develop the Fourier series in Section 6.8. Example 8 is used to motivate the inner product on $C[a, b]$. The Cauchy-Schwarz and triangle inequalities are not used here, but they should be part of the training of every mathematics student.

1. The inner product is $\langle x, y \rangle = 4x_1 y_1 + 5x_2 y_2$. Let $\mathbf{x} = (1, 1)$, $\mathbf{y} = (5, -1)$.

    a. Since $\| \mathbf{x} \|^2 = \langle x, x \rangle = 9$, $\| \mathbf{x} \| = 3$. Since $\| \mathbf{y} \|^2 = \langle y, y \rangle = 105$, $\| \mathbf{x} \| = \sqrt{105}$. Finally,

        $| \langle x, y \rangle |^2 = 15^2 = 225$.

    b. A vector $\mathbf{z}$ is orthogonal to $\mathbf{y}$ if and only if $\langle x, y \rangle = 0$, that is, $20z_1 - 5z_2 = 0$, or $4z_1 = z_2$. Thus all

    multiples of $\begin{bmatrix} 1 \\ 4 \end{bmatrix}$ are orthogonal to $\mathbf{y}$.

2. The inner product is $\langle x, y \rangle = 4x_1 y_1 + 5x_2 y_2$. Let $\mathbf{x} = (3, -2)$, $\mathbf{y} = (-2, 1)$. Compute that $\| \mathbf{x} \|^2 = \langle x, x \rangle = 56$, $\| \mathbf{y} \|^2 = \langle y, y \rangle = 21$, $\| \mathbf{x} \|^2 \| \mathbf{y} \|^2 = 56 \cdot 21 = 1176$, $\langle x, y \rangle = -34$, and $| \langle x, y \rangle |^2 = 1156$. Thus $| \langle x, y \rangle |^2 \le \| \mathbf{x} \|^2 \| \mathbf{y} \|^2$, as the Cauchy-Schwarz inequality predicts.

3. The inner product is $\langle p, q \rangle = p(-1)q(-1) + p(0)q(0) + p(1)q(1)$, so $\langle 4 + t, 5 - 4t^2 \rangle = 3(1) + 4(5) + 5(1) = 28$.

4. The inner product is $\langle p, q \rangle = p(-1)q(-1) + p(0)q(0) + p(1)q(1)$, so $\langle 3t - t^2, 3 + 2t^2 \rangle = (-4)(5) + 0(3) + 2(5) = -10$.

5. The inner product is $\langle p, q \rangle = p(-1)q(-1) + p(0)q(0) + p(1)q(1)$, so
$\langle p, q \rangle = \langle 4 + t, 4 + t \rangle = 3^2 + 4^2 + 5^2 = 50$ and $\| p \| = \sqrt{\langle p, p \rangle} = \sqrt{50} = 5\sqrt{2}$. Likewise
$\langle q, q \rangle = \langle 5 - 4t^2, 5 - 4t^2 \rangle = 1^2 + 5^2 + 1^2 = 27$ and $\| q \| = \sqrt{\langle q, q \rangle} = \sqrt{27} = 3\sqrt{3}$.

6. The inner product is $\langle p, q \rangle = p(-1)q(-1) + p(0)q(0) + p(1)q(1)$, so $\langle p, p \rangle = \langle 3t - t^2, 3t - t^2 \rangle = (-4)^2 + 0^2 + 2^2 = 20$ and $\| p \| = \sqrt{\langle p, p \rangle} = \sqrt{20} = 2\sqrt{5}$. Likewise $\langle q, q \rangle = \langle 3 + 2t^2, 3 + 2t^2 \rangle = 5^2 + 3^2 + 5^2 = 59$ and $\| q \| = \sqrt{\langle q, q \rangle} = \sqrt{59}$.

7. The orthogonal projection $\hat{q}$ of q onto the subspace spanned by p is

$$\hat{q} = \frac{\langle q, p \rangle}{\langle p, p \rangle} p = \frac{28}{50}(4 + t) = \frac{56}{25} + \frac{14}{25}t$$

8. The orthogonal projection $\hat{q}$ of q onto the subspace spanned by p is

$$\hat{q} = \frac{\langle q, p \rangle}{\langle p, p \rangle} p = -\frac{10}{20}(3t - t^2) = -\frac{3}{2}t + \frac{1}{2}t^2$$

9. The inner product is $\langle p, q \rangle = p(-3)q(-3) + p(-1)q(-1) + p(1)q(1) + p(3)q(3)$.

   a. The orthogonal projection $\hat{p}_2$ of p_2 onto the subspace spanned by p_0 and p_1 is

$$\hat{p}_2 = \frac{\langle p_2, p_0 \rangle}{\langle p_0, p_0 \rangle} p_0 + \frac{\langle p_2, p_1 \rangle}{\langle p_1, p_1 \rangle} p_1 = \frac{20}{4}(1) + \frac{0}{20}t = 5$$

   b. The vector $q = p_3 - \hat{p}_2 = t^2 - 5$ will be orthogonal to both p_0 and p_1 and $\{p_0, p_1, q\}$ will be an orthogonal basis for $\text{Span}\{p_0, p_1, p_2\}$. The vector of values for q at $(-3, -1, 1, 3)$ is $(4, -4, -4, 4)$, so scaling by 1/4 yields the new vector $q = (1/4)(t^2 - 5)$.

10. The best approximation to $p = t^3$ by vectors in $W = \text{Span}\{p_0, p_1, q\}$ will be

$$\hat{p} = \text{proj}_W\, p = \frac{\langle p, p_0 \rangle}{\langle p_0, p_0 \rangle} p_0 + \frac{\langle p, p_1 \rangle}{\langle p_1, p_1 \rangle} p_1 + \frac{\langle p, q \rangle}{\langle q, q \rangle} q = \frac{0}{4}(1) + \frac{164}{20}(t) + \frac{0}{4}\left(\frac{t^2 - 5}{4}\right) = \frac{41}{5}t$$

11. The orthogonal projection of $p = t^3$ onto $W = \text{Span}\{p_0, p_1, p_2\}$ will be

$$\hat{p} = \text{proj}_W\, p = \frac{\langle p, p_0 \rangle}{\langle p_0, p_0 \rangle} p_0 + \frac{\langle p, p_1 \rangle}{\langle p_1, p_1 \rangle} p_1 + \frac{\langle p, p_2 \rangle}{\langle p_2, p_2 \rangle} p_2 = \frac{0}{5}(1) + \frac{34}{10}(t) + \frac{0}{14}(t^2 - 2) = \frac{17}{5}t$$

12. Let $W = \text{Span}\{p_0, p_1, p_2\}$. The vector $p_3 = p - \text{proj}_W\, p = t^3 - (17/5)t$ will make $\{p_0, p_1, p_2, p_3\}$ an orthogonal basis for the subspace $\mathbb{P}_3$ of $\mathbb{P}_4$. The vector of values for p_3 at $(-2, -1, 0, 1, 2)$ is $(-6/5, 12/5, 0, -12/5, 6/5)$, so scaling by 5/6 yields the new vector $p_3 = (5/6)(t^3 - (17/5)t) = (5/6)t^3 - (17/6)t$.

13. Suppose that A is invertible and that $\langle \mathbf{u}, \mathbf{v} \rangle = (A\mathbf{u}) \cdot (A\mathbf{v})$ for $\mathbf{u}$ and $\mathbf{v}$ in $\mathbb{R}^n$. Check each axiom in the definition on page 428, using the properties of the dot product.

   i. $\langle \mathbf{u}, \mathbf{v} \rangle = (A\mathbf{u}) \cdot (A\mathbf{v}) = (A\mathbf{v}) \cdot (A\mathbf{u}) = \langle \mathbf{v}, \mathbf{u} \rangle$

   ii. $\langle \mathbf{u} + \mathbf{v}, \mathbf{w} \rangle = (A(\mathbf{u} + \mathbf{v})) \cdot (A\mathbf{w}) = (A\mathbf{u} + A\mathbf{v}) \cdot (A\mathbf{w}) = (A\mathbf{u}) \cdot (A\mathbf{w}) + (A\mathbf{v}) \cdot (A\mathbf{w}) = \langle \mathbf{u}, \mathbf{w} \rangle + \langle \mathbf{v}, \mathbf{w} \rangle$

   iii. $\langle c\mathbf{u}, \mathbf{v} \rangle = (A(c\mathbf{u})) \cdot (A\mathbf{v}) = (c(A\mathbf{u})) \cdot (A\mathbf{v}) = c((A\mathbf{u}) \cdot (A\mathbf{v})) = c\langle \mathbf{u}, \mathbf{v} \rangle$

   iv. $\langle c\mathbf{u}, \mathbf{u} \rangle = (A\mathbf{u}) \cdot (A\mathbf{u}) = \| A\mathbf{u} \|^2 \geq 0$, and this quantity is zero if and only if the vector $A\mathbf{u}$ is $\mathbf{0}$. But $A\mathbf{u} = \mathbf{0}$ if and only $\mathbf{u} = \mathbf{0}$ because A is invertible.

14. Suppose that T is a one-to-one linear transformation from a vector space V into $\mathbb{R}^n$ and that $\langle \mathbf{u}, \mathbf{v} \rangle = T(\mathbf{u}) \cdot T(\mathbf{v})$ for $\mathbf{u}$ and $\mathbf{v}$ in $\mathbb{R}^n$. Check each axiom in the definition on page 428, using the properties of the dot product and T. The linearity of T is used often in the following.

   i. $\langle \mathbf{u}, \mathbf{v} \rangle = T(\mathbf{u}) \cdot T(\mathbf{v}) = T(\mathbf{v}) \cdot T(\mathbf{u}) = \langle \mathbf{v}, \mathbf{u} \rangle$

   ii. $\langle \mathbf{u} + \mathbf{v}, \mathbf{w} \rangle = T(\mathbf{u} + \mathbf{v}) \cdot T(\mathbf{w}) = (T(\mathbf{u}) + T(\mathbf{v})) \cdot T(\mathbf{w}) = T(\mathbf{u}) \cdot T(\mathbf{w}) + T(\mathbf{v}) \cdot T(\mathbf{w}) = \langle \mathbf{u}, \mathbf{w} \rangle + \langle \mathbf{v}, \mathbf{w} \rangle$

   iii. $\langle c\mathbf{u}, \mathbf{v} \rangle = T(c\mathbf{u}) \cdot T(\mathbf{v}) = (cT(\mathbf{u})) \cdot T(\mathbf{v}) = c(T(\mathbf{u}) \cdot T(\mathbf{v})) = c\langle \mathbf{u}, \mathbf{v} \rangle$

   iv. $\langle \mathbf{u}, \mathbf{u} \rangle = T(\mathbf{u}) \cdot T(\mathbf{u}) = \| T(\mathbf{u}) \|^2 \geq 0$, and this quantity is zero if and only if $\mathbf{u} = \mathbf{0}$ since T is a one-to-one transformation.

15. Using Axioms 1 and 3, $\langle \mathbf{u}, c\mathbf{v} \rangle = \langle c\mathbf{v}, \mathbf{u} \rangle = c\langle \mathbf{v}, \mathbf{u} \rangle = c\langle \mathbf{u}, \mathbf{v} \rangle$.

16. Using Axioms 1, 2 and 3,

$$\| \mathbf{u} - \mathbf{v} \|^2 = \langle \mathbf{u} - \mathbf{v}, \mathbf{u} - \mathbf{v} \rangle = \langle \mathbf{u}, \mathbf{u} - \mathbf{v} \rangle - \langle \mathbf{v}, \mathbf{u} - \mathbf{v} \rangle$$
$$= \langle \mathbf{u}, \mathbf{u} \rangle - \langle \mathbf{u}, \mathbf{v} \rangle - \langle \mathbf{v}, \mathbf{u} \rangle + \langle \mathbf{v}, \mathbf{v} \rangle = \langle \mathbf{u}, \mathbf{u} \rangle - 2\langle \mathbf{u}, \mathbf{v} \rangle + \langle \mathbf{v}, \mathbf{v} \rangle$$
$$= \| \mathbf{u} \|^2 - 2\langle \mathbf{u}, \mathbf{v} \rangle + \| \mathbf{v} \|^2$$

Since $\{\mathbf{u}, \mathbf{v}\}$ is orthonormal, $\| \mathbf{u} \|^2 = \| \mathbf{v} \|^2 = 1$ and $\langle \mathbf{u}, \mathbf{v} \rangle = 0$. So $\| \mathbf{u} - \mathbf{v} \|^2 = 2$.

17. Following the method in Exercise 16,

$$\| \mathbf{u} + \mathbf{v} \|^2 = \langle \mathbf{u} + \mathbf{v}, \mathbf{u} + \mathbf{v} \rangle = \langle \mathbf{u}, \mathbf{u} + \mathbf{v} \rangle + \langle \mathbf{v}, \mathbf{u} + \mathbf{v} \rangle$$
$$= \langle \mathbf{u}, \mathbf{u} \rangle + \langle \mathbf{u}, \mathbf{v} \rangle + \langle \mathbf{v}, \mathbf{u} \rangle + \langle \mathbf{v}, \mathbf{v} \rangle = \langle \mathbf{u}, \mathbf{u} \rangle + 2\langle \mathbf{u}, \mathbf{v} \rangle + \langle \mathbf{v}, \mathbf{v} \rangle$$
$$= \| \mathbf{u} \|^2 + 2\langle \mathbf{u}, \mathbf{v} \rangle + \| \mathbf{v} \|^2$$

Subtracting these results, one finds that $\| \mathbf{u} + \mathbf{v} \|^2 - \| \mathbf{u} - \mathbf{v} \|^2 = 4\langle \mathbf{u}, \mathbf{v} \rangle$, and dividing by 4 gives the desired identity.

18. In Exercises 16 and 17, it has been shown that $\| \mathbf{u} - \mathbf{v} \|^2 = \| \mathbf{u} \|^2 - 2\langle \mathbf{u}, \mathbf{v} \rangle + \| \mathbf{v} \|^2$ and $\| \mathbf{u} + \mathbf{v} \|^2 = \| \mathbf{u} \|^2 + 2\langle \mathbf{u}, \mathbf{v} \rangle + \| \mathbf{v} \|^2$. Adding these two results gives $\| \mathbf{u} + \mathbf{v} \|^2 + \| \mathbf{u} - \mathbf{v} \|^2 = 2\| \mathbf{u} \|^2 + 2\| \mathbf{v} \|^2$.

19. let $\mathbf{u} = \begin{bmatrix} \sqrt{a} \\ \sqrt{b} \end{bmatrix}$ and $\mathbf{v} = \begin{bmatrix} \sqrt{b} \\ \sqrt{a} \end{bmatrix}$. Then $\| \mathbf{u} \|^2 = a + b$, $\| \mathbf{v} \|^2 = a + b$, and $\langle \mathbf{u}, \mathbf{v} \rangle = 2\sqrt{ab}$. Since a and b are nonnegative, $\| \mathbf{u} \| = \sqrt{a + b}$, $\| \mathbf{v} \| = \sqrt{a + b}$. Plugging these values into the Cauchy-Schwarz inequality gives

$$2\sqrt{ab} = |\langle \mathbf{u}, \mathbf{v} \rangle| \leq \| \mathbf{u} \| \| \mathbf{v} \| = \sqrt{a + b}\sqrt{a + b} = a + b$$

Dividing both sides of this equation by 2 gives the desired inequality.

20. The Cauchy-Schwarz inequality may be altered by dividing both sides of the inequality by 2 and then squaring both sides of the inequality. The result is

$$\left(\frac{\langle \mathbf{u}, \mathbf{v} \rangle}{2}\right)^2 \le \frac{\|\mathbf{u}\|^2 \|\mathbf{v}\|^2}{4}$$

Now let $\mathbf{u} = \begin{bmatrix} a \\ b \end{bmatrix}$ and $\mathbf{v} = \begin{bmatrix} 1 \\ 1 \end{bmatrix}$. Then $\|\mathbf{u}\|^2 = a^2 + b^2$, $\|\mathbf{v}\|^2 = 2$, and $\langle \mathbf{u}, \mathbf{v} \rangle = a + b$. Plugging these values into the inequality above yields the desired inequality.

21. The inner product is $\langle f, g \rangle = \int_0^1 f(t)g(t)dt$. Let $f(t) = 1 - 3t^2$, $g(t) = t - t^3$. Then

$$\langle f, g \rangle = \int_0^1 (1 - 3t^2)(t - t^3)\, dt = \int_0^1 3t^5 - 4t^3 + t\, dt = 0$$

22. The inner product is $\langle f, g \rangle = \int_0^1 f(t)g(t)\, dt$. Let $f(t) = 5t - 3$, $g(t) = t^3 - t^2$. Then

$$\langle f, g \rangle = \int_0^1 (5t - 3)(t^3 - t^2)dt = \int_0^1 5t^4 - 8t^3 + 3t^2 dt = 0$$

23. The inner product is $\langle f, g \rangle = \int_0^1 f(t)g(t)\, dt$, so $\langle f, f \rangle = \int_0^1 (1 - 3t^2)^2 dt = \int_0^1 9t^4 - 6t^2 + 1\, dt = 4/5$, and $\|f\| = \sqrt{\langle f, f \rangle} = 2/\sqrt{5}$.

24. The inner product is $\langle f, g \rangle = \int_0^1 f(t)g(t)\, dt$, so $\langle g, g \rangle = \int_0^1 (t^3 - t^2)^2 dt = \int_0^1 t^6 - 2t^5 + t^4 dt = 1/105$, and $\|g\| = \sqrt{\langle g, g \rangle} = 1/\sqrt{105}$.

25. The inner product is $\langle f, g \rangle = \int_{-1}^1 f(t)g(t)dt$. Then 1 and t are orthogonal because $\langle 1, t \rangle = \int_{-1}^1 t\, dt = 0$. So 1 and t can be in an orthogonal basis for $\text{Span}\{1, t, t^2\}$. By the Gram-Schmidt process, the third basis element in the orthogonal basis can be

$$t^2 - \frac{\langle t^2, 1 \rangle}{\langle 1, 1 \rangle} 1 - \frac{\langle t^2, t \rangle}{\langle t, t \rangle} t$$

Since $\langle t^2, 1 \rangle = \int_{-1}^1 t^2 dt = 2/3$, $\langle 1, 1 \rangle = \int_{-1}^1 1\, dt = 2$, and $\langle t^2, t \rangle = \int_{-1}^1 t^3 dt = 0$, the third basis element can be written as $t^2 - (1/3)$. This element can be scaled by 3, which gives the orthogonal basis as $\{1, t, 3t^2 - 1\}$.

26. The inner product is $\langle f, g \rangle = \int_{-2}^2 f(t)g(t)dt$. Then 1 and t are orthogonal because $\langle 1, t \rangle = \int_{-2}^2 t\, dt = 0$. So 1 and t can be in an orthogonal basis for $\text{Span}\{1, t, t^2\}$. By the Gram-Schmidt process, the third basis element in the orthogonal basis can be

$$t^2 - \frac{\langle t^2, 1 \rangle}{\langle 1, 1 \rangle} 1 - \frac{\langle t^2, t \rangle}{\langle t, t \rangle} t$$

Since $\langle t^2, 1 \rangle = \int_{-2}^2 t^2 dt = 16/3$, $\langle 1, 1 \rangle = \int_{-2}^2 1\, dt = 4$, and $\langle t^2, t \rangle = \int_{-2}^2 t^3 dt = 0$, the third basis element can be written as $t^2 - (4/3)$. This element can be scaled by 3, which gives the orthogonal basis as $\{1, t, 3t^2 - 4\}$.

27. **[M]** The new orthogonal polynomials are multiples of $-17t + 5t^3$ and $72 - 155t^2 + 35t^4$. These polynomials may be scaled so that their values at $-2, -1, 0, 1,$ and 2 are small integers.

28. **[M]** The orthogonal basis is $f_0(t) = 1$, $f_1(t) = \cos t$, $f_2(t) = \cos^2 t - (1/2) = (1/2)\cos 2t$, and $f_3(t) = \cos^3 t - (3/4)\cos t = (1/4)\cos 3t$.

6.8   SOLUTIONS

Notes: The connections between this section and Section 6.7 are described in the notes for that section. For my junior-senior class, I spend three days on the following topics: Theorems 13 and 15 in Section 6.5, plus Examples 1, 3, and 5; Example 1 in Section 6.6; Examples 2 and 3 in Section 6.7, with the motivation for the definite integral; and Fourier series in Section 6.8.

1. The weighting matrix W, design matrix X, parameter vector β, and observation vector $\mathbf{y}$ are:

$$W = \begin{bmatrix} 1 & 0 & 0 & 0 & 0 \\ 0 & 2 & 0 & 0 & 0 \\ 0 & 0 & 2 & 0 & 0 \\ 0 & 0 & 0 & 2 & 0 \\ 0 & 0 & 0 & 0 & 1 \end{bmatrix}, X = \begin{bmatrix} 1 & -2 \\ 1 & -1 \\ 1 & 0 \\ 1 & 1 \\ 1 & 2 \end{bmatrix}, \beta = \begin{bmatrix} \beta_0 \\ \beta_1 \end{bmatrix}, \mathbf{y} = \begin{bmatrix} 0 \\ 0 \\ 2 \\ 4 \\ 4 \end{bmatrix}$$

The design matrix X and the observation vector $\mathbf{y}$ are scaled by W:

$$WX = \begin{bmatrix} 1 & -2 \\ 2 & -2 \\ 2 & 0 \\ 2 & 2 \\ 1 & 2 \end{bmatrix}, W\mathbf{y} = \begin{bmatrix} 0 \\ 0 \\ 4 \\ 8 \\ 4 \end{bmatrix}$$

Further compute

$$(WX)^T WX = \begin{bmatrix} 14 & 0 \\ 0 & 16 \end{bmatrix}, (WX)^T W\mathbf{y} = \begin{bmatrix} 28 \\ 24 \end{bmatrix}$$

and find that

$$\hat{\beta} = ((WX)^T WX)^{-1}(WX)^T W\mathbf{y} = \begin{bmatrix} 1/14 & 0 \\ 0 & 1/16 \end{bmatrix}\begin{bmatrix} 28 \\ 24 \end{bmatrix} = \begin{bmatrix} 2 \\ 3/2 \end{bmatrix}$$

Thus the weighted least-squares line is $y = 2 + (3/2)x$.

2. Let X be the original design matrix, and let $\mathbf{y}$ be the original observation vector. Let W be the weighting matrix for the first method. Then $2W$ is the weighting matrix for the second method. The weighted least-squares by the first method is equivalent to the ordinary least-squares for an equation whose normal equation is

$$(WX)^T WX \hat{\beta} = (WX)^T W\mathbf{y} \tag{1}$$

while the second method is equivalent to the ordinary least-squares for an equation whose normal equation is

$$(2WX)^T (2W) X \hat{\beta} = (2WX)^T (2W)\mathbf{y} \tag{2}$$

Since equation (2) can be written as $4(WX)^T WX \hat{\beta} = 4(WX)^T W\mathbf{y}$, it has the same solutions as equation (1).

3. From Example 2 and the statement of the problem, $p_0(t) = 1$, $p_1(t) = t$, $p_2(t) = t^2 - 2$,

$p_3(t) = (5/6)t^3 - (17/6)t$, and $g = (3, 5, 5, 4, 3)$. The cubic trend function for g is the orthogonal projection $\hat{p}$ of g onto the subspace spanned by p_0, p_1, p_2, and p_3 :

$$\hat{p} = \frac{\langle g, p_0 \rangle}{\langle p_0, p_0 \rangle} p_0 + \frac{\langle g, p_1 \rangle}{\langle p_1, p_1 \rangle} p_1 + \frac{\langle g, p_2 \rangle}{\langle p_2, p_2 \rangle} p_2 + \frac{\langle g, p_3 \rangle}{\langle p_3, p_3 \rangle} p_3$$

$$= \frac{20}{5}(1) + \frac{-1}{10}t + \frac{-7}{14}\left(t^2 - 2\right) + \frac{2}{10}\left(\frac{5}{6}t^3 - \frac{17}{6}t\right)$$

$$= 4 - \frac{1}{10}t - \frac{1}{2}\left(t^2 - 2\right) + \frac{1}{5}\left(\frac{5}{6}t^3 - \frac{17}{6}t\right) = 5 - \frac{2}{3}t - \frac{1}{2}t^2 + \frac{1}{6}t^3$$

This polynomial happens to fit the data exactly.

4. The inner product is $\langle p, q \rangle = p(-5)q(-5) + p(-3)q(-3) + p(-1)q(-1) + p(1)q(1) + p(3)q(3) + p(5)q(5)$.

a. Begin with the basis $\{1, t, t^2\}$ for $\mathbb{P}_2$. Since 1 and t are orthogonal, let $p_0(t) = 1$ and $p_1(t) = t$. Then the Gram-Schmidt process gives

$$p_2(t) = t^2 - \frac{\langle t^2, 1 \rangle}{\langle 1, 1 \rangle} 1 - \frac{\langle t^2, t \rangle}{\langle t, t \rangle} t = t^2 - \frac{70}{6} = t^2 - \frac{35}{3}$$

The vector of values for p_2 is $(40/3, -8/3, -32/3, -32/3, -8/3, 40/3)$, so scaling by $3/8$ yields the new function $p_2 = (3/8)(t^2 - (35/3)) = (3/8)t^2 - (35/8)$.

b. The data vector is $g = (1, 1, 4, 4, 6, 8)$. The quadratic trend function for g is the orthogonal projection $\hat{p}$ of g onto the subspace spanned by p_0, p_1 and p_2 :

$$\hat{p} = \frac{\langle g, p_0 \rangle}{\langle p_0, p_0 \rangle} p_0 + \frac{\langle g, p_1 \rangle}{\langle p_1, p_1 \rangle} p_1 + \frac{\langle g, p_2 \rangle}{\langle p_2, p_2 \rangle} p_2 = \frac{24}{6}(1) + \frac{50}{70}t + \frac{6}{84}\left(\frac{3}{8}t^2 - \frac{35}{8}\right)$$

$$= 4 + \frac{5}{7}t + \frac{1}{14}\left(\frac{3}{8}t^2 - \frac{35}{8}\right) = \frac{59}{16} + \frac{5}{7}t + \frac{3}{112}t^2$$

5. The inner product is $\langle f, g \rangle = \int_0^{2\pi} f(t)g(t)dt$. Let $m \neq n$. Then

$$\langle \sin mt, \sin nt \rangle = \int_0^{2\pi} \sin mt \sin nt \, dt = \frac{1}{2}\int_0^{2\pi} \cos((m-n)t) - \cos((m+n)t)dt = 0$$

Thus $\sin mt$ and $\sin nt$ are orthogonal.

6. The inner product is $\langle f, g \rangle = \int_0^{2\pi} f(t)g(t)dt$. Let m and n be positive integers. Then

$$\langle \sin mt, \cos nt \rangle = \int_0^{2\pi} \sin mt \cos nt \, dt = \frac{1}{2}\int_0^{2\pi} \sin((m+n)t) + \sin((m-n)t)dt = 0$$

Thus $\sin mt$ and $\cos nt$ are orthogonal.

7. The inner product is $\langle f,g \rangle = \int_0^{2\pi} f(t)g(t)dt$. Let k be a positive integer. Then

$$\| \cos kt \|^2 = \langle \cos kt, \cos kt \rangle = \int_0^{2\pi} \cos^2 kt \, dt = \frac{1}{2} \int_0^{2\pi} 1 + \cos 2kt \, dt = \pi$$

and

$$\| \sin kt \|^2 = \langle \sin kt, \sin kt \rangle = \int_0^{2\pi} \sin^2 kt \, dt = \frac{1}{2} \int_0^{2\pi} 1 - \cos 2kt \, dt = \pi$$

8. Let $f(t) = t - 1$. The Fourier coefficients for f are:

$$\frac{a_0}{2} = \frac{1}{2}\frac{1}{\pi} \int_0^{2\pi} f(t) \, dt = \frac{1}{2\pi} \int_0^{2\pi} t - 1 \, dt = -1 + \pi$$

and for $k > 0$,

$$a_k = \frac{1}{\pi} \int_0^{2\pi} f(t)\cos kt \, dt = \frac{1}{\pi} \int_0^{2\pi} (t-1)\cos kt \, dt = 0$$

$$b_k = \frac{1}{\pi} \int_0^{2\pi} f(t)\sin kt \, dt = \frac{1}{\pi} \int_0^{2\pi} (t-1)\sin kt \, dt = -\frac{2}{k}$$

The third-order Fourier approximation to f is thus

$$\frac{a_0}{2} + b_1\sin t + b_2\sin 2t + b_3\sin 3t = -1 + \pi - 2\sin t - \sin 2t - \frac{2}{3}\sin 3t$$

9. Let $f(t) = 2\pi - t$. The Fourier coefficients for f are:

$$\frac{a_0}{2} = \frac{1}{2}\frac{1}{\pi} \int_0^{2\pi} f(t) \, dt = \frac{1}{2\pi} \int_0^{2\pi} 2\pi - t \, dt = \pi$$

and for $k > 0$,

$$a_k = \frac{1}{\pi} \int_0^{2\pi} f(t) \cos kt \, dt = \frac{1}{\pi} \int_0^{2\pi} (2\pi - t) \cos kt \, dt = 0$$

$$b_k = \frac{1}{\pi} \int_0^{2\pi} f(t) \sin kt \, dt = \frac{1}{\pi} \int_0^{2\pi} (2\pi - t) \sin kt \, dt = \frac{2}{k}$$

The third-order Fourier approximation to f is thus

$$\frac{a_0}{2} + b_1\sin t + b_2\sin 2t + b_3\sin 3t = \pi + 2\sin t + \sin 2t + \frac{2}{3}\sin 3t$$

10. Let $f(t) = \begin{cases} 1 & \text{for } 0 \le t < \pi \\ -1 & \text{for } \pi \le t < 2\pi \end{cases}$. The Fourier coefficients for f are:

$$\frac{a_0}{2} = \frac{1}{2}\frac{1}{\pi} \int_0^{2\pi} f(t) \, dt = \frac{1}{2\pi} \int_0^{\pi} dt - \frac{1}{2\pi} \int_\pi^{2\pi} dt = 0$$

and for $k > 0$,

$$a_k = \frac{1}{\pi} \int_0^{2\pi} f(t) \cos kt \, dt = \frac{1}{\pi} \int_0^{\pi} \cos kt \, dt - \frac{1}{\pi} \int_\pi^{2\pi} \cos kt \, dt = 0$$

$$b_k = \frac{1}{\pi} \int_0^{2\pi} f(t) \sin kt \, dt = \frac{1}{\pi} \int_0^{\pi} \sin kt \, dt - \frac{1}{\pi} \int_\pi^{2\pi} \sin kt \, dt = \begin{cases} 4/(k\pi) & \text{for } k \text{ odd} \\ 0 & \text{for } k \text{ even} \end{cases}$$

The third-order Fourier approximation to f is thus

$$b_1\sin t + b_3\sin 3t = \frac{4}{\pi}\sin t + \frac{4}{3\pi}\sin 3t$$

11. The trigonometric identity $\cos 2t = 1 - 2\sin^2 t$ shows that

$$\sin^2 t = \frac{1}{2} - \frac{1}{2}\cos 2t$$

The expression on the right is in the subspace spanned by the trigonometric polynomials of order 3 or less, so this expression is the third-order Fourier approximation to $\cos^3 t$.

12. The trigonometric identity $\cos 3t = 4\cos^3 t - 3\cos t$ shows that

$$\cos^3 t = \frac{3}{4}\cos t + \frac{1}{4}\cos 3t$$

The expression on the right is in the subspace spanned by the trigonometric polynomials of order 3 or less, so this expression is the third-order Fourier approximation to $\cos^3 t$.

13. Let f and g be in $C[0, 2\pi]$ and let m be a nonnegative integer. Then the linearity of the inner product shows that

$$\langle (f+g), \cos mt \rangle = \langle f, \cos mt \rangle + \langle g, \cos mt \rangle, \langle (f+g), \sin mt \rangle = \langle f, \sin mt \rangle + \langle g, \sin mt \rangle$$

Dividing these identities respectively by $\langle \cos mt, \cos mt \rangle$ and $\langle \sin mt, \sin mt \rangle$ shows that the Fourier coefficients a_m and b_m for $f+g$ are the sums of the corresponding Fourier coefficients of f and of g.

14. Note that g and h are both in the subspace H spanned by the trigonometric polynomials of order 2 or less. Since h is the second-order Fourier approximation to f, it is closer to f than any other function in the subspace H.

15. [M] The weighting matrix W is the 13×13 diagonal matrix with diagonal entries 1, 1, 1, .9, .9, .8, .7, .6, .5, .4, .3, .2, .1. The design matrix X, parameter vector β, and observation vector $\mathbf{y}$ are:

$$X = \begin{bmatrix} 1 & 0 & 0 & 0 \\ 1 & 1 & 1 & 1 \\ 1 & 2 & 2^2 & 2^3 \\ 1 & 3 & 3^2 & 3^3 \\ 1 & 4 & 4^2 & 4^3 \\ 1 & 5 & 5^2 & 5^3 \\ 1 & 6 & 6^2 & 6^3 \\ 1 & 7 & 7^2 & 7^3 \\ 1 & 8 & 8^2 & 8^3 \\ 1 & 9 & 9^2 & 9^3 \\ 1 & 10 & 10^2 & 10^3 \\ 1 & 11 & 11^2 & 11^3 \\ 1 & 12 & 12^2 & 12^3 \end{bmatrix}, \beta = \begin{bmatrix} \beta_0 \\ \beta_1 \\ \beta_2 \\ \beta_3 \end{bmatrix}, \mathbf{y} = \begin{bmatrix} 0.0 \\ 8.8 \\ 29.9 \\ 62.0 \\ 104.7 \\ 159.1 \\ 222.0 \\ 294.5 \\ 380.4 \\ 471.1 \\ 571.7 \\ 686.8 \\ 809.2 \end{bmatrix}$$

The design matrix X and the observation vector $\mathbf{y}$ are scaled by W:

$$WX = \begin{bmatrix} 1.0 & 0.0 & 0.0 & 0.0 \\ 1.0 & 1.0 & 1.0 & 1.0 \\ 1.0 & 2.0 & 4.0 & 8.0 \\ .9 & 2.7 & 8.1 & 24.3 \\ .9 & 3.6 & 14.4 & 57.6 \\ .8 & 4.0 & 20.0 & 100.0 \\ .7 & 4.2 & 25.2 & 151.2 \\ .6 & 4.2 & 29.4 & 205.8 \\ .5 & 4.0 & 32.0 & 256.0 \\ .4 & 3.6 & 32.4 & 291.6 \\ .3 & 3.0 & 30.0 & 300.0 \\ .2 & 2.2 & 24.2 & 266.2 \\ .1 & 1.2 & 14.4 & 172.8 \end{bmatrix}, \mathbf{Wy} = \begin{bmatrix} 0.00 \\ 8.80 \\ 29.90 \\ 55.80 \\ 94.23 \\ 127.28 \\ 155.40 \\ 176.70 \\ 190.20 \\ 188.44 \\ 171.51 \\ 137.36 \\ 80.92 \end{bmatrix}$$

Further compute

$$(WX)^T WX = \begin{bmatrix} 6.66 & 22.23 & 120.77 & 797.19 \\ 22.23 & 120.77 & 797.19 & 5956.13 \\ 120.77 & 797.19 & 5956.13 & 48490.23 \\ 797.19 & 5956.13 & 48490.23 & 420477.17 \end{bmatrix}, (WX)^T \mathbf{Wy} = \begin{bmatrix} 747.844 \\ 4815.438 \\ 35420.468 \\ 285262.440 \end{bmatrix}$$

and find that

$$\hat{\beta} = ((WX)^T WX)^{-1}(WX)^T \mathbf{Wy} = \begin{bmatrix} -0.2685 \\ 3.6095 \\ 5.8576 \\ -0.0477 \end{bmatrix}$$

Thus the weighted least-squares cubic is $y = g(t) = -.2685 + 3.6095t + 5.8576t^2 - .0477t^3$. The velocity at $t = 4.5$ seconds is $g'(4.5) = 53.4$ ft./sec. This is about 0.7% faster than the estimate obtained in Exercise 13 of Section 6.6.

16. **[M]** Let $f(t) = \begin{cases} 1 & \text{for } 0 \le t < \pi \\ -1 & \text{for } \pi \le t < 2\pi \end{cases}$. The Fourier coefficients for f have already been found to be $a_k = 0$

for all $k \ge 0$ and $b_k = \begin{cases} 4/(k\pi) & \text{for } k \text{ odd} \\ 0 & \text{for } k \text{ even} \end{cases}$. Thus

$$f_4(t) = \frac{4}{\pi}\sin t + \frac{4}{3\pi}\sin 3t \quad \text{and} \quad f_5(t) = \frac{4}{\pi}\sin t + \frac{4}{3\pi}\sin 3t + \frac{4}{5\pi}\sin 5t$$

A graph of f_4 over the interval $[0, 2\pi]$ is

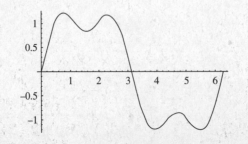

A graph of f_5 over the interval $[0, 2\pi]$ is

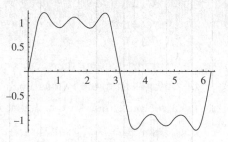

A graph of f_5 over the interval $[-2\pi, 2\pi]$ is

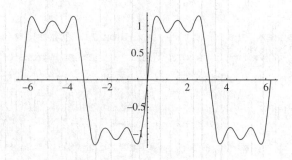

Chapter 6   SUPPLEMENTARY EXERCISES _____

1. **a**. False. The length of the zero vector is zero.

    b. True. By the displayed equation before Example 2 in Section 6.1, with $c = -1$, $\| -\mathbf{x} \| = \| (-1)\mathbf{x} \| = |-1| \|\mathbf{x}\| = \|\mathbf{x}\|$.

    c. True. This is the definition of distance.

    d. False. This equation would be true if $r\|\mathbf{v}\|$ were replaced by $|r| \|\mathbf{v}\|$.

    e. False. Orthogonal *nonzero* vectors are linearly independent.

    f. True. If $\mathbf{x} \cdot \mathbf{u} = 0$ and $\mathbf{x} \cdot \mathbf{v} = 0$, then $\mathbf{x} \cdot (\mathbf{u} - \mathbf{v}) = \mathbf{x} \cdot \mathbf{u} - \mathbf{x} \cdot \mathbf{v} = 0$.

    g. True. This is the "only if" part of the Pythagorean Theorem in Section 6.1.

    h. True. This is the "only if" part of the Pythagorean Theorem in Section 6.1 where $\mathbf{v}$ is replaced by $-\mathbf{v}$, because $\|-\mathbf{v}\|^2$ is the same as $\|\mathbf{v}\|^2$.

    i. False. The orthogonal projection of $\mathbf{y}$ onto $\mathbf{u}$ is a scalar multiple of $\mathbf{u}$, not $\mathbf{y}$ (except when $\mathbf{y}$ itself is already a multiple of $\mathbf{u}$).

    j. True. The orthogonal projection of any vector $\mathbf{y}$ onto W is always a vector in W.

    k. True. This is a special case of the statement in the box following Example 6 in Section 6.1 (and proved in Exercise 30 of Section 6.1).

    l. False. The zero vector is in both W and $W^\perp$.

    m. True. See Exercise 32 in Section 6.2. If $\mathbf{v}_i \cdot \mathbf{v}_j = 0$, then $(c_i\mathbf{v}_i) \cdot (c_j\mathbf{v}_j) = c_i c_j (\mathbf{v}_i \cdot \mathbf{v}_j) = c_i c_j 0 = 0$.

    n. False. This statement is true only for a *square* matrix. See Theorem 10 in Section 6.3.

    o. False. An orthogonal matrix is square and has *orthonormal* columns.

p. True. See Exercises 27 and 28 in Section 6.2. If U has orthonormal columns, then $U^T U = I$. If U is also square, then the Invertible Matrix Theorem shows that U is invertible and $U^{-1} = U^T$. In this case, $U^T U = I$, which shows that the columns of U^T are orthonormal; that is, the rows of U are orthonormal.

q. True. By the Orthogonal Decomposition Theorem, the vectors $\text{proj}_W \mathbf{v}$ and $\mathbf{v} - \text{proj}_W \mathbf{v}$ are orthogonal, so the stated equality follows from the Pythagorean Theorem.

r. False. A least-squares solution is a vector $\hat{\mathbf{x}}$ (not $A\hat{\mathbf{x}}$) such that $A\hat{\mathbf{x}}$ is the closest point to $\mathbf{b}$ in Col A.

s. False. The equation $\hat{\mathbf{x}} = (A^T A)^{-1} A^T \mathbf{b}$ describes the *solution* of the normal equations, not the matrix form of the normal equations. Furthermore, this equation makes sense only when $A^T A$ is invertible.

2. If $\{\mathbf{v}_1, \mathbf{v}_2\}$ is an orthonormal set and $\mathbf{x} = c_1 \mathbf{v}_1 + c_2 \mathbf{v}_2$, then the vectors $c_1 \mathbf{v}_1$ and $c_2 \mathbf{v}_2$ are orthogonal (Exercise 32 in Section 6.2). By the Pythagorean Theorem and properties of the norm

$$\| \mathbf{x} \|^2 = \| c_1 \mathbf{v}_1 + c_2 \mathbf{v}_2 \|^2 = \| c_1 \mathbf{v}_1 \|^2 + \| c_2 \mathbf{v}_2 \|^2 = (c_1 \| \mathbf{v}_1 \|)^2 + (c_2 \| \mathbf{v}_2 \|)^2 = |c_1|^2 + |c_2|^2$$

So the stated equality holds for $p = 2$. Now suppose the equality holds for $p = k$, with $k \geq 2$. Let $\{\mathbf{v}_1, \ldots, \mathbf{v}_{k+1}\}$ be an orthonormal set, and consider $\mathbf{x} = c_1 \mathbf{v}_1 + \ldots + c_k \mathbf{v}_k + c_{k+1} \mathbf{v}_{k+1} = \mathbf{u}_k + c_{k+1} \mathbf{v}_{k+1}$, where $\mathbf{u}_k = c_1 \mathbf{v}_1 + \ldots + c_k \mathbf{v}_k$. Observe that $\mathbf{u}_k$ and $c_{k+1} \mathbf{v}_{k+1}$ are orthogonal because $\mathbf{v}_j \cdot \mathbf{v}_{k+1} = 0$ for $j = 1, \ldots, k$. By the Pythagorean Theorem and the assumption that the stated equality holds for k, and because $\| c_{k+1} \mathbf{v}_{k+1} \|^2 = |c_{k+1}|^2 \| \mathbf{v}_{k+1} \|^2 = |c_{k+1}|^2$,

$$\| \mathbf{x} \|^2 = \| \mathbf{u}_k + c_{k+1} \mathbf{v}_{k+1} \|^2 = \| \mathbf{u}_k \|^2 + \| c_{k+1} \mathbf{v}_{k+1} \|^2 = |c_1|^2 + \ldots + |c_{k+1}|^2$$

Thus the truth of the equality for $p = k$ implies its truth for $p = k + 1$. By the principle of induction, the equality is true for all integers $p \geq 2$.

3. Given $\mathbf{x}$ and an orthonormal set $\{\mathbf{v}_1, \ldots, \mathbf{v}_p\}$ in $\mathbb{R}^n$, let $\hat{\mathbf{x}}$ be the orthogonal projection of $\mathbf{x}$ onto the subspace spanned by $\mathbf{v}_1, \ldots, \mathbf{v}_p$. By Theorem 10 in Section 6.3, $\hat{\mathbf{x}} = (\mathbf{x} \cdot \mathbf{v}_1) \mathbf{v}_1 + \ldots + (\mathbf{x} \cdot \mathbf{v}_p) \mathbf{v}_p$. By Exercise 2, $\| \hat{\mathbf{x}} \|^2 = |\mathbf{x} \cdot \mathbf{v}_1|^2 + \ldots + |\mathbf{x} \cdot \mathbf{v}_p|^2$. Bessel's inequality follows from the fact that $\| \hat{\mathbf{x}} \|^2 \leq \| \mathbf{x} \|^2$, which is noted before the proof of the Cauchy-Schwarz inequality in Section 6.7.

4. By parts (a) and (c) of Theorem 7 in Section 6.2, $\{U\mathbf{v}_1, \ldots, U\mathbf{v}_k\}$ is an orthonormal set in $\mathbb{R}^n$. Since there are n vectors in this linearly independent set, the set is a basis for $\mathbb{R}^n$.

5. Suppose that $(U\mathbf{x}) \cdot (U\mathbf{y}) = \mathbf{x} \cdot \mathbf{y}$ for all $\mathbf{x}$, $\mathbf{y}$ in $\mathbb{R}^n$, and let $\mathbf{e}_1, \ldots, \mathbf{e}_n$ be the standard basis for $\mathbb{R}^n$. For $j = 1, \ldots, n$, $U\mathbf{e}_j$ is the jth column of U. Since $\| U\mathbf{e}_j \|^2 = (U\mathbf{e}_j) \cdot (U\mathbf{e}_j) = \mathbf{e}_j \cdot \mathbf{e}_j = 1$, the columns of U are unit vectors; since $(U\mathbf{e}_j) \cdot (U\mathbf{e}_k) = \mathbf{e}_j \cdot \mathbf{e}_k = 0$ for $j \neq k$, the columns are pairwise orthogonal.

6. If $U\mathbf{x} = \lambda \mathbf{x}$ for some $\mathbf{x} \neq \mathbf{0}$, then by Theorem 7(a) in Section 6.2 and by a property of the norm, $\| \mathbf{x} \| = \| U\mathbf{x} \| = \| \lambda \mathbf{x} \| = |\lambda| \| \mathbf{x} \|$, which shows that $|\lambda| = 1$, because $\mathbf{x} \neq \mathbf{0}$.

7. Let $\mathbf{u}$ be a unit vector, and let $Q = I - 2\mathbf{u}\mathbf{u}^T$. Since $(\mathbf{u}\mathbf{u}^T)^T = \mathbf{u}^{TT}\mathbf{u}^T = \mathbf{u}\mathbf{u}^T$,

$$Q^T = (I - 2\mathbf{u}\mathbf{u}^T)^T = I - 2(\mathbf{u}\mathbf{u}^T)^T = I - 2\mathbf{u}\mathbf{u}^T = Q$$

Then

$$QQ^T = Q^2 = (I - 2\mathbf{u}\mathbf{u}^T)^2 = I - 2\mathbf{u}\mathbf{u}^T - 2\mathbf{u}\mathbf{u}^T + 4(\mathbf{u}\mathbf{u}^T)(\mathbf{u}\mathbf{u}^T)$$

Since $\mathbf{u}$ is a unit vector, $\mathbf{u}^T\mathbf{u} = \mathbf{u} \cdot \mathbf{u} = 1$, so $(\mathbf{u}\mathbf{u}^T)(\mathbf{u}\mathbf{u}^T) = \mathbf{u}(\mathbf{u}^T)(\mathbf{u})\mathbf{u}^T = \mathbf{u}\mathbf{u}^T$, and

$$QQ^T = I - 2\mathbf{u}\mathbf{u}^T - 2\mathbf{u}\mathbf{u}^T + 4\mathbf{u}\mathbf{u}^T = I$$

Thus Q is an orthogonal matrix.

8. **a.** Suppose that $\mathbf{x} \cdot \mathbf{y} = 0$. By the Pythagorean Theorem, $\|\mathbf{x}\|^2 + \|\mathbf{y}\|^2 = \|\mathbf{x} + \mathbf{y}\|^2$. Since T preserves lengths and is linear,

$$\|T(\mathbf{x})\|^2 + \|T(\mathbf{y})\|^2 = \|T(\mathbf{x} + \mathbf{y})\|^2 = \|T(\mathbf{x}) + T(\mathbf{y})\|^2$$

This equation shows that $T(\mathbf{x})$ and $T(\mathbf{y})$ are orthogonal, because of the Pythagorean Theorem. Thus T preserves orthogonality.

b. The standard matrix of T is $\begin{bmatrix} T(\mathbf{e}_1) & \cdots & T(\mathbf{e}_n) \end{bmatrix}$, where $\mathbf{e}_1,\ldots,\mathbf{e}_n$ are the columns of the identity matrix. Then $\{T(\mathbf{e}_1),\ldots,T(\mathbf{e}_n)\}$ is an orthonormal set because T preserves both orthogonality and lengths (and because the columns of the identity matrix form an orthonormal set). Finally, a square matrix with orthonormal columns is an orthogonal matrix, as was observed in Section 6.2.

9. Let $W = \text{Span}\{\mathbf{u}, \mathbf{v}\}$. Given $\mathbf{z}$ in $\mathbb{R}^n$, let $\hat{\mathbf{z}} = \text{proj}_W \mathbf{z}$. Then $\hat{\mathbf{z}}$ is in $\text{Col } A$, where $A = \begin{bmatrix} \mathbf{u} & \mathbf{v} \end{bmatrix}$. Thus there is a vector, say, $\hat{\mathbf{x}}$ in $\mathbb{R}^2$, with $A\hat{\mathbf{x}} = \hat{\mathbf{z}}$. So, $\hat{\mathbf{x}}$ is a least-squares solution of $A\mathbf{x} = \mathbf{z}$. The normal equations may be solved to find $\hat{\mathbf{x}}$, and then $\hat{\mathbf{z}}$ may be found by computing $A\hat{\mathbf{x}}$.

10. Use Theorem 14 in Section 6.5. If $c \neq 0$, the least-squares solution of $A\mathbf{x} = c\mathbf{b}$ is given by $(A^TA)^{-1}A^T(c\mathbf{b})$, which equals $c(A^TA)^{-1}A^T\mathbf{b}$, by linearity of matrix multiplication. This solution is c times the least-squares solution of $A\mathbf{x} = \mathbf{b}$.

11. Let $\mathbf{x} = \begin{bmatrix} x \\ y \\ z \end{bmatrix}$, $\mathbf{b} = \begin{bmatrix} a \\ b \\ c \end{bmatrix}$, $\mathbf{v} = \begin{bmatrix} 1 \\ -2 \\ 5 \end{bmatrix}$, and $A = \begin{bmatrix} \mathbf{v}^T \\ \mathbf{v}^T \\ \mathbf{v}^T \end{bmatrix} = \begin{bmatrix} 1 & -2 & 5 \\ 1 & -2 & 5 \\ 1 & -2 & 5 \end{bmatrix}$. Then the given set of equations is

$A\mathbf{x} = \mathbf{b}$, and the set of all least-squares solutions coincides with the set of solutions of the normal equations $A^TA\mathbf{x} = A^T\mathbf{b}$. The column-row expansions of A^TA and $A^T\mathbf{b}$ give

$$A^TA = \mathbf{v}\mathbf{v}^T + \mathbf{v}\mathbf{v}^T + \mathbf{v}\mathbf{v}^T = 3\mathbf{v}\mathbf{v}^T, A^T\mathbf{b} = a\mathbf{v} + b\mathbf{v} + c\mathbf{v} = (a + b + c)\mathbf{v}$$

Thus $A^TA\mathbf{x} = 3(\mathbf{v}\mathbf{v}^T)\mathbf{x} = 3\mathbf{v}(\mathbf{v}^T\mathbf{x}) = 3(\mathbf{v}^T\mathbf{x})\mathbf{v}$ since $\mathbf{v}^T\mathbf{x}$ is a scalar, and the normal equations have become $3(\mathbf{v}^T\mathbf{x})\mathbf{v} = (a + b + c)\mathbf{v}$, so $3(\mathbf{v}^T\mathbf{x}) = a + b + c$, or $\mathbf{v}^T\mathbf{x} = (a + b + c)/3$. Computing $\mathbf{v}^T\mathbf{x}$ gives the equation $x - 2y + 5z = (a + b + c)/3$ which must be satisfied by all least-squares solutions to $A\mathbf{x} = \mathbf{b}$.

12. The equation (1) in the exercise has been written as $V\lambda = \mathbf{b}$, where V is a single nonzero column vector $\mathbf{v}$, and $\mathbf{b} = A\mathbf{v}$. The least-squares solution $\hat{\lambda}$ of $V\lambda = \mathbf{b}$ is the exact solution of the normal equations $V^TV\lambda = V^T\mathbf{b}$. In the original notation, this equation is $\mathbf{v}^T\mathbf{v}\lambda = \mathbf{v}^TA\mathbf{v}$. Since $\mathbf{v}^T\mathbf{v}$ is nonzero, the least squares solution $\hat{\lambda}$ is $\mathbf{v}^TA\mathbf{v}/(\mathbf{v}^T\mathbf{v})$. This expression is the Rayleigh quotient discussed in the Exercises for Section 5.8.

13. **a.** The row-column calculation of $A\mathbf{u}$ shows that each row of A is orthogonal to every $\mathbf{u}$ in $\text{Nul } A$. So each row of A is in $(\text{Nul } A)^\perp$. Since $(\text{Nul } A)^\perp$ is a subspace, it must contain all linear combinations of the rows of A; hence $(\text{Nul } A)^\perp$ contains $\text{Row } A$.

b. If $\text{rank } A = r$, then $\dim \text{Nul } A = n - r$ by the Rank Theorem. By Exercsie 24(c) in Section 6.3, $\dim \text{Nul } A + \dim(\text{Nul } A)^\perp = n$, so $\dim(\text{Nul } A)^\perp$ must be r. But $\text{Row } A$ is an r-dimensional subspace of $(\text{Nul } A)^\perp$ by the Rank Theorem and part (a). Therefore, $\text{Row } A = (\text{Nul } A)^\perp$.

c. Replace A by A^T in part (b) and conclude that Row $A^T = (\text{Nul } A^T)^\perp$. Since Row $A^T = \text{Col } A$, Col $A = (\text{Nul } A^T)^\perp$.

14. The equation $A\mathbf{x} = \mathbf{b}$ has a solution if and only if $\mathbf{b}$ is in Col A. By Exercise 13(c), $A\mathbf{x} = \mathbf{b}$ has a solution if and only if $\mathbf{b}$ is orthogonal to Nul A^T. This happens if and only if $\mathbf{b}$ is orthogonal to all solutions of $A^T\mathbf{x} = \mathbf{0}$.

15. If $A = URU^T$ with U orthogonal, then A is similar to R (because U is invertible and $U^T = U^{-1}$), so A has the same eigenvalues as R by Theorem 4 in Section 5.2. Since the eigenvalues of R are its n real diagonal entries, A has n real eigenvalues.

16. **a.** If $U = \begin{bmatrix} \mathbf{u}_1 & \mathbf{u}_2 & \cdots & \mathbf{u}_n \end{bmatrix}$, then $AU = \begin{bmatrix} \lambda_1\mathbf{u}_1 & A\mathbf{u}_2 & \cdots & A\mathbf{u}_n \end{bmatrix}$. Since $\mathbf{u}_1$ is a unit vector and $\mathbf{u}_2,\ldots,\mathbf{u}_n$ are orthogonal to $\mathbf{u}_1$, the first column of $U^T AU$ is $U^T(\lambda_1\mathbf{u}_1) = \lambda_1 U^T\mathbf{u}_1 = \lambda_1\mathbf{e}_1$.

   b. From (a),

   $$U^T AU = \begin{bmatrix} \lambda_1 & * & * & * & * \\ 0 & & & & \\ \vdots & & A_1 & & \\ 0 & & & & \end{bmatrix}$$

   View $U^T AU$ as a 2×2 block upper triangular matrix, with A_1 as the $(2, 2)$-block. Then from Supplementary Exercise 12 in Chapter 5,

   $$\det(U^T AU - \lambda I_n) = \det((\lambda_1 - \lambda)I_1) \cdot \det(A_1 - \lambda I_{n-1}) = (\lambda_1 - \lambda) \cdot \det(A_1 - \lambda I_{n-1})$$

   This shows that the eigenvalues of $U^T AU$, namely, $\lambda_1,\ldots,\lambda_n$, consist of λ_1 and the eigenvalues of A_1. So the eigenvalues of A_1 are $\lambda_2,\ldots,\lambda_n$.

17. **[M]** Compute that $\| \Delta\mathbf{x} \|/\| \mathbf{x} \| = .4618$ and $\text{cond}(A) \times (\| \Delta\mathbf{b} \| / \| \mathbf{b} \|) = 3363 \times (1.548 \times 10^{-4}) = .5206$. In this case, $\| \Delta\mathbf{x} \|/\| \mathbf{x} \|$ is almost the same as $\text{cond}(A) \times \| \Delta\mathbf{b} \|/\| \mathbf{b} \|$.

18. **[M]** Compute that $\| \Delta\mathbf{x} \|/\| \mathbf{x} \| = .00212$ and $\text{cond}(A) \times (\| \Delta\mathbf{b} \|/\| \mathbf{b} \|) = 3363 \times (.00212) \approx 7.130$. In this case, $\| \Delta\mathbf{x} \|/\| \mathbf{x} \|$ is almost the same as $\| \Delta\mathbf{b} \|/\| \mathbf{b} \|$, even though the large condition number suggests that $\| \Delta\mathbf{x} \|/\| \mathbf{x} \|$ could be much larger.

19. **[M]** Compute that $\| \Delta\mathbf{x} \| / \| \mathbf{x} \| = 7.178 \times 10^{-8}$ and $\text{cond}(A) \times (\| \Delta\mathbf{b} \| / \| \mathbf{b} \|) = 23683 \times (2.832 \times 10^{-4}) = 6.707$. Observe that the realtive change in $\mathbf{x}$ is *much* smaller than the relative change in $\mathbf{b}$. In fact the theoretical bound on the realtive change in $\mathbf{x}$ is 6.707 (to four significant figures). This exercise shows that even when a condition number is large, the relative error in the solution need not be as large as you suspect.

20. **[M]** Compute that $\| \Delta\mathbf{x} \|/\| \mathbf{x} \| = .2597$ and $\text{cond}(A) \times (\| \Delta\mathbf{b} \| / \| \mathbf{b} \|) = 23683 \times (1.097 \times 10^{-5}) = .2598$. This calculation shows that the relative change in $\mathbf{x}$, for this particular $\mathbf{b}$ and $\Delta\mathbf{b}$, should not exceed .2598. In this case, the theoretical maximum change is almost acheived.

7 Symmetric Matrices and Quadratic Forms

7.1 SOLUTIONS

Notes: Students can profit by reviewing Section 5.3 (focusing on the Diagonalization Theorem) before working on this section. Theorems 1 and 2 and the calculations in Examples 2 and 3 are important for the sections that follow. Note that *symmetric matrix* means *real symmetric matrix*, because all matrices in the text have real entries, as mentioned at the beginning of this chapter. The exercises in this section have been constructed so that mastery of the Gram-Schmidt process is not needed.

Theorem 2 is easily proved for the 2×2 case:

$$\text{If } A = \begin{bmatrix} a & b \\ c & d \end{bmatrix}, \text{ then } \lambda = \frac{1}{2}\left(a + d \pm \sqrt{(a-d)^2 + 4b^2}\right).$$

If $b = 0$ there is nothing to prove. Otherwise, there are two distinct eigenvalues, so A must be diagonalizable.

In each case, an eigenvector for λ is $\begin{bmatrix} d - \lambda \\ -b \end{bmatrix}$.

1. Since $A = \begin{bmatrix} 3 & 5 \\ 5 & -7 \end{bmatrix} = A^T$, the matrix is symmetric.

2. Since $A = \begin{bmatrix} -3 & 5 \\ -5 & 3 \end{bmatrix} \neq A^T$, the matrix is not symmetric.

3. Since $A = \begin{bmatrix} 2 & 2 \\ 4 & 4 \end{bmatrix} \neq A^T$, the matrix is not symmetric.

4. Since $A = \begin{bmatrix} 0 & 8 & 3 \\ 8 & 0 & -2 \\ 3 & -2 & 0 \end{bmatrix} = A^T$, the matrix is symmetric.

5. Since $A = \begin{bmatrix} -6 & 2 & 0 \\ 0 & -6 & 2 \\ 0 & 0 & -6 \end{bmatrix} \neq A^T$, the matrix is not symmetric.

6. Since A is not a square matrix $A \neq A^T$ and the matrix is not symmetric.

7. Let $P = \begin{bmatrix} .6 & .8 \\ .8 & -.6 \end{bmatrix}$, and compute that

$$P^T P = \begin{bmatrix} .6 & .8 \\ .8 & -.6 \end{bmatrix}\begin{bmatrix} .6 & .8 \\ .8 & -.6 \end{bmatrix} = \begin{bmatrix} 1 & 0 \\ 0 & 1 \end{bmatrix} = I_2$$

Since P is a square matrix, P is orthogonal and $P^{-1} = P^T = \begin{bmatrix} .6 & .8 \\ .8 & -.6 \end{bmatrix}$.

8. Let $P = \begin{bmatrix} 1/\sqrt{2} & -1/\sqrt{2} \\ 1/\sqrt{2} & 1/\sqrt{2} \end{bmatrix}$, and compute that

$$P^T P = \begin{bmatrix} 1/\sqrt{2} & 1/\sqrt{2} \\ -1/\sqrt{2} & 1/\sqrt{2} \end{bmatrix}\begin{bmatrix} 1/\sqrt{2} & -1/\sqrt{2} \\ 1/\sqrt{2} & 1/\sqrt{2} \end{bmatrix} = \begin{bmatrix} 1 & 0 \\ 0 & 1 \end{bmatrix} = I_2$$

Since P is a square matrix, P is orthogonal and $P^{-1} = P^T = \begin{bmatrix} 1/\sqrt{2} & 1/\sqrt{2} \\ -1/\sqrt{2} & 1/\sqrt{2} \end{bmatrix}$.

9. Let $P = \begin{bmatrix} -5 & 2 \\ 2 & 5 \end{bmatrix}$, and compute that

$$P^T P = \begin{bmatrix} -5 & 2 \\ 2 & 5 \end{bmatrix}\begin{bmatrix} -5 & 2 \\ 2 & 5 \end{bmatrix} = \begin{bmatrix} 29 & 0 \\ 0 & 29 \end{bmatrix} \neq I_2$$

Thus P is not orthogonal.

10. Let $P = \begin{bmatrix} -1 & 2 & 2 \\ 2 & -1 & 2 \\ 2 & 2 & -1 \end{bmatrix}$, and compute that

$$P^T P = \begin{bmatrix} -1 & 2 & 2 \\ 2 & -1 & 2 \\ 2 & 2 & -1 \end{bmatrix}\begin{bmatrix} -1 & 2 & 2 \\ 2 & -1 & 2 \\ 2 & 2 & -1 \end{bmatrix} = \begin{bmatrix} 9 & 0 & 0 \\ 0 & 9 & 0 \\ 0 & 0 & 9 \end{bmatrix} \neq I_3$$

Thus P is not orthogonal.

11. Let $P = \begin{bmatrix} 2/3 & 2/3 & 1/3 \\ 0 & 1/\sqrt{5} & -2/\sqrt{5} \\ \sqrt{5}/3 & -4/\sqrt{45} & -2/\sqrt{45} \end{bmatrix}$, and compute that

$$P^T P = \begin{bmatrix} 2/3 & 0 & \sqrt{5}/3 \\ 2/3 & 1/\sqrt{5} & -4/\sqrt{45} \\ 1/3 & -2/\sqrt{5} & -2/\sqrt{45} \end{bmatrix}\begin{bmatrix} 2/3 & 2/3 & 1/3 \\ 0 & 1/\sqrt{5} & -2/\sqrt{5} \\ \sqrt{5}/3 & -4/\sqrt{45} & -2/\sqrt{45} \end{bmatrix} = \begin{bmatrix} 1 & 0 & 0 \\ 0 & 1 & 0 \\ 0 & 0 & 1 \end{bmatrix} = I_3$$

Since P is a square matrix, P is orthogonal and $P^{-1} = P^T = \begin{bmatrix} 2/3 & 0 & \sqrt{5}/3 \\ 2/3 & 1/\sqrt{5} & -4/\sqrt{45} \\ 1/3 & -2/\sqrt{5} & -2/\sqrt{45} \end{bmatrix}$.

12. Let $P = \begin{bmatrix} .5 & .5 & -.5 & -.5 \\ -.5 & .5 & -.5 & .5 \\ .5 & .5 & .5 & .5 \\ -.5 & .5 & .5 & -.5 \end{bmatrix}$, and compute that

$$P^T P = \begin{bmatrix} .5 & -.5 & .5 & -.5 \\ .5 & .5 & .5 & .5 \\ -.5 & -.5 & .5 & .5 \\ -.5 & .5 & .5 & -.5 \end{bmatrix}\begin{bmatrix} .5 & .5 & -.5 & -.5 \\ -.5 & .5 & -.5 & .5 \\ .5 & .5 & .5 & .5 \\ -.5 & .5 & .5 & -.5 \end{bmatrix} = \begin{bmatrix} 1 & 0 & 0 & 0 \\ 0 & 1 & 0 & 0 \\ 0 & 0 & 1 & 0 \\ 0 & 0 & 0 & 1 \end{bmatrix} = I_4$$

Since P is a square matrix, P is orthogonal and $P^{-1} = P^T = \begin{bmatrix} .5 & -.5 & .5 & -.5 \\ .5 & .5 & .5 & .5 \\ -.5 & -.5 & .5 & .5 \\ -.5 & .5 & .5 & -.5 \end{bmatrix}$.

13. Let $A = \begin{bmatrix} 3 & 1 \\ 1 & 3 \end{bmatrix}$. Then the characteristic polynomial of A is $(3-\lambda)^2 - 1 = \lambda^2 - 6\lambda + 8 = (\lambda - 4)(\lambda - 2)$, so

the eigenvalues of A are 4 and 2. For $\lambda = 4$, one computes that a basis for the eigenspace is $\begin{bmatrix} 1 \\ 1 \end{bmatrix}$, which

can be normalized to get $\mathbf{u}_1 = \begin{bmatrix} 1/\sqrt{2} \\ 1/\sqrt{2} \end{bmatrix}$. For $\lambda = 2$, one computes that a basis for the eigenspace is $\begin{bmatrix} -1 \\ 1 \end{bmatrix}$,

which can be normalized to get $\mathbf{u}_2 = \begin{bmatrix} -1/\sqrt{2} \\ 1/\sqrt{2} \end{bmatrix}$. Let

$$P = [\mathbf{u}_1 \quad \mathbf{u}_2] = \begin{bmatrix} 1/\sqrt{2} & -1/\sqrt{2} \\ 1/\sqrt{2} & 1/\sqrt{2} \end{bmatrix} \text{ and } D = \begin{bmatrix} 4 & 0 \\ 0 & 2 \end{bmatrix}$$

Then P orthogonally diagonalizes A, and $A = PDP^{-1}$.

14. Let $A = \begin{bmatrix} 1 & 5 \\ 5 & 1 \end{bmatrix}$. Then the characteristic polynomial of A is $(1-\lambda)^2 - 25 = \lambda^2 - 2\lambda - 24 = (\lambda - 6)(\lambda + 4)$,

so the eigenvalues of A are 6 and -4. For $\lambda = 6$, one computes that a basis for the eigenspace is $\begin{bmatrix} 1 \\ 1 \end{bmatrix}$,

which can be normalized to get $\mathbf{u}_1 = \begin{bmatrix} 1/\sqrt{2} \\ 1/\sqrt{2} \end{bmatrix}$. For $\lambda = -4$, one computes that a basis for the eigenspace is

$\begin{bmatrix} -1 \\ 1 \end{bmatrix}$, which can be normalized to get $\mathbf{u}_2 = \begin{bmatrix} -1/\sqrt{2} \\ 1/\sqrt{2} \end{bmatrix}$.

Let

$$P = \begin{bmatrix} \mathbf{u}_1 & \mathbf{u}_2 \end{bmatrix} = \begin{bmatrix} 1/\sqrt{2} & -1/\sqrt{2} \\ 1/\sqrt{2} & 1/\sqrt{2} \end{bmatrix} \text{ and } D = \begin{bmatrix} 6 & 0 \\ 0 & -4 \end{bmatrix}$$

Then P orthogonally diagonalizes A, and $A = PDP^{-1}$.

15. Let $A = \begin{bmatrix} 16 & -4 \\ -4 & 1 \end{bmatrix}$. Then the characteristic polynomial of A is $(16 - \lambda)(1 - \lambda) - 16 = \lambda^2 - 17\lambda = (\lambda - 17)\lambda$,

so the eigenvalues of A are 17 and 0. For $\lambda = 17$, one computes that a basis for the eigenspace is $\begin{bmatrix} -4 \\ 1 \end{bmatrix}$,

which can be normalized to get $\mathbf{u}_1 = \begin{bmatrix} -4/\sqrt{17} \\ 1/\sqrt{17} \end{bmatrix}$. For $\lambda = 0$, one computes that a basis for the eigenspace

is $\begin{bmatrix} 1 \\ 4 \end{bmatrix}$, which can be normalized to get $\mathbf{u}_2 = \begin{bmatrix} 1/\sqrt{17} \\ 4/\sqrt{17} \end{bmatrix}$. Let

$$P = \begin{bmatrix} \mathbf{u}_1 & \mathbf{u}_2 \end{bmatrix} = \begin{bmatrix} -4/\sqrt{17} & 1/\sqrt{17} \\ 1/\sqrt{17} & 4/\sqrt{17} \end{bmatrix} \text{ and } D = \begin{bmatrix} 17 & 0 \\ 0 & 0 \end{bmatrix}$$

Then P orthogonally diagonalizes A, and $A = PDP^{-1}$.

16. Let $A = \begin{bmatrix} -7 & 24 \\ 24 & 7 \end{bmatrix}$. Then the characteristic polynomial of A is $(-7 - \lambda)(7 - \lambda) - 576 = \lambda^2 - 625 =$

$(\lambda - 25)(\lambda + 25)$, so the eigenvalues of A are 25 and –25. For $\lambda = 25$, one computes that a basis for the

eigenspace is $\begin{bmatrix} 3 \\ 4 \end{bmatrix}$, which can be normalized to get $\mathbf{u}_1 = \begin{bmatrix} 3/5 \\ 4/5 \end{bmatrix}$. For $\lambda = -25$, one computes that a basis

for the eigenspace is $\begin{bmatrix} -4 \\ 3 \end{bmatrix}$, which can be normalized to get $\mathbf{u}_2 = \begin{bmatrix} -4/5 \\ 3/5 \end{bmatrix}$. Let

$$P = \begin{bmatrix} \mathbf{u}_1 & \mathbf{u}_2 \end{bmatrix} = \begin{bmatrix} 3/5 & -4/5 \\ 4/5 & 3/5 \end{bmatrix} \text{ and } D = \begin{bmatrix} 25 & 0 \\ 0 & -25 \end{bmatrix}$$

Then P orthogonally diagonalizes A, and $A = PDP^{-1}$.

17. Let $A = \begin{bmatrix} 1 & 1 & 3 \\ 1 & 3 & 1 \\ 3 & 1 & 1 \end{bmatrix}$. The eigenvalues of A are 5, 2, and –2. For $\lambda = 5$, one computes that a basis for the

eigenspace is $\begin{bmatrix} 1 \\ 1 \\ 1 \end{bmatrix}$, which can be normalized to get $\mathbf{u}_1 = \begin{bmatrix} 1/\sqrt{3} \\ 1/\sqrt{3} \\ 1/\sqrt{3} \end{bmatrix}$. For $\lambda = 2$, one computes that a basis for the eigenspace is $\begin{bmatrix} 1 \\ -2 \\ 1 \end{bmatrix}$, which can be normalized to get $\mathbf{u}_2 = \begin{bmatrix} 1/\sqrt{6} \\ -2/\sqrt{6} \\ 1/\sqrt{6} \end{bmatrix}$. For $\lambda = -2$, one computes that a

basis for the eigenspace is $\begin{bmatrix} -1 \\ 0 \\ 1 \end{bmatrix}$, which can be normalized to get $\mathbf{u}_3 = \begin{bmatrix} -1/\sqrt{2} \\ 0 \\ 1/\sqrt{2} \end{bmatrix}$. Let

$$P = \begin{bmatrix} \mathbf{u}_1 & \mathbf{u}_2 & \mathbf{u}_3 \end{bmatrix} = \begin{bmatrix} 1/\sqrt{3} & 1/\sqrt{6} & -1/\sqrt{2} \\ 1/\sqrt{3} & -2/\sqrt{6} & 0 \\ 1/\sqrt{3} & 1/\sqrt{6} & 1\sqrt{2} \end{bmatrix} \text{ and } D = \begin{bmatrix} 5 & 0 & 0 \\ 0 & 2 & 0 \\ 0 & 0 & -2 \end{bmatrix}$$

Then P orthogonally diagonalizes A, and $A = PDP^{-1}$.

18. Let $A = \begin{bmatrix} -2 & -36 & 0 \\ -36 & -23 & 0 \\ 0 & 0 & 3 \end{bmatrix}$. The eigenvalues of A are 25, 3, and –50. For $\lambda = 25$, one computes that a basis

for the eigenspace is $\begin{bmatrix} -4 \\ 3 \\ 0 \end{bmatrix}$, which can be normalized to get $\mathbf{u}_1 = \begin{bmatrix} -4/5 \\ 3/5 \\ 0 \end{bmatrix}$. For $\lambda = 3$, one computes that a

basis for the eigenspace is $\begin{bmatrix} 0 \\ 0 \\ 1 \end{bmatrix}$, which is of length 1, so $\mathbf{u}_2 = \begin{bmatrix} 0 \\ 0 \\ 1 \end{bmatrix}$. For $\lambda = -50$, one computes that a

basis for the eigenspace is $\begin{bmatrix} 3 \\ 4 \\ 0 \end{bmatrix}$, which can be normalized to get $\mathbf{u}_3 = \begin{bmatrix} 3/5 \\ 4/5 \\ 0 \end{bmatrix}$. Let

$$P = \begin{bmatrix} \mathbf{u}_1 & \mathbf{u}_2 & \mathbf{u}_3 \end{bmatrix} = \begin{bmatrix} -4/5 & 0 & 3/5 \\ 3/5 & 0 & 4/5 \\ 0 & 1 & 0 \end{bmatrix} \text{ and } D = \begin{bmatrix} 25 & 0 & 0 \\ 0 & 3 & 0 \\ 0 & 0 & -50 \end{bmatrix}$$

Then P orthogonally diagonalizes A, and $A = PDP^{-1}$.

19. Let $A = \begin{bmatrix} 3 & -2 & 4 \\ -2 & 6 & 2 \\ 4 & 2 & 3 \end{bmatrix}$. The eigenvalues of A are 7 and –2. For $\lambda = 7$, one computes that a basis for the

eigenspace is $\left\{ \begin{bmatrix} -1 \\ 2 \\ 0 \end{bmatrix}, \begin{bmatrix} 1 \\ 0 \\ 1 \end{bmatrix} \right\}$. This basis may be converted via orthogonal projection to an orthogonal basis for the eigenspace: $\left\{ \begin{bmatrix} -1 \\ 2 \\ 0 \end{bmatrix}, \begin{bmatrix} 4 \\ 2 \\ 5 \end{bmatrix} \right\}$. These vectors can be normalized to get $\mathbf{u}_1 = \begin{bmatrix} -1/\sqrt{5} \\ 2/\sqrt{5} \\ 0 \end{bmatrix}$,

$\mathbf{u}_2 = \begin{bmatrix} 4/\sqrt{45} \\ 2/\sqrt{45} \\ 5/\sqrt{45} \end{bmatrix}$. For $\lambda = -2$, one computes that a basis for the eigenspace is $\begin{bmatrix} -2 \\ -1 \\ 2 \end{bmatrix}$, which can be

normalized to get $\mathbf{u}_3 = \begin{bmatrix} -2/3 \\ -1/3 \\ 2/3 \end{bmatrix}$. Let

$$P = \begin{bmatrix} \mathbf{u}_1 & \mathbf{u}_2 & \mathbf{u}_3 \end{bmatrix} = \begin{bmatrix} -1/\sqrt{5} & 4/\sqrt{45} & -2/3 \\ 2/\sqrt{5} & 2/\sqrt{45} & -1/3 \\ 0 & 5/\sqrt{45} & 2/3 \end{bmatrix} \text{ and } D = \begin{bmatrix} 7 & 0 & 0 \\ 0 & 7 & 0 \\ 0 & 0 & -2 \end{bmatrix}$$

Then P orthogonally diagonalizes A, and $A = PDP^{-1}$.

20. Let $A = \begin{bmatrix} 7 & -4 & 4 \\ -4 & 5 & 0 \\ 4 & 0 & 9 \end{bmatrix}$. The eigenvalues of A are 13, 7, and 1. For $\lambda = 13$, one computes that a basis for

the eigenspace is $\begin{bmatrix} 2 \\ -1 \\ 2 \end{bmatrix}$, which can be normalized to get $\mathbf{u}_1 = \begin{bmatrix} 2/3 \\ -1/3 \\ 2/3 \end{bmatrix}$. For $\lambda = 7$, one computes that a

basis for the eigenspace is $\begin{bmatrix} -1 \\ 2 \\ 2 \end{bmatrix}$, which can be normalized to get $\mathbf{u}_2 = \begin{bmatrix} -1/3 \\ 2/3 \\ 2/3 \end{bmatrix}$. For $\lambda = 1$, one computes

that a basis for the eigenspace is $\begin{bmatrix} 2 \\ 2 \\ -1 \end{bmatrix}$, which can be normalized to get $\mathbf{u}_3 = \begin{bmatrix} 2/3 \\ 2/3 \\ -1/3 \end{bmatrix}$. Let

$$P = \begin{bmatrix} \mathbf{u}_1 & \mathbf{u}_2 & \mathbf{u}_3 \end{bmatrix} = \begin{bmatrix} 2/3 & -1/3 & 2/3 \\ -1/3 & 2/3 & 2/3 \\ 2/3 & 2/3 & -1/3 \end{bmatrix} \text{ and } D = \begin{bmatrix} 13 & 0 & 0 \\ 0 & 7 & 0 \\ 0 & 0 & 1 \end{bmatrix}$$

Then P orthogonally diagonalizes A, and $A = PDP^{-1}$.

21. Let $A = \begin{bmatrix} 4 & 1 & 3 & 1 \\ 1 & 4 & 1 & 3 \\ 3 & 1 & 4 & 1 \\ 1 & 3 & 1 & 4 \end{bmatrix}$. The eigenvalues of A are 9, 5, and 1. For $\lambda = 9$, one computes that a basis for

the eigenspace is $\begin{bmatrix} 1 \\ 1 \\ 1 \\ 1 \end{bmatrix}$, which can be normalized to get $\mathbf{u}_1 = \begin{bmatrix} 1/2 \\ 1/2 \\ 1/2 \\ 1/2 \end{bmatrix}$. For $\lambda = 5$, one computes that a basis

for the eigenspace is $\begin{bmatrix} -1 \\ 1 \\ -1 \\ 1 \end{bmatrix}$, which can be normalized to get $\mathbf{u}_2 = \begin{bmatrix} -1/2 \\ 1/2 \\ -1/2 \\ 1/2 \end{bmatrix}$. For $\lambda = 1$, one computes that a

basis for the eigenspace is $\left\{ \begin{bmatrix} -1 \\ 0 \\ 1 \\ 0 \end{bmatrix}, \begin{bmatrix} 0 \\ -1 \\ 0 \\ 1 \end{bmatrix} \right\}$. This basis is an orthogonal basis for the eigenspace, and these

vectors can be normalized to get $\mathbf{u}_3 = \begin{bmatrix} -1/\sqrt{2} \\ 0 \\ 1/\sqrt{2} \\ 0 \end{bmatrix}$, $\mathbf{u}_4 = \begin{bmatrix} 0 \\ -1/\sqrt{2} \\ 0 \\ 1/\sqrt{2} \end{bmatrix}$. Let

$$P = \begin{bmatrix} \mathbf{u}_1 & \mathbf{u}_2 & \mathbf{u}_3 & \mathbf{u}_4 \end{bmatrix} = \begin{bmatrix} 1/2 & -1/2 & -1/\sqrt{2} & 0 \\ 1/2 & 1/2 & 0 & -1/\sqrt{2} \\ 1/2 & -1/2 & 1/\sqrt{2} & 0 \\ 1/2 & 1/2 & 0 & 1/\sqrt{2} \end{bmatrix} \text{ and } D = \begin{bmatrix} 9 & 0 & 0 & 0 \\ 0 & 5 & 0 & 0 \\ 0 & 0 & 1 & 0 \\ 0 & 0 & 0 & 1 \end{bmatrix}$$

Then P orthogonally diagonalizes A, and $A = PDP^{-1}$.

22. Let $A = \begin{bmatrix} 2 & 0 & 0 & 0 \\ 0 & 1 & 0 & 1 \\ 0 & 0 & 2 & 0 \\ 0 & 1 & 0 & 1 \end{bmatrix}$. The eigenvalues of A are 2 and 0. For $\lambda = 2$, one computes that a basis for the

eigenspace is $\left\{ \begin{bmatrix} 1 \\ 0 \\ 0 \\ 0 \end{bmatrix}, \begin{bmatrix} 0 \\ 1 \\ 0 \\ 1 \end{bmatrix}, \begin{bmatrix} 0 \\ 0 \\ 1 \\ 0 \end{bmatrix} \right\}$. This basis is an orthogonal basis for the eigenspace, and these vectors can be normalized to get $\mathbf{u}_1 = \begin{bmatrix} 1 \\ 0 \\ 0 \\ 0 \end{bmatrix}$, $\mathbf{u}_2 = \begin{bmatrix} 0 \\ 1/\sqrt{2} \\ 0 \\ 1/\sqrt{2} \end{bmatrix}$, and $\mathbf{u}_3 = \begin{bmatrix} 0 \\ 0 \\ 1 \\ 0 \end{bmatrix}$. For $\lambda = 0$, one computes that a basis for

the eigenspace is $\begin{bmatrix} 0 \\ -1 \\ 0 \\ 1 \end{bmatrix}$, which can be normalized to get $\mathbf{u}_4 = \begin{bmatrix} 0 \\ -1/\sqrt{2} \\ 0 \\ 1/\sqrt{2} \end{bmatrix}$. Let

$$P = \begin{bmatrix} \mathbf{u}_1 & \mathbf{u}_2 & \mathbf{u}_3 & \mathbf{u}_4 \end{bmatrix} = \begin{bmatrix} 1 & 0 & 0 & 0 \\ 0 & 1/\sqrt{2} & 0 & -1/\sqrt{2} \\ 0 & 0 & 1 & 0 \\ 0 & 1/\sqrt{2} & 0 & 1/\sqrt{2} \end{bmatrix} \text{ and } D = \begin{bmatrix} 2 & 0 & 0 & 0 \\ 0 & 2 & 0 & 0 \\ 0 & 0 & 2 & 0 \\ 0 & 0 & 0 & 0 \end{bmatrix}$$

Then P orthogonally diagonalizes A, and $A = PDP^{-1}$.

23. Let $A = \begin{bmatrix} 3 & 1 & 1 \\ 1 & 3 & 1 \\ 1 & 1 & 3 \end{bmatrix}$. Since each row of A sums to 5,

$$A \begin{bmatrix} 1 \\ 1 \\ 1 \end{bmatrix} = \begin{bmatrix} 3 & 1 & 1 \\ 1 & 3 & 1 \\ 1 & 1 & 3 \end{bmatrix} \begin{bmatrix} 1 \\ 1 \\ 1 \end{bmatrix} = \begin{bmatrix} 5 \\ 5 \\ 5 \end{bmatrix} = 5 \begin{bmatrix} 1 \\ 1 \\ 1 \end{bmatrix}$$

and 5 is an eigenvalue of A. The eigenvector $\begin{bmatrix} 1 \\ 1 \\ 1 \end{bmatrix}$ may be normalized to get $\mathbf{u}_1 = \begin{bmatrix} 1/\sqrt{3} \\ 1/\sqrt{3} \\ 1/\sqrt{3} \end{bmatrix}$. One may also

compute that

$$A \begin{bmatrix} -1 \\ 1 \\ 0 \end{bmatrix} = \begin{bmatrix} 3 & 1 & 1 \\ 1 & 3 & 1 \\ 1 & 1 & 3 \end{bmatrix} \begin{bmatrix} -1 \\ 1 \\ 0 \end{bmatrix} = \begin{bmatrix} -2 \\ 2 \\ 0 \end{bmatrix} = 2 \begin{bmatrix} -1 \\ 1 \\ 0 \end{bmatrix}$$

so $\begin{bmatrix} -1 \\ 1 \\ 0 \end{bmatrix}$ is an eigenvector of A with associated eigenvalue $\lambda = 2$. For $\lambda = 2$, one computes that a basis for

the eigenspace is $\left\{ \begin{bmatrix} -1 \\ 1 \\ 0 \end{bmatrix}, \begin{bmatrix} -1 \\ -1 \\ 2 \end{bmatrix} \right\}$. This basis is an orthogonal basis for the eigenspace, and these vectors

can be normalized to get $\mathbf{u}_2 = \begin{bmatrix} -1/\sqrt{2} \\ 1/\sqrt{2} \\ 0 \end{bmatrix}$ and $\mathbf{u}_3 = \begin{bmatrix} -1/\sqrt{6} \\ -1/\sqrt{6} \\ 2/\sqrt{6} \end{bmatrix}$.

Let

$$P = \begin{bmatrix} \mathbf{u}_1 & \mathbf{u}_2 & \mathbf{u}_3 \end{bmatrix} = \begin{bmatrix} 1/\sqrt{3} & -1/\sqrt{2} & -1/\sqrt{6} \\ 1/\sqrt{3} & 1/\sqrt{2} & -1/\sqrt{6} \\ 1/\sqrt{3} & 0 & 2/\sqrt{6} \end{bmatrix} \text{ and } D = \begin{bmatrix} 5 & 0 & 0 \\ 0 & 2 & 0 \\ 0 & 0 & 2 \end{bmatrix}$$

Then P orthogonally diagonalizes A, and $A = PDP^{-1}$.

24. Let $A = \begin{bmatrix} 5 & -4 & -2 \\ -4 & 5 & 2 \\ -2 & 2 & 2 \end{bmatrix}$. One may compute that

$$A \begin{bmatrix} -2 \\ 2 \\ 1 \end{bmatrix} = \begin{bmatrix} -20 \\ 20 \\ 10 \end{bmatrix} = 10 \begin{bmatrix} -2 \\ 2 \\ 1 \end{bmatrix}$$

so $\mathbf{v}_1 = \begin{bmatrix} -2 \\ 2 \\ 1 \end{bmatrix}$ is an eigenvector of A with associated eigenvalue $\lambda_1 = 10$. Likewise one may compute that

$$A \begin{bmatrix} 1 \\ 1 \\ 0 \end{bmatrix} = \begin{bmatrix} 1 \\ 1 \\ 0 \end{bmatrix} = 1 \begin{bmatrix} 1 \\ 1 \\ 0 \end{bmatrix}$$

so $\begin{bmatrix} 1 \\ 1 \\ 0 \end{bmatrix}$ is an eigenvector of A with associated eigenvalue $\lambda_2 = 1$. For $\lambda_2 = 1$, one computes that a basis

for the eigenspace is $\left\{ \begin{bmatrix} 1 \\ 1 \\ 0 \end{bmatrix}, \begin{bmatrix} 1 \\ 0 \\ 2 \end{bmatrix} \right\}$. This basis may be converted via orthogonal projection to an

orthogonal basis for the eigenspace: $\{\mathbf{v}_2, \mathbf{v}_3\} = \left\{ \begin{bmatrix} 1 \\ 1 \\ 0 \end{bmatrix}, \begin{bmatrix} 1 \\ -1 \\ 4 \end{bmatrix} \right\}$. The eigenvectors $\mathbf{v}_1$, $\mathbf{v}_2$, and $\mathbf{v}_3$ may be

normalized to get the vectors $\mathbf{u}_1 = \begin{bmatrix} -2/3 \\ 2/3 \\ 1/3 \end{bmatrix}$, $\mathbf{u}_2 = \begin{bmatrix} 1/\sqrt{2} \\ 1/\sqrt{2} \\ 0 \end{bmatrix}$, and $\mathbf{u}_3 = \begin{bmatrix} 1/\sqrt{18} \\ 1/\sqrt{18} \\ 4/\sqrt{18} \end{bmatrix}$. Let

$$P = \begin{bmatrix} \mathbf{u}_1 & \mathbf{u}_2 & \mathbf{u}_3 \end{bmatrix} = \begin{bmatrix} -2/3 & 1/\sqrt{2} & 1/\sqrt{18} \\ 2/3 & 1/\sqrt{2} & -1/\sqrt{18} \\ 1/3 & 0 & 4/\sqrt{18} \end{bmatrix} \text{ and } D = \begin{bmatrix} 10 & 0 & 0 \\ 0 & 1 & 0 \\ 0 & 0 & 1 \end{bmatrix}$$

Then P orthogonally diagonalizes A, and $A = PDP^{-1}$.

25. a. True. See Theorem 2 and the paragraph preceding the theorem.

   b. True. This is a particular case of the statement in Theorem 1, where $\mathbf{u}$ and $\mathbf{v}$ are nonzero.

   c. False. There are n real eigenvalues (Theorem 3), but they need not be distinct (Example 3).

   d. False. See the paragraph following formula (2), in which each $\mathbf{u}$ is a unit vector.

26. a. True. See Theorem 2.

   b. True. See the displayed equation in the paragraph before Theorem 2.

   c. False. An orthogonal matrix can be symmetric (and hence orthogonally diagonalizable), but not every orthogonal matrix is symmetric. See the matrix P in Example 2.

   d. True. See Theorem 3(b).

27. Since A is symmetric, $(B^T AB)^T = B^T A^T B^{TT} = B^T AB$, and $B^T AB$ is symmetric. Applying this result with $A = I$ gives $B^T B$ is symmetric. Finally, $(BB^T)^T = B^{TT} B^T = BB^T$, so BB^T is symmetric.

28. Let A be an $n \times n$ symmetric matrix. Then

$$(A\mathbf{x}) \cdot \mathbf{y} = (A\mathbf{x})^T \mathbf{y} = \mathbf{x}^T A^T \mathbf{y} = \mathbf{x}^T A\mathbf{y} = \mathbf{x} \cdot (A\mathbf{y})$$

since $A^T = A$.

29. Since A is orthogonally diagonalizable, $A = PDP^{-1}$, where P is orthogonal and D is diagonal. Since A is invertible, $A^{-1} = (PDP^{-1})^{-1} = PD^{-1}P^{-1}$. Notice that D^{-1} is a diagonal matrix, so A^{-1} is orthogonally diagonalizable.

30. If A and B are orthogonally diagonalizable, then A and B are symmetric by Theorem 2. If $AB = BA$, then $(AB)^T = (BA)^T = A^T B^T = AB$. So AB is symmetric and hence is orthogonally diagonalizable by Theorem 2.

31. The Diagonalization Theorem of Section 5.3 says that the columns of P are linearly independent eigenvectors corresponding to the eigenvalues of A listed on the diagonal of D. So P has exactly k columns of eigenvectors corresponding to λ. These k columns form a basis for the eigenspace.

32. If $A = PRP^{-1}$, then $P^{-1}AP = R$. Since P is orthogonal, $R = P^T AP$. Hence $R^T = (P^T AP)^T = P^T A^T P^{TT} = P^T AP = R$, which shows that R is symmetric. Since R is also upper triangular, its entries above the diagonal must be zeros to match the zeros below the diagonal. Thus R is a diagonal matrix.

33. It is previously been found that A is orthogonally diagonalized by P, where

$$P = \begin{bmatrix} \mathbf{u}_1 & \mathbf{u}_2 & \mathbf{u}_3 \end{bmatrix} = \begin{bmatrix} -1/\sqrt{2} & -1/\sqrt{6} & 1/\sqrt{3} \\ 1/\sqrt{2} & -1/\sqrt{6} & 1/\sqrt{3} \\ 0 & 2/\sqrt{6} & 1/\sqrt{3} \end{bmatrix} \text{ and } D = \begin{bmatrix} 8 & 0 & 0 \\ 0 & 6 & 0 \\ 0 & 0 & 3 \end{bmatrix}$$

Thus the spectral decomposition of A is

$$A = \lambda_1 \mathbf{u}_1 \mathbf{u}_1^T + \lambda_2 \mathbf{u}_2 \mathbf{u}_2^T + \lambda_3 \mathbf{u}_3 \mathbf{u}_3^T = 8\mathbf{u}_1 \mathbf{u}_1^T + 6\mathbf{u}_2 \mathbf{u}_2^T + 3\mathbf{u}_3 \mathbf{u}_3^T$$

$$= 8\begin{bmatrix} 1/2 & -1/2 & 0 \\ -1/2 & 1/2 & 0 \\ 0 & 0 & 0 \end{bmatrix} + 6\begin{bmatrix} 1/6 & 1/6 & -2/6 \\ 1/6 & 1/6 & -2/6 \\ -2/6 & -2/6 & 4/6 \end{bmatrix} + 3\begin{bmatrix} 1/3 & 1/3 & 1/3 \\ 1/3 & 1/3 & 1/3 \\ 1/3 & 1/3 & 1/3 \end{bmatrix}$$

34. It is previously been found that A is orthogonally diagonalized by P, where

$$P = \begin{bmatrix} \mathbf{u}_1 & \mathbf{u}_2 & \mathbf{u}_3 \end{bmatrix} = \begin{bmatrix} 1/\sqrt{2} & -1/\sqrt{18} & -2/3 \\ 0 & 4/\sqrt{18} & -1/3 \\ 1/\sqrt{2} & 1/\sqrt{18} & 2/3 \end{bmatrix} \text{ and } D = \begin{bmatrix} 7 & 0 & 0 \\ 0 & 7 & 0 \\ 0 & 0 & -2 \end{bmatrix}$$

Thus the spectral decomposition of A is

$$A = \lambda_1 \mathbf{u}_1 \mathbf{u}_1^T + \lambda_2 \mathbf{u}_2 \mathbf{u}_2^T + \lambda_3 \mathbf{u}_3 \mathbf{u}_3^T = 7\mathbf{u}_1 \mathbf{u}_1^T + 7\mathbf{u}_2 \mathbf{u}_2^T - 2\mathbf{u}_3 \mathbf{u}_3^T$$

$$= 7\begin{bmatrix} 1/2 & 0 & 1/2 \\ 0 & 0 & 0 \\ 1/2 & 0 & 1/2 \end{bmatrix} + 7\begin{bmatrix} 1/18 & -4/18 & -1/18 \\ -4/18 & 16/18 & 4/18 \\ -1/18 & 4/18 & 1/18 \end{bmatrix} - 2\begin{bmatrix} 4/9 & 2/9 & -4/9 \\ 2/9 & 1/9 & -2/9 \\ -4/9 & -2/9 & 4/9 \end{bmatrix}$$

35. a. Given $\mathbf{x}$ in $\mathbb{R}^n$, $b\mathbf{x} = (\mathbf{uu}^T)\mathbf{x} = \mathbf{u}(\mathbf{u}^T\mathbf{x}) = (\mathbf{u}^T\mathbf{x})\mathbf{u}$, because $\mathbf{u}^T\mathbf{x}$ is a scalar. So $B\mathbf{x} = (\mathbf{x} \cdot \mathbf{u})\mathbf{u}$. Since $\mathbf{u}$ is a unit vector, $B\mathbf{x}$ is the orthogonal projection of $\mathbf{x}$ onto $\mathbf{u}$.

b. Since $B^T = (\mathbf{uu}^T)^T = \mathbf{u}^{TT}\mathbf{u}^T = \mathbf{uu}^T = B$, B is a symmetric matrix. Also,

$B^2 = (\mathbf{uu}^T)(\mathbf{uu}^T) = \mathbf{u}(\mathbf{u}^T\mathbf{u})\mathbf{u}^T = \mathbf{uu}^T = B$ because $\mathbf{u}^T\mathbf{u} = 1$.

c. Since $\mathbf{u}^T\mathbf{u} = 1$, $B\mathbf{u} = (\mathbf{uu}^T)\mathbf{u} = \mathbf{u}(\mathbf{u}^T\mathbf{u}) = \mathbf{u}(1) = \mathbf{u}$, so $\mathbf{u}$ is an eigenvector of B with corresponding eigenvalue 1.

36. Given any $\mathbf{y}$ in $\mathbb{R}^n$, let $\hat{\mathbf{y}} = B\mathbf{y}$ and $\mathbf{z} = \mathbf{y} - \hat{\mathbf{y}}$. Suppose that $B^T = B$ and $B^2 = B$. Then $B^T B = BB = B$.

a. Since $\mathbf{z} \cdot \hat{\mathbf{y}} = (\mathbf{y} - \hat{\mathbf{y}}) \cdot (B\mathbf{y}) = \mathbf{y} \cdot (B\mathbf{y}) - \hat{\mathbf{y}} \cdot (B\mathbf{y}) = \mathbf{y}^T B\mathbf{y} - (B\mathbf{y})^T B\mathbf{y} = \mathbf{y}^T B\mathbf{y} - \mathbf{y}^T B^T B\mathbf{y} = 0$, $\mathbf{z}$ is orthogonal to $\hat{\mathbf{y}}$.

b. Any vector in $W = \text{Col } B$ has the form $B\mathbf{u}$ for some $\mathbf{u}$. Noting that B is symmetric, Exercise 28 gives
$$(\mathbf{y} - \hat{\mathbf{y}}) \cdot (B\mathbf{u}) = [B(\mathbf{y} - \hat{\mathbf{y}})] \cdot \mathbf{u} = [B\mathbf{y} - BB\mathbf{y}] \cdot \mathbf{u} = 0$$
since $B^2 = B$. So $\mathbf{y} - \hat{\mathbf{y}}$ is in $W^\perp$, and the decomposition $\mathbf{y} = \hat{\mathbf{y}} + (\mathbf{y} - \hat{\mathbf{y}})$ expresses $\mathbf{y}$ as the sum of a vector in W and a vector in $W^\perp$. By the Orthogonal Decomposition Theorem in Section 6.3, this decomposition is unique, and so $\hat{\mathbf{y}}$ must be $\text{proj}_W \mathbf{y}$.

37. [M] Let $A = \begin{bmatrix} 5 & 2 & 9 & -6 \\ 2 & 5 & -6 & 9 \\ 9 & -6 & 5 & 2 \\ -6 & 9 & 2 & 5 \end{bmatrix}$. The eigenvalues of A are 18, 10, 4, and –12. For $\lambda = 18$, one

computes that a basis for the eigenspace is $\begin{bmatrix} -1 \\ 1 \\ -1 \\ 1 \end{bmatrix}$, which can be normalized to get $\mathbf{u}_1 = \begin{bmatrix} -1/2 \\ 1/2 \\ -1/2 \\ 1/2 \end{bmatrix}$. For

$\lambda = 10$, one computes that a basis for the eigenspace is $\begin{bmatrix} 1 \\ 1 \\ 1 \\ 1 \end{bmatrix}$, which can be normalized to get $\mathbf{u}_2 = \begin{bmatrix} 1/2 \\ 1/2 \\ 1/2 \\ 1/2 \end{bmatrix}$.

For $\lambda = 4$, one computes that a basis for the eigenspace is $\begin{bmatrix} 1 \\ 1 \\ -1 \\ -1 \end{bmatrix}$, which can be normalized to get

$\mathbf{u}_3 = \begin{bmatrix} 1/2 \\ 1/2 \\ -1/2 \\ -1/2 \end{bmatrix}$. For $\lambda = -12$, one computes that a basis for the eigenspace is $\begin{bmatrix} 1 \\ -1 \\ -1 \\ 1 \end{bmatrix}$, which can be

normalized to get $\mathbf{u}_4 = \begin{bmatrix} 1/2 \\ -1/2 \\ -1/2 \\ 1/2 \end{bmatrix}$. Let $P = \begin{bmatrix} \mathbf{u}_1 & \mathbf{u}_2 & \mathbf{u}_3 & \mathbf{u}_4 \end{bmatrix} = \begin{bmatrix} -1/2 & 1/2 & 1/2 & 1/2 \\ 1/2 & 1/2 & 1/2 & -1/2 \\ -1/2 & 1/2 & -1/2 & -1/2 \\ 1/2 & 1/2 & -1/2 & 1/2 \end{bmatrix}$ and

$D = \begin{bmatrix} 18 & 0 & 0 & 0 \\ 0 & 10 & 0 & 0 \\ 0 & 0 & 4 & 0 \\ 0 & 0 & 0 & -12 \end{bmatrix}$. Then P orthogonally diagonalizes A, and $A = PDP^{-1}$.

38. **[M]** Let $A = \begin{bmatrix} .38 & -.18 & -.06 & -.04 \\ -.18 & .59 & -.04 & .12 \\ -.06 & -.04 & .47 & -.12 \\ -.04 & .12 & -.12 & .41 \end{bmatrix}$. The eigenvalues of A are .25, .30, .55, and .75. For $\lambda = .25$,

one computes that a basis for the eigenspace is $\begin{bmatrix} 4 \\ 2 \\ 2 \\ 1 \end{bmatrix}$, which can be normalized to get $\mathbf{u}_1 = \begin{bmatrix} .8 \\ .4 \\ .4 \\ .2 \end{bmatrix}$. For

$\lambda = .30$, one computes that a basis for the eigenspace is $\begin{bmatrix} -1 \\ -2 \\ 2 \\ 4 \end{bmatrix}$, which can be normalized to get

$\mathbf{u}_2 = \begin{bmatrix} -.2 \\ -.4 \\ .4 \\ .8 \end{bmatrix}$. For $\lambda = .55$, one computes that a basis for the eigenspace is $\begin{bmatrix} 2 \\ -1 \\ -4 \\ 2 \end{bmatrix}$, which can be normalized

to get $\mathbf{u}_3 = \begin{bmatrix} .4 \\ -.2 \\ -.8 \\ .4 \end{bmatrix}$. For $\lambda = .75$, one computes that a basis for the eigenspace is $\begin{bmatrix} -2 \\ 4 \\ -1 \\ 2 \end{bmatrix}$, which can be normalized to get $\mathbf{u}_4 = \begin{bmatrix} -.4 \\ .8 \\ -.2 \\ .4 \end{bmatrix}$. Let $P = \begin{bmatrix} \mathbf{u}_1 & \mathbf{u}_2 & \mathbf{u}_3 & \mathbf{u}_4 \end{bmatrix} = \begin{bmatrix} .8 & -.2 & .4 & -.4 \\ .4 & -.4 & -.2 & .8 \\ .4 & .4 & -.8 & -.2 \\ .2 & .8 & .4 & .4 \end{bmatrix}$ and

$D = \begin{bmatrix} .25 & 0 & 0 & 0 \\ 0 & .30 & 0 & 0 \\ 0 & 0 & .55 & 0 \\ 0 & 0 & 0 & .75 \end{bmatrix}$. Then P orthogonally diagonalizes A, and $A = PDP^{-1}$.

39. [M] Let $A = \begin{bmatrix} .31 & .58 & .08 & .44 \\ .58 & -.56 & .44 & -.58 \\ .08 & .44 & .19 & -.08 \\ .44 & -.58 & -.08 & .31 \end{bmatrix}$. The eigenvalues of A are .75, 0, and -1.25. For $\lambda = .75$, one

computes that a basis for the eigenspace is $\left\{ \begin{bmatrix} 1 \\ 0 \\ 0 \\ 1 \end{bmatrix}, \begin{bmatrix} 3 \\ 2 \\ 2 \\ 0 \end{bmatrix} \right\}$. This basis may be converted via orthogonal

projection to the orthogonal basis $\left\{ \begin{bmatrix} 1 \\ 0 \\ 0 \\ 1 \end{bmatrix}, \begin{bmatrix} 3 \\ 4 \\ 4 \\ -3 \end{bmatrix} \right\}$. These vectors can be normalized to get $\mathbf{u}_1 = \begin{bmatrix} 1/\sqrt{2} \\ 0 \\ 0 \\ 1/\sqrt{2} \end{bmatrix}$,

$\mathbf{u}_2 = \begin{bmatrix} 3/\sqrt{50} \\ 4/\sqrt{50} \\ 4/\sqrt{50} \\ -3/\sqrt{50} \end{bmatrix}$. For $\lambda = 0$, one computes that a basis for the eigenspace is $\begin{bmatrix} -2 \\ -1 \\ 4 \\ 2 \end{bmatrix}$, which can be

normalized to get $\mathbf{u}_3 = \begin{bmatrix} -.4 \\ -.2 \\ .8 \\ .4 \end{bmatrix}$. For $\lambda = -1.25$, one computes that a basis for the eigenspace is $\begin{bmatrix} -2 \\ 4 \\ -1 \\ 2 \end{bmatrix}$,

which can be normalized to get $\mathbf{u}_4 = \begin{bmatrix} -.4 \\ .8 \\ -.2 \\ .4 \end{bmatrix}$.

Let $P = \begin{bmatrix} \mathbf{u}_1 & \mathbf{u}_2 & \mathbf{u}_3 & \mathbf{u}_4 \end{bmatrix} = \begin{bmatrix} 1/\sqrt{2} & 3/\sqrt{50} & -.4 & -.4 \\ 0 & 4/\sqrt{50} & -.2 & .8 \\ 0 & 4/\sqrt{50} & .8 & -.2 \\ 1/\sqrt{2} & -3/\sqrt{50} & .4 & .4 \end{bmatrix}$ and $D = \begin{bmatrix} .75 & 0 & 0 & 0 \\ 0 & .75 & 0 & 0 \\ 0 & 0 & 0 & 0 \\ 0 & 0 & 0 & -1.25 \end{bmatrix}$. Then P

orthogonally diagonalizes A, and $A = PDP^{-1}$.

40. [M] Let $A = \begin{bmatrix} 10 & 2 & 2 & -6 & 9 \\ 2 & 10 & 2 & -6 & 9 \\ 2 & 2 & 10 & -6 & 9 \\ -6 & -6 & -6 & 26 & 9 \\ 9 & 9 & 9 & 9 & -19 \end{bmatrix}$. The eigenvalues of A are 8, 32, –28, and 17. For $\lambda = 8$, one

computes that a basis for the eigenspace is $\left\{ \begin{bmatrix} 1 \\ -1 \\ 0 \\ 0 \\ 0 \end{bmatrix}, \begin{bmatrix} -1 \\ 0 \\ 1 \\ 0 \\ 0 \end{bmatrix} \right\}$. This basis may be converted via orthogonal

projection to the orthogonal basis $\left\{ \begin{bmatrix} 1 \\ -1 \\ 0 \\ 0 \\ 0 \end{bmatrix}, \begin{bmatrix} 1 \\ 1 \\ -2 \\ 0 \\ 0 \end{bmatrix} \right\}$. These vectors can be normalized to get

$\mathbf{u}_1 = \begin{bmatrix} 1/\sqrt{2} \\ -1/\sqrt{2} \\ 0 \\ 0 \\ 0 \end{bmatrix}$, $\mathbf{u}_2 = \begin{bmatrix} 1/\sqrt{6} \\ 1/\sqrt{6} \\ -2/\sqrt{6} \\ 0 \\ 0 \end{bmatrix}$. For $\lambda = 32$, one computes that a basis for the eigenspace is $\begin{bmatrix} 1 \\ 1 \\ 1 \\ -3 \\ 0 \end{bmatrix}$, which

can be normalized to get $\mathbf{u}_3 = \begin{bmatrix} 1/\sqrt{12} \\ 1/\sqrt{12} \\ 1/\sqrt{12} \\ -3/\sqrt{12} \\ 0 \end{bmatrix}$. For $\lambda = -28$, one computes that a basis for the eigenspace is

$\begin{bmatrix} 1 \\ 1 \\ 1 \\ 1 \\ -4 \end{bmatrix}$, which can be normalized to get $\mathbf{u}_4 = \begin{bmatrix} 1/\sqrt{20} \\ 1/\sqrt{20} \\ 1/\sqrt{20} \\ 1/\sqrt{20} \\ -4/\sqrt{20} \end{bmatrix}$. For $\lambda = 17$, one computes that a basis for the

eigenspace is $\begin{bmatrix} 1 \\ 1 \\ 1 \\ 1 \\ 1 \end{bmatrix}$, which can be normalized to get $\mathbf{u}_5 = \begin{bmatrix} 1/\sqrt{5} \\ 1/\sqrt{5} \\ 1/\sqrt{5} \\ 1/\sqrt{5} \\ 1/\sqrt{5} \end{bmatrix}$.

Let $P = \begin{bmatrix} \mathbf{u}_1 & \mathbf{u}_2 & \mathbf{u}_3 & \mathbf{u}_4 & \mathbf{u}_5 \end{bmatrix} = \begin{bmatrix} 1/\sqrt{2} & 1/\sqrt{6} & 1/\sqrt{12} & 1/\sqrt{20} & 1/\sqrt{5} \\ -1/\sqrt{2} & 1/\sqrt{6} & 1/\sqrt{12} & 1/\sqrt{20} & 1/\sqrt{5} \\ 0 & -2/\sqrt{6} & 1/\sqrt{12} & 1/\sqrt{20} & 1/\sqrt{5} \\ 0 & 0 & -3/\sqrt{12} & 1/\sqrt{20} & 1/\sqrt{5} \\ 0 & 0 & 0 & -4/\sqrt{20} & 1/\sqrt{5} \end{bmatrix}$ and

$D = \begin{bmatrix} 8 & 0 & 0 & 0 & 0 \\ 0 & 8 & 0 & 0 & 0 \\ 0 & 0 & 32 & 0 & 0 \\ 0 & 0 & 0 & -28 & 0 \\ 0 & 0 & 0 & 0 & 17 \end{bmatrix}$. Then P orthogonally diagonalizes A, and $A = PDP^{-1}$.

7.2   SOLUTIONS

Notes: This section can provide a good conclusion to the course, because the mathematics here is widely used in applications. For instance, Exercises 23 and 24 can be used to develop the second derivative test for functions of two variables. However, if time permits, some interesting applications still lie ahead. Theorem 4 is used to prove Theorem 6 in Section 7.3, which in turn is used to develop the singular value decomposition.

1. a. $\mathbf{x}^T A \mathbf{x} = \begin{bmatrix} x_1 & x_2 \end{bmatrix} \begin{bmatrix} 5 & 1/3 \\ 1/3 & 1 \end{bmatrix} \begin{bmatrix} x_1 \\ x_2 \end{bmatrix} = 5x_1^2 + (2/3)x_1 x_2 + x_2^2$

b. When $\mathbf{x} = \begin{bmatrix} 6 \\ 1 \end{bmatrix}$, $\mathbf{x}^T A \mathbf{x} = 5(6)^2 + (2/3)(6)(1) + (1)^2 = 185$.

c. When $\mathbf{x} = \begin{bmatrix} 1 \\ 3 \end{bmatrix}$, $\mathbf{x}^T A \mathbf{x} = 5(1)^2 + (2/3)(1)(3) + (3)^2 = 16$.

2. a. $\mathbf{x}^T A \mathbf{x} = \begin{bmatrix} x_1 & x_2 & x_3 \end{bmatrix} \begin{bmatrix} 4 & 3 & 0 \\ 3 & 2 & 1 \\ 0 & 1 & 1 \end{bmatrix} \begin{bmatrix} x_1 \\ x_2 \\ x_3 \end{bmatrix} = 4x_1^2 + 2x_2^2 + x_3^2 + 6x_1 x_2 + 2x_2 x_3$

b. When $\mathbf{x} = \begin{bmatrix} 2 \\ -1 \\ 5 \end{bmatrix}$, $\mathbf{x}^T A \mathbf{x} = 4(2)^2 + 2(-1)^2 + (5)^2 + 6(2)(-1) + 2(-1)(5) = 21$.

c. When $\mathbf{x} = \begin{bmatrix} 1/\sqrt{3} \\ 1/\sqrt{3} \\ 1/\sqrt{3} \end{bmatrix}$, $\mathbf{x}^T A \mathbf{x} = 4(1/\sqrt{3})^2 + 2(1/\sqrt{3})^2 + (1/\sqrt{3})^2 + 6(1/\sqrt{3})(1/\sqrt{3}) + 2(1/\sqrt{3})(1/\sqrt{3}) = 5$.

3. a. The matrix of the quadratic form is $\begin{bmatrix} 10 & -3 \\ -3 & -3 \end{bmatrix}$.

b. The matrix of the quadratic form is $\begin{bmatrix} 5 & 3/2 \\ 3/2 & 0 \end{bmatrix}$.

4. a. The matrix of the quadratic form is $\begin{bmatrix} 20 & 15/2 \\ 15/2 & -10 \end{bmatrix}$.

b. The matrix of the quadratic form is $\begin{bmatrix} 0 & 1/2 \\ 1/2 & 0 \end{bmatrix}$.

5. a. The matrix of the quadratic form is $\begin{bmatrix} 8 & -3 & 2 \\ -3 & 7 & -1 \\ 2 & -1 & -3 \end{bmatrix}$.

b. The matrix of the quadratic form is $\begin{bmatrix} 0 & 2 & 3 \\ 2 & 0 & -4 \\ 3 & -4 & 0 \end{bmatrix}$.

6. a. The matrix of the quadratic form is $\begin{bmatrix} 5 & 5/2 & -3/2 \\ 5/2 & -1 & 0 \\ -3/2 & 0 & 7 \end{bmatrix}$.

b. The matrix of the quadratic form is $\begin{bmatrix} 0 & -2 & 0 \\ -2 & 0 & 2 \\ 0 & 2 & 1 \end{bmatrix}$.

7. The matrix of the quadratic form is $A = \begin{bmatrix} 1 & 5 \\ 5 & 1 \end{bmatrix}$. The eigenvalues of A are 6 and -4. An eigenvector for $\lambda = 6$ is $\begin{bmatrix} 1 \\ 1 \end{bmatrix}$, which may be normalized to $\mathbf{u}_1 = \begin{bmatrix} 1/\sqrt{2} \\ 1/\sqrt{2} \end{bmatrix}$. An eigenvector for $\lambda = -4$ is $\begin{bmatrix} -1 \\ 1 \end{bmatrix}$, which may be normalized to $\mathbf{u}_2 = \begin{bmatrix} -1/\sqrt{2} \\ 1/\sqrt{2} \end{bmatrix}$. Then $A = PDP^{-1}$, where $P = \begin{bmatrix} \mathbf{u}_1 & \mathbf{u}_2 \end{bmatrix} = \begin{bmatrix} 1/\sqrt{2} & -1/\sqrt{2} \\ 1/\sqrt{2} & 1/\sqrt{2} \end{bmatrix}$ and

$D = \begin{bmatrix} 6 & 0 \\ 0 & -4 \end{bmatrix}$. The desired change of variable is $\mathbf{x} = P\mathbf{y}$, and the new quadratic form is

$$\mathbf{x}^T A \mathbf{x} = (P\mathbf{y})^T A(P\mathbf{y}) = \mathbf{y}^T P^T A P \mathbf{y} = \mathbf{y}^T D \mathbf{y} = 6y_1^2 - 4y_2^2$$

8. The matrix of the quadratic form is $A = \begin{bmatrix} 9 & -4 & 4 \\ -4 & 7 & 0 \\ 4 & 0 & 11 \end{bmatrix}$. The eigenvalues of A are 3, 9, and 15. An

eigenvector for $\lambda = 3$ is $\begin{bmatrix} -2 \\ -2 \\ 1 \end{bmatrix}$, which may be normalized to $\mathbf{u}_1 = \begin{bmatrix} -2/3 \\ -2/3 \\ 1/3 \end{bmatrix}$. An eigenvector for $\lambda = 9$ is

$\begin{bmatrix} -1 \\ 2 \\ 2 \end{bmatrix}$, which may be normalized to $\mathbf{u}_2 = \begin{bmatrix} -1/3 \\ 2/3 \\ 2/3 \end{bmatrix}$. An eigenvector for $\lambda = 15$ is $\begin{bmatrix} 2 \\ -1 \\ 2 \end{bmatrix}$, which may be normalized to $\mathbf{u}_3 = \begin{bmatrix} 2/3 \\ -1/3 \\ 2/3 \end{bmatrix}$. Then $A = PDP^{-1}$, where $P = \begin{bmatrix} \mathbf{u}_1 & \mathbf{u}_2 & \mathbf{u}_3 \end{bmatrix} = \begin{bmatrix} -2/3 & -1/3 & 2/3 \\ -2/3 & 2/3 & -1/3 \\ 1/3 & 2/3 & 2/3 \end{bmatrix}$ and

$D = \begin{bmatrix} 3 & 0 & 0 \\ 0 & 9 & 0 \\ 0 & 0 & 15 \end{bmatrix}$. The desired change of variable is $\mathbf{x} = P\mathbf{y}$, and the new quadratic form is

$$\mathbf{x}^T A\mathbf{x} = (P\mathbf{y})^T A(P\mathbf{y}) = \mathbf{y}^T P^T AP\mathbf{y} = \mathbf{y}^T D\mathbf{y} = 3y_1^2 + 9y_2^2 + 15y_3^2$$

9. The matrix of the quadratic form is $A = \begin{bmatrix} 3 & -2 \\ -2 & 6 \end{bmatrix}$. The eigenvalues of A are 7 and 2, so the quadratic

form is positive definite. An eigenvector for $\lambda = 7$ is $\begin{bmatrix} -1 \\ 2 \end{bmatrix}$, which may be normalized to $\mathbf{u}_1 = \begin{bmatrix} -1/\sqrt{5} \\ 2/\sqrt{5} \end{bmatrix}$.

An eigenvector for $\lambda = 2$ is $\begin{bmatrix} 2 \\ 1 \end{bmatrix}$, which may be normalized to $\mathbf{u}_2 = \begin{bmatrix} 2/\sqrt{5} \\ 1/\sqrt{5} \end{bmatrix}$. Then $A = PDP^{-1}$, where

$P = \begin{bmatrix} \mathbf{u}_1 & \mathbf{u}_2 \end{bmatrix} = \begin{bmatrix} -1/\sqrt{5} & 2/\sqrt{5} \\ 2/\sqrt{5} & 1/\sqrt{5} \end{bmatrix}$ and $D = \begin{bmatrix} 7 & 0 \\ 0 & 2 \end{bmatrix}$. The desired change of variable is $\mathbf{x} = P\mathbf{y}$, and the

new quadratic form is

$$\mathbf{x}^T A\mathbf{x} = (P\mathbf{y})^T A(P\mathbf{y}) = \mathbf{y}^T P^T AP\mathbf{y} = \mathbf{y}^T D\mathbf{y} = 7y_1^2 + 2y_2^2$$

10. The matrix of the quadratic form is $A = \begin{bmatrix} 9 & -4 \\ -4 & 3 \end{bmatrix}$. The eigenvalues of A are 11 and 1, so the quadratic

form is positive definite. An eigenvector for $\lambda = 11$ is $\begin{bmatrix} 2 \\ -1 \end{bmatrix}$, which may be normalized to $\mathbf{u}_1 = \begin{bmatrix} 2/\sqrt{5} \\ -1/\sqrt{5} \end{bmatrix}$.

An eigenvector for $\lambda = 1$ is $\begin{bmatrix} 1 \\ 2 \end{bmatrix}$, which may be normalized to $\mathbf{u}_2 = \begin{bmatrix} 1/\sqrt{5} \\ 2/\sqrt{5} \end{bmatrix}$. Then $A = PDP^{-1}$, where

$P = \begin{bmatrix} \mathbf{u}_1 & \mathbf{u}_2 \end{bmatrix} = \begin{bmatrix} 2/\sqrt{5} & 1/\sqrt{5} \\ -1/\sqrt{5} & 2/\sqrt{5} \end{bmatrix}$ and $D = \begin{bmatrix} 11 & 0 \\ 0 & 1 \end{bmatrix}$. The desired change of variable is $\mathbf{x} = P\mathbf{y}$, and the

new quadratic form is

$$\mathbf{x}^T A\mathbf{x} = (P\mathbf{y})^T A(P\mathbf{y}) = \mathbf{y}^T P^T AP\mathbf{y} = \mathbf{y}^T D\mathbf{y} = 11y_1^2 + y_2^2$$

11. The matrix of the quadratic form is $A = \begin{bmatrix} 2 & 5 \\ 5 & 2 \end{bmatrix}$. The eigenvalues of A are 7 and -3, so the quadratic

form is indefinite. An eigenvector for $\lambda = 7$ is $\begin{bmatrix} 1 \\ 1 \end{bmatrix}$, which may be normalized to $\mathbf{u}_1 = \begin{bmatrix} 1/\sqrt{2} \\ 1/\sqrt{2} \end{bmatrix}$. An

eigenvector for $\lambda = -3$ is $\begin{bmatrix} -1 \\ 1 \end{bmatrix}$, which may be normalized to $\mathbf{u}_2 = \begin{bmatrix} -1/\sqrt{2} \\ 1/\sqrt{2} \end{bmatrix}$. Then $A = PDP^{-1}$, where $P = [\mathbf{u}_1 \quad \mathbf{u}_2] = \begin{bmatrix} 1/\sqrt{2} & -1/\sqrt{2} \\ 1/\sqrt{2} & 1/\sqrt{2} \end{bmatrix}$ and $D = \begin{bmatrix} 7 & 0 \\ 0 & -3 \end{bmatrix}$. The desired change of variable is $\mathbf{x} = P\mathbf{y}$, and the new quadratic form is

$$\mathbf{x}^T A\mathbf{x} = (P\mathbf{y})^T A(P\mathbf{y}) = \mathbf{y}^T P^T A P\mathbf{y} = \mathbf{y}^T D\mathbf{y} = 7y_1^2 - 3y_2^2$$

12. The matrix of the quadratic form is $A = \begin{bmatrix} -5 & 2 \\ 2 & -2 \end{bmatrix}$. The eigenvalues of A are -1 and -6, so the quadratic

form is negative definite. An eigenvector for $\lambda = -1$ is $\begin{bmatrix} 1 \\ 2 \end{bmatrix}$, which may be normalized to $\mathbf{u}_1 = \begin{bmatrix} 1/\sqrt{5} \\ 2/\sqrt{5} \end{bmatrix}$.

An eigenvector for $\lambda = -6$ is $\begin{bmatrix} -2 \\ 1 \end{bmatrix}$, which may be normalized to $\mathbf{u}_2 = \begin{bmatrix} -2/\sqrt{5} \\ 1/\sqrt{5} \end{bmatrix}$. Then $A = PDP^{-1}$,

where $P = [\mathbf{u}_1 \quad \mathbf{u}_2] = \begin{bmatrix} 1/\sqrt{5} & -2/\sqrt{5} \\ 2/\sqrt{5} & 1/\sqrt{5} \end{bmatrix}$ and $D = \begin{bmatrix} -1 & 0 \\ 0 & -6 \end{bmatrix}$. The desired change of variable is $\mathbf{x} = P\mathbf{y}$,

and the new quadratic form is

$$\mathbf{x}^T A\mathbf{x} = (P\mathbf{y})^T A(P\mathbf{y}) = \mathbf{y}^T P^T A P\mathbf{y} = \mathbf{y}^T D\mathbf{y} = -y_1^2 - 6y_2^2$$

13. The matrix of the quadratic form is $A = \begin{bmatrix} 1 & -3 \\ -3 & 9 \end{bmatrix}$. The eigenvalues of A are 10 and 0, so the quadratic

form is positive semidefinite. An eigenvector for $\lambda = 10$ is $\begin{bmatrix} 1 \\ -3 \end{bmatrix}$, which may be normalized to

$\mathbf{u}_1 = \begin{bmatrix} 1/\sqrt{10} \\ -3/\sqrt{10} \end{bmatrix}$. An eigenvector for $\lambda = 0$ is $\begin{bmatrix} 3 \\ 1 \end{bmatrix}$, which may be normalized to $\mathbf{u}_2 = \begin{bmatrix} 3/\sqrt{10} \\ 1/\sqrt{10} \end{bmatrix}$. Then

$A = PDP^{-1}$, where $P = [\mathbf{u}_1 \quad \mathbf{u}_2] = \begin{bmatrix} 1/\sqrt{10} & 3/\sqrt{10} \\ -3/\sqrt{10} & 1/\sqrt{10} \end{bmatrix}$ and $D = \begin{bmatrix} 10 & 0 \\ 0 & 0 \end{bmatrix}$. The desired change of

variable is $\mathbf{x} = P\mathbf{y}$, and the new quadratic form is

$$\mathbf{x}^T A\mathbf{x} = (P\mathbf{y})^T A(P\mathbf{y}) = \mathbf{y}^T P^T A P\mathbf{y} = \mathbf{y}^T D\mathbf{y} = 10y_1^2$$

14. The matrix of the quadratic form is $A = \begin{bmatrix} 8 & 3 \\ 3 & 0 \end{bmatrix}$. The eigenvalues of A are 9 and -1, so the quadratic

form is indefinite. An eigenvector for $\lambda = 9$ is $\begin{bmatrix} 3 \\ 1 \end{bmatrix}$, which may be normalized to $\mathbf{u}_1 = \begin{bmatrix} 3/\sqrt{10} \\ 1/\sqrt{10} \end{bmatrix}$. An

eigenvector for $\lambda = -1$ is $\begin{bmatrix} -1 \\ 3 \end{bmatrix}$, which may be normalized to $\mathbf{u}_2 = \begin{bmatrix} -1/\sqrt{10} \\ 3/\sqrt{10} \end{bmatrix}$. Then $A = PDP^{-1}$, where

$P = [\mathbf{u}_1 \quad \mathbf{u}_2] = \begin{bmatrix} 3/\sqrt{10} & -1/\sqrt{10} \\ 1/\sqrt{10} & 3/\sqrt{10} \end{bmatrix}$ and $D = \begin{bmatrix} 9 & 0 \\ 0 & -1 \end{bmatrix}$. The desired change of variable is $\mathbf{x} = P\mathbf{y}$, and the

new quadratic form is

$$\mathbf{x}^T A\mathbf{x} = (P\mathbf{y})^T A(P\mathbf{y}) = \mathbf{y}^T P^T A P\mathbf{y} = \mathbf{y}^T D\mathbf{y} = 9y_1^2 - y_2^2$$

15. **[M]** The matrix of the quadratic form is $A = \begin{bmatrix} -2 & 2 & 2 & 2 \\ 2 & -6 & 0 & 0 \\ 2 & 0 & -9 & 3 \\ 2 & 0 & 3 & -9 \end{bmatrix}$. The eigenvalues of A are 0, –6, –8,

and –12, so the quadratic form is negative semidefinite. The corresponding eigenvectors may be computed:

$$\lambda = 0: \begin{bmatrix} 3 \\ 1 \\ 1 \\ 1 \end{bmatrix}, \lambda = -6: \begin{bmatrix} 0 \\ -2 \\ 1 \\ 1 \end{bmatrix}, \lambda = -8: \begin{bmatrix} -1 \\ 1 \\ 1 \\ 1 \end{bmatrix}, \lambda = -12: \begin{bmatrix} 0 \\ 0 \\ -1 \\ 1 \end{bmatrix}$$

These eigenvectors may be normalized to form the columns of P, and $A = PDP^{-1}$, where

$$P = \begin{bmatrix} 3/\sqrt{12} & 0 & -1/2 & 0 \\ 1/\sqrt{12} & -2/\sqrt{6} & 1/2 & 0 \\ 1/\sqrt{12} & 1/\sqrt{6} & 1/2 & -1/\sqrt{2} \\ 1/\sqrt{12} & 1/\sqrt{6} & 1/2 & 1/\sqrt{2} \end{bmatrix} \text{ and } D = \begin{bmatrix} 0 & 0 & 0 & 0 \\ 0 & -6 & 0 & 0 \\ 0 & 0 & -8 & 0 \\ 0 & 0 & 0 & -12 \end{bmatrix}$$

The desired change of variable is $\mathbf{x} = P\mathbf{y}$, and the new quadratic form is

$$\mathbf{x}^T A\mathbf{x} = (P\mathbf{y})^T A(P\mathbf{y}) = \mathbf{y}^T P^T AP\mathbf{y} = \mathbf{y}^T D\mathbf{y} = -6y_2^2 - 8y_3^2 - 12y_4^2$$

16. **[M]** The matrix of the quadratic form is $A = \begin{bmatrix} 4 & 3/2 & 0 & -2 \\ 3/2 & 4 & 2 & 0 \\ 0 & 2 & 4 & 3/2 \\ -2 & 0 & 3/2 & 4 \end{bmatrix}$. The eigenvalues of A are 13/2

and 3/2, so the quadratic form is positive definite. The corresponding eigenvectors may be computed:

$$\lambda = 13/2: \left\{ \begin{bmatrix} -4 \\ 0 \\ 3 \\ 5 \end{bmatrix}, \begin{bmatrix} 3 \\ 5 \\ 4 \\ 0 \end{bmatrix} \right\}, \lambda = 3/2: \left\{ \begin{bmatrix} 4 \\ 0 \\ -3 \\ 5 \end{bmatrix}, \begin{bmatrix} 3 \\ -5 \\ 4 \\ 0 \end{bmatrix} \right\}$$

Each set of eigenvectors above is already an orthogonal set, so they may be normalized to form the columns of P, and $A = PDP^{-1}$, where

$$P = \begin{bmatrix} 3/\sqrt{50} & -4/\sqrt{50} & 3/\sqrt{50} & 4/\sqrt{50} \\ 5/\sqrt{50} & 0 & -5/\sqrt{50} & 0 \\ 4/\sqrt{50} & 3/\sqrt{50} & 4/\sqrt{50} & -3/\sqrt{50} \\ 0 & 5/\sqrt{50} & 0 & 5/\sqrt{50} \end{bmatrix} \text{ and } D = \begin{bmatrix} 13/2 & 0 & 0 & 0 \\ 0 & 13/2 & 0 & 0 \\ 0 & 0 & 3/2 & 0 \\ 0 & 0 & 0 & 3/2 \end{bmatrix}$$

The desired change of variable is $\mathbf{x} = P\mathbf{y}$, and the new quadratic form is

$$\mathbf{x}^T A\mathbf{x} = (P\mathbf{y})^T A(P\mathbf{y}) = \mathbf{y}^T P^T AP\mathbf{y} = \mathbf{y}^T D\mathbf{y} = \frac{13}{2}y_1^2 + \frac{13}{2}y_2^2 + \frac{3}{2}y_3^2 + \frac{3}{2}y_4^2$$

17. [M] The matrix of the quadratic form is $A = \begin{bmatrix} 1 & 9/2 & 0 & -6 \\ 9/2 & 1 & 6 & 0 \\ 0 & 6 & 1 & 9/2 \\ -6 & 0 & 9/2 & 1 \end{bmatrix}$. The eigenvalues of A are $17/2$

and $-13/2$, so the quadratic form is indefinite. The corresponding eigenvectors may be computed:

$$\lambda = 17/2 : \left\{ \begin{bmatrix} -4 \\ 0 \\ 3 \\ 5 \end{bmatrix}, \begin{bmatrix} 3 \\ 5 \\ 4 \\ 0 \end{bmatrix} \right\}, \lambda = -13/2 : \left\{ \begin{bmatrix} 4 \\ 0 \\ -3 \\ 5 \end{bmatrix}, \begin{bmatrix} 3 \\ -5 \\ 4 \\ 0 \end{bmatrix} \right\}$$

Each set of eigenvectors above is already an orthogonal set, so they may be normalized to form the columns of P, and $A = PDP^{-1}$, where

$$P = \begin{bmatrix} 3/\sqrt{50} & -4/\sqrt{50} & 3/\sqrt{50} & 4/\sqrt{50} \\ 5/\sqrt{50} & 0 & -5/\sqrt{50} & 0 \\ 4/\sqrt{50} & 3/\sqrt{50} & 4/\sqrt{50} & -3/\sqrt{50} \\ 0 & 5/\sqrt{50} & 0 & 5/\sqrt{50} \end{bmatrix} \text{ and } D = \begin{bmatrix} 17/2 & 0 & 0 & 0 \\ 0 & 17/2 & 0 & 0 \\ 0 & 0 & -13/2 & 0 \\ 0 & 0 & 0 & -13/2 \end{bmatrix}$$

The desired change of variable is $\mathbf{x} = P\mathbf{y}$, and the new quadratic form is

$$\mathbf{x}^T A \mathbf{x} = (P\mathbf{y})^T A(P\mathbf{y}) = \mathbf{y}^T P^T A P \mathbf{y} = \mathbf{y}^T D \mathbf{y} = \frac{17}{2} y_1^2 + \frac{17}{2} y_2^2 - \frac{13}{2} y_3^2 - \frac{13}{2} y_4^2$$

18. [M] The matrix of the quadratic form is $A = \begin{bmatrix} 11 & -6 & -6 & -6 \\ -6 & -1 & 0 & 0 \\ -6 & 0 & 0 & -1 \\ -6 & 0 & -1 & 0 \end{bmatrix}$. The eigenvalues of A are $17, 1, -1$,

and -7, so the quadratic form is indefinite. The corresponding eigenvectors may be computed:

$$\lambda = 17 : \begin{bmatrix} -3 \\ 1 \\ 1 \\ 1 \end{bmatrix}, \lambda = 1 : \begin{bmatrix} 0 \\ 0 \\ -1 \\ 1 \end{bmatrix}, \lambda = -1 : \begin{bmatrix} 0 \\ -2 \\ 1 \\ 1 \end{bmatrix}, \lambda = -7 : \begin{bmatrix} 1 \\ 1 \\ 1 \\ 1 \end{bmatrix}$$

These eigenvectors may be normalized to form the columns of P, and $A = PDP^{-1}$, where

$$P = \begin{bmatrix} -3/\sqrt{12} & 0 & 0 & 1/2 \\ 1/\sqrt{12} & 0 & 2/\sqrt{6} & 1/2 \\ 1/\sqrt{12} & -1/\sqrt{2} & 1/\sqrt{6} & 1/2 \\ 1/\sqrt{12} & 1/\sqrt{2} & 1/\sqrt{6} & 1/2 \end{bmatrix} \text{ and } D = \begin{bmatrix} 17 & 0 & 0 & 0 \\ 0 & 1 & 0 & 0 \\ 0 & 0 & -1 & 0 \\ 0 & 0 & 0 & -7 \end{bmatrix}$$

The desired change of variable is $\mathbf{x} = P\mathbf{y}$, and the new quadratic form is

$$\mathbf{x}^T A \mathbf{x} = (P\mathbf{y})^T A(P\mathbf{y}) = \mathbf{y}^T P^T A P \mathbf{y} = \mathbf{y}^T D \mathbf{y} = 17 y_1^2 + y_2^2 - y_3^2 - 7 y_4^2$$

19. Since 8 is larger than 5, the x_2^2 term should be as large as possible. Since $x_1^2 + x_2^2 = 1$, the largest value that x_2 can take is 1, and $x_1 = 0$ when $x_2 = 1$. Thus the largest value the quadratic form can take when $\mathbf{x}^T \mathbf{x} = 1$ is $5(0) + 8(1) = 8$.

20. Since 5 is larger in absolute value than –3, the x_1^2 term should be as large as possible. Since $x_1^2 + x_2^2 = 1$, the largest value that x_1 can take is 1, and $x_2 = 0$ when $x_1 = 1$. Thus the largest value the quadratic form can take when $\mathbf{x}^T\mathbf{x} = 1$ is $5(1) - 3(0) = 5$.

21. a. True. See the definition before Example 1, even though a nonsymmetric matrix could be used to compute values of a quadratic form.

    b. True. See the paragraph following Example 3.

    c. True. The columns of P in Theorem 4 are eigenvectors of A. See the Diagonalization Theorem in Section 5.3.

    d. False. $Q(\mathbf{x}) = 0$ when $\mathbf{x} = \mathbf{0}$.

    e. True. See Theorem 5(a).

    f. True. See the Numerical Note after Example 6.

22. a. True. See the paragraph before Example 1.

    b. False. The matrix P must be orthogonal and make $P^T AP$ diagonal. See the paragraph before Example 4.

    c. False. There are also "degenerate" cases: a single point, two intersecting lines, or no points at all. See the subsection "A Geometric View of Principal Axes."

    d. False. See the definition before Theorem 5.

    e. True. See Theorem 5(b). If $\mathbf{x}^T A\mathbf{x}$ has only negative values for $\mathbf{x} \neq \mathbf{0}$, then $\mathbf{x}^T A\mathbf{x}$ is negative definite.

23. The characteristic polynomial of A may be written in two ways:

$$\det(A - \lambda I) = \det \begin{bmatrix} a - \lambda & b \\ b & d - \lambda \end{bmatrix} = \lambda^2 - (a+d)\lambda + ad - b^2$$

and

$$(\lambda - \lambda_1)(\lambda - \lambda_2) = \lambda^2 - (\lambda_1 + \lambda_2)\lambda + \lambda_1\lambda_2$$

The coefficients in these polynomials may be equated to obtain $\lambda_1 + \lambda_2 = a + d$ and $\lambda_1\lambda_2 = ad - b^2 = \det A$.

24. If $\det A > 0$, then by Exercise 23, $\lambda_1\lambda_2 > 0$, so that λ_1 and λ_2 have the same sign; also, $ad = \det A + b^2 > 0$.

    a. If $\det A > 0$ and $a > 0$, then $d > 0$ also, since $ad > 0$. By Exercise 23, $\lambda_1 + \lambda_2 = a + d > 0$. Since λ_1 and λ_2 have the same sign, they are both positive. So Q is positive definite by Theorem 5.

    b. If $\det A > 0$ and $a < 0$, then $d < 0$ also, since $ad > 0$. By Exercise 23, $\lambda_1 + \lambda_2 = a + d < 0$. Since λ_1 and λ_2 have the same sign, they are both negative. So Q is negative definite by Theorem 5.

    c. If $\det A < 0$, then by Exercise 23, $\lambda_1\lambda_2 < 0$. Thus λ_1 and λ_2 have opposite signs. So Q is indefinite by Theorem 5.

25. Exercise 27 in Section 7.1 showed that $B^T B$ is symmetric. Also $\mathbf{x}^T B^T B\mathbf{x} = (B\mathbf{x})^T B\mathbf{x} = \| B\mathbf{x} \| \geq 0$, so the quadratic form is positive semidefinite, and the matrix $B^T B$ is positive semidefinite. Suppose that B is square and invertible. Then if $\mathbf{x}^T B^T B\mathbf{x} = 0$, $\| B\mathbf{x} \| = 0$ and $B\mathbf{x} = 0$. Since B is invertible, $\mathbf{x} = \mathbf{0}$. Thus if $\mathbf{x} \neq \mathbf{0}$, $\mathbf{x}^T B^T B\mathbf{x} > 0$ and $B^T B$ is positive definite.

26. Let $A = PDP^T$, where $P^T = P^{-1}$. The eigenvalues of A are all positive: denote them $\lambda_1, \ldots, \lambda_n$. Let C be the diagonal matrix with $\sqrt{\lambda_1}, \ldots, \sqrt{\lambda_n}$ on its diagonal. Then $D = C^2 = C^T C$. If $B = PCP^T$, then B is positive definite because its eigenvalues are the positive numbers on the diagonal of C. Also

$$B^T B = (PCP^T)^T(PCP^T) = (P^{TT}C^T P^T)(PCP^T) = PC^T CP^T = PDP^T = A$$

since $P^T P = I$.

27. Since the eigenvalues of A and B are all positive, the quadratic forms $\mathbf{x}^T A\mathbf{x}$ and $\mathbf{x}^T B\mathbf{x}$ are positive definite by Theorem 5. Let $\mathbf{x} \neq \mathbf{0}$. Then $\mathbf{x}^T A\mathbf{x} > 0$ and $\mathbf{x}^T B\mathbf{x} > 0$, so $\mathbf{x}^T (A + B)\mathbf{x} = \mathbf{x}^T A\mathbf{x} + \mathbf{x}^T B\mathbf{x} > 0$, and the quadratic form $\mathbf{x}^T (A + B)\mathbf{x}$ is positive definite. Note that $A + B$ is also a symmetric matrix. Thus by Theorem 5 all the eigenvalues of $A + B$ must be positive.

28. The eigenvalues of A are all positive by Theorem 5. Since the eigenvalues of A^{-1} are the reciprocals of the eigenvalues of A (see Exercise 25 in Section 5.1), the eigenvalues of A^{-1} are all positive. Note that A^{-1} is also a symmetric matrix. By Theorem 5, the quadratic form $\mathbf{x}^T A^{-1}\mathbf{x}$ is positive definite.

7.3   SOLUTIONS

Notes: Theorem 6 is the main result needed in the next two sections. Theorem 7 is mentioned in Example 2 of Section 7.4. Theorem 8 is needed at the very end of Section 7.5. The economic principles in Example 6 may be familiar to students who have had a course in macroeconomics.

1. The matrix of the quadratic form on the left is $A = \begin{bmatrix} 5 & 2 & 0 \\ 2 & 6 & -2 \\ 0 & -2 & 7 \end{bmatrix}$. The equality of the quadratic forms

implies that the eigenvalues of A are 9, 6, and 3. An eigenvector may be calculated for each eigenvalue and normalized:

$$\lambda = 9: \begin{bmatrix} 1/3 \\ 2/3 \\ -2/3 \end{bmatrix}, \lambda = 6: \begin{bmatrix} 2/3 \\ 1/3 \\ 1/3 \end{bmatrix}, \lambda = 3: \begin{bmatrix} -2/3 \\ 2/3 \\ 1/3 \end{bmatrix}$$

The desired change of variable is $\mathbf{x} = P\mathbf{y}$, where $P = \begin{bmatrix} 1/3 & 2/3 & -2/3 \\ 2/3 & 1/3 & 2/3 \\ -2/3 & 2/3 & 1/3 \end{bmatrix}$.

2. The matrix of the quadratic form on the left is $A = \begin{bmatrix} 3 & 1 & 1 \\ 1 & 2 & 2 \\ 1 & 2 & 2 \end{bmatrix}$. The equality of the quadratic forms

implies that the eigenvalues of A are 5, 2, and 0. An eigenvector may be calculated for each eigenvalue and normalized:

$$\lambda = 5: \begin{bmatrix} 1/\sqrt{3} \\ 1/\sqrt{3} \\ 1/\sqrt{3} \end{bmatrix}, \lambda = 2: \begin{bmatrix} -2/\sqrt{6} \\ 1/\sqrt{6} \\ 1/\sqrt{6} \end{bmatrix}, \lambda = 0: \begin{bmatrix} 0 \\ -1/\sqrt{2} \\ 1/\sqrt{2} \end{bmatrix}$$

The desired change of variable is $\mathbf{x} = P\mathbf{y}$, where $P = \begin{bmatrix} 1/\sqrt{3} & -2/\sqrt{6} & 0 \\ 1/\sqrt{3} & 1/\sqrt{6} & -1/\sqrt{2} \\ 1/\sqrt{3} & 1/\sqrt{6} & 1/\sqrt{2} \end{bmatrix}$.

3. (a) By Theorem 6, the maximum value of $\mathbf{x}^T A\mathbf{x}$ subject to the constraint $\mathbf{x}^T\mathbf{x} = 1$ is the greatest eigenvalue λ_1 of A. By Exercise 1, $\lambda_1 = 9$.

   (b) By Theorem 6, the maximum value of $\mathbf{x}^T A\mathbf{x}$ subject to the constraint $\mathbf{x}^T\mathbf{x} = 1$ occurs at a unit eigenvector $\mathbf{u}$ corresponding to the greatest eigenvalue λ_1 of A. By Exercise 1, $\mathbf{u} = \pm \begin{bmatrix} 1/3 \\ 2/3 \\ -2/3 \end{bmatrix}$.

   (c) By Theorem 7, the maximum value of $\mathbf{x}^T A\mathbf{x}$ subject to the constraints $\mathbf{x}^T\mathbf{x} = 1$ and $\mathbf{x}^T\mathbf{u} = 0$ is the second greatest eigenvalue λ_2 of A. By Exercise 1, $\lambda_2 = 6$.

4. (a) By Theorem 6, the maximum value of $\mathbf{x}^T A\mathbf{x}$ subject to the constraint $\mathbf{x}^T\mathbf{x} = 1$ is the greatest eigenvalue λ_1 of A. By Exercise 2, $\lambda_1 = 5$.

   (b) By Theorem 6, the maximum value of $\mathbf{x}^T A\mathbf{x}$ subject to the constraint $\mathbf{x}^T\mathbf{x} = 1$ occurs at a unit eigenvector $\mathbf{u}$ corresponding to the greatest eigenvalue λ_1 of A. By Exercise 2, $\mathbf{u} = \pm \begin{bmatrix} 1/\sqrt{3} \\ 1/\sqrt{3} \\ 1/\sqrt{3} \end{bmatrix}$.

   (c) By Theorem 7, the maximum value of $\mathbf{x}^T A\mathbf{x}$ subject to the constraints $\mathbf{x}^T\mathbf{x} = 1$ and $\mathbf{x}^T\mathbf{u} = 0$ is the second greatest eigenvalue λ_2 of A. By Exercise 2, $\lambda_2 = 2$.

5. The matrix of the quadratic form is $A = \begin{bmatrix} 5 & -2 \\ -2 & 5 \end{bmatrix}$. The eigenvalues of A are $\lambda_1 = 7$ and $\lambda_2 = 3$.

   (a) By Theorem 6, the maximum value of $\mathbf{x}^T A\mathbf{x}$ subject to the constraint $\mathbf{x}^T\mathbf{x} = 1$ is the greatest eigenvalue λ_1 of A, which is 7.

   (b) By Theorem 6, the maximum value of $\mathbf{x}^T A\mathbf{x}$ subject to the constraint $\mathbf{x}^T\mathbf{x} = 1$ occurs at a unit eigenvector $\mathbf{u}$ corresponding to the greatest eigenvalue λ_1 of A. One may compute that $\begin{bmatrix} -1 \\ 1 \end{bmatrix}$ is an eigenvector corresponding to $\lambda_1 = 7$, so $\mathbf{u} = \pm \begin{bmatrix} -1/\sqrt{2} \\ 1/\sqrt{2} \end{bmatrix}$.

   (c) By Theorem 7, the maximum value of $\mathbf{x}^T A\mathbf{x}$ subject to the constraints $\mathbf{x}^T\mathbf{x} = 1$ and $\mathbf{x}^T\mathbf{u} = 0$ is the second greatest eigenvalue λ_2 of A, which is 3.

6. The matrix of the quadratic form is $A = \begin{bmatrix} 7 & 3/2 \\ 3/2 & 3 \end{bmatrix}$. The eigenvalues of A are $\lambda_1 = 15/2$ and $\lambda_2 = 5/2$.

   (a) By Theorem 6, the maximum value of $\mathbf{x}^T A\mathbf{x}$ subject to the constraint $\mathbf{x}^T\mathbf{x} = 1$ is the greatest eigenvalue λ_1 of A, which is 15/2.

(b) By Theorem 6, the maximum value of $\mathbf{x}^T A \mathbf{x}$ subject to the constraint $\mathbf{x}^T \mathbf{x} = 1$ occurs at a unit eigenvector $\mathbf{u}$ corresponding to the greatest eigenvalue λ_1 of A. One may compute that $\begin{bmatrix} 3 \\ 1 \end{bmatrix}$ is an eigenvector corresponding to $\lambda_1 = 7$, so $\mathbf{u} = \pm \begin{bmatrix} 3/\sqrt{10} \\ 1/\sqrt{10} \end{bmatrix}$.

(c) By Theorem 7, the maximum value of $\mathbf{x}^T A \mathbf{x}$ subject to the constraints $\mathbf{x}^T \mathbf{x} = 1$ and $\mathbf{x}^T \mathbf{u} = 0$ is the second greatest eigenvalue λ_2 of A, which is 5/2.

7. The eigenvalues of the matrix of the quadratic form are $\lambda_1 = 2$, $\lambda_2 = -1$, and $\lambda_3 = -4$. By Theorem 6, the maximum value of $\mathbf{x}^T A \mathbf{x}$ subject to the constraint $\mathbf{x}^T \mathbf{x} = 1$ occurs at a unit eigenvector $\mathbf{u}$ corresponding to the greatest eigenvalue λ_1 of A. One may compute that $\begin{bmatrix} 1/2 \\ 1 \\ 1 \end{bmatrix}$ is an eigenvector corresponding to $\lambda_1 = 2$, so $\mathbf{u} = \pm \begin{bmatrix} 1/3 \\ 2/3 \\ 2/3 \end{bmatrix}$.

8. The eigenvalues of the matrix of the quadratic form are $\lambda_1 = 9$, and $\lambda_2 = -3$. By Theorem 6, the maximum value of $\mathbf{x}^T A \mathbf{x}$ subject to the constraint $\mathbf{x}^T \mathbf{x} = 1$ occurs at a unit eigenvector $\mathbf{u}$ corresponding to the greatest eigenvalue λ_1 of A. One may compute that $\begin{bmatrix} -1 \\ 0 \\ 1 \end{bmatrix}$ and $\begin{bmatrix} -2 \\ 1 \\ 0 \end{bmatrix}$ are linearly independent eigenvectors corresponding to $\lambda_1 = 2$, so $\mathbf{u}$ can be any unit vector which is a linear combination of $\begin{bmatrix} -1 \\ 0 \\ 1 \end{bmatrix}$ and $\begin{bmatrix} -2 \\ 1 \\ 0 \end{bmatrix}$. Alternatively, $\mathbf{u}$ can be any unit vector which is orthogonal to the eigenspace corresponding to the eigenvalue $\lambda_2 = -3$. Since multiples of $\begin{bmatrix} 1 \\ 2 \\ 1 \end{bmatrix}$ are eigenvectors corresponding to $\lambda_2 = -3$, $\mathbf{u}$ can be any unit vector orthogonal to $\begin{bmatrix} 1 \\ 2 \\ 1 \end{bmatrix}$.

9. This is equivalent to finding the maximum value of $\mathbf{x}^T A \mathbf{x}$ subject to the constraint $\mathbf{x}^T \mathbf{x} = 1$. By Theorem 6, this value is the greatest eigenvalue λ_1 of the matrix of the quadratic form. The matrix of the quadratic form is $A = \begin{bmatrix} 7 & -1 \\ -1 & 3 \end{bmatrix}$, and the eigenvalues of A are $\lambda_1 = 5 + \sqrt{5}$, $\lambda_2 = 5 - \sqrt{5}$. Thus the desired constrained maximum value is $\lambda_1 = 5 + \sqrt{5}$.

10. This is equivalent to finding the maximum value of $\mathbf{x}^T A\mathbf{x}$ subject to the constraint $\mathbf{x}^T\mathbf{x} = 1$. By Theorem 6, this value is the greatest eigenvalue λ_1 of the matrix of the quadratic form. The matrix of the quadratic form is $A = \begin{bmatrix} -3 & -1 \\ -1 & 5 \end{bmatrix}$, and the eigenvalues of A are $\lambda_1 = 1 + \sqrt{17}$, $\lambda_2 = 1 - \sqrt{17}$. Thus the desired constrained maximum value is $\lambda_1 = 1 + \sqrt{17}$.

11. Since $\mathbf{x}$ is an eigenvector of A corresponding to the eigenvalue 3, $A\mathbf{x} = 3\mathbf{x}$, and $\mathbf{x}^T A\mathbf{x} = \mathbf{x}^T(3\mathbf{x}) = 3(\mathbf{x}^T\mathbf{x}) = 3\|\mathbf{x}\|^2 = 3$ since $\mathbf{x}$ is a unit vector.

12. Let x be a unit eigenvector for the eigenvalue λ. Then $\mathbf{x}^T A\mathbf{x} = \mathbf{x}^T(\lambda\mathbf{x}) = \lambda(\mathbf{x}^T\mathbf{x}) = \lambda$ since $\mathbf{x}^T\mathbf{x} = 1$. So λ must satisfy $m \le \lambda \le M$.

13. If $m = M$, then let $t = (1 - 0)m + 0M = m$ and $\mathbf{x} = \mathbf{u}_n$. Theorem 6 shows that $\mathbf{u}_n^T A\mathbf{u}_n = m$. Now suppose that $m < M$, and let t be between m and M. Then $0 \le t - m \le M - m$ and $0 \le (t - m)/(M - m) \le 1$. Let $\alpha = (t - m)/(M - m)$, and let $\mathbf{x} = \sqrt{1 - \alpha}\,\mathbf{u}_n + \sqrt{\alpha}\,\mathbf{u}_1$. The vectors $\sqrt{1 - \alpha}\,\mathbf{u}_n$ and $\sqrt{\alpha}\,\mathbf{u}_1$ are orthogonal because they are eigenvectors for different eigenvectors (or one of them is $\mathbf{0}$). By the Pythagorean Theorem

$$\mathbf{x}^T\mathbf{x} = \|\mathbf{x}\|^2 = \|\sqrt{1-\alpha}\,\mathbf{u}_n\|^2 + \|\sqrt{\alpha}\,\mathbf{u}_1\|^2 = |1-\alpha|\,\|\mathbf{u}_n\|^2 + |\alpha|\,\|\mathbf{u}_1\|^2 = (1-\alpha) + \alpha = 1$$

since $\mathbf{u}_n$ and $\mathbf{u}_1$ are unit vectors and $0 \le \alpha \le 1$. Also, since $\mathbf{u}_n$ and $\mathbf{u}_1$ are orthogonal,

$$\mathbf{x}^T A\mathbf{x} = (\sqrt{1-\alpha}\,\mathbf{u}_n + \sqrt{\alpha}\,\mathbf{u}_1)^T A(\sqrt{1-\alpha}\,\mathbf{u}_n + \sqrt{\alpha}\,\mathbf{u}_1)$$

$$= (\sqrt{1-\alpha}\,\mathbf{u}_n + \sqrt{\alpha}\,\mathbf{u}_1)^T (m\sqrt{1-\alpha}\,\mathbf{u}_n + M\sqrt{\alpha}\,\mathbf{u}_1)$$

$$= |1-\alpha|\,m\mathbf{u}_n^T\mathbf{u}_n + |\alpha|\,M\mathbf{u}_1^T\mathbf{u}_1 = (1-\alpha)m + \alpha M = t$$

Thus the quadratic form $\mathbf{x}^T A\mathbf{x}$ assumes every value between m and M for a suitable unit vector $\mathbf{x}$.

14. **[M]** The matrix of the quadratic form is $A = \begin{bmatrix} 0 & 1/2 & 3/2 & 15 \\ 1/2 & 0 & 15 & 3/2 \\ 3/2 & 15 & 0 & 1/2 \\ 15 & 3/2 & 1/2 & 0 \end{bmatrix}$. The eigenvalues of A are $\lambda_1 = 17$, $\lambda_2 = 13$, $\lambda_3 = -14$, and $\lambda_4 = -16$.

   (a) By Theorem 6, the maximum value of $\mathbf{x}^T A\mathbf{x}$ subject to the constraint $\mathbf{x}^T\mathbf{x} = 1$ is the greatest eigenvalue λ_1 of A, which is 17.

   (b) By Theorem 6, the maximum value of $\mathbf{x}^T A\mathbf{x}$ subject to the constraint $\mathbf{x}^T\mathbf{x} = 1$ occurs at a unit eigenvector $\mathbf{u}$ corresponding to the greatest eigenvalue λ_1 of A. One may compute that $\begin{bmatrix} 1 \\ 1 \\ 1 \\ 1 \end{bmatrix}$ is an eigenvector corresponding to $\lambda_1 = 17$, so $\mathbf{u} = \pm\begin{bmatrix} 1/2 \\ 1/2 \\ 1/2 \\ 1/2 \end{bmatrix}$.

   (c) By Theorem 7, the maximum value of $\mathbf{x}^T A\mathbf{x}$ subject to the constraints $\mathbf{x}^T\mathbf{x} = 1$ and $\mathbf{x}^T\mathbf{u} = 0$ is the second greatest eigenvalue λ_2 of A, which is 13.

15. **[M]** The matrix of the quadratic form is $A = \begin{bmatrix} 0 & 3/2 & 5/2 & 7/2 \\ 3/2 & 0 & 7/2 & 5/2 \\ 5/2 & 7/2 & 0 & 3/2 \\ 7/2 & 5/2 & 3/2 & 0 \end{bmatrix}$. The eigenvalues of A are

$\lambda_1 = 15/2$, $\lambda_2 = -1/2$, $\lambda_3 = -5/2$, and $\lambda_4 = -9/2$.

(a) By Theorem 6, the maximum value of $\mathbf{x}^T A\mathbf{x}$ subject to the constraint $\mathbf{x}^T\mathbf{x} = 1$ is the greatest eigenvalue λ_1 of A, which is 15/2.

(b) By Theorem 6, the maximum value of $\mathbf{x}^T A\mathbf{x}$ subject to the constraint $\mathbf{x}^T\mathbf{x} = 1$ occurs at a unit

eigenvector $\mathbf{u}$ corresponding to the greatest eigenvalue λ_1 of A. One may compute that $\begin{bmatrix} 1 \\ 1 \\ 1 \\ 1 \end{bmatrix}$ is an

eigenvector corresponding to $\lambda_1 = 15/2$, so $\mathbf{u} = \pm \begin{bmatrix} 1/2 \\ 1/2 \\ 1/2 \\ 1/2 \end{bmatrix}$.

(c) By Theorem 7, the maximum value of $\mathbf{x}^T A\mathbf{x}$ subject to the constraints $\mathbf{x}^T\mathbf{x} = 1$ and $\mathbf{x}^T\mathbf{u} = 0$ is the second greatest eigenvalue λ_2 of A, which is $-1/2$.

16. **[M]** The matrix of the quadratic form is $A = \begin{bmatrix} 4 & -3 & -5 & -5 \\ -3 & 0 & -3 & -3 \\ -5 & -3 & 0 & -1 \\ -5 & -3 & -1 & 0 \end{bmatrix}$. The eigenvalues of A are $\lambda_1 = 9$,

$\lambda_2 = 3$, $\lambda_3 = 1$, and $\lambda_4 = -9$.

(a) By Theorem 6, the maximum value of $\mathbf{x}^T A\mathbf{x}$ subject to the constraint $\mathbf{x}^T\mathbf{x} = 1$ is the greatest eigenvalue λ_1 of A, which is 9.

(b) By Theorem 6, the maximum value of $\mathbf{x}^T A\mathbf{x}$ subject to the constraint $\mathbf{x}^T\mathbf{x} = 1$ occurs at a unit

eigenvector $\mathbf{u}$ corresponding to the greatest eigenvalue λ_1 of A. One may compute that $\begin{bmatrix} -2 \\ 0 \\ 1 \\ 1 \end{bmatrix}$ is an

eigenvector corresponding to $\lambda_1 = 9$, so $\mathbf{u} = \pm \begin{bmatrix} -2/\sqrt{6} \\ 0 \\ 1/\sqrt{6} \\ 1/\sqrt{6} \end{bmatrix}$.

(c) By Theorem 7, the maximum value of $\mathbf{x}^T A\mathbf{x}$ subject to the constraints $\mathbf{x}^T\mathbf{x} = 1$ and $\mathbf{x}^T\mathbf{u} = 0$ is the second greatest eigenvalue λ_2 of A, which is 3.

17. [M] The matrix of the quadratic form is $A = \begin{bmatrix} -6 & -2 & -2 & -2 \\ -2 & -10 & 0 & 0 \\ -2 & 0 & -13 & 3 \\ -2 & 0 & 3 & -13 \end{bmatrix}$. The eigenvalues of A are $\lambda_1 = -4$, $\lambda_2 = -10$, $\lambda_3 = -12$, and $\lambda_4 = -16$.

(a) By Theorem 6, the maximum value of $\mathbf{x}^T A \mathbf{x}$ subject to the constraint $\mathbf{x}^T \mathbf{x} = 1$ is the greatest eigenvalue λ_1 of A, which is -4.

(b) By Theorem 6, the maximum value of $\mathbf{x}^T A \mathbf{x}$ subject to the constraint $\mathbf{x}^T \mathbf{x} = 1$ occurs at a unit eigenvector $\mathbf{u}$ corresponding to the greatest eigenvalue λ_1 of A. One may compute that $\begin{bmatrix} -3 \\ 1 \\ 1 \\ 1 \end{bmatrix}$ is an eigenvector corresponding to $\lambda_1 = -4$, so $\mathbf{u} = \pm \begin{bmatrix} -3/\sqrt{12} \\ 1/\sqrt{12} \\ 1/\sqrt{12} \\ 1/\sqrt{12} \end{bmatrix}$.

(c) By Theorem 7, the maximum value of $\mathbf{x}^T A \mathbf{x}$ subject to the constraints $\mathbf{x}^T \mathbf{x} = 1$ and $\mathbf{x}^T \mathbf{u} = 0$ is the second greatest eigenvalue λ_2 of A, which is -10.

7.4 SOLUTIONS

Notes: The section presents a modern topic of great importance in applications, particularly in computer calculations. An understanding of the singular value decomposition is essential for advanced work in science and engineering that requires matrix computations. Moreover, the singular value decomposition explains much about the structure of matrix transformations. The SVD does for an arbitrary matrix almost what an orthogonal decomposition does for a symmetric matrix.

1. Let $A = \begin{bmatrix} 1 & 0 \\ 0 & -3 \end{bmatrix}$. Then $A^T A = \begin{bmatrix} 1 & 0 \\ 0 & 9 \end{bmatrix}$, and the eigenvalues of $A^T A$ are seen to be (in decreasing order) $\lambda_1 = 9$ and $\lambda_2 = 1$. Thus the singular values of A are $\sigma_1 = \sqrt{9} = 3$ and $\sigma_2 = \sqrt{1} = 1$.

2. Let $A = \begin{bmatrix} -5 & 0 \\ 0 & 0 \end{bmatrix}$. Then $A^T A = \begin{bmatrix} 25 & 0 \\ 0 & 0 \end{bmatrix}$, and the eigenvalues of $A^T A$ are seen to be (in decreasing order) $\lambda_1 = 25$ and $\lambda_2 = 0$. Thus the singular values of A are $\sigma_1 = \sqrt{25} = 5$ and $\sigma_2 = \sqrt{0} = 0$.

3. Let $A = \begin{bmatrix} \sqrt{6} & 1 \\ 0 & \sqrt{6} \end{bmatrix}$. Then $A^T A = \begin{bmatrix} 6 & \sqrt{6} \\ \sqrt{6} & 7 \end{bmatrix}$, and the characteristic polynomial of $A^T A$ is $\lambda^2 - 13\lambda + 36 = (\lambda - 9)(\lambda - 4)$, and the eigenvalues of $A^T A$ are (in decreasing order) $\lambda_1 = 9$ and $\lambda_2 = 4$. Thus the singular values of A are $\sigma_1 = \sqrt{9} = 3$ and $\sigma_2 = \sqrt{4} = 2$.

4. Let $A = \begin{bmatrix} \sqrt{3} & 2 \\ 0 & \sqrt{3} \end{bmatrix}$. Then $A^T A = \begin{bmatrix} 3 & 2\sqrt{3} \\ 2\sqrt{3} & 7 \end{bmatrix}$, and the characteristic polynomial of $A^T A$ is

$\lambda^2 - 10\lambda + 9 = (\lambda - 9)(\lambda - 1)$, and the eigenvalues of $A^T A$ are (in decreasing order) $\lambda_1 = 9$ and $\lambda_2 = 1$. Thus the singular values of A are $\sigma_1 = \sqrt{9} = 3$ and $\sigma_2 = \sqrt{1} = 1$.

5. Let $A = \begin{bmatrix} -3 & 0 \\ 0 & 0 \end{bmatrix}$. Then $A^T A = \begin{bmatrix} 9 & 0 \\ 0 & 0 \end{bmatrix}$, and the eigenvalues of $A^T A$ are seen to be (in decreasing order) $\lambda_1 = 9$ and $\lambda_2 = 0$. Associated unit eigenvectors may be computed:

$$\lambda = 9: \begin{bmatrix} 1 \\ 0 \end{bmatrix}, \lambda = 0: \begin{bmatrix} 0 \\ 1 \end{bmatrix}$$

Thus one choice for V is $V = \begin{bmatrix} 1 & 0 \\ 0 & 1 \end{bmatrix}$. The singular values of A are $\sigma_1 = \sqrt{9} = 3$ and $\sigma_2 = \sqrt{0} = 0$. Thus the matrix Σ is $\Sigma = \begin{bmatrix} 3 & 0 \\ 0 & 0 \end{bmatrix}$. Next compute

$$\mathbf{u}_1 = \frac{1}{\sigma_1} A\mathbf{v}_1 = \begin{bmatrix} -1 \\ 0 \end{bmatrix}$$

Because $A\mathbf{v}_2 = \mathbf{0}$, the only column found for U so far is $\mathbf{u}_1$. Find the other column of U is found by extending $\{\mathbf{u}_1\}$ to an orthonormal basis for $\mathbb{R}^2$. An easy choice is $\mathbf{u}_2 = \begin{bmatrix} 0 \\ 1 \end{bmatrix}$.

Let $U = \begin{bmatrix} -1 & 0 \\ 0 & 1 \end{bmatrix}$. Thus

$$A = U\Sigma V^T = \begin{bmatrix} -1 & 0 \\ 0 & 1 \end{bmatrix}\begin{bmatrix} 3 & 0 \\ 0 & 0 \end{bmatrix}\begin{bmatrix} 1 & 0 \\ 0 & 1 \end{bmatrix}$$

6. Let $A = \begin{bmatrix} -2 & 0 \\ 0 & -1 \end{bmatrix}$. Then $A^T A = \begin{bmatrix} 4 & 0 \\ 0 & 1 \end{bmatrix}$, and the eigenvalues of $A^T A$ are seen to be (in decreasing order) $\lambda_1 = 4$ and $\lambda_2 = 1$. Associated unit eigenvectors may be computed:

$$\lambda = 4: \begin{bmatrix} 1 \\ 0 \end{bmatrix}, \lambda = 1: \begin{bmatrix} 0 \\ 1 \end{bmatrix}$$

Thus one choice for V is $V = \begin{bmatrix} 1 & 0 \\ 0 & 1 \end{bmatrix}$. The singular values of A are $\sigma_1 = \sqrt{4} = 2$ and $\sigma_2 = \sqrt{1} = 1$. Thus the matrix Σ is $\Sigma = \begin{bmatrix} 2 & 0 \\ 0 & 1 \end{bmatrix}$. Next compute

$$\mathbf{u}_1 = \frac{1}{\sigma_1} A\mathbf{v}_1 = \begin{bmatrix} -1 \\ 0 \end{bmatrix}, \mathbf{u}_2 = \frac{1}{\sigma_2} A\mathbf{v}_2 = \begin{bmatrix} 0 \\ -1 \end{bmatrix}$$

Since $\{\mathbf{u}_1, \mathbf{u}_2\}$ is a basis for $\mathbb{R}^2$, let $U = \begin{bmatrix} -1 & 0 \\ 0 & -1 \end{bmatrix}$. Thus

$$A = U\Sigma V^T = \begin{bmatrix} -1 & 0 \\ 0 & -1 \end{bmatrix}\begin{bmatrix} 2 & 0 \\ 0 & 1 \end{bmatrix}\begin{bmatrix} 1 & 0 \\ 0 & 1 \end{bmatrix}$$

7. Let $A = \begin{bmatrix} 2 & -1 \\ 2 & 2 \end{bmatrix}$. Then $A^T A = \begin{bmatrix} 8 & 2 \\ 2 & 5 \end{bmatrix}$, and the characteristic polynomial of $A^T A$ is

$\lambda^2 - 13\lambda + 36 = (\lambda - 9)(\lambda - 4)$, and the eigenvalues of $A^T A$ are (in decreasing order) $\lambda_1 = 9$ and $\lambda_2 = 4$. Associated unit eigenvectors may be computed:

$$\lambda = 9: \begin{bmatrix} 2/\sqrt{5} \\ 1/\sqrt{5} \end{bmatrix}, \lambda = 4: \begin{bmatrix} -1/\sqrt{5} \\ 2/\sqrt{5} \end{bmatrix}$$

Thus one choice for V is $V = \begin{bmatrix} 2/\sqrt{5} & -1/\sqrt{5} \\ 1/\sqrt{5} & 2/\sqrt{5} \end{bmatrix}$. The singular values of A are $\sigma_1 = \sqrt{9} = 3$ and

$\sigma_2 = \sqrt{4} = 2$. Thus the matrix Σ is $\Sigma = \begin{bmatrix} 3 & 0 \\ 0 & 2 \end{bmatrix}$. Next compute

$$\mathbf{u}_1 = \frac{1}{\sigma_1} A \mathbf{v}_1 = \begin{bmatrix} 1/\sqrt{5} \\ 2/\sqrt{5} \end{bmatrix}, \mathbf{u}_2 = \frac{1}{\sigma_2} A \mathbf{v}_2 = \begin{bmatrix} -2/\sqrt{5} \\ 1/\sqrt{5} \end{bmatrix}$$

Since $\{\mathbf{u}_1, \mathbf{u}_2\}$ is a basis for $\mathbb{R}^2$, let $U = \begin{bmatrix} 1/\sqrt{5} & -2/\sqrt{5} \\ 2/\sqrt{5} & 1/\sqrt{5} \end{bmatrix}$. Thus

$$A = U \Sigma V^T = \begin{bmatrix} 1/\sqrt{5} & -2/\sqrt{5} \\ 2/\sqrt{5} & 1/\sqrt{5} \end{bmatrix} \begin{bmatrix} 3 & 0 \\ 0 & 2 \end{bmatrix} \begin{bmatrix} 2/\sqrt{5} & 1/\sqrt{5} \\ -1/\sqrt{5} & 2/\sqrt{5} \end{bmatrix}$$

8. Let $A = \begin{bmatrix} 2 & 3 \\ 0 & 2 \end{bmatrix}$. Then $A^T A = \begin{bmatrix} 4 & 6 \\ 6 & 13 \end{bmatrix}$, and the characteristic polynomial of $A^T A$ is

$\lambda^2 - 17\lambda + 16 = (\lambda - 16)(\lambda - 1)$, and the eigenvalues of $A^T A$ are (in decreasing order) $\lambda_1 = 16$ and $\lambda_2 = 1$. Associated unit eigenvectors may be computed:

$$\lambda = 16: \begin{bmatrix} 1/\sqrt{5} \\ 2/\sqrt{5} \end{bmatrix}, \lambda = 1: \begin{bmatrix} -2/\sqrt{5} \\ 1/\sqrt{5} \end{bmatrix}$$

Thus one choice for V is $V = \begin{bmatrix} 1/\sqrt{5} & -2/\sqrt{5} \\ 2/\sqrt{5} & 1/\sqrt{5} \end{bmatrix}$. The singular values of A are $\sigma_1 = \sqrt{16} = 4$ and

$\sigma_2 = \sqrt{1} = 1$. Thus the matrix Σ is $\Sigma = \begin{bmatrix} 4 & 0 \\ 0 & 1 \end{bmatrix}$. Next compute

$$\mathbf{u}_1 = \frac{1}{\sigma_1} A \mathbf{v}_1 = \begin{bmatrix} 2/\sqrt{5} \\ 1/\sqrt{5} \end{bmatrix}, \mathbf{u}_2 = \frac{1}{\sigma_2} A \mathbf{v}_2 = \begin{bmatrix} -1/\sqrt{5} \\ 2/\sqrt{5} \end{bmatrix}$$

Since $\{\mathbf{u}_1, \mathbf{u}_2\}$ is a basis for $\mathbb{R}^2$, let $U = \begin{bmatrix} 2/\sqrt{5} & -1/\sqrt{5} \\ 1/\sqrt{5} & 2/\sqrt{5} \end{bmatrix}$. Thus

$$A = U \Sigma V^T = \begin{bmatrix} 2/\sqrt{5} & -1/\sqrt{5} \\ 1/\sqrt{5} & 2/\sqrt{5} \end{bmatrix} \begin{bmatrix} 4 & 0 \\ 0 & 1 \end{bmatrix} \begin{bmatrix} 1/\sqrt{5} & 2/\sqrt{5} \\ -2/\sqrt{5} & 1/\sqrt{5} \end{bmatrix}$$

9. Let $A = \begin{bmatrix} 7 & 1 \\ 0 & 0 \\ 5 & 5 \end{bmatrix}$. Then $A^T A = \begin{bmatrix} 74 & 32 \\ 32 & 26 \end{bmatrix}$, and the characteristic polynomial of $A^T A$ is

$\lambda^2 - 100\lambda + 900 = (\lambda - 90)(\lambda - 10)$, and the eigenvalues of $A^T A$ are (in decreasing order) $\lambda_1 = 90$ and $\lambda_2 = 10$. Associated unit eigenvectors may be computed:

$$\lambda = 90 : \begin{bmatrix} 2/\sqrt{5} \\ 1/\sqrt{5} \end{bmatrix}, \lambda = 10 : \begin{bmatrix} -1/\sqrt{5} \\ 2/\sqrt{5} \end{bmatrix}$$

Thus one choice for V is $V = \begin{bmatrix} 2/\sqrt{5} & -1/\sqrt{5} \\ 1/\sqrt{5} & 2/\sqrt{5} \end{bmatrix}$. The singular values of A are $\sigma_1 = \sqrt{90} = 3\sqrt{10}$ and

$\sigma_2 = \sqrt{10}$. Thus the matrix Σ is $\Sigma = \begin{bmatrix} 3\sqrt{10} & 0 \\ 0 & \sqrt{10} \\ 0 & 0 \end{bmatrix}$. Next compute

$$\mathbf{u}_1 = \frac{1}{\sigma_1} A\mathbf{v}_1 = \begin{bmatrix} 1/\sqrt{2} \\ 0 \\ 1/\sqrt{2} \end{bmatrix}, \mathbf{u}_2 = \frac{1}{\sigma_2} A\mathbf{v}_2 = \begin{bmatrix} -1/\sqrt{2} \\ 0 \\ 1/\sqrt{2} \end{bmatrix}$$

Since $\{\mathbf{u}_1, \mathbf{u}_2\}$ is not a basis for $\mathbb{R}^3$, we need a unit vector $\mathbf{u}_3$ that is orthogonal to both $\mathbf{u}_1$ and $\mathbf{u}_2$. The vector $\mathbf{u}_3$ must satisfy the set of equations $\mathbf{u}_1^T \mathbf{x} = 0$ and $\mathbf{u}_2^T \mathbf{x} = 0$. These are equivalent to the linear equations

$$\begin{array}{rcl} x_1 + 0x_2 + x_3 &=& 0 \\ -x_1 + 0x_2 + x_3 &=& 0 \end{array}, \text{so } \mathbf{x} = \begin{bmatrix} 0 \\ 1 \\ 0 \end{bmatrix}, \text{and } \mathbf{u}_3 = \begin{bmatrix} 0 \\ 1 \\ 0 \end{bmatrix}$$

Therefore let $U = \begin{bmatrix} 1/\sqrt{2} & -1/\sqrt{2} & 0 \\ 0 & 0 & 1 \\ 1/\sqrt{2} & 1/\sqrt{2} & 0 \end{bmatrix}$. Thus

$$A = U\,\Sigma\,V^T = \begin{bmatrix} 1/\sqrt{2} & -1/\sqrt{2} & 0 \\ 0 & 0 & 1 \\ 1/\sqrt{2} & 1/\sqrt{2} & 0 \end{bmatrix} \begin{bmatrix} 3\sqrt{10} & 0 \\ 0 & \sqrt{10} \\ 0 & 0 \end{bmatrix} \begin{bmatrix} 2/\sqrt{5} & 1/\sqrt{5} \\ -1/\sqrt{5} & 2/\sqrt{5} \end{bmatrix}$$

10. Let $A = \begin{bmatrix} 4 & -2 \\ 2 & -1 \\ 0 & 0 \end{bmatrix}$. Then $A^T A = \begin{bmatrix} 20 & -10 \\ -10 & 5 \end{bmatrix}$, and the characteristic polynomial of $A^T A$ is

$\lambda^2 - 25\lambda = \lambda(\lambda - 25)$, and the eigenvalues of $A^T A$ are (in decreasing order) $\lambda_1 = 25$ and $\lambda_2 = 0$. Associated unit eigenvectors may be computed:

$$\lambda = 25 : \begin{bmatrix} 2/\sqrt{5} \\ -1/\sqrt{5} \end{bmatrix}, \lambda = 0 : \begin{bmatrix} 1/\sqrt{5} \\ 2/\sqrt{5} \end{bmatrix}$$

Thus one choice for V is $V = \begin{bmatrix} 2/\sqrt{5} & 1/\sqrt{5} \\ -1/\sqrt{5} & 2/\sqrt{5} \end{bmatrix}$. The singular values of A are $\sigma_1 = \sqrt{25} = 5$ and

$\sigma_2 = \sqrt{0} = 0$. Thus the matrix Σ is $\Sigma = \begin{bmatrix} 5 & 0 \\ 0 & 0 \\ 0 & 0 \end{bmatrix}$. Next compute

$$\mathbf{u}_1 = \frac{1}{\sigma_1} A\mathbf{v}_1 = \begin{bmatrix} 2/\sqrt{5} \\ 1/\sqrt{5} \\ 0 \end{bmatrix}$$

Because $A\mathbf{v}_2 = \mathbf{0}$, the only column found for U so far is $\mathbf{u}_1$. Find the other columns of U found by extending $\{\mathbf{u}_1\}$ to an orthonormal basis for $\mathbb{R}^3$. In this case, we need two orthogonal unit vectors $\mathbf{u}_2$ and $\mathbf{u}_3$ that are orthogonal to $\mathbf{u}_1$. Each vector must satisfy the equation $\mathbf{u}_1^T \mathbf{x} = 0$, which is equivalent to the equation $2x_1 + x_2 = 0$. An orthonormal basis for the solution set of this equation is

$$\mathbf{u}_2 = \begin{bmatrix} 1/\sqrt{5} \\ -2/\sqrt{5} \\ 0 \end{bmatrix}, \mathbf{u}_3 = \begin{bmatrix} 0 \\ 0 \\ 1 \end{bmatrix}.$$

Therefore, let $U = \begin{bmatrix} 2/\sqrt{5} & 1/\sqrt{5} & 0 \\ 1/\sqrt{5} & -2/\sqrt{5} & 0 \\ 0 & 0 & 1 \end{bmatrix}$. Thus

$$A = U \Sigma V^T = \begin{bmatrix} 2/\sqrt{5} & 1/\sqrt{5} & 0 \\ 1/\sqrt{5} & -2/\sqrt{5} & 0 \\ 0 & 0 & 1 \end{bmatrix} \begin{bmatrix} 5 & 0 \\ 0 & 0 \\ 0 & 0 \end{bmatrix} \begin{bmatrix} 2/\sqrt{5} & -1/\sqrt{5} \\ 1/\sqrt{5} & 2/\sqrt{5} \end{bmatrix}$$

11. Let $A = \begin{bmatrix} -3 & 1 \\ 6 & -2 \\ 6 & -2 \end{bmatrix}$. Then $A^T A = \begin{bmatrix} 81 & -27 \\ -27 & 9 \end{bmatrix}$, and the characteristic polynomial of $A^T A$ is

$\lambda^2 - 90\lambda = \lambda(\lambda - 90)$, and the eigenvalues of $A^T A$ are (in decreasing order) $\lambda_1 = 90$ and $\lambda_2 = 0$. Associated unit eigenvectors may be computed:

$$\lambda = 90 : \begin{bmatrix} 3/\sqrt{10} \\ -1/\sqrt{10} \end{bmatrix}, \lambda = 0 : \begin{bmatrix} 1/\sqrt{10} \\ 3/\sqrt{10} \end{bmatrix}.$$

Thus one choice for V is $V = \begin{bmatrix} 3/\sqrt{10} & 1/\sqrt{10} \\ -1/\sqrt{10} & 3/\sqrt{10} \end{bmatrix}$. The singular values of A are $\sigma_1 = \sqrt{90} = 3\sqrt{10}$ and

$\sigma_2 = \sqrt{0} = 0$. Thus the matrix Σ is $\Sigma = \begin{bmatrix} 3\sqrt{10} & 0 \\ 0 & 0 \\ 0 & 0 \end{bmatrix}$. Next compute

$$\mathbf{u}_1 = \frac{1}{\sigma_1} A\mathbf{v}_1 = \begin{bmatrix} -1/3 \\ 2/3 \\ 2/3 \end{bmatrix}$$

Because $A\mathbf{v}_2 = \mathbf{0}$, the only column found for U so far is $\mathbf{u}_1$. The other columns of U can be found by extending $\{\mathbf{u}_1\}$ to an orthonormal basis for $\mathbb{R}^3$. In this case, we need two orthogonal unit vectors $\mathbf{u}_2$ and $\mathbf{u}_3$ that are orthogonal to $\mathbf{u}_1$. Each vector must satisfy the equation $\mathbf{u}_1^T\mathbf{x} = 0$, which is equivalent to the equation $-x_1 + 2x_2 + 2x_3 = 0$. An orthonormal basis for the solution set of this equation is

$$\mathbf{u}_2 = \begin{bmatrix} 2/3 \\ -1/3 \\ 2/3 \end{bmatrix}, \mathbf{u}_3 = \begin{bmatrix} 2/3 \\ 2/3 \\ -1/3 \end{bmatrix}.$$

Therefore, let $U = \begin{bmatrix} -1/3 & 2/3 & 2/3 \\ 2/3 & -1/3 & 2/3 \\ 2/3 & 2/3 & -1/3 \end{bmatrix}$. Thus

$$A = U\Sigma V^T = \begin{bmatrix} -1/3 & 2/3 & 2/3 \\ 2/3 & -1/3 & 2/3 \\ 2/3 & 2/3 & -1/3 \end{bmatrix} \begin{bmatrix} 3\sqrt{10} & 0 \\ 0 & 0 \\ 0 & 0 \end{bmatrix} \begin{bmatrix} 3/\sqrt{10} & -1/\sqrt{10} \\ 1/\sqrt{10} & 3/\sqrt{10} \end{bmatrix}$$

12. Let $A = \begin{bmatrix} 1 & 1 \\ 0 & 1 \\ -1 & 1 \end{bmatrix}$. Then $A^T A = \begin{bmatrix} 2 & 0 \\ 0 & 3 \end{bmatrix}$, and the eigenvalues of $A^T A$ are seen to be (in decreasing order) $\lambda_1 = 3$ and $\lambda_2 = 2$. Associated unit eigenvectors may be computed:

$$\lambda = 3 : \begin{bmatrix} 0 \\ 1 \end{bmatrix}, \lambda = 2 : \begin{bmatrix} 1 \\ 0 \end{bmatrix}$$

Thus one choice for V is $V = \begin{bmatrix} 0 & 1 \\ 1 & 0 \end{bmatrix}$. The singular values of A are $\sigma_1 = \sqrt{3}$ and $\sigma_2 = \sqrt{2}$. Thus the matrix Σ is $\Sigma = \begin{bmatrix} \sqrt{3} & 0 \\ 0 & \sqrt{2} \\ 0 & 0 \end{bmatrix}$. Next compute

$$\mathbf{u}_1 = \frac{1}{\sigma_1} A\mathbf{v}_1 = \begin{bmatrix} 1/\sqrt{3} \\ 1/\sqrt{3} \\ 1/\sqrt{3} \end{bmatrix}, \mathbf{u}_2 = \frac{1}{\sigma_2} A\mathbf{v}_2 = \begin{bmatrix} 1/\sqrt{2} \\ 0 \\ -1/\sqrt{2} \end{bmatrix}$$

Since $\{\mathbf{u}_1, \mathbf{u}_2\}$ is not a basis for $\mathbb{R}^3$, we need a unit vector $\mathbf{u}_3$ that is orthogonal to both $\mathbf{u}_1$ and $\mathbf{u}_2$. The vector $\mathbf{u}_3$ must satisfy the set of equations $\mathbf{u}_1^T\mathbf{x} = 0$ and $\mathbf{u}_2^T\mathbf{x} = 0$. These are equivalent to the linear equations

$$\begin{array}{rcl} x_1 + x_2 + x_3 &=& 0 \\ x_1 + 0x_2 - x_3 &=& 0 \end{array}, \text{so } \mathbf{x} = \begin{bmatrix} 1 \\ -2 \\ 1 \end{bmatrix}, \text{and } \mathbf{u}_3 = \begin{bmatrix} 1/\sqrt{6} \\ -2/\sqrt{6} \\ 1/\sqrt{6} \end{bmatrix}$$

Therefore let $U = \begin{bmatrix} 1/\sqrt{3} & 1/\sqrt{2} & 1/\sqrt{6} \\ 1/\sqrt{3} & 0 & -2/\sqrt{6} \\ 1/\sqrt{3} & -1/\sqrt{2} & 1/\sqrt{6} \end{bmatrix}$. Thus

$$A = U \Sigma V^T = \begin{bmatrix} 1/\sqrt{3} & 1/\sqrt{2} & 1/\sqrt{6} \\ 1/\sqrt{3} & 0 & -2/\sqrt{6} \\ 1/\sqrt{3} & -1/\sqrt{2} & 1/\sqrt{6} \end{bmatrix} \begin{bmatrix} \sqrt{3} & 0 \\ 0 & \sqrt{2} \\ 0 & 0 \end{bmatrix} \begin{bmatrix} 0 & 1 \\ 1 & 0 \end{bmatrix}$$

13. Let $A = \begin{bmatrix} 3 & 2 & 2 \\ 2 & 3 & -2 \end{bmatrix}$. Then $A^T = \begin{bmatrix} 3 & 2 \\ 2 & 3 \\ 2 & -2 \end{bmatrix}$, $A^{TT}A^T = AA^T = \begin{bmatrix} 17 & 8 \\ 8 & 17 \end{bmatrix}$, and the eigenvalues of $A^{TT}A^T$

are seen to be (in decreasing order) $\lambda_1 = 25$ and $\lambda_2 = 9$. Associated unit eigenvectors may be computed:

$$\lambda = 25: \begin{bmatrix} 1/\sqrt{2} \\ 1/\sqrt{2} \end{bmatrix}, \lambda = 9: \begin{bmatrix} -1/\sqrt{2} \\ 1/\sqrt{2} \end{bmatrix}$$

Thus one choice for V is $V = \begin{bmatrix} 1/\sqrt{2} & -1/\sqrt{2} \\ 1/\sqrt{2} & 1/\sqrt{2} \end{bmatrix}$. The singular values of A^T are $\sigma_1 = \sqrt{25} = 5$ and

$\sigma_2 = \sqrt{9} = 3$. Thus the matrix Σ is $\Sigma = \begin{bmatrix} 5 & 0 \\ 0 & 3 \\ 0 & 0 \end{bmatrix}$. Next compute

$$\mathbf{u}_1 = \frac{1}{\sigma_1} A^T \mathbf{v}_1 = \begin{bmatrix} 1/\sqrt{2} \\ 1/\sqrt{2} \\ 0 \end{bmatrix}, \mathbf{u}_2 = \frac{1}{\sigma_2} A^T \mathbf{v}_2 = \begin{bmatrix} -1/\sqrt{18} \\ 1/\sqrt{18} \\ -4/\sqrt{18} \end{bmatrix}$$

Since $\{\mathbf{u}_1, \mathbf{u}_2\}$ is not a basis for $\mathbb{R}^3$, we need a unit vector $\mathbf{u}_3$ that is orthogonal to both $\mathbf{u}_1$ and $\mathbf{u}_2$. The vector $\mathbf{u}_3$ must satisfy the set of equations $\mathbf{u}_1^T \mathbf{x} = 0$ and $\mathbf{u}_2^T \mathbf{x} = 0$. These are equivalent to the linear equations

$$\begin{aligned} x_1 + x_2 + 0x_3 &= 0 \\ -x_1 + x_2 - 4x_3 &= 0 \end{aligned}, \text{so } \mathbf{x} = \begin{bmatrix} -2 \\ 2 \\ 1 \end{bmatrix}, \text{and } \mathbf{u}_3 = \begin{bmatrix} -2/3 \\ 2/3 \\ 1/3 \end{bmatrix}$$

Therefore let $U = \begin{bmatrix} 1/\sqrt{2} & -1/\sqrt{18} & -2/3 \\ 1/\sqrt{2} & 1/\sqrt{18} & 2/3 \\ 0 & -4/\sqrt{18} & 1/3 \end{bmatrix}$. Thus

$$A^T = U \Sigma V^T = \begin{bmatrix} 1/\sqrt{2} & -1/\sqrt{18} & -2/3 \\ 1/\sqrt{2} & 1/\sqrt{18} & 2/3 \\ 0 & -4/\sqrt{18} & 1/3 \end{bmatrix} \begin{bmatrix} 5 & 0 \\ 0 & 3 \\ 0 & 0 \end{bmatrix} \begin{bmatrix} 1/\sqrt{2} & 1/\sqrt{2} \\ -1/\sqrt{2} & 1/\sqrt{2} \end{bmatrix}$$

An SVD for A is computed by taking transposes:

$$A = \begin{bmatrix} 1/\sqrt{2} & -1/\sqrt{2} \\ 1/\sqrt{2} & 1/\sqrt{2} \end{bmatrix} \begin{bmatrix} 5 & 0 & 0 \\ 0 & 3 & 0 \end{bmatrix} \begin{bmatrix} 1/\sqrt{2} & 1/\sqrt{2} & 0 \\ -1/\sqrt{18} & 1/\sqrt{18} & -4/\sqrt{18} \\ -2/3 & 2/3 & 1/3 \end{bmatrix}$$

14. From Exercise 7, $A = U\Sigma V^T$ with $V = \begin{bmatrix} 2/\sqrt{5} & -1/\sqrt{5} \\ 1/\sqrt{5} & 2/\sqrt{5} \end{bmatrix}$. Since the first column of V is unit eigenvector

   associated with the greatest eigenvalue λ_1 of $A^T A$, so the first column of V is a unit vector at which $\| A\mathbf{x} \|$ is maximized.

15. **a.** Since A has 2 nonzero singular values, rank $A = 2$.

   b. By Example 6, $\{\mathbf{u}_1, \mathbf{u}_2\} = \left\{ \begin{bmatrix} .40 \\ .37 \\ -.84 \end{bmatrix}, \begin{bmatrix} -.78 \\ -.33 \\ -.52 \end{bmatrix} \right\}$ is a basis for Col A and $\{\mathbf{v}_3\} = \left\{ \begin{bmatrix} .58 \\ -.58 \\ .58 \end{bmatrix} \right\}$ is a basis

   for Nul A.

16. **a.** Since A has 2 nonzero singular values, rank $A = 2$.

   b. By Example 6, $\{\mathbf{u}_1, \mathbf{u}_2\} = \left\{ \begin{bmatrix} -.86 \\ .31 \\ .41 \end{bmatrix}, \begin{bmatrix} -.11 \\ .68 \\ -.73 \end{bmatrix} \right\}$ is a basis for Col A and $\{\mathbf{v}_3, \mathbf{v}_4\} = \left\{ \begin{bmatrix} .65 \\ .08 \\ -.16 \\ -.73 \end{bmatrix}, \begin{bmatrix} -.34 \\ .42 \\ -.84 \\ -.08 \end{bmatrix} \right\}$ is

   a basis for Nul A.

17. Let $A = U\Sigma V^T = U\Sigma V^{-1}$. Since A is square and invertible, rank $A = n$, and all of the entries on the
   diagonal of Σ must be nonzero. So $A^{-1} = (U\Sigma V^{-1})^{-1} = V\Sigma^{-1} U^{-1} = V\Sigma^{-1} U^T$.

18. First note that the determinant of an orthogonal matrix is ± 1, because $1 = \det I = \det U^T U =$
   $(\det U^T)(\det U) = (\det U)^2$. Suppose that A is square and $A = U\Sigma V^T$. Then Σ is square, and
   $\det A = (\det U)(\det \Sigma)(\det V^T) = \pm\det \Sigma = \pm\sigma_1 \ldots \sigma_n$.

19. Since U and V are orthogonal matrices,

   $$A^T A = (U\Sigma V^T)^T U\Sigma V^T = V\Sigma^T U^T U\Sigma V^T = V(\Sigma^T\Sigma)V^T = V(\Sigma^T\Sigma)V^{-1}$$

   If $\sigma_1, \ldots, \sigma_r$ are the diagonal entries in Σ, then $\Sigma^T\Sigma$ is a diagonal matrix with diagonal entries $\sigma_1^2, \ldots, \sigma_r^2$
   and possibly some zeros. Thus V diagonalizes $A^T A$ and the columns of V are eigenvectors of $A^T A$ by
   the Diagonalization Theorem in Section 5.3. Likewise

   $$AA^T = U\Sigma V^T(U\Sigma V^T)^T = U\Sigma V^T V\Sigma^T U^T = U(\Sigma\Sigma^T)U^T = U(\Sigma\Sigma^T)U^{-1}$$

   so U diagonalizes AA^T and the columns of U must be eigenvectors of AA^T. Moreover, the
   Diagonalization Theorem states that $\sigma_1^2, \ldots, \sigma_r^2$ are the nonzero eigenvalues of $A^T A$. Hence $\sigma_1, \ldots, \sigma_r$
   are the nonzero singular values of A.

20. If A is positive definite, then $A = PDP^T$, where P is an orthogonal matrix and D is a diagonal matrix.
   The diagonal entries of D are positive because they are the eigenvalues of a positive definite matrix.
   Since P is an orthogonal matrix, $PP^T = I$ and the square matrix P^T is invertible. Moreover,

$(P^T)^{-1} = (P^{-1})^{-1} = P = (P^T)^T$, so P^T is an orthogonal matrix. Thus the factorization $A = PDP^T$ has the properties that make it a singular value decomposition.

21. Let $A = U\Sigma V^T$. The matrix PU is orthogonal, because P and U are both orthogonal. (See Exercise 29 in Section 6.2). So the equation $PA = (PU)\Sigma V^T$ has the form required for a singular value decomposition. By Exercise 19, the diagonal entries in Σ are the singular values of PA.

22. The right singular vector $\mathbf{v}_1$ is an eigenvector for the largest eigenvector λ_1 of $A^T A$. By Theorem 7 in Section 7.3, the second largest eigenvalue λ_2 is the maximum of $\mathbf{x}^T(A^T A)\mathbf{x}$ over all unit vectors orthogonal to $\mathbf{v}_1$. Since $\mathbf{x}^T(A^T A)\mathbf{x} = \|A\mathbf{x}\|^2$, the square root of λ_2, which is the second largest singular value of A, is the maximum of $\|A\mathbf{x}\|$ over all unit vectors orthogonal to $\mathbf{v}_1$.

23. From the proof of Theorem 10, $U\Sigma = [\sigma_1\mathbf{u}_1 \quad \cdots \quad \sigma_r\mathbf{u}_r \quad \mathbf{0} \quad \cdots \quad \mathbf{0}]$. The column-row expansion of the product $(U\Sigma)V^T$ shows that

$$A = (U\Sigma)V^T = (U\Sigma)\begin{bmatrix} \mathbf{v}_1^T \\ \vdots \\ \mathbf{v}_n^T \end{bmatrix} = \sigma_1\mathbf{u}_1\mathbf{v}_1^T + \ldots + \sigma_r\mathbf{u}_r\mathbf{v}_r^T$$

where r is the rank of A.

24. From Exercise 23, $A^T = \sigma_1\mathbf{v}_1\mathbf{u}_1^T + \ldots + \sigma_r\mathbf{v}_r\mathbf{u}_r^T$. Then since $\mathbf{u}_i^T\mathbf{u}_j = \begin{cases} 0 & \text{for } i \neq j \\ 1 & \text{for } i = j \end{cases}$,

$$A^T\mathbf{u}_j = (\sigma_1\mathbf{v}_1\mathbf{u}_1^T + \ldots + \sigma_r\mathbf{v}_r\mathbf{u}_r^T)\mathbf{u}_j = (\sigma_j\mathbf{v}_j\mathbf{u}_j^T)\mathbf{u}_j = \sigma_j\mathbf{v}_j(\mathbf{u}_j^T\mathbf{u}_j) = \sigma_j\mathbf{v}_j$$

25. Consider the SVD for the standard matrix A of T, say $A = U\Sigma V^T$. Let $B = \{\mathbf{v}_1, \ldots, \mathbf{v}_n\}$ and $C = \{\mathbf{u}_1, \ldots, \mathbf{u}_m\}$ be bases for $\mathbb{R}^n$ and $\mathbb{R}^m$ constructed respectively from the columns of V and U. Since the columns of V are orthogonal, $V^T\mathbf{v}_j = \mathbf{e}_j$, where $\mathbf{e}_j$ is the jth column of the $n \times n$ identity matrix. To find the matrix of T relative to B and C, compute

$$T(\mathbf{v}_j) = A\mathbf{v}_j = U\Sigma V^T\mathbf{v}_j = U\Sigma\mathbf{e}_j = U\sigma_j\mathbf{e}_j = \sigma_j U\mathbf{e}_j = \sigma_j\mathbf{u}_j$$

so $[T(\mathbf{v}_j)]_C = \sigma_j\mathbf{e}_j$. Formula (4) in the discussion at the beginning of Section 5.4 shows that the "diagonal" matrix Σ is the matrix of T relative to B and C.

26. [M] Let $A = \begin{bmatrix} -18 & 13 & -4 & 4 \\ 2 & 19 & -4 & 12 \\ -14 & 11 & -12 & 8 \\ -2 & 21 & 4 & 8 \end{bmatrix}$. Then $A^T A = \begin{bmatrix} 528 & -392 & 224 & -176 \\ -392 & 1092 & -176 & 536 \\ 224 & -176 & 192 & -128 \\ -176 & 536 & -128 & 288 \end{bmatrix}$, and the eigenvalues of $A^T A$ are found to be (in decreasing order) $\lambda_1 = 1600$, $\lambda_2 = 400$, $\lambda_3 = 100$, and $\lambda_4 = 0$. Associated unit eigenvectors may be computed:

$$\lambda_1: \begin{bmatrix} -.4 \\ .8 \\ -.2 \\ .4 \end{bmatrix}, \lambda_2: \begin{bmatrix} .8 \\ .4 \\ .4 \\ .2 \end{bmatrix}, \lambda_3: \begin{bmatrix} .4 \\ -.2 \\ -.8 \\ .4 \end{bmatrix}, \lambda_4: \begin{bmatrix} -.2 \\ -.4 \\ .4 \\ .8 \end{bmatrix}$$

Thus one choice for V is $V = \begin{bmatrix} -.4 & .8 & .4 & -.2 \\ .8 & .4 & -.2 & -.4 \\ -.2 & .4 & -.8 & .4 \\ .4 & .2 & .4 & .8 \end{bmatrix}$. The singular values of A are $\sigma_1 = 40$, $\sigma_1 = 20$,

$\sigma_3 = 10$, and $\sigma_4 = 0$. Thus the matrix Σ is $\Sigma = \begin{bmatrix} 40 & 0 & 0 & 0 \\ 0 & 20 & 0 & 0 \\ 0 & 0 & 10 & 0 \\ 0 & 0 & 0 & 0 \end{bmatrix}$. Next compute

$$\mathbf{u}_1 = \frac{1}{\sigma_1} A\mathbf{v}_1 = \begin{bmatrix} .5 \\ .5 \\ .5 \\ .5 \end{bmatrix}, \mathbf{u}_2 = \frac{1}{\sigma_2} A\mathbf{v}_2 = \begin{bmatrix} -.5 \\ .5 \\ -.5 \\ .5 \end{bmatrix},$$

$$\mathbf{u}_3 = \frac{1}{\sigma_3} A\mathbf{v}_3 = \begin{bmatrix} -.5 \\ .5 \\ .5 \\ -.5 \end{bmatrix}$$

Because $A\mathbf{v}_4 = \mathbf{0}$, only three columns of U have been found so far. The last column of U can be found by extending $\{\mathbf{u}_1, \mathbf{u}_2, \mathbf{u}_3\}$ to an orthonormal basis for $\mathbb{R}^4$. The vector $\mathbf{u}_4$ must satisfy the set of equations $\mathbf{u}_1^T\mathbf{x} = 0$, $\mathbf{u}_2^T\mathbf{x} = 0$, and $\mathbf{u}_3^T\mathbf{x} = 0$. These are equivalent to the linear equations

$$\begin{aligned} x_1 + x_2 + x_3 + x_4 &= 0 \\ -x_1 + x_2 - x_3 + x_4 &= 0, \text{ so } \mathbf{x} = \begin{bmatrix} -1 \\ -1 \\ 1 \\ 1 \end{bmatrix}, \text{ and } \mathbf{u}_4 = \begin{bmatrix} -.5 \\ -.5 \\ .5 \\ .5 \end{bmatrix}. \\ -x_1 + x_2 + x_3 - x_4 &= 0 \end{aligned}$$

Therefore, let $U = \begin{bmatrix} .5 & -.5 & -.5 & -.5 \\ .5 & .5 & .5 & -.5 \\ .5 & -.5 & .5 & .5 \\ .5 & .5 & -.5 & .5 \end{bmatrix}$. Thus

$$A = U\Sigma V^T = \begin{bmatrix} .5 & -.5 & -.5 & -.5 \\ .5 & .5 & .5 & -.5 \\ .5 & -.5 & .5 & .5 \\ .5 & .5 & -.5 & .5 \end{bmatrix} \begin{bmatrix} 40 & 0 & 0 & 0 \\ 0 & 20 & 0 & 0 \\ 0 & 0 & 10 & 0 \\ 0 & 0 & 0 & 0 \end{bmatrix} \begin{bmatrix} -.4 & .8 & -.2 & .4 \\ .8 & .4 & .4 & .2 \\ .4 & -.2 & -.8 & .4 \\ -.2 & -.4 & .4 & .8 \end{bmatrix}$$

27. [M] Let $A = \begin{bmatrix} 6 & -8 & -4 & 5 & -4 \\ 2 & 7 & -5 & -6 & 4 \\ 0 & -1 & -8 & 2 & 2 \\ -1 & -2 & 4 & 4 & -8 \end{bmatrix}$. Then $A^TA = \begin{bmatrix} 41 & -32 & -38 & 14 & -8 \\ -32 & 118 & -3 & -92 & 74 \\ -38 & -3 & 121 & 10 & -52 \\ 14 & -92 & 10 & 81 & -72 \\ -8 & 74 & -52 & -72 & 100 \end{bmatrix}$, and the

eigenvalues of A^TA are found to be (in decreasing order) $\lambda_1 = 270.87$, $\lambda_2 = 147.85$, $\lambda_3 = 23.73$, $\lambda_4 = 18.55$, and $\lambda_5 = 0$. Associated unit eigenvectors may be computed:

$$\lambda_1 : \begin{bmatrix} -.10 \\ .61 \\ -.21 \\ -.52 \\ .55 \end{bmatrix}, \lambda_2 : \begin{bmatrix} -.39 \\ .29 \\ .84 \\ -.14 \\ -.19 \end{bmatrix}, \lambda_3 : \begin{bmatrix} -.74 \\ -.27 \\ -.07 \\ .38 \\ .49 \end{bmatrix}, \lambda_4 : \begin{bmatrix} .41 \\ -.50 \\ .45 \\ -.23 \\ .58 \end{bmatrix}, \lambda_5 : \begin{bmatrix} -.36 \\ -.48 \\ -.19 \\ -.72 \\ -.29 \end{bmatrix}$$

Thus one choice for V is $V = \begin{bmatrix} -.10 & -.39 & -.74 & .41 & -.36 \\ .61 & .29 & -.27 & -.50 & -.48 \\ -.21 & .84 & -.07 & .45 & -.19 \\ -.52 & -.14 & .38 & -.23 & -.72 \\ .55 & -.19 & .49 & .58 & -.29 \end{bmatrix}$. The nonzero singular values of A are

$\sigma_1 = 16.46$, $\sigma_1 = 12.16$, $\sigma_3 = 4.87$, and $\sigma_4 = 4.31$. Thus the matrix Σ is

$$\Sigma = \begin{bmatrix} 16.46 & 0 & 0 & 0 & 0 \\ 0 & 12.16 & 0 & 0 & 0 \\ 0 & 0 & 4.87 & 0 & 0 \\ 0 & 0 & 0 & 4.31 & 0 \end{bmatrix}.$$ Next compute

$$\mathbf{u}_1 = \frac{1}{\sigma_1} A\mathbf{v}_1 = \begin{bmatrix} -.57 \\ .63 \\ .07 \\ -.51 \end{bmatrix}, \mathbf{u}_2 = \frac{1}{\sigma_2} A\mathbf{v}_2 = \begin{bmatrix} -.65 \\ -.24 \\ -.63 \\ .34 \end{bmatrix},$$

$$\mathbf{u}_3 = \frac{1}{\sigma_3} A\mathbf{v}_3 = \begin{bmatrix} -.42 \\ -.68 \\ .53 \\ -.29 \end{bmatrix}, \mathbf{u}_4 = \frac{1}{\sigma_4} A\mathbf{v}_4 = \begin{bmatrix} .27 \\ -.29 \\ -.56 \\ -.73 \end{bmatrix}$$

Since $\{\mathbf{u}_1, \mathbf{u}_2, \mathbf{u}_3, \mathbf{u}_4\}$ is a basis for $\mathbb{R}^4$, let $U = \begin{bmatrix} -.57 & -.65 & -.42 & .27 \\ .63 & -.24 & -.68 & -.29 \\ .07 & -.63 & .53 & -.56 \\ -.51 & .34 & -.29 & -.73 \end{bmatrix}$. Thus

$A = U\Sigma V^T$

$$= \begin{bmatrix} -.57 & -.65 & -.42 & .27 \\ .63 & -.24 & -.68 & -.29 \\ .07 & -.63 & .53 & -.56 \\ -.51 & .34 & -.29 & -.73 \end{bmatrix} \begin{bmatrix} 16.46 & 0 & 0 & 0 & 0 \\ 0 & 12.16 & 0 & 0 & 0 \\ 0 & 0 & 4.87 & 0 & 0 \\ 0 & 0 & 0 & 4.31 & 0 \end{bmatrix} \begin{bmatrix} -.10 & .61 & -.21 & -.52 & .55 \\ -.39 & .29 & .84 & -.14 & -.19 \\ -.74 & -.27 & -.07 & .38 & .49 \\ .41 & -.50 & .45 & -.23 & .58 \\ -.36 & -.48 & -.19 & -.72 & -.29 \end{bmatrix}$$

28. **[M]** Let $A = \begin{bmatrix} 4 & 0 & -7 & -7 \\ -6 & 1 & 11 & 9 \\ 7 & -5 & 10 & 19 \\ -1 & 2 & 3 & -1 \end{bmatrix}$. Then $A^T A = \begin{bmatrix} 102 & -43 & -27 & 52 \\ -43 & 30 & -33 & -88 \\ -27 & -33 & 279 & 335 \\ 52 & -88 & 335 & 492 \end{bmatrix}$, and the eigenvalues of

$A^T A$ are found to be (in decreasing order) $\lambda_1 = 749.9785$, $\lambda_2 = 146.2009$, $\lambda_3 = 6.8206$, and

$\lambda_4 = 1.3371 \times 10^{-6}$. The singular values of A are thus $\sigma_1 = 27.3857$, $\sigma_2 = 12.0914$, $\sigma_3 = 2.61163$, and

$\sigma_4 = .00115635$. The condition number $\sigma_1 / \sigma_4 = 23{,}683$.

29. **[M]** Let $A = \begin{bmatrix} 5 & 3 & 1 & 7 & 9 \\ 6 & 4 & 2 & 8 & -8 \\ 7 & 5 & 3 & 10 & 9 \\ 9 & 6 & 4 & -9 & -5 \\ 8 & 5 & 2 & 11 & 4 \end{bmatrix}$. Then $A^T A = \begin{bmatrix} 255 & 168 & 90 & 160 & 47 \\ 168 & 111 & 60 & 104 & 30 \\ 90 & 60 & 34 & 39 & 8 \\ 160 & 104 & 39 & 415 & 178 \\ 47 & 30 & 8 & 178 & 267 \end{bmatrix}$, and the eigenvalues

of $A^T A$ are found to be (in decreasing order) $\lambda_1 = 672.589$, $\lambda_2 = 280.745$, $\lambda_3 = 127.503$, $\lambda_4 = 1.163$,

and $\lambda_5 = 1.428 \times 10^{-7}$. The singular values of A are thus $\sigma_1 = 25.9343$, $\sigma_2 = 16.7554$, $\sigma_3 = 11.2917$,

$\sigma_4 = 1.07853$, and $\sigma_5 = .000377928$. The condition number $\sigma_1 / \sigma_5 = 68{,}622$.

7.5 SOLUTIONS

Notes: The application presented here has turned out to be of interest to a wide variety of students, including engineers. I cover this in Course Syllabus 3 described above, but I only have time to mention the idea briefly to my other classes.

1. The matrix of observations is $X = \begin{bmatrix} 19 & 22 & 6 & 3 & 2 & 20 \\ 12 & 6 & 9 & 15 & 13 & 5 \end{bmatrix}$ and the sample mean is

$M = \dfrac{1}{6}\begin{bmatrix} 72 \\ 60 \end{bmatrix} = \begin{bmatrix} 12 \\ 10 \end{bmatrix}$. The mean-deviation form B is obtained by subtracting M from each column of X, so

$B = \begin{bmatrix} 7 & 10 & -6 & -9 & -10 & 8 \\ 2 & -4 & -1 & 5 & 3 & -5 \end{bmatrix}$. The sample covariance matrix is

$S = \dfrac{1}{6-1} BB^T = \dfrac{1}{5}\begin{bmatrix} 430 & -135 \\ -135 & 80 \end{bmatrix} = \begin{bmatrix} 86 & -27 \\ -27 & 16 \end{bmatrix}$

2. The matrix of observations is $X = \begin{bmatrix} 1 & 5 & 2 & 6 & 7 & 3 \\ 3 & 11 & 6 & 8 & 15 & 11 \end{bmatrix}$ and the sample mean is $M = \dfrac{1}{6}\begin{bmatrix} 24 \\ 54 \end{bmatrix} = \begin{bmatrix} 4 \\ 9 \end{bmatrix}$.

The mean-deviation form B is obtained by subtracting M from each column of X, so

$B = \begin{bmatrix} -3 & 1 & -2 & 2 & 3 & -1 \\ -6 & 2 & -3 & -1 & 6 & 2 \end{bmatrix}$. The sample covariance matrix is

$S = \dfrac{1}{6-1} BB^T = \dfrac{1}{5}\begin{bmatrix} 28 & 40 \\ 40 & 90 \end{bmatrix} = \begin{bmatrix} 5.6 & 8 \\ 8 & 18 \end{bmatrix}$

3. The principal components of the data are the unit eigenvectors of the sample covariance matrix S. One computes that (in descending order) the eigenvalues of $S = \begin{bmatrix} 86 & -27 \\ -27 & 16 \end{bmatrix}$ are $\lambda_1 = 95.2041$ and

$\lambda_2 = 6.79593$. One further computes that corresponding eigenvectors are $\mathbf{v}_1 = \begin{bmatrix} -2.93348 \\ 1 \end{bmatrix}$ and

$\mathbf{v}_2 = \begin{bmatrix} .340892 \\ 1 \end{bmatrix}$. These vectors may be normalized to find the principal components, which are

$\mathbf{u}_1 = \begin{bmatrix} .946515 \\ -.322659 \end{bmatrix}$ for $\lambda_1 = 95.2041$ and $\mathbf{u}_2 = \begin{bmatrix} .322659 \\ .946515 \end{bmatrix}$ for $\lambda_2 = 6.79593$.

4. The principal components of the data are the unit eigenvectors of the sample covariance matrix S. One computes that (in descending order) the eigenvalues of $S = \begin{bmatrix} 5.6 & 8 \\ 8 & 18 \end{bmatrix}$ are $\lambda_1 = 21.9213$ and

$\lambda_2 = 1.67874$. One further computes that corresponding eigenvectors are $\mathbf{v}_1 = \begin{bmatrix} .490158 \\ 1 \end{bmatrix}$ and

$\mathbf{v}_2 = \begin{bmatrix} -2.04016 \\ 1 \end{bmatrix}$. These vectors may be normalized to find the principal components, which are

$\mathbf{u}_1 = \begin{bmatrix} .44013 \\ .897934 \end{bmatrix}$ for $\lambda_1 = 21.9213$ and $\mathbf{u}_2 = \begin{bmatrix} -.897934 \\ .44013 \end{bmatrix}$ for $\lambda_2 = 1.67874$.

5. [M] The largest eigenvalue of $S = \begin{bmatrix} 164.12 & 32.73 & 81.04 \\ 32.73 & 539.44 & 249.13 \\ 81.04 & 249.13 & 189.11 \end{bmatrix}$ is $\lambda_1 = 677.497$, and the first principal

component of the data is the unit eigenvector corresponding to λ_1, which is $\mathbf{u}_1 = \begin{bmatrix} .129554 \\ .874423 \\ .467547 \end{bmatrix}$. The fraction

of the total variance that is contained in this component is $\lambda_1 / \text{tr}(S) = 677.497/(164.12 + 539.44 + 189.11) = .758956$, so 75.8956% of the variance of the data is contained in the first principal component.

6. [M] The largest eigenvalue of $S = \begin{bmatrix} 29.64 & 18.38 & 5.00 \\ 18.38 & 20.82 & 14.06 \\ 5.00 & 14.06 & 29.21 \end{bmatrix}$ is $\lambda_1 = 51.6957$, and the first principal

component of the data is the unit eigenvector corresponding to λ_1, which is $\mathbf{u}_1 = \begin{bmatrix} .615525 \\ .599424 \\ .511683 \end{bmatrix}$. Thus one

choice for the new variable is $y_1 = .615525x_1 + .599424x_2 + .511683x_3$. The fraction of the total variance that is contained in this component is $\lambda_1 / \text{tr}(S) = 51.6957/(29.64 + 20.82 + 29.21) = .648872$, so 64.8872% of the variance of the data is explained by y_1.

7. Since the unit eigenvector corresponding to $\lambda_1 = 95.2041$ is $\mathbf{u}_1 = \begin{bmatrix} .946515 \\ -.322659 \end{bmatrix}$, one choice for the new variable is $y_1 = .946515x_1 - .322659x_2$. The fraction of the total variance that is contained in this component is $\lambda_1 / \text{tr}(S) = 95.2041/(86+16) = .933374$, so 93.3374% of the variance of the data is explained by y_1.

8. Since the unit eigenvector corresponding to $\lambda_1 = 21.9213$ is $\mathbf{u}_1 = \begin{bmatrix} .44013 \\ .897934 \end{bmatrix}$, one choice for the new variable is $y_1 = .44013x_1 + .897934x_2$. The fraction of the total variance that is contained in this component is $\lambda_1 / \text{tr}(S) = 21.9213/(5.6+18) = .928869$, so 92.8869% of the variance of the data is explained by y_1.

9. The largest eigenvalue of $S = \begin{bmatrix} 5 & 2 & 0 \\ 2 & 6 & 2 \\ 0 & 2 & 7 \end{bmatrix}$ is $\lambda_1 = 9$, and the first principal component of the data is the unit eigenvector corresponding to λ_1, which is $\mathbf{u}_1 = \begin{bmatrix} 1/3 \\ 2/3 \\ 2/3 \end{bmatrix}$. Thus one choice for y is

$y = (1/3)x_1 + (2/3)x_2 + (2/3)x_3$, and the variance of y is $\lambda_1 = 9$.

10. [M] The largest eigenvalue of $S = \begin{bmatrix} 5 & 4 & 2 \\ 4 & 11 & 4 \\ 2 & 4 & 5 \end{bmatrix}$ is $\lambda_1 = 15$, and the first principal component of the data is the unit eigenvector corresponding to λ_1, which is $\mathbf{u}_1 = \begin{bmatrix} 1/\sqrt{6} \\ 2/\sqrt{6} \\ 1/\sqrt{6} \end{bmatrix}$. Thus one choice for y is

$y = (1/\sqrt{6})x_1 + (2/\sqrt{6})x_2 + (1/\sqrt{6})x_3$, and the variance of y is $\lambda_1 = 15$.

11. **a.** If $\mathbf{w}$ is the vector in $\mathbb{R}^N$ with a 1 in each position, then $\begin{bmatrix} \mathbf{X}_1 & \ldots & \mathbf{X}_N \end{bmatrix} \mathbf{w} = \mathbf{X}_1 + \ldots + \mathbf{X}_N = \mathbf{0}$ since the $\mathbf{X}_k$ are in mean-deviation form. Then

$$\begin{bmatrix} \mathbf{Y}_1 & \ldots & \mathbf{Y}_N \end{bmatrix} \mathbf{w} = \begin{bmatrix} P^T \mathbf{X}_1 & \ldots & P^T \mathbf{X}_N \end{bmatrix} \mathbf{w} = P^T \begin{bmatrix} \mathbf{X}_1 & \ldots & \mathbf{X}_N \end{bmatrix} \mathbf{w} = P^T \mathbf{0} = \mathbf{0}$$

Thus $\mathbf{Y}_1 + \ldots + \mathbf{Y}_N = \mathbf{0}$, and the $\mathbf{Y}_k$ are in mean-deviation form.

b. By part a., the covariance matrix $S_{\mathbf{Y}}$ of $\mathbf{Y}_1, \ldots, \mathbf{Y}_N$ is

$$S_{\mathbf{Y}} = \frac{1}{N-1} \begin{bmatrix} \mathbf{Y}_1 & \ldots & \mathbf{Y}_N \end{bmatrix} \begin{bmatrix} \mathbf{Y}_1 & \ldots & \mathbf{Y}_N \end{bmatrix}^T$$

$$= \frac{1}{N-1} P^T \begin{bmatrix} \mathbf{X}_1 & \ldots & \mathbf{X}_N \end{bmatrix} (P^T \begin{bmatrix} \mathbf{X}_1 & \ldots & \mathbf{X}_N \end{bmatrix})^T$$

$$= P^T \left(\frac{1}{N-1} \begin{bmatrix} \mathbf{X}_1 & \ldots & \mathbf{X}_N \end{bmatrix} \begin{bmatrix} \mathbf{X}_1 & \ldots & \mathbf{X}_N \end{bmatrix}^T \right) P = P^T S P$$

since the $\mathbf{X}_k$ are in mean-deviation form.

12. By Exercise 11, the change of variables $\mathbf{X} = P\mathbf{Y}$ changes the covariance matrix S of X into the covariance matrix $P^T S P$ of $\mathbf{Y}$. The total variance of the data as described by $\mathbf{Y}$ is $\text{tr}(P^T S P)$. However, since $P^T S P$ is similar to S, they have the same trace (by Exercise 25 in Section 5.4). Thus the total variance of the data is unchanged by the change of variables $\mathbf{X} = P\mathbf{Y}$.

13. Let $\mathbf{M}$ be the sample mean for the data, and let $\hat{\mathbf{X}}_k = \mathbf{X}_k - \mathbf{M}$. Let $B = \begin{bmatrix} \hat{\mathbf{X}}_1 & \cdots & \hat{\mathbf{X}}_N \end{bmatrix}$ be the matrix of observations in mean-deviation form. By the row-column expansion of BB^T, the sample covariance matrix is

$$S = \frac{1}{N-1} BB^T$$

$$= \frac{1}{N-1} \begin{bmatrix} \hat{\mathbf{X}}_1 & \cdots & \hat{\mathbf{X}}_N \end{bmatrix} \begin{bmatrix} \hat{\mathbf{X}}_1^T \\ \vdots \\ \hat{\mathbf{X}}_N^T \end{bmatrix}$$

$$= \frac{1}{N-1} \sum_{k=1}^N \hat{\mathbf{X}}_k \hat{\mathbf{X}}_k^T = \frac{1}{N-1} \sum_{k=1}^N (\mathbf{X}_k - \mathbf{M})(\mathbf{X}_k - \mathbf{M})^T$$

Chapter 7 SUPPLEMENTARY EXERCISES

1. **a.** True. This is just part of Theorem 2 in Section 7.1. The proof appears just before the statement of the theorem.

   b. False. A counterexample is $A = \begin{bmatrix} 0 & -1 \\ 1 & 0 \end{bmatrix}$.

   c. True. This is proved in the first part of the proof of Theorem 6 in Section 7.3. It is also a consequence of Theorem 7 in Section 6.2.

   d. False. The principal axes of $\mathbf{x}^T A\mathbf{x}$ are the columns of any *orthogonal* matrix P that diagonalizes A. *Note*: When A has an eigenvalue whose eigenspace has dimension greater than 1, the principal axes are not uniquely determined.

   e. False. A counterexample is $P = \begin{bmatrix} 1 & -1 \\ 1 & 1 \end{bmatrix}$. The columns here are orthogonal but not orthonormal.

   f. False. See Example 6 in Section 7.2.

   g. False. A counterexample is $A = \begin{bmatrix} 2 & 0 \\ 0 & -3 \end{bmatrix}$ and $\mathbf{x} = \begin{bmatrix} 1 \\ 0 \end{bmatrix}$. Then $\mathbf{x}^T A\mathbf{x} = 2 > 0$, but $\mathbf{x}^T A\mathbf{x}$ is an indefinite quadratic form.

   h. True. This is basically the Principal Axes Theorem from Section 7.2. Any quadratic form can be written as $\mathbf{x}^T A\mathbf{x}$ for some symmetric matrix A.

   i. False. See Example 3 in Section 7.3.

   j. False. The maximum value must be computed over the set of *unit* vectors. Without a restriction on the norm of $\mathbf{x}$, the values of $\mathbf{x}^T A\mathbf{x}$ can be made as large as desired.

k. False. Any orthogonal change of variable $\mathbf{x} = P\mathbf{y}$ changes a positive definite quadratic form into another positive definite quadratic form. Proof: By Theorem 5 of Section 7.2., the classification of a quadratic form is determined by the eigenvalues of the matrix of the form. Given a form $\mathbf{x}^T A\mathbf{x}$, the matrix of the new quadratic form is $P^{-1}AP$, which is similar to A and thus has the same eigenvalues as A.

l. False. The term "definite eigenvalue" is undefined and therefore meaningless.

m. True. If $\mathbf{x} = P\mathbf{y}$, then $\mathbf{x}^T A\mathbf{x} = (P\mathbf{y})^T A(P\mathbf{y}) = \mathbf{y}^T P^T AP\mathbf{y} = \mathbf{y}^T P^{-1}AP\mathbf{y}$.

n. False. A counterexample is $U = \begin{bmatrix} 1 & -1 \\ 1 & -1 \end{bmatrix}$. The columns of U must be *orthonormal* to make $UU^T\mathbf{x}$ the orthogonal projection of $\mathbf{x}$ onto Col U.

o. True. This follows from the discussion in Example 2 of Section 7.4., which refers to a proof given in Example 1.

p. True. Theorem 10 in Section 7.4 writes the decomposition in the form $U\Sigma V^T$, where U and V are orthogonal matrices. In this case, V^T is also an orthogonal matrix. Proof: Since V is orthogonal, V is invertible and $V^{-1} = V^T$. Then $(V^T)^{-1} = (V^{-1})^T = (V^T)^T$, and since V is square and invertible, V^T is an orthogonal matrix.

q. False. A counterexample is $A = \begin{bmatrix} 2 & 0 \\ 0 & 1 \end{bmatrix}$. The singular values of A are 2 and 1, but the singular values of $A^T A$ are 4 and 1.

2. a. Each term in the expansion of A is symmetric by Exercise 35 in Section 7.1. The fact that $(B+C)^T = B^T + C^T$ implies that any sum of symmetric matrices is symmetric, so A is symmetric.

b. Since $\mathbf{u}_1^T\mathbf{u}_1 = 1$ and $\mathbf{u}_j^T\mathbf{u}_1 = 0$ for $j \neq 1$,

$$A\mathbf{u}_1 = (\lambda_1\mathbf{u}_1\mathbf{u}_1^T)\mathbf{u}_1 + \ldots + (\lambda_n\mathbf{u}_n\mathbf{u}_n^T)\mathbf{u}_1 = \lambda_1\mathbf{u}_1(\mathbf{u}_1^T\mathbf{u}_1) + \ldots + \lambda_n\mathbf{u}_n(\mathbf{u}_n^T\mathbf{u}_1) = \lambda_1\mathbf{u}_1$$

Since $\mathbf{u}_1 \neq \mathbf{0}$, λ_1 is an eigenvalue of A. A similar argument shows that λ_j is an eigenvalue of A for $j = 2, \ldots, n$.

3. If rank $A = r$, then $\dim \text{Nul } A = n - r$ by the Rank Theorem. So 0 is an eigenvalue of A with multiplicity $n - r$, and of the n terms in the spectral decomposition of A exactly $n - r$ are zero. The remaining r terms (which correspond to nonzero eigenvalues) are all rank 1 matrices, as mentioned in the discussion of the spectral decomposition.

4. a. By Theorem 3 in Section 6.1, $(\text{Col } A)^\perp = \text{Nul } A^T = \text{Nul } A$ since $A^T = A$.

b. Let $\mathbf{y}$ be in $\mathbb{R}^n$. By the Orthogonal Decomposition Theorem in Section 6.3, $\mathbf{y} = \hat{\mathbf{y}} + \mathbf{z}$, where $\hat{\mathbf{y}}$ is in Col A and $\mathbf{z}$ is in $(\text{Col } A)^\perp$. By part a., $\mathbf{z}$ is in Nul A.

5. If $A\mathbf{v} = \lambda\mathbf{v}$ for some nonzero λ, then $\mathbf{v} = \lambda^{-1}A\mathbf{v} = A(\lambda^{-1}\mathbf{v})$, which shows that $\mathbf{v}$ is a linear combination of the columns of A.

6. Because A is symmetric, there is an orthonormal eigenvector basis $\{\mathbf{u}_1, \ldots, \mathbf{u}_n\}$ for $\mathbb{R}^n$. Let $r = \text{rank } A$. If $r = 0$, then $A = O$ and the decomposition of Exercise 4(b) is $\mathbf{y} = \mathbf{0} + \mathbf{y}$ for each $\mathbf{y}$ in $\mathbb{R}^n$; if $r = n$ then the decomposition is $\mathbf{y} = \mathbf{y} + \mathbf{0}$ for each $\mathbf{y}$ in $\mathbb{R}^n$.

Assume that $0 < r < n$. Then $\dim \text{Nul } A = n - r$ by the Rank Theorem, and so 0 is an eigenvalue of A with multiplicity $n - r$. Hence there are r nonzero eigenvalues, counted according to their multiplicities.

Renumber the eigenvector basis if necessary so that $\mathbf{u}_1, \ldots, \mathbf{u}_r$ are the eigenvectors corresponding to the nonzero eigenvalues. By Exercise 5, $\mathbf{u}_1, \ldots, \mathbf{u}_r$ are in Col A. Also, $\mathbf{u}_{r+1}, \ldots, \mathbf{u}_n$ are in Nul A because these vectors are eigenvectors corresponding to the eigenvalue 0. For $\mathbf{y}$ in $\mathbb{R}^n$, there are scalars $c_1, \ldots, c_n$ such that

$$\mathbf{y} = \underbrace{c_1\mathbf{u}_1 + \ldots + c_r\mathbf{u}_r}_{\hat{\mathbf{y}}} + \underbrace{c_{r+1}\mathbf{u}_{r+1} + \ldots + c_n\mathbf{u}_n}_{\mathbf{z}}$$

This provides the decomposition in Exercise 4(b).

7. If $A = R^T R$ and R is invertible, then A is positive definite by Exercise 25 in Section 7.2.

   Conversely, suppose that A is positive definite. Then by Exercise 26 in Section 7.2, $A = B^T B$ for some positive definite matrix B. Since the eigenvalues of B are positive, 0 is not an eigenvalue of B and B is invertible. Thus the columns of B are linearly independent. By Theorem 12 in Section 6.4, $B = QR$ for some $n \times n$ matrix Q with orthonormal columns and some upper triangular matrix R with positive entries on its diagonal. Since Q is a square matrix, $Q^T Q = I$, and

   $$A = B^T B = (QR)^T (QR) = R^T Q^T Q R = R^T R$$

   and R has the required properties.

8. Suppose that A is positive definite, and consider a Cholesky factorization of $A = R^T R$ with R upper triangular and having positive entries on its diagonal. Let D be the diagonal matrix whose diagonal entries are the entries on the diagonal of R. Since right-multiplication by a diagonal matrix scales the columns of the matrix on its left, the matrix $L = R^T D^{-1}$ is lower triangular with 1's on its diagonal. If $U = DR$, then $A = R^T D^{-1} DR = LU$.

9. If A is an $m \times n$ matrix and $\mathbf{x}$ is in $\mathbb{R}^n$, then $\mathbf{x}^T A^T A\mathbf{x} = (A\mathbf{x})^T (A\mathbf{x}) = \| A\mathbf{x} \|^2 \geq 0$. Thus $A^T A$ is positive semidefinite. By Exercise 22 in Section 6.5, rank $A^T A = $ rank A.

10. If rank $G = r$, then dim Nul $G = n - r$ by the Rank Theorem. Hence 0 is an eigenvalue of G with multiplicity $n - r$, and the spectral decomposition of G is

   $$G = \lambda_1\mathbf{u}_1\mathbf{u}_1^T + \ldots + \lambda_r\mathbf{u}_r\mathbf{u}_r^T$$

   Also $\lambda_1, \ldots, \lambda_r$ are positive because G is positive semidefinite. Thus

   $$G = \left(\sqrt{\lambda_1}\mathbf{u}_1\right)\left(\sqrt{\lambda_1}\mathbf{u}_1^T\right) + \ldots + \left(\sqrt{\lambda_r}\mathbf{u}_r\right)\left(\sqrt{\lambda_r}\mathbf{u}_r^T\right)$$

   By the column-row expansion of a matrix product, $G = BB^T$ where B is the $n \times r$ matrix $B = \left[\sqrt{\lambda_1}\mathbf{u}_1 \quad \ldots \quad \sqrt{\lambda_r}\mathbf{u}_r\right]$. Finally, $G = A^T A$ for $A = B^T$.

11. Let $A = U\Sigma V^T$ be a singular value decomposition of A. Since U is orthogonal, $U^T U = I$ and

   $$A = U\Sigma U^T UV^T = PQ \text{ where } P = U\Sigma U^T = U\Sigma U^{-1} \text{ and } Q = UV^T.$$ Since Σ is symmetric, P is symmetric, and P has nonnegative eigenvalues because it is similar to Σ, which is diagonal with nonnegative diagonal entries. Thus P is positive semidefinite. The matrix Q is orthogonal since it is the product of orthogonal matrices.

12. **a.** Because the columns of V_r are orthonormal,

   $$AA^+\mathbf{y} = (U_r DV_r^T)(V_r D^{-1}U_r^T)\mathbf{y} = (U_r DD^{-1}U_r^T)\mathbf{y} = U_r U_r^T\mathbf{y}$$

Since $U_r U_r^T \mathbf{y}$ is the orthogonal projection of $\mathbf{y}$ onto $\operatorname{Col} U_r$ by Theorem 10 in Section 6.3, and since $\operatorname{Col} U_r = \operatorname{Col} A$ by (5) in Example 6 of Section 7.4, $AA^+\mathbf{y}$ is the orthogonal projection of $\mathbf{y}$ onto $\operatorname{Col} A$.

b. Because the columns of U_r are orthonormal,

$$A^+ A\mathbf{x} = (V_r D^{-1} U_r^T)(U_r DV_r^T)\mathbf{x} = (V_r D^{-1} DV_r^T)\mathbf{x} = V_r V_r^T \mathbf{x}$$

Since $V_r V_r^T \mathbf{x}$ is the orthogonal projection of $\mathbf{x}$ onto $\operatorname{Col} V_r$ by Theorem 10 in Section 6.3, and since $\operatorname{Col} V_r = \operatorname{Row} A$ by (8) in Example 6 of Section 7.4, $A^+ A\mathbf{x}$ is the orthogonal projection of $\mathbf{x}$ onto $\operatorname{Row} A$.

c. Using the reduced singular value decomposition, the definition of A^+, and the associativity of matrix multiplication gives:

$$AA^+ A = (U_r DV_r^T)(V_r D^{-1} U_r^T)(U_r DV_r^T) = (U_r DD^{-1} U_r^T)(U_r DV_r^T)$$

$$= U_r DD^{-1} DV_r^T = U_r DV_r^T = A$$

$$A^+ AA^+ = (V_r D^{-1} U_r^T)(U_r DV_r^T)(V_r D^{-1} U_r^T) = (V_r D^{-1} DV_r^T)(V_r D^{-1} U_r^T)$$

$$= V_r D^{-1} DD^{-1} U_r^T = V_r D^{-1} U_r^T = A^+$$

13. a. If $\mathbf{b} = A\mathbf{x}$, then $\mathbf{x}^+ = A^+\mathbf{b} = A^+ A\mathbf{x}$. By Exercise 12(a), $\mathbf{x}^+$ is the orthogonal projection of $\mathbf{x}$ onto Row A.

b. From part (a) and Exercise 12(c), $A\mathbf{x}^+ = A(A^+ A\mathbf{x}) = (AA^+ A)\mathbf{x} = A\mathbf{x} = \mathbf{b}$.

c. Let $A\mathbf{u} = \mathbf{b}$. Since $\mathbf{x}^+$ is the orthogonal projection of $\mathbf{x}$ onto Row A, the Pythagorean Theorem shows that $\|\mathbf{u}\|^2 = \|\mathbf{x}^+\|^2 + \|\mathbf{u} - \mathbf{x}^+\|^2 \geq \|\mathbf{x}^+\|^2$, with equality only if $\mathbf{u} = \mathbf{x}^+$.

14. The least-squares solutions of $A\mathbf{x} = \mathbf{b}$ are precisely the solutions of $A\mathbf{x} = \hat{\mathbf{b}}$, where $\hat{\mathbf{b}}$ is the orthogonal projection of $\mathbf{b}$ onto Col A. From Exercise 13, the minimum length solution of $A\mathbf{x} = \hat{\mathbf{b}}$ is $A^+\hat{\mathbf{b}}$, so $A^+\hat{\mathbf{b}}$ is the minimum length least-squares solution of $A\mathbf{x} = \mathbf{b}$. However, $\hat{\mathbf{b}} = AA^+\mathbf{b}$ by Exercise 12(a) and hence $A^+\hat{\mathbf{b}} = A^+ AA^+\mathbf{b} = A^+\mathbf{b}$ by Exercise 12(c). Thus $A^+\mathbf{b}$ is the minimum length least-squares solution of $A\mathbf{x} = \mathbf{b}$.

15. [M] The reduced SVD of A is $A = U_r DV_r^T$, where

$$U_r = \begin{bmatrix} .966641 & .253758 & -.034804 \\ .185205 & -.786338 & -.589382 \\ .125107 & -.398296 & .570709 \\ .125107 & -.398296 & .570709 \end{bmatrix}, D = \begin{bmatrix} 9.84443 & 0 & 0 \\ 0 & 2.62466 & 0 \\ 0 & 0 & 1.09467 \end{bmatrix},$$

and $V_r = \begin{bmatrix} -.313388 & .009549 & .633795 \\ -.313388 & .009549 & .633795 \\ -.633380 & .023005 & -.313529 \\ .633380 & -.023005 & .313529 \\ .035148 & .999379 & .002322 \end{bmatrix}$

So the pseudoinverse $A^+ = V_r D^{-1} U_r^T$ may be calculated, as well as the solution $\hat{\mathbf{x}} = A^+\mathbf{b}$ for the system $A\mathbf{x} = \mathbf{b}$:

$$A^+ = \begin{bmatrix} -.05 & -.35 & .325 & .325 \\ -.05 & -.35 & .325 & .325 \\ -.05 & .15 & -.175 & -.175 \\ .05 & -.15 & .175 & .175 \\ .10 & -.30 & -.150 & -.150 \end{bmatrix}, \hat{\mathbf{x}} = \begin{bmatrix} .7 \\ .7 \\ -.8 \\ .8 \\ .6 \end{bmatrix}$$

Row reducing the augmented matrix for the system $A^T\mathbf{z} = \hat{\mathbf{x}}$ shows that this system has a solution, so $\hat{\mathbf{x}}$

is in $\text{Col } A^T = \text{Row } A$. A basis for Nul A is $\{\mathbf{a}_1, \mathbf{a}_2\} = \left\{ \begin{bmatrix} 0 \\ 0 \\ 1 \\ 1 \\ 0 \end{bmatrix}, \begin{bmatrix} -1 \\ 1 \\ 0 \\ 0 \\ 0 \end{bmatrix} \right\}$, and an arbitrary element of Nul A is

$\mathbf{u} = c\mathbf{a}_1 + d\mathbf{a}_2$. One computes that $\| \hat{\mathbf{x}} \| = \sqrt{131/50}$, while $\| \hat{\mathbf{x}} + \mathbf{u} \| = \sqrt{(131/50) + 2c^2 + 2d^2}$. Thus if $\mathbf{u} \neq \mathbf{0}, \| \hat{\mathbf{x}} \| < \| \hat{\mathbf{x}} + \mathbf{u} \|$, which confirms that $\hat{\mathbf{x}}$ is the minimum length solution to $A\mathbf{x} = \mathbf{b}$.

16. **[M]** The reduced SVD of A is $A = U_r D V_r^T$, where

$$U_r = \begin{bmatrix} -.337977 & .936307 & .095396 \\ .591763 & .290230 & -.752053 \\ -.231428 & -.062526 & -.206232 \\ -.694283 & -.187578 & -.618696 \end{bmatrix}, D = \begin{bmatrix} 12.9536 & 0 & 0 \\ 0 & 1.44553 & 0 \\ 0 & 0 & .337763 \end{bmatrix},$$

$$\text{and } V_r = \begin{bmatrix} -.690099 & .721920 & .050939 \\ 0 & 0 & 0 \\ .341800 & .387156 & -.856320 \\ .637916 & .573534 & .513928 \\ 0 & 0 & 0 \end{bmatrix}$$

So the pseudoinverse $A^+ = V_r D^{-1} U_r^T$ may be calculated, as well as the solution $\hat{\mathbf{x}} = A^+ \mathbf{b}$ for the system $A\mathbf{x} = \mathbf{b}$:

$$A^+ = \begin{bmatrix} .5 & 0 & -.05 & -.15 \\ 0 & 0 & 0 & 0 \\ 0 & 2 & .5 & 1.5 \\ .5 & -1 & -.35 & -1.05 \\ 0 & 0 & 0 & 0 \end{bmatrix}, \hat{\mathbf{x}} = \begin{bmatrix} 2.3 \\ 0 \\ 5.0 \\ -.9 \\ 0 \end{bmatrix}$$

Row reducing the augmented matrix for the system $A^T\mathbf{z} = \hat{\mathbf{x}}$ shows that this system has a solution, so $\hat{\mathbf{x}}$

is in $\text{Col } A^T = \text{Row } A$. A basis for Nul A is $\{\mathbf{a}_1, \mathbf{a}_2\} = \left\{ \begin{bmatrix} 0 \\ 1 \\ 0 \\ 0 \\ 0 \end{bmatrix}, \begin{bmatrix} 0 \\ 0 \\ 0 \\ 0 \\ 1 \end{bmatrix} \right\}$, and an arbitrary element of Nul A is

$\mathbf{u} = c\mathbf{a}_1 + d\mathbf{a}_2$. One computes that $\| \hat{\mathbf{x}} \| = \sqrt{311/10}$, while $\| \hat{\mathbf{x}} + \mathbf{u} \| = \sqrt{(311/10) + c^2 + d^2}$. Thus if $\mathbf{u} \neq \mathbf{0}$, $\| \hat{\mathbf{x}} \| < \| \hat{\mathbf{x}} + \mathbf{u} \|$, which confirms that $\hat{\mathbf{x}}$ is the minimum length solution to $A\mathbf{x} = \mathbf{b}$.